The Blackwell Dictionary of W

For my grandson Louis Bunnin
N.B.

In memory of my grandparents
J.Y.

The Blackwell Dictionary of Western Philosophy

NICHOLAS BUNNIN AND JIYUAN YU

WILEY-BLACKWELL

A John Wiley & Sons, Ltd., Publication

This paperback edition first published 2009
© 2009 by Nicholas Bunnin and Jiyuan Yu

Edition history: Blackwell Publishing Ltd (hardback, 2004)

Blackwell Publishing was acquired by John Wiley & Sons in February 2007. Blackwell's publishing program has been merged with Wiley's global Scientific, Technical, and Medical business to form Wiley-Blackwell.

Registered Office
John Wiley & Sons Ltd, The Atrium, Southern Gate, Chichester, West Sussex, PO19 8SQ, United Kingdom

Editorial Offices
350 Main Street, Malden, MA 02148-5020, USA
9600 Garsington Road, Oxford, OX4 2DQ, UK
The Atrium, Southern Gate, Chichester, West Sussex, PO19 8SQ, UK

For details of our global editorial offices, for customer services, and for information about how to apply for permission to reuse the copyright material in this book please see our website at www.wiley.com/wiley-blackwell.

The right of Nicholas Bunnin and Jiyuan Yu to be identified as the author of this work has been asserted in accordance with the Copyright, Designs and Patents Act 1988.

Library of Congress Cataloging-in-Publication Data

Bunnin, Nicholas.
The Blackwell dictionary of Western philosophy / Nicholas Bunnin and Jiyuan Yu.
    p. cm.
Includes bibliographical references
ISBN 978–1–4051–9112–8 (alk. paper)
1. Philosophy – Dictionaries.   I. Yu, Jiyuan.   II. Title.
        B41.B79 2004
        190′.3—dc22
        2004000107

A catalogue record for this book is available from the British Library.

Set in Dante 9.5/12pt
by Graphicraft Limited, Hong Kong
Printed in Singapore by Ho Printing Pte Ltd

2 2009

Contents

Preface

Although the Dictionary covers a wide historical range and explores many subject areas, it focuses on terms and individuals at the center of current philosophical discussion. Many readers will consult the Dictionary for help in understanding individual terms and the contributions of individual philosophers, but others will explore a given philosophical issue or area by reading a range of related entries. A philosopher browsing through the text will learn much about the history and structure of Western philosophy and its sources of creative dispute. We hope that the Dictionary will be an invitation to further thought and that it will not be taken as the last word on any topic.

Entries for philosophical terms are intended to provide clear and challenging expositions that give access to major philosophical issues. Queries and objections are often included to capture the perplexity arising from philosophical questions and to encourage readers to be active and critical in their response to the Dictionary as a whole. Many entries give the derivations from Greek, Latin, French, or German. Entries for terms state the areas of philosophy in which the terms have their main use, provide cross-references to entries on philosophers and other terms, and conclude with illustrative quotations from a classical or modern source. The reference section at the end of the book gives details of the works cited in these quotations. Biographical entries discuss the philo-

sophical contributions and list at least some of the major works of their subjects.

In preparing the Dictionary, we aimed to provide a clear, balanced, and sophisticated picture of philosophy derived from primary works, leading scholarly authorities, and our own philosophical insights. Citations indicate the extensive range of primary sources consulted, but the entries themselves also reflect our gratitude to an excellent range of contemporary philosophical encyclopedias, dictionaries, reference works, and textbooks, including Paul Edwards (ed.), *Encyclopedia of Philosophy*, 8 vols. (Macmillan, 1967); J. O. Urmson and Jonathan Rée (eds.), *The Concise Encyclopedia of Western Philosophy and Philosophers* (Routledge, 1989); Edward Craig (ed.), *Routledge Encyclopedia of Philosophy*, 10 vols. (Routledge, 1998); Stuart Brown et al. (eds.), *Biographical Dictionary of Twentieth-Century Philosophers* (Routledge, 1996); Robert Audi (ed.), *The Cambridge Dictionary of Philosophy* (Cambridge University Press, 1995); G. Vesey and P. Foulkes, *Collins Dictionary of Philosophy* (Collins, 1990); Antony Flew (ed.), *A Dictionary of Philosophy* (Pan, 1979); A. R. Lacey, *A Dictionary of Philosophy*, 2nd edn. (Routledge, 1986); Thomas Mautner (ed.), *A Dictionary of Philosophy* (Blackwell, 1996); Peter A. Angeles, *The HarperCollins Dictionary of Philosophy*, 2nd edn. (HarperCollins, 1992); Simon Blackburn, *The Oxford Dictionary of Philosophy* (Oxford University Press, 1994); J. O. Urmson, *The Greek Philosophical Vocabulary*

(Duckworth, 1990); A. C. Grayling (ed.), *Philosophy: A Guide Through the Subject* (Oxford University Press, 1995); Nicholas Bunnin and E. P. Tsui-James (eds.), *The Blackwell Companion to Philosophy* (Blackwell, 1996); Ted Honderich (ed.), *The Oxford Companion to Philosophy* (Oxford University Press, 1995); the *Blackwell Companions to Philosophy* series; the *Blackwell Philosopher Dictionaries* series; and the Cambridge *Companions to Philosophers* series.

In addition to those mentioned above, we wish to thank the Leverhulme Trust and the People's Publishing House, Beijing. A grant from the Leverhulme Trust supported our preparation of the *Dictionary of Western Philosophy: English–Chinese* (People's Publishing House, Beijing, 2001). The present Dictionary is a revised and augmented version of that earlier work. The Philosophy Library and the Bodleian Library at the University of Oxford made their philosophical riches available to us. Edward Craig and Chad Hansen were referees for our Leverhulme Trust project, and Sir Peter Strawson assessed our initial list of headwords. Finally, we thank Nick Bellorini and Kelvin Matthews of Blackwell Publishing for their encouragement and support, and Valery Rose and Caroline Richards for their excellent editing. We both enjoyed our intensive work in compiling this Dictionary, and each learned so much from the philosophical insights of the other.

Nicholas Bunnin
Jiyuan Yu

A

abandonment

MODERN EUROPEAN PHILOSOPHY An experience gained through realizing that there are no objective principles or authorities to guide one's life. According to **existentialism**, this experience helps us to recognize that one cannot attain **authenticity** by appeal to God or to philosophical systems. We should each understand our own unique existential condition, reject bad faith, and assume full responsibility for life. The conception of abandonment is hence related to the existentialist account of the autonomy of the agent.

> "When we speak of 'abandonment' – a favourite word of Heidegger – we only mean to say that God does not exist, and that it is necessary to draw the consequence of his absence right to the end."
> **Sartre, *Existentialism and Humanism***

abduction

PHILOSOPHY OF SCIENCE **C. S. Peirce**'s term for the logic of discovery, a creative process that is one of the three fundamental types of reasoning in science, along with **induction** and **deduction**. When we encounter a new phenomenon that cannot be explained through the application of a general law, we should pick out certain characteristic features of this new phenomenon and attempt to find relations among these features. After forming several theories or hypotheses that might explain the phenomenon, we should select one of them to test against experience. Such a process of reasoning to form empirical theories or hypotheses for testing is called abduction. Peirce also called it retroduction, hypothesis or presumption, but other philosophers have normally called it induction. Peirce distinguished abduction from induction by defining induction as the experimental testing of a theory. He held that abduction is what Aristotle discussed as *apagago* (Greek, leading away, substituting a more likely premise for a less acceptable one).

> "Presumption, or more precisely, abduction... furnishes the reasoner with the problematic theory which induction verifies." **Peirce, *The Collected Papers*, vol. II**

Abelard, Peter (1079–1142)

Medieval French philosopher, born near Nantes, Brittany. Abelard, whose main concern was logic, made valuable contributions to discussion of issues such as inference, negation, predicate-expressions, and transitivity. He sought to discuss theological problems by analyzing the propositions used to state these problems. He steered a middle course between realism and nominalism and maintained that the reference of a universal term is not necessarily something that exists. In ethics, he focused on the intention of the agent rather than on the action itself and considered sin to be an intention to act against God's will and virtue to be living in love with God. His major works include *Dialectica, Theologian Scholarium, Ethics (Scito te ipsum,* or *Know Thyself)* and *Dialogue between a Christian, a Philosopher and a Jew.* He also wrote commentaries on Porphyry's *Isagoge* and Aristotle's *Categories* and *De Interpretatione.* The story of love between Abelard and Heloise has fascinated many later generations.

abortion

ETHICS The intentional killing of a fetus or fertilized human egg by causing its expulsion from the mother's womb before its birth. Whether abortion should be morally permitted has been intensively debated in the past few decades and has become a major political and legal issue in many industrialized countries. One focus of the debate is on the moral status of a fetus. Is a fetus a person with a substantive right to life? The anti-abortion argument holds that a fetus is already a person and therefore should be within the scope of the moral rule that "you should not kill." This view leads to a discussion concerning the concept of personhood, that is, at what stage between conception and birth does a fetus becomes a person? Another focus concerns the rights of the pregnant woman. Does she have a right to bodily autonomy, including the right to decide what happens to her own body? Even if a fetus is a person, how shall we balance its rights and the woman's rights? Still another problem concerns the extent to which we should take into account the undesirable consequences of the prohibition of abortion, such as poverty and overpopulation. Different sides of the debate hold different positions resulting in part from the moral principles they accept. There is currently no common basis to solve all the disagreement. Nevertheless, abortion, which was legally permitted only in Sweden and Denmark until 1967, has become accepted in the majority of Western countries.

"Induced abortion is the termination of unwanted pregnancy by destruction of the fetus." **Rita Simon,** *Abortion*

Absolute, the

METAPHYSICS [from Latin *absolutus,* in turn originating from *ab,* away, from and *solvere,* free, loosen; free from limitations, qualifications or conditions] To call something absolute is to say that it is unconditional or universal, in contrast to what is relative,

comparative or varying according to circumstances. In metaphysics, the Absolute, as a technical term, is a single entity that is ultimate, unchanging, overriding and all-comprehensive. **Nicholas of Cusa** uses this expression to refer to **God**. Subsequently, the Absolute is always associated with concepts such as the one, the perfect, the eternal, the uncaused, and the infinite and has been regarded as the reality underlying appearance and providing rational ground for appearance.

The revival of the notion of the Absolute in modern philosophy derives from the debate in the 1770s between Mendelssohn and Jacob about **Spinoza**'s definition of substance. **Schelling**, employing Spinoza's notion of substance, defines the Absolute as a neutral identity that underlies both subject (mind) and object (nature). Everything that is mental or physical is an attribute of the Absolute or of "indefinite substance." He further claims that the Absolute is a living force, an organism, and something that is self-generating rather than mechanistic. **Hegel** claimed that the Absolute is the unity of substance and its modes, of the infinite and the finite. Such an Absolute is both a substance and a subject, developing from the underlying reality to the phenomenal world and reaching absolute knowledge as its highest phase. Thus, the Absolute is a self-determining activity, a spirit, and a concrete dynamic totality. Its development mirrors the development of knowledge. Hegel's metaphysics sought to work out the process and implications of this development.

In the twentieth century, this term is particularly associated with **Bradley**, who conceives the Absolute to be a single, self-differentiating whole. Anti-metaphysical thought argues for the elimination of the Absolute as an entity that cannot be observed and that performs no useful function in philosophy.

"Absolutes are the limits of explanation, and as such they have been the main theme of traditional philosophy." **Findlay,** *Ascent to the Absolute*

absolute conception

METAPHYSICS A term introduced by Bernard **Williams** in his study of **Descartes** for a conception of reality as it is independent of our experience and to which all representations of reality can be related. To gain such a conception requires overcoming the limitations of our enquiry and any systematic bias, distortion, or partiality in our outlook. Such a conception may enable us to view our representations as one set among others and to avoid assessing the views of others from our own standpoint. Williams claims that our notion of knowledge implies that such a conception is possible.

"This notion of an absolute conception can serve to make effective a distinction between 'the world as it is independent of our experience' and 'the world as it seems to us'." **B. Williams,** *Ethics and the Limits of Philosophy*

absolute idea

METAPHYSICS The absolute idea, for **Hegel**, is equivalent to absolute truth in his *Phenomenology of Mind* and to **the absolute** in his *Logic*. It is also called absolute spirit. For Hegel, an idea is not something mental or separate from particulars, but is the categorical form of spirit. The absolute idea is the idea in and for itself, an infinite reality and an all-embracing whole. It exists in a process of self-development and self-actualization. As a metaphysical counterpart of the Christian God, it is the basis for the teleological development of both the natural and social worlds. Its determinate content constitutes reality. The absolute idea is what truly is, and the final realization of truth. For Hegel, the absolute idea is a dynamic self, involving inner purposiveness and normative ideals. By characterizing reality as the absolute idea, Hegel showed that his notion of reality is fundamentally conceptual. It is a unity of the ideal of life with the life of cognition. The core of Hegel's idealism is the claim that the being of all finite things is derived from the absolute idea. In terms of this notion, Hegel integrated ontology, metaphysics, logic, and ethics into one system.

"The defect of life lies in its being only the idea implicit or natural, whereas cognition is in an equally one-sided way the merely conscious idea, or the idea for itself. The unity and truth of these two is the Absolute Idea, which is both in itself and for itself." **Hegel,** *Logic*

absolute identity

LOGIC As traditionally understood, identity is a rigorous notion that cannot have variant forms, and the identity relation is taken absolutely. According to **Frege**, this absolute notion of identity can be expressed in two theorems: (1) **reflexivity**: x = x (everything is identical with itself) and (2) the **indiscernibility of identicals** (or **Leibniz**'s law): if a and b are identical, whatever is true of a is true of b, and vice versa. Hence, "a is identical with b" means simply "a is the same as b."

Peter **Geach** calls this account the classical theory of identity and believes that it is mistaken. Instead, he claims that identity is always relative, so that *a* is not simply the same as *b*, but rather that *a* can be the same as *b* relative to one concept but not the same as *b* relative to another concept. In response, some argue that relative identity is qualitative identity, while numerical identity remains absolute.

"Absolute identity seems at first sight to be presupposed in the branch of logic called identity theory." **Geach,** *Logic Matters*

absolute rights, see rights, absolute

absolute spirit, another term for absolute idea

absolutism

METAPHYSICS, ETHICS, POLITICAL PHILOSOPHY A term with different references in different areas. In metaphysics, it is opposed to subjectivism and relativism and claims that there is an ultimate, eternal, and objective principle that is the source and standard of truth and value. Ethical absolutism holds that there is a basic universal principle of morality that every rational being should follow, despite their different empirical circumstances. Moral absolutism is opposed to moral relativism, which denies that any single moral principle has universal validity. In political theory, it is the view that the government's power and rights are absolute and that they always have priority when they come into conflict with the rights, interests, needs, preferences, or desires of citizens or groups in society.

"In ethics, the rejection of absolutism leads initially to the recognition of multiple moral authorities, each claiming its own local validity." **Toulmin,** *Human Understanding*

abstract/concrete

EPISTEMOLOGY, METAPHYSICS [from Latin *abstrahere*, to remove something from something else and *concrescere*, to grow together] At the outset of a process of recognition our concepts are likely to be vague or superficial. We must first abstract them in order to understand their diverse determinations. Being abstract is the product of abstraction, that is, of drawing away something common from diverse perceptible or sensory items and disregarding their relatively inessential features. Concepts and universals are thus formed. To say that something is abstract means that it is conceptual, universal, essential, or a matter of principle, while to say that something is concrete means that it is contextual, particular, personal, sensible. To be concrete is equivalent to being rich and vivid. Since what is abstract is drawn from what is concrete, to be abstract is equated with lacking the detail and individuality of the concrete and is thought to be meager, dependent, and lifeless. The existence and nature of abstract entities such as numbers and universals has long been a matter of dispute.

In another usage, which is especially prominent in **Hegel**'s philosophy, being abstract means being cut off from thoughts or from other sensory items, while being concrete is to be relational. Hence, a particular is abstract if it is isolated from other particulars, while a concept or universal is concrete if it is related to other concepts or universals and is one item in an organic system. Hegel called such a concept a "concrete concept" or "concrete universal."

> "What we abstract from are the many other aspects which together constitute concrete objects such as people, economies, nations, institutions, activities and so on." **Sayer,** *Method in Social Science*

abstract entities

METAPHYSICS Objects that are not actualized somewhere in space and time, that is, non-particulars such as numbers, properties, relations, proposition, and classes. They stand in contrast to spatio-temporal physical objects. Whether these entities actually exist – whether we should ascribe reality to them – is a question of persistent dispute in philosophy. Empiricists and nominalists try to conceive of abstract entities as having merely a linguistic basis. However, if mathematics embodies general truths about the world and has abstract entities as its subject matter, abstract entities would be objects of reference and hence real existents. This is the claim of Platonism and is also a position admitted by **Quine**'s criterion of ontological commitment. The

discussion of abstract entities is related to the problem of being, to the problem of universals, and also to the theory of meaning.

> "Empiricists are in general rather suspicious with respect to any kind of abstract entities like properties, classes, relations, numbers, propositions, etc." **Carnap,** *Meaning and Necessity*

abstract ideas

EPISTEMOLOGY, PHILOSOPHY OF LANGUAGE How can an **idea** stand for all individuals of a given kind even though the individuals vary in their properties? How can we form general statements about kinds of things and reason with regard to them? **Locke** introduced the notion of abstract ideas, also called general ideas, and claimed that they are **universal** concepts generated as a result of a process of abstraction from our ideas of individual exemplars of a kind, by leaving out their specific features and keeping what is common to all. As an **empiricist**, Locke believed that only particulars exist in the world. An abstract idea does not refer to something individual or particular, but is a special kind of mental image. This image is the meaning of the abstract general term. The function of abstract ideas is to classify individuals into different kinds for us. As classically understood in Locke, abstraction is something in the mind between reality and the way we classify it. He believed that an abstract idea encompasses a whole kind of thing. This claim was rejected by **Berkeley**, who insisted that all ideas are particular and only become general through our use of them. Berkeley's criticism of Locke's notion of abstract ideas, like his criticism of Locke's theory of real essence, has been very influential, but it is a matter of dispute whether his criticism is sound.

> "This is called abstraction, whereby ideas taken from particular beings become general representatives of all of the same kind; and their name general names, applicable to whatever exists conformable to such abstract ideas." **Locke,** *An Essay Concerning Human Understanding*

abstract particular

METAPHYSICS An individual **property** that is peculiar to the individual or particular possessing it, for example the white color possessed only by Socrates and not shared by any other white things. A property is generally regarded as being **universal**, that is, capable of being exemplified in many individuals or particulars. But some philosophers believe that there are also particularized qualities or property-instances. These are abstract particulars.

The issue can be traced to **Aristotle**. He classified all the realities into four kinds in his *Categories*: (1) that which is neither predicated of a subject nor inherent in a subject, namely, primary substances; (2) that which is predicated of a subject but not inherent in a subject, namely, secondary substances such as species and genus; (3) that which is predicated of a subject and also inherent in a subject, namely, universal attributes or properties; and (4) that which is not predicated of a subject, but which is inherent in a subject. For this last kind of reality, Aristotle's example is a particular piece of grammatical knowledge. He seems to be distinguishing universal properties and particular properties. In contemporary metaphysics, some philosophers claim that individual properties are constitutive of concrete particulars, that is, of events and physical objects, while others apply **Ockham's razor** to deny their existence. Alternative terms for abstract particulars are perfect particulars, particularized qualities, unit of properties, tropes, cases, and property-instances.

"Stout calls particulars which he postulates 'abstract particulars'. In calling them 'abstract' it is not meant that they are other-worldly . . . It is simply that these particulars are 'thin' and therefore abstract by comparison with the 'thick' or concrete particulars which are constituted out of the abstract particulars." **D. Armstrong, *Universals and Scientific Realism*, vol. 1**

abstract terms

PHILOSOPHY OF LANGUAGE, PHILOSOPHY OF SCIENCE, PHILOSOPHY OF MATHEMATICS The terms naming **abstract entities**, such as "natural number," "real number," "class," or "property." Different abstract terms can name the same abstract entity, and abstract terms can be either singular or general. Such terms have been used in mathematics and physics. In relation to the problem of the **ontological** status of abstract entities, it is also disputed whether the use of these terms will indicate the truth of Platonic realism. For according to **Quine**'s theory, to admit names of abstract entities commits us to the existence of the abstract entities named by them.

"The distinction between meaning and naming is no less important at the level of abstract terms." **Quine, *From a Logical Point of View***

abstracta

METAPHYSICS [plural of Latin *abstractum*] Abstract entities or objects, which are not perceptible and have no spatio-temporal location. Because we cannot point to them, *abstracta* are not objects of **ostensive definitions**. It is generally thought that *abstracta* do not have causal powers, but this point is controversial in contemporary epistemology. *Abstracta* are contrasted with *concreta* (plural of Latin *concretum*), which are the things that make up the observable world. It is widely held that *abstracta* are dependent on *concreta*.

"Abstracta . . . are combinations of concreta and are not directly observable because they are comprehensive totalities." **Reichenbach, *The Rise of Scientific Philosophy***

abstraction

EPISTEMOLOGY [from Latin *abs*, away from + *trahere*, draw, draw away from] A mental operation that forms a **concept** or **idea** (an abstract idea) by picking out what is common to a variety of instances and leaving out other irrelevant properties. This is a process of deriving universals and establishing classifications. From this mental act we may form concepts, and then build them up into judgments involving combinations of concepts, and further join judgments into inferences. In ancient philosophy there was a persistent problem about the ontological status of abstract things, and this is also the central point in **Aristotle**'s criticism of **Plato**'s Theory of Forms. Aristotle also refers to abstraction as a mental analysis that separates form from matter. **Locke** takes abstraction as the means of making ideas represent all objects of the same kind by separating ideas from other existence. For him it is the capacity for abstraction that distinguishes between human beings and animals. His theory of abstract ideas is criticized by **Berkeley**.

"This is called abstraction, whereby ideas taken from particular beings become general representatives of all of the same kind; and their names general names, applicable to whatever exists

absurdity

EPISTEMOLOGY, MODERN EUROPEAN PHILOSOPHY [from Latin *absurdus*, out of tone] Used as a synonym for "the irrational." In epistemology, an obvious and undeniable **contradiction** or incoherence in a belief or a proposition, such as "the square is a circle." Absurdity is stronger than an error arising from a misapplication of a name to an object. The aim of a *reductio ad absurdum* argument is to reveal the absurdity of a proposition and by these means to show the truth of its negation. Absurdity is associated primarily with language and hence with human beings. Philosophical absurdities can arise from using terms belonging to one category as though they belonged to another category. Gibert **Ryle** called such absurdities "**category mistakes.**"

For **existentialism,** there are two other uses of "absurdity." The first concerns the meaninglessness of human existence that derives from its lack of ground or ultimate purpose. In the second use, absurdity transcends the limitations of the rational and requires our whole power of conviction and feeling to be embraced. As an equivalent of the transcendental, the absurd is profound and valuable. Absurdity in this latter sense is derived from existentialist criticism of the absolute claims of reason and displays the characteristic irrationalism of existentialism.

"This divorce between man and his life, the actor and his setting, is properly the feeling of absurdity." **Camus,** *The Myth of Sisyphus*

academic freedom

ETHICS The free performance of academic activities, especially research and teaching, without externally imposed constraints. Academic freedom is a necessary condition for the pursuit of unknown truths and for passing them on by teaching. Academic freedom needs protection because the search for new ideas and knowledge is crucial for the development of any society. Historically, academic activities, especially regarding controversial and unpopular subjects, have always been interfered with by authorities and other forces, who characteristically claim that developing this kind of knowledge is harmful to society. Various original and creative scholars in each generation have therefore been suppressed and even prosecuted for the new ideas they have developed. But history has repeatedly proved that such interference is mistaken. Since nobody and no organization can decide beforehand which knowledge is harmful, we have no reason to censor any scholarly performance on the grounds that it will produce harm. Academic freedom also requires justice in distributing research and teaching facilities, including job security for academics, research support, publication space, and appropriate ways of evaluating teaching.

"The greatest external threats to academic freedom come from ideologies and governments; and most of all from governments in the service of ideologies." **Kenny,** *The Ivory Tower*

Academy

ANCIENT GREEK PHILOSOPHY The school that **Plato** founded around 385 BC, so named because it was located near a park with a gymnasium sacred to the hero Academus. The Academy was like a college in an ancient university, with all members sharing the same religious connections and the ideal of a common life. It was a progenitor of European educational institutions. The curriculum of the Academy is generally believed to have been similar to the scheme presented by Plato in the *Republic* for training rulers.

"Academy" is a term also used to refer to the philosophy of Plato and his followers. Historians differ regarding the history of the Academy. Some divide it into the Old Academy (Plato, 427–347 BC, Speusipus, 407–339 BC, and Xenocrates, 396–314 BC) and the New Academy (Arcesilaus of Pitane, 316–241 BC and Carneades, *c.*214–129 BC). Some prefer to ascribe Arcesilaus to the Middle Academy, and Carneades to the New Academy. Others want to add a Fourth Academy (Philo of Larissa, 160–80 BC), and a Fifth Academy (Antiochus of Ascalo, 130–68 BC). The general position of the Academy was to explain and defend Plato's doctrines. Plato's successors in the Old Academy were more interested in his "Unwritten Doctrines." The leaders of the Middle and New Academies were skeptics. Philo tried to reconcile their position with that of the Old Academy, and Antiochus is known for his eclecticism.

Aristotle studied with Plato in the Academy for 19 years and left only when Plato died in 347 BC. Much of our information about the Old Academy comes from his writings. The Academy should be distinguished from Middle Platonism and **Neoplatonism**, although it was one of the main proponents of Neoplatonism. Along with other pagan schools, the Academy was closed by the Eastern Roman emperor, Justinian I, in 529.

During the Renaissance, the intellectual circle led by Ficino in Florence was also called the Platonic Academy. Most of its activities involved commenting on Plato's works. From the eighteenth century, all societies organized for advanced learning, and subsequently all universities and colleges, have also been called academies.

"The Academy that Aristotle joined in 367 was distinguished from other Athenian schools by two interests: mathematics . . . and dialectic, the Socratic examination of the assumptions of mathematicians and cosmologists." **G. Owen,** *Logic, Science and Dialectic*

accedie

ETHICS, MEDIEVAL PHILOSOPHY [Latin, generally, but inadequately, translated as sloth; also spelled *accidie*] One of the "seven deadly sins," a spiritual attitude that rejects all the pleasures of life and turns away from what is good. In *accedie* the mind is stagnant and the flesh a burden. *Accedie* resembles apathy, but they are not the same. *Accedie* concerns the lack of feeling and has a negative sense, while apathy concerns mental states in which emotion is governed by reason and is regarded as a virtue.

"Accedia . . . is sadness over a spiritual value that troubles the body's ease." **Aquinas,** *Summa Theologiae*

acceptability

PHILOSOPHY OF SCIENCE Philosophers of science disagree about what it means for a **theory** to be acceptable and about what determines degrees of acceptability. In this debate, the degree of acceptability is closely associated with issues concerning the degree of **confirmation** and the degree of **probability**. Some hold that to be acceptable a theory has to be proven. Others claim that a theory is acceptable if it is rendered probable by the available **evidence**. Others argue that the acceptability has

nothing to do with reliability, but is simply related to the fact that a theory performs more successfully than its competitors when undergoing testing.

"If we mean by the degree of acceptability of a theory the degree to which it is satisfactory from the point of view of empirical knowledge – that is, from the point of view of the aims of empirical science – then acceptability will have to become topologically equivalent to corroboration." **Popper,** *Realism and the Aims of Science*

accident

METAPHYSICS [from Latin *accidens*, something that happens, related to the Greek *sumbebekos*, from the verb *sumbainein*, to come together, to happen, and better translated coincident or concomitant] For **Aristotle**, a technical term that contrasts with **essence** and has three major meanings: (1) the permanent features of a thing that are inherent and inseparably bound up with it, but that do not constitute part of its essence. Aristotle sometimes called these features **properties** (Greek, *idia*); (2) the features that belong to the subject only for a time, with their addition or loss not affecting whether the subject remains the same thing. These correspond to the modern notion of accidental properties, which contrast with essential properties, the loss of which will change the identity of a thing; (3) the secondary categories (categories other than substance) that are accidents to substance. In another sense, they are essential, for example white is an accident to Socrates, but it is essentially a color. Accidents of this sort are more properly called attributes or properties, although they still do not contribute to the identity of individual substances. They can only inhere in a substance and do not have independent existence.

Medieval philosophers distinguished accident *per se*, which as an attribute is itself an entity, from accident *per accidens*, which is a way of talking about something inessential to an object. Modern philosophy has tended to reject the distinction between substance and accident and has understood accident, in a manner similar to Aristotle's third sense, as an attribute, quality, or property. Accordingly, **Descartes** claimed that there is no science except the accidental, **Locke** distinguished primary qualities from secondary qualities, and **Berkeley** claimed that substance itself is nothing but a set of accidents.

"Accident means that which attaches to something and can be truly asserted, but neither of necessity nor usually." **Aristotle,** *Metaphysics*

accidental property

METAPHYSICS A **property** that is not a defining or essential feature of a **particular**. The identity of a particular is not affected by the change or loss of its accidental properties. For instance, the color of a wall or roof is an accidental property of a house. The relationship between an accidental property and the particular of which it is a property is external rather than internal. Accidental properties are contrasted to "**essential properties**," the change or loss of which alters the identity of the particular. Traditionally, rationality has been taken to be an essential property of being a human being. When people mention a particular, it is its essential properties rather than its accidental properties that are crucial in determining the identity of that particular and the kind of thing that it is. Although the discussion of accidental and essential properties goes back to **Aristotle**, the revival of essentialism in the work of **Kripke** and **Putnam** has renewed interest in the distinction.

"P is an accidental property of members of class A, if 'A' is not defined in terms of 'p'." **Pap,** *Elements of Analytic Philosophy*

achievement verbs

PHILOSOPHY OF LANGUAGE, PHILOSOPHY OF ACTION For **Ryle**, some verbs merely signify actions, such as reading or hunting. Ryle calls these task verbs. Other verbs not merely signify actions, but also indicate that the actions are suitable or correct. Not only has some performance been gone through, but also something has been brought off by the agent in going through it. These acts and operations, which have had certain positive results, are called achievement verbs by Ryle. A mark of an achievement verb such as "see" is that as soon as it is correct to say that a person sees something it is also correct to say that he has seen it. Such verbs are also called success verbs or success words. Correspondingly, there are failure verbs, such as lose or misspell. All perception verbs are achievement verbs since they involve an acquiring of knowledge about the physical world.

"There was another motive for desiderating a mistake-proof brand of observation, namely that it was half-realised that some observation words, such as 'perceive', 'see', 'detect', 'hear', and 'observe' (in its 'final' sense) are what I have called 'achievement verbs'." **Ryle,** *The Concept of Mind*

Achilles and the tortoise

LOGIC, METAPHYSICS, ANCIENT GREEK PHILOSOPHY The most widely discussed of **Zeno's paradoxes**, which were designed to show that the concept of motion is incoherent. Achilles, the Olympic champion in running, can never catch up with the slow-moving tortoise if the latter is given a head start. Achilles has to take some time to reach the place where the tortoise started, but when he reaches that place, the tortoise will have moved to a further point. The same is true when Achilles reaches that further point, because the tortoise will again have moved on. This process will be repeated endlessly, and the gap, which may get smaller and smaller, will remain. So as long as the tortoise keeps moving forward, Achilles cannot possibly overtake it, yet the paradox arises because we know that faster runners do overtake slower ones. The difficult problem is to explain the concepts of space, time, and motion in a way that shows what goes wrong in Zeno's reasoning. This paradox, which is closely connected with the dichotomy paradox, depends on the assumption that space and time are continuous and infinitely divisible. Our source for all of Zeno's paradoxes is Aristotle's account in *Physics*.

"Zeno's paradoxes of motion, such as his 'Achilles and the Tortoise', revealed grave and subtle difficulties in the notion of infinite divisibility." **Copi,** *The Theory of Logical Types*

acosmism

METAPHYSICS, PHILOSOPHY OF RELIGION [from Greek, *a*, not + *cosmos*, world, order] **Spinoza's** identification of God and world has often been interpreted as an assertion of **atheism**, but **Hegel** interpreted Spinoza as claiming that God rather than the world really exists. He entitles this position "acosmism." This position does not mean that God and the world are two distinct entities, but Hegel believed that it left unsolved questions about the **appearance** of the world and of the philosophizing **metaphysical subject**.

"[T]he system of Spinoza was not Atheism but acosmism, defining the world to be an appearance lacking in true reality." **Hegel,** *Logic*

acquaintance

EPISTEMOLOGY The way in which a knowing subject is aware of an **object** by experiencing it directly and immediately. Acquaintance contrasts with **description**, where an object is known through an intermediary process of **inference**. There is controversy over what are the objects of acquaintance. Among the items proposed for this role are **sense-data**, **memories**, and **universals** such as redness, roundness. The notion of acquaintance has been used to constrain what we can be said to experience. **Russell** calls the knowledge derived through acquaintance knowledge by acquaintance, which is the direct knowledge of things and is distinguished from knowledge by description, which reaches truth through inference.

"Acquaintance: an animal is said to be acquainted with an object when the object, or an image of it, is part of the animal at the moment." **Russell,** *Collected Papers of Bertrand Russell*

acroama

PHILOSOPHICAL METHOD [from Greek *akroama*, a thing heard] For **Kant**, a basic principle, especially of philosophy. In contrast, an axiom is a basic principle of mathematics or science. This is a distinction between **axioms** and discursive principles or between mathematical and philosophical principles. An axiom requires the intuition of objects and thus considers the universal in the particular, while an acroama is discursive and considers the particular in the universal. All principles of pure understanding are acroama, for they are established by the analysis of language and a discursive process of proof. Kant drew this distinction to criticize the tendency in traditional metaphysics to apply mathematical principles to philosophy.

"I should therefore prefer to call the first kind acroamatic (discursive) proofs, since they may be conducted by the agency of words alone (the object in thought), rather than demonstrations which, as the term itself indicates, proceed in and through the intuition of the object." **Kant,** *Critique of Pure Reason*

act, see action

act and omission

PHILOSOPHY OF ACTION, ETHICS, PHILOSOPHY OF LAW To act is to do something, while an omission is a failure to act in circumstances where one has the ability and opportunity to act. In **euthanasia**, one acts if one actively kills a patient, but this can be distinguished from omitting to act, where not acting allows a death that intervention could have prevented. In contrast to killing, an omission lets die or does not strive to keep alive. To send poisoned food to the starving is an act that kills them, while failing to aid them is an omission that lets them die. In these and other similar moral situations, objectionable acts are open to moral condemnation. What then is the moral status of apparently parallel omissions? Are they equally wrong or are they permissible? Are such omissions something that morally ought not to be allowed? This question gives rise to a complex debate regarding the moral significance of the distinction between act and omission. **Consequentialism** denies the importance of the distinction, while **deontology** holds on to it.

"It [the acts and omissions doctrine] holds that there is an important moral distinction between performing an act that has certain consequences – say, the death of a disabled child – and omitting to do something that has the same consequences." **P. Singer,** *Practical Ethics*

act-centered, see agent-centered morality

act-consequentialism

ETHICS **Consequentialism** is generally divided into act-consequentialism and **rule-consequentialism**. Act-consequentialism holds that an action is right if it produces a better consequence than alternative actions available to the agent. Rule-consequentialism, on the other hand, claims that the rightness of an action depends not on its direct consequences but on whether it conforms to a set of rules that lead to better consequences than other alternative rules. Act-**utilitarianism** is the most typical and familiar form of act-consequentialism. But there are also other forms of act-consequentialism that hold that pleasure or happiness are not the only factors by which we assess the goodness of the consequences.

Like act-utilitarianism, act-consequentialism is criticized for considering all things from an impersonal standpoint.

> "Different act-consequentialist theories incorporate different conceptions of the overall good . . . but all such theories share the same conception of the right which requires each agent in all cases to produce the best available outcome overall." **Scheffler,** *The Rejection of Consequentialism*

act-object theory

THEORY OF KNOWLEDGE An analysis of **sensation** introduced by **Moore** and **Russell** in their **sense-data** theory, which suggests that sensation consists of sense-data (objects) and the act of sensing. Sense-data are entities that are distinct from the act of seeing. A sensation is a genuine relation between a subject and a really existent object. Objects exist independently of acts. Moore uses this distinction in criticizing **Berkeley**'s idealist thesis that *esse est percipi* by saying that it fails to distinguish between the object sense-datum and the act of consciousness that is directed upon it. "Yellow" is an object of experience, and the sensation of "yellow" is a feeling or experience. **Russell** claims that perceiving and other cognitive processes are acts of attention, directed at some object. But under the influence of adverbial analysis, Russell later abandons this act-object analysis. For **Broad**, sensa-data cannot exist independent of the act of sensing, and he call them "sensa."

> "The sensum theory . . . holds that this [sensation] is a complex, and that within it there can be distinguished two factors: X itself, which is the sensum and is an object, and a subjective factor, which is called the 'act of sensing'." **Broad,** *Scientific Thought*

act token

PHILOSOPHY OF ACTION, ETHICS Alvin **Goldman** has distinguished between act tokens and **act types**. An act type is a kind of **action**, such as driving a car or writing a paper. An act token is a particular act or action that is performed by a particular person in a particular circumstance: for instance, driving my Ford Escort yesterday afternoon or writing my paper about Aristotle's concept of substance. An act type is an action property, while an act token is an exemplification of such a type. An act token is the performance of an act. If an act type is wrong, all

act tokens that belong to it are wrong. There has been a debate about the identity conditions for actions. Generally, two act tokens are thought to be identical if and only if they involve the same agent, the same property, and the same place and time.

> "A particular act, then, consists in the exemplifying of an act-property, by an agent at a particular time. I shall call such particular acts 'act tokens'." **Goldman,** *A Theory of Human Action*

act type, see act token

action

PHILOSOPHY OF MIND, PHILOSOPHY OF ACTION, ETHICS [from Latin *agere*, to do] Some philosophers draw a distinction between acts and actions and suggest that while an act is the deed that is done, an action is the doing of it. But most believe that this distinction is hard to maintain and take an act as a synonym for an action.

Although there are actions in nature, such as the action of a river on its bank, an action is generally defined as what is intentionally done by a human rational agent. Natural action is described as a mere process, happening, or occurrence. Action has been the focus of much discussion in recent philosophy of mind, especially concerning human **intention** and **deliberation**. Many theories have been developed to explain what it means to act intentionally and to show how to distinguish actions from other **events** involving persons. On one standard account, an action is an event by which an agent brings about changes through bodily movement. A rival mental action theory argues that not all actions involve bodily movement and identifies actions with primary mental events in the causal chain between the agent and behavioral events. According to the causal theory of action developed by **Davidson**, **Searle**, and **Goodman** among others, actions are the effects of primary mental events. Other philosophers reject such primary mental events and deny that actions are events at all.

One bodily movement can bring about, directly and indirectly, many changes and the consequences of this for identifying and explaining actions are unclear. X moves his hand; by moving his hand, he turns the steering wheel; and by turning the steering wheel, he drives his car; and so on. Is there one action in this case or are there many? When should we distinguish an action from its consequences? Some philosophers suggest that we can deal with these problems by identifying **basic actions** that cause other actions but that are not themselves caused by actions. But there is much dispute regarding how to identify basic action.

Actions can be discussed in isolation, but they often occur in a pattern of activity either in a single life or involving others. **Social action** was profoundly explored by **Weber**.

If we seek a causal account of action, are actions caused by reason, desire, or both? Would another framework be more appropriate for explaining or understanding action either within a causal account or as a rival to it? It is unclear whether an explanation by **reasons** that is not a form of **causal explanation** is coherent. Answering such questions requires the analysis of many key notions, such as **motives**, intentions, **voluntary and involuntary** action, **practical reason**, wants, and **desires**. The question of explaining action is closely associated with the problem of free will and determinism and the problem of responsibility.

Another much debated problem in philosophy of law and moral philosophy is the relation between action and omission, inaction or negligence.

"The word 'action' does not very often occur in ordinary speech, and when it does it is usually reserved for fairly portentous occasions. I follow a useful philosophical practice in calling anything an agent does intentionally an action, including intentional omission." **Davidson**, *Essays on Actions and Events*

action (Aristotle)

ANCIENT GREEK PHILOSOPHY, ETHICS [Greek, *praxis*, from the verb *prattein*, to do] Broadly, everything that an **agent** does intentionally, in contrast to speech and to being acted upon. Humans, including children, and some non-human animals are capable of this sort of action. More strictly, action is confined to carrying out rational choice, something that non-humans cannot do. It is doing what is or could be the outcome of **deliberation** on the part of the agent or for what the agent is held responsible. This sense, which is central to moral philosophy, is related to the problem of **free will** and **responsibility**. Only in this sense is action open to moral praise and blame. Aristotle also used *praxis* narrowly

for rational action that is its own end, and that is not done merely for the sake of some further end. This sense contrasts with production (Greek, *poiesis*), which is for the sake of some end product. According to this contrast, ethical actions, unlike technical performances, are done and valued for their own sake. Philosophers also discuss the conceptual relations between these sorts of action and action in nature that does not involve intention, reason, or purpose, such as the action of a river on its bank.

"[An unconditional goal is] what we achieve in action, since doing well in action is the goal." **Aristotle**, *Nicomachean Ethics*

action at a distance

METAPHYSICS, PHILOSOPHY OF PHYSICS Action at a distance is contrasted to action by contact or local action. Whether one thing can act on another at a distance without postulating some kind of intervening medium as involved in the interaction has been a topic of debate in physics and philosophy since ancient Greece. The dominant tendency is to reject any such possibility. **Atomism** claims that atoms cannot interact without contact. Aristotle believes that every object in local motion must have a conjoined mover. This is also the main attitude in physics and philosophy of the seventeenth and eighteenth centuries. **Descartes**, **Newton**, **Locke**, and **Leibniz** all reduce actions at a distance to actions through a medium of some sort, yielding actions that are continuous, although there is no agreement about what the medium is. In contemporary field theory the question is still disputed. The problem of action at a distance is related to the question of whether causality is something more than correlation.

"The formula by which we determine what will happen in a given region will contain references to distant regions, and it may be said that this is all we can mean by 'action at a distance'." **Russell**, *The Analysis of Matter*

active intellect

METAPHYSICS, PHILOSOPHY OF MIND, ANCIENT GREEK PHILOSOPHY, MEDIEVAL PHILOSOPHY **Aristotle** claimed in *De Anima* III, 5 that, as with anything else, one can draw a distinction between **form** and **matter** and between **actuality** and **potentiality** within the soul. The formal and actual aspect of the soul is active intellect, and the material and potential aspect of the soul is passive intellect. Passive intellect amounts to ordinary apprehension that is receptive of the sensible and intelligible forms of objects. This kind of knowing is only potential. Passive intellect will perish at the death of an individual. Active intellect is the agent that brings the passive intellect's potential knowledge of objects to actuality. Active intellect is separable, unmixed, and impassable. The distinction between active and passive intellect and the nature and function of active intellect are ambiguous in Aristotle's writings and gave rise to many debates among commentators in the later Hellenistic and medieval periods and in contemporary Aristotelian scholarship as well. Controversial questions include: Is the distinction between active and passive intellect realized only within the human soul, or does active intellect exist outside human beings? Is active reason identical with God as described in the *Metaphysics*? If active intellect is entirely independent of body, how can we reconcile it with Aristotle's standard view that soul is the form of body?

"Intellect in this sense of it is separable, impassable, unmixed, since it is in its essential nature activity (for always the active is superior to the passive factor, the originating force to the matter which it forms)." **Aristotle, *De Anima***

active reason, another name for active intellect

actual idealism, see actualism

actualism

METAPHYSICS, PHILOSOPHY OF ACTION, ETHICS Actualism has several senses. First, it is the actual **idealism** of the Italian philosopher Giovanni **Gentile**. This theory claims that the pure act of **spirit** (that is, the transcendent subject as opposed to the empirical subject) is the only real thing in the dialectical process. Such acts are acts of self-affirmation and constitute a synthesis of the self and the world.

Secondly, actualism (also called factualism) is the view, proposed by **Plantinga**, **Stalnaker**, and **Armstrong**, that only the actual world exists. The world is wholly composed of actual entities, including concrete individuals and instantiated abstractions. All sorts of potentialities, tendencies, forces, and unexampled essences are not admitted. This view contests those theories of **possible worlds** that accept the existence of possible worlds and their contents as well as the existence of the actual world.

Thirdly, actualism as a theory of choice claims that an agent should choose the best option that he or she *will actually* do, rather than the best option that he or she *can* do. This latter view is called **possibilism**.

"I assume the truth of what may be called actualism. According to this view, we should not postulate any particular except actual particulars, nor any properties and relations (universals) save actual, or categorical, properties and relations." **D. Armstrong, *What is a Law of Nature?***

actuality/actualization

Ancient Greek philosophy [Greek, *energeia*, actuality, from *ergon*, function or action, etymologically associated with motion or activity; *entelecheia*, actualization (Greek), from *enteles echein*, having an end within, etymologically associated with the completion of an action or a process] Aristotle used these two terms interchangeably and ignored their different etymologies. In many places, he contrasted *energeia* with **motion** (*kinesis*) saying that motion is an incomplete activity that aims at some end beyond itself, while *energeia* is a complete activity which is its own end. Both *energeia* and *entelecheia* are used in contrast to potentiality for the fulfillment or realization of different kinds of potentiality. In Aristotle's discussion of substantial change, actuality or actualization is identical with form, and sometimes even with the composite of matter and form, that which has been shaped out of the matter.

"The word 'actuality' which we connect with actualisation has in the main been extended from motion to other things; for actuality in the strict sense is thought to be identical with motion." **Aristotle, *Metaphysics***

actuality (Hegel)

METAPHYSICS [German, *Wirklichkeit*, from *wirken*, to be active, or effectual] In the preface to *Philosophy of Right*, **Hegel** claimed that "what is rational is actual, and what is actual is rational." This has been criticized as a conservative doctrine that allows no attack on existing political systems and institutions, however tyrannical or perverse they might be. But this response is based on a mistaken understanding of Hegel's notion of actuality. Hegel employed the standard contrast between actuality and possibility or **potentiality**, but also contrasted actuality to mere existence or appearance, so that not everything existing is actual. In his *Logic*, actuality is the unity of **existence** and **essence**, of inward reality and outward reality. Something actual is fully developed according to the inner rationality of the **species** to which it belongs. For Hegel, everything has its own teleological necessity and can be said to be actual only when this necessity has been fully worked out. Hence, an infant, although it exists, is not actual with respect to the essence of human species.

"Actuality is the unity, become immediate, of essence with existence, or of inward with outward." **Hegel,** *Logic*

actualization, see actuality/actualization

actus reus, see *mens rea*

additive fallacy, an alternative expression of the additivity assumption

additivity assumption

ETHICS Also called the additive fallacy. **Utilitarianism** argues that we can add individual **utilities** together to make up a total utility and that any action that results in a larger amount of total utility is morally more acceptable than other actions that result in less total utility. Here a working hypothesis is assumed that individual utilities can be quantitatively measured, compared, and combined into an overall outcome. This is the additivity assumption. It is not only central to utilitarianism, but is also active in many other moral theories, insofar as they appeal to notions such as "balancing," "weighing," and "simple-complex." Critics, however, maintain that individual utilities are always qualitatively different and incommensurable and therefore that it is impossible to compare and contrast them. Furthermore, even if an aggregation is possible, this would not be sufficient to establish the moral status of an action, for a larger amount of utility does not entail an equal or just distribution.

"The view that the moral status of an act is the sum of individual positive and negative contributions – the particular reasons for and against performing the act – is, as I suggested, a familiar and attractive one. Nonetheless, I believe that the additive assumption should be rejected." **Kagan, "Additive Fallacy,"** *Ethics* **99**

adequacy conditions on definitions of truth, see material adequacy

adequate ideas

EPISTEMOLOGY For **Spinoza**, adequate ideas are the **ideas** from the second grade of **cognition**, **reason**, and from the third grade of cognition, intuitive knowledge, in contrast to the ideas formed from the first grade of cognition, sense **experience**. Adequate ideas are wholly caused from within individual minds, either by seeing them to be **self-evident** or by deriving them from other ideas that are self-evident. Adequate ideas are coextensive with true ideas, and bear all the internal marks of **truth**. In **Leibniz**, adequate ideas are those that are clearly and distinctly conceived.

"By adequate idea I understand an idea which, in so far as it is considered in itself, without reference to the object, has all the properties or internal marks of a true idea." **Spinoza,** *Ethics*

ad hoc hypothesis

EPISTEMOLOGY, PHILOSOPHY OF SCIENCE [Latin, *ad hoc*, for this, to this] Something that is *ad hoc* is only for the purpose at hand. A theory might be saved from a challenge that is inspired by contrary evidence if we introduce an additional hypothesis. Such a hypothesis, if it has no independent rationale but is used merely to preserve the theory, is called an *ad hoc* hypothesis. An *ad hoc* hypothesis is generally rejected by a satisfactory scientific explanation, for it is not testable independently of the effect to be explained, and hence does not have any theoretical power. In another sense, *ad hoc* also means an explanation introduced to account for some fact after that fact had been established.

"A satisfactory explanation is one which is not *ad hoc*." **Popper,** *Objective Knowledge*

Adorno, Theodor (1903–69)

German philosopher, sociologist, and musicologist, born in Frankfurt, a leading member of the Frankfurt School of critical theory. Adorno joined the Institute for Social Research before emigrating to the United States in 1934 following Hitler's rise to power. He rejoined the Institute in 1938 in New York, but returned to Frankfurt in 1953 and became director of the Institute in 1959. His most important work, *Negative Dialectics* (1966), is a critique of thinking based on identity and the presentation of a negative dialectic of non-identity that has exerted great influence on postmodern and post-structuralist thought. He was co-author of *The Authoritarian Personality* (1950), a study of the psychological origins of fascism and Nazism. With Horkheimer, he published *Dialectic of the Enlightenment* (1947), which traces totalitarianism and scientism in modern society to the Enlightenment conception of reason. He criticized Husserl in *Against Epistemology* (1956) and Heidegger in *The Jargon of Authenticity* (1965). His *Aesthetic Theory* was left unfinished at his death.

adventitious ideas

EPISTEMOLOGY [from Latin *ad*, to + *venire*, to come] **Descartes**'s term for those ideas that we get through senses and that are caused by things existing outside one's mind. Adventitious ideas contrast both to **innate ideas** and to fictitious ideas. Innate ideas are not obtained by experience, but are carried by the mind from birth. Fictional ideas are created by mind in **imagination**. Descartes argued that it is impossible for all ideas to be adventitious. In contrast, British empiricists claimed that all ideas can be reduced to adventitious ideas and specifically denied the existence of innate ideas. On their account, all universals result from the operation of mind on the basis of adventitious ideas. The treatment of adventitious and innate ideas became one of the major divergences between rationalism and empiricism.

"I marvel indeed at the train of reasoning by which you try to prove that all our ideas are adventitious and none of them constructed by us, saying – because the mind has the power not only of perceiving these very adventitious ideas, but, besides this, of bringing together, dividing, reducing, enlarging, arranging, and everything similar to this." **Descartes,** *Meditations, Reply to Objection V*

adverbial materialism

PHILOSOPHY OF MIND A theory of mind that combines the adverbial analysis of sense-experience with **materialism** or **physicalism**, developed by the American philosopher J. W. Cornman. In the spirit of adverbial analysis, the theory claims that when people perceive something red in the appropriate conditions, they do not sense red sense-data, but rather they sense red-ly. It further takes this sensing event to be identical with a brain event. Every sensing event is reduced to a physical event. The theory is opposed to **phenomenalism** and is compatible with direct materialism. Critics suggest that this analysis leaves out the most central element of perception, the perceptual **experience** itself.

"This [theory of adverbial materialism] is the theory that each sensory experience consists in an objectless sensing event that is not only identical with but also nothing but some physical event, presumably a neuronal brain event." **Cornman,** *Perception, Common Sense, and Science*

adverbial theory

EPISTEMOLOGY An analysis of sensing that intends to convert the objects of sensation into sense-experience characterized in an adverbial way. An adverb is introduced to describe the way a sensing activity is taking place; thus, "I sense a red color patch" should be regarded as a statement of how I sense, that is "I sense red-ly." The purpose of this analysis is to deny that sense-data are independent entities; rather, it takes them as sense-contents that cannot exist independent of the act of sensing of them. **Sense-data** are considered as modes of awareness instead of internal objects of awareness. The starting-point of this theory is the idea that sensations cannot exist when not sensed. It eliminates mental objects by reducing all statements about sensations to statements about the way or mode in which a subject is sensing. The analysis influenced both **Moore** and **Russell** with regard to their act-object theory of sensation and was later advocated by C. J. **Ducasse**, **Ayer**, and **Chisholm**. The analysis becomes difficult once a complex sensation is involved, such as, "I sense a red color patch to the left of a blue color patch." It is also challenged for its inability to distinguish sense-experience from purely mental imaging.

"If the adverbial theory is right, it tells us how I am sensing and does not require for its truth that there be an object being sensed." **Jackson,** *Perception*

aesthetic attitude

AESTHETICS A special attitude with which to approach art, nature, and other objects. First, it differs from a practical attitude and has no concern with practical (sensual, intellectual, or moral) **utilities**. An aesthetic attitude takes nature or a work of art "for its own sake." In this sense it is "disinterested," as **Kant** emphasized in his *Critique of Judgement*. Secondly, it does not involve personal desires, motives, or feelings in dealing with an object. This freedom from desire or emotion is called "aesthetic distance" or "aesthetic detachment." Thirdly, in contrast to a cognitive or scientific attitude, it is indifferent to the real existence, the content or the meaning of a thing. It does not appreciate an object through bringing it under concepts. Instead it is a pure appreciation or contemplation of the perceptual qualities of an object as an object of sensation. It is claimed that in this way we can live in the work of art as an embodiment of our feeling. **Schopenhauer** and **Heidegger** ascribe a metaphysical importance to the aesthetic attitude by saying that it can reveal the essence of reality more profoundly than conceptualization. The possible existence and role of a pure aesthetic attitude are topics of dispute.

"All appreciation of art – painting, architecture, music, dance, whatever the piece may be – requires a certain detachment, which has been variously called the 'attitude of contemplation', the 'aesthetic attitude', or the 'objectivity' of the beholder." **Langer,** *Feeling and Form*

aesthetic autonomy

AESTHETICS The idea that art has its own sphere demarcated from other human activities and determines its own principles or rules. Art cannot be replaced by other activities without loss. Aesthetic experience should be explained by aesthetic terms or attributes, and art should be valued by itself alone. The idea is intended to protect art from being assimilated to scientific, religious, or moral functions and to insist that art has a different domain from science and morality. The position demands that human beings should be liberated from various instrumental attitudes towards art and that the development of art should not be unjustifiably subjected to the service of extra-aesthetic concerns. In this century, aesthetic autonomy has gained popularity in the face of the danger of submerging the aesthetic attitude into the cognitive attitude.

"The only answer, in short, is in terms of aesthetic value beyond which we cannot go. We assume the autonomy of aesthetics and all we can do is to see where this assumption will lead to." **Saw,** *Aesthetics*

aesthetic detachment, see aesthetic attitude

aesthetic distance, see aesthetic attitude

aesthetic education

ETHICS, AESTHETICS Education directed at developing a person's aesthetic capacities and experiences of art. Its purpose is to educate a person's feeling and to enhance the harmony between **emotion** and **reason** in order to elevate our character. Its function regarding one's soul is analogous to the function of physical education for one's body. As early as **Plato**'s *Republic*, there is a detailed discussion to show that education should have an aesthetic concern. An account of this education is most systematically developed in **Schiller**'s *Letters on the Aesthetic Education of Man*. There are contrasting views of what such an education should be, according to different theories of art.

"Aesthetic education is possible only if it involves criticism; and edifies only when its mirror images are not merely produced or consumed, but when they are critically grasped and appropriated." **Shusterman,** *Pragmatist Aesthetics*

aesthetic imagination

AESTHETICS The **imagination** that plays a role in the production and appreciation of artworks. Aesthetic imagination explores the possibilities suggested by the connection of aesthetic experience. It accompanies indispensably our interactions with art. While scientific imagination is bound by agreement with reality and is in the service of theoretical work, aesthetic imagination is free and operates in the service of aesthetic feeling. Its purpose is the satisfaction of the feeling that inspires it. It broadens our understanding, gives rise to emotional identification with the object, and enables us to experience a wider range of feelings than we can experience in actual life. For **Kant**, aesthetic experience involves a free play of the imagination and the understanding.

"Aesthetic imagination can perceive the ennobling beauty and truth of past art produced in more harmonious times." **Shusterman,** *Pragmatist Aesthetics*

aesthetic judgment

AESTHETICS The ascription of an aesthetic property or value to an object, as distinguished from cognitive or logical judgment that gives us knowledge. The determining ground for such an ascription has been hotly disputed. For objectivism, an aesthetic judgment attributes an objective property to a thing judged and does not essentially involve the feelings of the person who is judging. It is hence a universal judgment. For subjectivism, the feelings, such as liking or disliking, of the person who judges are the decisive ground, and hence aesthetic judgment is not universal. The most influential frameworks of analysis of aesthetic judgments were developed by **Hume** and **Kant**. According to Hume, although aesthetic properties are not inherent in things, aesthetic judgments are not merely an expression of personal pleasure or displeasure. Like judgments of color, they are determined by contingent causal relations between object and subject, although their ultimate ground is the sensibility of human beings. Kant claims that aesthetic judgments do not depend on a set of formulated rules or principles. Unlike objective knowledge claims, they rest on subjective response and personal acquaintance. He suggests that in a broad sense aesthetic judgments include empirical aesthetic judgment and "judgments of taste." An empirical aesthetic judgment judges the agreeable or the pleasant and concerns that which simply gratifies desire. A judgment of taste is an aesthetic judgment in its narrow sense. It is the judgment of beauty and is "disinterested," in the sense that it is independent of all personal desires and motivations. Hence, a person making such a judgment expects other people to have similar responses under the same circumstance. Hence, judgments of **taste** have a type of subjective validity or universality.

"Aesthetic judgements, just like theoretical (i.e. logical) ones, can be divided into empirical and pure. Aesthetic judgements are empirical if they assert that an object or a way of presenting it is agreeable or disagreeable; they are pure if they assert that it is beautiful. Empirical aesthetic judgements are judgements of science (material aesthetic judgements); only pure aesthetic judgements (since they are formal) are properly judgements of taste." **Kant,** *Critique of Judgement*

aesthetic pleasure

AESTHETICS Distinguished from both sensual pleasure and intellectual pleasure, aesthetic pleasure or aesthetic enjoyment is the emotional element in our response to works of art and natural beauty. It can vary from **pleasure** in its mildest form to rapturous enthusiasm. To characterize the peculiar nature of aesthetic pleasure has been a challenging job for aesthetics. Since **Kant**, many theorists have accepted that aesthetic pleasure is a result of a disinterested and non-conceptual engagement with an object. But it is a point of dispute whether this pleasure arises from apprehending the formal character of the object, its content, or both. It is also unclear how much subjective elements contribute to this process. Other major issues concern the relation between aesthetic pleasure and the aesthetic attitude and the distinction, if there is one, between aesthetic pleasure in response to nature and to art.

"Aesthetic pleasure is manifested in a desire to continue or repeat the experience." **Sheppard,** *Aesthetics*

aesthetic property

AESTHETICS A quality that contributes to determining the **aesthetic value** of an artwork. Such properties can be subject either to positive evaluation, such as being beautiful, charming, elegant, sublime, balanced, graceful, or majestic, or to negative evaluation, such as being ugly, boring, clumsy, garish, or lifeless. There can, of course, be beautiful depictions of ugly objects or lifeless depictions of beautiful ones. Some aesthetic qualities, such as being sad or joyful, can be non-evaluative. It is widely agreed that we require a special sensitivity, "taste," to perceive them. Aesthetic properties are the ultimate sources of "aesthetic value," and contribute to determining the nature of artworks. Positively aesthetic properties make artifacts into works of art and figure in a subject's account of why an artwork pleases him. Some philosophers argue that as **emergent properties** aesthetic properties **supervene** on non-aesthetic properties, but others insist that aesthetic properties must be seen as entirely independent of non-aesthetic properties.

> "I imagined explaining my emotional response to the painting by pointing out some of its aesthetic properties; the colours, although pastel, are warm rather than faded, the faces of the saints 'sweet and gentle.'" **Mothersill,** *Beauty Restored*

aesthetic value

AESTHETICS The properties rendering a work of art good or successful, such as balance, charm, elegance, grace, harmony, integrity, or unity. Aesthetic value is whatever contributes to the "**beauty**" of a piece of art, in contrast to that which contributes to its usefulness, truth, or moral goodness. "Beauty" is the supreme name for aesthetic value, and "ugliness" is the supreme name for aesthetic disvalue. The history of aesthetics has been characterized by disputes about whether aesthetic value is waiting to be discovered objectively in the objects, independent of the responses of observers, or exists subjectively in the experiences of human agents, or lies in the connection between the object and the feelings of its observers.

> "Instead of saying that an aesthetic object is 'good', they [philosophers] would say that it has aesthetic value. And correspondingly, instead of saying that one object is better than another, but not because it has a higher cognitive or moral value, they would say that it has a higher aesthetic value, or is aesthetically more valuable." **Beardsley,** *Aesthetics*

aestheticism

AESTHETICS The position that art should be valued only according to its intrinsic **aesthetic properties**, such as **beauty**, harmony, unity, grace, or elegance. It maintains the supreme value of art over everything else. A work of art is nothing more than a work of art and should not be viewed as a means to further ends. Its internal aesthetic value is supreme. Pure beauty has nothing to do with **utility**. The pursuit of such beauty is the supreme source of human happiness and should not be constrained by moral or other considerations. In its extreme form, aestheticism claims that any art that has external functions or purposes is ugly. The slogan of aestheticism is "art for art's sake" (French, *L'art pour l'art*). An art critic should not be concerned with art for the sake of citizenship, patriotism, or anything else. Aestheticism is rooted in **Kantian** aesthetic formalism and flourished in the nineteenth century, first in French literature, represented by Flaubert, and then in English literature, represented by Walter Pater and Oscar Wilde. Aestheticism opposes society's interference with artistic creation, for artworks characterized by adventurousness are always subject to criticism based on customs and established modes of thought and feeling. But it is problematic whether an artwork can be completely isolated from its environment and social consequences. The opposite view, which can be called "instrumentalism," proposes that art should serve the needs of the people and the community.

> "[Aestheticism] is the view that aesthetic objects are not subject to moral judgements, that only aesthetic categories can be, or ought to be, applied to them." **Beardsley,** *Aesthetics*

aesthetics

AESTHETICS Although many problems discussed in contemporary aesthetics as a branch of philosophy can be traced to **Plato**'s dialogues (especially *Ion, Symposium, Phaedrus, Republic,* and *Philebus*) and **Aristotle**'s *Poetics*, aesthetics did not become an independent discipline until the eighteenth century. The term was coined by the German philosopher Alexander **Baumgarten** in his *Reflections in Poetry* (1735), based on the Greek word *aisthesis* (sensation, perception). Baumgarten defines it as "the science of sensitive knowing," which studies both art and sensible knowledge. **Kant** inherited these two senses. The first part of *Critique of Pure Reason*, the "Transcendental Aesthetic," deals with *a priori* sensible form; the first part of *Critique of Judgement*, called "Critique of Aesthetic Judgement," is a critique of taste, concerning the judgment of beauty and the sublime and the "autonomy of taste."

Nowadays the word "aesthetics" is confined to the study of experience arising from the appreciation of artworks and covers topics such as the character of aesthetic attitude, aesthetic emotions, and aesthetic value; the logical status of aesthetic judgments; the nature of beauty and its allied notions; and the relation between moral education and works of art. It also encompasses problems dealt with by the "philosophy of art" such as the nature of art and the perception, interpretation, and evaluation of artworks. Philosophy of art is thus a part of aesthetics. The development of aesthetics in the twentieth century has been deeply influenced by developments in the philosophy of mind, theories of meaning, and hermeneutics.

"The Germans are the only people who currently make use of the word 'aesthetic' in order to signify what others call the critique of taste. This usage originated in the abortive attempt made by Baumgarten, that admirable analytical thinker, to bring the critical treatment of the beautiful under rational principles, and so to raise its rules to the rank of a science." **Kant,** *Critique of Pure Reason*

Aeterni Patris, see neo-scholasticism

aether

ANCIENT GREEK PHILOSOPHY, PHILOSOPHY OF SCIENCE A rarified element believed to fill the heavens. **Anaxagoras** considered aether to be derived from *aithein* (Greek, to ignite, to blaze) and identified it with fire. Some other pre-Socratic philosophers considered aether to be derived from *aei thein* (Greek, runs always), and took it to be a divine element, different from other basic elements. **Aristotle** developed their idea by arguing that aether is a fifth element in addition to the usual four elements: fire, air, earth, and water. He divided the cosmos into two levels. While the lower world, which is within the sphere of the moon, is composed out of the four elements, the upper world, from the moon upwards to the first heaven, is composed of aether. Aether has no property in common with the four simple elements in the lower world and cannot be transformed into them, and the four elements cannot go up to the outer region. Aether as a divine body has no movement except uniform circular motion and is indestructible. This cosmology became the foundation of the Ptolemaic system of astronomy. Seventeenth-century science postulated aether as the medium of interactions in the heavens. Nineteenth-century science postulated aether as the medium of transmission in the wave theory of light. This term is also retained in contemporary **quantum field theory**.

"They [natural philosophers], believing that the primary body was something different from earth and fire and air and water, gave the name aether to the uppermost region, choosing its title from the fact that it 'runs always' and eternally." **Aristotle,** ***De Caelo***

affirmative method

PHILOSOPHY OF RELIGION [from Latin *via affirmativa* or *via positiva*] A Christian theological method for obtaining knowledge of God, in contrast to negative method (***via negativa***). The affirmative method rejects the claim of the *via negativa* that God cannot be apprehended by human concepts and discourse. On the basis of the doctrine that man is made in the image of God, it claims that the highest human qualities are pointers and signs of the perfection of God. We can, therefore, deduce divine attributes through analogy to these qualities. The basic procedure is to start with the highest human categories and to proceed through intermediate terms to particular divine titles. In this way we can indicate how human terms such as goodness, wisdom, and power are applicable to God in a manner that transcends our experience. Because knowledge obtained in this way is pre-eminent, the *via positiva* is also called the *via eminentiae*. Some theologians, such as **Aquinas**, claim that the *via negativa* cannot be used in isolation, but is a necessary preliminary step to the *via positiva*. There are difficulties in applying a method of analogy like the affirmative method beyond the possibility of our experience.

"The affirmative method means ascribing to God the perfections found in creatures, that is, the perfections which are compatible with the spiritual nature of God, though not existing in Him in the same manner as they exist in creatures." Copleston, *A History of Philosophy*, vol. II

affirming mode, another term for *modus ponens*

affirming the consequent

LOGIC A logical **fallacy** of the form "If p then q; q; therefore p," that is, the categorical premise affirms the consequent of the conditional premise, while the conclusion affirms its antecedent. For instance, "if he is sick, he does not come to work; he does not come to work; therefore he is sick." This is invalid because in the conditional premise the truth of the consequent does not entail the truth of the antecedent. The correct form should infer from the antecedent of a true implication to its consequent; that is, it should be of the form "If p then q; p; therefore q." This was called *modus ponens* by the medieval logicians and is also called the affirming mood.

> "'P ⊃ Q, Q, therefore P' bears a superficial resemblance to the valid argument form modus ponens and was labelled the fallacy of affirming the consequent." **Copi,** *Introduction to Logic*

a fortiori

LOGIC [Latin: for a stronger reason, even more so or with more certainty] An argument that if everything that possesses A will possess B, then if a given thing possesses A to a greater degree, it has a stronger reason (*a fortiori*) to possess B. For example, if all old men who are healthy can run, then *a fortiori* a young man who has greater health than old men can run.

> "All the so-called relational (or *a fortiori*) syllogisms depend on the transitivity of the relations." **Cohen and Nagel,** *An Introduction to Logic and Scientific Method*

afterlife, see disembodiment

agape

ANCIENT GREEK PHILOSOPHY, ETHICS [Greek, love; its Latin translation, *caritas*: hence charity] In contrast to other terms for love, such as *eros* and *philia*, *agape* is used for Christian love and is one of the primary **virtues** in Christian ethics. Its content is expressed in two biblical injunctions: "Love the lord your God with all your heart, and all your soul, and all your mind" (Matthew 22: 9, but adapted from Leviticus 19:18) and "Love your neighbor as yourself" (Matthew 22:37, but previously Deuteronomy 6:5). *Agape* is wholly unselfish, but there has been some dispute whether it includes rational self-love. The relationship of *agape* to justice is also problematic. In comparative religion, *agape* has been compared with Confucian *jen*, humanity.

> "Agape is that form of love in which God loves us, and in which we are to love our neighbour, especially if we do not like him." **Tillich,** *Ultimate Concern*

age of adventure, another name for the Renaissance

age of reason, another name for the Enlightenment

agent

PHILOSOPHY OF ACTION, ETHICS [from Latin *agens*, what is acting, referring to a rational human being who is the subject of action] An agent can decide to act or not. Having decided to act, an agent can **deliberate** how to act. Once the means of acting are chosen, an agent can apply the means to bring about certain changes. The kind of capacity intrinsic to an agent is called agency. The change caused by an agent is called agent-causation, in contrast to event-causation in which one thing is caused externally by another. In ethics, only agents are members of a moral community and bearers of moral responsibility.

> "The way a cause operates is often compared to the operation of an agent, which is held responsible for what he does." **von Wright,** *Explanation and Understanding*

agent-centered morality

ETHICS Also called agent-related ethics. It demands that moral consideration should be given to moral agents rather than merely to the consequences of the agent's acts. It is a thesis opposed to **consequentialism**, in particular to **utilitarianism**, which it labels outcome-centered ethics. It accuses consequentialism of ignoring the **integrity** of the characters of moral agents, for consequentialist ethics requires that what an agent is permitted to do in any situation is limited strictly to what would have the best overall outcome impersonally judged. In contrast, agent-centered morality focuses on the agent's **rights**, **duties**, or **obligations**. It holds that our primary **responsibility** as agents is to guarantee that our actions conform to moral rules and do not violate our obligations towards others. Agents should perform such actions even if they know that the consequences of what they do would be better if they were willing to compromise their principles. Major issues for this view are to classify the forms of agent-relativity, to justify agent-relative principles, and to offer an adequate rationale for agent-centered restrictions.

"Agent-centred morality gives primacy to the question of what to do, a question asked by the individual agent, and does not assume that the only way to answer it is to say what it would be best if he did." **T. Nagel,** *Mortal Questions*

agent-neutral reason

ETHICS The evaluation of something objectively, independently of one's own **interests**. This is in contrast to "agent-relative reason," which values things by taking one's situations into consideration. Agent-neutral reason cares about everyone, while an agent-relative reason cares more particularly about oneself. The introduction of this dichotomy of reasons for acting is credited to Derek **Parfit**, but Thomas **Nagel** borrows it (using the terms objective reason and subjective reason) and uses it widely. It plays a great role in the contemporary debate between "**consequentialism**" and "**agent-related ethics**." Consequentialism is generally characterized as "agent-neutral," for it requires that everyone should act so as to maximize the amount of happiness for all involved. Some philosophers therefore claim that it asks moral agents to consider their actions from an impersonal point of view and is thus in conflict with common sense. On the other hand, agent-related ethics is believed to be based on "agent-relative reason" because it allows moral agents to base their moral aims on their moral characters. Consequentialism is also called "agent-neutral morality" or "act-centered ethics," and its opposite is called "agent-related ethics" or "agent-centered morality."

"Nagel calls a reason objective if it is not tied down to any point of view. Suppose we claim that there is a reason to relieve some person's suffering. This reason is objective if it is a reason for everyone – for anyone who could relieve this person's suffering. I call such reasons agent-neutral. Nagel's subjective reasons are reasons only for the agent. I call these agent-relative." **Parfit,** *Reasons and Persons*

agent-related ethics, another expression for agent-centered morality

agent-relative reason, see agent-neutral reason

agglomeration principle

ETHICS, LOGIC A term introduced by Bernard Williams and now used as a rule of inference in deontic logic. According to the principle, if one has a duty to do a and if one also has a duty to do b, then one has a duty to do a and b. The principle also extends to cover all situations in which a property can be conjoined out of two other properties. The validity of the principle has been a matter of controversy because it needs to be reconciled with the principle that ought implies can. In some cases, a person can do a and can do b separately, but cannot do both of them and will therefore not have a duty to do both.

There is a converse to the principle of agglomeration, called the division principle, which states that if one has a duty to do both a and b, then one has a duty to do a and has a duty to do b.

". . . that 'I ought to do a' and 'I ought to do b' together imply 'I ought to do a and b' (which I shall call the *agglomeration principle*) . . ." **B. Williams,** *Problems of the Self*

agnosticism

PHILOSOPHY OF RELIGION [from Greek *a*, not + *gnostikos*, one who knows] A term used by T. H. Huxley for a position that neither believes that **God** exists nor believes that God does not exist and denies that we can have any knowledge about the nature of God. Agnosticism is contrasted both to **theism**, which holds that we can know the existence and nature of God, and to **atheism**, which denies the existence of God. Many agnostics argue that human reason has inherent and insuperable limitations, as shown by **Hume** and **Kant**. Therefore, we cannot justify any claims supporting either theism or atheism and should suspend our judgment over these issues. The attitude of agnosticism has persisted in many periods, but it became important philosophically in nineteenth-century debates concerning science and religious belief. Agnosticism is also used more generally for the suspension of judgment about the truth or falsity of claims going beyond what we directly sense or commonly experience.

"Agnosticism: this is the theory that we have no means of telling what are the characteristics of those relatively permanent things and processes which manifest themselves partially to us by the interrelated sensa which we from time to time sense." **Broad,** *The Mind and its Place in Nature*

agreeable

AESTHETICS [German, *das Angenehme*] For **Kant**, what the senses find pleasurable in sensation, that is, the feeling of **pleasure** evoked by the presence of a sensible object. Whatever is liked is agreeable. This feeling gratifies desire and offers a pathologically conditioned delight, not only for man, but also for non-rational animals. In contrast, the good evokes delight by pure rational determination. Kant believed that the nature of this delight is both agreeable and good. Judgment about the agreeable implies no universality, but universal agreement is required where the judgment is transferred to the morally good.

> "Agreeable is what the senses like in sensation."
> **Kant,** *Critique of Judgement*

AI, abbreviation of artificial intelligence

Ajdukiewicz, Kazimierz (1890–1963)

Polish analytical philosopher, born in Tarnopoi. Ajdukiewicz continued the development of twentieth-century Polish logic initiated by Twardowski and Lukasiewicz. He combined work on semantic categories, syntax, and meaning with a conventionalism in ontology and a pluralist epistemology. His conception of categorical grammar brought together his interests in logic and ontology. His major works include *Problems and Theories of Philosophy* (1949) and *Language and Knowledge*, 2 vols. (1960–5).

Albert the Great (c.1206–80)

Medieval Dominican Aristotelian, born in Germany. Albert the Great taught in Cologne and Paris. Under the influence of Neoplatonism, he attempted to reconcile Greek and Islamic philosophy and science with Christianity, a project that led to the great medieval synthesis of his student Aquinas. Albert's major works, including commentaries on Aristotle and *Summa Theologiae*, appear in his *Opera Omnia*.

Albo, Joseph (c.1380–1444)

Jewish philosopher, born in Spain. Albo used Jewish, Islamic, and Christian sources to provide a rational justification for Judaism. In his major work *The Book of Principle* (1425), he examined religious and philosophical discussions of the existence of God, providence, and the Torah as revelation, and developed a doctrine of natural, conventional, and divine law as a basis for political and social life.

d'Alembert, Jean Le Rond (1717–83)

French Enlightenment mathematician and philosopher, born in Paris, member of the Académie des Sciences, co-editor of the *Encyclopédie* (with Diderot). In his *Discourse préliminaire* to the great Enlightenment project of the *Encyclopédie* (1751–65), d'Alembert showed the influence of Bacon, Locke, and Newton as well as Descartes in laying down the methods of establishing human knowledge within a single rational framework of principles. He argued that these principles could be known through scientific investigation rather than through metaphysical argument.

algorithm

EPISTEMOLOGY, LOGIC [from the name of the Islamic mathematician al-Khuwarizmi (*c*.830)] A step-by-step procedure for reaching a sound result. The steps are finite in number, and each has instructions for its proper implementation, so that the whole procedure can be carried out in a mechanical fashion. An algorithm can be a calculative procedure to compute the value of a **function** for any **argument** within a domain. It can also be a decision procedure to determine whether a specific object has a particular property. The **truth table** test of the truth-value of a formula is one paradigm of an algorithm. It is important to know whether an algorithm is possible for a given kind of problem.

> "An algorithm is a procedure, brutish or not, that guarantees solution." **Boden,** *Artificial Intelligence and Natural Man*

alienation

PHILOSOPHY OF RELIGION, POLITICAL PHILOSOPHY, ETHICS, MODERN EUROPEAN PHILOSOPHY [German, *Entfremdung*, from *fremd*, alien or *Entäusserung*, from *entäussern*, to make outer or external, which is associated with Latin, *alius*, another. Also translated as estrangement] A state in which a thing is separated, through its own act, from something else that used to belong to it, so that this other thing becomes self-sufficient and turns against its original owner.

The idea of alienation may be traced to the Christian doctrine of **original sin** and to **Rousseau**'s theory of the **social contract**, in which individuals in a state of nature relinquish their natural freedom in favor of civil freedom upon entering a social state. It is explicated by **Hegel**, **Feuerbach**, and **Marx**.

For Hegel, the development of the absolute idea is a process of alienating or eternalizing ideas in the natural world and then de-alienating or recovering them at a higher stage. Each category develops into its contrary, which is originally contained in it. It thus enters a state of alienation, followed by reconciliation into a higher unity. This unity itself proceeds to further alienation. Nature is an alienation of the absolute idea. Each individual will be alien to social substance and also to his particular self although he is identified with the universal substance. The process of alienation and de-alienation corresponds to the process of the growth of human knowledge. Feuerbach held that God is nothing but the alienated human self. Marx claimed that alienation is a universal phenomenon of capitalist societies, rooted in the alienation of workers from the products of their labor. In capitalism these products take the form of commodities, money, and capital. For Marx, alienation can only be overcome by replacing capitalism by communism. The concept of alienation gained wide currency in the twentieth century, largely due to the influence of Marx's *Economical and Political Manuscripts*, which was written in 1844 and published in 1932. Neo-Marxists, especially **Lukács**, used the notion to provide a new interpretation of Marxism. **Existentialism** and the **Frankfurt school** take alienation to be a basic malaise of modern society and some Marxist theorists have looked for theoretical grounds to explain alienation in socialist societies. Alienation is discussed not only in philosophy, but also in other social sciences and daily life, to deal with disunities, bifurcations, or dichotomies affecting human well-being.

Alienation has various forms, but the self-alienation of human beings has attracted particular attention. Self-alienation refers to the separation of individuals from their real self, their nature, and their consciousness. It is a state in which a person loses individual integrity and independence and becomes a stranger to oneself.

"This 'otherness', this acting of a role imposed upon one, imposed perhaps by the unintended consequences of the behaviour of one's self or one's fellows in the past, which comes to threaten and coerce one as if it were a real entity menacing one from outside – this is the phenomenon of alienation, to which Rousseau and Hegel, Kierkegaard and Marx, and much modern psychology and sociology have given a central role." **Berlin, *The Magus of the North***

alternation

LOGIC A complex statement in the form "p or q," also called **disjunction** in contrast to conjunction. The logical word "or" in such a statement admits of both exclusive or non-exclusive interpretations in ordinary language. When it is used in an exclusive sense, "p or q" is true if only one of its components is true. It means either p or q, but not both. In a non-exclusive sense, "p or q" is true if at least one of its components is true. It means either p or q, or both. While alternation can include both senses of "or," some logicians prefer to confine alternation to the exclusive sense of "or," and others prefer to confine it to the non-exclusive sense.

"Whereas a conjunction is true if and only if its components are all true, an alternation is false if and only if its components are all false." **Quine, *Methods of Logic***

Althusser, Louis (1918–90)

Algerian-French structural Marxist, born in Birmendreis, Algeria. Under the influence of Lévi-Strauss's structuralism and Bachelard's notion of an epistemological break, Althusser stressed the importance of Marx's mature views and rejected Marx's earlier humanistic writings as ideological rather than scientific. He sought to understand historical processes in structural terms without theoretical recourse to the human subjects filling the roles determined by structures. He nevertheless saw the base and superstructure of Marx's social theory as mutually influential, with changes in the overdetermined superstructure capable of initiating revolution. His major writings include *For Marx* (1965) and *Reading Capital* (with Étienne Balibar, Pierre Macherey, and others) (1965).

altruism

ETHICS, POLITICAL PHILOSOPHY [from Latin *alter*, other or another] A term introduced into ethics by Auguste **Comte** and imported into England by Herbert **Spencer**. Altruism is the disinterested or benevolent concern for other people, that is, a regard to promote the welfare of others for their own sake rather than to promote one's own interest or a placing of the interests of others ahead of those of oneself. It opposes **egoism**, which tries to reduce morality to self-interest. Altruism has been a perennial problem for ethics. Greek ethics believed that it is one among many equally important values, but the mainstream of modern moral theory claims that it is the most important concern of ethics. On the other hand, some anti-traditionalist philosophers like **Nietzsche** and **Kierkegaard** condemn altruism on the grounds that it will lead to low self-esteem and self-negation.

The strength of altruism lies in the facts that altruistic acts undeniably occur in any society and that moral codes universally advocate altruism or benevolence and condemn selfishness. The issues surrounding altruism include the following. Given the self-preserving tendency of human nature, how are we to account for the existence of altruism? Even if we can understand how altruism occurs, is it morally justified? Are altruistic acts merely apparent and really motivated by self-interest? Since one should reasonably pursue one's own interests, does the good of others itself provide reason for an agent to promote that good? Given the difficulty in understanding another person, how can altruism really serve the good of others? Is there an adequate distinction between altruism and paternalism?

> "'Altruism' means, not 'doing good to others for a duty's sake', but 'doing good to others for its own sake' or 'doing good to others for the sake of doing good to others'." **Nowell-Smith,** *Ethics*

ambiguity

PHILOSOPHY OF LANGUAGE To say that a word or expression is ambiguous means that different **senses** or **references** are associated with the word or expression, and that it is not clear from the given context which of these senses is meant. This is called lexical or semantic ambiguity. To say a sentence or statement is ambiguous means that the sentence is confusing in its whole meaning, although each word in it is clear, because of the grammatical structure among the words. This is ambiguity of construction which is also called structural or syntactic ambiguity or amphiboly. The grammatical relations that most often produce syntactic ambiguity include misplaced modifiers, loosely applied adverbs, elliptical constructions and omitted punctuation. Other major types

of ambiguity include process–product ambiguity arising from the confusion between a process (behavior or movement) and a corresponding product; act–object ambiguity, in which a statement can refer to either an act or an object and it is not clear which is intended in the given context; and type–token ambiguity, in which an expression can refer to either a type or a token and it is not clear which is intended in the given context. The ideal language philosophers such as **Frege** and **Carnap** claim that natural language is full of ambiguities, and hence that it must be replaced by a **logically perfect language** that is free of ambiguity. In literature, ambiguity is a prized feature rather than something to be eliminated.

> "Semanticists and philosophers usually call a word 'ambiguous' only when there is some uncertainty about which meaning is being used in a particular instance. A word is not ambiguous by itself, it is used ambiguously." **Hospers,** *An Introduction to Philosophical Analysis*

ambiguous middle, fallacy of, another term for four-term fallacy

âme collective, see group mind

amoralism

ETHICS In Greek, *a* is a negative prefix, and "amoral" literally means not moral. Amorality is distinguished from immorality (evil, wrong), where "amoral" is synonymous with "non-moral," referring to actions that are morally value-free and that are neither moral nor immoral and neither right nor wrong. In another sense, the amoral is distinguished from both the immoral and the non-moral, referring to actions that are not the concern of standard moral or social concepts of good or bad. Generally "amoralism" is used in this latter sense for an attitude that ignores or rejects the ways in which morality governs human lives and is skeptical of the necessity of ethical life. Hence it becomes a task of ethics to justify morality by showing that ethical life is rational.

> "[W]hen an amoralist calls ethical considerations into doubt, and suggests that there is no reason to follow the requirements of morality, what can we say to him?" **B. Williams,** *Ethics and the Limits of Philosophy*

amour de soi

ETHICS, PHILOSOPHY OF ACTION, POLITICAL PHILOSOPHY [French, self-love or love of self] Rousseau's term for the instinctive sentiment or disposition of self-preservation which human beings have in the state of nature. It is born to humans, but also belongs to other animal creatures. *Amour-propre* and the natural feeling of pity are two supreme principles governing human behavior prior to the formation of society. Acts out of *amour de soi* tend to be for individual well-being. They are naturally good and not malicious because *amour de soi* as self-love does not involve pursuing one's self-interest at the expense of others. The sentiment does not compare oneself with others, but is concerned solely with oneself as an absolute and valuable existence. It is related to an awareness of one's future and can restrain present impulse. For Rousseau, *amour de soi* contrasts with *amour-propre*, a self-love that presupposes a comparison between oneself and others and consequently generates all the vicious and competitive passions.

"Amour de soi-même is a natural feeling which leads every animal to look to its own preservation, and which, guided in man by reason and modified by compassion, creates humanity and virtue." **Rousseau,** *Discourse*

amour-propre

ETHICS, PHILOSOPHY OF ACTION, POLITICAL PHILOSOPHY [French, literally self-love, although self-aggrandizement might be better] A term introduced by **Rousseau** in contrast to *amour de soi* [French, self-love]. *Amour de soi* is an instinctive disposition of self-preservation that is possessed by human beings in the state of nature and that contains no desire to surpass others. *Amour-propre* is generated after the formation of society or association and leads one to pursue superiority over others, even at the expense of the interests of others. For *amour-propre*, the well-being of the self relies on one's standing relative to other selves and on comparisons between oneself and others. It impels one to seek power and dominance, giving rise to relentless competition and conflict. It engenders deception, aggression, hypocrisy, malice, and all other evils that appear in human relationships. The immorality of *amour-propre* leads to the corruption of society. To avoid this,

according to Rousseau, one should withdraw from society and return to nature.

"Amour-propre is only a relative and factitious sentiment which is born in society, which leads each individual to make more of himself than of every other, which inspires in men all the evils they perpetrate on each other, and is the real source of the sense of honour." **Rousseau, in Ritter and Bondanella (eds.),** *Rousseau's Political Writings*

amphiboly

PHILOSOPHY OF LANGUAGE, LOGIC A kind of sentential ambiguity arising from the different combinations of the words in a sentence. For instance, the sentence "The brave son's mother is kind" can be understood either as saying that the son is brave or that the son's mother is brave. Hence this sentence is amphibolous. Amphiboly is also called syntactical or structural ambiguity. Under many circumstances an amphibolous sentence is true on one interpretation and false on another. If in one argument, a person uses the correct interpretation of the sentence as a premise, but infers using the false interpretation, he is committing the **fallacy of ambiguity**.

"A statement is amphibolous when its meaning is indeterminate because of the loose or awkward way in which its words are combined." **Copi,** *Introduction to Logic*

ampliative induction

LOGIC, PHILOSOPHY OF SCIENCE [from Latin *ampliatio*, broadening] A term introduced by Kneale for reasoning that proceeds from the observed to the unobserved or from the particular to the universal. Since its conclusion goes beyond what is contained in the premises, it is ampliative. Kneale claims that this is the method characteristic of natural sciences in establishing general propositions and that it is distinguished from summative **induction**, which characterizes work in social sciences; intuitive induction; and recursive induction, which operates in mathematics.

"One of the most striking characteristics of the induction used in natural sciences is that it goes in some sense beyond its premises, which are the singular facts of experience; I propose, therefore, to call it ampliative induction." **Kneale,** *Probability and Induction*

ampliative judgment, see ampliative reasoning

ampliative reasoning

LOGIC [from Latin *ampliatio*, broadening; in contrast to *restrictio*, narrowing] In medieval logic, the broadening of a term's extension. For **Peirce**, ampliation is ampliative reasoning in which the conclusion goes beyond what is contained in the premises. For example, we infer from "some x are y" to "all x are y." Ampliative induction, in contrast to other forms of induction, reasons in this way. In contrast, the conclusion of deductive reasoning is generally thought to be already contained in the premises. For **Kant**, a synthetic judgment is an ampliative judgment, because its predicate adds something new to its subject, in contrast to analytic or clarificatory judgments, in which the predicate can be derived through analysis of the subject term.

> "In ampliative reasoning the ratio may be wrong, because the inference is based on but a limited number of instances; but on enlarging the same the ratio will be changed till it becomes approximately correct." **Peirce,** *Collected Papers,* **vol. II**

analogies of experience

EPISTEMOLOGY, METAPHYSICS Kant introduced four groups of **categories**, with each group having principles or rules to show its objective validity in employment. Analogies of experience are these rules for the categories of relation, that is, the categories of substance, causality, and interaction. The analogies correspond to three temporal modes, namely duration, succession, and coexistence. The first analogy is the principle of the permanence of substance; the second is the principle of the fixed order of succeeding states; and the third is the law of reciprocity or community. Kant held that these principles are necessary conditions for the possibility of temporal experience. They enable our perceptions of objects in time to relate necessarily to one another, and hence make experience possible. The analogies of experience are merely regulative, not constitutive, principles, and they do not tell us whether there is an objective substance, causal relation, or interaction.

> "An analogy of experience is, therefore, only a rule according to which a unity of experience may arise from perception." **Kant,** *Critique of Pure Reason*

analogy

PHILOSOPHY OF LANGUAGE, EPISTEMOLOGY, PHILOSOPHY OF RELIGION [From Greek, *ana*, up, throughout + *logos*, reason] Originally meaning a mathematical proportion between different things, the term has been extended to refer to similarities and likenesses between different things. An expression has an analogical sense when it extends its application to additional things that are similar in certain respects to the original things covered by the term. An analogical argument states that because a thing a is like another thing b in some respect, it is possible that a is like b in other respects as well. Typical examples include the argument from design and certain responses to the other minds problem. In religion it is often held that a transcendent God can only be described analogically by human language. Analogical argument is metaphorical and correlative. It is suggestive but not conclusive.

> "Analogy is the inference that a not very large collection of objects which agree in various respects may very likely agree in another respect." **Peirce,** *Collected Papers,* **vol. I**

analysandum, see analysis

analysans, see analysis

analysis

PHILOSOPHICAL METHOD [from Greek *ana*, up + *lyein*, loose, untie] The mental process of dissolving a whole into its components and the relations between its components. The analysis into constituents is called material analysis, while the analysis of the manner of combination of the constituents is called formal analysis. The item to be analyzed is called the *analysandum*, and the item that does the analysis is called the *analysans*.

In this century, analysis has become the central method of Anglo-American analytical philosophy shaped by the development of modern logic. Its central characteristic is that we must investigate our language to make clear our thinking about the world. We approach the world through thought, and on this view the only way to approach the structure of our thought is to study what we say. Analysis is not a set of unified doctrines, but a style or manner of philosophy. Because different philosophers have different notions of analysis, there are different schools in analytical philosophy itself. For **Frege**, **Moore**, **Russell**, and early **Wittgenstein**, analysis aimed to overcome traditional philosophical problems through replacing the apparent structure of statements by their real and underlying logical structure. For them, as for **logical positivism**, analysis involves a reduction of complex discourse to simple elementary propositions. This sort of analysis is also called logical analysis. For later Wittgenstein and Oxford ordinary language philosophers, the notion of an underlying logical structure of language is unnecessary, but we still need to analyze our ways of talking to establish an understanding of our conceptual scheme. This sort of analysis is also called linguistic analysis.

> "Analysis may be defined as the discovery of the constituents and the manner of combination of a given complex." **Russell, *Collected Papers of Bertrand Russell*, vol. VII**

analysis, paradox of

LOGIC, PHILOSOPHY OF LANGUAGE A **paradox**, originally formulated by C. H. Langford in his discussion of **Moore**'s notion of **analysis**, leads to the conclusion that all analysis is either trivial or false. An analysis states relations between an *analysandum* (the expression to be analyzed) and an *analysans* (the analyzing expression). These expressions are either synonymous or not synonymous. If they are synonymous, the analysis does not convey any information and is trivial. If they are not synonymous, the analysis is false. Therefore, analysis is either trivial or false and is not a significant philosophical or logical procedure. This paradox involves an analysis of the notion of analysis. The standard response to it involves the use of **Frege**'s distinction between **sense** and **reference**. The truth of the analysis is a matter of the different expressions having the same reference, but triviality is avoided if the expressions have difference senses.

> "And the paradox of analysis is to the effect that, if the verbal expression representing the analysandum has the same meaning as the verbal expression representing the analysans, the analysis states a bare identity and is trivial; but if the two verbal expressions do not have the same meaning, the analysis is incorrect." **Langford, in Schilpp (ed.), *Philosophy of G. E. Moore***

analytic (Kant)

LOGIC, EPISTEMOLOGY, METAPHYSICS Analytic is a term **Aristotle** used for his syllogism and for the discussion of the conditions of demonstrative knowledge presented in his *Prior Analytics* and *Posterior Analytics*. In contrast, Aristotle presented what he called **dialectic** in the *Topics*, another part of his *Organon*. Since the sixteenth century, it has been common practice to divide logic into two parts: analytic, which concerns the elements of judgment, and dialectic, which concerns the persuasive force of syllogism, and this practice influenced German philosophy. In *Critique of Pure Reason*, **Kant** adopted this usage and divided his transcendental logic into the transcendental analytic and the transcendental dialectic. Analytic, in his understanding, is an analysis of the form of **understanding** and of **reason**. It seeks to determine the necessary rules of all formal truth and is a canon for deciding on the formal connectives of our knowledge. Kant practiced such an analytic in all of his three *Critiques*. In the first *Critique*, the transcendental analytic, including an analytic of concepts and an analytic of principles, seeks to uncover the concepts and principles of theoretical reason. In the second and third *Critique*, Kant used analytic to discover the principles of pure practical reason and of the power of aesthetic judgment.

> "The analytic brings to light, by sundering them, all acts of reason that we exercise in thinking." **Kant, *Logic***

analytic ethics

ETHICS A term for any analysis of moral concepts, but as a distinct approach it starts with G. E. **Moore**'s *Principia Ethica* (1913). It claims that the fundamental task of ethics is not to discuss substantive moral questions and to seek solutions for them, but rather to examine the meaning of moral terms such as "**good**," "**duty**," "**right**," "**ought**" and to make them as clear and precise as possible. It then evolved into the linguistic analysis of **moral judgments**, their types and their functions. This development was represented by **Ayer**'s account of morality, **Stevenson**'s **emotivism**, and **Hare**'s **prescriptivism**. Another dimension of analytic ethics is to examine **moral reasoning** and the basis for distinguishing **moral judgments** from other value judgments. This is represented especially in the work of Stephen

Toulmin. Analytic ethics can be viewed as synonymous with **meta-ethics**. In the 1960s, as the distinction between meta-ethics and normative ethics came into question, analytic ethics as a distinctive approach also lost favor. Many moral philosophers now believe that ethics should investigate both moral terms and moral questions. Nevertheless, analytic ethics, through its sharply defined analysis of moral terms, has had a lasting influence on ethics through raising the precision and theoretical level of ethical discussion.

"Analytic ethics as a branch of philosophy should, then, be clearly distinguished from empirical ethics, from a genetic or descriptive study of moral valuations, and from propagandistic morals." **Pap,** *Elements of Analytic Philosophy*

analytic Marxism

PHILOSOPHY OF SOCIAL SCIENCE, POLITICAL PHILOSOPHY A term not for a body of doctrine, but for a tendency or style developed during the past decade that attempts to bring Marxism into the web of contemporary political theory in order to benefit from rigorous critical standards and further development. It characteristically employs the conceptual tools and methods of **analytical philosophy**, **game theory**, and **decision theory** in its discussion of Marxism. Analytic Marxism is inspired by Marxist questions such as alienation, exploitation, class, social theory, theory of justice, theory of history, and Marx's theory of surplus value. Unlike conventional Marxism or Western Marxism, analytic Marxism does not stress Marxist exegesis, but it does seriously consider Marx's ideas as philosophy and discusses them with clarity and rigor. It is mainly directed to the underlying principles of Marxist theory and examines questions such as: "Is socialism in the interest of workers in modern capitalism?" "Why is exploitation wrong?" In general, it rejects Marx's methodological collectivism in favor of methodological individualism, which seeks to explain social arrangements and life by appeal to the rational behavior of differently endowed individuals. The major representatives of analytic Marxism include G. A. **Cohen**, Jon **Elster**, John Roemer, and Alan Wood. The tendency is also called neoclassical Marxism, rational choice Marxism and game theory Marxism. Analytic Marxists might in principle reject many of the main features of the traditional theory of Marxism, but proponents argue

that this pattern of development through rational criticism is characteristic of science in general.

"The project of Analytic Marxism is to clarify, criticise and develop the theory of Marxism, using the methods and techniques of analytical philosophy." **Sayers, in Ware and Nielsen (eds.),** *Analysing Marxism*

analytic philosophy

PHILOSOPHICAL METHOD Also analytical philosophy, analytic philosophy arose from **Russell** and **Moore**'s criticism of **Bradley**'s absolute idealism at the beginning of the twentieth century and developed out of the combination of **Frege**'s logic and the British empirical tradition. The philosophers of the first generation of analysis held on to the distinction between fact and value and between analytic and synthetic propositions. They rejected traditional metaphysics and normative ethics as the products of confusions generated by the surface grammar of language, and concentrated on the reductive logical analysis of the deep structure of language. Philosophy was understood as nothing but conceptual analysis. The early **Wittgenstein**, who did not share Russell's **empiricism**, held that such analysis also revealed the structure of the world. For **logical positivists**, analysis was focused on the **logical forms** of scientific discourse and much traditional philosophical discourse was rejected as **nonsense**.

After the Second World War, the main object of logical analysis became **ordinary language**, the view being that philosophy should concern itself with language *per se* rather than with its alleged essence. This tendency was influenced by the later Wittgenstein, but was mainly developed in Oxford through the work of such figures as **Ryle**, **Austin**, and **Strawson**. Ryle's behavioristic analysis of mind set the agenda for the philosophy of mind. Austin's speech act theory made the philosophy of language and the philosophy of mind interrelated disciplines. Strawson's notion of descriptive metaphysics restored the position of metaphysics in analytic philosophy. From the middle of the 1940s to the 1960s, analytic philosophy was regarded by many as synonymous with Oxford philosophy or **linguistic philosophy**, though this is not precisely correct. Ayer, for example, was critical of the emphasis on ordinary language, especially in Austin's work. In the United States, **Quine** rejected the distinction between analytic and synthetic propositions that was essential to early analytic philosophy and saw philosophy as a continuing enterprise of science. This has changed the landscape of analytic philosophy.

As a movement, analytic philosophy carries with itself a large variety of methods and doctrines. What unifies this movement is the spirit of the respect for rationality, the suspicion of dogmatic assumptions, and the pursuit of argumentative rigor and clarity on the model of the natural sciences. On these grounds, many recent innovations in philosophy, such as functionalism, the causal theory of reference, various theories of meaning and truth, the post-positivist philosophy of science, **Rawls**'s theory of justice and virtue ethics, can be seen as developments within analytic philosophy.

Analytic philosophy is often contrasted with continental philosophy, but this distinction should not be understood to be a geographical one. Although analytic philosophy is the dominant tendency in English-speaking countries, it is also practiced in many European countries, and was also contributed to greatly by continental philosophers such as **Brentano**, Frege, and the members of the **Vienna Circle**. The single most influential analytic philosopher, Wittgenstein, was from Austria.

"The basic tenet of analytical philosophy, common to such disparate philosophers as Schlick, early and later Wittgenstein, Carnap, Ryle, Ayer, Austin, Quine and Davidson, may be expressed as being that the philosophy of thought is to be equated with the philosophy of language." **Dummett**, *The Interpretation of Frege's Philosophy*

analytic philosophy of history, see philosophy of history

analytic-synthetic

LOGIC, PHILOSOPHY OF LANGUAGE This dichotomy is first explicated by **Kant**. In an analytic **judgment** the concept of the **predicate** is contained in the concept of the **subject**, and we can tell that the **proposition** is true by analyzing the relevant subject concept. An analytic judgment is **tautologous**, and its negation involves self-contradiction. In a **synthetic** judgment, the concept of the predicate adds something new to the concept of the subject, and the truth or falsity of the proposition cannot be

determined by analysis. Such a judgment provides a synthesis of two concepts and tells us something about the world. Kant connects this dichotomy with the distinction between the *a priori* and the *a posteriori*. He claims that all analytic judgments are *a priori*, and he is concerned with how **synthetic *a priori* judgment** is possible.

The adequacy of Kant's account of this distinction has been a topic of much dispute, in particular because it is unclear what it means to say that a predicate is "contained" or "included" in the subject and because the distinction thus formulated can only be applied to the sentential structure "S is P." Various other accounts have been developed this century. Many of them concentrate on the idea that a negation of an analytic proposition is self-contradictory, and that an analytic proposition cannot be false. Others suggest that a proposition P is analytic iff P is true by virtue of the meaning of the constituents of P, or that P is analytic iff it is true in all possible worlds, or that P is analytic iff P can be proved by logic and definition alone, or that P is analytic in a Language L iff P is true in virtue of the semantic rules of L.

Quine famously criticizes this distinction as a dogma of empiricism. He argues that the explication of the notion of analyticity is unsatisfactory since it appeals to the equally unclear notions of "necessity," "semantic rules," "synonym," etc. The explanation of these later notions either involves circularity or Platonic realism. He does not believe that this distinction, which plays such a great role in the development of modern philosophy, is sound. But P. F. **Strawson** and others argue that it is valid since the use we make of semantic meanings is indispensable.

"In all judgements in which the relation of a subject to the predicate is thought . . . , this relation is possible in two different ways. Either the predicate B belongs to the subject A as something which is (covertly) contained in this concept A; or B lies outside the concept A, although it does indeed stand in connection with it. In the one case I entitle the judgement analytic, in the other synthetic." **Kant**, *Critique of Pure Reason*

analytical behaviorism

PHILOSOPHY OF MIND A type of behaviorism, proposed by **Hempel** and others, in which all sentences containing sensation terms or psychological terms can be translated or reformulated into sentences containing only physicalistic terms. Hence, psychological terms do not refer to mental objects, events, or states. This theory extensively employs meaning analysis and contextual definition, and its goal is to deny the existence of mental substance. The major problem it faces is its difficulty in analyzing some psychological sentences in behavioral terms.

"Analytical behaviourism is the theory that all sentences using psychological or mentalistic terms are transformable by analysis of what they mean into sentences using no psychological terms, but containing only terms used to describe bodily behaviour and bodily dispositions to behave." **Cornman, *Materialism and Sensations***

analytical definition

LOGIC, PHILOSOPHY OF LANGUAGE A definition of a word that can be derived purely by explaining the property ascribed to the word in linguistic usage. For example, an analytical definition of "uncle" is "a man who has the same parents as a parent of another person," because this *definiens* gives the property that English ascribes to the word "uncle." Such a definition is necessarily true. To reject an analytical definition involves a violation of a rule of meaning for the language.

"Analytic definitions of concepts can give rise to analytic statements." **Arthur Pap, "Theory of Definition,"** *An Introduction to the Philosophy of Science,* **vol. I**

analytical jurisprudence

PHILOSOPHY OF LAW John **Austin** first brought out the distinction between analytical jurisprudence and **normative jurisprudence**. Analytical jurisprudence is the branch of legal theory or philosophy that is concerned with the linguistic and logical elucidation of legal concepts. It deals with the articulation and analysis of concepts, rules, and structures of law as it is. **Normative jurisprudence**, on the other hand, is concerned with the evaluative criticism of legal practices and with the prescription of what law ought to be. Analytical jurisprudence does not aim at ascertaining the meaning of a term in a particular text. It intends to reveal the conceptual framework that is common to all properly constituted legal systems and thus to achieve an improved understanding of legal ideas and legal rules. After John

Austin, the approach was further developed in this century by the American jurist W. N. Hohfeld and by the Oxford legal philosopher H. L. A. **Hart** in association with the development of linguistic philosophy.

"Analytic jurisprudence is concerned with the logical analysis of the basic concepts that arise in law, e.g. duty, responsibility, excuse, negligence, and the concept of law itself." **Murphy and Coleman,** *The Philosophy of Law*

analytical phenomenalism, see phenomenalism

analytical priority

PHILOSOPHICAL METHOD The priority in the order of philosophical analysis. If X must be appealed to in explaining Y, while the explanation of X itself does not need to involve Y, then X has analytical priority over Y. One of the main characteristics of analytical philosophy is the view that language is analytically prior to thought, and that we should focus on the analysis of language. The philosophy of thought, on the other hand, holds that thought is analytically prior to language. That is, the meaning of a language should be explained in terms of the thought that the language is used to express. Analytical priority is distinguished from ontological priority in which X is prior to Y because Y depends on X for its existence, while X does not exist because of Y. It is also distinguished from epistemological priority in which X is prior to Y because the knowledge of Y presupposes the knowledge of X, but not vice versa.

"To say that the notion of X is analytically prior to the notion of Y is to say that Y can be analysed or elucidated in terms of X, while the analysis or elucidation of X itself does not have to advert to Y." **Davies, in Bunnin and Tsui-James (eds.),** *The Blackwell Companion to Philosophy*

analytical Thomism, see Thomism

anamnesi, Greek term for recollection

anarchism

POLITICAL PHILOSOPHY [from Greek *a*, not + *arche*, ruling, governing, literally the lack of government] In a popular sense, pejoratively understood as a position opposing all existing authority and institutions and associated with lawlessness, chaos, violence, and terrorism.

Proudhon (1809–65) was the first to identify himself as an anarchist. In his sense, anarchism is a theory that advocates that voluntary and contractual social and economic organizations should replace the existing authoritarian and coercive state and state-like institutions. Accordingly, anarchism is a political theory that rejects authoritarianism and demands the establishment of a better society on the basis of free competition, cooperation, and equality. For anarchism, state power is not legitimate and does not have satisfactory justification. Authority involves oppression and domination and entails the promotion of privilege and wealth for a certain minority of the population. It is not helpful in achieving social goals, but produces undesirable consequences. Hence, a society may need certain forms of organization, but should remove all authoritarian and coercive regulations. **Political obligation** to the **state** should vanish. Such a view can be traced to Greek Stoicism and Chinese Taoism. It was fully expressed in modern times in William **Godwin**'s *An Inquiry Concerning Political Justice* (1793). With regard to the means to realize the desired anarchic state, different anarchists have different plans. For example, Proudhon and Max **Stirner** (1806–56) believed that anarchism should be achieved through the peaceful change of the existing coercive institutions, while M. **Bakunin** (1814–76) called for a violent revolution to destroy the current machinery of the state.

Anarchism has met tremendous difficulties, for it cannot find an acceptable means of maintaining social order and rectifying degenerate or evil societies. But in theoretical terms it is a significant source for the critique of authoritarianism. It also poses fundamental questions about the justification of political power and political obligation.

"The forms of anarchism anchored in social and philosophical theories do not deny the value of security and order, but they believe that these are maintainable without a state, without a government, without a monopoly of power." **Gans,** *Philosophical Anarchism and Political Disobedience*

anarchism (scientific)

PHILOSOPHY OF SCIENCE A position concerning the growth of science, associated in particular with Paul

Feyerabend, who denied that there is an overall methodology of science. It is an illusion to believe that there are transcultural norms of rationality of science that guide scientific activities. Hence all attempts to seek universal paradigms of scientific development and its rules are futile. The success of science depends on rhetoric, persuasion, and propaganda, rather than on rational argument. To adhere to a set of theories and to demand consistency and invariable meaning discourages development. We should rather advocate the proliferation of conflicting and competing theories. Science should be an anarchistic enterprise that proceeds according to the maxim "anything goes." Feyerabend also called his position theoretical pluralism and claimed that pluralism is essential for the growth of knowledge.

"Science is an essentially anarchic enterprise: theoretical anarchism is more humanitarian and more likely to encourage progress than its law-and-order alternatives." **Feyerabend,** *Against Method*

anarchy, see anarchism

anatomic property

METAPHYSICS [from Greek *ana*, up + *atomos*, indivisible, not atomic] If a property of something is not peculiar to that thing, but is also possessed by at least one more thing, this property is anatomic. For instance, weighing 70 pounds is an anatomic property, for it is not the case that there is only one thing in the world that weighs 70 pounds. An anatomic property contrasts with an **atomic** or **punctuate property**, which can be instantiated only by one thing, but is the same as a holistic property, which is a property such that if anything has it, then other things have it. The distinction between anatomic and atomic properties is significant for the discussion of meaning **holism**. While traditional British **empiricism**, logical positivism, and **behaviorism** emphasize the relation between a symbol and what is symbolized in the non-linguistic world and hence treat properties atomistically, contemporary semantic holism claims that the meaning of a symbol is determined by its role in a language and is accordingly anatomic.

"A property is anatomic just in case if anything has it, then at least one other thing does." **Fodor and Lepore,** *Holism*

Anaxagoras (500–428 BC)

Pre-Socratic natural philosopher, born in the small Ionian city of Clazomenae, and emigrated to Athens in 480 BC. Anaxagoras claimed that in the beginning the world comprised an original boundless and indeterminate mixture containing all ultimate constituents or seeds. All other things in the cosmos are generated out of this mixture through rotation, and every stuff contains a portion of every other stuff. The theory was a result of his attempt to answer Parmenides' denial of change. Anaxagoras also suggested that the mind (*nous*), as an all-powerful and omniscient agency, ordered the cosmos. This teleological idea excited Plato and Aristotle, although they complained that Anaxagoras failed to develop it.

Anaximander (flourished *c*.550 BC)

Pre-Socratic natural philosopher, born in Miletus, a student of Thales. Anaximander was said to have been the first person to construct a map of the world. He believed that there was one material stuff out of which everything in the cosmos came and into which everything returned in the end. Probably thinking that every ordinary material element could be destroyed by its opposite, he took the single cosmic stuff to be something boundless or indeterminate (*apeiron* in Greek). The *apeiron* is eternal and encompasses all the opposites. He held that the generation and destruction of things follow a principle of cosmic justice.

Anaximenes (flourished *c*.550 BC)

Pre-Socratic Greek philosopher, born in Miletus, a student of Anaximander. Following Thales and Anaximander, Anaximenes believed that there was one underlying principle from which everything comes and to which everything returns. For him, this principle is air. Air is boundless, but not as indeterminate as Anaximander's *apeiron*. It is through the process of condensation and rarefaction that air is transformed into everything else.

Anderson, John (1893–1962)

Scottish-Australian philosopher, born in Scotland, Professor of Philosophy at University of Sydney. Anderson was a crucial figure in establishing a distinctive school of Australian philosophy. He considered philosophy to be concerned with spatio-temporal states of affairs, events, and processes and to be continuous with science. He was an empiricist committed to the real existence of material objects in epistemology and was a naturalist in ethics and aesthetics. Several of his most influential essays are included in *Studies in Empirical Philosophy* (1962).

androcentrism

FEMINIST PHILOSOPHY [from Greek *andro*, the stem of the word man] Androcentrism is a male-centered perspective. According to many feminists, Western culture is androcentric because it is preoccupied with theoretical rather than practical issues and with reason rather than experience. It devalues women's experience and does not take women's concerns seriously. On this view, an androcentric bias is implicit in virtually every aspect of social life. One of the goals of **feminism** is to deconstruct the traditional androcentric philosophical framework. Androcentrism is opposed by gynocentrism [from Greek *gene*, woman], a female-centered perspective.

"The radical feminist position holds that the epistemologists, metaphysicians, ethics, and politics of the dominant forms of science are androcentric."
Harding, *The Science Question in Feminism*

Anglo-American philosophy, another term for analytic philosophy

Angst, German term for anxiety

anguish

MODERN EUROPEAN PHILOSOPHY [French, *angoisse*, also translated as dread] One of the typical **existentialist** attitudes toward the world, similar to **anxiety**. A person is both free to act as he or she chooses and to be conscious of this **freedom**. The feeling of anguish arises when a person is brought face to face with this consciousness or recognition of freedom. If a choice is original and cannot be justified by reasons outside one's own choice, then a person will always enter upon self-questioning concerning the rightness of the choice or the failure to choose and, hence, will experience a sort of uncertainty. Anguish is connected with the absurdity of the world, rather than directed at any particular danger. Most people flee from anguish through **bad faith**, while an **authentic** person is aware, through this feeling, of the gap between what is present and what is possible for him or her, and proceeds to increased creativity in the use of his own potentiality. Some existentialists also call this feeling "ontological guilt," a sense of guilt arising not from the violation of some particular prohibitions, but from the self-awareness of free choice. Both the moral psychology and the **ontology** of this central existentialist notion can be called into question.

> "It is by anguish that man becomes conscious of his freedom, or in other words, anguish is the manner of existence of freedom as consciousness of existing." **Sartre,** *Being and Nothingness*

anima, Latin term for soul

anima mundi, Latin term for world-soul

animal
PHILOSOPHY OF SCIENCE, PHILOSOPHY OF MIND [from Latin *anima*, soul, corresponding to Greek, *psyche*; Aristotle's *Peri Psyche* (On the Soul) is generally translated as *De Anima*] The distinction between living and non-living things lies, according to **Aristotle**, in the fact the former have **souls**, although there is a hierarchy of souls, from vegetative, locomotive, and sensory to rational souls. Only man has a rational soul, and plants have no more than vegetative souls. The Bible says that living things are animated with "the breath of life." Thus, the mark of living things is that they are animated or ensouled. Nowadays we distinguish between plants and animals, with humans considered to be a special kind of animal. **Descartes**, as a consequence of his dualism, described animals as mechanical automata and preferred to call them beasts rather than animals. The normal way to distinguish between human beings and non-human animals appeals to the fact that humans alone are self-conscious and genuine language users.

> "In my opinion the main reason for holding that animals lack thought is the following . . . It has never been observed that any brute animal has attained the perfection of using real speech, that is to say, of indicating by word or sign something relating to thought alone and not to natural impulse." **Descartes,** *The Philosophical Writings*

animal-centered ethics, see animal liberation, environmental ethics

animal liberation
ETHICS The term comes from the title of a book by Peter **Singer** in 1975. The movement to liberate slaves demanded the cessation of prejudice and discrimination against black people on the grounds of skin color. The women's liberation movement demanded the cessation of prejudice and discrimination against women on the grounds of gender. Analogically, the animal liberation movement calls for an end to prejudice and discrimination against animals on the grounds of species. Traditional ethics excludes animals from the ethical community because they lack the full range of human rationality, and animals have been exploited for food, in experiments, and as the victims of hunting. Singer accuses this tradition of speciesism. He argues that animals are capable of suffering and should be included in the community of beings that merit moral consideration. We need a new ethics to deal with human relationships with non-human animals. He claims that abusing and killing animals is not morally justified. Although there is controversy whether animals can have rights and whether these rights would entail that humans should be vegetarians, the animal liberation movement has greatly influenced human attitudes and behavior toward animals. It is widely accepted that we should at least avoid unnecessary animal suffering and avoid killing animals in brutal ways.

> "Animal liberation is human liberation too." **P. Singer,** *Animal Liberation*

animal rights, see rights, animal

animal spirits
PHILOSOPHY OF ACTION A term **Descartes** adopted from **scholasticism** for the principle of movement in automata rather than something spiritual. It was a key term in his theory of animal movement. "Animal" here included both humans and other animals. "Animal spirits" were claimed to be a subtle matter, something in the blood that is distributed through the pineal gland and moves the limbs causing various internal muscular motions. They were likened to "the fire without light in the heart." Animal spirits could be lively or sluggish, coarse or

fine, and it was claimed that due to this fact an animal machine could move itself.

> "The parts of the blood which penetrate as far as the brain serve not only to nourish and sustain its substance, but also and primarily to produce in it a certain very fine wind, or rather a very lively and pure flame, which is called the animal spirits." **Descartes,** *The Philosophical Writings*

animal symbolicum

METAPHYSICS, PHILOSOPHY OF MIND A term used by the German neo-Kantian Ernst **Cassirer**. The tradition since Aristotle has defined a human being as *animal rationale* (a rational animal). However, Cassirer claimed that man's outstanding characteristic is not in his metaphysical or physical nature, but rather in his work. Humanity cannot be known directly, but has to be known through the analysis of the symbolic universe that man has created historically. Thus man should be defined as *animal symbolicum* (a symbol-making or symbolizing animal). On this basis, Cassirer sought to understand human nature by exploring symbolic forms in all aspects of a human being's experience. His work is represented in his three-volume *Philosophie der Symbolischen Formen* (1923–9, translated as *The Philosophy of Symbolic Forms*) and is summarized in his *An Essay on Man*.

> "Hence, instead of defining man as an *animal rationale*, we should define him as an *animal symbolicum*." **Cassirer,** *An Essay on Man*

animism, another term for panpsychism

anomalous monism

PHILOSOPHY OF MIND [from Greek *a*, not + *nomos*, law, order] Donald **Davidson**'s term for his theory about the relationship between the mental and the physical. There is only one fundamental kind of thing, physical objects, upon which all mental events are **supervenient**. Hence this theory is a type of **monism** rather than a dualism. This theory asserts that there are no psychophysical laws that relate mental phenomena to physical ones. It is therefore impossible to reduce all mental phenomena to physical phenomena, or to explain **mental events** fully in terms of the physical structure of the brain. For this reason, Davidson calls this monism anomalous. Davidson contrasts his theory with three possible alternative theories about the mind–body relationship: nomological monism, which affirms the existence of laws correlating the mental and the physical; nomological dualism, which is ontologically dualist and which assumes a conceptual correlation between mind and body; and anomalous dualism, which is ontologically dualist but denies the possibility of mental reduction. Anomalous monism is a combination of ontological monism and conceptual non-reductionism. It considers mental events not as types but as particulars, as individual token events, and therefore replaces the widely accepted type-type identity theory by the token-token identity theory.

> "Anomalous monism resembles materialism in its claim that all events are physical, but rejects the thesis usually considered essential to materialism, that mental phenomena can be given purely physical explanations." **Davidson,** *Essays on Actions and Events*

Anscombe, G(ertrude) E(lizabeth) M(argaret) (1919–2001)

British philosopher, born in Limerick, Ireland, taught in Oxford and Cambridge. Anscombe was a student and friend of Wittgenstein and one of his literary executors. Her translation of *Philosophical Investigations* (1953) and her study *An Introduction to Wittgenstein's Tractatus* (1959) helped to bring Wittgenstein's views to a wider public. She was a major philosopher in her own right. *Intention* (1957), which founded contemporary philosophy of action, was considered by Davidson to be "the most important treatment of action since Aristotle." Her paper "Modern Moral Philosophy" (1958) offered penetrating criticism of modern philosophical ethics and led to the contemporary revival of virtue ethics. Her many important papers were included in the *Collected Philosophical Papers*, 3 vols. (1981). As a committed Catholic, she published numerous influential articles on contemporary moral issues.

Anselm of Canterbury, St (1033–1109)

Medieval Italian philosopher, theologian, and archbishop of Canterbury, born in Aosta, Piedmont. As a founder of scholasticism, Anselm held that reason is essential to understanding faith. He is most famous for devising the ontological argument for the existence of God, which infers from the premise that God is a being than which nothing greater can be conceived to the conclusion that God must exist in reality as well as in thought. Consideration of this and later formulations of the ontological argument have been continued to the present. Anselm's most important works are *Monologion* and *Proslogion*.

anthropological holism

PHILOSOPHY OF LANGUAGE A thesis derived from the later **Wittgenstein**, **Austin**, and others, claiming that there is an internal relation between a symbol and its non-linguistic role in **conventions**, rituals, practices, and performances. Hence, language cannot be narrowly understood as a set of sentences and linguistic philosophers should not concentrate only on establishing phrase-structure trees for sentences. Instead, they should take language as belonging to **forms of life** and explore the relation between linguistic symbols and their cultural and practical background.

"Anthropological holism is distinct from semantic holism only in so far as it concerns the relation between language and its intentional background – that is, the relation between language and the cultural background of beliefs, institutions, practices, conventions, and so forth upon which, according to anthropological holists, language is ontologically dependent." **Fodor and Lepore,** *Holism*

anthropomorphism

PHILOSOPHY OF RELIGION [from Greek *anthropos*, man, human kind + *morphe*, shape, form, figure] The ascription of human forms and qualities to non-human things, in particular **God**. In Homer and Hesiod, gods are described in terms of human characteristics and feelings. This type of religious anthropomorphism was first attacked by the Greek philosopher Xenophanes, who claimed that if horses or oxen had hands and could produce works of art, they too would represent the gods after their own fashion. Others replied to this objection by claiming that we can talk of God in terms of human attributes because man is made in the image of God. Man is the medium through which God manifests or reveals himself. According to this understanding, anthropomorphism, while explaining God in terms of man, ascribes man a theomorphic nature. The Christian doctrine of the incarnation is a typical example of anthropomorphism because God himself becomes

a human being. According to G. H. Lewes (1817–78), anthropomorphism describes animals, plants, and the universe in terms of such attributes as consciousness, feelings, thought, and communication, which are ordinarily thought to belong only to human beings.

"Anthropomorphism, . . . is the attribution to things not human of characteristics that apply only to humans." **Regan,** *The Case for Animal Rights*

anticipation

MODERN EUROPEAN PHILOSOPHY [German *Vorlaufen*, an existential attitude towards one's death and the future] **Heidegger** distinguished anticipation from expectation [German, *Erwarten*]. In the face of death, that is, in confronting that one's existence is limited and finite, expectation seeks a secure and stable relationship with other human beings and the world of the "they," forgetting one's past and passively awaiting the occurrence of death. Anticipation, on the other hand, views death as revealing one's uttermost possibility and seeks the meaning of what lies ahead. In anticipation *Dasein* finds itself moving toward itself as its ownmost potentiality-for-Being. It faces up to one's past. Rather than maintaining or continuing the process already dominant in the past and present, anticipation contains the possibility of drastic changes in one's future life. While the authentic future is called "anticipation," the authentic present is called "moment-of-vision," and the authentic past is called "repetition."

"Anticipation turns out to be the possibility of understanding one's ownmost and uttermost potentiality-for-Being – that is to say, the possibility of authentic existence." **Heidegger,** *Being and Time*

anticipations of perception

EPISTEMOLOGY, METAPHYSICS [German, *Antizipatione*, Kant's translation of Epicurus' Greek, *prolepsis*, a preconception that renders perception possible] For **Kant**, the rules intended to show the objective employment of the categories of quality: reality, negation, and limitation. Kant extended the meaning of anticipations to all knowledge that determines *a priori* the qualitative form of empirical knowledge. The leading principle for these categories is that any given perception will have an intensive magnitude, that is, a degree of reality. The qualities we sense must come in degrees, for example, the acuteness of a pain or the loudness of a noise. According to Kant, it is impossible for us to perceive appearances unless they possess this intensive magnitude. Anticipations of perception are contrasted to axioms of intuition, whose leading principle is that any perception has extensive magnitude. Both anticipations of perception and axioms of intuition are mathematical principles, in contrast to the dynamic principles of the analogies of experience and the postulate of empirical thought. By anticipations of perception, Kant claimed that the mathematics of intensity must apply to our experience. However, he did not specify what these anticipations are, and his discussion linking the principles to the categories remained vague.

"The principle which anticipates all perceptions as such is as follows: In all appearances sensation, and the real which corresponds to it in the object (*realitas phaenomenon*), has an intensive magnitude, that is, a degree." **Kant, *Critique of Pure Reason***

anti-individualism

POLITICAL PHILOSOPHY, PHILOSOPHY OF MIND A term used in contrast to individualism. In social philosophy, it is the claim that the value of **community** is prior to individual **freedom**. In political theory, it is the view that a society should have a common goal and that the individual should be subordinate to this goal. Social coherence and uniformity of view are emphasized, rather than diverse individual voices. Anti-individualism does not accept the value of individual experience and is intolerant of difference. In some versions, the existence of an individual is regarded as being determined by his place in society, and individual existence is considered to be a fiction. This position is reinforced through combination with **social Darwinism**, which suggests that individual experience contributes little to the progress of mankind. Other anti-individualist positions also involve claims limiting the role of individuals in social explanation as well as claims limiting the value of individuals.

In another use, anti-individualism in the philosophy of mind is the view that a person's mental events are fundamentally related to his social and linguistic contexts and hence cannot be individuated solely by appeal to the properties of their owner.

"His [Comte's] 'organic' interpretation of society involves the extremist anti-individualism, derealization of the human individual, worship of Humanity as the only real individual." **Kolakowski, *The Alienation of Reason***

antilogism

LOGIC A term for any situation in which three propositions cannot all be true simultaneously and at least one of them must be false. In a strict sense, it involves syllogistic reasoning whereby the conjunction of two premises implies the negation of the conclusion. Seeking an antilogism was a basic method to test the validity of a syllogism. A syllogism can only be valid when its two premises and the negation of its conclusion are inconsistent. Such an inconsistency is also called an inconsistent triad.

"When limited to three propositions constituting a disjunctive trio, the antilogism may be formulated in terms of illustrative symbols as follows: 'the three propositions p, q, and r cannot be true together.'" **Johnson, *Logic***

antinomianism

PHILOSOPHY OF RELIGION, ETHICS [from Greek *anti*, against + *nomos*, law or rule, hence, against law] A term introduced by **Luther** for the position that rejects the legitimacy of all regulations and laws. The position was embraced by certain early Christian sects, which believed that divine grace enables Christians to determine which conduct is right or wrong. Hence law should be superseded by the gospel. The term is now also used for the extreme relativist position that rejects all moral norms and claims that only sensitivity to a particular given situation can provide it with an ethical solution. The resolution of moral conflicts should depend upon the circumstances. **Existentialist** ethics is sometimes described as a type of antinomianism.

"Antinomianism . . . is the approach with which one enters into the decision-making situation armed with no principles or maxims whatever, to say nothing of rules." **Fletcher, *Situation Ethics***

antinomy

EPISTEMOLOGY [from Greek *anti*, against + *nomos*, law, an extreme form of paradox] A pair of opposed propositions, called a thesis and antithesis, each of which seems to be supported by formally valid argument, but which are inconsistent with one another. Guintilian (AD 35–100) presented antinomies as conflicting arguments side-by-side. **Kant** used this form, which was widely adopted in sixteenth-century jurisprudence, in the **dialectic** of all three *Critiques* to show that reason will inevitably lead to antinomies when it extends beyond the limits of experience in the hope of finding completeness and unity in explanation. Kant's most influential account of antinomies appears in the Transcendental Dialectic of his first *Critique*. He claimed that the rational cosmology of traditional metaphysics inevitably leads to antinomies. These are four sets of dialectical inferences about the nature of the world, corresponding to the four groups of categories. (1) Quantitative antinomy: thesis: the world is finite in space and time; antithesis: the world is infinite. (2) Qualitative antinomy: thesis: everything is made up of simple constituents; antithesis: nothing is made up of simple constituents. (3) Relational antinomy: thesis: everything has a cause, and there is no freedom; antithesis: not all things have a cause, and there is freedom. (4) Modal antinomy: thesis: a necessary being exists that explains the universe; antithesis: no necessary being exists.

In the second *Critique*, Kant presented the practical antinomy: thesis: the desire for happiness must be the motive for maxims of virtue; antithesis: the maxim of virtue must be the efficient cause for happiness. In the third *Critique*, he presented the antinomy of aesthetic judgment: the judgment of taste is not based on concepts; antithesis: the judgment of taste is based on concepts. All of these Kantian antinomies are drawn from opposing positions in the history of philosophy. According to Kant, once we show how these antinomies are generated from malfunctions of reason, they are shown to be illusory and preventable. Logical positivists were indebted to this aspect of Kant's thought.

Hegel claimed that antinomies are not confined to those uncovered by Kant, but appear in each area of thought. This contributed to the development of **Marx**'s materialist account of dialectic, and the notion of antinomy continues to be employed by Western Marxists and others as a tool for criticizing society.

> "The second kind of pseudo-rational inference is directed to the transcendental concept of the absolute totality of the series of conditions for any given . . . The position of reason in these dialectical inferences I shall entitle the antinomy of pure reason." **Kant,** *Critique of Pure Reason*

Antiochus (*c.*130–68 BC)

Hellenistic philosopher, born in Ascalon. He claimed to return to authentic Platonism by reviving the doctrines of the Old Academy, although his thought combined Stoicism with Platonism. He abandoned Academic skepticism and argued that Plato's epistemological stance was consistent with the Stoic doctrine of cognitive certainty. All of his works were lost.

anti-realism

METAPHYSICS, LOGIC, PHILOSOPHY OF LANGUAGE, EPISTEMOLOGY, PHILOSOPHY OF SCIENCE, PHILOSOPHY OF MATHEMATICS, MORAL PHILOSOPHY, AESTHETICS Anti-realism opposes **realism**, but its meaning varies according to how we formulate realism. Various sorts of realism argue for the objective existence of different objects and properties, such as the external world, mathematical objects, universals, moral and aesthetic properties, other minds, scientific laws, or theoretical entities. Correspondingly, anti-realism has many forms involving the denial of the objective existence of these objects and properties. Realism claims that the items under dispute exist independently of our experience, knowledge, and language and that the world is more than we can know. Anti-realism argues that since we know the world only through our mind-related perceptual and conceptual faculties, we cannot sensibly talk about a mind-independent world. The debate between realism and anti-realism takes different forms for different issues. For example, materialists and idealists debate the existence of the external world, and realists and nominalists debate the existence of universals.

An influential kind of anti-realism, particularly associated with M. **Dummett**, C. **Wright**, and J. **McDowell**, is sometimes called semantic anti-realism. According to this view, realism has an arbitrary metaphysical assumption that an objective reality exists independent of our knowledge. The position is characterized by following **intuitionist logic** in denying the principle of bivalence. Truth and falsity are not exhaustive, as they would be according to realism, because truth or falsity are determined by the conditions under which we can correctly assert or deny a sentence. Because there are circumstances in which neither assertion nor denial is justified, bivalence and realism fail. This position is influenced by **Frege** and by later **Wittgenstein**'s use of the theory of meaning and is seen by critics as being closely related to verificationism.

> "The general argument Dummett has given for anti-realism starts from the following thesis: that the content of a sentence is determined by the class of recognizable situations with respect to which it would be acknowledged as true and the class of recognizable situations with respect to which it would be acknowledged as false."
> **Peacocke, *Thoughts: An Essay on Content***

Antisthenes (c.444–c.366 BC)

Greek philosopher, born in Athens, one of the founders of the Cynic school. As a follower of Socrates, Antisthenes claimed that definition was a major goal of philosophy. He emphasized the role of education and self-improvement. Although accepting that pleasure resulting from labor was good, he condemned luxury and advocated a simple life. He argued that virtue is sufficient for happiness. Only a few fragments of his many works survived.

anti-theory

ETHICS A contemporary ethical movement represented by figures such as Annette **Baier**, Bernard **Williams**, John **McDowell**, Martha **Nussbaum**, Charles **Taylor**, Alasdair **MacIntyre**, Richard **Rorty**, and Stuart **Hampshire**. The "theory" that this movement opposes is modern **moral theory**, which takes it as its central task constructing and justifying a set of abstract universal moral rules and principles to guide and evaluate the moral behavior of all rational beings. These principles are completely context-free and can be applied in an almost computational way to any particular case. Correct moral judgments and practices seem to be deducible from these timeless principles, and all moral values are commensurable with respect to a single standard. Any moral conflict can be solved in a rational way. The anti-theory movement claims that moral theory of this sort is unnecessary, narrow, and impossible, for it cannot

specify moral norms embedded in cultural and historical traditions, it cannot account for virtue that is culturally informed and it is incompatible with the fact that there are irresolvable moral conflicts and dilemmas. In contrast, this movement suggests that ethics should return to Aristotelian virtue ethics, claims the primacy of social moral practice over rational principles and the primacy of ethical perception over rules, and emphasizes the plurality of social conventions and customs. It is united in its opposition to modern moral theory, but varies in its positive doctrines. Authors supporting this movement have their own versions of what ethics should be. In many cases, this movement leads to moral contextualism, conservatism, or communitarianism.

> "The expression 'anti-theory' emphasises opposition to any assertion (whether in the form of a substantive moral principle or a meta-ethical theory about the nature of moral claims) that morality is rational only insofar as it can be formulated in, or grounded on, a system of universal principles."
> **S. G. Clarke and E. Simpson (eds.), *Anti-Theory in Ethics and Moral Conservatism***

anxiety

MODERN EUROPEAN PHILOSOPHY [German, *Angst*, also translated as dread or uneasiness] A type of existential experience similar to **Sartre**'s "anguish." The topic was introduced into philosophy by **Kierkegaard** in his *The Concept of Dread* (1844). **Heidegger** distinguished anxiety from fear. Fear arises from a specific threat, and there is some external entity about which to be afraid. Anxiety, on the other hand, is a state of mind arising not from any particular and determinate affliction, but from one's own indefinite existence. Anxiety comes to us from nowhere and in the face of nothing. For Heidegger, it is simply concerned with our "thrownness in the world," that is, with **Being-in-the-world** itself. Anxiety reveals to us how we are in the world and brings us to face the alienated, not-home-like world. The framework in which we make sense of our own existence and of the world is not given once and for all. For each of us, anxiety makes our individuality, our determinate self and our own possibility. In particular, it reveals to us that no individual can escape death with the aid of the public. For Heidegger, anxiety is closely related to *Dasein* (the Being of human beings, which is Being-in-the-world). Thus through individuating *Dasein*, anxiety is a distinctive way in which *Dasein* is disclosed. Anxiety discloses *Dasein* as Being-possible, and in the meantime, as a state of mind it is also a basic kind of Being-in-the-world. The affirmative or passive attitude toward anxiety may lead respectively to authentic or inauthentic existence.

"That in the face of which one has anxiety is Being-in-the-world as such." **Heidegger,** *Being and Time*

apathy

ETHICS [from Greek *a*, not + *patheia*, affection, passion, emotion] A state of indifference to pleasure or pain in which one gains peace of mind or tranquillity by being emotionally unaffected by the external sensible world. In apathy, the control of emotion by reason is justified on the grounds that emotion is irrational, and it therefore stands in contrast to ordinary indifference or insensitivity. For Stoicism, apathy is the highest virtue, with the Stoic sage characterized as being emotionally detached and acting purely out of reason. This ideal is echoed in religions that despise worldly pleasures and in philosophical systems that devalue the role of emotion. Critics claim that at least some emotions are rational, thus undermining the general claim for the value of indifference.

"Apathy is a sort of depression which stops us doing anything, a weariness with work, a torpor of spirit which delays getting down to anything good." **Aquinas,** *Summa Theologiae*

apeiron

METAPHYSICS, PHILOSOPHY OF NATURE, ANCIENT GREEK PHILOSOPHY [Greek, from *a*, not + *peras*, limit or boundary, hence unbounded, infinite] The unbounded was contrasted with *peras* or *kosmos* (world), which was widely believed by the Greeks to be bounded. The Milesian philosopher **Anaximander** took the unbounded to be the first principle or ultimate generative force for all the things and events in the world. The *apeiron* is immortal and imperishable, unbounded both in space and in time, and does not have the characteristics of ordinary elements and their composites. **Aristotle** interpreted the *apeiron* of Anaximander as a material cause, analogous to **Thales'** water or **Anaximenes'** air.

But because *apeiron* appears to be more abstract than other material elements, what Anaximander meant by this term has been a subject of debate. **Pythagoreans** took *apeiron* and *peras* as two principles from which the world evolved and considered *peras* to be good and *apeiron* to be evil. **Parmenides** believed that what is cannot be incomplete and infinite and thus confined his **ontology** to *peras* and denied *apeiron*. For **Anaxagoras**, mind is *apeiron*, which is infinite or indefinite in extent.

"[Anaximander] said that the *apeiron* was the principle and element of things." **Simplicius,** *Physics*

apodeictic

LOGIC [from Greek *apo*, from + *deiktikos*, to be able to show] Also spelled apodictic, that which is demonstrable, necessarily true or absolutely certain. **Aristotle** contrasted the apodeictic (beyond dispute) with the eristic (subject to dispute). **Kant** distinguished the apodeictic (necessary) from the problematic (possible) and the assertoric (actual). All three belong to the modal categories. An apodeictic judgment has the form of "X must be Y" or "X cannot be Y."

"Geometric propositions are one and all apodeictic, that is, are bound up with the consciousness of their necessity." **Kant,** *Critique of Pure Reason*

apodeictic practical principle, another expression for categorical imperative

apodictic, another expression for apodeictic

Apollonian, see Dionysian

apologetics

PHILOSOPHY OF RELIGION [from Greek *apologia*, defence against a charge, answering back; hence **Plato**'s *Apology* describes **Socrates**' defence against accusations in an Athenian court] A dimension of Christian theology aimed at defending orthodox theistic beliefs against external criticism or against other world views. While theology is a rational inquiry by the faithful for the faithful, apologetics is a discourse between the faithful and those outside the faith that seeks to defend the validity of belief with reasons that will be meaningful to those who do not share the same faith. Historically, apologetics has had different forms and has employed different standards of judgment in expounding and defending religious belief according to its intended audience. Each generation has developed an apologetics in response to the criticism of religion of its time. For example, **Augustine**'s *City of God* was written in reply to the pagans; **Aquinas**' *Summa contra Gentiles* is an argumentative work directed at Muslim theology; and **Butler** wrote *The Analogy of Religion* to refute deism. The contemporary apologetic, represented by Paul **Tillich**, is characterized by its appeal to value as against fact. The practice of apologetics has impact upon hermeneutics.

> "The essential task of apologetics is the defence or 'answering back' of religion, and particularly the Christian faith against the doubts or accusations of its 'cultured despisers'." **Ferré**, *Basic Modern Philosophy of Religion*

apophatic theology, another expression for apophaticism

apophaticism

PHILOSOPHY OF RELIGION Also called apophatic theology or negative theology, a doctrine rejecting our capacity to know God. It belongs mainly to **Neoplatonism** and eastern Christian thought. **Clement of Alexandria** is credited with its formulation, and its major exponents include Meister Eckhart and Moses **Maimonides**. Apophaticism claims that God cannot be conceptualized in any way, nor can God be an object of intellect or sense. No language provides us with real knowledge of God, for he is beyond positive human understanding. The soul can come close to God only through faith and prayer.

> "Apophaticism teaches us to see above all a negative meaning in the dogmas of the church; it forbids us to follow natural ways of thought and to form concepts that would usurp the place of spiritual realities." **Lossky**, *The Mystical Theology of the Eastern Church*

aporia

PHILOSOPHICAL METHOD, ANCIENT GREEK PHILOSOPHY [from Greek *a*, not + *poros*, path, passage; literally, no way through, a puzzle or perplexity] In the early Platonic dialogues, **Socrates** raises various problems without offering solutions to them, whilst showing that the people he questions are unable to offer acceptable solutions either. This aporetic method leads to the development of the dialectical method, by which Socrates elicits truth through questioning. The term "aporia" is introduced by **Aristotle** for puzzles concerning incompatibilities that arise either among the views we hold without prompting, or among the reputable beliefs adopted commonly or by the wise. His approach is to seek the minimal adjustments needed to reconcile these conflicting views. According to him, philosophy exists to solve these kinds of aporia. Recently, "aporia" has also been used to refer to a text or an approach that contains contradictory lines of thinking.

> "The aporia of our thinking points to a knot in the object; for in so far as our thought is in aporia, it is in like case with those who are bound; for in either case it is impossible to go forward." **Aristotle**, *Metaphysics*

apparent variable, Russell and Whitehead's term for bound variable

appeal to authority

LOGIC [Latin: *argumentum ad verecundiam*, argument to reverence or respect] A fallacious argument that tries to establish its conclusion by appeal to the opinion of an expert or authority. It is a misuse of authority. For instance, "Something is true because some expert says that it is true." This argument is widely employed in everyday life, but it is logically fallacious because it uncritically accepts anything an expert or a great figure says rather than proving the conclusion by appeal to positive evidence. The view of a trained or legitimate expert nevertheless carries some weight although it is open to challenge. An argument of this form is especially poor if its conclusion goes beyond the field for which the authority has expertise.

> "The appeal to authority typically involves three persons: the arguer, the listener or reader, and the person whom the arguer cites as an authority." **Hurley**, *A Concise Introduction to Logic*

appearance

METAPHYSICS, EPISTEMOLOGY [from Latin *a*, *as*, to, toward + *parere*, come forth, become visible; what

is seen or what is immediately given to consciousness, equivalent to Greek, *phainomenon*, to appear
to be so, but also to be so manifestly. Thus Aristotle
took the opinion of the majority, especially of wise
men, as *phainomenon*] Appearance, what things seem
to be, is often contrasted to reality, what things are
themselves. It is a major distinction in philosophy;
and different philosophers offer different accounts
of the relationship between appearance and reality.
Some philosophers, such as **Plato**, say that appearance is an incomplete and imperfect copy of reality.
Some, such as **Aristotle**, say that reality is in appearance. Some, such as **Descartes**, say that appearance is regrettable and even spurious. Some, such
as **Kant**, say that our knowledge is restricted to
appearance (phenomena), but that for morality
we can make sense of a more fundamental reality
(noumena). And some, such as **Hegel** and **Bradley**,
say that appearance is a partial aspect of reality.
In metaphysics appearance is generally regarded as
less valuable than reality. Contemporary linguistic
philosophers distinguish two groups of appearance
idioms. Seeming idioms, such as "appears to be" or
"gives the appearance," are not strictly related to
senses, while looking idioms, such as "looks" or
"feels," are strictly related to senses.

> "Appearance means that one perceives it so." **Plato,**
> *Theatetus*

appearance (Kant)

METAPHYSICS, EPISTEMOLOGY Traditionally, appearance (*phenomenon*) is contrasted to reality. Appearance is thought to be the object of perception or
belief, while reality is characterized as the object of
knowledge. **Kant** transformed this contrast in his
distinction between appearance (*phenomenon*) and
thing-in-itself (*noumenon*). Appearances are objects
as we experience them with our spatial and temporal
forms of sensibility and our categories of understanding, while things-in-themselves are those objects
as they might be in themselves and known by a
pure intellect. He further claimed that appearance
(German, *Erscheinung*) should be distinguished from
illusion (*Schein*). Illusion is an abnormal perception
of an actually present object and signifies a representation to which nothing real corresponds. In
contrast, appearance is always the appearance of a
given object and is constant and universal. Contrary
to the traditional view, he argued that appearance is
the only object of science and is that to which the
concepts of the understanding apply. In contrast,
the thing-in-itself is beyond knowledge, although
Kant argued that its existence is a necessary condition for an object of one's awareness to count as an
appearance, for appearance itself presupposes that
there is something that appears. He held that if the
objects of experience were not appearances, then
all the problems of reason falling into conflict with
itself would re-emerge. Nevertheless, this claim and
the relation between appearance and thing-in-itself
remain matters of dispute.

> "The undetermined object of an empirical intui-
> tion is entitled appearance." **Kant,** *Critique of Pure
> Reason*

apperception

EPISTEMOLOGY, PHILOSOPHY OF MIND [from Latin
ad, to, towards + *percipere*, perceive] In contrast to
perception, which refers to the external world,
apperception is **introspection**, conscious thought,
or the **consciousness** of **internal states**. It is at the
same time consciousness of, or reflection on the
"I" or the **self**, that is the subject of these states.
In apperception the self is aware of itself as being
a unity and as possessing the power to act. For
Leibniz, all monads have perception, but only a
special kind of monad, which he called "rational
soul," has apperception. According to him, it is by
virtue of this consciousness that we become persons,
or members of a moral world. Leibniz's distinction
implies that there can be unconscious perception.
The concept of apperception played a central role
for **Kant**. Kant distinguished between empirical
apperception (inner sense), which amounts to
introspection, and the transcendental unity of
apperception (I think) that accompanies all of our
representations and combines concepts and intuitions in knowledge.

> "It is well to make the distinction between
> perception, which is the internal state of the monad
> representing external things, and apperception,
> which is consciousness or the reflexive knowledge
> of this internal state itself and which is not given
> to all souls nor at all times to the same soul."
> **Leibniz,** *Principles of Nature and Grace*

application

MODERN EUROPEAN PHILOSOPHY Application in the scientific world applies general knowledge or a universal law to particular instances by subsuming the instances under a general concept and rule. In the humanities, on the other hand, application is not so straightforward, for the distance between general laws (if there are any) and their instances is very great. Application is rather a process of intertwining theory and practice. Traditional **hermeneutics** classifies application as the third fundamental element in the act of understanding, besides "**understanding**" and "**interpretation**." In **Gadamer**'s hermeneutics, application becomes an essential and integral part involved in all interpretative understandings. Aristotle argues that ethical or practical knowledge must be tied to particular circumstances and modified to suit these circumstances. The meaning of an ethical norm can only be shown in a concrete situation of action. Analogically, Gadamer claims that all understanding must be historically situated. A text can only be understood in relation to the present and through modifications in accordance with changed historical circumstances. This is the moment of application in understanding. Understanding is always applied understanding, even when application is not the intended purpose. Understanding that is independent of the particular situation to which it is applied must be abstract and reductive. Since the situations in which applications occur are constantly changing, an historical text must be understood in every situation in a new and different way. According to Gadamer, application therefore involves the distinction between past and present, rather than the distinction between general and particular.

> "We consider application to be as integral a part of the hermeneutical act as are understanding and interpretation." **Gadamer,** *Truth and Method*

applied ethics

ETHICS Also called practical ethics. The study of how to apply ethical principles, rules, and reasons to analyze and deal with moral concerns arising in practical and social areas. Such a practical application of ethical theory has been a dimension of traditional ethics. **Aristotle** claimed that all universal moral standards must be adjusted and modified through their application to particular circumstances. However, applied ethics as a distinctive discipline, in contrast to other aspects of ethics, such as metaethics, normative ethics, and ethical theory, started to flourish in the middle of the twentieth century. Thus far, relatively well-established branches of applied ethics include academic ethics, agricultural ethics, **bioethics**, **business ethics**, **environmental ethics**, legal ethics, **medical ethics**, and nursing ethics. Since the moral principles to be applied are derived from different ethical systems, and are hence various and subject to conflict, applied ethics can seldom provide fixed answers to practical problems. It can, however, contribute to making discussion of these problems as clear and rigorous as possible. The development of applied ethics has also led philosophers to involve themselves in committees dealing with policy making, decision making, and evaluation.

> "While some saw 'applied ethics' as a straightforward task of applying moral principles to particular situations and professions, others were working out complex modes of interrelation." **Edel, Flower, and O'Connor (eds.),** *Morality, Philosophy, and Practice*

apprehension

EPISTEMOLOGY, ANCIENT GREEK PHILOSOPHY [from Greek *katalepsis*, holding or grasping, also translated as cognition, an important epistemological concept for Stoicism and Epicureanism] In Stoicism, recognition has four stages: reception of visual appearance (represented by an open hand); perception or attention, which results from the conjunction of visual appearance and the assent of mind (represented by a closed hand); apprehensive impression, which is accurate perception (represented by a fist); and knowledge (represented by grasping the fist with the other hand). At the third stage, apprehension instantaneously grasps an impression that reveals the real object and results in apprehensive or cognitive impression (Greek, *phantasia kataleptike*). **Epicurus** used apprehension as the criterion of truth by guaranteeing the clarity of an image. Because of ambiguity in the extant writings, some scholars interpret this as a kind of intuition, while others explain it as concentration or attention.

"Zeno did not attach reliability to all impressions but only to those which have a peculiar power of revealing their objects. Since this impression is discerned just by itself, he called it 'apprehensive'; . . . But once it had been received and accepted, he called it an apprehension, resembling things grasped by the hand." **Cicero,** *Academic*

apprehensive impression, see apprehension

appropriate act
ETHICS, ANCIENT GREEK PHILOSOPHY [Greek, *kathekon*, fitting] A key Stoic ethical term for an action that accords with nature and can be rationally justified. An appropriate act is a virtuous act and is the opposite of an inappropriate or vicious act. Other acts, for example walking, are neither inappropriate and vicious nor appropriate and virtuous, but intermediate between these two by being for natural ends that are indifferent as to virtue and vice. An intermediate act, however, can be either virtuous or vicious in some particular instance according to the disposition of the agent. The behavior of a good man is a continuous series of appropriate selections and rejections, and such a man knows that by the performance of appropriate acts he makes virtuous progress.

"Zeno was the first to use this term 'appropriate act', the name being derived from *kata tinas hekein*, 'to have arrived in accordance with certain persons'; appropriate act is an activity appropriate to constitutions that accords with nature." **Diogenes Laertius,** *Lives of Eminent Philosophers*

appropriation
EPISTEMOLOGY, PHILOSOPHY OF MIND William **James**'s technical term for the hanging together or continuity of **experience**. For James, experience is a continuous stream or chain, each link of which is inseparable from its predecessors and successors. Our present experience constitutes one point, but one point in a chain. It appropriates past experience, and is appropriated by future experience. This appropriating capacity of one's experience forms one's self-consciousness, representative of the entire past stream. It is hence the basis of **personal identity**. Other than this, there is no independent self. The relationship between appropriation and the self

has been charged with circularity, for appropriation allegedly presupposes an existence of a self. But James claimed that what performs appropriation is not an ego, but only the passing experience that one's body feels.

"Its appropriations are therefore less to itself than to the most intimately felt part of its present object, the body, and the central adjustments, which accompany the act of thinking, in the head. These are the real nucleus of our personal identity." **W. James,** *Principles of Psychology*

a priori/a posteriori
EPISTEMOLOGY [Latin, *a priori*, from what is earlier; *a posteriori*, from what comes after] This epistemological distinction was originally applied to two kinds of arguments in **Aristotle** and in medieval logic. If an argument proceeds from a cause to its effect, it is called *a priori*, and if it proceeds from an effect to its cause it is *a posteriori*. The distinction was later applied to concepts, propositions, knowledge, and truth. **Leibniz** distinguishes truth *a priori* (truth of reason) from truth *a posteriori* (truth established by experience). This corresponds to **Hume**'s distinction between knowledge about matters of fact and knowledge about relations of ideas. For **Kant**, knowledge is *a priori* if it is independent of experience and does not require experience to establish its truth, and is *a posteriori* if it is based on experience. He also connects this dichotomy with the distinction between the **analytic** and the **synthetic**, and claims that all analytic judgments are *a priori*. His major concern in the *Critique of Pure Reason* is how synthetic *a priori* judgment is possible. The distinction between the *a priori* and the *a posteriori* is also related to the distinction between the "necessary" and the "contingent." But the relations among these distinctions pose various problems. Philosophers have been debating whether *a priori* propositions must be necessary, or universal, and whether *a posteriori* propositions must be contingent. **Kripke** argues that *a posteriori* necessity is logically possible.

"There are two kinds of cognition. An *a priori* one, which is independent of experience; and an *a posteriori* one, which is grounded on empirical principles." **Kant,** *Lectures on Logic*

a priori knowledge

EPISTEMOLOGY Knowledge that is believed to be universally certain and necessarily true. It is known and justified independently of experiential evidence. *A priori* knowledge is in contrast to empirical or *a posteriori* knowledge. Rationalism assumes the existence of *a priori* knowledge mainly from the necessity of mathematical and logical truths. This is elaborated in detail by **Kant**, who also argues that *a priori* knowledge can be synthetic. His three distinctions, i.e. *a priori/a posteriori*, **necessary/contingent**, **analytic/synthetic**, have been the focus of the contemporary discussion of *a priori* knowledge.

Some empiricists admit the existence of *a priori* knowledge, but claim that it is trivial and only expresses the relations between our ideas (**Locke**), or that it can only be analytic truth based on the meanings of the words rather than knowledge about the world. Other empiricists tend to reject the existence of this form of knowledge, by claiming that prominent examples of *a priori* knowledge such as mathematical truths can be inductively justified (**Mill**), or that the distinction between analytic and synthetic is not tenable, and that no necessity can be known other than empirically (**Quine**). **Kripke** and **Putnam** also deny the internal relation between necessity and the *a priori*.

The proponents of *a priori* knowledge usually claim that we have a faculty of intuition by which we may ascertain the truth of *a priori* propositions. On the other hand, the opponents of *a priori* knowledge insist that there is no psychological evidence to suggest that we have such a mysterious cognitive faculty.

> "An instance of knowledge is *a priori* if and only if its justification condition is *a priori* in the sense that it does not depend on evidence from sensory experience." **Moser (ed.),** *A Priori Knowledge*

a priori proposition

EPISTEMOLOGY A proposition or statement whose truth is not based on empirical investigation. In contrast to empirical or *a posteriori* propositions, which are known through experience. Mathematical axioms, logical laws, and metaphysical propositions are generally regarded as examples of *a priori* propositions. If all the concepts in an *a priori* proposition are *a priori* concepts, the proposition is called an absolutely *a priori* proposition. Otherwise, it is called a relatively *a priori* proposition. **Empiricism** holds that all knowledge must be based on experience. Consequently, it tends to reject speculative metaphysics, although it then becomes a major task to provide a satisfactory empiricist account of mathematical and logical truths.

> "It is traditional to say that an *a priori* proposition is a proposition that is 'independent of experience', and is such that 'if you understand it, then you can see that it is true'." **Chisholm,** *Person and Object*

A-proposition

LOGIC In **syllogisms**, **categorical propositions** are divided into four kinds, according to their quality (affirmative or negative) and quantity (universal or particular). The medieval logicians designated them by letter names corresponding to the first four vowels of the Roman alphabet: A, E, I, O. An A-proposition is the universal affirmative (All S are P), meaning that every member of the S class is a member of the P class. An E-proposition is the universal negative (No S are P), meaning that no member of the S class is a member of the P class. An I-proposition is the particular affirmative (Some S are P), meaning that at least one member of the S class is a member of the P class. An O-proposition is the particular negative (Some S are not P), meaning that at least one member of the S class is not a member of the P class.

> "The central concern of traditional logic is the investigation of the logical relations of four propositional forms – Universal affirmative (A), Universal Negative (E), Particular Affirmative (I), Particular Negative (O)." **D. Mitchell,** *An Introduction to Logic*

Aquinas, St Thomas (1224/5–74)

Medieval Italian philosopher and theologian, the greatest scholastic thinker, born at Roccasecca, near Aquino, Naples, studied under Albertus Magnus in Paris and Cologne, taught at the University of Paris from 1252 to 1259 and again from 1266 to 1272, canonized in 1323. Aquinas systematically interpreted and defended Aristotle's thought and sought to reconcile it with Christian doctrines. He held that faith in God's existence could be justified by human reason and proposed the famous "**five ways**" to prove the existence of God on the basis of Aristotle's account of causes. Because he held that reason could not have complete knowledge of the nature of God, Aquinas argued that faith and reason must supplement each other. Aquinas constructed the most comprehensive Christian philosophical system and also contributed an important theory of natural law. Among his voluminous works, the most important are the two encyclopedic syntheses of philosophy and theology: *Summa contra Gentiles* (1259–64) and *Summa Theologiae* (1266–73). He also composed commentaries on Aristotle that are of great philosophical interest.

arbitrariness of grammar, another term for autonomy of language

Arcesilaus (*c.*315–240 BC)

Hellenistic skeptic philosopher, born in Pitane, Aeolis, the founder of the Middle Academy. He rejected Stoic dogmatism and claimed that nothing could be known, including the knowledge that one knows nothing. Hence, no one should assert anything, and life can be guided only by probability. For this reason, he did not write a single book, but his views were recorded by Cicero and Sextus Empiricus.

archaeology of knowledge

MODERN EUROPEAN PHILOSOPHY A term introduced by the French philosopher and historian Michel **Foucault**. Archaeology here is not a study of origin (*arche* in Greek), but is rather a study of what Foucault calls an "archive," that is, the deep structure or form that determines the conditions of possibility of knowledge in a particular period. An archive, which is also called the "historical *a priori*," is time-bound and factual. It is discovered rather than deduced. Archaeology is hence a distinct approach to the analysis of the history of thought, in contrast to the standard history of ideas. While the history of ideas is an interpretative discipline and defines the thoughts, themes and representations that are revealed in discourse, archaeology is concerned with the discourses themselves, taking them as practices obeying certain rules. While the history of ideas seeks continuity and coherence to relate discourses

to their predecessors, their backgrounds, and their impacts, archaeology seeks to show the specificity of discourses and the irreducibility of the sets of rules that govern the operations of particular discourses. While the history of ideas places emphasis on individual thinkers and their relations, archaeology of knowledge claims that the consciousness and statements of individual thinkers are determined by the underlying conceptual structures at a given time. Accordingly, we should aim to delineate this structure, which is beyond the beliefs and intentions of individual thinkers. Finally, while the history of ideas intends to identify what has been said and bring back the distant, archaeology seeks to provide a systematic description of discourse. Archaeology has four basic methodological principles: attribution of innovation, the analysis of contradictions, comparative descriptions, and the mapping of transformations. These principles are fully discussed in Foucault's *The Archaeology of Knowledge*.

> "The rights of words – which is not that of the philologists – authorises, therefore, the use of the term archaeology to describe all these searches. This term does not imply the search for a beginning; it does not relate analysis to geological excavation. It designates the general theme of a description that questions the already-said at the level of its existence: of the enunciative function that operates within it, of the discursive formation, and the general archive system to which it belongs." **Foucault,** *The Archaeology of Knowledge*

arche

PHILOSOPHICAL METHOD, ANCIENT GREEK PHILOSOPHY [from Greek *archein*, to start; hence archê the starting-point or beginning, first principle or origin; plural, *archai*] **Aristotle** claimed that philosophy should investigate the fundamental *archai* and causes of generation, existence, and knowledge. He described how at the very beginning of philosophy **Thales** sought the *arche* to account for the generation of the world. Thales believed this to be water. **Anaximander** is said to be the first person to use the word *arche* to name such a first entity. Aristotle called each of his four causes *arche*. He also called the basic premises for scientific deduction *archai*, discoverable by an intuitive faculty *nous*. In ethics the end, that is, the good to be pursued, is called *arche* as well.

"It is common, then, to all *archei* to be the first point from which a thing either is or comes to be or is known." **Aristotle,** *Metaphysics*

archetype

METAPHYSICS [from Greek *arche*, first + *typos*, pattern or stamp, the original model or pattern from which things are formed or from which they become copies] One of the main claims of **Plato**'s Theory of Forms or Ideas is that Ideas are archetypes for sensible things. **Locke**, like **Descartes**, took archetypes as the referents or external causes of ideas. Real ideas conform to real beings or archetypes, and adequate ideas are those that perfectly represent their archetypes. However, complex ideas of **modes** and **relations** are not copies, but are themselves originals or archetypes. Berkeley considered archetypes to be ideas in the mind of God. In **Kant**, archetypes in metaphysics can only be **regulative principles**. Hence, he criticized Plato for hypostatizing Ideas by making them into the constitutive principles of the origin of things. On the other hand, archetypes in ethics are ideals for imitation. In the analytical psychology of Carl **Jung**, archetypal images and symbols are said to emerge from the collective unconscious of humankind.

"Adequate ideas are such as perfectly represent their archetypes." **Locke,** *An Essay Concerning Human Understanding*

architectonic

PHILOSOPHICAL METHOD **Kant**'s conception for the systematic relations of all human knowledge and for the art of constructing such a system. These two senses are interconnected, for he believed that human reason possesses by nature such a function of construction and that all knowledge arising from pure reason belongs to one system. Architectonic is contrasted with the technical, for while a technical investigation starts from empirical criteria, architectonic anticipates these criteria. Kant himself designed an architectonic system. He began by distinguishing first (pure) philosophy from empirical philosophy and then subdivided pure philosophy into a propaedeutic investigation of pure reason (criticism) and the system of pure reason (metaphysics). He divided metaphysics in turn into the metaphysics of morals, dealing with what ought

to be, and the metaphysics of nature, dealing with what is. He further divided the metaphysics of nature into transcendental philosophy, which is concerned with the understanding and reason, and the physiology (natural science) of given objects. This rational physiology again had two branches, transcendental and immanent. Transcendental physiology includes rational cosmology and rational theology. For Kant, this framework was supported by traditional logic.

The notion of architectonic has been used to oppose attempts to break up human knowledge into different independent branches, although some critics claim that overemphasizing the demands of system can frustrate philosophical work that is critical of a particular system or philosophical systems in general. The idea of architectonic was developed by **Hegel** and also by the **Logical Positivists** in their ideal of **unified science**.

"By an architectonic I understand the art of constructing systems. As systematic unity is what first raises ordinary knowledge to the rank of science, that is, makes a system out of a mere aggregate of knowledge, architectonic is the doctrine of the scientific in our knowledge." **Kant,** *Critique of Pure Reason*

archive, see archaeology of knowledge

Arendt, Hannah (1906–75)

Jewish political philosopher, born in Hanover, Germany, a student of Martin Heidegger at Marburg and Karl Jaspers at Heidelberg. Arendt moved to the USA in 1941 as a refugee from the Nazis and taught at a number of universities. Her work started from reflections on the moral and social issues raised by the catastrophic history of modern Europe. She examined Nazism and communism as major forms of totalitarianism and sought to explore politics as a distinct sphere of human activity. Her major works include *The Origins of Totalitarianism* (1951), *The Human Condition* (1958), *On Revolution* (1963), *Eichmann in Jerusalem: a Report on the Banality of Evil* (1963), *On Violence* (1970). She planned a three-volume work, *Life of the Mind*, as a systematic examination of the faculties of thinking, willing, and judging, but lived to complete only the first two volumes.

aretaic judgment, another name for judgment of value

arête, Greek term for virtue or excellence

argument

LOGIC [from Latin *arguere,* to make clear] The reasoning in which a sequence of **statements** or **propositions** (the premises) are intended to support a further statement or proposition (the conclusion). The passage from the premises to the conclusion is justified through following acceptable patterns of **inference** and often marked by means of locutions such as "so," "hence," "it follows that," or "because." Generally, arguments are divided into two types: deductive arguments, in which the conclusion makes clear something implied in the premises, and inductive arguments, in which the conclusion goes beyond what the premises provide. While a statement is said to be true or false, an argument is said to be valid or invalid, sound or unsound. To discriminate valid from invalid forms of argument is precisely the task of logic. In another technical use, especially in mathematics and logic, an argument, in contrast to a function, is a member of the domain of a function.

"The aim of argument is conviction; one tries to get someone to agree that some statement is true or false." **Strawson,** *Introduction to Logical Theory*

argument *a posteriori*

LOGIC, PHILOSOPHY OF RELIGION An argument *a posteriori* proceeds from an effect to its cause, in contrast to an argument *a priori*, which proceeds from a cause to its effect. The pair of terms *a priori* and *a posteriori* are used here in their pre-Kantian sense. The distinction between these two types of arguments or demonstrations was made by the scholastic philosopher **Albert the Great**, but the idea can be traced to Aristotle's view that we may either proceed from what is evident to us to what is evident in nature or proceed from what is evident in nature to what is evident to us. In the philosophy of religion, arguments that seek to prove God's existence from the current condition of the world are called proof *a posteriori* (a typical example being the argument from design), while the proofs that start from our concepts of God's nature are *a priori*.

"Since therefore the effects resemble each other, we are led to infer, by all the rules of analogy, that the causes also resemble, and that the Author of nature is somewhat similar to the mind of man . . . By this argument *a posteriori*, and by this argument alone, do we prove at once the existence of a Deity and his similarity to human mind and intelligence." **Hume,** *Dialogues Concerning Natural Religion*

argument *a priori*, see argument *a posteriori*

argument by analogy

EPISTEMOLOGY, PHILOSOPHY OF RELIGION, PHILOSOPHY OF MIND An inference from certain similarities between two things to the conclusion that these things are also alike in other respects. Such a form of inference is not decisive, for it depends upon an implicit premise that the fact that two things are similar in some given respects entails that they are similar in other respects as well, and this premise is not obviously true. Arguments of this form can, however, be suggestive and are therefore widely employed. The **argument from design** is a version of an argument by analogy. It infers analogically from the relationship between human agents and artifacts (for example between a watch-maker and a watch) to the existence of God as the designer of the world. Indeed, analogical argument is represented in various forms of **teleological arguments** for God's existence. In the philosophy of mind, some philosophers adopt this form of argument to attribute a mind and mental phenomena, which are generally assumed to be private, to other individuals.

"The following is the structure of an analogical argument. Two objects A and B share several properties, say, a, b, c; A has an additional property d, therefore B has the property d also." **Pap,** *Elements of Analytic Philosophy*

argument from design

PHILOSOPHY OF RELIGION A traditional and popularly accepted argument for the existence of God. Natural phenomena present a complex and intricate order, like that of a machine or a work of art. This provides evidence for thinking that there must be a designer who is responsible for the structural and adaptive order of natural things and who has capacities far exceeding human abilities. Hence, we may reasonably presume that God exists as this designer. The argument from analogy, a version of this argument, argues that since the world is like a clock, it must derive from something like a clock-maker, which is God. The argument from design can be traced to the Stoics and is the fifth of **Aquinas**' Five Ways of proving the existence of God. It was attacked by **Hume**, who introduced many other possible explanations for natural order, thus providing methodological objections to the dogmatic acceptance of the divine origin of the world, especially where experience cannot test our judgment. **Kant** also rejected the validity of the argument from design. The argument was further challenged when **Darwin**'s theory of evolution explained by natural selection the adaptive features of living things that were cited to prove that the world might be designed.

"The argument from design reasons, from the fact that nature's laws are mathematical, and her parts benevolently adapted to each other, that its cause is both intellectual and benevolent." **W. James**, *The Varieties of Religious Experience*

argument from differential certainty

EPISTEMOLOGY An argument for the existence of **sense-data**. Suppose I perceive something, for example a tomato, but I do not know what it is. What I *can* be certain that I am perceiving are some sense-data such as red, round shape. These sense-data are the objects of my direct awareness and are infallible. But I cannot be certain that I am perceiving a real tomato, or even a material thing, for what I am perceiving may be a fake, an illusion, or an hallucination. That of which I can be certain cannot be identical with that of which I cannot be certain; therefore there are sense-data whose existence is distinct from that of material things. Critics of this argument maintain that, even though it is true that there are different degrees of certainty in perceptions and statements, this does not entail that there are ontologically different kinds of things corresponding to my different levels of certainty.

"It might be true that for the speaker in our argument from differential certainty, the statement 'I see a tomato', in the conditions specified, is less certain than statements such as 'I am directly aware of something red and with a tomato-ish shape'." **Pitcher,** *A Theory of Perception*

argument from religious experience

PHILOSOPHY OF RELIGION An argument for the existence of God in terms of the inner, emotional experience of the presence and activity of something divine and transcendent. Some people have this kind of experience in daily life, but unless there is indeed something that is divine and transcendent, we cannot have experience of it. Hence God must exist. This kind of argument was developed in the nineteenth and twentieth centuries by philosophers of religion as a result of dissatisfaction with the traditional theistic arguments. Since religious experience provides a non-inferential mode of knowledge of God, analogous to sense perception of the external world, this argument is presented as the main proof of the existence of God. Critics argue that religious experience might be explained reductively through sociology, psychology, or other fields and as a consequence it begs the question to ascribe independent cognitive value to it. We can have the experiences without being obliged to explain them by the existence of God. However, we often accept reductive explanation in terms of other fields where the primary belief is irrational, but the rationality or irrationality of religious belief must be determined before this objection to the argument for religious experience can be assessed. Further, it is argued that because religious experience is inherently mysterious and untestable, it cannot constitute persuasive evidence for those who do not have similar experiences.

"As a method of showing the existence of a God not otherwise known or believed to exist the Argument from Religious Experience is indeed absurd. It is not absurd if considered as a method of getting to know something about a God already known, or believed, to exist." **McPherson,** *The Philosophy of Religion*

argument from the relativity of perception

EPISTEMOLOGY Under certain circumstances, the ways that things are perceived by us are not the ways that they really are. For instance, a straight oar with one end in water looks bent. When the conditions of a perceiver change, the same thing that he perceived before will be different from what he perceives now. For instance, the same food will taste differently when one is healthy and when one is sick. Hence, what is perceived to be and what really is are different. This argument has been employed by many philosophers from **Plato**, **Descartes**, **Locke**, and **Hume** to **Russell** and **Ayer**, but for different purposes. **Rationalism** makes use of it to prove the unreliability of sense-experience and to show the ontological difference between reality and **phenomena**. **Empiricism**, on the other hand, suggests that the properties we perceive are **sense-data** and are not properties of physical objects themselves. This argument is similar to the argument from illusion.

"[A]rguments from the relativity of perception . . . start from the familiar observation that how things look to us is heavily dependent on the lighting, our angle of vision or whether we are wearing spectacles." **Smith and Jones**, *The Philosophy of Mind*

argumentum ad baculum

LOGIC [Latin, argument to a stick, meaning appeal to force] An attempt to win assent for a conclusion by appealing to force or by issuing threats concerning the consequence that will follow if the conclusion is not accepted. This sort of argument is frequently employed in international politics and in lobbying campaigns. It is a **fallacy** because the conclusion is not justified on a rational basis. It is perhaps not an argument at all, but a way to get one's position accepted, in particular when rational arguments in support of the position fail.

"The *argumentum ad baculum* is the fallacy committed when one appeals to force or the threat of force to cause the acceptance of a conclusion." **Copi**, *Introduction to Logic*

argumentum ad hominem

LOGIC [Latin, argument against or directed to the man] Rejecting a person's argument or view by attacking the person who is maintaining the view. There are various ways of making such an attack, and the standard way is to abuse the character of the opponent, for instance by claiming that he is a liar. Although in practical life the opinion of a person with a bad record regarding truthfulness is generally not respected, this argument is logically fallacious because even a person with a history of dishonesty can speak the truth. That a person is untrustworthy does not entail that his opinion is always mistaken. This **fallacy** is close to the genetic fallacy, which focuses on the source of a view rather than on the view itself.

"This is traditionally called the *ad hominem* argument – an argument, that is, directed against the man (*ad hominem*) rather than to the point (*ad rem*)." **Sullivan**, *Fundamentals of Logic*

argumentum ad ignorantiam

LOGIC [Latin, argument to ignorance] The inference that a conclusion A is false from the fact that A is not proved to be true or known to be true, or that A is true from the fact A is not proved to be false or known to be false. This kind of argument can be used to shift the burden of proof or to reach a tentative conclusion, but the conclusion cannot have much strength. Our ignorance of A entails neither that A is false nor that A is true. Truth is one thing, and whether or not the truth is known by us is another.

"The *argumentum ad ignorantiam* is committed whenever it is argued that a proposition is true simply on the basis that it has not been proved false or it is false because it has not been proved true." **Copi**, *Introduction to Logic*

argumentum ad misericordiam

LOGIC [Latin, argument to pity] An argument making use of an appeal to the pity, sympathy, and compassion of the audience in order to establish its conclusion. This widely employed argument is logically **fallacious** because it puts an emotional burden on the audience rather than concentrating on the argument itself. The fact that an argument is accepted out of pity or charity does not entail that it is logically strong. Argument is a matter of reason. Often, an argument *ad misericordiam* is offered to sway an audience in defiance of factual evidence and sound reasoning.

"The *argumentum ad misericordiam* is the fallacy committed when pity is appealed to for the sake of getting a conclusion accepted, where the conclusion is concerned with a question of fact rather than a matter of sentiment." **Copi**, *Introduction to Logic*

argumentum ad populum

LOGIC [Latin, argument to the people] An argument that seeks to get its conclusion accepted by appeal to popular opinion, mass enthusiasm, group interests or loyalties, or customary ways of behaving. For example, "Since most people believe that this thing is true, it is true." This kind of argument is widely used in social life, but it is logically **fallacious** because it does not establish its conclusion on the basis of facts and relations between premises and the conclusion. Broadly conceived, this argument contains an *argumentum ad misericordian* if the enthusiasm appealed to is based on pity.

"We may define the *argumentum ad populum* fallacy a little more narrowly as the attempt to win popular assent to a conclusion by arousing the emotions and enthusiasms of the multitude rather than by appeal to the relevant facts." **Copi,** *Introduction to Logic*

argumentum ad verecundiam, the Latin term for appeal to authority

argumentum ex consensu gentium
LOGIC [Latin, argument from the consensus of the nations, an argument that supports a conclusion by appeal to common human consent] An argument that because all people consent that this is the case, so it is. The argument has been widely used in the history of philosophy to attempt to establish divine existence (the common consent argument for the existence of God) or to establish a variety of general moral principles. Sometimes it is treated as an instance of *argumentum ad populum*. It is difficult to distinguish cases in which common consent might have some weight in justifying claims or show that no justification is necessary from cases in which common consent cannot provide needed justification.

"The argument *ex consensu gentium* is that the belief in God is so widespread as to be grounded in the rational nature of man and should therefore carry authenticity with it." **W. James,** *The Varieties of Religious Experience*

Aristippus (*c.*435–356 BC)
Greek philosopher, born in Cyrene, North Africa, a follower of Socrates and the founder of the Cyrenaic school of hedonism. He claimed that pleasure was the highest end of life and that pleasure and suffering were the criteria of good and evil. All pleasures are equal in value, but differ in degree and duration. However, he also emphasized that

happiness consists in the rational control of pleasure and not in the slavery of subordination to pleasure. His grandson, also named Aristippus, was said to have systematized the theory of the Cyrenaic school.

aristocracy
POLITICAL PHILOSOPHY [from Greek *aristos*, best + *kratia*, rule, hence rule by the best] The form of constitution that appoints the best people to the offices of government. In ancient Greek society, the best people were determined by their good birth, property, education, and merit. Thinkers such as **Plato** and **Aristotle** believed that because aristocracy carries with it a high sense of honor, responsibility, and duty, it is better than its rivals, that is, monarchy (rule by one) and democracy (rule by the people). The degenerate form of aristocracy is **oligarchy** (rule by a rich minority), which regards only the interest of the ruling class. Aristocracy has been widely rejected by modern liberal egalitarianism.

"The sovereign may confine the government to the hands of a few, so that there are more ordinary citizens than there are magistrates: this form of government is called aristocracy." **Rousseau,** *The Social Contract*

Aristotelian logic, see traditional logic

Aristotelian principle
ETHICS, PHILOSOPHY OF ACTION, POLITICAL PHILOSOPHY A principle of motivation or a psychological thesis that everyone's central goals in life are bound up with the exercise of one's natural or acquired abilities or faculties. The greater our ability, the greater satisfaction we can expect to get from the exercise of our skill. Believing that this idea is implicit in **Aristotle**'s ethics, **Rawls** has introduced this term and uses the principle to explain both why certain things are recognized as primary goods and how to rank primary goods in importance. Hence this principle is essential for Rawls's thin theory of the good and its role in his theory of justice. Basing his theory of the good upon this psychological principle strikingly distinguishes his theory from **utilitarianism**, which is based on psychological **hedonism**.

"It will be recalled that the Aristotelian principle runs as follows: other things equal, human beings enjoy the exercise of their realised capacities (their innate or trained abilities), and this enjoyment increases the more the capacity is realised, or the greater its complexity." **Rawls**, *A Theory of Justice*

Aristotelianism

PHILOSOPHICAL METHOD The tradition of translation, commentary, and interpretation of Aristotle's doctrines by various groups in different historical periods. Each group or period has read into Aristotle its own preoccupations and has focused on different aspects of Aristotle's thought. Hence Aristotelianism presents different and even contradictory outlooks. It is sometimes also called peripateticism, after the Aristotelian *peripatikos* (Greek, walking) school whose members liked to discuss philosophical issues while walking.

The interpretation of Aristotle starts with Aristotle's disciple and successor **Theophrastus**. In the first century BC, Andronicos of Rhodes edited and published the first Complete Works of Aristotle, containing all the esoteric works. Other exoteric works survive only in the form of fragments, which were first collected by V. Rose in the nineteenth century.

The **Neoplatonists Plotinus** and **Proclus** took Aristotle's thought as a preface to Plato's philosophy and attempted to reconcile them. Plotinus' disciple **Porphyry** wrote a famous commentary to Aristotle's *Categories* that set the stage for the subsequent long-standing discussion between realism and nominalism regarding the nature of universals. This tendency was further reinforced in the sixth century by Boethius's commentary to Porphyry's *Isogage*, a book that was based on Aristotle's *Organon*. **Boethius** also translated the *Categories* and *On Interpretation*, which were the only primary Aristotelian materials that were available to Western Europeans until the twelfth century, and constituted the major basis for the development of medieval logic. Arabic Aristotelianism developed in the ninth century, largely through the work of **Avicenna** (Ibn Sina) and **Averroes** (Ibn Rushd), who translated Aristotle's works into Arabic and commented on them. They paid much attention to Aristotle's doctrine of active intellect in the *De Anima*. Their work helped Western Europeans to understand Aristotle, particularly through the study of their commentaries in the arts faculties of Paris and Oxford during the thirteenth century. Their influence led to the condemnation of Aristotle's philosophy by the Bishop of Paris in 1277 and to a short-lived prohibition of the study of Aristotle. In the late twelfth and early thirteenth centuries, Aristotle's texts in Greek reached Paris and Oxford and stimulated a renaissance of interest in Aristotle. Aristotle's works were systematically translated and studied. The major contributors to this movement included Roger **Bacon**, Robert **Grosseteste**, St **Bonaventura**, and, above all, St Thomas **Aquinas**. Aquinas, the most important philosopher of the medieval age, was preoccupied with justifying the claims of Christian teachings in terms of Aristotle's doctrines. Aristotelianism is therefore associated with scholasticism and Thomism. Aristotle was simply called the philosopher, or in Dante's words, the master of those who know.

The scientific revolution launched by **Copernicus** and **Galileo** in the sixteenth and seventeenth centuries attacked Aristotle's system as an obstacle to the progress of learning, although this claim is more justly leveled at the Aristotle of the scholastics rather than Aristotle himself. Nowadays Aristotle's views about the physical and animal world have been superseded, but much of his writing over a wide range of fields can still inspire important philosophical work.

In the early part of the twentieth century, the study of Aristotle benefited from the Oxford translation of his works edited by W. D. **Ross** and was influenced methodologically by W. Jaeger's genetic method. The study has developed greatly since the middle of this century, stimulated by the work of excellent scholars, such as G. E. L. **Owen** and John Ackrill, and many other Oxford and Cambridge philosophers have been influenced by the study of Aristotle. Recent developments in metaphysics, philosophy of mind, philosophy of language, and virtue ethics, have generated a new revival of Aristotelianism, sometimes called neo-Aristotelianism.

Philosophically, Aristotelianism is contrasted with the contrary tendency of Platonism. The distinction between them has been roughly portrayed as being that between empiricism and rationalism or naturalism and idealism, although the real relationships linking the thought of Plato and Aristotle are still a matter of scholarly debate.

> "'Aristotelianism' certainly means an emphasis on the primacy of the subject matter, the experienced world encountered." **Randall,** *Aristotle*

Aristotle (384–322 BC)

Greek philosopher, born in Stagira in Macedon, moved to Athens in 367 to become Plato's student until Plato's death at 347, tutor of Alexander the Great. In 355, Aristotle established his own school in Athens, the Lyceum. He believed that by nature human beings desire to know, and classified knowledge into theoretical sciences (including mathematics, physics or natural philosophy, and theology or first philosophy), practical sciences (including ethics and political science), and productive sciences (including poetics and rhetoric). Although most of his writings were reported to be lost, the surviving works contain great contributions to nearly all of these areas.

In theoretical sciences, the major works include *Physics*; *De Caelo*; *De Anima*; *De Partibus Animalium*; *De Motu Animalium*; *De Generatione Animalium*; and *Metaphysics*. He claimed that philosophy is a science of being *qua* being. The primary being is substance, while all other beings are attributes of substance. Hence the study of substance, the primary being, is the core of the science of being. Substance can be analyzed into form, matter, and the composite of form and matter. Of these, form (which is identified with essence) is primary substance or ultimate reality. Each thing has its own nature, that is, its inner principle of motion, and form and matter are two natures. The relation between soul and body should be understood in terms of the relation between form and matter. To know each thing, one needs to know its four causes (the material cause, the formal cause, the efficient cause, and the final cause). In natural things, the formal cause, efficient cause, and final cause coincide, and they are different operations of the same form. Natural things develop from potentiality to actuality. The whole universe is ordered, for everything in the world, in its pursuit of eternity, is moved by the Prime Mover.

In practical sciences the important works include *Nicomachean Ethics* and *Politics*. According to Aristotle, ethics should focus on character and virtue and should address the issue of how to lead a good or flourishing life. Furthermore, ethics and politics are inseparable, for human beings are political animals and politics should mainly concern the best constitution in which citizens can develop their character. Aristotle's ethics is the intellectual source of the contemporary revival of virtue ethics.

In productive sciences, Aristotle left us *Rhetoric* and *Poetics*. In addition, Aristotle's six treatises on logic (*Categories*; *De Interpretatione*; *The Prior Analytics*; *The Posterior Analytics*; *Topics*; and *The Sophistical Elenchi*) were grouped together by later commentators under the title of "Organon" (literally, tool, or instrument). In the *Organon* Aristotle developed syllogistic logic and an analysis of demonstrative science. For a long time in the history of Western philosophy, Aristotle was referred to simply as "The Philosopher." Scholars differ over understanding Aristotle's philosophy in terms of a process of development involving different stages or as a unified system.

Armstrong, David (1926–)

Australian philosopher of knowledge, philosopher of mind, philosopher of science, and metaphysician, born Melbourne, Professor of Philosophy at University of Sydney. Armstrong is an empiricist and realist. His early work on epistemology was followed by his influential formulation of a non-reductionist materialist theory of mind. Armstrong's ontology, based on states of affairs, accepts the reality of individuals, properties, and relations on the grounds that what is real is a matter of what has causes and effects. He is committed to the reality of universals, although it is an empirical question which predicates stand for universals and which do not. Laws of nature are empirically discovered relations of non-logical necessity between universals. Among his prolific writings are *Perception and the Physical World* (1961), *A Materialist Theory of Mind* (1968), *Universals and Scientific Realism* (1978), and *What is a Law of Nature?* (1983).

Arnauld, Antoine (1612–94)

French theologian, mathematician, and philosopher. Arnaud was a leading figure among the Port-Royal Jansenists. His objections to Descartes's *Meditations* raised the problem of the Cartesian circle, namely, we know that God exists because we have a clear and distinct idea of God, but what we perceive clearly and distinctly is guaranteed to be true only if God exists. His major work is *Port-Royal Logic* (with Pierre Nicole, 1662).

Arrow, Kenneth (1921–)

American economist and theorist of social choice, Professor of Economics at Stanford University, winner of Nobel Prize in 1972. Arrow is best known to philosophers for Arrow's paradox, which shows that there is no function meeting certain common-sense conditions that can order options for a society in terms of the preferences of individual members of that society. This insight, discussed in his work *Social Choice and Individual Values* (1951), has important consequences for democratic theory.

arrow of time

METAPHYSICS, PHILOSOPHY OF SCIENCE One of the central notions in the philosophy of time. We ordinarily believe that time is inherently directional. Time seems to be asymmetric, for we can affect the future in a way that we cannot affect the past. The past is fixed and the future is open. This is why we can talk about **free will**. This seems to suggest that natural processes have a natural temporal order. We talk about this directionality of time as the arrow of time. However, physics claims that time as such does not have an intrinsic orientation. It does not move toward the future as it does not move toward the past. The philosophical basis of the so-called arrow of time has been a topic of dispute.

> "It has become an almost universal practice to refer to the direction of time or the arrow of time in physics, with the implicit meaning of the direction of flow or movement of the now from past to future." **Davies, *The Physics of Time Asymmetry***

Arrow's impossibility theorem

PHILOSOPHY OF SOCIAL SCIENCE, POLITICAL PHILOSOPHY Also called Arrow's paradox, first formulated by the American economist Kenneth J. **Arrow** in *Social Choice and Individual Values* (1951). Intuitively, a social choice can be obtained through the aggregation of individual preferences. Such a choice, if acceptable, must satisfy the following reasonable formal conditions: (a) a social ordering can be obtained from any set of individual orderings and preferences; (b) if at least one individual prefers A to B and nobody

else objects to it, then the society should choose A (Pareto optimality); (c) the social choice cannot be determined dictatorially; (d) the choice with regard to A and B should be decided between them alone, independent of irrelevant alternatives. But Arrow proves that on these conditions there is no method to determine social ordering through the aggregation of individual preferences. Various attempts have been made to get out of this paradox, but none turns out to be satisfactory. The theorem indicates that the notion of general will conceived by **Rousseau** and prominent in social and political debate cannot easily be determined in practice. The **voting paradox** is an example of this theorem.

> "'Arrow's impossibility theorem' brings about, in a dramatic way, the tension involved in ruling out the use of interpersonal comparisons of utility, in aggregating individual preferences into consistent and complete social choice, satisfying some mild-looking conditions of reasonableness." **Sen, *On Ethics and Economics***

Arrow's paradox another expression for Arrow's impossibility theorem

art

AESTHETICS [from Latin *ars*, *artis*, skill, human products that can arouse aesthetic experience] Starting from the eighteenth century, art replaced "**beauty**" to become the central notion of aesthetics. However, it has been difficult to provide a suitable definition of art to enable one to distinguish artworks from other objects and to bring all artistic activities, such as painting, sculpture, architecture, music, and literature, under one heading. In an objective object-centered account, **Plato** defined art as *mimesis*, that is, the representation or display of certain aspects of reality. However, not all arts are representational. Another traditional definition claims that art is the **expression** of emotions, feelings, and moods. Art-expression is a specific form of self-expression. This is a subjective artist-centered notion. Other accounts include art as **significant form** (aesthetic formalism); art as what is recognized by an institution (**institutional theory of art**); art as creation; and art as play. Another major issue dividing theories of art concerns the function of art. Some theorists hold that art is functional, serving psychological, moral, social, and other practical purposes, while others claim that art is autonomous and not-functional. In their view art should be pursued for its sake and for pure aesthetic value.

> "Art is the creation of forms symbolic of human being." **Langer,** *Feeling and Form*

art for art's sake, see aestheticism

artificial intelligence

PHILOSOPHY OF MIND, LOGIC, PHILOSOPHY OF LAN-GUAGE, EPISTEMOLOGY, PHILOSOPHY OF ACTION Often abbreviated as AI. The use of programs to enable machines to perform tasks that human beings perform using their intelligence, and to simulate on a computer human thinking and problem solving. Artificial intelligence aims to bypass the human brain and body and to achieve a fuller understanding of rationality. The idea can be traced to **Turing**'s intelligent machine. In 1956, the first AI program, called "Logical Theorist," devised by Herbert Simon and others, was capable of proving on its own 38 of the first 52 theorems from *Principia Mathematica*. Today, AI has developed into a domain of research, application, and instruction within computer science and other disciplines, focusing on issues such as new programming languages, methods of inference and problem solving, visual recognition, and expert systems. Early AI avoided human psychological models, but this orientation has been altered due to the development of **connectionism**, based on theories of how the brain works. In connectionism, complex functions, including learning, involve the transmission of information along pathways formed among large arrays of simple elements. AI seeks to understand human intelligent processes in terms of symbol manipulation and raises questions about the conditions, if any, in which we would be justified in ascribing mental attributes to purely physical systems. It has also contributed to the development of cognitive science and to some controversies in the philosophy of mind. There is a distinction between the strong thesis of AI and the weak thesis of AI. The weak thesis, which proposes only that a computer program is helpful for understanding the human mind, is widely accepted. The strong thesis, that computer "minds" instantiate human psychological processes, is highly controversial. It is chal-

lenged by John **Searle**'s argument that the syntactic manipulation of symbols by a machine is not complemented by a semantic understanding of the meaning of the symbols for the machine, as it is for human beings.

> "Artificial intelligence is not the study of computers, but of intelligence in thought and action. Computers are its tools, because its theories are expressed as computer programs that enable machines to do things that would require intelligence if done by people." **Boden,** *Artificial Intelligence and Natural Man*

artificial virtue, see natural virtue

artworld

AESTHETICS A word transformed into a technical term by the American philosopher Arthur **Danto** in his 1964 paper "The Artworld." For Danto, an artworld provides an atmosphere or context in which artworks are embedded. It is mainly constituted by the history and theory of art. Such a world varies according to time and place. According to Danto, this theoretical context takes an artwork up into the world of art and keeps it from collapsing into the real object that it is. Another American philosopher, George Dickie (1926–), developed the notion of an artworld from a figure of speech to something having an ontological status. He first defines it as a formal institution comprising such things as museums, galleries, and art journals on the one hand, and artists, art critics, organizers of exhibitions and others possessing relevant authority about art and the art market, on the other. Representatives of an artworld can confer upon an artifact the status of an artwork. This account of an artworld has become essential for his "**institutional theory of art**." Later Dickie modified his notion into one of an art circle, an interrelated structure of relationships among artists and their audiences. Dickie's notion of an artworld is more concrete than Danto's. Nevertheless, their common idea is that art has its own environment and is the product of a type of specialized and unique institutionalized activity. Accordingly, art does not serve human life, as Plato and Aristotle claim, but is disengaged from worldly concerns. Art is a world in which one can apply one's own set of practices. The theory may explain the transcultural and transhistorical nature of artworks.

"To see something as art requires something the eye cannot descry – an atmosphere of artistic theory, a knowledge of the history of art: an artworld." **Danto, "Artworld," in** *The Journal of Philosophy* **61**

asceticism

ETHICS, PHILOSOPHY OF MIND, PHILOSOPHY OF RELIGION [from Greek *askesis*] Originally meaning a course of self-discipline such as that undertaken by athletes, and later associated with rigorous self-discipline, abstinence, simplicity, and the solitary and contemplative life, popular in ancient society, early Christianity, and some forms of Buddhism and Hinduism. Some ascetics also follow exercises that consist in many means of tormenting themselves. Philosophically, asceticism proposes that a person should repress desires. A strong version requires one to relinquish one's desires totally, while a weaker version demands only that one denies bodily or worldly desires. There have been various grounds for advocating this unnatural style of life. Morally, asceticism is seen as the way to free one's soul from the body's pollution. Epistemologically, it is considered to be the way to gain truth or virtue. Religiously, it is claimed that the ascetic life will be rewarded by God. For every grain of pain now, we shall have a hundred grains of pleasure by and by. Asceticism, in contrast to hedonism, approves of actions that tend to diminish present pleasure or to augment present pain.

"Asceticism has commonly assumed that the impulses connected with the body are base and are to be treated accordingly." **Blanshard,** *Reason and Goodness*

ascriptivism

PHILOSOPHY OF ACTION A position regarding the meaning of statements about the voluntariness of acts. It claims that in saying that "This act is **voluntary**," we are ascribing **responsibility** for the act to its agent, rather than describing the act as being caused by its agent in a certain way. Thus, to call an act voluntary or intentional is not a causal statement. Such statements are not matters of fact, but are matters of practical (legal or moral) decision. They are not true or false. The idea of ascriptivism was introduced by H. L. A. **Hart** and belongs to a more general position of non-cognitivism. Peter **Geach**, who named the view, rejects ascriptivism and insists that to ascribe an act to an agent is a causal description of an act.

"Ascriptivists hold that to say an action X was voluntary on the part of an agent A is not to describe the act X as caused in a certain way, but to ascribe it to A, to hold A responsible for it." **Geach, "Ascriptivism,"** *Philosophical Review* **LXIX**

aseity

METAPHYSICS, PHILOSOPHY OF RELIGION, MODERN EUROPEAN PHILOSOPHY [from Latin *aseitas*, *a*, from + *se*, itself] The property of being completely and absolutely independent of anything distinct from oneself and deriving solely from oneself. As self-determination of the self as itself, it is absolute freedom. In the later medieval **scholasticism**, **God** was thought to be the only entity that has this status. God is responsible for his own existence and does not depend on anything else. Everything else, on the contrary, relies for existence on God. Based on aseity, God is ascribed various other perfections. In modern times, **Schopenhauer** used the term for the ontological status of Will. In **existentialism**, since God is dead, man comes to have aseity as absolute freedom. Nothing should be in man that is not by him. The problem of reconciling absolute freedom with the place of man in society was explored by **Sartre** in *Critique of Dialectical Reason*.

A related property perseity (from Latin *per*, by + *se*, itself, intrinsically) is a state in which a thing acts out of its own inner structure. Any substance, in contrast to its attributes, is in a state of perseity. However, only God can be in a perfect state of perseity, because through aseity God alone is completely independent of anything else, while other substances rely on God for their existence.

"Men have occasionally claimed that God is the cause of his own existence or of his being the kind of being which he is, although this is not a claim normally made by traditional Theologians. Etymology would suggest that this is what is meant when God is said to have 'aseity' (his existence deriving from himself, a se)." **Swinburne,** *The Coherence of Theism*

A-series of time

METAPHYSICS A term introduced by **McTaggart** for the temporal ordering of events according to whether they are past, present, or future, in contrast to the B-series of time, which orders events according to whether they are before or after one another or earlier or later than one another in time. These two kinds of temporal series are different. Events in the B-series of time will not change their ordering over time. Plato's time is always earlier than Hegel's time, and this relationship will never change. According to the A-series, every event will successively be future, present, and past. Although McTaggart admitted that the tense-distinctions in the A-series are essential to understanding the nature of temporality, he uses the A-series to introduce his famous argument against the reality of time. Since past, present, and future are contradictory attributes and since the A-series ascribes possession of these contradictory attributes to the same events, McTaggart concluded that time is not real. On this basis one is led to argue that the past and the future are not realms of true existence. Even if this time-series were not real, however, we always perceive it as though it were real. McTaggart called this perceptible time-series the C-series.

> "For the sake of brevity I shall give the name of the A-series to that series of positions which runs from the far past through the near past to the present, and then from the present through the near future to the far future, or conversely." **McTaggart**, *The Nature of Existence*

as if

METAPHYSICS, ETHICS, AESTHETICS For **Kant**, a form of analogical argument as a maxim of regulative judgment. In theoretical philosophy, traditional metaphysical entities such as God and the soul are beyond the limits of experience, and we cannot really know their nature. Nevertheless we may still suppose them as if they were working principles. We take them as guidance for determining the constitution and connection of empirical objects. This regulative principle can also be applied to practical philosophy and aesthetics. A moral agent should act as if he were a legislator in the kingdom of ends. A finished work of art should appear as if it were a product of nature, but without the constraint of rules.

> "We declare, for instance, that the things of the world must be viewed *as if* they received their existence from a highest intelligence." **Kant**, *Critique of Pure Reason*

assertion

LOGIC A term used synonymously with **judgment** for affirming or denying what can be true or false. Traditionally, an asserted sentence is composed of a subject-expression, a predicate-expression, and a copula. On this view, the copula is essential to unite any pair of terms into an assertion, but **Frege**, **Wittgenstein**, and others have offered different accounts of how a proposition or assertion has unity. An asserted **sentence** is contrasted to other sentences in terms of its **assertoric force**. In traditional logic assertoric force is bound up with the grammatical predicate. Assertion does not merely express a thought or hypothesis and does not issue a command or ask a question, but is committed to the truth of the sentence or puts forward a thought as being true. Wittgenstein criticized Frege's proposal of an **assertion-sign** to indicate whether a thought is asserted. Important questions arise about the asserted and non-asserted occurrence of sentences that are part of other sentences. If we assert "P and Q," we also assert both component sentences, but this is not the case in asserting "P or Q." In asserting "John believes that P," we do not assert "P." To reason is to infer any assertion from assertions already admitted.

> "It is one thing merely to express a thought and another simultaneously to assert it. We can often tell from the external circumstances which of the two things is being done . . . This is why I distinguish between thoughts and judgements, expressions of thought and assertions." **Frege**, *Philosophical and Mathematical Correspondence*

assertion-sign

The symbol "⊢" that **Frege** placed in front of a **sentence** to indicate that the sentence is asserted (that is affirmed or denied) or is a judgment. Frege needed this symbol to distinguish asserted propositions from unasserted ones, because while in traditional logic assertoric form is marked by the grammatical predicate, Frege's concept-script disassociated assertoric force from **predication**. In this symbol, "|" is called the judgment-stroke and "—" is called the content-stroke or horizontal stroke. "|" is crucial because without it, "—" only expresses a content, without being committed to its truth. In modern logic this symbol has two further uses. When it is written between sets of sentences, it indicates that the sentences following it can be derived from the sentences preceding it; for example, "[$A_1 \ldots A_n$] ⊢B" means that B may be deduced from the premises $A_1 \ldots A_n$. Furthermore, ⊢B also means that B is a theorem in a system, that is, it may be assumed without any proof.

"The assertion-sign – what Frege called the 'judgment-stroke' – can be attached only to the name of a truth-value, i.e. to a sentence." **M. Dummett**, *The Interpretation of Frege's Philosophy*

assertoric

A judgment or proposition by which one asserts that something is or is not the case. An affirmative assertoric judgment has the form: "X is Y," while a negative assertoric judgment has the form: "X is not Y." An assertoric is a **modal** form of proposition or judgment, in contrast to two other modal categorical judgments: problematic (possible) and **apodeictic** (necessary). Expressed adverbially, an assertoric judgment can be stated: "X is actually Y," or "X is actually not Y."

"In assertoric judgements affirmation or negation is viewed as real (true)." **Kant**, *Critique of Pure Reason*

assertoric force

Frege's term for the force that makes a sentence an assertion rather than a hypothetical, interrogative, or imperative sentence. Assertoric force is distinguished from assertoric sense. The former is the act of asserting, and is represented using the "**assertion-sign**," while the latter is the thought or judgeable content contained in a sentence. In English, the indicative mood of the main verb has assertoric force, for it makes the expression of a thought into an assertion. The idea of assertoric force inspired Austin to develop his **speech act** theory.

"Assertoric force can most easily be eliminated by changing the whole into a question; for one can express the same thought in a question as in an assertoric sentence, only without asserting it." **Frege**, *Collected Papers*

association of ideas

EPISTEMOLOGY, PHILOSOPHY OF MIND A view, especially important in **Hume**, explaining the patterned occurrence of ideas in our minds. The human mind can synthesize and combine various simple ideas into complex ones that are previously unknown. Exploiting the analogy of the principle of universal gravitation in the natural world, Hume believes that there are certain principles according to which the mind operates to connect all sorts of ideas. The occurrence of one idea will lead the mind to its correlative. These principles are three in number: resemblance, contiguity in time and place, and causation. They were used by Hume to explain all the complicated operations of the mind that unify **thought** in the **imagination**. This constructive mechanism of the human mind became the basis for **associationism**, but was undermined by its own internal problems and by rival views, such as **behaviorism**.

"We have already observed that nature established connexions among particular ideas, and that no sooner one idea occurs to our thoughts than it introduces its correlative, and carries our attention towards it, by a gentle and insensible movement. These principles of connexion or association we have reduced to three, namely, resemblance, contiguity and causation." **Hume**, *Enquiries Concerning the Human Understanding and Concerning the Principles of Morals*

associationism

PHILOSOPHY OF MIND A position claiming that the association of elementary mental contents and representations is sufficient to account for complex mental states and processes, because the latter can be broken into or reduced to the elements of their association. Hence, all postulations of external entities that are supposed to explain mental phenomena are unnecessary. The position has been favored by British **empiricism**, including **Berkeley**, **Hume**, and J. S. **Mill**. Hume believed that there are three fundamental principles of association, that is, contiguity, resemblance, and causation based on constant conjunction. Associationism refers also to the psychological program, called associationistic psychology, developed by **Hartley** and in modern times by B. F. Skinner. Associationism is generally connected with ethical hedonism and metaphysical reductionism.

"Classical Associationists – Hume, say – held that mental representations have transportable constituents and, I suppose, a combinational semantics: the mental image of a house contains, as proper parts, mental images of proper parts of houses." **Fodor, in** *Mind and Action*

astrology

PHILOSOPHY OF SCIENCE As a theory, astrology is related to ancient cosmology and Ptolemaic astronomy, but it is mainly known as a divinatory art, to foretell one's future life according to the pattern of the heavenly bodies at birth or to predict future human events on the basis of current celestic movements. Astrology presupposes that a person's fate has been determined and written in the stars and leaves no place for human freedom. It has been a target of criticism in the Western rationalist tradition and is now presented as a prime example of a **pseudo-science**.

"Astrology . . . pretends to discover that correspondence or concatenation which is between the superior globe and the inferior." **Bacon,** *The Philosophical Works of Francis Bacon*

asymmetric relation, see symmetric relation

atheism

PHILOSOPHY OF RELIGION [from Greek *a*, not + *theos*, God, the absence of belief in God] The belief that **God** – especially a personal, **omniscient**, **omnipotent**, benevolent God – does not exist. Throughout much of Western history, atheism has been a term of abuse, and atheists have been attacked for impiety and immorality. The non-believers of a particular religion have also been called atheists by the believers of that religion. As a philosophical position, atheism is supported by several arguments. Because science proves that matter is eternal, there is no need for God to be the creator of the material universe. The existence of so many evils and defects in the world is incompatible with the existence of a God with the traditional supreme attributes. God is claimed to exist necessarily, but it is difficult to make sense of the notion of necessary existence. These arguments contest important arguments for the existence of God. Of significant philosophers, **Holbach**, **Feuerbach**, **Marx**, **Nietzsche**, and **Sartre** were all atheists. Atheism should be distinguished

from **pantheism**, which claims to identify God with the world, and from **agnosticism**, which claims that we do not know whether God exists.

In another sense, atheism is the position of not being a **theist**. God might exist, but does not govern or care for the world. This view, which is faithful to the Greek etymology of the term, is sometimes called negative atheism, in contrast to the positive atheism discussed above.

". . . the controversy between atheists and non-atheists in Western society has usually been about the question of whether an all-good, all knowing, all-powerful being exists." **M. Martin,** *Atheism*

a this

METAPHYSICS, ANCIENT GREEK PHILOSOPHY [Greek *tode ti*, sometimes translated as thisness] Unlike *tode* (this), which is simply a pronoun that can refer to everything, *tode ti* is a technical term introduced by **Aristotle**. In the *Categories* he defines it as "individual and numerically one" and takes it as a mark of a primary **substance** (sensible particular). In contrast, a secondary substance (species and genus) is marked by *poion ti* (a kind). In the *Metaphysics*, *tode ti* is one criterion for primary substance. In contrast, the universal is not substance and is labeled *toionde* (Greek, such, the equivalent of *poion ti*). Aristotle claimed that among **form**, **matter**, and the composite of form and matter, form best meets the criterion of *tode ti*, with the composite second. Since *tode ti* seems straightforwardly to denote a particular thing, Aristotle's form appears to be a particular. But this is a disputable point, for many who believe that Aristotelian form is a kind of universal maintain that *tode ti* is not necessarily a particular, but can mean a determination and that an *infirma species* can also be *tode ti*. The morphology *tode ti* suggests that one of its two constituent words is a class-name and that the other restricts the class to a single member, but it is disputable which function should be assigned to which word.

"Everything that is common indicates not 'a this', but 'such', but substance is 'a this'." **Aristotle,** *Metaphysics*

atom

METAPHYSICS, ANCIENT GREEK PHILOSOPHY, PHILOSOPHY OF SCIENCE [from Greek *atomos*, in turn from *a*, not + *temos*, cut, hence the smallest unit, which cannot be further cut or divided] The central conception of the Greek atomists, such as Leucippus and **Democritus**, who claimed that atom and **void** are the principles from which everything else in the world is composed. Atoms are ungenerated, imperishable, indivisible, homogeneous, and finite. The attributes ascribed to an atom are similar to the properties that **Parmenides** ascribed to his "is." Atoms move in the void and differ only in size, shape, and position. Thus sensible features like color, taste, and smell do not belong to external bodies but are the result of the interaction between atoms and ourselves. The conception of the atom is broadly viewed as one of the greatest achievements of ancient natural philosophy; and it has been a subject of dispute in the later development of philosophy and science, especially in the **corpuscularian** philosophy of the seventeenth and eighteenth centuries. In Greek philosophy, Aristotle also used the term atom for the *infirma* species.

"By convention are sweet and bitter, hot and cold, by convention is colour; in truth are atoms and the void." **Democritus, in Sextus Empiricus'** *Adversus Mathematicos (Against the Grammarians)*

atomic fact

METAPHYSICS, LOGIC, PHILOSOPHY OF LANGUAGE A term introduced by **Russell** and also employed by **Wittgenstein** in his *Tractatus*. For Russell, atomic facts are the simplest kind of facts given in experience, but Wittgenstein is less interested in this epistemological aspect than in the role of atomism in logic and in the possibility of language. Atomic facts consist in the possession of a quality by some particular thing (i.e. "This is white") or in a relation among some particulars (i.e. "A gives B to C"). The relation can be dyadic (between two things), triadic (among three things), tetradic (among four things), and so on. Russell also calls a quality a "monadic relation," allowing the integration of predication into his general account of relations. Each atomic fact contains a relation and one or more terms of the relation. Those propositions expressing atomic facts are called **atomic propositions** and assert that a certain thing has a certain quality or that certain things have a certain relation. Atomic facts determine the truth or falsity of atomic propositions, and there is a logical isomorphism between them. Atomic

facts are the terminating points of logical analysis. A "molecular fact," that is, complex facts such as "p or q", is constituted by more than one atomic fact. Molecular facts are represented by the **truth-functional** compound propositions of atomic propositions, called molecular propositions.

"There you have a whole infinite hierarchy of facts – facts in which you have a thing and a quality, two things and a relation, three things and a relation, four things and a relation, and so on. That whole hierarchy constitutes what I call atomic facts, and they are the simplest sort of facts." **Russell,** *Logic and Knowledge*

atomic proposition

LOGIC A proposition asserting that a certain thing has a certain quality, or that certain things have a certain relation, such as "This is white," or "This is between a and b." Atomic propositions can be either positive ("This is white") or negative ("This is not white"). They express atomic facts and have their truth or falsity determined by atomic facts. An atomic proposition itself cannot be further analyzed into other component propositions, but the combination of two or more atomic propositions through logical connectives forms a **molecular proposition**.

"We may then define an atomic proposition as one of which no part is a proposition, while a molecular proposition is one of which at least one part is a proposition." **Russell,** *Collected Papers of Bertrand Russell,* **vol. VII**

atomism

METAPHYSICS, PHILOSOPHY OF SCIENCE, PHILOSOPHY OF LANGUAGE [from Greek *atom*, the indivisible] A position holding that the world is composed of a infinite number of indivisible small elements and the **void**. It was first proposed as a metaphysical hypothesis by the Greek philosophers Leucippus and **Democritus** in order to account for the phenomenon of **change** denied by **Parmenides**. This ancient atomism, which was later developed by **Epicurus**, claimed that there are an infinite number of imperceptible material **atoms**, differing in quantitative properties. The atoms meet in the void and join together to form various compounds that may again divide into atoms. Their quantitative differences determine the qualitative differences of the compounds. All movement in the world can be reduced to the arrangement and rearrangement of atoms in the void.

This metaphysical doctrine was revived in modern philosophy by **Gassendi** in the form of **corpuscularism**. Such speculation about the structure of the world was supported by the chemical investigations of John Dalton (1766–1844) and then in physics. In this century, **Russell** and early **Wittgenstein** developed a kind of logical atomism, claiming that the world is ultimately composed of elementary or atomic facts, to which elementary propositions correspond. Semantic atomism, developed by F. **Dretske** and J. **Fodor** and others, proposes that the meaning of a concept is determined by its relation to the thing to which it applies, rather than by its relation to other concepts.

> "The logic which I will advocate is atomistic . . . When I say that my logic is atomistic, I mean that I share the common-sense belief that there are many separate things." **Russell, *Logic and Knowledge***

atomistic property, another term for punctuate property

atonement

PHILOSOPHY OF RELIGION, ETHICS Originally, the condition of being at one after two parties have been estranged from one another, but later an act or payment through which harmony is restored. The Jewish Day of Atonement (Hebrew *Yom Kippur*) is a holy day requiring abstinence and repentance from all believers. In Christianity, the primary act of atonement was the self-sacrificial death of Jesus Christ in order to redeem humankind from sin, leading to the reunion of God and men. This mysterious account represents a primitive morality of paying back what one owes, but understanding the nature of this sacrifice has been a topic of debate. Interpretations include paying a ransom exacted by the devil, satisfying an outraged God, restoring God's honor insulted by sin, repaying what is our debt to God, substituting for us and giving an example of love that inspires repentance. It is difficult to render any of these theories coherent with the notion of a perfect deity. Jesus is innocent and human beings are sinful. How can the sacrifice of the former

substitute for that of the latter? If God accepts that sacrifice, how can he be just? The Resurrection of Christ and the identity between the Son and the Father make atonement even more problematic.

> "Atonement, following our view, is a 'sheltering' or 'covering', but a profounder form of it." **Otto, *The Idea of the Holy***

attitude

ETHICS, PHILOSOPHY OF ACTION A mental state of approval or disapproval, favoring or disfavoring. It is associated with emotion and feeling, but is contrasted to **belief**. While belief is concerned with fact and is cognitive, attitude is concerned with evaluation and emotional response. People having the same beliefs might have different attitudes, or have the same attitudes although they have different beliefs toward the same object. Hence the distinction between attitude and belief amounts to the distinction between **value** and **fact**. Subjectivist ethics claims that attitude is more directly related to motivation and behavior and that ethical and other value judgments are matters of attitude rather than of cognition.

> "The term 'attitude' . . . designates any psychological disposition of being for and against something." **Stevenson, *Facts and Values***

attribute

METAPHYSICS, LOGIC [from Latin *ad*, upon + *tribure*, assign, bestow] In contrast to the notion of **substance**, attributes are things that can be predicated of or attributed to a substance and are represented by **predicates** in logic. The development of metaphysics further distinguishes between essential and accidental attributes. An essential attribute is a characteristic a thing must possess during its existence, while an accidental attribute is a characteristic that a thing may or may not possess, and the alteration of which will not affect the nature of that thing. This distinction corresponds to that between essence and accident. An attribute is generally taken to be the same thing as a property, quality, or characteristic.

The basic description of attribute is from **Aristotle**'s philosophy. Attributes are ontological complements to objects. While an object is concrete and independent, an attribute is abstract and metaphysically incomplete. Attributes are the different ways of existing that an object exhibits. The notion of attribute also plays an important role in rationalism, especially in the philosophy of **Spinoza**. For him, attributes were the things that constitute, express, or pertain to the essence or nature of God or substance. Substance has an infinite number of attributes, each of which expresses one infinite and eternal essence. However, human intellect knows only two attributes, thought and extension. This account differed from **Descartes**, who claimed that thought and extension actually form two independent substances. However, Spinoza thought that there is a real distinction between thought and extension, and he developed a theory of **psycho-physical parallelism** to explain their interactions. Contemporary philosophy considers a state of affairs as comprising the having of an attribute by an object. Various discussions regarding the notion of attribute are based on the identification of attributes with **universals**. Philosophers debate questions such as the ontological status of attributes, whether there are uninstantiated attributes and how an attribute is related to an object. There is also a view that can be traced to Aristotle according to which an attribute can be a particular. The white color of Socrates' skin might be peculiar to Socrates himself and vanish along with his death. A universal attribute, according to this view, is merely a resemblance among particular attributes.

"By attributes I understand that which the intellect perceives of substance as constituting its essence." **Spinoza,** *Ethics*

attribute theory of mind, an alternative term for the double-aspect theory

attributive adjective

LOGIC, ETHICS Peter Geach distinguishes attributive adjectives from predicative adjectives. While predicative adjectives have the same application to different nouns to which they are attached, attributive adjectives can yield various applications with regard to different nouns. If X can be both A (a singer), and B (a criminal), and if X can be a CA (an intelligent singer) and CB (an intelligent criminal), then C is a predicative adjective. If X can be both A (a singer) and B (a criminal), and X can be DA (a nice singer),

but cannot be DB (a nice criminal), then D is an attributive adjective. The purpose of the distinction is to illuminate the meaning of the concept good by showing that good is an attributive rather than a predicative adjective.

"I shall say that in a phrase 'an A B' ('A' being an adjective and 'B' being a noun) 'A' is a (logically) predicative adjective if the predication 'is an A B' splits up logically into a pair of predications 'is a B' and 'is A'; otherwise I shall say that 'A' is a (logically) attributive adjective." **Geach, in Foot (ed.),** *Theories of Ethics*

aufheben, German word for sublation

Augustine of Hippo, St (354–430)
Medieval theologian and philosopher, born in Thagaste, North Africa, moved in 383 to teach in Rome and Milan, converted from Manichaeism to Neoplatonism and then to Christianity, and, after returning to North Africa, became Bishop of Hippo in 395. Augustine played a crucial role in the transition from classical antiquity to the Middle Ages. For him, Neoplatonism is a preparation for Christianity, and philosophy can discover wisdom and help to achieve human blessedness. He provided Neoplatonic interpretations of major Christian teachings and made significant contributions to topics such as the corruption of human nature, free will, predestination, sin, love, grace, Divine law, and time. His masterpiece *Confessions* (397–400) is both a spiritual autobiography and a philosophical classic. His other important works include *City of God* (413–26) and *The Trinity* (420).

Augustinian picture of language
PHILOSOPHY OF LANGUAGE A view that **Wittgenstein** attributed to St **Augustine** and criticized at the beginning of *Philosophical Investigations*. According to this view, each word has a **meaning** which is the **object** for which it stands, and so it has a meaning in virtue of its being correlated with some entity. This view is criticized as being oversimplified because it concentrates excessively on **names** and ignores other kinds of words that function very differently from names. Furthermore, even in the case of names the meaning-relation is more complicated. From this view Wittgenstein himself

proceeded to develop an alternative approach to language that emphasizes the multiplicity of different kinds of words and uses of language.

> "In this [Augustinian] picture of language we find the roots of the following idea: Every word has a meaning. This meaning is correlated with the word. It is the object for which the word stands."
> **Wittgenstein,** *Philosophical Investigations*

Augustinianism

PHILOSOPHY OF RELIGION, MEDIEVAL PHILOSOPHY A philosophical and theological tradition based on the thought of St **Augustine** and defended by his followers. Augustine applied **Plato**'s teaching to Christian dogmas. The main elements of Augustinianism are its doctrines of **grace** and **predestination**. Human beings have inherited the **sin** of Adam and Eve, and have lost the capacity that they had in the original paradisal state to **will** and do **good**. Individuals themselves are incapable of ameliorating the situation, and only God's grace can save them. God's grace provides humanity with the knowledge of the good and the capacity to will the good and the joy in doing the good. The Scriptures constitute a special **revelation** that is beyond the reach of philosophy and **reason**. Faith in Christ alone enables man to understand the world and his own position in it on a rational basis. This later became the official doctrine of grace in the Latin Christian Church. Augustine also claimed that the chance of salvation is predestined and that man's will is impotent to attain it. The choice of God as to who would be saved and who would be condemned is hidden from us. This view of predestination gives rise to much debate in medieval philosophy. Augustinianism dominated medieval thought until the time of **Aquinas**. In the twelfth and thirteenth century it became the main rival of Aristotelianism and Thomism and has remained a major part of Western theology.

> "The gulf between nature and God can be bridged only by grace. This is the governing principle of Augustinianism." **Leff,** *Medieval Thought*

Austin, John (1790–1859)

British legal philosopher, born in Creeting Mill, Suffolk, legal positivist. Austin was appointed to the chair of jurisprudence at the newly founded University College, London, in 1826. He founded analytic jurisprudence, which examines the concepts and terminology common to any legal system, rather than focusing on the historical and sociological dimensions of the law. Influenced by his friend Bentham, his view of law was utilitarian, and his command theory of law initiated legal positivist accounts of the distinctive nature and normativity of the law. His masterpiece is *The Providence of Jurisprudence Determined* (1832).

Austin, J(ohn) L(angshaw) (1911–60)

British philosopher, born in Lancaster, educated and taught at Oxford. As a leading figure of Oxford ordinary language philosophy, Austin maintained that the main task of philosophical investigation is to examine and elucidate the concepts of ordinary language. His most significant contribution to philosophy is the speech act theory, according to which what an utterance is used to do is a main factor in determining its meaning. He understood saying something as performing linguistic acts and classified speech acts into three kinds: locutionary, illocutionary, and perlocutionary. According to him, we can remove many traditional philosophical problems by distinguishing these acts. His papers are collected in *Philosophical Papers* (1961), *How to Do Things with Words* (1961), and *Sense and Sensibilia* (1962).

authenticity

MODERN EUROPEAN PHILOSOPHY [German *Eigentlichkeit*, from *eigen*, own, literally, my ownness, what is mine] **Anxiety**, the feeling arising from our sense of **freedom**, reveals to us that each person is uniquely himself or herself and no one else. According to **Heidegger**, each of us has our own potentialities to fulfill and has to face our death on our own. If, as Heideggerian *Dasein*, one has a resolute attitude in facing this lonely condition and holds a responsible position toward one's uniqueness and individuality, that person is said to lead an authentic existence and to be aware of what this condition means. Authenticity holds onto both the future and the past and provides a constancy of the self. It also requires *Dasein* to accept its own death. Indeed, Heidegger claims that the real authentic self is revealed when one encounters one's own death. In authenticity, "I" always comes first, although this "I" is not a Subject. If one is led by anxiety to protect oneself through absorption into the mass and the anonymous "they," as people generally do, then that person leads an inauthentic existence. In inauthenticity, "they" comes first, and one's own existence is lost. This attitude is what Heidegger calls *Dasein's* "fallingness," that is, *Dasein's* turning away from itself and allowing itself to be engrossed in day-to-day preoccupations and to drift along with trends of the crowd.

"As modes of Being, authenticity and inauthenticity (these expressions have been chosen terminologically in a strict sense) are both grounded in the fact that any *Dasein* whatsoever is characterized by mineness." **Heidegger,** *Being and Time*

authoritarianism

POLITICAL PHILOSOPHY A political view that claims that subjects should obey some authority whose excellence or legitimacy is not open to question. In practice, within an authoritarian political system the government has unlimited power and lacks proper constitutional constraint. The authority can make decisions without needing to consult or negotiate with those to whom the decisions will apply. Such a society is ruled by a person or persons rather than by law. **Hobbes**'s *Leviathan* provides a rationale for subjects to obey an authoritarian ruler. In modern times, authoritarianism has been displayed in various forms of dictatorship. It is opposed to liberal **individualism** and is widely condemned for suppressing individuality and encroaching upon personal rights. Defenders of authoritarianism claim that it can provide security and order for society and that it is preferable to the limitations and corruption of a liberal **democratic** system. In ethics, authoritarianism is an ethical system that presupposes that the majority are ethically incompetent and need to obey ethically competent authority.

"Authoritarianism in its pure form . . . states its basic prescription of obedience in such a way that there is no need for a higher validating principle." **Ladd,** *The Structure of Moral Code*

authority

POLITICAL PHILOSOPHY, PHILOSOPHY OF LAW The right possessed by a person, organization or state to issue commands and have them obeyed. This right implies an obligation upon those who are subject to the authority to respect and obey the commands.

Authority is a kind of **power**, but not every kind of power is authority. Several kinds of power are merely coercive and do not have any **legitimacy**. A major problem in political philosophy is to justify the grounds of state authority that provides the final appeal in settling dispute. **Social contract** theory is one attempt to provide a solution. It claims that legitimate authority among men can come only through covenants. The scope and limits of state authority also need explanation. Authority can hold in some areas but not in others or over some people but not over others. Max **Weber** distinguished three kinds of authority: rational-legal authority, which is from reason and law; traditional authority, which is from tradition; and charismatic authority, which is from some special qualities a person has [Greek *charisma*, divine gift]. Outside political and legal contexts, an authority is a reliable source of information.

"To have authority to do something is to have the right to do it." **Raphael,** *Problems of Political Philosophy*

authority *de facto,* see authority *de jure*

authority *de jure*

POLITICAL PHILOSOPHY, PHILOSOPHY OF LAW Legitimate authority that is derived from **rules** that people are legally or morally obliged to obey. In contrast, *de facto* authority is based on power rather than legitimacy. For authority to be stable, power and legitimacy must be combined, and in practice there is no clear way of distinguishing between *de jure* and *de facto* authority. Authority *de jure* is a normative concept that is intrinsically related to the notion of **rights**. In contrast, authority *de facto* is a causal concept based on tradition or power. The distinction plays a central role in contemporary discussions of authority and brings together the characteristic concerns of political philosophy with legitimacy and political science with power. The validity of the distinction is questioned by theorists, who hold that one kind of authority is basic and that the other kind of authority must be reduced to it.

"So long as men believe in the authority of states, we can conclude that they possess the concept of *de jure* authority." **Wolff,** *In Defense of Anarchism*

automaton

PHILOSOPHY OF MIND, PHILOSOPHY OF ACTION A moving thing whose motion is due to the internal structure of its parts rather than to an external cause. **Descartes** uses automaton as a synonym of self-moving machine. For him, the whole world is an automaton, for it contains in itself the corporeal principle of the movements for which it is designed. All animated bodies (including human bodies) are automata and they are not essentially different from inanimate matter but simply exhibit greater complexity in the disposition and function of their parts. Non-human animals are automata pure and simple. All their actions and reactions can be accounted for in terms of the automatic movements of their organs, which are essentially like those performed by any artificially constructed machine. Humans are distinguished from automata because some of their actions are initiated freely by the will. Currently "automaton" may refer either to a machine that imitates human intelligence or to a machine running according to a program.

"We do not praise automatons for accurately producing all the movements they were designed to perform, because the production of these movements occurs necessarily. It is the designer who is praised for constructing such carefully-made devices." **Descartes, *The Philosophical Writings***

autonomy

POLITICAL PHILOSOPHY, ETHICS [from Greek *auto*, self + *nomos*, law, self-rule] A term traced to **Machiavelli**, who used it to mean both free from dependence and self-legislation. **Rousseau** claimed that the people of a politically autonomous society are bound only by the laws that they legislate themselves. **Kant** applied this notion to the moral domain and established it as a central concept in his ethical theory. A moral **agent** is autonomous if his **will** is not determined by external factors and if the agent can apply laws to itself in accordance with reason alone. Such agents respect these laws and are bound only by them. In Kant, autonomy contrasts with **heteronomy** (from Greek *hetero*, other + *nomos*, law, ruled by others) in which one's will is controlled by outside factors, including one's desires. Autonomy is linked to **freedom** and is a necessary condition for ascribing **responsibility** to an agent. Respect for

a person as a self-determined being is a common moral theme. However, since each of us lives in a society and is inevitably constrained by various external elements, it is possible to dispute the extent to which true individual autonomy is possible and practical. In other areas, autonomy is logical or conceptual independence.

"Autonomy is the ground of the dignity of human nature and of every rational nature." **Kant, *Groundwork for the Metaphysics of Morals***

autonomy of grammar, another term for autonomy of language

autonomy of language

PHILOSOPHY OF LANGUAGE, METAPHYSICS Also called arbitrariness of grammar, or autonomy of grammar. The view that the grammar of language and its constituent linguistic rules do not mirror the essence of reality or the world, as held by linguistic foundationalism. If language is autonomous, it does not correspond to extra-linguistic reality, nor is it constrained by such a reality, and an account of reality cannot be justified by what is represented in language. Language is not a product of the rational representation of an external reality. This idea has led **Leibniz**, **Frege**, and **Russell** to attempt to invent an ideal language to construct a better representation of the world than ordinary language.

Wittgenstein disagrees with the autonomy of language in his *Tractatus*, but later embraces and develops it in great detail in his account of **language games**. He argues that the meaning of a word is determined by grammatical **rules** governing its use rather than by the external metaphysical nature of the world. Language is like a game, which is determined by its rules. The aims of language are fixed by the rules of grammar. If we change the rules, a word has a different meaning. The autonomy of language does not imply that what a term means is a matter of personal choice, but indicates that language is not merely an instrument to depict what is outside language. In this sense of autonomous, Wittgenstein claims that speaking a language is part of a communal activity and is embedded in a **form of life**. The idea of the autonomy of language is criticized by essentialists such as **Kripke** and **Putnam**, who argue that the meaning of a word is determined by the nature of that to which it refers, and that our understanding of the meaning of a word changes in accordance with the development of scientific knowledge of that nature.

> "The analogies of language with chess are useful in that they illustrate the autonomy of language. Thus in the case of chess there is no temptation to think that it is essential to point outside to some object as the meaning." **Wittgenstein,** *Manuscript*

autonomy of morals

ETHICS The claimed independence of morality or ethics as a discipline from other fields such as biology, psychology, sociology, or religion, and even from other disciplines of philosophy such as metaphysics, epistemology, or political philosophy. Instead, morality is claimed to have its own internal rational methods of justification and criticism. Moral terms do not refer to natural properties and hence cannot be defined by them. Moral judgments cannot be judged by any objective principles outside morality. Value judgments are not derived from statements of fact. The distinction between **fact** and **value,** between is and ought, and the alleged naturalistic fallacy are all derived from attempts to justify the autonomy of morals.

> "The fundamental term of normative evaluation, the one in terms of which the others are defined, must itself be indefinable. This thesis, which many philosophers find quite plausible, may be called the doctrine of the autonomy of morals." **F. Feldman,** *Introductory Ethics*

auxiliaries

POLITICAL PHILOSOPHY, ANCIENT GREEK PHILOSOPHY [Greek *epikoupoi*] In the *Republic*, the class of warriors in **Plato**'s Ideal State or its executive branch of government. It was the second class, separated from the class of **guardians,** which was composed of noble young men. The function of the auxiliaries was to carry out the executive orders of the guardians for the preservation and maintenance of the city. While the guardians had knowledge, the auxiliaries only had true beliefs. Their virtue was courage, and they corresponded to the spirited element in the soul.

> "Those young men whom we have called guardians hitherto we shall call auxiliaries to help the rulers in their decisions." **Plato,** *Republic*

averageness, another expression for everydayness

Averroes (*c.*1126–98)

The Latin name for Ibn Rushd, medieval Islamic philosopher, born in Cordoba, Spain. Averroes composed a massive set of commentaries on the whole corpus of Aristotle's works. The Latin translations of his commentaries formed an integral part of the educational curriculum in European universities of his time, and, as a result, he was simply called "the commentator." His careful explication and original discussion of Aristotle's doctrines, such as those of the soul and of active and passive intellect, exerted great influence on Western medieval philosophy from the thirteenth to the seventeenth centuries, although church leaders frequently condemned some Islamic aspects of teachings. His name is often associated with the doctrine of double truth. His own major work is *The Incoherence of the Incoherence* (*c.*1180).

Avicenna (980–1037)

The Latin name of Ibn Sina, medieval Islamic philosopher and physician, born near Bukhara, Persia. Avicenna introduced Aristotle to the Islamic world and developed a system that combined the philosophy of Aristotle and Plotinus with Islamic thought. God is necessary being and the necessitating cause of all existents. Essence and existence are identical only in God. Avicenna also described the spiritual journey to God in terms of Islamic mysticism. He wrote more than a hundred works on philosophy, religion, and science. His most important philosophical works are *Healing: Directives and Remarks* and *Deliverance*, and his *Canon of Medicine* was a standard textbook until the seventeenth century. The translation of his writings into Latin initiated the Aristotelian revival of the twelfth and thirteenth centuries and had profound effects on the Latin West, particularly through the writings of Aquinas. His works were a major influence on Christian theology.

avowal

PHILOSOPHY OF MIND, PHILOSOPHY OF LANGUAGE A term associated with **Wittgenstein**'s later account of the mind and introduced into philosophy by **Ryle**. Along with expression and utterance, it is an English translation of the German word *Ausdruk*. An avowal is the utterance of a first-person present-tense sentence to express a mental state (for example "I am in pain") rather than to describe something. For Wittgenstein, an avowal is not a cognitive claim that can be true or false, and it makes no sense to justify what I avow by reference to further grounds. Rather, an avowal is an act that characterizes being in the inner state which it expresses. It is nonsense to say that "I know that I am in pain." This notion is associated with Wittgenstein's **private language** argument. This argument rejects the traditional Cartesian claim that an expression of mind is a description of inner mental states and raises many issues in contemporary philosophy of mind. However, it remains controversial whether first-person psychological sentences must be understood as something other than reports of facts about ourselves.

> "Not many unstudied utterances embody explicit interest phrases, or what I have elsewhere been calling 'avowals', like 'I want', 'I hope', 'I intend', 'I dislike' . . . ; and their grammar makes it tempting to misconstrue all the sentences in which they occur as self-descriptions. But in its primary employment 'I want . . .' is not used to convey information, but to make a request or demand." **Ryle**, *The Concept of Mind*

awareness, direct and indirect, see immediate perception

axiarchism

ETHICS, METAPHYSICS [from Greek *axis*, value + *arche*, rule, rule by what is good and valued] A term invented by John Leslie for the belief that the world is largely or entirely determined by what is ethically valuable, and that things in this world have an intrinsic desire for the good. It is thought that this optimistic metaphysical outlook has been held by many philosophers throughout history. The belief that the universe is the product of a directly ethical requirement is extra axiarchism.

> "Axiarchism is my label for theories picturing the world as ruled largely or entirely by value." **Leslie**, *Value and Existence*

axiological ethics, see axiology

axiology

ETHICS [from Greek *axios*, worthy + *logos*, theory or study] The general study of value and valuation, including the meaning, characteristics, and classification of value, the nature of evaluation, and the character of value judgments. The topics have traditionally been attached to the general study of ethics, but have developed into a special branch since the last century. Axiology is also called the theory of value and is mainly an **epistemology** of value. The word "axiology" was first introduced into philosophy by Urban as a translation of the German *Werttheorie*. Major contributors to axiology as a special discipline include Ehrenfels, **Meinong**, **Brentano**, Max **Scheler**, N. **Hartmann**, G. E. **Moore**, R. B. **Perry**, H. Rashdall, W. D. **Ross**, and C. I. **Lewis**. The ethics that extends the analysis of value to practical demands is called "axiological ethics."

> "'Axiology' meant the study of the ultimately worthwhile things (and of course of the ultimately counterworthwhile things) as well as the analysis of worthwhileness (or counterworthwhileness) in general." **Findlay**, *Axiological Ethics*

axiom

PHILOSOPHY OF MATHEMATICS, LOGIC [from Greek *axioma*, something worthy of acceptance or esteem] An initial set of propositions selected as the foundations of a systematic field of knowledge. Axioms serve as the basis for a mathematical or logical system, although they themselves cannot be proved within the system. A system in which certain propositions are inferred from axioms in accordance with a set of inferring rules is called an **axiomatic system**. The propositions derived from axioms are called theorems. Traditionally, a proposition is chosen as an axiom because it is basic, in that it cannot be derived from other propositions in the system, self-evident and intuitively true. Axioms can be divided into non-logical axioms, which are propositions with non-logical contents, and logical axioms, which contain only logical constants and variables. A logical axiom is also called axiom schema, which is a distinctive form of axiom that can be embodied in an infinite number of specific statements.

axiom of choice

LOGIC, PHILOSOPHY OF MATHEMATICS An axiom of set theory formulated by Zermelo. It states that for any infinite set, A, of non-empty subsets, no two of which having a common member, there is a set composed of choosing exactly one member from each of the subsets of the set A. Alternatively, it can be formulated that for a given class of classes, each of which has at least one number, there always exists a selector-function that selects one number from each of these classes. This axiom is independent of other axioms of set theory and many mathematical principles turn out to be equivalent to it. The axiom implies the existence of a set that we are unable to specify and hence challenges mathematical **constructivism**, which identifies the existence of a mathematical object with its construction by a rule. This axiom is essential for the development of set theory.

"The axiom of choice asserts that for every set S there is a function f which associates each non-empty subset A of S with a unique number f (A) of A." **Moore,** *Zermelo's Axiom of Choice*

axiom of infinity

LOGIC, PHILOSOPHY OF MATHEMATICS An axiom that is introduced by **Russell** to define the series of natural numbers in response to difficulties for such a definition arising from his **theory of types**. The axiom is a hypothesis that there is some type (the lowest type of individuals) with an infinity of instances. This axiom is widely criticized because its commitment to contentious claims about the world seem to exclude it from being a truth of logic. This in turn undermines Russell's original programme of deriving arithmetic from logic alone.

"It cannot be said to be certain that there are in fact any infinite collections in the world. The assumption that there are is what we call the 'axiom of infinity'." **Russell,** *Introduction to Mathematical Philosophy*

axiom of reducibility

LOGIC, PHILOSOPHY OF MATHEMATICS **Russell**'s ramified **theory of types** imposes too many restrictions upon mathematics, with the result that substantial mathematical theorems cannot be formulated and proved. To save them, Russell introduces the axiom of reducibility, which sorts **propositional functions** into levels and claims that for every propositional function of a higher order there exists a corresponding function of the first order which is extensionally equivalent to it. This axiom meets many difficulties, but Russell himself does not take it as a self-evident truth of logic.

"The axioms of reducibility, . . . could perfectly well be stated as a hypothesis whenever it is used, instead of being assumed to be actually true." **Russell,** *Introduction to Mathematical Philosophy*

axiom schema, see axiom

axiomatic method

LOGIC, PHILOSOPHY OF MATHEMATICS The basic procedure of the axiomatic method is (1) the assumption of a set of propositions, **axioms**, or fundamental truths that are logically independent of one another, and (2) the deduction of theorems (that is, propositions that are logically implied or proven by the axioms) from them in accordance with a set of rules of inference, as we infer a conclusion validly from a set of premises. Its result is to produce an axiomatic system. Axiomatic method has powerfully influenced philosophy, although each feature of the method has been criticized as inappropriate for philosophy.

"Familiar in mathematics is the axiomatic method, according to which a branch of mathematics begins with a list of undefined terms and a list of assumptions or postulates involving these terms, and theorems are to be derived from the postulates by the methods of formal logic." **Church,** *Introduction to Mathematical Logic*

axiomatic system

LOGIC, PHILOSOPHY OF MATHEMATICS A system in which a series of propositions are derived from an initial set of propositions in accordance with a set of formation rules and transformation rules. The members of the initial set of propositions are called **axioms**. They are independent, that is, not derivable from within the system. The derived series of propositions are called theorems. The formulation rules specify what symbols are used and what combinations of the symbols are to count as axioms and propositions directly derived from axioms. It is thus a system in which all axioms and theorems are ordered in a hierarchical arrangement and the relations between them are necessarily deductive. All propositions conforming to formation rules are called **well-formed formulae** (wff). The transformation rules determine how theorems are proved. If there is a decision procedure with respect to which all theorems of the system are provable, the system is said to be sound. If all provable formulae are theorems of that system, the system is said to be **complete** with respect to that decision procedure. If a system does not involve contradiction, it is said to be **consistent**. Soundness, completeness, and consistency are the characteristics required of an axiomatic system.

"In an axiomatic system a change anywhere ramifies into a change everywhere – the entire structure is affected when one of its supporting layers is removed." **Rescher,** *Cognitive Systematization*

axioms of intuition

EPISTEMOLOGY, METAPHYSICS For **Kant**, in order for quantitative experience to be possible, we must apply the **categories** of quantity, unity, plurality, and totality. We need rules to make these categories conform to the conditions of **intuitions** of objects. These rules for showing the objective validity of the

categories of quantity are the axioms of intuitions. The leading principle for these axioms is that all intuitions are extensive magnitudes, meaning that they have magnitudes that are spatially or temporarily extended. This principle is purported to explain the application of geometry to empirical objects and to render possible the measurement of the experiential world. Kant did not, however, specify what these axioms are. This omission raises questions about the relations between the axioms of intuition and their leading principle and about the relation between the axioms of intuition and the categories of quantity.

"Axioms of intuition. Their principle is: All intuitions are extensive magnitudes." **Kant,** *Critique of Pure Reason*

Ayer, Sir A(lfred) J(ules) (1910–89)

British philosopher, born in London, taught at Oxford and London, knighted in 1970. Ayer's widely read *Language, Truth and Logic* (1936) linked logical positivism to the British tradition of linguistic analysis, especially Hume's philosophy, and effectively introduced this anti-metaphysical philosophical movement to the English-speaking world. Ayer discussed various philosophical topics, such as perception, memory, other minds, personal identity, and skepticism and was a pioneer of ethical emotivism. His other books include the *Foundations of Empirical Knowledge* (1940), *Thinking and Meaning* (1947), *The Problem of Knowledge* (1956), *The Central Questions of Philosophy* (1972).

B

Bachelard, Gaston (1884–1962)
French philosopher of science and critic, born in Bar-sur-Aube, Professor of the History and Philosophy of Science at the Sorbonne. Bachelard rejected the positivist account of the progress of science by steady incremental accumulation and argued for the role of creative discontinuities or breaks in science and art. He stressed the importance of rejecting fixed orthodoxies and of replacing a static rationalism by a mutable conception of reason. Similar themes appear in his later critical writings. Among his major works are *The New Scientific Spirit* (1934) and *The Psychoanalysis of Fire* (1938).

backward causation

METAPHYSICS, PHILOSOPHY OF SCIENCE **Causation** is normally taken to be forward causation, in which a cause brings about an effect occurring at the same time as the cause or later. However, philosophers such as David **Pears** and Michael **Dummett** argue that backward causation is logically possible, with the ordinary temporal direction of causality reversed and the effect preceding its cause. If this is true, a current happening might bring about an earlier event and what happens in the present can affect the past.

The plausibility of backward causation depends upon our account of causation. Let us suppose that a cause is a sufficient condition for an event to take place. On this account, if an event occurring at a later time is a sufficient condition for a previous event, then the later event should be seen as a cause of the earlier event. As an example of backward causation, we can consider Aristotelian final causation, according to which an end determines something to act or move in order to realize that end. The end comes into existence later as a result of the earlier action that it determines. Backward causation can also explain many phenomena in **quantum** mechanics. However, such a notion does not entail that we can interfere with an earlier event, for we can only be an observer rather than an agent for this type of causation. Even so, there is still controversy whether what already exists can be caused by what does not yet exist.

> "We can conceive of a world in which a notion of causality associated with the opposite direction would have been more appropriate and, so long as we consider ourselves as mere observers of such a world, there is no particular conceptual difficulty about the conception of such a backward causation." **Dummett, "Bringing about the Past," in** *Philosophical Review 73*

Bacon, Francis (1561–1626)
British philosopher and statesman, born in London, educated at Cambridge. Bacon was a man of great learning and a complex personality. Through his deep conviction that science, as a systematic study of nature, could positively transform man's estate,

he became a prophet of modern science. He attacked Aristotelian and Platonic traditions and summarized the prejudices and false ways of thinking that hindered the acquisition of knowledge as the "four idols" of the mind. He attempted to construct a new method of scientific discovery, which he called the Great Instauration. Although he did not complete his project, his systematic presentation of the method of scientific induction remains a remarkable achievement. His important philosophical works are *The Advancement of Learning* (1605) and *Novum Organum* (1620). His other influential works include *Essays* (1597) and *New Atlantis* (1624).

Bacon, Roger (c.1215–c.1292)

English medieval philosopher, scientist, and theologian, born in Somerset, taught in Oxford and Paris. Bacon's rejection of Aristotelian thought and his project for a unified science based on mathematics and experiment anticipated developments in early modern science, but he held that philosophy, mathematics, and the study of language were most importantly devoted to theology and gaining knowledge of God. He held that the role of reason was to formulate hypotheses that could be confirmed only by experimental methods. His major work is *Opus Maius* (1267).

bad faith

MODERN EUROPEAN PHILOSOPHY, PHILOSOPHY OF MIND [French *mauvaise foi*, a kind of self-deception; for Sartre not merely a lie to oneself, but a lie about one's freedom] A person in bad faith takes a negative attitude with respect to himself or herself. This existential phenomenon is highlighted by **Sartre** in *Being and Nothingness* and illustrated in his literary works, although his discussion is ambiguous and is subject to much dispute in interpretation. Human reality lies in the intricate relationship between **freedom** and **responsibility**. Bad faith ignores their inner relationship, and is an attempt to evade responsibility for what one has freely chosen, by pretending to oneself and others that things are predetermined and could not have been otherwise. A person who falls into bad faith regards himself as merely a passive subject of outside influences. Bad faith refuses to acknowledge that human beings are self-determining and hence differ from things in the world. Bad faith is rooted in our freedom of consciousness and is possible

because human consciousness brings **nothingness** and non-being into the world. The phenomenon reveals the discrepancy inherent in human reality between the human condition and human behavior, between our abstract awareness of our nature and our concrete acts. According to Sartre, a person in bad faith is playing, and the instability of play makes bad faith possible in the face of the apparently paradoxical nature of **self-deception**. In contrast to bad faith, good faith acknowledges oneself as a self-conscious human being freely and responsibly acting within the world.

> "It is best to choose and to examine one determined attitude which is essential to human reality and which is such that consciousness instead of directing its negation outward turns it toward itself. This attitude, it seems to me, is bad faith."
> **Sartre, *Being and Nothingness***

bad infinity

METAPHYSICS, PHILOSOPHY OF RELIGION **Hegel**'s term for an endless series advancing from one thing to another, like a straight line with no end. It is an infinite series of causes and effects and is separated from the finite. A bad infinity contrasts with true infinity, which is closely associated with the finite, for something that is infinite in one perspective can also be finite in another. True infinity is like a circle, finite but unbounded, and it is associated in Hegel's system with the negation of the negation. From the perspective of bad infinity, **God** is infinite and the world is finite, and hence there arises a contrast between God and the world. Hegel claims that this division is overcome in the perspective of true infinity.

> "Something becomes an other; this other is itself somewhat; therefore it likewise becomes an other, and so on ad infinitum. This infinity is the bad or negative infinity: it is only a negation of an infinite; but the finite rises again the same as ever, and is never got rid of and absorbed." **Hegel, *Logic***

Baier, Annette (1929–)

New Zealander moral philosopher, born in Queenstown, New Zealand, Professor of Philosophy, University of Pittsburgh. Baier seeks to understand mental and moral phenomena, including reason and intentionality, in terms of human social being.

As a scholar of Hume, she stresses the importance of sentiment and custom in moral life and argues against a conception of moral philosophy that attempts to find a system of universal moral rules. Her main work is *Postures of the Mind: Essays on Mind and Morals* (1985).

Baier, Kurt (1917–)

Australian moral philosopher, born in Vienna, Austria, Professor of Philosophy, University of Pittsburgh. Baier argues for the truth and falsity of normative moral judgments and for the objectivity and verifiability of ethics as a rational system governing human interaction, based on the moral point of view rather than egoism. Within this framework, he has developed theories of fairness, obligation, punishment, law, and applied ethics. His main work is *From a Moral Point of View* (1955).

Bain, Alexander (1818–1903)

Scottish psychologist and philosopher, born in Aberdeen and Professor of Logic and Rhetoric at University of Aberdeen. Bain sought to unite associationist psychology, reflex physiology and empiricist philosophy in a single theory of the mind and founded the journal *Mind* to promote this project. His understanding of belief in terms of action prepared the ground for the development of pragmatism. His major works include *The Senses and the Intellect* (1855) and *The Emotions and the Will* (1859).

Bakunin, Michael (1814–76)

Russian political thinker, exponent of anarchism. Bakunin was the major figure of nineteenth-century anarchism as a revolutionary activist and thinker. He argued for a negative revolt against the positive institutions of church and state in order to establish a society based on free cooperation without private property. He rejected the control of society by a scientific elite, including a Marxist elite committed to scientific socialism. His major works include *Revolutionary Catechism* (1865) and *Federalism, Socialism and Anti-Theologism*.

bald man paradox, see sorites paradox

barber paradox

LOGIC There is a barber in a remote village who claims to shave all and only those villagers who do not shave themselves. Does the barber shave himself? If he does, then he does not, because he shaves only those who do not shave themselves; if he does not, then he does, because he shaves all those who do not shave themselves. The barber shaves himself if and only if he does not shave himself. This **paradox** was recounted by **Russell**, although he attributed it to an unknown source. It is similar in form to **Russell's paradox**, that is, whether the set of all sets that are not members of themselves is a member of itself, but it is different in nature. For while Russell's paradox has deep implications for logic and mathematics, we may dismiss the existence of such a barber (because there cannot be one). It is for this reason that the barber paradox, together with others of this sort, is called a pseudo-paradox, in contrast to logical and semantic paradoxes.

"We respond to the barber paradox simply by saying that there is no such barber." **Sainsbury,** *Paradoxes*

Barcan formula

LOGIC A principle in quantified modal logic, introduced by the American logician Ruth Barcan **Marcus**. It states that if possibly there exists something that is A, then there is something that is possibly A. That is, $\Diamond(\exists x)A$ strictly implies $(\exists x)\Diamond A$. This is also true for its converse: $(\exists x)\Diamond A$ strictly implies $\Diamond(\exists x)A$. The Barcan formula also includes the following thesis: If everything is necessarily A, necessarily everything is A. That is, $(\forall x) \Box A \supset \Box (\forall x)A$. The formula is rejected by **Kripke** and **Rescher** by appeal to the theory of **possible worlds**, for in this formula the antecedent might be true of the actual world, but its consequent might be false in certain possible worlds.

"... The Barcan Formula stipulating the implication from $\Diamond(\exists x)\phi x$ to $(\exists x)\Diamond\phi x$." **Rescher,** *A Theory of Possibility*

bare fact, another term for brute fact

bare particular

METAPHYSICS A thing changes its **properties** over time while remaining the same thing. The traditional explanation is that the **substance** or **essence** of a thing remains or endures and does not involve change unless the thing itself is destroyed. An alternative account can be provided on the basis of the notion of bare particular. On this view, instead of being a continuing entity, an individual is a series of momentary objects that stand in contingent relations to other objects in the series. These relations guarantee that the thing endures. Each momentary object comprises universal properties, relations, and a further element called a bare particular. The bare particular is the instantiation of the universal properties and serves as the bearer of the characteristics co-present with it. The bare particular is different from either properties or relations, is without characteristics (hence, bare), and is even more basic than time and space. Since a bare particular cannot be a constituent of two different momentary objects, it confers individuality upon substances by being the basis for their numerical oneness.

The difference between a basic particular and the usual notion of substance is that it is momentary rather than continuing. The theory of basic particulars is opposed to the cluster theory, according to which a substance is the sum of the characteristics we associate with them. It further opposes the principle of the **identity of indiscernibles** by allowing the logical possibility of two or more substances having all of their characteristics in common. The notion of bare particulars is disputable. It is suspect epistemologically, for a thing without characteristics is neither perceivable nor knowable. Many philosophers, while finding difficulties in accepting the claim that a particular is a bundle of universals, also reject the notion that a particular can exist without properties.

"The bare particular and the pure universal are vicious abstractions from states of affairs." **D. Armstrong,** *What is a Law of Nature?*

bargaining
PHILOSOPHY OF SOCIAL SCIENCE, POLITICAL PHILOSOPHY A procedure for deciding disputes and negotiating an optimal solution for two or more parties. Bargaining is an important social fact. It is widely used in market economies and daily civil affairs, and the notion has been borrowed by political theorists as a strategy of coalition formation in politics. Bargaining is always a process during which a series of outcomes appear, each yielding some level of utility for the bargaining parties, until a final outcome is reached

that is acceptable to each party. It is essential in bargaining to consider carefully what risks one can afford to take as well as the advantages that are offered.

"I shall therefore extend 'bargaining' to cover any situation where one party offers another either some advantage or the removal of the threats of some disadvantage in return for the other party's performing some specific action." **Barry,** *Political Argument*

Barth, Karl (1886–1968)
Swiss theologian, born in Basle, Professor, University of Basle. The sole object of Barth's theology is the God who addresses fallen human beings with his Word through Jesus Christ. His theology is dialectical rather than metaphysical because it focuses on this revelation and the human response to it rather than focusing on natural theology or an analogy of being between God and human beings. His major works include *Romans* (1919), *Anselm* (1931), and *Church Dogmatics* (1932).

basic action
PHILOSOPHY OF ACTION Some actions are done by performing other actions. In some sense, the latter actions cause the former actions. If I am driving a car, the action of driving a car is accomplished by such things as turning the steering wheel, depressing the accelerator or brake, and checking the road and the mirror. These actions in turn are accomplished by moving my hands, feet, and eyes. The chain of actions that are responsible for other actions must terminate in actions that are not accomplished by performing other actions. **Danto** calls these actions basic actions and calls actions performed by means of other actions non-basic actions. In many cases it is unclear how to identify basic actions. Discussion concerning the nature of basic actions has been a central focus of action theory.

"B is a basic action of a if and only if (i) B is an action and (ii) whenever a performed B, there is no other action A performed by a such that B is caused by A." **A. C. Danto, "What We Can Do,"** *Journal of Philosophy* **60**

basic norm
PHILOSOPHY OF LAW A term introduced by the Austrian legal philosopher Hans **Kelsen**. As a **legal**

positivist, Kelsen objected to the reduction of the validity of law to morality. How, then, are we to account for the source of legal validity? Kelsen claims that law is a system of norms. Each lower-level norm derives its authority from norms at a higher level. This chain of validation will eventually lead to an ultimate norm, that is, a basic norm (German *Grundnorm*) which, at the historical starting-point of norm creation conferred legislative power on the fathers of the first constitution. A basic norm is a presupposition that must be assumed by anyone who seeks to explain our knowledge of positive law. As the ultimate power-conferring source, the basic norm corresponds to **Austin**'s command of the sovereign and **Hart**'s **rule of recognition**.

> "Coercive acts ought to be carried out only under the conditions and in the way determined by the 'fathers' of the constitution or the organs delegated by them. This is, schematically formulated, the basic norm of the legal order of a single state." **Kelsen,** *General Theory of Law and State*

basic particulars

METAPHYSICS, EPISTEMOLOGY **Strawson**'s term for a distinguishable class of **particulars** that can be identified and re-identified without reference to particulars of other kinds. Other particulars are identifiable only through making identifying **reference** to basic particulars. As constituents of our conceptual framework, basic particulars bestow their characteristics upon this scheme. Because the possibility of identifying particulars lies in locating these particulars in a single unified spatio-temporal system, and because material bodies are three-dimensional objects that endure through time and are accessible to observation and experience, Strawson argues that material bodies are the best candidates for basic particulars.

> "The assertion that material bodies are basic particulars in our actual conceptual scheme, then, is now to be understood as the assertion that, as things are, identifying thought about particulars other than material bodies rests in general on identifying thought about material bodies, but not vice versa." **Strawson,** *Individuals*

basic proposition

EPISTEMOLOGY For **logical positivists**, a **proposition** or statement that describes the content of one's present experience, such as "I feel a headache." Propositions of this kind are considered to be basic because of their privileged epistemological position. They are incorrigible, that is, their truth cannot be denied by other evidence. Further, they can provide the test for the truth or falsity of other propositions and are the terminus of any process of empirical verification. In these respects, they are claimed to provide the foundations of all knowledge. But for there to be such incorrigible propositions would require that I have private experiences to which I can give private descriptions, a view sharply disputed in Wittgenstein's discussion of the possibility of a private language. Other logical positivists call basic propositions "protocol propositions," "experiential propositions," observational proposition, or "elementary proposition."

> "It is characteristic of these propositions, which I have elsewhere called 'basic propositions,' that they refer solely to the content of a single experience." **Ayer,** *Language, Truth and Logic*

basic sentence, another term for basic proposition

Bataille, George (1897–1962)

French Nietzschean thinker, born in Billom, curator and librarian. Bataille embraced Nietzsche's rejection of external authority and certainty to develop an atheistic mysticism that explored the ego and the limits of interior experience. He used the techniques of yoga to replace rational conscious thought with horrific visions of an ineffable beyond. His main works include *Theory of Religion* (1948), *Literature and Evil* (1957), and *Eroticism* (1957).

Bauer, Bruno (1809–82)

German philosopher, theologian, and historian, Professor at University of Bonn. Bauer became a leading Left Hegelian, who argued that the Christ of the New Testament was a fiction and that political life must be freed from oppressive religious authority. His understanding of Hegel focused on the development of human self-consciousness toward freedom. His main works include *The Good Cause of Freedom* (1842).

Baumgarten, Alexander (1714–62)

German aesthetician, taught at Berlin and Frankfurt an der Oder. Baumgarten developed Wolff's systematic philosophy in studies of metaphysics and ethics, but his most important work gave the name to the modern study of aesthetics. His major work was *Aesthetica*, 2 vols. (1750–8).

Bayes, Thomas (1702–61)

English clergyman and theorist of probability. Bayes established the basis of an account of confirmation, explaining how evidence can support hypotheses by altering the prior probability of the hypotheses being true. Bayesian philosophy of science has flourished in recent decades. His most important work is *An Essay towards Solving a Problem in the Doctrine of Chances* (1763).

Bayes's theorem

LOGIC, PHILOSOPHY OF SCIENCE A theorem of the **probability** calculus, named after the eighteenth-century English mathematician Thomas Bayes, which compares the degree of support for a **hypothesis** prior to acquiring new **evidence** and after obtaining that evidence. As such it provides the basis for a general account of science. The theorem can be formulated as follows: Prob (H/E) = Prob (H) x Prob (E/H)/Prob (E), where H is the hypothesis whose probability is to be evaluated, and E is new evidence; Prob (H) is the probability of H prior to acquiring the evidence; Prob (E) is the prior probability of acquiring that evidence; Prob (H/E) is the probability of H given the new evidence; and Prob (E/H) is the prior probability of acquiring the evidence given the assumption that H is true. The theory states that the conditional probability of H given E is greater than the unconditional probability of H to the extent that E is improbable in itself, but probable given H. This theorem indicates rational grounds for altering one's assessment of probability for a hypothesis in the face of new evidence. On the assumption that belief can vary by degrees, evidence that is improbable on other hypotheses but probable on this hypothesis will raise the degree of belief for this hypothesis more than evidence that is similarly probable on this and other hypotheses.

"Bayes' theorem can be used to justify the assignment of a comparatively high . . . posterior probability to a hypothesis provided the latter's antecedent probability is not too small." **Pap,** *An Introduction to the Philosophy of Science*

Bayesian epistemology, another expression for Bayesianism

Bayesianism

EPISTEMOLOGY, PHILOSOPHY OF SCIENCE Also called Bayesian epistemology, a theory of epistemic justification, claiming that a belief P is justified if and only if the **probability** of P is reasonably high and that the probability for changing epistemic justification through the acquisition of new data can be calculated and predicated according to the probability calculus, including **Bayes's theorem**. On a Bayesian view, the assignment of probability to belief is both subjective and rational. Different investigators can subjectively hold hypotheses with different initial degrees of belief. The operation of Bayes's theorem in rationally altering these subjective assignments in the light of new evidence will tend toward convergence in the beliefs held by the investigators. In using evidence, evidence that is unlikely in itself but likely on a given hypothesis will increase the degree of belief in that hypothesis more than evidence that is likely in itself or equally likely on this and competing hypotheses. Because of its emphasis on the role of new evidence, the theory does not deal so well retrospectively with old evidence, and the prior assignment of likelihood can also be arbitrary. Also the balance between subjectivity and rationality can be questioned, with parallel tracks of investigation rather than convergence being a possible outcome.

"Bayesianism is like probabilism in maintaining that: scientists' (and others') degrees of belief are measured by probabilities, but unlike probabilism, it sees no significance in very high or low probabilities." **Miller,** *Critical Rationalism*

Bayle, Pierre (1647–1706)

French skeptic. Bayle argued with wit and scholarship against the presumptions of reason to establish religious and philosophical truth. He examined a wide range of historical thinkers as well as biblical and mythological figures to support his skeptical conclusions. His views were widely influential among eighteenth-century Enlightenment thinkers. His most important work is *Historical and Critical Dictionary* (1697).

beatific vision

PHILOSOPHY OF RELIGION A term introduced by Thomas **Aquinas** for the vision of **God**. This vision does not use the senses, concepts, or any mental structures or processes. Instead it is meant to be an intimate and direct union with God. It is a kind of supernatural light by which one sees God face to face. All reasoning and deliberation is eliminated, although the certitude of judgment remains. Within it, God's essence is manifested. This is what man's ultimate beatitude consists in, as the consummation of the union with God. By nature, the vision belongs to God alone, but he grants it to human beings when he embraces them. Philosophers examine what the epistemological implications of beatific vision would be.

"In order that a person comes to the full, beatific vision, the first requisite is that he believes God, as a learner believing the master teaching him." **Aquinas,** *Summa Theologiae*

beauty

AESTHETICS An object's capacity to arouse pleasant experiences for its observer. For **Plato**, whose dialogues *Hippias Major, Symposium, Phaedrus,* and *Philebus* concentrate on the notion of beauty (Greek *kalon*), it is an objective **form**, a paradigm shared and imitated by all things that we call beautiful. Beauty is thus knowable and measurable. For others, beauty lies in the "eye of the beholder" and is not inherent in objects. On this view, beauty must be linked to human apprehension, and different individuals may respond differently to the same object. Accordingly, beauty is subjective. Other positions claim that beauty is produced through the relation between an object and its observer.

Philosophers also disagree whether beauty is a unifying notion. Some claim that beauty is a general notion of aesthetic value, encompassing all other aesthetic experiences. To be beautiful amounts to "to be recommendable aesthetically." Consistent with this understanding, beauty cannot be defined in terms of other qualities, and can only be intuited. Others believe that beauty is merely one species of aesthetic value, alongside such qualities as elegance, harmony, or uniformity.

Until the eighteenth century, beauty was considered to be the central notion of aesthetics, as good was the central notion of ethics. The most important question for aesthetics was, "What is beauty?" Then aesthetics becomes more concerned with the notion of art. While for ancient thinkers, all works of art were beautiful, this ceased to be true in modern times. Many modern artworks are thought to be ugly according to the common standard, although they might still be beautiful according to some peculiar theories of art or within some aesthetic practices. The notion of beauty is still not fully explored in contemporary aesthetics.

"For beauty includes three conditions: integrity or perfection, since these things which are impaired are by that very fact ugly; due proportion or harmony; and lastly, brightness or clarity, whence things are called beautiful which have a bright colour." **Aquinas,** *Summa Theologiae*

Beauvoir, Simone de (1908–86)

French existentialist and feminist, born in Paris. De Beauvoir was Sartre's life-long companion and an independent and original thinker in her own right. She was best known for her book *The Second Sex* (1949), which explored women's social situation and historical predicament and provided a systematic analysis of gender and sexual difference. The book is the most important classic in the development of contemporary feminism. Her other philosophical work includes *The Ethics of Ambiguity* (1947). She was a well-known novelist and autobiographical writer, with works including *Memoirs of a Dutiful Daughter* (1958), *The Prime of Life* (1960), *The Force of Circumstance* (1963), *A Very Easy Death* (1964), *All Said and Done* (1972), and *A Farewell to Sartre* (1981).

becoming

METAPHYSICS [from Greek *gignesthai*, coming to be, the generation of something new] **Aristotle**'s term for substantial **change** in which a new composite of form and matter is generated. In contrast, *kinesis* (Greek, motion) is reserved for non-substantial changes in quality, quantity, or place. *Gignesthai* is also contrasted with *phthora* (Greek, ceasing to be), and one of Aristotle's books is entitled *Peri geneseos kai phthoras* (*On Coming to Be and Ceasing to Be*, Latin *De Generatione et Corruptione*). However, Aristotle did not always observe the distinction between *gignesthai* and *kinesis* and sometimes uses these terms interchangeably.

In contemporary philosophy, becoming is generally understood in the sense of Aristotelian substantial change, that is, a change involving something coming into existence from the present to the future rather than a change in the attributes of some existing thing. Some philosophers such as **McTaggart** claim that the distinction between present and future is not real. On this view, it becomes difficult to answer the questions of what the thing is that becomes and what becoming itself is. C. D. **Broad** proposed that becoming is a *sui generis* type of change that defies analysis.

"Whether we would think becoming, or express it, or ever perceive it, we hardly do anything else than set going a kind of cinematography inside us." **Bergson,** *Creative Evolution*

Bedeutung, see sense and reference

beetle in a box

PHILOSOPHY OF LANGUAGE, EPISTEMOLOGY Part of **Wittgenstein**'s argument against the possibility of a **private language**. Suppose every language user has a private box into which no one else is allowed to look, and suppose that we refer to the contents of these boxes as beetles. Since the contents of different boxes are different, the word "beetle" plays no role in the language-game at all, for other language users have no idea what it means. They use the same word "beetle," but it may refer to totally different things. By analogy, if one ascribes a private definition or name to one's private sensations, it is semantically irrelevant, for it has no genuine sense and cannot be used as a name.

"Suppose everyone had a box with something in it: we call it 'beetle'. No one can look into anyone else's box, and everyone says he knows what a beetle is only by looking at his beetle . . . If so it would not be used as a name of a thing." **Wittgenstein,** *Philosophical Investigations*

begging the question

LOGIC Also called *petitio principii* or circular reasoning. A kind of informal logical **fallacy** that assumes implicitly as a premise in an argument something to be proved. That is, at least one premise needs support from the conclusion to be argued for. Sometimes the circularity can only be exposed after a series of intermediate arguments. For instance, one uses S_1 to argue for S_2, and uses S_2 to argue for S_3, and so on until S_n, but then one uses S_n to argue for S_1. Since it is a general requirement that the evidence used to establish a conclusion should have prior and independent reliability, circular reasoning seriously undermines the acceptability of an argument. However, not all circularities are vicious.

"Since the aim of a proof is to bring knowledge, the conditions for a proof's being circular or begging the question are stated in terms of knowledge." **Nozick,** *Philosophical Explanations*

behavior

PHILOSOPHY OF MIND Broadly, all actions and reactions and the workings and performances of all kinds of material things. For the purposes of behaviorism, it is restricted to animal or specifically human **actions** comprising all publicly observable ordinary voluntary or involuntary acts, such as running, walking, talking, or eating. Behavior normally implies a relationship with **mind** or **consciousness**, but includes mere physical movements or passions of the body. Sometimes philosophers call the former behavior proper and the latter physical behavior. Behavior is the central notion of behaviorism, which seeks to eliminate any mentalistic entity or property in the explanation of what we do or to reduce these mental things to physical entities or properties.

"'Behaviour proper' entails 'physical behaviour', but not all 'physical behaviour' is 'behaviour proper', for the latter springs from the mind in a certain particular way." **D. Armstrong,** *A Materialist Theory of the Mind*

behavioral theory of meaning

PHILOSOPHY OF LANGUAGE **Behaviorism** rejects any account of the mental that requires positing inner and publicly inaccessible items and claims that overt behavior, construed in terms of a stimulus-response model, provides the basis for understanding mental life. By applying this approach to analyze the concept of meaning, some philosophers suggest that the meaning of an utterance is the response it evokes in an audience in a particular context. The forerunner of this tendency was John B. Watson. The linguist L. Bloomfield put forward a simple version of such a theory that claims that meaning can be identified with regularly evoked behavioral responses. Charles **Morris**, who assumed that every meaningful expression is a sign for something, elaborated a more sophisticated version of this theory, based on dispositions to respond rather than actual overt responses. According to Morris, meaning is identified with considered dispositions to response produced by utterances. A certain level of behavioral disposition is sufficient for a mental life. Charles L. **Stevenson**'s discussion of the emotive meanings of evaluative terms also falls within this theory. However, the theory does not leave room for the relation between a sentence and the sorts of things it is used to talk about. Moreover, behavior does not always carry with it mental states. The theory ceased to be a focus of philosophical debate with the decline of behaviorism.

"The behavioural theory of meaning also concentrates on what is involved in using language in communication, but it differs from the ideational theory in focusing on publicly observable aspects of the communication situation." **Alston**, *Philosophy of Language*

behaviorism

PHILOSOPHY OF MIND Contemporary behaviorism had its origins in psychology, with the Russian psychologist Ivan Pavlov (1849–1936) and especially the American psychologist J. B. Watson (1878–1958). It was extended by B. F. Skinner and others as an attempt to explain psychological functioning in terms of observed behavioral data. It stands in contrast to introspective psychology, which appeals to the notion of a mental state. Behaviorism was introduced to philosophy, particularly by G. **Ryle** in *The Concept of Mind*, as a new approach to dealing with the relationship between mind and body. Philosophical behaviorism is a type of reductive **materialism** that proposes that all our talk about **mental states** and process can be explained by a set of statements about people's overt behavior or disposition to behave. Accordingly, there is no need to appeal to an inner life or to mental phenomena such as desires, beliefs, moods, or emotions as separately existing entities. **Descartes**'s mental substance, which is contrasted to physical substance, constitutes the myth of the ghost in the machine. The later **Wittgenstein**'s private language argument is also

said by some to be a version of behaviorism, although others deny this interpretation. Through its criticism of the dominant mind–body dualism of modern philosophy, behaviorism avoids certain intrinsic difficulties of dualism, such as the interaction between mind and body, but its total repudiation of inner mental states makes it unable to explain many phenomena. Two persons with completely similar behavior could nevertheless differ psychologically. This and other theoretical problems led to the emergence of the identity theory of mind and functionalism as anti-dualist strategies.

"According to philosophical behaviourism, for something to 'have a mind' is simply for it to be a material object that behaves, or is disposed to behave, in certain complicated ways." **Shoemaker**, *Self-Knowledge and Self-Identity*

being

METAPHYSICS, LOGIC A participle from the verb "to be." Its Greek equivalent is *on*, so **ontology** means a theory of being. Being can be ascribed to everything that can be talked about. Whatever we say using language must involve the verb "to be" in some form, and in this sense, as **Hegel** says, it is the widest but also the emptiest of all notions. Merely to say that something is amounts to saying nothing about it. But when **Parmenides** took being as a kind of subject-matter, his speculation about the nature of being was an attempt to locate the object of knowledge and to explain that it is the simple and unchanging ultimate reality behind the changing sensible world. Starting from Parmenides, metaphysics takes "what being is" as its central question. Different metaphysical systems can be viewed as different answers to this question.

Plato claimed that only the universal forms are beings, while sensible things are both being and not being. His distinction initiates the lasting dichotomies between reality and phenomenon and between **universal** and **particular**. He eventually identified being in the truest sense with the Good.

Aristotle thought that being is not a genus divisible into species, but rather that it has many senses. In his *Categories*, he discusses ten senses of being and argues that **substance** is the primary sense, while other categories such as quality, quantity, and relation are secondary senses. Thus, in seeking to determine "what is being" Aristotle focused his investigation on substance. Primary being is primary substance, which in turn is primary **essence**. Aristotle's ontology is the source of the dichotomy between substance and attributes and between essential and accidental properties. In some of his discussion, he ascribed primary substance, that is, primary being, to **God**.

The medieval metaphysicians distinguished between existence (that it is) and essence (what it is) on the basis that everything is created by God. God alone is the unity of existence and essence, while all other existing things have their essence necessarily grounded in God.

Descartes claimed, "I think, therefore I am," and **Berkeley**'s slogan was "To be is to be perceived." These theses essentially determine the development of modern philosophy. The discussions of substance and essence in modern philosophy are all discussions about being. Contemporary **existentialism** is also mainly concerned with the relation between existence and essence in the search for authentic meaning in the contingency of human life. **Heidegger** claimed that we are still not clear about the word "being," and launches a new investigation into the meaning of Being in his *Being and Time*.

However, many other philosophers, such as **Hume, Kant, Frege, Moore, Wittgenstein**, and the logical positivists believe that it is a mistake to ask questions about what is being. Traditional metaphysics fails to notice that the verb "to be" has a number of different uses, as copula, as sign of identity, as a sign of existence. Being or existence, that is, the existential sense of "to be," is argued by contemporary philosophical logicians not to be a first-order predicate that ascribes a property to an object, but rather to be a second-order predicate that ascribes a property to a concept.

The tendency to reject the pursuit of necessary existential grounds for contingent things does not imply that the question "what being is" disappears. **Quine** believes that in asking about being we are asking what it is for an entity of any given kind to exist. His answer is that "to be is to be the value of a variable." What exists is anything that can be substituted for a variable of an acceptable quantified formula if that formula could form part of a scientifically acceptable theory about the world. A major focus of current discussion of being in analytic philosophy concerns what we should say about the existence of abstract entities such as possibilities, numbers, and classes and what we should say about the existence of fictitious entities, such as characters in a novel.

Another version of the question "what being is" asks what is the distinguishing mark of an existing thing and leads on to questions of the distinguishing features of identity.

> "And indeed the question which was raised of old and is raised now and always, and is always the subject of doubt, viz what being is, is just the question, what is substance?" **Aristotle,** *Metaphysics*

being (Aquinas)

METAPHYSICS, MEDIEVAL PHILOSOPHY [Latin *esse* or *ens*] Following **Aristotle**, **Aquinas** believed that the word "being" is used in many ways and distinguished the actually existent in its own right (*ens per se*), the actually existent coincidentally (*ens per accidens*), potential and actual existents, and existence in the sense of the true (*esse ut verum*). In addition to restating Aristotle's doctrines of being, Aquinas distinctively held that the existent in its own right is the predicate that is genuinely predicated of an individual, and is therefore a first-order predicate. In contrast, existence in the sense of true is ascribed to the predicate that indicates the nature of a kind and can therefore be applied to any subject of that kind, but does not belong to an individual. Thus existence in the sense of true is a second-order predicate that does not carry existential import. This idea was taken by **Frege** for his diagnosis of existence according to which existence is not a predicate. Aquinas clearly stated the distinction between existence (the fact that it is) and essence (what a being is), a contrast that originated in **Avicenna**'s distinction between necessary and possible being. All finite things owe their existence to the creation of God and do not exist necessarily in virtue of their essence. Only in God is there a unity of existence and essence.

> "We use the verb 'is' to signify both the act of existing, and the mental uniting of predicate to subject which constitutes a proposition." **Aquinas,** *Summa Theologiae*

being (Hegel)

METAPHYSICS [German *Das Sein*] The **existence** of things in general, in contrast to their inner **essence** and also to the antithesis of thought. More specific-ally, being serves as the first **category** in Hegel's logic. In this sense, being is pure, without any determination, although it can be thought. To say of something that it is means merely that it is and nothing more. Being is thus in contrast to *Dasein* (determinate being). Since for Hegel there is noth-ing to think about regarding pure being, it passes into nothingness. To think about being amounts to thinking about nothing and vice versa. Being and nothing are synthesized in the category of becom-ing, which in a sense is being and in another sense is nothing. Being, nothing, and becoming form the first triad of Hegel's dialectic. Hegel associated being with **Parmenides** and becoming with **Heraclitus**. While Greek philosophy generally valued being over becoming, Hegel emphasized becoming as the development of spirit rather than being. This change of focus has exerted profound influence upon German philosophy.

> "Being is the notion implicit only: its special forms have the predicate 'is'; when they are distinguished they are each of them an 'other'; and the shape which dialectic takes in them, i.e. their further specialisation, is a passing over into another."
> **Hegel**, *Logic*

being (Heidegger)

METAPHYSICS, CONTEMPORARY EUROPEAN PHILOSOPHY
Like **Plato** and **Aristotle**, **Heidegger** particularly emphasizes being as the subject-matter of philo-sophy. However, the meaning of being for him differs considerably from traditional conceptions. The Western metaphysical tradition has been centered on the question, "What is Being?". For Heidegger, the question up to his time not only lacks an answer, but is also obscure and without direction. All traditional approaches to being, Heidegger says, are concerned not with *Sein* (Being itself), but *Seinede* (beings). *Seinede* is translated as "existents," "entities," "beings," or "assents," that is, as individual existents or as essential properties. Thus a concern with beings has led to a forgetfulness of Being. The distinction between Being and entities is prior to the traditional distinction between being as essence and being as existent. Thus we not only lack a proper answer to the meaning of Being, but the question of Being as well is not properly

constructed. Traditional metaphysics or ontology since Plato and Aristotle has changed the study of being into the study of entities. Heidegger's distinc-tion leads him to reinterpret the history of Western philosophy, in particular to destroy the history of ontology. His *Being and Time* seeks to provide a disclosure of Being through unlocking what the forgetfulness of Being hides from us.

For Heidegger himself, Being is the Being of entities, but it is not itself a kind of entity. Rather it determines entities as entities. He never gives an explicit answer to what Being itself is, but says that this inquiry should proceed through an analysis of an entity that enjoys a privileged relationship with Being in general. This entity is *Dasein*, the only entity that can question its own existing and raises the question of Being. To distinguish his own philo-sophy from traditional **metaphysics** and **ontology**, he calls his own metaphysics "fundamental onto-logy," that is, philosophy that is concerned with the foundations of any other ontology. The study of *Dasein* is supposed to be preliminary to understand-ing Being in general. But Heidegger never finished his work to show how such a general understanding is reached.

> "Do we in our time have an answer to the ques-tion of what we really mean by the word 'being'? Not at all. So it is fitting that we should raise anew the question of the meaning of Being." **Heidegger**, *Being and Time*

being-for-itself

METAPHYSICS, CONTEMPORARY EUROPEAN PHILOSOPHY
[French *l'être-pour-soi*] In **Sartre**'s distinction between two regions of being, being-for-itself is human consciousness or conscious being, in contrast to being-in-itself [French *l'être-en-soi*], a thing or non-conscious being. Here, "for-itself" means being that has presence to itself. The distinction is essentially a distinction between mind and body, consciousness and things. Sartre employs different words to avoid the impression of dualism. Being-for-itself is also being-in-itself insofar as its "is" is concerned, but it is characterized by the negative activity of conscious-ness, that is, by the freedom of choice. A human being, as a being-for-itself, is the only being that can detach itself from the rest of the world and thereby cause "**Nothingness**" to emerge. In this sense, the

distinction between being-for-itself and being-in-itself corresponds to the distinction between nothingness and being.

"... the being of the *cogito* has appeared to us as being-for-itself". **Sartre, *Being and Nothingness***

being-in-itself, see being-for-itself

being-in-the-world

CONTEMPORARY EUROPEAN PHILOSOPHY [German *In-der-Welt-sein*] A central term in **Heidegger**'s *Being and Time*. To say that *Dasein* is being-in-the-world does not mean that *Dasein* is spatially contained in the world. The world here does not mean the universe or the connections of real things, but is an existential-ontological concept, referring to the historical and cultural contexts in which *Dasein* exists or is formed. This world is not external, but belongs to *Dasein's* own structure. *Dasein*, as Being-there, must have a place. Being-in-the-world is the basic state or the fundamental existential constitution of *Dasein*. It is a unitary phenomenon. By this term Heidegger indicated the inseparability of human being from the world and was thus opposed to the traditional approach to a human being an isolated agency. The structure of Being-in-the-world is characterized by care, and is revealed by existential analysis.

"In the preparatory stage of the existential analytic of *Dasein*, we have for our leading theme this entity's basic state, Being-in-the-world." **Heidegger, *Being and Time***

being *qua* being

METAPHYSICS, ANCIENT GREEK PHILOSOPHY **Aristotle**'s term for the subject-matter of metaphysics, in which *qua* being specifies the aspect of being to be treated. Mathematicians deal with number *qua* number, namely, the numerical character of number. Philosophers are concerned with being *qua* being by investigating things with respect to the nature of their being. Since Aristotle divided being into many categories, being *qua* being deals with being in each category. **Ontology**, as the science of being *qua* being, considers how each of these categories can be a kind of being and how different senses of beings are related to each other.

A study of being *qua* being does not involve questions of content but addresses only the nature

of being itself. Therefore it is a universal science, contrasted with the special sciences that study distinct classes of being. Because according to the focal meaning pattern all senses of being are related to substance, the study of **substance** (ousiology) is the chief and central subject-matter of the science of being *qua* being. Aristotle's description of being *qua* being is ambiguous, giving rise to several major disputes, for example concerning whether being *qua* being can be reduced to substance and concerning how the science of being *qua* being can be connected to theology – Aristotle's other account of the subject-matter of metaphysics.

"There is a science which investigates being qua being and the attributes which belong to this in virtue of its own nature." **Aristotle, *Metaphysics***

being-with

CONTEMPORARY EUROPEAN PHILOSOPHY [German *Mitsein*] A central feature of **Heidegger**'s *Dasein*, according to which we are not isolated from other humans, but are so constituted that our being is available in principle to one another even prior to our experience of others. Being-with aims to reject the isolation of the individual in the social world through the constitution of *Dasein*, in the way that the concept of **being-in-the-world** rejects the isolation of the individual in the world. Being-with thus seeks to overcome the account of the isolated self in the Cartesian tradition and especially in the works of **Husserl**.

"Being-in-the-world, the world is always the one that I share with Others. The world of *Dasein* is a *with-world* [*Mitwelt*]. Being-in is *being-with* Others . . ." **Heidegger, *Being and Time***

belief

EPISTEMOLOGY Since **Plato** defined **knowledge** as justified belief plus a *logos*, belief has been a central concept in epistemology. Many discussions in the theory of knowledge take belief rather than knowledge as their starting-point. It is generally thought that belief is inherently relational and thus needs an object. Belief has often been represented as a state available to introspection with a certain relation to a present image or complex of images. The object of belief has been variously understood to be an actual or possible sensory state, a state of affairs, or a proposition. "I believe that P" means that I have an attitude of acceptance toward P, with some (possibly inconclusive) reason. But **functionalism** disputes the view that belief must have an object. Traditionally, belief is considered as a state of mind serving as a causal factor in behavior, but **Ryle** argued that belief is a tendency to say or to do something, rather than a state of mind. Most analyses of belief hold that beliefs are either true or false, although intuitionists hold that some beliefs are neither true nor false. In addition, **probabilism** or probability theory holds that belief comes in degrees. There is also an **eliminativist** rejection of belief as a postulated entity in outdated folk psychology. Major philosophical issues about belief include the possibility of infallible belief as the ultimate justification of other beliefs, the relation of belief with acceptance, reason, conceptual and linguistic capacity, the relation between justified true belief and knowledge and the distinction between belief *de re* and belief *de dicto*. Moore's paradox, which arises from the absurdity of uttering "P, but I do not believe that P," and the intentionality of belief sentences raise important questions about the nature of belief.

> "To believe is thus nothing but to accept something of which I am not yet logically certain. Belief, furthermore, is also a practically sufficient holding-to-be-true." **Kant,** *Lectures on Logic*

belief *de dicto*

EPISTEMOLOGY, LOGIC [Latin *dicto*, proposition] Belief *de dicto*, or *de dicto* belief, is the acceptance of a proposition and has the form "I believe that P." In contrast, belief *de re*, or *de re* belief, is belief about an individual object [Latin *res*, thing], and has the form "I believe of A that it is X." Belief *de re* puts the believer in a particular relation to the believed object or person. The believer is ascribing something to that object. It implies that there must be an object that the belief is about. Belief *de dicto*, on the other hand, does not involve such a relation. The distinction is drawn for the purpose of determining the nature of belief attributions. Some argue that belief *de re* can be characterized as a species of belief *de dicto*, because belief *de re* can be thought to be a belief about a singular proposition, or because a belief *de re* must presuppose a *de dicto* belief. In contrast, some philosophers argue that belief *de re* ascribes a real relation between believers and the object of their belief.

> "There are two varieties of belief – *de re* beliefs, which are somehow 'directly' about their objects, and *de dicto* beliefs, which are about their objects only through the mediation of a dictum, a definite description (in a natural language, or in some 'language of thought')." **Dennett,** *Kinds of Minds*

belief *de re*, see belief *de dicto*

belief/desire thesis

PHILOSOPHY OF ACTION A thesis that originated with **Hume** and provides an answer to the question what it is for an **agent** to have a reason to act. The thesis states that there are two factors that motivate us to act: **desire** and **belief**. Joining these two factors gives a sufficient condition for an agent to act in a certain way. However, Hume maintained that desire is an essentially motivating state, for it is internally related to motivation, but that belief motivates in a contingent way, because it can only fulfill its motivating function with the help of desire. The desire to drink a cup of water provides the motivational push but cannot determine whether the water is drinkable. This sort of information is supplied by belief, although belief does not have motive force in itself. Desires without beliefs are blind, and beliefs without desires are inert. There have been recent attempts to give alternatives to the belief/desire thesis as an account of motivation.

> "A complete motivating state – a state which is sufficient for action – must be a combination of belief and desire. This is the belief/desire thesis." **Dancy,** *Moral Reasons*

belief in

PHILOSOPHY OF RELIGION Traditionally, "belief in" is seen to be an evaluative attitude to a person, whether human or divine, while "belief that" is a cognitive attitude to a proposition. "Belief that" is also called propositional belief. The standard modern analysis of belief suggests that the object of belief is a proposition P and that all belief can be reduced to "belief that," for "I believe P" amounts to "I believe that P is true." In line with this program there has been an attempt to eliminate the distinction between "belief in" and "belief that." But this turns out to be difficult. "Belief in" includes "belief that," but possesses an additional proattitude.

That "I believe in God" not only implies that "I believe that God exits," but also involves commitment or trust toward God. "Belief in" in such cases is identical with faith. While "belief that" can be corrected or removed easily, "belief in" is often unshakeable by counter-experience. Whether this approach to reducing "belief in" to "belief that" can succeed is still a matter of dispute in epistemology.

"The question whether belief-in is or is not reducible to 'belief-that' is by no means trivial, nor is it at all an easy question to answer." **Price,** *Belief*

belief that, see belief in

beneficence

ETHICS [from Latin *bene*, well or good + *facio*, to do] Literally doing something to promote the **good** or interest of somebody else, due to a benevolent character. The word "benefit" comes from the same root. Beneficence is to act in a way that benefits others, and it is supplemented by non-maleficence [from Latin *male*, bad + *facio*, to do], that is, doing no harm. Beneficence has been recognized as a basic obligation or duty. To deal with possible conflicts between the principle of beneficence and other duties, such as the respect for autonomy, is a major topic in various areas of applied ethics.

"[I]t must be remembered that 'duty of beneficence' means an obligation to do good to others." **Nowell-Smith,** *Ethics*

benevolence

ETHICS Affection for others, a desire for the good of others, or a disposition to act to promote their welfare. Benevolence is associated with **love,** compassion, charity, and **altruism.** Benevolence is an altruistic sentiment that motivates us to act for the interests of others for their own sake. Some moral philosophies, such as Christian ethics, **Hume**'s ethics, and especially **utilitarianism,** ascribe benevolence fundamental importance in ethics. Nevertheless, humans generally give priority to the pursuit of their own interests, and the explanation of the general presence of benevolence in human nature and attempts to explain altruism in terms of benevolence remain matters of dispute.

"The term ['benevolence'] stands for a positive reaction to other people's desire and satisfactions, which the benevolent person has only because they are the desires and satisfactions of others." **B. Williams,** *Ethics and the Limits of Philosophy*

Benjamin, Walter (1892–1940)

German Marxist cultural and literary theorist, born in Berlin, a member of the Frankfurt School. Benjamin's ironic writings on art and culture initiated many themes at the center of current philosophical assessments of modernity. He was drawn to popular culture, especially theater, photography, and cinema, and to the experience of European urban life in a period of crisis. His critical and theoretical originality grew from close attention to social and aesthetic phenomena that he explored. His main works include *The Origin of German Tragic Drama* (1928) and *Illuminations* (1968).

Bentham, Jeremy (1748–1832)

English political, legal, and moral philosopher and social reformer, founder of utilitarianism, born in London. Bentham sought to promote "the greatest happiness of the greatest number" as the aim of both action and legislation, and he developed a "hedonistic calculus" to determine the amount of happiness, that is, the quantities of pleasure and pain, brought about by alternative courses of action. He sought to use utilitarianism to design a perfect legal and political system, rather than as an ethics to guide personal action. Major works are: *A Fragment on Government* (1776) and *An Introduction to the Principles of Morals and Legislation* (1789).

Berdyaev, Nikolai (1874–1948)

Russian religious philosopher, born in Kiev, Professor of Philosophy at University of Moscow before exile in Paris. Berdyaev's religious philosophy emphasized human subjective ethical creativity in a fallen world, although he held that human individuals can achieve their full personality through mystical access to inexpressible knowledge of a noumenal world of values. His existentialist account of the priority on freedom recognizes evil, but links human creativity to the creativity of God. His main works include *The Meaning of History* (1923) and *The Destiny of Man* (1931).

Bergson, Henri (1859–1941)

French philosopher, born in Paris, Professor at the Collège de France from 1900 to 1921, the recipient of the 1927 Noble Prize for literature. For Bergson, whereas science is based on intellect and concerns the inert physical world, metaphysics is based on intuition and concerns spirit. In his *Time and Free Will* (1889), Bergson distinguished between the scientific concept of spatialized time and continuous duration, the time of direct experience. He used duration to criticize mechanism and determinism and to explain the nature of human freedom. In *Creative Evolution* (1907), he combined Darwin's theory of evolution, Plotinus, and traditional French vitalism, holding that there is a creative impetus of life (*élan vital*) that underlies and determines the whole evolutionary process to make the world dynamic rather than static. Bergson believed that his views explained the dominant features of evolution better than Darwin's theory of natural selection. Other major works include *Matter and Memory* (1896) and *Two Sources of Morality and Religion* (1932).

Berkeley, George (1685–1753)

Irish philosopher, born at Kilkenny, Ireland, a fellow at Trinity College, Dublin in 1707, Anglican bishop of Cloyne from 1734. As an immaterialist, Berkeley rejected the existence of inert material substance and attacked the doctrine of abstract ideas. He also rejected Locke's distinction between primary and secondary qualities and argued that sensible objects are not mind-independent, but are a collection of perceived qualities. His highly original thesis "to be is to be perceived" (*esse est percipi*) made him the most important representative of subjective idealism. Whatever is not actually perceived by human beings is an object of perception of God. His view that natural sciences should focus on what experience reveals to us and on predicting human experience has great influence on nineteenth- and twentieth-century positivism. His main works are: *An Essay Towards a New Theory of Vision* (1709), *A Treatise Concerning the Principles of Human Knowledge* (1710), *Three Dialogues between Hylas and Philonous* (1713), *De Motu* (1721), and *Siris* (1744).

Berlin, Sir Isaiah (1909–97)

British philosopher and historian of ideas, born in Riga, Latvia, educated and taught at Oxford,

knighted in 1957. Berlin was a leading liberal thinker who turned from analytic philosophy to the history of ideas. He was an important figure in the contemporary revival of political philosophy in the English-speaking world. His commitment to the diversity of incompatible ultimate values led him to reject claims that there is a single ideal of the good life. He also rejected Hegelian and Marxist claims of the inevitability of objective progress of history. He envisaged a liberal society in which a variety of ends of life are pursued and social organization is based on small autonomous communities. He famously distinguishes two senses of liberty: the negative liberty characterized as the absence of obstructions, and the positive liberty characterized by self-mastery, and claimed that the latter was liable to lead to totalitarianism. His major works include *Historical Inevitability* (1954), *Two Concepts of Liberty* (1959), *Vico and Herder* (1976), *Concepts and Categories* (1979), *Against the Current* (1980), *The Crooked Timbers of Humanity* (1991), and *Magus of the North* (1993).

Bernoulli's theorem

LOGIC A theorem about the probability of the frequency of occurrence of events in a sequence of independent trials, first proved by the Swiss mathematician Jakob Bernoulli (1654–1705). Suppose that we have a sequence of n trials. If there is a possible outcome, A, of each trial, and the probability P of A in each trial is the same, then as the number n of trials increases and approaches infinity, the probability of the relative frequency of As in the sequence lies within the range $P \pm x$, where x is an arbitrary small number. This is also called the weak law of large numbers.

"Bernoulli's theorem in its classical form holds as an approximation for the direct inference, if the sample is larger and the population still larger or even infinite." **Carnap, *Logical Foundations of Probability***

Berry's paradox

LOGIC A **paradox** formulated in *Principia Mathematica* by **Russell** and **Whitehead** and attributed by Russell to Berry, a librarian at the Bodleian Library in Oxford. Names of integers consist of a finite sequence of syllables in English. Some of them can be named in one syllable (such as 2, 5), and others need at least two (such as 7, 14). All the names of some integers must consist of at least 19 syllables and among these there must be a least. Now the phrase *The least integer not nameable in fewer than nineteen syllables* expresses a finite integer. Although any name of this integer must contain at least 19 syllables, the words printed above in italics amount to a name for it and they contain only 18 syllables. This is contradictory.

> "A third [semantical paradox] is Berry's, concerning the least number not specifiable in less than nineteen syllables. That number has just now been specified in eighteen syllables." **Quine, *From a Logical Point of View***

Bertrand's paradox

Logic A **paradox** proposed by the French mathematician Joseph Bertrand (1822–1900). How can we find the probability that a randomly drawn chord to a given circle is longer than one side of an equilateral triangle inscribed in the same circle? It is longer if its midpoint falls at the inner half of the radius that bisects the chord. Its probability is 1/2. It is also longer if its midpoint lies in the area of the inner circle with radius bisecting the original; since this circle occupies one quarter of the area of the original, its probability is 1/4. There are further possibilities. This paradox shows that the principle of indifference cannot be simply used in choosing among alternatives in such cases.

> "It is one of three problems formulated by Bertrand in his *calcul des probabilités* of 1889, pp. 4–5 in order to show that it is senseless to speak of choosing at random from an infinity of alternatives . . . The name 'Bertrand paradox' was given to this particular problem by Poincaré." **Kneale, *Probability and Induction***

best of all possible worlds

Metaphysics, philosophy of religion **Leibniz** claimed that because **God** is the most perfect being, the world he chose to create must be the most perfect and best among all possible worlds. To choose to create a lesser world would have been a sign of imperfection in God. Furthermore, since God, as an **omnipotent** and **omniscient** being, not only

intends to create a **possible world**, but also knows what is the best and has the capacity to actualize it, our world must actually be the best. Accordingly, it is a logical consequence of orthodox theism that our world is the best possible world. This idea is satirized by **Voltaire** in *Candide* through his protagonist's claim that "everything is for the best in the best of all possible worlds."

> "This supreme wisdom, united to a goodness that is no less infinite, cannot but have chosen the best . . . There would be something to correct in the actions of God if it were possible to do better . . . So it may be said that if this were not the best of all possible worlds, God would not have created any." **Leibniz, *Theodicy***

biconditional

Logic Also called material equivalence. The combination of the conditional proposition "If p then q" and its reversal "If q then p." It is written as "p if and only if q," and is symbolized in standard predicate calculus by a triple-bar sign "$p \equiv q$" or a double-headed arrow "$p \leftrightarrow q$." "If and only if" is often abbreviated as "iff." In the truth-functional treatment, "p iff q" is true when p and q are both true or both false, and is false if one of them is true while the other is false. Hence p and q are taken to be logically equivalent.

> "A biconditional $[\phi \equiv \iota]$ is true just in case ϕ and ι are alike in truth value." **Quine, *Mathematical Logic***

bifurcation of nature

Metaphysics **Whitehead**'s term for a tendency in modern philosophy to divide reality into two parts and then assign to them different degrees of reality. One version distinguishes **primary qualities** from **secondary qualities** (such as color), and then assigns primary qualities to the physical world and secondary qualities to subjective experience. Another version separates nature apprehended in awareness and nature that is the cause of awareness. A further version distinguishes between sensations or **sense-data** and things. Whitehead claimed that this practice is mechanistic and a fallacy of modern philosophy. His philosophy of process is intended to overcome these divisions by exhibiting in one system the interrelations of all that is observed.

"What I am essentially protesting against is the bifurcation of nature into two systems of reality, which, in so far as they are real, are real in different senses." **Whitehead,** *The Concept of Nature*

bioethics

ETHICS [From Greek *bios*, life] A branch of **applied ethics** dealing with the moral issues about life and death arising from modern biological and medical research and health care practice. These issues include the allocation of scarce medical resources, the extent of the autonomy of the patient and the scope and limits of the authority of doctors and nurses, **abortion** and **euthanasia**, experiments with human subjects, genetic research and its applications, birth control, exogenesis, new medical techniques in human reproduction, prenatal screening, surrogate motherhood, and tissue or organ donation. Additional topics will arise as research advances. Many discussions surround such key moral notions of autonomy, equality, beneficence, justice, and responsibility. Bioethics is generally regarded as a synonym of "medical ethics" or "health care ethics," although it covers many issues beyond the sphere of medically related matters. Since its central focus is health-related matters, bioethics provokes great public interest.

"It is through applying the language of bioethics that health care understands its place in a culture, and the culture comprehends the significance of health care practices and the biomedical sciences it sustains." **Engelhardt,** *The Foundations of Bioethics*

biography

PHILOSOPHY OF MIND In **Russell**'s use of the term, all of the percepts perceived by one percipient throughout a life. This total experience and complete data of one's experience is distinguished from momentary data as part of one's experience, which Russell calls a "perspective." Wryly, Russell designates a biography not lived by anyone an "official" biography. Questions of biography also arise in relation to **hermeneutics**, **personal identity**, and **responsibility**.

"The sum-total of all particulars that are (directly) either simultaneous with or before or after a given particular may be defined as the 'biography' to which the particular belongs." **Russell,** *Mysticism and Logic*

biological naturalism

PHILOSOPHY OF MIND **Materialism** claims that all mental states and events are determined by physical processes. **Dualism** claims that mental phenomena cannot be reduced to physical properties. John **Searle** believes that these two seemingly irreconcilable positions are not in fact inconsistent. He develops a position called biological naturalism, according to which all mental phenomena including **intentionality** and **consciousness** are higher-level characteristics of the brain. They are caused by lower-level neurobiological processes in the brain, although these lower-level elements do not themselves possess the features of mental phenomena. In terms of this view, Searle claims that all difficulties arising from attempts to reconcile the natures of mind and body can be solved.

"Mental phenomena are caused by neurophysiological processes in the brain and are themselves features of the brain. To distinguish this view from the many others in the field, I call it 'biological naturalism'." **Searle,** *The Rediscovery of the Mind*

biomedical ethics, see bioethics

bipolarity

LOGIC **Wittgenstein**'s principle, meaning that every **proposition**, like a magnet, has two poles. It must be capable of both being true or being false. If a proposition is to be capable of **truth**, it must also be capable of falsehood. This is different from the principle of **bivalence**, which states that a proposition is either true or false. While the principle of bivalence can be symbolized as "(p) (p $\vee \neg$p)," the principle of bipolarity can be symbolized as "(p) ($\lozenge$p $\wedge$ $\lozenge\neg$p)." Wittgenstein puts forward this principle in order to distinguish between names and propositions. While a name has a reference, and has only a one-way relationship with reality, a proposition has sense and has a two-way relationship with reality. For a proposition can have sense if it can determine a possibility that reality either satisfies or not. Even if a proposition is not true, it is still meaningful. In his later period, Wittgenstein seems to give up this principle.

"To understand a proposition p it is not enough to know that p implies 'p is true', but we must also know that ~p implies 'p is false'. This shows the bi-polarity of the proposition." **Wittgenstein,** *Notebooks*

bivalence

LOGIC A basic principle of classical or standard logic, according to which every statement or proposition must be either true or false. It is closely associated with the **law of the excluded middle**, but its status is controversial in modern non-standard logic. Many logicians and philosophers claim that some statements or propositions (for example, **future contingents**, mathematical claims without constructive proofs, or paradoxical, **vague**, or **modal** statements) are neither true nor false, but rather have an intermediate truth-value. Modern systems of multi-valued logic, partly motivated by such claims and partly developed as important formal investigations in their own right, are truth-valueless or have from three truth-values to an infinite number of truth-values. Since **Dummett**, this principle has become the focus of the debate between **realism** and **anti-realism**. According to anti-realism, the basic position of realism is to hold that a statement must be either true or false, no matter whether we know it.

> "The principle that every statement is true or false is called the principle of Bivalence." **Kneale and Kneale, *The Development of Logic***

black box

PHILOSOPHY OF MIND A system or entity whose internal organization, mechanism, or structure is either unknown or viewed as insignificant. We know about it through its input-output functions rather than through its internal mechanism. In other words, we know what it does, but not how it works. In the philosophy of mind, **behaviorism** holds that knowing the functions of the mind exhausts our knowledge of the mind. We can leave aside questions about the nature of the internal mechanisms if we know these functions. This view can be called the black box theory of mind. There is also a black box theory of science that holds that a theory should be taken as a device for predicting without any need to know the inner mechanisms of the phenomena performing the functions.

> "So far we have actually been treating consciousness itself as something of a black box. We have taken its 'behaviour' (= phenomenology) as 'given' and wondered about what sort of hidden mechanism in the brain could explain it." **Dennett, *Consciousness Explained***

Black, Max (1909–88)

British-American philosopher of language and philosopher of science, born in Baku, Russia, Professor of Philosophy, Cornell University. Black wrote a wide range of influential essays using conceptual analysis to illuminate topics such as vagueness, scientific method, inductive inference, paradox, justification, metaphor, and practical reason. He accepted the philosophical importance of common sense in his search for intellectual clarity. His main works include *The Nature of Mathematics* (1933), *Language and Philosophy* (1949), and *The Labyrinth of Language* (1968).

Blackburn, Simon (1944–)

British philosopher of language and metaphysician, Professor of Philosophy, University of North Carolina and University of Cambridge. Blackburn is best known for his quasi-realism about items whose reality is disputed. He holds, for example, that values supervene on natural properties through their projection on the world of patterned human perception and activity and can be discussed in judgments that are true or false. Their status, therefore, lies between independently existing properties of the world and subjective expressions that have no place in reality. His main works include *Spreading the Word* (1984) and *Essays in Quasi-Realism* (1993).

blindsight

EPISTEMOLOGY Some visual cortex-damaged patients claim that although they can see nothing in a portion of their visual field, they can take in visual information from the environment and act on that information. For instance, such persons can have beliefs about how items are located in this field and move according to their beliefs. This phenomenon suggests that such people can have a visual capacity without a conscious visual experience, for they are blind with respect to those items in the blind-sighted region of their environment. This phenomenon is, paradoxically, called blindsight. The philosophical interest of this case is that it reveals that the relation between perception and consciousness is more complicated than we thought. It indicates that perceptual experience is not the same as the mere obtaining and processing of information.

> "The person sees with the blind-sighted part of his eye, and so takes in perceptual information, and

can form beliefs on the basis of the information, but has no visual experience." **Lyons,** *Approaches to Intentionality*

Bloch, Ernst (1885–1977)

German Marxist metaphysician and humanist, born in Ludwigshofen, taught in Leipzig and University of Tübingen. Bloch's heterodox Marxist views understood reality as a teleological development toward a utopian end of human society and consciousness unmarred by exploitation. This development does not involve objective forces, but takes place subjectively in individual minds according to a principle of hope that is the human expression of a fundamental hunger of existence. His main works include *The Principle of Hope*, 3 vols. (1954–9) and *Natural Law and Human Dignity* (1961).

Block, Ned (1942–)

American philosopher of mind and of psychology, Professor of Philosophy, New York University. Block is best known for a series of ingenious articles that criticize behaviorism and functionalism in the philosophy of mind and discuss related questions of images, qualia, consciousness, and causality. His thought experiments claim that we would not ascribe intelligence to computers whose human-like capacities can be explained without recourse to consciousness and experience. An influential article is "Trouble with Functionalism" in Savage (ed.), *Minnesota Studies in the Philosophy of Science*, vol. IX: Perception and Cognition (1978).

Blondel, Maurice (1861–1941)

French metaphysician, theologian, and philosopher of action, born in Dijon, Professor of Philosophy, University of Aix-en-Provence. Blondel's phenomenological study of willing and doing allowed human action to be intelligible only if directed toward a transcendent deity. He used his concrete analysis of action and morality to criticize the emerging neoscholasticism of his time and, as a Catholic philosopher, sought to explore metaphysical and moral themes in dialogue with non-believers. His main works include *Action* (1893).

Bodin, Jean (1530–96)

French political theorist and early economist. Bodin established a theory of sovereignty in which the sovereign ruler has absolute authority to establish laws governing subjects and regulating interests. The sovereign's rule is constrained only by divine law, natural law, and the constitution and is properly employed to achieve the common good. His main works include *Six Books on the Republic* (1576).

body

PHILOSOPHY OF MIND, PHILOSOPHY OF SCIENCE [Greek *soma* and Latin *corpus*] The material composition of a human, in contrast to mind or soul. Body does not rely for its existence upon human thought. Yet traditionally, especially in religious doctrines, the body is viewed as a tomb, an obstacle to the soul's aspiration to a purely spiritual existence. Many contemporary philosophers have tried to explain the **mind–body relationship** in terms of **identity**, **reduction**, or **supervenience**. Body is also a synonym for "**material object**," and even more generally for "**matter**." While for **Descartes**, body as matter is identified with extension, **Hobbes** believed that body is coextensive with space.

"The substance which is the immediate subject of local extension and of the accidents which presuppose extension, such as shape, position, local motion, and so on, is called body." **Descartes,** *The Philosophical Writings*

body (Merleau-Ponty)

PHILOSOPHY OF MIND, CONTEMPORARY EUROPEAN PHILOSOPHY The Cartesian tradition views a human being as a combination of body and mind. The former was considered to be a passive object, while the latter was an active **subject** and the source of all knowledge. To overcome this dualism, **Merleau-Ponty** claimed that the human body is itself a subject in dialogue with the world and with others. Body and mind are not opposed to one another, but together form one reality that is at the same time material and spiritual. Body is certainly corporeal, but also provides us with the power of existence or transcendence, which enables us creatively to modify our corporeity. Traditional thinking only paid attention to the subjective ego, but ignored the fact that both the voluntary ego and objective things implicitly depend on an actual body living in the world. Our perception takes up a sense that is already latent in what is given because the body originally animates in its own way the spectacle of what is perceived. Our perception depends on our body's place in the world. Body is in primordial contact with **being** and is the common texture of all objects. We should live with and experience body rather than taking it as a mere object. Since everything should be embodied or incarnated in the body, purely subjective phenomena are impossible, and body has an **intentionality** as well as the mind. Merleau-Ponty's conception of body is the key term for his phenomenology of perception.

> "I am my body, at least wholly to the extent that I possess experience, and yet at the same time my body is as it were a 'natural' subject, a provisional sketch of my total being. Thus experience of one's own body runs counter to the reflective procedure which detaches subject and object from each other, and which gives us only the thought about the body, or the body as an idea, and not the experience of the body or body in reality." **Merleau-Ponty,** *Phenomenology of Perception*

Boethius, Anicius Manlius Severinus (*c.*480–524)

Roman philosopher, born in Rome. Boethius was Theodoric's principal minister for many years, but was imprisoned in 523 and executed on a charge of treason. His Latin translations of and commentaries on Aristotle's logical writings were the major sources of medieval philosophy. His commentaries on **Porphyry**'s *Introduction to Aristotle's Categories* stimulated the scholastic controversy on the ontological status of universals. His *De Consolatione Philosophiae* (*The Consolation of Philosophy*), composed in prison, is a dialogue between the figure of Philosophy and the author that seeks to show that true happiness consists in virtue and is not affected by changes in earthly fortune.

Boltzmann, Ludwig (1844–1906)

Austrian physicist and philosopher of science, born in Vienna, and taught in various German and Austrian universities. Boltzmann used statistical methods to defend atomism against contemporary critics and argued against phenomenalists that unobservable entities and properties must be posited in science. His fallibilist epistemology rejected foundational claims put forward for experimental facts by empiricist programs in science. His major works include *Theoretical Physics and Physical Problems* (1974).

Bolzano, Bernard (1781–1848)

Bohemian philosopher, theologian, mathematician, and logician, Professor of the Science of Religion, Charles University, Prague. Bolzano argued that the existence of abstract entities, such as ideas, propositions, and truths, must be accepted to establish the objectivity of knowledge against the claims of skepticism and the dangers of subjectivity. His accounts of logical derivation and of substitution of propositions and their parts were precursors of later developments in the theory of logic and quantification. His realist ontology and semantics influenced Husserl. His major works include *Wissenschaftslehre*, 4 vols. (1837).

Bonaventura, St (1221–74)

Medieval Italian theologian and philosopher, born in Bagnorea, Tuscany, with the real name of Giovanni di Fidanza. Bonaventura was professor of theology of the University of Paris (1253–7) and became minister-general of the Franciscan order in 1257. He sought to reconcile philosophy and theology, and developed many arguments for the existence of God. He held that the culmination of human wisdom is quasi-experiential knowledge of God. His main works are: *Breviloquium* (1257), *De Reductione Artium ad Theologiam* (*On the Reduction of the Arts to Theology*), *Itinerarium mentis in Deum* (*The Mind's Journey to God*, 1259), *Biblia Pauperum* (*Poor Man's Bible*), *Commentary on the Sentences of Peter Lombard*.

boo-hurrah theory

ETHICS A nickname for **emotivism**, because emotivism claims that ethical judgments, rather than being statements of facts, are only expressions of emotion, and are neither true nor false. Moral judgments are attitudes rather than beliefs. In this way, to say something is right is to have a favorable attitude toward it and amounts to saying "Hurrah!" To say something is wrong is to have an unfavorable attitude toward it and is equivalent to saying "Boo!"

"On that [non-cognitivist] view, to say that stealing is wrong is merely to voice one's disapproval of stealing, so the remark could be more revealingly rewritten as 'stealing-Boo'. Similarly, 'God is good' could be translated as 'Hurrah for God'. Not surprisingly, this view was dubbed the Boo-Hurrah theory of ethics." **McNaughton,** *Moral Vision*

Boole, George (1815–64)

English mathematician and logician, born in Lincoln. Boole was largely self-educated and taught at the University of Cork from 1849. Boolean algebra translated symbols expressing logical relations into algebraic equations and then manipulated them in accordance with a set of algebraic laws. This work is the foundation of the development of modern symbolic logic. His principal works are: *The Mathematical Analysis of Logic* (1847) and *An Investigation of the Laws of Thought* (1854).

Boolean algebra

LOGIC The algebraic treatment of logic, first discussed by the Irish mathematician and logician George **Boole** in *The Mathematical Analysis of Logic* (1847). He translated symbols expressing logical relations into algebraic equations, and then manipulated them in accordance with a set of algebraic laws that he took as **axioms** governing the operations. This has become the central idea in modern mathematical logic. The characteristic axioms Boole's system contains are as follows: for every term there exists a complement; for any two terms there exists a sum; for any two terms there exists a product; for any term there exists a universal class; for any term there exists a null class; any two classes are commutative with regard to disjunction and conjunction; and any three classes are distributive with regard to disjunction and conjunction. The variables in this algebra are unquantified and can be read as schematic one-place predicate letters. Boolean algebra has been developed and applied to many areas. Any abstract structure constitutes such an algebra if its appropriate operations satisfy these axioms.

"The Boolean algebra of unions, intersections, and complements merely does in another notation what can be done in that part of the logic of quantification which uses only one-place predicate letters." **Quine,** *Philosophy of Logic*

borderline case

LOGIC, PHILOSOPHY OF LANGUAGE A term for cases at the margin of application for expressions lacking a clear-cut **extension**, where there is no sharp boundary to mark the field of its application. This **vagueness** is not due to our ignorance or imprecise knowledge, but is intrinsic to the word itself. For instance, the concept of a person leaves it undetermined whether a fetus or a brain-damaged human being is a person. Our concept of ought leaves the boundary between prudential judgments and moral judgments uncertain. Some philosophers wish to replace our current terms with others that have sharp boundaries, but others argue that new borderline cases can always arise.

"Most words admit of what are called borderline cases. What this means is that for most words there are things which are such that we are uncertain (not as a result of lack of knowledge) whether to call them w or non-w." **Carney and Scheer,** *Fundamentals of Logic*

Bosanquet, Bernard (1848–1923)

British neo-Hegelian philosopher and aesthetician, born at Alnwick, taught at Oxford (1871–81) and St Andrews (1903–8). Bosanquet claimed that reality or the Absolute is systematic and that truth is comprehensible only within systems of knowledge. He focused in particular on the notion of individuality in the idealist tradition. An individual is a concrete universal or the harmony of differences, and the expression of individuality, through imagination, is beauty. Ultimately, the only real individual is the Absolute itself. In social philosophy, he emphasized the influence of the community upon the individuals and defined freedom as self-mastery. The most important of his many books are: *Knowledge and Reality* (1885), *Logic or the Morphology of Knowledge* (1888), *History of Aesthetics* (1892), *The Philosophical Theory of the State* (1899), *The Principle of Individuality and Value* (1912), and *Three Lectures on Aesthetics* (1915).

bound variable

LOGIC If a variable occurs in a quantified sentence (for example "There exist a number of Xs such that . . ."), it falls within the scope of its prefixed **quantifier** and is therefore bound. This contrasts with a free variable, which is a variable occurring in an unquantified sentence (for example "X is . . ."). Substitution is not permissible for a bound variable. One cannot take individual expressions as values. It is possible that the same variable may be bound in a whole sentence and free in some part. **Russell** and **Whitehead** call bound variables apparent variables. For Quine, a bound variable involves **ontological commitment**.

"Among the contexts provided by our primitive notation, the form of context $(\alpha)\phi$ is peculiar in that the variable α lends it no indeterminacy or variability . . . A variable in such a context is called bound; elsewhere, free." **Quine, *From a Logical Point of View***

Boyle, Robert (1627–91)

English natural philosopher and chemist. Boyle argued for a scientific method that explained phenomena in terms of physical atomism, although he also saw the activity of God in natural phenomena. His account of science was based on hypothesis and experiment, and he was hostile to the claims of rationalist theory in science. His major works include *The Origin of Forms and Qualities according to the Corpuscular Philosophy* (1666) and *A Disquisition about the Final Causes of Natural Things* (1688).

bracketing, method of

MODERN EUROPEAN PHILOSOPHY The crucial step in **Husserl**'s **phenomenological reduction**. In our cognitive relationship with the world we naturally assume the existence of the external spatio-temporal world and the existence of ourselves as psycho-physical individuals. Husserl claims that we should bracket or "put between quotation marks" this natural attitude. This does not entail that the world is no longer thematic, but only that we should prohibit naive natural assertions and the use of any objective judgments. Husserl held that through using this method we can confine ourselves to the region of transcendentally pure **experiences**, wherein **consciousness** is strictly considered as intentional agency. We are accordingly in a position to obtain **eidetic** or essential intuitions toward intentional structures of experiences.

"The true significance of the method of phenomenological 'bracketing' (Einklammerung) does not lie absolutely in the rejection of all transcendent knowledge and objects of knowledge, but in the rejection of all naively dogmatic knowledge in favour of the knowledge that is alone in the long run justified from the phenomenological point of view of essence." **Husserl, *Shorter Works***

Bradley, F(rancis) H(erbert) (1846–1924)

British neo-Hegelian idealist, born in Glasbury, Brecknockshire, a fellow at Merton College, Oxford, from 1870. In his most important work, *Appearance and Reality* (1893), Bradley conceived absolute reality to be a single, self-differentiating whole and the only subject of predicates. The Absolute includes appearances but also transcends them. Many common categories, such as relation and time, are self-contradictory and hence are mere appearances. In *Ethical Studies* (1876), he criticized Mill's utilitarianism from a Hegelian point of view and took self-realization as the end of morality. His other works are the *Principles of Logic* (1883) and *Essays on Truth and Reality* (1914). Bradley was one of the major targets of Moore and Russell in their turn from absolute idealism to philosophical analysis.

brain writing, see language of thought

brains in a vat

EPISTEMOLOGY A thought-experiment imitating **Descartes**'s **argument from dreaming**. Suppose we remove a person's brain from his body and keep it alive in a vat, and then wire the vat to a computer that provides the normal stimuli. The result would be that this brain in a vat would have a mental life that merges perfectly with its past life so that it is not aware of what has happened. There is no basis for the brain to distinguish between its present situation and its previous situation. The conceptual possibility of this experiment leads to skepticism about the reliability of experience and empirical knowledge in our actual lives. Some philosophers, however, challenge the value of such "science fiction" examples in philosophy.

"Suppose we (and all other sentient beings) are and always were 'brains in a vat'. Then how does it come about that our word 'vat' refers to noumenal vats and not to vats in the image?" **Putnam, *Meaning and the Moral Sciences***

Brandt, Richard (1910–97)

American moral philosopher, born in Wilmington, Ohio, Professor of Philosophy, Swarthmore College and University of Michigan. Brandt's moral philosophy addresses the question of what moral code fully rational persons would endorse for their own society. His utilitarian answer to this question is empirically grounded in psychological studies as well as in philosophy. He is also ready to redefine crucial terms such as "rational" in ways answerable to empirical evidence. His main works include *Ethical Theory* (1959) and *A Theory of the Good and the Right* (1979).

Brentano, Franz (1838–1917)

German-Austrian philosopher and psychologist, born at Marienburg, taught at the universities at Wurzburg and Vienna. Brentano developed a descriptive psychology to classify mental phenomena without prior assumptions as a basis for all philosophy. His program deeply influenced Meinong, Husserl, and later phenomenology. Brentano is best known for his revival of the medieval doctrine of intentionality, according to which the fundamental feature of a mental act is its directedness toward objects or its possession of contents. The objects of mental acts are characterized by "intentional inexistence," that is, they need not exist. For Brentano, intentionality distinguishes the mental from the physical. His major works are: *Psychology from an Empirical Standpoint* (1874), *The Origin of Our Knowledge of Right and Wrong* (1889), and *The True and the Evident*.

Brentano's thesis

PHILOSOPHY OF MIND, MODERN EUROPEAN PHILOSOPHY A thesis ascribed to the German philosopher and psychologist Franz **Brentano** on the basis of his *Psychology from an Empirical Standpoint* (1874). Brentano revived the medieval notion of **intentionality** as the fundamental feature of mental phenomena, in contrast to physical phenomena. An intentional state has contents by being directed upon an object or a state of affairs. The contents of intentional states are characterized by inexistence, that is, they need not exist or be true. On this basis, Brentano claims that all and only mental phenomena are intentional. They are peculiar and cannot be reduced to physical properties or states. As a result, psychology

should be autonomous from physical science. This thesis has exerted a great influence upon modern and contemporary philosophy of mind and epistemology, although it has been challenged by the identity theory of mind and its physicalist successors. Intentionality is also central to **Husserl**'s phenomenology.

> "A consequence of this [Brentano's] thesis (or another way of putting it) is that intentional concepts such as belief, which might relate to the 'inexistence', cannot be defined except in other terms of psychology, that is to say, in other intentional terms." **Nelson,** *The Logic of Mind*

Bridgman, Percy (1882–1962)

American physicist and operationalist philosopher of science, born in Cambridge, Massachusetts, taught at Harvard University. Bridgman's instrumentalist philosophy of science accepted only those concepts that could be reduced to experimental operations, although he accepted constructs if they could be experimentally correlated with other constructs out of operations. His operationalism was influenced by Einstein's treatment of time in the theory of relativity. His main work is *The Logic of Modern Physics* (1927).

Broad, Charles Dunbar (1887–1971)

English empiricist philosopher of mind, science, and psychical research, born in Harlsden, Professor of Moral Philosophy, University of Cambridge. Broad provided careful, balanced assessments of competing positions in the areas of philosophy drawing his interest. His scrupulous examinations provide one model of philosophical method, but Broad lacked the brilliant insight of his Cambridge contemporaries Moore, Russell, and Wittgenstein. His main works include *The Mind and Its Place in Nature* (1925), *Five Types of Ethical Theory* (1930), and *An Examination of McTaggart's Philosophy* (1933).

broad content, see narrow content

Brouwer, Luitzen Egbertus Jan (1881–1966)

Dutch intuitionist philosopher of mathematics, born in Overschie, Professor of Mathematics, University of Amsterdam. Brouwer's intuitionism sought foundations of mathematics that avoided antinomies and paradoxes, especially concerning infinite classes. His interpretation of Kant's constructivist demands on mathematical proof led to his rejection of the law of excluded middle and the principle of double negation of classical logic in his intuitionist mathematics. Even those who accept classical mathematics and look to other means to avoid contradiction recognize the importance of Brouwer's formal system, and his intuitionism has influenced accounts of meaning and truth in contemporary anti-realism. His writings are contained in *Collected Works* (1975–6).

Brownson, Orestes (1803–76)

American transcendentalist philosopher, born Stockbridge, Vermont. Brownson was an important figure in New England Transcendentalism, who later converted to Catholicism. He saw the need to base reform on changes in the political and social system rather than solely on the moral development of individual citizens. His main works include *The American Republic: Its Constitution, Tendencies, and Destiny* (1865).

Bruno, Giordano (1548–1600)

Italian Renaissance philosopher, born at Nola. Influenced by Hermetic writings, Bruno developed a version of pantheism that he combined with Greek atomism. He held that the universe is infinite in extent and diversity, but united in the One and identical with God. He also defended the Copernican theory of heliocentricity. His unorthodox views, in particular his works on magic, led to his arrest in 1592 by the Inquisition. He was condemned as a heretic and was burned to death on the Campo de'Fiori in Rome. His major works include *On the Infinite Universe and Worlds* (1584), *On Cause, Principle and Unity* (1584), and *On Heroic Enthusiasms* (1585). He has been regarded as a martyr, and his philosophy of nature exerted influence on seventeenth-century cosmology and metaphysics.

Brunschvicg, Léon (1869–1944)

French idealist theologian and historian of philosophy and science, Professor of Philosophy at the Sorbonne and École Normale Supérieure. Brunschvicg rejected Kant's transcendental deduction of the categories as an abstract universal account of the conditions of knowledge in favor of a Hegelian reflective understanding of the progress of human consciousness in history. In applying this approach to the philosophy of science, he sought to reconcile idealism and positivism. His main works include *The Progress of Consciousness* (1927).

brute fact

METAPHYSICS, EPISTEMOLOGY Also called bare fact. In an absolute sense, a fact that is obtained or explained by itself rather than through other facts and that has a fundamental or underlying role in a series of explanations. We normally cannot give a full account why the fact should be what it is, but must accept it without explanation. The first principles of systems of thought generally possess such a status. Brute facts correspond to *causa sui* or necessary existence in traditional metaphysics and are ultimately inexplicable. For **empiricism**, what is given in sense-perception is brute fact and provides the incorrigible basis of all knowledge.

In a relative sense, any fact that must be contained in a higher-level description under normal circumstances is brute in relation to that higher-level description, although in another situation the fact could itself become a higher-level description containing its own brute fact.

> "There is something positive and ineluctable in what we sense: in its main features, at least, it is what it is irrespective of any choice of ours. We have simply to take it for what it is, accept it as 'brute fact'." **Walsh, *Reason and Experience***

B-series of time, see A-series of time

Buber, Martin (1878–1965)

Austrian-born Israeli existentialist religious and social philosopher, born in Vienna, Professor at University of Frankfurt am Main and Hebrew University of Jerusalem. Buber's philosophy centered on relations between the self and others, which he radically contrasted to relations between the self and objects. He argued that central features of our ethical, social, and religious life become unintelligible if we understand human relations and relations to God in terms of our relations to objects. In human relations, we respond to the presence and individuality of others in forming joint human projects rather than seeing others as objects to manipulate. His theology understood God as the ultimate "Thou." His main works include *I and Thou* (1922) and *Paths in Utopia* (1949).

bulk term, another expression for mass term

Bultmann, Rudolf (1884–1976)

German demythologizing existentialist theologian, born in Wiefelstede, Professor at University of Marburg. Bultmann drew on Heidegger's ontology to develop a theology suitable for modernity. He sought to demythologize the scriptures by translating biblical language into terms of human fallenness and God's call to authentic existence. His main works include *Faith and Understanding* (1969), *History and Escatology* (1957), and *Theology of the New Testament*, 2 vols. (1948–53).

bundle dualism, see bundle theory of mind

bundle theory of mind

PHILOSOPHY OF MIND A theory associated with **Hume**. After contemplating the difficulties of Cartesian dualism, Hume rejected the existence of an enduring, substantial **self** that remains the same throughout one's life. We cannot discern any continuing spiritual principle within ourselves. All one can observe is a sequence or a bundle of experiences occurring in succession from birth to death. The mind is nothing more than a bundle of perceptions. It is a theater in which different perceptions successively make their appearance. Since perceptions or impressions cannot endure, there cannot be an enduring self. Only because there is resemblance, contiguity, and regularity in the bundle of perceptions, do we attribute a self or an **identity** to ourselves, but this is a customary association of ideas rather than a real connection among perceptions. The position is popular among empirical philosophers, and is also called the serial theory (because it claims that the self is a series of experiences), the **associationist** theory, or the **logical construction** theory. Since the mind is a succession of non-physical items distinct from the body, this theory also implies a kind of dualism that is called bundle dualism. The theory contrasts with the pure ego theory. Hume not only proposed the bundle theory, but also saw grave difficulties in it.

> "I may venture to affirm of the rest of mankind, that they are nothing but a bundle or collection of different perceptions, which succeed each other with an inconceivable rapidity, and are in a perpetual flux and movement." **Hume,** *A Treatise of Human Nature*

Burali-Forti's paradox

LOGIC This **paradox** of the greatest ordinal was the first paradox discovered in modern **set theory** and was formulated by Cesare Burali-Forti. An ordinal number can be assigned to every well-ordered set, that is, a set for which every subset has at least one member. Such ordinals can be compared for size, and the set of these ordinals is a well-ordered set. The ordinal of this set must be larger than any ordinal contained within the set, but because the set is of all ordinals of well-ordered sets, the ordinal of the set must be contained within it. The ordinal of this set is therefore larger than and not larger than any ordinal within the set. According to **Russell**, the way of solving this paradox is to deny that the set of all ordinal numbers is well-ordered.

> "It is that in order to avert Burali-Forti's paradox the authors of *Principia* felt called upon to suspend typical ambiguity and introduce explicit type indices at the crucial point." **Quine,** *Selected Logical Papers*

burden of proof

PHILOSOPHICAL METHOD [Latin *onus probandi*] Originating in classical Roman law, an adversary proceeding where one party tries to establish and another to rebut some charge before a neutral adjudicative tribunal. The term has come to refer to a rule concerning the division of the labor of argumentation. Suppose A and B represent two competing views. If A has a favorable position, B will be required to produce strong arguments to defend its less favorable position. This is to say, A sets the burden of proof on B. If B cannot shift this burden, its position is defeated, even though it might be right. On the other hand, if B puts forward arguments that show that its position is stronger than A's, then it transfers the burden of proof to A. It is a basic rule of dealing with evidence. Normally any position that argues for or against something has the burden. For instance, because common sense usually has an intuitive appeal prior to argument, any philosophical position standing against common sense bears the burden of proof.

> "To say that the burden of proof rests with a certain side is to say that it is up to it to bring in the evidence to make out the case." **Rescher,** *Methodological Pragmatism*

Buridan, Jean (c.1295–c.1358)
French medieval logician and natural philosopher, born in Béthune, taught at the University of Paris. Buridan proposed a nominalist account of language in which universals have no real existence and an ontology that accepted only particular substances and qualities. His theory of propositions and discussion of paradoxes were the main features of his logic. He explained projectile motion in terms of impetus rather than through final causes, and his theory of action allowed freedom through deferring action in the absence of a compelling reason to choose what to do. His main works include *Compendium Logicae* (1487) and *Consequentiae* (1493).

Buridan's ass
METAPHYSICS, PHILOSOPHY OF ACTION The fourteenth-century French philosopher Jean Buridan proposed that **reasons** determine our choice between two alternatives and that we will do what our reason tells us is best. To argue against this theory, a case was devised to the effect that a starving ass is placed between two haystacks that are equidistant and equally tempting. There is no more reason to go toward one stack than the other, without additional relevant information. Thus, according to Buridan's theory, the ass would starve to death. This thought experiment has been influential in the discussion of **free will** and **determinism**. It is also related to the principle of indifference. But decision theory suggests that although the ass cannot decide which stack it should choose, it surely can decide between starving to death and having either of the stacks.

> "Buridan's ass, which died of hunger being unable to decide which of the two haystacks in front of it happened to be superior, could have rationally chosen either of the haystacks, since it has good reason for choosing either rather than starving to death." **Sen,** *On Ethics and Economics*

Burke, Edmund (1729–97)
British political philosopher and aesthetician, born in Dublin. In *A Philosophical Inquiry into the Origin of our Ideas of the Sublime and the Beautiful* (1757), Burke criticized the rationalist emphasis on intellectual clarity in art and argued that the most powerful quality of an artwork is its obscurity. He distinguished between the beautiful and the sublime in terms of the finite and the infinite. Burke was an active politician who wrote widely on politics. He supported the Irish Movement and American Independence, but preferred the inherited wisdom of tradition to political innovation allegedly justified by reason. His classic work of political conservatism, *Reflections on the Revolution in France* (1790), condemned the French Revolution for tearing apart the established social fabric and introducing a new set of values based on false rationalistic philosophy.

business ethics
ETHICS Business ethics is a branch of **applied ethics** developed largely in the second half of the twentieth century. Business, in spite of its profit-seeking nature, is believed neither to be unethical by its very nature nor to have its own special code. Rather, it is subject to the constraints of social responsibility and should be conducted in accordance with general ethical rules. Business ethics addresses three levels of concern: business persons, business enterprises, and the business community. With regard to business persons, it deals with the moral **responsibilities** and **rights** of individual employees, such as those involving honesty and integrity, job discrimination, and working conditions. With regard to business enterprises, it deals with corporate governance, responsibilities concerning consumers, product safety, and the environment, and relations among owners, managers, and employees. Since enterprises are the main business entities, this level is the primary concern of business ethics. With regard to the business community, it deals with the moral justification of economic systems. Along with the development of international business, this level involves wider consideration of cultural and social background.

> "Business ethics is a specialised study of moral right and wrong. It concentrates on how moral standards apply particularly to business policies, institutions, and behaviour." **Velasquez,** *Business Ethics*

Butler, Joseph (1692–1752)

English moral philosopher and natural theologian, born in Wantage, Berkshire. Butler was the Bishop of Bristol (1738–50) and Bishop of Durham (1750–2). In his ethical work *Fifteen Sermons* (1726), he claimed that human nature is complex, containing many affections, including both the self-love and benevolence that Hobbes and Shaftsbury respectively took to be the foundation of morality. He held that the distinctive human faculty of reflection or conscience is superior to affections and is our guide to right conduct. In *Analogy of Religion* (1736), he defended revealed religion against the deists, holding that nature and revelation are complementary and that the revealed doctrines of Christianity can be confirmed through the study of nature.

C

Cajetan, Thomas de Vio (1468–1534)
Italian scholastic philosopher, born in Gaeta, taught at Padua and Rome, became a Cardinal. Cajetan promoted revived interest in Aquinas and scholasticism, but his most important original work dealt with the role of analogy in human knowledge of God. He distinguished improper analogy of inequality and analogy of attribution from acceptable analogy of proportion. Analogy of proportion allows us to use the same terms to characterize God and ourselves without equivocation. This discussion is contained in *De Nominum Analogia* (1498).

calculus
LOGIC [from Latin for pebbles (plural: calculi)] A rule-governed formal symbolic system that can be mechanistically applied for calculation and reasoning in mathematics and logic. The word was adopted because in ancient times calculation was done with pebbles. All axiomatic systems, together with other systems of calculation, measurement, or comparison, are calculi. As a branch of mathematical analysis, calculus was principally developed by **Leibniz**, **Newton**, Lagrange, Cauchy, **Cantor**, and Peano. Leibniz also developed calculus as a formal system of reasoning, that is, to reduce valid argument forms or structures to a calculus by whose rules we can construct and criticize arguments. This is what he called *calculus ratiocinatur* (a calculus of reasoning), or what we generally mean by a logical calculus.

Based on the work of **Frege**, modern logical calculus is generally divided into propositional calculus, which deals with the truth functions of propositions, and predicate calculus, which is concerned with items such as the quantifiers, variables, and predicates of first-order languages.

> "A calculus is, in fact, any system wherein we may calculate." **Langer, *An Introduction to Symbolic Logic***

calculus of classes, another term for set theory

calculus of individuals, another term for mereology

calculus ratiocinatur, see calculus

Calvin, John (1509–64)
French Protestant reformer and theologian, born in Noyon, taught in Geneva. Calvin argued that knowledge of God and knowledge of ourselves are jointly grounded in our recognition of misery and corruption in our lives. Without a sense of our own limitations, we cannot know God, and without knowing God and acknowledging his benevolence and love, we have false estimates of ourselves. Conscience is the subjective aspect of knowing, worshiping, and obeying God and sin is a wilful resistance to this knowledge, worship, and

obedience. In his social and political teachings, Calvin argued for the separation of church and state and for justice in civic affairs, ideally through a republic. His major work, *Institutes of the Christian Religion* (1536), was repeatedly revised and developed throughout his life.

Calvinism

PHILOSOPHY OF RELIGION The theological teaching and political views developed by the French theologian and church reformer John **Calvin** and defended by seventeenth-century Calvinist scholars. Calvin rejected Aristotelian scholasticism and advocated a kind of natural theology in which our belief in God is rooted in our innate instinct. Scripture is the norm as well as the source by which the faithful can attain certitude with regard to the content of revelation without the need of an infallible ecclesiastical interpretation. Calvin emphasized the doctrine of predestination and claimed that humans have not had freedom since the Fall. He claimed that church and state have different tasks and should be constructed independently of each other. Church is not a supernatural instrument for salvation. It should be reformed and corrected by each of the faithful according to the scriptures. A resistance to the rulers rather than passive submission is also advocated. Calvin's thinking exerted great influence in the Renaissance and Reformation era throughout Western Europe.

"For Calvinists, the question of whether or not their souls were predestined to salvation was of the utmost significance." **Keat and Urry, *Social Theory as Science***

Cambridge change

METAPHYSICS The Cambridge philosophers **Russell** and **McTaggart** argued that the criterion of change for an entity X is that the sentence "X is F" is true at time t_1, and false at time t_2. Peter **Geach** called a change according to this criterion a Cambridge change and argued that it need not be a real change. Suppose that the sentence "Socrates is taller than Theaetetus" was true when Socrates was 55 and Theaetetus was 15, but false five years later. Because Theaetetus grew taller, there was a Cambridge change in Socrates even if his height remained the same over this period. Socrates did not undergo a real change. A Cambridge change can occur because there is a real change elsewhere. Whenever there is a mere Cambridge change there must be a real change somewhere, but the converse is not true. Geach used this notion to explain the ascription of change to an unchanging God in virtue of God's relation to a changing created world.

"An object O is said to 'change' in this sense if and only if there are two propositions about O, differing only in that one mentions an earlier and the other a later time, and one is true, and the other false. I call this an account of 'Cambridge change'." **Geach, *Truth, Love and Immortality***

Cambridge Platonists

METAPHYSICS, ETHICS, PHILOSOPHY OF RELIGION A group of philosophers and theologians in the seventeenth century, mainly associated with the University of Cambridge, who took **Plato** and **Neoplatonism** as their authorities. The chief representatives included B. Whichcote (1609–82), J. Smith (1618–52), R. **Cudworth** (1617–80) and H. **More** (1614–87). The Cambridge Platonists characteristically emphasized the role of reason and consciousness, which they acclaimed to be "the candle of the Lord" (Whichcote's phrase). Metaphysically, this position is antagonistic toward mechanism and materialism, especially that of **Hobbes**. In anticipation of **Kant**, it claimed that consciousness is not secondary and derivative, but is rather the architect of reality. Ethically, the Cambridge Platonists stressed love, character, and motivation, rather than external and universal creed and moral principle. It paved the way for the eighteenth-century British moral philosophers, such as **Hume** and **Hutcheson**, for moral sense theory and the intuitionist moral tradition. In religious terms, these philosophers opposed **Calvinism**, sectarianism, and fanaticism. They argued that people accept the existence of God due neither to some doctrine nor to the supreme will of God, but out of one's inner rational love. It proposed a rational theology and broad toleration.

"English seventeenth-century philosophy seems to us dominated by the rise of empiricism. But the Erasmian tradition was still alive and fighting, most notably in a group of thinkers loosely referred to as the 'Cambridge Platonists'." **C. Taylor, *Sources of the Self***

Campanella, Tommaso (1586–1639)

Italian Renaissance theologian and philosopher, born in Stilo, imprisoned for heresy and conspiracy. Campanella sought knowledge in scripture and nature and anticipated Descartes in articulating a method of doubt and founding knowledge and certainty on self-consciousness. He is best known for his account in *The City of the Sun* (1623) of a utopian egalitarian society that is without private property and is ruled by philosophers.

Camus, Albert (1913–60)

French existentialist philosopher and novelist, born in Mondovi, Algeria. The central theme of Camus's writing is that human existence is absurd. The world is meaningless, and there is no metaphysical guarantee of the validity of human values. The problem of suicide is the focus of his most influential philosophical work, *The Myth of Sisyphus* (1943). His early value-nihilism was replaced by a humanistic ethic in his second philosophical work, *The Rebel* (1951). His existentialist novels include *The Outsider* (1942), *The Plague* (1947), and *The Fall* (1956). In 1957 Camus was awarded the Nobel Prize for literature.

Canguilhem, Georges (1904–95)

French philosopher and historian of science, Professor of the History and Philosophy of Science, the Sorbonne. Canguilhem's work on the history of biology focused on epistemological breaks between the conceptual frameworks of science in different periods, and the radical changes of perspective accompanying these breaks. He understood change in scientific disciplines as emerging from attempts to deal with problems that could not be solved within existing conceptual frameworks. His major works include *The Normal and the Pathological* (1943) and *Ideology and Rationality in the History of the Life Sciences* (1977).

canon

LOGIC, EPISTEMOLOGY [from Greek *kanon*, a rule to measure or set a limit] For **Epicurus**, the rule for distinguishing between true and false judgments, in contrast to Aristotle's *Organon*, which deals with rules for attaining demonstrative knowledge and hence can extend one's knowledge. Later, both organon and canon became terms for logic, in contrast to **dialectic**. **Mill**'s five rules of induction are also called five canons of induction. **Kant**'s whole project of critical philosophy is based on the contrast

between canon and organon. He takes an organon to be an instruction about how knowledge may be extended and how new knowledge may be acquired. Critical philosophy is not an organon, but is rather a canon in the sense of setting the limit for human understanding and reason. His transcendental analytic provides a canon for the understanding in its general discursive or analytic employment. Reason in its speculative employment does not have a canon, because it cannot be correctly applied. In its practical employment, however, reason deals with two problems: "Is there a God?" and "Is there a future life?" and has two criteria for its canon: "What ought I to do?" and "What may I hope?"

> "I understand by a canon the sum-total of the a priori principles of the correct employment of certain faculties of knowledge." **Kant, *Critique of Pure Reason***

canonical notation

LOGIC **Quine**'s term for a notation that reflects the simplest kind of grammatical or logical framework that is adequate for all our propositional thinking, whatever its subject-matter. This simplest structure is supposed to reveal the broadest features of reality, and is the framework shared by all the sciences. To seek to construct such a notation is the same as the quest for ultimate **categories**, a project that has been the aim of many philosophers, as we can explicitly see in **Aristotle, Kant, Peirce, Frege, Carnap**, and Quine.

> "The quest of a simplest, clearest overall pattern of canonical notation is not to be distinguished from a quest for ultimate categories, a limning of the most general traits of reality." **Quine, *Word and Object***

Cantor, Georg (1845–1918)

German mathematician, born in St Petersburg, Russia, Professor, University of Halle. Cantor's account of set theory and transfinite arithmetic established the basis of the logicist program of deriving mathematics from set theory and the mathematics of infinity. His treatment of the ordering of infinite sets, continuity and discontinuity, and the paradoxes of set theory have all had major consequences for mathematics and philosophy. His works are contained in *Gesammelte Abhandlungen* (1932).

Cantor's paradox

LOGIC A **paradox** showing that we cannot treat the set of all sets as a set-theoretical entity. It was discovered by Georg **Cantor** through comparing the number of **sets** contained in the set of all sets S and the number of sets contained in PS (the power set of S), where the power set of a set is the set of all the subsets of that set. Cantor's theorem shows that for any set A, its power set PA contains more sets than A. The paradox arises because no set can contain more sets than the set of *all* sets S, yet the power set of S does contain more sets than S. Cantor's paradox and **Burali-Forti's paradox** together are called the paradoxes of size.

> "In Cantor's paradox it is argued that there can be no greatest cardinal number and yet that the cardinal number of the class of cardinal number . . . must be the greatest." **Quine,** *Selected Logical Papers*

capital punishment

ETHICS, POLITICAL PHILOSOPHY The death penalty, or the execution according to the law of murderers and in some societies others who have committed serious crimes. The killing is done by officials in the name of society and on its behalf. The morality of capital punishment has been a puzzling problem for philosophers, especially against the background of the humanism of the **Enlightenment**. Granted the sanctity of human life, would not the punishment of the death penalty be a violation of the murderer's right to life? The defenders of capital punishment usually follow **Locke**'s view that although the human right to life is natural, whenever a person violates the right to life of another, he forfeits his own right and it thus need not be respected. This position faces many theoretical difficulties, for it actually denies that the human right to life has absolute value and asserts that it can be yielded in the name of social defense and retributive justice. Philosophers who oppose capital punishment argue that punishment is necessary in order to reduce crime rates, but that it is not necessary to take a person's life to achieve this end. To forfeit one's right to life is not identical with forfeiting one's life. They point to many cases in which innocent people have been executed in miscarriages of justice that cannot be corrected. Because human life has an over-

riding worth, we must find an alternative form of punishment, such as long-term imprisonment, which does not compromise its value. Many countries have indeed abolished capital punishment. But this position would also have difficulties if it turned out that other forms of punishment were less effective than capital punishment in crime prevention and deterrence and that they increased the economic burdens on society. Weighing the importance of moral principles, empirical findings, and democratic preferences in deciding the question of adopting or maintaining capital punishment involves many important disputes.

> "Capital punishment has its own special cruelties and horrors, which change the whole position. In order to be justified, it must be shown, with good evidence, that it has a deterrent effect not obtainable by less awful means, and one which is quite substantial rather than marginal." **Glover,** *Causing Death and Saving Lives*

cardinal virtues

ETHICS [from Latin *cardo*, hinge] Cardinal virtues are presented as the highest ideals or forms of conduct for human life. **Plato** in his *Republic* listed four cardinal virtues: **temperance**, **courage**, **wisdom**, and **justice**. This doctrine is associated with his theory of the tripartite soul. Temperance is the virtue of appetite, courage is the virtue of emotion, and wisdom is the virtue of reason. If each of the three parts of soul realizes its respective virtue, the whole soul has the virtue of justice. In medieval philosophy, Thomas **Aquinas** called these virtues natural or human virtues and added three other theological virtues: **faith**, hope, and **love**. Together they form seven cardinal virtues. In modern time, philosophers such as **Schopenhauer** claimed that there are only two cardinal virtues: **benevolence** and justice. This diversity raises questions concerning why different cardinal virtues have been recognized in different times and circumstances and concerning the kinds of justification that are appropriate in distinguishing cardinal virtues from other virtues.

> "By a set of cardinal virtues is meant a set of virtues such that (1) they cannot be derived from one another and (2) all other moral virtues can be derived from or shown to be forms of them." **Frankena,** *Ethics*

care

MODERN EUROPEAN PHILOSOPHY [German *Sorge*] For **Heidegger**, care is the state in which *Dasein* is concerned about its Being. Since *Dasein*'s essence lies in its existence, that is, in fulfilling its possibilities, its concern with the movement from any present actuality to another future condition must raise the question, "What shall I do?" This is care, which lies in the capacity of *Dasein* to choose its Being. Care is viewed as the fundamental relationship between *Dasein* and the world and is the basis of *Dasein*'s significance in the world. It is the state that underlies all of *Dasein*'s experiences. Since all choice has to be made in the world, care characterizes *Dasein*'s Being as **Being-in-the-world**. Care comprises existence (Being-ahead-of-itself), facticity (Being-already-in), falling (Being-alongside), and discourse and shows *Dasein* in its entirety. It is essentially connected with temporality, that is, the time structure of human life. The division *"Dasein* and Temporality" in *Being and Time* attempts to reveal temporality as the basis of all the elements of care.

"We have seen that care is the basic state of *Dasein*. The ontological signification of the expression 'care' has been expressed in the 'definition': 'ahead-of-itself-Being-already-in (the world)' as Being-alongside entities which we encounter (within-the-world)." **Heidegger,** *Being and Time*

caring

ETHICS Caring or care is a moral **sentiment** and concern for the **well-being** of others. As an emotional attitude toward other individuals as individuals, care differs from benevolence or sympathy, which concerns other individuals as human beings in accordance with abstract moral principles. Hence, caring is much deeper and particularized than sympathy. It is certainly not merely a feeling, but also has a cognitive element, that is, understanding another person's real needs, welfare, and situation. Care has generally been taken as one among many important attitudes. Heidegger, however, saw **care** as the fundamental attitude of *Dasein* or human being. In the second half of the twentieth century, feminist thinkers have considered care to be the fundamental ethical phenomenon and have attempted to construct an entire ethical approach on its basis, that is, the ethics of care or the caring perspective.

"The caring so central here is partly emotional. It involves feelings and requires high degrees of empathy to enable us to discern what morality recommends in our caring activities." **Held,** *Feminist Morality*

Carlyle, Thomas (1795–1881)

Scottish historian, critic, philosopher of culture, and political thinker, born in Ecclefechan. Carlyle conceived history in terms of biography, especially the biography of the heroes of an age, and understood biography in terms of critical moral assessment. His cultural criticism rejected the mechanical understanding of nineteenth-century materialist, democratic, industrial society and sought deeper personal and cultural self-understanding. Among his major works are *Sartor Resartus* (1833–4), *History of the French Revolution* (1837), and *On Heroes, Hero Worship, and the Heroic in History* (1840).

Carnap, Rudolf (1891–1970)

German-American philosopher, a leading member of the Vienna Circle, born in Ronsdorf, Germany and emigrated to the United States in 1935, where he taught at University of Chicago and UCLA. Influenced by Frege and Wittgenstein, Carnap held that metaphysical problems are pseudo-problems and that philosophy should proceed by applying the methods of modern logic and mathematics. The analysis of syntax is especially significant in solving philosophical disputes, and Carnap also sought philosophical clarification by distinguishing between the material questions about the world and formal questions about our framework of concepts. In his long and productive career, he made many influential contributions on topics such as logical syntax, perception, the philosophy of science, the theory of meaning, the foundations of mathematics, formal semantics, the foundations of modal logic, physicalism, probability and confirmation, induction and the unity of science. With Reichenbach, he founded the journal *Erkenntnis*, and edited the *International Encyclopedia of Unified Science* with Neurath and Morris. His major works include *The Logical Construction of the World* (1928), *The Logical Syntax of Language* (1934), *Meaning and Necessity* (1947), and *The Logical Foundations of Probability* (1950).

Carroll, Lewis (1832–98)

Pen name of Charles Dodgson. English mathematician, logician, and writer, born in Daresbury, taught at Christ Church, Oxford. Carroll's puzzles of logic, metaphysics, epistemology, and philosophy of language, often articulated at the point of absurdity, contribute life and humor to his classic writings for children and provide an informal introduction to many modern philosophical preoccupations. His major works include *Alice in Wonderland* (1865), *Through The Looking-Glass* (1871), and *The Hunting of the Snark* (1876).

Cartesian circle

EPISTEMOLOGY, METAPHYSICS, PHILOSOPHY OF RELIGION
A challenge to **Descartes**'s program to establish a scientific system on a purely metaphysical basis. Descartes tried to prove that whatever we perceive clearly and distinctly must be true and can serve as the **foundation** of a science. His argument goes like this: We have a clear and distinct idea that an omnipotent and benevolent **God** exists; the existence of such a deity entails that we cannot be subject to deception; therefore, our **clear and distinct** ideas must be reliable. This argument involves a circle. On the one hand, the existence of a perfect and non-deceiving God is the sole guarantee of the truth of what we perceive clearly and distinctly. On the other hand, Descartes claims that our intellect's power of clear and distinct perception is the sole guarantee of the truth of God's existence. Hence, what is to be proved has been taken for granted during the proof. The circle was noticed by his contemporary critics **Arnauld** and **Gassendi**. Descartes's answer to this challenge is to say that God only warrants the veracity of our memory, while clear and distinct perception is a self-sufficient guarantee of our immediate ideas. But his answer is generally considered to be unsatisfactory.

> "Since it is only by relying on the validity of clear and distinct ideas that he proves the existence of God, to rely on God for the validation of clear and distinct ideas seems to be arguing in a circle. This is the famous Cartesian Circle, of which he has repeatedly been accused." **B. Williams,** *Descartes*

Cartesian dualism

METAPHYSICS, PHILOSOPHY OF MIND **Descartes** divided the world into extended **substance**, or matter, and thinking substance, or **mind** or **soul**. He claimed that the nature of the mind is completely alien to the nature of matter. Accordingly, the soul is entirely distinct from the body. Although it joins the body during life, the soul is incorporeal, not extended, and can survive the death of the body. This is Descartes's most famous metaphysical doctrine and, as the main form of dualism, it has greatly influenced modern European philosophy. The doctrine is a criticism of **Aristotle**'s account of soul according to which the soul is the function or **form** of the body. In contrast to his own account of physical nature, Descartes held that mental phenomena cannot be mechanistically explained on the basis of physical properties. His theory also provided a metaphysical basis for the Christian doctrine of immortality. Its major problem is that since mind and matter are distinct, it is unclear how the mental and the physical are related, and how subjective cognition can attain reliable knowledge of objective reality. This becomes the famous **mind–body problem** that has dominated subsequent philosophy of mind.

> "Cartesian dualism results from trying to put these forces in equilibrium: the subjectivity of the mental is (supposedly) accommodated by the idea of privileged access, while the object of that access is conceived, in conformity with the supposed requirement of objectivity, as there independently – there in a reality describable from no particular point of view – rather than as being constituted by the subject's special access to it." **McDowell, in Lepore and McLaughlin (eds.),** *Actions and Events*

Cartesianism

PHILOSOPHICAL METHOD, METAPHYSICS, EPISTEMOLOGY
Cartesian is an adjective deriving from *Cartesius*, the Latin version of the name **Descartes**. Cartesianism is a philosophical tradition in the spirit of the philosophy of Descartes. Its main features include (1) Cartesian **doubt**, that is, starting from an attitude of universal doubt in order to find secure foundations for the epistemic edifice; (2) the Cartesian **ego**, established through the argument *cogito ego sum*, the indubitable awareness we have of our own existence that serves as the first principle of metaphysics; (3) **clear and distinct** ideas that **God** implants in us

and that serve as the starting-points of a solid scientific enterprise. They also provide the foundation of epistemic justification. The use of God to validate clear and distinct ideas and the use of clear and distinct ideas to justify belief in God constitute the **Cartesian circle**; (4) **Cartesian dualism**, according to which mind and body are two heterogeneous entities. Various important discussions in contemporary philosophy have started from the criticism of one or more aspects of Cartesianism.

> "'Cartesianism' aptly labels the radically foundationalist view that a belief is cognitively justified if and only if its object either (a) is manifest in itself to the believer in the absence of any but manifest presuppositions (amounting thus to something given), or (b) is arrived at through deductive proof from ultimate premises all of which are thus manifest." **Sosa, *Knowledge in Perspective***

Cartwright, Nancy (1943–)

American philosopher of science, born in Pennsylvania, Professor at Stanford University and the London School of Economics. Cartwright's philosophy of science derives from her detailed understanding of scientific practice. She is a realist about scientific entities and their capacities, but rejects realism about scientific laws and models. The real causal powers of entities, therefore, have precedence over imperfect causal generalizations. She has also argued against the need for a single theoretical structure for science and holds that science can better be seen as a patchwork, with different theories developed in different fields. Her major works include *How the Laws of Physics Lie* (1983), *Nature's Capacities and Their Measurement* (1989), and *The Dappled World: A Study of the Boundaries of Science* (1999).

cash-value

EPISTEMOLOGY William **James**'s term. The test of the truth of an idea or a proposition lies in its agreement with reality. This amounts to asking for its cash-value, that is, the fulfillment of the sense-experience that the proposition either records or predicts. We must put each concept to work in practical contexts. If an idea or a proposition operates, its cash-value is actualized. We may ascribe truth to it, in particular on the occasions on which it works. The notion of cash-value corresponds to **Peirce**'s **pragmatic maxim**, which holds that the **meaning** of a scientific concept is its practical bearing.

> "Matter is known as our sensations of colour, figure, hardness and the like. They are the cash-value of the term. The difference matter makes to us by truly being is that we then get such sensations; by not being, is that we lack them." **W. James, *Pragmatism***

Cassirer, Ernst (1874–1945)

German philosopher, a representative of the Marburg neo-Kantian school, born in Breslau, Silesia, taught at various universities in Germany, Britain, Sweden, and the United States. Cassirer defined man as the symbolizing animal and maintained that symbolic representation is the fundamental function of human consciousness. His philosophy is a Kantian transcendental analysis of the nature and function of symbolic representation, with the aim of examining the organizing principles of the human mind in all its aspects, including science, art, religion, and language. His most important work is *The Philosophy of Symbolic Forms* (3 vols. 1923–9). Other works include *The Problem of Knowledge in the Philosophy and Science of Modern Times* (4 vols, 1906–20), *Language and Myths* (1925), *An Essay on Man* (1945), and *The Myth of the State* (1947).

casuistry

ETHICS [from Latin *casus*, case] The study of individual moral cases to which general **moral principles** cannot be directly applied in order to decide whether they can be brought into the scope of general norms. Its major procedures include appeal to **intuition**, **analogy** with **paradigm cases**, and the assessment of particular cases. Casuistry has a derogatory sense as a species of **sophistry** by which any conduct might be justified. Casuistry has traditionally been seen to be a part of rhetoric and was widely practiced in the medieval period in the elaboration of church creed and practice. It developed into **probabilism**, that is, the view that if a practical counsel is possibly true, then it is wise to follow it. Casuistry in this sense was attacked by **Pascal**. However, casuistry also has a positive meaning in ethics. **Aristotle**'s ethics established that practical reason is crucial for adjusting universal moral norms to make them suit particular circumstances. Casuistry is the art of **practical reasoning**, in contrast to the mechanistic application of rigid rules of conduct. In the second half of the twentieth century, with the flourishing of applied ethics, casuistry has also been revived.

> "There can be rational discussion whether a given extension of the term properly bears the spirit or underlying principle of its application to the core cases. Arguments in this style are, in the Catholic tradition, known as arguments of casuistry (the unfriendly use of that term was a deserved reaction to devious use made of the technique)." **B. Williams,** *Ethics and the Limits of Philosophy*

categorematic, see syncategorematic

categorical imperative
ETHICS According to **Kant**, the fundamental absolute formal demand (or set of demands) on our choice of **maxims** or **principles** on which to act. He proposed a number of formulations of the categorical imperative that on the surface differ radically from one another, although Kant himself believed that the different formulations are equivalent. On the first version, the principle on which one acts should also be capable of becoming a universal law. As a rational agent, I must accept that a sufficient reason for me is a sufficient reason for another rational being in an exactly similar situation. The second formulation requires that one should treat humanity in oneself and others never simply as means but also as ends. One should never simply use people, for rational beings have an intrinsic worth and dignity. The third formulation requires that we treat others as autonomous and self-determining agents. To treat people as ends in themselves is to respect their autonomy and freedom. In choosing principles, one should act as though one were legislating as a member of a **kingdom of ends**. The core of Kant's **deontology** is to ground all duties in the categorical imperative. Unlike the categorical imperative, hypothetical imperatives have force only if we have certain desires or inclinations. Recent expositions have tried to show the unity of Kant's formulations and have defended the categorical imperative against the traditional criticism that it produces an empty formalism.

> "Now all imperatives command either hypothetically or categorically. The former represent the practical necessity of a possible action as a means for attaining something else that one wants (or may possibly want). The categorical imperative would be one which represented an action as objectively necessary in itself, without reference to another end." **Kant,** *Groundwork for the Metaphysics of Morals*

categorical proposition
LOGIC The basic subject-predicate proposition in which a **predicate** is used to affirm or negate all or some of what a subject indicates. The subject and the predicate are the terms of the proposition. In traditional logic, there are four categorical propositions: (1) the universal affirmative, "All S are P"; (2) the universal negative, "All S are not P"; (3) the particular affirmative, "Some S are P"; and (4) the particular negative, "Some S are not P." They are respectively abbreviated as A, E, I, O. Categorical propositions are so called in order to distinguish them from **modal** propositions (which express possibility or necessity), conditional propositions, and other complex propositions. If both of the premises and the conclusion of a syllogism are expressed in the form of a categorical proposition, then the syllogism is called a categorical syllogism.

> "In a categorical proposition, there is always something, the 'predicate', which is either affirmed or denied of something else, the 'subject'." **Prior,** *Formal Logic*

categorical syllogism, see categorical proposition

categoricity
LOGIC **Dewey**'s term, although the idea is much older, for a **semantic** property ascribed to a theory or an axiomatic system, according to which any two of its satisfying interpretations (or models) are isomorphic. That is, any two models, M and N, of a theory T have the same structure, and there is a one-to-one correspondence between the domain of M and the domain of N. A theory with such a standard structure or model is categorical. Categoricity is an ideal property for the axiomatic method, but its application is very limited.

"Categoricity, as thus defined for the first-order language x, is a relatively trivial notion. None of the usual axiomatically formulated mathematical theories will be categorical, because any set of sentences of x with an infinite model will have models that are of differing cardinality and hence are not isomorphic." **Mates,** *Elementary Logic*

category

LOGIC, METAPHYSICS, PHILOSOPHY OF LANGUAGE [from Greek *kategorein*, to accuse] The basic and general concepts of thought, language, or reality. **Aristotle** and **Kant** provided the classical discussions of categories, although categories play different roles in their thought. Aristotle introduced the term in a logical-philosophical context, meaning "to assert something of something" or "to be predicated of something." Thus, his notion of category is closely connected to the subject-predicate form. Categories are, in the first instance, kinds of **predicates**. In the *Categories* and the *Topics* 1.9, Aristotle introduced ten kinds of categories: substance, quantity, quality, relation, place, time, position, state, action, and affection. As kinds of predicate, they reveal different ways in which a subject can be. Because there is a corresponding kind of **being** for each category, each category can also be considered to be a kind of being. Some categories come from ordinary interrogatives (what, when, where, how); others are derived from grammatical structures (for instance, the active and the passive). Only in two places does Aristotle list all ten categories; in other places he gives a shorter list, often ended by "and so on." Through his classification of categories, Aristotle explained many difficulties in the philosophy of **Parmenides** and **Plato**, and greatly influenced the later development of metaphysics.

Categories for Kant are pure non-empirical concepts of the understanding by which we must structure and order the objects of experience in order for experience itself to be possible. They are the concepts under which things intuited must fall or the concepts that give unity to the synthesis of intuition. Aristotle set forth the first table of categories as our basic structure of talking about the world. Kant revived Aristotle's approach, but criticizes him

for identifying the categories haphazardly and took it upon himself to identify them exhaustively, systematically, and with certainty. Kant believed that categories stem from the act of **judgment**, that is, the logical function of thought in judgment. While the act of judgment holds representations in a unity, categories are precisely the pure concepts according to which we organize experience in a given intuition. Categories and acts of judgment are therefore one and the same thing in the sense that both give unity to the synthesis of intuition. For Kant there are as many categories as there are acts of judgment. Traditional logic classified four kinds of judgment, each kind containing three moments: (1) *Quantity*: Universal, Particular, Singular; (2) *Quality*: Affirmative, Negative, Infinite; (3) *Relation*: Categorical, Hypothetical, Disjunctive; and (4) *Modality*: Problematic, Assertoric, Apodictic. Accordingly, Kant's table of categories has four headings, each of which has three members: (1) *Quantity*: Unity, Plurality, Totality; (2) *Quality*: Reality, Negation, Limitation; (3) *Relation*: Substance/Accidents, Cause/Effect, Reciprocity between Agent/Patient; (4) *Modality*: Possibility/Impossibility, Existence/Non-Existence, Necessity/Contingency. Within each heading, the first two members constitute a dichotomy, and the third member arises from their combination. Together these twelve categories form the grammar of thinking.

Kant's table of categories has been a subject of controversy. Some agree that categories should be derived from fundamental principles of thinking, but propose to emend it either because it is not exhaustive or because it does not reflect modern developments in logic. For other critics, philosophical reflection on judgment should be concerned not with its basic structure, but with its actual use, thus requiring non-Kantian grounds for identifying the categories. Some philosophers accept that categories are non-empirical concepts that we must use for experience or language to be possible, but seek to understand categories outside a systematic context. **Ryle**'s notion of category sees a relatively open-ended set of categorical distinctions.

"The kinds of essential being are precisely those that are indicated by the figure of categories; for the sense of being are just as many as these figures." **Aristotle,** *Metaphysics*

category mistake

PHILOSOPHICAL METHOD, LOGIC **Ryle**'s term for a kind of error typically involved in the generation of philosophical problems and in attempts to solve them. The logical type or **category** to which a concept belongs is constituted by the set of ways in which it is logically legitimate to operate with that concept. When one ascribes a concept to one logical type or category when it is in fact of another, a category mistake is committed. For instance, to say "time is red" is to commit such a mistake, for time is not the sort of thing that could have a color. In another example, it is a mistake to assign the Average Man to the same category as actual individual men like Smith and Jones. According to Ryle, the Cartesian dogma of the ghost in the machine commits a category mistake by describing the **mind** as belonging to the category of **substance**, when it actually belongs to the category of **disposition**. The way to expose a category mistake is through a *reductio ad absurdum* argument, showing the conceptually unacceptable consequences of treating an item as belonging to an inappropriate category.

> "It is, namely, a category mistake. It represents the facts of mental life as if they belonged to one logical type or category (or range of types or categories), when they actually belong to another."
> **Ryle,** *The Concept of Mind*

catharsis

AESTHETICS, ANCIENT GREEK PHILOSOPHY [Greek, cleansing or purging] **Aristotle** defined the function of tragedy as the catharsis of such emotions as pity and fear. In contrast, **Plato** claimed that tragedy encourages the emotions. Aristotle did not give an exact explanation of what he meant by catharsis. In Greek, the word can mean either religious purification from guilt or pollution or medical purgation of various bodily evils. Accordingly, there developed two dominant interpretations of this term. One view tends to translate it as "purification" and takes Aristotle to mean that tragedy has a moral effect of achieving psychological moderation and refinement. It can relieve tensions and quiet destructive impulses. The other view tends to translate it as "purgation" and believes that Aristotle proposed that tragedy arouses relaxation and amusement rather than having moral significance. The debate between these

two accounts has persisted over the whole history of philosophy. But it is generally agreed that tragedy has the function of catharsis because of its inherent value or worth. In the twentieth century, this term became more complicated through association with Freudian psychoanalysis.

> "There is often a very special refreshing feeling that comes after aesthetic experience, a sense of being unusually free from inner disturbance or unbalance. And this may testify to the purgative or cathartic, or perhaps sublimative, effect."
> **Beardsley,** *Aesthetics*

causa sui

METAPHYSICS, PHILOSOPHY OF RELIGION [Latin, self-cause, cause of itself] **Spinoza** introduces *causa sui* as one of the major characteristics of **substance** or **God**. God is caused not by anything else, but by itself. Here "cause" is not used in its ordinary sense as the agency that brings something into being. Thomas **Aquinas** has pointed out that to say that God is self-caused in the ordinary sense of "cause" is self-contradictory. For the idea of such a causal power implies the separation between the cause itself and its effect. But the meaning of Spinoza's *causa sui* is that the reason for God's existence lies in his **nature** or **essence**. God or substance does not owe its existence to anything else, but is rather the source of its own existence. This is in a sense an abbreviation of the **ontological argument** for God's existence.

> "By causa sui I understand that whose essence involves existence, or that whose nature cannot be conceived unless existing." **Spinoza,** *Ethics*

causal analysis of mental concepts

PHILOSOPHY OF MIND The initial step in D. **Armstrong**'s **central-state materialism**. A token **behavior** must have a cause within the person, and the cause is that person's mental states. Unlike a behaviorist analysis, mind is not behavior but is the cause of behavior. According to Armstrong, the concept of a mental state is primarily "the concept of a state of the person apt for bringing about a certain sort of behavior." On the basis of his causal analysis, Armstrong moves to the second step of his theory, which is to identify mental states with states in the brain. The central task of his book

A Materialist Theory of the Mind is to work out this analysis of mental concepts. The major challenge to this theory is the claim that it is inadequate as an explanation of consciousness.

> "Indeed, it is startling to observe that Wittgenstein's dictum, 'An "inner process" stands in need of outward criteria', might be the slogan of a Causal analysis of mental concepts." **D. Armstrong, *A Materialist Theory of the Mind***

causal determinism

METAPHYSICS The view that the world is governed by the principle of **causality**, that is, for anything that happens, there must be a cause. Nothing can exist and cease to exist without a cause. Causality is the objective and necessary connection that exists and functions universally. To understand a phenomenon is to understand its causal relations. The view is also called causalism.

> "While the causal principle states the form of the causal bond (causation), causal determinism asserts that everything happens according to the causal law." **Bunge, *Causality***

causal deviance, another term for wayward causal chain

causal dualism, see dualism

causal explanation

METAPHYSICS, PHILOSOPHY OF SCIENCE The explanation of an event or state of affairs as an effect of another preceding or concurrent event or state of affairs, which is the cause. On most accounts, the cause and effect must be linked by a causal law that holds universally between items of their types in a specified range of initial conditions. Some philosophers require causal accounts to explain why an effect must take place, while others reject causal necessity and see the universality of causal explanation merely as a limiting condition of statistical explanation. Causal explanation can be given materially in terms of events or states of affairs and initial conditions, or formally in terms of the truth of relevant propositions.

Causal explanation is the most important type of **deductive-nomological** or **covering law** explanation. Historically, the theory of deductive-nomological explanation was developed out of the theory of causal explanation. To provide a causal explanation is to specify the cause in terms of the necessary and sufficient conditions of the effect. Causal explanations can be complex, with the choice over what is a cause and what is a background condition determined in part by the interests of the investigator. Necessary and sufficient conditions can be nested within one another, as in **Mackie**'s account of a cause as an insufficient but necessary element of an unnecessary but sufficient condition of the effect. Establishing a causal law determined an invariable sequential order of dependence between kinds of events or states of affairs in certain initial conditions, but there is controversy whether there could be causal laws of backward causation.

> "To give a causal explanation of a certain event means to derive deductively a statement (it will be called a prognosis) which describes that event, using as premises of the deduction some universal laws together with certain singular or specific sentences which we may call initial conditions." **Popper, *The Open Society and Its Enemy*, vol. II**

causal theory of action

PHILOSOPHY OF ACTION A theory of action which proposes that the distinguishing feature of free action is that it is caused by appropriate antecedent mental events and episodes such as desires, beliefs, rememberings, and so on. It is a necessary condition for **behavior** to be an **intentional** action that it be caused by a mental event. Hence to explain action is to specify the prior mental events that are the proximate cause of the action. This is to reject the view, held by the later **Wittgenstein**, **Anscombe**, and **Hampshire** that explanations of actions by **reasons** are not causal explanations. The classic discussion of the causal theory of action can be found in **Davidson**'s paper, "Actions, Reasons and Causes" (1963). Davidson claims that there is a primary reason that explains an action by rationalizing it. Primary reason has two components: a pro-attitude toward so acting and a belief that acting in this way is to promote what the pro-attitude is directed upon. This is the agent's reason for performing the action and the cause of that action. Finding the reason for so acting is a species of causal explanation, and freedom can be explained in terms of causal power. The causal theory of action is now the most influential account of action. Other proponents include **Goldman**, **Searle**, and Castaneda. The major problem it faces arises from the possibility of a wayward or deviant causal chain, in which a non-standard causal chain between a mental event and an action calls into question the intentionality of the action.

"According to causal theories of intentional action, if one has appropriate reasons for doing something and if these reasons cause one to do that, what is done is an intentional action." **Moya**, *The Philosophy of Action*

causal theory of knowledge

EPISTEMOLOGY An attempt to modify the traditional definition of knowledge as justified true belief in the light of challenges such as "**Gettier's problem**." The theory suggests that the justification condition should be conceived as a causal condition between the believer and the fact that he believes. Hence knowledge is true belief that bears a proper relationship with the believed fact. This is an **externalist** position, for the subject need not necessarily be aware that this causal condition is fulfilled. The theory has different formulations depending on how one conceives of the causal criterion. The theory also intends to reject Platonist abstract entities and substitute causal connection. The classical position is expressed by Alvin **Goldman** in his paper "A Causal Theory of Knowing." Different versions by other philosophers such as **Armstrong** and **Dretske** are developed as a rejection of Goldman's position. The areas of debate regarding this theory include issues involving the sort of causal relationship that can be sufficient for knowledge, how to account for knowledge of future events, and whether it is possible to have knowledge without causation.

"The spirit of any account worthy of the name [of causal theory of knowledge] will include the idea that to know about something one must have some sort of causal connection with the thing known." **J. Brown**, *The Laboratory of the Mind*

causal theory of meaning, another term for the causal theory of reference

causal theory of perception, an alternative term for representationism

causal theory of reference

LOGIC, PHILOSOPHY OF LANGUAGE Also called the causal theory of **meaning**. Most traditional theories of reference depend on the distinction of **intension** (a list of properties) and **extension** (reference) and then claim that intension is the ground for describing the meaning of a term, while extension or reference is decided by the description of meaning. The causal theory of reference, developed recently in the United States by Keith Donnellan, David **Kaplan**, Hilary **Putnam**, and, more influentially, Saul **Kripke**, is a rebellion against such a tradition. Although each of these philosophers presents a different version of theory, the common attribute of the theory is that referential expressions are neither connotative appellations nor disguised or abbreviated **descriptions**. **Proper names** and **natural kind** terms (such as "gold" or "water") have no intension as understood by these theorists, and accordingly do not have their reference fixed by the concepts or descriptions associated with them. They acquire meaning through the causal linguistic or non-linguistic circumstances of their initial use and maintain it through a historical chain of communication. Although we may fix the reference of a term by giving descriptions, this is not the same as giving the meaning of that term. A speaker uses a name correctly if his usage is causally linked in an appropriate way to the chain of communication. Hence what we need is a definite theory of reference that would capture this causal relation. This theory is, to some extent, an updated version of **Mill**'s view that proper names have denotations but no connotations. It introduces social and contextual considerations into semantic theory that traditionally focuses on the semantic relations that hold between certain linguistic expressions and the objects for which they stand.

"[There] is the idea that certain real (usually causal) relations between our words and the world may make an essential contribution to the content of utterance without in any way figuring in the knowledge of those who utter them. Causal theories of the references of singular terms and essentialist theories of the extension of natural-kind words both advance such a claim." **von Wright,** *Realism, Meaning and Truth*

causalism, another expression for causal determinism

causality, see causation

causality, principle of

METAPHYSICS, PHILOSOPHY OF SCIENCE A common and deeply held belief that every event or state of affairs has a **cause** and that every **proposition** about the world can be derived from other propositions about the world in virtue of causal relations among the items given in the propositions. If we knew enough relevant facts, we could infer any other fact about the world. The principle is also called the principle of **determinism**. The justification of this principle is a matter of dispute. For **physicalism**, it is based on the uniformity of nature. For **Hume**, it is based subjectively on the habit of associating like events. In **Kant**'s version of the principle, every event follows upon a preceding event in accordance with a rule. But his characterization is regarded as too narrow, since not all causality involves succession.

"The principle of causality, . . . asserts, to put it in a simple, unsophisticated way, that every event has a cause." **Pap,** *Elements of Analytic Philosophy*

causation

METAPHYSICS, EPISTEMOLOGY, PHILOSOPHY OF SCIENCE One of the fundamental topics in metaphysics, also called causality. Causation is the firm and constant relation between **events** such that if an event of the first kind occurs, an event of the second kind will or must occur. The occurrence of the first event, the cause, explains the occurrence of the second event, the effect. Some philosophers believe that items other than events, such as **objects, states of affairs,** and **facts** can also enter into causal relations. The traditional view before **Hume** claimed that causation is an actual trait, which involves objective interdependence among real events. Hence, causation was seen as an ontological category, for necessary connection is a relation objectively holding between objects or happenings that are said to be causally related. But according to the British

empiricists, causation is only an epistemological category. **Locke** took it to be a connection between sensation and the sensed object, while for Hume it was purely a relation of ideas, and was just a matter of our imposing our mental habits upon the world. Hume argued that the traditional conception of causation is mistaken. Because nothing but experience can teach us of the orderliness of nature and because we do not experience instances of necessary connection, the phrase "necessary connection" is meaningless. We can verify spatial contiguity and temporal priority in our impressions, but not necessary connection. The real basis for our idea of causation is observed regularity. Events of type a have always been followed by events of type b, and so when a new a-type event occurs we predict by custom that a b-type event will follow. This is not a logical, demonstrable, or self-evident connection, but concerns our habitual attitudes and what happens in our minds. Hence Hume claimed that predictions of causation can have only an inductive basis, not a necessary or certain one. Hume's theory was established on the basis of his principle of the association of ideas and it has been the focus of much debate. **Kant**'s attempt to establish causation as a category, or as a condition for the possibility of experience, provides a major rival to the Humean account. What, then, is the distinctive feature of cause and effect? Various approaches have been presented. Among them, the most influential include the regularity theory, which claims that causal relations are instances of a kind of regularity; the **counterfactual** theory, which claims that a cause is a cause because without its occurrence the effect would not have occurred; and the manipulation analysis, which proposes that a cause is a cause because by manipulating it we can produce something else. Other problems widely discussed include: the possibility of **backward causation**, where an effect precedes cause; the relations between causation and **explanation**, between causation and **determinism**, and between causation and **necessity**; the role of causation in **natural laws**; causal deviance; and the **eliminativist** possibility of science getting rid of the notion of causation.

"The term causation . . . signifies causingness and causedness taken together." *The Collected Works of John Stuart Mill*

cause

METAPHYSICS In modern usage, a cause normally involves an **agent** or **event** that exerts **power** and effects a **change**. A cause produces or brings about an effect. If X occurs and Y invariably follows, then X is the cause and Y is its effect, and the relationship between them is called causation or causality. A cause is often regarded as a sufficient condition for the occurrence of its effect, but there are complex arguments over the role of **sufficient and necessary conditions** in an adequate account of causes and effects. The existence of causal chains is a necessary condition for the possibility of science. A cause is generally taken to precede its effect, but some argue that there could be **backward causation** (where a cause follows its effect), and concurrent causation (where a cause is simultaneous with its effect). According to **Davidson**, the reason for an **action** is a mental act that is causally linked to the action and that explaining an action by giving a reason is a sort of causal explanation. Cause is also employed to translate the Greek term *aitia*. Hence, **Aristotle**'s theory of four *aitia* is translated as "four **causes**." However, *aitia* as cause means more broadly explanatory feature. Of Aristotle's four causes, only efficient cause bears some resemblance to the modern notion of cause, while all of the other three (material, formal, and final causes) are inactive and cannot be agents.

> "Power being the source from whence all action proceeds, the substances wherein these powers are, when they exert this power into act, are called causes, and the substances which thereupon are produced, or the simple ideas which are introduced into any subject by the exerting of that power, are called effects." **Locke, *An Essay Concerning Human Understanding***

causes, four

ANCIENT GREEK PHILOSOPHY [Greek *aition*, cause or explanatory factor, from the adjective *aitos*, responsible] **Aristotle** held that we know by means of causes, of which there are four sorts: material causes (out of which things come to be), formal causes (what things essentially are), efficient causes (sources of movement and rest), and final causes (purposes or ends). He claimed that all his predecessors sought after these causes, but only vaguely and incompletely. In modern use, a cause is an agent or event exerting power and effecting a change, and a cause must do something to bring about an effect. Of Aristotle's four causes, only efficient cause resembles this modern notion, and even here there are differences. What Aristotle was distinguishing are different sorts of answers that can be given to the questions "Why?" or "Because of what?" Aristotelian causes are four types of explanatory factors or conditions necessary to account for the existence of a thing. Aristotle sometimes said that formal and final causes are identical, especially in his natural teleology, and sometimes went further, to say that formal, final, and efficient causes are identical.

> "Evidently we have to acquire knowledge of the original causes (for we say we know each thing only when we think we recognise its first cause), and causes are spoken of in four senses." **Aristotle, *Metaphysics***

cause in fact, see *sine qua non*

cave, simile of the

ANCIENT GREEK PHILOSOPHY, METAPHYSICS, EPISTEMOLOGY A fundamental image of human **knowledge** and reality described by **Plato** in the *Republic* (514–21). Imagine prisoners in an underground cave who have been there since their childhood. They are chained in such a way that they cannot turn their heads but can only see the shadows on the cave wall in front of them. The shadows are cast by a fire behind them and by the artifacts that men carry and pass along a track across the cave, like the screen at a puppet show. The prisoners naturally believe that the shadows are the only real things. If one of them happens to be released and turns round to the fire and to see the objects themselves, he will initially be bewildered, his eyes will be in pain, and he will think that the shadows are more real than their originals.

If he is further dragged upward through the entrance of the cave and to the sunlight, he will be even more dazzled and angry. At first, he will only be able to see the reflections of the real things in the water, and then the things themselves in the light of the sun, and finally even the sun itself. At that time, he will be in a condition of real liberation and will pity his fellow-prisoners and his old beliefs and life.

If he goes back to save his fellow-prisoners, it will take time for him to get used to the darkness in the cave, and he will find it hard to persuade the prisoners to follow him upward.

This simile is connected with the simile of the **Sun** and the simile of the **Line**, with the world inside the cave corresponding to the perceptible world and the world outside the cave corresponding to the intelligible world, but the text has been subjected to a variety of divergent interpretations.

Plato explicitly stated that the prisoners are like us and serve as a representation of the human condition, and the prisoner being dragged out of the cave is analogous to a process of enlightenment by education. We can interpret the upward journey and the contemplation of things above as the upward journey of the soul to the intelligible realm. The Cave simile exerted great influence on later political and educational theories.

> "Socrates is meant to tell us in the [simile of the] cave that the general condition of mankind is one of seeing things indirectly through their images."
> **Crombie,** *An Examination of Plato's Doctrines*

cement of the universe

METAPHYSICS, PHILOSOPHY OF MIND **Hume**'s term for what he took to be the most basic principles of the **association of ideas**, that is, resemblance, contiguity in time or in place, and causation. These are the links that connect us with any person or object exterior to ourselves. For Hume, the human mind operates according to these principles to construct various complex **ideas** and consequently to build up our picture of the universe. These principles are themselves associated, and the presence of one will introduce the other two to the mind. The contemporary philosopher John **Mackie** took "The Cement of the Universe" to be the title for his influential book about **causation** (1974).

> "As it is by means of thought only that any thing operates upon our passions, and as these are the only ties of our thoughts, they [the principles of association] are really to us the cement of the universe, and all the operations of the mind must, in a great measure, depend on them." **Hume,** *A Treatise of Human Nature*

censorship

ETHICS, POLITICAL PHILOSOPHY The inspection and restriction of the contents of publications, films, and performances by a religious or government office or some other body. There are generally two kinds of censorship. The first examines works for illegitimate or immoral contents, such as hard-core **pornography**; the other concerns political and ideological content and seeks to prohibit or alter what is offensive to the government or other censoring body. **Liberalism** especially condemns political censorship on the grounds that such a practice violates the basic **right** of free speech. This gives rise to the problem of how and to what extent free speech must be protected. The prior restraint of publication or performance is considered more difficult to justify than providing penalties afterwards, but there is also the possibility that afterwards penalties will contribute to self-censorship. In some circumstances, such as wartime, there is a greater tolerance of censorship than in ordinary times.

> "If we recognise the general value of free expression, therefore, we should accept a presumption against censorship or prohibition of any activity when that activity even arguably expresses a conviction about how people should live or feel, or opposes established or popular convictions."
> **Dworkin,** *A Matter of Principle*

central-state materialism

PHILOSOPHY OF MIND Also called the central-state theory of mind and synonymous with the **identity theory**, a **materialist** or **physicalist** theory of mind that holds that mental states, such as visual perceptions, pains, and beliefs are inner states that cause **behavior**. These inner mental states, however, are identified with states or processes occurring in the brain and central nervous system. Mind is in brain. That is not to say that it is a substance, but that it is possessed by a substance. This theory can be traced to Thomas **Hobbes**, and in contemporary philosophy has been developed by **Feyerabend**, Place, **Putnam**, and especially by the Australian philosophers J. J. C. **Smart** and D. **Armstrong**. In the standard version, the identity between mental states and physical states is contingent, not necessary. The theory, which occupies the middle ground between dualism and **Ryle**'s behaviorism, emerged as an attempt to overcome one of the major difficulties faced by the latter, that is, the denial of the existence of inner mental states. But the theory itself has trouble in analyzing the **intentionality** of mental states, how they can have content and be about something. Some critics also object that it has difficulty in accounting for the logical possibility of disembodied existence.

"For the most part these who profess physicalism (or materialism) are advocating a physicalism of substance combined with something like a dual aspect theory of events. They assert that mental events are identical with physical events within an organism's central nervous system or brain. The theory is sometimes called central state materialism." **Hodgson**, *The Mind Matters*

central-state theory of mind, another term for central-state materialism

certainty

EPISTEMOLOGY, LOGIC [from Latin *certus*, sure] Either a state of mind (psychological certainty), such as acceptance, trust, taking as reliable, and not disputing or questioning, or a property of a proposition of being incapable of being doubted and being undeniable (propositional certainty). Psychological certainty is opposed to **doubt** and **skepticism**, and propositional certainty contrasts to **probability**. Psychological certainty regarding truth is insufficient to establish propositional certainty without further justification. What is known to be certain is a kind of true knowledge, but certainty is different from truth because "certainly true" is stronger than "true" and because we can also judge that a proposition is "certainly false." The distinction between certainty and probability can be compared to the distinction between necessity and contingency. Certainty admits varying degree according to the nature and extent of the testimony.

Modern philosophy has sought to ground knowledge on certainty, which was understood by **Descartes** in terms of the impossibility of doubt. Some have located certainty in thoughts or experiences that could not be denied and that could provide the basis for the acceptance of riskier items. Others, like **Peirce**, proposed a general **fallibilism**, according to which knowledge was possible without

the requirement of certainty. In response to **Moore**'s discussion of certainty in terms of common sense, **Wittgenstein**'s account in *On Certainty* distinguishes between certainty and knowledge. What is certain provides a partially changing array of "hinge" propositions, on which our whole system of belief in ordinary propositions depends.

"Certain, possible, impossible: here we have the first indication of the scale that we need in the theory of probability." **Wittgenstein**, *Tractatus*

ceteris paribus

PHILOSOPHY OF SCIENCE [Latin other things being equal] The generalization of a scientific law or regularity is reached on the assumption that normal conditions obtain, and its application also generally assumes normal circumstances or conditions. All abnormal and exceptional conditions are ruled out. Hence all generalizations imply an unstated *ceteris paribus* clause, which may be stated "other things being equal," or "if conditions are normal, then . . ." The existence of *ceteris paribus* clauses suggests the limitation of the validity and the scope of general explanations. The development of science reduces the scope of *ceteris paribus* clauses by including some previously excluded circumstances within more complex and comprehensive theories. Some philosophers hold that science will always deal with simplified models of reality and that *ceteris paribus* clauses will never be fully eliminated.

"In actual causal arguments in the social sciences, it will often emerge that the claim that C is sufficient for E rests upon an unstated *ceteris paribus* clause: *c* is sufficient for *e* under normal circumstances." **Little**, *Varieties of Social Explanation*

chance

ANCIENT GREEK PHILOSOPHY, METAPHYSICS [Greek *tuche*, from *tunchanein*, to happen; also translated as fortune, luck] In a broad sense, *tuche* is used as a synonym of *automaton* (spontaneous). Sometimes **Aristotle** distinguished the two terms, but the distinction was neither important nor always observed. Something happening by chance does not happen for any reason. Its cause cannot be accounted for, and it is an exception to the general rule. Chance can be either good or bad, that is, either good luck or bad luck, fortunate or unfortunate. In ethics, matters of chance or luck are uncontrolled events that are beneficial or harmful to somebody. In modern philosophy, chance contrasts with **determinism** and is discussed without ethical aspects in statistics and **probability** theory.

> "Thus to say that chance is a thing contrary to rule is correct." **Aristotle,** *Physics*

change

METAPHYSICS [Greek *metabole, alloiosis, gignesthai* or *kinesis*, which are also be translated by other terms, such as alteration, generation, becoming, motion and movement] Any transition to something. **Aristotle** analyzed three elements in a change: a pair of opposites: the lack of a character prior to the change (privation) and the character after the change (form); and the subject or substratum that underlies the opposites. He held that all change is from the potential to the actual. He also distinguished two types of change on the basis of his theory of **categories**. First, a non-substantial change occurs if a definite thing changes its attributes and comes to be such-and-such a thing, with the substratum of change being an individual. For example, there is a non-substantial change if a man changes from being unmusical to being musical. Non-substantial change includes change of place, qualitative change and quantitative change. Secondly, substantial change occurs if the subject itself, rather than its attributes, changes, with the substratum of change being matter. Substantial change is coming-into-being, the generation of a new composite of form and matter. Sometimes Aristotle distinguished among *kinesis* (non-substantial change); *gignesthai* (substantial change) in contrast with *phthora* (ceasing to be); and *metabole* (the whole change), but did not always observe these distinctions. His theory of change is a criticism of **Parmenides**, who claimed that change is impossible because being cannot be generation from not-being. According to Aristotle, not-being is an absence that changes through being replaced by a positive characteristic.

Contemporary philosophers understand change as the difference between a thing T at time t_1 and at time t_2; as the replacement of one thing T by another thing T' at time t; or as the occurrence of an event at time t. **Cambridge change**, which need not involve a real change in a thing, occurs if some predicate is true of T at t_1 but false of T at t_2. This has provoked much debate, for in such cases T can undergo a Cambridge change without really altering. Since change involves time, philosophers who deny the reality of time deny the existence of change as well. There is also a tradition, starting from **Heraclitus** and represented in the twentieth century by **Whitehead**, that reduces physical objects to changes or processes.

> "If change proceeds . . . from the contrary, there must be something underlying changes into the contrary state; for the contraries do not change." **Aristotle,** *Metaphysics*

character

ETHICS [Greek *êthos*, character or disposition] A state of desiring and feeling resulting from early habituation. The notion is closely connected with habit and custom. From *êthos* we derive the name of the philosophical discipline "ethics," literally meaning "concerned with the character." The character of a person makes that person the sort of person he is. The cultivation of character requires the education of the non-rational parts or aspects of the soul. **Aristotle** divides virtue (excellence) into **virtues** of intelligence and virtues of character. A large part of his ethics concerns the formation of virtues of character.

> "Virtue of character results from habit; hence its name ethics, slightly varies from Êthos." **Aristotle,** *Nicomachean Ethics*

characterizing term, Strawson's term for mass term

charity

ETHICS, PHILOSOPHY OF RELIGION [from Latin *caritas*, generally translated as love] The benevolent love for **God** and one's neighbors (others). Charity, along with **faith** and hope, is one of the three cardinal Christian theological **virtues**. Among them, faith is first in order of origin, while charity is the highest in order of perfection. Charity is the fundamental and underlying spiritual orientation for Christian life, and determines all other moral and intellectual virtues. For Christians, this is because we come from God and will go back to God. Charity is not instrumental but is unconditional and is pursued beyond the present life. Currently, charity is the voluntary provision for the poor and suffering and the pursuit of other good causes. It is taken to mean the same as philanthropy.

"Charity is the mother and root of all the virtues in as much as it is the form of them all." **Aquinas,** *Summa Theologiae*

Chinese room argument

PHILOSOPHY OF MIND A thought experiment devised by John **Searle** in his 1980 paper "Minds, Brains and Programs." It is designed to demonstrate that software cannot make a computer conscious or give it a mind that is anything like a human mind. Suppose an English speaker, who cannot speak Chinese, is locked in a room with two windows and an instruction book in English. Pieces of paper with questions in Chinese written on them are put into the room through one window. The person matches these pieces of paper with other pieces of paper with Chinese symbols according to the instructions in the book and then passes these other pieces of paper through the other window. Searle believes that this is basically what the set-up inside a computer is like and that the non-Chinese-speaking person is like the computer. He processes everything received from the input according to a program, and his output might, as a matter of fact, take the form of answers to the Chinese questions he received. Hence he passes the **Turing test**, but still does not gain an understanding of Chinese. Similarly, a computer only operates according to designed formal rules, and cannot be aware of the contents of the symbols it manipulates. Searle then concludes that a program is not a mind, for the former is formal or syntactical, while the latter has semantic content. **Semantics** is not intrinsic to **syntax**, and syntax is not sufficient for semantics. The Chinese room argument is a powerful criticism of the position of strong **artificial intelligence**, which claims that a mind is nothing more than a computer program. The logic and implications of this Chinese room argument have been hotly debated over the past decade.

"I believe the best-known argument against strong AI was my Chinese room argument that showed a system could instantiate a program so as to give a perfect simulation of some human cognitive capacity, such as the capacity to understand Chinese, even though that system had no understanding of Chinese whatever." **Searle,** *The Rediscovery of the Mind*

Chisholm, Roderick (1916–99)

American philosopher, born in North Attleboro, Massachusetts, educated at Harvard, taught at Brown. Chisholm was heavily influenced by Brentano and revived the notion of intentionality in analytic philosophy. His *Theory of Knowledge* is one of the most widely used textbooks of epistemology. Chisholm contributed many original positions on issues in epistemology, philosophy of mind, ontology, and ethics. His views on the primacy of the intentional over semantics, the problem of criteria, foundationalism, internalism, the adverbial theory of sensory experiencing, agent causality, ontological categories, intrinsic value, and mereological essentialism provoked lively debates in metaphysics and epistemology. His works include *Perceiving: A Philosophical Study* (1957), *Person and Object* (1976), *The First Person* (1981), *The Foundations of Knowing* (1982), *On Metaphysics* (1989), and *A Realistic Theory of Categories* (1996). He edited the journal *Philosophy and Phenomenological Research*.

choice, see decision

Chomsky, Noam (1928–)

American theorist of linguistics, philosopher of language and mind, and political thinker, born in Philadelphia, Professor at Massachusetts Institute of Technology. Chomsky radically altered the development of theoretical linguistics by introducing transformational and generative grammar and by claiming that our acquisition and use of language shows that the human mind has innate genetically given linguistic features. In keeping with a program of minimalism, his later linguistic writings have sought to reduce a range of transformational rules to a single abstract transformational principle. His work has deeply influenced philosophy of language, philosophy of mind, and cognitive science. His major works include *Syntactic Structures* (1957), *Cartesian Linguistics* (1966), *Knowledge of Language* (1986), *Deterring Democracy* (1992), and *Language and Thought* (1993).

chronological logic, another name for tense logic

Chrysippus (*c.*280–*c.*208 BC)
Stoic philosopher, born in Soli, Asia Minor. After studying in Athens under Zeno and Cleanthes, he became the third head of the Stoa. None of his complete works survived, although he was extensively quoted by Plutarch and other secondary sources. He is credited with systematizing and defining Stoic philosophy and defending it against Academic attack. He developed Stoic logic that anticipated modern prepositional calculus and is considered to be the first to formulate truth conditions for conditional statements. Diogenes Laertius remarked that "If there had been no Chrysippus there would have been no Stoa."

Church, Alonzo (1903–95)
American mathematical logician, born in Washington, DC, Professor at Princeton and UCLA. In mathematical logic, **Church's theorem** proved the undecidability of first-order logic, and **Church's thesis** linked the notion of effective computation to recursiveness. Church argued for realism regarding abstract objects and contributed to the theory of probability as well as playing a major role in the development of mathematical logic. His works include *Introduction to Mathematical Logic*, vol. 1 (1956).

Church's theorem, see Church's thesis

Church's thesis
LOGIC "That the notion of an effectively calculable function of positive integers should be identified with that of a recursive function . . ." This thesis was proposed by the American mathematical logician Alonzo **Church** in 1935. It combines **Gödel**'s notion of recursiveness with the notion of computability. A function is computable if and only if it is recursive and **Turing**-computable. Since this thesis is closely related to the concept of Turing-computability, it is sometimes called the Church–Turing thesis. The notion of effective computability in Church's thesis is an intuitive rather than proven notion. For this reason, Church's thesis is a thesis rather than a theorem. There is, however, Church's theorem, proved by Church in 1936, which states that there is no decision procedure for determining whether an arbitrary formula of predicate

calculus is a theorem of the calculus. It is a negative solution to the decision problem. Church's thesis serves as one of the premises of Church's theorem.

> "Church's thesis, if true, guarantees that a Turing machine can compute any 'effective' procedure."
> **Baker,** *Saving Belief*

Cicero, Marcus Tullius (106–43 BC)
Roman philosopher and orator, born at Arpinum in Latium. His writings include the *Academica, De finibus, Tusculan Disputations, De fato, De Officiis* (*On Duties*), *De Re Publica* (*On the State*), and *De Legibus* (*On the Laws*). Cicero sought to make Greek philosophy available to Latin speakers and was the creator of philosophical vocabulary in Latin. He was a trained Academic skeptic, but was inclined toward Stoicism in moral philosophy. His writings show the influence of Stoicism, Epicurus, and Skepticism. His exposition of the Stoic concepts of natural law and justice greatly influenced Roman law.

circular definition
LOGIC A definition is circular if its *definiens* has to be explained by appeal to its *definiendum*, or if its *definiendum* appears in its *definiens*. This is in violation of the rule in formal logic that the *definiens* should not contain any part of the *definiendum*. A more common form of circularity occurs in a set of definitions, if a term A is defined by B, and B by C, and then C by A.

> "If a definition contains the definiendum in the definiens, the definition is said to be circular."
> **Adams,** *The Fundamentals of General Logic*

circular reasoning, another term for begging the question

citizenship
POLITICAL PHILOSOPHY The legal status of being a member of a nation or state. In contemporary political philosophy, citizenship is both a duty-related and rights-related concept. As a citizen, one has a **duty** to promote and defend the interest of the state, even, if necessary, at the expense of one's own life. Citizens are also obliged to sacrifice some of their private life to engage in public activity. Citizens, however, are recognized as having a **right** to participate in public life, rights to vote and to

stand for public office, rights to education and other welfare, and rights to legal protection. Other rights, such as those involving free speech, free association, and access to a free press, also derive from the notion of citizenship. Citizenship has been described as a democratic ideal that distinguishes free individuals from mere subjects who live under various forms of undemocratic regimes. The equality of democratic citizenship is a central topic in the political discussion of equality.

> "Democratic citizenship is a status radically disconnected from every kind of hierarchy." **Walzer,** *Spheres of Justice*

civil disobedience

POLITICAL PHILOSOPHY, PHILOSOPHY OF LAW Activity engaged in openly but deliberately against the law in order to express some conscientious and deeply held convictions in the hope of changing perceived injustices in the law and government policies. The laws broken need not be the laws against which protest is raised. Civil disobedience must be distinguished from militant actions and organized forcible resistance. As a mode of address or protest for a vital social purpose, civil disobedience generally occurs in a well-ordered, democratic society and against a constitutional regime. The activity itself is in violation of law, but it is performed by people who accept the basic principles of a democratic society. Problems arise regarding questions such as the grounds on which these acts can be justified and how the legal systems might legitimately respond to them. The discussion of civil disobedience is closely related to the question of political obligation.

> "I shall begin by defining civil disobedience as a public, non-violent, conscientious yet political act contrary to law usually done with the aim of bringing about a change in the law or policies of the government." **Rawls,** *A Theory of Justice*

civil duty, see civil rights

civil liberties, see civil rights

civil rights

POLITICAL PHILOSOPHY, PHILOSOPHY OF LAW Civil matters pertain to the dealings of the **state** with its citizens as citizens. Civil rights are the rights granted to the citizens by the constitution and laws of a state and must be protected by the constitution and laws. These rights, or civil liberties, generally include freedom of speech, freedom of assembly, freedom of the press, freedom of religious belief, and freedom of political participation. In this sense, they cover the rights stated in articles 1–21 of the *Universal Declaration of Human Rights* (1948). The right to due process in the law and other legal protections are also included. It is a matter of dispute whether fundamental economic and social rights, such as the rights to education, work, shelter, and health care, should also be regarded as civil rights. Questions arise concerning the relations among civil rights. Are they all on a par, or are some more fundamental than others? What should be done if the rights conflict? Can each stand on its own or are they interdependent? Civil rights are correlated with civil duties. If A has a right to X, then other citizens and the state have an obligation not to interfere with A's right. The United States enacted a Civil Rights Act in 1964, which addressed in particular the problem of racial equality. Here "civil rights" means the equal rights of black people to education, employment, and the vote.

> "The liberal, therefore, needs a scheme of civil rights whose effect will be to determine those political decisions that are antecedently likely to reflect strong external preferences and to remove those decisions from majoritarian political institutions altogether." **Dworkin,** *A Matter of Principle*

civil society

POLITICAL PHILOSOPHY [German *burgerliche Gesellschaft*] A major term in **Hegel**'s political philosophy for an economic organization of independent persons. Civil society is distinguished from an autonomous and sovereign political **state**. It includes a system of needs, that is, the institutions and practice involved in the economic activities that meet a variety of needs, the administration of **justice**, public authority, and corporations. A political state makes one a **citizen**, while a civil society makes one a bourgeois. In a civil society, the individual pursues his own private good and has equal civil rights. However, there is also a determinate system that guarantees both the **freedom** of the individual and the harmony of individual needs and the collective needs of the **community**. Hence civil society characterizes modern ethical life (*Sittlichkeit*). Hegel's original distinction between civil society and the political state helps to understand the central role of the economic market in modern society.

"Civil society – an association of members as self-subsistent individuals in a universality which because of their self-subsistence, is only abstract. Their association is brought about by their needs, by the legal systems – the means to security of person and property – and by an external organisation for attaining their particular and common interests." **Hegel,** *Philosophy of Right*

civitas, see commonwealth

Clarke, Samuel (1675–1729)

English rationalist philosopher and natural theologian, born in Norwich, rector of St James, Westminster. Clarke was an early exponent of Newton's scientific achievements and defended them in correspondence with Leibniz. In his ethical writings, he argued for the objectivity of moral qualities and relations and held that we could have rational knowledge of these on the analogy of our mathematical knowledge. His works include *A Demonstration of the Being and Attributes of God* (1704–5), *A Discourse concerning the Unchangeable Obligations of Natural Religion and the Truth and Certainty of Christian Revelation* (1706), and *The Leibniz–Clarke Correspondence* (1717).

class

LOGIC A collection of entities satisfying a condition for membership in the class, that is, having certain common properties. The notion of a class or set is fundamental to **set theory**. A class is said to be open if it has infinite members and closed if its members are numerable. According to the axiom of extensionality, if two classes are exactly alike with respect to their members, they are identical. If a class has no members, it is called the null class or empty class. Class is usually used interchangeably with set, but some suggest that while set covers only those classes that are members of other classes, class covers collections that are not members of any other classes. The distinction is thought to be significant for solving **Russell's paradox**, which is also called the class paradox.

"By 'class' I mean things that have members." **D. Lewis,** *Parts of Classes*

classical Aristotelian conception of truth

LOGIC, PHILOSOPHY OF LANGUAGE Tarski asserted that his task was to enunciate the conception of truth in **Aristotle**'s formula: "To say of what is that it is not, or of what is not that it is, is false, while to say of what is that it is, or of what is not that it is not, is true." Aristotle's conception is the standard version of the **correspondence theory of truth**: "The truth of a sentence consists in its agreement with reality." This formula is equivalent to the **semantic** notion of truth: "A sentence is true if it designates an existing state of affairs." This is in turn the same as Tarski's (T) schema: "'p' is true iff p."

"We should like our definition to do justice to the intuitions which adhere to the classical Aristotelian conception of truth." **Tarski, "The Semantic Conception of Truth," in Feigl and Sellars (eds.),** *Readings in Philosophical Analysis*

class-inclusion

LOGIC A transitive relationship such that if an individual S (or a class A) is included in a class B, and B is in turn included in a higher class C, then if S (or class A) belongs to class B, S (or class A) also belongs to class C. For instance, if Socrates is a human being, and human beings are animals, then Socrates is an animal. In contrast, class-membership is an intransitive relationship. If A is a member of B, and B is a member of C, it does not follow that A is a member of C. For instance, Smith is a member of Oxford University, and Oxford University is a member of the National Union of Universities. But Smith is not a member of the National Union of Universities.

"The relation of class-inclusion is to be distinguished from the relation of class-membership, most importantly because class-membership is non-transitive." **Alexander,** *A Preface to the Logic of Science*

class-membership, see class-inclusion

Cleanthes (*c*.331–232 BC)

Greek Stoic philosopher, born in Assos. He succeeded Zeno of Citium as the second head of the Stoic school in 262 BC. Of his writings, only *Hymn to Zeus* is extant. He was credited to have made important contributions to Stoic theology and cosmology.

clear and distinct

EPISTEMOLOGY **Descartes**'s general criterion of
the **certainty** of knowledge or truth. It is based on
methodological **doubt** and attached to the intellectual perception of **ideas**. Clarity is in contrast to
obscurity. A perception or idea is clear if it contains
no implications that might subsequently cause us to
doubt them. This requires the attentiveness of the
mind. An idea is distinct if it is separated from
everything else and contains absolutely nothing
else but clear ideas. Distinctness is contrasted to
confusion and is a stricter notion than clarity.
An idea may be clear without being distinct, but a
distinct idea is always clear. Descartes claimed that
sorting out what is clear and distinct from what is
obscure and confused is a laborious task. However,
since this criterion relies on the intellect's power, it
is usually criticized as failing to provide a genuine
solution to the problem of the validation of human
knowledge, for it simply declares that truth is
self-manifesting to the human mind.

> "I call a perception 'clear' when it is present and
> accessible to the attentive mind . . . I call a percep-
> tion 'distinct' if, as well as being clear, it is so
> sharply separated from all other perceptions that
> it contains within itself only what is clear."
> **Descartes,** *The Philosophical Writings*

Clement of Alexandria (c.150–c.219)

Alexandrian Christian theologian, probably born
in Athens. Clement argued that philosophy was in
harmony with Christian doctrine and could help
to understand it. He emphasized a Neoplatonic
contrast between simple and complex unity. God is
a simple unity who can not be named or discussed
in terms of the Aristotelian categories. The Son,
however, is knowable as a complex unity. Clement
used further philosophical doctrines to discuss
God's goodness and human virtue, truth, and faith.
His major philosophical work was *Stromateis*.

closed sentence, see open sentence

closed society, see open society

cogito ergo sum

METAPHYSICS, EPISTEMOLOGY, PHILOSOPHY OF MIND
[Latin, I think, therefore I am] The first principle or
first truth of **Descartes**'s metaphysical system. I can
doubt everything, including whether I have a body.
But as long as I am engaged in the process of thinking, I exist. Even if I doubt my existence, there must
exist an "I" who can doubt. It would be a contradiction to deny the existence of something that is thinking. Thus this proposition is certain and indubitable.
It is the first limitation to the agnostic doubt, and
the starting-point of strict knowledge. It implies, of
course, some prior knowledge of the meaning of
the terms involved and their logical implications,
but it is the first matter of existence of which one
can be sure. The proposition might be construed
syllogistically as presupposing a major premise
that everything that thinks exists. But Descartes
emphasized that the certainty of my existence is not
a logical inference; rather it is an individual and
immediate act of thinking.

> "Observing that this truth 'I am thinking, there-
> fore I exist' (*Ego cogito ergo sum*) was so firm and
> sure that all the most extravagant suppositions of
> the sceptics were incapable of shaking it, I decided
> that I could accept it without scruple as the first
> principle of the philosophy I was seeking."
> **Descartes,** *Discourse on Method*

cognition

EPISTEMOLOGY [from Latin *cognitio*, awareness, or the
formation of the ideas of something] *Cognitio* is
usually translated as "knowledge"; but this is not
precise. While "knowledge" is also used to translate
"scientia," **Descartes** distinguished cognition from
knowledge (*scientia*), for much of our cognition is
confused and inadequate. **Spinoza** distinguished
among three grades of cognition. The first grade is
composed of mere second-hand opinion, imagination and cognition derived from shifting experience.
This kind of cognition admits of falsity. The second
grade is reason (*ratio*), which seeks the underlying
reason or cause of phenomena, and to find necessary truths. The third and highest grade is intuitive
knowledge (*scientia intuitive*), which advances from
adequate ideas of the essence of attributes to the
adequate knowledge of the essence of things. The
distinction between intuitive knowledge and reason
roughly corresponds to **Aristotle**'s distinction between *nous*, which grasps the first principles, and
apodeixis (demonstration), which involves **deduction**
from the established first principles.

In general philosophical usage, cognition comprises those states and processes leading to knowledge and is distinguished from sensation, feeling, and volition. In contemporary cognitive psychology and **cognitive science**, cognition is viewed as the representational state and process of the mind, including not only thinking, but also language-using, symbol-manipulating, and behavior-controlling.

> "Cognition of the first kind alone is the cause of falsity; cognition of the second and third orders is necessarily true." **Spinoza, *Ethics***

cognitive science

PHILOSOPHY OF MIND An interdisciplinary investigation of human cognition and cognitive processes such as thinking, reasoning, memory, attention, learning, mental representation, perception, and problem solving. It emerged in the 1970s, and psychology, linguistics, philosophy, neuroscience, computer science, and artificial intelligence all contribute to this enterprise. While **artificial intelligence** attempts to get computing machines to approximate a human mind, the basic idea of cognitive science is to view the human mind as a computer-like information processing system. It is hence an attempt to understand the human cognition system in terms of the developments of computer science and artificial intelligence. Initially cognitive science viewed computation as the manipulation of symbols, but its recent development has taken the form of **connectionism** or neural network modeling.

> "The basic inspiration of cognitive science went something like this: human beings do information processing." **Searle, in Bunnin and Tsui-James (eds.), *The Blackwell Companion to Philosophy***

cognitive value

LOGIC, PHILOSOPHY OF LANGUAGE A term **Frege** introduced to contrast with **truth-value**. The truth-value of a sentence is its truth or falsity and does not vary if we substitute for one of its components another term having the same reference. However, the substitution might result in a different understanding of the sentence. For the substitute term might have the same reference (that is, what it designates) but a different sense (that is, what it means). Hence, the substantial information the sentence

conveys will be changed. This sense is the cognitive value of a sentence, which we understand when we understand the sentence. Cognitive value is also called epistemic value.

> "a = a and a = b are obviously statements of differing cognitive value." **Frege, *Collected Papers***

cognitivism

ETHICS, PHILOSOPHY OF MIND Ethical theories that hold that there is knowledge of moral facts and that normative ethical judgments can be said to be true or false. Cognitivism includes the majority of traditional ethical theories. In contrast, **non-cognitivism**, represented by **emotivism** and **prescriptivism**, holds that moral statements do not possess truth-values and cannot be known. Outside of ethics, cognitivism is a psychological theory that explains behavior by appeal to the information-processing states of the physical brain.

> "Roughly, cognitivists hold that there is ethical knowledge; non-cognitivists deny it." **Hancock, *Twentieth-Century Ethics***

Cohen, Gerald Alan (1941–)

Canadian-British analytical Marxist political philosopher, born in Montreal, Chichele Professor of Social and Political Theory at University of Oxford. Cohen is a leading exponent of analytical Marxism, using rigorous analytic methods to explicate, reconstruct, and criticize Marx's theoretical claims. In particular, he defended Marx's account of history by reconstructing Marx's historical determinism in terms of functional explanation. His works include *Karl Marx's Theory of History: A Defense* (1978) and *History, Labour and Freedom: Themes from Marx* (1988).

Cohen, Hermann (1842–1918)

German-Jewish neo-Kantian philosopher, born in Coswig, Professor at University of Marburg and Lecturer at the High School for the Science of Judaism. Cohen founded the Marburg school of neo-Kantianism with Paul Natorp and interpreted Kant's theory of knowledge in psychological terms. He later turned to questions of religion. He interpreted Judaism as an ethical system based on biblical prophecy, giving priority to ethics over ritual. He argued for the integration of Jews in

European society and against Zionism. His main works include *The Concept of Religion in the Philosophical System* (1915) and *The Religion of Reason Taken from Jewish Sources* (1918).

Cohen, Morris Raphael (1889–1947)

American legal philosopher, philosopher of science, and logician, born Minsk, Russia. Professor, City College of New York. Cohen argued that as part of science, logic was based on the nature of things rather than forming a set of abstract tautologies. He was a realist regarding abstract entities, but held that claims about their existence and the principles of science, ethics, and law were fallible and always open to further testing. His principle of polarity, that opposite qualities must involve each other, supported a dialectical practice of reasoning from opposing views. His major works include *Reason and Nature* (1931), *Law and Social Order* (1933), and *An Introduction to Logic and Scientific Method* (with Ernest Nagel, 1934).

coherence theory of truth

LOGIC, EPISTEMOLOGY, PHILOSOPHY OF LANGUAGE A theory taking truth to consist in coherent relations among the members of a set of beliefs and propositions, rather than in relations between a proposition and a corresponding fact. This theory arises due to the failure of the **correspondence theory of truth** to provide a satisfactory explanation of the nature of correspondence. The coherence of a proposition with other propositions is the ultimate criterion of truth. Truth is defined in terms of the coherence of propositions. Coherence usually means consistency and independence. Generally speaking, the proponents of this theory have their philosophical outlook shaped by an admiration for mathematics. For many **rationalists**, this theory of truth is an essential ingredient in their epistemology. In the twentieth century, this theory was proposed by the idealist **Bradley** and the logical positivist **Neurath**, and was most recently defended by **Rescher**. Its major problem is that it generally goes beyond one's power to put a proposition into a holistic system of beliefs. Furthermore, a proposition might be coherent with others in its system, but the system as a whole might be incompatible with another system of beliefs. Accordingly, coherence and truth do not seem to be the same.

> "A coherence theory of truth may be seen in an essentially regulative role governing the considerations relating to the classification of empirical propositions as true, rather than claiming to present the constitutive essence of truth as such." **Rescher,** *The Coherence Theory of Truth*

coherentism

EPISTEMOLOGY [from Latin *cohaerere*, to adhere together, stick together] Coherentism is a theory of epistemic justification, in opposition to **foundationalism**. It denies the view that there is a set of self-warranting perceptual beliefs that serve as the ultimate justification for all other beliefs. Instead, it suggests that all beliefs form a network within which each has equal epistemic status. A cognitive system is a family of interrelated theses that are linked to one another by an interlacing network of connections. These connections are inferential in nature but not necessarily deductive. Justification is a matter of coherence. A belief is justified if and only if it coheres with the background system of beliefs. There are various ways of understanding the nature of coherence; and different views of what coherence is form different versions of coherentism. Since coherence is essentially an internal relation among beliefs, there is a major difficulty for coherentism to deal with, that is, how to fill the gap between justified belief and external reality. It is also difficult for this theory to accommodate perceptual knowledge. In another usage, coherentism means the view that a complete inductive logic is restricted to a principle of credal coherence.

> "Coherentism . . . views the network-interrelatedness of factual theses as the criterial standard of their acceptability." **Rescher,** *Cognitive Systematization*

collective predicate, Goodman's term for mass noun

collective responsibility

ETHICS, POLITICAL PHILOSOPHY Modern ethics has been traditionally individualistic in the sense that only the individual can be the focus of ethical consideration and that an action of a group can be morally meaningful only when it can be reduced to the actions of individuals. But there is a tendency to believe that in certain circumstance we can have a notion of group or collective responsibility that cannot be reduced to individual responsibility. For example, some seek to ascribe responsibility or blame collectively to white South Africans under apartheid and to Germans as a whole under the Nazi regime. The problem is how to talk about this group responsibility. It does not seem correct to model it on the discourse of individual responsibility. What is important is to define what the group is. It is generally thought that the group in question should not be a random collection of individuals, but must be one that has a group cohesion and identity. All its members should have common interests and a sense of pride and shame in the group. Blame or responsibility should be ascribed to this kind of group not only when all of its members do something wrong, but also when some of its members commit significant blameworthy actions in virtue of their membership. The issue, along with similar questions regarding group interest, group rights, and group justice, remains open and is unlikely to be settled until we have a better understanding of the metaphysical nature of social entities and the relationship between groups and their members.

"My account makes it a necessary condition for the ascription of collective responsibility to unorganised groups that each member of a group engage in acts or omissions which contribute to the harmful consequences for which the group is held collectively responsible." May, *The Morality of Groups*

collectivism

POLITICAL PHILOSOPHY, PHILOSOPHY OF SOCIAL SCIENCE In contrast to **individualism**, which gives priority to individual interests over collective interests, the view that the common interests of a group or society are more important than the interests of its individual members. The significance of an individual cannot be considered apart from the group or state to which he belongs, and an individual can flourish or develop freedom only within the necessary background conditions provided by some collectivity. When the interests of an individual and society clash, the individual should concede in order to allow the society to meet its goals. Like individualism, collectivism has ethical, metaphysical,

explanatory, and methodological versions, which need not all be accepted. One can accept the claim that there are collective entities like families or states that have some kind of metaphysical priority over their individual members without accepting a moral priority for the goals of the collective over the aims of the individuals.

Often collectivism is equated with socialism, on the basis of **Marx**'s explanation of social and historical phenomena in terms of class conflict based on the forces and relations of production, and of his understanding of individualism as a product of the capitalist mode of production. Socialism proposes the use of the apparatus of state and government power to control, command, and regulate the economy and various other sectors of civil society for the good of the proletariat and ultimately other social classes until class-based society is superseded by communism. This sophisticated theory and its criticism raises many fundamental questions about the claims of collectivism.

"I use the term 'collectivism' only for a doctrine which emphasises the significance of some collective or group, for instance, the state (or a certain state; or a nation; or a class) as against that of the individual." Popper, *The Open Society and Its Enemies* I

Collingwood, R(obin) G(eorge) (1889–1943)

British philosopher and archaeologist of Roman Britain, born in Coniston, Lancaster, studied and taught in Oxford. Collingwood made significant contributions to metaphysics, aesthetics, and the Philosophy of history. He held that metaphysics should explicate the absolute presuppositions of the thought of a given society in a particular period and study their changes. These presuppositions cannot be assessed as true or false, but can only be shown historically. Influenced by Croce, he systematically developed an expression theory of art. He held that history, being concerned with the world of human activity, should seek to reconstruct in imagination the reasons that historical agents acted as they did. He was a prolific writer, and representative works include *The Principles of Art* (1938), *An Essay on Metaphysics* (1940), *The Idea of Nature* (1945), and *The Idea of History* (1946). He also wrote a widely read *Autobiography* (1939).

command

ETHICS, PHILOSOPHY OF LANGUAGE, LOGIC As a central concept in **Kant**'s moral philosophy, a law that must be obeyed and followed even in opposition to inclination. A command is formulated through an **imperative** and is expressed as an **ought**. It is the subjection or conformity of the inclinations of the **will** to objective **moral law**. **Categorical imperatives** are commands in the absolute sense, while hypothetical imperatives are commands that are subject to certain conditions regarding the aims of those to whom they are addressed. In contemporary philosophy of language, a command is a kind of **speech act** which, when addressed to other people, expresses a mandate and involves a prescription. The logic of commands or imperatives has been part of a more general development of contemporary logic.

"The representation of an objective principle insofar as it necessitates the will is called a command (of reason)." **Kant**, *Groundwork for the Metaphysics of Morals*

command theory of law

PHILOSOPHY OF LAW A theory that can be traced to Jeremy **Bentham**, but which became widely known through the work of his disciple John **Austin**, who elaborated the theory in *The Province of Jurisprudence Determined* (1832). Austin rejected the claim of **natural law** theory that positive law is derived from natural law. Instead, he defined law as a species of command issued by a **sovereign** person or body that has purpose or power to inflict punishment. Law is a coercive method of social control, and we do not have an option to avoid following legal requirements. In his understanding, a command has two aspects: (1) it signifies a desire or wish conceived by a rational being; (2) it can inflict evil or harm on those who fail to satisfy this desire. Accordingly, his definition of law excludes customary law, constitutional law, and international law, because they are not commands in his sense. If the sovereign has stipulated a sanction, one is under a legal duty. Austin's command theory of law is generally criticized as being too narrow, for law does more than merely command. In recent times, his definition of law is examined by H. L. A. **Hart** in *The Concept of Law*.

"Austin's particular theory is often called 'the command theory of law' because he makes the concept of command central in his account of law and maintains that all laws are commands, even when they do not take a form that appears imperative in nature." **Murphy and Coleman**, *The Philosophy of Law*

commensurability, see incommensurability

common consent argument, another term for *consensus gentium* argument

common good

ETHICS, POLITICAL PHILOSOPHY The public and shared interests of a **community**, such as peace, order, and security, the enjoyment of which by some community members does not prevent enjoyment of it by others. The common good is contrasted to individual or private goods, the enjoyment of which precludes the rights of others to them. The common good is essential for human happiness and every member of the community is obliged to pursue it. In the traditional theory of **natural law**, protecting and promoting the common good is the sufficient and necessary condition for the authenticity of the law. The existence of the common good demands that the individual should be subordinate to the community and that in certain circumstances individual interests should be sacrificed to secure the common good. A major issue in contemporary ethical and political theory is to justify the rationality and scope of this subordination and sacrifice.

"Government is assumed to aim at the common good, that is, at maintaining conditions and achieving objectives that are similarly to everyone's advantage." **Rawls**, *A Theory of Justice*

common notion

EPISTEMOLOGY, LOGIC [Greek *koine ennoia*] A Stoic term for notions that refer to the most basic features of a conceived object and that arise naturally in the minds of all sensible men. These notions are thought to be self-validating, self-evident, and are the starting-point of all reasoning and investigation. In Euclid's geometry, common notions are **axioms** or first principles. In modern philosophy, some philosophers such as Thomas **Reid** consider them as intuitively known and unquestionable beliefs that are generally accepted and arise out of natural instinct. **Descartes** used the conception of common notion for fundamental logical truths or axioms, such as "It is impossible for the same thing to be and not to be at the same time." The truth of a common notion is completely assured. According to Descartes, we do not arrive at these notions out of natural instinct. They are rather acquired by the natural light of reason, though some people whose natural light is obstructed would not perceive them properly. Common notions form a part of the content of the mind and are a condition of knowledge.

"Common notions, . . . are, as it were, links which connect other simple natures together and whose self-evidence is the basis for all the rational inferences we make." **Descartes,** *The Philosophical Writings*

common sense

EPISTEMOLOGY The natural and ordinary beliefs that are taken for granted by people independent of philosophical training. While rationalistic philosophy often starts by challenging and rejecting common sense, there is a kind of philosophy that argues that the general consent that exists regarding the views of common sense offers justification for accepting them in preference to skeptical or revisionary doctrines. Historically, Thomas **Reid**, the main figure in the Scottish school of common sense, argued with great subtlety against **Hume**'s **skepticism** and his associated theory of ideas. G. E. **Moore**, the leading defender of common sense in the last century, claims in his famous paper "A Defense of Common Sense" that a philosopher's common sense convictions are more certain that any of the arguments purporting to establish skepticism.

Another meaning of common sense, initiated by **Aristotle** (Greek, *koine aisthesis*), refers to a faculty that integrates the data from the five specialized senses. This meaning is accepted by the **scholastics** and also elaborated in the philosophy of **Descartes**. **Kant** adapted the Aristotelian notion to form an account of common sense as reflective, public, and critical, in contrast to what he saw as Reid's vulgar account of common sense.

"Both common sense and physics supplement precepts by the assumption that things do not cease to exist when unperceived." **Russell,** *Human Knowledge*

common sense morality

ETHICS Pre-theoretical moral convictions, held by ordinary people. Its value in ethics has been a subject of dispute. While some philosophers, such as **Plato** and **Aquinas**, believe that ordinary morality must be subject to theoretical examination and guidance, others, such as **Aristotle, Kant, Hegel**, those in the British **moral sense** tradition, moral **intuitionists**, **Rawls** and applied ethical theorists, believe that an adequate ethics must lie primarily in systematizing our common sense moral judgments. If the conclusions derived from a moral theory deeply conflict with common sense, the theory itself must be defective. Common sense morality denies that we need moral experts to guide our daily life, but it must combat moral relativism and can face a demand to provide a criterion to test the adequacy of common sense moral beliefs.

"I submit that analogous to this internal common sense of law there is an internal common sense of morality which every rational morality ought to respect." **Cooper,** *The Diversity of Moral Thinking*

common sense psychology, another term for folk psychology

commonwealth

POLITICAL PHILOSOPHY In a broad sense, a commonwealth contrasts with the **state of nature** and is identical with a civil state or *civitas*. In a narrow sense, it is government, in particular democratic government. Both **Hobbes** and **Locke** endorsed the broad sense. A commonwealth as a civil state is formed when people in a state of nature consent to give up some of their **rights** and **powers** in exchange for the protection of other rights and powers. It is generally believed that in a commonwealth people can live in a peaceful and orderly manner. A commonwealth must have some form of government, that is, some system of subjection and obedience. In this regard, it is different from a community in which there is no system of subjection. Both Hobbes and Locke held that a commonwealth should be one coherent living body. Among the various forms of governments a commonwealth might have, Hobbes preferred monarchy, while Locke proposed democracy.

"By common-wealth, I must be understood all along to mean, not a Democracy, or any form of government, but any independent community which the *Latines* signified by the word *civitas*, to which the word which best answers in our language, is commonwealth, and most properly expresses such a Society of Man, which Communities or city in English does not, for there may be subordinate Communities in a Government." **Locke, *Two Treatises on Government***

communicative action

ETHICS, POLITICAL PHILOSOPHY For **Habermas**, a distinct and crucially important type of social interaction that is oriented toward reaching mutual understanding through a process of argumentation. Within such action, participants harmonize their respective plans on the basis of having a common understanding of the situation and make claims that all concerned can accept as valid. Communicative action seeks public agreement rather than private advantage: agents do not seek to influence others to act in ways solely favoring their own interests and plans. Communicative action is opposed to strategic action, in which individual participants are oriented toward achieving their own goals by manipulating their opponents. Strategic action is instrumental and egoistic, with individual agents seeking to achieve their ends by any effective means. Communicative action is a matter of dialogue and is characterized by reciprocity. There are implicit canons of normative validity in communicative action, and each side acts out of unforced obligations based upon mutual understanding. Discourse is the idealization of communicative action. Philosophy should reveal the universal conditions determining the possibility of communicative action. It should show how communicative actions of different types are embedded in historical situations and how they change in historical time. The theory of communicative action is inspired by speech act theory.

"The concept of communicative action presupposes languages as the medium for a kind of reaching understanding, in the course of which participants, through relating to a world, reciprocally raise validity claims that can be accepted or contested." **Habermas, *The Theory of Communicative Action* I**

communicative ethics, another name for discourse ethics

communicative rationality

PHILOSOPHY OF LANGUAGE, ETHICS **Habermas**'s term for the rationality that is implicitly contained in the structure of human speech and shared by all competent speakers. Standard accounts of rationality represent it as involving one-dimensional logical relations between propositions and as centered in the thought and action of individual subjects. In contrast, communicative rationality is two-dimensional and involves a dialogical relationship between different speakers. The traditional conception of rationality is represented in the paradigm of our knowledge of objects, while communicative rationality is expressed in the paradigm of mutual understanding between subjects who are capable of speech and action and in an understanding of the world that is decentered away from the individual subject. It is the life-world rationality, dealing with the intersubjectivity of valid claims. Its sphere of validity corresponds to the sphere of human speech. For Habermas, the notion of communicative rationality is the basis for communicative action. He calls the process by which communicative action replaces strategic action communicative rationalization.

"This communicative rationality recalls older ideas of logos, inasmuch as it brings along with it the connotations of a noncoercively unifying, consensus-building force of a discourse in which the participants overcome their at first subjectively biased views in favour of a rationally motivated agreement." **Habermas, *The Philosophical Discourse of Modernity***

communicative rationalization, see communicative rationality

communitarianism

POLITICAL PHILOSOPHY A family of positions that stand in contrast to liberal **individualism**. While liberal individualism, which developed from **utilitarian** and **Kantian** thought to **Rawls** and **Nozick**, focuses on the individual as the bearer of rights and as the center of moral and political analysis, communitarianism shifts this focus to the **community**. It insists that the individual is embedded into a concrete moral, social, historical, and political context that is constitutive of individual identity. Hence communitarianism replaces the atomistic conception of the person with a contextualist view of human identity and agency. It emphasizes the social nature of life and the relationships constituting it rather than freedom of choice. It claims that communal good is prior to individual rights and that there is no single distributive principle that is applicable to all social goods. The intelligibility and justification of justice must be connected to tradition and the shared conception of the good. We cannot stand outside the discourse and traditions of particular societies. The major proponents of communitarianism include A. **MacIntyre**, M. **Sandel**, C. **Taylor**, and R. **Rorty**, but the position has not yet been systematized and does not have a common manifesto. The major charge facing at least some communitarian positions is that they have conservative social and political implications and that they make cross-cultural criticism difficult.

"As the name suggests, communitarianism is concerned with community, and more particularly its absence from the liberal account." **Archard, in Bunnin and Tsui-James (eds.), *Blackwell Companion to Philosophy***

community

ETHICS, POLITICAL PHILOSOPHY, PHILOSOPHY OF SOCIAL SCIENCE In ethics, community is not an institution that is organized for any special purpose in accordance with rules. Instead, it is the social context in which members are united by mutual cooperation and reciprocity. Community in this sense has been seen as a virtue in traditional conceptions of the good or ideal society. Liberal **individualism** places priority on the individual in contrast to community by isolating individuals from their historical and social context and treating individuals as abstract bearers of rights. Contemporary communitarianism argues that community rather than the individual should be the basis of ethics and political theory. The community is constitutive of the individual's identity. It is a formative context and an organic whole rather than an aggregate of atoms. This idea can be traced to **Aristotle's** emphasis on the role of the *polis* in the cultivation of virtues and **Hegel's** doctrine of *Stattlichkeit*. Since

in a contemporary society, national identity and historical, ethical, or religious identities do not coincide, the boundaries of political communities have become unclear.

"Integrity demands that the public standards of the community be both made and seen, so far as this is possible, to express a single, coherent scheme of justice and fairness in the right relation." **Dworkin, *Law's Empire***

compatibilism

METAPHYSICS, PHILOSOPHY OF ACTION Also called soft determinism, a position that holds that **determinism** and **free will** are compatible. Hence human actions can be caused, but still be free. Free actions are not uncaused actions, but are actions that are closely linked with an agent's inner causation through one's own beliefs and desires. On this view, I did X freely means that if I had wanted to I could have done otherwise and that I did X as a result of my own desire and deliberation rather than as a result of being compelled and coerced. Accordingly, the study of human beings can yield some predictability within the terms of an inexact science, although complete accuracy is not possible. The truth of determinism carries no threat to moral responsibility. For freedom is in contrast with coercion or constraint, rather than with having a cause. That my action is causally determined does not entail that I am constrained to do it and does not entail that I am not free. The proponents of this view include **Hume** and **Mill**. In contrast, **incompatibilism**, also called hard determinism, holds that determinism and free will are not compatible and that the truth of determinism will destroy the grounds of moral responsibility.

"Compatibilist philosophers ascribe to us a single conception of the initiation of action, and a kind of belief as to the sufficiency of this initiation in so far as moral approval and disapproval are concerned. The conception is that of a voluntary action, and here a determinism is taken to affect moral responsibility not at all." **Honderich, *The Consequence of Determinism***

competence and performance

PHILOSOPHY OF LANGUAGE A distinction drawn by **Chomsky**. Competence is a person's acquaintance with a set of grammatical **rules**, which are abstracted to a considerable degree from actual linguistic activities. It is the person's underlying linguistic ability. Performance applies this competence in actual circumstances to produce grammatical sentences. According to Chomsky, a linguist should be concerned with linguistic competence rather than the non-regularities of actual performance. A suitable grammar should be a description of an ideal speaker-hearer's intrinsic competence. The distinction between competence and performance is related to **Saussure**'s distinction between *langue and parole*. It is also said to be close to **Ryle**'s distinction between knowing how and knowing that, but this claim is controversial.

> "We thus make a fundamental distinction between competence (the speaker-hearer's knowledge of his language) and performance (the actual use of language in concrete situations)." **Chomsky,** *Aspects of the Theory of Syntax*

complete notion

METAPHYSICS, LOGIC, PHILOSOPHY OF LANGUAGE For **Leibniz**, a **concept** of an **object** that contains all the **predicates** truly attributable to that object. The objects of such a concept can only be the individuals that are the real subjects of categorical judgments. Correspondingly, an entity is an individual substance if and only if its concept is complete. An individual is nothing but the object of a complete concept. In comparison, an accident is a being whose notion does not include everything that can be attributed to the subject to which the notion is attributed. Since an individual contains all the predicates in itself, and is a complete world, many other propositions in Leibniz's metaphysics are derived directly from his account of a complete notion, such as the thesis of the **identity of indiscernibles**, the thesis that individuals are ungenerable and indestructible, the thesis that individuals are incapable of real interaction, and the thesis that each substance is quasi-omniscient and quasi-omnipotent since each is a micro-cosmos.

> "We can say that the nature of an individual substance or of a complete being is to have a notion so complete that it is sufficient to contain and to allow us to deduce from it all the predicates of the subject to which this notion is attributed." **Leibniz,** *Discourse on Metaphysics*

completeness

LOGIC A property ascribed to a system of formal logic, an axiomatic system or a theory, generally meaning that all truths of the system or the theory can be derived or proved within the system or theory. A logical system is **semantically** complete if and only if all of its semantically valid formulae are theorems of the system. It is **syntactically** complete if an addition of a non-theorem will lead to inconsistency. Syntactical completeness is the stronger sense of completeness. A theory is complete or negation-complete if any of its statements or the negation of that statement is provable within the theory. However, according to **Gödel's theorem**, none of the systems of ordinary arithmetic is complete for it must either be inconsistent or contain at least one truth that is not provable within the system itself. This thesis of incompleteness effectively undermines **Hilbert**'s program of providing mathematical proofs of its own consistency.

> "The notion of completeness of a logical system has a semantical motivation, consisting roughly in the intention that the system shall have all possible theorems not in conflict with the interpretation." **Church,** *Introduction to Mathematical Logic*

complex ideas

EPISTEMOLOGY **Locke** distinguished between simple and complex ideas. While simple ideas come directly from **sensation** or **reflection**, complex ideas are compounded by the mind from simple ideas and can also be decomposed into them. Complex ideas are the results of mental operation on simple ideas, and their existence indicates that we are not entirely passive in experience. In the first edition of his *Essay*, Locke divided complex ideas into **modes**, **substances** (ideas), and **relations**. Modes, such as triangle or gratitude, are said not to contain the supposition of subsisting by themselves, but are dependent on substances. Substances, ideas such as man or sheep, are taken to represent distinct particular things subsisting by themselves. Relations consist in the consideration and comparison of one idea with another. However, in the fourth edition of the *Essay*, relations became products of the mind's power of comparing both simple and complex ideas with one another. In that edition Locke added a new category, that is, general ideas or **universals**, which are the results of abstraction in which the mind separates ideas from all other ideas that accompany them in their real existence.

> "When the understanding is once stored with these simple *ideas*, it has the power to repeat, compare, and unite them, even to an almost infinite variety, and so can make at pleasure new complex *ideas*."
> **Locke**, *An Essay Concerning Human Understanding*

compositionality

PHILOSOPHY OF LANGUAGE A language is compositional if its syntactically complex expressions, for example sentences, derive their meanings from their syntactic structures and the meanings of their lexical constituents. For instance, the meaning of the sentence "Snow is white" is a function of the meaning of "snow," the meaning of "white," and the places that these expressions occupy in the subject-predicate structure of the sentence. The **semantic** feature of compositionality has a wide application in the philosophy of language. It also forms the basis for the truth-conditional theory of meaning. A satisfactory semantic theory should explain how the meanings of small expressions contribute to the meanings of larger ones that contain them. It has become the principle that the meaning of an expression is a function of the meaning of its parts and the **syntactic** structure of these parts. This principle is generally ascribed to **Frege** and is also called the **Fregean principle**.

> "The principle of compositionality: The meaning of an expression is a monotonic function of the meaning of its parts and the way they are put together." **Cann**, *Formal Semantics*

compound thought

LOGIC, PHILOSOPHY OF LANGUAGE Analogous to a compound sentence, which consists of two or more sentences. **Frege** introduced the notion of compound thought, which is a whole combined out of two or more thoughts by something that is not a thought. As a compound sentence is itself a sentence, a compound thought is itself a **thought**, and it can also be compounded into other thoughts. Frege distinguishes six different types of compound thought. With A and B representing different single thoughts, they are: (1) A and B; (2) (not A) and (not

B); (3) (not A) and B; (4) not (A and B); (5) not (not A) and (not B); and (6) not ((not A) and B). Frege believed that in a mathematical compound thought, if one component is replaced by another thought having the same truth-value, the new compound thought has the same true-value as the original. The idea is central to propositional logic.

> "By 'compound thought' I shall understand a thought consisting of thoughts, but none of thoughts alone." **Frege**, *Collected Papers*

compromise

ETHICS, POLITICAL PHILOSOPHY The agreement reached through joint negotiations by contending parties after each party makes some concessions from its initial demands. Compromise is based on the premise that for each party cooperation in dealing with the issues in question is better than the breakdown of the relationship. Surrender of some goals is seen by each as helping to secure other and perhaps more important goals. When compromise in this sense applies to conflicts arising from rationally irreconcilable ethical commitments, it is called moral compromise. Moral compromise is necessary for people within a society where conflicting moral principles and interests prevail. Otherwise, a peaceful and non-coercive agreement on a single course of action by proponents of opposing principles cannot be achieved. However, because moral compromise involves sacrificing basic principles and can damage the integrity of the moral agents, it normally carries a derogatory sense. Compromise always involves a tension between uniting with people with different moral convictions and maintaining loyalty to one's principles and oneself. This tension leads to discussion of how we should understand the role of moral principles and integrity.

> "Compromise is both something 'reached' and a 'way of reaching'. As something reached, a compromise is a certain type of outcome of a conflict or disagreement; as a way of reaching, it is a process for resolving conflict or disagreement." **Benjamin**, *Splitting the Difference*

computational model of mind

PHILOSOPHY OF MIND While **artificial intelligence** attempts to get computing machines to approximate the abilities of minds, **cognitive science** is based on the assumption that mind is a machine, with the implication for the philosophy of mind that the mind is viewed as a computational information-processing system. Philosophers who accept this analogy attempt to solve problems regarding the mind/body relationship in terms of this analogy. They try to reveal facts about human functional and representational organization by modeling them on the basis of a computer's internal set-up. This is the project of assimilating mind to computer. Advocates of different understandings of computation develop different models. However, various aspects of the whole project have been criticized. One of the most influential objections is presented in **Searle**'s **Chinese room argument**, which seeks to show that the mind is not merely a kind of software or program.

> "That causal relations reconstruct inferential relations is a foundational assumption of computational theories of mental processes." **Fodor and Lepore,** *Holism*

computer functionalism, another term for the strong thesis of AI

Comte, Auguste (1798–1857)

French philosopher, the founder of positivism, born in Montpellier. Comte maintained that the progress of human mind goes through three stages: the theological, the metaphysical, and the positive or scientific. These three stages offer explanations respectively in terms of gods, abstractions, and observations. He held that sociology is the crowning empirical science and applied his law of three stages to social and political development. He was a pioneer of methodological individualism, the idea that social scientific explanation of collective behavior is ultimately based on the explanation of individual behavior. In his later years he also sought to establish a universal religion of humanity, based on his positivism. His main works are: *Course on the Positive Philosophy* (6 vols. 1830–42), *System of Positive Polity* (4 vols. 1851–4), *Catechism of Positivism* (1852), and *The Subjective Synthesis* (1856).

concept

LOGIC, EPISTEMOLOGY, PHILOSOPHY OF MIND, PHILO-SOPHY OF LANGUAGE A general notion or **idea** that may apply to a multiplicity of things and that is expressed by general words. It is the simplest content of our thinking. Concepts are contrasted to **proper names**, which refer only to one individual thing. Individuals fall under concepts, and we talk about individuals in terms of concepts. Concepts themselves admit a degree of generality. A **genus** concept is wider in extension than a **species** concept. A concept is a component of **propositions**. It mediates between the mind and physical reality, and is a psychological entity with a non-psychological content. Hence it belongs to what **Frege** called the third realm. A central concern for **analytical philosophy** is to classify our most fundamental concepts by analyzing their contents and their logical relations with other concepts. Philosophy is concerned with analyzing concepts such as truth, meaning, person, mind, body, justice, goodness, object, cause, matter, motion, space, time, beauty, and their logical relations. Such concepts have wide applications and are crucial in expressing and understanding. Often, their analysis takes place within the context of sophisticated theories using many basic concepts rather than in isolation. Concepts themselves do not admit of truth or falsity, but the propositions of which concepts are components are the bearers of truth value. Frege distinguished concepts from objects, suggesting that the former are expressed by predicates, the latter by subjects or names.

> "A representation through reason is a concept . . . Universal representations are concepts, and concepts are universal representations." **Kant,** *Lectures on Logic*

concept and object

LOGIC, PHILOSOPHY OF LANGUAGE A distinction based by **Frege** on an analogy between functional expressions in mathematics and subject-predicate **propositions**, according to which such propositions can be analyzed in terms of argument and function. Concepts are given through the functional aspect or the predicate part of a proposition. Predicate expressions are concept words. The argument of the function or the subject part of a proposition stands for an individual object. In the subject-predicate formula, predicates are taken formally, referring not to an individual but to a form or essence. In mathematics, each function is incomplete and contains an empty space to be filled by the argument. Similarly, in propositions a concept is unsaturated, and can be completed by various objects picked out by subject terms. For Frege, this combination of predicate and subject terms to introduce concepts and to pick out objects to complete them is the way that language works.

Frege also distinguished between first-order concepts (under which objects fall) and second-order concepts (under which concepts fall) and derived a corresponding distinction between first-order and second-order predicates. Frege claimed that the major fault in the **ontological argument** for the existence of God is that it treats existence as a first-order concept when it is actually a second-order concept.

The distinction between concepts and objects suggests that predicates correspond to concepts rather than to objects and that the abstract objects expressed by the concept are parasitic upon concrete objects. This position can claim to correct **Aristotle**'s view that predicates correspond to objects. Aristotle's ten categories (ten forms of predication) can be regarded as ten kinds of concepts under which concrete objects fall. The notions of concept and object reflect more precisely the roles performed in language by **predicates** and subjects. But they also create a **paradox** that "the concept *horse*" is not a concept, but an object for it is a definite entity that is not incomplete and that can be referred to. This paradox leads **Wittgenstein** to distinguish formal concepts from ordinary concepts.

"The concept (as I understand the word) is predicative. On the other hand, a name of an object, a proper name, is quite incapable of being used as a grammatical predicate." **Frege,** *Philosophical Writings of Gottlob Frege*

concepts of reflection, see transcendental reflection

concepts of the understanding, pure, another Kantian term for categories

conceptual analysis

PHILOSOPHICAL METHOD The activity of attempting to clarify the **meanings** of **concepts** or ideas by employing logical devices. It tries to discover what elements a concept is composed of and how these elements are related. It also states the relations between certain concepts and the necessary and sufficient conditions of the application of given concepts. Conceptual analysis is the basis for propositional analysis. Only when we understand the meaning of a word can we employ it in formulating precise questions and thus provide correct solutions. For **analytical philosophy**, this activity of reaching the understanding of a given concept is vital. In its early period, conceptual analysis was taken as a synonym of philosophy.

"So his (i.e., the analytical philosopher's) self-awarded title of 'analytical philosopher' suggests 'conceptual analysis' as the favoured description of his favoured activity." **Strawson,** *Analysis and Metaphysics*

conceptual content, see judgeable content

conceptual polarity, another expression for polar-related concept pair

conceptual relativism

METAPHYSICS, EPISTEMOLOGY, ETHICS The claim that truth is relative to a **conceptual scheme**, and that there are different conceptual schemes in different cultures and traditions. Different people can and sometimes do adopt and use different specific notions of being true, being moral, and being right. Each of these different notions has its own rationality, and there is no common measurement among them. The position does not entail that the fact that one believes something automatically makes it true, but it advocates a pluralist attitude.

"Conceptual relativism . . . apparently implies that conceptual variability admits of no rational assessment." **Moser,** *Philosophy after Objectivity*

conceptual role theory

PHILOSOPHY OF LANGUAGE, PHILOSOPHY OF MIND A **semantic** theory that claims that the **meaning** of a linguistic expression is determined by its role in a language or theory. What a person means by an utterance depends on the network of associated beliefs that the person has. There are various ways of understanding the notion of conceptual role, and hence there are a number of versions of the theory.

It is called variously the cognitive role theory, the causal role theory, the functional role theory, and the network theory of meaning. The general idea concerns the way an expression associates with other expressions in a language. The theory originated with Wilfrid **Sellars** and has been developed by Ned **Block**, Paul Churchland, Devitt, **Harman**, and Lycan. It criticizes the traditional view that the meaning of an expression involves a word–world relation and argues that the same word can mean a number of different things because it has a number of linguistic roles although it has the same reference. The theory contributes to the understanding of the meaning of some expressions such as **logical constants**. Applied to mental representations, it suggests that something is a representation and has the content it does in virtue of its cognitive role. Hence one can locate a mental representation in a cognitive network by considering the possible cognitive consequences of occurrences of that mental representation in the system. Its main problem, according to **Fodor**, is that the conceptual role theory cannot account for truth and reference conditions. Furthermore, an expression that belongs to different languages will be different in meaning and this leads to linguistic relativism.

> "The meaning of an expression for an individual is a function of the role that expression plays in his internal representational economy – that is, of how it is related to sensory input and behavioural output and of its inferential/computational role within the internal economy. Sparing the niceties, this is the network theory of meaning, otherwise known as the holistic theory or the conceptual-role theory." **Churchland**, *Neurophilosophy*

conceptual scheme

METAPHYSICS, EPISTEMOLOGY, PHILOSOPHY OF SCIENCE A scheme itself has a structure. It contains some basic concepts that can explain anything else, but that are not explained by others. A conceptual scheme, also called a "conceptual framework," is a network of concepts and propositions by which we organize, describe, and explain our experience. Each discipline has its own conceptual scheme, and it changes along with the development of the science. A conceptual scheme is the backbone of a language. Philosophers such as **Aristotle**, **Kant**, and **Strawson**

believe that reality is represented in our conceptual scheme, and to understand what there is we must understand our conceptual scheme. Strawson therefore characterizes **descriptive metaphysics** as a study of conceptual schemes, believing that it is an instrument of conceptual change and a means of furthering new directions or styles of thought. However, each of these three philosophers believes that at the deepest level human beings all share one common conceptual scheme. Belief in the existence of a global conceptual scheme is in contrast to "**conceptual relativism**," which claims that truth is relative to a conceptual scheme, and that there are different conceptual schemes in different cultures and traditions. **Davidson** claims that although there appear to be many conceptual schemes, if we are to understand an alternative conceptual scheme, we must translate it, at least partially, into our present conceptual scheme. The availability of such a translation suggests that the translated scheme might not be a genuine alternative.

> "Conceptual schemes, we are told, are ways of organizing experience; they are systems of categories that give form to the data of sensation; they are points of view from which individuals, cultures or periods survey the passing scene." **Davidson**, *Inquiries into Truth and Interpretation*

conceptualism

METAPHYSICS A theory of **universals** that claims that universals exist as thoughts or concepts formed by the knowing mind. It is one of the three positions about the nature of universals mentioned in **Porphyry**'s *Introduction to Aristotle's Categories*. The other two are **nominalism**, which claims that universals are merely common names, and **realism**, which claims that universals exist in some mind-independent fashion. Conceptualism holds a position midway between realism and nominalism and argues that universals neither exist merely as names nor exist in their own right. A universal is a predicate, but predicates can be truly or falsely predicated of things only because they stand for concepts. As a product of mind, universals can be instantiated by many particulars at the same time. They are mental representations or ideas, conceptualized out of the particular things to which they apply. Their main function is to serve as principles of classification.

"Conceptualism holds that there are universals but they are mind-made." **Quine**, *From a Logical Point of View*

concreta, see *abstracta*

concrete/abstract, see abstract/concrete

concrete concept, another expression for concrete universal

concrete essence

MODERN EUROPEAN PHILOSOPHY **Merleau-Ponty's** term for the meaning or sense of a thing or its non-sensory presence. According to his account of our existential hold on things, a thing is given or acquired through contact. As a consequence, essence can be grasped only through its actualization within the world. Hence essence must be concrete, and pure essence is impossible. This account stands in opposition to **Husserl's** notion of essence (*eidos*).

"The concrete essence of the triangle . . . is not an essence of objective 'properties', but the formula of an attitude, a certain modality of my hold on the world, a structure." **Merleau-Ponty**, *Phénoménologie de la Perception*

concrete other

ETHICS, POLITICAL PHILOSOPHY In the self–other relationship, a standpoint from which to understand others as concrete, historical, and emotional individuals, with their own needs, capacities, and life plans. Such a view pays attention to the private sphere of life and emphasizes complementary reciprocity in one's relations with others. In contrast, we treat individuals from the standpoint of the generalized other by dealing with them as abstract and rational entities with a set of rights and duties. According to feminist critics, the standpoint of the generalized other has dominated the history of Western moral and political theory, with the consequence of focusing ethics on the public sphere of justice and ignoring the private sphere of care. Hence, the experience of women has been excluded from the consideration of moral theory. According to these critics, the remedy for this prejudice is to establish a new type of ethics that recognizes the concrete as well as the generalized other.

"The standpoint of the concrete other, by contrast, requires us to view each and every rational being as an individual with a concrete history, identity, and affective-emotional constitution." **Benhabib, in Kittay and Meyers (eds.),** *Women and Moral Theory*

concrete universal

METAPHYSICS A term introduced by **Hegel** to correct the traditional view that a universal is abstract through referring to the common nature of a kind of entity by abstraction. Hegel held that a universal is concrete rather than an abstract form. A true universal is not a mere sum of features common to several things, but is self-particularizing or self-specifying. A universal is not isolated from particulars, nor does it transcend them. Rather it inheres in particulars as their essential determination. Hegel even claimed that particulars are nothing but dialectical relations among universal concepts. Further, a universal concept is not isolated from other universals, but can be derived from them and, hence, is one item in a system. In Hegel's logic, each category contains its contrary and develops into that contrary. Together, the category and its contrary are synthesized into a third category, which becomes a member of a new triad. The absolute idea is the culmination of this development as the largest concrete universal.

"End . . . is the concrete universal, which possesses in its own self the moment of particularity and externality and is therefore active and the urge to repel itself from itself." **Hegel**, *Science of Logic*

concretism, another term for reism

concupiscence

ETHICS [from Latin *con*, with + *cupere*, desire] Sexual and other bodily desires, or the human faculty that generates these desires, which are traditionally seen as not being derived from reason. For **Augustine**, concupiscence is the incentive to **sin** that baptism cannot take away. Unlike its opposite love or **charity**, it is something with which we must always struggle. Concupiscence is the first step in the chain of evil, but it will diminish as charity grows. **Aquinas** used concupiscence as equivalent to *epithumia* (Greek *epi*, upon + *thumos*, desire).

He held that these desires are in the part of the soul that we share with other kinds of animals and that this part should be morally subjected to regulation by the rational part of the soul. Because of concupiscence, the incontinent man will act contrary to a decision he had reached through reason about a course of action.

> "Concupiscence is a general cause of sin." **Aquinas,** *Summa Theologiae*

concurrence of God

PHILOSOPHY OF RELIGION [from Latin *concursus dei*] A thesis in medieval theology that proposes that **God** has the power to preserve the existence of things and activate them once he created them, a power that is essentially identical with his divine act of **creation**. All created substances are active and have causal powers, but the exercise of their causal powers must have the concurrence of God. If God withdrew his concurrence, created substances would collapse into nothing. A human action is the effect of one's own deliberation and choice and God's causal endorsement. **Descartes** sometimes used the phrase "regular concurrence" to account for the conservation of motion in the world whose quantity was imparted to matter when it was created. He also used the phrase "divine concurrence" to express the view that things are allowed by God to act under their own systems as they were created.

> "Created substances ... are things which need only the concurrence of God to exist." **Descartes,** *Principles of Philosophy*

concursus dei, Latin term for concurrence of God

Condillac, Etienne Bonnot de (1715–80)

French Enlightenment philosopher, born in Grenoble. Condillac developed an empiricist account of the human mind in which complex powers, such as attending, judging, and reasoning, were analyzed by being broken down and reconstituted in terms of sensations. His analytic method was linked to a conception of a lucid and complete well-made language of simples that would be adequate to express all knowledge. In a thought experiment, he added our senses one by one to a marble statue until the sense of touch gave grounds for the existence of

the external world. His major works include *Treatise on Sensations* (1754).

conditio sine qua non, see *sine qua non*

conditional

LOGIC A conditional, or a conditional statement, is a complex sentence of the form: "if p then q." Both p and q are statements, with p the antecedent and q the consequent. The logical relation between the antecedent and consequent is called implication. The converse of the conditional, that is, "if not q then not p," is called the contrapositive. Conditionals are also called hypotheticals. In propositional logic, a conditional is generally symbolized as "p→q" or "p⊃q." The major problem associated with conditionals is determining their **truth condition**. Most commonly a conditional is treated as a truth-function such that "if p then q" is false if and only if p is true and q is false. This is called the **material conditional** or material implication. But there is a **paradox** associated with the material conditional that has led to a revision called the strict conditional, which claims that a conditional is true if and only if when p is true, q is necessarily true. There are, however, also problems associated with **strict conditionals**. A much-debated issue concerns the truth conditions of the **counterfactuals** in which the antecedent is false. For example, "If Kennedy had not been killed, he would have won the next election." The problem of counterfactuals is also closely associated with the discussion of possible worlds.

> "A sentence of the form 'If ... then ...', where the blanks are to be filled with other sentences, is called a conditional." **Mates,** *Elementary Logic*

conditional duty, see *prima facie* duties

conditional probability

LOGIC The probability of an event e′ occurring after the occurrence of another event e. The value of this probability is determined by the effect of the probability of e on the probability of e′ before e occurred.

A related notion is conditional proof. If B is deduced from a set of premises that includes A_n, then in a deductive system we can infer from the remaining premises the conditional if A_n then B. This rule of conditional proof is presented as the following: If $A_1 \ldots A_n \lozenge B$, then $A_1 \ldots A_{n-1} \lozenge A_n \supset B$. This rule is also called the rule of $\supset$ introduction.

> "Crudely, the expected frequency of a kind of outcome, B, given that a kind of outcome, A, has occurred, is the probability of B conditional on A or the conditional probability of B given A." **Sklar,** *Philosophy of Physics*

Condorcet, Marquis de (1743–94)

French encyclopedist, born in Ribemont, secretary of the Académie des Sciences and member of the Académie Française. Condorcet saw human history as a history of progress and hoped that the French Revolution would lead to a new stage that abolished inequalities through rational government. His most important work foreshadowed the later development of philosophy of the social sciences through the application of the calculus of probability and statistics to social and political questions, such as voting and rational decision making. His major works include *Essay on the Application of Analysis to the Probability of Majority Decisions* (1785) and *The Sketch for a Historical Picture of the Progress of the Human Mind* (1795).

confirmation

LOGIC In ordinary language, to confirm is to verify. As a logical term, confirmation is the measurement of the extent to which evidence raises the **probability** of a **hypothesis**. Hence, it is closely related to probability and to the problem of **induction**. A confirmation proposition assesses the probability of a hypothesis. **Carnap** in his *Logical Foundations of Probability* claims that a confirmation-proposition can be classificatory (e[vidence] confirms h[ypothesis]), comparative (e confirms h more than e_1 confirms h_1), or quantitative (the confirmation of h given e is c). Confirmation theory examines how different evidence renders different hypotheses probable and how much the evidence affects the probability.

Confirmation (or affirmation) is a translation of *Konstatierung* (German), a term used by **Schlick** to denote what he takes to be the peculiar characteristic of observation statements, namely that one may be absolutely certain of their truth. Unlike many other **logical positivists**, he denies that observations are fundamental in the edifice of knowledge, since they are always of the form "here now so and so."

Instead, their place in the system comes at the end rather than at the beginning of knowledge. Other statements are hypotheses, which in a sense depend upon the fleeting confirmations but not in the sense of being built up from them.

> "Many writers use the term 'confirms' or some technical term for describing the extent to which evidence renders hypotheses probable." **Swinburne,** *An Introduction to Confirmation Theory*

conjecture

PHILOSOPHY OF SCIENCE For Karl **Popper**, science does not start with **observations**, but with practical problems and an existing problematic theory. We attempt to offer tentative solutions to the problems. These tentative solutions are conjectures or **hypotheses** that can be subjected to severe testing or trial, whose object is to refute them. If a conjecture is refuted in testing, it must be rejected. Because Popper denied that **induction** can lead to conclusive verification, he rejected a central role for induction in science. He held, however, that conclusive refutation is possible through falsification and that a hypothesis is corroborated by withstanding serious attempts to refute it. Popper views science as a dynamic enterprise that grows from old problems to new problems by means of conjectures and refutations. This is the main point of his **falsificationism**.

> "The way in which knowledge progresses, and especially, our scientific knowledge, is by unjustified (and unjustifiable) anticipations, by guesses, by tentative solutions to our problems, by conjectures." **Popper,** *Conjectures and Refutations*

conjunction

LOGIC A complex proposition of the form "p and q." Both p and q are **propositions** and are called conjuncts. In **propositional calculus**, a conjunction is symbolized either as "p·q," "p∧q," or "p&q." Taking it as **truth-functional**, "p and q" is true if and only if each of p and q is true. If either conjunct is false, or both are false, then the conjunction is false. We may infer from the premise p and the premise q to the conclusion p and q. This is called the rule of conjunction or conjunction introduction. We may also infer from the premise "p and q" to the conclusion p or to the conclusion q. This is called conjunction elimination. Conjunction can also be used to join together more than two statements in the process of asserting them all.

"A conjunction of statements all of which are true is true; and a conjunction of statements not all of which are true is false." **Quine**, *Methods of Logic*

conjunction elimination, see conjunction

conjunction introduction, see conjunction

connectionism

PHILOSOPHY OF MIND A program in **artificial intelligence** and **cognitive science** that is designed to help us understand how the brain operates in terms of computer models of brain functioning. The theory considers the brain as a network of neural units that interact until they reach a stable state in response to external inputs. The information-process is parallel and distributed, that is to say that a lot of information is processed simultaneously and each connection contributes to many contents. Connectionism is also called parallel distributed processing (PDP) or neural network modeling. This approach, pioneered by F. Rosenblatt and O. Selfridge, contrasts with the traditional approach in cognitive science, which treats the brain as a rule-governed linear manipulator. The central philosophical implication of connectionism is that human intelligence can be understood to arise out of the whole structure of neural systems in the brain. Such a philosophical approach is sometimes called neuro-philosophy.

"Connectionism (or PDP, for parallel distributed processing) is a fairly recent development in AI that promises to move cognitive modelling closer to neural modelling, since the elements that are its bricks are nodes in parallel networks that are connected up in ways that look rather like neural networks in the brain." **Dennett**, *Consciousness Explained*

connective, see logical constant

connotation

LOGIC, PHILOSOPHY OF LANGUAGE J. S. **Mill** distinguishes connotation from **denotation**. A connotation is the signification or conception of a term that indicates those attributes we really mean to predicate of the object. Denotation, in contrast, is the scope for which a term is truly predicated. The term "red," for instance, denotes all red things, but connotes the attribute of redness. Mill claims that we must distinguish connotative terms from non-connotative terms. The former denote a subject and imply an attribute; and therefore have a meaning. A **proper name** has denotation, but has no connotation; hence it is not a connotative term. This idea is fully developed in **Russell**'s theory of **definite description**. Other logicians use **intension** to name what Mill calls connotation, and **extension** to name denotation.

"Whenever the names given to objects convey any information – that is, where they have properly any meaning – the meaning resides not in what they denote but in what they connote." *Collected Works of John Stuart Mill*, **vol. VII**

conscience

ETHICS [from Latin *con*, with + *scire*, know] The immediate and intuitive human moral consciousness, the inborn restraining or directing force by which an individual judges what he ought to do or what is morally permissible. Conscience has been held to be one of the main sources of morality. Different philosophers describe it as a human faculty of moral sense, as the voice of **God**, as a personal demon, or as the voice of reason. The British philosopher Bishop **Butler** claimed that conscience is a **sentiment** of the understanding and treated it as the basis for his whole moral system. But others, especially Christian moralists, believe in the existence of erring or bad conscience, for moral agents may have mistaken ideas about what they ought to do, and they are liable to be deceived. Hence we need to distinguish between voluntary bad conscience, which is blameworthy, and involuntary bad conscience, which should be forgiven. In a question related to the problem of the **weakness of will**, we may ask whether an agent may act against his conscience.

"If obeying and disobeying a mistaken conscience are both bad, it seems that men with mistaken consciences are caught in a trap, and cannot avoid sin." **Aquinas**, *Summa Theologiae*

consciousness

PHILOSOPHY OF MIND Various forms of subjective experience such as sensation, mood, emotion, retrospection, memory, thought, and self-consciousness. There are grave difficulties in all attempts to develop a philosophical account of what consciousness is or how it might be explained. If we concentrate on what it is like to be a conscious human being, we have no explanation; if we try to explain consciousness in terms of what goes on in our brains, the sheer feel of consciousness itself is left aside. **Descartes** believed that consciousness is the essence of mind or the general property of mental states, implying that all mental states are conscious. On a Cartesian view, consciousness is irreducibly subjective in the sense that the individual with that consciousness appears to have privileged access to it in a way that no one else can achieve. Various versions of behaviorism, functionalism, and naturalism challenge these Cartesian points and try to explain consciousness in physical, functional, or neurological terms. But the problem of how we can understand consciousness on a physical or neural basis, the so-called explanatory gap, still remains. Major contemporary issues concerning consciousness include: Does consciousness have a causal role? If so, what is it? Are all **mental states** conscious? What is the relation between consciousness and **intentionality**? What is the philosophical importance of the raw feel of conscious states? Do persons have **privileged access** to their conscious states?

"Consciousness: a person is said to be conscious of a circumstance when he uses words, or images of words, to others or to himself, to assert the circumstance." **Russell,** *Collected Papers of Bertrand Russell,* vol. IX

consensus gentium argument

PHILOSOPHY OF RELIGION Also known as the common consent argument for the existence of **God**, this argument is based on the premise that belief in God is virtually, if not strictly, universal. According to the version of the Stoic philosopher **Seneca,** the near universality of this belief suggests that it is innate and instinctive and that it must therefore be true. This biological version of the argument was severely attacked by **Locke** in *An Essay Concerning Human Understanding* (iv, 9). Locke rejected the claim that the belief is universal and also argued that universality would not entail that the idea of God is innate. **Mill** challenged the link between the innateness of the belief that God exists and its truth.

Another version was formulated by the British philosopher G. H. Joyce. The universality of a belief suggests that human reason assures us that it is true. If human reason is trustworthy, which is obviously the case, then the belief that God exists must be true. Setting aside the dubious premise of the universality of this belief, this version has been criticized on the grounds that most believers come to their belief in God by traditional indoctrination. The *consensus gentium* argument appears to lack logical force. It was once universally believed that the earth is flat, but the universality of this belief does not show that it was true. Nevertheless, this argument raises questions of whether some of our universal beliefs do not need external justification and whether religious beliefs could be among these.

"The argument for *consensus gentium* is a fallacy, which means only that we can't be sure that a belief is true just because it may be true that everyone, or nearly everyone, holds it. But we certainly can't be sure that it is false either." **Penelhum,** *Problems of Religious Knowledge*

consent

PHILOSOPHY OF RELIGION, POLITICAL PHILOSOPHY Epistemologically identical with assent, that is, believing or accepting some propositions. **Locke** described how consent is involved in the formation of beliefs, and he attacked the universal consent argument for God's existence. Consent is more often used in a political context, where it is contrasted with coercion or exploitation and is offered as grounds for the legitimation of social and political practice. In the state of nature there is no consent regarding the standard of right and wrong. To gain security, people consent to form a **social contract** and create a single body politic in which each individual agrees to give some of his liberty to the government and to obey the laws, and in return enjoys the rights of being protected. The consent of individuals is what constitutes the **community**; but for a society to act as a living body, it must be run according to the consent of the majority. This is because the aim of the social contract, which is based on consent, is to preserve the lives, freedom, and property of all, and not merely of a minority of rulers. However, there are many occasions on which we do not give our express consent to the decisions of a government. To cope with this problem, Locke put forward a notion of tacit consent, that is, consent without any verbal or behavioral expression. There has been debate about what constitutes tacit consent. In contemporary political philosophy, express and tacit consent are also called actual and potential consent. Potential consent is ascribed to a person if a normal subject would rationally consent to something in a given situation.

> "The beginning of political society depends upon the consent of the individuals, to join into, and make one society." **Locke, *Two Treatises on Government***

consequential characteristics, see supervenience

consequentialism

ETHICS The term may be traced to G. E. M. **Anscombe**'s 1958 paper "Modern Moral Philosophy." It is now a general practice to divide moral theory into consequentialism and non-consequentialism, also called teleological and non-teleological ethics. Consequentialism or **teleological ethics** holds that the value of an action is determined entirely by its consequences and thus proposes that ethical life should be forward-looking, that is, concerned with maximizing the good and minimizing the bad consequences of actions. **Utilitarianism** and **pragmatism** are important representatives of consequentialism. Sometimes consequentialism is divided into restricted or **rule-consequentialism**, according to which an action is right if it accords with rules that lead to better consequences than alternative rules, and extreme or **act-consequentialism**, according to which an action is right if it produces better consequences than alternative actions open to the agent. Another form of consequentialism is **motive-consequentialism**, which holds that a motive is good if it intends to bring about the best consequences.

Consequentialism has been subjected to criticism in contemporary ethics. Its major demerits are claimed to be the following. First, it is agent-neutral in that it ignores the interests, projects, and personal relationships of the moral agents themselves and can require the unlimited sacrifice of any one of them. It is thus an impersonal and disinterested standpoint. This feature is condemned by common sense morality, intuitionism, and in particular, agent-centered virtue ethics. Secondly, consequentialism overemphasizes the importance of good consequences and hence implies the possibility that any act, no matter how immoral it is, can be justified as long as it can bring about the best consequences. The claim that consequences are prior to morality strongly violates moral common sense. In its defense, proponents of consequentialism have formulated various notions of consequence in an attempt to answer some of the criticism.

> "Any form of consequentialism locates ethical value ultimately in states of affairs." **B. Williams, *Ethics and the Limits of Philosophy***

conservatism

POLITICAL PHILOSOPHY A political position that accords primacy in politics to upholding traditional, inherited, and established values and practices. Conservatism opposes large and sudden social and cultural change, especially violent revolution, because it holds that any large-scale radical reform will bring unforeseen and unintended adverse consequences. Conservatism does not absolutely reject change, but requires that change must be continuous, gradual, and tested against experience. In Britain, conservatism was first systematically developed by Edmund **Burke** in his response to the violence of the French Revolution.

Conservatism generally distrusts any abstract theory that seeks to establish universal and objective political principles on the basis of an allegedly universal human nature. In contrast, it holds that the nature of human beings is correlated with the societies and circumstances in which humans find themselves. A society has its distinct history and cultural setting. Political theory should articulate the knowledge and rules that are presupposed in political practice. This approach to political philosophy, mainly represented in the twentieth century by Michael **Oakeshott** and Roger Scruton, has some common features with **communitarian** thought. A major objection facing conservatism is that existing values and institutions might have arisen historically from violent revolution or radical reform. In addition, even flexible and imaginative conservatives sometimes must deal with a radically defective historical inheritance.

"By 'conservatism' I intend here to refer to any view to the effect that all attempts to transform societies in accordance with principles (whether they be want-regarding or ideal-regarding principles) are pernicious: dangerous and self-defeating at once." **Barry,** *Political Argument*

consilience of inductions

PHILOSOPHY OF SCIENCE [from Latin *con,* together + *salire,* to jump] A term introduced by the British philosopher of science William **Whewell** to describe a feature of the best kind of induction. In the process of induction, seemingly diverse and apparently unrelated phenomena may provide evidence that leaps in the same direction to support an unforeseen and uncontemplated scientific hypothesis. According to Whewell, a theory formed on the basis of the consilience of induction might not only explain different phenomena but also uncover their underlying cause. It is hence more general and credible than induction without consilience and has deductive force. One example is Newton's theory of gravitation, which applies not only to the motions of the heavenly bodies but also to the motions of the tides.

"Accordingly the cases in which inductions from classes of facts altogether different have thus jumped together, belong only to the best established theories which the history of science contains . . . I will take the liberty of describing it by a particular phrase; and will term it the 'consilience of inductions'." **Whewell,** *Philosophy of the Inductive Sciences*

consistency

LOGIC Propositions are consistent if they can all be true. A system of propositions can be shown to be inconsistent if it contains a **contradiction** (a proposition and its negation). No proposition is consistent with its own denial. If two propositions are true, then they must be consistent. However, it

does not follow from the fact that two propositions are consistent that both are true. The relation of consistency is symmetrical. Consistency and **completeness** are two key concerns of modern logic.

"When we speak of two propositions as 'consistent', we mean that it is not possible, with either one of them as premise, to deduce the falsity of the other." **Lewis and Langford,** *Symbolic Logic*

constant

LOGIC As a technical logical term, any operator with a fixed meaning. In predicate logic, the **quantifiers** some (symbolized as ∃) and all (symbolized as ∀) are constants. In **modal logic**, the **operators** necessarily (□) and possibly (◊) are constants. In **propositional logic**, the **truth-functional** operators, that is, the connectives which indicate the **logical form** of a proposition, such as not (∼), and (∧), or (∨), if . . . then (→) and if and only if (↔) are constants. More generally, constants contrast with **variables**, which range over a domain, with constants (a, b, c) distinguished from the variables (x, y, z) that they instantiate. It is difficult to determine a principle distinguishing logical constants from non-logical constants, although philosophers agree on their enumeration.

"The expressions which occur in formulae, but are not variables, are constants." **Strawson,** *Introduction to Logical Theory*

constant conjunction

METAPHYSICS **Hume**'s term for the relation that exists when the occurrence of an event of one kind A is invariably attended by the occurrence of an event of another kind B. Fire is generally followed by heat; hence there is a constant conjunction between fire and heat. The experience of constant conjunction between two or more kinds of event conveys to our mind the idea of a **necessity connection** between these events, and leads us to label the precedent events as causes and the attendant events as effects. On the basis of such an experience, when we observe A, we infer the existence of B. Thus Hume claimed that our idea of **causation** is derived from constant conjunction.

". . . the constant conjunction of objects determines their causation." **Hume,** *A Treatise of Human Nature*

constative

PHILOSOPHY OF LANGUAGE J. L. **Austin**'s term for utterances such as "John is running," which state, report, or describe **facts** in the world. The utterance "John is running," depends for its truth or falsity on whether it is the case that John is running. Here the act or fact and the utterance are distinct and the former decides the truth of the latter. Most language clearly belongs to this kind of utterance. Constative utterances are contrasted with **performative** utterances, which have a similar linguistic structure but do not issue true or false statements about the world. However, Austin was not satisfied with this distinction, and he later replaced it with his theory of **illocutionary acts**.

"Not all true or false statements are descriptions, and for this reason I prefer to use the word 'Constative'." **Austin,** *How to Do Things with Words*

constitutive principles

METAPHYSICS **Kant**'s term for the principles that objectively state what is present in the object itself, that is, what is the constitution of **appearance**. Constitutive principles are principles of **pure** understanding that are laid down by us as standard and necessary constituents of the world of appearance. Constitutive principles are contrasted with **regulative principles**, which are rules to show how experience may be organized or regulated without reference to the constitution of the object. Regulative principles, such as **transcendental ideas**, play no part in determining the objective character of the world of appearance. They are maxims, neither provable nor disprovable, and are not to be understood as true or false. They serve to guide our inquiry within experience and can lead us to transgress the limits of reason from the conditioned to the unconditioned. For Kant we must observe the distinction between these two kinds of principles. If we use regulative principles as constitutive, dialectical illusions or errors arise. Kant's **transcendental dialectic** is a presentation of what these errors are.

"The principles of pure understanding, whether constitutive a priori, like the mathematical principles, or merely regulative, like the dynamical, contain nothing but what may be called the pure schema of possible experience." **Kant,** *Critique of Pure Reason*

constructionism

PHILOSOPHY OF HISTORY An idealist view of history, developed by L. J. Goldstein and J. W. Meiland. They claim that there is no real **past** consisting of events that exist independent of our knowledge of them. The task of historians, therefore, is not to discover what happened in the past but to construct a past or a **narrative** of the past on the basis of present evidence and in accordance with certain methodological rules. Consequently, if historians come to possess new evidence or change their methodology, their historical account could be greatly altered. Constructionism contests the objectivity of historical statements by denying that these statements refer to an actual past.

"Constructionism is just the thesis that whatever historians do is to be conceived not as discovering but as constructing the past." **Atkinson,** *Knowledge and Explanation in History*

constructivism

PHILOSOPHY OF MATHEMATICS The view that mathematics should confine itself only to the entities that it can construct, that is, which it can prove systematically in virtue of things we already accept. Thus, constructivism opposes mathematical **Platonism**, which treats mathematical objects as entities independent of cognitive operations and treats the facts concerning mathematical objects as not depending on the possibilities of verification. Constructivism is a term covering many different doctrines: finitism rejects abstract notions such as set and operation; predicativism claims definitions of mathematical objects should be predicative; and Bishop's constructive mathematics takes it that the statements of mathematics should have numerical meaning; Markov's constructive recursive mathematics and the mathematical **intuitionism** of **Brouwer** and Heyting belong to the center of constructivist thought.

"Constructivism in the broad sense is by no means homogeneous, and even the views expressed by different representatives of one school, or by a single mathematician at different times, are not always homogeneous." **Troelstra and Dalen,** *Constructivism in Mathematics*

contemporaneity

MODERN EUROPEAN PHILOSOPHY, PHILOSOPHY OF HISTORY According to **Kierkegaard**, there are two kinds of history: one is secular and the other sacred. Secular history consists of past events and a process of temporal becoming. Sacred history, for Kirkegaard Christian history, also has temporal becoming, but, paradoxically, it is also always present in virtue of its **eternity**. Eternity knows neither past nor future, but is the everlasting now. Christ is not merely an historical person. By accepting his existence, a believer is always contemporary with him. In relation to him, there is only one situation of contemporaneity, and to believe in him is to become contemporary with him. This conception attempts to answer a question arising from the incarnation: if Christ lived in human form at a particular time, what bond is there to sustain his relationship to later generations of believers?

"The person who actually became a Christian on the presupposition of the contemporaneity of the transitional situation with Christianity's coming into the world indeed knew what Christianity is." **Kierkegaard,** *Concluding Unscientific Postscript to Philosophical Fragments*

content

PHILOSOPHY OF LANGUAGE, PHILOSOPHY OF MIND [from Latin *continere*, contain] That which a mental or **propositional attitude** is about or means, and hence also called mental content or propositional content. The content of a belief, intention, hope, and other attitude is typically expressed in language by a that-clause, for example, "I believe *that it will rain tomorrow*" or "I fear *that you will be late*." The logical structure of such sentences is puzzling. For most attitudes the sentences are not extensional, and it is difficult to understand their structure and why they have it. Content seems to be abstract and language-dependent and to have truth conditions, but it is also generally considered to be a distinctive feature of thought.

We can distinguish between the **narrow content** and the **broad** or wide **content** of what we say or think. Narrow content is about the same objects and properties whatever the circumstances, whilst broad or wide content incorporates certain aspects of one's embedding situation or environment

and can vary in what it is about according to these circumstances. Suppose two liquids seem exactly similar in surface properties, but have different internal constitutions. According to narrow content, we should use different terms for the two liquids, but according to broad content, the situation in which they both could be used alike could allow us to use the same term for them.

Some philosophers believe that content can be understood as a set of **possible worlds** in which certain objects and properties are realized, while others believe that content should be understood in terms of a structured composite of substance and attributes. There is also debate about what makes a token mental state a belief and about the relation between the acceptability conditions and the truth conditions of a content.

"Content is typically attributed in English by 'that' clauses and this feature permits an ontologically and theoretically neutral way to distinguish one belief from another (or one desire from another, and so on)." **Baker,** *Saving Belief*

content holism

PHILOSOPHY OF LANGUAGE A type of **semantic holism**, which claims that an expression can have a content only as a part of a whole language. It cannot have a content unless many other expressions have contents. If I believe a proposition P, then I would have to believe various propositions that are in the context of P. Content holism contrasts with linguistic **atomism**, which believes that an expression can have a meaning by itself through its relation to an extra-linguistic entity.

"What we will call content holism is the claim that properties like having content are holistic in the sense that no expression in a language can have them unless many other (nonsynonymous) expressions in that language have them too." **Fodor and Lepore,** *Holism*

content stroke, see assertion-sign

context principle

LOGIC, PHILOSOPHY OF MATHEMATICS, PHILOSOPHY OF LANGUAGE Introduced by **Frege** in *The Foundations of Arithmetic* as a fundamental methodological principle, it asserts that a word has meaning only in the context of a **sentence**. Frege's original intention was to solve the problem of how numbers are given to us. By this principle, he transferred the question from an epistemological approach to a linguistic investigation into how we are able to fix the senses of sentences containing numeric terms. According to **Dummett**, the context principle is significant in the linguistic turn of philosophy and is essential to the whole movement of **analytic philosophy**. On the basis of this principle, Dummett himself derived the **dependence thesis**. If it is impossible to grasp the sense of a word independent of the sentence in which it occurs, then it is also impossible to grasp a constituent of a **thought** without apprehending the whole thought of which it is a constituent.

"The context principle . . . is . . . the thesis that it is only in the context of a sentence that a word has meaning." **Dummett**, *Origins of Analytic Philosophy*

contextual definition

LOGIC, PHILOSOPHY OF LANGUAGE A definition conveying the sense of a term by defining the sentence or the text in which it occurs. Excellent examples are provided by **Russell**'s analyses of **definite descriptions**, which amount to definitions of the sentences in which the definite descriptions occur. According to Russell, all **incomplete symbols** have their meanings by contextual definitions, for incomplete symbols are not denoting expressions that stand for something, and they have **meaning** only in a context of a sentence or a formula. In employing contextual definitions, Russell had a device for eliminating unwanted entities. **Ayer** claimed that philosophical **analysis** in its entirety is a matter of contextual definition. But this is generally regarded as an inadequate account of philosophical analysis, for contextual definition only reveals the logical structure of language and is applied only to linguistic complexes. Philosophical analysis, on the other hand, is applied also to mental and other complexes. Contextual definition is also called definition in use, and **Bentham** called it **paraphrasis**.

"Contextual definition of a term showed how to translate sentences containing the term into equivalent sentences lacking the term." **Quine**, *Ontological Relativity and Other Essays*

contextual implications

ETHICS Nowell-Smith's term for a distinctive use of ethical language. The proper use of ethical language in a given context authorizes certain inferences that the original ethical sentences cannot be said to assert or state, but which their use implies in that context. Any **logical implication** can be said to be a sub-class of contextual implication, but not vice versa. The denial of contextual implications is logically odd. The proper use of ethical language itself implies that the speaker believes his statement is true and conforms with the relevant recognized moral **rules** or his own **moral principles**. It also implies that what the speaker says may be assumed to be relevant to the interests of his audience and that he would make the same statement in similar situations.

"I shall say that a statement P contextually implies a statement Q if anyone who knew the normal conventions of the language would be entitled to infer Q from P in the context in which they occur." **Nowell-Smith**, *Ethics*

contextual relativism, an alternative term for contextualism

contextualism

ETHICS, PHILOSOPHY OF LANGUAGE Also called contextual relativism, a position in both ethics and the philosophy of language that claims that various sorts of contexts should be taken into account when we consider a moral position or the meaning of a term. Both ethical contextualism and linguistic contextualism are directed against **formalism**, which claims that we can establish a set of abstract moral principles that have universal application without regard to particular situations (ethical formalism) or that we may determine the meaning of a statement through the study of its logical structure (linguistic formalism).

Ethical contextualism holds that we cannot deal with ethical problems in detachment from the particular practical situations in which the problems arise. Instead, ethics should be concerned with ethical problems in given contexts. Historically, **Aristotle, Aquinas, Hume**, and **Hegel** are considered to be contextualists to some degree. In the twentieth century, influenced by **pragmatism** and **logical**

positivism, contextualism has been used specifically for the view that in any given context there are always some ethical premises that are themselves unquestioned, although they may be questioned in another context. These premises, conjoined with the result of common experience or science, can lead to a suitable resolution of the problems that arise in that context. On this view, abstract ahistorical principles are dispensable. **Dewey, Austin**, and **Wittgenstein** are claimed as representatives of this kind of position. Ethical **feminism** also endorses this position, but it claims, controversially, that universal principles are masculine illusions, while women's moral consideration is contextual and concrete.

In the philosophy of language, contextualism proposes that the meaning of a word is determined by its use or occurrence in a sentence, that is, by its contribution to the content of the sentence. Accordingly, sentences or propositions are prior to words or concepts in the explanation of meaning. To understand a word is to understand how it can be employed in a sentence. Contextual definition, which means explaining a word by appeal to the sentence in which it occurs, is based on contextualism. By analogy with contextualism, **Quine** and **Davidson** developed what is called **semantic holism**, that is, the view that the meaning of a sentence is determined by its use in a whole language. Contextualism is also used for the claim that the meaning of a **theory** varies according to its placement in different non-logical contexts. Meaning must be qualified by certain historical, semantic, social, and political perspectives.

> "The contextualists . . . felt that there was much more to theory than its being a logical calculus which merely enabled the scientists to make predictions." **Aronson, *A Realist Philosophy of Science***

contiguity

PHILOSOPHY OF MIND, METAPHYSICS If two objects are next to or succeed each other, they are contiguous. For **Hume**, contiguity is one of the three basic principles of the **association of ideas** (the other two are resemblance and causation). If we experience the **constant conjunction** of two contiguous objects, this experience will lead the mind to infer the existence of one of them from the presence of the other. This is a necessary condition for us to establish that

there is a relation of cause and effect between these two objects. Hence, for Hume, contiguity is essential for our notion of **causation**. For **Leibniz**, the principle of contiguity is a natural law that each natural change is continuous rather than abrupt. It can be summarized by the slogan *natura non facit saltum* (Nature makes no leaps).

> " 'Tis likewise evident, that as the senses, in changing their objects, are necessitated to change them regularly, and take them as they lie *contiguous* to each other, the imagination must by long custom acquire the same method of thinking, and run along the parts of space and time in conceiving its objects." **Hume, *A Treatise of Human Nature***

contingent identity

LOGIC A crucial notion for **central-state materialism** or the **identity theory**. This theory in the philosophy of mind claims that mental states or processes are nothing other than processes in the brain. But linguistics argued that the logic of statements about brain states and the logic of statements about mental states are different and that brains and minds cannot therefore be identical. To deal with this objection, physicalism introduced the notion of contingent identity to say that the identity between mental states and brain states is not logical or necessary identity. Expressions for the states are not identical in meaning, but pick out the same items contingently or accidentally, and the identity holds as a matter of contingent fact. The identity is not a conceptual truth. The world could have been otherwise, but it happens to be the case that mental states are brain states. The notion of contingent identity has been attacked by **Kripke**, who claims that contingent statements involving descriptions do not reflect any genuine identity. Identity statements must be made using **names** rather than **descriptions**, but then, following **Leibniz**'s **law**, if an identity statement is true, it must be necessarily true.

> "Everyone agrees that descriptions can be used to make contingent statements . . . Certainly when you make an identity statement using description – when you say 'the x such that φx and the x such that ψx are one and the same' – that can be a contingent fact." **Kripke, *Naming and Necessity***

contingent/necessary

LOGIC, METAPHYSICS A basic philosophical distinction. Contingent **propositions** happen to be true or happen to be false, but could be otherwise. According to a **possible world** account, a proposition is contingent if and only if it is true in at least one possible world and false in at least one other possible world. Necessary propositions are true whatever the circumstances. Necessary propositions are true in all possible worlds. Philosophers disagree whether there are any necessary propositions. Some restrict necessary propositions to propositions that are **analytic** or true because of their **logical form**, including logical and mathematical propositions. Others argue that some propositions can be metaphysically, transcendentally, or naturally necessary. A contingent event is one that does not necessarily take place. If there are necessary events, natural rather than logical necessity is involved. The provision of a **semantics** for **modal** terms (such as necessary and possibly) and the revival of **essentialism** has led to renewed interest in the distinction between what is necessary *de dicto* (of a statement) and what is necessary *de re* (of a thing).

"Classical metaphysics depreciated the contingent . . . As late as Hegel, 'necessary' is a word for laudation, and 'contingent' of denigration." **Hartshorne,** *Creative Synthesis and Philosophical Method*

contingentism, see necessitarianism

continuum, see continuum hypothesis

continuum hypothesis

PHILOSOPHY OF MATHEMATICS, PHILOSOPHY OF SCIENCE A continuum is a collection of points, such that between any two points there are distinct points. Classical examples of continua are lines, planes, and spaces. This notion can be traced to **Aristotle**'s definition of continuity in *Physics* V, which states that "things are called continuous when the touching limits of each become one and the same and are, as the word implies, contained in each other." In his theory of infinite cardinal numbers (the numbers measuring the size of infinite sets), **Cantor** postulates the continuum hypothesis that the cardinality of any power set of an infinite set (the set of all of its subsets) is the second highest cardinality after that of the set itself. **Gödel** proved in 1938 that this hypothesis is compatible with the most popular system of the **set theory** (the Zermelo–Fraenkel–Skolem system). However, Paul Cohen proved in 1963 that its negation is also compatible with that system. Hence this hypothesis is independent of the accepted axioms of set theory. The question of the truth or falsity of this hypothesis constitutes the so-called continuum problem.

"It is now known that the truth or falsity of the continuum hypothesis and other related conjectures cannot be determined by set theory as we know it today." **P. Cohen,** *Set Theory and the Continuum Hypothesis*

contractarianism

ETHICS, POLITICAL PHILOSOPHY An approach to ethics on the basis of **social contract** theory. It has two forms: **Hobbesian** contractarianism and **Kantian** contractarianism. Hobbesian contractarianism starts from the assumption that people have a natural equality of physical power and proceeds to infer that to prevent harm to one another it is mutually advantageous to reach an agreement that protects each person's interests. Accordingly, there is no inherent right or wrong, and morality flows from the constraints necessary for mutually beneficial cooperation. This position is criticized because it does not take morality as a value in itself, and, furthermore, the pursuit of mutual advantage itself requires some prior moral claims. Kantian contractarianism, which is also called contractualism, argues that people have a natural equality of moral status. John **Rawls** is the most influential contemporary proponent of this position. According to Rawls, if a contract is negotiated from an original position of equality, it can give equal consideration to each of its contractors. Thus, moral thinking is about what agreements people could make in such circumstances. An action is wrong if its performance is disallowed by a system of rules that is set by informed, unforced, and general agreement and that no one could reasonably reject in those circumstances. Some critics argue that this position offers an intellectual account of morality, but fails to uncover any real motivation for acting morally. They claim that it does not give any reason for persons possessing greater power to avoid using it to harm others in the pursuit of their own interests, and that it does not give any reason to give moral consideration to the interests of future generations.

"A disturbing feature of Contractarianism is the way it ties people's moral claims to their bargaining power." **Glover,** *What Sort of People Should There Be?*

contractualism, another name for contractarianism

contradiction

LOGIC [*from Latin* contra *against* + *dicere* speak] A contradiction conjoins a statement and its negation ("p and not p"), ascribes and denies the ascription of the same feature to an individual ("a is f and not f"), or, more broadly, is false on logical grounds alone. According to the **law of non-contradiction,** "p" and "not p" cannot both be true. They are logically exclusive and logically exhaustive and cannot be true or false together. These two inconsistent statements are called contradictories. Contradictories are distinguished from **contraries** because while contradictories can neither be both true nor both false, contraries cannot both be true but can both be false. In the square of oppositions, the universal affirmative judgment (A) "All S are P" and the particular negative judgment (O) "Some S are not P" are contradictories, and so are the universal negative (E) "All S are not P" and the particular affirmative (I) "Some S are P."

Traditionally, finding a contradiction has been a way of showing that a system must be rejected. Accepting contradictions has been considered intellectually ruinous because every proposition follows from a contradiction. But there have been recent explorations of logical systems that seem able to tolerate some contradictions. **Hegel** and **Marx** understood contradictions to be conflicts necessary to the dialectical development of spirit or history. Their accounts should not be confused with other discussions of contradiction.

"A contradiction cancels itself and leaves nothing." **Strawson,** *Introduction to Logical Theory*

contradictories, see contradiction

contrafactuals

LOGIC, PHILOSOPHY OF SCIENCE Also called counterfactuals or contrary-to-fact conditionals. Propositions expressed in the form: "if P had been the case, then Q would have been the case." The antecedent is presupposed or known to be false and hence describes a contrary to fact or contrafactual state of affairs. The consequent claims how things would have been were the antecedent state of affairs to be realized. For example, "If I had been the president of the United States at that time, I would not have got involved in the Vietnam War." All contrafactuals are subjunctive, but not all subjunctive **conditionals** are counterfactual.

The peculiarity of counterfactuals is that they are not **truth-functional.** Their truth-value cannot be determined by the truth-values of their components. They involve neither **material implication** nor **strict implication.** Thus there arises a problem about how to determine the truth conditions of counterfactuals. Currently there are three main positions. One, held by **Chisholm, Goodman,** and **Rescher,** suggests that a counterfactual is true if its antecedent P, when conjoined with law-like generalizations and statements of background conditions, will logically entail the consequent Q. The second, held by D. **Lewis** and **Stalnaker,** has been developed on the basis of **possible world** theory and claims that a counterfactual is true if its consequent Q is true in the nearest possible world in which the antecedent P is true. The third argues that a counterfactual should be treated as an argument and should be judged as valid or invalid, but not as true or false. Each solution has some difficulties and the problem of counterfactual conditionals is still a subject of lively debate.

"Any adequate analysis of the contrafactual conditional must go beyond mere truth values and consider causal connections, or kindred relationships, between matters spoken of in the antecedent of the conditional and matters spoken of in the consequent." **Quine,** *Methods of Logic*

contraposition

LOGIC In traditional logic, an immediate inference formed by negating both the subject term and the predicate term of a proposition and exchanging their positions. The result is called the contrapositive, in which the predicate of the original proposition becomes the subject. Thus, contraposition is the operation of converting the obverse of a proposition or of obverting its converse. Of the four basic categorical propositions in traditional logic, the contrapositive of SAP ("All s are p") is "all not p are not s"; that of SEP ("All s are not p") is "all not p are not not s"; that of SIP ("Some s are p") is "Some not p are not s," and that of SOP ("Some s are not p") is "some not not p are not s." The contrapositions of SAP and SIP are valid, while that of SEP and SOP are invalid.

In modern logic, contraposition is an inference consisting in negating both the antecedent and the consequent of a conditional, and exchanging their positions. For instance, from the premise "If p then q," contraposition yields "if not q then not p." This is a valid inference.

"Contraposition may be defined as a process of immediate inference in which from a given proposition another proposition is inferred having for its subject the contradictory of the original predicate." **Keynes,** *Formal Logic*

contraries

LOGIC Two statements that cannot both be true but may both be false. For example, "this cat is black" and "this cat is white" are contrary statements or contraries because a cat cannot be both completely black and completely white. It might, however, be neither black nor white, but, say, tan. Contraries differ from **contradictions** because in a pair of contrary statements, the negation of one does not entail the other. In traditional logic, the universal affirmative judgment "all S are P" and the universal negative judgment "all S are not P" are contraries.

"To say of two statements that they are contraries is to say that they are inconsistent with each other, while leaving open the possibility that there is some statement inconsistent with both." **Strawson,** *Introduction to Logical Theory*

contrary, see contraries

contrary-to-fact conditional, see contrafactual

contributor's dilemma

ETHICS, POLITICAL PHILOSOPHY Should I contribute to public goods? If I help, I will add to the sum of benefits. But only a very small portion of the benefit I add will come back to me. Since my share of what I add will be very small, it may not repay my contribution. It may thus be better for me if I do not contribute. This can be true whatever others do. But it will be worse for everyone if fewer people contribute. This is the contributor's dilemma, and it raises the question of what difference a single **altruistic** choice would make in cases that involve many people and whether it is rational to contribute in such cases. In rational choice theory this dilemma is related to the problem of the **free rider**.

"It is often claimed that, in those contributor's dilemmas that involve very many people, what each person does would make no difference." **Parfit,** *Reasons and Persons*

convention

PHILOSOPHY OF SOCIAL SCIENCE, PHILOSOPHY OF LANGUAGE [from Latin *conveniens*, suitable, proper; related to Greek *nomos*, laws, social customs, in contrast to *physis*, nature] Conventions are acceptable regularities or patterns in a **community** or population group, with examples including such things as moral rules, laws, and traffic rules. Conventions arise either unconsciously or from specific agreement. They are inherited, imitated, and taught explicitly within a community. Philosophy of language holds that many words gain their **meaning** by convention, rather than being determined by the nature of the objects they refer to. What it is for a sentence S to mean X is explained in terms of the existence of a convention in a population of speakers that S should be used to mean X. There is a convention relation between sentences in general and the propositions they express. According to **logical positivism**, a language framework is also determined by convention. There are various discussions about the precise mechanism that gives rise to a convention and the way it is maintained.

"Conventions are to be explained in terms of the patterns of beliefs and intentions of the members of the population." **Stalnaker,** *Inquiry*

conventional implicature, see conversational implicature

conventionalism

PHILOSOPHY OF MATHEMATICS, PHILOSOPHY OF SCIENCE, ETHICS The view that human conventions rather than independent realities or necessities shape our basic concepts of the world, scientific theories, ethical principles, and the like. On this view, scientific laws and theories are conventions or postulates, rather than absolute and independent. They depend on our choices from among alternative ways of organizing and explaining experience. Human arrangements are the measure and final source of their authority. We choose a given theory on the basis of its convenience or simplicity, but it is not any more true than the rival theories. This position developed out of **Kant**'s claims that the laws we find in the natural world are dependent on the character of our rational human minds and on our conceptual structure, although Kant argued that the basic concepts and principles so originating were unique and not open to successful challenge. The major proponent of conventionalism was H. **Poincaré**, who held that mathematical theorems are relative to our framework of knowledge, are subject to revision, and may even be totally abandoned. The difference between Euclidean and **non-Euclidean geometry** is not factual but conventional. The only necessary limitation on our choice of theorems and laws is the avoidance of contradiction. Other proponents include E. **Mach**, P. **Duhem**, and, in some respects, the later **Wittgenstein**. Conventionalism is close to **instrumentalism** and **pragmatism**, but is opposed to **realism**. Its difficulty is that it must admit that alternatives to our accepted principles are also workable conventions and that the choice between rival principles is arbitrary. Among its critics are M. **Schlick**, K. **Popper**, and E. **Nagel**. In moral philosophy, conventionalism is the view that moral rules are due to social conventions.

"Conventionalism . . . tries to show that most of the epistemological questions contain no questions of truth-character, but are to be settled by arbitrary decisions." **Reichenbach, Experience and Prediction**

conventionality of language forms, see principle of tolerance

conversational implicature
PHILOSOPHY OF LANGUAGE **Grice**'s term for a structure of **implications** based on features governing conversation and its context that supplements and

at times overrides implications licensed by logic and the conventional meaning of terms. This notion is central to Grice's influential theory of language.

A person by saying a statement S implicates another statement T if he is aware that T is required to complete what he is saying and is also aware that his cooperative hearer s can normally work out the implied T from the spoken S according to certain principles governing a conversation. In this case, the conversation has an implicature, and T is the *implicatum*. One of the most important principles of conversational implicature is the cooperative principle, which states that you should "make your conversational contribution such as is required at the stage at which it occurs, by the accepted purpose or direction of the talk exchange in which you are engaged." Conversational implicature is contrasted to conventional implicature, which is derived from the conventional meanings of the lexical terms occurring in the sentence and the sentential structure.

"I wish to present a certain subclass of non-conventional implicatures, which I shall call conversational implicatures, as being essentially connected with certain features of discourse." **Grice, Studies in the Ways of Words**

conversion
LOGIC In traditional logic, an operation that obtains a proposition by interchanging the subject term and **predicate** term of another proposition. The resultant proposition is called the converse of the original proposition. For instance, the converse of SAP ("All s are p") is "All p are s." Of the four basic categorical propositions in traditional logic, the converse of SEP and that of SIP are valid, for they do not involve a change of quantity. Hence, they are also called simple conversions. The converse of SAP and of SOP are invalid, for they involve a change of quantity. They are also called conversion *per accidens*.

In modern logic, conversion refers to an operation that infers a conclusion by interchanging the positions of the antecedent clause and the consequent clause, that is, from "If p then q" to "If q then p." This is invalid.

"We convert a proposition when we transpose the terms of the original proposition." **D. Mitchell, An Introduction to Logic**

Cook Wilson, John (1849–1915)

English philosopher of logic and epistemology, born in Nottingham, Professor of Logic, University of Oxford. Cook Wilson rejected the neo-Hegelian absolute idealism of his Oxford contemporaries and argued for a common-sense logical realism based on grammar and on the ordinary understanding of terms undistorted by logical or philosophical theory. His method had influence through his students on later ordinary language philosophy. His major work is *Statement and Inference* (1926).

Copernican revolution

METAPHYSICS, EPISTEMOLOGY In opposition to the traditional geocentric, Ptolemaic framework for explaining the appearance of planetary motion, Nicolaus **Copernicus** established a new mode of thought that claims that the earth is in motion and that the sun is immovable at the center of the planetary system. This hypothesis was confirmed by Kepler and **Newton**, and represents a fundamental transformation in the development of modern science.

In opposition to the traditional metaphysical claim that knowledge must conform to the objects, **Kant** in his critical philosophy sought to establish that objects must conform to our knowledge and that understanding is the lawgiver of nature. He drew a famous analogy in the preface to the second edition of the first *Critique*, comparing his new mode of thought in philosophy to what Copernicus did in astronomy. In proposing that objects must conform to our knowledge, he claimed to proceed "precisely on the lines of Copernicus' primary hypothesis." Apparent features of our experience can be ascribed to ourselves rather than to the objects of our experience. Commentators accordingly take Kant's philosophy to be a Copernican revolution in metaphysics. Moreover, while Copernicus' thesis is only a hypothesis, Kant claimed that he has demonstrated his thesis apodeictically by examining the nature of the forms of intuition and categories.

> "This indeed is the essence of the 'Copernican Revolution' which Kant proudly announced as the key to a reformed and scientific metaphysics. It is only because objects of experience must conform to the constitution of our minds that we can have the sort of a priori knowledge of the nature of experience which is demonstrated, in outline, in the Critique itself." **Strawson, *The Bounds of Sense***

Copernicus, Nicolaus (1473–1543)

Polish astronomer and physician, born in Torun, canon of the Cathedral of Frauenburg. Copernicus revolutionized traditional astronomy by placing the sun, rather than the earth, at the center of the planets. His theory seemed to contradict our common experience of seeing the sun rise and set and also contradicted scriptural authority. His account raised questions about the role of theory and experience in scientific knowledge and about the grounds for choice among rival theories in terms of different measures of simplicity, scope, and power. His major work is *On the Revolutions of the Heavenly Orbs* (1543).

copula

LOGIC The function of the verb "to be" when it joins the subject-expression and predicate-expression in an assertion to show that there is affirmation or denial. Sometimes the copula is also viewed as a part of the predicate itself. "To be" also serves as an identity-sign between expressions, but that is a different function from that of the copula. While the expressions are reversible when "to be" serves as an identity-sign, the subject and predicate cannot exchange positions when "to be" serves as a copula. As a copula it may be eliminated without affecting the meaning of a statement, but as an identity-sign it may not. In the philosophy of logic, there is discussion as to whether the copula divides every elementary proposition into "S-P" form, and whether the copula involves a commitment to the existence of various sorts of entities and structures.

> "A copula is the link of connexion between the subject and the predicate, and indicates whether the latter is affirmed or denied of the former." **Keynes, *Formal Logic***

corporatism

POLITICAL PHILOSOPHY A system in which interests are represented and policies are determined through the activities of organized groups in society acting as legitimate intermediaries between their members and the state. Corporate groups seek to limit or modify the activity and effect of market forces and the **state** and to bargain for the interests of their members in terms of class compromise. Many theorists believe that corporatist interference with the market offers short-term comfort at the expense of long-term inefficiency and stagnation. Corporatism has a long history, and its different forms correspond to different stages of economic development and different ideological motivations. Corporatism that is imposed by a centralized state, as in the case of **fascism**, can become a part of an authoritarian system, but corporatism can also be a relatively autonomous product of pressures from the working class.

Corporatism resembles the **syndicalism** of the **anarchist** tradition, which seeks to free workers from all capitalist and state controls and to establish a society with a decentralized system of worker-owned and worker-managed economic organizations.

> "Corporatism can be defined as a system of interest representation in which the constituent units are organised into a limited number of singular, compulsory, non-competitive, hierarchically ordered and functionally differentiated categories, recognised or licensed (if not created) by the state and granted a deliberation representational monopoly within their respective categories in exchange for observing certain controls on their selection of leaders and articulation of demands and supports."
> **Schmitter in Schmitter and Lehmbruch (eds.),** *Trends Toward Corporatist Intermediation*

corpuscularianism

METAPHYSICS, PHILOSOPHY OF SCIENCE A metaphysical view of the world in the spirit of the Greek **atomism** of **Democritus**. It holds that everything is composed of indivisible corpuscles or atoms, which are the units at the last stage of the analysis of material things into their components. This theory accepts the distinction between **primary and secondary qualities** and claims that corpuscles differ intrinsically in their primary qualities such as size, shape, mutual arrangement, and motion. With these differences, they form various kinds of materials and things. Every change can be reduced to mechanical action, with geometry and mechanics as the paradigms of science. Modern corpuscularianism was developed by the Irish scientist Robert **Boyle** in the middle of the seventeenth century as an attempt to replace the **Aristotelian** world view of **hylomorphism**, but it is also associated with **Galileo, Descartes, Locke, Newton**, and chemical atomism. The dominance of the theory declined

with the emergence of the field theory in the middle of the nineteenth century, but it still exerts great influence on contemporary philosophy of science.

> "Corpuscularians, although disagreeing quite substantially about specific details, held that the things we experience are in fact made up of small material particles and the way we experience them is a product of the action of these small particles on our sense organs." **Tiles and Tiles,** *An Introduction to Historical Epistemology*

corrective justice,

an alternative expression for rectificatory justice

correspondence rules

PHILOSOPHY OF SCIENCE In the double language model developed by **Carnap** and Ernest **Nagel**, the language of science is divided into **theoretical language** and **observation language**. Correspondence rules serve to relate these two languages. These rules are statements containing both theoretical terms and observational terms. By means of these rules, a theoretical term can be partially and indirectly explained empirically. These rules are also called by different authors "mixed sentences," "operational definitions," or "correlative definitions."

> "[C]orrespondence rules, as I call them . . . connect the theoretical terms with the empirical ones." **Carnap,** *Philosophical Foundations of Physics*

correspondence theory of truth

LOGIC, PHILOSOPHY OF LANGUAGE The most widely held theory of truth, taking truth to consist in a relation of correspondence between **propositions** and the way things are in reality. A proposition is true if it states what is the case, and false otherwise. It is a kind of replica or map of reality. This theory can be traced to **Aristotle**'s dictum in the *Metaphysics* that "to say of what is that it is, and of what is not that it is not, is true." **Locke** provided an empirical foundation for it, because if sense-experience is the main source of our knowledge, truth must consist in a kind of correspondence. **Russell** and **Wittgenstein**, during their logical atomism periods, offered versions of the theory, according to which truth is correspondence and correspondence is a relation of structural isomorphism between propositions and facts. A true proposition is one where the elements of the propositional sign correspond to the objects of the thought. The correspondence theory has been attacked because it presupposes a controversial metaphysics of things and **facts**. Moreover, the notion of correspondence is ambiguous. Various words have been employed to convey the meaning of correspond, such as accord with, fit in with, agree with and tally with, yet the sort of relation alleged to exist between a sentence and fact is still unclear. To avoid this criticism **Austin** developed a version that explains correspondence in terms of two kinds of correlation involving descriptive conventions and demonstrative conventions between words and world. His theory is also controversial. **Tarski**'s **semantic theory of truth** is also an attempt to reconstruct the essence of the traditional notion of correspondence.

> "The property of being a mother is explained by the relation between a woman and her child; similarly, the suggestion runs, the property of being true is to be explained by a relation between a statement and something else . . . I shall take the licence of calling any view of this kind a correspondence theory of truth." **Davidson**, *Inquiries into Truth and Interpretation*

corroboration

LOGIC, PHILOSOPHY OF SCIENCE **Popper**'s term for the support obtained by a **hypothesis** or conjecture that survives serious testing and is not superseded by another hypothesis or conjecture. Popper preferred to call the testable degree of a hypothesis its degree of corroboration rather than its probability. Corroboration is introduced to distinguish Popperian testing from **confirmation** and to show that the probabilistic theory of **induction** is wrong. Corroboration is a measurement or report of the past performance of a theory and does not make a theory universal or more reliable. Hence, the degree of corroboration of theory has nothing to do with **prediction** or future decision making. For Popper, a theory can never be established beyond doubt. The aim of science is not to verify, but to falsify.

> "The term 'confirmation' has lately been so much used and misused that I have decided to surrender it to the verificationists and to use for my own purposes 'corroboration' only." **Popper**, *Conjectures and Refutations*

cosmogony

ANCIENT GREEK PHILOSOPHY, PHILOSOPHY OF SCIENCE The theory of the genesis and growth of the cosmos, the main theoretical form of **pre-Socratic** philosophy. There were many pre-philosophical mythical and religious cosmogonies among the ancient Greeks, Egyptians, and Babylonians, but the pre-Socratics differed fundamentally from all of them by seeking the origin of the world on a rational basis, rather than by appealing to a supernatural force. Nevertheless, their cosmogony was deeply influenced by Hesiod's theogony or genealogical account of the divine kingdom. All of the pre-Socratics held that the cosmos has a beginning. Some set up one or more elements as fundamental principles, claiming that the primary opposites, hot and cold, wet and dry, evolved from these principles and that the other parts of the cosmos evolved from these opposites. Other philosophers claimed that there was an original mixture from which evolved first the four basic elements and then natural substances and the organic world. Although views differed about the process, the whole picture was evolutionary rather than creative and involved no design. Compared with scientific cosmogony, the theories of the pre-Socratics were largely speculative, but they nevertheless demonstrated rational intelligence, which yielded many profound insights.

> "Practically all that we know about the philosophy of the Milesians concerns their cosmogony, their account of how the world came into being." **A. Armstrong**, *An Introduction to Ancient Philosophy*

cosmological argument

PHILOSOPHY OF RELIGION A family of arguments advanced to prove the existence of **God**. These arguments are based not on the analysis of God's essential nature, but on the nature of the cosmos or universe. Different versions argue respectively from the empirical facts that the universe is in motion, causally organized, contingent, or ordered to the conclusions that there must be an unmoved mover, an uncaused cause, a necessary being, or an orderer. God is then identified with the being that is shown to be necessary in order to explain the selected features of the world. In the history of philosophy, **Plato, Aristotle, Aquinas, Descartes, Leibniz**, and **Locke** are among the defenders of one or more versions of the cosmological argument, while **Hume, Kant, Mill,** and **Russell** are among the critics. A major difficulty facing all versions of the argument lies in the ambiguous nature of their key notions, such as **necessity** or **causality**. Even if the argument succeeds, it shows the existence of a divine object, whereas religion requires God to be known primarily as a person.

> "In the widest sense of the term, any theistic argument that proceeds from the world to God can be described as cosmological." **Hick,** *Arguments for the Existence of God*

cosmology

METAPHYSICS, PHILOSOPHY OF SCIENCE [from Greek *kosmos*, the world or universe + *logos*, theory or study] A study of the universe as a whole, especially its constitution and structure. Philosophical cosmology is a rational inquiry that combines some scientific evidence and substantial speculation. It is also called rational cosmology, in contrast to mythic cosmology and to modern cosmology, which is a branch of astronomy. **Wolff** took rational cosmology to be one of three branches of specific metaphysics, with the others being rational theology and rational psychology. The most general issues discussed in philosophical cosmology include **space, time, causality, necessity**, contingency, **change, eternity**, and infinity.

Cosmology was the dominant concern of the **pre-Socratics**. It also played a significant role in the philosophy of **Plato** and **Aristotle** and in medieval philosophy. Most claims of traditional cosmology were undermined by Renaissance science, but the subject was revived by **Leibniz** and **Newton**. **Kant** applied his critical philosophy to cosmology, claiming that cosmological problems can never be solved because we cannot apply **categories** beyond their spatio-temporal limits. Attempts to resolve such problems result in **antinomies**. According to Kant, cosmology arises from a natural inclination of human reason to seek absolute knowledge of the world, and he claimed that a positive critical cosmology is needed to set the limit of reason in this regard. Later, **Schelling** and **Hegel** turned rational cosmology into the philosophy of nature.

Contemporary cosmology is grounded in empirical natural sciences, particularly modern physics. Since few observations are available in this area,

metaphysical theories still play an important role. The main problems of contemporary cosmology include the origin, size, and development of the universe, the possibility of other universes, the nature of space, time, matter, and energy, and the kinds of logic needed for cosmological theory.

> "Cosmology seeks to understand the nature of brute matter, considered as the cause of phenomena and as the foundation of physical laws." **Duhem,** *Essays in the History and Philosophy of Science*

cost–benefit analysis

ETHICS, POLITICAL PHILOSOPHY, PHILOSOPHY OF SOCIAL SCIENCE A type of **practical reasoning** that analyzes or evaluates an issue by calculating how much cost we need to put in and how much interest or benefit the outcome is going to produce. We then choose the alternative that, measured by some common scale, costs least but gains most. It is a standard **utility calculus** and is widely employed in economic affairs and social policy. In order to apply this sort of reasoning, the goals of an action must be well defined. Furthermore, it must be possible to compare costs of alternative policies in terms of some definite unit and to quantify benefits in a way that renders them commensurable with one another. This approach is therefore limited regarding those moral and social issues that resist quantitative analysis. Not all significant costs and benefits can be measured or can be brought into a system of commensurability.

> "Cost-benefit analyses are not popular now in some quarters; and they have indeed been misused, by failing to include very important costs and benefits (often because they are not measurable in terms of money)." **Hare,** *Essays on Political Morality*

count noun

PHILOSOPHY OF LANGUAGE, METAPHYSICS A noun used for a kind of countable thing such as "table," "river," or "body." A count noun has grammatical plural forms and can be modified by an indefinite article. The question "How many Cs are there?" has an answer if C is a count noun. A count noun can replace a **variable** in **predicate logic**. A count noun corresponds to a **sortal**, but contrasts with a **mass term**, which refers to an uncountable thing or substance such as wood, water, or flesh. Mass nouns do not have plural forms and are not modified by an indefinite article. They are used to answer the question "How much M is there?"

> "Count nouns have plurals; in the singular they admit of the indefinite article, and it is appropriate where c is a count-noun to ask the question 'How many Cs are there?'" **C. Williams, *Being, Identity and Truth***

counterexample

LOGIC, PHILOSOPHICAL METHOD A counterexample to a generalization is a case that is an instance of the kind to which the generalization applies but which does not have the property that the generalization asserts that things of that kind possess. For instance, "All swans are white" is a generalization. But if there is one swan that is not white, that non-white swan becomes a counterexample. A counterexample to an argument is a case in which all premises are true but the conclusion is false. The discovery of a counterexample to an argument indicates that the argument is not logically valid, or at least that its conclusion cannot be universally applied. Hence the absence of a counterexample becomes a mark of the **validity** of an argument. A valid inference is one that has no counterexample. Otherwise, it is invalid.

> "To find an interpretation which shows that an argument is logically invalid is the same thing as finding a counterexample to the argument." **Suppes, *Introduction to Logic***

counterfactuals, see contrafactuals

counterfactuals of freedom, another expression for middle knowledge

counterpart theory

METAPHYSICS A theory that can be traced to **Leibniz**, but has recently been developed by D. **Lewis** to cope with the problem of **trans-world identity**. For Lewis, an individual can exist only in one of the plurality of **possible worlds**, because a thing can only be in one place at a time. There is nothing that inhabits more than one world. Hence, individuals are worldbound, and there are no identical individuals

in different worlds. How, then, are we to analyze what is possible or impossible for a worldbound individual? Lewis claims that individuals have counterparts in other worlds. Even though they are not identical with their actual-world counterparts, they resemble them more closely than do other things in their worlds. They are such that for anything X in the actual world W, its counterpart X-in-W_n is just as X-in-W would have been, had things been different in the way things are different between W and W_n. Trans-world resemblance is the counterpart relation, and is a substitute for trans-world identity.

> "In general, something has for counterparts at a given world those things existing there that resemble it closely enough in important respects of intrinsic quality and extrinsic relations, and that resemble it no less closely than do other things existing there." **D. Lewis, *Counterfactuals***

courage

ETHICS [Greek *andreia*, related to *aner*, an adult man; hence manliness or bravery, corresponding to Latin *virtus*] One of the prominent **virtues** in ancient Greece. In the ancient world, a good man had to be courageous or brave in battle and in the face of other dangers. **Socrates** argued that courage as a virtue must involve knowledge of what is and what is not truly to be feared. Moreover, courage is not only fortitude in the face of physical danger, but also involves enduring in one's convictions against all adversity and temptation. Courage is the subject of **Plato**'s dialogue *Laches* and is further discussed in the *Republic*. It corresponds to the spirited element in the tripartite of the soul, and is the virtue of the auxiliaries. **Aristotle** considered courage to be a mean between fear and confidence.

> "Hence whoever stands firm against the right things and fears the right things, for the right end, in the right way, at the right time, and is correspondingly confident, is a courageous person." **Aristotle, *Nicomachean Ethics***

covering law model

PHILOSOPHY OF SCIENCE, PHILOSOPHY OF SOCIAL SCIENCE A term for an account of scientific **explanation**, according to which an event is explained through deduction from a general law and certain initial conditions. In an explanation, the event is subsumed or covered by the general law. This is called the **deductive-nomological model** of explanation (D-N model). The model can also apply to the covering law itself, that is, the law can be explained by deducing it from a higher order covering law or body of laws. Such a theory of explanation was elaborated by **Hempel**. In an extended sense, the covering law model can employ statistical laws to explain an event by showing that it is highly probable. This model of explanation, which is usually inductive, is called the inductive-probabilistic model. The term "covering law model" was used by **Dray** for the first model in *Law and Explanation in History* (1957). Hempel extended the term to the second model as well. Many disputes have arisen concerning each model. For the deductive-nomological model, some critics claim that in some cases a law is not needed to provide an explanation, while at least some accounts satisfying the model do not have explanatory force. On one diagnosis, these problems arise because the formal approach of the model does not leave room for contextual elements in explanation. There is also debate about the nature of the statistical model and whether a purely statistical law can explain. The covering law model is also called the subsumption theory of explanation.

"The Hempelian theory of explanation has become known as the Covering Law model (or theory)." **von Wright**, *Explanation and Understanding*

Craig's theorem

LOGIC, PHILOSOPHY OF SCIENCE A theorem in mathematical logic put forward and proved by the American logician William Craig in his paper "On Axiomatizability within a System" (*Journal of Symbolic Logic*, 1953). The theorem states that if we separate the vocabulary of a formal system into the T (theoretical) terms and the O (observational) terms, there is a formalized system T′ such that (a) the axioms of T′ contain only the observational terms, and (b) T and T′ imply the same O-sentences. This theorem shows that **theoretical terms** are in principle eliminable from empirical theories. It is thus a method by which we may formulate all connections between observables without having to make use of theoretical terms. To apply this method,

one needs first to distinguish the essential expressions of the system from the auxiliary expressions, and to take the content of the system to be identical with the class of essential expressions and then to construct a new axiomatized system that contains all the essential expressions and none of the auxiliary expressions. This system has the same observational consequences as the original one. Craig himself does not think that this method really dissolves the problem of analyzing the empirical meaning of theoretical terms and holds that this method applies only to completed deductive systems. Nevertheless, his theorem has greatly influenced discussion in the philosophy of science of the relationship between theoretical terms and observational terms. The method is close in spirit to the notion of the **Ramsey sentence**.

"What Craig's theorem provides is a general method of eliminating a selected group of terms from a formalised system without changing the content of the system." **H. Brown**, *Perception, Theory and Commitment*

creation *ex nihilo*

PHILOSOPHY OF RELIGION Creation out of nothing, in contrast to the claim that *ex nihilo nihil fit* (nothing comes out of nothing). Christian theists held the doctrine that **God** created the world out of nothing, contrary to the view of the relation between God and the world expressed by **Plato** and **Neoplatonism**. The doctrine of creation *ex nihilo* maintains that **matter** is not eternal and that no matter existed prior to a divine creative act at the initial moment of the cosmic process. Whilst the pre-existence of matter would restrict God to the role of a formal cause or an agent that orders or arranges pre-existing stuff, the doctrine of creation *ex nihilo* holds that matter was created instantaneously by God out of nothing, in the strict sense of absolute non-being. On this view, creation is absolutely without determination. For example, God did not create the world because he needed this action to complete his nature. God is held to be necessary and is not confronted with any alien and rival necessity that might determine or constrain his acts.

"According to classical theism God created the world 'out of nothing' (*ex nihilo*)." **H. Owen**, *Concepts of Deity*

creativity

AESTHETICS Generally, to create is to make something new, including both material objects and ideas.
Creativity has a wide application in human activities,
but is of particular significance in the production
of art. In Greek thought, a poet is called "maker"
(Greek *poietes*). **Aristotle**'s masterpiece on aesthetics,
what is usually translated as *"poetics"*, is in its Greek
original *"poietikos"* ("concerned with making").
Art has long been seen as a creative activity, but
there have been disagreements regarding what it
means to say that an activity is a creative artistic
activity. Creativity implies novelty and involves
producing something different from what has been
produced before, but also extends beyond mere
novelty. In creation, an artist seeks to assimilate
within a design recalcitrant features of a subject
and to keep and enhance the subject's initiative and
freedom. There is disagreement whether the process
of artistic creation is explicable. For **Plato**, artists
themselves lack knowledge and are under the influence of divine inspiration. Hence artistic creativity
is associated with madness. For others, although
artistic creation derives from inspiration, it is also
subject to rational analysis.

"Creative activity in art, that is to say, is not a
paradigm of purposive activity, that is, of activity
engaged in and consciously-controlled so as to produce a desired result." **Tomas (ed.), Creativity in
the Arts**

credo ut intelligam

PHILOSOPHY OF RELIGION [Latin, I believe in order
that I may understand] An avowal from St **Anselm**'s
Proslogion, in which the **ontological argument** was
first expressed. Anselm claimed that it is impossible to understand Christian doctrines without
faith or belief. **Reason** itself cannot discover anything intelligible about **God**. The view has inspired
other explorations of non-intellectual or non-rational
conditions of understanding. Outside theology, it is
popular to affirm that one must use the practical
means of living in a culture in order to understand
that culture, and that detached rational understanding of a culture is impossible.

"I do not seek to understand in order that I may
believe, but I believe in order that I may understand (*credo ut intelligam*). For this I also believe;
that if I did not believe, I could not understand."
Anselm, *Proslogion*

criterion, problem of the

EPISTEMOLOGY A criterion is a test or standard by
which truth, existence, identity, or meaning can be
determined. There is an influential question concerning the relation between criteria and that for
which they are criteria, called the problem of the
criterion. The problem was originally formulated
by **Sextus Empiricus** in the *Outline of Pyrrhonism* (II,
4). To know the truth, one needs a proof that what
one knows is the truth. How, then, can a proof be
true? It seems that any proof requires a criterion to
confirm it, and the criterion needs a proof to demonstrate its truth. That involves a circular process of
reasoning. This **paradox** has historically had various
formulations and has been a subject of wide discussion. **Chisholm** presents the problem in this way:
We have two general questions in epistemology:
(A) "What do we know?" and (B) "How do we know
anything?" Question A concerns the extent of
our knowledge, and B the criterion for knowledge.
However, if we try to answer A, we must answer B
first. To know whether things are really as they seem
to be, we need to have a procedure for distinguishing appearance from reality. On the other hand, if
we want to answer question B, we must answer
question A first. For to know whether a procedure
is good or proper, we must first know the distinction
between appearance and reality. To get out of this
circle, we must show that we can justify our criteria
of knowledge without appealing to what these
criteria countenance as knowledge. This involves
the distinction of different levels of knowledge and
different levels of justification. Fulfilling this task has
become one of the major problems of epistemology
and of philosophy in general.

"The problem of the criterion seems to me to be
one of the most important and one of the most
difficult of all the problems of philosophy. I am
tempted to say that one has not begun to philo-
sophise until one has faced this problem and has
recognised how unappealing, in the end, each of
the possible solutions is." **Chisholm, *The Foundations of Knowing***

criterion of verifiability

PHILOSOPHICAL METHOD, EPISTEMOLOGY, PHILOSOPHY
OF LANGUAGE A test proposed by **logical positivists**
to distinguish genuine **propositions** from pseudo-
propositions. By virtue of demonstrating that
metaphysics is composed of pseudo-propositions,
they attempted to show that philosophy, as a genuine branch of knowledge, must be distinguished
from metaphysics. What purports to be a factual
proposition has cognitive sense if and only if it is
empirically verifiable. If it cannot be shown to
be true or false, it is factually insignificant, although
it can perhaps have emotive meaning for those
who utter it. We can distinguish between practical
verifiability and verifiability in principle. Many
propositions could, with sufficient effort, be verified
in practice. For others, such as "there are planets
of stars in other galaxies," we can conceive of an
observation allowing us to decide its truth or falsity,
but lack the means which would enable us actually
to make such an observation. Because we know that
being in a position to make the observation would
allow verification, this kind of proposition is verifiable in principle.

There is a further distinction between a strong and
a weak sense of verifiable. According to the strong
sense, held by **Schlick**, a proposition is verifiable
if and only if its truth is conclusively or practically
established in experience; according to the weak
sense, developed by **Ayer**, a proposition is verifiable
if it is possible for experience to render it probable.

> "The criterion which we use to test the genuine-
> ness of apparent statements of fact is the criterion
> of verifiability." **Ayer,** *Language, Truth and Logic*

critical cognitivism

EPISTEMOLOGY A term introduced by Roderick
Chisholm for an approach to the problem of how
to formulate the criterion that determines disputed
knowledge claims, such as knowledge of ethical facts,
religious knowledge, knowledge of other minds, or
knowledge of the past and future. The difficulty with
this kind of knowledge is to show how we can infer
from what is directly evident to what is indirectly
evident. We may reasonably assume that we have
just four sources that yield knowledge, that is, external perception, inner consciousness, memory, and
reason. None of them can individually and directly

provide us with knowledge of the disputed type. We
have also induction and deduction, but they do not
help either. Chisholm then attempts to establish the
existence of principles of evidence other than the
principles of induction and deduction and called this
approach critical cognitivism. It tells us under what
conditions cognitive states will confer evidence or
reasonableness upon propositions about external
things. It takes the knowledge produced by other
approaches as sign or evidence for more dubious
knowledge and reaches the latter from the former
facts of experience.

> "The other type of answer might be called critical
> cognitivism. If we take this approach, we will
> not say that there are empirical sentences that
> might serve as translations of the sentences
> expressing our ethical knowledge; but we will say
> that there are empirical truths which enable us
> to know certain truths of ethics." **Chisholm,** *Theory
> of Knowledge*

critical ethics, another name for meta-ethics

critical idealism, another term for transcendental idealism

critical realism

EPISTEMOLOGY, METAPHYSICS An American epistemological movement that flourished in the early
twentieth century. Its representatives include
George **Santayana**, Roy Wood **Sellars**, and Arthur
O. Lovejoy. The movement took its name from
Sellars's book *Critical Realism* (1916). A volume,
*Essays in Critical Realism: A Cooperative Study of
the Problem of Knowledge* (1920), became the
manifesto of the school. By claiming that there is
an objective and independent physical world that
is the object of knowledge, critical realism opposed
idealism. It also opposed the naive version of
direct realism proposed by the new realists,
specifically their claim that we directly perceive
the objective things themselves. Critical realism is
called "critical" because it claims that what is present directly in consciousness are mental states
and not the physical things as such. They held
that the mind knows the external world via the
mediation of the mental. Critical realists tried to
account for the relationship between the mediating

elements and what they represent. They believed their accounts to be the most reasonable way to explain phenomena such as error, illusion, and perceptual variation. However, critical realists had many disagreements over the nature of the mediating elements and the roles they filled. Candidates for the mediating elements ranged over **essences, ideas**, and **sense-data**. Because of differences, critical realism did not survive as a school.

> "Critical realism accepts physical realism. Like common sense, it holds to the belief that there are physical things; and, like enlightened common sense, its idea of the physical world is moulded by the conclusions of science. It is a criticism of naive realism, and an attempt to free it from its presupposition that knowledge is, or can be, an intuition of the physical thing itself." **Sellars**, *Essays in Critical Realism*

critical theory

ETHICS, POLITICAL PHILOSOPHY, PHILOSOPHY OF SOCIAL SCIENCE A type of social theory that originated with Western Marxist thinkers attached to the Institute of Social Research at the University of Frankfurt. Leading critical theorists included Max **Horkheimer**, Theodor W. **Adorno**, and Herbert **Marcuse**. The Institute moved to Geneva and during the Second World War to the United States, but it returned to Germany in 1950. The original proponents of critical theory are also called the **Frankfurt school**.

The project of critical theory was inspired by **Marx**'s "Theses on Feuerbach," in which Marx said, "Philosophers have given different interpretations of the world; the point is to change it." Critical theory rejected the attempt of logical positivism to find universal laws in the human sciences. It held that modern science and technology have been totally reduced to an administrative system governed by a purely technological rationality. To counteract this, critical theory focused on the **superstructure** rather than the economic base of societies and emphasized moral, political, and religious values. It claimed that knowledge is relative to human interest and introduced a wide range of cultural criticism into Marxist social theory. It sought to reveal the false embodiment of the ideals of reason in the social and political conditions of capitalist

societies. Critical theory sought to identify the possibility of social change and to promote a self-reflective, domination-free society.

Critical theory developed into a new phase with the work of Jürgen **Habermas**, who was based at the same Institute. Habermas's ambition was to replace the technological rationality predominant in modern societies with **communicative rationality**, which reaches conclusions through discussion and dialogue. He tries to achieve this goal by shifting philosophical emphasis from the subject–object relation to the process of intersubjective communication. He believes that the act of communication anticipates the goal of critical theory and also establishes a universalistic discourse ethics as the evaluative foundation of social critique.

> "The expression 'critical theory' has been applied to a wide range of different theoretical standpoints. In its narrowest sense, it refers to the views advocated by members of the Frankfurt school, especially in the early writings of Max Horkheimer and Herbert Marcuse." **Keat and Urry**, *Social Theory as Science*

critical thinking, another term for informal logic

Critique of Judgement

AESTHETICS, PHILOSOPHY OF SCIENCE The third and last critique in **Kant**'s critical philosophy. First published in 1790, the *Critique of Judgement* is an examination of the power or faculty of **judgment**, that is, the possibility of making judgments. This issue is related to the schematism of the first critique. Kant divides judgment into two kinds: a determinant judgment applies a rule or concept to particular instances, and a reflective judgment (or judgment of reflection) discovers the rule or concept under which a given particular instance falls. The thinking in determinant judgment is from the universal to the particular, but in reflective judgment, the thinking is from the particular to the universal. The *Critique of Judgement* concerns reflective judgment, especially its two most problematic forms: **aesthetic judgment** and teleological judgment. The book is divided into two parts: the critique of aesthetic judgment of **taste**, and the critique of teleological judgment. Each has its own analytic and dialectic.

There are generally two approaches to the third *Critique*. One approach emphasizes its role in the whole critical enterprise. The first critique discussed the realm of nature, the second the realm of freedom, and the third is viewed as a bridge that combines these two realms and completes the critical philosophy. The other approach focuses on the critique of aesthetic judgment of taste. The analytic of this part includes an analytic of the beautiful and an analytic of the **sublime**, which are viewed as the origin of modern aesthetics. On this approach, these questions of aesthetics are considered independently.

> "A Critique of pure reason, i.e. of our faculty of judging on a priori principles, would be incomplete if the critical examination of judgement, which is a faculty of knowledge, and as such, lays a claim to independent principles, were not dealt with separately." **Kant, *Critique of Judgement***

Critique of Practical Reason

ETHICS The second critique of **Kant**'s critical philosophy, first published in 1788. The book was divided into two parts: the doctrine of the elements of pure **practical reason** and the methodology of pure practical reason. The former part was further divided into the Analytic and the Dialectic. The Analytic sought to determine **synthetic *a priori* principles** about what we ought to do and to demonstrate the legitimacy of these principles. The Dialectic dealt with an **antinomy** concerning the definition of the highest good, with the conflicting theses represented by **Epicurus** and the Stoics. While the first critique rejected the traditional metaphysical notions of **God, freedom**, and **immortality** as objects of knowledge, the *Critique of Practical Reason* justified them for **morality** as postulated objects of **faith**. The book elaborated and developed the central ideas about morality that Kant established in the *Groundwork for the Metaphysics of Morals* (1785).

> ". . . reason, which contains constitutive a priori principles solely in respect of the faculty of desire, gets its holding assigned to it by the *Critique of Practical Reason*." **Kant, *Critique of Judgement***

Critique of Pure Reason

EPISTEMOLOGY, METAPHYSICS **Kant**'s greatest masterpiece, one of the most important books in the

history of Western philosophy. It fundamentally shaped the development of modern philosophy. For Kant, a critique was a critical examination, and pure reason was contrasted with empirical reason, with pure reason seeking to provide knowledge independent of experience. Kant saw a critique of pure reason as a critical examination of these claims of pure reason conducted by pure reason itself. While the logical use of reason unifies knowledge already gained through other faculties, pure reason tries to add to our knowledge through its own labors, and thus becomes the source of dialectical error. Pure reason is also the name that followers of **Wolff** gave to their philosophy, which was dominant in Kant's time. Kant's criticism of pure reason has both of these aspects in mind.

The first *Critique* is an examination of the limits and conditions of human theoretical reason. It was first published in 1781, but very extensively revised for its second edition in 1787. The first edition is designated A and the second edition B. In modern editions and translations, the page numbers of both editions are normally marked in the margin. The book is divided into two parts: the Transcendental Doctrine of Elements and the Transcendental Doctrine of Methods. The former occupies five-sixths of the book, and the Doctrine of Methods is merely a systematic presentation of the basic elements of knowledge discovered in the previous part. The Doctrine of the Elements is divided into the Transcendental Aesthetic and the Transcendental Logic, which is further divided into the Transcendental Analytic and the Transcendental Dialectic.

The first *Critique* purported to carry out a **Copernican revolution** in philosophy by proposing that objects must conform to our knowledge rather than our knowledge to objects. This position is related to the complex and controversial claims of Kant's **transcendental idealism**, which he sought to combine with empirical realism. The Transcendental Aesthetic deals with **sensibility**. Kant sought to demonstrate that sensibility has *a priori* forms, **space** and **time**, that are subjective forms of intuition. He also offered influential claims about the nature of mathematics. The Transcendental Analytic deals with **understanding**. Kant proposed his table of **categories** as pure concepts of the understanding and a **schematism** for the application of the categories to sensible objects. The claim that **judgment** and **perception** involve both sensibility and understanding is a major theme of the first *Critique*. The crucially important **transcendental deduction** of the categories attempted to justify our use of the categories as conditions for the possibility of experience. Kant also provided important examinations of individual categories and of ourselves as subjects of experience. These two parts attempt to answer Kant's central question of how **synthetic *a priori* judgments** are possible. Kant tried to provide a metaphysical foundation for Newtonian physics. The pure concepts of understanding can only be applied to a spatiotemporal phenomenal world. Once human reason attempts to make use of them beyond our experience to **things-in-themselves**, illusions, errors, or antinomies are generated. According to Kant, this is the source of the errors of traditional metaphysics. The task of the transcendental dialectic, which is concerned with reason, is to expose these errors.

> "I do not mean by this [the critique of pure reason] a critique of books and systems, but of the faculty of reason in general, in respect of all knowledge after which it may strive independently of all experience." **Kant, *Critique of Pure Reason***

Croce, Benedetto (1866–1952)

Italian idealist philosopher and historian, born in Pescasseroli, Abruzzi. Deeply influenced by Hegel, Croce maintained that philosophy and history are unified. His philosophy of spirit distinguished four levels of mental activity: the aesthetic, the logical, the economic, and the ethical. His most influential philosophical work is in the field of aesthetics. He claimed that aesthetics is the science of intuitive cognition and that all art is lyrical in character. He pioneered the expression theory of art, which was later developed by Collingwood. Croce founded the journal *La Critica* in 1904. From 1925, he was the main anti-fascist Italian intellectual, and he was also active in public life after the Second World War. His most important book is *Aesthetics as Science of Expression and General Linguistics* (1902). Other works include *Logic as the Science of Pure Concept* (1905), *Philosophy of the Practical, the Economical, and the Ethical* (1909), *Poetry and Literature: An Introduction to Its Criticism and History* (1936).

crucial experiment

PHILOSOPHY OF SCIENCE [Latin *experimentum crucis*] A term introduced by Francis **Bacon** in *Novum Organon*. At a certain stage of scientific development, two rival **hypotheses** appear to have equal explanatory power. When this occurs, it is of great importance that scientists should devise an experiment that can play a decisive role in determining which one of rival scientific theories should be refuted or accepted. Eddington's measurement of the gravitational bending of light rays during a solar eclipse was crucial in the debate between **Einstein**'s general relativity and Newtonian mechanics. In the nineteenth and twentieth centuries, the notion of a crucial experiment has become an important topic in the discussion of scientific methodology. Some, like **Duhem**, argue that a crucial verifying experiment is impossible. Others, like **Popper**, believe that a crucial experiment functions decisively in falsifying one of the rival theories. Still others, like **Lakatos**, suggest that a crucial experiment cannot be final in overthrowing a theory, although it may be an indication of the progress or demise of a research program.

> "In most cases we have, before falsifying a hypothesis, another one up our sleeves; for the falsifying experiment is usually a crucial experiment designed to decide between the two. That is to say, it is suggested by the fact that the two hypotheses differ in some respect; and it makes use of this difference to refute (at least) one of them." **Popper, *The Logic of Scientific Discovery***

cruelty

ETHICS [from Latin *cruor*, spilled blood] Cruelty is traditionally conceived as an activity of inflicting pain upon other persons. In addition to physical pain, which is related to spilling blood, it also covers mental or psychological pain. It is opposed to care and beneficence, and is regarded as a paradigmatic evil. Cruelty can be committed by individual persons or by institutions (for example, by the slave system or by Nazi Germany), although in many cases they are difficult to separate. Institutional cruelty involves a relationship between the strength of the institution and the weakness of its victims. There are issues concerning the complicity of the individual agents or members of the institution and the extent to which they are responsible for such cruelty. In some cases, questions of assessment arise because persons believe themselves to be caring, but those affected by their actions consider them to be cruel. There is dispute whether and to what extent cruelty to evil doers can be justified. One important case concerns whether **capital punishment** is cruel. In contemporary **environmental ethics**, cruelty as an evil extends from the human community to human relationships with animals. The **animal liberation** movement demands that we stop cruelty to non-human animals.

"Cruelty or savageness is the desire whereby any one is incited to work evil to one whom we love or whom we pity." **Spinoza,** *Ethics*

C-series of time, see A-series of time

Cudworth, Ralph (1617–88)

English philosopher and theologian, one of the leading Cambridge Platonists, born in Aller, Somerset. Cudworth sought to refute atheistic determinism and Hobbes's materialism. He held that all knowledge and virtue participate in eternal ideas of truth and goodness in the mind of God. God works through the spiritual plastic natures that exist between the conscious mind and material objects. There are eternal moral truths and distinctions in ethics. His major works are: *The True Intellectual System of the Universe* (1678), *A Treatise Concerning Eternal and Immutable Morality* (1731), and *A Treatise of Free Will* (1838).

cultural relativism

EPISTEMOLOGY, ETHICS, PHILOSOPHY OF SOCIAL SCIENCE A theory that holds that each **culture** is a unique and arbitrary system of thought and behavior. What is considered to be a reasonable claim in one society is not necessarily thought to be so in another culture, and consequently it is impossible to compare and rank different cultures. Any behavior has to be explained in terms of the society and context in which it occurs. Any attempt to compare different cultures would inevitably have to appeal to some assumptions universally found in human cultures, but cultural relativism denies that there are such significant cultural universals. Cultural relativism was the dominant conviction in anthropology in the 1930s and 1940s and is still employed in many studies of the social sciences, including studies of ethics. Many philosophers reject cultural relativism as incoherent, on the grounds that it undermines our concepts of **truth**, **objectivity**, and **meaning**.

"The reason cultural relativism is so crucial is that it challenges the orthodoxies of our civilisation. To the confirmed relativist, the ideas of our society (whether moral or existential) are a matter of convention and are not rooted in absolute principles that transcend time and place." **Hatch,** *Culture and Morality*

culture

PHILOSOPHY OF SOCIAL SCIENCE In its most central sense, culture refers to the forms of life and the tools, symbols, customs, and beliefs that are characteristic of a distinct historical group of people. This sense of culture, associated with the notion of society, provides much of the subject-matter of sociology and anthropology. The variety of cultures has led some thinkers to endorse "**cultural relativism,**" the claim that the culture of any society must be judged in its own terms and not by standards provided by the culture of another society. Others have accepted the importance of culture while rejecting cultural relativism. Culture may also refer to the system of value and ways of thinking peculiar to a society. This amounts to "the consciousness of a society." In its widest sense, culture refers to the totality of human thoughts, behaviors, and the products of human activities. Culture in this sense, which stands in contrast to biological nature and has been used to distinguish humans from animals, belongs to the subject of philosophical anthropology. More selectively, culture comprises art, sports, entertainment, and other leisure activities. High culture, containing the most significant and accomplished works of visual art, music, dance, and literature, has often been contrasted with popular culture, although the two in some circumstances influence one another. Culture also means personal cultivation through education and training. The science of culture seeks to understand that which is defined by the creation of values.

"A culture is an interrelated network of customs, traditions, ideals and values." **M. Singer (ed.),** *American Philosophy*

Cumberland, Richard (1632–1718)

English moral philosopher, born in London, fellow of Magdalene College, Cambridge, Bishop of Peterborough. Cumberland argued that there is a foundation of morality in nature and rejected the Hobbesian claim that morality derived from the decree of a sovereign and the claim that morality derived from the decree of God. His claim that there is a universal human inclination toward benevolence and that an action is morally right through promoting the general good anticipated later utilitarian theory. His main philosophical work is *On the Laws of Nature* (1672).

cunning of reason

METAPHYSICS, PHILOSOPHY OF HISTORY According to **Hegel**, the **absolute idea** or spirit accomplishes its end through the interactions and competitions of particular things, although reason itself cunningly avoids being dragged into the struggle. It remains in the background to control the whole process without being the object of explicit awareness. Reason does not work directly on the subject or lower itself to becoming a particular thing, but nevertheless achieves its goal. Particular things are merely means used for the end of reason, but are themselves parts of a necessary process. The play of contingency serves to realize the necessary plan or the inner **teleology** of the world. In the area of history, everyone pursues his own purpose and falls into battle with others, but eventually history develops its own pattern out of particular and selfish human actions.

"It is not the universal idea which places itself in opposition and struggle, or puts itself in danger; it holds itself safe from attack and uninjured in the background and sends the particular of passion into the struggle to be worn down. We can call it the cunning of reason that the Idea makes passions work for it, in such a way that whereby it posits itself in existence it loses thereby and suffers injury." **Hegel, *Die Vernunft in der Geschichte***

curve-fitting problem

PHILOSOPHY OF SCIENCE A problem first proposed by Legendre (1753–1833) and Gauss (1777–1855). Curve-fitting to the data on a graph is a method of inferring from observed data. If a scientist tries to connect two variables on the grounds of a set of n data points, he will join them with a curve. There might be a family of curves that fit these n points to any desirable degree. How, then, can the scientist locate the best-fitting curve? Intuitively, and also based on common sense, a smooth curve will be chosen. But why is this one the best fitting? Philosophically, there is a problem of **simplicity**, that is, how we determine the simplest curve from all those curves that pass through every one of a set of data points on a graph, and how we justify choosing it. This problem is relevant not only to the definition of simplicity but also to the problem of **induction**.

"The curve-fitting problem: two different curves are defined at all points and pass exactly through each data point, why should we think that the smooth curve is more probably true?" **Sober, *Simplicity***

cybernetics

PHILOSOPHY OF SCIENCE, PHILOSOPHY OF MIND [from Greek *kybernetes*, pilot, helmsman, governor] A term introduced by Norbert Wiener in 1947 for the study of communication and the manipulation of information in self-regulating systems and control systems, both in machines and in living organisms. Its central notion is control. Cybernetic theory is closely related to communication theory and biology, and in the popular understanding is the simulation of human data-processing and regulative functions in a digital computer. The philosophical interest in this field concerns computers that are developed by combining simple components through complex and goal-directed cybernetic processes.

"In the present content, the term [cybernetics] is used to designate the study of communication and central function of living organisms, in particular human beings, in view of their possible simulation in mechanical terms." **Syre, *Cybernetics and Philosophy of Mind***

Cynics

ANCIENT GREEK PHILOSOPHY, ETHICS [from Greek *kunikos*, dog-like, in turn from *kuon*, dog] A Greek school founded by **Socrates**' disciple **Antisthenes**, and represented by **Diogenes of Sinope**. The school got its name because it was opposed to the existing civil life and against any cultural constraints (*norm*), requiring instead that we conform to nature (*physis*), and live like dogs, that is, live shamelessly from the point of view of civil life. They not only advocated an ascetic lifestyle, but actually practiced it. Nevertheless, the Cynics were not moral nihilists. They believed that virtue is sufficient for a happy life, which lies in the freedom to do what reason requires, self-mastery of desires and feelings, and indifference to external disturbances such as wealth, social status, pleasure, and pain. They held that virtue is independent of fate and fortune and that a virtuous life is intrinsically better than a non-virtuous life. This position seeks to isolate human nature from social and historical contexts. Animal behavior is taken as a criterion of naturalness. It deeply influenced the Hellenistic ideal of sagacity and, in particular, Stoic ethics.

"One omnipresent figure since the mid-fourth century had been that of the itinerant Cynic, whose main tenets would be the absolute self-sufficiency of virtue and the total inconsequentiality of all social norms, physical comforts, and gifts of fortune." **Long and Sedley,** *The Hellenistic Philosophers*

Cyrenaics

ANCIENT GREEK PHILOSOPHY A Greek philosophical school, noted for its radical hedonism. Its origin can be traced to **Socrates'** disciple **Aristippus**, and the name is derived from his native city, the North African Greek colony of Cyrene. The founder of this school was his grandson, referred to as **Aristippus** junior (about 340 BC), and other major exponents included Anniceris, Hegesias, and Theodorus, all of whom were contemporaries of **Epicurus**. Cyrenaics claimed that because the past is gone and the future is not certain, the present enjoyment of sensual **pleasure**, that is, what they called "the smooth motion of the flesh," is the supreme good in life. Their view thus contrasted with the **hedonism** of Epicurus, which emphasized recollection and anticipation. The epistemological basis of the Cyrenaic position was their claim that momentary **perception** and feeling are the only authentic source of guidance. Its metaphysical ground is that all living creatures pursue pleasure and avoid pain by nature. The school has been criticized for ignoring those deep long-term needs that go beyond sensory gratification.

"Aristippus, a native of Cyrene (whence the name of his followers, Cyrenaics) was said to have been brought to Athens by the fame of Socrates." **Guthrie,** *A History of Greek Philosophy*

D

daimon

ANCIENT GREEK PHILOSOPHY [Greek, spirit, divinity] In Greek philosophy, sometimes **god** and sometimes an immortal spirit, that is, the divine **soul** which is incarnated in a mortal **body** but which may return to its god-like state. In another use, a *daimon* is guardian angel which looks after an individual both in life and after death. Happiness in Greek is *eudaimonia*, having a good *daimon*. **Socrates** claimed that he had a *daimon*, which ordered him to do what he did, although his *daimon* was his reason.

> "When anyone dies, his own daimon, which was given charge over him in his life, tries to bring him to a certain place where all must assemble."
> **Plato**, *Phaedo*

Dante Alighieri (1265–1321)

Italian philosophical poet, born in Florence. Although not an original philosopher himself, Dante's works provide an enduring model of the expression of philosophy in literature. His writings are infused with philosophical thought and reflections, from *Convivio*, in which he argues for the consolation of philosophy, to his ideal of peaceful secular rule to free the human intellect in *De Monarchia* and the Augustinian vision of his masterpiece *Divine Comedy*.

Danto, Arthur (1924–)

American philosopher of art, history, action, epistemology, born in Ann Arbor, Michigan, Professor of Philosophy, Columbia University. Danto has extended the range of analytic philosophy to discuss art, history, and contemporary European philosophy. His discussion of the artworld explores the context in which works can be seen as artworks. His main works include *Analytic Philosophy of History* (1965), *Analytic Philosophy of Action* (1973), and *The Transfiguration of the Commonplace* (1981).

Darwin, Charles (1809–82)

English biologist and theorist of evolution, born in Shrewsbury. Darwin's theory of evolution through natural selection brought about a revolution in our understanding of science and provided a naturalistic account of the complexity and capacities of organisms, including human beings. Discussion of his work is at the center of philosophy of biology and has influenced evolutionary approaches to psychology, society, and ethics. His major works include *On the Origin of Species by Means of Natural Selection* (1859) and *The Descent of Man* (1871).

Darwinism

PHILOSOPHY OF SCIENCE A scientific doctrine based on the work of the British naturalist, Charles **Darwin**, and in particular on his book *On the Origin of Species by Means of Natural Selection* (1859). It claims that the organic world, including the human species, came into being through a natural and gradual process of **evolution** and its major mechanism of

natural selection. Nature selects those **species** and those members of the same species that are best adapted to the environment in which they live. When we notice that members of the species S' have feature F for the sake of advantage G, we should understand this to be a result of evolution. For some members of a preceding species S had F and other members of S did not have F, but members of S that had F thereby had advantage G, and members of S without F did not have advantage G. In the long run, only members of S with F survived, so now all members of the successor species S' have F.

Because it can explain functional adaptation and the variety of species in natural terms, Darwinism rejects the **argument from design** for the existence of God and the theory of genesis. It also rejects **teleology**, since the development of an organism is determined by the environment and environment changes, hence there is no final goal for each organism other than adaptation to its environment. It also suggests that distinctions between species or natural kinds are not absolute and challenges traditional essentialism. Darwinism deprives humankind of its alleged superiority over other species by locating the species in terms of natural evolution. All the central features of Darwin's theory have provoked long-lasting debates and have dramatically changed our view of the world. The questionable attempt to introduce the notion of the survival of the fittest into an account of human society through **social Darwinism** has generated various ethical and social controversies. Darwin himself did not have an adequate theory about the nature of heredity and genetic change, and this gap has been filled by the modern science of genetics. Contemporary evolutionary theory is a neo-Darwinian synthesis of the theory of natural selection and genetic theory.

> "The one criterion for Darwinism is the abstract success or prevalence of whatever happens to prevail, without any regard for its character."
> **Bradley, *Essays on Truth and Reality***

Dasein

MODERN EUROPEAN PHILOSOPHY, METAPHYSICS [German being-there] A crucial term for **Heidegger**, but it is generally left untranslated. In traditional German philosophy, *Dasein* is broadly every kind of being or existence, and narrowly the kind of being that belongs to persons. Heidegger uses the term solely for the modes of human being. Human being must have a place *there* in the world and must be considered as **Being-in-the-world**. This Being is a human structure rather than the being of this or that particular man (*der Mensch*). Heidegger claimed that the meaning of **Being** is the subject-matter of philosophy. *Dasein* is the only kind of Being that can raise the question about Being and wonder about itself as existing. By making the understanding of Being possible, it is ontologically distinctive. Rather than being an object of some sort, *Dasein* is defined as being-in-the-world. By being viewed as a life story unfolding between birth and death, it is associated with the conception of "historicity" or "temporality." For Heidegger, any inquiry about Being must start with the investigation of *Dasein*. The analysis of *Dasein* is the inquiry into the conditions for the possibility of understanding Being in general. Instead of being an epistemological study that is concerned with our way of knowing Being, the study is an ontological investigation into what Being is. The study of *Dasein*, which is the theme of Heidegger's *Being and Time*, constitutes a necessary preliminary to the question of Being in general. The book begins with an examination of the static or formal structure of *Dasein*, and then discusses its temporal structures. To describe ourselves as *Dasein* is sharply distinct from the Cartesian view of human beings as an external combination of **mind**, as an isolated subject, and **body**.

> "This entity which each of us is himself and which includes inquiring as one of the possibilities of its Being, we shall denote by the term '*Dasein*'."
> **Heidegger, *Being and Time***

data

EPISTEMOLOGY [The singular datum from Latin *datum*, given] The materials or information from which any inquiry or inference begins. Data are the beliefs that need no further reason and that are the indispensable minimum of premises for our knowledge of the world. The data have different degrees of certainty and can be further divided into hard data and soft data. The former are the beliefs which are certain, self-evident, and are believed on their own account, and the latter are the beliefs that are found upon examination not to have this status but which are inferred from other beliefs. **Russell** always uses "data" and "hard data" as synonymous. This distinction also corresponds to another of Russell's distinctions between primitive knowledge and derivative knowledge.

> "I give the name 'data' or rather 'hard-data' to all that survives the most severe critical scrutiny of which I am capable, excluding what, after the scrutiny, is only arrived at by argument and inference." **Russell,** *Our Knowledge of the External World*

Davidson, Donald (1917–2003)

American analytic philosopher of mind and language, born in Springfield, Massachusetts, Professor of Philosophy, University of California, Berkeley. Davidson has made major contributions on a wide range of philosophical topics. His discussion of the logical form of causal and action sentences places events at the center of his ontology. He argued for a causal account of the role of reasons in explaining actions, and defended physicalism in the philosophy of mind in terms of anomalous monism rather than through systematic relations between types of mental events and types of physical events. He adopted a holistic approach to the ascription of beliefs and other propositional attitudes to individuals and supplemented Quine's theory of radical translation with a theory of radical interpretation governed by a principle of charity. He also employed this principle to counter skepticism and relativism. In philosophy of language, he adapted Tarski's theory of truth for formalized languages to provide a semantic theory of meaning for natural languages, with special attention to the difficulties arising from indexical expressions and indirect speech contexts. His major works include *Essays on Actions and Events* (1980), *Inquiries into Truth and Interpretation* (1984), and *Subjective, Intersubjective, Objective* (2001).

death

ETHICS, METAPHYSICS Death is the final cessation of life. Murder, **suicide, euthanasia, capital punishment**, and war all raise complicated moral questions about death. Questions in **medical ethics** arise because different criteria of death can come into conflict. In addition, there are moral questions concerning the death of animals. The unnatural and unwilled death of an innocent person is regarded as a harm because it deprives that person of future experiences. But it is difficult to determine whether some other deaths are straightforward harms, harms outweighed by additional concerns, or not harms at all. One can consider, for example, self-chosen death, natural death, or death legally imposed as punishment for certain major crimes, such as murder.

It is possible to ask when the harm of death takes place. Before death, the person is not yet dead, although he is capable of suffering from the anticipation of death. After death, the person is already dead and cannot suffer. Harm restricted to the moment of death would lack the weight that we normally ascribe to the harm of death.

The experience of death has been a chief concern for **existentialism**. In **Heidegger**'s analysis of *Dasein*, death reveals the terrible temporality of our existence. In this revelation, he claimed, we find the ground of our authentic existence. Everyone dies his or her own death. As an experience entirely of one's own, death cannot be shared. This experience makes one focus on one's finitude, on one's uniqueness and on one's determinate self. The analysis of death is not only the ground of **authenticity** and **freedom**, but also the ground for the totality of *Dasein*. A total perspective of *Dasein* can only be reached when one is dead. This complete account is not possible until my death actually takes place. But we may provide an account of the required sort from the first-person standpoint by being aware that "I am going to die." Death is hence characterized as Being-towards-the-end. This Being is the way one comports oneself in pondering when and how this possibility of death may be actualized. It has been widely proposed that the finitude imposed by death is part of what gives life meaning and that an immortal life is morally meaningless.

> "Death reveals itself as that possibility which is one's ownmost, which is non-relational, and which is not to be outstripped." **Heidegger,** *Being and Time*

death instinct

PHILOSOPHY OF MIND, PHILOSOPHY OF SOCIAL SCIENCE The biological basis of **Freud**'s **psychoanalysis** postulates that in mental life there are two classes of instinct, which correspond to the contrary processes of dissolution and construction in the organism. These two classes of instinct are the death instinct and the life instinct. He also expresses this contrast as the contrast between *thanatos* (Greek, death) and *eros* (Greek, love), a pair of notions that can be traced to the cosmology of **Empedocles**. The life instinct, or *eros*, establishes order and prolongs one's life. The death instinct, which is also called the destructive impulse, ego-instinct, or even the aggressive instinct, is an impulse to destroy order and to return to a pre-organic state. According to Freud, these two kinds of instinct are present in living beings in regular mixtures, and life consists in the manifestation of the conflict or interaction between them. For the individual, reproduction represents the victory of the life instinct, while death is the victory of the death instinct. Their conflict and interaction also dynamically promote the development of **culture**. The idea of the death instinct is influenced by **Schopenhauer**'s idea that the goal of life is death. There are problems with both life and death instincts. Although the life instinct could be explained in Darwinian terms, it is more difficult to see how the death instinct could be explained by **natural selection** within the process of **evolution**.

"The one set of instincts, which work essentially in silence, would be those which follow the aim of leading the living creature to death and therefore deserve to be called the 'death instincts'; those would be directed outwards as the result of the combinations of numbers of unicellular elementary organisms, and would manifest themselves as destructive or aggressive impulses." **Freud, *Standard Edition of the Complete Psychological Works of Sigmund Freud*, vol. 18**

death of art

AESTHETICS Also called end of art. On the basis of **Hegel**'s theory, the American philosopher Arthur C. **Danto** believes that art has an ultimate goal of self-realization through self-comprehension. He argues that because twentieth-century art fulfilled this goal and realized its destiny, the history of art has come to an end. In art, there is no longer a distinction between subject and object. Knowledge becomes its own object. Rather than seeking to understand the external world directly, art depends more and more on theory for its existence. Things

that are hardly works of art can now become artworks by means of an atmosphere of theory in an **artworld**. The quest for itself transforms the character of the object. Questions about what art is and what art means seem to have been answered. The traditional boundaries between art forms are no longer stable. In this situation, art is alienated more and more from the public and becomes philosophy. Artistic activities lose direction. Certainly, we continue to produce artworks, but they now miss the historical importance that art once possessed. We make works of art only by habit. Danto calls contemporary art "post-historical art." Danto has been criticized for basing the alleged death of art on a very narrow notion of art. Critics argue that because art meets the demands of human nature, so long as human nature does not come to an end, art will continue its history.

"It supposes that its own philosophy is what art aims at, so that art fulfils its destiny by becoming philosophy at last. Of course art does a great deal more or less than this, which makes the death of art an overstatement. That ours is a post-historical art, however, is a recognition deepened with each succeeding season." **Danto, *The Philosophical Disenfranchisement of Art***

death penalty, an alternative name for capital punishment

decidability

LOGIC A theory (system or set) is decidable if there is an **algorithm** for determining whether an arbitrary **well-formed formula** is or is not a theorem of the theory. If the solution is positive, there is a **decision procedure** that enables one to determine this mechanically by following a rule within a finite number of steps. The **truth-table** is a decision procedure for **propositional calculus**. **Gödel's theorem** proved that in any axiomatic system there are well-formed formulae which are not decidable within the system itself.

"A set of sentences G is decidable just in case there is a decision procedure – an effective finitary method – for determining any sentence in the language whether or not it is in G." **Chellas, *Modal Logic*** decision

decision

ETHICS [Greek *prohairesis*, decision, from *pro*, before in the sense of temporal and preferential priority + *hairesis*, choosing] In Aristotle's ethics, the origin of **action**. His theory of decision is viewed as a predecessor of the modern theory of **will**. Choice may be based on emotion and appetite, while *prohairesis* is rational choice. Decision is a **mental act** that combines both thinking and desiring and comprises both a rational desire for some good as an end in itself and deliberation about how to achieve the end. It is an impulse following upon a judgment reached by deliberation. Action or decision can be the outcome of **practical reason** in deliberation.

"For it is our decision to do what is good and bad, not our beliefs that make the characters we have." **Aristotle,** *Nicomachean Ethics*

decision procedure

LOGIC A mechanistic procedure for determining whether an arbitrary **well-formed formula** is a **theorem** of a given formal system or theory by following a rule within a finite number of steps or a procedure to determine its semantic validity. A decision procedure determines whether a well-formed formula is true under any **interpretation**. A decision procedure is an **algorithm**. For instance, the truth-table is a decision procedure for **propositional calculus**. A proof that such a procedure exists for a theory provides a positive solution to the decision problem for that theory. Otherwise, there is a negative solution. A decision procedure is also a way of finding whether a concept can be applied in any given case. A concept connected with such a procedure is called definite and is regarded as meaningful.

"A procedure of decision for a class of sentences is an effective procedure either, in semantics, for determining for any sentence of that class whether it is true or not . . . or, in syntax, for determining for any sentence of that class whether it is provable in a given calculus." **Carnap,** *Logical Foundations of Probability*

decision theory

ETHICS, PHILOSOPHY OF ACTION, PHILOSOPHY OF SOCIAL SCIENCE, POLITICAL PHILOSOPHY The mathematically oriented theory of rational choice or decision making, which aims to make clear what is the best thing to do in a given situation. There are many situations in which an agent is faced with a set of alternatives that have various degrees of risk and various probabilities of possible outcomes being realized. Sometimes the agent has only limited knowledge of the consequences of possible **actions**. Decision theory helps an agent confronted with such a situation to decide the most rational way to act given the relevant available information. The common approaches include assigning probability to the outcomes of each possible action and then either to choose the action with the maximum expected **utility** or to choose the action that is least bad compared with other alternatives. Decision theory is philosophically interesting, because it is closely associated with notions such as **preference**, **choice**, and **deliberation** and is hence widely applicable in moral and political theory. **Game theory** is one part of decision theory, for while decision theory must take into account all factors involved, including natural and blind chance, game theory only involves interactions with the choices of other rational agents.

"Decision theory as an empirical theory holds that there is some specification of alternative actions, outcomes, and beliefs about these and their probabilities, and preferences among these, such that the person acts so as (for example) to maximise expected utility." **Nozick,** *Philosophical Explanations*

deconstruction

MODERN EUROPEAN PHILOSOPHY A term introduced by the French philosopher Jacques **Derrida**, and characteristic of his thought. He believes that preceding Western metaphysical systems were established on the basis of fundamental conceptual oppositions, such as speech/writing, soul/body, transcendent/empirical, nature/culture, and good/evil. For each conceptual pair, one term was allegedly superior to the other. Deconstruction is a philosophical practice that aims to remove our thinking from the domination of these opposites by asking how they are possible. It is an analysis or critique of the meaning of linguistic expressions by attending to their use or to the role that they play in human activities. Derrida begins by demonstrating that the supposedly inferior concept within each pair has the same defining characteristics as the allegedly superior one and that there is no ground for giving priority to one over the other. He then displaces the opposition by introducing an overarching concept that avoids having the fixity or determinateness that a concept normally possesses. To a limited extent, deconstruction is similar to **Hegel**'s procedure of following the **dialectic** of thesis, antithesis, and synthesis, although Derrida repeatedly emphasizes that deconstruction is not a scientific procedure. The term can be traced to **Husserl**'s *Abbau* [German, dismantling] and **Heidegger**'s destruction of the history of **ontology**. Some commentators compare deconstruction to **Kant**'s critique of reason. Both Kant and Derrida are concerned with the possibility of **metaphysics** and the possibility of objectivity discoverable by reason. Deconstruction is not purely negative, but seeks to attain the ultimate foundation of concepts. In addition to its influence in philosophy, deconstruction has had a great impact on literary criticism.

> "All sentences of the type 'deconstruction is x' or 'deconstruction is not x', a priori, miss the point, which is to say that they are at least false. As you know, one of the principal things at stake in what is called in my texts 'deconstruction', is precisely the delimiting of ontology and above all of the third-person present indicative: 'S is P'." **Derrida, in Wood (ed.),** *Derrida and Difference*

de dicto

LOGIC [Latin, about a proposition] The distinction between *de dicto* and *de re* (about a thing) propositions gained currency with St Thomas **Aquinas**. *De dicto* propositions predicate certain terms of a subject-predicate proposition as a whole, thus forming a second-order statement. *De re* propositions predicate certain terms of a subject. This distinction has a wide application, but is particularly important in the analysis of modal propositions, that is, propositions concerning **necessity** and possibility. *De dicto* modality concerns the ascription of "necessary" or "possible" to a proposition, for example, "it is possible that Socrates is running." *De re* modality concerns the ascription of these modal terms to a subject or object, such as, "Socrates is possibly running." A *de dicto* interpretation and a *de re* interpretation will result in different truth-values for a

proposition. Controversy over the distinction has revived with the renewal of interest in modal logic and **essentialism**.

> "These terms are often explained by saying that in a modality *de dicto* necessity (or possibility) is attributed to a proposition (or *dictum*), but that in a modality *de re* it is attributed to the possession of a property by a thing (*res*)." **Hughes and Cresswell,** *An Introduction to Modal Logic*

de dicto **belief,** another term for belief *de dicto*

deduction

LOGIC [from Latin *de*, away, from + *ducere*, lead, draw] An inference which proceeds from a more general to the less general, or from the necessary to the contingent. It contrasts with **induction**, which is an inference proceeding from the particular or less general to the more general. A conclusion derived deductively is the logical consequence of the premises; hence deduction is also a process of making explicit the logical implications of general statements. A deduction is valid if it is impossible that all the premises are true while the conclusion is false. Deductive logic reveals the inferential relationship of **entailment** existing between premises and conclusions and codifies the rules of deduction. A deductive system that has been viewed as the paradigm of scientific knowledge is one in which all other rules can be deduced from a small set of **axioms** or theorems. In jurisprudence, deduction means the establishing of a legal rather than factual ground for an action. It is this meaning that **Kant** borrows in his **transcendental deduction**.

> "In deduction, a proposition is proved to hold concerning every member of a class, and may then be asserted of a particular member." **Russell,** *The Principles of Mathematics*

deduction (Kant)

PHILOSOPHICAL METHOD, EPISTEMOLOGY, METAPHYSICS
Deduction is normally used in a logical or geometrical sense for the derivation of a conclusion from premises, but **Kant** adopted a different use from the practice of jurists. The law distinguishes between the question of right (*quid juris*) and the question of fact (*quid facti*). Both these questions need to be

proved. While questions of fact are proved through experience, the proof of questions of right is called deduction. In this sense, a deduction is a proof of the legitimacy of something. In his critical philosophy, Kant set out various *a priori* intuitions and concepts, but argued that he needed to provide justification and explanation of how they can be validly applied to objects. This procedure is what he called deduction. He further distinguished three types of deduction: metaphysical deduction, which is the argument that derives the categories from the twelve forms of judgment; empirical deduction, which shows the legitimacy of applying an empirical concept in terms of our experience of empirical objects; and **transcendental deduction**, which is carried out by a **transcendental argument**. The transcendental deduction is the central argument of the *Critique of Pure Reason*.

"Now among the manifold concepts which form the highly complicated web of human knowledge, there are some which are marked out for pure a priori employment, in complete independence of all experience; and their right to be so employed always demands a deduction." **Kant,** *Critique of Pure Reason*

deductive logic

LOGIC Deductive logic analyzes the logical concepts related to deduction and classifies propositions in terms of their **logical forms**. It seeks to formulate logic explicitly by analyzing the logical forms of arguments and the relationship of valid **entailment** in deductive argument in order to reveal the forms of argument in which the conclusion is necessarily inferred from the premises. A proposition that implies a false conclusion cannot be true. An argument is valid if premises and the negation of the conclusion involve a self-contradiction.

"The task of deductive logic is often defined as the explicit formulation of the implicitly recognised rules of deductive inference." **Pap,** *Elements of Analytic Philosophy*

deductive-nomological model

PHILOSOPHY OF SCIENCE A theory of **explanation** developed by **Hempel**. On this model, an event is explained by logically deducing the sentence describing it from a law-like generalization and a statement of certain initial conditions. The law-like generalizations are called nomological generalizations or **covering laws**. This model of explanation, abbreviated as the D-N model, can also apply to the covering laws themselves. A covering law can be explained by deducing it from a higher-order covering law or body of laws. The D-N model is a sub-model of the covering law model, with the inductive-statistical model considered to be another sub-model. Because it is the variant of greatest importance and most frequent employment, the deductive-nomological model is often taken as synonymous with the covering law model.

"The general conception of explanation by deductive subsumption under general laws or theoretical principles . . . will be called the deductive nomological model, or the D-N model of explanation." **Hempel,** *Aspects of Scientific Explanation*

deep structure

PHILOSOPHY OF LANGUAGE The distinction between deep structure and surface structure is one of the most influential and significant features of **Chomsky's** theory of language. Deep structure is actually the abstract features of grammatical structure. It has some affinity with the logical structure of sentences and is closely associated with **meaning**. For Chomsky, deep and surface structure do not distinguish between profound and superficial linguistic features, but between what is **abstract** and what is **concrete** in language. Surface structure is present in the sensory or observational characterization of an utterance and is closely associated with the phonetic structure of the spoken language. This structure, according to Chomsky, cannot reveal the ambiguity of a sentence. In some cases, two sentences may mean the same but differ in their surface structures; in other cases, two sentences may have the same surface structure but differ in their syntax. Since surface structure is a poor guide to the meaning of a sentence, we need to postulate the existence of deep structure, that is, the underlying abstract structure that determines the semantic interpretation of a sentence. Deep structure does not cause surface structure. They are generally distinct, but in some cases they may coincide. However, Chomsky does not say how we can detect or identify deep structure. There has been much debate about this notion amongst linguists. Historically this distinction can be traced to **von Humboldt**'s notions of inner form and outer form, and **Wittgenstein**'s distinction of surface grammar and deep grammar in his *Philosophical Investigations*, although the latter distinction is only concerned with the use of a word.

"The syntactic component of a grammar must specify, for each sentence, a deep structure that determines its semantic interpretation and a surface structure that determines its phonetic interpretation. The first of these is interpreted by the semantic component; the second by the phonological component." **Chomsky, *Aspects of the Theory of Syntax***

defeasibility

ETHICS, PHILOSOPHY OF LAW, EPISTEMOLOGY A term for the liability of certain legal or moral principles and rules to be overridden in appropriate circumstances. In the face of **Gettier's problem**, which challenges the traditional definition of knowledge as justified true belief, a defeasibility theory of knowledge has also developed. This theory maintains that for a belief to count as knowledge, it is necessary, but not sufficient, for it to be true and justified. Because a currently justified belief might be defeated in the face of new evidence, the belief is defeasible, and its justification is merely *prima facie* justification. New evidence that overcomes justified belief can be called a defeater. It renders doubtful the connection between the belief and the original justification. Epistemologists argue whether we should define knowledge as undefeated justified true belief. A defeasible knowledge claim can be made confidently, but should recognize the possibility in principle that further evidence could give reason to withdraw the claim. A concept can also be defeasible. The standard criteria for the correct application of a defeasible concept allow for that application to be retracted in the light of further evidence. Verification of claims using defeasible concepts is never conclusive and is always open to the possibility of revision.

"The notion of defeasibility was first introduced in moral philosophy where it was applied to concepts such as duty, obligation, and responsibility.

Such concepts were said to be defeasible in that their applicability could be negated or overridden by one or other of a set of circumstances." **O'Connor and Carr, *Introduction to the Theory of Knowledge***

definiendum, see definition

definiens, see definition

definist fallacy

LOGIC Frankena's term for the mistake of defining one predicate by means of another predicate which cannot properly define it. This is the fallacy of identifying two distinct properties. He regards **Moore**'s "**naturalistic fallacy**" – the practice that attempts to define general ethical terms such as "good" in terms of some supposedly identical natural property – as a species of definist fallacy. In logic, "definist fallacy" refers more generally to a tactic in argument that defines a term in a way favorable to one's position, and then insists that the debate should continue on that basis. For example, an anti-abortion activist insists on defining a fetus as a person, and turns the debate about the morality of abortion into a debate about the morality of killing a person. Sometimes "definist fallacy" also refers to an attitude that requires that a term must be defined before it can be employed.

"The definist fallacy is the process of confusing or identifying two properties, of defining one property by another, or of substituting one property for another." **Frankena, "Naturalist Fallacy," *Mind* XLVIII**

definite description

LOGIC, PHILOSOPHY OF LANGUAGE, METAPHYSICS An expression that picks out something as the sole individual having a certain set of properties and has the form "the so-and-so." In contrast, an indefinite or ambiguous description is an expression that may apply to many different objects and has the form "a so-and-so." A definite description is not a **name**, but a complex symbol such as "The author of *Waverley*." **Russell**'s theory of definite descriptions provides a classic analysis of definite descriptions. A proposition containing definite descriptions can be analyzed into three parts: an existence condition, a uniqueness condition, and a predication. A proposition "the F is G" can be presented as "there is one and only F and it is G." In such a case, a definite description is analyzed through a contextual definition. Russell held that his theory can solve a number of **semantic** problems about the apparent reference to non-existents, as with the expression "the present King of France." It removes the burden of finding objects to which these expressions seem to refer and was seen as the central paradigm of **analytic philosophy**. But Russell's analysis was criticized by Peter **Strawson** for failing to distinguish between **sentences** and the **statements** made by the speaker in uttering the sentences.

> "I want you to realize that the question whether a phrase is a definite description turns only upon its form, not upon the question whether there is a definite individual so described." **Russell, *Logic and Knowledge***

definition

LOGIC [from Latin *definire*, limit; equivalent to Greek *horismos* or *horos*, boundary or setting a boundary] The use of an expression (Latin *definiens*, the part of the definition which does the defining) to clarify the meaning of some other expression (Latin *definiendum*, the word or expression which is to be defined). In Greek philosophy the canonical form of definition gives the **essence** or **species** of something by stating its *genus* and the *differentia* of the *genus*, thus marking off the defined species from other species of same genus. To define "man," for example, we say that it is a rational (*differentia*) animal (*genus*).

Definition increases information and prevents ambiguity and is essential for various kinds of intellectual investigation, but its nature and status are themselves a topic of philosophical debate. While essentialists like **Plato**, **Aristotle**, **Kant**, and **Husserl** hold that essential definitions reveal the essence of what is defined, **nominalists** or **prescriptivists** like **Hobbes**, **Russell**, **Quine**, and **Carnap** reject the notions of essence and real definition and hold that nominal or verbal definitions are only a matter of symbolic **convention**, and that the *definiendum* is just a word and not a **concept** as understood by realists.

Further common types of definition are: (1) lexical or reportive definitions, which clarify the meaning of an already existing term; (2) stipulative definitions, which show how an author intends to use a term; (3) functional definitions, which define something by showing what functions it performs; (4) extensional or denotative definitions, which provide a list of members to which the *definiens* can be correctly applied; and (5) intensional or connotative definitions, which reveal the common property shared by all things to which the *definiens* can be applied, although many terms lack a common property and instead have patterns of likeness which link the items to which they can be applied. In addition, there are other types of definition that are philosophically useful, such as contextual definitions, recursive definitions, inductive definitions, ostensive definitions, and persuasive definitions.

> "A definition is a phrase signifying a thing's essence." **Aristotle, *Topics***

definition by genus and difference

LOGIC [from Latin *genus et differentia*] The most generally applicable form of **intensional** definition, which conveys the meaning of a term by picking out the genus or larger class to which it belongs and the difference or attribute which distinguishes it from the other members of its genus. Hence what is achieved is a genus qualified by a specific difference. For instance, "man" is defined by "the rational" (the difference) and "animal" (the genus).

> "A definition by genus and difference assigns a meaning to a term by identifying a genus term and one or more difference words that, when combined, convey the meaning of the term being defined." **Hurley, *A Concise Introduction to Logic***

definition in use, another term for contextual definition

deflationary theory of truth, see truth

degree of belief

LOGIC, EPISTEMOLOGY, PHILOSOPHY OF SCIENCE The central notion of an account holding that belief comes in degrees rather than being a simple matter of "yes" or "no." That we have different degrees of subjective confidence in our beliefs is a basic tenet of **Bayesianism**, which argues that the subjective **probability** or degree of belief of propositions can be altered by new **evidence**, according to a procedure recommended by **Bayes's theorem**. Beliefs can be compared in the sense that the degree of belief or subjective probability of one belief is greater than another. Degrees of belief can be analyzed in terms of the degree of belief with which a belief is actually held or of the degree of belief with which it rationally should be held. Bayesian theory allows purely subjective initial assignments of degrees of belief, but applies rational discipline to the alteration of beliefs in light of new evidence, with the expectation that there will be convergence in the degrees of belief assigned to beliefs by different investigators. For **personalists** such as **Ramsey** and **de Finetti**, the consistent degrees of beliefs must conform to the rules of **probability calculus**. This notion implies a perspective from which we may quantify beliefs and suggests a possible approach to a rigorous science of behavior.

> "The degree of belief that a person S has in the sentence P is a numerical measure of S's confidence in the truth of P, and is manifested in the choices S makes among bets, actions, etc." **Garber, "Old Evidence and Logical Omniscience in Bayesian Confirmation Theory," in** *Minnesota Studies in the Philosophy of Science*, **vol. X**

degree of confirmation

LOGIC, PHILOSOPHY OF SCIENCE A term introduced by **Carnap**. If one knows what observations would be relevant to the truth or falsity of a statement, the statement is said to be confirmable. How much evidence, then, is required for one to say that the statement is actually confirmed? The degree of confirmation is the measure by which generalized statements may be ranked in order of acceptability. It is a quantitative concept of confirmation and of **probability**. If we take h to be a statement, e to be evidence, q to be a real number between 0 and 1, and c to be a symbol for degree of confirmation, then $c(h.e) = q$ or the degree of confirmation of h with respect to e is q.

> "Given certain observations e and a hypothesis h (in the form, say, of a prediction or even of a set of laws), then I believe it is in many cases possible to determine, by mechanical procedures, the logical probability, or degree of confirmation, of h on the basis of e." **Carnap,** *Philosophical Foundations of Physics*

deism

PHILOSOPHY OF RELIGION [from Latin *deus*, god] A doctrine of natural, as distinct from revealed, religion claiming that reason assures us that **God** exits, but that the mode of divine existence is absolute and transcendent. This account denies all of God's mystical relations to the world and human affairs. Divine revelations, dogma, and religious superstitions should also be excluded as fictions. Once God set the universe in motion, he intervened no more and left it to its own laws, just as a watch maker leaves a watch which has been set in motion. Although both **theism** and deism are associated with belief in the existence of God, deism is less orthodox than theism. The idea of deism can be traced to **Aristotle**'s notion of a **prime mover**, but in Christianity the term was first used by the **Calvinists** during the latter part of the sixteenth century, and developed over the following two centuries. Deism was a reaction against the attempt of medieval theology to subordinate philosophy to theology, and represented an attempt to place religion within the framework of reason. **Voltaire, Locke**, and **Kant** all took a deistic position. In modern times, deism has led to anti-authoritarian political and social positions and has promoted a growth of the spirit of **tolerance**.

> "Deism . . . uses the word 'God' . . . to refer to the great force who initially caused the universe to function but who has since that time withdrawn from any active participation or 'interference' with his artefact." **Ferré,** *Basic Modern Philosophy of Religion*

Deleuze, Gilles (1925–95)

French post-structuralist philosopher, taught at University of Paris VIII (Vincennes). Deleuze approached philosophical questions through culture, art, literature, and psychology, with a focus on desire, difference, and liberation. His account of language and thought centered on desire and the irrational. His main works include *Nietzsche and Philosophy* (1962), *Difference and Repetition* (1968), and *The Logic of Sense* (1969).

deliberation

ETHICS, PHILOSOPHY OF ACTION [Greek *bouleusis*, a prerequisite of *prohairesis*, decision] **Aristotle** discussed deliberation in the *Nicomachean Ethics*, Book 3, Ch. 3. The objects of deliberation are the things that can be calculated with probability and can be brought about by our efforts. Starting from an assumed end, that is, an accepted object of **desire** or wish, deliberation analyzes the ways and means by which the end can be achieved, and terminates in a rational choice and appropriate action. In Greek "means to the end" are things related to a goal, and the term is broader than the modern conception of instrumental means to an end. Deliberation, which enables a person to know what he must do if he is to achieve his objective, is a major feature in Aristotle's ethics and in contemporary **virtue ethics**.

"We deliberate not about ends, but about what promotes ends." **Aristotle,** *Nicomachean Ethics*

demarcation, criterion of

PHILOSOPHY OF SCIENCE **Popper** maintained that the demarcation problem, that is, the problem of distinguishing genuine scientific theories from pseudo-scientific theories, is one of the most fundamental problems for the philosophy of science. To deal with this problem, it is crucial to establish a criterion of demarcation. Popper proposed **falsifiability** as the criterion. Unless scientists state the conditions under which their theories can be refuted, their theories belong to pseudo-science. For Popper, the problem of demarcation is precisely the problem of scientific rationality and his criterion of demarcation determines the **logic of scientific discovery** and the definition of science. Critics argue that some pseudo-scientific claims satisfy the criterion and are indeed falsified, but that their proponents ignore their refutation. On this view, the demarcation becomes a matter of scientific **integrity** rather than a formal test of falsifiability. **Lakatos** argued that all theories from their inception are surrounded by falsifying instances. For this reason, demarcation cannot be sharply drawn in terms of falsification, and scientific rationality involves pursuing potentially fruitful theories. Others argue that scientific theories have histories and that only at some stages is the question of falsifiability appropriate. On this view, the question of demarcation is dealt with historically.

"... I tentatively introduced the idea of the falsifiability (or testability or refutability) of a theory as a criterion of demarcation." **Popper, in** *The Philosophy of Karl Popper*

Demiurge

ANCIENT GREEK PHILOSOPHY In **Plato**'s *Timaeus*, the divine craftsman, who made the lower gods, the soul of the universe, and the immortal part of the human soul. The lower gods in turn made all physical things. In creating, the Demiurge uses the **Forms** or Ideas as his model, works on given existing or material elements, and must persuade necessity to cooperate in order to finish the job ideally well. Although the idea of the Demiurge had great influence on Christianity, the Demiurge is thus not identical with the biblical Creator. For Plato, it is a literary device to symbolize the rational element in the world order.

"The work of the Demiurge, whenever he looks to the unchangeable and fashions the form and nature of his work after an unchangeable pattern, must necessarily be made fair and perfect." **Plato,** *Timaeus*

democracy

POLITICAL PHILOSOPHY [from Greek *demos*, people + *kratia*, mighty, powerful, literally, rule by the people] A form of government, traditionally contrasted to **aristocracy** (rule by the best), **oligarchy** (rule by the few), and **monarchy** (rule by the one). Ideally, democracy requires all citizens to join in making governmental decisions, but such pure democracy, excluding women and slaves, was only practiced for a short period in ancient Athens. The standard democratic form is representative democracy, that is, rule by a group of representatives who are elected for limited periods directly or indirectly by the people. A representative democracy governs through discussion and persuasion rather than by force. Decisions are generally made by majority vote in order that policies will reflect at least to some degree the will or interests of the people. In order to prevent the over-concentration of power, the main legislative, executive, and judicial functions of government are separated. The values and principles underlying this form of government are **liberty** and **equality**, sometimes called the democratic ideals. According to the principle of liberty, individuals should make decisions for themselves, rather than allowing decisions to be made on their behalf and imposed on them. The principle of equality requires all citizens to have an equal right to select those holding governmental office and to stand for office themselves. The active role of citizens in a democracy underlies the recognition of certain rights and liberties that shape their personality outside political life and ground the **rule of law**. Among these rights are the freedom of speech, freedom of the press, freedom of association, freedom of assembly, and protection against arbitrary arrest. It is widely believed, especially by members of Western societies and by contemporary political theorists, that representative democracy can secure a maximum of freedom and rights for citizens and a minimum of the abuse of political power. Nonetheless, there are difficulties in maintaining an authentic democratic system in the face of the overwhelming influence of wealth and power, indifference, ideological fixations, mutual hatred, and corruption. **Rousseau**'s democratic theory has clearly totalitarian aspects, and J. S. **Mill** recognized that the rights of a minority in a democracy could be violated by the majority. Part of the theory of democracy deals with the transition from lesser to greater democracy and with determining the institutional contexts in which democracy can function with stability and effectiveness.

"The sovereign may put the government in the hands of the whole people, or of the greater part of the people, so that there are more citizens-magistrates than there are ordinary private citizens. This form of government is known as democracy." **Rousseau, The Social Contract**

Democritus (c.460–370 BC)

Greek philosopher, born in Abdera. Together with his teacher Leucippus, Democritus founded ancient atomism, holding that the ultimate constituents of the universe are atoms, literally "indivisible things" or "things that could not be further divided." Atoms are real beings that are unlimited in number. They move about in the void (also called "the nothing" or "not being"). Changes among atoms are causally determined. Souls are composed of fine atoms and are not immortal. Only atoms and the void are real, although we recognize other things as a matter of

convention. Democritus was said to have written many books, but only a few fragments on ethics survive. His ethics was based on his conception of *eudaimonia*.

demonstration

LOGIC, EPISTEMOLOGY [from Latin *de*, away, from + *monstrare*, show; its Greek counterpart is *apo*, away + *deixis*, show] For **Aristotle**, demonstration was the inference of new knowledge from certain previously established knowledge or **axioms**, in contrast to intuition, which directly apprehends first principles. All **syllogism** is demonstration, although not all demonstration is syllogism. For **Descartes** and **Locke**, demonstration was the discovery of the connections of ideas and the comparison of ideas by reason alone. It amounts to rational justification and contrasts with immediate knowledge. **Hume** proposes that demonstrative knowledge is indubitable knowledge, in contrast to contingent knowledge about matters of fact. In contemporary philosophy, demonstration amounts to proof, that is, the deduction of a conclusion from one or more accepted premises by means of a set of valid rules of inference.

"In the nature of the case the essential elements of demonstration are three: the subject, the attributes, and the basic premises." **Aristotle, Posterior Analytics**

De Morgan, Augustus (1806–71)

British mathematician and logician, born in Madura, India, Professor of Mathematics, University of London. De Morgan sought to codify the principles of logic as an independent system of symbols on the model of mathematics. He contributed to the study of fallacies, logical sums and products, paradoxes, probability and rational partial belief, predication, relations, and unorthodox syllogistic reasoning. His main works include *Essay on Probabilities* (1838), *Formal Logic* (1847), *On the Syllogism* (1864), and *Budget of Paradoxes* (1872).

De Morgan rule

LOGIC A valid rule of inference for conjunction and disjunction which shows how we can move negation signs inside and outside of parentheses. It states that we can proceed from the negation of a conjunctive proposition to the disjunction of the negations of its parts, and conversely that we can proceed from the negation of a disjunctive proposition to the conjunction of the negations of its parts. To symbolize, ~(P∧Q) (not both P and Q) = ~P∨~Q (either not P or not Q); and ~(P∨ Q) (not either P or Q) = ~ P∧~Q (not P and not Q). We must notice that "not both" is not equivalent to "both . . . not," and that "not either" is not equivalent to "either . . . not." The rule is named after the nineteenth-century logician Augustus **De Morgan**, but it occurred earlier in **William of Ockham**'s work.

> "De Morgan rule . . . may be summarised as follows: when moving a negation sign inside or outside a set of parentheses, 'and' switches to 'or', and conversely." **Hurley,** *A Concise Introduction to Logic*

Dennett, Daniel (1942–)

American philosopher of mind, Professor at Tufts University. Dennett argues that many problems in the philosophy of mind arise from confusing the "intentional stance" of folk psychology and the "design stance" of a scientific cognitive psychology. Beliefs, desires, and the self are useful abstractions rather than real entities and events. In his examples and doctrines, Dennett ranges beyond philosophy to neurophysiology, artificial intelligence, and evolution. His major works include *Content and Consciousness* (1969), *Brainstorms* (1978), *The Intentional Stance* (1987), and *Consciousness Explained* (1991).

denominatio extrinseca

METAPHYSICS A **scholastic** term used in contrast to *denominatio intrinseca*. *Denominatio intrinseca* (intrinsic denomination) means a reference to a thing's intrinsic property or its inherent properties, while *denominatio extrinseca* (extrinsic denomination) is a reference to a thing's accidental properties. More narrowly, an extrinsic denomination is an experiential determination directed at a thing. For instance, being seen or being talked about is an extrinsic denomination of a thing when someone sees or talks about that thing. Thomas **Aquinas** proposes that of **Aristotle**'s ten **categories**, the first four, substance, quality, quantity, and relation, are intrinsic denom-

inations, and all others are extrinsic denominations. But the distinction is controversial, especially with regard to the status of relation. An accepted notion in contemporary philosophy is that if a relation is internal, it is an intrinsic denomination; if it is external, it is an extrinsic denomination.

> "Extrinsic denominations: denominations which have absolutely no function in the very thing denominated." **Leibniz,** *Philosophical Essays*

denominatio intrinseca, see *denominatio extrinseca*

denotation

LOGIC, PHILOSOPHY OF LANGUAGE The distinction between denotation and **connotation** was introduced by J. S. **Mill**, and corresponds to what other logicians call the distinction between **extension** and **intension**, or that between **reference** and **meaning**. Denotation is the object designated by a singular term or the class of objects referred to by a general term. Connotation is the attribute of an object, which permits the term to apply correctly to the object. Words with different connotations can have the same denotation. For instance, "the capital of the United Kingdom" and "the largest city in the United Kingdom" denote the same object, although they connote different attributes. A name, such as a **proper name**, may have a denotation but no connotation. The idea that some terms denote but do not connote and therefore do not have meaning is crucial for **Russell**'s theory of definite description.

> "If we know that the proposition 'a is the so-and-so' is true, i.e. that a is so-and-so and nothing else is, we call a the denotation of the phrase 'the so-and-so'." **Russell,** *Collected Papers of Bertrand Russell,* **vol. VI**

denoting phrases

LOGIC, PHILOSOPHY OF LANGUAGE Term introduced and analyzed in **Russell**'s important article "On Denoting." It refers to definite and indefinite **descriptions**, including those which may denote one definite object, e.g. "the present King of England," those which may be denoting phrases but do not denote anything, e.g. "the present King of France," and those which may denote ambiguously, e.g. "a man," "some men." According to Russell, denoting phrases do not have meaning in themselves, but contribute to the meaning of the whole proposition in which they occur. Thus these phrases are also called **incomplete symbols**.

> "A denoting phrase is essentially part of a sentence, and does not, like most single words, have any significance on its own account." **Russell,** *Logic and Knowledge*

denying mode, another term for *modus tollens*

denying the antecedent
Logic A logical **fallacy** of the form "if p then q, not p, therefore not q." The categorical premise denies the antecedent of the conditional premises, while the conclusion denies its consequent. For instance, "If he is sick, he does not come to work"; "he is not sick"; therefore, "he comes to work." The inference is not valid because being sick is a sufficient rather than a necessary condition for not coming to work. Hence it is not sound to deny the consequent on the basis of a denial of the antecedent. The correct form should be from the denial of the consequent of the conditional to the denial of its antecedent; that is, "if p then q; not q; therefore not p." This is called by the medieval logicians *modus tollens*, and is also called the denying mode.

> "The truth of the premises does not require the truth of the conclusion. This means that denying the antecedent is an invalid form of the simple conditional argument." **Adams,** *The Fundamentals of General Logic*

deontic concept, another term for deontic modality

deontic judgment, another name for judgment of obligation

deontic logic
Logic, ethics A kind of formal logic, also called the logic of obligation, which concerns the logical relations between propositions containing deontic modalities or concepts such as obliged, permitted, or forbidden. It was motivated by the development of **modal logic** in the twentieth century, and the observation by logicians that the words obligatory and permissible parallel the roles of **necessary** and **possible** in arguments. Deontic logic can be traced to the medieval logicians, and to **Leibniz**, **Bentham**, and Ernst Mally, but in contemporary logic it started with G. H. **von Wright**'s seminal paper "Deontic Logic" (*Mind* 60, 1951). The most systematic treatment of this logic so far is in the works of von Wright. In a sense, deontic logic is the application of formal logic to ethical notions and tends to codify the rules of **practical reasoning**. Although the discovery of **paradoxes** in formal deontic systems has led to proposals for their radical reformulation, many logicians still endorse this part of logic, anticipating the contribution of deontic logic to the development of both ethical and logical theory.

> "There are several families of concepts, the members of which exhibit in their mutual relations the same formal pattern as the modalities. An example are the deontic or normative notions: obligation, permission, and others. The formal theory of these has become known as deontic logic." **von Wright,** *Philosophical Logic*

deontic modality
Logic, ethics [from Greek *deontos*, fitting, proper or as it should be] Deontic modalities, also called deontic concepts, are the concepts implying obligation (ought to), permission (may), and forbidding (ought not to). Sentences in which these concepts occur are called deontic sentences. This term was introduced by G. H. **von Wright**, and he contrasts them with **normative** concepts such as "right" or "wrong," and **axiological** concepts such as "good" or "bad." The logic that is concerned with the logical relations between propositions containing deontic modalities is **deontic logic** or the logic of obligation.

> "The deontic modalities are about the mode or way in which we are permitted or not to perform an act." **von Wright,** *An Essay in Modal Logic*

deontology
Ethics [from Greek *to deon*, what is proper, what ought to be, or duty] An ethics based on acting according to **duty**. It concentrates on moral motives and takes **obligation** or duty as its central notion.

Deontology holds that there are certain things that are right or wrong intrinsically. We should do them or not do them simply because of the sorts of things they are, regardless of the consequences of doing them. Hence, deontology is contrasted to teleological or **consequentialist** ethics (represented by **utilitarianism**), which claims that the rightness of an action depends on whether it brings about good consequences. To lie is wrong simply because it is a lie, no matter how much happiness it can produce. There is a set of moral principles and rules that a moral agent must observe absolutely. Deontology maintains that consequentialism is wrong because the goodness of the consequences of an action does not guarantee the rightness of an action. But it is difficult for deontology to explain why certain sorts of things are wrong in themselves. Generally deontology attempts to answer this question by appeal to common sense moral intuition or to human rationality, but a satisfactory account of what makes an act wrong is still required.

Kant is the most important deontological theorist. Other major deontologists include Samuel **Clarke**, W. D. **Ross**, **Prichard**, **Butler**, and, in contemporary philosophy, Alan **Donagan**, C. Fried, and Thomas **Nagel**. Some theorists have tried to distinguish rule-deontology and act-deontology. The former determines what is right in accordance with a set of universally applied moral rules, while the latter maintains that given changing circumstances we should act in accord with particular moral judgments regarding particular situations. This distinction is not presently in fashion. Deontology and utilitarianism have been the two major trends in modern Western ethics.

The term was introduced by **Bentham**, in a manuscript entitled "Deontology," to refer to the ethics which has "for its object the learning and showing for the information of each individual, by what means the net amount of his happiness may be made as large as possible." Bentham's deontology is equivalent to utilitarianism, but this usage is largely ignored.

> "Deontological ethics . . . is any system which does not appeal to the consequences of our actions, but which appeals to conformity with certain rules of duty." **Smart and Williams**, *Utilitarianism: For and Against*

dependence thesis, see context principle

de re, see *de dicto*

de re **belief,** another expression for belief *de re*

derivative belief, see primitive knowledge

derivative knowledge, see primitive knowledge

Derrida, Jacques (1930–)
Algerian-born French post-structuralist and phenomenologist deconstructionist philosopher, born in Algiers, Professor of Philosophy at the Sorbonne and École Normale Supérieure. Derrida rejects the metaphysics of presence that he claims characterizes Western philosophy since Plato. He applies his method of deconstruction to philosophical and other texts to reveal the indeterminacy and instability of meaning. The implications of his hostility to metaphysics and to foundationalist programs in general are still being explored, and his studies of language, metaphysics, and aesthetics have been influential in cultural and literary criticism. His main works include *Speech and Phenomena* (1967), *Of Grammatology* (1967), *Writing and Difference* (1967), and *Margins of Philosophy* (1972).

Descartes, René (1596–1650)
French philosopher and mathematician, regarded as the father of modern philosophy, born at La Haye. Descartes rejected the methods and assumptions of scholasticism and sought to set knowledge on a firm basis by demanding certainty in the justification of our beliefs. His philosophical system, based on his method of systematic doubt, accepted nothing as true that could not be clearly and distinctly perceived to be true. He held that for each of us the first indubitable truth is "I am thinking, therefore I exist" (Latin *cogito ergo sum*). Descartes's focus on the primacy of epistemology shaped subsequent understanding of the nature of the philosophy. Since doubt is an imperfect state, he inferred the existence of God as a Perfect Being. Cartesian dualism argues that mind and body are distinct substances and that a human being is a union of an extended body and a thinking mind. The relation between mind and body remains a basic question

in philosophy of mind. His rationalism, search for certainty and conception of mind have also influenced phenomenology and other movements in modern European philosophy. Descartes's philosophy is best understood in relation to his contributions to the emerging modern science of his time. His major works include *Discourse on the Method* (1637), *Meditations on First Philosophy* (1641), *Principles of Philosophy* (1644), and *The Passions of the Soul* (1649). He died in Stockholm while tutoring Queen Christina in philosophy.

description, attributive use of, see description, referential use of

description, referential use of

LOGIC, PHILOSOPHY OF LANGUAGE Donnellan distinguishes between the attributive and the referential use of descriptions. In the **attributive** use, a speaker makes an assertion about whatever or whoever fits the description, without necessarily having any idea what that thing or person is. In the referential use, a speaker has a definite individual in mind and uses the description to refer to it, thus enabling his audience to pick out or identify what he is talking about. In the referential use, the description is merely a tool for achieving reference, and the reference can succeed even if the thing referred to does not fit the description. This distinction shows that our use of descriptions is complex and that descriptions do not always refer to whatever happens to fit them. Donnellan uses his distinction to criticize the analyses of descriptions offered by **Russell** and **Strawson**. Russell ignores the referential use, while Strawson seems to ignore the attributive.

"I will call the two uses of definite descriptions I have in mind the attributive use and the referential use. A speaker who uses a definite description attributively in an assertion states something about whoever or whatever is the so-and-so. A speaker who uses a definite description referentially in an assertion, on the other hand, uses the description to enable his audience to pick out whom or what he is talking about and states something about that person or thing." **Donnellan, "Reference and Definite Description," in Schwarz (ed.), *Naming, Necessity and Natural Kinds***

description, theory of

LOGIC, EPISTEMOLOGY, PHILOSOPHY OF LANGUAGE **Russell** divided description into two kinds: indefinite description, that is, phrases of the form "a so-and-so," and definite description, that is, phrases of the form "the so-and-so." He claimed that descriptions are not referring expressions, and they do not need to **denote** anything in order to be meaningful. A description is an **incomplete symbol** and is meaningful only in a sentence that contains it ("contextual definition"). Both kinds of description can be analyzed away, and can be replaced by **quantifiers** and **variables**. We can replace an indefinite description with an existential quantifier ("There is one thing that is . . .) and we can replace a definite description with a uniqueness quantifier ("There is exactly one thing such that. . . .). Russell's theory of definite descriptions has greatly influenced contemporary epistemology and logic, and has been cited as a model of philosophical **analysis**. The theory, however, is challenged by Peter **Strawson**, who argues that descriptions are, at least sometimes, referring expressions that can single out something. Keith Donnellan further argues that both Russell and Strawson are one-sided, for they fail to notice that description can be used either attributively or referentially.

"Russell appears to claim for the Theory of Description that it gives an exact account of the working of one class of definite singular terms, viz. singular descriptions, and I am bound to deny this." **Strawson, in Davidson and Hintikka (eds.), *Words and Objections***

descriptive ethics

ETHICS, PHILOSOPHY OF SOCIAL SCIENCE The description of the moral views and moral principles held by people at a particular time in a particular community. Descriptive ethics also examines resemblances and differences among these moral views, but does not commit itself to preferring one view to another. It seeks to explain ethical discourse and statements as well. While **meta-ethics** specifies the proper use of ethical terms and lays down certain rules of ethical discourse, descriptive ethics does not move beyond an account of ethical discourse by placing it within a general cultural background. Descriptive ethics is more properly a branch of anthropology rather than a branch of ethics, and some philosophers believe that one cannot gain insight in descriptive ethics without testing the ethical views and principles philosophically.

> "I shall call the investigation of the moral code and accompanying ethical conceptions of a person or group descriptive ethics." **Ladd,** *The Structure of a Moral Code*

descriptive fallacy

PHILOSOPHY OF LANGUAGE, ETHICS J. L. **Austin**'s term for the practice in the traditional theory of statements of taking all statements to be descriptive and claiming that to understand the meaning of a sentence is to understand its **truth condition**. However, Austin argued that there are many sentences, such as those used in **performative** utterances, whose meanings are not determined by their truth-conditions. They are not subjects of truth and falsity, for they do not specify or report features of reality, but are used to do something. To say "I swear . . ." is not to report that one swears, but is the act of swearing itself. This point is well developed by **non-cognitivism**, whose major theme is to distinguish factual statements from ethical statements.

> "To overlook these possibilities in the way once common is called the 'descriptive fallacy'." **Austin,** *How to Do Things with Words*

descriptive meaning

PHILOSOPHY OF LANGUAGE, ETHICS Some philosophers suggest that we distinguish between two kinds of **meaning** of expressions. Descriptive meaning contributes to a bare presentation of facts, as in the claim "This strawberry is sweet." **Evaluative meaning** functions in a different way by offering an assessment, as in the claim "This strawberry is good." The descriptive meaning of a statement can be determined by its **truth conditions**, while the evaluative meaning cannot. This is because the descriptive meaning is constant while the evaluative meaning varies with the reactions of those using the expression. For instance, "war" has a fixed and translatable descriptive meaning, but its emotive associations can give it different evaluative meanings. For some "war" evokes a feeling of terror, and for others it evokes a feeling of heroic courage. The distinction between these two kinds of meaning is crucial for the distinction between ethical

descriptivism (**cognitivism**) and non-descriptivism (**non-cognitivism**). Non-descriptivism, such as **emotivism** and **prescriptivism**, holds that ethical judgments have an element of descriptive meaning, but chiefly have evaluative meaning. In contrast, descriptivism holds that the entire meaning of moral judgments is descriptive. Descriptive meaning is also called **semantic meaning**.

> "As the descriptive meaning of 'good' in 'good apple' is different from its meaning in 'good cactus'; but the evaluative meaning is the same – in both cases we are commending." **Hare,** *The Language of Morals*

descriptive metaphysics

METAPHYSICS A term introduced by P. F. **Strawson** in *Individuals*, in contrast to revisionary metaphysics. Descriptive metaphysics aims to describe the most general features of our **conceptual scheme**, that is, to describe reality as it manifests itself to the human understanding. Conceptual analysis is its main method. Revisionary metaphysics, on the other hand, attempts to revise our ordinary way of thinking and our ordinary conceptual scheme in order to provide an intellectually and morally preferred picture of the world. Hence, revisionary metaphysicians generally like to establish a well-organized system beyond the world of experience. Strawson claims that the history of metaphysics can be broadly divided into these two kinds of metaphysics. **Aristotle** and **Kant** are considered to be the forerunners of descriptive metaphysics, and Strawson's own *Individuals* is also subtitled *An Essay in Descriptive Metaphysics*, while **Descartes**, **Leibniz**, and **Berkeley** are representatives of revisionary metaphysics. This distinction may not cover all metaphysical systems, but it has been greatly influential in reviving work in metaphysics.

> "Descriptive metaphysics is content to describe the actual structure of our thought about the world, revisionary metaphysics is concerned to produce a better structure." **Strawson,** *Individuals*

descriptive psychology

PHILOSOPHY OF MIND, MODERN EUROPEAN PHILOSOPHY The name that the German philosopher Franz Brentano gave to his psychology, in which he sought to give a pure description of the constituents of human **consciousness** and their modes of combination, in order to present a general notion of the entirety of human consciousness. According to Brentano, such a psychology enables us to know directly the human mind as it actually is. It is distinguished from genetic psychology because it is not concerned with the physiological genesis of psychological phenomena. However, Brentano considered it to be the basis for genetic psychology. Brentano's descriptive psychology had great impact on **Husserl**'s **phenomenology** and **Meinong**'s philosophy. It has also played a significant role in the philosophy of mind.

"Descriptive psychology, we said, sets itself the task of an analysing description of our phenomena, i.e., of our immediate experiential facts, or, what is the same, of the objects which we apprehend in our perception." **Brentano,** *Descriptive Psychology*

descriptivism

PHILOSOPHY OF LANGUAGE, METAPHYSICS **Hare** calls the division between descriptive and non-descriptive ethical theories a division between cognitive and non-cognitive ethical theories. Descriptivism or **cognitivism** holds that ethical statements are obtained in the same way as factual statements and accordingly that we understand the meaning of ethical judgments by determining their **truth conditions**. Both **naturalism** and **intuitionism** belong to descriptivism. Non-descriptivism or **non-cognitivism**, on the other hand, argues that ethical judgments are not the same as factual statements and that they generally are neither true nor false. Their meaning contains a descriptive element which may be decided by their truth conditions, but they are chiefly emotive or prescriptive. **Emotivism** and **prescriptivism** are both varieties of non-descriptivism.

"[T]hat moral judgements are a kind of descriptive judgements, i.e. that their descriptive meaning exhausts their meaning. This is descriptivism." **Hare,** *Freedom and Reason*

de se belief

EPISTEMOLOGY [from Latin *de*, of + *se*, self] First-person belief involving a form of self-attribution in which we recognize properties as belonging to ourselves independent of the grounds on which we ascribe properties to external things or persons, such as under descriptions or through perception. The existence of this kind of belief has raised philosophical questions about the analysis of what is believed and about our knowledge of what is ascribed to ourselves in this way. It contrasts with *de re* belief, which is about external particulars and about myself when seen as an external object.

"Perceptual beliefs of a certain sort – what philosophers call *de se* belief (e.g. that is moving) – are often silent about what it is they represent, about what topic it is on which they comment, about their reference." **Dretske,** *Explaining Behavior*

desert

ETHICS, POLITICAL PHILOSOPHY What a person ought to get or what he deserves to get according to some facts about him, such as his actions, character, or state. Virtuous persons should be rewarded by happiness in proportion to their virtue, and evil persons should be punished in proportion to the degree of evil in their actions. The idea of desert is associated with **fairness** and **justice**, but conflicts with egalitarian and utilitarian principles. Legitimate claims to desert do not always entail that others must guarantee that the claimants get their desert. However, by accepting the idea of desert, one is likely to hold that desert is essential for morality. One is also likely to hold that a just political system should promote the provision of just deserts by distributing benefits and harms according to desert. On this basis, desert is an important element in determining how we should treat persons, especially where no explicit moral principles or rules give us guidance. In contemporary political philosophy, meritarianism is the view that advocates the importance of considering deserts.

"To ascribe desert to a person is to say that it would be a good thing if he were to receive something (advantageous or disadvantageous) in virtue of some action or effort of his or some result brought about by him." **Barry,** *Political Argument*

desire

ETHICS, PHILOSOPHY OF MIND, PHILOSOPHY OF ACTION [Greek *orexis*] **Aristotle** distinguished three forms of desire: (1) *boulesis*: a wish or rational desire for objects conceived as good; (2) *thumos*: an emotional or non-rational desire for objects that appear good. Because Aristotle frequently associated it with self-assertive feelings involving pride and anger, *thumos* can also be translated as "spirit" or "temper"; (3) *epithumia*: an appetite or irrational desire for an object believed to be pleasant. These desires are associated especially with basic biological needs, such as desires for food or sex. Aristotle's classification is apparently based on **Plato**'s tripartite division of the soul, ascribing different desires to different parts of the soul. Desire, in each form, is a motive force leading to movement.

In contemporary philosophy, desire includes all kinds of wants and interests that lead one to act in order to satisfy them, in particular the wants related to bodily pleasure or certain dispositions. As a source of motion, desire is a prominent but complicated concept in moral philosophy and theory of action. Desire can be divided into intrinsic desire (a desire of something for its own sake as an end) and extrinsic desire (a desire of something as a means to further ends). This roughly corresponds to the distinction between basic and derivative desires. Desire is a basic psychological state, which is distinguished from belief because a desire never purports to represent the way the world is and because believing something to be true or good need not rationally affect our desires. This raises a matter of dispute, whether a desire is simply a fact that cannot be assessed in terms of truth and falsehood and that is not subject to rational criticism. Desire is usually ascribed to the appetitive part of the soul, but Plato believed that even reason itself has a desire for the **Good**. **Hume** argued that desire is neither true nor false, neither rational nor irrational. Another long-standing debate concerns the relationship between desire and reason in the initiation of action. Aristotle believed that both of them are involved. Hume held that reason is motivationally inert and that ethics must be based on desire. **Kant** argued that reason can itself lead one to act and that moral laws should be independent of contingent desires.

> "Desire: an animal engaged in pursuing a purpose is said to desire the condition in which it will be in relative equilibrium." **Russell,** *Collected Papers of Bertrand Russell,* **vol. IX**

despair

MODERN EUROPEAN PHILOSOPHY In ordinary language, despair is the feeling based on the belief that one cannot get what one desires. **Kierkegaard** took despair as the starting-point of his positive philosophy

of existence or his anthropological contemplation. Despair is the sense of emptiness one feels in finding that one can neither ignore nor face up to a spiritual goal. As doubt is a despair of thought, despair is a doubt of personality. It is typically presented in one's defiance of God. A person feels that he is right against God, but also that he cannot be right against God. In despair, one feels a contradictory or paradoxical existence, involving an interplay of finitude and infinitude, of the divine and the human and of freedom and necessity. It presents a contradiction between certainty that death is the end and belief that life transcends death. The opposite of despair is faith. For Kierkegaard, a person destroyed by despair is superficial. An authentic feeling of despair initiates a process by which one cultivates one's real self. Despair about one's life and its foundation is necessary if one is to move from a sensuous life to a higher form of existence. Kierkegaard's discussion of despair is a direct source of later **existentialism**.

> "If there is to be any question of a sickness unto death in the strictest sense, it must be a sickness of which the end is death and death is the end. This is precisely what despair is." **Kierkegaard,** *Sickness unto Death*

determinables and determinates

LOGIC A pair of terms introduced in the twentieth century by the British philosopher and logician W. E. **Johnson** and further specified by A. N. **Prior** and J. **Searle**. The relation between determinates and determinables is one between the special and the general. For instance, "red" is a determinate of the determinable "color," and Plato is a determinate of the determinable "man." However, the relation is significantly different from the relation between **genus** and **species**. While a species is defined by adding an independent property (differentia) to a genus, a determinate cannot be specified by conjoining a differentia with the determinable. A determinate has a distinctively positive content. If it is correct to predicate a determinate of an object, the object must fall under the corresponding determinable term. Only if a thing can be colored, for example, may we predicate red of it. Thus, the determinable is a necessary and sufficient condition of predicability of the determinate. Determinates emanate from determinables as members of mutually exclusive groups, so that all determinates under the same determinable are incompatible.

> "I propose to call such terms as colour and shape determinables in relation to such terms as red or circular which will be called determinates." **W. E. Johnson,** *Logic*

determinant judgment, see *Critique of Judgement*

determinates, see determinables and determinates

determination

METAPHYSICS, LOGIC A term for a property or characteristic, such that what is determinate can be clearly and precisely specified, whilst an indeterminate thing can be specified only vaguely and without precision.

Determination also refers to **relations** between objects, including material things, events, ideas, and states of affairs, such that the existence, occurrence, or character of the items that are determined is fixed by the items that determine them. Accordingly, we may infer from knowledge of certain items in such relations to knowledge of certain other items related to them. Some philosophers claim that determination in this sense is identical with **causation**, for "A causes B" amounts to "A determines B." Others claim that determination is a relation between mathematically idealized states, while causation involves relations between observable changes of state. Still others argue that causation is only one form of determination. The relationship between determination and causation depends largely on how one understands the notion of "causation." Some philosophers also propose that there can be a relation of determination between a thing and itself, that is "self-determination."

> "As for 'determination', I do not mean final discovery of truth, but only enough examination to reach a decision as to whether a given statement or its negate is to be admitted as evidence for the hypothesis in question." **Goodman,** *Fact, Fiction and Forecast*

determinism

METAPHYSICS The theory that every event has a **cause**, and that all things in the universe, including human beings, are governed by causal laws and operate in accordance with them. Given such and such conditions, some specified thing must happen. There are many versions of determinism in addition to causal determinism. Ethical determinism, which can be found in **Plato, Aquinas,** and **Leibniz,** claims that human voluntary actions are determined by the true end or good. Logical determinism claims that a given future event must either occur or not occur. The prediction before the event that whatever happens would happen will turn out to have been correct, as can be shown purely by logical considerations of **future contingents**. Theological determinism, which can be found in **Augustine, Spinoza,** and **Leibniz,** infers from God's will that the existing world is the only possible world, so we have to accept it and find our own places in it. It also infers from God's **omniscience** and **omnipotence** that everything that happens is inevitable. There are also varieties of causal determinism. Physical determinism, advocated by the **Epicureans** and especially by **Hobbes,** holds that all things, including human actions, are determined by eternal and inviolable laws of nature. Psychological determinism, which is elaborated by **Hume** and others, considers that human behavior is caused by psychological events within the mind of the agent. Each version of determinism has its opponents. The discussion of determinism is as old as philosophy itself and has produced a vast literature. The principal problem concerns the relation between determinism and **free will** or human **choice**. If determinism is true, how can we account for freedom and moral **responsibility**? Soft determinism claims that free action is still possible in a deterministic world, whilst hard determinism regards free will as illusory.

> ". . . if there is a coherent thesis of determinism, then there must be a sense of 'determined' such that, if that thesis is true, then all behaviour whatever is determined in that sense." **Strawson,** *Freedom and Resentment*

determinism, hard, see determinism, soft and hard

determinism, principle of, another term for causality, principle of

determinism, soft and hard

METAPHYSICS, PHILOSOPHY OF ACTION A distinction between soft determinism and hard determinism is drawn by William **James**. By soft determinism, he means all those theories, like those of **Hobbes**, **Hume**, and **Mill**, that affirm that determinism is true, but deny that determinism has the implication that people are not morally responsible. These theories, then, seek somehow to reconcile determinism with morals. By hard determinism, on the other hand, he means those theories holding that people are completely governed by natural laws and are therefore not responsible for what they are or for what they do. On this view, freedom is only an illusion. Representatives of hard determinism are philosophers such as Baron **D'Holbach**, **Schopenhauer**, and Hospers. In short, while hard determinism contrasts determinism with **free will**, soft determinism thinks that they are compatible. Hard determinism belongs to **incompatibilism**, and soft determinism to **compatibilism**. Currently most defenders of determinism argue for soft determinism.

> "Old-fashioned determinism was what we may call hard determinism . . . Nowadays we have a soft determinism which abhors harsh words, and repudiating fatality, necessity, and even predetermination, says that its real name is freedom."
> **W. James**, *Essays in Pragmatism*

deterrence

ETHICS, POLITICAL PHILOSOPHY The threat or warning that retaliation will follow if another party commits a transgression. Its purpose is to prevent harmful and unjust offense. The morality of deterrence is a heatedly debated topic due to its connection with **capital punishment** and especially with nuclear strategy. The arguments that seek to justify the necessity of capital punishment are chiefly based on its function as a deterrent, that is, on the expected reduction of murders and other violent crimes in a society in which murderers are executed. The major ground for the justification of the possession of nuclear weapons is also its function as a deterrent, that is, the expected consequence of preventing war. However, deterrence itself involves many paradoxes. Should deterrence be sincere, so that retaliation will be carried out if the threat fails, or insincere, so that retaliation will not be carried out if the threat fails? If it is insincere, is it morally ruled out as a form of lying? If it is sincere, would retaliation carry the risk of violating any conception

of a just war by punishing innocent people and punishing the offense disproportionately? Should we only threaten what we may morally do? If this is the case, the function of deterrence in maintaining the real goods of peace and stability will be undermined. But if we must threaten to do what is morally wrong, then how can deterrence itself be permissible? Different and conflicting moral principles will lead to different and conflicting answers to these questions about deterrence.

> "It is doubtful whether threats of punishment have as much deterrent value as it is often supposed."
> **Brandt**, *Ethical Theory*

deus sive natura

METAPHYSICS, PHILOSOPHY OF RELIGION [Latin, God or nature] **Spinoza** claimed that there is only one **substance** in which all **attributes** and **modes** inhere, but that this substance has two names: **God** or **nature**. This is the first principle of Spinoza's metaphysical system and the chief characteristic of his **pantheism**. God might be conceived to be the creator of the world, and nature might be conceived to be that which God created, but God is nature, and nature is God. There is no formal distinction. Spinoza thus denied the contrast between God and the world, a thesis essential for Christianity. Philosophers have discussed the consequences of his position, as well as the methodological basis of his metaphysical arguments.

> "There can only be one substance, and this Spinoza called 'God or Nature' (Deus sive Natura)." **N. Smart**, *Historical Selections in the Philosophy of Religion*

developmentalism

ANCIENT GREEK PHILOSOPHY Also called the genetic method, Werner Jaeger's method for dealing with **Aristotle**'s thought, elaborated in *Aristotle: Fundamentals of the History of His Development* (1923). Aristotle's thought is traditionally interpreted as a unified organic system. Jaeger, however, claimed that there was an intellectual development in Aristotle from his early **Platonism** to the **empiricism** of his later period. He believed that it was impossible to explain the peculiar state of Aristotle's extant writings without the supposition that they belonged to different stages in his evolution of thought. His interpretation greatly influenced Aristotelian scholarship in the twentieth century and still offers a major approach to reading Aristotle. Nevertheless, Jaeger's own developmental picture has been widely criticized, especially by G. E. L. **Owen**, who argued that Aristotle started by attacking Platonism and later developed a position closer to Platonism.

> "Despite the number of developmental studies that have been carried out the complex task of reassessing Aristotle has still only just begun. So far other scholars have hardly been much more successful than Jaeger was in gaining acceptance for their interpretations of the way Aristotle's thought developed." **Lloyd,** *Aristotle*

deviant causal chain, another name for wayward causal chain

deviant logic

LOGIC A term for a non-classical or non-standard logic. These logic systems establish different sets of theorems or valid inferences from those established by classical or standard logic, and are proposed as rivals to the latter. Some deviant logics, for example, reject the principle of **bivalence** in classical logic. Deviant logics include **many-valued logic**, **intuitionist logic**, quantum logic, and **free logic**. They contrast with extended logics, which introduce new vocabulary and new theorems to classical logic and hence are extensions rather than rivals to it. Examples of extended logics are **modal logic**, **tense logic**, **deontic logic**, and epistemic logic.

> "A 'deviant logic' is a system which is a deviation of classical logic." **Haack,** *Philosophy of Logics*

Dewey, John (1859–1952)

American philosopher and a theorist of education, born in Burlington, Vermont, taught at Michigan, Chicago, and Columbia. Dewey was a leading exponent of pragmatism, although he preferred to call his own philosophy "instrumentalism" or "experimentalism." Rather than building a system or seeking to establish abstract truth, philosophy is a method to solve problems and to guide and transform our experiential situations. The standard of knowledge is "warranted assertibility," according to which a judgment is warranted if it does the work which it is supposed to do. Any warranted assertion is fallible and must be revised and refined by being subjected to continuous testing in experience. We begin with experience and return to experience. Different ways of understanding the world, such as science, art, and religion, can be seen to be mutually complementary. Dewey's theory of education sought the individual's development of problem-solving skills to deal with an ever-changing world. The ideal social structure allows for the maximum self-development of all individuals. Dewey's main philosophical works include *Experience and Nature* (1925), *The Quest for Certainty* (1929), *Art as Experience* (1933), and *Liberalism and Social Action* (1935).

dialectic (Hegel)

METAPHYSICS, LOGIC, PHILOSOPHY OF MIND **Hegel's** conception of dialectic was influenced by **Kant's antinomies** and **Fichte's** triadic process of thesis, antithesis, and synthesis. Hegel claimed that **contradictions** are universally present and account for all **change** and movement in both thought and the world. Through dialectic, thought as understanding first holds a **category** as a concept that is finite and independent of other concepts; secondly, thought as negative reason recognizes that the initial concept depends for its meaning on being contrasted with its negation; and thirdly, thought as positive reason reaches a higher category, which embraces both earlier contradictory categories in a unity of opposites, but also contains a contradiction in itself. This tripartite structure of opposition and subsequent reconciliation keeps repeating until the complete system of concepts is reached. Hegel claimed that dialectic is not merely a process of thinking, but is a development conducted by concepts themselves and by the **absolute idea**. More important, dialectic also constitutes the autonomous self-development of the world. He claimed that a thing develops by changing into its opposite and then resolves the contradiction into a synthesis. The process continues until it arrives at complete perfection. This tripartite structure is also the architectonic structure of Hegel's philosophy. Some philosophers seek to retain Hegel's attempt to understand change and development in thought and the world, but reject the rigidity of his dialectical structure.

"It is customary to treat Dialectic as an adventitious art, which for very wantonness introduces confusion and a mere semblance of contradiction into definite notions . . . But by Dialectic is meant the indwelling tendency outwards by which the one-sidedness and limitation of the predicates of understanding is seen in its true light, and shown to be the negation of them." **Hegel,** *Logic*

dialectic (Kant), see canon, transcendental dialectic

dialectical materialism

METAPHYSICS, EPISTEMOLOGY, PHILOSOPHY OF SOCIAL SCIENCE The general name for Marxist philosophy, although it is sometimes distinguished from **historical materialism** in virtue of its focus on ontology and epistemology. Dialectical materialism provides the fundamental principles of **Marxism**, with historical materialism showing how these principles are worked out in society and history. Influenced by **Hegel**'s dialectic and Ludwig **Feuerbauch**'s materialism, it seeks to provide an organic combination of dialectic and materialism. In opposition to **idealism**, it holds that **matter** is the primary being and that mind is subordinate. Matter can exist without mind, but mind cannot exist without matter. Sense-experience reveals the existence of an external and objective world. In contrast to mechanistic materialism, it holds that the material world is not static. Things are full of **contradictions** or opposites, which drive them into a continuous process of development. This development is progressive through recognizing and reconciling the inherent contradictions. The basic principles of development include the law of the transformation of quantity into quality, the law of the interpenetration of opposites, and the law of negation of the negation. Dialectic materialism is the basis of Marxist theories of social change and revolution and has formed an essential part of communist ideology. The theory was founded by Marx and expounded in detail by Engels in *Anti-During* (1879) and *Ludwig Feuerbach and the Outcome of Classical German Philosophy* (1888). It was further developed by Lenin in *Materialism and Empiriocriticism* (1909). Neither Marx nor Engels used the term "dialectical materialism" to refer to their materialism. **Plekhanov** first adopted the term to refer to the metaphysical framework of Marxism.

"The latest discoveries of natural science – radium, electrons, the transmutation of elements – have remarkably confirmed Marx's dialectical materialism." **Lenin, "The Three Sources and Three Component Parts of Marxism,"** *Collected Works*

dianoia

ANCIENT GREEK PHILOSOPHY, PHILOSOPHY OF MIND [Greek, intelligence, mind, thinking, reasoning, from the verb *dianoeisthai*] A term used in different related ways. First, *dianoia* is mind or thinking in general, in contrast to body (*soma*). Secondly, it is thought or intelligence, divided by **Aristotle** according to whether it is concerned with study (*theoria*), with production (*techne*), and with action (*phronesis*). Thirdly, it is rational understanding or discursive thinking, in contrast to intuitive thinking (*nous* or *noesis*). Fourthly, in **Plato**'s simile of the line, it is the state of mind that is concerned with mathematical entities, that reasons from hypothesis, and that reaches conclusions with the aid of the sensible objects rather than reasoning from unhypothetical first principles.

"When *dianoia* is concerned with study, not with action or production, its good or bad state consists in being true or false." **Aristotle,** *Nicomachean Ethics*

dichotomy, paradox of

ANCIENT GREEK PHILOSOPHY, LOGIC Also called the stadium or racetrack paradox, one of **Zeno of Elea**'s arguments to show that **motion** is impossible. If somebody wants to move from A to B, he must first reach the halfway point between A and B; but before reaching the halfway point, he must reach the halfway point between A and that halfway point, and so *ad infinitum*. Thus to move any distance at all, one must cover an infinite number of halfway points, which is impossible in any finite time. Therefore, it is logically impossible for someone to move from A to B. **Aristotle**'s first diagnosis of this paradox was that a finite time is also infinitely divisible and that will be sufficient for someone to move an infinitely divisible distance. He later decided that that response was not adequate, and claimed instead that the infinite number of halves is only a potential, rather than an actual, infinity. Contemporary philosophers and mathematicians are still inquiring whether it is really impossible to complete an infinite series of tasks; if it is impossible, whether the impossibility is a logical one or merely a physical one and what the impossibility really consists in. Many answers have been proposed, but none is generally accepted.

> "For we have many arguments contrary to accepted opinion, such as Zeno's that motion is impossible and that you cannot traverse the stadium." **Aristotle, *Topics***

dictum de omni et nullo

LOGIC [Latin, said of all and none] A principle which some medieval logicians believed to be the principle of the first figure of **syllogism**, and which others even thought to be a principle underlying all valid syllogistic reasoning. Among its various formulations, one version is that "whatever is affirmed or denied universally of something is also affirmed or denied of anything of which that thing is predicated of." This is alleged to be derived from **Aristotle**, *Prior Analytics*, 24b26. A related version is "what qualifies an attribute qualifies a thing possessing it." This is claimed to be based on Aristotle's *Categories* 1b10. But modern logicians believe that Aristotle never intended such a principle for his syllogism, even for its first figure. Indeed, it is impossible that this principle covers all valid moods of syllogism.

> "The *dictum de omni* [*et nullo*] defines the relation of subject and predicate, so that 'Any A is B' is to be understood as meaning 'To whatever A is applicable, B is applicable'." **Pierce, *Collected Papers*, vol. II**

Diderot, Denis (1713–84)

French Enlightenment philosopher and writer, born in Langres. Diderot was a follower of Locke, and advocated an anti-religious, materialist, and scientific world view. He wrote novels, satires, and critical essays on art, science, commerce, religion, and politics. He is best known as the principal editor of the *Encyclopédie*, or *Critical Dictionary of Sciences, Arts and Trades* (35 vols., 1751–76), a work that became the centerpiece of the French Enlightenment. His other works include *Philosophical Thoughts* (1746), *An Essay on Blindness* (1749), *Thoughts on the Interpretation of Nature* (1754), and *Rameau's Nephew* (1767).

differance

MODERN EUROPEAN PHILOSOPHY, PHILOSOPHY OF LANGUAGE, METAPHYSICS [French *différance*] A term introduced by **Derrida** from the French verb "*différer*," meaning both "to differ" (to be other, not to be identical) and "to defer" (to temporize, to take recourse in the temporal mediation of a detour that suspends the fulfillment of desire). Differing, corresponding to the Greek *diapherein*, is related to spatiality and is the root of all conceptual oppositions. Deferring, on the other hand, is related to temporality and involves the perceptual change in the relationship of determining meaning between the linguistic chain and the extralinguistic world. With this neologism, Derrida tries to suggest that while traditional **metaphysics** is concentrated on "**presence**," the meaning of language is always deferred because linguistic meaning is associated with the use of language and cannot be present in language as structure. In a productive movement, differance is an oscillation between differing and deferring. It is the condition for the possibility of all objects and the condition for the opening of **Heidegger**'s ontological difference between Being and beings. It is the irreducible difference of all differences. For Derrida, differance indicates the impossibility of achieving a theoretical account of a thing's inner structure and serves as the condition for the deconstruction of metaphysics.

> "In a conceptuality adhering to classical strictures, 'differance' would be said to designate a constitutive, productive, and originary causality, the process of scission and division which would produce or constitute different things or differences. But because it brings us close to the infinitive and active kernel of differer, differance (with an a) neutralizes what the infinitive denotes as simply active." **Derrida, *Margins of Philosophy***

difference principle

POLITICAL PHILOSOPHY **Rawls**'s second principle of **justice** includes two parts, the first requiring fair equality of opportunity and the second, called the difference principle, constraining the distribution of social and economic inequalities so that the position of the least advantaged members of society will be as good as it can be. Inequalities in income, wealth, and office can be tolerated so long as they involve a continuous mutual improvement. The operation of this principle does not aim to reduce the advantage of more-favored individuals, but rather to improve the situation of less-favored ones. The principle involves a basic contrast with the **utilitarian** pursuit of social arrangements that promote the **greatest happiness** of the greatest number, and sharply conflicts with the **social Darwinist** suggestion that the unfit should be eliminated for the advantage of society. Commentators have raised problems concerning the relations between the difference principle and the other principles of justice advanced by Rawls. The principle has been vigorously debated by those who seek a more egalitarian principle and by those who argue that it is unjust to enforce Rawlsian constraints on the distribution of goods. In particular, Robert **Nozick** argues that individuals are entitled to goods that they have legally acquired whatever the pattern of distribution turns out to be.

"Then the difference principle is a strongly egalitarian conception in the sense that unless there is a distribution that makes both persons better off (limiting ourselves to the two-person case for simplicity), an equal distribution is to be preferred." **Rawls,** *A Theory of Justice*

differentia, see genus, definition

dignity
ETHICS, POLITICAL PHILOSOPHY A prominent attribute of human beings, an object of respect that is independent of such factors as race, gender, talent, wealth, or social rank, and is purely rooted in human reason and autonomy. The notion of human dignity was emphasized in the Renaissance, and is fully elaborated in **Kant**'s ethics. Any agent who is morally authentic has personal dignity. Since human beings have dignity, they must be treated as ends in themselves, rather than merely as a means to other ends. Traditionally, human dignity has been considered to be the basis of moral worth, and human beings have been held to be the only objects of moral consideration. In contemporary ethics, the notion of human dignity is challenged. According to behaviorists and **Freud**, the noble account of humanity is false, because the majority of human actions are determined by desires and dispositions rather than being guided by reason. Proponents

of animal ethics accuse this notion of being the product of **speciesism**. **Utilitarians** also believe that human dignity is not supreme and can be overridden to obtain the best consequences. In spite of these challenges, human dignity is widely upheld, in part because it provides intelligible grounds for human **rights** and self-respect.

"That which constitutes the condition under which alone anything can be an end in itself, this has not merely a relative worth, i.e. value, but has an intrinsic worth, that is dignity." **Kant,** *Critique of Practical Reason*

dilemma
LOGIC In ordinary language, a dilemma is a situation in which one has to make a choice between two or more conflicting but equally important alternatives. **Ryle** used the term for theoretical situations in which a thinker is strongly inclined to support different positions and embracing one of these positions would seemingly oblige him to repudiate the others. In logic, a dilemma is a form of argument consisting of two conditionals and one disjunction. They are divided into constructive dilemmas and destructive dilemmas. Each is subdivided into one complex form and one simple form. The simple constructive form is: if p then q; if r then q; p or r; therefore q. The complex constructive form is: if p then q; if r then s; p or r; therefore q or s. The simple destructive form is: if p then q; if p then s; not-q or not-s; therefore not-p. The complex destructive form is: if p then q; if r then s; not-q or not-s; therefore not-p or not-r.

"A dilemma is a formal argument containing a premise in which two or more hypotheticals are conjunctly affirmed, and a second premise in which the antecedents of these hypotheticals are alternatively affirmed or their consequences alternatively denied." **Keynes,** *Formal Logic*

dilemma of attention
EPISTEMOLOGY A problem for the notion of a **sense-datum**. A sense-datum is generally conceived as being what is directly present in perception and as being incorrigible. However, it is a fact that what is present in perception will be different according to whether one perceives inattentively or carefully. For instance, when we look at a speckled hen, at

first glance it is perceived vaguely as being speckled, but a close look will show the color and shape of the speckles and we may also come to know their size and number. The sense-datum theory faces a dilemma in explaining this phenomenon: it is forced either to admit that the sense-data change with the change of attention, or to say that the accuracy of sense-data varies. If it admits the former, we have difficulty in understanding how the change in attention, which is merely a change in the mode of awareness, can affect a change in the object. If it says the latter, then sense-data cannot be incorrigible. While **Ayer** insists on the incorrigibility of sense-data, and hence admits that sense-data are different in different situations, **Price** maintains that sense-data are consistent at the expense of their incorrigibility. Since the example of the speckled hen is widely employed to illustrate the problem, this dilemma is also called the problem of the speckled hen.

"Apart from the weakness of those arguments [for the existence of sense-data] the final conception of sense-data involves serious difficulties. The first is the dilemma of attention." **Hirst,** *The Problem of Perception*

Dilthey, Wilhelm (1833–1911)

German philosopher, born at Biebrich, Professor at the University of Berlin 1882–1905. Dilthey's main work concerned hermeneutics and the philosophy of history. His philosophy of life understood philosophy to be the systematic interpretation of human experience. He sought to answer the question "How is meaningful experience possible?" and took meaning to be a category that is peculiar to life and the historical world. Since the *Geisteswissenschaften* (human or cultural sciences), with a common subject of man, provide the broadest possible knowledge of the wealth and variety of life, clarifying the nature and methodology of the human sciences became the central theme of Dilthey's philosophy. He claimed that, in contrast to the natural sciences, human sciences have a distinct methodology, namely *Verstehen*, the interpretative understanding of the subject's purposes, values, and meaning. His principal writings include *Introduction to the Human Sciences* (1883), *Experience and Poetry* (1905), *Formation of the Historical World in the Human Sciences* (1910), *The Types of World Views* (1911).

diminished responsibility

PHILOSOPHY OF LAW Some defendants who satisfy the *mens rea* criterion can still provide evidence to prove that they committed a crime when their mentality was abnormal. Such mental conditions do not constitute insanity, but substantially impair the defendant's powers of control, judgment, and reasoning. Hence, the defendant is not fully accountable for his action. If such an excuse is acceptable, the defendant's responsibility for the crime is also diminished and this can reduce a conviction to a less severe crime, although it does not justify total acquittal. The idea of diminished responsibility was introduced in England by statute in 1957. This partial defense applies mainly in murder cases. If a plea of diminished responsibility is successful, a person accused of murder might be found guilty only of manslaughter.

"[T]he doctrine of diminished responsibility . . . provides that a person who kills should not be convicted of murder if he was suffering from such abnormality of mind as 'substantially impaired his mental responsibility', but only of manslaughter carrying a maximum penalty of imprisonment for life." **Hart,** *Punishment and Responsibility*

Ding an sich, the German term for thing-in-itself

Diogenes of Sinope (*c*.400–*c*.325 BC)

Greek philosopher, born in Sinope, a major figure of the Cynic movement. Diogenes maintained that the true way of life is living according to nature. Because society is artificial, we should reject conventional values and social establishments. He claimed that, rather than being a citizen of any given society, he was a citizen of the universe. He argued that virtue is sufficient for happiness and lies in self-sufficiency and that physical asceticism is a means to attain virtue. Diogenes' doctrines greatly influenced every aspect of Stoic philosophy.

Dionysian/Apollonian

MODERN EUROPEAN PHILOSOPHY, AESTHETICS In the *Birth of Tragedy*, **Nietzsche** characterized the Dionysian and Apollonian as two natural artistic powers. The Apollonian is associated with dreams and illusions and is the impulse to create harmony and measure and to establish proportionate form amid the flux of change. The Dionysian, in contrast, is associated with intoxication and is the impulse to disrupt and to change established orders and norms. This duality developed in Nietzsche from the basic impulses operative in art into the basic tendencies discernible in human life and in nature. He viewed the two tendencies as different expressions of a single fundamental impulse: the **will to power**. In his later usage, the Dionysian is no longer opposed to the Apollonian, but becomes a synthesis of both gods. The world itself is described as a Dionysian one, which is eternally self-creating and eternally self-destroying, that is, a world characterized by the process of eternal recurrence.

> "Much will have been gained for esthetic once we have succeeded in apprehending directly – rather than merely ascertaining – that art owes its continuous evolution to the Apollonian–Dionysiac duality, even as the propagation of the species depends on the duality of the sexes, their constant conflicts and periodic acts of reconciliation." **Nietzsche,** *The Birth of Tragedy*

direct intention

PHILOSOPHY OF ACTION, ETHICS, POLITICAL PHILO-SOPHY **Bentham** distinguished between direct intention and oblique intention. Direct intention is what is directly or strictly aimed at, including both the ends and the means to achieve the ends. These are the agent's deliberate and voluntary **choices**, for which he claims direct **responsibility**. Oblique intention, on the other hand, is the foreseen consequences of the agent's voluntary actions, which lie outside the range of what is strictly pursued. This distinction is closely related to the problem of **double effect**, which contrasts the deliberate effects produced by an action and its foreseen but undesired effects.

> "A consequence, when it is intentional, may either be directly so, or only obliquely. It may be said to be directly or linearly intentional, when the prospect of producing it constituted one of these links in the chain of causes by which the person was determined to do that act." **Bentham,** *An Introduction to the Principles of Morals and Legislation*

direct realism

EPISTEMOLOGY A type of perceptual realism that claims that the physical world is independent of perceivers and that what we perceive directly is the nature of the physical objects themselves. This position contrasts with **anti-realist** positions such as **phenomenalism**, which claims that there is no real physical world outside of experience. It also contrasts with another type of perceptual realism – **indirect realism** – which argues that the physical world is only perceived indirectly and that **sense-data** are what we immediately experience. There are two main versions of direct realism. **Naive realism** believes that all perceptual properties are in the physical objects, while scientific direct realism suggests, on the basis of **Locke**'s distinction between ideas of **primary and secondary qualities**, that our ideas of secondary qualities are relative to the existence and sensory capacities of a perceiver.

> "Direct realism holds that in sense-perception we are directly aware of the existence and nature of the surrounding physical world." **Dancy,** *Introduction to Contemporary Epistemology*

dirty hands

ETHICS, POLITICAL PHILOSOPHY A term that was derived from the title of **Sartre**'s 1948 play *Dirty Hands* (*Les Mains Sales*) and which is widely used by contemporary moral and political philosophers in describing political activities that violate the common demands of morality. It is not clear whether dirty hands can be avoided in politics and whether immoral acts considered necessary to govern can be excused. According to ideas developed by **Machiavelli**, **Hobbes**, and Max **Weber**, it is necessary for political rule to be violent, deceitful, and immoral, and a politician would be naive to act on the assumption that others will comply with morality. Furthermore, it is necessary sometimes for a politician to do evil in order to achieve a greater good for the community. Because political reasons must sometimes override moral considerations, the demands of politics are incompatible with private virtue. **Aristotle**, on the other hand, held that political activity is necessary to achieve the full development of virtue and consequently politics cannot stand outside of ethics.

"It is cases where the politician does something morally disagreeable, that I am concerned with: the problem that has been called that of dirty hands. The central question is: how are we to think about the involvement of politicians in such actions, and about the dispositions that such involvement requires?" **Williams, in Hampshire (ed.),** *Public and Private Morality*

disappearance theory of mind, another name
for eliminative materialism

discourse

PHILOSOPHY OF LANGUAGE, ETHICS, POLITICAL PHILO-
SOPHY, MODERN EUROPEAN PHILOSOPHY Generally,
discourse is a linguistic sequence longer than a single sentence, and containing sentences or statements as its minimal unit. Conversation, dialogue, narrative, and argument are all considered forms of discourse. The study of discourse takes account of speakers and hearers involved in the discourse and the temporal and spatial placement of the discourse. In contemporary continental philosophy, discourse is viewed as the basis on which to defend the legitimacy of social and political practices, in contrast to traditional accounts of such legitimacy based on reason or a theory of human nature. On some views, the aim of discourse is to achieve consensus about those interests that are generalizable. Through showing how sentences are related through various types of relations, discourse analysis seeks to uncover the norms governing our language and institutions. An ethics based on discourse tends to offer a set of norms and practices that are fully acceptable to those subject to them. **Discourse ethics** aims at a **community** based not on imposition, but on the agreement of free and equal persons.

"The word 'discourse' will be used to refer to a string of statements regardless of what type these statements may be. An argument is an example of discourse." **Ladd,** *The Structure of a Moral Code*

discourse ethics

ETHICS, POLITICAL PHILOSOPHY, PHILOSOPHY OF LAN-
GUAGE The ethical theory that **Habermas** attempts to establish in *The Theory of Communicative Action*. According to the theory, the search for fundamental ethical principles should focus on the structure of practical discourse or on the fundamental norms of rational argumentative speech. Moral practice is fundamentally structured around the imperatives of a species that is dependent upon linguistically coordinated action. Communication has its own rationality and normative content, which will inevitably involve the reciprocal recognition of validity claims. Any claims about what is **right** can be justified when challenged only through argumentative discourse leading to rationally motivated consensus. This argumentation is understood as a procedure for the exchange and assessment of information and reasons. Discourse is the medium in which the ethical aspects of our idealizing suppositions are most transparent and most easily reflected upon. This character of discourse allows us to transcend strategic action and to act according to obligations based upon mutual understanding. The approach of discourse ethics is **deontological**, **cognitive**, and **universalistic**, and is hence opposed to **communitarian** moral theory. To some extent, discourse ethics is regarded as a reconstruction of **Kantian** ethics by shifting the basis from our reflecting moral consciousness to a **community** of subjects in dialogue. It is also called **communicative ethics**.

"Whereas the communitarians appropriate Hegel's legacy in the form of an Aristotelian ethics of the good and abandon the universalism of rational natural law, discourse ethics takes its orientation for an intersubjective interpretation of the categorical imperative from Hegel's theory of recognition but without incurring the cost of a historical dissolution of morality in ethical life." **Habermas,** *Justification and Application*

discrimination

ETHICS [from Latin *discrimen*, that which separates]
To discriminate may simply be to make a distinction. In ethics, it involves distinguishing a group of people from others for unfair and harmful treatment on some unjustified grounds, often on the basis of bias or prejudice. Discrimination conflicts with the principles of **justice** and **equality**. Discrimination against women on the grounds of gender is called **sexism**. Discrimination against black people and other minorities on the grounds of race is called **racism**. Some groups, like women and minorities, have long been unfairly treated and remain disadvantaged even

after beginning to receive equal treatment. In recent years, in Western countries there has been a movement to correct entrenched injustice based on past discrimination and to establish equality of opportunity by deliberately making policies to treat these groups preferentially in such areas as employment and education. However, this approach, sometimes called **reverse discrimination**, has been subject to bitter dispute and legal challenge. Opponents argue that it violates the principle of equal competition and that the injustices of earlier generations cannot be put right by unjustly punishing members of the present generation. Animal ethics attempts to extend the scope of the ethical community and calls discrimination against animals on the grounds that they are not rational, **speciesism**.

"Impartiality is undoubtedly a requirement of justice, and . . . it is a form of equality as contrasted with the discrimination of equity." **Raphael,** *Problems of Political Philosophy*

disembodiment

PHILOSOPHY OF MIND, PHILOSOPHY OF RELIGION The existence of a **person** after bodily death and disintegration. It is one account that has been proposed for the afterlife or life after death. It presupposes that life need not terminate on the death of the body. The conditions for disembodied personal existence include the maintenance of a person's identity with that of one's pre-mortem state, and the maintenance of psychological awareness, especially memory, of one's experience before death. The mental life of a disembodied individual might be extremely austere if embodiment is needed to have new experiences. Re-embodiment occurs if a disembodied soul becomes united with another body. Resurrection is the return to life of a body that has been reunited with its original soul. Some Christian doctrine supports the actuality of disembodied existence, but other Christian accounts require a renewed embodiment with one's earthly body or with another special body for survival to be possible. Philosophically, the arguments in favor of disembodiment are drawn from **Cartesian dualism**, which claims that mind and body are independent entities. Some philosophers are also interested in the implications of apparent near-death out-of-body experiences. But many philosophers who accept the logical possibility of disembodied life after death reject it as physically impossible. Nevertheless, some philosophers claim that any suitable theory of mind should allow disembodied existence to be a logical possibility.

"The term used to refer to reunion is 're-embodiment'. The term used to refer to a person or mind capable of disembodiment is 'soul'." **Graham,** *Philosophy of Mind*

disguised description theory

PHILOSOPHY OF LANGUAGE A theory about the meaning of egocentric facts, such as "I am having such and such an experience." It is based on **Russell**'s theory of description and holds that the word "I" is an abbreviation for a definite description denoting a particular that is known by description rather than by acquaintance. So the word "I" in each of its occurrences can be replaced by a descriptive phrase of the form "the self having such and such properties." For instance, the statement "I see an image" is taken to state that a self having the appropriate description sees an image.

"According to disguised description theory, the person who knows an ego-centric fact is not prehending any particular as a self and is not using the word 'I' as a proper name in the logical sense." **Broad,** *Examination of McTaggart's Philosophy*

disinterest, see aesthetic attitude

disjunction

LOGIC Also called an alternation. A complex proposition of the form "p or q," where p and q are component propositions and are called disjuncts. The connective "or" has an inclusive sense and an exclusive sense. In its inclusive sense, sometimes called inclusive disjunction, "p or q" means "p or q or both." In **propositional calculus**, such a disjunction is symbolized as "$p \vee q$." It is true if p is true, if q is true, or if both disjuncts are true; it is false if and only if both disjuncts are false. From the premise p or q and the premise not p, we may infer the conclusion q, and this is called a disjunctive **syllogism**. In its exclusive sense, sometimes called exclusive disjunction, "p or q" means "either p or q but not both." In propositional calculus, it is symbolized as "[(p ∨ q) ∧ ~ (p ∧ q)]." It is true if p and q have opposite truth-values and is false if they have the same truth-values.

> "We may take next disjunction, 'p or q'. This is a function whose truth-value is truth when p is true and also when q is true, but is falsehood when both p and q are false." **Russell,** *Introduction to Mathematical Philosophy*

dispositional property

METAPHYSICS, PHILOSOPHY OF SCIENCE Properties of material things have, since **Locke**, been traditionally divided into primary and secondary qualities. Recent philosophers further divide primary qualities into substantial and dispositional properties. A dispositional property is the capacity of an object to affect or to be affected by other things. An active capacity of a thing to affect others is also called a **power**. For instance, falling down is a dispositional property of a thing that has weight, and being poisonous is a dispositional property of arsenic. Dispositional properties are analyzable into nothing but dispositions, and hence they can be distinguished from substantial properties, which are independent particulars. Substantial properties might provide a basis for dispositional properties, but some philosophers hold that all properties are dispositional.

> "It is a dispositional property of a paper that it will burn." **Joske,** *Material Objects*

dispositions

LOGIC, PHILOSOPHY OF SCIENCE, PHILOSOPHY OF MIND [from Latin *dis*, away + *ponere*, place] The tendency, habit, ability, or proneness to act or react in a certain way in certain circumstances. It is not an entity, a state of affairs, or an instance of behavior, but a behavioral pattern. One will display this pattern through a number of instances of behavior. To attribute a disposition to X is to say that X is prone to do Y in circumstance C. Sentences embodying dispositional claims are always hypothetical in form: "If circumstance C occurs, then X will do Y." The term "disposition" is prominent in **Ryle's** philosophy of mind, for his strategy is to replace the Cartesian mental substance and its activities with behavioral dispositions. He claims that the Cartesian concept of mind commits a **category mistake**, for it takes the mind to be one sort of ontological category, substance, when in fact the mental belongs to the category of disposition. He analyzes the majority of mental states in terms of dispositions. Since **Descartes** does not think of the mind as a disposition, any dispositional account of the mind is incompatible with Cartesian dualism. However, there are various views about dispositions. For Ryle, a disposition does not involve any hidden internal cause and is simply manifested in the circumstances specified. **Armstrong**, on the other hand, argues that dispositions are derivative and that their existence requires the prior existence of an underlying state of affairs. He attempts to identify dispositions with their bases. Others think that dispositions have categorical bases, but are not identical with them.

> "To possess a dispositional property is not to be in a particular state, or to undergo a particular change; it is to be bound or liable to be in a particular state, or to undergo a particular change, when a particular condition is realised. The same is true about specifically human dispositions such as qualities of character." **Ryle,** *The Concept of Mind*

disquotational theory of truth

LOGIC, PHILOSOPHY OF LANGUAGE The claim that truth is nothing more than a simplifying linguistic device, with the truth-predicate understood as having a distinctive role according to the principle of disquotation. According to this principle, for any appropriate sentence p, "*p*" is true if and only if p. The sentences "*p*" and "'*p*' is true" are in some sense equivalent in meaning, and "so and so is true" amounts to "so and so" and no more. The truth-predicate produces a sentence that can be used to say the very same thing and to perform the very same propositional acts as the original sentence. Accordingly, truth is a matter of the linguistic role of an expression rather than an external relation of **correspondence** with the world or a property. The major problem confronting the disquotational theory is to explain the fact that not all utterances are treated as having truth-values.

> "Disquotational theory of truth: on this theory, we understand the word 'true' not by associating that word with a property, or a correspondence, but by learning such facts as the obvious fact that 'Snow is white' is true if and only if snow is white." **Putnam,** *Realism and Reason*

distinct, see clear and distinct

distributed

LOGIC A way of characterizing how a term occurs in categorical propositions. A term is distributed if it refers to all members of the **class** to which it is referring and is explicitly or implicitly prefixed by a **universal quantifier**. For instance, in "Every man is mortal," "man" is distributed, for it covers every man. "All" and "none" are called distributive signs. In traditional logic, all subject terms of universal categorical propositions and all predicate terms of negative propositions are said to be distributed. But the predicate terms of affirmative propositions and the subject terms of particular propositions are not distributed. The distribution of terms is important in **syllogistic** inference. A valid syllogism requires that (a) if a term is distributed in the conclusion, it must be distributed in a premise, and (b) the middle term must be distributed in at least one premise.

"A term is said to be distributed, when it is used in reference to its whole extension, or to all that it can denote; undistributed, when not so used." **Joseph, *An Introduction to Logic***

distributive law

LOGIC Two principles of modern logic concerning the interchange of the connectives "and" and "or": (1) $p \wedge (q \vee r) \equiv (p \wedge q) \vee (p \wedge r)$; (2) $p \vee (q \wedge r) \equiv (p \vee q) \wedge (p \vee r)$. In (1) the operator "and" distributes over the operator "or" and expresses the distributivity of conjunction into disjunction or alternation. In (2) "or" distributes over "and" and expresses the distributivity of disjunction into conjunction. The spirit of these laws is similar to mathematical algebra's $p(q + r) = pq + pr$. In opposition to distributive laws are associative laws: (1) $p \vee q \vee r = (p \vee q) \vee r = p \vee (q \vee r)$; (2) $p \wedge q \wedge r = (p \wedge q) \wedge r = p \wedge (q \wedge r)$. These laws plus the communitive law ($p \vee q = q \vee p$, and $p \wedge q = q \wedge p$) are called the usual formal laws.

"By the usual formal laws, we mean the following, ... (iii) the distributive law: $a(b + g) = ab + ag$." **Russell, *Introduction to Mathematical Philosophy***

divided reference, Quine's term for a sortal

divine attributes

PHILOSOPHY OF RELIGION Properties attributed to **God**, which are believed to be essential for God as the creator of the universe and the supreme being and which distinguish him from other kinds of being. These properties include **omnipotence** (God has maximal power), **omniscience** (God has unlimited knowledge), **eternity** (God is not bounded by time), absolute goodness (God is wholly benevolent), infinity (God is free from any limitation), unity (God cannot be divided), **simplicity** (God is not composite but absolutely simple), incorporeality (God is not material), immutability (God is not subject to change), and impassability (God is not affected). Contemporary discussions of these attributes reveal that many of them imply **paradoxes**. Some of these have been included in this dictionary as separate entries, such as the paradox of omnipotence, paradox of omniscience, and the **problem of evil**. Other problems arise from ascribing versions of human attributes, such as reason, intelligence, or perceptual knowledge, to a being that is not embodied and does not exist temporally.

"The main problem in connection with the divine attributes is how to reconcile their multiplicity with the simplicity of God." **Mascall, *He Who Is***

divine command theory

ETHICS, PHILOSOPHY OF RELIGION Also called theological voluntarism, a position which claims that **God**'s command is the ultimate source of moral **obligation** or that God's **will** is the basis of moral laws. An action is said to be good because it conforms to divine commands. An action is said to be bad or evil because it is performed even though the agent knows that such an act breaches God's commands. This position was held by the medieval theologians and philosophers **Anselm**, **Abelard**, **Duns Scotus**, and **William of Ockham**. It was endorsed by **Locke** and **Berkeley**, and in the modern age it has been especially elaborated by **Kierkegaard** and **Barth**. It was criticized by **Aquinas**, who emphasized God's intellect rather than his will. The theory faces several major problems: How can we gain access to God's commands? If God is dead, are there any constraints on how we should behave? The theory is also challenged by **Plato**'s **Euthyphro dilemma**: Does God command that a thing is good because it is good, or is a thing good because God commands it? If it is the former, God is not the authority and we should be able to determine our morality without reference to God; if it is the latter, we have a tautology: A thing is what God commands because it is what God commands. In neither case do we seem to have explained the nature of goodness. This theory has difficulty in explaining how God's command can have moral force. If a moral law is justified in terms of God's will, it is not clear how we can determine that God's will is good. If we have other grounds for finding out what is morally good, we might determine that God's will is good, but we do not need his commands to know our moral obligations.

> "According to a divine command theory of morality, obligations are to be explained in terms of what God wills or commands: we have such obligations because God wills or commands the content of the obligation." **Kvanvig,** *The Problem of Hell*

divine illumination

PHILOSOPHY OF RELIGION **Augustine**, deeply influenced by **Plato**, believed that the universality, immutability, and necessity of eternal truths cannot be grasped by reference to sense-experience. How then can our mortal and fallible minds know them? Plato answered this question in terms of his theory of reminiscence, which Augustine replaced with his theory of divine illumination. According to this theory, the glimpses that human minds have of eternal truth are illuminated by the divine mind. The notion of illumination comes from Plato's analogy of the **Sun** in the *Republic*. Plato held that by analogy to the Sun as the author of the light illuminating the sensibility of the world, the idea of the Good is the source of intelligibility of the idea of the world. For Augustine, illumination is direct **intuition** whereby the mind comes to know the truth, analogous to the act by which the eye sees a body. As objects must be made visible by natural light before they can be perceived, so truths must be made intelligible before they can be known. Augustine claimed that God is the source of this spiritual light. Hence, the theory of divine illumination

constitutes a proof of God's existence as well as an explanation of human knowledge. The notion of divine illumination is not only epistemological, but also indicates the dependence of human rationality upon God. However, Augustine did not offer a clear account of the precise nature and operation of divine illumination, and that has given rise to much dispute among commentators.

> "They [Platonists] have declared that the light which illumines the intellects of men in all things that may be learned is this selfsame God by whom all things were made." **Augustine,** *City of God*

division

ANCIENT GREEK PHILOSOPHY [Greek *diairesis*] Also called **dialectic**, a method of definition employed by **Plato**, especially in his later dialogues. It consists of a complete and exact division of a **genus** into a series of subgenera or **species**. The classification corresponds to a **Form** in nature and was compared to dissection according to the joints. Plato used it in an attempt to find an answer to the problem of the one and the many. As an exploration of the relation between genus and species, the method contributed to the formation of **Aristotle**'s logic.

> "Unless one is capable of dividing things into their kinds and embrace each individual thing under a single form, he will never become skilled in discussion as is within the limit of human capacity." **Plato,** *Phaedrus*

division of linguistic labor

PHILOSOPHY OF LANGUAGE A hypothesis introduced by **Putnam** in his article "The Meaning of 'Meaning.'" Language is used in a community, and a community is divided into many subsets. A word in a language may have different **meanings** and **extensions**, depending on its different references and the occasions on which it is used. The expert speakers may know all facets of the word and be aware of its various distinctions, but this will not be the case for average speakers. Not all of them can know all the distinctions or the exact extension. They use the word in the way that is accepted by the subset of the community to which they belong. By virtue of this principle, Putnam tries to indicate that not every term is a **description**, and that the extension of each term is at least partly determined socially rather than in the mind of the individual speaker.

"Every linguistic community exemplifies the sort of division of linguistic labour just described, that is, possesses at least some terms whose associated 'criteria' are known only to a subset of the speakers who acquire the terms, and whose use by the other speakers depends upon a structured cooperation between them and the speakers in the relevant subsets." **Putnam, "The Meaning of 'Meaning,'" in** *Minnesota Studies in the Philosophy of Science,* **vol. VII**

division principle, see agglomeration principle

dogma

PHILOSOPHY OF RELIGION, EPISTEMOLOGY [from Greek *dogma,* that which seems to be, later meaning public decree or ordinance] Originally, any peculiar doctrine, but subsequently used as a term of abuse. Historically, a dogma is a religious doctrine proclaimed by scripture or the Church, which requires popular acceptance without rational justification. For its supporters, a dogma is indisputable and unchallengeable. According to skeptical critics, any metaphysical proposition is a dogma because, although there may be a rational argument for it, this argument itself relies on some unproved first principles and is therefore unreliable. Hence, any metaphysical doctrine is allegedly open to the charge of dogmatism.

"The concept of 'dogma', through historical and especially canonical development, has taken on a heteronomous character. Dogma is the central object of attack for autonomous culture." **Tillich,** *What is Religion?*

dogmatism

EPISTEMOLOGY [from Greek *dogma,* belief, public decree] Ancient **skepticism** charged all non-skeptical philosophies with dogmatism, meaning that they were committed to some doctrines which they believed to be indubitably true. This does not entail that all knowledge is false or skepticism would turn out to be a negative form of dogmatism. For ancient skepticism, we should suspend our judgment because knowledge is neither possible nor impossible. For classical German philosophy, dogmatism is the position that knowledge arises from the effect of independent reality on the mind and contrasts with **Kantian transcendental idealism**. In modern times, dogmatism is the uncritical, partial, and possibly irrational persistence of some opinion.

"Those who are properly called dogmatists . . . think that they have discovered the truth." **Sextus Empiricus,** *Outline of Pyrrhonism*

domain, see range

dominion thesis

ETHICS The position that human beings should dominate over animals as decided by God in the Bible. After the Creation, God told human beings that they "have dominion over the fish of the sea and over the birds of the air and over every living thing that moves upon the earth." This was repeated after the Flood. These passages have been understood to indicate that God grants the right of humans to take animal life, and that animals exist to serve the needs or interests of human beings. The thesis, although subjected to various interpretations, has been widely taken to support traditional anthropocentrism or human chauvinism, and is opposed by **environmental ethics**.

"Dominion thesis, the view that the earth and all its nonhuman contents exist and are available for man's benefit and serve his interests and, hence, that man is entitled to manipulate the world and its systems as he wants, that is, in his interest." **Routley and Routley, "Against the Inevitability of Human Chauvinism," in Goodpaster and Sayre (eds.),** *Ethics and Problems of the 21st Century*

Donagan, Alan (1925–91)

Australian-American moral philosopher and historian of philosophy, born in Melbourne, Professor of Philosophy, University of Chicago. Donagan derived a natural law conception of a moral system that is binding on all rational agents from Aquinas and Kant. His sophisticated defense of a distinction between event-causation and agent-causation allowed him to explain how free human agents making choices fit into this system. His main works include *The Theory of Morality* (1977) and *Choice: The Essential Element in Human Action* (1987).

double-aspect theory, see dual-aspect theory

double contingency, see social action

double effect, doctrine of

ETHICS In some cases an action will inevitably bring about double effects: the intended good results and the foreseen undesirable effects. Can such an action be permitted? Starting with Thomas **Aquinas** and developed by Catholic theologians, the principle of double effect was formulated. Under the circumstances of such double effect, an action is permissible if the evil result is not directly intended, the good result is not achieved through the evil result, and the good result outweighs the bad one. But these conditions can themselves come into conflict. Some contemporary moral philosophers have tried to revise the formulation, and others deny this principle on the grounds that it is difficult to distinguish between the intentional and the foreseen and between the directly and indirectly intended consequences. Nevertheless, this principle is widely used to justify responses to many difficult cases in ethics, such as killing in self-defense, killing a fetus in order to save the life of its mother and inflicting civilian causalities during a military action.

"By 'the doctrine of the double affect' I mean the thesis that it is sometimes permissible to bring about by oblique intention what one may not directly intend." **Foot,** *Virtues and Vices*

double language model

PHILOSOPHY OF SCIENCE A model developed by **Carnap** and **Nagel,** among others, to suggest that the language of science can be divided into theoretical and observational languages. They are semiautonomous. **Observational language** is directly related to sense impressions while **theoretical language** cannot be analyzed in the standard empirical way. Theoretical terms used by theoretical languages neither are nor should be definable in the observation language. The experiential content of theoretical terms is obtained through correspondence rules, which connect the two languages by sentences containing both theoretical terms and observational terms. This model gives rise to much debate regarding, for example, how an observational term can fix its meaning independent of its relation with

theoretical terms, and how to assess the truth of a theoretical sentence.

"[The] well-known double language model [consists] of an observational language, Lo and a theoretical language, Lt, the latter containing a postulate system, T. The languages are connected to each other by correspondence rules, i.e. by sentences containing observational terms and theoretical terms." **Feyerabend, "Against Method,"** in *Minnesota Studies in the Philosophy of Science,* **vol. III**

double negation, see negation of a negation

double truth theory

PHILOSOPHY OF RELIGION A position ascribed to the medieval philosopher Siger of Brabant and the **Averroists,** according to which the truth of **faith** and the truth of philosophy belong to two different domains. While a proposition is true from the philosophical point of view and can be demonstrated by reason, an incompatible proposition, which is therefore false philosophically, can be true by revelation in religion. This theory was an attempt to retain **Aristotle**'s metaphysical doctrines when they contradicted Christian teaching, but was condemned as heretical in the thirteenth century by the Bishop of Paris.

"A double-truth theory, namely that a proposition could at the same time be true in theology and false in philosophy." **Copleston,** *A History of Medieval Philosophy*

doubt

EPISTEMOLOGY Doubt in its ordinary sense is an uncertain state of mind. It contributes substantially to **skepticism,** whose purpose is the questioning of knowledge claims and the suspension of belief. **Descartes**'s **method** of doubt differs from this sense and also from traditional skepticism. It is a procedure by which he attempted to demolish all prejudices and preconceived opinions for the purpose of establishing a firm and stable metaphysical basis for his system. In other words, Descartes established the method of doubt in order to eliminate doubt and find something indubitable. Doubt is employed in order to lead the mind away from the senses and toward rational truth. It is only a means to an end, and not an end in itself. The method of doubt plays a central role in Descartes's first philosophy. It comprised a succession of arguments, from the unreliability of the senses, the possibility that one is dreaming, the possible error of mathematical reasoning, and finally to the malicious demon.

> "Because in this case I wish to give myself entirely to the search after truth, I thought that it was necessary for me to take an apparently opposite course, and to reject as absolutely false everything as to which I could imagine the least ground of doubt, in order to see if afterwards there remained anything in my belief that was entirely certain." **Descartes, *Discourse on Method***

doxa

ANCIENT GREEK PHILOSOPHY, METAPHYSICS, EPISTEMO-LOGY [Greek, usually translated as belief or opinion, from the verb *dokein* or *doxazein*, to appear, to believe or to seem] A term used in connection with seeming, the immediate awareness of or direct acquaintance with objects in contrast with *episteme* (**knowledge**). For **Plato**, *doxa* is not only opinion, but also the faculty or capacity to produce opinion. It is the state of mind of the non-philosopher (the lover of opinion, *philo-doxos*), and its object is the perceptible world of becoming, which is both to be and not to be, and things that are copies of the **Forms**. In contrast, *episteme* is not only knowledge as a consequence of **cognition**, but also the faculty to produce knowledge. It is a state of mind of the philosopher (the lover of wisdom, *philo-sophos*), and its object is the world of the Forms itself, which really is. The distinction is discussed in detail in the *Republic* Book V, and is essential for Plato's separation of the world of the Forms from the sensible world. It has had a lasting influence on Western metaphysics and epistemology.

> "We clearly agree that *doxa* is different from knowledge." **Plato, *Republic***

doxastic theory

EPISTEMOLOGY [from Greek *doxa*, opinion or belief] A doxastic state refers to one's belief. Doxastic theory claims that epistemic **justification** is only a function of such a state. We can determine what to believe on the basis of the overall beliefs we possess, without needing to take into account anything else, including perceptual states. Both **foundationalism**

and **coherentism** are doxastic theories. This theory is thus opposed to non-doxastic theory, which claims that in order to justify one's beliefs it is not enough to examine the beliefs themselves. Rather we must refer to the cognitive process of belief-forming and belief-preserving. Non-doxastic theory is divided into **internalism**, which suggests that justification is a function of one's internal states, and **externalism**, which argues that justification must involve factors that are external to one's consciousness.

> "Doxastic theories take the justifiability of a belief to be a function exclusively of what else one believes." **Pollock and Cruz, *Contemporary Theories of Knowledge***

doxastic virtue, see epistemic virtue

Dray, William (1921–)

Canadian philosopher of history, born in Montreal, Professor of Philosophy, University of Ottawa. Dray challenged the covering law model of scientific explanation as suitable for historical explanation. He argued that we are interested in how historical developments are possible rather than in why they are necessary. He compared understanding rational human action to literary narrative rather than to scientific explanation. His main works include *Laws and Explanation in History* (1957) and *Perspectives on History* (1980).

dread, see *Angst*

dreaming, argument from

EPISTEMOLOGY One of the principal arguments against the certainty of **perception** in **Descartes**. Dreaming is taken by Descartes to be a kind of experience we have when we sleep, with a content consisting mainly of imagery. In a dream, while I am actually lying undressed in bed, I can think that I am dressed and seated near the fireplace. Now I think that I am awake, and am reading this book with a pen in my hand. But since I have been deceived by similar illusions whilst asleep, I cannot know with certainty that these apparent perceptions do not belong to a dream. There seems to be no logical criterion to distinguish waking experience from dream experience. I have reason to doubt any of my perceptions on the grounds that it could be an illusion from my dreams. We cannot distinguish between deception and non-deceptive perception. Thus my perceptions on any given occasion might not be veridical, and could be merely illusory. Any perceptual beliefs I form on their basis could be false. This argument raises the problem of the external world and has played a great role in modern Western philosophy.

"In the dream argument Descartes recognises that conflicts may occur among perceptions of any sort – even among those that bear the sensory marks of perception under the most ideal conditions." **Frankfurt, *Demons, Dreamers and Madmen***

Dretske, Fred (1932–)

American philosopher of mind, epistemologist and philosopher of science, born in Waukegan, Illinois, Professor of Philosophy at Stanford University and Duke University. Dretske distinguishes between simple seeing (without belief) and epistemic seeing (with belief) and relates this account to analog and digital modes of encoding information. Digital encodings have prepositional content and allow beliefs and desires to have causal powers. His main works include *Knowledge and the Flow of Information* (1981) and *Explaining Behaviour: Reasons in a World of Causes* (1988).

dual-aspect theory

PHILOSOPHY OF MIND As an alternative to **Cartesian dualism** of mind and body, this theory holds that mind and body are not two independent things, but two attributes of the same underlying **substance**; hence they cannot be actually separate, but can only be abstracted from one another in thought. **Spinoza**'s philosophy of mind, which is often called **parallelism**, is sometimes said to be more adequately called a dual-aspect or double-aspect theory, for he claims that mind and body are attributes of one and the same substance, and sometimes even says that a **mode** of thought and a mode of extension are one and the same thing, only being expressed in two ways. The problem for this theory is that it replaces the problems of substance dualism with those of property dualism, for the interaction between these two attributes remains unclear. The best example of dual-aspect theory in modern philosophy of mind is **functionalism**, as held by **Strawson, Hampshire**, and **Davidson**.

"The double aspect theory 'explains' psychophysical correlations by saying that one and the same event, which in itself is neither mental or physical, may be apprehended introspectively or perceptively; in so far as it is apprehended in the former way it is mental, in so far as it is apprehended in the latter way, it is physical." **Pap, *Elements of Analytic Philosophy***

dualism

METAPHYSICS, PHILOSOPHY OF MIND Any metaphysical theory which, in contrast to monism, holds that reality is composed of two kinds of fundamental entities, neither of which can be reduced to the other. **Descartes** divided the world into extended substance (matter) and thinking substance (mind), and these two have mutually incompatible properties. Accordingly, the soul is entirely distinct from the body. This standard mental–physical dualism is called **Cartesian dualism**. Aside from the above "substance dualism," there is also "property dualism," called **dual-aspect theory**, which suggests that the mental and the physical are two mutually irreducible types of properties of one and the same thing. **Russell** holds a kind of "causal dualism," according to which the dualism is not between two entities or properties, but rather between two fundamental kinds of law: physical causal laws and psychological causal laws.

Traditional dualism, implying that the mind or soul is independent of body, has difficulty in accounting for interaction between body and mind and has become the focus of many disputes in contemporary philosophy of mind. **Ryle** accuses dualism of making the mind a ghost in the machine. Various theories about the relationship between mind and body have been proposed to avoid the problems of dualism.

In its wider sense, dualism refers to philosophical systems that are established on some sharp fundamental distinction, such as **Plato**'s distinction between the sensible world and ideal world or **Kant**'s distinction between the phenomenal world and the noumenal world.

"Dualism: this theory holds that there are both mental and physical particulars. It is the Cartesian view, the view of educated common sense, and the view of Christian theology." **Russell, *Collected Papers of Bertrand Russell*, vol. IX**

Ducasse, Curt (1881–1969)

French-American analytic philosopher, born in Angouleme, France, Professor of Philosophy, Brown University. Ducasse was a pioneer of analytic philosophy in the United States and wrote on causality, perception, aesthetics, and paranormal phenomena. His dualism allowed minds to enter into causal relations with physical things and with other minds. He argued for an adverbial account of seeing that did not require sensa. His major works include *Truth, Knowledge and Causation* (1969).

duck-rabbit

EPISTEMOLOGY, PHILOSOPHY OF MIND The psychologist J. Jastrow draws an ambiguous picture in his *Fact and Fable in Psychology*, which can be viewed either as the head of a duck, or as the head of rabbit, although one cannot perceive the picture as both at the same time. **Wittgenstein** appeals to this picture in his *Philosophical Investigations* to illustrate the point that if the same object can be seen as two different things, it shows that **perception** is not purely sensory and that we must attend to aspects in our account of perception. A report of perception is concept-laden, a combination of experience and thought.

> "I may, then, have seen the duck-rabbit simply as a picture-rabbit from the first." **Wittgenstein,** *Philosophical Investigation*

Duhem, Pierre (1861–1916)

French physicist and philosopher and historian of science, born in Paris, Professor at University of Bordeaux, member of the Académie des Sciences. Duhem argued for a holistic account of scientific theory, according to which the whole body of theory has empirical consequences rather than a single theory or theoretical claim. This implies that alterations in theory in the face of conflicting observations can be made anywhere in the body of theory and are not restricted to claims that are most closely associated with the observations. His studies of medieval science led Duhem to argue for the fallibility of any system of natural classification. His main works include *The Aim and Structure of Physical Theory* (1906) and *To Save the Phenomena* (1908).

Duhem–Quine thesis

PHILOSOPHY OF SCIENCE Also called the Quine–Duhem thesis. The view that any single **hypothesis** or theoretical sentence is not conclusively refuted when predictions derived from it turn out to be false, that is, when it is apparently incompatible with observation. Predictions may also rest upon other hypotheses, which serve as background knowledge. We can always revise this background knowledge to save the hypothesis in question. Empirical tests can only be applied to the whole system of hypotheses, not to single theoretical sentences. The unit of empirical significance is the whole of science. The confirmation conditions of a single sentence are determined by the sentence's role in the language or in the theory in which it occurs. This thesis was defended by the French philosopher of science, P. **Duhem**, and by **Quine**. This thesis is also called epistemological **holism**, and is related to Quine's denial of the distinction between analytic and synthetic propositions.

> "The Quine/Duhem thesis says that confirmation is holistic; that is, that every statement in a theory partially determines the level of confirmation of every other statement in the theory." **Fodor and Lepore,** *Holism*

Dummett, Michael (1925–)

British philosopher of language and mathematics, born in London, Professor of Logic, University of Oxford. Dummett is a major commentator on the work of Frege and a leading analytic philosopher in his own right. Under the influence of Brouwer's intuitionism, he has articulated and defended anti-realist positions in the philosophy of mathematics and explored the legitimacy of anti-realism in other areas of philosophy. His main works include *Frege: Philosophy of Language* (1973), *Truth and Other Enigmas* (1978), *The Logical Basis of Metaphysics* (1991), and *Origins of Analytic Philosophy* (1993).

Duns Scotus, John (c.1266–1308)

Scholastic philosopher and theologian, probably born at Duns in Scotland, lectured in Oxford and Paris, died in Cologne. Duns Scotus used Avicenna, Augustine, and earlier Franciscan thought to engage with medieval Aristotelian philosophy and theology. He asserted the primacy of the will over the intellect and the freedom of the individual will. Faith and reason supplement each other, and theology is practical rather than theoretical. He recognized formal distinctions as well as real distinctions and conceptual distinctions. Distinctions among God's attributes and the distinction between a particular thing's common nature and its individuality are instances of formal distinctions. He was a moderate realist about universals and called the individuality of a particular thing its *haecceitas* (thisness), a notion revived by Chisholm in contemporary metaphysics. His major works include *Opus Oxoniense* (the Oxford lectures), *Quaestiones quodlibetales*, *On the First Principles*, *Opus Parisiense* (the Paris lectures).

duration

METAPHYSICS, PHILOSOPHY OF MIND A notion of time, generally meaning the temporal distance between the beginning of an event and its end. **Bergson** contrasts duration to physical time and places it as a central conception of his philosophy. Physical time (*le temps*) is our ordinary idea of time, which is conceived as being an unbounded line composed of units or moments. Physical time is spatialized and intellectualized, and it can be measured by some measuring device or tool. This spatialized or mathematical idea of time enables us to fix the occurrence of events, but is itself empty and homogeneous. In contrast, duration (*durée*) or pure duration is the time of inner experience, a non-spatial stream of consciousness in which before and after interpenetrate one another. Duration is constituted by deep-seated conscious states, applies only to persons and not to external things, and leads to **free will**. We can only be aware of duration by **intuition**. It is a series of qualitative changing with no quantitative differentiation. It is heterogeneous and not homogenous. If we take the concept of the **self** as a succession of states, it is the superficial self as seen from physical time. Duration expresses the nature of the life of the deeper self. Only acts starting from duration are free. The distinction between physical time and duration, according to Bergson, can avoid **determinism**. His account of duration and physical time influenced the **existentialist** distinction between **authentic** and inauthentic existence.

"Pure duration is the form which the succession of our conscious states assumes when our ego lets itself live, when it refrains from separating its present state from its former states." **Bergson, *Time and Free Will***

Durkheim, Émile (1858–1917)

French sociologist and philosopher, born in Épinal, taught at the universities of Bordeaux and Paris, a principal founder of modern sociology. Durkheim's sociological work is philosophically important through its methodological collectivism or holism. He held that social facts or social phenomena cannot be reduced to facts about individuals, and should be treated as things that are explained solely by reference to other social facts. Society as a whole has its own life and is the proper object of social study. Society is held together by collective representations that exist independent of individual consciousness and can be examined through social facts. He applied this methodology to studies of suicide and religion. His major works include *The Rules of Sociological Method* (1895), *Suicide* (1897), and *The Elementary Forms of Religious Life* (1912).

Dutch book

EPISTEMOLOGY, PHILOSOPHY OF SCIENCE A combination of bets on which a person will suffer a collective loss no matter what happens. Suppose you are betting on a coin toss and accept odds of 3:2 that the coin lands heads and 3:2 that the coin will land tails. On this basis, you will never win and will always lose. Whatever the outcome of the coin toss, your bets will total 4 and you will gain only 3. The notion of the Dutch book was introduced into epistemology by **Ramsey** and **de Finetti** to show that it is irrational to put oneself in a no-win situation by accepting beliefs that have an incoherent combination of degrees of belief. Hence, rational degrees of belief must conform to the **probability calculus**. The validity of this argument is controversial, for what it proves is a prudential rationality rather than an epistemic rationality.

"The Dutch Book argument . . . entails that if your degrees of belief . . . do not satisfy the probability calculus, then there are positive and negative stakes . . . which you would accept in bets at the odds determined by your degree of belief and which, once accepted, would cause you to lose money come what may." **Howson and Urbach, *Scientific Reasoning***

duty

ETHICS [German *die Pflicht*] What is owed or due to others or to oneself. In an ordinary sense, duty comprises the requirements, **obligations**, or assignments ascribed to any occupant of a social position, such as the position of parent, citizen, or jobholder, for which the person occupying that position is responsible. Duty as an ethical conception can be traced to the Stoics, but came to prominence in **Kant**'s ethics as the central concept of morals. Kant's ethics is therefore a **deontological** theory (from Greek *deon*, duty).

For Kant, duty is what ought to be done and thus constrains action. It is distinctive of conscientious conduct and is a concept that must be apprehended *a priori*. A **good will** is the basis of morality, and to have a good will is always to act from a sense of duty. Only an action performed out of a sense of duty can have moral worth. Duty is what we are obliged to do out of respect for the universal law. Kant distinguished duties chiefly into duties of **justice** (juridical duties) and duties of **virtue** (ethical duty). A duty of justice is external in the sense that it applies to action that we can be compelled to do by an appropriate legal authority, while a duty of virtue is internal in the sense that its constraint or compulsion regarding action originates from our awareness of the moral law. This distinction roughly corresponds to his earlier distinction between acting in accordance with duty and acting from duty. He also distinguished between positive duty (what one ought to do) and negative duty (what one ought not to do); between perfect duty (which must be fulfilled under any circumstance and which specifies a particular action) and imperfect duty (which may be overridden and for which we have a significant degree of freedom in deciding how to comply).

"Duty is the necessity of an action done out of respect for the law." **Kant, *Groundwork for the Metaphysics of Morals***

Dworkin, Ronald (1931–)

American political and legal philosopher, Professor of Philosophy, New York University and Professor of Jurisprudence, University of Oxford. Dworkin gives priority to rights in his account of law and argues that rights must be respected even if they conflict with general social or political welfare. He argues that the law should not be conceived as a determinate system of rules, but that in making decisions judges must take account of standards regarding rights or welfare that are not rules. This is shown by the existence of hard cases, which can not be settled by the application of rules. His main works include *Taking Rights Seriously* (1977), *A Matter of Principle* (1985), and *Law's Empire* (1986).

dyadic

LOGIC [from Greek *dyas*, two, a pair] A *dyad* is a group consisting of two parts. In logic, a dyadic relational predicate, such as "is higher than" or "is better than," requires two terms to make a complete sentence. A dyadic predicate expresses a relation between two items and is symbolized as Rxy. The order of the letters after the predicate matters, and Rxy cannot in general be equated with Ryx. A dyadic or two-place predicate expresses a two-term relation. In contrast, monadic or one-term predicates do not express relations, and polyadic many-term predicates, such as triadic or three-term predicates and tetradic or four-term predicates, express relations among more than two terms.

"Predicative expressions used to form sentences exemplifying simple predicative formulae with more than one individual variable are sometimes called relational predicates, and are distinguished into dyadic ('two-place'), triadic ('three-place'), &c. predicates, according to the number of individual expressions they commonly require to form a sentence." **Strawson, *Introduction to Logical Theory***

E

écart

MODERN EUROPEAN PHILOSOPHY [French, splitting off or separation from itself] For **Merleau-Ponty**, the primordial action or movement of **Being**. Being, which is dynamic, possesses itself to some degree and gains some hold, but then is removed from itself (*écart*), due to its finitude and its insufficiency for ever-renewed attempts to overcome separation. The result of this movement is **temporality**. *Écart* implies that Being is at the same time one and many. It is thus consistent with the lapse, flux, or *ekstase* of Being. *Écart*, which characterizes Merleau-Ponty's understanding of Being, is the character of Being that we experience with necessary indeterminacy in all situations.

"Look in a completely different direction: the for itself itself is an incontestable, but derived, characteristic: it is the culmination of separation (écart) in differentiation . . . the perceptual separation (écart) as making up the 'view' such as it is implicated in the reflex, for example – and enclosing being for itself by means of language as differentiation." **Merleau-Ponty**, *The Visible and the Invisible*

ecocentrism

ETHICS An approach to **environmental ethics**, proposing that its central concern should be the ecological system or biotic community and its sub-systems, rather than the individual members it contains. Ecocentrism is based on the claim that ecology has revealed human beings and the rest of nature to be related both diachronically (through time) and synchronically (at one time) and to be part of the web of life. Proponents argue that we should therefore consider the whole ecosystem rather than its individual members in isolation from the matrix in which the individuals are embedded. Unlike the major modern moral traditions, which focus on the interests or rights of the individual, ecocentrism is a holistic, or even totalitarian, approach. It judges the moral worth of human behavior in terms of its impact on the environment. Hence, while other approaches try to extend traditional Western moral norms to issues concerning animals and the environment, ecocentrism attempts to establish a new ethical paradigm. Land ethics and deep ecology are the most important representative forms of this trend. A fundamental problem facing ecocentrists is how to provide an appropriate place for human individuals within their account of the welfare of the environment.

"Those philosophers, among whom I count myself, have been called 'ecocentrists' since we have advocated a shift in the locus of intrinsic value from individuals (whether individual human beings or individual higher 'lower animals') to terrestrian nature – the ecosystem – as a whole." **Callicott**, *In Defense of the Land Ethic*

economic base, see relations of production

economic determinism

PHILOSOPHY OF SOCIAL SCIENCE The basic thesis of Marx's **historical materialism**, that the modes of production determine the legal/political **superstructure** and ideological superstructure of a society. Although some scholars use the term as a neutral description, many critics employ it pejoratively to accuse the theory of claiming that non-economic phenomena are mechanically determined by the economic structure in a way that is incompatible with the existence of human freedom and moral responsibility. But Marx never claimed that there is a monocausal relation between the economical structure and superstructure. Instead, he emphasized in his later life that superstructure, although fundamentally determined by the economical structure, is not ineffectual, but plays an active role in maintaining the economic base. Engels shared this view. Some commentators are uncertain how well the distinction between base and superstructure survives a more robust role for the superstructure, even if in the last analysis the base is allocated explanatory priority.

"It used to be said more often than it is now that Marx was an 'economic determinist'. Some critics held this against him, while others reckoned it a point in his favour." **Plamenatz,** *Karl Marx's Philosophy of Man*

economic structure, see relations of production

ecstacy, see temporality

effective historical consciousness, see effective history

effective history

MODERN EUROPEAN PHILOSOPHY EPISTEMOLOGY, PHILOSOPHY OF HISTORY [German *Wirkungsgeschichte*] **Gadamer** claims that history or **tradition** is not simply the past, but is in a process of realization. History has effects in terms of conditioning our historical **understanding**. An interpreter is subject to the way in which an object has already been understood in the tradition to which the interpreter belongs. Any understanding is historically situated and is rooted in prejudice. Understanding is thus not the act of a subject, but rather an aspect of effective history. A pure "objective" understanding, free from any special vantage point, does not exist. History limits our **knowledge**, but also aids our development by means of determining what we can understand. Accordingly, no rejection of the tradition can be as completely radical as claimed by its proponents. The consciousness that is affected by history, through having a pre-history, and will in turn affect history, through having a post-history, is called effective historical consciousness. History is a unity of history with the understanding of it.

"The true historical object is not an object at all, but the unity of the one and the other, a relationship in which exist both the reality of history and the reality of historical understanding. A proper hermeneutics would have to demonstrate the effectivity of history within understanding itself. I shall refer to this as 'effective-history'." **Gadamer,** *Truth and Method*

effective procedure

EPISTEMOLOGY, PHILOSOPHY OF SCIENCE, PHILOSOPHY OF MIND In contrast to a random procedure, an effective procedure is a mechanical step-by-step process with a finite number of steps before reaching an answer or calculating a solution. An effective procedure can be given as a finite set of instructions that determine what is to be done at each step. The notion of effective procedure is crucial for computer science. A **Turing machine** employs an effective procedure because in such a machine a computer program effectively specifies the information processing to be carried out by the machine. This mechanical procedure is a type of **algorithm**.

"[An effective procedure] denotes a set of rules (the program) specifying certain processes, which processes can be carried out by a machine processor built in such a way as to accept these rules as instructions determining its operations." **Boden,** *Artificial Intelligence and Natural Man*

efficiency

POLITICAL PHILOSOPHY, PHILOSOPHY OF SOCIAL SCIENCE A term for assessing means to achieve ends. In contemporary philosophy, efficiency is mainly used as a welfare criterion to measure the condition of a society. A society is efficient if the institutions within it can work cooperatively to generate the greatest possible welfare. **Hobbes** claimed that virtually everyone is better off if there is a political-legal order and that a society is more efficient if it has a government than if it lacks one. Under **Pareto optimality**, a distribution of goods is efficient if any alternative distribution would make some individual better off at the cost of making another individual worse off. The notion of efficiency attracts a widespread interest in contemporary political philosophy, in debates about conflicts between equity and efficiency and between stability, coordination, and efficiency.

> "An arrangement of the basic structure is efficient when there is no way to change this distribution so as to raise the prospects of some without lowering the prospects of others." **Rawls**, *A Theory of Justice*

egalitarianism

ETHICS, POLITICAL PHILOSOPHY Also equalitarianism. The doctrine that all men are equal in the sense that they should receive equal treatment or consideration in moral, political, and even economic life. The position, which is opposed to inegalitarianism, denies that any individual or group should be accorded prior moral concern over others. Each individual is to be counted as one. One aim of **liberalism** is to respect and advance equality, although different liberal doctrines give different weight to the claims of equality. Strict egalitarianism would insist upon an equal distribution of all **primary goods**, but many egalitarians allow different rewards to be attached to different positions so long as the positions are open to all on the basis of fair equality of opportunity.

> "Egalitarianism: . . . the doctrine that all human beings have the right to equal respect and consideration." **Haksar**, *Equality, Liberty and Perfectionism*

ego (Freud)

PHILOSOPHY OF MIND **Freud** rejected the view that the mind is a unity. Instead, he divides it into three parts: id [German *Es*, literally, "it"], ego [German *Ich*, literally, "I"], and superego [German *Überich*]. For Freud, the id contains bodily appetites and unconscious instincts. It is not subjected to logical processing or to time, and it represents the resistance of human nature and what should be checked.

The id replaced what Freud earlier called the **unconscious**. The superego is a human's moral faculty and is the agent of conscience. It is the location of ego-ideal, that is, what one desires but cannot have. It represents an individual's social personality, and acts as a deputy for the **culture** outside oneself. It is a judge and a censor. The presence of the superego explains how it is possible for us to act in a way that serves something beyond our own self-interest. The ego, the subject of intentional actions and decisions, is the mediator between id and superego, and is the real "I" or genuine **self**. It has a conscious part and an unconscious part. It tries to measure itself by the ideal set by the superego and to act on the demands of the superego to subdue the unsociable chaos of the id's desires. The ego also tries to keep its own perceptual responses free from the constraints of morality. The contents of the id can find expression in consciousness only through the ego, through the approval of the ego, or by the ego falling prey to the id's manipulation. Freud compares the relation between the ego and id to the relation between a rider and horse. In all, the ego represents characteristic human values of prudence and rationality. It is the layer of the id that has been modified by the influence of the external world of reality.

Freud's tripartite picture does not simplify the function of mind into a conflict between rational and irrational. In a sense, it can be traced to **Plato**'s division of the soul into reason, spirit, and appetite, although Freud locates reason in the area of ego. As with all the major elements of Freudian theory, it is tempting to accept Freud's account of the ego, id, and superego without suitable scrutiny.

> "Putting ourselves on the footing of everyday knowledge, we recognise in human beings a mental organisation which is interpolated between their sensory stimuli and the perception of their somatic needs on the one hand and their motor acts on the other, and which mediates between them for a particular purpose. We call this organisation their 'Ich' ('ego', literally, 'I')." **Freud**, *Standard Edition of the Complete Psychological Works of Sigmund Freud*, vol. 23

egocentric particulars

LOGIC, PHILOSOPHY OF LANGUAGE, PHILOSOPHY OF MIND A term introduced by **Russell**, which he also called emphatic particulars. Items designated by words such as "this," "I," "here," "now," "past," "future," "near," or "far," whose **denotation** is relative to the speaker and his position in space and time and depends on the contexts of their utterances. In a sense, all of them can be defined in terms of an ostensive "this." These words are neither **proper names**, nor terms for general concepts, nor **descriptions** and therefore are not easy to fit into the usual logical and **semantic** categories. They will affect the truth of the propositions in which they occur, for such propositions cannot have a constant truth-value. They may be said to denote without connoting anything. It therefore becomes a fundamental problem how to avoid egocentric particulars in the formulation of epistemologically basic propositions. Since the use of egocentric terms must involve the selective activity of the mind, the existence of such terms is also supposed to be a criticism of the **no-ownership theory** of mental states. Other authors call egocentric particulars token-reflexives, indicator terms, or indexicals.

> "There is also difficulty about 'egocentric particulars', i.e. 'I', 'this', 'now', 'here'." **Russell**, *An Inquiry into Meaning and Truth*

egocentric perceptual statements

PHILOSOPHY   OF   LANGUAGE,   EPISTEMOLOGY
Shoemaker's term for statements that make use of egocentric terms such as "this," "here," "near," "far," "left," or "right" to describe events or objects in relation to the speaker. The truth or falsity of these statements is decided with reference to such circumstances as the speaker's location, orientation, and point of view.

> "It is just because egocentric perceptual statements can be false, and can be discovered to be false by reference to the speaker's point of view, that they are informative in the way they are." **Shoemaker**, *Self-Knowledge and Self-Identity*

egocentric predicament

EPISTEMOLOGY The term, coined by the American philosopher R. B. **Perry**, refers to the situation according to which everyone's knowledge is limited by his or her own **experience** and cannot go beyond that experience. This situation has already been expressed in **Berkeley**'s dictum "to be is to be perceived." Because of this predicament, we cannot have empirical knowledge of **other minds**, for we cannot share their experience. We also cannot have empirical knowledge of the mind-independent **external world**, for any recognition of the world must be formed on the basis of one's experience. **Idealism**, although widely criticized in this regard, generally takes this predicament as a strong proof of its truth.

> "The fallacious argument from the egocentric predicament is to confuse the redundant statement that 'everything which is known, is known' with the statement that 'everything which is, is known'; or to infer the second statement from the first." **Perry**, *Realms of Value*

egoism, ethical

ETHICS Also called normative egoism or rational egoism. An ethical view that holds that satisfying some desire of mine is a necessary and sufficient condition for me to act. This theory places the **self** at the center of ethical life in relation to other persons. According to this view, people will naturally behave unjustly and reject fundamental moral rules, if they can do so without any negative consequences for themselves. It then follows that we do not have a natural regard for the public interest, and that a rational person will act to maximize selfish satisfactions. For an ethical theory based on this account of human psychology, moral life is the life that maximizes the good-for-me. Psychological egoism provides a theoretical basis for ethical egoism, but the failure of psychological egoism would not entail that ethical egoism is false. It only shows that ethical egoism must find another basis. Egoism stands in contrast to altruism, which claims that morality must be based on our desire to help others. Egoism was explicitly argued for by Thrasymachus in **Plato**'s *Republic* and developed by **Hobbes**. To explain obvious acts of **altruism** and **benevolence** in many situations, egoists argue that altruism or the observance of the general moral order is disguised self-seeking, for it will create a stable society, which can preserve us and promote our long-term interests. The main difficulty of egoism is that it takes morality as an external bond, rather than being an internal feature of our moral personality. The **prisoner's dilemma** indicates that cooperative action may achieve better results than selfish action and has been offered as a serious basis for rejecting ethical egoism. However, it is also argued that egoism will allow us to act cooperatively as long as this promotes deeply based long-term self-interest. On this view, the prisoner's dilemma only shows that people should not pursue egoistic ends directly and does not entail the rejection of egoism itself.

"There is a theory of how we should act which has been called, confusingly enough, ethical egoism. This claims that each person ought to pursue his or her own self-interest." **B. Williams, *Ethics and the Limits of Philosophy***

eidetic imagery
EPISTEMOLOGY [from Greek *eidos*, the thing to be seen] Persons are capable of having eidetic imagery if they can form an **image** of something as if that thing were really in front of them, and if they can manipulate that image in some way. Such images are phenomenologically indistinguishable from **perceptions**, but are not illusory perceptions. Just as we can read off features of our visual phenomena, the person with eidetic images can project them upon physical surfaces and can read off their features. The existence of this kind of phenomenon suggests that we cannot easily dispense with the notion of inner-perception.

"In the unusual phenomenon of 'eidetic imagery', the subject can read off or count off the details of his memory image." **Dennett, *Content and Consciousness***

eidetic intuition, see eidetic reduction

eidetic reduction
MODERN EUROPEAN PHILOSOPHY **Husserl**'s term for an intuitive act toward an **essence** or universal, in contrast to an empirical intuition or **perception**. He also called this act an essential intuition, eidetic intuition, or eidetic variation. In Greek, *eideo* means "to see" and what is seen is an *eidos* (Platonic **Form**), that is, the common characteristic of a number of entities or regularities in experience. For Plato, *eidos* means what is seen by the eye of the soul and is identical with essence. Husserl also called this act "ideation," for *ideo* is synonymous with *eideo* and

also means "to see" in Greek. Correspondingly, *idea* is identical to *eidos*.

Eidetic reduction is the stage subsequent to transcendental or phenomemological reduction and is sometimes viewed as the second stage of **phenomenological reduction** itself. Transcendental reduction lifts us to the transcendental realm, and turns empirical consciousness to transcendental or pure consciousness. For Husserl, eidetic reduction of an act of transcendental consciousness penetrates to essence. It is a procedure for acquiring insight into essence and places us in cognitive contact with general or universal knowledge. The result of this reduction is a clearer and more distinct consciousness of the universal. This reduction or intuition is a rule-governed act, which direct intuition often resists. In eidetic reduction, we do not concentrate on the perceived instance, but the essence that the instance exemplifies. Understanding this reduction, therefore, provides an explanation of how we transcend the contingency of our basic experience and extract what is essential.

"If the phenomenological reduction contrived a means of access to the phenomenon of real and also potential inner experience, the method found in it of 'eidetic reduction' provides the means of access to the invariant essential structures of the total sphere of pure mental process." **Husserl, *Shorter Works***

eidetic variation, an alternative expression for eidetic reduction

Einstein, Albert (1879–1955)
German-Swiss-American physicist and philosopher, born in Ulm, Professor at the Institute for Advanced Studies, Princeton. Einstein's theory of relativity unified and revolutionized our account of the physical world according to a four-dimensional theory of space-time that replaced the Newtonian understanding of phenomena within a fixed three-dimensional spatial system. His theory's holistic methodological grounds and its implications for science, epistemology, and metaphysics raise central questions in the philosophy of physics, as does his insistence in debates with Born on a realistic interpretation of quantum theory. His major works include *The Meaning of Relativity* (1921), *The Born–Einstein Letters* (1971), and *Collected Papers*, 2 vols. (1987–9).

élan vital

PHILOSOPHY OF SCIENCE [French *élan*, force or impetus] A central notion of the French philosopher Henri **Bergson**, introduced in *Creative Evolution* and translated as "impetus of life" or "vital impetus." Bergson was influenced by **Darwin**'s theory of **evolution**, but claimed that evolution cannot be a process of random **natural selection**. He argued that the theory fails to explain why biological evolution leads toward greater and greater complexity. He therefore postulated the existence of an *élan vital* underlying and determining the course of evolution. *Élan vital* is a force which is not capable of scientific explanation, but which pervades the whole of nature and presents itself in innumerable forms. By pushing nature to evolve into new but unforeseen forms of organic structures, it makes evolution a creative process rather than a mechanistic one. Bergson denied that introducing *élan vital* as a theoretical entity makes evolution teleological, but claimed that *élan vital* finds its most complete expression in human intelligence. Accordingly, human reason is at the highest level of evolution.

"The impetus of life [élan vital], of which we are speaking, consists in a need of creation. It cannot create absolutely, because it is confronted with matter, that is to say with the movement that is the universe of its own. But it seizes upon this matter, which is necessity itself and strives to introduce to it the largest possible amount of indetermination and liberty." **Bergson,** *Creative Evolution*

elementary proposition

LOGIC, PHILOSOPHY OF LANGUAGE, METAPHYSICS In **Wittgenstein**'s early philosophy, an elementary proposition is the simplest kind of proposition. It is the basis for analyzing other kinds of propositions but cannot itself be analyzed in terms of other propositions. Hence, elementary propositions are where the **analysis** of propositions terminates. Elementary propositions, which give language the fundamental capacity to picture the world, consist of **names**. The way in which the names are combined represents the way in which **objects** hang together in a **state of affairs**. Elementary propositions are meant to be logically independent of each other and not to contradict or entail one another, although Wittgenstein later recognized overwhelming difficulties with this

requirement. What elementary propositions depict are always positive **facts**. By depicting the totality of possible states of affairs as the world, the totality of elementary propositions forms a complete description of the world. Wittgenstein never gives an example of what such a proposition would be, and elementary propositions lose their importance in his later period.

For some **logical positivists**, an elementary proposition is also called a basic proposition or protocol sentence.

"The simplest kind of proposition, an elementary proposition, asserts the existence of a state of affairs." **Wittgenstein,** *Tractatus*

elenchus, see Socratic elenchus

elimination of metaphysics

EPISTEMOLOGY, PHILOSOPHY OF LANGUAGE, METAPHYSICS A slogan of **logical positivism**, representing the culmination of the anti-metaphysical tradition in the history of Western philosophy. **Hume** wanted to burn all books whose contents cannot be checked by our experience or by abstract reasoning concerning quantity or number. **Kant** criticized traditional metaphysics on the grounds of his examination of the nature and limits of knowledge. The attack by logical positivism, on the other hand, was based on a theory of language that was partly inherited from **Wittgenstein**'s *Tractatus*. Logical positivists claim that there are only two kinds of meaningful propositions: formal propositions, which are logical and mathematical principles, and factual propositions, which are empirically verifiable. Metaphysical propositions, which are about such things as the **absolute**, **essences**, **transcendent** entities, and **fate**, are literally nonsensical or **meaningless**, because they contain pseudo-words or because they are pseudo-statements, with an arrangement of words violating the rules of **logical syntax**, and lack any criteria of application. Thus, metaphysics breaks the rules that any utterance must satisfy if it is to be literally significant. All metaphysical questions and answers are irreconcilable with logic and scientific thinking. The root of the problem is that metaphysics establishes an impossible task for itself, that is, to discover a kind of knowledge that is beyond experience. Yet if something is beyond any possible experience, it could be neither said nor thought nor asked. Hence, according to logical positivists, metaphysics, though it has poetic merit and emotional value, does not contribute to knowledge. If philosophy wants to be a genuine branch of knowledge, it must emancipate itself from metaphysics. This position of the **Vienna Circle** is itself criticized, in part because its division between two kinds of meaningful propositions is not exhaustive. Furthermore, its attack ignores the detailed analysis of various metaphysical arguments, some of which have every appearance of being meaningful.

The elimination of metaphysics is a major theme in the work of **Heidegger** and **Derrida**, but these authors have found their successive attempts to exclude metaphysics from their work to have failed.

> "Logical analysis yields the negative result that the alleged statements in this domain are entirely meaningless. Therewith a radical elimination of metaphysics is attained, which was not yet possible from the earlier anti-metaphysical standpoints." **Carnap, "The Elimination of Metaphysics Through Logical Analysis of Language," in Ayer (ed.),** *Logical Positivism*

eliminative induction, another expression for induction by elimination

eliminative materialism

PHILOSOPHY OF MIND Also called the disappearance theory of mind, or eliminativism, the view that our standard mental concepts, such as belief and desire, are inappropriate for a serious scientific account of human beings. Our talk about **propositional attitudes** is misleading and should, or will be, eliminated. The mental phenomena to which these concepts are supposed to refer do not exist. **Folk psychology**, which employs these mental concepts, does not have the status of a serious theory. Instead, we must use the language of physics and neurophysiology to replace these notions. The leading advocates of this controversial theory include Paul Churchland, Patricia Churchland, Richard **Rorty**, and Stephen Stich. Eliminative materialism should be distinguished from the **identity theory** of mind, which believes in the existence of mental phenomena but insists that they are contingently identical with neuro-physical states.

> "[T]he eliminative materialists . . . have said, in effect, that our talk about the propositional attitudes is indeed just talk, but have then gone on to say that it is not only dispensable but should be dispensed with as soon as possible." **Lyons,** *Approaches to Intentionality*

eliminativism, another term for eliminative materialism

elite

ETHICS, POLITICAL PHILOSOPHY, PHILOSOPHY OF SOCIAL SCIENCE A group of persons who are pre-eminent according to some ideal of status or performance in a given society. Elites of various kinds occur in society, for example, scholarly elites contain the most learned academics, artistic elites contain the best writers and artists, and moral elites contain the most virtuous. The membership of an elite is generally regarded as providing the paradigm of achievement in a given area. On epistemological grounds, **Plato** claimed that the moral elite and the political elite are identical. He held that the most learned are also the most just and should be the rulers. Each moral theory generally has an ideal of the hero who best exemplifies its moral principles. For **Nietzsche**, a member of an elite is someone who best exercises the will of power and overcomes resentment. The word "elite" itself does not imply any special or unjustified privilege, although elites are liable to defend their own position rather than serving the wider society. The existence of elites in various fields is a fact, reflecting individual differences in talent and power. In contemporary liberal moral and political theory, an elite is understood to hold certain powers and privileges that mark it off from the rest of society. Elitism is contrasted to egalitarianism and promotes the role of elites, in some cases with anti-egalitarian consequences for the distribution of goods.

> "Majoritarian democracy, it is said, is therefore the most effective safeguard against the rule of a hypocritically self-interested elite." **Wolff,** *In Defense of Anarchism*

elitism

ETHICS, POLITICAL PHILOSOPHY The claim that society should train a group of pre-eminent individuals for positions of political leadership. The view was first elaborated by **Plato** in his *Republic*. He held that political power should be given to **philosopher-kings**, who would be the wisest and most intelligent members of society. An elite of the best people would make laws and determine policy, but an elitist program faces many difficulties. First, unless there were indeed a special wisdom of political leadership, choosing an elite would be arbitrary. Secondly, if there were such wisdom, it would be necessary to identify those possessing it to receive a suitable education. Thirdly, there would be problems in installing these experts in ruling positions and in protecting their rule against those who see it as illegitimate. Finally, a procedure would be needed for the regular and peaceful replacement of members of the elite. Elitism seems incompatible with democratic **liberalism**, which promotes **equality** and **liberty** and proposes that leadership should be elected from the general citizenry, but many liberal systems have chosen their political leadership from a privileged social and economic elite that has been educated for leadership.

"To advance an elitist hypothesis today it is not enough merely to argue . . . that an elite always or usually exist and that they are probably of decisive importance. In addition to this, it is now necessary to refute the widely held assumption that values such as equality, liberty, and freedom are universal and objective." **Field and Higley,** *Elitism*

Elster, Jon (1940–)
Norwegian social and political philosopher, Professor of Social Science, Columbia University. Elster's interdisciplinary approach to explaining social phenomena, combining philosophy, economics, and the theory of rational choice, has contributed to the development of analytic Marxism and has contributed to wider issues in normative political and social philosophy. His major works include *Sour Grapes* (1983) and *Making Sense of Marx* (1985).

emanation
METAPHYSICS A term in **Plotinus**' *Enneads*, a metaphorical description of the manner in which a lower-level reality is derived from a higher-level reality.

The supreme One is perfect, and its perfection is inevitably productive and creative. It spreads its goodness abroad by generating an external image of its internal activity. Thus, there is a necessary and spontaneous downward procession from the One to the Divine Mind, and then in turn to the Soul or Form, and finally to the material universe. This procession is one of emanation, like the radiation of heat from a fire or the diffusion of scent from a flower. It is simply a giving-out, which involves no change or diminution in the higher reality. The lower reality is at first produced as an unformed potentiality, but then turns back to the higher reality in contemplation and is thus informed and filled in content. According to Plotinus, the process of emanation is not temporal, but only indicates the relations of priority and dependence. Plotinus's poetic vision and his attempt to explain priority have both influenced later philosophers.

"The generation of reality by the One is described by the Neo-platonists in terms of their well-known image of emanation." **Wallis,** *Neo-platonism*

embodiment
PHILOSOPHY OF MIND The existence of states of the mind or soul caused by or identical with states of the body. In contrast, disembodiment is the existence of a person after bodily death. For **materialists**, a person can exist only in an embodied form. In the philosophy of mind, embodiment raises a problem about how **consciousness** relates to the brain and to the physical world more generally. If conscious states are causally determined by physical states, it is not clear how these physically caused states are governed. There are other difficulties in explaining why mental states are so different from the physical states that determine them. Another sense of embodiment is associated with the French philosopher **Merleau-Ponty**, who distinguished between one's objective body as a physiological entity, and one's phenomenal body, that is, one's own body as one experiences it. He considered such experience to be an experience of embodiment.

"This is the puzzle of how conscious states relate to the physical world, specifically to the body: the problem of embodiment." **McGinn,** *The Problem of Consciousness*

embraced desire

PHILOSOPHY OF ACTION, PHILOSOPHY OF MIND Actions are the results of human desires and intentions. If these desires and intentions are those that we desire or like ourselves to have, they are called embraced desires. Embraced desires enable us to do what is desired happily and willingly. In contrast are reluctant desires, which are the desires we do not wish to have. Reluctant desires push us to do something we do not really want to do. They emerge especially when we are frustrated or in situations where we are being obstructed.

"Reluctant desires and intentions, we can say, are those which operate in situations to which the agent is somehow opposed. Embraced desires and intentions satisfy the condition that they operate in situations which the agent at least accepts." **Honderich,** *A Theory of Determinism,* **vol. 2**

emergence

PHILOSOPHY OF SCIENCE, PHILOSOPHY OF SOCIAL SCIENCE Based on the assumption that a whole is more than the sum of all its parts, the doctrine of emergence holds that the whole has properties which cannot be explained in terms of the properties of its parts. Such a property is called an **emergent property**. The enormous complexity of the interactions among parts leads to the generation of a property of the whole that cannot be deduced from the properties of parts. This position, which was held historically by C. L. Morgan and S. Alexander, objects to the **reductionist** interpretation of organization. One of its contemporary variants is **methodological holism**, which holds that facts about a society cannot be reduced to facts about individuals. A society or group has some characteristics that cannot be defined or explained by the characteristics of its members. This theory, also called emergentism, is also useful in explaining psychological and biological phenomena. An important version of anti-emergentist views is **methodological individualism**.

"The doctrine of emergence is sometimes formulated as a thesis about the hierarchical organisation of things and processes, and the consequent occurrence of properties at 'higher' levels of organisation which are not predictable from properties found at 'lower' levels." **Nagel,** *The Structure of Science*

emergent property

PHILOSOPHY OF SCIENCE, AESTHETICS Complex systems such as a living organism seem to possess some properties that cannot wholly be reduced to the characteristics of its individual components or be predicted from them. These properties seem not to be the sum of the components of that system, but to be something new and different that emerges from their combination. They are called emergent properties. The thesis that there are such properties is called the doctrine of **emergence** or emergentism. Aesthetic qualities are often held to be emergent from the combination of other properties of aesthetic objects, such as shape, color, texture, and size. In contrast, additive properties can be reduced to the properties of the components of a system. It is a matter of dispute whether ultimately all properties are additive.

"It may seem that we should make a further distinction between two sorts of regional property, which are sometimes called summative (or additive) and emergent . . . We might say that the brightness of a white light made up of two white lights is summative; the colour of a light made up of two different coloured lights is emergent." **Beardsley,** *Aesthetics*

emergentism, see emergence

Emerson, Ralph Waldo (1803–82)

American philosopher and essayist, born in Boston, educated at Harvard, the leading figure of New England Transcendentalism. Influenced by German romanticism and absolute idealism, Emerson claimed that nature is a higher spiritual reality. There is a correspondence between the human soul and the universe, and man should live his life in conformity to nature. He rejected contemporary American commercialism and advocated self-reliance and the self-development of the individual. His major books include *Nature* (1836), *Representative Men* (1850), *The Conduct of Life* (1860), *Society and Solitude* (1870), and *Letters and Social Aims* (1876).

emotion

PHILOSOPHY OF MIND, PHILOSOPHY OF ACTION, ETHICS [from Latin *e*, out + *movere*, move, agitating motions] Aristotle claimed that emotion, which he called

passion [Greek *pathos*, being acted upon] is a process or motion. Emotions are complex mental states with various degrees of intensity. Unlike moods, they are about some real or imagined objects. They give rise to actions or reactions. In this respect, they are associated with the **will**, but are distinguished from feeling in general because not all kinds of feeling are action-causing. Emotions are accompanied or expressed by bodily symptoms or external behavior. Typical emotions include love, anger, fear, joy, anxiety, pride, contempt, compassion, and indignation, and can occur alone or in combination.

It is difficult to determine both the place and the role of emotions. **Plato** divided the human soul into three parts and held that emotion, as the state characteristic of the intermediate part, lies between appetite and reason. It can either help reason to control appetite or take the side of appetite to rebel against reason. This ambivalent position led to two contrary attitudes toward emotion in the later development of ethics. Rational ethics considers emotion to be a threat to morality and requires it to be governed by reason, while others, represented by **Hume** and **Nietzsche**, believe that emotion rather than reason is the center of moral life. **Descartes**'s study of the passions initiated important seventeenth-century discussion of the emotions.

William **James** and Carl G. Lange independently developed a position according to which emotion is a brute fact, a specific feeling caused by characteristic bodily changes in response to external stimuli. This thesis, which is called the "**James–Lange view**," initiated the modern discussion of emotion. If emotion is the mental expression of bodily change, is it subject to the assessment of reason? Many traditional philosophers deplore the arationality of emotion, according to which emotion is neither rational nor irrational, but **emotivism** holds that emotion can cause cognition. Others consider that emotion can lead us to apprehend things in certain ways and is complementary to reason. According to this view, emotion has moral, aesthetic, and religious value.

Emotion is associated with both **virtues** and vices. Some types of emotion, such as jealousy and pride, are vices, while others, such as love and benevolence, are virtues. It is disputed whether emotions are objective or subjective. For example, when we love something, is it because the object is loveable in itself, or because we project a subjective

feeling upon it? **Freud** claimed that emotion is a reaction to something in our **unconscious**, rather than to something external. Many other modern writers have explored the diversity, complexity, and opacity of the emotions.

> "Emotions do not form a natural class. After a long history of quite diverse debates about their classification, emotions have come to form a heterogeneous group: various conditions and states have been included in the class for quite different reasons and on different grounds, against the background of shifting contrasts." **Rorty (ed.),** *Explaining Emotions*

emotive meaning

ETHICS, PHILOSOPHY OF LANGUAGE A term introduced by the **logical positivists** in their discussions of the verifiability criterion. According to that criterion, only statements that can be checked by empirical evidence are meaningful. However, there are many apparently meaningful statements, such as those associated with moral discourse, which cannot be tested by experience. The logical positivists claimed that such statements are not factually or cognitively meaningful, but have emotive meaning, that is, emotive force. A detailed discussion of emotive meaning was developed by C. K. Ogden and I. A. Richards, who distinguish the symbolic (referential) and emotive functions of language. In their symbolic function, statements refer to things; in their emotive function, they express and evoke feelings and attitudes. In his emotivism, C. L. **Stevenson** distinguished between the **descriptive meaning** and emotive meaning of expressions. The distinction lies in the kind of states of mind expressed or aroused. If the state of mind is cognitive, the meaning of the term conveys information and is descriptive. If the state of mind is affective or emotional, the meaning of the expression is emotive. Expressions in emotive meanings do not refer to the qualities of things, but prescribe a particular action or course of conduct. According to Stevenson, the meaning of ethical terms is descriptive in a sense, but primarily and chiefly emotive.

> "The emotive meaning of a word or phrase is a strong and persistent tendency, built up in the course of linguistic history, to give direct expression

"(quasi-interjectionally) to certain of the speaker's feelings or emotions or attitudes; and it is also a tendency to evoke (quasi-imperatively) corresponding feelings, emotions, or attitudes in those to whom the speaker's remarks are addressed."
Stevenson, *Facts and Values*

emotivism

ETHICS, AESTHETICS, PHILOSOPHY OF LANGUAGE Also called the emotive theory of ethics. An account of the function of evaluative utterances in terms of the expression of the speaker's emotion and the evoking of the hearer's **emotion**, and a theory of evaluative fields such as ethics and aesthetics in terms of this account. The position can be traced to **Berkeley**, who claimed that evaluative terms such as "good" serve to raise some **passion** rather than to convey information. The view was developed in the twentieth century by the **logical positivists**, particularly **Ayer**, who claimed that ethical judgments are neither statements of non-ethical scientific facts nor statements of non-scientific ethical facts, but are only expressions of emotion that can be neither true nor false. In this way, to say that something is right or wrong amounts to saying "Hoorah!" or "Boo!" Hence, this version of emotivism is nicknamed the "**boo-hoorah theory**." A full and sophisticated theory of emotivism is elaborated by C. L. **Stevenson** in his classical work *Ethics and Language* (1944). It argues that traditional moral theories generally but mistakenly take moral judgments to be nothing but descriptive expressions. Ethical utterances might be descriptive, but their main or primary meaning is emotive, for they do not refer to qualities in things, but function like interjections ("Alas!"), imperatives ("Do such and such!"), optatives ("Would that this were so"), prescriptions ("You should such and such"), or **performatives** ("I apologize"). An ethical statement is chiefly used to express (but not to report) one's attitude and to try to influence the attitudes and conduct of others. Hence any purely descriptive account of evaluative judgments must be deficient. Other major proponents of emotivism include P. H. Nowell-Smith, Paul Edwards, and R. M. **Hare**. Hare's theory has been called "**prescriptivism**" or, by Stevenson himself, "near-emotivism." Emotivism was a major ethical theory in the twentieth century, but has lost its dominant position in recent decades, partly through changing

understanding of the role of language and **analysis** in philosophy and partly because of its failure to connect morality with reason.

"Emotivism is the doctrine that all evaluative judgements and more specifically all moral judgements are nothing but expressions of preference, expressions of attitude or feeling, insofar as they are moral or evaluative in character." **MacIntyre, *After Virtue***

empathy

ETHICS, AESTHETICS, PHILOSOPHY OF HISTORY [from Greek *en*, in, into + *pathos*, feeling or passion, literally being in or into a state of emotion] A term introduced by the psychologist E. B. Titchener (1867–1927). In aesthetics, empathy is the unconscious projection of one's own inner feelings into an aesthetic object or activity. In ethics, it is a person's insightful understanding of the inner feelings of another person on the basis of a sympathetic imaginative identification with that person, although the role of empathy in our ethical responses is much debated. Empathy corresponds to the German term *Einfühlung*, and is used in **hermeneutics** for a method characteristic of the humanities, involving the re-creation in the mind of the scholar of the thoughts, feeling, and motivations of the objects of his study.

"The operations of sympathetic understanding or, as it is often now called, 'empathy', have been much discussed in the history of moral philosophy." **B. Williams, *Ethics and the Limits of Philosophy***

Empedocles (*c*.490–430 BC)

Greek natural philosopher, born in Acragas, Sicily. Empedocles wrote two long philosophical poems (*On the Nature of Things* and *Hymns of Purification*), but only fragments of them survive. He held that things in the world were formed out of four roots or elements (earth, water, air, and fire). Alongside these elements are two principles, Love and Strife. Love unites the elements, whereas Strife separates them. Love and Strife alternate in periods of domination of the kosmos as a whole. Empedocles used understanding of generation and destruction in terms of the combination and separation of several ultimate constituents to respond to Parmenides' rejection of the possibility of change.

emphatic particulars, another term for egocentric particulars

empiricism

EPISTEMOLOGY, METAPHYSICS A philosophical approach to knowledge and reality. Its central contentions are that all **knowledge** or all meaningful discourse about the world is related to sensory experience (including inner sense or introspection), and that the boundaries of possible sense-experience are the boundaries of possible knowledge. Different empiricists have different views about how knowledge is based on sensation. The major interest of empiricism is in the sphere of sense-perception, and it offers detailed examinations of problems concerning **perception**, the relation between **sense-data** and material **objects**, the problem of the **external world**, and the results and methodology of the sciences. This approach embraces concreteness and particularity, and encourages rigorous standards of clarity and precision. Empiricism claims that the sciences provide our best knowledge of reality. It is suspicious of abstraction and generalization and rejects all irrational and superstitious claims. The major difficulty empiricism faces is to provide a satisfactory account of **universals**, and of *a priori* **necessary truths** in mathematics and logic. Empiricism contrasts with **rationalism**, taken as an epistemological approach that gives a lesser role to sense-experience and emphasizes the centrality of the faculty of reason itself in knowledge. When rationalism is taken broadly as respect for reason and a rejection of irrationality, empiricism is a type of rationalism. Modern scholarship rejects too sharp a distinction between rationalism and empiricism among some of the great seventeenth-century philosophers.

Empiricism as a tradition can be traced to **Aristotle**, and has been deeply rooted in the British intellectual tradition since the Middle Ages. The classical British empiricists include **Hobbes, Locke, Berkeley**, and **Hume**, and in the twentieth century **Russell, Ayer**, and the **Vienna Circle** (also called logical empiricists) are its major representatives.

"Modern empiricism has been conditioned in large part by two dogmas. One is a belief in some fundamental cleavage between truths which are analytic, or grounded in meanings independently of matter of fact, and truths which are synthetic, or grounded in fact. The other dogma is reductionism: the belief that each meaningful statement is equivalent to some logical construct upon terms which refer to immediate experience." **Quine,** *From a Logical Point of View*

empirio-criticism

EPISTEMOLOGY A rigorously **positivist** and radically empirical philosophy, established by the German philosopher Richard Avenarius and developed by the Austrian scientist and philosopher Ernst **Mach**. Developing the thought of **Berkeley** and **Hume**, empirio-criticism claims that all we can know is our **sensations** and that knowledge should be confined to pure **experience**. Any metaphysical claims, such as the objective existence of the **external world** or of **causation**, which transcends experience and cannot be verified by experience, must be rejected as a construct of the mind. Philosophy should be based on scientific principles. This position influenced **logical positivism** and **James's pragmatism**. Lenin severely attacked it in his *Materialism and Empirio-Criticism* (1908) and even claimed that this type of philosophy represents the interests of capitalism. What he criticized was the espousal of Mach's views by his fellow Bolsheviks Bogdanov, Bazarov, and others.

"I shall refer to those arguments by which materialism is being combated . . . Machians. I shall use this latter term throughout as a synonym for 'empirio-criticists'. . . ." **Lenin,** *Materialism and Empirio-Criticism*

empty class, another term for null class

empty name

LOGIC, PHILOSOPHY OF LANGUAGE A name which does not have a bearer or does not refer to any particular. These names are grammatical realities of a type that **Russell** called **logical** fictions. Empty names such as "Santa Claus" are intelligible, even when they have no bearer, but the explanation for this is uncertain. Russell rejected **Frege's** account in terms of his distinction between **sense and reference** and gave his own account in terms of names and associated **descriptions**.

"Philosophers have thought that . . . there can be names without bearers – what have been called 'empty names'." **C. Williams**, *Being, Identity and Truth*

enantiomorphs, another term for incongruent counterparts

encompassing

MODERN EUROPEAN PHILOSOPHY A basic term of the German **existentialist** Karl **Jaspers**. We always think within a **horizon**, and a horizon itself indicates something that goes beyond it. The Encompassing is the horizon within which every particular horizon is enclosed and from which the closed whole of **Being** can be reached. The Encompassing transcends the division of subject and **object**, and its basic structure is the simultaneity of subject-being and object-being. The Encompassing is a philosophical operation, which is directed from totality toward the phenomenological totality of being in all its fullness and richness. With the Encompassing, our consciousness of being is free from any specific knowing. The Encompassing is prior to reason and is the source of all knowing and all being. It has seven modes: *Existenz*, **transcendence**, *Dasein*, consciousness-as-such, spirit, world, and reason. The basic difficulty with Jaspers's notion is to show how the Encompassing can be conceived while maintaining its special fundamental status. For once we think about the Encompassing, it becomes an object and a special kind of being.

"What is neither object nor act of thinking (subject), but contains both within itself, I have called the Encompassing." **Jaspers**, *The Philosophy of Karl Jaspers*

end-in-view

PHILOSOPHY OF MIND, PHILOSOPHY OF ACTION A term used by **Dewey** to criticize the mechanistic view of the **means–end** relationship popular in motivational psychology. Dewey claimed that although there is a fixed actual end, at the moment of deliberation one acts in terms of an end-in-view rather than the actual end. The end-in-view is a plan or a hypothesis that guides present activity and is to be evaluated by its consequences and revised throughout the activity guided by it. Its appraisal springs from the fact that

there is something lacking or wanting in the existing situation. Things can be anticipated as ends only in terms of the conditions by which they are brought into existence. Thus, an end-in-view is also a means of organizing actions. The term reflects the reciprocal characters of ends and means. With this term, Dewey attempted to extend the notion of a hypothesis, which is usually limited to science, to the domains of morality, education, and other social theories in order to include all act-guiding ideas.

"The end-in-view is formed and projected as that which, if acted on, will supply the existing need or lack and resolve the existing conflict." **Dewey**, *Theory of Evaluation*

end of art, another expression for death of art

end/means, see means/end

endoxa

ANCIENT GREEK PHILOSOPHY, EPISTEMOLOGY, PHILOSOPHICAL METHOD [Greek, a commonly held opinion or common belief, in this sense a kind of *phainomenon*] Beliefs that can be the beliefs of ordinary people, but are especially the views of any notable group or wise person worth attending to. In **Aristotle**'s **dialectic** procedure, he always began his argument with the opinions of his predecessors or the beliefs held by most people. After stating the conflicts among these beliefs, he tried to clarify what could justifiably be retained from them and then tried to reach an acceptable position reconciling as far as possible the views he considered.

"Endoxa are those opinions which are accepted by everyone or by the majority or by the wise – that is, by all, or by the majority, or by the most notable and reputable of them." **Aristotle**, *Topics*

enforcement of morals

ETHICS, POLITICAL PHILOSOPHY, PHILOSOPHY OF LAW A thesis that society should make use of criminal law to solve moral issues such as **pornography** and **homosexuality**. It presupposes that the law can justifiably act to shape or restrict private morality. We should not draw a clear-cut distinction between law and morality or between crime and sin. On this view, by softening these distinctions society will promote the development of noble morality and create suitable conditions for human flourishing. Representatives of this position included Sir J. F. Stephen and Lord Devlin. Their claims are based on natural law theory and on the belief that morality is a divine command. The position contrasts with **Mill**'s **harm principle**, which suggests that law exists in order to protect one from demonstrable harm at the hands of others, and that the only reason for society to restrict an individual's **liberty** in terms of law is that the individual's action causes harm to others. Supporters of **legal positivism** maintain that law and morality are independent and that it is therefore wrong to employ the criminal law to uphold morality. Major problems facing the thesis concern which morality the law should enforce in a morally complex society, and how to strike a balance between individual freedom and the integrity of society.

> "The morals which he [the law-maker] enforces are those ideas about right and wrong which are already accepted by the society for which he is legislating and which are necessary to preserve its integrity." **Devlin**, *The Enforcement of Morals*

enlightened self-interest, see self-interest

Enlightenment
EPISTEMOLOGY, METAPHYSICS, ETHICS, POLITICAL PHILOSOPHY, PHILOSOPHY OF RELIGION A broad and powerful intellectual movement in seventeenth- and eighteenth-century Europe, particularly in Britain, France, and Germany, characterized by a rejection of superstition and mystery and an optimism concerning the power of human reason and scientific endeavor. Because of these features, it is also called the Age of Reason. The movement placed secular reason as the ultimate judge of all sorts of dogma or authority and attempted to overcome the control of the Catholic Church over human affairs. According to major Enlightenment thinkers, everyone is equal and has the same status in virtue of his rationality. The movement advocated investigating everything openly and freely in accordance with the methods of natural sciences. Everything that could not sustain rational investigation had to be abandoned. The slogan for this movement was "Have courage to use your reason!" (Latin *sapere aude!*).

Theologically, the Enlightenment developed the doctrines of "**deism**," which claimed that religious doctrines should meet the standards of reason. Politically, it emphasized natural **liberty** and human **rights** and advocated religious **toleration**. Philosophically, the Enlightenment produced various forms of **materialism** and **determinism**. The *Encyclopaedia*, edited by the French philosophers **Diderot** and **d'Alembert**, was the representative document of the Enlightenment.

The movement completely rejected the role of **tradition** and **culture**. Critics claimed that by over-emphasizing the role of reason, it ignored the value of **community** and commitment. Hence the movement came to be criticized by many schools of counter-Enlightenment and post-Enlightenment thinking.

> "In the most general sense of progressive thought, the Enlightenment has always aimed at liberating men from fear and establishing their sovereignty. Yet the fully enlightened earth radiates disaster triumphant. The program of the Enlightenment was the disenchantment of the world; the dissolution of myths and the substitution of knowledge for fancy." **Adorno and Horkheimer**, *Dialectic of Enlightenment*

enlightenment project
ETHICS, POLITICAL PHILOSOPHY Alasdair **MacIntyre**'s term for the pattern of thought that underlies the entirety of moral and political philosophy since the Enlightenment. This pattern seeks to provide us with a neutral ground of morality and political principles. It appeals to pure reason and establishes an abstract and ruled-governed ethics that attempts to justify particular actions by applying universal standards. Yet it rejects teleology and denies that the human race has its own *telos* to fulfill. Consequently, the distinction between what is and what should be is abolished, and the universal standards and principles themselves lose their necessary framework of values and their grounds of evaluation. The enlightenment project, especially in its **liberal** individualistic form, emphasizes the free choices and **rights** of the individual, but disregards the social and historical context in which actual individuals are embedded. According to MacIntyre, the enlightenment project has failed to fulfill its promise, and its failure has led to the chaos of moral values in

contemporary Western culture. His *After Virtue* (1981) aims to identify this failure and argues that the remedy is to replace rule-governed ethics with **virtue ethics**, and to replace asocial **individualism** with **communitarianism**. His characterization and criticism of the enlightenment project has stirred wide debates and has in some sense shaped the development of moral and political philosophy in the past decade.

> "A central thesis of this book is that the breakdown of this [enlightenment] project provided the historical background against which the predicaments of our own culture can become intelligible." **MacIntyre,** *After Virtue*

ens ab alio, see *ens a se*

ens a se

METAPHYSICS, PHILOSOPHY OF RELIGION [Latin, being from itself and in itself] A medieval term for a kind of **being**, which contrasts with being out of itself (*ens ex se*) and with being that depends upon another thing as the ground of its existence (*ens ab alio*). In medieval philosophy, *ens a se* is a thing that is completely self-sufficient and depends on nothing else for its existence, and this description is ascribed solely to God. The idea is derived from the biblical teaching that **God** is the Creator. God is *ens a se* by existing independent of anything else, but all created things, including human beings, are *ens ex se* because they depend on God for their existence. The term **aseity** (Latin *aseitas*) was formed from *ens a se* for the abstract property of being completely independent. Some scholastics used the distinction between *ens a se* and *ens ab alio* as the basis of a proof of the existence of God. They argued that since we experience the things in this world as *ens ab alio*, which depend on another thing for the ground of their existence, there must be something which is *ens a se* on which they depend. Otherwise, an infinite regress would ensue. An account of God as *ens a se*, on which we depend for our being, poses the problem of how to reconcile the existence of God with human **free will**. **Spinoza** transformed the notion of *ens a se* into *causa sui* (self-cause), which he identified with **substance**, that is, God or nature. He also transformed the notion of *ens ab alio* into his concept of **mode**.

> "As well as being *a se*, I understand God to be 'metaphysically necessary'. By this I mean that he is the or a cause of every logically contingent 'fact', or state of affairs, at any time and at any place." **Padgett,** *God, Eternity and the Nature of Time*

ens ex se, see *ens a se*

ens irreale, see *ens reale*

ens necessarius

METAPHYSICS, PHILOSOPHY OF RELIGION [Latin, a necessary being] A necessarily existing being, whose **essence** necessarily and directly implies its **existence**. It is the only being in which essence and existence coincide. This being is not constrained by reason and is self-sufficient because it is free from both rational motives and external causes. **God** is claimed to be such a being and moreover to be the only being of this kind. **Spinoza** argued that his substance is such a being and is identical with God or nature. Some philosophers argue that the notion of a necessary being is philosophically confused because only propositions or sentences can be necessary. Because existence is not a predicate, "X necessarily exists" does not say anything that could be true. Other philosophers reply that there can be *de re* **necessity** ascribed to things and that something would exist necessarily if it existed in all **possible worlds**.

> "*Ens necessarius*, i.e. an entity of which the essence is such that it would not be what, qua essence, it is, if it did not also exist." **Lovejoy,** *The Great Chain of Being*

ens rationis

METAPHYSICS, LOGIC, PHILOSOPHY OF MIND, PHILOSOPHY OF LANGUAGE A thing which has only rational or mental being (plural, *entia rationis*). An *ens rationis* can be thought or said, but does not really exist in the world. For example, **abstract entities**, **universals**, **possibilities**, fictions, and **ideal** things are *entia rationis*. They exist as objects of knowledge and as mental constructs. The nature of beings of this kind is a topic of everlasting concern for metaphysicians and logicians. For **Kant**, an *ens rationis* was a concept without an object, excluded from the possibilities, but not on those grounds rendered impossible.

Brentano, who calls an *ens rationis* an object-type that is conventionally introduced to express what there is, claims that we can call it being only in a loose and improper sense. Other writers defend a more robust ontological status for some sorts of *ens rationis*.

"*Entia rationis*, things which somehow exist in the mind." **Brentano**, *Psychology from an Empirical Standpoint*

ens reale

METAPHYSICS, PHILOSOPHY OF MIND **Brentano** divided things into *ens reale* (plural, *entia realia*) and *ens irreale* (plural, *entia irrealia*). The former is ordinarily translated as "real (or actual) thing" and the latter as "unreal thing." But this is not precise. *Entia realia* are not only real things such as dogs, human beings, and tables, but also imaginary things such as unicorns. Hence, **Chisholm** suggests translating this term as "individuals." *Entia irrealia* are such things as privations, possibilities, properties, concepts, and propositions, and Chisholm translates the term as "non-individuals." An alternative translation renders *ens reale* as "concretum" and *ens irreale* as "non-concretum." Brentano's **realism** holds that *entia realia* are the only things that exist and are the only things of which we can think. On this view, all statements about *entia irrealia* can be reduced upon **analysis** into statements about *entia realia*.

"Brentano's more general point may be put this way: we can think only of *entia realia*; and to think of an *ens reale* is to think of something which, if it existed, would be an individual." **Chisholm**, *Brentano and Intrinsic Value*

ens successivam

METAPHYSICS [Latin, successive being] An entity which changes one or another of its parts as it endures through time. The term was introduced by **Augustine**, who claimed that the universe is such an entity, in that it is composed of successively existing parts. For **Aquinas**, it is a thing with some parts that do not exist at the same time as other of its parts. The term was revived in **mereological essentialism**, which claims that the parts of an object are essential to its identity and cannot change so long as the object maintains its identity. The

succeeding parts of a thing, therefore, are not parts in any real sense.

"This is what might be called the ens successivum – the 'successive table' that is made up of different parts at different times." **Chisholm**, *Person and Object*

entailment

LOGIC The relationship between **statements**, by which one statement (the conclusion) follows logically from another statement or statements (the premises). Entailment permits the conclusion to be logically, necessarily, or validly deduced from the premises. The traditional and classical criterion of entailment is that S entails Q if and only if to assert S while denying Q would result in inconsistency. Because this criterion involves the paradoxes of **strict implication**, some logicians have been trying to find a more precise criterion.

"'S_1 entails S_2' may be defined as 'S_1 and not-S_2 is inconsistent'." **Strawson**, *Introduction to Logical Theory*

entelechy

ANCIENT GREEK PHILOSOPHY, METAPHYSICS [from Greek *enteles*, end + *echein*, having within, having an end within] **Aristotle**'s term, normally translated as actualization but often merely transliterated as entelechy. It is etymologically associated with the completion or perfect state toward which an action or a process internally leads. Entelechy is the form that becomes the end of motion for each thing or potential matter realized within itself. Aristotle used the term interchangeably with *energeia* (generally rendered as actuality). **Leibniz** used this term for the primitive active force in **monads**. The vitalist Hans Driesh held that all organisms have an entelechy as an inner goal-directed, non-material life-force which promotes their development toward becoming perfect adults.

"The term 'actuality' [*energeia*] is derived from 'activity' [*ergon*], and points to *entelechy* [actualization]." **Aristotle**, *Metaphysics*

enthusiasm

EPISTEMOLOGY, PHILOSOPHY OF MIND [from Greek *enthousiatikos*, to be inspired] **Plato** characterized poets in terms of *enthousiatikos* because their works proceed from inspiration by God rather than from rational knowledge. Thus they do not have knowledge regarding their works. Later enthusiasm was understood to be emotional zeal or impulse manifested in irrational behavior. It is taken by John **Locke** as a third source of assent besides faith and reason, but was used pejoratively as a synonym of fanaticism by **Leibniz** and **Kant**.

> "This I take to be properly enthusiasm, which, though founded neither on reason nor divine revelation, but rising from the conceits of a warmed or overweening brain, works yet, where it once gets footing, more powerfully on the persuasions and actions of men than either of those two, or both together, men being most forwardly obedient to the impulse they receive from themselves." **Locke,** *An Essay Concerning Human Understanding*

enthymene
LOGIC [Greek, an inference based on a probable or an unstated premise or with an unstated conclusion] In **Aristotle**'s original use, an **inference** based on a probable premise, but later a **syllogism** or other form of inference in which one premise or conclusion is not explicitly stated. The omitted premise or conclusion is in general easily supplied. For example, "Every person is mortal, so Smith is mortal." This is an enthymene, for the premise "Smith is a person" is not stated. An enthymene can produce a false conclusion if the supplied premise is false or if it does not render the argument valid.

> "These syllogisms are expressed as enthymenes, i.e. with the omission of one at least of the requisite propositions." **Johnson,** *Logic*

entia per alio
METAPHYSICS [singular, *ens per alio*] A **scholastic** term for things which, like parasites, derive all their properties from other things. The grounds of existence for them is not in themselves. They cannot persist through time, and they evaporate if the things that sustain them disappear. *Entia per alio* are in contrast to *entia per se*, which are entities that have their own independent identities.

> "An *ens per alio* never is or has anything on its own. It is what it is in virtue of the nature of something other than itself." **Chisholm,** *Person and Object*

entia per se, see *entia per alio*

entia rationis, Latin term for entities of reason

entity
METAPHYSICS [from Latin *ens*, being, thing] A term generally used interchangeably with thing or object. Joseph Owens has proposed that entity should be used to translate the Greek *ousia*, which is usually translated as **substance**, because *ousia* is derived from the Greek copula *estin* and entity is similarly derived from the Latin copula *ens*. Hence, this translation would maintain an important etymological relation. However, his suggestion has difficulties. While *ousia* can be used both independently and as "*ousia* of . . . ," in English we cannot say "entity of . . ."

> "In consequence of this perversion of the word Being, philosophers looking about for something to supply its place, laid their hands upon the word entity, a piece of barbarous Latin, invented by the schoolmen to be used as an abstract name, in which class its grammatical form would seem to place it, but being seized by logicians in distress to stop a leak in their terminology, it has ever since been used as a concrete name." *The Collected Works of John Stuart Mill,* **vol. VII**

entity of reason
METAPHYSICS, EPISTEMOLOGY [Latin *ens rationis*, also called an ideal entity] In **Scholastic** philosophy, there are things which do not really exist, but which are apprehended by reason, that is, conceptual entities such as **relations**, orderings, or general notions. A relation does not exist like a **substance** or **accident**, but is a conception obtained by **abstraction** from a consideration of things having certain associations to each other. An entity of reason is not an actual thing, but is an object of knowledge and has its foundations in actual things.

> "If 'nothing' means something imaginary, or what they commonly call an entity of reason [*ens rationis*], then this is not 'nothing' but something real and distinctly conceived. Nevertheless, since it is merely conceived and is not actual, although it can be conceived, it cannot in any way be caused." **Descartes,** *The Philosophical Writings*

entrenchment

LOGIC, PHILOSOPHY OF LANGUAGE A term introduced
by **Goodman**, in association with **Goodman's paradox** or the **new riddle of induction**, as a function
of the frequency and success of projection in producing true statements. If a **predicate** has been projected
frequently in past generalizations, it is entrenched
for future generalizations of the same sort and
has high **projectibility**. For example, all observed
emeralds have been both green and grue (green to
some future time T and blue thereafter), and any
evidence confirming the generalization that all
emeralds are green also confirms that all emeralds
are grue. Nevertheless, we call them green rather
than grue because "green" is better entrenched and
more projectible than "grue," and we will conclude
that future emeralds will be green, not grue.
Entrenchment is not identical with familiarity, for
relatively unfamiliar predicates can also be well
entrenched. The entrenchment of a predicate
results not only from the actual projection of that
predicate alone, but also from the projection of all
predicates coextensive with it. Entrenchment is the
decisive factor for projectibility, and the degree
of entrenchment of a predicate provides us with a
criterion for deciding between projectible predicates.
A predicate is unprojectible if it is not entrenched.

> "Entrenchment depends upon frequency of pro-
> jection rather than upon mere frequency of use."
> **Goodman,** *Fact, Fiction and Forecast*

entropy

PHILOSOPHY OF SCIENCE In physics, the measure
of disorder, which is defined either in terms of the
interchange of heat and other forms of energy or as
proportional to the statistical probability of the random arrangement of particles in a physical system.
According to the second law of thermodynamics,
entropy always increases in an isolated system, that
is, the system becomes more and more disordered.
Entropy is also employed in information theory as a
measure of information content, defined by a formal
probability function called Shannon entropy.

> "In a qualitative interpretation the law of entropy
> asserts that a gas to which no energy is added and
> from which no energy is subtracted (an 'isolated
> system') will approach a state of uniform density
> and uniform temperature." **Pap,** *An Introduction to
> the Philosophy of Science*

enumerative induction, another expression for
induction by enumeration

environmental ethics

ETHICS An ethics motivated by contemporary
environmental crises such as air and water pollution,
the degradation of ecosystems, the extinction of
species, and soil erosion. The basis of environmental
ethics is an opposition to the historical anthropocentrism (also called **speciesism** or human chauvinism)
of traditional ethics, which takes non-human living
things and nature as objects of exploitation and
as means to human ends, rather than as ends in
themselves. Environmental ethics tries to establish
human responsibility toward these entities and
nature as a whole. It is not simply a branch of
applied ethics, but involves establishing a new and
distinctive theoretical framework.

There are various approaches to environmental
ethics. Weak anthropocentrism accepts that human
interest is still primary, but argues that human
beings should cultivate an attitude of noble obligation toward the environment. Animal-centered
ethics, also called the **animal liberation** movement
or zoocentrism, claims that we must extend the
scope of ethical consideration from human beings
alone to members of all animal species, on the
grounds that animals are sentient beings (Peter
Singer) or "subjects-of-a-life" (Tom Regan). On this
view, rationality is rejected as the criterion for
membership of the moral community. Life-centered
ethics or biocentrism, represented by K. E. Goodpaster and Paul Taylor, argues that all classes of
living beings, including plants as well as animals,
should be included in the moral community. Weak
anthropocentrism, animal-centered ethics, and life-
centered ethics all hold that traditional human
ethical theory is sound and with alterations can be
applied to areas other than human society. Other
versions of environmental ethics argue against the
extension of human ethics to non-human beings and
claim that we need a new ethics because human
ethics is inescapably anthropocentric. Furthermore,
traditional human ethics is **individualistic**, while an
adequate **holistic** ethics should be concerned with
the ecosystem as a whole and with relations amongst
entities within the ecosystem. On this view, the
integrity, diversity, and stability of the ecosystem
should be the primary standard by which the morality of an action is judged. This holistic approach,

or **ecocentrism**, is sometimes accused of being an environmental fascism. Its major schools include land ethics, represented by Aldo Leopold, J. B. Callicott, and H. Rolston III, deep ecology, represented by A. Naess, and ecofeminism, which argues that the subjection of nature to human beings corresponds to the subjection of women to men and sees the liberation of nature and the liberation of women as aspects of the same process.

> "Environmental ethics is the field of inquiry that addresses the ethical responsibilities of human beings for the natural environment." **Armstrong and Botzler (eds.),** *Environmental Ethics*

environmental fascism

ETHICS Tom Regan's epithet for the land ethics of Aldo Leopold and others, which proposes an **holistic** approach to the biotic community and claims that the criterion for the morality of an action is whether it promotes the integrity, diversity, and stability of the biotic community. Regan, who stresses the central position of human individuals in moral considerations, claims that if land ethics faces a conflict between human interests and the interests of the environment, it would require the sacrifice of human interests for the greater biotic good. Since there are too many people and too few trees on this planet, for example, land ethics might demand that we eliminate much of the human population and plant many more trees. But defenders of land ethics have replied that this is by no means an inevitable consequence of this theory.

> "It is difficult to see how the notion of the rights of the individual could find a home within a view that, emotive connotations to one side, might be fairly dubbed 'environmental fascism'." **Regan,** *The Case for Animal Rights*

envy

ETHICS, POLITICAL PHILOSOPHY A negative feeling that arises from perceiving others as having some good which one desires but lacks or has to a lesser degree. Envy, which can lead to hostile and destructive actions aimed at harming the person one envies, is a major theme in literature. Envy is often due to a threat to one's self-esteem. **Egalitarianism** is proposed partly to reduce the phenomenon of envy, but opponents of egalitarianism often claim that its demand for equality is based on envy. Another

proposal argues that strengthening the self-esteem of members of society will allow them to accept greater goods held by others without envy, although this outcome might depend on a shared conception of a just distribution of goods.

> "We may think of envy as the propensity to view with hostility the greater good of others even though their being more fortunate than we does not detract from our advantages." **Rawls,** *A Theory of Justice*

Epictetus (c.55–135)

Roman Stoic philosopher, born as a slave in Hierapolis. Having been expelled from Rome with all other philosophers by the Emperor Domitian, Epictetus set up a school in Nicopolis in 89. His major works include *Discourses* and *Manual*. He held that the aim of philosophy is to cure moral defects. All men have an inherent capacity for virtue. We should regard slavery and freedom with indifference, although freedom is preferable. We need to distinguish between what is in our power and what is beyond our control. Will and inner freedom are within our power and are the basis for our happiness. Freedom consists in having one's desires fulfilled, and the sage accepts whatever happens as ordained for the best. Good men cannot be harmed, and one should love one's enemy.

Epicureanism

ANCIENT GREEK PHILOSOPHY, EPISTEMOLOGY, META-PHYSICS, ETHICS, PHILOSOPHY OF RELIGION The philosophy founded by **Epicurus**, who established his Garden school in Athens in 306 BC. Metaphysically, Epicurus endorsed the **atomism** of **Democritus**, but revised the theory in accord with **Aristotle**'s criticisms of it. Epistemologically, Epicurus proposed that all **sensations** are true. Ethically, he held that internal tranquility and the absence of pain are the chief goods. He opposed the competitive nature of conventional society and advocated absolute **egalitarianism**, believing that real happiness is having peace of mind and a healthy body. His basic teachings about the guidance of life, presented in a fourfold remedy, include: the gods present no fears, death presents no worries, good is easy to attain, and evil is readily endurable. Other major representatives of Epicureanism include Hermarchus of Mytileme (c.290 BC) and Polystratus (c.275 BC). However, the school was a quasi-religious community and there was little development of his teaching. Most writings of Epicurus were lost, but his doctrines were preserved by **Lucretius**. Epicureanism itself advocated an austere way of life, but the nature of the theory provoked many polemicists to argue against it, in particular the Stoics. They charged that it led to lives based on unchecked sensual enjoyment, and hence for many centuries Epicureanism carried the connotation of vulgar hedonism or atheism. The original Epicureanism was resuscitated in modern times by Pierre **Gassendi** and deeply influenced the development of **utilitarianism** in England.

> "Like Utilitarianism, Epicureanism reduces all virtue to personal well-being understood hedonistically, but it differs from Utilitarianism in tying the virtue of any given individual not to the pleasure (or freedom of pain) of mankind generally but, in an egoistic manner, to the pleasure of the individual said to be virtuous." **Slote, *From Morality to Virtue***

Epicurus (341–270 BC)

Hellenistic atomist philosopher. Of his writings, only about 80 aphorisms, various fragments, and three letters survive, but his philosophy was systematically presented in Lucretius' epic poem *De Rerum Natura*. Happiness, our final end, lies in pleasure, but the ultimate good of pleasure comprises peace of mind and tranquility rather than sensual gratification. The greatest disturbance to the peace of mind is the fear of death. To help get rid of the source of this fear, Epicurus developed the atomism of Leucippus and Democritus to demonstrate that all natural processes are the necessary results of atomic movements, with no external interference from God. Furthermore, the soul is not immortal, but is composed of atoms. Epicurus' hedonism has deeply influenced utilitarianism.

Epimenides (6th century BC)

Greek logician, possibly author of the liar paradox.

epiphenomenalism

PHILOSOPHY OF MIND [epiphenomenon, from Greek *epi*, on or above + *phainein*, appear, meaning literally a by-product or incidental product of some process which has no effects of its own] Epiphenomenalism is a theory about the relationship between **mind and body** first defended by Thomas Huxley, and adopted in various versions of **mechanistic materialism**. On this view, conscious **mental states** or events are by-products of the brain processes of the central nervous system, as a shadow is to the body of which it is a shadow. Mental states themselves have no causal powers, and can affect neither bodily behavior nor other mental states. The **mind** is not a thing, but a string of **events**. Each mental event can be fully explained by some bodily event or events. Mind cannot exist without body. Unlike **dualism**, epiphenomenalism denies that the mind is a fundamental entity.

> "The thesis that they [the mental events] are not causal factors is known as epiphenomenalism." **Ayer, *Philosophy in the Twentieth Century***

episteme

ANCIENT GREEK PHILOSOPHY, EPISTEMOLOGY [Greek, knowledge] **Knowledge**, from which the word epistemology is formed. **Plato** regarded knowledge as a cognitive state of the **soul** concerned solely with unchanging and necessary objects, the Ideas or **Forms**. Knowledge contrasts with belief (*doxa*), the cognitive state concerned with sensible things. For Plato, the contrast between *episteme* and *doxa* is essential for establishing the theory of Ideas. **Aristotle** normally confined knowledge to the demonstrative sciences, which provide necessary and invariant truths about necessary and invariable states of affairs. These sciences start from necessary premises, proceed through **syllogistic** deduction, and reach necessary conclusions. The necessary premises that form the first principles of these sciences are not grasped by *episteme*, but by *nous* (intuition).

> "Episteme then is by its nature directed to what is, to know it as it is." **Plato, *Republic***

epistemic holism

PHILOSOPHY OF SCIENCE The core of this position is the **Duhem–Quine thesis**. According to Duhem, statements about physical things cannot be verified or falsified in isolation from the theory to which they belong. Quine further suggested that what should be tested against experience is not a sentence, not even a theory in isolation, but the whole of science, since all branches of science share logic and mathematics. Epistemic holism is the ground for Quine's rejection of the distinction between synthetic and analytic statements. It also paves the way for **semantic holism** which focuses on the essential interconnectedness that exists between thoughts.

"The central factor underlying it [epistemic holism] is the potential complex interconnectedness of things, both causally and evidentially." **Heal, in Carruthers and Smith (eds.),** *Theories of Theories of Mind*

epistemic justification

EPISTEMOLOGY Although epistemic justification may concern objective justification regarding what we should believe given what is in fact true, it mainly concerns subjective justification. This seeks to determine what we should believe or should not believe, given what we actually do believe, even though what we do believe may not be correct. If and only if one is justified in believing that a proposition is true, is one justified in believing that proposition. To believe what is true one needs to believe what is justified, and to avoid believing what is false one must not accept what is not justified. Justification of belief requires specification of the norms under which one may hold a belief. Determining what to believe is a fundamental problem for epistemology. "Acceptance," "being beyond reasonable doubt," "being evident," "being certain," "having some proposition in its favor," etc. are all different senses of epistemic justification.

"Epistemic justification, unlike truth, is capable of degrees of the things that we are justified in believing; some are more justified than others." **Chisholm,** *The Foundations of Knowing*

epistemic modality

LOGIC, EPISTEMOLOGY The mode in which a thing is said to be known to be true (**verified**), known to be untrue (**falsified**), or neither known to be true nor false (**undecided**). G. H. **von Wright** claimed that these epistemic modalities are related to each other logically as the alethic **modalities** (necessary, assertible, and possible). Each of these modal concepts can either be *de dicto*, when it is about the mode in which a proposition is known to be true or false (for instance "It is known that Socrates taught Plato"), or *de re*, when it is about the mode in which

an individual is known to have or not have certain attributes (for instance, "Socrates is known to be poor"). The study of the logical relations between epistemic modalities is the subject of modal epistemic logic, developed mainly by von Wright and Jaakko **Hintikka**.

"The basic epistemic modalities are: verified (known to be true), falsified (known to be false) and undecided (neither known to be true nor known to be false)." **von Wright,** *An Essay in Modal Logic*

epistemic value, an alternative expression for cognitive value

epistemic virtue

EPISTEMOLOGY The personal disposition of character, which tends to lead to the attainment of true knowledge and the avoidance of error, such as the desire to seek the truth, impartiality in scientific activities, and the courage to question orthodox views. It is also the internalized standard of belief-acceptance and belief-rejection. The opposite of epistemic virtue is epistemic vice. Since epistemic virtue is related to personal character, and does not involve empirical data, virtuously formed knowledge is not necessarily justified knowledge. In this context, virtue means simply doing well, a notion of efficiency rather than morality. A person of epistemic virtue is more likely to be successful in his inquiry, but that does not mean that he is a morally good person. The concept is derived from **Aristotle**'s notion of intellectual **virtue**. Epistemologists also talk about doxastic virtue, which is the disposition leading to the formation of reliable beliefs. Its content is the same as epistemic virtue.

"Such concepts as epistemic character or epistemic virtue seem to have their natural home in the conduct of inquiry project, since they focus on what it is to have the good judgement required by guidelines for going about inquiry." **Haack,** *Evidence and Inquiry*

epistemics, see epistemology

epistemological atomism

EPISTEMOLOGY Sluga's term for the view that there is a direct acquaintance with objects and that knowledge is not in the first instance knowing that or a matter of judging, but knowledge of objects and their properties. This term plays a role mainly in the interpretation of **Frege**'s philosophy and the claim that Frege is committed to such a view, as many interpreters have held.

"Sluga connects my saying that, for Frege, the referent of a proper name is its bearer with what he calls 'epistemological atomism', which he accuses me of ascribing to Frege." **Dummett,** *The Interpretation of Frege's Philosophy*

epistemological dualism

EPISTEMOLOGY, METAPHYSICS Any theory of **sense-data** that maintains that sense-data are distinct from the **physical objects** that they represent. Physical objects are constant, but different perceivers may have different sense-data regarding the same object. Physical objects are public, while **sense-data** are private. Furthermore, not all of what we perceive, in particular **secondary qualities**, are inherent in physical objects. A change of sense-data is not a real physical change. Since sense-data are not identical to physical objects, doubt arises with regard to the reliability of perception as the source of knowledge about the external world. According to this view, we do not really know physical objects themselves, although they are the cause of sense-data. From this position, **Berkeley**'s **immaterialism** and **phenomenalism** are derived by denying the existence of unknown **substances**.

"Epistemological dualism, . . . according to it, the sense-datum, i.e. that which is directly perceived, is always distinct from the physical object, even though it may be exactly similar to it like a faithful mirror image." **Pap,** *Elements of Analytic Philosophy*

epistemological necessity

EPISTEMOLOGY A necessity that can be deduced from a thinker's other beliefs, and is generally associated with the "must" of certainty. It is a relation between certain features, showing the dependence of one thing on another. Enquiry establishes such an epistemological necessity between the phenomenon to be explained and its necessary conditions. For instance, we will say, "it must be painful" if we see somebody struck by a stone.

"When it is shown that certain features are equally essential; when it is shown that certain features are interconnected so that some are necessary for others; when it is shown that certain features are not so closely connected as might be assumed, it is epistemological necessity, closeness, or lack of connection that is being demonstrated." **Harrison,** *On What There Must Be*

epistemology

EPISTEMOLOGY [from Greek *episteme*, knowledge + *logos*, theory; literally, theory of knowledge] The adjective "epistemic" pertains to knowledge. Epistemics is sometimes used as equivalent to epistemology or is used to denote a scientific approach to knowledge. Epistemology is also equivalent to gnoseology (from Greek *genoskein*, to know). Epistemology generally starts with attempts to refute **skepticism** by justifying the claim that knowledge is possible, and then proceeds to clarify the nature and the scope of knowledge. The standard analysis of knowledge claims that it is justified true belief, a definition initiated essentially by **Plato**, although it is challenged most recently by **Gettier's problem**. Because of this definition, philosophers have been working to analyze the relation between **knowledge** and **belief**, between knowledge and **truth**, and between knowledge and **justification**. The last issue is especially central. In a sense, epistemology pays more attention to the problem of what it is to be justified in believing than to knowledge *per se*. Another main task of epistemology concerns the origin of knowledge, that is, to assess the role of **sense** and **reason** in the acquisition of knowledge. Philosophers are divided into rationalists and empiricists with respect to this issue. **Rationalism**, represented by **Plato**, **Descartes**, and **Leibniz**, takes reason to be the source of knowledge, while **empiricism**, represented by **Locke** and **Hume**, argues that experience is the source of truth. **Kant** attempted to reconcile both by claiming that knowledge is possible only by the combination of our *a priori* **intuitions** and **concepts** of the **understanding** and **appearances**. Contemporary epistemology is dominated by Anglo-American philosophy and is largely empirical. Corresponding to the development of the **philosophy of language**, speech and meaning become important issues. Since epistemology is closely associated with psychology and the philosophy of mind, perception, memory, imagination, other minds, and error are major topics. The discussions of induction and *a priori* knowledge are also prominent, in part through the association of epistemology with philosophy of science.

"Questions such as these, about the nature, origin, and limits of human knowledge, motivated the enterprise of epistemology, past and present." Moser and Nat, *Human Knowledge*

epithumia, see concupiscence

epoche, see suspension of judgment

E-proposition, see A-proposition

equalitarianism, an alternative expression for egalitarianism

equality

POLITICAL PHILOSOPHY That all men are equal is a basic democratic principle, but it is not a statement of fact, for people differ in virtually all of their mental and physical capacities. The principle of equality, rather, claims that all persons have a right to equal treatment. For Kant, this equality is based on our human rationality and gives humans the dignity of being moral ends, who are not merely means to the ends of others. Equal treatment entitles all persons to equal consideration and equal opportunity. In a democratic society, all members are equally assured of basic rights to freedom and political participation, regardless of factors such as their race, gender, or religion. The vast gap separating the rich and poor today has led some egalitarian philosophers to extend the notion of equality from the equality of democratic citizenship to the equality of condition. On this latter claim, each person should have the same amount of goods or the same level of social and economic benefit. This simple equality seems to conflict with widely accepted principles of justice and liberty. Attempts at reconciliation have produced a better understanding of the equality of condition. Traditionally, equality has been limited to human being, but some recent environmental philosophers have criticized the alleged anthropocentrism of this restriction and have sought to extend equality of concern to non-human animals or to nature as a whole.

"The essential equality is thought to be equality of consideration." Rawls, *A Theory of Justice*

equity

POLITICAL PHILOSOPHY A basic requirement of social justice, involving fairness or fair shares, in contrast to equality or equal shares. Unlike strict equality, which does not take account of relevant difference, equity requires like cases to be treated equally and unlike cases to be treated unequally. The distribution of resources in society must be determined according to the merit, need, and capacity of the recipients. Only persons within the same category, for whom all relevant conditions are the same, should receive the same treatment. Plato and Aristotle distinguished arithmetical equality from proportionate equality. According to arithmetic equality, everybody receives an equal share irrespective of worth. Proportionate equality corresponds to equity and calls for distribution according to morally relevant differences. Equity requires the modification of general rules to meet special situations and seeks to provide just decisions in particular cases. Normally, what is equitable is equivalent to what is just, although some theorists see equity as no more than one aspect of justice. The principle of equity, with its emphasis on merit and worth, can come into conflict with consequentialist moral theories.

"The principle of equity is that equals should be treated equally, and unequals unequally." Barry, *Political Argument*

equivalence

LOGIC, PHILOSOPHY OF LANGUAGE For words and expressions, equivalence can be divided into extensional and intensional equivalence. Words or expressions that have the same meaning (that is, are synonymous) are intensionally equivalent; words or expressions that have the same reference or extension are extensionally equivalent. Words and expressions may be extensionally equivalent without being intensionally equivalent; but if two terms are intensionally equivalent, then they are extensionally equivalent as well.

Two statements or propositions p and q are equivalent if they have the same truth-value (either both true or both false). A distinction can be drawn between material equivalence (p and q have the same truth-value) and logical equivalence (p and q are mutually entailing). The sign for material equivalence is "↔" or "≡"; "p ↔ q" or "p ≡ q" means "if p then q, and if q then p." That is, p is both a necessary and sufficient condition of q, and q is both a necessary and sufficient condition of p. If p and q are logically equivalent, each entails the other.

> "'S₁ is logically equivalent to S₂' = df 'S₁ entails S₂ and S₂ entails S₁'." **Strawson, *Introduction to Logical Theory***

equivalence relation

LOGIC An equivalence relation is transitive (that is, if the relation R exists between a and b and exists between b and c, then it also exists between a and c), symmetric (that is, if a has the relation R to b, then b also has the relation R to a), and reflexive (a bears the relation R to itself). An equivalence relation holds between equivalent things or between things that are exactly similar in some respect. "Being the same age as" and "having the same length as" are typical equivalence relations. The equivalence relation is essential for establishing certain measurements in mathematical logic. If there is a **class** of objects within which each member has an equivalence relation to every other member, and does not have this relation with anything in a different class, this class is called the equivalent class of the relation.

> "Not only does every sameness predicate express an equivalence relation, but every equivalence relation is expressed by some sameness predicate." **Hodges, *Logic***

Erasmus, Desiderius (1466–1536)

Dutch humanist and scholar, born in Rotterdam. Erasmus was a leading figure in the revival of the study of Greek texts, including his edition of the New Testament, and in Renaissance hostility to scholasticism. He is best known for his masterpiece of irony, *In Praise of Folly* (1509), and for his attack on Luther's rejection of free will in *On Free Will* (1524).

ergon

ANCIENT GREEK PHILOSOPHY, METAPHYSICS, ETHICS [Greek, work or what we do] A term having various translations, including process of production,

product, achievement, action, task, activity, and function. In philosophy, it is mainly used for a characteristic **function** or activity uniquely ascribed to a thing or kind of thing. Both **Plato** and **Aristotle** appeal to such functions to explain the **essence** of a thing and the **good** for man. It is thus connected with **virtue** (*arete*), "the excellence in performing one's *ergon*." The *ergon* of a knife is cutting. If it cuts well, it is a good knife and has virtue. Analogously, Aristotle argued, man has an *ergon*, rational activity, which is the feature distinguishing man from non-human animals and plants. He held that human virtue or human good, therefore, is performing rational activities rightly and well.

> "... that is the ergon of each thing which it only or it better than anything else can perform." **Plato, *Republic***

eristic

ANCIENT GREEK PHILOSOPHY, PHILOSOPHICAL METHOD, LOGIC [from Greek *eris*, fight, conflict] For **Plato** and **Aristotle**, the art of dispute which makes use of invalid and fallacious arguments to persuade the audience. It is aimed at winning a debate rather than seeking the truth. According to its basic method, an interlocutor is required to answer yes or no and cannot qualify his reply. The eristic method, which was developed by the **sophists** and the Megarian school, was popular in the debates of the Athenian court and the assemblage. It is a sort of reasoning, but not genuine. The art is employed for nothing else but victory. The Megarian school called it **dialectic**, but Aristotle distinguished it from dialectic. Eristic is associated with words, while dialectic is concerned with reality. Eristic refutes everything that is said and is destructive, while dialectic is aimed at the truth and is constructive. In the *De Sophistic Elenchis*, Aristotle examined various types of eristic argument, and identified many general **fallacies** that they commit.

> "When an argument seems to prove a conclusion but does not, which is called an eristic reasoning." **Aristotle, *Topics***

Eriugena, John Scot (c.810–c.877)

Irish-born medieval philosopher. Eriugena established a metaphysical system influenced by Neoplatonism, in which God is both nature that is not created and creates and nature that is neither created nor creates. In between God the creator and God to whom all things return are primordial causes and the created world. His dual account of God allows for positive as well as negative theology, with God being ultimately a mystery to himself as well as to his creatures. His major works include *De Praedestinatione* and *De Divisione Naturae*.

eros

ETHICS, EPISTEMOLOGY, PHILOSOPHY OF MIND [Greek love or erotic love, but not a mere appetite for sexual gratification] Sexual desire is a component of *eros*, but there are other elements as well. For **Socrates**, **Plato**, and **Aristotle**, *eros* was normally confined to an older man's pederastic desire for a younger man, as sanctioned by the institutions and fashions of aristocratic circles of many cities in ancient Greece. Eros included intense interest in the beloved and desire for his presence and company. In *Phaedrus* and *Symposium*, Plato saw this love for the beauty of a fair young body as only the earthly version of something far higher. It led successively to the love of a fair soul and character, the love of study, the love of a way of life, the love of the social order, and finally ascended to the very presence of the **Form** of Beauty itself, of which all other kinds of beauty are only imperfect copies. Thus, *eros* is a way of grasping spiritual truth. Philosophers, poets, and artists are all inspired by the divine power of *eros* as madness. This is Platonic spiritual love, although platonic love has also come to mean companionship without sexual desire. Hence, *eros* is distinguished from Christian love (*agape*) or romantic love. For Aristotle, erotic love was a source of **friendship**. **Freud** borrowed the term and claimed that his doctrine of *eros* was closer to that of Plato. However, while Plato's *eros* is a longing for a true version of reality, Freud's love is the hope of recapturing a sexual bliss allegedly lost in infancy.

> "If we are to make this gift our own, Eros will help our mortal nature more than all the world." **Plato, Symposium**

eros (Freud)

PHILOSOPHY OF MIND [Greek *eros*, love, desire] **Freud** claimed that there are two classes of ultimate instinct in the id. Our mental world contains *eros*, which is our life-preserving instinct, and *thanatos* (from Greek, death), which is our **death instinct**. *Eros*, which replaced Freud's earlier notion of libido, is in the tradition of **Plato** and **Spinoza**, a never-satisfied desire and effort. *Eros* inspires us to strive for individual happiness and forms our wishes to unite with others. It drives living organisms to develop. *Thanatos* drives us toward a return to the inorganic. According to Freud, these two forces fight each other, and their conflict and interaction determine the development of individual life and culture. This pair of notions, *eros* and *thanatos*, can be traced to the cosmology of **Empedocles**.

> "The other set of instincts would be those which are better known to us in analysis – the libidinal, sexual or life instincts, which are best comprised under the name of Eros; their purpose would be to form living substance into ever greater unities, so that life may be prolonged and brought to higher development." **Freud, Standard Edition of the Complete Psychological Works of Sigmund Freud, vol. 18**

error theory

ETHICS J. L. **Mackie**'s term for his position rejecting **ethical naturalism**. Ethical naturalism claims that all moral judgments refer to some objective moral property, are capable of truth and falsity, and have their truth-value determined by an external objective meaning. According to naturalism, moral judgments are true through reflecting what is the case in nature. Mackie rejects ethical naturalism because he holds that there are no objective values or moral facts to determine the truth-value of moral judgments. Hence, all ethical theories that presuppose the existence of objective moral truth are systematically wrong. Mackie claimed that morality is a matter of free choice, rather than something imposed on us by an objective moral reality. His **non-cognitivist** position echoes **Moore**'s **naturalistic fallacy** and **Hume**'s **is/ought gap**.

> "The denial of objective values will have to be put forward not as the result of an analytic approach, but as an 'error theory', a theory that although most people in making moral judgements implicitly claim, among other things, to be pointing to something objectively prescriptive, these claims are all false." **Mackie, Ethics**

ersatzism

METAPHYSICS, LOGIC, PHILOSOPHY OF LANGUAGE [from German *ersatz*, substitute or fake] A theory which is intended to modify the **modal realism** of David **Lewis**. The claim of modal realism that there are countless concrete worlds has been criticized as being incompatible with common sense. Ersatzism suggests instead that we have only one concrete world, but that there are countless **abstract entities**, which represent ways that this world might have been. We talk about what is the case according to these abstract entities, and they form an abstract realm. There are various versions of this theory, but in general the role played by these abstract entities is similar to that played by Lewis's plurality of concrete worlds. Lewis himself rejects these attempts to retain the benefit of his modal realism while making concessions in favor of common sense.

"According to ersatzism, we have a well-established division of all there is into the concrete and the abstract." **D. Lewis,** *On the Plurality of Worlds*

eschatology

PHILOSOPHY OF RELIGION [from Greek *eschatos*, last, final + *logos*, theory, the theory about what is ultimate and final] A branch of theology that is concerned with the last things for humankind: death, resurrection, and the last judgment of God. It is also concerned with the end of the world and the final moment of history. It aims to make full sense of the contingency of our existence and attempts to grasp the upper reaches of unified experience that we detect in the things around us. Some eschatologians argue that in our present life there are states analogous to states of an afterlife. This kind of belief is called realized eschatology.

"The eschatology we have elaborated is a rational and an a priori, not an empirical, eschatology: it bases itself on the philosophical surds of our present existence, and suggests the supplementation necessary to resolve them." **Findlay,** *Ascent to the Absolute*

esoteric, see exoteric

esse est percipi

EPISTEMOLOGY, METAPHYSICS [Latin, to be is to be perceived] The central thesis or *a priori* ground for the subjective **idealism** or **immaterialism** of the Anglo-Irish empiricist, George **Berkeley**. It claims that the ordinary objects of experience exist if and only if they are perceived. Hence, things cannot be independent of our minds and are what they appear to us to be. The major argument for this proposition is as follows: (1) every corporeal object is a collection or association of sensible qualities; (2) every sensible quality is relative to the percipient and is therefore an idea; (3) an idea cannot exist without our mind or sensation; (4) hence every physical object is an association of ideas and cannot exist in its own right. However, in this argument, premises (1) and (2) are controversial. The problem with (1) is that it denies the traditional distinction between underlying **substance** and peripheral **accidents**. Berkeley attempted to refute the notion of substance or substratum, but with uncertain success except against **Locke**'s minimal account. Moreover, the achievements of physics in his time seemed to prove, contrary to his thesis, that external things have their properties intrinsically and are the basis for the laws of physics. Against this, Berkeley argued that scientific theories are not descriptive but predictive. This insight is surprisingly echoed by many twentieth-century philosophers of science. The problem with (2) is that it denied Locke's distinction between **primary qualities** and **secondary qualities**. There is no strong argument to suggest that primary qualities are relative to perceivers in the way Berkeley suggested. Furthermore, ideas as things perceived must be caused, and should be accounted for by another ground. Berkeley denied that they are caused by external objects and argued that they are caused by God. There are also other arguments (including the **master argument**) for the thesis *essse est percepi*, but each faces serious difficulties. In general, this thesis is ill founded, and does not constitute the defense of **common sense** against **skepticism** that Berkeley intended it to be. Nevertheless, it is of deep philosophical interest. Berkeley's direct object is to deny the existence of anything unknowable behind the perceived corporeal world. His sensing should be understood not as my accidental sensing, but as sensing as such. We might be able to think coherently of a table as not seen by this or that man, but difficulties arise if we try to think of it as not seen at all. Modern **phenomenalism** moves from the actual perceptions of God at the basis of Berkeley's account to the possible perceptions that we would have in appropriate circumstances as crucial to our account of objects.

"For as to what is said of the absolute existence of unthinking things without any relation to their being perceived, that seems perfectly unintelligible. Their *esse* is *percipi*, nor is it possible they should have existence, out of the minds of thinking things which perceive them." Berkeley, *The Principles of Human Knowledge*

essence

METAPHYSICS [from Latin *esse*, to be, a translation of Greek *ousia* or, more properly, *to ti en einai*, what it was for a thing to be, in an attempt to retain a relation with the term to be] Aristotle introduced the phrase *to ti en einai*. Instead of using the present tense *esti* (is), the Greek expression uses the philosophical imperfect *en* (was), which implies something remaining or eternal, although this implication is interpreted variably. Aristotle's **ontology** begins with **being** and proceeds to what-it-is, to **substance** (primary being), and finally to essence, which is primary substance identical to **form**. The expression *to ti en einai* is derived from the formal structure of a question asking for a **definition**. Thus, essence is the ontological correlate and primary object of definition. Traditionally essence is taken to be a common nature shared by things of a certain kind, with the function of essence being to identify species membership or to place individuals into a species. But there are also many passages in Aristotle suggesting that essence and form as primary substance is particular. This gives rise to much controversy about how to understand the ontological status of essence. In general, essence is the property of a thing without which the thing could not be what it is. As **essential property**, it is distinguished from **accidental properties**.

"What, then, you are by your very nature is your essence." Aristotle, *Metaphysics*

essential occurrence, see vacuous occurrence

essential property, see accidental property

essentialism

METAPHYSICS, EPISTEMOLOGY, LOGIC, PHILOSOPHY OF LANGUAGE The doctrine that among the properties which a thing X possesses, we can distinguish between its **essential properties** and its **accidental properties**. According to this view, some of the properties of X form its **essence**, while the remaining properties are accidental. According to different kinds of essentialism, an essential property makes X the individual it is, the kind of thing it is, or a member of its kind. Essential properties are revealed by a **real definition**, although it is disputed whether there can be definitions either of individuals or of particular essences. Essentialism originated from **Parmenides**, **Plato**, and especially **Aristotle**, but has been in decline since the criticisms of British **empiricism** beginning in the seventeenth century. It was revived in the middle of the twentieth century and is represented in particular by **Kripke**. Contemporary essentialism claims that some properties of an object are essential to it and that so long as it existed the object could not fail to have them. If essence is inherent in things, then there are **necessary truths** about objects and their properties (**necessity de re**). Essentialism is focused on the relationship between essence and individual **identity**, as well as on the relationship between essence and **natural kinds**. It is closely related to the **causal theory of reference** and the theory of **modality** in terms of **possible worlds**. Various versions of anti-essentialism claim that the notion of essence is trivial or that we are never in a position to specify what properties of a thing are essential or accidental. **Popper** refers to essentialism as the view that the aim of science is to provide explanations in terms of things and properties that are not themselves susceptible of any further explanation.

"Understood Platonistically, essentialism holds, at the very least, that some things have some of their properties essentially." **Slote,** *Metaphysics and Essence*

estrangement, see alienation

eternal recurrence

MODERN EUROPEAN PHILOSOPHY **Nietzsche** held that the world is cyclical, with everything that has occurred repeated over again in a process that extends to infinity. In eternal recurrence, the simplest forms strive toward the most complex, and then the most complex returns to the simple starting-point. The world oscillates between these extremes in a never-ending cycle. This idea, which is influenced by **Heraclitus** and other Greek philosophers, was presented by Nietzsche to be his fundamental conception. He characterized himself as the teacher of eternal recurrence. This position is certainly not merely **a cosmological** theory. It is intended to banish all **teleology** from our account of the world and to reject all views that the world develops in a linear manner toward some final and perfect end. Further, it establishes the grounds for the claim that all purposes, aims, and means are only different modes expressing a single principle inherent in the world, that is, the **will to power**. Rather than being pessimistic, belief in the idea of eternal recurrence shows willingness for life to extend eternally, against the ascetic ideal. On this view, the meaningful is repeated eternally, and life is not consigned to a meaningless eternity. With Nietzsche's emphasis on striving, the valued life is seen as a process of living rather than as a fixed state.

> "Behold, we know what you teach: that all things recur eternally, and we ourselves too; and we have already existed an eternal number of times, and all things with us." **Nietzsche,** *Thus Spoke Zarathustra*

eternal sentence

LOGIC A sentence whose truth or falsity is fixed once and for all, without regard to the passage of time, the varying of circumstances, and the speaker. If it is true, it is true forever; if it is false, it is false forever. Examples of this sort of sentence include laws of mathematics, of logic, and of nature, as well as reports of passing events. A **proposition** is said to be the meaning of a sentence, but, strictly speaking, it is the cognitive meaning of an eternal sentence.

> "By incorporating additional information into the sentence such as dates and the names of persons and places, we can obtain an eternal sentence: one that is fixedly true or false." **Quine,** *Ontological Relativity and Other Essays*

eternal Thou

MODERN EUROPEAN PHILOSOPHY, PHILOSOPHY OF RELIGION A term for **God** used by Martin **Buber** in *I and Thou*, in contrast to a human and temporal Thou. God, as the eternal Thou, is the grounds of all **I–Thou** relations, but is not merely an abstract power. According to Buber, we can meet Him in the concrete reality of the divine presence. God is inherent or implicit within the scope of human life. Our relation to God is an extension of the human I–Thou relation. The eternal Thou can never be limited by another Thou, and its nature prevents it from even becoming an it. With this term, Buber hoped to clarify what people mean in using the term "God" and to indicate how God can be reached.

> "In every sphere in its own way, through each process of becoming that is present to us, we look out toward the eternal Thou, in each we are aware of a breath from the eternal Thou; in each Thou we address the eternal Thou." **Buber,** *I and Thou*

eternity

METAPHYSICS, PHILOSOPHY OF RELIGION One of the divine attributes, which has been interpreted in two different ways. According to the first, **God** is eternal by not being bound by **time**. He exists outside of or beyond time. He is timeless but is the creator of time. Since he is not in time, all events occurring in time are for him simultaneous. While our "now" designates changing time and sempiternity, God's "now" is abiding, unmoved, and immovable. It makes no sense to ask how long God has existed or to divide up his life into periods of time. Although this understanding of eternity can account for God's **foreknowledge**, immutability, and **immortality**, it creates a **paradox**. If the Trojan War and my writing this entry are simultaneous for God, these two events must be simultaneous. But how can they be? Further, if our experience is essentially temporal, it does not seem to make sense to take the content of this experience non-temporally. According to the second interpretation, God has **temporality**, that is, a past, present, and future, but is eternal because he has always existed in the past, exists at present, and will always exist in the future. Eternity amounts to the totality of time. This understanding of eternity cannot account for God's being the creator of time and his immutability. Many philosophers tend to reserve eternity for existence outside of time and use everlasting for existence throughout time. On either interpretation, God's eternity implies that he is free from those imperfections that make the passage of time for us a matter of regret.

"To say that God is eternal is to say that he is not in time." **Helm**, *Eternal God*

ether, see aether

ethical individualism

ETHICS The position that only individual persons are the subject of moral predicates and values and are the central concern of moral concern. On this view, the choice of moral values is up to the **individual**, and the individual should be the final authority and arbiter of morality. This position is implied by the suggestion of **Hume**'s fact–value dichotomy that moral evaluations are not constrained by factual descriptions of the world. Ethical individualism became prominent in the nineteenth century through the criticism of Christianity as a basis for morality in the works of **Nietzsche** and **Kierkegaard**. In the twentieth century, it was represented by **existentialism**, which holds that the individual is the only legislator of his or her morality, and by **emotivism** and **prescriptivism**, which claim that morality is nothing more than the expression of personal attitudes.

"According to this doctrine [of ethical individualism], the source of morality, of moral values and principles, the creator of the very concern of moral evaluation, is the individual." **Lukes**, *Individualism*

ethical knowledge

ETHICS, EPISTEMOLOGY Also called moral knowledge. Knowledge of moral truths or principles from which moral prescriptions can be derived, but it is a matter of dispute whether there is such a kind of knowledge. **Ethical relativism**, **skepticism**, and **nihilism** reject the existence of moral knowledge by denying that there are moral facts or moral truths to be known. Non-objective moral theorists hold that moral language expresses only sentiments, approval or disapproval or other emotional attitudes, without involving truths. They claim that ethical problems are in principle insoluble and that ethical statements are incapable of being true or false. Other philosophers insist on the existence of moral knowledge, but must explain how we can recognize a complete and correct set of rules for human conduct. Some philosophers suggest that general moral rules can be derived from reason, according to Kantian **ethical rationalism**, or by intuition, according to ethical

intuitionism. Other moralists argue that we may start from particular moral facts and move up to wider principles, as in **Ross**'s intuitive induction and the common sense theory. Another problem is how to justify a moral belief or how to change moral belief into knowledge. Many disputes arise from using both **foundationalism** and **coherentism** to justify moral views. The attempts to support the possibility of moral knowledge by showing how we can establish and justify moral truths provide the content of moral epistemology.

"In the last decade or two serious doubts about the very possibility of ethical knowledge have become widespread." **Baylis**, *Ethics*

ethical life

ETHICS, POLITICAL PHILOSOPHY, PHILOSOPHY OF LAW [German *Sittlichkeit*, also called ethical order or ethical principles] For **Hegel**, the system of recognized ethical norms and principles of a **culture** and society, which constitutes a communal end for all of its members and which all members recognize and accept. Individuals can guarantee their **freedom** and happiness by conforming to this system of ethical norms. It is not purely transcendent and is not merely a social substance of which individuals are accidents. Hegel's paradigm of ethical life in this sense is Greek culture. The concept of ethical life is distinguished from *Moralität*, which for Hegel is typified by Kantian ethics and concerns the **individual** and private morality of the modern bourgeoisie, who are **alienated** from public life. In *Sittlichkeit*, one's **duty** is derived from one's relations to the concrete social order. It is the morality of a social order whose rational institutions and laws provide the content of conscientious conviction. In ethical life, moral sense and social sense are unified. Hegel claims that in *Moralität* they are severed, for in this abstract morality one's duty is derived from one's own abstract moral reflection and not from relations to a concrete social order. Thus, the distinction between *Sittlichkeit* and *Moralität* reflects the difference between Hegel's ethics and **Kant**'s ethics. In modern society, ethical life is characterized by **civil society**.

"Ethical life is the idea of freedom in that on the one hand it is the good become alive – the good endowed in self-consciousness with knowing and willing and actualised by self-conscious action – while on the other hand self-consciousness has in the ethical realm its absolute foundation and the end which actuates its effort." **Hegel,** *Philosophy of Right*

ethical naturalism, see naturalistic ethics

ethical objectivism

ETHICS In contrast to ethical **subjectivism, skepticism**, and relativism, ethical objectivism or objectivistic ethics argues that ethical judgments are not about the speaker or solely about the speaker and holds that at least some ethical judgments are concerned with moral facts and can be rationally justified. They are true or false independent of subjective matters such as the speaker's own feelings, desires, attitudes, and beliefs. Ethical objectivism has many versions. Ethical logicism claims that the truth-value of ethical judgments can be determined by logical rules. Ethical intuitionism holds that ethical generalizations are obtained by insight. **Moral sense** theories hold that we can gain knowledge through the perception of the difference between right and wrong, just as we can gain knowledge through the perception of the difference between red and blue. Theological theories argue that God provides an objective criterion of what is right or wrong. Ethical naturalism holds that ethical judgments can be based on some scientific, empirical investigation of the natural or social world. According to **Ideal Observer** theories, ethical judgments are about what some ideal being would determine if such a being existed. The common difficulty for all forms of ethical objectivism is to justify the source of objectivity and hence the existence of objective moral values.

"To be an (ethical) objectivist is to hold that whether something is or is not morally right is independent of the attitudes or inclinations of any particular speaker or set of speakers." **B. Mitchell,** *Morality: Religious and Secular*

ethical rationalism

ETHICS A term describing Kantian moral theory and its claim that moral judgments are purely rational and do not concern the emotions or the development of character. Ethical rationalism is a formal and universalist position. It is related to ethical cognitivism, which believes that morality has cognitive

elements instead of being a matter of personal attitude and preference.

"By 'ethical rationalism', by contrast, I mean a theoretical position which views moral judgements as the core of moral theory, and which neglects that the moral self is not a moral geometrician but is an embodied, finite, suffering and emotive being." **Benhabib,** *Situating the Self*

ethical relativism

ETHICS The view that ethical terms and principles are relative to cultures, societies, and even persons. There are different ethical judgments about the same subject, and there is no decisive method of reasoning that can adjudicate between these conflicting judgments. Accordingly, there is no objective ethical truth. Moral principles are not valid universally, and can do no more than follow the conventions of the societies to which we belong. The position can be traced to the ancient Greek philosopher **Protagoras** and has subsequently had various proponents. Ethical relativism may be used to justify moral **toleration**, but it has major theoretical difficulties. Its claim that all conflicting moral judgments have equal values is implausible. Furthermore, even if moral values are relative to societies, problems still arise. A given society may lack consistency in its principles. In addition, individuals may belong to different societies or other collective groups, such as families, communities, political parties, or nations, which may adhere to conflicting principles.

"A Greek philosopher who lived in the fifth century BC, named Protagoras, seems to have believed two things: first, that moral principles cannot be shown to be valid for everybody; and second, that people ought to follow the conventions of their own group . . . Views roughly similar to those of Protagoras may be classified as forms of ethical relativism." **Brandt,** *Ethical Theory*

ethical subjectivism

ETHICS In contrast to **ethical objectivism**, ethical subjectivism or subjective ethics claims that ethical judgments are about the speaker's feelings concerning something rather than about independent moral facts. In calling an action right, speakers state that they approve of it. In calling an action wrong, speakers state that they disapprove of it. Consequently, there are no moral truths independent of our feelings. This kind of approach to moral philosophy is explicitly expressed by **Hume**, who argued that morality is a matter of feeling, not reason. Ethical subjectivism is right in emphasizing the connection in morality between the meaning of "good" and the **pro-attitude** of the speaker, but it also faces many difficulties. A person's feelings are changeable, and different persons may have different feelings. Thus, subjectivism makes moral evaluation unstable and also makes moral disagreements insoluble. In the twentieth century, more refined versions of ethical subjectivism were introduced, such as **Stevenson**'s **emotivism**, **Hare**'s **prescriptivism**, and John Dewey's theory that moral statements do not express one's feelings *per se*, but rather express one's feelings after thinking things through. In a further refinement, it is claimed that one should think as reasonably and impartially as possible. Subjectivism hence has developed into **non-cognitivism** or non-descriptivism.

"The best course is therefore to retain the term 'subjectivist' for those who think that moral judgements state facts about the states of mind etc. of person, and use some new term ('non-descriptivist' is the most perspicuous) for those who don't think that their central function is to state facts at all." **Hare**, *Essays in Ethical Theory*

ethical theory
ETHICS Used by **Williams** as a technical term, opposed to the distinction between ethics and **meta-ethics**. According to this distinction, ethics concerns what one should do and how one should live, while meta-ethics concerns the status of ethical claims. They are separable and meta-ethics may involve only the **analysis** of ethical terms without ethical implications. For Williams this distinction is untenable. An ethical theory should combine both parts, which are inherently not separable. The consideration of the subject-matter of ethics will affect the position about what tests for the correctness of basic ethical beliefs and principles are appropriate, and this will in turn affect substantively ethical consequences. Ethical theory can be either positive or negative. A positive one believes that there is a general test for the acceptability of basic ethical principles, while a negative one thinks that holding an ethical position simply consists of choosing one and sticking to it. Williams himself takes a more complicated version of negative

ethical theory, which argues that there may be tests in some cultural circumstances and not in others. He claims that his position implies a **skepticism**, not about ethics, but about what philosophy can do in determining how we should think in ethics.

"An ethical theory is a theoretical account of what ethics thought and practice are, which account either implies a general test for the correctness of basic ethical beliefs and principles or else implies that there cannot be such a test." **B. Williams**, *Ethics and the Limits of Philosophy*

ethical virtue
ANCIENT GREEK PHILOSOPHY, ETHICS, PHILOSOPHY OF MIND, PHILOSOPHY OF ACTION [from Greek *ethike arete*, also translated as moral virtue or excellence of character] According to **Aristotle**, the kind of virtue which belongs to the part of the **soul** that is not rational in itself but which obeys reason. In contrast, **intellectual virtue** is the virtue of the rational part of the soul. Ethical virtue is concerned with feelings and actions. It is a settled disposition of character willingly to do things admired by society in a regular way, and is acquired through constant practice that creates a habit of action. Aristotle held that ethical virtue is a **mean** between two opposite vices. The mean is relative to us, that is to say, it is to be determined by **practical wisdom**. Aristotle tried to bring all ethical virtues under the doctrine of the mean. Practical wisdom is itself an intellectual virtue, but according to Aristotle, it cannot be a full virtue without ethical virtues. He also held that ethical virtues cannot be full virtues without practical wisdom.

"[Ethical] virtue is a state that decides, consisting in a mean, the mean relative to us, which is defined by reference to reason, i.e. to the reason by reference to which the person of practical wisdom would define it." **Aristotle**, *Nicomachean Ethics*

ethics, axiological, see axiology

ethics, emotive theory of, an alternative expression for emotivism

ethics, intuitionistic
ETHICS, EPISTEMOLOGY Also called ethical intuitionism. One kind of objective ethical theory that has

a long tradition in Britain. Its major proponents have included **Shaftesbury, Hutcheson**, Bishop **Butler, Reid, Sidgwick, Moore, Prichard**, and **Ross**. In a general sense, it is a thesis concerning the epistemological status of moral statements and claims that ethical knowledge is known to be true by immediate awareness or necessary insight. This position is established mainly through the rejection of alternative positions. It argues against moral **skepticism**, which holds that there is no moral truth. It denies the practice of defining basic ethical terms such as "**good**" and "**right**" in terms of natural properties. It claims that the position that ethical generalization is a process of ratiocination involves an infinite regress or a vicious circle. Accordingly, fundamental moral judgments must be neither inductively nor deductively justified, and they must be **self-evident**. In a narrow sense, ethical intuitionism is the view that we can immediately know that certain actions are morally right or wrong without consideration of their consequences.

Ethical intuitionism is also called non-naturalism in the sense that it is opposed to the claim of **naturalism**, that we know the truth or falsity of ethical statements by experience. However, since both intuitionism and naturalism claim that there is ethical knowledge, both are types of moral **cognitivism** and are opposed to **non-cognitivism**. It is sometimes associated with ethical **pluralism**, which holds that there is more than one non-reducible moral principle. **Rawls** sees this as allowing unacceptable indeterminacy in ethics, but others embrace the flexibility such pluralism provides. The difficulty of intuitionistic ethics is that there are no criteria for checking the validity of our intuitions, and for solving the conflicts between intuitions.

"The intuitional view of ethics consists in the supposition that certain rules, stating that certain actions are always to be done or to be omitted, may be taken as self-evident premises." **G. Moore,** *Principia Ethica*

ethics, normative

ETHICS A type of ethics, usually contrasted with **meta-ethics**. Its central concern is not with moral concepts or moral methods, but with substantive moral questions. Its basic aim is to determine what the moral principles are by which all moral **agents**

ought to be guided for morally right actions, and thus to provide ways of resolving existing ethical disagreements. Normative ethics is usually divided into two parts. One is called **consequentialism**, which claims that actions are not right or wrong in themselves, but are morally determined by the good or evil consequences they cause. The right action is that which brings about the best possible balance of good over evil consequences. Consequentialist normative ethics includes ethical **egoism, contractarianism**, ethical **altruism**, and **utilitarianism**. It is also called teleological ethics. The other part of normative ethics is called non-consequentialist or non-teleological ethics, for it holds that moral right and wrong are not determined, or at least are not solely determined, by appeal to the consequences of actions. Another name for this view is **deontology** [from Greek *deon*, duty], since it takes duty to have prior and independent value. The distinction between normative ethics and meta-ethics appeared in the early to middle part of the twentieth century, but has recently come to be less favored, for a clearcut distinction between these two types of ethics is very difficult to determine. Many ethical questions are both meta-ethical and normative.

"We may reasonably ask about ethical statements, 'Which ethical statements are true or valid?' and 'Why?'. A person's answer to these questions may be called his 'normative ethical theory'." **Brandt,** *Ethical Theory*

ethics and morality

ETHICS Ethics in Greek is *êthikos*, literally meaning something concerned with *êthos* (Greek, character), which in turn is connected with *ethos* (social custom, habit). **Cicero** employed the Latin *moralis* to translate the Greek *êthikos*. *Moralis* literally means something concerned with *mores* (Latin, character, manner, custom, and habit). Hence, etymologically ethics and morality mean the same thing.

Both ethics and morality can refer to social regulations that are embedded in cultural and historical traditions governing people's character and behavior. Different societies have different moralities and the same society can have different morality at different times or conflicting moralities at the same time, but the overriding purpose of all moralities is to preserve social harmony.

Both ethics and morality also refer to a branch of philosophy that studies these social regulations, to answer the questions "How should a person live?" or "How should a person act?" In this usage, ethics is also called **ethical theory**, and morality is called moral philosophy or moral theory. This study can be further divided into **meta-ethics**, that is, the study of moral language and central moral terms such as **right, duty, obligation, virtue, value**, and **freedom**; normative ethics, the establishment of moral principles and rules which people should follow; and **applied ethics**, the application of moral rules to solve practical issues arising in various social areas.

Starting from the middle of the twentieth century, there has been a tendency to distinguish ethics from morality. Morality (and therefore moral theory) is confined to the scope of modern ethical theories such as utilitarianism and deontology, which try not only to incorporate diverse rules into a coherent system, but also to set up certain universal rules applicable to all societies. It is closely associated with the emphasis of duty or obligation, a strict demand of responsibility, and an impartial concern for the non-instrumental goods of others. On the other hand, ethics is used to cover, in addition, the Aristotelian approach of emphasizing the formation of virtues in the agent rather than his actions, and is concerned with the happiness of agents rather than their duty or obligation. Such a distinction between ethics and morality is associated with the rise of contemporary virtue ethics and of the anti-theory movement. The value of the distinction is still in dispute.

> "From now on, therefore, I shall for the most part use 'ethical' as the broad term to stand for what this subject is certainly about, and 'moral' and 'morality' for the narrower system." **B. Williams,** *Ethics and the Limits of Philosophy*

ethics of belief

EPISTEMOLOGY The study of what we ought to believe, what we have a right to believe, or how we can know that what we believe is certain. As ethics seeks to evaluate ethical behavior, ethics of belief seeks to determine rules for the evaluation of doxastic states. It is called ethics of belief because what we ought to believe is not a private matter, but is a public concern with social consequences,

and is hence a matter of morality. Nevertheless, as a part of epistemology, this type of belief formulation is different from the formulation of genuinely moral belief. This part of epistemic activity can be traced to **Locke**, but the term is introduced by the British philosopher W. K. Clifford, who insisted that what determines belief choice is sufficient **evidence**. R. M. **Chisholm** claims that the rule of determination is logical consistency. Alternatively, William **James** believed that we can appeal to other elements beyond epistemological consideration in order to decide what we should believe.

> "We can simplify Locke's rather complicated formulation of his 'ethics of belief' as follows: the degree of our assent to a proposition ought to be proportioned to the strength of the evidence for that proposition." **Price,** *Belief*

ethics of care

ETHICS The **feminist ethics** that attempts to construct an entire ethical approach on the basis of **caring** or care. Care has been taken to be a central value and a fundamental ethical phenomenon. Care is not merely a feeling, but also an understanding of another person's real needs, welfare, and situation. The ethics of care focuses on specific individuals rather than on universal principles. It extends from caring for children to care about the globe. In terms of this approach, feminism labels all modern ethical theories, the ethics of **justice**. The ethics of justice is characterized as male-biased because it emphasizes rational moral law and ignores the role of feeling and the experience of women. Feminism claims that care ethics is modeled on the family, while the male ethics of justice or rights ethics is modeled on the **social contract**. Carol Gilligan, in her book *In a Different Voice*, argues that women speak in a different voice, the voice of care. However, care is generally involved in one-to-one encounters. It is still to be elaborated how the ethics of care can be elevated to a general and public level, and how it can be reconciled with the requirements of justice and **rights**. Besides, it is also disputed how much we should care, and what is the relation between care and self-interest. It is realized that the voices of justice and of care should be presented as complementary ones. Justice is related to institutions, care to characters. Some argue that we should combine them rather than idealizing an ethic of care at the expense of the ethics of justice.

"In advocating an ethic of care these critics, we have seen, come close both to traditional misogynist positions and to ethical relativism. When the 'voices' of justice and of care are presented as alternatives between which we must choose, each is viewed as a complete approach to moral issues. However, the two in fact focus on different aspects of life." **Valdes, in Nussbaum and Sen (eds.),** *The Quality of Life*

ethics of justice, see ethics of care

ethnocentrism

ETHICS, EPISTEMOLOGY, PHILOSOPHY OF SOCIAL SCIENCE [from Greek *êthos*, custom] The position of using the traditions of one's own **culture** or society as a starting-point for judging any practice. In a sense, ethnocentrism is inevitable, because we are deeply shaped by the beliefs and values of the **communities** in which we are raised. We become people in the abstract by becoming members of such particular concrete groups. If this contingent fact is given too much weight, however, ethnocentrism will collapse into **cultural relativism**, chauvinistic **conservatism**, and **racism**. One can balance ethnocentrism with an attempt to find a universal and more objective point of view. Even if this **Enlightenment** ideal cannot be achieved, ethnocentrism need not confine our outlook to narrow limits. One must have an open mind to converse with people who have grown up with a different Êthos, and it remains a fallacy to take one's own Êthos as objectively and universally correct.

"Ethnocentrism only involves taking one's language, beliefs, desires and the interests of one's community as a starting point." **D. Hall,** *Richard Rorty*

ethnology

PHILOSOPHY OF SOCIAL SCIENCE [from Greek *êthnos*, nations, people] J. S. **Mill**'s term for a theory about the laws of the formation of character, including both national and individual character. These laws are hypothetical and affirm tendencies. They are based neither on simple observation nor on the highest generalizations, but constitute a system of

corollaries from experimental psychology. This science is supposed to contribute to educational improvements. Mill claimed that it is a deductive science and the "exact science of human nature."

"Ethnology will serve for the ulterior science which determines the kind of character produced in conformity to these general laws, by any set of circumstances, physical and mental." **Mill, "On the Logic of the Moral Sciences," in Ayer (ed.),** *A System of Logic,* **vol. VI**

ethnomethodology

PHILOSOPHY OF SOCIAL SCIENCE An approach to sociology initiated by Garfunkel, so called because it emphasizes the study of the methodologies of people (*ethnos*) in daily life in contrast to scientific method. Empirical sociology claims that sociology can establish firm connections between social facts on the grounds that social life is actually not regulated by rules and that social action has no intrinsic identity. Ethnomethdology rejects this position and claims that any imputation of beliefs and desires is incorrigibly contextual, depends on indexicals, and is marked by uncertainty. Any purported sociological generalizations are based on the analyst's unexamined assumptions. Social facts should be dealt with by ethnomethodology, the characteristic of which is *ad hoc* rationality. It does not subject a social action to rigorous definition and does not set criteria for adequacy of its account. Instead, ethnomethodology holds that the properties of social life lie in the mutual dependence of **meanings** on their context and on the actor's motives. Rather than being generally endowed with a store of social knowledge that describes their surroundings, people constantly exercise their social knowledge and are forever theorizing about each other's actions. In a word, people are fundamentally their own sociologists. Ethnomethdology is hence interested in the properties of **intersubjectivity** as exhibited by social factors in the day-to-day world.

"[Ethnomethodology] aims to examine the ordinary, common-sense, mundane world in which members live and do so in a way that remains faithful to the methods, procedures, practices, etc., that members themselves use in constructing and making sense of this social world." **Benson and Hughes,** *The Perspectives of Ethnomethodology*

ethos, see *êthos*

êthos

ANCIENT GREEK PHILOSOPHY, ETHICS [Greek, character, disposition, from *êthos*, habit, custom; the transliteration of its adjective *êthikos* is ethics and literally means being concerned with character] *Êthos* is not the same as ethos. Aristotle divided *arête* (**virtue** or excellence) into two kinds: intellectual virtues and *êthika arête*. The latter is generally translated as moral virtues, although excellence of character or virtue of character might be more accurate. According to Aristotle, *êthos* is a significant element for us to gain *êthika arête*, but **practical reason** is also indispensable.

> "Virtue of character [of *êthos*] results from habit [*ethos*], hence its name ethical, slightly varies from ethos." **Aristotle,** *Nicomachean Ethics*

etiquette

PHILOSOPHY OF SOCIAL SCIENCE, ETHICS The set of manners and hypothetical imperatives governing social behavior, which is inherited through oral tradition rather than written code, and is manifested in virtually every aspect of social life in a community. To know the **culture** of a society is essentially to know its etiquette. Etiquette helps in establishing communal harmony, although its requirements are not as strict as those of morality. It changes continuously over time and helps to form the cultural **tradition** of a society.

> "The rules of governing the least socially important customs are the rules of etiquette for that society." **Feldman,** *Introductory Ethics*

Eubulides

Ancient Greek logician from Miletus, member of the Megarian school, author of the sorites paradox and possibly author of the liar paradox.

eudaemonism

ETHICS [from Greek *eudaimonia*, happiness or well-being] An ethical stance which claims that happiness is the property by which all intrinsic goods are **good** and by which all our rational behavior is ultimately justified. Hence we ought to seek happiness as our ultimate end in life and pursue everything else for the sake of happiness. This ethical eudaemonism is related to psychological eudaemonism, but not identical with it. Psychological eudaemonism proposes that all intentional behavior of an agent aims at the agent's own happiness. Although happiness has been taken in the history of Western ethics to be the ultimate good, there is no agreement about what constitutes happiness. For example, for **Aristotle** happiness is rational activity, but for the **Epicureans** and the **utilitarians**, happiness is a life of greatest pleasure and least pain. Through its concern for ends, eudaemonism is teleological in nature. It was criticized by **Kant**, but has been revived in contemporary **virtue ethics**.

> "It [the moral theory which prevailed in Kant's time] may be generally described as a system of eudaemonism which, when asked what man's chief end ought to be, replied Happiness. And by happiness eudaemonism understood the satisfaction of the private appetites, wishes, and wants of the man: thus raising the contingent and particular into a principle for the will and its actualization." **Hegel,** *Logic*

eudaimonia

ETHICS, PHILOSOPHY OF MIND [Greek, human flourishing, from *eu*, good + *daimon*, a divinity or spirit, having a good divinity to look after one] The highest **good** for humans. *Eudaimonia* is normally translated as happiness, but this is not precise, because happiness tends to be identified with **pleasure** or the satisfaction of our sentient nature, and this is only one element in Greek *eudaimonia*. Another, and philosophically more important, element is the satisfaction of our nature as active beings. In this sense, it is equivalent in Greek to living well or doing well. Because *eudaimonia* concerns the shape of one's whole life rather than particular moments or parts of one's life, it is also translated as well-being. For many Greek philosophers, including **Plato, Aristotle**, and **Epicurus**, *eudaimonia* is the state of life which is most worth living.

For Aristotle *eudaimonia* is the state of life in which man deeply fulfils his nature, and it is the complete end or *telos* of one's life. He defined *eudaimonia* as activity in accordance with **virtue**, so the genuine pursuit of happiness and the virtuous life are one and the same. In practical life, *eudaimonia* is generally activity in accordance with moral virtue and **practical reason**, but ideally it is activity in accordance with the virtue of the theoretical part of the soul, although we take part in this activity not insofar as we are men, but only insofar as there is something divine in us. Attempts to reconcile these claims affect our reading of Aristotle's ethics.

> "As far as its name goes, most people virtually agree [about what the good is], since both the many and the cultivated call it happiness (*eudaimonia*), and suppose that living well and doing well are the same as being happy." **Aristotle,** *Nicomachean Ethics*

euthanasia

ETHICS [from Greek *eu*, good + *thanatos*, death] The death of B brought about by A for B's sake, typically to terminate B's unbearable suffering caused by an incurable and terminal disease, B's serious paralysis, B's grotesque disfigurement, B's irreversible comatose state, and so on. It is also called mercy killing.

There are two ways of distinguishing various types of euthanasia. One is to divide it into voluntary, non-voluntary, and involuntary acts. Euthanasia is voluntary if B requests it whilst in a rational state; non-voluntary if B has lost the capacity of choosing death or life, but is killed or allowed to die; and involuntary if B does not consent to end his life but is still killed. The other way is to divide it into active and passive euthanasia. Euthanasia is active if B is deliberately killed by some action and passive if B is not killed but is deliberately allowed to die.

Involuntary euthanasia is generally regarded as murder and as being morally wrong. Passive euthanasia is considered by many to be permissible. The debate about the morality of euthanasia usually surrounds active euthanasia. The arguments for it include mainly the principle of mercy (**beneficence**) and respect for **autonomy**. The arguments against it mainly concern the sanctity of life, and the **slippery slope argument**. In many countries, the moral debate about euthanasia has become a legal debate about whether we should legalize euthanasia.

> "Let us insist, then, that when we talk about euthanasia we are talking about a death understood as a good or happy event for the one who dies." **Foot,** *Virtues and Vices*

Euthyphro dilemma

ETHICS, PHILOSOPHY OF RELIGION **Plato**'s dialogue *Euthyphro* is named after a person who engaged in dialogue with **Socrates**. Euthyphro wanted to sue his father, who had caused a peasant's death, in the belief that God would punish him if he did not sue. But Socrates found it outrageous that a person should prosecute his own father, and the two of them started to discuss the nature of piety. In response to Euthyphro's claim that an action is pious because it is loved by the gods, Socrates asks: "Is 'what is pious' pious because the gods approve of it, or do they approve of it because it is pious?" This issue, whether a man's moral code ought to be influenced by beliefs about divine commands, is not solved in the dialogue. This dilemma reveals a structure that lies at the heart of various justifications of moral and other necessary truths by appeal to a divine authority or an ultimate rational authority. If a thing is good because some authority approves of it, then we need a further justification of the worth of the authority's approval or must accept vacuously that what the authority approves is good. If an authority approves of a thing because it is good, then the approval of authority may be a guide to what is good, but it offers no justification of its goodness. The question raised by the dilemma has been a topic of intensive discussion, especially in theology, ethics, and political theory.

> "The difficulty here is commonly stated in the form of this dilemma: Given that it is right to do X, and that it is God's will that we should do X: is X right because God wills it, or does God will it because it is right? The classical statement of this problem is the Euthyphro dilemma in Plato's dialogue of that name." **Mayo,** *The Philosophy of Right and Wrong*

evaluative meaning

ETHICS, PHILOSOPHY OF LANGUAGE The force of an expression which conveys the speaker's positive or negative attitude toward what the expression is describing, and is in contrast to **descriptive meaning**, which is a bare description of the fact and picks out the range to which the expression applies. Evaluative meaning varies with the reaction of the user of the expression and lacks truth conditions. Evaluative meaning is related to advising and prescribing what should and should not be done. **Emotivism** and **prescriptivism** pay particular attention to the evaluative meaning of ethical terms, for they believe that morality is a matter of emotional attitude rather than belief.

> "A word has evaluative meaning if its use implies a favourable or unfavourable attitude on the part of the speaker." **McNaughton,** *Moral Vision*

Evans, Gareth (1946–80)

British philosopher of language and philosopher of mind, born in London, taught at University of Oxford. Evans's subtle discussion of questions of reference and intentionality focused on the conditions under which a thought can be about an object. His own views often sought to reconcile aspects of major rival approaches to issues of thought, reference, and meaning. His main works include *The Varieties of Reference* (1982) and *Collected Papers* (1985).

event

METAPHYSICS, PHILOSOPHY OF SCIENCE, PHILOSOPHY OF ACTION [from Latin *ex*, out + *venire*, to come] A happening or occurrence that does not persist in the relations of a thing, but occurs in a certain place during a particular interval of time. This is a widely used but very ambiguous conception. No agreement has been achieved with regard to its simple nature, its qualities, or its relations. Scholars are divided whether an event should be classified as an **object**, a **fact**, a **state of affairs**, or simply a **change**, whether it is **universal** or **particular**, and over the criteria to individuate events. They also disagree whether events or objects should be more basic in our **ontology**. **Davidson** used to hold a position that two events are identical if their causes and effects are identical, but then are causes and effects themselves events? **Quine** claims that two events are identical if they happen in the same temporal-spatial location. But then several things could happen in the same temporal-spatial location. Are they one or several events? Because of Davidson's work, the discussion of events is now closely associated with accounts of **action**.

> "An 'event' is supposed to occupy some continuous portion of space-time, at the end of which it ceases, and cannot occur." **Russell,** *Human Knowledge*

everlasting, see eternity

everydayness

MODERN EUROPEAN PHILOSOPHY **Heidegger**'s term, also called averageness, for the ordinary and undifferentiated way in which human beings exist over most of their lifetime, taking everything that comes to them from the world. It is the average manner of human being, in which *Dasein* is blind to its own possibilities. The first division of *Being and Time*, entitled "the preparatory fundamental analysis of *Dasein*," attempts to reveal the complex and mysterious character of this most familiar way of one's being. The analysis of *Dasein*'s everydayness serves as a path for uncovering the essential structure of *Dasein*. For in our everyday lives we already have some vague and average understanding of **Being**. Heidegger portrayed our everyday situation in terms of **Being-in-the-world**. Everydayness is constituted by three modes of fallingness, that is, idle talk (groundless understanding and interpretation), curiosity (a tendency to move from average intelligibility to closing off the understanding in idle talk), and ambiguity (the failure to distinguish what is genuinely known from what is not).

> "Accordingly, *Dasein*'s 'average everydayness' can be defined as 'Being-in-the-world which is falling and disclosed, thrown and projecting, and for which its ownmost potentiality-for-Being is an issue, both in its Being alongside the "world" and in its Being-with-others'." **Heidegger,** *Being and Time*

evidence

EPISTEMOLOGY, PHILOSOPHY OF LAW [from Latin *e*, out + *videre*, see] Originally meaning evident or obvious, the term has developed into meaning evidence for, rather than self-evident. Evidence is something or some consideration that is used to support or reject some claim, to confer a certain degree of **probability** upon a proposition, or to decrease its probability. If a piece of evidence is supportive, it is favorable; otherwise it is unfavorable. In the law, evidence is governed by the rules of evidence and includes physical evidence as well as testimony. In epistemology, evidence comprises beliefs or propositions that may be used to justify other beliefs or propositions. If S has adequate evidence for h, it would be unreasonable for S not to accept h. There are many disputes regarding the nature of the beliefs that can provide evidential justification. A theory of **epistemic justification**, which claims that a belief is justified if and only if it is supported by evidence, is called **evidentialism**.

> "'Evidence' eventually came to mean not just considerations which make a proposition evident or obvious, but any considerations which make it in any degree probable." **Price, *Belief***

evidentialism

EPISTEMOLOGY A theory about **epistemic justification**. It claims that a belief or a doxastic attitude toward proposition P is epistemologically justified for a person S at the time t if and only if this belief fits the evidence S has at t, and the evidence S possesses is certainly well supported epistemologically and is properly arrived at. The position is implicit in the philosophy of **Chisholm** and is explicitly expressed by Feldman and Conee. The major problem it faces is to provide a satisfactory account of the relations between experience and introspective or perceptual belief.

> "What we call evidentialism is the view that the epistemic justification of a belief is determined by the quality of the believer's evidence for the belief." **Feldman and Conee, "Evidentialism,"** *Philosophical Studies* 48

evil

ETHICS, PHILOSOPHY OF RELIGION Evil is divided into moral evil and natural evil. While natural evil results from unusual natural occurrences such as earthquakes, disease, or famine, moral evil is due to deliberate human action and its origin and nature are the concerns of ethics. Moral evil is the extreme form of moral wrong and causes much suffering and pain. **Socrates** believed that nobody rationally chooses evil and that evil is the result of ignorance. This raises a question about the relation between reason and evil. Orthodox theologians hold that evil can be intentional, for human beings have a fallen nature. Another major problem regarding evil is the compatibility between the existence of an **omnipotent** and perfectly good **God** and the fact that the world is full of evil. For if God knows everything and is all-powerful and benevolent, he can easily do

something to prevent evil from happening. This is the so-called problem of evil, which atheism takes as evidence for denying the existence of God. Some theists argue that God deliberately allows some evil to make possible greater goods. Evil results from human **free will**. If God denies evil, he would have to deny human freedom of will first, but the possession of free will is definitely a greater good. Others argue that the existence of evil is an illusion, or that evil is the privation of goodness proper to something.

> "Many philosophers believe that the existence of evil constitutes a difficulty for the theist, and many believe that the existence of evil (or at least the amount and kinds of evil we actually find) make belief in God unreasonable or rationally unacceptable." **Plantinga, *God, Freedom and Evil***

evil spirit, see malicious demon

evolution

PHILOSOPHY OF SCIENCE, ETHICS, EPISTEMOLOGY [from Latin *evolutio*, unrolling, unfolding, developing] A theory that the world and its contents, in particular the organic world, are subject to a developmental process, on some theories of evolution from the simple to the complex. The idea gained popularity in the **Enlightenment** as an alternative to the Christian theory of creation and design. Philosophically, it also challenged Greek **essentialism**. But it was not until **Darwin** published *On the Origin of Species* (1859) that evolution became a well-established scientific theory. The theory of evolution is hence virtually synonymous with Darwinism. Darwin's central tenet is that the organic world develops through a process of **natural selection**, in which the members of a **species** that are best adapted to the environment are most able to survive and reproduce. The theory has had an enormous impact on subsequent intellectual history. Many philosophers have attempted to use the framework of evolutionary thought to explain social phenomena and to deal with traditional philosophical issues, although many of these uses of the theory are controversial. The contemporary theory of evolution combines Darwin's insight with the new science of genetics, and there is debate whether the species, the individual, or the gene is the unit of survival in evolution. Two philosophical fields based on the theory of evolution, **evolutionary epistemology** and **evolutionary ethics**, have attracted support.

> "By 'evolution' I mean the natural unfolding and change of organisms down through the generations from earlier forms, widely different." **Ruse, *Taking Darwin Seriously***

evolutionary epistemology

EPISTEMOLOGY The analysis of human knowledge and of its development in evolutionary terms. It has two basic approaches. The first considers the growth of knowledge as analogical to the growth of organisms, and holds that the acceptance of knowledge is the result of selection among ideas. The ideas that gain attention and allegiance in the course of struggle will be established until displaced by a challenger. Advocates of this approach include Campbell and Toulmin. **Popper** claimed that this approach amounts to his theory of falsification. The other approach, represented by Lorenz and Ruse, claims that the human cognitive structure itself is a result of **natural selection** and, hence, is equipped with innate dispositions incorporating our principles of thought and reasoning. Evolutionary epistemology is part of a broader program of **naturalized epistemology**. Rather than seeking to secure our knowledge claims against skeptical doubts, it tries to explain major features of our knowledge as necessary or inevitable features of ourselves as natural beings.

> "[Evolution] has taught us appropriate intellectual responses to various contacts and collisions, by structuring the brain of the mind that responds. This is the central claim of evolutionary epistemology." **Schilcher and Tennant, *Philosophy, Evolution and Human Nature***

evolutionary ethics

ETHICS An ethics established on the basis of biological evolutionary theory. It claims that ethical principles can be derived from understanding the process of **evolution**. There are two major approaches. The first claims that the evolutionary process itself is morally positive and progressive. The good is whatever is the fittest for survival, that is, whatever can contribute to maintaining and developing the human species. Hence, it is morally wrong to do anything that might hinder the evolutionary process. A crude version of this claim, which is associated

with **social Darwinism**, advocates competition and liberty and rejects equality and the provision of welfare. Social Darwinism has been widely rejected, but other versions of this approach suggest that we should help those who are most fit for life. The second approach is associated with **sociobiology**, which suggests that organisms within the same species are not necessarily in conflict and that cooperation is sometimes a better biological strategy than conflict. Some sociobiologists claim that **altruism** is a human evolutionary adaptation and that we are determined to be moral by our genes. Such an approach seems compatible with some versions of **social contract** theory and might help to explain how naturally selected tendencies can supplement rationality in explaining obligation. However, the empirical study of evolutionary altruism suggests that we tend naturally to cooperate with our closest kin and with those in a position to cooperate. This contrasts with any universal and equal obligation, and its altruism is rather narrow. Evolutionary ethics is also criticized for its attempt to derive ought directly from is. Even if its current evolutionary conjectures were established more firmly, it is unclear that its alleged moral consequences would also become established.

> "A system of evolutionary ethics is one based on a criterion of value purportedly derived from the evolutionary theory of the origin and proliferation of life on earth." **Schilcher and Tennant, *Philosophy, Evolution and Human Nature***

ex nihilo nihil fit

METAPHYSICS [Latin, nothing can be made or emerge out of nothing] A metaphysical principle that was first employed by **Parmenides** against the theory of **change** proposed by earlier natural philosophers. The principle implies that nothing in the world can arise without a **cause**. Christian theologians defended the doctrine of God's creation *ex nihilo* (from nothing) by claiming that this Parmenidean principle can be applied only to natural things and not to the activity of the supreme deity who exists outside nature.

> "When we apprehend that it is impossible that anything can be formed of nothing, the proposition *ex nihilo nihil fit* . . . is a common notion or axiom." **Descartes, *Principles of Philosophy***

examination paradox, see surprise examination paradox

excellence, an alternative translation of *arête* (virtue)

excellence of character, another expression for ethical virtue

excuse

ETHICS, PHILOSOPHY OF LAW The condition or reason that can free an **agent** who commits a wrong from censure or responsibility. Excuse is different from **justification**, for while an excuse implies that the agent's action is morally wrong or not permissible, justification is the condition or reason which makes an action not a wrongdoing but positively permissible. Strictly speaking, an excuse should also be distinguished from mitigating circumstance, which can reduce the degree of reprehension or severity of punishment for a wrongdoing agent, but which cannot fully eliminate the blame. For example, an extremely hungry man commits a robbery. His hunger is a mitigating circumstance, but not an excuse for his impermissible action. What conditions or reasons may, then, excuse a wrongdoing? According to **Aristotle**, if an action is caused by some uncontrollable external force, it is excusable. According to **Hume**, if an action is not caused by a defect of character, for example by evil motivation at the time of action, it is excusable. Generally, the conditions that may serve as excuses include, among others, ignorance, immaturity, insanity, compulsion, coercion, and accident.

"An excuse is a statement, claim or plea, used to mitigate some true charge that tends to discredit a person in some way." **Brandt,** *Ethical Theory*

exegesis

PHILOSOPHY OF RELIGION, PHILOSOPHY OF HISTORY [from Greek *eksêgêsis*, explanation, interpretation] **Interpretation**, particularly biblical interpretation. In the medieval period, exegesis became a subdiscipline of theology, dealing with the interpretation of holy scripture, biblical criticism, and biblical history. Because it presupposed **faith** and aimed at defending Catholic dogma, it was also called biblical theology. Exegesis tries to interpret a text by clarifying its authorship and earlier sources, by understanding it in its original context, and by bringing out the author's meaning from the text itself. It contrasts with *eisegesis*, which reads meaning into a text. Exegesis is a predecessor of **hermeneutics**.

"The systematic understanding of fixed life-expressions we shall call Exegesis. Since mental life is capable of being objectively understood only when it is completely and creatively, i.e. verbally, expressed, so is the task of exegesis that of interpreting the written records of human existence." **Dilthey, in Gardiner (ed.),** *Theories of History*

existence

METAPHYSICS, LOGIC, PHILOSOPHY OF LANGUAGE [from Latin *ex*, out of + *sistere*, cause to stand, meaning something there] Medieval philosophers, influenced by the doctrine that everything is created by God, distinguished between existence (*that* it is) and essence (*what* it is). Thomas **Aquinas** applied this contrast to interpret **Aristotle**'s doctrine of **substance** as meaning that a substance is brought to be by conferring existence to an essence. God alone is the unity of essence and existence, while everything else has its existential ground in God. Against this background, later philosophers have continued to discuss the relationship between essence and existence. Existence is the fact that there is a thing, while essence is the nature of that thing and is the necessary ground for the contingent being of the thing. The central theme of **existentialism** is that for human beings existence precedes essence.

Although "**being**" has three distinct meanings, existence, the copula, and the sign of identity, existence and being are often taken as equivalent. "What exists?" is considered by many to be the central question in philosophy. When traditional metaphysics asks "What is being?," it asks about being in the sense of existence. We can begin with the claim that things which exist are those that can bring about effects in the behavior of other things and can in turn be affected by them. However, we can also talk about the existence of fictitious entities and **abstract entities**, and these do not seem to have such powers; philosophers have disputed what "existence" means in these contexts. Also, it is not clear what to say when our minds seem to be affected by things that do not exist, such as by apparent objects in dreams, illusions, or delusions.

The modern anti-metaphysical tradition, in attacking the quest for being in traditional metaphysics, focuses on the thesis that existence is not a **property**. This thesis, initiated by **Hume** and **Kant**, has been discussed in great detail in the twentieth century. According to it, the **existential propositions** share the same grammatical form with attributive propositions but are logically different from them. Existential propositions do not ascribe a property to a subject, and in spite of its grammatical role existence is a not a logical predicate. For **Russell**, **Wittgenstein**, and the **logical positivists**, misunderstanding the nature of existential propositions is the root of traditional metaphysics.

Contemporary philosophical logic and philosophy of language offer further intensive discussion of what we mean by saying that existence is a grammatical predicate, but not a logical predicate. Various theories have been advanced concerning our talk about existence and its existential implications and assumptions, such as Russell's theory of **descriptions**, **Pears**'s distinction between **referential tautologies** and referential contradictions, and **Strawson**'s criticism of Russell's theory of descriptions. **Quine**'s widely influential account of the quantificational apparatus of logic and his formula "to be is to be the value of a bound variable" raises questions about where quantification is possible and about the relations between logic and **ontology**.

> "I think an almost unbelievable amount of false philosophy has arisen through not realising what 'existence' means." **Russell, *Logic and Knowledge***

existence (Heidegger)

MODERN EUROPEAN PHILOSOPHY Etymologically, existence (*existere*) means "standing out" or "standing outside." On this basis, **Heidegger** claimed that not all actual entities can be said to exist. Existence is not, as traditionally conceived, something one simply encounters or comes across in the world (what Heidegger called presence-at-hand). Rather, it is the mode of being of *Dasein* (human existence), for only *Dasein* can stand out from its own occurrence in the world and reflect on itself. For Heidegger, existence is *Dasein*'s awareness that it is. *Dasein*'s essence lies in its existence because we make

ourselves be what we are in the course of living out our possibilities. For Heidegger, existence in this sense is also the ground of **presence**, that is, the mode of being of the world.

> "That kind of Being towards which *Dasein* can comport itself in one way or another, and always does comport itself somehow, we call 'existence' [*Existenz*]." **Heidegger, *Being and Time***

existence proposition, another term for existential proposition

existential generalization

LOGIC A rule of inference in predicate calculus that introduces **existential quantifiers**. If a statement *fa* contains a free variable *a*, it can be generalized into $(\exists x)fx$. Using an example in ordinary language, we can generalize from "Socrates is mortal" to "Someone is mortal." Existential generalization is a process that generates an existentially quantified statement from one instance of it. This is valid on the assumption of predicate logic that at least one thing exists in the universe. Existential generalization contrasts with **existential instantiation**, which generates one instance, say *fa*, from an existentially quantified statement like $(\exists x)fx$.

> "Existential generalization . . . carries us from a theorem φ to a theorem $(\exists x)\psi$ where φ is like ψ except for containing free occurrences of 'y' in all the positions in which ψ contains free occurrences of 'x'." **Quine, *From a Logical Point of View***

existential import

LOGIC Also called existential presupposition, a sentence, statement, or proposition has existential import if it implies a commitment to the existence of something. In Aristotelian logic, all universal propositions in the form of "all A's are B's" have existential import since they imply that there is at least one A that is B, that is, that an A exists. Such propositions imply the existence of at least one object to which the subject-term A applies. However, this implication is not accepted in modern predicate calculus. **Universal quantification** is formalized as $\forall x\ (fx{\to}gx)$, "for all x, if x is f, then x is g." The proposition does not have existential import, because the proposition can be true even if there is no x, unlike propositions containing existential quantification.

"An expression 'a' may occur in a theory, we saw, with or without purporting to name an object. What clinches matters is rather the quantification (∃x) (x = a). It is the existential quantifier, not the 'a' itself, that carries existential import." **Quine,** *Ontological Relativity*

existential instantiation

LOGIC A rule of inference in predicate logic that removes the **existential quantifier** by proceeding from an existentially quantified statement (∃x)fx to fa, which is an existential instantiation of it. Using an example in ordinary language, it is a procedure to infer from "Someone is mortal" to "Socrates is mortal." Existential instantiation contrasts with **existential generalization**, which generates an existentially quantified statement from one of its instances.

"To substitute 'This girl is' for 'There is a girl' in 'There is a girl in father's chair' is to produce an existential instantiation of the latter." **C. Williams,** *What is Existence?*

existential presupposition, another name for existential import

existential proposition

LOGIC, METAPHYSICS In the traditional **syllogism** a proposition of the "I" form (Some P is Q) or the "O" form (Some P is not Q), which says that something having a particular property or lacking a particular property exists. **Russell** analyzes existential propositions by appealing to the notion of a **propositional function** and saying that such propositions assert or deny the truth of at least one value of a propositional function and that their subject phrases are not referring terms. For instance, "some men are mortal" can be analyzed into "there is at least one x, such that x is a man and x is mortal," and "some men are not mortal" can be analyzed into "there is at least one x, such that x is a man and x is not mortal." The subject-term in the original proposition moves to a predicate position in the analysis and thus loses its referring function. Sometimes Russell calls existential propositions negative general propositions, and they are also called existential statements.

"In ordinary language, the words 'some', 'a', and 'the' (in the singular) indicate existence propositions." **Russell,** *Human Knowledge*

existential quantifier

LOGIC, METAPHYSICS According to **Frege**, a particular categorical proposition in traditional logic of the form "Some s are p," can be analyzed as "There is at least one thing x, such that x is s and x is p." This can be symbolized as (∃x) (sx ∧ px). (∃x) is called the "existential quantifier," and means "There is at least one thing x such that . . ." or "Something is . . ." An existential quantifier binds an **open sentence** into an **existential proposition**. Along with the **universal quantifier**, it is one of the two major operators in predicate logic. For **Quine**, the only satisfactory or intelligible sense of existence involves being an object that is a value of a variable bound by an existential quantifier. His claim raises questions about whether quantification and hence existence are limited to objects in **first-order predicate** calculus.

"The existential quantifier (∃x) may be read "At least one object x is such that . . ." **Quine,** *Theories and Things*

existential statement, see existential proposition

existentialism

MODERN EUROPEAN PHILOSOPHY As a type of philosophy, existentialism began with the works of **Kierkegaard** and **Nietzsche**, although the term "existentialism" was introduced by the French philosopher Gabriel **Marcel** at the end of the Second World War. At that time, existentialism became a major philosophical movement in continental Europe. It grew from hostility toward the modern rationalism that characterized the Age of Reason. This rationalism claimed that reason is our highest faculty and that it is capable of solving any problem. It held that the universe is a coherent and intelligible system, which can be comprehended in a deductive conceptual system. The rationalism culminated in **Hegel**'s Absolute Reason. Existentialism suggests that such belief in reason is itself irrational and rejects all purely abstract thinking. Instead of **abstraction**, it holds that philosophy should deal with the lives and experiences of individuals and their historical situations. Existentialism draws a fundamental distinction between **essence** and **existence**. Rationalist philosophy emphasizes essence as the abstract common nature of things. In contrast, existentialism argues that existence precedes essence and starts its philosophical work from individual and particular existence. This doctrine is the source of its name. Existentialism is characterized by its concern with individuality and concreteness.

Existentialism further distinguishes two kinds of existence or being. One is the existence of things in the world that lack free will; the other, which **Heidegger** called *Dasein*, is human existence, characterized by reflection upon itself and free choice. Belief in the **freedom** of human beings is the most fundamental thesis of existentialism, which claims that the possibility of choice is the central fact of human nature. Existentialism takes human freedom as the basic subject-matter of its philosophical analysis. In relation to this freedom, **intentionality**, emotion, the **absurdity** of the world, and basic human experiences of **anxiety**, **dread**, and **death** become recurrent themes of existentialism. Major exponents of existentialism include Karl **Jaspers**, Gabriel **Marcel**, Martin Heidegger, Jean-Paul **Sartre**, Maurice **Merleau-Ponty**, and Albert **Camus**. These authors present different existentialist perspectives. They are even divided into Christian existentialists (Jaspers and Marcel) and atheistic existentialists (the others mentioned above). Existentialism had important influence in literature and other art forms in Europe. Sometimes, existentialism is called philosophy of existence.

> "What is at the very heart and centre of existentialism is the absolute character of the free commitment, by which every man realises himself in realising a type of humanity – a commitment always understandable, to no matter whom in no matter what epoch – and its bearing upon the relativity of the cultural pattern which may result from such absolute commitment." **Sartre**, *Existentialism & Humanism*

existentiell-existentiale **distincton,** see ontico-ontological distinction

Existenz

MODERN EUROPEAN PHILOSOPHY A German term having a different meaning from its English equivalent "existence." Its specific connotations may be traced to **Schelling** and **Kierkegaard**, but it was brought to prominence by Karl **Jaspers**, who contrasted *Existenz* and *Dasein*. Contrary to **Heidegger**, he characterized *Dasein* as the empirical nature of a human being and the object of theoretical reflection. On his view, *Existenz* is authentic being or the genuine self. It is what is just mine. This authentic and unique self is infinitely open to new possibilities and cannot be thought conceptually by means of **clear and distinct** ideas. It is a self that is experienced and lived. *Existenz* is internally related to **transcendence**, on which it is directed, and it is realized through **freedom**. For Jaspers, *Existenz* and freedom are always interchangeable. *Existenz* is the ground for being, for freedom of thought, and for action.

> "*Existenz* is what never becomes object, the origin from which issues my thinking and acting, that whereof I speak in ideas which discern nothing." **Jaspers**, *Philosophie*

exoteric

ANCIENT GREEK PHILOSOPHY [from Greek *exoterikos*, outer, external] **Aristotle** called his polished and published writings, most of which were in the style of Platonic dialogues, his exoteric writings. They were intended to be read by the public and non-specialists outside his school. In contrast, the **Hellenistic** Aristotelian commentators introduced the term esoteric (from Greek *esoterikos*, inner) for Aristotle's treatises, which were not published except as textbooks within the school and which were accessible only to a small circle of his own disciples. When Andronics edited Aristotle's completed works in the first century AD, he did not include the exoteric writings. This might be the reason for their loss, and they survive only in a few fragments. Later on, exoteric doctrines and rituals were easily accessible and understood by the public, while esoteric doctrines and rituals were secret and mysterious, and conveyed only to a small inner circle.

> "There are external goods and goods of the soul, . . . a distinction which we also draw in exoteric writings." **Aristotle**, *Eudemian Ethics*

expected utility

ETHICS, PHILOSOPHY OF ACTION, PHILOSOPHY OF SOCIAL SCIENCE The likelihood of the various possible outcomes of an act and their value for the agent. Under many circumstances, an agent may be faced with several possible courses of action. To decide which course of action he should take, the agent, if he is rational, should calculate the expected utility of each act and then perform the available action with the highest expected utility. Expected utility thus serves as a major reason for a rational act. But the calculation of expected utility involves some **paradoxes**, such as **Newcomb's problem** and the **St Petersburg paradox**.

"The expected utility of an act is the sum of all the utilities that might accrue from its performance, each multiplied by the probability that the act will produce that utility." **Ackermann,** *Belief and Knowledge*

experience

EPISTEMOLOGY, PHILOSOPHY OF MIND [from Greek *empirie* and Latin *experientia*] That which contrasts to what is merely thought or to what is accepted on the basis of authority or tradition. In philosophy, experience is generally what we perceive by the senses (sensory experience), what we learn from others, or whatever comes from external sources or from inner **reflection**. In this sense, experience is associated with observation and experiment. **Empiricism** stresses that our knowledge must be based on experience, but **rationalism** claims that experience is a potential source of error and prefers rational certainty to mere empirical generalization. In ordinary usage, for every experience there must be something experienced that is independent of the subject of experience. But in philosophy, the relation between experience as a state of **consciousness** and independent **objects** of experience becomes a focus of debate. There must be something **given** in experience, yet the status of the given is very controversial. Different answers respectively ground positions such as **realism**, **idealism**, and **skepticism**. The different ways of understanding the given also involve different ways of understanding the notion of **sense-data**. There is also debate about the relation between experience and theory. Starting with **Kant**, there has been a tendency to deny an account of experience as bare sensation that is unprocessed by **thought**. In modern philosophy of mind a major theme, which bears on many theoretical issues,

concerns the alleged **privacy** of an experience as an event knowable only to its possessor and the possibility of public access to that experience.

"Whence has it all the materials of reason and knowledge? To this I answer, in one word, from *experience*; in that all our knowledge is founded, and from that it ultimately derives itself." **Locke,** *An Essay Concerning Human Understanding*

experiential proposition another term for basic proposition or protocol sentence

experimentalism

PHILOSOPHY OF SCIENCE, EPISTEMOLOGY A term for **Dewey**'s form of **pragmatism**, which he also called **instrumentalism** or practicalism. Dewey believed that the pattern and standard for knowledge should be modern science and modern scientific methods, in particular the method of experiment. His thinking focuses on the analysis and evaluation of experiment. He claimed that the task of philosophy is the critical evaluation of belief and that the function of concepts is practical. Problem solving is an experiment in coping with ever new situations. **Knowledge** can only be understood within its context and must be justified in practical matters. Experimentalism is a theory of knowledge. It places emphasis on direct action and scientific control, and concerns methods and consequences. Dewey's claims have played an important role in American intellectual culture. His emphasis on experiment corrects an excessive concentration on theory and observation in rival approaches to science.

"Since the method of modern science culminates in experimentation, Dewey's philosophy becomes pre-eminently the philosophy of experiment. It becomes experimentalism." **Werkmeister,** *A History of Philosophical Ideas in America*

explanandum, see explanation

explanans, see explanation

explanation

PHILOSOPHY OF SCIENCE, EPISTEMOLOGY An account characteristically telling us why something exists or happens or must exist or happen. To explain is to increase knowledge, remove perplexity, and diminish surprise. All theories have the function of explaining, but the nature of explanation is a philosophical issue. In an explanation, the thing being explained is called the *explanandum*, and the things used to explain it are called the *explanans*. An explanation is a general conclusion about the *explanandum* derived from the *explanans*. The standard view about the nature of scientific explanation is the **covering law model** of explanation. This view was proposed by **Mill** and fully elaborated by **Hempel**, and it holds that to explain is to put a particular event under a general law. This model is further divided into two types. For **deductive-nomological explanation**, if a law is deterministic, we may deduce an explanation of an event from the law and the antecedent conditions. For statistical explanation, if a law is probabilistic or statistical, the explanation is probabilistic. One difficulty faced by the covering model is how to explain the highest level of general laws. Various alternative views about explanation have been developed. Some philosophers suggest a causal approach, claiming that to explain is to identify the underlying mechanisms that produce events, states, and regularities. Others believe that to explain is provide a coherent unification of phenomena. Still others argue that explanation needs to be adjusted to the epistemic or practical needs of the audience. There is debate about whether explanation requires **necessity** (thus ruling out statistical explanation) and about how claims to natural necessity could be justified. There is also debate over **Dilthey**'s contrast between scientific explanation and historical **understanding**. Some argue that particularistic historical explanation and **narrative** explanation differs in kind from explanation in terms of laws. To explain a human action is normally to appeal to the **beliefs** and **desires** that provide the agent's **reasons** for so acting. Whether this kind of explanation can conform to the covering law model is also a matter of controversy.

"An individual fact is said to be explained, by pointing out its cause, that by stating the law or laws of causation, of which its production is an instance."
The Collected Works of John Stuart Mill, **vol. VII**

explanation sketch

PHILOSOPHY OF SCIENCE, PHILOSOPHY OF HISTORY A term introduced by Carl **Hempel**, who argues that the paradigm of scientific explanation is given by the **covering law model**. According to this model, we explain a particular event by bringing it under a general covering law. Hempel claims that **historical explanation** also conforms to this pattern. However, there are rarely general laws in history in the way that there are general natural scientific laws, and normally historians do not explain particular actions by appealing to any universal law. Therefore, there seems to be a limitation to applying a model of scientific explanation to the work of historians. Hempel recognizes this limitation, but maintains that historical explanation and scientific explanation remain the same type in principle. They differ only because scientists seek to offer full explanations, while historians offer explanation sketches, which vaguely and incompletely approximate fully warranted scientific explanations. An explanation sketch is an outline of what a full explanation would be if it could be discovered. The validity of an explanation sketch relies on its capacity to indicate what must be done in order to transform it into a completely satisfactory explanation. In spite of the attractions of a unified account of explanation, many philosophers of history have questioned the adequacy of the explanation sketch model and have explored alternative accounts of historical explanation.

"What the explanatory analysis of historical events offers is, then, in most cases not an explanation in one of the meanings developed above, but something that might be called an *explanation sketch*. Such a sketch consists of a more or less vague indication of the laws and initial conditions considered as relevant, and needs 'filling out' in order to turn into a full-fledged explanation." **Hempel, "The Function of General Law in History," in Gardiner (ed.),** *Theories of History*

explanation/understanding, see understanding/explanation

explication

PHILOSOPHY OF LANGUAGE, LOGIC A term introduced by **Carnap** for the modification or replacement of an expression of **natural language** or a pre-theoretic concept by a logically or theoretically more explicit expression or concept. The purpose of explication is to reduce or eliminate **vagueness** or **ambiguity**, or to establish the logical relation between an expression and other explicit expressions in a domain. What is to be modified is called the *explicandum*, and it is replaced by the *explicatum*. In analytic philosophy, explication, as a synonym for **analysis** or explanation, has been considered to be the main task of logical analysis.

> "By the explication of a familiar but vague concept we mean its replacement by a new exact concept." **Carnap**, *Meaning and Necessity*

explicit definition

LOGIC, PHILOSOPHY OF LANGUAGE An explicit definition defines a term by means of other terms and states directly and explicitly its **intension**, the necessary and sufficient conditions for the term's applicability. An explicit definition is equivalent to the word being defined. As a result, the definiendum and the definiens become interchangeable in any context without a change of meaning. For instance, that "man is a rational animal" is an explicit definition. So, wherever we use the term "man," we can substitute "rational animal" for it. An explicit definition is what we normally understand a definition to be. It can be contrasted to an implicit definition, which defines a term by stating that it is implied by certain axioms rather than by directly stating its intension.

> "An explicit definition is a rule legitimising substitution of one symbol for another, and in virtue of such a rule the defined symbol may always be eliminated and replaced by the definiens without change of meaning of the sentence in which it occurs." **Pap**, *Elements of Analytic Philosophy*

exportation

LOGIC A principle of inference, which states that a conditional statement having conjunctive antecedents can be replaced by a conditional statement having conditional consequents. From the premise "If p and q, then r" $[(p \wedge q) \rightarrow r]$, we can conclude "if p, then if q then r" $[(p \rightarrow (if q \rightarrow r)]$. This inference is indeed a strict implication and can therefore be expressed as $[(p \wedge q) \rightarrow r] \leftrightarrow [(p \rightarrow (if q \rightarrow r)]$. The reverse of this inference is also true and is called **importation**.

> "If p implies p and q implies q, then if pq implies r, then p implies that q implies r. This is . . . called exportation." **Russell**, *Principles of Mathematics*

expression theory

AESTHETICS A theory, developed by **Croce**, **Cassirer**, **Santayana**, **Dewey**, **Collingwood**, and **Ducasse**, holding that all works of art are expressions of the emotions and feelings of their artists. The properties of an artwork can be designated by the same words that designate the feelings, emotions, attitudes, and moods of human beings. Artistic creation originates with the highly specific but chaotically indeterminate emotional states of an artist. Such a state drives an artist to endeavor to articulate, clarify, and stabilize this emotion or feeling. An artwork is the intuitionalizing of this feeling and the embodiment of it in some definite and tangible concrete form. Hence, artistic creation is a process of achieving self-expression. **Beauty** is successful expression. For instance, the meaning of a musical work is its expression of a psychological state or quality, such as fortitude, melancholy, or gaiety. The appreciation of art requires us to retrieve the psychological states undergone by the artist during creation.

The expression theory rejects any instrumentalist view of art. It argues that the production of art is not a matter of technique, which is essential only for crafts rather than for art proper. The concrete form of an artwork is merely a vehicle for communicating artistic feeling. This theory is influenced by **Hegel**'s idealism and a version of it has been associated with Freudian psychological theory. It has been criticized for ignoring the capacity for art to express religious and philosophical ideas as well as the artist's emotions, and for ignoring the individuality and peculiarities of artworks. Critics also point out that judging a work of art does not require one to recreate the psychological processes involved in its production.

> "Expression theory, in replacing the beauty theory of art and the concept of art as imitation, whether of a naturalistic reality or a beautiful reality, found the essence of art to lie in the very process of expression itself." **Hofstadter**, *Truth and Art*

extended logic, see deviant logic

extended substance, see thinking substance

extension

LOGIC, PHILOSOPHY OF LANGUAGE In contrast to **intension**, **connotation**, or **meaning**, but sometimes used as a synonym for **denotation** or **reference**. The extension of a general term or a predicate expression is the **class** or the range of entities of which the general term or predicate expression is true or to which this term applies. For example, the extension of the general term "green" is the whole set of things of which it is true to say that they are green. The extension of a proper name is the individual object to which it refers. For instance, England is the extension of the term "England." **Frege** held that a **proposition** is also an extension, namely its **truth-value**. Something is called extensional if it pertains to extension.

> "The extension of a term . . . is the set of things to which it is applicable." **Kneale and Kneale,** *The Development of Logic*

extension (metaphysics)

METAPHYSICS, PHILOSOPHY OF SCIENCE For **Descartes**, geometric extension in length, breadth, and depth is the defining characteristic of **matter** or corporeal **substance**, just as thought is of thinking substances. Extension and thought are respectively the principal properties or attributes of the two substances, for they constitute the **essence** of matter and mind. A body may extend in many ways and this is the grounding of the various properties of matter. But all these are simply modes of extension. This idea is echoed by **Spinoza**, who also believed that extension and thinking are two attributes of substance. To explain physical phenomena in terms of the modifications of the simple geometrical attributes of extension is to replace the **scholastic** notion of **substantial form**.

> "By 'extension' we mean whatever has length, breadth and depth, leaving aside the question whether it is a real body or merely a space." **Descartes,** *The Philosophical Writings,* **vol. 1**

extensional logic, see intensional logic

extensionalism

LOGIC, PHILOSOPHY OF LANGUAGE, PHILOSOPHY OF SCIENCE An approach in the philosophy of logic and **semantics**, associated with **Frege, Russell, Carnap,** and especially **Quine**, that reduces the **intensional** to the extensional. Intensional meaning presupposes the existence of meant entities and is definable only in terms of other intensional ideas. In contrast, extensional meaning implies that terms solely designate existent objects and that co-designating terms are interchangeable in any syntactical context without loss of truth-value (*salva veritate*). Extensionalism argues that the idea of intensional meaning is obscure and a myth and suggests that legitimate scientific theory can only be extensional. It rejects reference to non-existent objects and **propositional attitudes** expressed in intensional terms. This theory is based on the thesis of extensionality formulated by Carnap, which states that once the obscurities and confusions of **ordinary language** are revealed and all non-existents are excluded, all sentences made in an intensional language can be translated entirely into an extensional language. Extensionalism has been further developed by Quine, who suggests that an adequate logic should eliminate all intensional contexts, such as propositional attitudes, quotational, and **modal** contexts because they fail to permit quantification and fail to support the substitution *salva veritate* of extensionally co-designating terms.

> "Extensionalism, as we are using this term, is a version of scepticism, about the scientific feasibility of attempting to explicate the concept of meaning. According to the extensionalist position, the logical form of sentences and expressions in natural language can be accounted for on the basis of the concept of extension, without recourse to the concept of meaning." **Katz,** *Semantic Theory*

extensionality, axiom of

LOGIC A postulate of **set theory** formulated by Zermelo, which states that two **sets** or **classes** are identical if and only if they have the same members. Any sets A and B that are alike in members are identical. Hence, a set is determined by its members. This **axiom** is a form of the **indiscernibility of identicals** or **Leibniz's law**, according to which if two things are identical, their properties are the same.

> "One axiom that we shall certainly want in some form or other is that of extensionality, also known as that of *Bestimmtheit* or definiteness: classes are the same whose members are the same." **Quine,** *Set Theory and Its Logic*

extensionality, thesis of

LOGIC, PHILOSOPHY OF LANGUAGE A thesis introduced by **Carnap** and providing the basis for **extensionalism**. It states that once the obscurities and confusions of **ordinary language** are revealed and all non-existents are excluded, all sentences formed in an **intensional** language can be translated entirely into an extensional language. For any non-extensional system there is an extensional system into which it can be translated. In an extensional system, given any statement *s* that contains a proposition *p* as a part, we can substitute for *p* any other proposition which has the same truth-value as *p* without altering the truth-value of *s*. Thus, in any statement about a **propositional function**, any formally equivalent function may be substituted without changing the truth-value of the statement. Accordingly, statements in any language can be translated while keeping the same truth-value. This thesis, however, is not true of propositions asserting **propositional attitudes**.

"We will now formulate the thesis of extensionality in a way which is at the same time more complete and less ambitious, namely, a universal language of science may be extensional; or, more exactly: for every given intensional language S_1, an extensional language S_2 may be constructed such that S_1 can be translated into S_2." **Carnap, *The Logical Syntax of Language***

extensive magnitude

METAPHYSICS, PHILOSOPHY OF SCIENCE For **Kant**, extensive magnitudes are the spatial-temporal dimensions that can be used to measure things of certain types. In contrast, **intensive magnitudes** are degrees of intensiveness of a sense experience and are matters of quality rather than quantity. A physical object has extensive magnitude, while beauty has an intensive magnitude. Kant held that the principal feature of the axioms of intuition is that "all intuitions are extensive magnitudes," and that the principal feature of the anticipations of perception is that "in all appearances, the real that is an object of sensation has intensive magnitude, that is, a degree."

"I entitled a magnitude extensive when the representation of the parts makes possible, and therefore necessarily precedes, the representation of the whole." **Kant, *Critique of Pure Reason***

external perception, see inner perception

external point of view, see internal point of view

external property, see right (Kant)

external questions, see internal questions

external relation

LOGIC, METAPHYSICS, EPISTEMOLOGY When A stands in relation R to B, if R is not a constitutive element of either A or B, it is an external and unessential relation, for it is a contingent matter for A and B to be related in this way. Otherwise, the relation is an intrinsic or **internal relation**. The distinction between external and internal relations can be traced to **Hume**'s distinction between relations of fact and relations of ideas, and became a major argument for the rejection of absolute idealism by **Moore** and **Russell** and a point of contention between **Royce**'s idealism and **neo-realism**. According to idealism, the existence of things depends on their being experienced, and hence the relation between the things and experience of them is internal. But realism claims that things exist outside of experience and are connected with consciousness by external relations. The contents of things are not made up of their relations to consciousness. The knowledge relation is not constitutive of the objects of knowledge. The nature of reality cannot be inferred merely from the nature of knowledge. For realism, the idealist view of the internal relation between knowing and known involves an **egocentric predicament**.

"A relation is internal, as I shall use the term, when given certain terms with certain natures, the relation must hold between the terms. It holds 'in every possible world' that contains those terms and where these terms have these natures. With an external relation there is no such necessity." **D. Armstrong, *Universals***

external world

METAPHYSICS, EPISTEMOLOGY The external world comprises the system of things and events external to our **perceptions**. Since perception is relative to one individual, other persons may also be parts of the external world. The central philosophical problem about the external world is as follows. Since perception is the only channel by which we as subjects are connected with the world, how do we know whether perception gives us correct reports about the world? Formulated another way, the problem becomes how to make sense of perceptual statements. Our experience does not seem to be any different when it correctly represents the external world and when it does not. Can we directly perceive the external world, or must there be a medium of **sense-data**? This is one of the most important philosophical issues, and various major philosophical doctrines, such as **realism**, **phenomenalism**, and **skepticism**, arise from our attempts to solve problems about our knowledge of the external world.

"The experient himself has no way of telling, internally to his experience, whether the relationship holds between the immediate content of his experience and what it represents. This makes acute the so-called problem of the external world." **Danto,** *Analytical Philosophy of Language*

externalism

EPISTEMOLOGY, PHILOSOPHY OF LANGUAGE A theory of **epistemic justification**, which is opposed to **internalism**. It denies that the justification of a belief requires the believer to be aware of the cognitive process of the given belief. Internalism, which holds that one must have this awareness, has difficulty in explaining the ascription of knowledge to unsophisticated adults or to young children, and in explaining some classical problems, such as **induction**. Externalism suggests instead that the nature of a belief is at least partly determined by the surrounding objective world, rather than solely subjectively. Therefore, justification requires the consideration of factors external to one's consciousness. Externalism thus links justification to **truth**. There are various forms of externalism, and the most influential include **reliabilism**, which claims that justification depends on the reliability of the cognitive process generating the belief, and **probabilism**, which claims that justification should be evaluated in terms of probability. In the philosophy of language, externalism claims that to understand a sentence S descriptively is to know under what conditions S is true.

"The externalist . . . insists that a belief can be justified even though the knower is ignorant of that justification." **Maddy,** *Realism in Mathematics*

externalism (ethics)

ETHICS Ethical externalism (also called motivational externalism) holds that the **justification** of an action is separate from the motivation, for the former is merely an issue about the degree to which an action conforms to the best moral principles. A person's belief that he ought to do something is the reason for him to do that thing, regardless of whether he has motivation. To recognize a moral truth is one thing, and to be motivated by it is quite another. Externalism is opposed to **internalism** (also called motivational internalism), which maintains that we accept a moral truth only if we have at least a *prima facie* motivation for acting under the guidance of that moral truth.

"Externalism holds . . . that the necessary motivation is not supplied by ethical principles and judgements themselves, and that an additional psychological sanction is required to motivate our compliance." **T. Nagel,** *The Possibility of Altruism*

extra-human fertilization, another expression for *in vitro* fertilization

extrinsic value

ETHICS Also called instrumental value or extrinsic good, the value which is pursued not for its own sake, but for the sake of something else, especially for the beneficial consequences it will bring about. It is contrasted with intrinsic value, which is pursued in and for itself. A thing has an extrinsic value because it is a means to the achievement of intrinsic value or because it in some sense contributes to such achievement. For instance, if we exercise for the sake of health, exercise is extrinsically valuable while health is intrinsically valuable. One thing can sometimes be both intrinsically and extrinsically valuable.

"The intrinsically valuable is usually described as that which is good in itself or good for its own sake; the extrinsically valuable, as that which has value as instrumental to something else." **C. Lewis,** *An Analysis of Knowledge and Valuation*

F

fact

METAPHYSICS, LOGIC, PHILOSOPHY OF LANGUAGE [from Latin *factum*, originally something done, a deed or an action] Starting in the seventeenth century, a fact is described as a set of **objects** in the objective world, related in certain ways that can be stated by a **proposition** or judgment. The constituents of facts are **things** and qualities or **relations**. While things are named but not asserted, facts are asserted but not named. Facts must be expressed by a sentence rather than by a single term. Facts are objects of propositions and decide their **truth** or falsity. **Wittgenstein** claims in his *Tractatus* that the world is the totality of facts, not of things, and that the ultimate constituents of the world are **atomic facts**.

Facts can be either positive (the s is p) or negative (the s is not p). We can also distinguish between particular facts (the s is p) and universal facts (all s's are p), and between **brute facts** (which involve no rules or institutions, such as the fact that I raise my hand) and institutional facts (which depend on rules or institutions, such as the fact that I promise). There is also a distinction between fact (what is) and **value** (what ought to be). The view that facts are independent of propositions and that the truth and falsity of propositions is determined by whether they are paired with the facts which they state is central to the **correspondence theory of truth**.

> "We express a fact, for example, when we say that a certain thing has a certain property, or that it has a certain relation to another thing; but the thing which has the property or the relation is not what I call a 'fact'." **Russell,** *Logic and Knowledge*

fact/value gap, see is/ought gap

facticity

MODERN EUROPEAN PHILOSOPHY **Heidegger** held that facticity comprises the concrete situations and the cultural and historical contexts into which *Dasein* finds itself thrown *a priori*, and which constitute the concrete limitations of human possibilities. As one component of care, facticity is a mode of **Being** of *Dasein*. In contrast, Heidegger called what are merely material and non-human conditions factuality. *Dasein* exists not factually, but factically. Its facticity indicates that *Dasein* cannot transcend its concrete situations as a free-floating spirit, but must have its Being in the world. Facticity is disclosed by one of *Dasein*'s existentiales, that is, its state of mind. For **Sartre**, facticity was the set of facts relevant or given to the person, for example his physical characteristics, his parents, and his unique position. It represents the contingency of human existence and belongs to **being-in-itself**. According to Sartre, this finitude of human existence does not determine our **freedom** or our fundamental project. Instead, it is the basis upon which we make our free choices. An infinite being does not need to exercise choice, and human choice consists precisely in discovering a person's facticity and seeking to negate or surpass its limitations toward existing as an ideal self-determinating being.

> "The concept of 'facticity' implies that an entity 'within-the-world' has Being-in-the-world in such a way that it can understand itself as bound up in its 'destiny' with the Being of those entities which it encounters within its own world." **Heidegger,** *Being and Time*

factual phenomenalism, see phenomenalism

faculty

PHILOSOPHY OF MIND [from Latin *facultas*, derived from *facilis*, easy + *facere*, make; Greek *dunamis*] **Aristotle** gave two definitions for faculty: (1) a **power** or **function** of **soul** to cause something, such as volition, sense, and intellect; and (2) a **potentiality** which would be actualized by **form**. Both Aristotelian senses persisted through medieval philosophy to modern philosophy, but faculty has come increasingly to be used in the first sense. Kant distinguished the faculties (German *Vermögen*) of the soul, which include the faculties of knowledge, feeling of pleasure and displeasure, and desire, and the faculties of cognition, which include the lower faculties of **sensibility** and the higher faculties of **reason**, **judgment**, and **understanding**. He then established analogies between the faculties of soul and the higher faculties of cognition. The faculty of knowledge is related to that of understanding, and both are applied to the area of nature. The faculty of reason is related to that of desire, and both are applied to the area of freedom. The faculty of judgment is related to the feeling of pleasure and displeasure, and both are applied to the area of art. Modern psychologists have criticized the use of the notion of faculty, but the extent to which this calls for revision in Kantian doctrine is uncertain. An appeal to the notion of faculty in doing philosophy was popular in German idealism, but was attacked by **Nietzsche**.

In an extended sense, since the Middle Ages a faculty has been a part of the structure of a university. In the seventeenth and eighteenth centuries, the faculties of law, medicine, and theology were considered to be the higher faculties and the faculty of philosophy was considered to belong to the lower faculties because it was only propaedeutic to the above studies.

> "It is best, I think, to confine the use of the word 'faculty' exclusively to ultimate and irreducible powers of the mind. Used in this way ... the reference of mental process to faculties, e.g. to faculties of cognition, conation, and feeling, seems unexceptionable." **Campbell,** *On Selfhood and Godhood*

fairness

POLITICAL PHILOSOPHY Equal, proportional, and impartial treatment, constituting a virtue of any institution that involves the distribution of goods and responsibilities. **Aristotle** distinguished between a general notion of justice, as the obedience to laws and regulations, and a particular notion of justice, as the fair distribution of honors and money. This particular notion of justice connects justice with fairness, a bond that is fully exploited by John **Rawls**, who claims in his 1958 paper "Justice as Fairness" that the most basic and important idea in the conception of justice is fairness. The contemporary discussion of fairness is directed against **utilitarianism**, which emphasizes the total amount of utility in a given consequential state of affairs, but ignores the issue of whether that utility is distributed fairly among individuals. In contrast to traditional **contractualism** which considers **consent** to be the only basis for **political obligation**, the notion of fairness also provides an independent source for obligation. For if a person participates in and benefits from a rule-governed, co-operative, and just society, that person has a duty to follow the rules. This is called the principle of fairness, but it is claimed by some critics to lead to tyrannical oppression of individuals.

> "Now by definition the requirements specified by the principle of fairness are the obligations. All obligations arise in this way." **Rawls,** *A Theory of Justice*

faith

PHILOSOPHY OF RELIGION [from Latin *fides*, also meaning trust or loyalty] Voluntary acceptance of views that are not supported rationally or empirically or that cannot be so supported, especially in association with religious belief. Faith is therefore contrasted with philosophical and scientific **knowledge**. The term became philosophically prominent with Paul, who took it as a Christian attitude of belief in the words or works of Christ. Paul's conception of faith as the gift of **God** was greatly developed by **Augustine** and **Aquinas**. How to reconcile the tension between faith and knowledge has been a major philosophical theme since medieval times. For **Kant**, faith is the acceptance of **transcendental ideas**, God, freedom, and immortality, which are beyond the realm of experience and are therefore not objects of theoretical knowledge. They nevertheless play a great role in moral affairs. **Hegel**, **Kierkegaard**, and **Nietzsche** all dealt extensively with the topic of faith. Faith is also an ethical term for keeping promises.

"For by grace you have been saved through faith; and this is not your own doing; it is the gift of God." **Paul, in** *New Testament*, **Ephesians 2:8**

fallacy

LOGIC [from Latin *fallax*, deceptive] A term for a seemingly valid but actually erroneous argument or piece of reasoning. An invalid inference which occurs as a result of mistakes in the **logical form** of an argument gives rise to **formal fallacy**. Formal fallacies are violations of the formal rules of inference and are dealt with in formal logic. More often, fallacies arise informally. They do not involve a mistake in formal inference, but arise from the misapplication of a contextual method or a tactic to get a conclusion accepted. The investigation of informal fallacies is an important part of logic because we must learn to avoid them if logic can be trusted. Each of the various principal types of informal fallacy receives an entry in this dictionary.

"A fallacy is an argument which appears to be conclusive when it is not." **Joseph,** *An Introduction to Logic*

fallacy of accent

LOGIC A **fallacy** originally noticed by **Aristotle**, in which an argument proceeds to a conclusion by changing the syllabic accent of a word and hence causing its meaning to be changed. Such an argument is, of course, invalid. It is later expanded to cover cases in which one argues by emphasizing different parts of a sentence hence changing its meaning. It is also called the fallacy of emphasis, and usually occurs in spoken language.

"The fallacy of accent is committed whenever a statement is accented in such a way as to change its meaning, and is employed in an argument." **Carney and Scheer,** *Fundamentals of Logic*

fallacy of accident

LOGIC **Aristotle** claimed that it is a **fallacy** to take an accidental property to be an essential one. The most often quoted example is: "This dog is yours; this dog is a father; therefore this dog is your father." A fallacy of accident later came to be considered erroneous reasoning from a general rule to a particular case having accidental circumstances which prevent the general rule from applying to it unless the general rule is qualified in some way. For instance, "It is a virtue to tell the truth; so I should tell John that he has cancer." In such a characterization, a fallacy of accident is always equated with a **fallacy of** *secundum quid*, although the latter covers a wider range.

"The fallacy of accident consists in applying a general rule to a particular case whose 'accidental' circumstances render the rule inapplicable." **Copi,** *Introduction to Logic*

fallacy of ambiguity

LOGIC Also called the **fallacy** of clearness, or for **Aristotle** a sophism. Aristotle held that this kind of fallacy arises from **ambiguity** in words or in the sentences that contain ambiguous words. It is a fallacy if during the course of argument the meanings of the ambiguous words shift so that the conclusion is not validly established. The major forms of this kind of fallacy include the **fallacy of accent**, fallacy of **amphiboly**, **fallacy of equivocation**, **fallacy of composition**, and **fallacy of division**. To avoid these fallacies, we need to distinguish the meanings of the words carefully.

"Fallacies of ambiguity are arguments which are incorrect or invalid because of some ambiguity in the language, for example, because a word, phrase, or statement can be understood in different ways." **Carney and Scheer,** *Fundamentals of Logic*

fallacy of clearness, see fallacy of ambiguity

fallacy of the complex question, another name for fallacy of many questions

fallacy of composition

LOGIC An erroneous kind of reasoning that argues that if each part of a whole has a certain property, then the whole has that property. For instance, "If each component of this car is of good quality, the car is of good quality." The term is also used for arguments from the premise that each individual member of a collection has a certain attribute, to the conclusion that the collection has that attribute. The argument is invalid because it mistakenly assumes that the whole or collection is a simple aggregation of the parts or individual members. The converse is the fallacy of division, which argues that if a whole or collection has a certain property, then each of its parts or members has that property. For example, "The United States is rich, so each citizen of the US is rich." This **fallacy** fails to realize that there is not such a transference relationship between a whole and its parts. Both the fallacy of composition and the fallacy of division are examples of the **fallacy of ambiguity,** for they often involve a confusion between the distributive use and the collective use of a word.

> "The fallacy of composition consists in reasoning from what is true only of the parts of some whole to what is true to the whole." **Carney and Scheer,** *Fundamentals of Logic*

fallacy of converse accident, see fallacy of *secundum quid*

fallacy of division, see fallacy of composition

fallacy of emphasis, another name for fallacy of accent

fallacy of equivocation

LOGIC The simplest form of **fallacy of ambiguity.** An ambiguous word or statement is used more than once in the same argument, with the meaning shifting implicitly but significantly between uses. It therefore leads to a misleading or mistaken conclusion.

For example, "Chinese is difficult. I am a Chinese, therefore I am difficult." This **fallacy** is different from the fallacy of accent, for words differently accented are not strictly the same word.

> "In the simplest case of fallacies dependent on language the ambiguity can be traced to double-meaning in a single word. This is the Fallacy of Equivocation." **Hamblin,** *Fallacies*

fallacy of false cause

LOGIC Also called the fallacy of *post hoc ergo propter hoc* (Latin, after this, therefore because of this). The argument reasons that of two correlated things A and B, because A is prior to B in time, A is the cause of B. For instance, "I usually drink tea after lunch; therefore, lunch is the cause of my drinking tea." This is incorrect because it confuses succession and **causation.** It moves from a merely temporal sequence of events to a causal sequence. The alleged cause is not really responsible for the consequence and is not the cause at all. Hence this **fallacy** is also called *non causa pro causa* because it mistakes what is not the cause for a real cause.

> "Any argument in which one mistakes what is not the cause of a given effect for its real cause is a false cause fallacy." **Carney and Scheer,** *Fundamentals of Logic*

fallacy of hasty generation, see fallacy of *secundum quid*

fallacy of many questions

LOGIC Also called the fallacy of the complex question. A asks B a question and demands a simple yes or no answer. But the question implies some unwarranted presupposition that needs to be answered separately. A simple yes or no answer will make B concede the unwarranted presupposition. For example, "Have you stopped beating your father?" No matter whether B answers yes or no, he concedes that he has beaten his father at some time, but that might not be true at all.

> "There remains lastly the fallacy of many questions. This consists in putting questions in such a form that any single answer involves more than one admission." **Joseph,** *An Introduction to Logic*

fallacy of scope, see scope

fallacy of *secundum quid*

LOGIC [Latin, derived from Greek *para to pe*, in a certain aspect] The fallacy of neglecting qualification, which trades on the mistaken idea that what is true with certain qualifications is also true without them. It is always identified with the **fallacy of accident**, which applies a general principle or rule without regard to the specific aspects of the circumstances of its application. *Secundum quid* has an additional form, which generalizes a rule from one instance that may be atypical or exceptional. In this form it is the fallacy of hasty generalization or the fallacy of converse accident, because contrary to the fallacy of accident, it moves from the particular to the general. For example, "Smith is British, and he is very cold toward other people; therefore all British people are cold."

"The fallacy of secundum quid . . . consists in using a principle or proposition without regard to the circumstances which modify its applicability in the case or kind of cases before us." **Joseph,** *An Introduction to Logic*

fallacy of the undistributed middle

LOGIC One basic rule for a valid syllogistic inference is that the term common to the two premises (the middle term) must be distributed in at least one premise, that is, the premise must imply every other premise formed by replacing the original term by other terms with part of its extension. If this rule is violated, the inference commits the fallacy of the undistributed middle, and is invalid. For example, "Smith is intelligent," and "All philosophers are intelligent," therefore "Smith is a philosopher." This **syllogism** is incorrect, because the middle term "intelligent" in both premises is a predicate of an affirmative proposition and is distributed in neither premise.

"Since people may be persuaded that syllogisms with undistributed middle terms are valid when they are not, the term 'fallacy' is used." **Carney and Scheer,** *Fundamentals of Logic*

fallibilism

EPISTEMOLOGY, PHILOSOPHY OF SCIENCE **Peirce**'s term for the view that none of our beliefs, even the apparently most fundamental, is certain and that any

of our beliefs can be revised. A false conclusion might be derived from inductive or deductive inferences. An individually held proposition that is considered to be certain might be false in a web of belief. Rightly understood, relinquishing **certainty** does not open the way to skeptical **doubt**, but is instead a motivation for further investigation. This attitude is opposed to infallibilism, which is held, for example, by religions that declare that their teachings are absolutely right and are not subject to error. All views that accept the possibility of error or hold that **knowledge** is in principle indeterminate and modifiable are fallibilist. Hence, **Reichenbach**, **Popper**, and **Quine** are all fallibilists.

"For years in the course of this ripening process, I used for myself to collect my ideas under the designation fallibilism; and indeed the first step toward finding out is to acknowledge you do not satisfactorily know already." **Peirce,** *Collected Papers*, **vol. I**

fallingness, see authenticity

falsifiability

LOGIC, PHILOSOPHY OF SCIENCE **Popper**'s term, also called testability or refutability, for the property of a theory that it is potentially refutable. In opposition to **logical positivism**, Popper held that science is not about verifying hypotheses or theories, but falsifying them. Falsifiability is the criterion of **demarcation** between science and pseudo-science. A genuine **explanation** must have falsifiable consequences. If a statement or a theory is unfalsifiable, it is pseudo-scientific. Any **hypothesis** or **conjecture**, once refuted, must be superseded by other hypotheses. This is the logic of scientific discovery. If a conjecture survives refutation, then it is temporarily corroborated, but that does not mean that it is confirmed. The theory of falsifiability expresses Popper's hostility to **justificationism**.

"Since a low probability means a high probability of being falsified, it follows that a high degree of falsifiability, or refutability, or testability, is one of the aims of science." **Popper,** *Conjectures and Refutation*

falsification

PHILOSOPHY OF SCIENCE **Popper**'s term for the rejection or refutation of a scientific **hypothesis** or theory on the basis of its confrontation with counter-examples. **Falsifiability**, which is opposed to verifiability, is a property of a theory itself. Falsification, which is opposed to verification, is an empirical **method** for testing the **truth** of a theory. Popper claimed that it is impossible to verify a theory, that is, to guarantee its truth, by the inductive method. A theory supported by confirming evidence has not been confirmed, but only corroborated. It is still open to countless chances of falsification. Scientific claims need the test of falsification rather than verification. A theory that is unfalsifiable is unscientific. Science develops through falsification.

"Thus, there is no induction: we never argue from facts to theories, unless by way of refutation or falsification." **Popper,** *The Philosophy of Karl Popper*

falsificationism, see justificationism

family resemblance

PHILOSOPHY OF LANGUAGE The term can be traced to **Nietzsche**, but becomes prominent through the later **Wittgenstein**'s discussion about the **essence** of language. Traditional essentialism holds that a general term such as "language" or "game" must have a single common property to connect all entities subsumed under it. But Wittgenstein rejects this view. Items under many general terms are like a family, the different members of which resemble one another in different ways with a whole series of overlapping similarities. These relationships and similarities are called family resemblance. This notion is meant to show that there is no need to depart from actual ordinary languages to search for a sublime underlying structure in which each term would have a uniform essence. Accordingly, we should trace out those relationships needed for any investigation, rather than seeking a definition specifying necessary and sufficient conditions for the application of a term. This account of family resemblance can be applied more generally as an attempted general solution to the traditional problem of **universals**.

"I can think of no better expression to characterise these similarities than 'family resemblance'." **Wittgenstein,** *Philosophical Investigations*

fascism

POLITICAL PHILOSOPHY [from Latin *fasces*, the bundle of ax and rods carried before Roman consuls as a symbol of authority] A political doctrine, in opposition to **liberalism** and socialism, which was originally proposed in early twentieth-century Italy by Mussolini and the **neo-Hegelian** philosopher Giovanni **Gentile**. The doctrine was deeply influenced by the Hegelian theory of the **state** and combined extreme **nationalism** with extreme **communitarianism**. Fascism rejects **individualism** by claiming that a nation is an organic entity rather than an aggregate of individuals with basic **rights**. It propounds irrationality and particularity in contrast to **rationality** and **universality**. It supports the role of the government as the upholder of moral integrity and the nation's collective purpose. It advocates an authoritarian state in which the government controls all aspects of social life. In practice, Mussolini's fascist government denied freedom of speech to individuals and appealed to violence. The term 'fascism' was later used to characterize Hitler's National Socialism (Nazi) and other European regimes influenced by Hitler and Mussolini. Through Hitler, fascism became associated with genocidal anti-Semitism, but other fascist regimes were militaristic. Since the Second World War, the term has been taken as a symbol of evil, which is applied to any oppressive and totalitarian political regime or action. Some political theorists seek to understand how fascist regimes arose in the context of **modernity**.

"Fascism is a genus of political ideology whose mythic core in its various permutations is a palingenetic form of populist ultranationalism." **Griffin,** *The Nature of Fascism*

fatalism

METAPHYSICS, PHILOSOPHY OF ACTION The doctrine that what will happen is predetermined and it will happen whatever attempt we make to intervene. Human action is ineffectual regarding these events. Fatalism might be derived from logical principles, especially about **future contingents**, from the assumption of perfect divine **foreknowledge**, or from the principle of **causality**, which claims that everything is causally determined. Fatalism is distinguished from **determinism** in the sense that determinism, although it is also based on the principle of causality, still admits that human action may effectively cause one event rather than another, while fatalism characteristically denies any human effect on the future. Stoicism is a typical representative of fatalism.

> "That the course of events will be what it will be is a logical truism; yet many people are reluctant to admit it, because they think that it commits them to some sort of fatalism." **Ayer,** *The Problem of Knowledge*

fate

ETHICS, PHILOSOPHY OF RELIGION [from Latin *fatum*, what is spoken or decreed] The necessity in things which makes them happen as they do and, in particular, a person's appointed lot, which is beyond his own control. Fate is usually personified as an agency acting according to its own will and not bound by **causation**. Fate is cursed or praised according to the bad luck or good fortune it brings to a person. In ancient Greece, Stoics claim that it is idle to speak of **free will** if a man's fate is not up to himself. In *On Fate*, **Cicero** argues that if there is free will, everything does not happen by fate; if everything does not happen by fate, there is no **predetermination**; but without predetermination, **God** has no **foreknowledge**. Medieval philosophers ask how we can be responsible for the evil we do if God predetermines our fate.

> "'Fate': a name given by some people not to the position of the stars but to a chain of causes dependent on God's will." **Augustine,** *City of God*

fear, see anxiety

feeling

PHILOSOPHY OF MIND [Greek *pathos*, feeling, passion, from *paschein*, to undergo, to be affected, to suffer] What happens to anything that suffers or is affected. As a reaction to external stimuli, *pathos* is a mode of passivity rather than activity. Feeling or **passion** is generally taken to be a synonym for **emotion**, that is, the intense impulses, such as anguish, rage, or love, which directly affect one's **perception** and **behavior**. From **Plato** onwards, the central tradition of Western philosophy has contrasted passion with **reason** and has regarded passion with suspicion, as something displaying a lack of discipline, exercising a corruptive power and distorting perception and deliberation. **Aristotle** usually confined *pathos* to states of the **soul** that involve pleasure or

pain, including the **desires** and feelings of the non-rational part of the soul. A virtuous person has feeling but can control it, whereas the young and the **incontinent** are always controlled by their feeling. Many philosophers believe that a good man should have reason as the master of his passions, and **Spinoza** especially had subtle and interesting things to say about the use of emotions in the rational management of emotion. **Hume** claimed that reason has no motivating role in action and is the slave of passion. There is a counter-discourse that positively evaluates the role of passion. This tendency is apparent in the irrationalism of **Schopenhauer** and **Nietzsche** and in the work of **Heidegger** and subsequent **existentialists**. The American philosopher Martha **Nussbaum** argues that passion has its own cognitive role, and other philosophers try to distinguish between rational and irrational passion.

> "I call feeling appetite, anger, fear, confidence, envy, joy, friendliness, hatred, longing, emulation, pity and in general what is accompanied by pleasure or distress." **Aristotle,** *Nicomachean Ethics*

Feigl, Herbert (1902–88)

Austro-Hungarian logical positivist philosopher of science and philosopher of psychology, born in Reicheburg, Professor at the University of Minnesota. Feigl was a major proponent of logical positivism in the Vienna Circle, which he helped to found, and after emigration in the United States. He argued on empirical grounds for the identity of mental states and physical states, but denied the reduction of mental concepts to physical concepts. His major works include "The 'Mental' and the 'Physical'" in H. Feigl et al. (eds.), *Minnesota Studies in the Philosophy of Science*, vol. 2 (1958) and *Inquiries and Provocations: Selected Writings 1929–1974* (1981).

Feinberg, Joel (1926–2004)

American moral, political, and legal philosopher, born in Detroit, Michigan, Professor of Philosophy at University of Arizona. Feinberg's work focuses on individual liberty and on the justification for state interference with a person's behavior. He allows criminal sanctions against harm and extreme offense to others, but rejects criminalizing self-harm or immorality. He also argues that the state should not require behavior solely on the grounds that it will

benefit the agent or others. His major works include
Doing and Deserving (1970), *Rights, Justice and the
Bounds of Liberty* (1980), and *The Moral Limits of the
Criminal Law*, 4 vols. (1984–8).

felicity calculus, see hedonistic calculus

feminism

ETHICS, POLITICAL PHILOSOPHY, EPISTEMOLOGY A
movement based on the belief that the traditional
relationship between men and women is one of male
domination over women. Feminism has the overall goal of removing all forms of subordination of
women to men and obtaining **equality** between
men and women in all fields, especially in terms of
political and legal rights. Feminist philosophy seeks
to understand the origin and various forms of this
domination and to explore its contemporary consequences for women, as a basis for its elimination.
It challenges various dualistic ontological dichotomies that associate women with their inferior or
negative terms, for example, linking men with logic
and rationality and woman with intuition and emotion. It rejects the traditional centrality of rational
principles and emphasizes interpersonal relationships, **caring**, and the role of **community**. From a
perspective of upholding the value of women's
experience and ways of thinking, it reassesses many
central notions of Western political philosophy,
such as **autonomy**, **equality**, **liberty**, **justice**, and
rights. Feminists generally support a sharp distinction between biologically determined sex and socially
constructed **gender** and the possibility that changing
gender roles will emerge. Feminism has influenced
recent developments in many areas of philosophy,
especially ethics, political and social philosophy, and
epistemology.

Because a diversity of experiences and preoccupations have led to different theoretical understandings
about women's experience, feminism has never been
a unified system but presents versions having significant differences among themselves. Feminist
philosophy in France, Britain, and the United States
reflects in part the broader philosophical contexts in
which they developed. Liberal feminism focuses on
equal opportunities in education and employment
for women. Marxist feminism argues that women
must socialize their family work and join the working class. Radical feminism argues that subordina-

tion has its deepest cause in the reproductive and
sexual roles of women and argues that women
should be autonomous in these regards. Existentialist
feminism contends that women must define themselves in terms of the Self, rather than in terms of
the Other in relation to men. Some psychoanalytic
feminists find the origin of women's subordination
in their early childhood experience, although others
look more to **Lacan** than to **Freud** for inspiration.
Different fields of philosophy have different forms
of feminism, such as **feminist ethics**, **feminist
epistemology**, and eco-feminism. A major challenge
to feminism is to determine how it can be systematized theoretically.

> "Feminism argues that women are oppressed
> or dominated by men and that the structural
> arrangements that initiate, support, and legitimate
> that systematic oppression constitute patriarchy."
> **Farganis,** *Situating Feminism*

feminist epistemology

EPISTEMOLOGY A feminist theory of knowledge which
claims that traditional mainstream epistemology
is **androcentric**, and is filled with gender biases. According to this view, the Enlightenment or Kantian
conception of **rationality** considers the epistemic
subject as an abstract individual, and authoritative
knowledge in Western societies is largely based on
the experiences of white males. Women have long
been in an epistemic underclass. The conceptual
frameworks and methods in all branches of knowledge are virtually androcentric. Feminists argue that
the central problem of epistemology should be
"Whose knowledge is it?" An adequate epistemology
should be free of all prejudices of androcentricity.
The acquisition of knowledge must take into account
the particularities of the subject, and hence is
essentially an historical, social, and political activity.
Accordingly, feminist epistemology joins the anti-
essentialism of **postmodernism**, and challenges the
traditional idea of **objectivity**. It claims that although
feminism is by nature a political movement, it
can still find a distinctive place in epistemology by
asking questions such as "Who are the subjects of
legitimate knowledge?" "Whose experience should
be used to test knowledge?" "What is the nature of
objectivity?" "How can a researcher be dispassion-
ate?" There are many versions of what a feminist

perspective of epistemology should be. Some feminists focus on criticizing the alleged traditional male-dominated nature of epistemology. Others believe that the oppressive position in which women have found themselves might provide a different perspective for examining the central issues of epistemology, and therefore endeavor to analyze women's experience. But others believe that there is no special female way of knowing.

> "Feminist epistemology consists rather in attention to epistemological concerns arising out of feminist projects, which prompt reflection on the nature of knowledge and our method for attaining it."
> **Lennon and Whitford (eds.),** *Knowing the Difference*

feminist ethics

ETHICS Feminist ethics contrasts with the allegedly male-biased traditional Western ethics. It argues that traditional ethics ignores women's issues and interests, fails to recognize feminine values and experience, and identifies human experience with male experience. The traditional lists of virtues are always gender-characterized. Hence, women's actual subordination is rationalized by traditional ethics, and this must be revealed and criticized for the liberation of women.

The criticism of the Western tradition concerning the position of women can be traced to figures such as **Wollstonecraft**, **Mill**, Engels, and Simone de **Beauvoir**. Carol Gilligan's *In a Different Voice* (1982) elaborates the different moral development of men and women. She argues that in opposition to the traditional ethic of **justice**, which emphasizes rights and rules, we should establish an ethic of **care**, that is, a women-centered ethics, based on women's experience and a new conceptual framework. It will replace male values with female values and stress responsibility, empathy, and the relationships between people. Motherhood is the paradigm of this ethic. Sometimes the contrast between an ethics of justice and an ethic of care is described as contrasting **rationality** and **emotion**. Feminist ethics expands from the general situation of women's subordination to almost every particular problem faced by women, such as abortion, equality, family planning, militarism, the environment, pornography and all sex-related issues. Its criticism of the traditional bias is remarkable, but the positive delineation of this

ethics is not yet clear, let alone systematic. It has been disputed whether women's experience is so strikingly different from men's and whether this difference can be seen as being more basic than the differences of class, race, and culture.

> "Feminist ethics is born in women's refusals to endure with grace the arrogance, indifference, hostility, and damage of oppressively sexist environments. It is fuelled by bonds among women, forged in experiments to create better environments now and for the future, and tried by commitments to overcome damage already done."
> **Card (ed.),** *Feminist Ethics*

Ferguson, Adam (1723–1816)

Scottish common sense moral and political philosopher, born in Logierait, Professor at University of Edinburgh. Ferguson's account of the origins of society and of the history of relations between individuals and society offered an empiricist sociological alternative to speculative social contract theories of his time. His major work is *Essay on the History of Civil Society* (1767).

Feuerbach, Ludwig (1804–72)

German left Hegelian naturalistic humanist, born in Landshut. Feuerbach used Hegel's concept of alienation to explain why imperfect humans ascribe perfections belonging to the essence of the human species to an illusory God. His main works include *The Essence of Christianity* (1841) and *Principles of the Philosophy of the Future* (1843).

Feyerabend, Paul (1924–94)

Austrian philosopher and historian of science, born in Vienna, taught in many universities, including University College London, University of California, Berkeley, and Zurich. Feyerabend argued for a historical rather than analytic account of the development of science. He held that scientific observations in different periods were fully theoretical according to radically incommensurable frameworks, and that there is no rational method for moving from one framework to another or for criticizing one framework from the standpoint of another. In place of objectivity, there are different traditions of enquiry that give coherence to fragments of intellectual life. His main works include *Against Method* (1974),

Science in a Free Society (1978), *Philosophical Papers*, 2 vols. (1981), and *Farewell to Reason* (1987).

Fichte, Johann Gottlieb (1762–1814)

German idealist philosopher, born in Rammenku, Saxony, taught at Jena (where he was dismissed in 1799 because of his unorthodox views on freedom and religion), Erlangen, and Berlin. Influenced by Kant, Fichte claimed that the absolute ego and its self-legislating activity are the ultimate subjective reality. Of its two interacting drives, practical and theoretical, the practical is more determining. In positing the non-ego, it makes self-consciousness possible through a dialectical process. Fichte argued that the non-ego is not a thing-in-itself and strongly rejected what he called the dogmatic view that there is an independent external world. For him, the idealist view that conscience alone is the root of all truth is the only doctrine that is compatible with human freedom. Fichte exerted a considerable impact on Hegel's dialectic. His most important work is *Foundation of the Science of Knowledge* (1794). Other works include *Critique of All Revelation* (1792), *The Foundation of Natural Rights* (1796), *The Vocation of Man* (1800), and *Addresses to the German Nation* (1807–8). By identifying the ego with the German nation, this last work played a major role in fostering later German nationalism and totalitarianism.

Ficino, Marsilio (1433–99)

Italian philosopher, born at Figline, appointed to head the Platonic Academy of Florence by Cosimo de' Medici. Ficino attempted to reconcile Platonism with Christianity by focusing on the role of love in both systems, and advocated an ascent to God through contemplation. His Latin translations of Plato made Plato accessible to the Latin West. He also translated Neoplatonist and Hermetic writings. His major works include *Symposium* (1469), *Theologia Platonica* (1473), and *Three Books on Life* (1489). He exerted considerable influence upon the Renaissance revival of Platonism.

fictional names

LOGIC, METAPHYSICS, PHILOSOPHY OF LANGUAGE Names of invented objects, characters, and places in novels, myths, and other forms of narration. Examples include "Hamlet" and "the Golden Mountain." These **names** do not refer to existing things, but they appear to refer to something rather than nothing. The existence of fictional names creates many philosophical puzzles. If a name obtains its meaning from the objects to which it refers, it is difficult to understand how fictional names gain their meaning. Various responses have been proposed. Some claim that fictional names refer to beings of a special kind, which subsist rather than exist. Others attempt to analyze the sentences in which fictional names occur into sentences in which they do not occur. Others suggest that fictional names do not refer, but merely pretend to refer. Others use the apparatus of **possible worlds** to claim that a fictional name refers to an individual in a possible world, with the unity of that individual given by the narratives in which its name occurs or in terms of a **causal theory of reference**. Understanding fictional names will help us to understand **meaning** and **reference** more generally as well as our response to fictional characters in novels and drama.

> "For each fictional name in a story, I suggest, a stylised sentence expressing its Story Line will contain a quantifier and a conjunct introducing that name." **Plantinga,** *The Nature of Necessity*

fideism

PHILOSOPHY OF RELIGION A position which holds that in establishing and accepting religious convictions, **faith** is primary and **reason** is either secondary or entirely dispensable. To avoid placing reason above **God**, we cannot on this view subject religious beliefs to the assessment of reason. Fideism has two versions. The extreme version claims that faith and reason are contrary, that only faith can grasp the profound mysteries of religion, and that according to rational assessment religious truths are impossible. This position is represented by Tertullian's dictum: *credo quia absurdum* (I believe because it is absurd). In modern time this view was developed by **Kierkegaard**, who claimed that the acceptance of religious truths requires a leap of faith beyond the rational. The moderate version of fideism claims that faith precedes reason in seeking and accepting fundamental religious beliefs, but that reason can play a role in explicating and comprehending these beliefs. This position has been held by the Christian Augustinian tradition and is represented by St **Anselm's** dictum: *credo ut intelligam* (I believe in order that I may understand). In recent times, some religious philosophers have developed a fideism based on **Wittgenstein**'s view that some claims have a fundamental role for us in making rational assessment of our ordinary beliefs possible. If religious claims had this special status, there would be no room for reason to justify or reject them. Others respond that there are no grounds for awarding this status to religious beliefs and that we should be suspicious of attempts to shelter them from rational examination.

"Fideism, the doctrine that faith alone determines whether a man recognises or fails to recognise the truth of a doctrine which is nevertheless an objectively true doctrine, independently of being believed or recognised to be true." **Bambrough,** *Reason, Truth and God*

fidelity

ETHICS [from Latin *fides*, faith, literally faithfulness or trustworthiness] The virtue of living up to the commitments or obligations acquired from one's participation in an institution or by one's promises or contracts. The former is identical with **loyalty**, while the latter is identical with honesty, or **fairness**, and is the traditional focus of fidelity. W. D. **Ross** considered fidelity to be one of his *prima facie* **duties**. Its opposite is infidelity, that is, the breaking of one's promises or faith. Adultery has been regarded as a paradigm of infidelity. **Feminist ethics**, due to its emphasis on human relationships, pays a great deal of attention to fidelity. Significant problems surrounding the notion of fidelity include such matters as the relation between the reasonableness of promises and fidelity and how intimate the personal relation should be in order to raise questions of faithfulness.

"The principle of fidelity is but a special case of the principle of fairness applied to the social practice of promising." **Rawls,** *A Theory of Justice*

"Fido"–fido theory of meaning

PHILOSOPHY OF LANGUAGE My dog Fido is an **entity**, and is designated by the **name** "Fido." On analogy, some theories of meaning claim that every meaningful expression refers to or designates an extralinguistic entity, including **abstract entities**, and

derives its **meaning** from what it designates. Gibert **Ryle** applied a derogatory label to this theory of meaning. According to him, this analogy is naive and incorrect. "Fido" stands in the relation of designation to my dog Fido. However, not every meaningful expression is a name that stands for some entity. For all expressions to be meaningful in this way, we would in the first place have to invent whole classes of abstract entities to which expressions that do not function in a designating way could seem to stand in a relation of designation. The expression "red" would, for example, give rise to the expression "redness" to stand for the objective **property** of redness. But this multiplication of entities would be futile. The central objection here is that having meaning is not identical with standing for. Other philosophers call this theory Platonic realism or **hypostatization**.

"I am still not quite sure why it seems so natural to assume that all words are names, and even that every possible grammatical subject of a sentence, one-worded or many-worded, stands to something as the proper name 'Fido' stands for the dog Fido, and what is a further point, that the thing it stands for is what the expression means." **Ryle,** *Collected Papers*, **vol. II**

Field, Hartry (1946–)

American logician and philosopher of mathematics, born in Boston, Professor of Philosophy, New York University. Field has attempted to provide a naturalistic causal account of semantic and intentional concepts like meaning and belief to supplement Tarski's theory of truth with physicalism regarding the mind. His nominalism in the philosophy of mathematics and philosophy of science dispenses with abstract entities at the cost of denying that mathematics and scientific theories are true. His major works include *Science without Numbers: A Defence of Nominalism* (1980) and *Realism, Mathematics and Modality* (1989).

fifth element, see aether

final cause

METAPHYSICS, PHILOSOPHY OF SCIENCE [from Latin *finis*, end or purpose, the equivalent of Greek *telos*] According to **Aristotle**'s theory of **explanation**, a final cause is one of four **causes**, the others being the material, formal, and efficient causes. His expression for a final cause is *to hou heneka* (Greek, for the sake of which). By appealing to a final cause, we explain a thing through its goal or end. An explanation based on a final cause is called a **teleological explanation** (from *telos*). In *Metaphysics*, Aristotle argued that **form**, as primary substance, is the final cause and that as final cause form is actuality. In his physical works, Aristotle made extensive use of final causes in explaining the generation and structure of natural things and their parts. He also claimed that as the **unmoved mover**, **God** is the final cause of the world. His teleology deeply influenced the later development of Western philosophy of science, although much modern philosophy of science has been hostile to teleology, either by denying it entirely or by reducing it to standard causal relations. Discussion of teleological or functional explanations remains active in philosophy of biology and philosophy of social science.

"The final cause is an end, and that sort of end which is not for the sake of something else, but for whose sake everything else is; so that if there is to be a last term of this sort, the process will not be infinite; but if there is no such term there will be no final cause." **Aristotle**, *Metaphysics*

final end, see final good

final good

ETHICS, PHILOSOPHY OF ACTION The notion of a final good is fundamental in ancient ethical systems. Every action is pursued for an end or *telos*, and this end is good for the agent. Some goods are themselves pursued for other higher goods, and hence there is a hierarchy of goods. To proceed in this way, there must be a single good that is sought for its own sake while all other goods are sought for the sake of it. This single good is the final (or best or highest) good, also called the final end. It should be terminal, comprehensive, and self-sufficient, although this final condition is in dispute. In ancient Greek philosophy, each ethical school agreed that this final good is *eudaimonia* (well-being or happiness), but differed with regard to what happiness is. Different schools respectively took it to be honor, pleasure, virtue, contemplation, or tranquillity. For an individual's

life, the final good is the direction of his or her life as a whole, that is, that person's life plan. To answer the fundamental ethical question "How should I live?", one needs first to deliberate and determine what the final good is for one's life, which will organize the priorities in life and make life a unity. The notion of final good fell into neglect in modern moral theory because the latter emphasizes the impartiality of moral agents rather than their life as a unity. However, it has been revived in contemporary **virtue ethics**.

"Suppose, then, that there is some end of the things we pursue in our actions which we wish for because of itself, and because of which we wish for the other things; and we do not choose everything because of something else, since if we do, it will go on without limit, making desire empty and futile; then clearly this end will be the good, i.e. the final good." **Aristotle**, *Nicomachean Ethics*

de Finetti, Bruno (1906–85)
Italian personalist philosopher of mathematics. De Finetti established the foundations of the subjectivist theory of probability, in which an agent can have degrees of belief between full belief and full disbelief, although the degrees of belief of different agents will converge as new evidence is introduced. His main works are *Foresight: Its Logical Laws, Its Subjective Sources* (1937) and *Theory of Probability*, 2 vols. (1970).

finite-state grammar
PHILOSOPHY OF LANGUAGE One of three models for the structure of a language (the other two are phrase structure grammar and transformational grammar). It is based on the **Turing machine** model. Suppose that we have a machine that is in one of a finite number of internal states, and operates by moving from one state to another by producing a symbol, for example a word. After producing a number of symbols, such as a sequence of words, which is called a **sentence**, the machine ends in a final state. **Chomsky** calls this machine finite-state grammar, and the language thus produced finite-state language. This model holds that a grammar is a finite set of rules and that an infinite number of sentences are generated in accordance with these rules. A speaker can be conceived of as a machine, producing one sentence,

or even one morpheme, at a time; and a hearer is also a machine that receives one sentence, or even one morpheme, at a time. This model can only be applied to some special cases and is not very useful in practice, for it can describe or specify only a finite number of sentences of finite length, but we must have more powerful internal generative capacities than such a machine to have our ability to use language.

"A finite-state grammar is the simplest type of grammar which, with a finite amount of apparatus, can generate an infinite number of sentences." **Chomsky,** *Syntactic Structures*

finite-state language, see finite-state grammar

Finnis, John (1940–)
British legal and moral philosopher, Professor of Law and Legal Philosophy, University of Oxford. Finnis argues for the normative assessment of the legal institutions of society in terms of natural law. Natural law is grounded in the pursuit among all societies of objective basic goods and can be used to criticize positive law as unjust. He holds that law and morality are both answerable to principles of practical reasonableness. His main works include *Natural Laws and Natural Rights* (1980), *Fundamentals of Ethics* (1983), and *Moral Absolutes* (1991).

first cause argument for the existence of God
PHILOSOPHY OF RELIGION One of the classic arguments for the existence of **God,** a variant of the cosmological argument and the second of **Aquinas'** **five ways** to prove the existence of God. Everything in the world has something else as its cause, and each cause has its own cause. This chain of **causation** could stretch to infinity. Because this is unintelligible, there must be a cause that is not caused by anything else and this is the first cause. This first cause is God. From the logical point of view, the argument does not show that there is only one first cause rather than many first causes. Also, it does not explain why a first cause is omnipotent or perfectly good. **Russell** pointed out that the argument starts from a premise that everything is caused by something else, but contradicts this in its conclusion that there is one thing, the first cause, which is not caused by something else.

"The first cause argument is itself of no value for the establishment of theism: because no cause is needed for the existence of that which has no beginning." *The Collected Works of John Stuart Mill,* **vol. X**

first entelechy, another term for substantial form

first-level concept
LOGIC, PHILOSOPHY OF MATHEMATICS, METAPHYSICS **Frege** distinguished between first-level concepts and second-level concepts, although he sometimes used the expressions "first-order concepts" and "second-order concepts" for the same purpose. Since Frege's distinction between **concept** and **object** corresponds to his distinction between **predicate** and subject, this is also a distinction between first-level predicates and second-level predicates. A first-level concept or predicate is applied to an object to ascribe a property to that object. A second-level concept or predicate is applied not to an object, but to a concept or a predicate. It is a concept of first-level concepts or a predicate of first-level predicates. A first-level concept is also called an nth-level concept, while a second-level concept is called an n+1th-level concept. This doctrine can be traced to **Kant**'s view that **existence** is not a real **property.** Accordingly, existence is a second-level rather than the first-level concept. To say "X exists" means that the concept X is instantiated. Analogously, number is also a second-level concept. When we say that X is a number, we do not mean that X is an object that has the property of being a number, but rather that the concept X has numerous instantiations. Frege's famous doctrine that existence is a second-level concept or predicate is inferred from his doctrine of number.

"The ontological proof of God's existence suffers from the fallacy of treating existence as a first-level concept." **Frege,** "Function and Concept," *Philosophical Writings of Gottlob Frege*

first-level predicate, see first-level concept

first-order language, see first-order logic

first-order logic
LOGIC, PHILOSOPHY OF MATHEMATICS If in a logical language the **quantifiers** only contain **variables**

ranging over **individuals**, this language is called a first-order language, and these variables are called first-order variables. The study of the rules of inference in a first-order language is called first-order logic. In this logic, individuals are the only arguments of **predicates**. If the variables range over **properties**, **relations**, **functions**, and **classes** of the individuals, they are called second-order variables. A language containing second-order variables is a second-order language, and the logic of this language is second-order logic. The domain of second-order logic is determined by the first-order logic. If the variables range over the domain of properties or the relations of properties, then we have third-order variables, language, and logic. This construction can go on to even higher orders. Any logic that is at least a second-order logic is called higher-order logic. Strictly speaking, first-order logic emerged with **Hilbert** in 1917. For most mathematicians, it is the proper and natural framework for mathematics.

"I have distinguished between a logician's use of first-order logic (where quantifiers range only over individuals), second-order logic (where quantifiers can also range over sets or relations), w-order logic (essentially the simple theory of types), and various infinitary logics (having formulas of infinite length or rules of inference with infinitely many premises)." **G. H. Moore, "The Emergence of First Order Logic," in** *Minnesota Studies in the Philosophy of Science*, **vol. XI**

first-order predicate, see predicate

first-person perspective

EPISTEMOLOGY, PHILOSOPHY OF MIND We may ascribe mental concepts either to ourselves (first-person ascriptions through our inner awareness of our mental states) or to others (third-person ascriptions through outer manifestations in behavior and speech). These two kinds of ascription give rise to puzzles about the unitary nature of mental phenomena, for given the special character of the subject, my description of my own mental states could be quite different in nature and content from my description of other minds. We can then ask whether, in order to offer a satisfactory account of mental phenomena, we should proceed from the perspective of the subject with the **mental states** or from the

perspective of forming judgments about the states of **other minds**. The former is the first-person perspective and is associated with **Cartesianism**, and the latter is called the third-person perspective and is associated with **behaviorism**. The first-person perspective is private and peculiar to the subject. Its advocates hold that this perspective affords **privileged access** to the mental states of the subject. The third-person perspective is public and observable. Its advocates believe that our conception of mental states is informed by the behavioral criteria we use to apply mental concepts to others. It is also possible to occupy the middle ground between these two positions. Different perspectives provide different theories about the nature and essence of mental states, and about the **mind–body** relationship. The dichotomy of the first-person perspective and the third-person perspective corresponds to the contrast between the subjective and the objective, and has been central in modern philosophy.

"It was the nature – indeed the very existence – of the allegedly public, physical world that was felt to be dubious, or at least doubtable, from within one's private movie theatre. This Cartesian first-person perspective dominated the philosophy of mind, as well as metaphysics and epistemology generally, from the seventeenth century through the first half of our time." **Lycan,** *Consciousness*

first philosophy

PHILOSOPHICAL METHOD, PHILOSOPHY OF RELIGION, METAPHYSICS, PHILOSOPHY OF SCIENCE In **Aristotle**, first philosophy is either the study of the highest type of being (the unmoved mover or **God**) in theology or the study of **being** *qua* **being** in **ontology**. Theology is called first philosophy because its object is superior to physical entities, the study of which is second philosophy. Ontology is called first philosophy because it investigates the principles and laws that all other branches of science presuppose and the first causes of the whole world of being. From this latter sense, the general meaning of first philosophy as the foundation of all science is derived. For Francis **Bacon**, first philosophy is the mother of other sciences. According to **Descartes**, first philosophy is the science of the principles of knowledge. For Christian **Wolff**, first philosophy is concerned with the first principles and concepts of thought.

For **Husserl**, first philosophy is the methodological and theoretical foundation of all other philosophical disciplines. Critics disagree whether there is first philosophy within philosophy or first philosophy prior to science.

> "All attempts at discovering ultimate foundations, in which the intentions of first philosophy live on, have broken down." **Habermas, *The Theory of Communicative Action*, vol. I**

first principle

PHILOSOPHICAL METHOD, EPISTEMOLOGY, METAPHYSICS, LOGIC, PHILOSOPHY OF MATHEMATICS [Greek *arche*, beginning, starting-point] A fundamental principle, rule, or law for a systematic enquiry. From first principles other principles, rules, or laws of that system are derived or explained, but first principles themselves cannot be derived or explained from any other principles within that system. Mathematical **axioms** and logical principles are recognized as having the status of first principles. First principles are regarded as being **self-evident**, *a priori*, or capable of being grasped only through **intuition**. Traditionally, it was thought that a system without first principles could not be coherent or **consistent**. Some philosophers argue that instead of offering justification to subordinate rules, first principles are themselves justified by their success in organizing or deriving the right set of subordinate rules. They also argue that in some cases, or in principle, we have a choice in deciding the first principles of a system. The study of first principles normally belongs to the domain of metaphysics. **Aristotle** claimed that a principle is the starting-point from which a thing is or comes to be or is known.

> "These [first] principles must satisfy two conditions. First, they must be so clear and so evident that the human mind cannot doubt their truth when it attentively concentrates on them; secondly, the knowledge of other things must depend on them, in the sense that the principles must be capable of being known without knowledge of other matters, but not vice versa." **Descartes, *The Philosophical Writings of Descartes***

Firstness

METAPHYSICS The metaphysics of **Peirce** claims that there are three universal **categories** of elements among **phenomena**, respectively Firstness, Secondness, and Thirdness. Firstness comprises the qualities of phenomena, such as red, bitter, tedious, and hard. These qualities merge into one another and have no perfect identities. Secondness includes the facts of experience, which we know by their resistance and consequences. They are not the mind's creation. Thirdness includes laws or thoughts that determine how facts may be. Firstness is an essential element of both Secondness and Thirdness. Secondness is an essential part of Thirdness. Thirdness is the mediation between Secondness and Firstness. Metaphysics deals with phenomena in their Thirdness. These three categories are also three modes of existence: possibility, **actuality**, and destiny.

> "A Firstness is exemplified in every quality of a total feeling . . . the word possibility fits it, except that possibility implies a relation which exists, while universal Firstness is the mode of being of itself." **Peirce, *Collected Papers*, vol. I**

fittingness

ETHICS We generally explain our moral actions in terms of **moral principles** or of long-term **self-interest**. However, many cases are not covered by either of these considerations. In these situations, we claim that an action is morally permissible if we assess that it is fitting, suitable, and appropriate to a particular agent in a particular situation. This is the moral consideration of fittingness, a common concern emphasized by **Cicero** and revived in contemporary **virtue ethics**. The practice of determining what is fitting requires a good character and consistency. The action of a virtuous person is always regarded as an example to follow, because it is fitting.

> "We often explain both why we did something and why we intend to do something by saying that it is fitting or appropriate to a situation or that it is in accordance with a moral rule." **Nowell-Smith, *Ethics***

five ways

PHILOSOPHY OF RELIGION [Latin *quinque viae*] **Aquinas'** five proofs for the existence of **God**. The five ways employ the different Aristotelian notions of **cause** or explanation in what can be seen as five formulations of one basic argument. All five ways are *a posteriori* in the sense that they start with empirical facts about the physical world and then argue to the existence of a **transcendent** cause to explain them. Thus they are distinct from *a priori* proofs, which start from the **essence** or **definition** of God. The first way argues from the fact that things move or **change** to the existence of an unmoved mover. The second way argues on the basis of a hierarchy of efficient causes existing in the world that there is an ultimate uncaused cause. The third way proceeds from the contingency of things, that is, their being subject to generation and corruption, to the conclusion that there must be an absolute being. The fourth way, also called the **henological argument**, moves from our experience of a gradation of perfection in the world to the conclusion that there must be an absolute perfection. The fifth way argues that since every natural body exists for some end, there must be an absolute **final cause**. The five ways employ the different kinds of Aristotelian cause or explanation to argue for the existence of God.

"If these 'five ways' are not singly or collectively wholly convincing, and . . . rest on an interpretation of causality which requires very considerable modification in the light of present day knowledge of the working of natural processes, nevertheless, they constitute an impressive rational demonstration of the existence and attributes of God." **E. James**, *The Concept of Deity*

flaccid designator

PHILOSOPHY OF LANGUAGE, LOGIC A term that contrasts with **Kripke**'s **rigid designator**. While a rigid designator designates the same thing in all **possible worlds**, a flaccid designator designates different things in different possible worlds. For example, the term "China's capital" currently designates Beijing, but it used to refer to Nanjing or Xian, and it could have referred to other cities had circumstances been different. The expression "the best seller" is another example of a flaccid designator, for the term refers to different books at different times and could have designated other different books had circumstances been different.

"There is no widely accepted name for terms such as these, which refer to different things in different possible worlds; but we might call them flaccid designators (because 'flaccid' is the opposite of 'rigid')." **R. Martin**, *The Meaning of Language*

flux

METAPHYSICS [from Greek *rhein*, to flow] The Greek philosopher **Heraclitus** claimed that the world is an ever-living fire and is hence in an unceasing process of flux or **change**. We are and are not at any given moment, and because of constant change "one cannot step into the same river twice." **Plato** accepted this view of the sensible world, but argued that if there were nothing more than such a changing world, we would be led to **ethical relativism** and no account of **truth** would be possible. He concluded that there must be another eternal world, the intelligible world of really existing **forms** or **ideas**, which is the primary source of **knowledge**. For Plato, the sensible world of flux participates in the world of ideas, and the contrast between these two worlds corresponds to the contrast between genesis and **being**.

"In his youth Plato first became acquainted with Cratylus and the Heraclitean doctrines that all perceptible things were in everlasting flux, and that there is no knowledge of them. He continued to hold these views later." **Aristotle**, *Metaphysics*

flying arrow, paradox of

LOGIC One of **Zeno's paradoxes**, designed to show the impossibility of **motion**. On the assumption that **time** is composed of atomic instants, Zeno inferred that motion is discontinuous. The flying arrow, at any given instant during its flight, occupies a space equal to itself. What occupies a space equal to itself is at rest. Hence, the arrow is at rest at every instant. Since time is composed of instants, if the arrow does not move at any instant, it is at rest throughout its flight.

"The third [paradox] is just given above, that the flying arrow is at rest." **Aristotle**, *Physics*

focal meaning

METAPHYSICS, PHILOSOPHY OF LANGUAGE [from Greek *pros hen legesthai*, being said in relation to one point] A term connected with **Aristotle**'s doctrine of the different senses of **being** in the different **categories**. Although being has many senses, these senses are not disconnected or isolated, but are all related to one central point, that is, being in the category of **substance**. Quality is said to be because it is quality of substance; quantity is said to be because it is quantity of substance, and so on for the other categories. In virtue of this pattern, Aristotle claimed that a universal science of being (the science of **being *qua* being**) is possible. Aristotle himself made use of this pattern only to connect substance with other categories. Influenced by Thomas **Aquinas**, some scholars have extended the account of focal meaning beyond Aristotle's own use to cover the relation between sensible substances and **God**, saying that God is the focal meaning of all substances. By these means, they intend to reconcile the tension between the science of being and theology in Aristotle.

> "There are many senses in which a thing may be said to 'be', but all that 'is' is related to one focal meaning, one definite kind of thing, and is not said to 'be' by a mere ambiguity." **Aristotle,** *Metaphysics*

Fodor, Jerry (1935–)

American philosopher of mind and language, born in New York, Professor at Rutgers University. Fodor has attempted to unify philosophy of mind and cognitive science. He is best known for his language of thought hypothesis, arguing for a theory of thought that posits a computational system realized in the neural structure of the brain that captures folk psychological concepts, such as belief, in individual mental states that have semantic and syntactic properties. Causal relations among these states are held to mirror the logical relations within the train of thought that they embody. His main works include *The Language of Thought* (1975), *The Modularity of Mind* (1983), *Psychosemantics* (1987), *A Theory of Content and Other Essays* (1990), and *Holism: A Shopper's Guide* (with Ernest Lapore) (1992).

folk psychology

PHILOSOPHY OF MIND, PHILOSOPHY OF SCIENCE Also called common sense psychology, a term for common sense understanding about intentional **mental states** and overt **behavior**, using such terms as "belief," "desire," "intention," "fear," "imagination," and "hope." In contrast to scientific or experimental psychology, or academic psychology in general, folk psychology is governed by a putative network of principles, which is taken to underlie our ability to explain and predict human behavior. It is familiar since childhood and is used effortlessly by all of us

in everyday life. It is folk psychology in the way that our common sense talk about material objects is called folk physics. **Eliminativism** in the philosophy of mind, presented in the 1980s by P. M. Churchland, claimed that folk psychology, as an outdated pre-scientific view of the world, should be replaced by a more scientific theory of the mind-brain. These claims provoked a continuing debate about the status and adequacy of folk psychology. In opposition to eliminativism, **Fodor** and **Dennett** argue that folk psychology can be vindicated, to a greater or lesser extent, by scientific psychology; others argue that folk psychology is not a theory, for it does not have generalizations about the relations among mental states and about the relations between mental states and behavior. Some philosophers argue about the claim that the central concepts of folk psychology, such as **belief** and **desire**, have features, such as **intentionality**, which exclude them from any scientific psychology.

Folk psychology in another sense flourished in Germany and was represented by the work of Wilhelm Wundt. Here the term means cultural psychology, that is, a study of the mentality of a people who share a social practice as that mentality is expressed in culture, myths, and customs.

> "Briefly, folk psychology is the tag given to ordinary talk about the mind." **Christensen and Turner (eds.),** *Folk Psychology and the Philosophy of Mind*

Follesdal, Dagfinn (1932–)

Norwegian philosopher of language and Husserl scholar, born in Askim, Professor of Philosophy at University of Oslo and Stanford University. Follesdal argues for a socially based normative theory of reference to explain how genuine singular terms, later called rigid designators by Kripke, function in modal contexts. He has also provided important links between Husserl's philosophy, particularly his theory of meaning and conception of justification, and analytic philosophy. His main works include *Referential Opacity and Modal Logic* (1966).

Foot, Philippa (1920–)

English moral philosopher, born in Owsten Ferry, taught at University of Oxford and University of California at Los Angeles. Foot has argued for naturalism and against prescriptivism in ethics, holding that a system of ethical requirements depends on the desires that we actually have. More recently, her work has led to a revival of interest in virtue ethics. Her major works include *Virtues and Vices* (1978), *Natural Goodness* (2001), and *Moral Dilemmas* (2002).

footnotes to Plato

PHILOSOPHICAL METHOD In a famous remark, A. N. **Whitehead** said that the development of Western philosophy is a series of footnotes to **Plato**. This was not a substantive claim that every subsequent development is nothing more than an expansion or exegesis of what Plato said in his works, but should be considered as a metaphor to indicate how powerfully Plato's thought has influenced the Western tradition. Various contemporary philosophical achievements are deeply indebted to him. Plato's works are an inexhaustible mine of suggestion. The remark also points to the reflective nature of philosophy, by which earlier thought remains crucially important for later work. In contrast, science generally supersedes its past.

"The safest general characterisation of the European philosophical tradition is that it consists of a series of footnotes to Plato." **Whitehead,** *Process and Reality*

force/sense, see sense/force

foreknowledge

PHILOSOPHY OF RELIGION, EPISTEMOLOGY, METAPHYSICS, PHILOSOPHY OF ACTION **Knowledge** about what will happen in the future before it actually happens. This knowledge is ascribed to **God** as a divine attribute and as a natural aspect of God's **omniscience**. God knows what is going to happen, and his knowledge admits no alternatives. God's foreknowledge implies that there is a fixed or predestined future. If this is the case, then all future human **actions** and the course of history are predestined rather than free. Humans will have to act in the predetermined way. The resulting conflict between foreknowledge and **free will** is a perennial problem in both philosophy and theology. To accept the existence of foreknowledge involves the rejection of free will. If we admit free action, then God's foreknowledge must be modified in some way. Some philosophers argue, for example, that because an omniscient God is unembodied and outside

time, he has knowledge of laws and universals, but lacks knowledge of particular things, such as human actions.

"There exists in the history of thought a deterministic idea . . . that the course of world-history is determined . . . by the foreknowledge of a supreme being. This being, as it were, 'sees' the world states follow one upon another in a linear succession." **von Wright,** *Causality and Determinism*

forgery

AESTHETICS A duplicate of an original work intended to be taken as that work, or a work in the style of an artist intended to be taken as the work of that artist. The problem of determining whether an artwork is genuine has been a troublesome issue for collectors and museums. Philosophers are interested in the issue of forgery because no matter how similar a forgery is to an original work, the forgery is regarded as having less **aesthetic value** and is sometimes denied having any aesthetic value at all. How can we explain this phenomenon? Some regard this rejection of forged works as merely a matter of snobbishness or financial self-interest of the art market. Some believe that the rejection is a response to the immorality of the forgers and dealers who lie about the identity of the work. Others claim, more reasonably, that the original artwork embodies its historical context and the artist's originality, which cannot be duplicated. Some believe that forgeries are another sort of artwork in their own right, not the same as their originals. Where, then, is the artistry of forgeries? All these problems raise important questions about the identity of artworks, aesthetic value, and aesthetic enjoyment. Some questions about forgery also arise concerning plagiarism, in which writers present as their own work material copied from others.

"The hard-headed question why there is any aesthetic difference between a deceptive forgery and an original work challenges a basic premise on which the very functions of collectors, museum, and art historian depend." **Goodman,** *Languages of Art*

forgiveness

ETHICS, PHILOSOPHY OF RELIGION A trait of character of a morally offended or injured person who overcomes a natural and generally proper resentment directed at the person who commits the offense and refuses to blame the latter. Forgiveness is neither a justification of the wrongdoing, nor an excuse for it. Forgiveness reflects one's benevolent disposition and is generally regarded as a virtue. It is emphasized in Christian ethics, which holds that the forgiveness of enemies corresponds to God's forgiveness of us. It is also widely discussed in contemporary **virtue ethics**, for it is a popular ethical phenomenon to offer forgiveness and to ask to be forgiven. However, forgiveness must have a limit, depending on the degree of remorse of the offender. For proper resentment is not a bad thing, but a manifestation of self-respect and a respect for **moral rules**. Unlimited and unprincipled forgiveness will turn out to be a kind of moral wickedness and even a manifestation of the vice of servility.

"To forgive is to accept the repudiation and to forswear the resentment." **Strawson,** *Freedom and Resentment and Other Essays*

for itself, see in itself

form

METAPHYSICS, ANCIENT GREEK PHILOSOPHY [Greek *eidos*, derived from the verb *idein*, to see, literally the sensible shape of a thing; has the same sense as Greek *morphe*] **Plato** and **Aristotle** use *eidos* to mean the inner structure or intelligible form of a thing, the shape grasped by the eye of the soul, which serves as the object of **knowledge** or thought. For Plato, forms exist in some way independently of **particulars**; they are paradigms, while the particulars are imperfect copies of them. He uses form (*eidos*) synonymously with **idea** (which is also derived from the verb *idein*). Hence, Plato's theory of Ideas is also called the theory of Forms (see idea, Plato).

Aristotle sometimes uses *eidos* in contrast to **genus**. *Eidos* in this sense is always translated as **species** rather than as form. As species, it is a common predicate and a kind of secondary **substance** in the *Categories*, but in the *Metaphysics* Aristotle denies that it is a substance. More often, form contrasts with **matter** in Aristotle's philosophy. It denotes the inner structure of a thing, which is expressed in its **definition**; it is in this sense that

form is synonymous with **essence** (*to ti en einai*), and is called primary substance. In Aristotle's doctrine of the four **causes**, form is designated the formal cause, which is responsible for unifying material elements into an organic thing. In this sense, form is usually identical with the final cause and sometimes also with the efficient cause, and is also identical with **actuality**. How these claims can be reconciled is a matter of controversy. There are also disputes concerning whether Aristotle asserts the existence of particular form as well as the existence of universal form. A doctrine of particular form is developed in **Plotinus**, and in medieval philosophy, especially by **Aquinas**.

"By form I mean the essence of each thing and its primary substance." **Aristotle,** *Metaphysics*

form of life

PHILOSOPHY OF LANGUAGE For later **Wittgenstein**, the context of practice or **culture** in which speaking a language is embedded in the form of **language games**. Since language is a set of social activities, speaking a language becomes part of a communal activity and a way of living in society. Wittgenstein calls the totality of communal activities, the culture into which language games are embedded, a form of life. A form of life comprises shared natural and linguistic responses, broad agreement in **definitions** and **judgments**, and corresponding **behavior**. Language is connected with our life through our shared playing of language games and is thus interwoven with non-linguistic contexts. To imagine language is to imagine a form of life that in itself can neither be justified nor unjustified. This indicates that grammatical rules are an integral part of human historical practice and are subject to change. Insofar as there are foundations for language for the later Wittgenstein, what must be accepted as given are forms of life. Wittgenstein's remarks about this term are not always consistent and clear and have consequently led to exegetical controversy. In particular, he sometimes speaks of multiple forms of life as specific patterns with limited scope.

"Hence the term 'language-game' is meant to bring into prominence the fact that the speaking of language is part of an activity, or of a form of life." **Wittgenstein,** *Philosophical Investigations*

form of proposition

LOGIC **Russell**'s term, referring to a formula that contains only **variables**, from which a **class** of **propositions** can be obtained by substituting other constituents for one or more constituents contained by the original proposition. Hence a form of proposition is the common structure which propositions of the same class share.

> "The form of a proposition is that which is in common between any two propositions of which the one can be obtained from the other by substituting other constituents for the original ones." **Russell,** *Collected Papers of Bertrand Russell,* **vol. VIII**

form of representation, another term for representational form

formal

LOGIC The adjective "formal" is derived from form, that is, the general nature or structure to which a type of thing belongs. In general, formal considerations or approaches have to do with the abstract structure, or pattern, of a subject, rather than with its **content** or **meaning**. It is thus opposed to factual or material considerations. Hence **formal logic**, for example, is concerned not with the content of particular sentences in an argument, but only with the structure of their **truth-values**. A **formal language** consists merely of variables and connectives.

> "A theory, a rule, a definition, or the like, is to be called formal when no reference is made in it either to the meaning of the symbols . . . or to the sense of the expressions . . . but simply and solely the kinds and order of the symbols from which the expressions are constructed." **Carnap,** *The Logical Syntax of Language*

formal analysis, see analysis

formal concept

LOGIC, PHILOSOPHY OF LANGUAGE, METAPHYSICS **Wittgenstein**'s term in the *Tractatus* for a variety of concepts which differ from ordinary concepts. Ordinary concepts reflect things independent of language. If formal concepts, such as **thing**, color, **fact**, **event**, **function**, **object**, **concept**, and **number**, were like ordinary concepts, they would denote arcane entities of which we could have a special logical experience, but this is not so. Formal concepts are used in relation to a diverse range of related phenomena and cannot be properly expressed by a **predicate** or general term. No analytical definition is available for a formal concept, and, like a **variable**, a formal concept must be understood through the **signs** which are its values.

> "When something falls under a formal concept as one of its objects, this cannot be expressed by means of a proposition. Instead it is shown in the very sign for this object." **Wittgenstein,** *Tractatus*

formal distinction

LOGIC, PHILOSOPHY OF LANGUAGE, PHILOSOPHY OF RELIGION A term associated with **Duns Scotus**. A distinction can be real, between two separate, non-identical entities, or mental or conceptual, drawn purely by reason and not existing objectively in things. A formal distinction, which is between different formulations of one and the same reality, is intermediate between a real distinction and a merely mental distinction. Form, in this sense, provides an objective basis for a concept, and Scotus used this notion to provide an objective basis for our knowledge of **God**. Traditionally, God was conceived as simple, and distinctions between his attributes were thought to exist merely from our human point of view rather than in reality. For this reason, our statements about God would have no **objectivity**. The notion of a formal distinction allowed God's attributes to be neither real nor merely mental. The notion was also used to explain the Trinity, by claiming that the three persons are formally distinct rather than really distinct. Furthermore, the notion gave insight into the validity of our universal conception of individuality by being intermediate between the **species** to which an individual belongs and its individual **form**, what Scotus called *haecceitas* (**haecceity**).

> "In the same real thing there are always formally distinct realities (be they in the same real part or the same real whole)." **Scotus, in** *Duns Scotus: Metaphysician*

formal fallacy

LOGIC Violations of logical rules of inference that result in invalid inference. They can be detected merely by checking the **logical form** of argument.

Formal fallacies are contrasted with informal fallacies, which can only be found through analysis of the content and context of an argument. Each branch of formal logic has many specific formal fallacies; for example, affirming the consequent and denying the antecedent in propositional logic, the undistributed middle term in syllogism, and the illicit quantifier shift in predicate logic.

"A formal fallacy is one that may be identified through mere inspection of the form or structure of an argument." **Hurley,** *A Concise Introduction to Logic*

formal language, another term for logical calculus

formal logic
LOGIC The systematic presentation of the valid patterns (forms) of inference and certain implications which hold among **propositions,** relying heavily on the meaning of structural words such as "all," "some," "if," "not," "and," and "or." It is divided into standard (or classical) logic, non-standard logic, and inductive logic. Standard logic includes traditional logic (Aristotelian syllogism) and modern classical logic, which is an expansion of traditional logic and is composed mainly of the **propositional calculus** and predicate **calculus.** Non-standard logics include the extensions of classical logic, sometimes called extended logic, and deviations from classical logic, sometimes called **deviant logic.** Extended logic includes logics such as **modal logic, tense logic, deontic logic,** epistemic logic, preference logic, and imperative logic. Deviant logic includes logics such as **many-valued logic, intuitionist logic,** and quantum logic. We can gain additional insight into the form of some systems of logic by seeing that they can be mapped onto one another. Systems of formal logic can be developed by proof from **axioms** or through **natural deduction,** which gives rules of inference from given assumptions. Formal logic contrasts with informal logic, which deals with the relations of implication arising from context-related words.

Logical systems seek to attain **consistency** and **completeness,** although **Gödel** showed that for any consistent logical system capable of expressing arithmetic there are true sentences that cannot be proved in the system, thus rendering the system incomplete. He also showed that such systems cannot prove their own consistency. Both results show the limitations of the procedures of any formal system.

"The subject-matter of formal logic will be the investigation of those general logical laws which hold in virtue of the meanings of the structural words and the syntax of natural languages." **D. Mitchell,** *An Introduction to Logic*

formal mode of speech, see material mode of speech

formal semantics
PHILOSOPHY OF LANGUAGE In contrast to general linguistic semantics, formal semantics is characterized by its appeal to the formal logical method in discussing the meaning of linguistic **signs.** Richard Montague laid down some foundational work in this field. Its main representative is truth-conditional **semantics,** developed by **Tarski** and **Davidson** on the basis of **Frege**'s logic. This approach ascribes semantic values to the basic symbols of a language, takes these symbols as elements of the structure of the language, and then derives the semantic values of complex expressions from these elements in accordance with formation rules. The meaning of every sentence is determined by the truth-conditions of its component sentences. Generally, a formal semantics proceeds by first setting up a language, and then laying down rules for matching up **sentences** of that language with **propositions** or **truth-values.** Formalization is used as a way of clarifying what the truth conditions are.

"Formal semantics itself was decided as a means of providing a precise interpretation for formal languages, i.e. the logical and mathematical languages that are opposed to natural languages that are spoken or written as the native languages of human beings." **Cann,** *Formal Semantics*

formal universal
PHILOSOPHY OF LANGUAGE One kind of linguistic **universal.** It is the **grammar** which expresses the formal conditions that the grammar of every language must meet, such as the sequence of rules for the phonological component of a grammar, the transformational rules that map semantically interpreted **deep structures** into phonetically interpreted surface structures, and the ways that the rules of a grammar can be interconnected. It seeks abstract

universal properties of languages in contrast to another kind of linguistic universal: the substantive universal.

> "The property of having a grammar meeting a certain abstract condition might be called a formal linguistic universal, if shown to be a general property of natural languages." **Chomsky, *Aspects of the Theory of Syntax***

formalism (aesthetic)

AESTHETICS A term for all theories of art which claim that the essence of art is given through the formal unity of an artwork, involving such features as structure, balance, harmony, and integrity. Our appreciation of art lies in recognizing these formal qualities and, furthermore, in responding to them. The content of an artwork and its relations with the outside world are subordinate to its formal features. Formalism tends to take a work of art to be a self-sufficient entity and has no concern with its content, meaning, and function. The beauty of a painting consists in the relations of color, line, and mass. In sculpture, beauty consists in the rhythms and symmetries of line and plane. Along with the **representational theory** and the **expression theory**, formalism, represented by **Kant** and Clive Bell (1881–1964), is a major theory of art. Objections to formalism include the claims that the conception of form is ambiguous and that form should be viewed as a vehicle through which an artwork expresses its **meaning**.

> "(Formalism) is the theory that all intrinsic value in art belongs to its 'form' – using this term to designate the organisation of the sensuous medium or 'surface' of the work of art." **Parker, *The Principles of Aesthetics***

formalism (ethics)

ETHICS Ethical formalism holds that to decide whether one is morally obliged to perform or to avoid a certain act, one should not focus on the nature of act itself, but should rather elaborate a set of highly abstract **moral principles** or laws that can be applied universally, without regard to the particular persons and diverse circumstances in which ethical problems arise. The essence of moral philosophy is to justify abstract moral laws, and moral reasoning is typically rule-governed. The main

proponents of formalism include Bishop Joseph **Butler**, **Kant**, and W. D. **Ross**. Sometimes formalism is used interchangeably with **deontology**. It is thus opposed to other ethical theories such as **contextualism**, **existentialism**, **intuitionism**, **feminism**, and **ethical relativism**, which claim that ethical thinking must attend to and judge particular cases. Formalism is the chief target of the contemporary **anti-theory** movement and **virtue ethics**, for virtue is generally regarded as being responsive to social and cultural contexts.

> "It is, for instance, an easy consequence of our principles that moral formalism – i.e. a rigid adherence to the letter, with no appeal to the spirit, of the rules – will tend to be at a maximum in a static and isolated society." **Strawson, *Freedom and Resentment and Other Essays***

formalism (legal)

PHILOSOPHY OF LAW A position in legal philosophy, which claims that law is a logically complete and coherent body of rules and that we can apply these rules universally to solve all particular cases, without need to refer to non-legal considerations, such as those arising from social and moral phenomena. This position flourished in the middle of the nineteenth century, but was bitterly attacked by **legal realism** or rule skepticism, which argued that legal rules are unimportant and that law is nothing more than the actual decisions of courts or legal officers. **Hart** agreed that law is a set of rules, but rejected the claim that rules can settle everything, for rules are often vague and indeterminate. In addition, because human knowledge is limited, we cannot formulate rules for all future cases. Formalism is also criticized by **Dworkin** in his rights thesis. He holds that there are **hard cases** that cannot be resolved by the simple application of rules.

> "The vice known to legal theory as formalism or conceptualism consists in an attitude to verbally formulated rules which both seeks to disguise and to minimise the need for such choice, once the general rule has been laid down." **Hart, *The Concept of Law***

formalism (mathematics)

PHILOSOPHY OF MATHEMATICS As a type of philosophy of mathematics, formalism is the view that mathematical knowledge is a formal system of **propositions**, that these propositions are meaningless formulae that are operated on by fixed rules, and that mathematics consists in knowing what formulae can be derived from the **axioms** according to the rules. There is no need to go beyond the **symbols** and the rules of combination to claim the existence of **abstract entities**. This theory is initiated in the **non-Euclidean geometry** of the nineteenth century and in the work of Peano. Its major development is D. **Hilbert**'s philosophy of mathematics. This position has been attacked, initially by **Frege** and then by **Russell**, for failing to analyze mathematical concepts and for failing to account for the practical use of mathematics.

> "Formalism, associated with the name of Hilbert, echoes intuitionism in deploring the logicist's unbridled recourse to universals." **Quine,** *From a Logical Point of View*

formalization

PHILOSOPHY OF LANGUAGE The practice of stipulating a correspondence scheme between **ordinary language** and a formal language, such as the **propositional** or predicate **calculus**, and translating the ordinary language into the formal language. The purpose of formalization is to make the implicit logical structure of ordinary language explicit in order to assess the validity of arguments in ordinary language. For example, consider "If Socrates is a man, he would be dead. Socrates is a man, so he would be dead." If we let "p" correspond to "Socrates is a man," and "q" to "He would be dead," the formalization is $(p \rightarrow q)$, p; q. Analytic philosophers such as **Russell** have claimed that most traditional philosophical problems arise from the confusing structure of ordinary language and hence that ordinary language should be replaced by an artificial language. But this remedy was criticized by the later **Wittgenstein** and by the Oxford ordinary language philosophers.

> "We stipulate that if a formalization is to be adequate, the associated correspondence scheme should be such that if we replace the P-letters by the corresponding English sentences, and then replace the P-connectives by the corresponding English connectives, the result is a sentence (argument) that says the same as the original English." **Sainsbury,** *Logical Form*

formally correct condition, see material adequacy

formula, see well-formed formula

Foucault, Michel (1926–84)

French philosopher and historian of ideas, born in Poitiers, Professor of the history of systems of thought at the Collège de France from 1970. Usually called a structuralist or post-structuralist, Foucault developed a distinctive approach to intellectual history, focusing on what he called the deep structure that determines the conditions of the possibility of knowledge in a particular period rather than on individual thinkers or human subjects. One of his major concerns was to trace how our present form of knowledge came to be. He held that the notion of the self is historically specific and that the order of words is more important than the order of things for our understanding. He sought to explain changes in systems of discourse by connecting knowledge with power or social control and held that prevailing social attitudes are manipulated by those in power. Foucault's methodology centered on his "archaeology of knowledge" and later his "genealogy of language." His major works include *Madness and Civilisation* (1961), *The Order of Things* (1966), *The Archaeology of Knowledge* (1969), *Discipline and Punish* (1975), *History of Sexuality* (3 vols., 1976–84).

foundationalism

EPISTEMOLOGY The term may be used in the rationalist sense, referring especially to **Descartes**'s project of constructing a system of **knowledge** on a foundation of **clear and distinct ideas** of reason. However, in contemporary philosophy it is a type of theory of **epistemic justification** in Anglo-American epistemology, which holds that knowledge can be exhibited as a structure, with a foundation and superstructure. Since the senses are our only contacts with the external world, some basic beliefs resulting directly from **perception** have a privileged epistemic status. They are self-warranting without standing in need of further **justification**, while all other non-basic beliefs must be justified ultimately by appeal to them. These basic perceptual beliefs provide the ultimate foundation of justification. There are various views among different versions of foundationalism about the nature of the basic, incorrigible perceptual beliefs, and the modes of the derivation of the superstructure from the foundations. In opposition to foundationalism are **coherentism** and other forms of anti-foundationalism, which deny that any beliefs are incorrigible or basic. The affirmation of foundational beliefs is attacked as **"the myth of the given."**

> "I assume that, for anything H that is evident for us, there is something E which is a basis of H for S. This assumption might be said to characterise 'foundationalism'." **Chisholm, *Person and Object***

four elements

ANCIENT GREEK PHILOSOPHY, METAPHYSICS In ancient Greek thought, water, air, fire, and earth. While **Thales**, **Anaximenes**, and **Heraclitus** took water, air, and fire respectively as the sole first principle for generating everything else in the cosmos, **Empedocles** was the first to consider these three plus earth as first principles with equal status and called them the "roots of everything." He held that the four elements were each ungenerated and indestructible and created all other things, together with the cosmic agents **Strife** and **Love**. **Plato** in the *Timaeus* made use of the doctrine of four elements, and **Aristotle**, taking it as a basis for his physics, claimed that the four elements are capable of mutual transformation and that their nature is decided by two pairs of opposites: hot and cold, wet and dry.

> "Empedocles was the first to speak of four material elements." **Aristotle, *Metaphysics***

four-term fallacy

LOGIC Also called in Latin *quaterno terminorum* (a quadruplet of term) or fallacy of the ambiguous middle. A normal **syllogism** carries with it three terms, with the middle term appearing twice in the premises. But sometimes the two appearances of the middle term have different meanings, although the word is the same. As a result, the syllogism has four rather than three terms, and there is no connection between two premises. Such a syllogism is defective and commits a four-term fallacy. For example, "Light is the absence of darkness," and "A pen is light," therefore, "A pen is the absence of darkness." This inference is wrong, because the word "light" has entirely different meanings in the premises. The four-term fallacy is a form of the **fallacy of equivocation** or ambiguity.

> "The tag 'fallacy of four terms' has usually been applied . . . to arguments involving an ambiguous middle term." **Hamblin, *Fallacies***

Frankena, William (1908–94)

American moral philosopher and philosopher of education, born in Montana, Professor of Philosophy, University of Michigan. Frankena's moral philosophy supports the legitimacy of adopting a moral point of view from which to make normative judgments based on what is good and evil for sentient beings. He has written on the virtues, education, and the environment. His main works include *Perspective on Morality* (1976) and *Thinking About Morality* (1980).

Frankfurt, Harry (1929–)

American Descartes scholar, metaphysician, and philosopher of action, born in Langhorne, Pennsylvania, Professor of Philosophy, Yale University and Princeton University. Frankfurt argues that freedom of the will and responsibility do not depend on our being able to do other than what we do, but rather requires that as persons we have a reflective capacity for second-order desires that some of our first-order desires are effective in action. His main works include *Demons, Dreamers and Madmen* (1970) and *The Importance of What We Care About* (1988).

Frankfurt school, see critical theory

fraternity

ETHICS, POLITICAL PHILOSOPHY A brotherhood or an emotionally intimate political relationship between members of a society or group dedicated to a common aim, and characterized by feelings of affection, mutual help, and looking after the weak. It has been regarded as a **virtue**, much like **friendship**, and is modeled on an idealized view of the relation that exists between siblings. As a political ideal, it attempts to subordinate people's fratricidal impulses through commitment to shared values and positive feelings. **Nationalism** generally advocates the nurturing of this kind of feeling among fellow-countrymen. Christianity regards fraternity as natural, for human beings are all brothers by nature. **Liberty**, **equality**, and fraternity were equally promoted as goals of the French Revolution. Marxism holds that this relationship exists between working classes all over the world. Fraternity is widely thought to be impractical and is ignored in much modern democratic theory. But **Rawls** argues that fraternity is required by his second principle of **justice**, which permits economic inequalities in a democratic society only if they benefit the least-favored group in the society.

> "The principle of fraternity [is] that in spite of all the divisions and distinctions between members of a community, they should treat one another as fellow members and individuals in their own rights." **Lucas,** *The Principles of Politics*

free logic
LOGIC The branch of the logic of terms that is free of existential assumptions or presuppositions with respect to both general terms and singular terms. Traditional logic permits inference from A-propositions to I-propositions or from E-propositions to O-propositions. That implies that no general term is empty. Modern predicate logic rejects this point, but still believes that singular terms refer. Free logic proposes that statements containing quantificational phrases have existential import if and only if there is an object g for all general terms G or there is an object s for all singular terms S. Hence free logic is also called "logic without existence assumptions." Technical study in this area started in the mid-1950s, and various systems have been proposed by Schock, Leonard, **Hintikka**, Lambert, and Leblanc.

> "In classical logic, individual constants carry existential commitment . . . In free logic, the constants do not carry this commitment. This is not to say that they may fail to denote, but rather, that their denotata may not be within the range of the ordinary existential quantifier – the denotata may be non-existent objects." **Forbes,** *Language of Possibility*

free rider
ETHICS, POLITICAL PHILOSOPHY, PHILOSOPHY OF SOCIAL SCIENCE A person who enjoys a benefit provided by a public good but who does not contribute to this good. Some of the free rider's consumption of the public good does not prevent the same consumption by others, for example the free enjoyment of radio broadcasts, but some will inevitably be at the expense of others, for example getting welfare benefits without paying taxes that support the system of welfare. Either way, if everybody contributes nothing, the public good will not exist. If a public good permits many free riders, it cannot be maintained. An ethical question thus arises about whether a free rider's consumption is just and about whether the public can be justified in getting rid of free riders or forcing them to contribute. There are difficulties in explaining why the behavior of the free rider is irrational.

> "A Free-rider obtains a benefit without paying all or part of its cost." **Gauthier,** *Morals By Agreement*

free variable
LOGIC A **variable** occurring in an unquantified sentence, without being prefixed by a **quantifier**. In contrast, a **bound variable** falls within the scope of a prefixed quantifier. A sentence containing one or more free variables is called an **open sentence**. **Russell** and **Whitehead** also called bound variables apparent variables, and free variables real variables.

> "An occurrence of a variable in a sentence is called free in that sentence in which it is unquantified." **Quine,** *Methods of Logic*

free will, problem of
METAPHYSICS, PHILOSOPHY OF ACTION There are threats to freedom involving the apparent determination of human action by factors independent of our **will**. These include divine **foreknowledge** and, in modern philosophy, the possibility that our actions are determined by causal laws. The problem seems to pose a dilemma whether one accepts or denies **determinism**. If determinism is true, one's acts are determined by events beyond one's control, and hence one has no free will. If determinism is false, one's acts are undetermined and due to **chance**, which is also beyond one's control, and hence one has no free will. One way out of the dilemma is to argue that free will is a dispositional causal power, which can exist in a wholly determined world and is thereby compatible with determinism. Another response attempts to show that determinism has weaker implications than any which would prevent it from being compatible with free will. Some philosophers argue that what we value in freedom is not challenged by determinism and is not aided by indeterminism. Rather, free will is constrained

by coercion rather than determinism. Some argue further that any account of action, choice, and free will would be incoherent without determinism. Nevertheless, some philosophers still claim that on a proper understanding of freedom and fore-knowledge or freedom and causal laws, we cannot have both. These philosophers tend to retain a strong notion of **necessity** linked to foreknowledge or causality and a distinctive account of agency that does not fall under causal laws.

"The problem of the freedom of the will is concerned with the question whether the human will is subordinated to the general principle of causality or whether it escapes from its constraints." **Ajdukiewicz,** *Problems and Theories of Philosophy*

freedom

PHILOSOPHY OF MIND, PHILOSOPHY OF ACTION, ETHICS, POLITICAL PHILOSOPHY A concept concerning thought and action which has two related aspects: **negative freedom**, or freedom from, is the power to act in the absence of external constraint, coercion, or compulsion; and positive freedom, or freedom to, is the power to choose one's own goals and course of conduct among alternatives. Under these general determinations, freedom has various forms, of which freedom of speech, freedom of conscience, freedom of the press, freedom of association, and various economic freedoms are historically the most important. If one can claim freedom regarding an interest, then one has a right to pursue that interest. Freedom is used as a synonym of **liberty**, and J. S. **Mill**'s *On Liberty* has had the greatest influence among books on the concept of freedom.

For **Plato**, a man is free if he is governed by **reason**, but a slave if he is ruled by **desires** and **passions**. **Kant** distinguished the theoretical sense of freedom, that is, the **spontaneity** of understanding as opposed to receptivity of the sensibility, from the practical sense of freedom, that is, the **autonomy** of the **will** as opposed to **heteronomy**. **Fichte** and **Schelling** transformed spontaneity and autonomy respectively into subjective or objective absolutes, a tendency inherited by **Sartre** but criticized by **Hegel**, **Nietzsche**, **Heidegger**, and **Adorno**. This latter position has claimed that freedom is intrinsically qualified. The **liberal** tradition generally connects freedom with our concept of humanity.

"That there is freedom in our will, and that we have power in many cases to give and withhold our assent at will, is so evident that it must be counted among the first and most common notions that are innate in us." **Descartes,** *The Philosophical Writings*, **vol. I**

freedom of speech

POLITICAL PHILOSOPHY The freedom to express one's own mind in speech, writing, or some other way without prior restriction, contemporary constraint, or subsequent punishment. The fundamental justifications for freedom of speech are its essential role in the pursuit of **truth** and in free political life, and its fundamental contribution to our **dignity** as rational and self-determining beings. Hence, freedom of speech has instrumental value. Freedom of speech has been regarded as one of the basic human **rights** that governments have a basic requirement to protect. Even those fully committed to maintaining freedom of speech recognize that some speech can rightly be restricted by law. Speech that seriously endangers individuals, groups, or the nation as a whole are often judged to lie outside the protection of freedom of speech. There are various conflicts over the kinds of speech that may be restricted and over the competing rationales for restricting them. While certain kinds of speech are recognized as being harmful, suppressing freedom of speech without rational grounds is seen as a greater evil. The discussion of free speech is related to questions about the rationality of **censorship** and to the consideration of other basic freedoms.

"We may take for granted that a democratic regime presupposes freedom of speech and assembly, and liberty of thought and conscience." **Rawls,** *A Theory of Justice*

freedom of the will

METAPHYSICS, ETHICS, PHILOSOPHY OF MIND, PHILOSOPHY OF ACTION The doctrine of freedom of the will or **free will** derives from the natural feeling that we can choose what we do according to the dictates of our own soul, without being compelled, and that in the conditions of our action we could have acted otherwise. Only because our will is free can we speak meaningfully of ethical conceptions such as **responsibility, duty, obligation, self-determination,** and commitment. The concept of free will is contrasted to the notion of **determinism**. If everything is causally determined, how can there be a free will? While free will is supported by our everyday consciousness, determinism gains its ground in science. With regard to their relation, philosophers are divided into **compatibilists**, who claim that there is some way to reconcile determinism and free will, and **incompatibilists**, who reject the possibility of reconciliation. Some incompatibilists reject determinism, while others claim that free will is illusionary.

> "The freedom of the will consists in the possibility of knowing actions that still lie in the future."
> **Wittgenstein,** *Tractatus*

Frege, Gottlob (1848–1925)

German philosopher, logician, and mathematician, the founder of modern mathematic logic and the philosophy of language, born in Weimar, Professor of mathematic at the University of Jena. In the *Begriffsschrift* (Concept-Script, 1879), *The Foundations of Arithmetic* (1884), and *Basic Laws of Arithmetic* (2 vols., 1893, 1903), Frege developed the logicist program of reducing arithmetic to logic. Although his own version of logicism was undermined by Russell's paradox, Frege's philosophical insights greatly influenced Russell, Wittgenstein, and contemporary logic, philosophy of mathematics, and philosophy of language. In logic, Frege's theory of quantification established the framework for modern logic. In his "Function and Concept" and "On Concept and Object" (1891) Frege analyzed sentences in terms of function and argument, and in "On Sense and Reference" (1892), he drew the distinction between sense (*Sinn*) and reference (*Bedeutung*) to show that the sense of an expression and its reference do not always vary together. These classic papers laid the grounds for the subsequent development of analytic philosophy. Frege's anti-psychologism involved realism regarding concepts and thoughts.

Fregean principle, an alternative term for compositionality

Freud, Sigmund (1856–1939)

Austrian psychologist, the founder of psychoanalysis, born in Freiburg, Moravia, educated in Vienna, and moved to England in 1938. Freud broadened the notion of the psyche to include unconscious as well as conscious states. He held that the unconscious mind and its repressed contents have a dynamic role in determining behavior and forming neurosis. He divided the mind into the "id" (the unconscious mind), the "ego," and the "super-ego." His psychoanalysis gave explanatory prominence to sexual instincts and the unconscious Oedipal fantasies of early childhood, and aimed to resolve neurosis through a "talking cure" that brought repressed thoughts to consciousness. He held that phenomena such as dreams, jokes, and slips of the tongue are disguised manifestations of repressed thoughts that can lead through psychoanalysis to uncover their origins with beneficial therapeutic effect. Freud applied his theory of individual psychology to the explanation of religion, morality, politics, and human history. In spite of powerful criticism of his theory, methodology, and therapy, Freud remains a source of inspiration, especially among contemporary European philosophers. His major works include *The Interpretation of Dreams* (1900), *Totem and Tabu* (1913), *Introductory Lectures on Psychoanalysis* (1915–16), *Beyond the Pleasure Principle* (1919–20), *The Ego and the Id* (1923), *The Future of an Illusion* (1927), *Civilisation and Its Discontents* (1930), and *New Introductory Lectures on Psychoanalysis* (1933).

friendship

ETHICS A prominent moral topic in Greek ethics from **Socrates** to the Stoics. The word is generally used to translate the Greek word *philia*, although the latter covers a broader area, including all personal relationships motivated by mutual **love** and the relationships amongst family members. **Aristotle**'s *Nicomachean Ethics* deals with the problem of friendship in detail. He divides friendship into three types: that based on mutual **pleasure**, that based on **utility**, and that based on the mutual appreciation of virtuous **character**. The last type is the real and genuine kind of friendship. Only a virtuous person can be a friend to another virtuous person, and a friend in this relationship is another **self**, a mirror of one's character. Aristotle characterizes friendship as involving the pursuit of the goods of one's friends for their own sake, and involving reciprocity of sentiment. The issue of friendship has fallen into neglect in modern ethics, for it believes that friendship is a private affair, a matter of personal choice, rather than a part of common morality. The topic has been revived with the emergence of contemporary **virtue ethics**, and especially of **feminist ethics**, both of which emphasize personal relationships rather than universalistic moral considerations.

> "Friendship is said to be reciprocated goodwill."
> **Aristotle,** *Nicomachean Ethics*

full theory of the good, see thin theory of the good

fully generalized proposition
LOGIC Also called a completely general proposition, a quite general proposition, or a logical proposition. A fully generalized **proposition** contains only **variables** and **truth-functional connectives**, and does not mention any particular thing at all. It thus provides a purely logical structure. **Russell** claims that such a proposition is **analytic** and *a priori*. **Wittgenstein** believes that a fully generalized proposition can also describe the world in virtue of its articulated or composite structure; but this claim has attracted the criticism that such a proposition cannot say anything about the world through its structure alone without saying of anything that it has some character.

> "We can describe the world completely by means of fully generalised propositions, i.e. without first correlating any name with a particular object."
> **Wittgenstein,** *Tractatus*

function
LOGIC, PHILOSOPHY OF MATHEMATICS In ordinary language, a function roughly means a purpose or role. In logic and mathematics, a function is a particular kind of **relation** in which given any **object** or objects (called an **argument** of the function), another object (called the **value** of the function for that argument) will be yielded. A function has one or more **variables**, which can take different arguments. Giving definite values to the variables of a function yields a definite value to the whole function. **Truth-functions** in **propositional logic** (also called functional calculus) are special functions in which the truth-value of a compound proposition is determined by the truth-values of its propositional components and by the logical terms

connecting them. A function is applicable to a certain **class** of objects. The class to which the function applies is called the domain of the function, and the class of values is called the range of the function. **Frege** held that **concepts** are functions that map objects onto **truth-values**.

> "A function is, as observed, a relation. But it is a relation of a special sort, having the peculiarity that no two elements bear it to the same element."
> **Quine,** *Mathematical Logic*

function and argument
LOGIC A mathematical function is an operational **relation** which can apply to a domain. An argument is an **object** to which a function is applied within this domain. An argument is a variable part within a function, for one argument can always be replaced by another object in the same domain. The output that results from applying a function to an argument is called the value of the function for that argument. For instance, for the function f = 2x and the argument 3, the value is 6. **Frege** introduced the concepts of function and argument into logic and claimed that a function is analogous to a **concept** or a **predicate** expression, while an argument is analogous to an **object** or a subject expression in a proposition. In applying these concepts to **propositions**, Frege used the terms **truth-function** and **truth-value** in light of the crucial importance of **truth** and falsity in assessing propositions.

> "Suppose that a simple or complex symbol occurs in one or more places in an expression (whose content need not be a possible content of judgment). If we imagine this symbol as replaceable by another (the same one each time) at one or more of its occurrences, then the part of the expression that shows itself invariant under such replacement is called the function; and the replaceable part, the argument of the function." **Frege,** *Begriffsschrift*

function stroke, see Sheffer function

functionalism
PHILOSOPHY OF SCIENCE, PHILOSOPHY OF MIND A term for any theory that takes the notion of function as the first explanatory principle. In the philosophy

of mind, it is currently a widely supported theory of the **mind–body relationship**. This theory was developed as a result of the recognition of the defects of the **identity theory** of mind. Its chief characteristic is that it asks what makes a **mental state** a mental state rather than asking about the intrinsic property of a mental state. According to functionalism, a mental state or event should be explained by its functional role, that is, its causal relationship with other mental states, with sensory inputs and the consequential output behavior of a subject. Unlike the identity theory of the mind, it does not claim that mental states are directly *per se* neural states, but sees mental states in terms of something more abstract, that is, the causal or functional roles some neural states possess. The theory can be traced to the later **Wittgenstein** and his account of use, and its major representatives include Hilary **Putnam** and Jerry **Fodor**. Functionalism is closely associated with **cognitive science**, **artificial intelligence**, and the computer model of the mind. There are various versions of functionalism in the philosophy of mind. Ned **Block** distinguishes between psycho-functionalism and conceptual functionalism. Psycho-functionalism views mental states not from the biological point of view, but from the organizational point of view. Mental states are analogous to the functional states of a computer, and the mind is a program that can be multiply realized, that is, shared by various physiochemical systems. Conceptual functionalism is a development of **analytical behaviorism** and considers a mental state to be a contribution to a **disposition** to behave. Another distinction is between **machine functionalism**, which understands function in terms of the operation of the whole organism, and teleological functionalism, which understands function as what the thing is for. **Homuncular functionalism** is one version of teleological functionalism. The main objections faced by functionalist accounts of the mind are that it cannot account for **qualia**, that is, what it is like to feel a **sensation**, and for **intentionality**.

> "According to functionalism, the behaviour of, say, a computing machine is not explained by the physics and chemistry of the computing machine. It is explained by the machine's program." **Putnam, *Mind, Language and Reality***

fundamental ontology, see being (Heidegger)

fundamental project
MODERN EUROPEAN PHILOSOPHY **Sartre** denied the **transcendental ego** and tried to account for our **identity** by means of the notion of fundamental project or original choice. A fundamental project is an act that is responsible for the whole mode of life of a person, which makes him recognizable in every particular situation. The project or choice is neither given nor fixed, but is actively constructed. It is manifested in various actions across many years. Because the project is a choice, we are not passively subjected to the external causal world. We always define ourselves by projecting beyond causality. In this way, our life history should be conceived as a coherent, long-term, and self-determining process of life experience. The project is fundamental and the choice is original through relation to a person's **being-in-the-world** in its entirety. The project is not related to any particular object in the world and is not empirical. We exist with this choice or project and are therefore responsible for our lives. The fundamental project is the expression of our **freedom** and is the ground of our **responsibility**.

> "This fundamental project must not of course refer to any other and should be conceived by itself. It can be concerned neither with death nor life nor any particular characteristic of the human condition; the original project of a for-itself can aim only at its being." **Sartre, *Being and Nothingness***

fusion of horizons
MODERN EUROPEAN PHILOSOPHY **Gadamer** follows **Husserl** and **Heidegger** in arguing that we live and understand within **horizons**, which provide a framework for the possibility of **meaning**. Although a horizon is formed in **tradition** and **culture**, there is, in interpreting a historical text, a tension between this horizon of the text and the horizon of the present and of the interpreter. In **understanding**, we need to acquire the historical horizon, but it is also impossible to eliminate our own criteria and **prejudices**. We should be aware of the particularities of both horizons and overcome them by establishing a relation that brings them together. Any real

understanding involves such a fusion of horizons in the course of which tradition acquires new life and our own prejudices are challenged. Since language is crucial to understanding, a fusion of horizons is essentially a fusion of language.

"In the process of understanding there takes place a real fusing of horizons, which means that as the historical horizon is projected, it is simultaneously removed." **Gadamer,** *Truth and Method*

future contingents

LOGIC, METAPHYSICS The problem of future contingents concerns ascertaining the truth-value of statements about future events. If we adhere to the classical principle of **bivalence** that every statement must be either true or false, then future contingent statements will be either true or false in advance of the event. This conclusion, which seems to commit us to **fatalism**, has led some to skepticism regarding the principle of bivalence, although other philosophers argue that a proper understanding of bivalence for future contingent statements does not ensnare us in fatalism. The problem, which originated in **Aristotle**'s discussion of the **sea-battle** tomorrow, was much disputed by medieval logicians, because if future contingent statements are neither true nor false, divine **foreknowledge** would come into question. In the twentieth century **Lukasiewicz** sought to deal with this problem by introducing **three-valued logic**, which in turn led to the development of various **many-valued logics**.

"Aristotle dismissed the truth-states of alternatives regarding future-contingent matters, whose occurrence – like that of the sea-battle tomorrow – is not yet determinate by us, and may indeed actually be undetermined." **Rescher,** *Topics in Philosophic Logic*

future generations

POLITICAL PHILOSOPHY, ETHICS Since certain actions of the present generation of human beings, such as natural resource depletion, chemical waste, birth control, and the use of nuclear weapons, have inevitable effects upon the life quality, identity, and the size of future generations, we feel we have moral duties and obligations toward the members of future generations. **Consequentialists** argue that we should promote the interests of future generations as we do those of our own generation, and **deontologists** claim that we should always act in ways that make people better off or at least not worse off than they would otherwise be. However, each position is open to question, because future generations are created by us and their sizes are determined by us. The major philosophical question concerns the basis of our **duty** to future generations. Some refer to the **rights** of the future generation. But how can we talk about the rights and interests of non-existent people? Others refer to intergenerational **justice**, according to which each generation should obtain its own share. But since the number of people belonging to future generations is uncertain, what is the ground for deciding equal shares? Some moralists object to the view that we have moral responsibility toward future generations, for ethical relations can only be between agents who can benefit or harm each other. The debate about moral issues regarding future generations indicates that important aspects of current moral theory are defective.

"It may be irrational to be less concerned about the further future. But we cannot be sure of this while we are undecided on the reason why." **Parfit,** *Reasons and Persons*

future-referring term, see past-referring term

G

Gadamer, Hans-Georg (1900–2002)
German philosopher, a student of Heidegger, the leading exponent of hermeneutics, born in Marburg, taught at Leipzig, Frankfurt, and Heidelberg. Gadamer developed philosophical hermeneutics to deal with the fundamental conditions that underlie understanding and interpretation. He took understanding to be the basic feature of human existence and held that hermeneutics should be ontological rather than methodological. All understanding and interpretation presupposes prejudices and involves a fusion of the present horizon of the interpreter and the historical horizon of the text. Interpretation is a virtual dialogue and a historical process. Because human studies are caught up in a hermeneutic circle, it is inappropriate to demand objectivity and neutrality in human sciences. Gadamer's hermeneutics have been applied in law, theology, and literature. His major work is *Truth and Method* (1960), and the other works include *Philosophical Hermeneutics* (1976), *Klein Schriften*, 4 vols. (1972–9), and *Reason in the Age of Science* (1981).

Gaia hypothesis

ETHICS, PHILOSOPHY OF SCIENCE [from Greek *Gaia*, the earth goddess] Lovelock's **hypothesis**, which sees the earth as a living self-regulating organism. On this view, the earth is a creature that is not merely the sum of its parts, but is a complex entity with properties extending beyond those of its constituents of biosphere, atmosphere, oceans, and soil. All of these components are related to the complex interactions of organisms. If the system loses its equilibrium, there could be disastrous consequences for life. The hypothesis emphasizes the interdependence between life and ecosphere. It is intended to challenge the view that nature is nothing but an object to be conquered, controlled, and exploited for human ends. Consequently, we should live with nature and shift our traditional bias of human-centrism. The hypothesis captures the spirit of deep ecology and has affected environmental philosophy and the environmental protection movement. It is a matter of dispute whether it is a serious new paradigm for understanding nature and our relation to it or merely a body of evocative and persuasive imagery.

> "The Gaia hypothesis is for those who like to walk or simply stand and stare, to wonder about the Earth and the life it bears, and to speculate about the consequences of our own presence here."
> **Lovelock, *Gaia: A New Look at Life on Earth***

Galileo Galilei (1564–1642)
Italian astronomer, physicist, and philosopher, born in Pisa. Galileo has a profound influence on the replacement of the Aristotelian system with modern science and philosophy through his experimental investigations, his use of mathematics and observation

in science, his introduction of the distinction between primary and secondary qualities, and his skeptical scientific methodology. His main works include *Dialogue Concerning the Two Chief World Systems* (1632) and *Dialogues Concerning Two New Sciences* (1638).

gambler's fallacy

LOGIC Also called the Monte Carlo fallacy. Two fallacious ways of reasoning starting from the same premise. The initial premise is that a particular given outcome has occurred many times in succession. From here one person infers that the same outcome will occur again next time; and the other infers that the opposite outcome will occur next time. Both are wrong because the system does not have a memory. A coin will not come up heads or tails because it has come up heads many times in succession. The **probability** of past outcomes does not affect the probability of a future event. It will neither increase nor decrease, but remains the same on each occasion.

"The simplest available explanation of the prevalence of the 'gambler's fallacy' is that it seems from a quite legitimate use of the counterfactualizable conception of probability in contexts where it is not assumed, or not taken as established, that pure chance is operating." **L. Cohen, *The Dialogue of Reason***

game theory

PHILOSOPHY OF ACTION, PHILOSOPHY OF SOCIAL SCIENCE, ETHICS, POLITICAL PHILOSOPHY The mathematical theory of game-like human situations in which each rational **agent** strategically acts so as to maximize preferred **utility** or outcome. However, the realization of this strategy depends on the actions of other players in the same situations, and on the assumption that each of them is equally rational in his or her choices. Each player must take the strategies of other players into account, since it is impossible for all players to maximize simultaneously their preferred utility. A situation which yields such a consequence that no agent can improve his or her position if such an agent unilaterally withdraws from it, is called the **Nash equilibrium**. Game theory tries to find what the most rational strategy should be in such situations. It was systematically developed by John **von Neumann** and Oskar Morgenstern in the 1940s, and has a wide application in the contemporary discussion of moral and political theory. Game theory is a part of **decision theory**.

"Game theory therefore starts with games where initial choices are to be made without prior communication and where any emergent conventions exist without being enforced by any kind of sanctions." **Hollis, in Bunnin and Tsui-James (eds.), *The Blackwell Companion to Philosophy***

Gassendi, Pierre (1592–1655)

French philosopher, born in Champtercier, Provence. Gassendi brought empiricist and skeptical criticism to bear on the philosophy of Descartes. His Objections were among those appended to the publications of Descartes's *Meditations* in 1641. In response to Descartes's replies, he further developed his criticism in *Disquisitio Metaphysica* (1644). Gassendi wrote extensively on Epicurus, and his major philosophical concern was to reconcile Greek atomism with Christian doctrine in order to provide an interpretation of the new sciences. His position was systematically expounded in *Syntagma Philosophicum*, published posthumously.

Gauthier David (1932–)

Canadian moral and political philosopher, born in Toronto, Professor of Philosophy at University of Toronto and University of Pittsburgh. In work influenced by Kant and Hobbes, Gauthier seeks to understand the agreements that would be reached through practical reason among rational agents as a basis for restraining self-interest through morality and politics. His main works include *The Logic of Leviathan* (1969) and *Morals by Agreement* (1986).

Geach, Peter (1916–)

British philosopher of logic, metaphysics, mind, religion, and ethics, born in London, Professor of Logic, University of Leeds. Geach has used his understanding of Aristotle, Aquinas, and modern formal logic to deal with a wide range of philosophical problems. His account of mental acts as sayings in the heart, his notion of identity as relative to kind terms, his investigation of the virtues, and his philosophical theology have been influential. His main works include *Mental Acts* (1956), *Reference and Generality* (1962), and *God and the Soul* (1969).

Geisteswissenschaften

PHILOSOPHY OF HISTORY, PHILOSOPHY OF SOCIAL SCI-
ENCE [German, human sciences or human studies,
but including social sciences as well as humanities]
A term particularly associated with Wilhelm **Dilthey**
and contrasted to *Naturwissenschaften* [German, natural sciences]. Natural sciences offer objective knowledge and can explain phenomena in terms of laws,
but these features are lacking in the humanities.
Hermeneutics, according to Dilthey, can defend the
human sciences as an integrated body of disciplines
with their own methods and principles in contrast
to those of the natural sciences. Their dependence
upon the cognitive capacity of **understanding** gives
them a distinct status as a source of **knowledge**. The
human sciences possess a peculiar relation to human
experience. Rather than establishing laws to explain
events, they describe historical facts and formulate
standards of **value** and practical imperatives. Some
philosophers propose hermeneutics as the methodology that is appropriate to provide **objectivity** for
humanities. This claimed objectivity is challenged
by those who wish to free **interpretation** from
the need to have an objective end-point and by the
positivist claim that human knowledge must meet
the standards for a **unified science** that are essentially set by the natural sciences.

> "All the disciplines that have socio-historical real-
> ity as their subject-matter are encompassed in this
> work under the name *Geisteswissenschaften* [human
> sciences]." **Dilthey,** *Selected Works,* **vol. I**

gender

ETHICS, POLITICAL PHILOSOPHY The distinction between sex and gender is a central feature of recent
feminist thought. While sexual distinctions between
male and female have been understood as being
biologically and anatomically determined, especially
with respect to reproductive roles, gender has been
understood as a variable social construction, with
gender difference determined socially and culturally.
Sex has to do with **facts**, while gender has to do with
values. These values, however, are generally those
of male domination and masquerade as a factual
basis for male social superiority. By distinguishing
between sex and gender, feminist theory provides a
standpoint from which alleged male superiority can
be challenged. Because some feminist theorists have

rejected the distinction between sex and gender on
the grounds that sex is also socially constructed, the
boundaries between the biological and the social
remains a matter of dispute in this domain. In addition, some feminists are seeking a new way to base
their critique of male-dominated society.

While discussion of gender is largely confined
to humans, questions about sex, sexual desire, and
sexual behavior can also be asked about members
of other animal species. Some theorists claim that
such investigations can also illuminate our understanding of human sexuality. The relationships
between sexual desire and reason and the role of sex
in explaining human behavior have been explored by
Freud, his successors, and his critics. Non-standard
forms of sexual activity, such as **homosexuality**,
have become major topics in **applied ethics**.

Gender is also a grammatical term. While many
languages distinguish nouns, pronouns, and adjectives into masculine and feminine gender, some
languages, such as Greek, Latin, and German,
distinguish these parts of speech into three genders:
masculine, feminine, and neutral, with each having
different patterns of inflection.

> "The concept of gender carries in one word both
> a recognition of the social aspect of the 'sexual'
> dichotomy and the need to treat it as such."
> **Delphy,** *Close to Home*

genealogy

MODERN EUROPEAN PHILOSOPHY, PHILOSOPHY OF HIS-
TORY An inquiry into origin and descent. **Nietzsche**
defined genealogy as the investigation of the origin
of moral prejudices in *On the Genealogy of Morals*
(1887). He traced the root of human morality back
to the most naked struggle for power. **Foucault** took
over this term and developed it into a concept of
history and a discipline. In contrast to the standard
historical approach, which traces a line of inevitability and demonstrates that the present is based on
the past, genealogy begins with the present and goes
backward in time until a difference is located. It
intends to break off the past from the present and
undercuts the legitimacy of the present. Genealogy
rejects the role of **cause** or **explanation** and rejects
the claim of a unitary body of **theory**. It focuses
instead on local, discontinuous **knowledge**, and
attempts to reveal the multiplicity of factors behind

an event and the fragility of historical forms. By demonstrating the foreignness of the past, it exposes the relativity of present phenomena that are taken for granted. Foucault in his *Archaeology of Knowledge* presents a genealogic approach to intellectual history, in order to account for the transition from one system to another by connecting them to their social, economical, and political backgrounds.

"What I would call genealogy . . . is a form of history which can account for the constitution of knowledge, discourses, domains of objects etc., without having to make reference to a subject which is either transcendental in relation to the field of events or runs in its empty sameness throughout the course of history." **Foucault, *Power/ Knowledge***

general proposition

LOGIC The "A" (all *p*s are *q*) and "E" (all *p*s are not *q*) propositions in the traditional **syllogism**, which assert or deny the truth of all values of a propositional function. They correspond to general facts and are also called universal propositions. General propositions might be **tautologies**, and they might also obtain through **induction** or complete enumeration. **Russell**'s account of general propositions also includes **existence** propositions, i.e. "I" (some *p* is *q*) or "O" (some *p* is not *q*) propositions in the traditional syllogism, for I is the denial of E, and O is the denial of A. He therefore names "A" and "E" as positive general propositions and "I" and "O" as negative general propositions.

"We will call propositions containing the word 'some' negative general propositions, and those containing the word 'all' positive general propositions." **Russell, *Our Knowledge of the External World***

general propositional form

LOGIC, METAPHYSICS Although different propositions have different **logical forms**, they share something in common with one another in virtue of each of them being a **proposition**. This common form underlying all superficial differences of propositions is what the early **Wittgenstein** calls the "general propositional form." It is the essence of being a proposition and is contained in every proposition. It is both the real logical **constant** and the most general propositional **variable**, whose range is the

totality of propositions. This form is implicit in the rules of logical **syntax**, but Wittgenstein sometimes also claims that the general propositional form indicates how things stand, and that the combination of the symbols for things and relations in this propositional form corresponds to the things having these relations in reality.

"It now seems possible to give the most general propositional form: that is, to give a description of the proposition of any sign-language whatsoever in such a way that every possible sense can be expressed by a symbol satisfying the description, and every symbol satisfying the description can express a sense, provided that the meanings of the names are suitably chosen." **Wittgenstein, *Tractatus***

general term

LOGIC **Quine**'s expression, in contrast to a **singular term**. While a singular term **denotes** an individual **object**, a general term denotes a kind or a type of individual thing. General terms include both adjectives such as "wise" and "human" and common nouns such as "man" and "horse." They can be predicated of more than one object and are also called **predicates**. For Quine, general terms fill a position in propositions that is not available to quantified **variables**. Common nouns as general terms can be divided into general **sortal** nouns, which are countable (for example "dog" and "car"), and general **mass terms**, which cannot be counted (for example "water" and "sugar").

"The general term is what is predicated, or occupies what grammarians call predicative position; and it can as well have the form of an adjective or verb as that of a substantive." **Quine, *Word and Object***

general will

POLITICAL PHILOSOPHY, ETHICS A term introduced by Jean-Jacques **Rousseau** for the collective will or the common interest, that is, what we all really and truly want. The general will derives from the sovereign body, which is composed of all the adult members of the **state** and provides the legitimate authority of the state. We have an obligation to accept the jurisdiction of the state because the authority of the state represents the general will directed to the common **good**. The general will, which is superior to the individual will, stands in contrast to the will of all. The will of all is the mere aggregate of private and individual wills, although the general will can be worked out from the will of all. Rousseau's theory of the general will is an alternative to the **social contract** as justification for the ground of **political obligation**. In subjecting oneself to the authority of the **community**, one is subjecting oneself to being directed by the general will. The general will is expressed in **laws**, which are established on the basis of majority vote by a general assembly composed of all adult men of the community. The notion of the general will was developed by **Hegel** and by British Hegelians such as **Green** and **Bosanquet**. The main objection to this theory is that it assumes that the state has its own will, which overrides the will of its individual members and which justifies ignoring these individual wills. Furthermore, it is not clear why membership in a society would necessarily give insight into its general will or whether the general will would necessarily provide the common good.

"The general will alone can direct the forces of the state in accordance with that end which the state has been established to achieve – the common good." **Rousseau,** *The Social Contract*

generalization

LOGIC A generalization is usually a universal statement that is true of all particular things of a certain kind. For instance, "all men are mortal," which can be read "for all x, if x is a man then x is mortal." Such a statement is made through **induction** and other logical procedures. A generalization is lawlike if it supports a **counterfactual conditional**. We say that "all men are mortal" is law-like because "for all x, if x were a man, then x would be mortal." In predicate **calculus**, if a **well-formed formula** X holds for any arbitrary individual, we may infer from X to $(\forall a)X$. This is called the rule of generalization.

"We mean by a generalisation a statement that all of a certain definable class of propositions are true." **Keynes,** *A Treatise on Probability*

generalization argument

ETHICS An argument and moral principle, which holds that if the results of everyone's doing a certain action are undesirable, no one has a **right** to do that action. Similarly, if the results of no one's doing a certain action are undesirable, every one ought to do it. The validity and the conditions of application of this argument are fully discussed by Marcus Singer in *Generalization in Ethics* (1961). According to him, the validity of this argument is established on two premises: one is called the principle of consequences, which states that if X's doing A has undesirable results, then X does not have a right to do A. The other, called the generalization principle, states that if some persons ought not to do A, then no one who is in a similar situation ought to do A.

"The generalization argument has the general form: 'if everyone were to do x, the consequences would be disastrous (or undesirable); therefore no one ought to do x.'" **M. Singer,** *Generalization in Ethics*

generalization principle

ETHICS A principle formulated by Marcus Singer, but traceable to **Sidgwick**, which states that what is right for one person must be right for every relevantly similar persons in relevantly similar circumstances. What is right for one person cannot be wrong for another unless there is some difference with respect to their natures or circumstances. The principle is similar in spirit to the **Golden Rule** or **Kant**'s **categorical imperative**. It is the basis for what Singer calls the "generalization argument," which infers from "not everyone has the right to . . ." to "no one has the right to . . ." This implies that there are general grounds for an act to be right or wrong. An act must be right or wrong for a class of relevantly similar people. The principle can be challenged because it is unclear how we can decide whether circumstances are similar or not similar.

"The principle that what is right (or wrong) for one person must be right (or wrong) for any similar person in similar circumstances. For obvious reasons, I shall refer to this principle as 'the generalization principle'." **M. Singer,** *Generalization in Ethics*

generalized other, see concrete other

generative grammar

PHILOSOPHY OF LANGUAGE **Chomsky**'s term for his own approach to **grammar** and language. He defines language as consisting of a set of **sentences**, and grammar as a device for producing or generating grammatical sequences. Generative grammar is the internalized capacity or set of **rules** that is acquired by a person unconsciously when he learns a language, by means of which he is able to formulate and understand an infinite number of grammatical utterances from finite observational materials. It assigns structural descriptions that indicate the ways of deriving perfectly well-formed sentences in a language. Thus, although a person is exposed to only a limited number of sentences, he can construct and understand many new ones without difficulty. What it is to be generative is not explicitly explained, but has to do with the notions of production, analysis, description, and specification. Chomsky's linguistics emphasizes especially the speaker or writer rather than the hearer or reader. Generative grammar is contrasted to traditional grammar, which gives only an enumeration of typical structures with common variants and relies on the intelligence and linguistic intuition of the hearer or reader.

"By a generative grammar I mean simply a system of rules that in some explicit and well-defined way assigns structural descriptions to sentences." **Chomsky,** *Aspects of the Theory of Syntax*

generosity

ETHICS [from Latin *generous*, noble, associated with *genus*, race or family] Generosity means literally noble-mindedness and is identical with the Greek virtue of **great-soulness** or magnanimity. In this sense, generosity is taken as a crowning virtue by **Descartes** and others. It is the knowledge that our will is free and responsible for every action and the firm resolution to carry out what we judge to be best. A generous person depends not on external circumstance, but on his own power. In another and probably more popular usage, generosity is taken as a special virtue: the disposition to give freely or let others share what one possesses. It is an overflow of good will.

"Generosity is the willingness to expend one's resources to help others." **Rachels,** *The Elements of Moral Philosophy*

genetic epistemology

EPISTEMOLOGY, PHILOSOPHY OF SCIENCE Genetic epistemology was founded as a distinct approach to epistemology on the basis of genetic psychology by J. M. Baldwin (1861–1934) and was fully developed by J. Piaget (1896–1980). In contrast to traditional epistemology, which emphasizes logical relations between belief, justification, and truth, genetic epistemology argues that **knowledge** is neither *a priori* nor **innate**, but results from a constant construction involving the human subject and the external object in a **dialectical** process of biological and intellectual transformation. It is essentially an **evolutionary theory of knowledge**, based on a combination of a structural conception of the human subject with an evolutionary theory of mental development. It still needs development as an independent discipline.

"In both Great Britain and America philosophers in the main stream of the philosophy of knowledge base themselves not on psychological but on logical and linguistic analysis, whereas genetic epistemology concerns itself with the psychological development of concepts and operations, that is, with psychogenesis." **Piaget,** *The Principles of Genetic Epistemology*

genetic fallacy

LOGIC An argument that judges, evaluates, or explains something in terms of its origin or the original context in which it was generated. Since it is very likely that there might be some essential differences between a thing's origin and its current state, such an argument is always considered as a **fallacy**, especially when it is used in rejecting an opposing view. That human beings originated from apes does not entail that they are still apes.

"The genetical fallacy [is that], according to which the nature of a phenomenon is determined entirely by its origin." **C. Evans,** *The Subject of Consciousness*

genetic method, see developmentalism

genidentity

METAPHYSICS, PHILOSOPHY OF SCIENCE An account of **objects** as sequences of **states** was initiated by **Heraclitus'** maxim that "one cannot step into the same river twice." This position raises the question of how we determine that different stages at different times belong to the history of the same object.

The German philosopher Kurt Lewin introduced the term genidentity in 1922 to characterize this problem. Different philosophers provide different criteria of genidentity. The most influential one, proposed by **Reichenbach** and **Carnap** in accordance with modern physics, suggests that genidentity is an equivalence relation established by a continuity of observation. It is a relation between world points, or moments of particles, holding in either temporal direction.

"Two world points of the same world line, we call genidentical; likewise, two states of the same thing." **Carnap,** *The Logical Structure of the World*

Gentile, Giovanni (1875–1944)

Italian Hegelian idealist, born at Castelvetrano, Sicily. In *The General Theory of the Spirit as Pure Act* (1916), Gentile developed actual idealism or actualism, holding that the act of thinking is the foundation of the world of human experience, and claiming that the task of philosophy is to exhibit the logical structure of actual experience. This theory was further developed in *System of Logic as Theory of Knowing* (vol. 1, 1917, vol. 2, 1923). His interest in education was expressed in *Summary of Education as Philosophical Science* (1913–14) and in his reform of the Italian education system as Mussolini's Minister of Education in the early 1920s. Gentile, who was the main philosophical elaborator of Italian fascism as a political doctrine, was assassinated in 1944.

Gentzen, Gerhard (1909–45)

German logician. Gentzen introduced the formalization of classical and intuitionistic logic through natural deduction. A system of natural deduction has rules of inference but does not treat any logical truths as axioms. His works appear in *Collected Papers* (1969).

genus

METAPHYSICS, LOGIC, PHILOSOPHY OF SCIENCE A kind or **class** of things that share a common nature and can therefore be predicated of each member within the given class. A genus (plural, genera) can be further divided into sub-classes, called **species**. A genus itself can be a species of a higher genus. The highest genus (Latin *genus summum*) is the most

inclusive and ultimate class that is not a sub-class of any further genus. The division of a genus into species is specified according to a **differentia**, which distinguishes the defined species from other species within the same genus. Genus plus differentia is the standard Aristotelian **definition** and is still the most typical form of definition.

Genus has both metaphysical and logical senses. **Plato** used genus synonymously with **Idea**, and in *Sophist* he discusses the relationship among the most universal genera, such as being/not being, sameness/difference, and motion/rest. **Aristotle** not only elaborated the pattern of genus plus differentia definition, but in *Categories* also took genus and species as secondary **substances** because both are predicated of, and reveal, the **essence** of **individuals**, that is, primary substances. His ten **categories** are indeed ten ultimate genera of **being**. The notions of genus and species are widely applied in biology.

"In a secondary sense those things are called substances within which, as species, the primary substances are included; also those which, as genera, include the species." **Aristotle,** *Categories*

genus summum, see genus

Gestalt psychology

EPISTEMOLOGY, PHILOSOPHY OF MIND [from German *Gestalt*, form, organized whole or figure] *Gestalt* psychology is a theory of **sensation** which suggests that we are primarily aware of organized wholes of our environment and not of the irreducible elements into which these wholes might in theory be analyzed. On this account, we can see nothing simpler than a figure, for it can be shown that we naturally organize a series of lines and dots into a coherent pattern. Thus, *Gestalt* psychology rejected British **empiricism**'s prevailing psychological atomism of sensations, according to which sensations are minute elements that we synthesize into patterns or wholes. The *Gestalt* school of psychology was founded in 1910 by Max Wertheimer, Kurt Koffka, and Wolfgang Kohler. Their work is philosophically important because of the insight it gives to the nature of **perception** and especially because it undermines the **myth of the given**.

> "The experiments made by gestalt psychologists are adduced to show that Locke . . . was mistaken in supposing either that the mind is actually supplied with unitary impressions or that it is a merely possible receptor." **Ayer, _The Problem of Knowledge_**

Gettier, Edmund (1927–)

American epistemologist, Professor of Philosophy, University of Massachusetts. In a paper, "Is Justified True Belief Knowledge?" _Analysis_ (1963), Gettier raised a variety of counter-examples against the analysis of knowledge as justified true belief, leading to a rich literature trying to supplement the analysis to make it satisfactory, adding additional counter-examples or providing other approaches to knowledge.

Gettier's problem

EPISTEMOLOGY Also called Gettier's paradox or Gettier's example. Since **Plato**'s _Theaetetus_, propositional **knowledge** has been standardly defined as justified true **belief**, whose analysis is as follows: A knows P if and only if (1) p is true, (2) A believes P, and (3) A is justified in believing P. This traditional tripartite analysis is challenged by **Gettier** in a paper entitled "Is Justified True Belief Knowledge?" (_Analysis_, 1963). Gettier constructs counter-examples to this definition. One of them is as follows. Smith applied for the same job as Jones. He believes that Jones will get the job and also that Jones has ten coins in his pocket. He is thus justified in deducing the belief that the person who will get the job has ten coins in his pocket. As it turns out, Smith himself gets the job and he happens to have ten coins in his pocket. Thus the belief that the person who will get the job has ten coins in his pocket is true, and Smith is justified in believing it. But he does not know it. It shows that the traditional analysis of knowledge is problematic, for A does not know P even though all three conditions are met.

Gettier's problem has caused a long-standing debate about the nature of propositional knowledge and has changed the course of epistemology to a considerable extent. There are many attempts to challenge the validity of Gettier's counter-examples. There are also many attempts to discard the tripartite analysis of knowledge. More scholars believe

that Gettier's paradox only shows that the traditional analysis is insufficient, and so they attempt to add a further condition. Various proposals have been made, but none has achieved consensus. The problem is still open.

> "We have learned from Gettier's paradox that not every sound justification for a true belief is sufficient to entitle the holder of the belief to claim knowledge; the justification must be suitably related to what makes the belief true." **Dummett, _The Seas of Language_**

Gewirth, Alan (1912–2004)

American moral philosopher, born in Union City, New Jersey, Professor of Philosophy, University of Chicago. Gewirth argues for the objectivity of morality on the grounds of a principle of generic consistency, holding that an agent's need for freedom and well-being ultimately implies that one must act with recognition of the need for freedom and well-being for others as well. His main works include _Reason and Morality_ (1978) and _Human Rights_ (1982).

ghost in the machine

PHILOSOPHY OF MIND **Ryle**'s phrase to characterize the Cartesian concept of mind. According to **Descartes**, the human **mind** and the human **body** are independent **substances** that are ordinarily harnessed together. Human bodies are in space and subject to mechanical laws. Their processes and states can be observed externally. Minds, on the other hand, are not in space, and are not subject to mechanical laws. Their processes and states are private and can be accessed only by their possessors. After the death of the body the mind may continue to exist and function. This dualistic account of human beings is caricatured by Ryle as the dogma of the ghost in the machine. For him the view is mistaken in construing the mind as an extra **object** situated in a body and controlling it by a set of unwitnessable activities. Ryle's object in _The Concept of Mind_ is to demolish this dogma.

> "Such in outline is the official theory. I shall often speak of it, with deliberate abusiveness, as 'the dogma of the Ghost in the Machine'." **Ryle, _The Concept of Mind_**

Gilson, Étienne (1884–1978)

French neo-Thomist, born in Paris, Professor at University of Toronto. Gilson was an outstanding historian of philosophy who explored the diversity and sophistication of medieval thought. He is especially known for his discussions of the Augustinian and Aristotelian strands of medieval philosophy, his account of the complex relations between reason and faith, and his exposition of the metaphysics and epistemology of Aquinas. His main works include *The Christian Philosophy of St. Thomas Aquinas* (1919), *The Unity of Philosophical Experience* (1937), and *The Philosopher and Theology* (1960).

given, the

EPISTEMOLOGY That which is presented immediately to **consciousness**, the direct content of **sense-experience**. For many empiricist philosophers, **sense-data** are the given, offering the basis of **certainty**, the ultimate foundation of knowledge and the material from which we infer the existence of other **objects**. What is given can be known non-inferentially and provides the basis presupposed by other forms of **knowledge**. It is the ultimate resort for all factual claims about the world. The existence of the given and its epistemic status are at the core of sense-datum theories of various forms. Other philosophers, although admitting an element that is given in our experience, reject the traditional place of the status of the given as "the myth of the given."

"For to say that an object is immediately 'given' is to say merely that it is the content of a sense-experience." **Ayer, *Language, Truth, and Logic***

gnoseology, another name for epistemology

Gnosticism

PHILOSOPHY OF RELIGION [from Greek *gnosis*, knowledge] A religious and philosophical movement prominent in the early Christian centuries, which drew on the doctrines of **Plato**'s *Timaeus* and the Judeo-Christian myth of Genesis. Gnosticism focused on the role of revealed knowledge in salvation. There are two worlds: the good spiritual world, and the evil material world created and ruled by a lower god or demiurge. **God** is **transcendent** and unknown. Man in his nature is essentially akin to the divine, with a spark of heavenly light imprisoned in a material body. A spiritual savior, normally Jesus, has come to impart *gnosis*, that is, revealed knowledge about the divine origin of the soul and about the way of redemption from the world. *Gnosis* is the redemption of the sinner who is a spiritual man. The human beings who possess this knowledge, called gnostics, will be saved, for by means of that knowledge they awaken to the recognition of their true origin and nature and can hence be liberated from the bondage of the material world. Faith is inferior to *gnosis*. The dualistic cosmological doctrine of Gnosticism and its belief that **salvation** is dependent upon **knowledge** rather than **faith** are incompatible with orthodox Christianity. Consequently it was banned by the Christian emperors as a heresy. Yet Gnosticism spread into the Middle East and was absorbed into **Manichaeism**. It also appeared frequently under different names in the Middle Ages. A number of gnostic texts were rediscovered in Nag Hammadi in Egypt in 1945.

"This is the first and most important point in defining Gnosticism. It is a religion of saving knowledge, and the knowledge is essentially self-knowledge, recognition of the divine element which constitutes the true self. To this recognition is added a bewildering variety of myths and cultic practices." **Grant, *Gnosticism and Early Christianity***

God

PHILOSOPHY OF RELIGION, METAPHYSICS It is difficult to offer a universal definition of this term, which has such a wide and varied application. In general usage, God is represented as being the ultimate source of all that is, the **omnipotent**, **omniscient**, perfectly **good** and loving creator of the world, who preserves the natural order of the world and sustains its moral order. The concept of God has both religious and metaphysical aspects. While religion proceeds on the assumption that God exists, metaphysics takes great pains to examine rational arguments for the existence of God. The account of God differs greatly according to religion and metaphysical system. Is there one supreme God or many lesser gods? What are the attributes of God, and are some **divine attributes** more fundamental than others? What are the implications of divine **perfection**? Is God immanent or **transcendent** in relation to the world? How can we have knowledge of God? Must God be a personal being in order to be a suitable object of worship? What is the place of **faith** and **revelation** in our relation to God? Does **evil** in the world show that there is no all-powerful, all-knowing, and perfectly good God? Does it matter whether we can prove or disprove God's existence? Can we explain belief in God in psychological or sociological terms? Various theological and philosophical doctrines have their origin in these and related problems.

> "By a theist I understand a man who believes that there is a God. By a 'God' he understands something like a 'person' without a body (i.e. a spirit) who is eternal, free, able to do anything, knows everything, is perfectly good, is the proper object of human worship and obedience, the creator and sustainer of the universe." **Swinburne**, *The Coherence of Theism*

God is dead

ETHICS, METAPHYSICS, PHILOSOPHY OF RELIGION **Nietzsche**'s formula for the cultural and intellectual crisis in traditional religious and metaphysical thinking, which is characterized by its attempt to explain the world and the meaning of life by appealing to **God** as an ultimate **transcendent** reality. Nietzsche's proclamation marked a rebellion against the interpretation of the world and ourselves in terms of Christian **morality** and also rejected the superiority of **reason**. According to Nietzsche, we should eliminate the idea of the existence of God and should destroy both our **faith** in God and our accustomed ways of thinking based on that faith. He sought to undermine Judeo-Christian morality and values and advocated a revaluation of all values. Through such a revaluation, we would reconsider everything in a manner faithful to the earth and free from any God-hypothesis. Nietzsche claimed that this will provide our greatest relief, but will also cause universal madness. This slogan has had great impact on **existentialism** and on other intellectual movements of the twentieth century.

> "God is dead. God remains dead. And we have killed him . . . There has never been a greater dead." **Nietzsche**, *The Gay Science*

Gödel, Kurt (1906–78)

Austrian-born American mathematical logician and philosopher of mathematics, born in Brunn,

Privatdocent at University of Vienna and Professor at the Institute for Advanced Studies, Princeton. Gödel is famous for his crucial proofs undermining assumptions about the possibility of proving the completeness and consistency of mathematical systems within the systems themselves. He is also known for his realist account of the philosophy of mathematics. His writings are contained in *Collected Works* (1986–).

Gödel's theorems

LOGIC, PHILOSOPHY OF MATHEMATICS Two fundamental theorems about incompleteness and consistency in formal systems, proved by the Austrian mathematical logician Kurt **Gödel** in work initiated in his paper "On Formally Undecidable Propositions in *Principia Mathematica* and Related Systems, I" (1931). According to the first, any formal system which is capable of expressing arithmetic must contain true sentences, which can be formulated in the system but which cannot be proven employing only the system's own resources, although their construction shows that the sentences are true. According to the second, no formal system is powerful enough to prove its own consistency. By showing that no formal system can prove every truth it can formulate or prove its own consistency, these theorems indicate the limits of purely formal methods in mathematics and undermine **Hilbert**'s formalist program. Gödel's theorems have deeply influenced our understanding of **consistency**, **completeness**, **truth**, provability, computable functions, and the relationship between arithmetic and metamathematics.

> "The 'incompleteness theorem' of Kurt Gödel showed that no set of logical relations can be established that does not also imply the existence of still other relations with which the set itself cannot cope." **S. Richards**, *Philosophy and Sociology of Science*

Godwin, William (1756–1836)

British moral and political philosopher, born in Wisbech. Godwin's radical political philosophy sought to free naturally good and equal human beings from corrupt government in order to establish an anarchist social order functioning according to utilitarian principles and respecting natural rights. His main work is *An Enquiry Concerning Political Justice* (1793).

Golden Rule

ETHICS The rule originates in Western culture with Jesus in Matthew 7:12 in the Bible. Its commonest formulation is: "Do unto others as you would have them do unto you." It has also a negative formulation, which is: "Do not do unto others as you would not have them do unto you." The word "golden" in the expression of "Golden Rule" is an early English usage, meaning "of inestimable value." The same rule had been formulated in the Oriental tradition by the Chinese philosopher Confucius. His version is: "What you do not like when done to yourself, do not do to others." The Golden Rule has been widely accepted as the first **principle** of conduct and is embodied in the core of many social and moral codes. However, many philosophers have questioned its nature and value. Both **Kant** and **Sidgwick** suggest that it is imprecise in formulation and cannot be a rule guiding action, for it is too formal and too general to be used in either moral or legal circumstances. There are many counter-examples to using it as a moral principle. Other moralists have tried to reformulate the rule in order to address such criticism, but no alternative formulation has won general acceptance. Now it is generally held that the Golden Rule must be used together with other principles of conduct. Another major problem concerns the essence of this rule. Some believe that it teaches **impartiality** through a role-reversal test; others consider it as a principle of **autonomy**, by which one judges one's own conduct by referring to the conduct others.

> "Ethical altruism . . . says that people ought to act with each other's interests in mind. That is, of course, a basic statement of morality, best summarized in the so-called Golden rule: 'Do unto others as you would have them do unto you'."
> **Solomon, Introducing Philosophy**

Goldman, Alvin (1938–)

American epistemologist and philosopher of mind and action, born in Brooklyn, New York, Professor of Philosophy, University of Arizona, and Rutgers University. Goldman responded to the Gettier problem by requiring causal links between beliefs and the facts known for justified true beliefs to constitute knowledge. His causal theory of action accounts for intentional action in terms of causal relations between mental states and behavior. He has argued more generally for the importance of cognitive psychology for epistemology. His main works include *A Theory of Human Action* (1970), *Epistemology and Cognition* (1986), and *Liaisons: Philosophy Meets the Cognitive and Social Sciences* (1992).

good

ETHICS Many approaches to ethics are centered on achieving what is good, although others are based on doing what is **right**. Giving priority to one goal need not exclude the other, but might shape its contents or limit how we pursue it. In either case, goodness has a place in **moral psychology**, motivating our **actions** and explaining our **emotions**. However, the notion of the good is extremely complex. **Plato**, in the *Republic*, claimed that the good, while being the source of **being** and **knowledge**, is beyond conceptual **analysis**. This position was developed by **Plotinus** and **Aquinas**. **Aristotle** suggested that the good is that to which everything aspires, but argued that the word is used in many ways and belongs to each **category**. In this respect it is similar to what **Wittgenstein** calls a family resemblance notion, and a unified definition is difficult to achieve. A good man and a good knife, for example, are good in different senses. Accounts of goodness can be divided into **cognitivist** and **non-cognitivist** theories. Cognitivist approaches take goodness to be a real property to which the term "good" applies. Non-cognitivist approaches claim that we construct what is good or use the term to express approval. For some ethical systems, goodness is reduced to one quality, like happiness or **pleasure** or satisfying **desire**. But G. E. **Moore** argued that goodness is a simple **non-natural property** that cannot be analyzed and is not subject to empirical investigation. It is indefinable and can only be grasped through **intuition**. Any attempt to define goodness in terms of natural properties is charged by Moore as committing the **naturalistic fallacy**. In spite of the influence of Moore's attack, naturalistic ethics has been revived. **Rawls's thin theory of the good** provides a basis for his theory of **justice** by specifying those things that all members of society will want whatever else they desire. His **liberalism** allows different fully elaborated theories of the good to be sought by different members of society so long as they are pursued within constraints established by the theory of justice. **Geach** drew a distinction between **attributive** and **predicative** adjectives. A phrase like "a red house" can be analyzed as "this is a house and it is red," while a phrase like "a good mother" cannot be analyzed as "she is a mother and she is good." For she might be good as a mother, but not good in other respects. Hence, the adjective "red" is predicative, while "good" is attributive. In a phrase "a good x," the meaning of "good" is intimately connected with the meaning of the noun it qualifies, and is at least partly determined by the latter. Geach argues that we should take "a good x" as a whole and understand it differently for different kinds of x.

"Every craft and every investigation, and likewise every action and decision, seems to me to aim at some good; hence the good has been well described as that at which everything aims." **Aristotle,** *Nicomachean Ethics*

good will

ETHICS **Kant**'s term for a self-conscious disposition to make morally commendable **choices**. The acts of a good will are done for the sake of **duty** or in accordance with the **categorical imperative**. For Kant, there will always be circumstances under which traditional moral **virtues** or **goods** will be misused. Only a good will is good without qualification. A good will is the only thing that can guarantee the correct use of traditional virtues. It is good not because of what it effects or accomplishes. Even if an action that it chooses causes harm, it is still good as a will. A good will constitutes the indispensable condition of our being worthy of happiness. Kant's notion provided a new foundation for moral philosophy. A good will can be achieved by a human being and is thus contrasted to a **holy will**, which is a spontaneous and willing acceptance of moral requirements without being disturbed by human sensuous **desire**.

"There is no possibility of thinking of anything at all in the world, or even out of it, which can regard as good without qualification, except a *good will.*" **Kant,** *Groundwork for the Metaphysics of Morals*

Goodman, Nelson (1906–98)

American nominalist philosopher of language, science, and art, born in Somerville, Massachusetts, Professor of Philosophy at University of Pennsylvania and Harvard University. Goodman endorsed an austere nominalism that rejects classes in favor of abstract individuals that combine at a time and place to constitute concrete individuals. His account of language is based on denotation of actual individuals rather than on meaning and counterfactual inferences about possible individuals. His new riddle of induction explains the use of predicates in terms of their entrenchment. He compares works of art as symbols to sentences with cognitive structures and allows science and art to be accompanied by many other ways of world-making. His major works are *The Structure of Appearance* (1951), *Fact, Fiction and Forecast* (1954), *The Languages of Art* (1968), and *Ways of World-Making* (1978).

Goodman's paradox, another name for the new riddle of induction

Gorgias (c.483–375 bc)

Greek sophist and rhetorician, born in Leontini, Sicily, and settled in Athens in 427 as a teacher of rhetoric. His book *On Not-Being* was an attempt to discredit Eleatic philosophy. Gorgias used Eleatic dialectical reasoning to establish three propositions that contradicted Eleatic views: (1) nothing is; (2) even if anything is, it is unknowable to man; (3) even if anything is knowable, it is inexpressible and incommunicable to others. Gorgias's main concern was rhetoric, which he defined as the art of persuasion. He developed a new style of prose writing that gained immense popularity in the early fourth century bc. He was portrayed in Plato's important dialogue *Gorgias*.

grace

PHILOSOPHY OF RELIGION In theology, **God**'s free gift by which sinful human beings are saved, for human beings cannot achieve **salvation** through their own efforts. While human gifts might be motivated by self-interest, God's grace is disinterested, for God does not need anything from human beings. Grace is given unilaterally, but there are theological disagreements whether we can act to gain or to deserve grace and whether grace is available for all humans or only for some predestined for salvation.

> "The grace of God could not be commended in a way more likely to evoke a grateful response, than the way by which the only Son of God . . . clothed himself in humanity and gave to men the spirit of his love by the mediation of a man, so that by this love men might come to him . . ." **Augustine,** *City of God*

grammar

PHILOSOPHY OF LANGUAGE, LOGIC A system of **rules** that structures a **natural language**. The traditional study of grammar contains two branches: morphology, which concerns word formation, word class, declensions, and conjunctions; and **syntax**, which concerns the principles governing sentence formation. A traditional grammar is generally prescriptive, that is, legislating over the correct use of a natural language. The contemporary study of grammar is more descriptive and aims to provide a general theory to account for the actual usage of natural languages. The **categories** and rules of a universal grammar are applicable to all human languages. Contemporary grammar is dominated by **Chomsky's** attempt to determine a universal grammar and his notion of a **generative grammar**, that is, a system of rules specifying all and only the grammatical sentences of a language, plus a specification of their relevant structural properties. A generative grammar focuses more on linguistic **competence** than on **performance**. Richard Montague developed a new approach to grammar that applies the techniques of model theory to natural languages and takes a categorical grammar as its syntactic component. Grammar, as a theory of natural languages, can be contrasted to the **logical grammar** of **Wittgenstein** and **Carnap**.

> "We use the term 'grammar' with a systematic ambiguity. On the one hand, the term refers to the explicit theory constructed by the linguist and proposed as a description of the speaker's competence. On the other hand, we use the term to refer to his competence itself." **Chomsky and Halle,** *The Sound Pattern of English*

grammatical predicate, see predicate

grammatical proposition

EPISTEMOLOGY, PHILOSOPHY OF LANGUAGE Many **propositions**, such as "I know I am in pain," or "Red is a color," are usually thought to be **empirical** and to represent what is the case in the world. The **meaning** of the proposition is determined by the nature of the **external world**. However, **Wittgenstein** claims that these seemingly empirical propositions are actually grammatical. They do not represent the world, but merely give **rules** in accordance with which their constituent words are used. The meaning of a word is determined by the rule. Hence, "I know whether I am in pain" means that "It is meaningless to say that 'I doubt whether I am in pain.'" "Red is a color" means "If something is red, it is colored."

> "'An order orders its own execution'. So it knows its execution, then, even before it is there? – But that was a grammatical proposition and it means: If an order runs 'Do such-and-such' then executing the order is called 'doing such-and-such'." **Wittgenstein,** *Philosophical Investigations*

grammatology

MODERN EUROPEAN PHILOSOPHY [from Greek *gramma*, that which is drawn or written + *logos*, theory, hence a science of writing] **Derrida's** term for a science of writing. Because the Western metaphysical tradition has ranked speech or voice over writing, it is charged by Derrida with **phonologism**. Derrida argues that we should reverse the priority between speech and writing and establish a science of writing, that is, grammatology. His wide definition of writing includes in general all that gives rise to an inscription, such as cinematography and choreography, as well as pictorial, musical, sculptural "writing." Grammatology can accommodate what **Lévi-Strauss** calls general linguistics. According to Derrida, **Hegel's** system is the end of the tradition of phonologism, but it is also the beginning of the era of grammatology. The positive details of grammatology need to be developed further before its implications can be assessed.

> "Science of 'the arbitrariness of the sign', science of the immotivation of the trace, science of writing before speech and in speech, grammatology

would thus cover a vast field within which linguistics would, by abstraction, delineate its own area." **Derrida,** *Of Grammatology*

Gramsci, Antonio (1891–1937)

Italian Marxist political philosopher and theorist of culture, born in Ales. Gramsci offered a less authoritarian and deterministic account of Marxism, in which the hegemony of ruling elites can be preserved when economic conditions for revolution exist by attracting the working class to the moral and cultural values of the elite. Cultural and moral questions and persuasion, rather than economic conditions, therefore become crucial to the possibility of revolutionary success. His main works include *Prison Notebooks* (1929–35) and *Letters from Prison* (1965).

gratitude

ETHICS [from Latin *gratus*, pleasing] A sentimental and thankful **emotion** on the part of the recipient of a favor directed at the benefactor and motivating actions that return some good to that person. The favor received must have proceeded from direct intentional good will on the part of the benefactor, rather than as an unintended consequence, or there is no reason to feel gratitude. The return of the favor is not bound to be a proportionate repayment, and the benefactor has no moral **right** to ask the beneficiary to return it. What counts in gratitude is to reciprocate love with love. It is a natural rather than imposed **desire** to benefit the benefactor and to do the latter a justice. Different philosophers emphasize respectively the elements of **love, beneficence,** and **justice** in the emotion of gratitude.

"Gratefulness or gratitude is the desire or zeal for love by which we endeavour to benefit him who has benefited from a similar emotion of love." **Spinoza,** *Ethics*

great chain of being

METAPHYSICS A term introduced by the American philosopher A. O. Lovejoy, according to which all beings in the world are not equal with regard to their metaphysical or **ontological** status. They are hierarchically ordered, with **absolute being** or **God** at the top and things of the slightest existence at the bottom. There are an infinite number of things with different existential grades between them. Absolute

being is pure **actuality,** whilst at the bottom of the hierarchy are pure **potentialities.** This idea of a great chain of being can be traced to **Plato**'s division of the world into the **Forms,** which are full beings, and sensible things, which are imitations of the Forms and are both being and not being. **Aristotle**'s **teleology** recognized a perfect being, and he also arranges all animals by a single natural scale according to the degree of perfection of their souls. The idea of the great chain of being was fully developed in **Neoplatonism** and in the Middle Ages. Dante's *Divine Comedy* presents a literary illustration of this hierarchy. The notion is connected with the **principle of plenitude,** which claims that every possibility is actualized.

"The result was the conception of the plan and structure of the world . . . the conception of the universe as a 'Great Chain of Being', composed of an immense, or . . . of an infinite number of links ranging in hierarchical order from the meagerest kind of existents (which barely escape non existence), through every possible grade up to the ens perfectissimum." **Lovejoy,** *The Great Chain of Being*

great year

METAPHYSICS Also called the perfect year. On the basis of observation, the ancient Greeks believed that **time** is cyclical, and they extended this idea to claim that the universe has a cyclical renewal. One cycle forms a great year, in which the sun, moon, and planets are all destroyed and begin again after returning together to the same positions that they had occupied at a given previous time. On this view, there is an everlasting repetition of history. This notion pervades Greek philosophy; and some philosophers like **Empedocles** and **Plato** even made the cycle of the **soul**'s incarnations parallel the cycle of the great year. **Heraclitus** claimed that the length of a great year is 10,800 years, but this length varies in different sources. Although rejected by modern astronomy, this idea has been expressed in modern times in the philosophy of **Nietzsche** and **Peirce.**

"And yet there is no difficulty in seeing that the perfect number of time fulfils the perfect [or great] year when all the eight revolutions . . . are accomplished together and attain their completion at the same time." **Plato,** *Timaeus*

greatest happiness principle

ETHICS, POLITICAL PHILOSOPHY A principle providing the central idea of classical **utilitarianism**. It is often considered another name for **Bentham's principle of utility**, although its well-known formulation was provided by **Hutcheson** in 1725. According to this principle, an **action** is moral if it produces the greatest happiness for the greatest numbers of people involved. The greatest happiness involves the maximization of **pleasure** and the minimization of **pain**. Classical utilitarianism derives from this principle the meaning of key moral terms, such as **good**, **right**, and **duty**. As it stands, however, the principle needs explanation because of a problem about the distribution of happiness in a population. An action is not necessarily good if it procures the greatest happiness for the greatest numbers by giving immense happiness to a small group and meager happiness to the rest. Furthermore, there are difficulties about how to measure quantities of happiness.

"The creed which accepts as the foundation of morals 'utility' or the 'greatest happiness principle' holds that actions are right in proportion as they tend to promote happiness; wrong as they tend to produce the reverse of happiness." **Mill**, *Utilitarianism*, **in Robson (ed.)**, *Collected Words*, **vol. X**

great-soulness

ETHICS [from Greek *megalo*, large, great + *psukhia*, soul] Also translated as magnanimity, a **virtue** that **Aristotle** describes in the *Nicomachean Ethics* as a virtue concerning greatness. A person who has a great soul, namely, a magnanimous person, is perfectly virtuous and is the best person. He will not be calculating or suspicious, and he is happy to give benefits but shamed to receive them. He is of a distinguished position and is indifferent to the opinions of his inferiors. He is aware that he is worthy of great things and is indeed worthy of them. He takes a suitable attitude toward honor for his virtues, not discarding it or pursuing it indiscriminately. He cannot have his life determined by others. The deficiency of this virtue is pusillanimousness, and its excess is vanity. Usually this virtue is taken to contrast with the Christian virtue of **humility**.

"Great-soulness seems, even going by the name alone, to be concerned with great things." **Aristotle**, *Nicomachean Ethics*

Green, Thomas Hill (1836–82)

English absolute idealist and political philosopher, born in Birkin, Fellow of Balliol College, Oxford and Professor of Moral Philosophy, University of Oxford. Green was a major expositor and critic of Hume's empiricism and naturalism from the standpoint of an idealism that gives priority to rationally determined relations rather than sense-experience. His liberal political philosophy allows the state to establish conditions in which each individual has maximum freedom consistent with an equal freedom for all others. His main works include *Prologomena to Ethics* (1883).

Grelling's paradox

LOGIC Also called the heterological paradox, formulated by Kurt Grelling in 1908. Some adjectives such as "English" may apply to themselves (for "English" is also an English word), while other adjectives such as "German" do not apply to themselves (for "German" is not a German word). The adjectives in the second group may be called **heterological**. Then is the adjective "heterological" itself heterological or not? If it is, then according to the definition of heterological it does not apply to itself and is not heterological; if it is not, then according to the definition it does apply to itself and is heterological. Grelling's paradox is a prime example of the **semantic paradoxes**. It inspires the distinction between an **object language** and its **metalanguage** and thus had great impact on **Tarski's semantic theory of truth**.

"In view of Grelling's paradox, we know a set which is determined by no sentence of the object language; namely, the set of all sentences of the object languages that do not satisfy themselves." **Quine**, *Philosophy of Logic*

Grice, Herbert Paul (1913–90)

English philosopher of language, metaphysics, and ethics, born in Birmingham, taught at University of Oxford and Professor of Philosophy at University of California, Berkeley. Grice provided an account of meaning and communication that is based on the priority of speaker's meaning to linguistic meaning and provides a major rival to truth-conditional theories of meaning. His distinction between saying and implying, where implying is governed by conventions of conversational implicature, has wide application, from the interpretation of logical connectives to the philosophy of perception, and has influenced understanding of the boundary between semantics and pragmatics. His main works are included in *Studies in the Ways of Words* (1989).

Grosseteste, Robert (c.1170–1253)

English medieval scientist, philosopher, and commentator on Aristotle, born in Suffolk, Chancellor of University of Oxford and Bishop of Lincoln. Grosseteste initiated the serious study of science and the methodology of science in England, commented on newly rediscovered Aristotelian texts, and was influenced by Augustinian Neoplatonism and Jewish and Muslim philosophers. Many of his philosophical views are related to his account of light as the cause of local motion, as the means of the soul acting on the body, and as the source of intelligibility in the universe. His major works include *De Luce* (On Light), *De Motu Corporali et Luce* (Corporal Motion and Light), and *Hexameron*.

Grotius, Hugo (1583–1645)

Dutch philosopher of law and statesman, born in Delft. Grotius was the founder of modern international law through his theory of just war. He argued that war is just in response to one or more wrongs committed by one state against another. Because there is no international agency to force states to right these wrongs, states can justly take the law into their own hands to rectify them. His major work is *On the Law of War and Peace* (1625).

group mind

PHILOSOPHY OF MIND, PHILOSOPHY OF SOCIAL SCIENCE
[French *âme collective*] **Durkheim**'s term for a descriptive property of a society or a group, represented through the statistically average rate of typical social interactions such as birth, marriage, and suicide among its members. Because all individual features are neutralized in such a rate, it cannot be determined by any single individual's **consciousness** or **behavior**. Accordingly, society is not merely a totality of individuals, and the behavior of the group is not determined by the behavior of its members. The group mind is the collective aspect of the **beliefs**, tendencies, and practices of a group that

characterize truly social phenomena. Durkheim held that this collective aspect is a natural consequence of individuals living together. The existence of group mind indicates that society is an organism, and it is a basic condition for sociology to be an independent discipline. It is further inferred that **methodological holism** should be the proper method for analyzing society. Whether there is such a super entity as a group mind and how it might be characterized have been important matters of dispute.

> "The average, then, expresses a certain state of the group mind (*l'âme collective*)." **E. Durkheim**, *The Rules of Sociological Method*

group responsibility, an alternative expression for collective responsibility

grue paradox, another name for the new riddle of induction

Grünbaum, Adolf (1923–)

German-born American philosopher of physics and psychoanalysis, born in Cologne, Professor of Philosophy at the University of Pittsburgh. Grünbaum has made significant contributions to the philosophy of space and time and scientific rationality. He criticized Popper's designation of Freudian theory as unfalsifiable and hence pseudoscience, but argued that the reasoning supporting the claims of psychoanalysis was scientifically flawed and required evidence outside the interaction between analyst and patient. His major works include *Philosophical Problems of Space and Time*, 2nd ed. (1973) and *Foundations of Psychoanalysis: A Philosophical Critique* (1984).

guardians

ANCIENT GREEK PHILOSOPHY, POLITICAL PHILOSOPHY
[Greek *phulakes*] In **Plato**'s *Republic*, initially the army or watch-dogs of the Ideal City, but from 412c the older and wiser rulers, as distinguished from the young ruled or **auxiliaries**. As the top administrators, the guardians were to look after the City as a whole and maintain its operation. Their **virtue** was **wisdom**, and they corresponded to the rational element in the soul. Plato's account of the guardians contained radical features. Women and men could both be guardians and would enjoy equality

in education and public duties. In order to secure the unity of the City, the guardians would not have families and would share their spouses and children. The Ideal City could be realized only if it were ruled by **philosopher-kings**, that is, if philosophers became the rulers or if the present rulers became genuine philosophers. Plato used the term philosopher here in its original sense of a lover of knowledge and not for a professional role. Through their training, the guardians beheld the **Form** of the Ideal City and possessed real **knowledge**. As philosophers, they ruled the City not because of their desire for power, wealth, or influence, but out of **duty**.

"Let us now boldly say that those who are our guardians in the most precise sense must be philosophers." **Plato,** *Republic*

guilt

ETHICS, PHILOSOPHY OF LAW, PHILOSOPHY OF MIND Guilt is the state of violating the legal or moral rules through wrongdoing and upon which **punishment** should be imposed. The absence of guilt is innocence, that is, the condition of moral purity. An innocent person is not culpably responsible for an action. The state of guilt usually arouses the sense of guilt in the agent, although not every guilty person has this feeling. The feeling of guilt results from wrongdoing and leads to the recognition of one's responsibility and to the state of remorse, which is the desire to expiate the wrong done.

A neighboring conception is **shame**, a state of failing to comply with the basic standard of worth or excellence that is endorsed both by oneself and by the public. Shameful states include the exposure of physical indelicacy and of intellectual and moral weakness. Feelings of shame result from defects of one's worth, honor, and integrity, arising from the violation of the sentiment of self-respect and the standard of public esteem. Sometimes guilt and shame overlap, for a sense of guilt generally accompanies a sense of shame. However, what is emphasized in guilt is wrongdoing and **responsibility**, while what is emphasized in shame is shortcoming or defect.

"When we go against our sense of justice we explain our feelings of guilt by reference to the principle of justice." **Rawls,** *A Theory of Justice*

Gyge's ring

ETHICS A story told in **Plato**'s *Republic* in order to illustrate the claim that no one is just willingly, but only under compulsion. If a just man could get away without the bad consequences of doing wrong, he would commit unjust acts. Gyges was a shepherd in the service of a king, who found a ring that made him invisible whenever he turned the hoop inwards. Gyges used this invisibility to do many things and eventually usurped the kingdom. Hence, it was claimed that if a just man came into possession of such a ring, he would use it to do exactly what the unjust man does. On this view, what is really valued is not being just, but only seeming to be just. The whole of the *Republic* is an argument against it, and Plato tried to show that it is not worth being unjust even if one has Gyges' ring.

"We have found that justice in itself is best for the soul itself, and that it must do what is right, whether it has the ring of Gyges or not." **Plato,** *Republic*

gynocentrism, see androcentrism

H

Habermas, Jürgen (1929–)
German political and social philosopher, born in
Düsseldorf, Professor of the History of Philosophy
at University of Frankfurt. Habermas is the leading
contemporary inheritor of the critical social philosophy of the Frankfurt School and its concern for
human emancipation. His conception of knowledge
is based on the rational human pursuit of theoretical, practical, and aesthetic interests, in contrast
to a positivist restriction of knowledge to science.
Knowledge emerges through dialogue in undistorted
speech situations, among speakers with radically
different intellectual commitments who nevertheless understand one another and can reach rational
consensus through argument. He defends a modernist conception of truth and meaning against postmodernist relativism. His major works include
Knowledge and Human Interests (1968), *The Theory of
Communicative Action*, 2 vols. (1981), and *The Philosophical Discourse of Modernity* (1985).

haecceitism, see haecceity

haecceity
METAPHYSICS [from Latin *haec*, this, *haecceitas*, thisness, individual essence] A term introduced by **Duns
Scotus**, much discussed by **Aquinas**, and revived in
contemporary metaphysics. Originally it was used
for an **individual essence** by which a thing is the
individual that it is, and by which one instance of

a **species** is distinguished from other members of
the same species. It was claimed to be the necessary
property which a thing must possess and which
no other thing could possibly have, for example,
Socrates' soul is peculiar to Socrates who possesses
it. A theory that claims the existence of haecceity
is called haecceitism. According to this theory,
individuals within the same species are not merely
numerically different, but each has a unique inner
essence after abstracting from their shared repeatable
properties. A haecceity to an individual corresponds
to a quiddity to a kind or a universal.

> "G is an individual essence (or haecceity) = df G is
> a property which is such that, for every X, X has
> G if and only if X is necessarily such that it has
> G, and it is impossible that there is a Y other than
> X such that Y has G." **Chisholm,** *Person and Object*

hallucination
EPISTEMOLOGY An **experience** that a subject has
about something, but the experienced thing does
not exist. In a typical example, a drunkard "sees"
snakes. Such an experience is private, that is,
available only to the subject. Hallucinations are
common in acute fevers, in madness, and in many
extreme physical and emotional conditions. One
major issue in the analysis of hallucinations is
whether what we apparently perceive exists in any
sense or is nothing at all. Hallucination is different

from **illusion**, where something material is seen but is presented other than it is. The occurrence of hallucination is used by **sense-datum** theorists, who call what is presented in hallucination wild sense-data, to reject **naive realism** and to support the existence of sense-data independent of material things. Hallucinations suggest that what we are aware of directly may have no relation to external things and that what we directly perceive are not material things. A possible objection to this argument allows that hallucination is a type of mental imagery, but rejects the claim that it is a form of perceptual consciousness.

> "I follow the fairly standard practice of using . . . 'hallucination' for cases where nothing material is seen." **Jackson,** *Perception*

Hampshire, Sir Stuart (1914–2004)
English moral philosopher and philosopher of mind, born in Lincolnshire, Professor at University College, London and Princeton University and Warden of Wadham College, Oxford. Hampshire combined humanistic sensibility, analytical power, and systematic ambition in an account of knowledge and morality that recognizes human beings as embodied agents acting in a complex social and physical world. He had a capacity to identify and illuminate real perplexities of moral life. His major works include *Spinoza* (1951), *Thought and Action* (1959), *Freedom of Mind* (1971), and *Morality and Conflict* (1983).

hard cases
PHILOSOPHY OF LAW Cases where established **rules** or laws cannot provide conclusive answers and about which informed people can reasonably disagree. If we view law as a body of rules, hard cases constitute indeterminacy in law or legal gaps. Dworkin therefore claims that we must understand law as comprising more than rules. To solve hard cases, judges must be guided by standards that are not rules, and these non-rule standards are either **principles** that concern the **rights** of individuals or policies that concern social or collective goals. In contrast to the traditional view, which claims that judges should be guided by appeal to policies in settling hard cases, Dworkin argues that the appropriate technique should involve appeal to principles, that is, to the consideration of the abstract

rights of individuals such as **liberty**, **equality**, respect, and **dignity**. According to his rights thesis, judicial reasoning about hard cases takes place against a background of assumptions about rights.

> "If the case at hand is a hard case, when no settled rule dictates a decision either way, then it might seem that a proper decision could be generated by either policy or principle." **Dworkin,** *Taking Rights Seriously*

hard data, see data

Hare, R(ichard) M(ervyn) (1919–2002)
British prescriptivist moral philosopher, born in Backwell, Professor of Moral Philosophy, University of Oxford and Professor, University of Florida at Gainesville. Hare had great influence through his account of rationality of moral judgments as imperatives constrained by Kantian demands of universality and consistency. He supported a sophisticated form of utilitarianism as the moral theory that meets these demands and applied his theoretical position to deal with a wide range of issues in applied ethics. His major works include *The Language of Morals* (1952), *Freedom and Reason* (1963), and *Moral Thinking* (1981).

harm
ETHICS, PHILOSOPHY OF LAW **Plato** in the *Republic* claims that harm is an internal moral defect due to the disharmony of the different elements of the **soul**. Harm is a mental illness for a person to whom we should give pity. Currently, harm generally refers to the external violation of one's interests, that is, some adverse effect caused by another person's wrongdoing. The person who produces harm should be condemned and even punished. To say somebody has been harmed amounts to saying that this person has been wronged or treated unjustly. However, while harm is morally wrong, the justified and deserved **punishment** of wrongdoing is not regarded as harm.

An associate conception is **offense**, which refers to an uncomfortable and resentful mental state arising from the wrongful conduct of someone else. An offense itself does not directly cause the impairment of one's interests, although an offense that leads to adverse effects becomes a harm.

Sometimes the distinction between harm and offense is challenged on the grounds that the unpleasant state of mind is itself a harm.

> "Our full paradigm of (wrongful) harm will include a person who acts on a victim, and the act of harming that produces the setback of the victim's interest." **Feinberg, *Harm to Others***

harm principle
ETHICS A principle proposed by J. S. **Mill** in *On Liberty*, claiming that the individual is sovereign over his mind and body and hence that the only proper ground for limiting his **liberty** is that his act concerns others and causes **harm** to others. This principle is considered to be essential for securing individual liberty against the interference of law. Mill denied that society is entitled to use law to uphold conventional moral standards or to restrict a person's liberty to act in ways that harm no one else. Society often violates the principle on the grounds that the person is not mature enough to realize his own real interests, or that the action, although affecting only himself, is intrinsically wrong. Mill argued that in these cases we may reason with the person or attempt to persuade him, but we have no right to compel him. Mill's position was criticized by Devlin, who proposed instead the thesis of the **enforcement of morals**, that is, that law should enforce publicly accepted standards of private morality.

> "The object of this essay is to assert one very simple principle . . . That principle is, that the sole end for which mankind are warranted, individually or collectively, in interfering with the liberty of action of any of their number, is self-protection. That the only purpose for which power can be rightly exercised over any member of a civilised community, against his will, is to prevent harm to others." **Mill, *On Liberty*, in Robson (ed.), *Collected Works*, vol. XVIII**

Harman, Gilbert (1938–)
American philosopher of mind, ethics, language, and epistemology, born in East Orange, New Jersey, Professor of Philosophy, Princeton University. In accord with his commitment to a scientific account of persons that combines philosophy and cognitive science, Harman's functionalist account of the mind explains the capacity of mental states to represent a language of thought through their role in a physically based functional system. Moral facts are determined by principles of social cooperation that are justified through providing long-term benefit to agents. His work on changes in systems of beliefs, desires, and intentions develops rules of reasoning that are useful for understanding human and artificial intelligence and are independent of logical rules of inference. His major works include *Thought* (1973) and *Change in View: Principles of Reasoning* (1986).

harmony
ANCIENT GREEK PHILOSOPHY, METAPHYSICS [from Greek *harmonie*, derived from the verb *harmozein*, to fit together, also translated as adjustment or concord] The mutual adjustment of different components according to rational principles to form an organic and coherent whole. It is a key word for the **Pythagoreans**, who used it to refer to the musical scale, and analogically to refer to the proportional movements on a cosmic scale of the sun, moon, and fixed stars. When they say that number is the first principle, they mean that all physical things are composed of elements harmonized in a certain ratio. This is the Pythagorean mathematics of harmony. **Heraclitus** also claims that everything is the harmony of the opposites. Ancient Greek medicine took health as a harmony of physical opposites.

> "It is clear that the theory that the movement of the stars produces a harmony . . . is nevertheless untrue." **Aristotle, *De Caelo***

Hart, H(erbert) L(ionel) A(dolphus) (1907–92)
English philosopher of law, born in Harrogate, Professor of Jurisprudence, University of Oxford. Hart's influential account of legal positivism, established through criticism of the legal positivism of Austin and Bentham, conceived the law in terms of primary rules of obligation that are formed in a system through secondary rules of recognition, change, and adjudication. His major works include *Causation in the Law* (with Tony Honoré) (1959), *The Concept of Law* (1961), and *Essays on Bentham: Studies in Jurisprudence and Political Theory* (1982).

Hartley, David (1705–57)

English associationist psychologist, physician, and philosopher, born in Halifax. Under the influence of Newton's theory of vibration, Hartley proposed an associationist theory of the mind based on speculative physiology. His main philosophical work is *Observations on Man, His Frame, His Duty and His Expectations* (1749).

Hartmann, Eduard von (1842–1906)

German pessimistic philosopher and critic of culture, born in Berlin. Hartmann followed Kant and Schopenhauer in his account of the misery of the world and claimed that although this is the best of all possible worlds, it would have been better had the world not existed. In a vitalist and pantheist system, he argues that the unconscious is the grounds of all being and that the world emerges from the unconscious irrational will and the unconscious rational idea. A positive note of pleasure is introduced through the advance of consciousness, but with the full emergence of consciousness the world will cease to exist. Hartmann's dynamic thus leads to annihilation rather than to Hegelian rational fulfillment. His major work is *The Philosophy of the Unconscious* (1869).

Hartmann, Nicolai (1882–1950)

German philosopher of ontology and ethics, born in Riga, Latvia, Professor of Philosophy at Universities of Marburg, Cologne, Berlin, and Göttingen. Hartmann pursued an aporetic method based on the exposition and clarification of antinomies, and argued for the priority of metaphysics over epistemology. His ontology recognizes levels of being, with his account of being concerned with some universal categories as well as with categories that are restricted to a given level. His ethical writings include a phenomenology of the virtues that reflects both Aristotle and Nietzsche. His major works include *Ethics*, 3 vols. (1926) and *New Ways of Ontology* (1940).

Hartshorne, Charles (1897–2000)

American process metaphysician and theologian, born in Kittaning, Pennsylvania, Research Fellow at Harvard University and Professor of Philosophy, University of Texas at Austin. Hartshorne employed Whitehead's scientific process philosophy to discuss questions in theology. He argued that vital feeling, although concentrated in individuals, permeates the universe in an affective continuum. He saw God as including the world but also transcending it. He offered an account of Anselm's ontological argument in terms of modal logic. His major works include *The Divine Relativity* (1947) and *Creative Synthesis and Philosophic Method* (1970).

Hayek, F(riedrich) A(ugust) von (1899–1992)

Austrian-born British economist and political philosopher, born in Vienna, Professor at Universities of London, Chicago, and Freiburg. Hayek argued in favor of the social and economic institutions that emerge from the accumulation of individual decisions within a market and against rational social and economic planning in order to defend the scope of liberty in society. His radical liberalism also opposed state interference to establish a redistributivist social justice. His major works include *The Road to Serfdom* (1944), *The Constitution of Liberty* (1960), *Law, Legislation and Liberty*, 3 vols. (1973–9), and *Economic Freedom* (1991).

health care ethics, see bioethics

heaven

PHILOSOPHY OF SCIENCE, PHILOSOPHY OF RELIGION [Greek *ouranos*] In Hesiod's theogony, an archaic cosmogonical concept. **Aristotle**, in his *On the Heavens* (Greek *Peri Ouranow*, Latin *De Caelo*), distinguishes three senses of heaven: (1) the outermost circumference of the universe; (2) the sky or heaven in general; (3) the universe as a whole, a synonym for *kosmos*. In Christian tradition, heaven is the place reserved for saved sinners after death, in contrast to **hell**, which is reserved for unrepentant sinners, and purgatory, an intermediate place for sinners to expiate sins before going to heaven. On this view, **God** is in heaven, which lies beyond the cosmos.

> "When the Westerner dreams of another world he very often dreams of heaven or purgatory or hell – these are bad dreams." **N. Smart,** *The Philosophy of Religion*

hedonism, ethical

ETHICS [from Greek *hedone*, pleasure] An ethical position which claims that **pleasure** or happiness is the highest or most intrinsic **good** in life, and that people should pursue as much pleasure and as little **pain** as possible. This position was defended by the Greek philosophers **Aristippus** and **Epicurus, Hobbes**, the British empiricists **Locke** and **Hume**, and the **utilitarians**. However, there are significant differences among hedonists concerning the meaning of pleasure. Different understandings yield different varieties of hedonism. Pleasure is in general an unfortunate word, for it is commonly associated with carnal **desires**. But sensual pleasure is not what hedonist philosophers intend. For Epicurus, pleasure was simply the absence of pain. Modern hedonists often include any experience that one enjoys. So thinking, reading, and creation are all included as pleasures. Some hedonists appeal to psychological hedonism in support of their position, for example, Epicurus based his view on the observed phenomenon that all living things are content with pleasure. Other hedonists, such as Locke, argued that hedonism is an analytic truth, for it is the main characteristic of good to be able to cause pleasure. Utilitarianism is the most systematic version of ethical hedonism. The thesis that pleasure and happiness are identical has been criticized since the time of **Socrates** and **Plato**. The difficulties of hedonism include the fact that some pleasures, such as pleasure in the suffering of other people, are intrinsically bad; furthermore, some things, such as medical treatment, are intrinsically good, but not positively pleasant. Since the pleasure in question is one's own pleasure, and pain is one's own pain, hedonism is usually related to **egoism**.

"Ethical hedonism may be, somewhat roughly, defined by the principle that 'x is good' is equivalent to 'x produces pleasure'." **Pap,** *Elements of Analytic Philosophy*

hedonism, paradox of

ETHICS A **paradox** showing that egoistic hedonism as a theory has a self-defeating limit. The more you deliberately pursue the maximization of pleasure, the less you can attain. If you go directly to seek pleasure, you tend to get less pleasure than those who seek pleasure indirectly by studying or making other efforts. The most profound pleasures, such as those obtained from child-raising and professional achievement, can only be obtained as a result of undertaking unpleasant tasks.

"... that a rational method of attaining the end at which it aims requires that we should to some extent put it out of sight and not directly aim at it. I have before spoken of this conclusion as the 'fundamental paradox of Egoistic Hedonism'." **Sidgwick,** *The Methods of Ethics*

hedonism, psychological

PHILOSOPHY OF MIND A psychological position which claims that human **actions** are determined by the **desire** to secure **pleasure** and to avoid **pain**. Everyone acts in order to gain the greatest possible personal satisfaction. There are many forms of this view, which respectively assert that a person is motivated to do A rather than B only because he thinks A is more pleasant to B, only because his thought of A is more attractive, or only because his choice of A is causally correlated with his past enjoyment. Psychological hedonism is the theoretical basis of many forms of **ethical hedonism**. However, the extent the former can support the latter is a matter of dispute, for psychological hedonism only asserts that something is more desirable because it is more pleasant, but never says that people only desire pleasure. In addition to its relation to ethical hedonism, psychological hedonism is also important as a theory of human motivation in psychology.

"Psychological hedonism ... is not a theory concerning the criterion of morality, but concerning the genetic question: what motivates human conduct? The psychological hedonist answers: expectation of pleasure or pains." **Pap,** *Elements of Analytic Philosophy*

hedonistic calculus

ETHICS Also called the utility calculus or felicity calculus, a device for calculating quantities of **pleasure** and **pain**, appealed to by Jeremy **Bentham**. When we need to choose between alternative courses of **action**, we should calculate the amount of pleasure or pain that each action can produce for all the people affected. The right action in the circumstances is the action that can contribute most to the sum of happiness. The criteria which one needs to consider in calculating the amount of pleasure include intensity, duration, certainty (or uncertainty), propinquity (or remoteness), fecundity (their tendency to promote or lead to more pleasure), purity (not mixed up with or followed by unappealing feelings), and extent (the number of persons who are affected by it). Bentham made it clear that he does not expect this process to be strictly pursued before every moral judgment or judicial operation, but these factors should always be kept in view. Bentham also described the implications of the hedonistic calculus on legal reform. However, this calculus is widely criticized because it is hard to compare different types of pleasure, a problem that has led to a reassessment of the nature of pleasure.

> "Bentham devised what is called the 'Hedonistic calculus' for calculating the amount of pleasure or pain that would occur as a result of one's actions."
> **Hospers,** *Human Conduct*

Hegel, Georg Wilhelm Friedrich (1770–1831)

German idealist philosopher, born in Stuttgart, taught at Jena, Heidelberg, and Berlin. Hegel built a speculative system that comprises the whole range of philosophy. The Absolute Spirit or Idea, which he understood as both subject and substance, is a reality underlying the phenomenal world that develops historically through a rationally intelligible succession of forms. In its final phase it reaches absolute knowledge. This development is structured by a triadic dialectical process, at each stage involving the resolution of two opposites (thesis, antithesis) in a higher unity (synthesis). Dialectic constitutes the autonomous self-development of both thought and the world. The world-spirit develops through various historical phases, culminating in the freedom and self-consciousness of humanity. Hegel's major works include *The Phenomenology of Mind* (1807), *The Science of Logic* (1812–16), *Encyclopedia of the Philosophical Sciences* (1817, expanded editions in 1827, 1830, and 1845), including the *Science of Logic*, the *Philosophy of Nature*, and the *Philosophy of Spirit* and *The Philosophy of Right* (1821). In addition, numerous volumes of his lectures on aesthetics, the history of philosophy, history, the philosophy of religion, were posthumously edited and published. Hegel's thinking has deeply influenced Marxism, positivism, neo-Hegelian idealism, and existentialism. His social morality has been revived in contemporary communitarianism. Moore and Russell turned to analytic philosophy through criticism of neo-Hegelianism.

Hegelianism

PHILOSOPHICAL METHOD, METAPHYSICS, AESTHETICS, ETHICS, PHILOSOPHY OF RELIGION, POLITICAL PHILOSOPHY A term for the philosophy of **Hegel** and for the various metaphysical, aesthetic, ethical, religious, and political theories developed by his followers in the spirit of his philosophy. The rich, complex, difficult, and ambivalent nature of Hegel's doctrines has generated divergent and even contradictory schools of Hegelian thought, each representing and developing one-sided interpretations or partial elements of his whole system. Right-wing "Old Hegelians," represented by Karl Göschel and Hermann Hinrishs, emphasized the Christian and conservative elements in Hegel's thought and tried to reconcile them with contemporary political conditions. Left-wing "Young Hegelians" were politically and religiously radical and developed Hegel's humanistic and historical dimensions. Their major representatives included Ludwig **Feuerbach**, Bruno Bauer, and David Friedrich Strauss. Among them, Feuerbach made important contributions to the history of philosophy. **Marx** and Engels were once Young Hegelians. Although Hegel's philosophy fell into neglect in Germany from the middle of the nineteenth century until its revival at the beginning of the twentieth century, it has since stimulated the development of philosophy in various schools, including neo-Marxism and **hermeneutics**. In Denmark Hegelian thought was introduced by J. Heinberg and provoked **Kierkegaard** to oppose Hegel's doctrines. In Britain, Hegelianism was initiated by J. H. Stirling's *The Secret of Hegel* (1865) and developed into absolute idealism, represented by T. H. **Green**, F. H. **Bradley**, Bernard **Bosanquet**, and John **McTaggart**. These philosophers embraced Hegel to challenge **empiricism** and **utilitarianism** in the so-called neo-Hegelian movement. This movement became a target of attack by **Russell, Moore**, and **Popper**. In the United States Hegelianism, represented by William Harris and Josiah **Royce**, had considerable influence on **pragmatism**. In Italy, Hegelianism, represented in liberal and conservative versions by Benedetto **Croce** and Giovanni **Gentile**, became a mainstream of philosophy. In France, Hegelianism was established by Victor Cousin and revived in the twentieth century through the Marxist-existentialist interpretation of Hegel. Currently, the English-speaking world has another wave of interest in Hegel, in part through the development of **communitarian** ethics and the writings of Alasdair **MacIntyre** and Charles **Taylor**.

> "The appropriation of Hegelianism by members of different historical generations living in different political and cultural environments naturally exacerbated existing tensions and produced new conflicts within the Hegelian school. But Hegelians remained convinced that there was an essential core of Hegelianism that they all shared." **Toews,** *Hegelianism*

Hegelians, young

METAPHYSICS, POLITICAL PHILOSOPHY, PHILOSOPHY OF RELIGION A Hegelian philosophical movement that flourished in Germany from 1830 to 1848, with the University of Berlin as its central base. It emerged through criticizing what came to be called the "Old Hegelians" or "right-wing Hegelians," who believed that the **absolute idea** achieved its actual end in Hegel's philosophy. Young Hegelians believed in **reason** as a continually unfolding process and took their task to be its herald. They claimed that philosophization did not end in Hegel and that the reflective **spirit** in its continuing development transcends any fixed system of thought, including Hegel's own. They took a critical attitude toward Hegel and believed that they could overcome or **sublate** Hegel and develop Hegelianism beyond Hegel. Young Hegelians were politically and religiously radical and focused their interest on developing the humanistic and historical dimensions of Hegel's thought. Active Young Hegelians included David Friedrich Strauss, Ludwig **Feuerbach**, Bruno Bauer, Arnold Ruge, Friedrich Engels, Karl **Marx**, Max Stirner, and Karl Schmidt. Marx and Engels quickly developed criticisms of this movement in *The German Ideology*. The Young Hegelian movement receives special attention at present due to interest in the origins of **Marxism**.

> "In sum, the Young Hegelian movement rests upon the belief that Hegelianism did not die with Hegel." **Stepelevich (ed.),** *The Young Hegelians*

hegemony

POLITICAL PHILOSOPHY [from Greek *hegomai*, to lead or command] Domination by force and, hence, a kind of domination by one country over another.

For **Plekhanov** and subsequent Western Marxist writers, hegemony is a form of social and political control that is based more on intellectual, moral, and cultural persuasion or consent than on physical coercion. In this way, the proletarian class can amalgamate all sections of the working class into a greater whole, which has a single unified aim. This sense of hegemony is fully developed by the Italian Marxist philosopher Antonio **Gramsci**. Gramsci took hegemony [Italian *diregere*] to be moral and intellectual leadership that allows a leading group to compromise with various allies who are unified into a whole. Political leadership in a democratic revolution should be based on an alliance with other sections that have similar goals. Gramsci used this concept to analyze all forms of class association, including those within a dominant social group. He even used it to explain the capacity of the bourgeoisie to hold power. For Gramsci, the concept of hegemony was central to Marxist philosophy, which he called the philosophy of **praxis** in his *Prison Notebooks* in order to escape the attention of the prison censor.

> "What we can do, for the moment, is to fix two major superstructural 'levels': the one that can be called 'civil society', that is the ensemble of organisms commonly called 'private', and that of 'political society', or 'the state'. These two levels correspond on the one hand to the function of 'hegemony' which the dominant group exercises throughout society and on the other hand to that of 'directed domination' or command exercised through the state and 'juridical government'." **Gramsci,** *Selections from the Prison Notebooks*

Heidegger, Martin (1889–1976)

German philosopher, born in Messkirch, Baden, studied under Husserl, taught at Marburg and Freiburg. Heidegger developed Husserl's phenomenology and was a central figure in the development of existentialism and hermeneutics. In *Being and Time* (1927), Heidegger sought to understand the meaning of being in general, but addressed this central question through revealing the fundamental features of the being of human beings, which he termed *Dasein* ("being there"). He held that *Dasein* is the only kind of being that can raise the question of being and wonder about itself as existing. Instead of being a thing-with-properties, *Dasein* is being-in-the-world.

One is authentic through living in a self-determining way rather than following the crowd. *Dasein* is historical and temporal, with a life story unfolding between birth and death. Within this context, authenticity, care, dread, finitude, and death become major themes of his philosophy. He intended his philosophical terminology, which he traced to pre-Socratic and German origins, to support a fundamental ontology to replace what he saw as a mistaken metaphysical tradition. Heidegger did not complete his original project. Important works of his later period include *Kant and the Problem of Metaphysics* (1929), "The Origin of the Work of Art" (1950), *An Introduction to Metaphysics* (1953), *What is Called Thinking?* (1954), *On the Way to Language* (1959) and *Nietzsche*, 2 vols. (1961). His accounts of poetry and technology have initiated extensive discussions. Heidegger's brief period as Rector of the University of Freiburg under Hitler and his membership of the Nazi Party raise questions about the relationship between his discredited political allegiance and his philosophical views. He was, nevertheless, one of the most original and influential philosophers of the twentieth century.

hell

PHILOSOPHY OF RELIGION In Christian doctrine, the place a person is sent after death if judged by **God** to be an unrepentant sinner. There the person will be cut off from the vision of God and will suffer all sorts of physical pain. Hell is described in the imaginative language of fire and brimstone and of weeping and gnashing of teeth. It is in contrast to **heaven**, which is reserved after death for persons judged by God to be worthy of **salvation**. The notion of hell warns people to behave well during their lives, but its existence is thought by many to be incompatible with God's goodness. Hence the problem of hell becomes a version of the problem of **evil**: how we can explain the evil of hell if God is **omnipotent**, **omniscient**, and perfectly **good**.

> "According to the standard tradition, being in hell is the worst thing that could ever happen to anyone." **Kvanvig,** *The Problem of Hell*

Hellenistic philosophy

ANCIENT GREEK PHILOSOPHY, LOGIC, ETHICS, PHILOSOPHY OF SCIENCE Hellenistic is a chronological term for the period dating from the death of Alexander the Great in 323 BC to the end of the Roman Republic in 31 BC. Hellenistic philosophy was the development of post-Aristotelian philosophy in a period that ended with the revival of interest in **Plato** and **Aristotle** in the first century BC, roughly corresponding to the political period. Its main philosophical trends were Stoicism, founded by **Zeno of Citium**, **Epicureanism**, founded by **Epicurus**, and **Skepticism**, founded by **Pyrrho**. Philosophy in this period narrowed its scope to logic, ethics, and philosophy of nature, and Hellenistic philosophy contributed significantly in each of these areas. Traditionally, Hellenistic philosophy has been thought to concentrate on ethics and to lack originality, but much recent scholarship has given a more positive account of its wide-ranging philosophical achievements.

> "These [Stoicism, Scepticism and Epicureanism] are the movements of thought which define the main line of philosophy in the Hellenistic world, and 'Hellenistic philosophy' is the expression I use . . . to refer to them collectively." **A. A. Long,** *Hellenistic Philosophy*

Heloise complex

PHILOSOPHICAL METHOD The French philosopher and writer Heloise was seduced and later betrayed by her private tutor, the scholastic philosopher Peter **Abelard**. Nevertheless, Heloise retained a strong passion for Abelard and wrote books and letters addressed to him. According to Michèle **Le Doeuff**, in the Heloise complex feminists tend to give priority to a male exponent of feminism or to a male philosopher whose ideas have been borrowed to justify feminist claims. As a result, we have, for example, Lacanian feminism or Foucaultian feminism. This tendency generally treats the philosophy of the male master as complete in itself and requiring no more than application to issues concerning women. Le Doeuff claims that the tendency contradicts the spirit of feminism and undermines the independence of feminist thinking about issues concerning women.

> "Since the days of antiquity, women have been admitted into the field of philosophy chiefly when they took on the role of the loving admirer: we can call this the 'Heloise Complex'." **Le Doeuff,** *Hipparchia's Choice*

Helvétius, Claude-Adrien (1715–71)

French Enlightenment philosopher, one of the leading encyclopedists, born in Paris. Helvétius argued that all men were originally equal and explained their later differences in terms of education and environment. His hedonist view that the desire to gain pleasure and avoid pain is the ultimate motive of all human actions influenced British utilitarians. His psychology claimed that sensation is the source of all intellectual activity. His views were presented in the *De l'esprit; or, Essays on the Mind and its Several Faculties* (1759) and developed in the *De L'homme* (On Man) (1772).

Hempel, Carl Gustav (1905–97)

German-American philosopher of science, born in Orianenberg, Germany, and moved to the United States in the 1930s. Hempel's covering law model of explanation, also called the deductive-nomological model, held that a statement is explained if and only if it can be deduced from a law-like generalization. His ravens paradox, also called Hempel's paradox or the paradox of confirmation, shows the incompatibility of three highly plausible principles of confirmation. His major works include *Aspects of Scientific Explanation* (1965) and *Philosophy of Natural Science* (1966).

Hempel's paradox

LOGIC, PHILOSOPHY OF SCIENCE Also called the ravens paradox or paradox of **confirmation**, a paradox concerning the nature of confirmation. There are three principles in the background of this paradox. First, **Nicod's criterion**, put forward by the French philosopher Jean Nicod (1893–1924), holds that for a generalization "All As are Bs," an instance of an A being B provides confirming **evidence**, and instances of something that is neither A nor B are irrelevant to it. Secondly, the equivalence principle holds that if a piece of evidence confirms a generalization G_1, it also constitutes confirming evidence for any generalization G_2 which is logically equivalent to G_1. Thirdly, a principle of deductive logic holds that "All As are Bs" is equivalent to "All non-Bs are non-As."

Hempel discovered that, whilst all these principles are valid separately, a **paradox** arises if they are taken together. Take the generalization "All ravens are black." According to the third principle,

it is equivalent to the generalization "All non-black things are non-ravens." Instances of non-black things include such items as white shoes and green leaves. According to Nicod's principle, white shoes and green leaves are among the confirming instances that provide evidence for the generalization "All non-black things are not-ravens," but are irrelevant to the generalization "All ravens are black." But according to the second principle, since these two generalizations are logically equivalent, white shoes and green leaves are paradoxically confirming instances that provide evidence for the generalization "All ravens are black." There are various attempts to find a solution, but none of them has achieved general approval.

> "Hempel's paradoxes of confirmation . . . are generated by the fact that three highly plausible principles of confirmation prove incompatible." **Swinburne, *An Introduction to Confirmation Theory***

henological argument

PHILOSOPHY OF RELIGION [from Greek *hen*, one] A type of theistic argument for the existence of **God** with a form resembling the fourth of **Aquinas' five ways**. From observations that there are various degrees of **goodness**, perfection, **truth**, and **reality** in the world, the argument infers that there must be one being which represents the highest degree of all these positive attributes as their full realization. This being is the best, most perfect, truest, and most real being and is God. If positive attributes can exist in different degrees without being realized in one being at the highest level or if there is no such highest level, the argument fails.

> "The henological argument is so called because in it we reason from multiplicity to unity (*hen*): from goodness, truth, reality in the various forms in which experience makes them known to us, to a Being who is the Good, the True, the Real." **Joyce, *Principles of Natural Theology***

henotheism

PHILOSOPHY OF RELIGION [from Greek *hen*, one + *theos*, god] Max Müller's term for a doctrine that allows many gods to exist, while claiming that one **God** is their supreme ruler who deserves their loyalty and obedience. It is a compromise between **polytheism**, the belief that many gods exist, and monotheism, the belief that there is only one God. Some religious philosophers consider henotheism to be an intermediate phase in the development from polytheism to monotheism.

> "Henotheism is the recognition of one God for purposes of devotion and worship without denying the existence of other Divine beings." **Taliaferro, in Bunnin and Tsui-James (eds.),** *The Blackwell Companion to Philosophy*

Heraclitus (*c.*540–475 BC)

Pre-Socratic philosopher, born in Ephesus. Only fragments of his book *On Nature* survive. Heraclitus claimed that the matter underlying natural phenomena is fire and that because everything is in flux, one cannot step into the same river twice. The changes occurring in fire, however, are not random, and *logos* is the single unchanging law governing the cosmic process of the changing universe. He held that the apparent unity and stability of the world are based on restless strife and war between opposites. Heraclitus critically examined the limits of sense-perception and attended to the role of language in philosophy. He was called by his contemporaries "the obscure," probably because of the abstract nature of his thinking.

Herder, Johann Gottfried (1744–1803)

German philosopher of language and of history, born in Mohrungen, senior church administrator of the Lutheran clergy in Weimar. Herder argued for the inseparability of language and thought and for an historical understanding and assessment of diverse cultures, with their different traditions and customs, as progressive embodiments of humanity. He criticized the rational universalism of the Enlightenment for ignoring the different possibilities of human fulfillment within these diverse cultures. His major works include *Treatise upon the Origin of Language* (1772) and *Outlines of a Philosophy of the History of Man* (1784–91).

heresy

PHILOSOPHY OF RELIGION [from Greek *hairein*, taking of something, later the taking or holding of an opinion] In ancient times, any school, whether the **Peripatetics**, Academics, **Epicureans**, or Stoics, was considered as a heresy. Hence, heresy was originally not a term of abuse. A heretic was a person who teaches his own view. Christianity at the very beginning also considered itself a heresy, but when it gained dominance, it used the term for any view that does not conform to orthodox Christian teaching or for any sect whose interpretation of the Bible was different from the official interpretation of the Church. The Church determined which beliefs were a heresy and, hence, who should be punished. Many heretics were burned in the Middle Age. Similar patterns of heresy, intolerance, and expulsion can arise in secular fields, especially where authority is more important than reason in resolving disputes about doctrine.

> "Heresy is a separation made in ecclesiastical communion between men of the same religion, for some opinions no way contained in the rule itself." **Locke,** *A Letter Concerning Toleration*

hermeneutic circle

MODERN EUROPEAN PHILOSOPHY, PHILOSOPHICAL METHOD, PHILOSOPHY OF RELIGION, PHILOSOPHY OF HISTORY, PHILOSOPHY OF SOCIAL SCIENCE A notion introduced by **Schleiermacher**, originally referring to the relation of the whole and the part in **interpretation**. The parts cannot be interpreted without an understanding of the whole, but the whole cannot be understood without an interpretation of the parts.

When **Heidegger** radically reinterpreted "**understanding**" from a species of human **cognition** to the primordial mode of *Dasein*'s being, the hermeneutic circle became the principal method for his fundamental **ontology**. Starting from our traditional understanding of **Being**, we assume that the analysis of *Dasein* serves as a basis for the understanding of Being. Thus, we have a pre-understanding of Being, derived from the practices and language of our culture. This characterization is still incomplete and serves only to guide further investigation. We then proceed to analyze all of *Dasein*'s characters of Being, the existentialia, and eventually reach a more primordial **horizon** for the understanding of Being. This investigation moves in a circle, but it is not a vicious one. Through it, philosophy makes explicit something that is implicitly known in life. Fundamental ontology is hence a back-and-forth movement between a pre-understanding of Being and the uncovering of the structural features of *Dasein*. Because both inquiry and **justification** are contextualized by a pre-understanding rooted in **tradition** and **culture**, the hermeneutic circle becomes a fundamental feature of all human activities. This idea is further developed by **Gadamer**. For him, the hermeneutic circle for human studies is similar to the *ad hoc* revision of **hypotheses** in the natural sciences. Human studies are caught up in this circle, for there are no **axioms** or self-evident truths upon which we can make linear progress in understanding. In proposing a basic role for the hermeneutic circle, Gadamer resists the application of **the hypothetico-deductive method** to human studies.

> "The [hermeneutic] circle, then, is not formal in nature, it is neither subjective nor objective, but describes understanding as the interplay of the movement of tradition and the movement of the interpreter." **Gadamer,** *Truth and Method*

hermeneutic phenomenology, see phenomenology

hermeneutics

PHILOSOPHICAL METHOD, PHILOSOPHY OF RELIGION, PHILOSOPHY OF HISTORY, PHILOSOPHY OF SOCIAL SCIENCE [from Greek *Hermeneia*, the god who conveys the messages of Zeus, thus associating hermeneutics with the problem of understanding and interpretation] Hermeneutics started as a methodology of **interpretation**, based by **Schleiermacher** on his own experience in studying **Plato** and the New Testament. Besides grammatical understanding, which concerns the written text, he claimed that we should seek a psychological understanding to uncover the living principles or ideas in the mind of the author of a text. **Dilthey** further developed hermeneutics as a methodology aiming to recreate an author's original process of creation and to provide grounds for **objectivity** in the human sciences, in contrast to the grounds for objectivity in the natural sciences.

Traditional hermeneutics in Schleiermacher and Dilthey took **understanding** to be a subspecies of knowing and took hermeneutics itself to be a technique rather than being philosophy. In contrast, **Heidegger** considered understanding to be a central mode of human existence, the projection of the possibilities of *Dasein* tied to the world. For him, hermeneutics should deal with human existence as "text-analogous," that is, as a meaningful text for which we uncover its underlying **meaning**. In this way hermeneutics becomes philosophy itself. The **hermeneutic circle** becomes involved in explaining *Dasein*'s being rather than in explicating literary texts.

Gadamer, on the basis of Heidegger's notion of understanding, developed a general hermeneutics that he called "philosophical hermeneutics." He claimed that understanding is not a methodological problem and does not aim to formulate a set of interpretative rules. Rather, understanding is the basic feature of human existence. Hence, hermeneutics is **ontological** rather than methodological and should seek to reveal the fundamental conditions that underlie the phenomenon of understanding in all its modes. The object of human sciences is part of our heritage. It is part of the **effective history** to which we already belong and it orients our normal understanding. It is irrelevant to demand objectivity in the human sciences, because all understanding must be prejudiced and is not purely objective. No interpretation can be final. Understanding is a constant play between the interpreters and the text.

Other major figures in hermeneutics include Emilio Berti and Paul **Ricoeur**. The emphasis on the contextuality of human knowing has influenced the work of Ronald **Dworkin**, Charles **Taylor**, Alasdair **MacIntyre**, and Richard **Rorty**.

> "The hermeneutics developed here is not, therefore, a methodology of the human sciences, but an attempt to understand what the human sciences truly are, beyond their methodological self-consciousness, and what connects them with the totality of our experience of world." **Gadamer,** *Truth and Method*

Herzen, Alexander (1812–70)

Russian social philosopher, emigrated to London. Herzen was a radical Westernizer who opposed Russian autocracy and defended individual liberty, yet combined the demand to see oneself as free with a physiological determinism. His philosophy of history focused on the contingency of human affairs and opposed Hegelian teleological rational interpretation of historical developments. He supported moral relativism and an account of moral judgments as changeable preferences. His major works include *From the Other Shore* (1850).

heterological paradox, another name for Grelling's paradox

heteronomy

ETHICS, POLITICAL PHILOSOPHY [from Greek *hetero*, other + *nomos*, law] Being bound by the legislating of other **agents**, not of oneself. A mode of **action** in which **reason** acts under a law that it has not prescribed. In ethics, a heteronomous **will** is controlled by an external cause or interest. In contrast, an autonomous will is free and decides actions itself. **Kant** considered most traditional moral theories to be based on heteronomous moral **principles**, whose validity depends upon the interests that we hold rather than being imposed by reason. They contain **hypothetical imperatives**, while Kant's own principle of autonomy is a **categorical imperative**. A person is heteronomous if his actions are determined by the **passions** or inclinations rather than by reason. A will is heteronomous if it follows the guide of **desire**.

> "If the will seeks the law that is to determine it anywhere but in the fitness of its maxims for its own legislation of universal laws, and if it thus goes outside of itself and seeks this law in the character of any of its objects, then heteronomy always results." **Kant, *Groundwork for the Metaphysics of Morals***

heuristic

EPISTEMOLOGY, PHILOSOPHY OF SCIENCE, LOGIC [from Greek *heuriskein*, to find out, to discover] An experimental process of discovery, which is conducive to an investigation or to understanding without the use of **algorithms**. A heuristic act requires originality and invention. In this sense, it contrasts with the process of mere routine application of established knowledge or to a teacher demonstrating the established results of the sciences. In modern **logic**, a heuristic procedure aims at problem solving, but offers no guarantee of providing a proof. In this sense, heuristic contrasts with proof. In education theory, a heuristic method trains students to find problems and solutions for themselves.

> "Intellectual acts of a heuristic kind make an addition to knowledge and are in this sense irreversible, while the ensuing routine performances operate within an existing framework of knowledge and are to this extent reversible." **Polanyi, *Personal Knowledge***

Hick, John (1922–)

English philosopher of religion, born in Scarborough, Professor, University of Birmingham and Claremont Graduate School. Hick has written on a wide range of issues in the philosophy of religion. He justifies the compatibility of evil and a loving God through the importance of our response to evil for the development of the soul. He accepts religious pluralism in terms of the diversity of human cultural renderings of a single transcendent noumenal reality. His major works include *Faith and Knowledge* (1957), *Evil and the God of Love* (1966), *Philosophy of Religion* (1966), and *An Interpretation of Religion* (1989).

highest good, English translation of *summun bonum*

Hilbert, David (1862–1943)

German formalist mathematician, born in Königsberg, Professor at the University of Göttingen. Hilbert proposed a formalist account of mathematics in which the complete and consistent axiomatic development of a mathematical calculus bypassed questions about the existence and nature of mathematical objects that were raised by Platonism and intuitionism. Although Gödel showed that the formalist program to provide a finitist proof of the consistency of an infinite arithmetic calculus is impossible to accomplish, Hilbert's approach to the metamathematical assessment of mathematical systems remains important. His major works include *Foundations of Geometry* (1899) and *Principles of Mathematical Logic*, 3rd ed. (with W. Ackermann) (1949).

Hintikka, Jaakko (1929–)

Finnish philosophical logician and epistemologist, born in Vantaa, Professor of Philosophy at University of Helsinki, the Academy of Finland, Florida State University, Stanford University, and Boston University. Hintikka is a principal developer of game theoretical semantics and the interrogative theory of enquiry. He has contributed to studies of the foundations of mathematics and logical theory, including the logic of knowledge and belief. His main works include *Knowledge and Belief* (1962).

historical determinism

PHILOSOPHY OF HISTORY, PHILOSOPHY OF SOCIAL SCIENCE The position that a fundamental factor is or must be responsible for the happening of all historical events. Events are determined by this factor and are functions of it. Because it is determined in this way, history develops according to objective historical **laws** and has an inevitable tendency or fixed direction. There are various versions of historical determinism, depending on what is regarded as filling the role of the fundamental factor. Historical determinists use their theory to make factual statements about actual historical events and tend to predict future developments on the basis of what they see as historical laws. For this reason, historical determinism is sometimes regarded as another name for speculative philosophy of history. Philosophers have challenged the claim that there must be an underlying factor and that there can be such a factor. Every proposal for the determining factor in history has attracted critical examination.

> "The advocates of such a [historical] determinism may fix on geography, climate, race, religion, philosophy, or the material conditions of life and may argue that one such variance is fundamental, that all the other variables of history are functions of it." **White,** *Foundations of Historical Knowledge*

historical explanation

PHILOSOPHY OF HISTORY The task of historians is to explain what happened in the past. When they claim to provide **understanding**, what is the form of their explanation and what is its character and nature? Philosophers are generally divided over this issue. Some believe that historical explanation is an application of a paradigm of scientific explanation, especially Carl **Hempel**'s **covering law model** or the **deductive-nomological model**. On this view, to explain a particular event is to bring it under some general causal law as an instance of that law. Accordingly, explaining an historical event is to subsume it under the general regularity to which it belongs. Because well-established causal laws are rarely found in history, Hempel concedes that historical explanations are **explanation**

sketches, that is, vague and incomplete preliminary accounts leading to fully supported explanations like those in science. New insights into the nature of science might lead to altered versions of Hempel's original argument using different **paradigms** of scientific explanation.

Other philosophers argue that explanations in history and science are distinct on the grounds that they address different subject-matters. While science is concerned with the general and universal in seeking to explain the regularities of the mechanical physical world, history deals with unique, spatio-temporally bounded, particular **events**. Historical events are made by human beings, and each individual human being has **beliefs**, **desires**, **motives**, and **intentions** that cannot be generalized. They argue that the covering law model is not applicable in history. As an alternative, R. G. **Collingwood** and William **Dray** developed a **rational explanation** model, according to which historical understanding requires historians to establish the relation between a particular historical event and the **reasons** for agents to cause that event.

Disputes over historical explanation sometimes turn to the examination of concrete examples to explore the strengths and weaknesses of rival approaches.

> "The term historical explanation is not as clear as one would like, and a brief cautionary note seems called for accordingly. For what I intend to discuss under this heading is only one of the main types of historical explanation, that whereby we explain actions by referring deeds to the 'thoughts' of individual agents (to their purposes, situation-conceptions, means/ends beliefs, and so on)." **R. Martin,** *Historical Explanation*

historical knowledge

PHILOSOPHY OF HISTORY, EPISTEMOLOGY Knowledge about the **past**, but derived from present **evidence**. It is often characterized as knowledge giving insight into particular past **events**, in contrast to scientific knowledge, which is concerned with discovering general **laws** applicable to the past, present, and future. Many philosophical problems arise concerning historical knowledge. Is there a real past beyond current experience that can determine the truth and falsity of historical statements? Some philosophers hold that there must be, for the existence of a real past is the best explanation of the present, but **Russell** questioned this claim. Even if there is a real past, many disputes concern the possibility of justifying our claims to have **knowledge** about it, partly because direct current experience of the past is apparently not available. Also, explanations proposed by historians seem to be inevitably subject to their own principles, beliefs, and sympathies, which can distort their claims. Historical accounts retain value for us even if they are conflicting or are shown to be mistaken, possibly because some aspects of historical knowledge are carried by features other than factual accuracy. Some philosophers are more inclined to characterize the main features of historical knowledge than to discuss skeptical questions about its possibility.

"Historical knowledge is the knowledge of what mind has done in the past, and at the same time it is the redoing of this, the perpetuation of past acts in the present." **Dilthey**, *The Construction of the Historical World in the Human Studies*

historical materialism

METAPHYSICS, PHILOSOPHY OF HISTORY, PHILOSOPHY OF SOCIAL SCIENCE The theory about human society and history proposed by **Marx** and Engels and developed by their followers. It is a model for **historical explanation**, based on **dialectical materialism**. A systematic exposition of this theory is not provided by its founders, but a framework is offered by Marx in *A Preface to The Critique of Political Economy* (1859). The theory holds that social being determines social consciousness. Human history is a developmental process of labor. The **forces of production**, by which humans obtain the material means of existence, are the real foundation of history. Humans, who enter into the **relations of production** in labor, are divided into different economical classes according to their place in these relations. The forces of production and the relations of production form the economical structure of a society, which determine the **superstructure**, including the social and political superstructure and the ideological superstructure. To understand features of the superstructure such as religion, philosophy, literature, or law, we must look to the productive or economic structure of society. When the forces of production develop to

a certain extent, they come into conflict with the existing relations of production, and the latter become a fetter constraining the further development of the former. Such conflicts lead to a period of social revolution, and **contradictions** between the forces and relations of production are solved by class struggle. This struggle will result in a new society, in which the relations of production correspond to the productive forces and the superstructure corresponds to the economical structure. According to orthodox interpretations, the development of human society will go through five phases: primitive, slave, and feudal society, and capitalism and communism. Each new stage is formed by overcoming the internal contradictions between the forces and relations of production in the previous stage. Historical materialism predicts that capitalism will eventually be replaced by an ideal communism, of which socialism is the preliminary stage.

Some critics question whether there can be any single explanatory scheme for historical development and others, on theoretical or empirical grounds, question the pattern of explanation offered by historical materialism. Within Marxism, many of the main features of historical materialism have been reassessed.

"I hope, even British respectability will not be overshocked if I use, in English as well as in so many other languages, the term, 'historical materialism', to designate that view of the course of history which seeks the ultimate cause and the great moving power of all important historic events in the economic development of society, in the consequent division of society into distinct classes, and in the struggles of these classes against one another." **Engels**, *Socialism: Utopian and Scientific*

historical objectivism, see historical relativism

historical relativism

PHILOSOPHY OF HISTORY, EPISTEMOLOGY The claim that **historical explanation** cannot be objective on the model of scientific explanation, which is based on a methodology of **theory**, **observation**, and experiment. Some philosophers agree that history does not have scientific objectivity, but claim that history and other subjects have their own appropriate notions of **objectivity**, while others explore the implications of the claim that historical explanation cannot be objective. Historians draw conclusions from documentation, but historical records may be neither faithful nor complete. In analyzing historical documentation, a historian is not a perfectly neutral investigator, but is equipped with an array of **horizons**, biases, and **prejudices** that can limit or distort historical work and also make it possible. For this reason, different historians may reach remarkably different conclusions from the same material. Historical knowledge apparently must be relative to the minds of different historians or to the wider factors that shape their minds. Unless we have reason to believe that some factors are more likely to produce truth than others, we can clarify the patterns of **relativity**, but we cannot choose among historical **interpretations** based on them. In contrast to historical relativism, historical objectivism claims that historical knowledge can provide an exact reconstruction of what really happened in the past, and historical **skepticism** denies the possibility of historical knowledge at all. These different attitudes toward historical knowledge lead to different attitudes toward the reality of the past and the nature of history. For objectivism, the past is what actually happened independent of our minds. For skepticism, we cannot justify the claim that such a past exists. For relativism, the past comprises the often conflicting constructions of historians on the basis of evidence.

"Now the fact that every historical work, like any intellectual endeavour, is limited by psychological and sociological conditions (to mention only two) is indisputable. The radical novelty in historical relativism lies in the fact that it claims that the truth of the work, its meaning and validity, can only be grasped by referring its content to these conditions." **Mandelbaum**, *The Problem of Historical Knowledge*

historical sentence

PHILOSOPHY OF HISTORY, METAPHYSICS, EPISTEMOLOGY A sentence that describes what happened in the **past**. It is the main type of sentence that historians employ in their writing. The subject of a historical sentence can either be an individual historical agent, such as Napoleon or Alexander, or a social entity, such as a class, group, religious organization, social movement, or political party. Why individual human beings and social entities can both be subjects of historical sentences and how they are related to one another are contested matters. They are central to the debate between **methodological individualism** and **methodological collectivism**, but they also enter disputes between **individualism** and **holism** at epistemological and metaphysical levels. Because historical sentences are based on **memory** and **evidence** rather than on current **observation**, their reliability is a main issue debated by supporters of historical objectivism, **historical relativism**, and historical skepticism.

"By historical sentence I shall mean: a sentence which states some fact about the past." **Danto**, *Analytical Philosophy of History*

historical skepticism, see historical relativism

historicality, see historicity

historicism

PHILOSOPHY OF HISTORY, PHILOSOPHY OF SOCIAL SCIENCE, METAPHYSICS, PHILOSOPHICAL METHOD In one use, the view that the nature of a thing can be understood only by tracing its position and role in the context of historical development. In continental philosophy, the term has metaphysical as well as methodological significance. Historical development is viewed as objectively necessary and governed by its own laws. For **Hegel**, this objective process is the self-development of the world **spirit** or absolute **self**. This view is also shared by Italian philosophers **Vico** and **Croce**. For **Marx** this process is purely objective and independent of human agency. This continental notion of historicism leads to the claim that the historical approach is distinct from the naturalistic approach. It is this notion that Karl **Popper** has in mind when he attacks historicism in his *The Open Society and its Enemies* and *The Poverty of Historicism*.

Analytical philosophy of history generally confines historicism to its methodological usage, claiming that an adequate **explanation** and evaluation must be historical. Many philosophers also believe that historical development can only be assessed relative to our outlooks or conceptual frameworks, and that these are historical in themselves. Consequently, any ahistorical and objective standpoint in evaluating human history is impossible. There is some dispute over how to distinguish historicity in this sense from **relativism**. This sense is close to what Popper calls "historism," that is, explaining the differences between various sociological doctrines and schools by referring to their connection with the predilections and interests prevailing in a particular historical period.

A further sense of "historicism" refers to the attitude which requires that inquiry concerning historical events must be purely historical, that is, not influenced by our current principles or beliefs. But there is little evidence for the practical possibility of this approach.

> "In strong opposition to methodological naturalism in the field of sociology, historicism claims that some of the characteristic methods of physics cannot be applied to the social sciences, owing to the profound differences between sociology and physics." **Popper, *The Poverty of Historicism***

historicity

MODERN EUROPEAN PHILOSOPHY [German *Geschichtlichkeit* or *Historizität*, also translated as historicality, a term in the phenomenological tradition denoting the feature of our human situation by which we are located in specific concrete temporal and historical circumstances] For **Dilthey**, historicity identifies human beings as unique and **concrete** historical beings. According to **Jaspers**, it involves an essential characteristic of everything that is concrete and not **universal** and represents a synthesis of **freedom** and **necessity**. For **Heidegger**, historicity has two senses. First, *Dasein* must be understood as contextualized by the stream of concrete events of world history. The second and more fundamental sense is based on Heidegger's claim that *Dasein* is not an **object**, but a life history, a happening, an unfolding between birth and death and a flowing outward into the future and backward into the past. Hence historicity is defined by Heidegger in terms of temporalization or structure of **temporality**. It denotes *Dasein's* way of taking up the possibilities of the past by projecting itself onto its ownmost possibility of being-as-whole. The human past is constitutive of the **self** and its future possibilities. Heidegger

himself saw difficulties in the harmonization of these two senses.

> "Authentic Being-towards-death – that is to say, the finitude of temporality – is the hidden basis of *Dasein's* historicality." **Heidegger, *Being and Time***

historism, see historicism

Hobbes, Thomas (1588–1679)

English philosopher, political theorist, and classicist, born in Malmesbury, Wiltshire. Hobbes is best known for his theory of human nature and his theory of the social contract. He held that man is ruled by self-interest and that the condition of human existence in the state of nature is, or is liable to become, a "war of every man, against every man." In order to overcome the dangers of this nasty and brutish state, men contract to surrender the right of aggression to a sovereign, whose overwhelming power allows the establishment and maintenance of peaceful order. Metaphysically, Hobbes held that all reality is corporeal. The world is a mechanistic system, composed ultimately of matter in motion, and all change, including human action, is explicable in mechanical and materialist terms. He was a nominalist in philosophy of language and an empiricist in epistemology. His magnum opus is *Leviathan* (1651), and other important works include *De Cive* (completed in 1641, but not published until 1647), *Human Nature, or the Fundamental Elements of Policy* (1650), *De Corpore* (1655), *Questions Concerning Liberty, Necessity, and Chance* (1656), and *De Homine* (1658).

Hocking, William Ernest (1873–1966)

American idealist philosopher of religion, born in Cleveland, Ohio, Professor of Philosophy, Harvard University. Hocking drew on pragmatism, idealism, and process philosophy in his philosophy of religion and argued for the importance of religion as the basis of morality and politics. His main works include *The Meaning of God in Human Experience* (1912) and *Human Nature and Its Remaking* (1923).

Holbach, Paul-Henri D' (Baron) (1723–89)

French materialist philosopher, born in Edesheim, Germany, a major contributor to the Encyclopédie. Holbach's most influential book, *The System of Nature* (1770), presents a system of atheistic materialism.

He held that the world is a machine governed by fixed laws of motion. All is necessity, and there is no chance in nature. Man is a product of nature, and because there is no mind independent of nature, free will is an illusion. In *Christianity Unveiled* (1756) and *Common Senses* (1772), Holbach attacked Christianity as a superstition. "God" is a meaningless term that is fabricated by the priests to dominate the populace. In the *Social System* (1773), *Natural Politics* (1774), and *Universal Morality* (1776), he attacked the state church and absolute monarchy and attempted to show that atheism and a virtuous life are fully compatible. To avoid punishment, his works were initially published in Holland anonymously.

holism

METAPHYSICS, EPISTEMOLOGY, PHILOSOPHY OF SCIENCE, PHILOSOPHY OF SOCIAL SCIENCE, PHILOSOPHY OF LANGUAGE The view that wholes have some metaphysical, epistemic, or explanatory priority over the elements, members, individuals, or parts composing them. A whole cannot be reduced to its parts. A part cannot be understood apart from the whole to which it belongs. Knowledge of the whole is not the simple aggregation of knowledge of its parts. Epistemological holism in the philosophy of science (the **Duhem–Quine thesis**) and semantic holism in the philosophy of language propose that the **meaning** and **truth** of our claims cannot be assessed one by one, but must be assessed as part of **theories**, bodies of theory, or everything we believe about the world. In the social sciences, **methodological holism**, in contrast to **methodological individualism**, claims that **individuals** can be understood only in terms of the practices or institutions in which they take part. It is a rival to some aspects of individualism, which seek to reduce statements about groups, institutions, and culture to statements about certain of their components. Metaphysical holism claims that wholes are distinct **entities**, whose existence cannot be reduced to that of the items composing them. On some views these wholes are prior to their parts, but on others they emerge from the interaction between parts.

"Holism blurs the supposed contrast between the synthetic sentence, with its empirical content, and the analytic sentence, with its null content." **Quine,** *Theories and Things*

holistic property, see anatomic property

holy

PHILOSOPHY OF RELIGION, ETHICS In the broad sense, anything that people worship. The holy is a religious quality that is distinguished from the ordinary by virtue of its mighty power. Human experience of the holy is parallel to the aesthetic experience of the **sublime**. Before Christianity, gods were not considered to be naturally friendly and hence the holy is associated with supernatural, unpredictable, fearful, or threatening power. The **God** of Christianity is **omnipotent** but also morally perfect. Although the holy is still associated with awesomeness, God, as a holy object, is the primary source of **beauty**, **love**, and moral reverence. The holy is thus used as a synonym of the sacred. The Bible refers to itself as holy books, and theology calls the Old and New Testaments the Holy Scriptures. The Trinity consists of the Holy Father, the Holy Son, and the Holy Spirit. For Christians, the holy family is Jesus, his mother Mary and St Joseph. On this basis, holy is also used for absolute and complete moral goodness and becomes a moral term as well. For **Kant**, a will that unconditionally obeys the **categorical imperative** out of a sense of **duty** is a holy will.

"'Holy' becomes 'good', and 'good' from that very fact in turn becomes 'holy', 'sacrosanct'; until there results a thenceforth indissoluble synthesis of the two elements and the final outcome is thus the fuller, more complex sense of 'holy', in which it is at once good and sacrosanct." **Otto,** *The Idea of the Holy*

holy will, see good will

Home, Henry, Lord Kames (1696–1782)

Scottish legal theorist and aesthetician, born in Kames, High Court Judge. Kames argued for a naturalist account of art and criticism in terms of the human capacity for pleasure and the nature of human emotions and passions. He held that works of art are agreeable or disagreeable through conforming to the natural course of our ideas or reversing this course. He also sought a naturalist account of the foundations of morality. His major works include *Essays on the Principles of Morality and Natural Religion* (1751) and *Elements of Criticism* (1763).

homonym

LOGIC, METAPHYSICS For **Aristotle** two different kinds of things are homonymous if they have the same **name**, but the name applies to them for different reasons. For example, a man and a picture of a man can both be called animal, but the man is so called because according to Aristotle's definition of animal it is a living thing that moves itself, and the picture is so called, not because it fits the definition of animal, but because it is a representation of something that is an animal. These meanings are obviously different. In Aristotle's metaphysics, a finger, in a normal sense, is a finger of a living body. Once it is separated from that body, it is dead and can only be called a finger homonymously. This point is important in his discussion of **matter** and **definition**.

"Things are said to be named 'homonymously' when, though they have a common name, the definition corresponding with the name differs for each." **Aristotle,** *Categories*

homosexuality, problem of

ETHICS, PHILOSOPHY OF LAW A homosexual relationship is an erotic relationship between persons of the same sex. It has historically been generally regarded as immoral, for it is disapproved of by the majority of social customs and the majority of the population. However, this wide disapproval seems merely a matter of opinion rather than something with a rational foundation. According to rational moralists, there is a distance between a mere opinion and moral truth. Another reason proposed to condemn homosexuality is the claim that it violates **natural law** and cannot lead to the fulfillment of the reproductive function of genitals. However, there are many ways to consider what a thing's nature is, and the body has more functions than reproduction. Moreover, progress in biology and psychology has indicated that homosexuality is a natural state rather than a freely chosen sinful condition.

"If I am right, then constraints on liberty that can be justified only on the ground that the majority finds homosexuality distasteful, or disapproves of the culture that it generates, are offensive to equality and so incompatible with a theory of representation based on equal concern and respect." **Dworkin,** *A Matter of Principle*

homunctionalism

PHILOSOPHY OF MIND Also called homuncular functionalism. A theory in the philosophy of mind and cognitive science, associated with W. G. **Lycan** and D. **Dennett**. In opposition to **reductionism**, it explains a **mind** or intelligent system by considering it to be a system made up of interconnecting departments. Each department can be seen as a **homunculus**, a small sub-personal **agent**, with its own function to perform. These homunculi are coordinated with each other to produce the overall behavioral response of a mind or an intelligent system to stimuli. Each department, or each homunculus, can in turn be viewed as a system composed of interconnected sub-departments or sub-homunculi. This process can go down to the neurological level. In this hierarchy, the task performed by lower-level units are simpler and easier than the task of the higher-level unit which they are supposed to explain.

"The irreducibility of institutional types makes for a mark in favour of homunctionalism as a philosophical theory of the mental." **Lycan,** *Consciousness*

homuncular functionalism, another term for homunctionalism

homunculus

PHILOSOPHY OF MIND [Latin, small man] Generally used for those fallacious theories in the philosophy of mind which explain **mental states** and processes in terms of the **hypothesis** that there is a further human-like agent within us who has the same mental states and processes as ourselves. This kind of theory involves a regress *ad infinitum*, for we may ask whether there is a further human-like agent within in this entity to whom we must appeal in order to explain our mental states. However, Dennett argues that the homunculus hypothesis can be a useful **explanation** if there is a hierarchy of homunculi, where each performs a simpler task than the task they are together employed to explain. He subscribes, on this basis, to the position of **homuncular functionalism.**

"Homunculi are bogeymen only if they duplicate entirely the talents they are run in to explain. If one can get a team or committee of relatively ignorant, narrow-minded, blind homunculi to produce the intelligent behaviour of the whole this is progress." **Dennett,** *Brain Storms*

homunculus fallacy, see homunculus

honor

ETHICS Honor is a state of being esteemed as a result of one's social position, one's achievements, or of one's excellence of any sort. The moral worth of honor and whether it should be morally pursued are matters of dispute. For **Aristotle**, the magnanimous person should seek honor for otherwise he shows a weakness or defect. In Christian ethics, **humility** is a chief virtue, and honor should be ascribed to **God. Hobbes** believed that the pursuit of honor is a basic human drive and is morally neutral. To honor someone is the same as respecting that person. We have a **duty** to honor others and to honor oneself.

"The desire to join others in friendship to himself, with which a man living according to the guidance of reason is possessed, I call 'honour'." **Spinoza,** *Ethics*

horizon

MODERN EUROPEAN PHILOSOPHY A term given a special philosophical meaning in the works of **Dilthey, Husserl, Heidegger,** and other **phenomenologist** and **hermeneutic** philosophers. A horizon is a framework or field of vision within which one understands. Everyone as an historical being is conditioned by a **tradition** and **culture** and hence dwells in some horizon. A horizon is one's **life-world.** An **understanding** that is purely objective and, hence, free from one's particular horizon cannot exist. The meaning of a text is determined within some horizon. To achieve historical understanding one must acquire a historical horizon and interpret in terms of historical being itself and of the horizon of the past tradition, rather than in terms of one's contemporary criteria and **prejudices.** A horizon itself is always in the process of formation. The phenomenon of horizons is the basis for the **hermeneutic circle.** It also suggests that since all understanding is achieved against the background of a horizon of intelligibility, no understanding is complete or free from error. The perspectival nature of the notion of

horizon is captured by the notion of a point of view, but this more modest notion, for better or worse, leaves out some deeper aspects.

"A horizon is not a rigid frontier, but something that moves with one and invites one to advance further." **Gadamer,** *Truth and Method*

horizontal stroke, see assertion-sign

Horkheimer, Max (1895–1973)

German social philosopher and critical theorist, born in Stuttgart, Professor and Director of the Institute of Social Research, University of Frankfurt. At the Frankfurt School, Horkheimer established an interdisciplinary program of critical theory that associated philosophy with the social sciences rather than with metaphysics. He used a conception of reason that extended beyond instrumental reason in his criticism of the social and cultural catastrophes of the twentieth century. His major works include *The Eclipse of Reason* (1947), *The Dialectic of Enlightenment* (with Adorno) (1947), and *Critique of Instrumental Reason* (1967).

horseshoe, the logical symbol "⊃"; see material implication

hule, Greek term for matter

human being

METAPHYSICS, ETHICS, PHILOSOPHY OF MIND [from Latin *homo*] For **Aristotle**, a human being is a rational animal. For **Descartes**, as a consequence of his dualism, a human being is not an organic whole, but the amalgam of two distinct elements, **mind** and **body.** In spite of this difference, however, both Aristotle and Descartes took **rationality** as the essential characteristic of human beings. "Human being" in this sense has been used as a synonym for "person," viewed as a being that possesses inalienable **rights** to life and liberty and that is superior to non-human animals. Contemporary moral philosophy tends to distinguish "persons" from "human beings," holding that the former is a self-conscious being, while the latter is simply a member of the species *Homo sapiens.* We can use this distinction to ask how notions such as "I," "**the self,**" "human being," "**person,**" and "**individual**" differ in their content and application.

"If deliberating with a view to action is what human beings who conceive themselves as rational agents take it to be, then anybody who acts deliberately is free either to gratify his instincts and desires or not to gratify them. And this is part of the traditional conception of what it is to be human." **Donagan,** *The Theory of Morality*

human chauvinism

ETHICS A term introduced by Val Routley and Richard Routley, referring to the traditional anthropocentrism existing in Western culture, according to which human beings are the only subjects of moral consideration and are the only objects with intrinsic values. Non-human species are not entitled to membership of the moral **community**, and they have value only insofar as they are instrumental to human interests or purposes. The ground for supporting this attitude is the belief that the human species has special characteristics, such as **reason**, which make it superior to other species. Human chauvinism, which is also called speciesism by other authors, is the target of criticism of **environmental ethics**. On this view, human beings should change their moral consciousness toward **animals** and include them in the moral community in certain ways.

"Western ethics still appears to retain, as its very heart, a fundamental form of chauvinism, namely, human chauvinism. For both popular Western thought and most Western ethical theories assume that both value and morality can ultimately be reduced to matters of interest or concern to the class of humans." **Routley and Routley, "Against the Inevitability of Human Chauvinism," in Goodpaster and Sayre (eds.),** *Ethical Problems of the 21st Century*

human nature

METAPHYSICS, ETHICS, POLITICAL PHILOSOPHY, PHILOSOPHY OF SOCIAL SCIENCE Starting with Greek **essentialism**, the philosophical tradition has generally held that there is a human **nature** and that it is made up of one or more qualities that determine what it is to be a human being and distinguish human beings from other kinds of animals. Different accounts of what qualities constitute human nature led to different views about how we should live. Greek philosophers such as **Plato** and **Aristotle** argued that a human is essentially a rational animal. This stand-

ard view has been challenged by such figures as **Hume**, evolutionary theorists, and **Freud**, who questioned the primacy of human rationality and in some cases found much continuity between humans and other animals. Some philosophers also reject rationality as the ultimate criterion to distinguish human from other animals because we accept persons lacking important rational capacities as human beings, yet exclude animals displaying significant rationality. The question of rationality in human nature has led to debates over many issues, concerning, for example, human **identity**, the distinction between the concept of a **person** and the concept of a **human being**, the human status of fetuses and infants, the senile, and humans whose rational capacities are radically damaged or diseased. Other issues include whether human nature is **benevolent**, sinful, or self-interested and the relationship between **freedom** and **rationality**. Modern political theory has been closely related to sharply contrasting views of human nature. In addition to offering different accounts of the contents of human nature, some philosophers have challenged the methodology of specifying human nature through finding a distinguishing essence.

The rise of anti-essentialism and the sociology of knowledge led to the rejection of human nature as a biologically fixed substratum that determines variable socio-cultural formations. On this view, all our human features are molded by our social environments or socially constructed within them. What seems to be a fixed human nature is a socio-cultural variable.

"It is from considering the relations which the several appetites and passions in the inward frame have to each other, and, above all, the supremacy of reflection or conscience, that we get the idea of the system or construction of human nature." **Butler,** *Fifteen Sermons*

human rights, see rights, human

human sciences, see *Geisteswissenschaften*

humanism

ETHICS, PHILOSOPHICAL METHOD In the early Renaissance, the disciplines of grammar, rhetoric, poetry, history, and philosophy were called *studia humanitatis*, that is, the humanities. A teacher of one of these disciplines was called a "humanist." At that time the study of these disciplines was stimulated by the newly discovered literature of classical Greece and Rome. These teachers found a human ideal involving features such as a unity between humans and **nature**, a confidence in the power of human **understanding**, the ability to enjoy the **pleasures** of life. They tried in their teaching to develop the human personality in accordance with this model. **Petrarch** is generally called the father of humanism, and **Erasmus** is regarded as its most outstanding representative. Hence humanism originally meant the pursuit of a desirable kind of humanity. Since this human ideal was believed to have been lost in medieval times, such an educational program became a movement aiming to liberate thought and was the most pervasive element of Renaissance culture.

In another sense, humanism was an American movement of thought in the early twentieth century. It was an attitude that emphasized the **dignity** of human beings by ascribing a fundamental set of human values to them. There were, however, significant variations among different versions of American humanism. Literary humanism accepted the dualism between humanity and nature and claimed that human value is derived from intuitive glimpses of a reality higher than nature. Scientific humanism argued that modern science can offer value and new meanings and claimed that by means of its knowledge and power we can achieve true enlightenment and progress. The main trend was religious humanism, which denied the distinction between the sacred and the secular. It claimed that man is a part of nature and has emerged as the result of a continuous process of **evolution**. The universe is not created, and religion consists of those actions, purposes, and experiences which are humanly significant. The British pragmatist and humanist thinker F. C. S. **Schiller** believed that humanism is a tradition that proceeds from **Protagoras'** maxim that man is the measure of all things.

"The term 'humanism' has been associated with the Renaissance and its classical studies for more than a hundred years, but in recent times it has become the source of much philosophical and historical confusion. In present discourse almost any kind of concern with human value is called 'humanistic'." **Kristeller,** *Renaissance Thought and Its Sources*

humanity

ETHICS, AESTHETICS [Latin *humanitas*] The idea of humanity originated with the Stoics, who referred to the unity of mankind as a whole. The **substance** and **essence** of **human beings** or of the human species determines human beings as human and distinguishes human beings from animals. Humanity, furthermore, involves a set of moral and aesthetic characteristics that are valuable in themselves. **Kant's categorical imperative**, which requires that one treat a person as an **end** and not merely as a means, is an expression of humanity as human **dignity**. Humanity is the object of respect in moral life. The moral and aesthetic characteristics of humanity are embodied in human expression and behavior. **Cicero** and **Seneca** established *humanitas* as a moral-aesthetic ideal or way of life, an idea that was revived in the Renaissance. The subjects that constitute an educational program to cultivate the ideal of humanity are called the humanities. In the twentieth century, **Cassirer** proposed that humanity should be understood in terms of the activities leading to its historical and cultural achievements.

"For the subject we wish to know is not the individual consciousness but the universal subject. If we refer to this subject by the term 'humanity', then we must affirm that humanity is not to be explained by man, but man by humanity." **Cassirer,** *An Essay on Man*

Humboldt, Wilhelm von (1767–1835)

German humanist, statesman, and linguistic scholar, born in Potsdam, founder of the University of Berlin. In questioning the universal rationality of the Enlightenment, Humboldt argued for the importance of historical experience and for an appreciation of the ideas that link the inner being of man to historical events. His philosophy of language claimed a formative role for different languages and their inner forms for diverse cultural responses to the world. His major works include *The Limits of State Action* (1791) and *On the Dual* (1828).

Hume, David (1711–76)

Scottish philosopher and historian, born in Edinburgh. Hume was a dominant figure of British empiricism and the Scottish Enlightenment. Hume sought to understand the nature and limits of our knowledge and to establish the foundation of a genuinely empirical science of human nature. Hume maintained that from our sensory experience we cannot found any knowledge of unperceived objects, such as the external world, innate ideas, God, free will, necessity, and uniformity in the nature, but his arguments can be seen to support either naturalism or skepticism. In his account of causality, Hume claimed that the necessary connection between a given cause and its effect is nothing but a habitual expectation of mind that is based upon repeated experience of the constant conjunction of events of given kinds. Induction is also based on habit, since we cannot prove from experience that the future resembles the past. We should distinguish between propositions regarding the relation of ideas and propositions regarding matters of fact (a distinction now referred to as "Hume's fork"). The former are demonstrative, but the latter can only be inferred with probability. We must learn to live with probabilities rather than certainties. The mind or the self is nothing but a bundle or collection of different perceptions, united together by certain relations. Hume emphasized the role of moral sentiment or sympathy in ethics and argued that passion rather than reason alone determined human action. He also argued that we can not legitimately infer "ought" from "is" or evaluation from description (this is also called "Hume's law"). Hume's *Dialogues Concerning Natural Religion* offer powerful criticism of major arguments for the existence of God, especially the argument from design. Hume's philosophical views, which are of fundamental importance in their own right, were regarded by Kant as waking him from his "dogmatic slumbers." Hume's major philosophical writings include *A Treatise of Human Nature* (1739–40), *Enquiry Concerning Human Understanding* (1748), and *Dialogues Concerning Natural Religion* (1799). Hume was more famous in his lifetime for his *History of England* (6 vols., 1754–62) than for his philosophy, and his economic writings influenced Adam Smith.

Hume's fork

LOGIC, ETHICS, EPISTEMOLOGY, METAPHYSICS A term used in two different senses. In one sense, it is **Hume**'s distinction between **ought** and **is** and his principle that if the premises are factual and do not contain normative elements, then no normative conclusion can be inferred. This follows from the more general principle that there can be nothing in the conclusion of a valid **argument** that is not already present in the premises.

In another sense, Hume's fork is his claim that there are only two valid kinds of reasoning: demonstrative reasoning concerning relations of **ideas** and empirical reasoning concerning matters of **fact**. This distinction provided a major argument against the validity of inductive reasoning in Hume's *Enquiries* (Sect. IV, Part 11). Inductive reasoning is not demonstrative reasoning, for demonstrative reasoning is *a priori* and implies no **contradiction**, while inductive reasoning admits contradictions. Nor is inductive reasoning empirical reasoning, which is based on **experience** and infers claims about the future on the assumption that the future will conform to the past. Because this assumption itself presupposes the validity of **induction**, a circularity is involved if induction is empirical reasoning. Therefore, induction is not a valid form of reasoning.

Both arguments based on kinds of Hume's fork have provoked deep and important philosophical controversy.

> "The argument, sometimes known as 'Hume's fork', claims that there is a logical gap in any argument which seeks to derive moral conclusions from purely factual descriptive premises." **Plant, *Modern Political Thought***

Hume's law see is/ought gap

humility

ETHICS Humility is the state of having a low opinion of oneself and of one's achievements. Humility seems to be a kind of inaccurate assessment of oneself, but it is still widely taken to be a virtue. For Christian ethics, we are from **God** and are determined by God, and every merit we achieve we owe to God. We should be grateful rather than proud. Accordingly, humility is viewed as a distinctive virtue in dealing with the relationship between God and human beings, and in putting human beings in their proper place. For other ethical theories, humility involves not crediting too much to oneself. As human beings, we are determined by nature, helped by the contributions of others and are subject to various kinds of luck. Humility reflects these facts and is therefore admired.

> "Humility is pain arising from the fact that man regards his want of power as weakness." **Spinoza, *Ethics***

humor
PHILOSOPHY OF MIND Humor is a psychological phenomenon, which has a variety of objects, modes, and institutional settings. Appreciation of humor characteristically involves laughter, although laughter can also express such things as pain, hysteria, or embarrassment. It has been notoriously unclear what makes something funny, amusing, or comical. One theory originated by Thomas **Hobbes** claims that humor arises if there is an insult to other people. We laugh because we feel a sense of superiority in some way to the object of humor. But this account is narrow and leaves out much that falls within the scope of humor. Another influential theory, developed by **Kant** and **Schopenhauer**, claims that humor arises if there is an insult to **reason**. Humor is a response to incongruities involving such things as logical impossibility, **ambiguity**, irrelevance, and general inappropriateness. A theory developed by **Freud** holds that humor provides a release of nervous and psychical energy. Humor is related to such phenomena as wit, sarcasm, and irony.

> "The capacity to see and feel what is loveable, admirable, in a thing, and what is laughable in it, at the same time, constitutes humour." *The Collected Works of John Stuart Mill*, vol. XX

Husserl, Edmund (1859–1938)
German philosopher, the father of phenomenology, born in Prossnitz, taught at Halle, Gottingen, and Freiburg. Husserl held that human mental phenomena are characterized by intentionality. Intentionality has a structure of *noesis* (the intentional act) and *noema* (the intended object), with the *noema* giving *noesis* its directness and meaning. The phenomena of phenomenology concern the meaning or essence internal to consciousness rather than sensory experience. To discover this essential structure, we need to bracket off the empirical world to discover the transcendental ego that is the unity of the empirical

ego's consciousness. The transcendental ego constituted in time is the starting-point for phenomenological reflection and the source of all intentional acts. In his later works, Husserl distinguished between the lived world and the scientific world and claimed the priority of the former as the basis for the latter. Husserl's thinking was influenced by Descartes, Kant, Brentano, and Frege, especially regarding anti-psychologism, and has in turn influenced both analytic philosophers and phenomenological and existentialist philosophers, particularly his student, Heidegger. Husserl's major works include *Logical Investigations* (1900–1), *Ideas: General Introduction to Pure Phenomenology* (1913), *Formal and Transcendental Logic* (1929), *Cartesian Meditations* (1931), *The Crisis of European Sciences and Transcendental Phenomenology* (1936), and *Experience and Judgement* (1939).

Hutcheson, Francis (1694–1746)
Scottish moral philosopher, born at Drumalig, Ireland, taught at University of Glasgow, a leading figure of the Scottish Enlightenment. In ethics, Hutcheson developed the moral sense theory originally stated by Shaftesbury. He held that human beings have a moral sense by which we perceive and approve virtue and perceive and condemn vice, and by which we are motivated to be virtuous. Hutcheson modeled the workings of moral sense on Locke's theory of perception. His view that virtue is that which pleases influenced Bentham's utilitarianism. Hutcheson's aesthetic theory resembled his moral theory in claiming that we have an internal reflective sense of beauty. His most important book is the *Inquiry into the Origins of Our Ideas of Beauty and Virtue* (1725, significantly revised in 1738). Other works include *An Essay on the Nature and Conduct of the Passions and Affections, with Illustrations on the Moral Sense* (1726), *A System of Moral Philosophy* (1755), and *Metaphysical Synopsis* (1742).

hylomorphism
METAPHYSICS, PHILOSOPHY OF MIND [from Greek *hule*, matter + *morphe*, form, the doctrine of form and matter] Also spelled *hylemorphism*, a theory first elaborated by **Aristotle**, who claimed that reality is constituted by **form** and **matter** and that each living thing is composed of **soul** as form and **body**

as matter. But hylomorphism had different senses in Aristotle. In one sense, the generation of a thing is the introduction of form into matter, but the pair of form and matter is not associated with the pair of **actuality** and **potentiality**. In the other sense, form is associated with actuality and matter is always understood as being potential. The generation of a thing on this account is the gradual development of potential matter, so that it becomes an **individual** upon obtaining form or actuality. This latter view of hylomorphism concerns the continuity of substantial **change**. Hylomorphism underwent further subtle development in medieval philosophy, especially in the metaphysics of **Aquinas**, and it was also the basis for **philosophical anthropology**.

> "Aristotle's theory of the soul and its relation to the body is sometimes called 'hylomorphism', from the word hyle (matter) and morphe (form)." **J. Ackrill,** *Aristotle*

hylozoism

METAPHYSICS, PHILOSOPHY OF MIND [from Greek *hule*, matter + *zoe*, life, the whole material world as endowed with life] A term credited to the seventeenth-century **Cambridge Platonist** Ralph **Cudworth**, to account for the relationship between the **soul** and the **body**, in contrast to **dualism, materialism**, and **hylomorphism**. Hylozoism, which denied any distinction between spirit and matter and between life and body, is generally used interchangeably with **panpsychism**. Nevertheless, some argue that while hylozoism claims that life is inherent in all matter, panpsychism proposes that there are different degrees of **consciousness** in all matter. Nowadays, this term is widely employed for the **cosmogony** of early Greek natural philosophers such as **Thales, Anaximander**, and **Anaximenes**, who believed that the world ultimately originated from living stuff.

> "Hylozoism, the doctrine that matter as such has the property of life and growth." **Furley,** *The Greek Cosmologists*

hypocrisy

ETHICS [Greek, answer, including the sort of answers actors give each other on the stage] A state in which one's outward appearance is not a sign of one's inner state. The outward appearance is in accordance with ethical requirements, while the inner and hidden state is morally blameworthy. Hypocrisy is morally condemnable because it is a kind of deception or pretence, a failure to live up to one's avowed moral principles. It is therefore associated with lack of trustworthiness, insincerity, and **inauthenticity**, and has generally undesirable consequences. Hypocrisy can also be directed at oneself, and in that case it is identical with **self-deception** or **bad faith**.

> "The word 'hypocrisy' . . . its present meaning is: the assumption of a false appearance of virtue or goodness, with dissimulation of real characters or inclinations." **Bok,** *Lying*

hypokeimenon, Greek term for substratum

hypostasis

METAPHYSICS [Greek *stasis*, standing + *hupo*, under] A key **Neoplatonist** term for ultimate **reality**, roughly a synonym of **being** or **substance**. **Plotinus** held that the One, Divine Mind, and Soul are three *hypostases*, and all other things are manifestations of them. A large part of his philosophy is devoted to explaining the nature of these hypostases and how other things manifest them. The idea influenced the Christian conception of the Trinity, according to which the Father, Son, and Holy Spirit are three **persons**. The term should not be confused with hypothesis.

> "We must affirm that they [One and Good] are the same – not, it is true, as venturing any predication with regard to that Hypostasis but simply as indicating it to ourselves in the best terms we find." **Plotinus,** *Enneads*

hypostatization

LOGIC A fallacy of confounding different types or **categories** of things. It arises as a result of treating **abstractions** and **relations** as if they were actually existing **objects**, as in the claim that ideas have an independent **subsistence**. Hypostatization is also called abstractionism, substantialization, or **reification**. This fallacy is severely criticized in **Frege**'s philosophy.

> "As I understand it, a hypostatization or substantialization or reification consists in mistaking as things entities which are not things." **Carnap,** *Meaning and Necessity*

hypothesis

EPISTEMOLOGY, PHILOSOPHY OF SCIENCE [from Greek *hypo*, under + *thesis*, position, supposition, assumption] A tentative and speculative **explanation** of a problem or a provisional affirmation before proof. Such an explanation is made because of its explanatory power regarding the phenomenon. A hypothesis is subject to revision or abandonment through observation, experiment, and argument. If it is shown to be acceptable after these further investigations, it may be elevated to the status of a scientific **theory** or **law**. The use of hypotheses is essential for the development of science.

"An hypothesis is a supposition which we make (either without actual evidence, or on evidence avowedly insufficient) in order to endeavour to deduce from it conclusions in accordance with facts which are known to be real." *The Collected Works of John Stuart Mill*, **vol. VII**

hypothetical fact

PHILOSOPHY OF LANGUAGE A term used by **Ryle** in his early discussion about **meaning** and **propositions**. What one knows is the meaning of a sentence expressing what one knows. If the sentence is a factual sentence, its meaning is the **fact** it states. Such a theory must also account for the meanings of **beliefs** that are not yet known to be true and for false beliefs. Ryle claims that the meaning of these beliefs is a hypothetical fact. Unlike a fact, a hypothetical fact is not a subsisting reality, and indeed is not a fact at all. A hypothetical fact specifies what the world would be like if the statement of one's belief were true. This is actually a would-be factual **statement**. Hence, a hypothetical fact is identical with the statement expressing it and is a **description**. Ryle's notion can be compared with **Kripke**'s later account of **possible worlds** as descriptions of how the world might be, in contrast to **Lewis**'s **realism** regarding possible worlds.

"By a hypothetical fact I do not of course mean something of which it is a matter of conjecture whether it is a fact or not, but simply a fact the statement of which is of the form 'if X then Y'." **Ryle**, *Collected Papers*, **vol. II**

hypothetical imperative

ETHICS For **Kant**, a form of **command** issued by the **will**, in contrast to another form of command, the **categorical imperative**. In his account of morality, the fundamental role is assigned to categorical imperatives rather than to hypothetical imperatives. While the categorical imperative commands an action as an objective necessity in itself, without regard to any inclination or **end**, a hypothetical imperative commands an action as the **means** for satisfying some inclination or purpose. The necessity of action it imposes is conditional or hypothetical on the given end that the agent wills: you must do something if a certain purpose is to be satisfied. Once the end is removed, there is no longer a command. It commands or counsels a man only if he has the **desire** in question. The dynamic element in obedience to such an imperative is desire or impulse, with a cognitive factor concerning the relation of means to end. Since the hypothetical imperative is concerned with the intended result of **action**, it is determined **heteronomously**. Hypothetical imperatives are divided into two kinds: problematic or technical practical principles point to the means of attaining a possible end; and assertoric practical principles point to the means of attaining a given end.

"A hypothetical imperative thus says only that an action is good for some purpose, either possible or actual." **Kant**, *Groundwork for the Metaphysics of Morals*

hypothetical induction, an alternative expression for inference to the best explanation

hypothetico-deductive method

PHILOSOPHY OF SCIENCE A model of scientific explanation, abbreviated as the H-D method. It proposes that in creating a scientific **theory**, we should first formulate a general theory or **hypothesis** that can immediately explain the results already obtained and from which further particular statements or predictions can be derived. These inferred predictions can be verified and falsified in experimental and observational tests. On this basis we decide whether to accept or to reject the general hypothesis. The hypothetico-deductive method contrasts with the inductive method. In the philosophy of science it has been regarded during the twentieth century as an ideal scientific method. Karl **Popper** and his followers have argued that the method is effective in testing a general theory by **falsification**, and concentrate on the formal relationship between hypothesis and its consequential statements. Some critics claim that this method oversimplifies the actual relation between theory and **observation**.

"As it is frequently characterised, the hypothetico-deductive method consists of (1) setting up a hypothesis, (2) deducing consequences from a hypothesis, and (3) checking by observation to see whether these consequences are true." **Salmon,** *Logic*

I

I think
METAPHYSICS, EPISTEMOLOGY, PHILOSOPHY OF MIND
[German *Ich denke*] **Kant**'s account of the "I think,"
which accompanies all our representations, originated
from **Descartes**'s *cogito*. **Leibniz** turned the *cogito*
into the conscious and self-conscious in general. Kant
denied that it is possible to prove the existence of the
self in terms of **consciousness**, but assigned a great
role to the "I think" in epistemology as the **form** of
transcendental apperception, the mind of a self-
conscious or self-aware being. The "I think" is neither
an **experience** nor a substantial subject of experiences. It is rather a necessary vehicle or accompaniment of experience, which precedes experience and
relates experiences to a numerically identical self. It
is an original or non-derivative **unity of consciousness** rather than an object of consciousness.

"All the manifold of intuition has, therefore, a
necessary relation to the 'I think' in the same subject in which this manifold is found." **Kant,** *Critique
of Pure Reason*

I think, therefore I am, the English translation of
Latin *cogito ergo sum*

Ibn Rushd, see Averroes

Ibn Sina, see Avicenna

icon
PHILOSOPHY OF SCIENCE, PHILOSOPHY OF HISTORY, EPI-
STEMOLOGY, PHILOSOPHY OF MIND [from Greek *eikon*,
image, likeness, picture] A **sign** or **symbol** that resembles or behaves similarly to the thing or process
it represents and is thus an analogue of that thing or
process. Scientific experiments can employ iconic
models for processes that do not exist under laboratory conditions. A cultural icon is a thing or individual that epitomizes the character of a particular
society or period. In psychology, an icon or iconic
memory is a visual image that lingers briefly after
its physical stimulus is removed. The icon for
hearing is called an echo. An icon can be stored
briefly in some medium. Before it disappears, it can
be read and explained as if the physical stimulus
were still present. This transient visual persistence
is also called an after-image.

"There seems no alternative but to introduce a
new term for the transient visual memory in question. I will call it 'the icon' or 'iconic memory'."
Neisser, *Cognitive Psychology*

iconoclasm
PHILOSOPHY OF RELIGION, ETHICS The demand that
images or **icons** must be destroyed or have their
putative power amputated. This position responds
to the ascription of a high spiritual, cultural, and
moral status to images in a way or to a degree considered inappropriate by the iconoclasts. The use of
images as objects of worship is called idolatry, and
has been widely condemned in Judaism, Christianity, and Islam, for the image is felt to substitute for

the real object of worship. Popular devotion to the social, religious, and sensuous power of images has led historically to many iconoclastic movements, especially in periods of social transition. This is unfortunate for art because many of the religious images destroyed by iconoclasts were works of art. Iconoclasm is used more generally to characterize those who would attack the most central features of their culture and society.

"You after all have to ask yourself why there has been at various times in history such intense controversy over the making of graven images, why there have been movements of iconoclasm at all." **Danto,** *The Philosophical Disenfranchisement of Art*

id, see ego (Freud)

idea (Hegel)

METAPHYSICS Hegelian ideas are similar to Platonic ideas, but unlike those of empiricism. For **Hegel**, an idea is not a mental representation of an object, but is actually present in things as the ground of their existence. An idea is equivalent to **truth** and exists in a primary sense that does not derive from the existence of things. It is the full realization of a **concept** and is the unity of concept and **object**. The identity between concept and object suggests that a concept can provide adequate **knowledge** of an object. When we know an object, we know its concept and its idea, rather than its material constituent. Hegel claimed that an idea is the nature of an object and that all finite things depend upon ideas for their being. In a sense, his philosophy is a kind of **idealism**. The idea which is in and for itself is the **absolute idea**.

"The idea is truth in itself and for itself, – the absolute unity of concept and objectivity." **Hegel,** *Logic*

idea (Hume)

METAPHYSICS, EPISTEMOLOGY While **Locke** called all objects of mind ideas, Hume thought that this use perverted the original meaning of the word "idea." Instead, he called all objects of the mind **perceptions** and divided perceptions into two kinds: **impressions** and ideas. Impressions are the **mental objects** involved when we are feeling and experiencing and can be **sensations, passions,**

or **emotions**. Impressions include Locke's ideas of sense and of **reflection**. Ideas, on the other hand, are the mental objects involved in thinking and reasoning. According to Hume, this distinction was based on the difference between thinking and feeling, of which everyone can naturally be aware. Impressions are what we have when we are actually perceiving something, while ideas are what we have when we think about the thing in its absence. Hume held that ideas are formed on the basis of impressions and are exact **representations** of the latter. Every simple idea is caused by its corresponding simple impression. The difference between impressions and ideas is not essential, but is a matter of the degree of force and liveliness with which perceptions strike upon the mind. Ideas are of two kinds: simple ideas that are derived directly from impressions and complex ideas that are combinations of simple ideas and need not represent the actual relation of impressions. Hume's view that there is a corresponding relationship between impressions and ideas is controversial. Nevertheless, he distinguished between ideas and impressions in order to defend the basic contention of **empiricism** that there can be no **thoughts** or ideas unless there are first some sensations or feelings.

"Those perceptions, which enter with most force and violence, we may name *impressions*; and under this name I comprehend all our sensations, passions and emotions, as they make their first appearance in the soul. By *ideas* I mean the faint images of these in thinking and reasoning." **Hume,** *A Treatise of Human Nature*

idea (Kant)

METAPHYSICS, EPISTEMOLOGY In contrast to the **categories** or pure concepts of the understanding corresponding to the various forms of **judgment**, there are ideas or pure concepts of reason corresponding to the various kinds of logical **inference**. There are three kinds of inference in traditional logic: the categorical, hypothetical, and disjunctive. Accordingly there are also three kinds of ideas, namely the idea of the soul as the absolute unity of the thinking subject, the idea of the absolute unity of the sequence of the condition of appearance, and the idea of the absolute unity of the conditions of objects of thought in general.

While categories can determine objects of **experience**, there are no corresponding empirical objects for ideas. Hence they are **transcendental** ideas. Ideas are only **regulative** and subjective in providing guidance to inquiry. They are orders or advice to the faculty of **reason** in its logical employment. However, reason has a propensity to take ideas as belonging objectively to **things in themselves**, hence generating dialectical errors. The three ideas provide spurious subject-matter for three spurious metaphysical disciplines: rational psychology, rational cosmology, and rational theology.

> "I understand by idea a necessary concept of reason to which no corresponding object can be given in sense-experience. Thus the pure concepts of reason, now under consideration, are transcendental ideas." **Kant, Critique of Pure Reason**

idea (Locke)

METAPHYSICS, EPISTEMOLOGY For **Plato** an Idea was something objective, an intelligible **archetype**. The Christian Platonists replaced the archetypes with inborn memories, which they call **innate ideas**. The possession of these innate ideas and reflection upon them are necessary conditions for obtaining necessary **truths**. **Locke** rejected the existence of innate ideas, but accepted the assumption that the mind forms its picture of the world through ideas. He used the word "idea" widely and not very carefully. His various uses of this word in his works are hard to render consistent with one another. Sometimes he identified idea with **perception**. In this sense, ideas are what we are immediately aware of when we are perceiving things through **senses** or when in **reflection** we are introspectively aware of our own feelings and **thoughts**. Sometimes they are the copies of such sensory or introspective items in **understanding**. For Locke, ideas are the contents of thought or sensory experience, the thoughts we have about some object. This interchangeable use of idea and thought is also found in **Hume**. Sometimes ideas are objects, the immediate objects of the mind. Ideas, not physical objects, are what we immediately perceive. Ideas are also said to be the objects of **memory** and **imagination**. This account offers a kind of **representative theory of perception**. Sometimes ideas are even explained as qualities or collections of qualities of which we may have ideas. Locke

divided ideas into simple ideas and complex ideas. Simple ideas cannot be broken down any further into component parts. Such ideas include our ideas of red, pain, and point. Complex ideas are ideas built up into combinations out of simple ideas, including **abstract ideas**, general ideas, **universals**, and some ideas of reflection. Locke defined **knowledge** as the perception of the connection and agreement of ideas.

> "I must here in the entrance beg pardon of my readers for the frequent use of the word *idea*, which he will find in the following treatise. It being that term which, I think, serves best to stand for whatsoever is the object of the understanding when a man thinks." **Locke, An Essay Concerning Human Understanding**

idea (Plato)

METAPHYSICS, EPISTEMOLOGY [from Greek *idea*, what a thing looks like, in turn from *idein*, to see, to look, a declension of *eidein*, to see, to look, from which comes *eidos*, form, the synonym of *idea*] **Plato** used *idea* and *eidos* interchangeably for the non-sensible entities that are unchanging, eternal, and universal **absolutes**, the objects of **knowledge**, and the **paradigms** from which sensible things derive their **reality**. He held that these supreme entities are the **essence** or inner structure of things. The transition of *idea* from outer look or shape to inner structure is by way of a metaphor. If you see with eyes, what you see is outer shape, but if you "see" with the soul – that is, think – what you get is essence or the common characteristic. Platonic ideas are objective, in contrast to ideas as subjective, mental ideas in modern philosophy. To avoid confusion, many modern scholars prefer to call Plato's doctrine the Theory of **Forms** rather than the Theory of Ideas.

> "You remember then that I did not ask you to indicate to me one or two of the many pious actions, but the very Form (eidos) itself by which all pious acts are pious. For you said, I think, that it is by one Idea (idea) that impious things are impious and pious pious." **Plato, Euthyphro**

ideal (Kant)

PHILOSOPHY OF RELIGION An ideal or transcendental ideal for **Kant** is a special kind of idea, the subject-matter of rational theology. When we try to think of the conditions for the complete determination of any individual thing, we are led inevitably to the concept of a supreme being as the pure rational idea of an individual possessing all realities, that is, **God**, which serves as an **archetype** for imitation and as a source of being. This is the ideal of **pure reason**. According to Kant, this ideal is a mere idea of a ground of all possibilities and a subjectively necessary **hypothesis** for our reason. But once we take it as an objective necessity and conclude the necessary existence of such a being, we commit a dialectical illusion. This occurs in the **ontological argument**, cosmological proof, and physico-theological proof.

"By the ideal I understand the idea, not merely in concreto, but in individuo, that is, as an individual thing, determinable or even determined by the idea alone." **Kant, *Critique of Pure Reason***

ideal language, another term for logically perfect language

ideal observer theory

ETHICS A theory originating with Adam **Smith** in *The Theory of Moral Sentiments*, although he himself used the term "impartial spectator." It was fully developed by Roderick Firth in his paper "Ethical Absolutism and the Ideal Observer." The theory holds that moral judgments should be analyzed by reference to the feelings of an ideal observer. To say "X is right" means that X would be approved of by such an observer," and to say "Y is wrong" means that Y would be disapproved of by him. This observer, as a hypothetical being, has all the relevant knowledge (he is well-informed), has equal **love** for all (he is impartial), is totally without passions toward persons and objects, is infallible, and is consistent. In other respects this observer is a "normal" **person**. This theory can overcome the difficulties of ethical subjectivism by avoiding the problem of fallible agents, and is also different from theological theories because it is not committed to asserting the existence of **God** but only assumes that an observer could have some god-like attributes, such as full knowledge and equal love. It is a form of **ethical naturalism** because what a fully informed being would probably approve of is empirically testable. Its problem is that all the characteristics ascribed to the ideal observer are themselves evaluative terms,

and therefore should also be analyzed by appeal to an ideal observer. This involves a regress *ad infinitum*.

"Using the term 'ideal observer', then, the kind of analysis which I shall examine in this paper is the kind which would construe statements of the form 'x is P', in which P is some particular ethical predicate, to be identical in meaning with statements of the form: 'Any ideal observer would react to x in such and such a way under such and such conditions.'" **Firth, "Ethical Absolutism and the Ideal Observer,"** *Philosophy and Phenomenological Research* **(1952)**

ideal type

PHILOSOPHY OF SOCIAL SCIENCE According to the sociologist Max **Weber**, a methodologically indispensable device in theory-construction for the social sciences. An ideal type is a theoretical construct abstracted and summarized from certain characteristic social phenomena of an epoch and presented either as a system of concepts or as a system of statements. It is not a description of social reality and cannot be observed, but is a conceptual pattern or an organizing principle for social scientists to establish certain relationships among social events and phenomena and conceive them as a consistent system. Unlike natural scientists employing natural **laws**, social scientists do not deduce social phenomena from the notion of ideal type, but apply an ideal type as a **heuristic** device in the analysis of concrete social events.

"An ideal type is formed by the one-sided accentuation of one or more points of view and by the synthesis of a great many diffuse, discrete, more or less present and occasionally absent concrete individual phenomena, which are arranged according to those one-sidedly emphasised viewpoints into a unified analytical construct." **Weber, *The Methodology of the Social Sciences***

idealism

METAPHYSICS, EPISTEMOLOGY Any philosophical position claiming that **ideas** are the true objects of **knowledge**, that ideas are prior to things, and that ideas provide the grounds of **being** to things. On this view, ideas have priority both metaphysically and epistemologically, and external reality as it is known to us reflects mental operations. Idealism does not suggest that **mind** creates **matter** or the material world in a substantive sense. Nor does this view confuse **thought** with the object of thought, but rather it claims that the **external world** can be grasped only by reference to the work of ideas and that all we can say about the external world is mediated by operations of the mind. The world in itself is certainly mind-independent, but the world as conceived by us must be constructed by mind. Idealism is a philosophical position about how the world as we know it can be the case and is not directly related to any political position. Since there are various understandings of the nature of idea, there are also correspondingly many types of idealism.

"Values exist, but their existence and their character are both somehow dependent upon us, upon our choices, attitudes, commitments, structures, or whatever. This position might be called philosophical idealism or creationism." **Nozick,** *Philosophical Explanations*

idealism, absolute

METAPHYSICS, EPISTEMOLOGY, ETHICS, PHILOSOPHY OF HISTORY A modern version of objective **idealism**, represented by **Hegel** and his followers. In contrast to the metaphysics and epistemology of **empiricism**, Hegel claimed that ideas are not formed by a human mind through experiencing objects. On the contrary, he claims that ideas or concepts come first and determine the **being** of things. Things are what they are in virtue of revealing the **concepts** or **ideas** immanent in them. Although ideas or concepts determine the structure of reality, the individual human mind is not the source of ideality. Ideas develop as a means of self-actualization. Their systematic development exhibits the whole structure of an **absolute idea**, which is also the structure of **reality**. As a result, the world has an inherent all-embracing rational order and value conforming to the structure of the absolute idea. Hegel's absolute idealism is an attempt to describe systematically both nature and human social existence. It does not deny the existence of an external and objective world, but explains the world by assuming that there is a purposive intelligence at the heart of nature, which controls nature just as our minds control our bodies.

Absolute idealism was popular in Britain from the 1860s to the 1920s, represented by **Bradley, Green, Bosanquet, Royce, McTaggart,** and the Oxford-trained American Blanshard. These figures disagreed over details, but all believed the **Absolute** to be the only true thing, with other things considered as being partial aspects of the Absolute or illusory appearances generated by the Absolute. Absolute idealism depends on the logical claim that all relations are internal. **Moore** and **Russell** initially accepted the claims of absolute idealism, but then rejected its account of **relations** and also other aspects of the position.

"Absolute idealism holds that there is only one particular, namely God or the Absolute, and only one kind of fact, namely the kind which attributes a property to the Absolute." **Russell,** *Collected Papers of Bertrand Russell,* **vol. IX**

idealism, critical, another term for transcendental idealism

idealism, objective

METAPHYSICS, EPISTEMOLOGY, ETHICS A type of idealism initiated by **Plato** and holding that the real, which is the object of **knowledge**, is constituted by the inner immaterial structure or **essence** of things, which Plato called **ideas** or **forms**. Objective idealism rejects the claim that we have knowledge of unstable **appearances** given as the objects of **experience**. By holding that the organization or form of the world is independent of our minds, this idealism is objective or absolute, rather than subjective. Platonic ideas provide the basis not only for knowledge, but also for **moral principle**. Absolute idealism is a variant of objective idealism. When **Leibniz** first employed the term "idealism," he was referring to Plato's theory of ideas.

"There are types of objective idealism which describe and explain the world in the same way as realism with only the additional assertion that the whole system is mental or spiritual." **D. Williams,** *Principles of Empirical Realism*

idealism, subjective

METAPHYSICS, EPISTEMOLOGY A form of idealism associated with **Berkeley**, although he himself called his own philosophy **immaterialism**. **Locke** distinguished **primary qualities** (such as size and shape) and **secondary qualities** (such as color and smell) and claimed that secondary qualities are not in material things but are mind-dependent. Berkeley argued that even primary qualities are mind-dependent and that both kinds of qualities as objects of experience are **ideas** in our mind. Material objects are simply collections of ideas, and do not exist independent of a perceiver. For Berkeley, "to exist" means to be perceived by some mind, thus leading to his dictum: *"esse et percipi."* Minds and ideas are the only real things, but this does not mean that the world disappears when I close my eyes and returns when I open them again. Berkeley thought that the natural world would still exist, because it is perceived by **God**. Some philosophers prefer a **phenomenalist** rendering of subjective idealism, according to which objects are determined by our actual experiences and by the experiences we would have were certain conditions fulfilled. In either religious or phenomenalist versions, subjective idealism accepts the existence of the ordinary world, but provides special ways of interpreting its existence. Opponents of idealism sometimes argue that subjective idealism collapses into **solipsism** and the claims that my ideas and I are the only reality. Berkeley's thought remains highly influential, however, because its arguments reveal in a negative way some of the deep philosophical problems which **empiricism** has difficulty in avoiding.

"It is extremely important to realise that the psychological reflection is a transcending of the given every whit as much as the physical; indeed even more, if anything. It was the failure to notice this which led Berkeley to subjective idealism." **Russell,** *Collected Papers of Bertrand Russell,* **vol. I**

idealism, transcendental

METAPHYSICS, EPISTEMOLOGY **Kant**'s description of his own basic philosophical position, which he also called critical idealism. In developing his position, Kant rejected both **rationalism** and **empiricism**, and claimed that it is impossible for us to gain **knowledge** of the world either by sense experience alone or solely by rational thought, and our knowledge must employ both **sensibility** and **understanding**. Knowledge is limited to the phenomenal world and cannot inform us about **noumena** or **things-in-**

themselves. Nevertheless, the world we experience is real, and Kant linked his transcendental idealism with **empirical realism**. His metaphysics explores the conditions of the possibility of **experience** rather than attempting to provide knowledge beyond the limits of our experience. For knowledge of the world to be possible, our sense experience must conform to the *a priori* **intuitions** of **space** and **time** and the **categories** of understanding. Space, time, and the categories are not features of things, but constitute the conditions of the possibility of experience. Their origin is not the empirical self, but what he calls the **transcendental unity of apperception** ("the 'I think' which accompanied all my representations"). About this "I" we know nothing except that it is, for it is a formal condition of knowledge rather than an **object** of knowledge. Objects in the natural world depend on the constitution of our sensibility and understanding. **Fichte** and **Schelling** drew on some Kantian texts to extend the metaphysical role of the **spontaneity** of the "I," but this was a departure from Kant's own orientation. Philosophers disagree over the value of transcendental idealism to Kant's philosophy. Some defend it as ineliminable, whilst others consider it to be incoherent.

"By transcendental idealism I mean the doctrine that appearances are to be regarded as being, one and all, representations only, not things in themselves, and the time and space are therefore only sensible forms of our intuition, not determinations given as existing by themselves, nor conditions of objects viewed as things in themselves." **Kant,** *Critique of Pure Reason*

ideas of ideas

METAPHYSICS, EPISTEMOLOGY, PHILOSOPHY OF RELIGION **Spinoza**'s theory, according to which **God** has an **idea** of everything that follows from any of his **attributes**. Because the ideas in God themselves are among the things following from his attribute of thought, there is necessarily in God an idea of every idea that there is in him. This process can go on *ad infinitum*. The levels of these ideas are distinct from one another because what they represent is different. Hence, besides mental–physical **parallelism** (extra-cognitive parallelism), there is infinite mental–mental parallelism (intra-cognitive parallelism). Spinoza intended this account to serve as a theory of self-knowledge. But an infinite hierarchy of ideas of ideas is criticized by many commentators as being profligate.

> "The ideas of the ideas of modifications follow in God and are related to God in the same way as the ideas themselves of modifications." **Spinoza,** *Ethics*

ideation, see eidetic reduction

ideational theory of meaning

PHILOSOPHY OF MIND, PHILOSOPHY OF LANGUAGE A theory holding that the **meaning** of a word is the **idea** with which it is regularly associated or for which it stands. According to the theory, ideas are private and independent of language. Language is a tool for providing publicly observable indications of private ideas and to convey these ideas to others. A linguistic expression gets its meaning by being used to indicate ideas. The classical version of this theory was elaborated by **Locke** in his *Essay Concerning Human Understanding*, I, 2, III. He says: "The use, then, of words is to be sensible marks of ideas; and the ideas they stand for are their proper and immediate signification." Since the ambiguous word "idea" for Locke refers to mental **images**, this theory is also called the "image theory of meaning." The strength of this theory is that it catches the insight that language is an instrument for the communication of **thought**. However, according to this theory, we do not understand what someone is saying until we get the idea. This is not usually the case. More often, an idea itself is derived from meaning rather than vice versa. Moreover, the theory must answer claims that either language and thought cannot be separated or, if they can, language has priority. **Fodor**'s language of thought thesis reasserts the thesis that thought is prior on the basis of a theory of thinking for which thought has the same kind of **syntactic** structure as language.

> "The ideational theory [of the meaning] would be that two expressions have the same use if and only if they are associated with the same ideas." **Alston,** *Philosophy of Language*

ideatum

METAPHYSICS, PHILOSOPHY OF LANGUAGE [Latin, plural, *ideata*, generally translated as object, although

object is also used to translate *objectum*] Originally a scholastic term for something produced by **God** as a copy of the **idea** which He himself has. In Spinoza's philosophy, an *ideatum* corresponds to an idea and is what an idea is of, that is, the thing which is presented in an idea.

> "A true idea must correspond with its ideatum, that is what it conceives." **Spinoza,** *Ethics*

identity

LOGIC, METAPHYSICS [from Latin *idem*, the same] Identity has been interpreted in two ways: as singleness over time and as sameness amid difference. These two notions are connected, for to identify something as the same over time cannot be separated from distinguishing one thing from others. However, each interpretation introduces its own peculiar problems.

Identity as singleness over time amounts to sameness amid **change**. Common sense suggests that a thing can remain itself in spite of alterations, yet it is difficult to explain how this can be so. Identity over time leads on to questions such as the nature of **substance**, the relationship of **appearance** to **reality**, and the conditions of **personal identity**. Identity as sameness amid diversity raises questions concerning kind identity, the sameness which is shared by a number of things, and questions concerning individual identity, the identity by which one thing is itself and can be distinguished from other things of the same kind. This latter question is called the problem of individuation.

To tell whether two or more things of a given kind are identical, we must specify their identity conditions or criteria of identity. Different kinds of things are determined according to different criteria of identity. In logic, identity is characterized by an **equivalence** relation and is determined by what is called **Leibniz's law**, or the **identity of indiscernibles**: two things are identical if every **property** belonging to one belongs to the other.

A major dimension of contemporary discussion of identity places the question of identity within the theory of **meaning**. Identity is considered as a **relation** rather than as a property and, furthermore, as a relation between **names** or **signs** of objects rather than a relation between **objects**. Many philosophers follow **Frege** in arguing that an identity sentence would be cognitively insignificant if it were about a relation between objects and that it is meaningful because it is about a relation between signs of objects. Frege made the brilliant but controversial claim that in order to understand how identity statements are meaningful we must distinguish between the **sense** and the **reference** of signs.

The claim that items can be contingently identical has been vigorously challenged by **Kripke**, who argues that identities, although open to empirical discovery, are matters of **necessity**.

> "Problems concerning identity have been extensively discussed in the history of philosophy at least since Heraclitus worried about how anything could persist through change." **Brody, *Identity and Essence***

identity, law of

LOGIC The law expressed in the formula A = A and stating that everything is what it is, or that if anything is A, then it is A. Something cannot be what it is and fail to be what it is at the same time. Along with the **law of contradiction** and the **law of excluded middle**, the law of identity is one of the three traditional **laws of thought** that are regarded as basic and fundamental to all thought.

> "The law of identity is 'If and only if p, then p'." **Prior, *Formal Logic***

identity, numerical

LOGIC, METAPHYSICS **Aristotle** distinguished three kinds of sameness or identity: (1) specific identity, according to which one thing is identical with another in respect of their **species**, that is, the two things belong to the same species; (2) generic identity, according to which one thing is identical with another in respect of their **genus**, that is, the two things belong to the same genus; and (3) numerical identity, according to which one thing is identical with another if the two things share the same **space** and **time** and have all their characteristics in common. If two things are numerically identical, they are in an **equivalence** relation and are actually one and the same thing, except for having different **names**. Numerical identity is sometimes called particular identity.

> "We generally apply the term [identity] numerically or specifically or generically – numerically in cases where there is more than one name but only one thing, for example 'doublet' and 'cloak'." **Aristotle, *Topics***

identity, the paradox of

LOGIC Identity, signified by expressions such as "the same as," is generally thought to be a **relation** either between two distinct things, or between one thing and itself. However, if it is the former, then the statement of identity must be false because two distinct things cannot be the same. If it is the latter, the statement of identity is true, but is the most trivial tautology. The **paradox**, which can be traced to **Plato** and **Aristotle**, was explicitly expressed by **Wittgenstein**: "to say of two things that they are identical is nonsense, and to say of one thing that it is identical with itself is to say nothing at all" (*Tractatus*, 5.5303). **Frege** attempted to solve the paradox by saying that a true meaningful identity statement involves expressions with the same **reference** but different **senses**. **Russell** claimed that the paradox is due to the confusion of two levels of **predicates**, and Wittgenstein denied that identity is a relation.

> "The paradox of identity similarly proceeds from an assumption – the assumption that a statement of identity asserts a relation." **C. Williams, *What is Identity?***

identity criteria

LOGIC, METAPHYSICS The conditions in accordance with which we determine whether items are the same at a given time or whether a given thing is the same over time. This notion can be traced to **Frege** and was examined by the later **Wittgenstein**. A criterion of identity is generally understood to provide logically necessary and sufficient conditions for determining the truth or falsity of an identity claim, but some philosophers take the criterial relation as being looser than one which provides necessary and sufficient conditions. Since identity admits of different kinds, there are various kinds of identity criteria.

> "That in accordance with which we judge whatever identity holds I call a criterion of identity." **Geach, *Reference and Generality***

identity of indiscernibles, see indiscernibility of identicals

identity statement

LOGIC A statement in which an expression of **identity**, such as "is" or "are," unites two expressions aiming to identify the same thing or kind of thing. All identity statements are symmetric, that is, if "A is B," then "B is A." An identity statement is not a kind of subject-predicate statement, for one cannot distinguish subject and predicate roles for the expressions to perform. There are various kinds of identity statements. For meaning identity, a statement presents two general nouns that are synonyms, for example "Motor cars are automobiles." For referential or name identity, a statement gives two proper names of a subject, for example "Mount Everest is Chomolungma." For **contingent identity**, a statement gives two expressions that accidentally and perhaps temporarily pick out the same individual, for example "Beijing is the Capital of the People's Republic of China." For necessary identity, a statement gives two expressions that necessarily designate the same individual. The necessity can be explained in terms of the kind of expressions used (**rigid designators**) or by logical, mathematical, metaphysical, or scientific theoretical considerations.

> "We may say that identity statements are a distinct class of statements, not to be assimilated to subject-predicate statements." **Strawson, *Individuals***

identity theory

PHILOSOPHY OF MIND A materialist account of the relationship between **mental states** and **events** and physical states and events, according to which mental states such as thinking, believing, feeling, and hoping as a matter of fact turn out to be identical to physical states in the brain. Although things could have been otherwise, to have a mind is to have a brain, and to be in a certain mental state is to be in a certain neural state. Mental states and events actually occur in their owners' central nervous systems. For example, **pain** is identical with a certain firing of c-fibres. Identity theory is a widely held version of **materialism** or **physicalism**. It is sometimes used as a synonym for **central-state materialism**. It originated in the late 1950s with Herbert **Feigl** and U. T. Place, and versions of it have been fully defended

by J. J. C. **Smart**, David **Armstrong**, Hilary **Putnam**, David **Lewis**, and Donald **Davidson**. The identity theory of mind shares the behaviorists' criticism of **dualism**, but it also accommodates the inner and the episodic and therefore overcomes important weaknesses of **behaviorism**. The earlier version of the theory, type-type identity theory, claims that every **type** of mental event is identical with some type of physical state. However, this turns out to be problematic since, for example, it is reasonable to assume that persons with the same beliefs need not always have similar neural states. This gives rise to the token-token identity theory, according to which there is no necessary correspondence between a given type of mental state and a certain type of bodily state. Instead an instance or **token** of a mental state is identical with a token physical state of some type or other. Some critics argue that the token-token theory lacks the explanatory power of the type-type theory. The notion of **contingent identity** employed by identity theory is severely criticized by **Kripke** and T. **Nagel**. **Functionalism** may be seen as a recent successor to the identity theory put forward by those continuing to seek a materialist or physicalist account of the mind.

> "The so-called 'identity theory' may be characterised roughly as the theory that the mind is a brain, or more concretely that mental events, states, and processes are brain events, states and processes." **J. Smart, *Essays Metaphysical and Moral***

ideology

POLITICAL PHILOSOPHY, PHILOSOPHY OF RELIGION, PHILOSOPHY OF SOCIAL SCIENCE [from Greek *idea* + *logos*, literally, the doctrine of ideas, but used both positively and negatively in the social sciences] A term introduced by Destutt de Tracy at the end of the eighteenth century and initially used in the modern critique of religion. His use led to a positive sense of ideology as any world view and body of philosophical thought. In this sense, ideology covers the whole sphere of culture, including science, and can be seen as a necessary intermediary between ourselves and the world. **Marx** made prominent use of the term, but in a pejorative or negative sense. For Marx, ideology is false consciousness: an interrelated set of value judgments which guide social and political actions, but which have not been subjected to rational scrutiny. These judgments are necessarily deceptive through distorting our understanding of social reality. Ideology, according to Marx, covers religion and all other forms of distorted consciousness. In this sense, ideology is the antithesis of science and functions politically as a specific element of the **superstructure** of society. The term is still used in both its positive and negative sense.

"In this, its origin, the term ideology has a positive connotation. It is the rigorous science of ideas which, by overcoming religions and metaphysical prejudices, may serve as a new basis for public education." **Larrain**, *The Concept of Ideology*

idiolect

PHILOSOPHY OF LANGUAGE, PHILOSOPHY OF MIND [from Greek *idio*, peculiar] A lect is a variety of some basic language. For example, a dialect is a variety of language based in a particular region. An idiolect is a language that is peculiar to an individual, in contrast to a language shared by a community or sociolect. For instance, you and I both speak and write English, but you and I may have different levels of English competence and performance. An idiolect is closely related to one's intentional states, and hence becomes the common object of study of the philosophy of language and the philosophy of mind.

"Idiolect [is] the dialect of a certain speaker at a certain time." **Bar-Hillel**, *Language and Information*

idol

EPISTEMOLOGY, PHILOSOPHY OF RELIGION, PHILOSOPHY OF SCIENCE, PHILOSOPHY OF SOCIAL SCIENCE [from Latin *idolum*, image] Anything which powerfully influences the common people but whose existence is really ungrounded. These kinds of idols widely exist in religion, culture, social, and economic life. Idol worship or idolatry has been condemned by orthodox Christianity and in contemporary philosophy by **Nietzsche**, **Marx**, **Freud**, and others.

The English philosopher Francis **Bacon** used the term in its original sense of an illusion or false appearance. He distinguished four idols, that is, four common hindrances to the acquisition of knowledge arising through **prejudice** or false ways of thinking. (1) The idols of the tribe (*idola tribus*), the tendency inherent in the human mind to take the human view of nature as the way the nature works in itself. (2) The idols of the cave (*idola specus*), prejudices caused by the nature of each individual's mind and the mental habits due, for example, to one's education. The term is borrowed from **Plato**'s allegory of cave. (3) The idols of the market-place (*idola fori*), caused by the daily intercourse of common life and by the influence exerted by one's language. (4) The idols of the theatre (*idola theatri*), influences exerted by **traditions** and authoritative theories or opinions. For Bacon, idols are the antithesis of ideas. Idols stand in the same relation to the true **interpretation** of nature as **fallacies** stand to ordinary logic. Roger **Bacon** had earlier put forward four hindrances to obtaining true knowledge in the beginning of his *Opus Maius*: the use of insufficient authority, custom, popular opinions, and the concealment of ignorance. Some argue that Francis Bacon derived his theory of idols from Roger Bacon. However, the work of Roger Bacon was not published when Francis Bacon was alive.

"The idols and false notions which are now in possession of the human understanding, and have taken deep root therein, not only beset men's minds that truth can hardly find entrance, but even after entrance obtained, they will again in the very instauration of the sciences meet and trouble us, unless men being fore-warned of the danger fortify themselves as far as may be against their assaults." **Bacon**, *Novum Organum*, in *The Philosophical Works*

idolatry, see iconoclasm

iff, abbreviation of if and only if, see biconditional

ignoratio elenchi

LOGIC [Latin, ignorance of refutation] An informal **fallacy** in traditional logic, in which one argues against something that is not really the position of the opponent. An advocate of such an argument is hence ignorant of what his opponent is trying to refute or prove. It is any fallacy of irrelevance in which one argues for or proves something that is not an issue at hand and is also called an irrelevant conclusion or missing the point. An argument involves this fallacy if it passes from one area of ideas to another.

"To pass in argument from the world of psychology to that of philosophy, or vice versa, or to subordinate either world to the other, cannot fail to involve us on every occasion in *ignoratio elenchi*." **Oakeshott,** *Experience and its Modes*

I–It

METAPHYSICS, MODERN EUROPEAN PHILOSOPHY According to Martin **Buber**, the world is twofold because the human attitude toward it is twofold. This twofold attitude is reflected in the formulations I–It and **I–Thou** (or I–You). For Buber, they are the two primary relationships between oneself and another. In the I–It relationship, It can be both non-human objects and other persons, covering everything with which the I comes into contact and uses for its own **utility**. This is a relation between a user and an object of use or between an observer and an object of observation. This is a one-sided relation, within which the I concentrates upon its own purposes and concerns and keeps the It at a distance, where it is measured and studied. Once there is personal engagement and commitment, the I–It relation becomes the I–Thou relation.

"It becomes unmistakably clear how the spiritual reality of the basic words emerges from a natural reality: that of the basic word I–you from a natural association, that of the basic word I–It from a natural discreteness." **Buber,** *I and Thou*

illicit major

LOGIC A rule for categorical **syllogisms** states that no term may be distributed in the conclusion which is not distributed in one of the premises. The violation of this rule leads to logical **fallacies**. If a major term that is undistributed in the premises becomes distributed in the conclusion, the fallacy is called the illicit process of the major term (or the illicit major). For example, "All persons are mortal; no tree is a person; therefore, no tree is mortal." This inference is erroneous because the major term "mortal" is asserted only partly in the premises but is asserted wholly in the conclusion. If it is the minor term that is undistributed in the premises but distributed in the conclusion, the logical fallacy is called the illicit process of the minor term (or the illicit minor). For example, "All persons are mortal; all persons are two-legged; therefore, all two-legged

things are mortal." This syllogism is incorrect because the conclusion asserts the whole of "two-legged" and hence goes beyond what is implied in the premises.

"When a syllogism contains its major term undistributed in the major premise but distributed in the conclusion, the argument is said to commit the fallacy of illicit process of the major term (or, more briefly, the illicit major)." **Copi,** *Introduction to Logic*

illicit minor, see illicit major

illocutionary act

PHILOSOPHY OF LANGUAGE **Austin**'s term, one of three ways in which saying something is doing something. To perform a **locutionary act** is to utter a meaningful utterance. But over and above this there is a further **act** that gives the **force** of the utterance, the way it is to be taken. An illocutionary act makes clear this aspect of an utterance and is the further act that is performed in performing a locutionary act. Asking or answering a question, giving an assurance or a warning, making an appeal or a criticism are only a few examples of this kind of speech act. The illocutionary force of an utterance is largely dependent on **conventions**, contexts, or a speaker's intention, rather than on the **truth** or falsity of an utterance. Unlike a **perlocutionary act**, according to Austin, an illocutionary act need not produce any effect on others, but is nevertheless a way of understanding the sentence uttered. Austin's chief interest lay in analyzing illocutionary acts on the grounds that they represent a dimension of language which is not **meaning** but which is at least equally important as meaning in **understanding** an utterance. Although some argue that illocution is still a kind of meaning, Austin's theory of illocution has exerted great influence on contemporary philosophy.

"To determine what illocutionary act is so performed we must determine in what way we are using the locution." **Austin,** *How to Do Things with Words*

illusion, argument from

EPISTEMOLOGY, METAPHYSICS An argument starting from the fact that our **senses** sometimes deceive us, for they vary with the physical and psychological condition of the observer and with the nature of the circumstances in which objects appear. From this common premise **rationalism** and **empiricism** derive different conclusions. For rationalists such as **Plato** and **Descartes**, the deceptive nature of the senses shows that **appearances** are not real and cannot be the true objects of **knowledge**. Thus an alternative metaphysical foundation of knowledge must be sought. Empiricists such as **Berkeley** claim that since sensible appearances are unstable, they cannot characterize material things and are the products of mind. If, however, we know nothing other than such appearances we have no grounds to believe in material things. This view leads to **phenomenalism** if we take the common objects of experience to comprise actual sensible appearances and the appearances that would exist were we to be in different circumstances. Philosophers object to the different versions of the argument. Although our senses sometimes deceive us, they do not, and perhaps could not, always do so.

"All that this argument from illusion proves is that the relationship of a sense-content to the material thing to which it belongs is not that of part to whole." **Ayer**, *Language, Truth and Logic*

image

EPISTEMOLOGY, PHILOSOPHY OF LANGUAGE [from Latin *imago*, a representation] A mental picture purportedly representing external **objects**, with certain visual similarities to the latter. This position is called the picture view and is associated with the notion of **introspection**. In this century with the rise of **behaviorism**, the notion of introspection came under attack, and the picture view of imagism became a matter of controversy. A once popular alternative was J. B. Watson's descriptionalism, according to which an image is a **representation** in the manner of a linguistic description. Recently, the picture view has been revived based on the data of empirical psychology. The issue of image is related to various modern forms of **representationalism**.

Traditionally, images are thought to have a close relationship with thinking, and **understanding** the meaning of a word was believed to bring to mind an appropriate image associated with the word.

But **Frege** established a contrast between image and **thought** and considered an image to be merely psychological, with no place in an account of **meaning**. **Wittgenstein** further attacked the supposed role of images in thought. If an image, as a picture of an external thing, can confer meaning on a word, then vividly seeing the external object should be an even better way of conferring meaning. But seeing an object does not settle matters of meaning. If a seeing of a red thing does not explain the meaning of redness, how can a red mental image do so?

"If you endeavor to recall the appearance of your mother, there will usually arise in your fancy a definite visual image, or picture, of a familiar face and figure, which can represent only your mother." **McCall**, *Basic Logic*

image theory of meaning, another term for ideational theory of meaning

imagination

EPISTEMOLOGY, PHILOSOPHY OF MIND, AESTHETICS The ability to represent **objects** or **states of affairs** that cannot exist, that do not exist, or that do not exist here and now. Imagination is both condemned for its link with falsity and prized for its role in artistic **creativity**, especially in romantic art. **Aristotle** suggested that imagination (Greek *phantasia*) lies in the middle between **perception** and **thought**. The British empiricists held an imagist conception of the imagination, according to which to image is to see with the mind's eye. They held that to image something is to have an **image** that represents its physical correspondent and that all **ideas** in the mind are mental images. In **Kant**'s account, imagination is not so crucial for forming **concepts**, but performs an indispensable role in **perception** as an intermediary between our **sensibility** and **understanding** that allows us to have knowledge of a unified world. **Wittgenstein** proposed that we should study how the word "imagination" is used. He also claimed that although mental images exist and are important for imagination, not all kinds of imagination involve them. He characterized imagination in terms of "seeing-as" and seeing under an aspect. His view raises problems about the status of images and the relation between imagination and perception.

> "Imagination is the reorganization of available memories in the light of a particular goal. It can be called creativity in the sense that every such reorganisation is original with the individual."
> **Arnold, in Mischel (ed.),** *Human Action*

imitation

EPISTEMOLOGY, METAPHYSICS, AESTHETICS [Greek *mimesis*] (1) **Plato** used imitation, like **participation**, to describe the relation between the **particulars** and **Forms**. Forms are the originals, analogous to painters' or sculptors' models, and the particulars are resemblances or copies of them. It shows that the particulars are inferior to Forms, as in general originals do not depend on copies, while copies must rely on the originals. Forms are not dependent on the particulars, while the latter cannot exist without Forms. (2) Plato also uses this word to describe the nature of art; art is mainly imitation of the particulars which are themselves imitations of Forms, so it is far away from the **truth**; furthermore, art as imitation has bad effects on the actor's personality; for these reasons Plato orders the expulsion of all imitative arts from his ideal state. Nevertheless his view that "art is imitation" has lasting influence in the theory of literature.

> "For imitation is surely a kind of production, though it be only a production of images, as we say, not of originals of every sort." **Plato,** *Sophist*

imitation game, see Turing test

imitation theory

AESTHETICS, METAPHYSICS, EPISTEMOLOGY The oldest theory of art, whose central claim is that the essence of art is to imitate or display things in the real world. "Imitation" is the translation of the Greek word *mimesis* (hence the theory is also called "mimetic theory of art"). *Mimesis* is sometimes translated as "**representation**" (hence the theory is also called the "representation theory of art"). This theory originated with **Plato** and **Aristotle** and was the dominant theory of art until the rise of Romanticism. It has retained a deep metaphysical concern for knowing how things are and argues that art has a cognitive role. However, there has been much debate about the precise meaning of "imitation" and "representation" and about questions relating to the

nature of representation. Some writers claim that to imitate is to portray the visible form of nature, while others believe that imitation requires idealization. The basic criticism of the imitation theory is that not all forms of art are imitation or representation. Music, for example, is not essentially representational. Contemporary abstract painting further stands outside the scope of this theory. Nevertheless, the theory still has able defenders. An influential version has been developed by Nelson **Goodman**, who argues that representation means **denotation**. On this view, the relation between an artwork and the thing it represents is analogous to the relation between a **description** and what it describes.

> "The imitation theory focused on a readily evident relational property of works of art, namely, art's relation to subject matter." **Dickie,** *Art and the Aesthetic*

immaterialism

METAPHYSICS, EPISTEMOLOGY **Berkeley**'s own designation for his philosophy, which is always taken as a synonym for subjective **idealism**. Berkeley referred to his opponents as **materialists**. Matter for him was not the corporeal as such, but rather that which is inaccessible by the finite perceiving mind or something whose existence has no bearing to any perceiving mind, such as **Descartes**'s material **substance** or **Locke**'s unknown underlying **essence**. Berkeley held that to be is to be perceived. The corporeal is exactly as it is perceived to be, and the existence of absolute and independent matter is unintelligible. What is real comprises **sense-impressions** and **ideas**.

> "If there are difficulties attending immaterialism, these are at the same time direct and evident proofs for it. But for the existence of matter, there is not one proof, and far more numerous and insurmountable objections lies against it." **Berkeley,** *Three Dialogues Between Hylas and Philonous*

immediate inference

LOGIC **Inference** must start with one or more premises. If we draw a conclusion simply from one single premise, one proposition from another single proposition, the inference is immediate. It does not use a middle term or any other means for reaching a conclusion. For instance, from the single premise "All humans are mortal," we can infer validly that "Some humans are mortal." This contrasts with mediate inference, in which a conclusion is drawn from more than one premise, such as a **syllogism** and polysyllogism. In the **square of opposition** of traditional logic, given the truth and falsity of one of the categorical propositions, we may immediately infer the truth or falsity of some or all of the other three categorical propositions. Other major forms of immediate inference include **conversion**, **obversion**, and **contraposition**.

"Where a conclusion is drawn from only one premise . . . the inference is said to be immediate." **Copi,** *Introduction to Logic*

immediate perception

EPISTEMOLOGY A distinction between immediate and mediate or indirect perception that originated with **Berkeley**, and is also called the distinction between direct and indirect awareness. One may say that "I hear a train," but what one actually hears is a sound. In this case the sound is what a person perceives immediately without any inference, while the train is perceived mediately, for the person may not perceive the train at all but only infer from hearing the sound that there is a train. We have mediate perception only when we have immediate perception, although the immediate perception need not be temporally prior. What, then, is the nature of this distinction between immediate and mediate perception? Different responses are the basis of a division in the philosophy of perception between **naive or direct realism** on the one hand, and **representationalism** and **phenomenalism** on the other. Both representationalism and phenomenalism take this distinction seriously, arguing that the objects of immediate perception are **sense-data** or sense-impressions, while the objects of mediate perception are physical existents that are represented by the sense-data (representationalism) or are constructed out of sense-data (phenomenalism). Naive or direct realism argues that what we immediately perceive are nothing but the physical objects themselves. According to this theory, both immediate and mediate perception is the acquiring of beliefs about the world by means of senses, and this distinction is not a sharp one. The analysis of immediate perception is indeed a central problem in contemporary philosophy of perception.

"Immediate perception, then, is perception which involves no element of inference, while mediate perception does involve such an inference." **D. Armstrong,** *Perception and the Physical World*

immortality

PHILOSOPHY OF RELIGION, METAPHYSICS, PHILOSOPHY OF MIND [from Latin *in*, not + *mors*, death] A state of existing eternally or timelessly, specifically regarding personal immortality through the **survival** of the **soul** after the **death** of the body. The immortality of the soul, an ancient idea found in almost every primitive religion, was fully developed in Christianity. It claims that a soul never dies and will be punished or rewarded according to its behavior in the earthly life. Immortality in this sense has served as a presupposition of morality, or, in **Kant**'s words, "a postulate of pure practical reason." Metaphysically, the soul's immortality was elaborated in **Plato**'s *Phaedo*. He argued that because the soul is immaterial and simple, in the sense of having no parts, and occupies no space, it can not be decomposed. This kind of argument was influential in the history of philosophy, but it has been opposed by the **Aristotelian** view that the soul is the **form** of the body and cannot exist separately. On some views, one's present body is no more than a temporary home for one's soul, and one is immortal through **reincarnation** or transmigration into another body when one's present body perishes.

Plato also claimed that human beings have a natural desire to seek immortality. There are two basic ways of pursuing this end. One is to have bodily offspring, and another, preferred by Plato, is to produce something that is eternal, especially through the discovery of truths. One's spiritual work can continue to exist in other people's minds after one's death.

"Immortality means endurance in time, deathless life on this earth." **Arendt,** *Human Condition*

impartial spectator, see ideal observer theory

impartialism

ETHICS A tendency reflected in every kind of **altruistic** moral theory, and especially **Kantian** ethics.

It advocates the view that moral consideration should be isolated from all forms of partiality and self-concern and emphasizes the universalizability of moral **reasons**. Moral **principles** are universally applicable and cannot be principles that favor oneself or those close to one on pain of being rationally unacceptable. Impartialism extensively employs the analogical argument that one should consider events from another person's point of view and should hypothetically put oneself in the position of those whom one's acts will affect.

> "The idea behind the Golden Rule is that of impartialism – that one should make no exception in one's own favour." **Boer and Lycan,** *Knowing Who*

impartiality

ETHICS, POLITICAL PHILOSOPHY If an agent is included in a group with regard to which the issue of impartiality arises, impartiality is the virtue of treating oneself and others on an equal basis. If one is not in the group regarding which one is impartial, impartiality is a virtue of being personally uninvolved with any party in the group. Impartiality is associated with **equality**, **justice**, and **fairness**. It is objective and impersonal. Since it is an essential requirement of moral behavior to consider each individual equally, impartiality is a basic feature of morality. There are various tests of impartiality, such as the **Golden Rule**, the reverse-role test, the **categorical imperative**, **universalizability**, and **Rawls**'s **veil of ignorance**.

> "What is it to be 'impartial'? It is to take an attitude that would not be changed if positions of individuals involved were reversed, or if the individuals were different from whom they are." **Brandt,** *Ethical Theory*

imperative

LOGIC, ETHICS, PHILOSOPHY OF LANGUAGE Originally the mood of sentences that issue commands or requests. **Kant** took it as the form of moral **commands** for determining an **action** in accordance with a certain principle of the **will**. It is expressed by an **ought**. According to him, there are fundamentally two kinds of imperatives: the hypothetical and the categorical. A **hypothetical imperative** commands an action with regard to the agent's ends.

If the end is only possible, it is a problematic or technical imperative, also called a rule of skill. If the end is actual, it is an assertoric imperative, also called a counsel of **prudence**. A **categorical imperative** commands an action as an objective necessity in itself, without regard to the agent's ends, and is also called the apodeictic imperative. It requires that one should act only on **maxims** that are **universalizable**.

An account of imperatives under Kantian influence is also important for **prescriptivism**. The philosophy of language is interested in the relationship between this commanding function of imperatives and other functions in language, such as communicating information. Contemporary logicians have attempted to develop an imperative logic.

> "The conception of an objective principle so far as it constrains a will, is a command (of reason), and the formula of this command is called an imperative." **Kant,** *Groundwork for the Metaphysics of Morals*

imperfect duty

ETHICS **Kant** drew a distinction between perfect and imperfect duties. A perfect duty must be fulfilled under any circumstances and specifies a particular action, while an imperfect duty may be overridden and allows a significant degree of freedom in deciding how to comply with it. A perfect duty, such as the duty not to lie, establishes a necessary goal for an action and is commanded apodeictically. An imperfect duty, such as the duty to support the poor, allows exceptions and various ways in which it may be satisfied. It allows contingently good action under a necessarily good **maxim**. The distinction can be traced to **scholasticism**, in which perfect duties could be enforced by external legislation, while imperfect duties could not.

> "Imperfect duties are, accordingly, only duties of virtue. Fulfilment of them is merit . . . but failure to fulfil them is not in itself culpability . . . but rather mere deficiency in moral worth, unless the subject should make it his principle not to comply with such duties." **Kant,** *The Metaphysics of Morals*

imperialism

POLITICAL PHILOSOPHY, ETHICS A term with many senses. In **Marxism**, imperialism is the world system of political domination and economic exploitation that emerged from the competition amongst highly developed capitalist powers, especially in the nineteenth and twentieth centuries. According to Lenin, imperialism is the highest stage of capitalism. On this view, capitalism entered the imperialist phase because surplus capital that could not be absorbed in the home market had to be invested in colonies and other dominated countries. A few imperialist countries divided the world into different spheres of influence. When the balance of the division of the world market was broken, world war resulted. There have been rival accounts of the origin and nature of imperialism. For Kautsky, imperialism is the oppression and exploitation of underdeveloped countries by developed countries. In contemporary ethics, imperialism is mainly used in a cultural sense to characterize the claim that the point of view of one special group, based on nation, culture, race, religion, gender, or other considerations, is privileged. According to a feminist version of this theory, it is cultural imperialism to hold that only the position of white bourgeois men is scientific.

"What we mean when we speak of empire or imperialism is the relationship of a hegemonial state to peoples or nations under its control." **Lichtheim,** *Imperialism*

impersonal verb

LOGIC, PHILOSOPHY OF LANGUAGE Verbs appearing in sentences such as "It is snowing." In this kind of sentence the word "it" does not have the logical function of a subject. The speaker does not intend to pick out something it designates. This sort of sentence is a subjectless sentence, and the standard subject-predicate distinction does not apply to it. Hence, the verb in it does not introduce an action performed by a subject, and we never significantly ask, for example, "What is snowing?"

"When verbs occur in phrases like 'It is raining' or 'It is freezing', they are traditionally called 'impersonal verbs'." **C. Williams,** *Being, Identity and Truth*

implication

LOGIC In its ordinary sense, implication is a synonym of **entailment**, a logical relation between one or a set of premises and a consequence deduced from this premise or set of premises. It is most commonly expressed in sentences of the form "if p

then q," when p is the implying proposition (also called the antecedent or protasis), and q is the implied proposition (also called the consequent or apodasis). **Russell** and **Whitehead** used the term **material implication** to express the relation between the antecedent and consequent of a true conditional proposition, which is symbolized as $p \supset q$ or as $p \to q$. In order to avoid the so-called paradoxes of material implication, C. I. **Lewis** introduced a notion of **strict implication**, saying that p strictly implies q if and only if it was impossible that p should be true and q false. Other attempts to further clarify the meaning relation between antecedent and consequent include **Carnap**'s L-implication and the system of entailment.

"In order to be able validly to infer the truth of a proposition, we must know that some other proposition is true, and that there is between the two a relation of the sort called 'implication', that is that (as we say) the premise 'implies' the conclusion." **Russell,** *Introduction to Mathematical Philosophy*

implicit definition

LOGIC, PHILOSOPHY OF MATHEMATICS, PHILOSOPHY OF SCIENCE Also called **definition** by **axioms** or definition by **postulates**. In contrast to an explicit definition, which gives the necessary and sufficient conditions for a term to be applied, an implicit definition of a term does not directly state the **extension** and **intension** of a term, but defines the term by showing that it satisfies certain axioms, the validity of which is strictly guaranteed. Thus the axioms of a system of geometry implicitly define the primitive geometrical signs that the axioms contain by delimiting the **interpretations** of the signs that satisfy it. This notion gains its importance in modern mathematics through the work of **Hilbert**. For he claims that the quest for explicit definitions for many mathematical terms such as "straight line," "point," and "plane" is extremely difficult and that we should define such terms implicitly as whatever entities satisfy the formal axioms formulated by means of them. As a result, although **non-Euclidean geometry** still uses Euclidean terms such as "point," "place," and "straight line," these terms do not mean the same in the two systems, since they are implicitly defined by the postulate set in which they occur. A similar use of implicit definitions in natural science, in which terms are defined through satisfy-ing the theories in which they are embedded, also raises questions of the stability of **meaning** in the face of changes in **theory**.

> "When the term 'implicit definition' is used in connection with formal postulational systems, it refers to a set of formal postulates, i.e. postulates whose extralogical terms, the 'primitives' of the system, are not interpreted. Such a set is said to implicitly define the primitive extralogical terms it contains." **Pap, Semantics and Necessary Truth**

importation
LOGIC A principle of **inference** which states that from the premise "If p, then q and r" $[(p \to (q \wedge r)]$, we can conclude "if p and q, then r" $[(p \wedge q) \to r]$. This inference is **a strict implication** and can be expressed in **propositional logic** as $[p \to (q \wedge r)] \leftrightarrow [(p \wedge q) \to r]$. The reverse of this inference, which is also valid, is called **exportation**.

> "If q implies q, and r implies r, and if p implies that q implies r, then pq implies r. This is the principle of importation." **Russell, Principles of Mathematics**

impredicative definition
LOGIC, PHILOSOPHY OF MATHEMATICS A **definition** of an object by reference to the totality to which the object belongs. The term is credited to **Russell** and **Poincaré**. Both argued that this kind of definition must be banned from the conceptual foundation of mathematics. No totality can contain members defined in terms of itself for they imply a **vicious circle** and lead to logical **paradox**. For example, it is an impredicative definition if we define a **set** A as "the set of all sets that are not members of them-selves." Then if asked whether A is a member of itself or not, the answer is paradoxical, that is, A is a member of itself if and only if A is not a member of itself. This is the famous **Russell's paradox**.

> "It appears that if one were seriously to outlaw all impredicative definitions, that is to say, definitions of an object by reference to a totality which in-cludes itself or object definable only in terms of itself, one would not only have to sacrifice a great deal of accepted mathematics but would also be jeopardising the complete programme of deriving mathematics from Logic." **Ayer, Russell and Moore**

impression (Hume), see idea (Hume)

in and for itself, see in itself

inauthenticity, see authenticity

incentive
ETHICS In **Kant**'s ethics, the subjective ground of **desire** that provides a subjective end for the **will**. In contrast, a **motive** is the objective ground of volition. An incentive is material and sensuous and is related to a particular subject. It does not always conform to the objective conditions of morality and can only supply grounds for **hypothetical imperat-ives**. On the other hand, a **categorical imperative** abstracts from incentives and is applicable to all rational subjects.

> "From what has gone before it is clear that the purposes which we may have in our actions, as well as their effects regarded as ends and incentives of the will, cannot give to actions any uncondi-tioned and moral worth." **Kant, Groundwork for the Metaphysics of Morals**

inclination
ETHICS [from Latin *in* + *clinare*, bend, lean] A kind of **incentive**, **disposition**, or tendency that will cause certain **action**. It is rooted in the world of sense and is material and subjective. In **Kant**'s ethics, inclination is the source of the **heteronomy** of the will. A will dominated by inclination does not give itself a law and only passively reacts to external stimuli. This is a state of slavery. Inclination cannot be **universalized** and can only be the basis of a **hypothetical imperative**. It also contrasts with **duty** and **reason**. For Kant, it is crucial to distinguish whether an action stems from duty or from inclina-tion in deciding whether an action has a genuine moral worth, although critics claim that his grounds for moral worth are too austere.

> "The dependence of the faculty of desire on sensations is called inclination, which accordingly always indicates a need." **Kant, Groundwork for the Metaphysics of Morals**

incommensurability
PHILOSOPHY OF SCIENCE Two **theories** are commen-surable if there is common ground to assess or

measure their merits and demerits. Some philosophers, such as **Popper**, have held that science develops through the successive replacement of commensurable theories, that is, old and relatively unsuccessful theories are superseded by new and relatively successful theories. However, in his account of **paradigm shifts** of scientific revolutions, **Kuhn** argued that any new **paradigm** will completely replace and destroy the old one and that they are incommensurable. The component statements of the rival paradigms are mutually untranslatable. They involve different **conceptual schemes**, different problems, and even alternative logics. The claims of one theory cannot be framed in the language of the other, and the whole network of thought and practice has to be reconstructed. The transition between paradigms involves a breakdown of communication. After a paradigm shift, scientists live in a totally different world. Science does not accumulate **truth** as time passes, and when a new paradigm replaces an older one, it dismisses all the results obtained within the old paradigm. We do not have common ground for resolving the disputes between different paradigms. This view was further developed by **Feyerabend**, but faces difficulty in explaining examples of evident continuity in the growth of scientific knowledge.

"We have already seen several reasons why the proponents of competing paradigms must fail to make complete contact with each other's viewpoints. Collectively these reasons have been described as the incommensurability of the pre- and postrevolutionary normal-scientific traditions." **Kuhn,** *The Structure of Scientific Revolutions*

incompatibilism, see compatibilism

incomplete symbol
LOGIC, METAPHYSICS, PHILOSOPHY OF LANGUAGE **Russell**'s term for an expression that has no significance on its own, but which acquires **meaning** in a context provided by other symbols. An incomplete symbol does not refer to actual **objects** directly. According to Russell, **definite descriptions**, class-symbols, and logical fictions are all incomplete symbols. Because appeal to this device removes the necessity to admit a domain of unreal entities, it is an important component of Russell's theory of descriptions. A full discussion of this term is provided by **Whitehead** and Russell, *Principia Mathematica*, I, 3.

"Thus all phrases (other than propositions) containing the word 'the' (in the singular) are incomplete symbols. They have a meaning in use, but not in isolation." **Whitehead and Russell,** *Principia Mathematica*

incompleteness, see completeness

incompleteness theorem, see Gödel's theorem

incongruent counterpart
METAPHYSICS A counterpart of an object is something that completely resembles it. For example, a left hand is a counterpart of the right hand. **Kant** set out the argument from incongruent counterparts, which states that counterparts cannot be congruent if, though formally identical, they differ in their relation to absolute **space**. Even if identical in shape, they cannot change their spatial orientation in a way that would allow one to fit into the limits of the other. Hence, they are incongruent. For example, in three dimensions a right hand cannot occupy the same spatial location as a left hand. This argument depends upon the claim that the properties of space are prior to the relations of bodies. Counterparts have spatial properties not susceptible to any relational analysis. This argument presupposes the **Newtonian** conception of absolute space and is at odds with the **Leibnizian** relativist view of space because his relational theory cannot capture the difference of spatial orientation of right and left hands. The problem is taken by some philosophers as proof that space is absolute, while others argue that in different spatial systems incongruent counterparts would be congruent. Incongruent counterparts are also called **enantiomorphs** (from Greek *enantion*, opposite + *morphe*, form).

"I shall call a body which is exactly equal and similar to another, but which cannot be enclosed in the same limits as that other, its incongruent counterpart." **Kant,** *Theoretical Philosophy*

inconsistent triad, another term for antilogism

incontinence
ETHICS [Greek *akrasia*, from *a*, not + *kratein*, to control or master] A lack of control over oneself,

especially over one's irrational **desires**. An incontinent man or *akrastic* does what he knows he ought not to do, or fails to do what he knows he should do. **Socrates** claimed that **virtue** is **knowledge** and that no man voluntarily does evil. He therefore denied the existence of incontinence and took what appeared as incontinence to be a kind of ignorance. Both **Plato** and **Aristotle** believed that incontinence exists and considered it to be a matter of great importance to understand how it is possible. Plato's account emphasized the clash between the different elements in the **soul**, with incontinence occurring when a person's **emotion** or appetite overcomes his **reason**. Aristotle offered two different interpretations. Along with Plato, he sought to explain incontinence in terms of a psychological conflict, but in a revision of Socrates' argument he also argued that an incontinent person does not properly know that what he is doing is bad. He knows some of the premises relating to his action only potentially, in the way that men who are asleep, mad, or drunk have knowledge. Aristotle's complex discussion has been the subject of much interpretation and debate.

Incontinence involves an important aspect of the conception of **human nature**. Its existence shows that sometimes **belief** is powerless before **passion**, and that **intellect** does not always determine **will**. Philosophers have taken great pains to explain this phenomenon, which separates moral beliefs and moral commitment.

> "For incontinence makes someone act contrary to what he supposes." **Aristotle**, *Nicomachean Ethics*

incorrigible

EPISTEMOLOGY, METAPHYSICS A **statement** or **proposition** is incorrigible in a strong sense if it is impossible to be mistaken or uncertain about its **truth** and is incorrigible in a weak sense if it cannot be corrected even if it may be mistaken. An example of the strong sense is given by the so-called **basic propositions**, which are meant merely to record one's present experience without relating it to anything else. I cannot doubt propositions such as "I have a headache," although this statement might be doubted by other persons or by myself at other times. An example for the weak sense is given by our reports of our dreams, which we are not in a position to correct even if they are mistaken. A search for an absolute ground in metaphysics and epistemology is a search for a starting-point that is incorrigible, but it is disputable whether there can be such a point.

> "I should now agree with those who say that propositions of this kind are 'incorrigible', assuming that what is meant by their being incorrigible is that it is impossible to be mistaken about them except in a verbal sense." **Ayer**, *Language, Truth and Logic*

independence, logical

LOGIC If neither a sentence S nor its negation not-S is deducible from a set of sentences T, then S is logically independent of T. That is, there is no logical relationship between S and T, and T does not determine the truth-value of either S or not-S. In an axiomatic system, an **axiom** is generally regarded to be independent of other axioms in the system. Hence independence amounts to non-deducibility. The **axiom of choice** and the **continuum hypothesis** are regarded as typical independent sentences.

> "Axiomatists are naturally concerned that their axioms be independent: that none be derivable as a theorem from the rest, and hence dispensable." **Quine**, *Methods of Logic*

indeterminacy in law

PHILOSOPHY OF LAW Also called the no right answer thesis. Lawyers debate about problems of indeterminacy in which the criteria for the application of legal **rules** are vague or in which a case falls under two or more conflicting rules. Many legal philosophers believe that in these cases it is uncertain which side of a legal dispute is stronger. They claim that legal rules in such **hard cases** provide no right answer and that informed people can reasonably disagree about them. For **natural law** theorists, hard cases arise because law is derived from moral **principles**, but moral principles themselves are sometimes in conflict. For **legal positivists**, there is indeterminacy because law is derived from the body of past legislation and conventions that cannot be expected always to apply in solving present issues. It is unlikely that a system contains in itself appropriate conflict-resolving rules for all cases. Accordingly, they argue that for hard cases lawyers and judges should develop the law on the basis of moral, social, or other extra-legal arguments.

indeterminacy of translation

PHILOSOPHY OF LANGUAGE, PHILOSOPHY OF SCIENCE, METAPHYSICS Different translators render an alien language into our own language in terms of different translation manuals. These manuals may all fit the totality of known speech dispositions, but are not compatible with each other. It is a natural assumption that in translating the translator discovers as an objective fact that an alien word is synonymous to some word in our language, and that we can decide which manual is correct or better. But **Quine** challenges this assumption by arguing that there is no matter of fact according to which we may determine which manual is correct. Our choice of the manual is not based on the belief that it alone assigns the true **meanings** to the expressions of the alien language, but is determined by the utility of the manual in facilitating conversation, that is, by subjective, **pragmatic** considerations. Any individual linguistic utterance may be given different **interpretations**. Any manual may fit the facts so long as it conforms to the **stimulus meaning**, but the stimulus meaning varies according to the **context**. Physical facts do not determine our talk about **synonymy**. This indeterminacy of translation leads to the indeterminacy of **reference**, of **truth**, and of **ontological commitment**. The thesis is consistent with Quine's denial of the distinction between **analytic and synthetic propositions**, because this distinction means little if there is no fact of the matter determining whether a sentence in another language should be translated into an analytical or synthetic claim. It is also consistent with Quine's **extensionalism**, for it shows that there is no basis for assigning determinate **intensional** contents to propositions. Because this thesis leads toward a general mistrust of determinate meaning and undermines many of the traditional aspirations of philosophy, it has been the subject of important disputes. On the other hand, **Chomsky** holds that it adds nothing essential to the accepted view that physical theory is itself indeterminate with regard to all possible empirical evidence.

indeterminism

METAPHYSICS, PHILOSOPHY OF SCIENCE, ETHICS A theory which claims, in opposition to **determinism**, that some **events** just happen without determining **causes** and that no prior conditions account for them. Such events can be characterized in terms of **chance**, randomness, or uncertainty. According to **quantum** mechanics, quantum events at the most fundamental level of reality are of this kind. The indeterminism of modern physics erodes any sharp demarcation between the **laws of nature** and the special facts of nature. This distinction can be understood only by placing it within the context of **statistical laws**. The contrast between indeterminism and determinism reflects a difference in the world views held by quantum mechanics and **Newtonian** physics.

Some philosophers apply indeterminism to ethics and suggest that human beings have uncaused free **actions**, with no antecedent events explaining their **choices**. It is difficult on this view to explain in what sense we can ascribe an uncaused action to an agent. Answers to this question will help to decide whether **freedom** is more compatible with random or chance actions or with causally determined ones.

indicative word

LOGIC, EPISTEMOLOGY, PHILOSOPHY OF LANGUAGE An indicative word signifies a sensible **object** and its **properties**. Such words include **names**, words denoting qualities, and words denoting perceptible **relations**. The meaning of indicative words can be given directly by **ostensive definitions**.

indicator terms, another term for egocentric particulars

indifference/spontaneity, see spontaneity/indifference

indirect perception, see immediate perception

indirect realism

EPISTEMOLOGY There are two types of perceptual realism, direct and indirect realism. Both claim that the physical world exists independently of perceivers and that the world is as science says it is. While direct realism believes that what we perceive is the physical world itself, indirect realism argues that what we immediately or directly perceive are **sense-data**, rather than the physical world itself, which can only be perceived indirectly. Thus, indirect realism sets up a field of sense-data between our **perception** and the physical world. But it contrasts with **phenomenalism**, for it denies that physical existents are composed out of sense-data. There are two main versions of indirect realism. One, called naive indirect realism, claims that sense-data have all the types of properties that physical objects have. The other, called scientific indirect realism, suggests that physical objects have **primary properties**, while **secondary properties**, such as color, smell, and taste, belong only to sense-data.

"The dispute between the direct realist and the indirect realist concerns the question of whether we are ever directly aware of the existence and nature of physical objects." **Dancy,** *Introduction to Contemporary Epistemology*

indiscernibility of identicals

LOGIC, METAPHYSICS, PHILOSOPHY OF LANGUAGE This principle, also called **Leibniz's law**, or the principle of substitutivity, states that for any two objects X and Y, if they are identical, all the properties that belong to X belong also to Y, and vice versa. Everything true of one will be true of the other. **Leibniz**'s formulation is: "To suppose two things indiscernible is to suppose the same thing under two names." Leibniz himself argues that there are not in nature two real beings that are indiscernible from one another. Two leaves in a garden can never be found perfectly alike. This principle plays a great role in the contemporary discussion of **intentionality**. A contrary form may say that if a property is true of

one thing but not of the other, they are not identical. But this is not always true in belief contexts or in other referentially **opaque contexts**.

A correlated principle, called the principle of the **identity of indiscernibles**, is sometimes also included as part of Leibniz's law. It states that if X and Y have all their properties in common, they are identical.

If we shift our focus to language, these principles are related to the principle of **extensionality**, which states that the **names** and **descriptions** of the same **object** can be substituted for one another in all contexts *salva veritate* (without changing the truth-value of the statements in which they appear). These principles apply within limits rather than universally, but it is difficult to explain what we should say outside these limits, for example, about intentional contexts, in which substitutivity *salva veritate* does not hold.

"One of the fundamental principles governing identity is that of *substitutivity* – or, as it might well be called, that of *indiscernibility of identicals*. It provides that, *given a true statement of identity, one of its two terms may be substituted for the other in any true statement and the result will be the same.*" **Quine,** *From a Logical Point of View*

individual

LOGIC, METAPHYSICS, PHILOSOPHY OF LANGUAGE, ETHICS, POLITICAL PHILOSOPHY [from Latin *individuus*, indivisible, employed by Boethius to translate Greek *atom*, uncuttable or undividable; a single distinct entity or unit which is incapable of being divided actually or conceptually while preserving its identity] In a standard sense, an individual is something that can be **individuated**, that is, counted or picked out in language and thus be distinguished from other things. In logic, individuals are things that can be subjects of sentences in the **first-order** predicate **calculus**, in contrast with **predicates** or **functions**. Individuals are often taken to be identical with **particulars**, but there is a significant difference. All particulars are individuals, but not all individuals are particulars. What we pick out in language are not merely various kinds of particular things, but also general things such as justice, wisdom, beauty. In moral, political, and social thought, an individual is a **person**, in contrast to a group or society.

individual essence

METAPHYSICS An essence is usually thought to be a **property** common to a kind of thing, to belong to a **species** and therefore to be **universal**. But there is also a tradition, starting from **Aristotle**'s notion of *tode ti* ("thisness"), which suggests that each individual member of a given species has its own unique essential property. For instance, Plato is a man. Man is a universal essence that Plato shares with other human beings. However, there might be a property of being Plato that distinguishes Plato from Socrates and Aristotle and from all other human beings. Such an essence is a distinct property that is unique to an object and possessed by nothing else. **Duns Scotus** called an individual essence *haecceity*. The idea of individual essence is controversial, but it has been revived in contemporary **essentialist** discussions of **modal logic** as the property by which a proper name has a referent. In **possible world** accounts of modality, an individual essence is the property of X such that in every possible world in which X exists, X has this property, and in no possible world is there is an object distinct from X that has it.

"We can even imagine that there is an essential property of being a particular individual, for example, property F, such that it is necessary that, if anything has that property, it is quantitatively identical with Fred. This sort of property is called an individual essence." **R. Martin,** *The Meaning of Language*

individual property, see abstract particulars

individual term, another expression for singular term

individualism

ETHICS, POLITICAL PHILOSOPHY, METAPHYSICS, EPISTEMOLOGY, PHILOSOPHY OF SOCIAL SCIENCE, PHILOSOPHY OF MIND Any theory or attitude which holds that **individuals** rather than wholes composed out of individuals are of central value and have fundamental existence. It claims that an individual can be understood apart from the physical environment, social relations, and historical traditions in which the individual is embedded. The notion of individualism has had different connotations in different stages of history and in different cultures, corresponding respectively to concerns for **egoism** and **self-interest**, **anarchy**, self-assertion, and **freedom**. In metaphysics, both ancient **atomism** and logical **atomism** are individualistic by holding that the world is constructed out of atoms, although their contents are distinct. In epistemology, classical **empiricism** is individualistic, for it believes that the private experience of individuals is the ultimate source of **knowledge**. In the philosophy of social science, **methodological individualism** is the view that inquiry into society should be based on the characteristics of individual persons. In the philosophy of mind, individualism proposes that mental semantic meaning is determined by the intrinsic properties of mental representations and does not depend upon their social and historical settings. This psychological individualism has been challenged by claims that the individuation of mental states involves the world and the linguistic community.

Generally, the central areas of the application of individualism have been in ethics and political philosophy. In these areas, individualism is related to the ideas of **autonomy** and self-development. Ethical individualism claims that only the individual person is the subject of moral predicates and values and the central focus of moral consideration. Hence it contrasts with moral **holism**. In political philosophy, as an essential feature of political **liberalism**, individualism claims that the individual is viewed as the bearer of **rights**, that a government can be legitimately formed only on the basis of the **consent** of individuals, and that political **representation** is the representation of individual interests. Society is a **logical construction** whose aim is to enable its individual members to pursue their respective interests without interference.

In opposition to individualism are various versions of holism, such as **totalitarianism**, **collectivism**, socialism, and **communitarianism**. All of these can be viewed as examples of anti-individualism.

"It is liberty and equality which are the cardinal ideals of individualism." **Lukes,** *Individualism*

individuality

METAPHYSICS [from Latin *individuum*, a translation of Greek *atom*, indivisible] The characteristic or property which makes something or someone the **individual** that it is. Different views result in different applications of the concept of an individual and different accounts of the relationship between individuals and **universals**. One popular view derived from the etymology of this term explains individuality in terms of indivisibility. Yet there are difficulties in determining what counts as a thing that cannot be divided. Logically, a **species** cannot be divided into its single members. Physically, a particular thing cannot be divided into its components without losing its nature. Metaphysically, simple entities cannot be divided into parts. The logical sense of indivisibility is compatible with universality and must be distinguished from **particularity**. Other approaches to the nature of individuality include the view that a thing is individual if it is distinct from other things, that an individual has a particular "thisness," that an individual has a spatio-temporal **identity**, that an individual is something that cannot be **predicated** of anything else, and that an individual is a thing that cannot be instantiated by anything else. In these senses individuality amounts to particularity. The discussion of individuality is related to issues such as the principle of individuation and the discernibility of individuals.

> "My major claim concerning the intensional analysis of individuality is that, contrary to the standard view among present day philosophers, who interpret individuality as some kind of distinction or difference, individuality must be understood primarily as non-instantiability." **Gracia,** *Individuality*

individuative term, another expression for sortal

indoctrination

POLITICAL PHILOSOPHY, PHILOSOPHY OF RELIGION One of the major aims of the philosophy of education is to distinguish between the superficially similar notions of teaching and indoctrination. While teaching encourages students and learners to develop their rational capacities and to have their own views on various disputed issues, indoctrination is regarded as the activity of conveying **dogma** to pupils who are expected to accept it without question. The beliefs that are taught are not open to rational criticism from the pupil. They are intended to be implanted in the minds of the students so that their subsequent experience will not change their beliefs. Indoctrination is typically represented in the preaching of religious doctrine or political opinion. It typically involves authoritarian methods and is open to manipulation by interested parties.

> "Perhaps the least contentious account would be that indoctrination is a form of teaching in which it is intended that certain beliefs should be accepted without question, either because it is thought that they are not only important but unquestionably true, or because, for various reasons, it is thought important that, true or not, they should not be questioned." **T. Moore,** *Philosophy of Education*

induction

LOGIC, PHILOSOPHY OF SCIENCE [from Latin *inducere*, *in*, into + *ducere*, lead, a translation of Aristotle's *epagoge*, leading to] For **Aristotle**, first, a form of reasoning in which we establish a generalization by showing that the reasoning holds for certain instances that are said to fall under it and, secondly, the process by which we apprehend a particular instance as exemplifying an abstract generalization. Nowadays, we call the first kind of reasoning simple or enumerative induction and the second kind **induction by intuition**. In addition, there is also **induction by elimination**, which reaches a generalization by eliminating competing generalizations. In **induction by enumeration**, the fundamental form of induction, the basic process of inference is that, if A_1 is P, A_2 is P, A_3 is P, then all As are P. An enumeration that covers all the instances falling under the generalization is called a complete enumerative induction.

Induction is contrasted with **deduction**, in which a particular conclusion is deduced from a universal premise as a matter of **logical necessity**. In induction, a **universal** is derived from what is **particular** and goes beyond the content of its premises. For this reason induction was called by **Peirce ampliative** argument. For this reason, the conclusion of an inductive argument is generally probable rather than necessary. The discussion of induction is closely associated with that of **probability** and **confirmation**. Francis **Bacon**, who called his theory of induction a **new organon**, in contrast to Aristotle's **syllogism**, held that all new **knowledge** must come from some form of induction. J. S. **Mill** established five **canons** of induction.

Hume proposed the deeply important problem of induction, which claims that we lack adequate grounds to infer from observed regularities to the probable continuance of those regularities. Inductive reasoning is based on the principle of uniformity of nature, according to which **events** that I have not observed are similar to events that I have observed, but this principle is itself a conclusion based on induction. The rational foundations of inductive reasoning have been a major topic in subsequent philosophy, especially in the **empiricist** tradition. Anti-inductivism emerged to deny that induction is a rational process. The **hypothetico-deductive method** was proposed as a rival to inductive method, with **Popper** claiming that science proceeds by tests of **falsification** of imaginative **hypotheses** rather than by inductive confirmation. **Goodman** put forward his **new riddle of induction** concerning how an induction could be characterized in terms of an inference to the continuation of previously observed similarities. His "green-grue" example showed that the same inductive process can confirm two opposite generalizations. The debate about the nature and rationality of induction continues.

"The so-called method of inductive inference is usually presented as proceeding from specific case to a general hypothesis of which each of the special cases is an 'instance' in the sense that it conforms to the general hypothesis in question, and thus constitutes confirming evidence for it." **Hempel,** *Aspects of Scientific Explanation*

induction, the problem of

LOGIC, PHILOSOPHY OF SCIENCE A problem originally formulated by **Hume** concerning the legitimacy of inductive **inference**. Typically, **induction** infers from limited observation that some As are B to the conclusion that all As are B. But how can we rationally accept that such an inference is valid? On what grounds can we claim that the conclusion thus reached is acceptable? The classic response to this problem is that the validity of inductive reasoning is based on the **uniformity of nature**. This principle of induction claims that the future will resemble the past, and hence a generalization from observed cases is applicable to unobserved cases. But Hume argued that this principle can be justified only by induction and that the justification of induction in terms of the principle thus involves **vicious circularity**. The answer that Hume provided to the problem is that induction is not a rational inference, but arises from custom and habit. A skeptical interpretation of his account argues that induction needs rational support that custom and habit cannot provide. A naturalistic interpretation of his account claims that our inductive practice does not need any **justification** outside itself or that custom and habit is all the justification that we need.

Recent generations of philosophers have also considered the problem of induction. **Reichenbach** claimed that induction is a method of reaching posits or **conjectures**, rather than an inference. **Popper** held a similar view. Some philosophers try to deny that justification in terms of the uniformity of nature involves circularity, by distinguishing different levels of induction. **Goodman** has proposed a **new riddle of induction**, suggesting that an appeal to the uniformity of nature is empty without grounds for preferring some uniformities to others. Some philosophers, including **Russell**, have held on the grounds of the possibility of knowledge that the justification of induction is *a priori*. An influential response, initiated by **Strawson**, suggests that the problem of induction is generated because we assess inductive reasoning by the standards of deductive reasoning, when in fact each of them has its own standard. Inductive reasoning is **defeasible** reasoning, that is, reasoning which reaches conclusions that can be overturned by further evidence.

"But whatever view we take of the problem of induction, it remains true that being able to derive it from some accepted causal law is the strongest justification for believing in the existence of any unobserved event." **Ayer,** *The Concept of a Person and Other Essays*

induction by elimination

LOGIC, PHILOSOPHY OF SCIENCE Also called eliminative induction or the method of elimination, a type of inductive reasoning which initially assumes several possible **hypotheses** for explaining the same phenomenon, and then eliminates those that are countered by new evidence through the progress of observation and experiment. The remaining hypothesis is then taken to be correct. By this procedure we establish an affirmative conclusion by rejecting all the rival hypotheses. The problem with this type of induction is that the number of competing hypotheses might be indefinite and potentially infinite, and hence elimination does not guarantee that the hypothesis surviving from those considered is correct. Neither does it ensure that only one of a finite set of alternatives is correct. Induction by elimination contrasts with **induction by enumeration**, which infers a general conclusion by enumerating the particular instances of that generalization.

"That type of inference in which one of the premises is a disjunction of several general statements, the other premises are singular statements which refute all the members of that disjunction except one, and the conclusion is the only member of the disjunction which is not refuted by the singular premises, is termed induction by elimination." **Ajdukiewicz,** *Pragmatic Logic*

induction by enumeration

LOGIC, PHILOSOPHY OF SCIENCE The **inference** to a **generalization** by the simple enumeration of the particular instances of the generalization. When we observe that $A_1, A_2, A_3, \ldots A_n$, all have a property B, and that no As have been found not to have B, we infer that all As have the property of B. Induction by enumeration, also called enumerative induction, is thought to be the fundamental form of inductive reasoning. It is non-demonstrative, and the truth of the conclusion is not guaranteed. Different causal factors and different circumstances may lead other As to lack the property B, and hence there is always the possibility of **counterexamples**. Furthermore, scientists generally have a **hypothesis** before enumerating its instances, and their active programs of experimental testing go beyond mere enumeration. Induction by enumeration is in contrast with **induction by elimination**.

"Induction by enumeration is any such inference in which a statement of a general regularity is accepted as the conclusion on the strength of accepting statements of particular cases of the regularity." **Ajdukiewicz,** *Pragmatic Logic*

induction by intuition

LOGIC, METAPHYSICS, PHILOSOPHY OF SCIENCE Also called intuitive induction, **induction** that moves from the observation of a single fact or a few facts to general statements. The implicit **universal** is exhibited in the clearly known particulars. This is the method of establishing propositions of restricted universality in philosophy, especially in metaphysics. In science, the result of this intuition is tested by further observation. Induction by intuition is an important means of forming **hypotheses** prior to testing them more systematically.

"'Induction by intuition', or 'imagination', the discovery of law by the construction of new concepts on the basis of relatively few observations and the confirming of the law by a great number of observations." **Frank,** *Philosophy of Science*

inductive definition, see recursive definition

inductivism

PHILOSOPHY OF SCIENCE A theory of science which holds that scientific **knowledge** consists of the **laws** or **principles** derived by inductive **canons** from accumulated facts. The knowledge grows if more facts are accumulated. The plausibility of a law increases with the observed numbers of instances of the phenomenon explained by that law. Accordingly what scientists do is to pile up relevant facts and generalize laws and principles from them. Critics of this theory of science claim that it ignores the function of **theory** and that its account of intellectual discovery and creation is oversimplified. Some philosophers accept **Popper**'s criticism of inductivism even if they also criticize his own **falsificationist** theory of science.

"The real reason why inductivism is so wrong is that it is so unrealistic. It is an attempt to codify a more or less mythical conception of science." **Harré,** *The Philosophies of Science*

ineffability

PHILOSOPHY OF LANGUAGE, METAPHYSICS, PHILOSOPHY OF RELIGION, AESTHETICS [from Latin *ineffabilis*, not expressible in words] Many theologians and philosophers believe that **God** is beyond our description and conceptualization, because human experience is finite and language has its limits. Some meta-physicians claim that the first principle of existence or ultimate reality also resists any linguistic speci-fication, such as **Plato**'s **Form** of the Good, and **Plotinus' One**. Consequently, some things are ineffable and can only be grasped through mystical **intuition** or **revelation**. There are also claims that works of art can convey what is ineffable by showing what can not be said, but critics argue that what can not be said, can not be expressed in any other way.

"Perhaps those who call the experience of what is beyond existence and non-existence ineffable merely mean that they cannot adequately describe it to those who have not had it." **Nozick, Philosophical Explanations**

inegalitarianism, see egalitarianism

inequality

POLITICAL PHILOSOPHY, PHILOSOPHY OF LAW, PHILO-SOPHY OF SOCIAL SCIENCE Differential possession of what is advantageous or desirable by different individuals or groups in political, legal, social, and economic areas. The main aim of **egalitarianism** is to reject any enforced policies leading to inequality, and to maintain that each **individual** or group has equal **rights** to political participation and legal protection. Egalitarianism also tries to narrow the wealth gap between different individuals through welfare and taxation policies. However, because we have natural differences in talent and merit, and because the society and its economic system require a hierarchic organization, it is unlikely that all sorts of inequalities can be eliminated. Accordingly, it becomes a matter of debate whether and to what degree a society is justified in narrowing inequalities. These debates focus on the relations between inequalities and **liberty, efficiency**, and **justice**. Some theorists reject the broad egalitarian consensus and argue that in many respects inequality is preferable to equality.

"It can be of little practical consequence that one regards inequality as bad – as many do – unless one is generally able to determine if one situation's inequality is worse than another's." **Temkin, Inequality**

inertia

METAPHYSICS, PHILOSOPHY OF SCIENCE [from Latin *inertia*, idle, not having its own active powers, or unable to move itself] For **Aristotle**, it is part of the nature of **motion** that it will come to an end. **Scholastics** developed this idea by claiming that it is the inherent tendency of terrestrial **matter** to be inert or sluggish. **Descartes** transformed the notion of inertia to mean the persistence of motion or rest. Other things being equal, matter will continue in a state of uniform motion or rest and change unless externally affected. This is viewed as an early for-mulation of the **Newtonian** principle of inertia (the first law of motion): every body maintains its state of rest, or of uniform motion in a straight line, unless it is compelled to change that state by forces imposed upon it.

"Inertia is a disposition to resist changes to a body's state of motion or rest." **Harré, Laws of Nature**

infallibility

EPISTEMOLOGY The impossibility of being mistaken. Some philosophers claim that certain perceptual **beliefs**, such as "I am in pain," are infallible and therefore may serve as the basis for justifying other beliefs. But others argue that even in such cases mistakes are possible through applying the wrong **concept** to a given item. Questions of infallibility have been discussed with the related notion of **incor-rigibility**. An infallible claim cannot be mistaken, while an incorrigible claim cannot be corrected and hence cannot be mistaken. Infallibility is also used for the view that it is impossible for **knowledge** to be wrong. A requirement that knowledge must be infallible would have the effect of excluding many legitimate questions from debate. Many philosophers do not think that this is acceptable, for it would reject all procedures liable to **error** and would radically narrow the scope of knowledge. The possibility of knowledge might vanish altogether because if **fallibilism** is correct, even propositions that we take to be **necessary truths** are in principle open to error. The notion of the infallibility of know-ledge can be traced to **Plato**'s philosophy and is one type of rationalist ideal. The idea that scientific knowledge should be infallible has been challenged by **Popper**'s claim that only when a theory can be falsified is it a real scientific theory.

"The one feature which is common to all versions of the doctrine that knowledge implies infallibility is that, in order for the concept of knowledge to be applicable, there must not be the possibility of error." **J. Evans,** *Knowledge and Infallibility*

inference

LOGIC The procedure of drawing one statement (as a conclusion) from another statement or statements, which have been established to be true or false. Inference is generally divided into **deductive** inference (from a general rule to a particular instance), and **inductive** inference (from particular data to a general rule). **Abductive** inference is sometimes listed as a third type of inference, but is more often regarded as a special case of inductive inference. The conclusion of deductive inference is necessary, while the conclusion of inductive inference is **probable**. An argument consists of at least one inference. Logic seeks to establish the rules of inference. An inference is **valid** if it conforms to the given rules, and is invalid if it fails so to conform. "To infer" should be distinguished from "to imply," for **implication** can be a relation between propositions themselves, while inference must involve the **belief** states of an epistemic agent.

"Inference is a method by which we arrive at new knowledge, and what is not psychological about it is the relation which allows us to infer correctively." **Russell,** *Introduction to Mathematical Philosophy*

inference to the best explanation

PHILOSOPHY OF SCIENCE A kind of reasoning that is common in both daily life and science. If we observe that a, b, c, . . . are true, and if there is a **hypothesis** H which can best explain all these cases, then it is **probable** that H is true. This is a non-demonstrative **deduction**, sometimes called a hypothetical deduction. The **confirmation** of a scientific theory is essentially an inference to the best explanation. This method of reasoning resembles the process that **Peirce** calls **abduction**. There are many discussions surrounding this method of reasoning, such as how to make it precise, whether it is really different from inductive reasoning, and what is the criterion for determining which of several competing hypotheses is the best.

"The standard presentation of the link between the empirical adequacy and truth of a theory is known as the inference to the best explanation. Since it aims to exploit the truth-conducive virtues of explanation it is most effectively applied to causal explanation." **Kosso,** *Reading the Book of Nature.*

inferred entity, another term for metaphysical entity

infima species

METAPHYSICS A determinate **form** of the lowest generality, which does not admit of any further differentiation. The things below *infima species* are particular instances that are identical in specific nature. An *infima species* is the common and stable nature of a **kind** of thing and is therefore the object of **definition** and **knowledge**. In **Aristotle**'s *Categories*, an *infima species* is a secondary **substance**. In his *Metaphysics*, its **ontological** status is ambiguous, depending on whether one understands it to be identical with form and also on whether one understands primary substance to be universal form or particular form. But Aristotle claimed that an *infima species* cannot mark off one individual from another and that **matter** should be the principle of individuation.

"An infima species, or lowest species, if there can be such a thing, would be a sort without any distinct sub-sort instantiating it." **Lowe,** *Kinds of Being*

infinite and finite

LOGIC, PHILOSOPHY OF MATHEMATICS, PHILOSOPHY OF SCIENCE, PHILOSOPHY OF RELIGION [from Latin *in*, not + *finire*, to limit, to stop, literally, not to have a limit or end, that is, unlimited, boundless or indeterminate; *finire*, literally, to have a limit or end. Greek counterparts: *apeiron*, unlimited or undetermined, *peras*, limit] A pair of concepts that is widely used in discussing the world, **God**, mathematics, and **space** and **time**. The concepts are used in metaphysical, theological, mathematical, and logical discussions.

The question whether the world is infinite or finite is one of the oldest questions of philosophy. The logical nature of infinity and finitude can be traced to **Zeno of Elea**'s **paradoxes** of **motion**.

Attempts to solve these paradoxes have stimulated inquiry into the nature of these terms. In general, the Greeks believed that the infinite is incomplete, imperfect, and indeterminate, and therefore put it into the category of the bad, while the finite is complete, perfect, and determinate and belongs to the category of the good. **Aristotle** discussed these conceptions in detail in his *Physics*. For him, the world must be finite, and the infinite can only be **potential**. The distinction between actual and potential infinity was revived in **Cantor**'s mathematics.

In Christian philosophy, the omnipotent God cannot be finite, but is an infinite and eternal being upon whom finite beings are dependent. Hence, contrary to the Greek notion, the infinite is seen as complete and perfect. The world is still finite, but it is conceived to be an imperfect creation of the infinite God.

Hegel distinguished between bad infinity and true infinity. Bad infinity is an endless series, like a straight line with no end in either direction. It is simply negative and is distinct from the finite. True infinity is closely associated with the finite. Like a circle, it is finite but unbounded. A thing can be infinite from one perspective, but finite from another. Hegel believed that the finite involves **negation** or limitation and claimed that the infinite is associated with the negation of a negation. Finite things have to depend on other things for their **being**, and their negation leads to another negation, producing an affirmation. The development of finite things is also the self-development of the **absolute idea**. In Hegel's sense of being self-contained and autonomous, the absolute idea is the only real true infinity.

"Dualism, in putting an insuperable opposition between finite and infinite, fails to note the simple circumstance that the infinite is thereby only one of two, and is reduced to a particular, to which the finite forms the other particular." **Hegel,** *Logic*

infinite regress argument
LOGIC An argument that occurs in many different branches of philosophy. An example from metaphysics may be found in **Plato**, who recognized that if there is one idea for many similar things, then when we consider the idea together with these other things, we may require a further idea, and so on *ad infinitum*. Plato's famous **Third Man argument**

is one version of this argument. **Aristotle** made use of an infinite regress argument in proving the existence of the **unmoved mover**. He claimed that if everything in **motion** is moved by a mover, there would be an infinite series of movers. Since this is impossible, there must be an unmoved mover. Aristotle also used the argument in ethics in seeking to show that if every rational action has a goal, there must be a final goal. An infinite regress argument is also used in epistemology. If we are to know a conclusion, we must know its premises, and to know the premises, we must seemingly know the premises of the premises *ad infinitum*. To avoid this infinite regress, it is claimed that there must be basic and non-demonstrable first **principles** or foundations that ground the rest of our knowledge.

"For it is impossible that there should be an infinite series of movements, each of which is itself moved by something else, since in an infinite series there is no first term." **Aristotle,** *Physics*

infinite-valued logic, see many-valued logic

informal fallacy
LOGIC The kind of **fallacy** which does not occur in the **logical form** or structure of an argument, but is committed in various other ways and can be identified through analysis of its content and its context. **Aristotle**'s *Sophistical Refutations* was the first systematic study of informal fallacies, although many other forms were added by later authors. Aristotle divided all fallacies into those dependent on language (Latin *in dictione*) and those outside of language (Latin *extra dictionen*). Modern logic textbooks accordingly generally divide informal fallacies into **fallacies of ambiguity** and material fallacies. Fallacies of ambiguity arise from the ambiguity of words or sentences in which ambiguous words occur, such as the **fallacies of accent, amphiboly, equivocation, composition, division, and** *secundum quid*. Material fallacies are due to reasons other than the ambiguity of language and are further divided into the fallacies of relevance and insufficient evidence. The fallacy of relevance occurs in those arguments whose premises are logically irrelevant to the truth of the conclusion and are hence incapable of establishing it. Many informal fallacies of this kind have a Latin name of the form *"argumentum ad . . . ,"* such as

argumentum ad baculum, *argumentum ad hominem*, *argumentum ad ignorantiam*, *argumentum ad misericordiam*, *argumentum ad populum*, and *argumentum ad verecundiam*. Other forms include the **fallacy of the complex question**, the **genetic fallacy**, *ignoratio elenchi*, *petitio principii* (**begging the question**), the **slippery slope argument**, and the **straw man fallacy**. The fallacy of insufficient evidence occurs in those arguments whose premises are relevant to the conclusions but are not strong or good enough to establishing the truth of the conclusions, such as the false cause or *post hoc* **fallacy** and hasty generalization. This dictionary has a single entry for each of the above fallacies.

> "Informal fallacies are frequently backed by some motive on the part of the arguer to deceive the reader or listener." **Hurley, *A Concise Introduction to Logic***

informal logic

LOGIC Also called logical **pragmatics**. Informal logic investigates the relations of **implication** arising from subject-matter words and the contents of a **discourse**. It concerns the nature and function of arguments or assertions in **natural language** whose richness cannot be exhausted in **formal logic**. Informal logic is not as precise as formal logic and its findings are relative to given contexts. Its major topics include matters such as incomplete patterns of arguments, **conversational implicature**, **informal fallacies**, and rhetorical techniques for persuasion. In contrast, formal logic deals with **semantic** rather than pragmatic relationships, especially with the **entailments** arising from the formal or structural words of propositions. While formal logic regards argument as a set of **propositions** and examines their **truth-value**, informal logic deals with the use of propositions to carry out the various aims of dialogue in everyday reasoning. Informal logic takes account of the wider context of dialogue and seeks to understand how we legitimately convince or persuade in reasonable discourse.

> "Generally the theory of informal logic must be based on the concept of question-reply dialogue as a form of interaction between two participants, each representing one side of an argument, on a disputed question." **Walton, *Informal Logic***

informed consent

ETHICS Informed consent is a moral requirement in **medical ethics**. In the process of medical treatment, competent patients are entitled to be informed in understandable language of the benefits of the treatment, its possible risks, and the alternative methods of treatment. No treatment should be given without the patient's voluntary **consent** on the basis of the information provided. The argument in support of this requirement is that a patient is in principle **autonomous** and self-determining. Patients have the **right** to refuse to allow their body to be touched. It is in the interest of the patients to participate in the process of making significant decisions affecting their lives. The problem is that knowing a diagnosis that patients prefer not to know does not necessarily serve their best interests.

> "The idea of 'informed consent' is based on the notion of autonomy . . . Autonomy rests on rationality. It is difficult to act rationally in the absence of relevant information. It is on the basis of benefits, risks and alternatives that we formulate reasons for a course of action." **Lee, *Law and Morals***

Ingarden, Roman (1893–1970)

Polish phenomenological philosopher and aesthetician, born in Cracow. Ingarden was a disciple of Husserl, but resisted Husserl's idealism and sought to combine phenomenology with realism. His ontology assumed that knowing is determined by the objects of cognition, and focused on the analysis of various objects and relationships. His ontology of art asks what it is for a literary work to exist and argues that works of art are pure intentional objects. His important works include *The Literary Work of Art* (1931), *The Controversy over the Existence of the World*, (1947–8), and *Studies in Aesthetics* (1957–8).

in itself

METAPHYSICS [German *an sich*, also translated as by itself or as such] **Hegel** contrasted in itself with **for itself** [German *für sich*]. In itself is essentially or intrinsically **potential**, unreflective, and underdeveloped, while for itself is **actual**, reflective, and developed. In itself is implicit and self-identical, while for itself is exteriorized and lies before itself. A baby is rational in itself but not for itself until its rationality is actualized. In and for itself [German *an und für sich*] is the completely developed state in which in itself and for itself are unified and a thing is at home with itself. A thing develops from **being-in-itself** to **being-for-itself** and ends up as being-in-and-for-itself. This development conforms to the Hegelian pattern of thesis-antithesis-synthesis. In this sense, in itself is implicit and does not imply the development of relations to something else.

Generally, in itself is not distinguished from for itself or from in and for itself, but is rather contrasted with for us or for others. To call something in itself means that it is at least mainly independent of other things and has its own **essence** apart from its **relations** with others. In itself corresponds to Greek *kath'hauto* or *to auto*, which Plato uses for his Idea or Form. In this sense, if we consider a thing to be in itself, we take it not to be related to our **consciousness**. **Kant** called an object that is beyond our possible **experience**, but can still be thought, a **thing-in-itself** [German *Ding-an-sich*].

> "The Notion itself is for us, in the first instance, like the universal that is in itself, and the negative that is for itself, and also the third, that which is both in and for itself, the universal that runs through all the moments of the syllogism; but the third is also the conclusion." **Hegel**, *Science of Logic*

innate ideas

EPISTEMOLOGY, PHILOSOPHY OF MIND There are several views regarding the conception of innate ideas. One takes them to be the **ideas** which are not derived from **experience** but which originate in the **mind** itself. Another holds that they are ideas that are potentially inherent in the mind at birth and are brought out by experience, which renders them manifest in some way. Still another regards them as ideas that we have an innate **disposition** to form. The concept has a long history. It can be traced to **Plato**'s theory of **recollection**, and becomes a pivotal issue in the debate between **rationalism** and **empiricism** in the seventeenth and eighteenth centuries, with **Descartes** and **Leibniz** defending innate ideas and **Locke** and **Hume** attacking them. The debate led to **Kant**'s view that our understanding has *a priori* **categories**, which are prerequisites for the organization of experience. The notion was revitalized in the twentieth century by **Chomsky**, who claims in his analysis of the human linguistic capacity that human beings have an innate universal **grammar** within them, which is the precondition of language acquisition.

> "I did . . . observe that there are certain thoughts within me which neither came to me from external objects nor were determined by my will, but which came solely from the power of thinking within me; so I applied the term 'innate' to the ideas or notions which are the forms of these thoughts in order to distinguish them from others, which I called 'adventitious' or 'made up'." **Descartes**, *Philosophical Writings*, **vol. I**

inner observation, see inner perception

inner perception

EPISTEMOLOGY, PHILOSOPHY OF MIND Franz **Brentano** claimed that there are two kinds of human **perception**, external perception through the sense organs and inner or internal perception, which is the awareness of **mental acts** present in us. While the object of external perception is a physical **phenomenon**, in particular sensible qualities, the object of internal perception is a mental phenomenon, including presentations, **judgments**, and acts of **will**. According to Brentano, internal perception is the basis of psychology. Internal perception is further characterized as being **immediate**, **infallible**, and **self-evident**. "Perception" here translates the German word *Wahrnehmung*, which literally means to take something to be true. Brentano claims that internal perception is perception in this real sense of the word. Internal perception differs from internal observation or **introspection**. While introspection directs full attention toward a phenomenon to gain a firm grasp of it, inner perception does not observe and does not take one's own mental activity as its object. For example, anger is a kind of internal perception, but when an angry person observes his own anger, it will diminish.

> "Note, however, that we said that inner perception [*Wahrnehmung*] and not introspection, i.e. inner observation [*Beobachtung*], constitutes this primary and essential source of psychology." **Brentano**, *Psychology from an Empirical Standpoint*

inner process

PHILOSOPHY OF MIND Mental **phenomena** such as **meaning**, **understanding**, remembering, **thinking**, and knowing are widely considered to be inner processes. They are within the **mind**, private, incorporeal, invisible, although they have a place in **time** and some have a temporal extent. In **Cartesian dualism**, which contrasts the public physical world with the private mental world, these mental phenomena are ascribed to the mental realm and at best have parallel phenomena in the physical world. **Wittgenstein** characterizes this traditional dualism in terms of "inner/outer," but believes that this dichotomy itself is problematic. By taking the mind as a world of mental entities, states, processes, or events, it has already considered the mind as something similar to the physical world. According to Wittgenstein, mental phenomena such as inner processes are actually not a realm at all. They should be explained in terms of the **grammar** of expressions for mental phenomena, a basic feature of which is that "an 'inner process' stands in need of outward criteria." Hence, "inner process," traditionally understood, is not a suitable term to describe the mental phenomena it was employed to describe, for these "phenomena" are actually not processes.

"What we deny is that the picture of the inner process gives us the correct idea of the use of the word 'to remember'." **Wittgenstein,** *Philosophical Investigations*

inner sense

EPISTEMOLOGY A distinction between outer and inner sense depends upon the **scholastic** distinction between external senses, such as touch and vision, and internal senses, which are directed toward the states of the mind itself. **Kant** considered these to be two distinct types of **sensibility**. We use outer sense to represent to ourselves **objects** outside us, and inner sense to make our own **representations** the objects of our thought. Kant further distinguished **form** and **matter** in both outer and inner sense. The form of outer sense is **space**, through which external objects are organized in terms of shape, magnitude, and mutual **relations**. The form of inner sense is **time**, through which representations of our inner state and the immediate condition of inner appearances are determined. Kant emphasized

that inner sense is not the pure **apperception** of the *cogito*, for the former is psychological and receptive, while the latter is **transcendental** and the **spontaneous** source of **synthesis**.

Although outer sense and inner sense are indispensable, the latter is more fundamental because all representations, whether their objects are internal or external, belong to inner sense. All sensory states are mediated by it. Thus the real contrast is not between outer and inner sense, but between outer and inner sense taken together and inner sense alone.

"Inner sense, by means of which the mind intuits itself or its inner state, yields indeed no intuition of the soul itself as an object; but there is nevertheless a determinate form [namely, time] in which alone the intuition of inner states is possible, and everything which belongs to inner determinations is therefore represented in relations of time." **Kant,** *Critique of Pure Reason*

innocence, see guilt

in obliquo

PHILOSOPHY OF MIND A mode of **thinking** (also called *modus oblique*) in contrast to *in recto* (also called *modus rectus*). According to this account, when a **mental act** is about a subject in relation to an **object**, a person is thinking of a subject and an object at the same time. One thinks of the subject *in recto* and thinks of the object *in obliquo*. For example, if I am thinking of X who loves flowers, then X is thought *in recto* and flowers are thought *in obliquo*.

"It is plain that a clarification of the presentation can come about through an analysis of its object both in recto and in obliquo." **Brentano,** *Psychology from an Empirical Standpoint*

in recto, see *in obliquo*

inscrutability of reference

LOGIC, PHILOSOPHY OF LANGUAGE Also referential inscrutability, a collateral thesis of the **indeterminacy of translation**. Traditionally, **meaning** and **reference** are closely associated and even inseparable. In attacking this assumption, **Quine** claims that in a hypothetical native language the reference of **general terms** is objectively and behaviorally inscrutable. For example, we have no objective reason for deciding that "gavagai" refers to rabbits instead of to undetached rabbit parts. This relation between us and a remote native language can also be applied to my understanding of my neighbor's linguistic behavior. Quine concludes that the referents of terms and the range of **quantifiers** are not determined by physical or behavioral facts. Absolute questions of reference are meaningless, and reference can only be relative to a coordinate system.

"The conclusion I draw is the inscrutability of reference. To say what objects someone is talking about is to say no more than how we propose to translate his terms into ours; we are free to vary the decision with a proxy function." **Quine,** *Theories and Things*

insolubilia, the term used by medieval logicians for paradoxes

institutional theory

AESTHETICS A theory of art developed by the American philosopher George Dickie, based on **Danto**'s notion of an **artworld**. The theory claims that an artwork is an artifact that possesses the status of a candidate for appreciation. This status is conferred by a suitable representative of a formal social institution, that is, the artworld. Accordingly, any artifact can be a work of art so long as it is admitted by the artworld. In other words, art is the consequence of social agreement rather than having intrinsic aesthetic features. In a later version, Dickie claims that a work of art is an artifact created for presentation to a group of persons (the artworld public) who are prepared to some extent to understand artworks. In contrast to the **imitation theory**, which emphasizes the relation between art and its subject matter, and the **expression theory**, which stresses the relation of an artwork to its creator, the institutional theory focuses on the established practice of art and its appreciation. The theory has the advantage of highlighting the social context through which art is generated and provided with properties that are not directly exhibited to the senses. Critics of the theory point out that its definition of art is circular, for it explains art in terms of an artworld and explains the artworld in terms of the artifacts it recognizes as art. In addition, critics claim that the theory cannot properly establish the criteria by which the artworld confers upon artifacts the status of candidate for appreciation.

"The institutional theory of art concentrates attention on the nonexhibited characteristics that works of art have in virtue of being embedded in an institutional matrix which may be called 'the artworld' and argues that these characteristics are essential and defining." **Dickie,** *Art and the Aesthetic*

institutional violence, see structural violence

instrumentalism

PHILOSOPHY OF SCIENCE, EPISTEMOLOGY An account of the nature of scientific **theory**, holding that scientific theory does not establish the **existence** of things and so can be neither true or false. We judge a theory not in terms of its **truth** or falsity, but in terms of its usefulness. Scientific theory is nothing more than a useful tool or instrument for research. The position was first expressed in the preface to **Copernicus**' book *De Revolutionibus*, with the aim of avoiding conflict with religious orthodoxy by claiming that his heliocentric theory was not to be regarded as true, but merely as a tool. Instrumentalism was developed by **Berkeley** and **Mach** and became a major formulation in **anti-realism**. **Pragmatism** in general is instrumentalist through its claim that all ideas are teleological or instrumental, and its emphasis on the continuity between **action** and **judgment**. One version of instrumentalism, associated with John **Dewey**'s pragmatism, is based on the theory of **evolution**. Dewey argued that **ideas, concepts,** and **propositions** are all tools or instruments for organizing human **experience** and predicting future consequences. The existence of ideas is bound up with the practical needs of life. He preferred to call this theory **experimentalism**. Criticism of instrumentalism is that it fails to distinguish real **belief** from acceptance in an instrumentalist spirit and fails to distinguish an epistemological account of the possession of **knowledge** from an account of the application of knowledge.

"Instrumentalism means a behaviouristic theory of thinking and knowing. It means that knowing is literally something which we do; that analysis is ultimately physical and active; and meanings in their logical quality are standpoints, attitudes and methods of behaving toward facts, and that active experimentation is essential to verification." **Dewey,** *Essays in Experimental Logic*

integrity

ETHICS In an ordinary sense, honesty or being upright. In contemporary ethics it is emphasized by Bernard **Williams** as a fundamental value underlying ethical behavior. It means wholeness or **harmony** of oneself, that is, a virtue that integrates various parts of life under the guidance of the central value or principle which one has chosen and to which one's life is committed. It is consistency and continuity across the various dimensions of one's life and hence amounts to moral **identity**. Integrity involves the relation between the **agent**'s sense of self and **action**. **Persons** of integrity are loyal to their chosen moral **principles**, which are in turn central to their self-understanding. Their actions and decisions flow from these internal attitudes, principles, and convictions. They are unwilling to yield them even in the face of great pressure. Opposed to integrity is the state of self-dividedness or disintegration. **Plato** in his *Republic* argued that **justice** is the harmony of **soul**, and this harmonious state is precisely the state of integrity. One of Williams's major criticisms of **utilitarianism** is that it cannot account for human integrity, for in some situations an action may have the best consequences but may violate a moral principle that the agent endorses. If we should act in accordance with the requirements of utilitarian calculation, we might have to abandon the principles to which we are committed, and thus alienate our actions from our beliefs.

"... we are partially at least not utilitarians, and cannot regard our moral feelings merely as objects of utilitarian value ... [T]o come to refer to those feelings from a purely utilitarian point of view, that is to say, as happenings outside one's moral self, is to lose sense of one's moral identity; to lose, in the most literal way, one's integrity." **B. Williams, in Smart and Williams (eds.),** *Utilitarianism: For and Against*

intellectual love

ETHICS, PHILOSOPHY OF RELIGION, PHILOSOPHY OF MIND In Spinoza's philosophy, the only love with a privileged status. In contrast to ordinary, non-intellectual love for visible and tangible things, intellectual love arises from the intuitive **knowledge** that **God** is the cause of all things, a knowledge that involves peace of mind. Intellectual love is directed toward an eternal and infinite thing, and is itself unmingled with any sadness. The human **mind** should seek for it with all its strength. In a sense, intellectual love is simply an expression of the love of **wisdom**, that is, philosophy. Spinoza also ascribes it to God himself. God has a kind of self-love that is identical with God's love for man and man's love for God. It is a state of joyful self-knowledge.

"The intellectual love of God which arises from the third kind of knowledge is eternal." **Spinoza,** *Ethics*

intellectual synthesis, see synthesis (Kant)

intellectual virtue

ETHICS, PHILOSOPHY OF MIND According to **Aristotle**, virtue is related to **soul** rather than **body**, and the human soul includes a part which has **reason** in itself and another part which is non-rational but obeys the rational part. He divided virtue into two kinds: the excellence of the exercise of the rational part is intellectual virtue, and the excellence of the exercise of the non-rational part is **ethical virtue**, also called excellence of **character** or moral virtue. Ethical virtue has another dimension, because it is cultivated out of social custom and habit. In *Nicomachean Ethics*, book VI, Aristotle discussed various forms of intellectual virtue, including technical wisdom (craft, *techne*), theoretical wisdom (science, *episteme*), **wisdom** (*sophia*), **understanding** (*nous*), and **practical wisdom** (*phronesis*). Aristotle claimed that contemplation, as the activity that expresses theoretical wisdom, is the route to greatest happiness, but he also suggested that a happy life should promote all virtues. How to reconcile these two inconsistent notions of happiness (*eudaimonia*) has been a matter of continuing controversy. Practical wisdom as a type of intellectual virtue is concerned with good and bad and is intrinsic also to ethical virtue.

"Intellectual virtue arises and grows mostly from teaching, and hence needs experience and time." **Aristotle,** *Nicomachean Ethics*

intellectus

PHILOSOPHY OF MIND, EPISTEMOLOGY, METAPHYSICS [Latin, intellect, mind, from the verb *interlegere*, *inter*, between + *legere*, collect, choose] Any **power** or act of the **mind**, including the capacity for **understanding** and the activity of current conscious **thought**. The exercise of intellect, which differentiates humans from animals, is expressed especially in the use of language. Intellect also specifically includes acts of **intuition**. As a power of **apprehension**, judging, and **reasoning**, it is a part of the mind which contrasts with the **will**, our capacity for appetite, **desire**, **choice**, and **action**. Echoing **Aristotle**'s distinction between **active reason** and passive reason, Aquinas distinguished between *intellectus possibilis* (possible or receptive mind) and *intellectus agens* (active mind). Active mind directly knows material things that exist outside the mind. These things are only potentially known, but active mind is the power to make them actually **intelligible** and provides an object of thinking for itself. Receptive mind is, on the other hand, a capacity for attending to what we have acquired through active mind.

> "The human intellect (*intellectus*) does not immediately, in first, apprehending a thing, have complete knowledge; rather, it first apprehends only one aspect of the thing – namely, its whatness, which is the primary and proper object of the intellect – and only then can it understand the properties, accidents and relationships incidental to the things' essence." **Aquinas,** *Summa Theologiae*

intelligible object, see intelligible world

intelligible world

METAPHYSICS, EPISTEMOLOGY [Latin *mundus intelligibilis*, in contrast to *mundus sensibilis*, sensible world] For **Kant**, the sum total of **noumena** or **things-in-themselves**, which are, as members of this world, also called intelligible **objects**. The intelligible world is conceived to be an essentially rational world, which we can think through **pure reason**. Although this world is thinkable, we do not know it and cannot even prove whether such a world exists. But as a moral world, a **kingdom of ends**, it is an area where the **moral law** is applicable, and its main object is **freedom**. As **space** and **time** are the **forms** of the sensible world, freedom is held to be the form of the intelligible world. There is much controversy over the meaning and justification of all of these Kantian claims.

> "The *mundus intelligibilis* [intelligible world] is nothing but the general concept of a world in general, in which abstraction is made from all conditions of its intuition, and inference to which, therefore, no synthetic proposition, either affirmative or negative, can possibly be asserted." **Kant,** *Critique of Pure Reason*

intension

LOGIC, PHILOSOPHY OF LANGUAGE What a **term** means, or the sum of **properties** comprehended in a term. It is a synonym of **connotation** and Frege's **sense**, in contrast to **extension**, which is a synonym of **denotation** or **reference**. In 1662 the Port Royal Logic introduced the distinction between extension and comprehension; and later Sir William **Hamilton** replaced comprehension by intension. J. S. **Mill** replaced this distinction with one between denotation and connotation. Intension is the characteristic that determines the applicability of a term, while extension is the set of **objects** to which a term is applicable. Different terms with different intensions, such as "unicorn" and "centaur," can have the same extension, in this case because there are no unicorns and there are no centaurs. Take care to distinguish "intension" from "**intention**."

The distinction between intension and extension has been applied to **predicates**, **singular terms**, **sentences**, and contexts. Following Frege, the extension of a sentence is its **truth-value**, while its intension is the **thought** or proposition that it expresses. An extensional context allows an expression to be replaced by any expression with the same extension without changing the truth-value of the sentence in which it occurs. Replacing an expression in an intensional context by an expression with the same extension risks changing the truth-value of the sentence in which it occurs. Many philosophers try to understand the use of intensional contexts, while others try to eliminate their use.

> "In logic, the totality of the characteristics of a concept is called its 'intension'." **Schlick,** *General Theory of Knowledge*

intensional logic

LOGIC **Formal logic** is generally concerned with **inference** on the basis of the **extensions** of the **concepts**, **predicate** expressions, and **propositions** employed, and is hence sometimes called **extensional logic**. It proposes that if two expressions have the same extension and **denotation**, then they are interchangeable without changing the **truth-value** of the propositions in which the expressions occur. But this is not true of propositions containing **propositional attitudes** (expressed in forms such as "a believes that p," "a supposes that p," and "a asserts that p") and propositions containing **modal terms** such as necessarily or possibly. In such contexts these expressions are **referentially opaque**. Intensional logic has been developed to deal with inference strictly upon the meaning or intension of the concepts, predicate expressions, and propositions. It is based on **Frege**'s distinction of **sense** and **reference**, and its major practitioners include Frege, **Russell**, **Church**, and Anderson.

"In the formal semantics of intentional logic, suppose we take a definite description to designate, in each world, the object which satisfies the description." **Kripke**, *Naming and Necessity*

intensionalism

PHILOSOPHY OF LANGUAGE In philosophy of language, the claim that in **natural languages** there are relationships at an independent level of **semantic** structure that determine the **denotations** and **truth conditions** of expressions, and that they cannot be reduced to the relationships at any other level of semantic structure. This position, which is proposed by **Frege** and **Church**, suggests that **sense** determines **reference**, but it is challenged by **Quine**'s attack on the **analytic/synthetic** distinction. Intensionalism is opposed by **extensionalism**, which rejects **intensional logic** and proposes that we should translate all statements containing intensional notions into statements containing only **extensional terms**. Recently, a weaker version of intensionalism has been developed. It distinguishes between type-reference (referring expressions as the words and phrases of a language) and token-reference (referring expressions as utterances or inscriptions of the words and phrases that are produced in the use of language). The weaker version then claims that sense determines type-reference, but not token-reference.

"Intensionalism claims that there is sense as well as reference, that sense can be complex, and that as a consequence of sense inclusion, there is special form of necessity, truth, analyticity, and a special form of valid inference, analytic entailment." **Katz,** *Cogitations*

intensive magnitude, see extensive magnitude

intention

PHILOSOPHY OF MIND, PHILOSOPHY OF ACTION A state of **mind** directed toward **action**. An action characterized as intentional is done with a certain intention. **Anscombe**'s *Intention* (1957) led to important debates by asking what the relation is between intention as a state of mind and as a characterization of action. Intention is not **desire**, for what one intends is what one can achieve, while one may desire anything. Nor is intention **belief** because, unlike belief, intention cannot be judged to be **true** or false. A traditional approach reduces intention to desire and **belief**. One intends to do something because one desires this thing and believes that one can achieve it. This reductionist approach has been much criticized recently. Alternatively, some characterize intention as a distinct psychological attitude over and above desire and belief, but what this attitude is has not been explicated. **Davidson** developed an evaluative notion of intention according to which to intend to do something is to evaluate this conduct as the best. M. Bratman offers a plan notion of intention according to which intention is the crucial ingredient in the notion of plan. A distinction between direct intention (what one intends to do directly) and oblique intention (the foreseen consequence of the directly intended action) can be traced back to **Bentham**. If an intention is directed at a present action, it is called action-related, and if it is directed at a future action, it is called future-directed. Another dispute concerns how these two kinds of intention are related. The problem of intention is intertwined with many important issues, such as **practical reasoning, deliberation, volition, weakness of the will**, and action, and is a major theme in the philosophy of mind.

"And we may be inclined to say that 'intention' has a different sense when we speak of a man's intentions simpliciter – i.e. what he intends to do – and of his intention in doing or proposing something – what he aims at in it. But in fact it is implausible to say that the word is equivocal as it occurs in these different cases." **Anscombe,** *Intention*

intentional fallacy

AESTHETICS A term introduced by W. K. Wimsatt and M. C. Beardsley in 1946, referring to the view that in interpreting and evaluating a work of art, particularly a literary work, we should mainly appeal to the author's intention in creating the work, that is, the plan or design in the author's mind. Wimsatt and Beardsley regarded this view as a **fallacy** because the author's intention and the work of art are two distinct entities. The author's private intention can be reliably grasped only through the statement of the author, but this kind of statement is another text open for **interpretation**. The work of art is public and has properties open to interpretation and assessment whatever the author's intention. The critics of art should be concerned with the artwork itself rather than the author's mind, which is irrelevant to the critical assessment of the work. Hence, the intentional fallacy can be classified as a fallacy of irrelevance. Opponents of the notion of the intentional fallacy argue that the sharp distinction between private minds and public artworks depend on an outmoded conception of **mind**. Some argue that every artwork is open to multiple interpretations. Either we must use the author's intention to help choose among interpretations or we must accept that there is no such thing as the correct interpretation of a work of art.

"Intentional fallacy ... occurs when the artist's intentions are given decisive say over the nature of the artwork." **Sorenson,** *Thought Experiments*

intentional inexistence, see intentionality; mental phenomenon

intentional stance

PHILOSOPHY OF MIND A term introduced by Daniel **Dennett**. In explaining an entity, we appeal either to its actual state determined by its **law of nature**, or to its designed **program**. To opt for the first is to adopt the physical stance and to choose the second is to adopt the design stance. But if the entity is too complex to be analyzed properly by these stances, such as a **person** or a chess-playing computer, we need to adopt an intentional stance, which presupposes that the entity is a **rational** and **conscious agent** (whether or not it actually is so), and then predict what it will do given the **beliefs** and information we ascribe to it. Dennett claims that in terms of this stance we may be able to reconcile the views of a system as a **responsible** and free agent, and as a complex of physical parts. An entity that is a proper object of the intentional stance might be called an intentional system.

"There is a third stance one can adopt toward a system, and that is the intentional stance ... In the case of a chess playing computer one adopts this stance when one tries to predict its response to one's move by figuring out what a good or reasonable response would be, given the information the computer has about the situation." **Dennett,** *Brain Storms*

intentional system, see intentional stance

intentionality

PHILOSOPHY OF MIND, PHILOSOPHY OF LANGUAGE, MODERN EUROPEAN PHILOSOPHY A characteristic feature of mental and linguistic states, according to which they have an **object** or **content** and are thus about something. The problem of intentionality is explicitly formulated in **Plato**'s *Theaetetus* with the question how we can think about things which are not. The term was introduced in modern philosophy by **Brentano**, as the fundamental characteristic of a **mental act** or **consciousness**, that is, its directedness toward objects and its reference to a content. Brentano characterized this feature in terms of intentional inexistence (existence-in-mind or immanent objectivity) because the objects of consciousness need not exist and some, like the round square, cannot exist. Intentionality is conceived as a **relation** between a mental act and an object or content, which is posited as the terminus of a mental act. However, although intentionality is directed toward some object or content, that object need not exist and that content need not be true. Accounting for this feature of intentionality has become a deeply perplexing philosophical issue. Brentano's student **Meinong** posited an elaborate array of unusual entities as objects of intentionality as a result of his distinction between the character of an object and its being. **Russell**'s theory of descriptions attempted to eliminate this ontological proliferation.

Husserl took the notion of intentionality from Brentano and turned it into an essential notion of **phenomenology**. For him, the intentionality of mental acts does not entail that they must have objects. The directedness of an **experience** is an intrinsic feature, which does not require us to posit an entity to be an object toward which it is directed. For Husserl, a *noema* gives a mental act its directedness and meaning. Husserl's study of intentionality has had great influence upon philosophy of language and of mind.

Contemporary philosophy of language distinguishes between intentional and non-intentional verbs. As a matter of logic, intentional verbs, like "to desire" or "to believe," do not require the existence of their objects or the truth of their content, whereas non-intentional verbs, including mental verbs like "to perceive" or "to know," do require the existence of their objects or the truth of their content. Some philosophers follow **Quine** in seeking to reduce or eliminate intentionality from our account of the world.

> "We understand under intentionality the unique peculiarity of experiences 'to be the consciousness of something'." **Husserl**, *Ideas*

interactionism

METAPHYSICS, PHILOSOPHY OF MIND A dualist position claiming that although **mind** and **body** are two separate **substances**, they causally affect one another. The mind and the body are two independent things, but throughout life they interact with each other. Interactionism contrasts with another dualist position, **parallelism**, which denies any **causal** relationship between mind and body. **Descartes** appealed to the pineal gland as the locus of mind–body interaction. The difficulties with his account led many of his followers to parallelism. Interactionism is compatible with common sense. However, if mind affects body, it must be through the brain, yet many scientists argue that physiology has not found any

non-physical causation in the activity of the brain. Others claim that we cannot understand the workings of the brain without introducing mental states within our theoretical framework.

> "Interactionism, in the mild sense, is the proposition that some material events occasion mental events and vice versa." **Wisdom**, *Problems of Mind and Matter*

internal point of view

PHILOSOPHY OF LAW For **Hart**, law is a union of **primary rules** and secondary rules. As in other rule-governed games, there can be two attitudes toward rules. First, one can take the rules merely as objects of observation and judgment, without accepting them. This is called the external point of view. In contrast, the second attitude is to treat oneself as a participant in the legal system and to appeal to these rules for guidance in one's own life, taking them as standards for making criticisms, demands, and acknowledgments. From the external point of view, one will make statements such as "In Country X they recognize as law . . . whatever the legislature enacts . . ." This is an external statement. From the internal point of view, one will make statements such as "It is the law that . . ." This is an internal statement.

> "For it is possible to be concerned with the rules, either merely as an observer who does not himself accept them, or as a member of the group which accepts and uses them as guides to conduct. We may call these respectively the 'external' and the 'internal points of view'." **Hart**, *The Concept of Law*

internal property, see right (Kant)

internal questions

METAPHYSICS, PHILOSOPHY OF LANGUAGE According to **Carnap**, philosophical problems concerning the **existence** of entities can be treated as either internal or external. Internal questions arise within a given conceptual framework and are settled by applying the criteria that the framework system supplies. Within the language of that framework, internal questions have the form "Are there Es?," "E" being the term for the relevant kind of entity.

Such questions can receive an analytical answer, whilst questions of the form "Are there Es conforming to such and such conditions?" can be settled either factually or analytically. External questions cannot be settled within a framework, but rather concern the status and legitimacy of the framework itself.

The problems of existence raising internal questions should not be subject to dispute, for it is obvious that there are such things as physical objects, numbers, or fictional characters. The reason that they are so debated is that they have been treated as external questions. Carnap suggests that such **ontological** questions should be interpreted as questions about a decision whether or not to accept a language containing expressions for these particular kinds of entity. The distinction between internal and external questions is challenged as arbitrary, but is defended by Ayer.

> "Questions of the existence of certain entities of the new kind within the framework, we call them internal questions; . . . questions concerning the existence or reality of the system of entities as a whole, [are] called external questions." **Carnap, Meaning and Necessity**

internal relation

LOGIC, METAPHYSICS An internal relation affects the nature of the related terms, for the relation is itself a constitutive part of the **essence** of the **objects** related. A thing that fails to possess this relation could not be what it is, just as it cannot fail to possess any of its **essential properties**. An internal relation is contrasted to an external relation, which belongs to individuals accidentally. An individual may have or lack an external relation depending upon contingent circumstances, but neither state will affect its **nature** because the external relation is not a constituent of its related terms. **Bradley** is usually taken to hold a doctrine of internal relations, according to which every object is internally related to all other objects and none is independent. As a result, **reality** is a connected totality, and the existence of every object can be deduced from the other objects. Since the relation of knowing and being known is also internal, the nature of reality can be inferred from the nature of **knowledge**. This becomes the main target of **Moore** and **Russell** in their criticism of

absolute idealism and in **neo-realism**'s criticism of **Royce**. Russell identifies the doctrine of internal relations with **monism**. In contrast, he identifies his own logical atomism, which allows only external relations, with **pluralism**. For **Wittgenstein**, internal relations are logical relations.

> "An internal relation is a relation which forms part of the description of a particular, such that the particular would, as it were, lose its identity if it ceased to stand in this relation to some other particular." **Pap, Elements of Analytic Philosophy**

internalism

EPISTEMOLOGY, PHILOSOPHY OF LANGUAGE A theory of **epistemic justification**, which claims that the justification of one's belief is determined by one's actual or potential awareness of the correct cognitive process that generates and sustains the given **belief**. Accordingly, justification is a function of one's internal states: one's perceptual states, memory states, and so on. This has been a major trend since **Descartes**, who identifies justification with having a reason for thinking that the belief is true. According to this theory, the justification of a belief is determined entirely by subjective characteristics, ignoring external factors, and is therefore opposed to **externalism**. In the philosophy of language, internalism refers to the position that denies that to **understand** a sentence is to understand its **truth conditions**, holding instead that the **meaning** of a sentence is its use.

> "[A] justification must always take the form of a convincing series of reasons available to the knower. In contemporary epistemology, this is called 'internalism'. The externalist, by contrast, insists that a belief can be justified even though the knower is ignorant of that justification." **Maddy, Realism in Mathematics**

internalism (ethics)

ETHICS Ethical internalism is a theory concerned with moral motivation. Internalism claims that motivation is internal for the **justification** of a moral action. Something can be a **reason** for action only if it is desired by the **agent** in question. Only if the agent believes that he ought to do something can this **obligation** be a reason for his action. Internalism hence objects to what is considered to be any psychologically unrealizable moral theory. It has two different versions. One was proposed by **Plato, Kant**, and their followers, and claims that rational consideration generates motivation, that is, knowing that something is right entails a motive for doing it. This version is also called cognitive or rational internalism. The other version, proposed by **Hume**, claims that the agent's **desires** produce motivation, while his rational **beliefs** motivate only in a contingent way. However, Hume believed that a combination of desire and belief forms a complete motivating state. This is his **belief/desire thesis**. Internalism is also called motivational internalism, and is opposed to ethical **externalism** (also called motivational externalism), which is the view that the justification of an action is separate from its motivation.

> "Internalism is the view that the presence of a motivation for acting morally is guaranteed by the truth of ethical propositions themselves." **T. Nagel,** *The Possibility of Altruism*

Interpretation (Heidegger)

MODERN EUROPEAN PHILOSOPHY **Heidegger** distinguished *Interpretieren* (Interpretation) from *Auslegung* (interpretation, literally laid out). For him, Interpretation corresponds to **understanding** as a primordial mode of *Dasein*'s **being** and seizes the possibilities opened by understanding. In contrast, interpretation corresponds to cognitive understanding and provides our day-to-day *existentiell* interpretations. The former grasps the being of all entities, while the latter provides our ordinary accounts of entities. According to Heidegger, Interpretation, as the discovery of the transhistorical and transcultural structures of *Dasein*, determines interpretation and makes it possible. Philosophical understanding is associated with Interpretation.

> "Thus by exhibiting the positive phenomenon of the closest everyday Being-in-the-world, we have made it possible to get an insight into the reason why an ontological Interpretation of this state of Being has been missing. This very state of Being, in its everyday kind of Being, is what proximally misses itself and covers itself up." **Heidegger,** *Being and Time*

intersubjectivity

PHILOSOPHY OF MIND, EPISTEMOLOGY, AESTHETICS, MODERN EUROPEAN PHILOSOPHY Something is intersubjective if its existence is neither independent of human **minds** (purely objective) nor dependent upon single minds or subjects (purely subjective), but dependent upon the common features of different minds. **Aesthetic properties** and Lockean **ideas** of **secondary qualities** belong to this category. The intersubjective, which contrasts mainly to the purely subjective, implies a sort of objectivity which derives from the common nature of different minds rather than from the nature of the object itself. Their common and shared nature implies an interaction and communication among different minds or subjects, and this is their intersubjectivity. On this view, a mind not only experiences the existence of other minds, but also carries within it an intention to communicate with these other minds.

For **Husserl**, these features of intersubjectivity indicate that we constitute the world as a shared world (*Lebenswelt*) rather than a solipsistic one. This view is further developed by **Merleau-Ponty**, who rejects the traditional dichotomy of **subject** and **object** and conceives intersubjectivity as intercorporeity. For analytical philosophy, intersubjectivity is the mutual accessibility between two or more minds. Each of them is aware not only the existence of the other, but also of its intention to convey information to the other. Intersubjectivity is fundamental to rejecting **solipsism** and proving the existence of **other minds**. The problem of other minds was at the center of philosophy of mind in the mid twentieth century, but no longer has a dominant role.

> "The principle of 'radical' idealism, namely of always going back to the constitutive acts of transcendental subjectivity, must obviously illuminate the universal horizon consciousness that is the 'world' and, above all, the intersubjectivity of this world – although what is constituted in this way, the world as what is common to many individuals, itself includes subjectivity." **Gadamer,** *Truth and Method*

intrinsic description

EPISTEMOLOGY, METAPHYSICS, PHILOSOPHY OF LANGUAGE **Ayer**'s term for a **description** that is peculiar to a **particular event** at a particular time. If two events are distinct, their intrinsic descriptions are different. One cannot infer from the description of one event the features and character of the other. Such a description is **atomistic**, for it does not carry any **causal** implication and it isolates an event from its actual and potential **relations** to other objects or events. Intrinsic descriptions are not common in ordinary language, since they are not very informative. Sometimes, this sort of description is thought to be possible only for private and fleeting **sense-impressions**. Ayer, however, claims that such descriptions are accepted by the **empiricist** tradition and should be sufficient to give an account of everything that happens. They are confined to the domain of actual **facts** and underlie **Hume's** principle that inference concerning matters of fact is not demonstrative.

"I shall introduce the concept of an intrinsic description. I shall say that such a description of the state of a subject S at a particular time t is intrinsic to S at t if and only if nothing follows from it with regard to the state of S at any time other than t, or with regard to the existence of any subject S' which is distinct from S, in the sense that S and S' have no common part." **Ayer, *Probability and Evidence***

introspection

EPISTEMOLOGY, PHILOSOPHY OF MIND [from Latin *intro*, inward, into + *specere*, look, to look into one's own mind] Direct awareness of or attending to one's **mental states** and activities. Traditionally, introspection is conceived on the model of **perception**, invoking a **faculty** of **inner sense**. While sense-perception enables us to be aware of current happenings in our environment and our body, introspection enables us to be aware of current happenings in our own **mind**. However, this analogy to sense-perception is questioned in contemporary philosophy of mind. Some philosophers take introspection to be no more than a capacity for making true statements about one's mental happenings. The **Cartesian** tradition holds that introspection is a major source of evidence for the existence of a substantial mind. However, **Ryle** and others have tried to replace introspection with **retrospection** by claiming that if introspection is a mental activity, and if each mental activity is introspectible, then introspection

will involve an **infinite regress**. The Cartesian tradition also holds that we logically cannot be mistaken about our current mental states, but this view is attacked by many philosophers and psychologists. Introspection is the same as **Locke's reflection**.

"The technical term 'introspection' has been used to denote a supposed species of perception. It was supposed that much as a person may at a particular moment be listening to a flute, savouring a wine, or regarding a waterfall, so he may be 'regarding', in a non-optical sense, some current mental states or process of his own." **Ryle, *The Concept of Mind***

introspective awareness, another term for introspection

intuition

EPISTEMOLOGY, PHILOSOPHY OF MIND, METAPHYSICS, PHILOSOPHY OF RELIGION, ETHICS, PHILOSOPHY OF MATHEMATICS, LOGIC [from Latin *intueri*, look at, look upon or inspect] The innate power of the **mind** to see or directly apprehend **truths**, without the aid of sensory stimuli, and without prior **inference** or discussion. It is knowing a **particular** in a **universal** in a single flash of insight. Intuitive **knowledge** is thus distinguished from inferential knowledge. Intuition can be empirical (a direct presentation of sensible **objects** in the mind), practical (a direct awareness of whether a particular circumstance fits with a general rule), or intellectual (an apprehension of universals, **concepts**, **self-evident** truths, or **ineffable** objects such as **God**). Practical intuition is a part of **practical reason** and was discussed by **Aristotle** in his ethics. Intellectual intuition, or reason's insight, is a crucial faculty for the **rationalist** tradition. For **Descartes**, it is the recognition of the starting-point of **deduction**. For **Spinoza**, it is scientific intuition and is the highest of the three modes of knowing. For **Kant**, it is a type of **experience** in which the normal antitheses of sense and thought, particular and universal, have been overcome.

Intuition plays an important role in mathematics, metaphysics, ethics, and logic, especially with regard to the fundamental **concepts** and **principles** of these areas. However, intuition as a **faculty** is impossible to check. It is viewed by some as non-rational or non-cognitive, and its claim to be a source of knowledge always faces suspicion. **Empiricism** in general rejects the existence of any faculty of intuition.

"In whatever manner and by whatever means a mode of knowledge may relate to objects, intuition is that through which it is in immediate relation to them, and to which all thought as a means is directed." **Kant, *Critique of Pure Reason***

intuitionism, ethical, see ethics, intuitionistic

intuitionism, mathematical
PHILOSOPHY OF MATHEMATICS, METAPHYSICS, EPISTEMOLOGY, PHILOSOPHY OF LANGUAGE A philosophy of mathematics founded by L. E. J. **Brouwer**. Influenced by Kantian philosophy, Brouwer claimed that mathematical **objects** are not mind-independent, but are products of mental construction. Mathematical **knowledge** lies in our capacity to construct proofs. A mathematical statement is true if and only if a proof can be constructed for it, and it is false if and only if it is shown that a proof cannot be constructed. Because there is a gap between proof and the denial that a proof can be constructed, intuitionism denies the **law of the excluded middle** and the law of double negation. Mathematical intuitionism is a species of mathematical **constructivism** and is opposed to the **Platonist** claim that the existence of mathematical objects is mind-independent. The reasoning of mathematical intuitionism was formalized by Brouwer's disciple Arend Heyting as **intuitionistic logic**. Its metaphysical and epistemological ideas have been developed and extended to areas outside mathematics by M. **Dummett** as **anti-realism** and the **warranted assertibility** theory of **meaning**.

"The conceptualist position in the foundations of mathematics is sometimes called intuitionism, in a broad sense of the term. Under stricter usage 'intuitionism' refers only to Brouwer and Heyting's special brand of conceptualism, which suspends the law of the excluded middle." **Quine, *From a Logical Point of View***

intuitionist logic
LOGIC A system of principles to formalize the types of reasoning allowed by mathematical **intuitionism**, after which this logic is named. It denies the principles of classical logic, which are not countenanced by mathematical intuitionism. In its most important formation, it is a calculus developed by Arend Heyting in 1930, inspired by his teacher **Brouwer**. It supposes that mathematical **objects** are products

of mental operations and that the **truth** of a mathematical statement is its provability, that is, the mental construction that would represent a proof of it. A mathematical statement is true if and only if we have a proof of it. Accordingly, no definite **truth-table** can be given for its **connectives** because a truth-table is based on the **law of the excluded middle** (or the principle of **bivalence**), which holds that a statement must be either true or false, whether or not we know it to be true or false. But intuitionist logic claims that if we do not have a proof of a statement or a denial that it can be proved, then we cannot say that it is true or false. Hence it rejects the law of the excluded middle as a **theorem**. It diverges from classical logic also by denying other laws of **negation**. Intuitionist logic is closely related to **anti-realism**, which does not admit any mind-independent truth.

"What is called intuitionist logic differs from the classical two-valued logic primarily over its treatment of negation." **Bostock, *Intermediate Logic***

intuitive induction, another expression for induction by intuition

inversion
LOGIC In traditional logic a form of immediate **inference** from a single premise, in which the subject of the inferred proposition is the **contradictory** of the subject of the premise. The original proposition is called the inverted, and the inferred proposition is called the inverse.

"Inversion may be defined as a process of immediate inference in which from a given proposition another proposition is inferred having for its subject the contradictory of the original subject." **Keynes, *Studies and Exercises in Formal Logic***

in vitro fertilization
ETHICS [Latin *in vitro*, in glass, in contrast to *in vivo*, in a living organism; normally abbreviated IVF, also called extra-human fertilization] A technique for fertilizing an egg outside the body and then implanting it in the womb of the woman providing it, or in the womb of another women, to develop into a fetus and a baby. The procedure was first carried out successfully for a human mother by the British scientists R. Edwards and P. Steptoe in 1978

and has now become a standard treatment for some forms of human infertility. Babies produced by this method are sometimes called test-tube babies, but the progress of the pregnancies and the children that are born are perfectly normal. Much ethical controversy has arisen because IVF has extended the range of human reproduction and has opened the way to surrogate motherhood and, more recently, to the possible genetic manipulation of embryos. Many theorists would welcome the correction of serious genetically based illnesses, but they would reject manipulation concerning gender, intelligence, strength, or appearance. The justification for these intuitive choices is difficult to determine. Some **feminists** view IVF as a means of liberating women from biological inequality, while others consider that it reinforces the male domination of female bodies. The debate is still going on about the conditions under which fertilization *in vitro* should be permitted.

> "'In vitro' is Latin for 'in glass'; so 'in vitro fertilization' simply means that the fertilization takes place in glass." **Singer and Wells,** *The Repro-duction Revolution*

I-proposition, see A-proposition

Irigaray, Luce (1932–)
Belgian-born French feminist philosopher and psychoanalyst, born in Blaton, attached to the Centre National de Recherches Scientifique and lecturer at the École des Hautes Études en Sciences Sociales. Irigaray argues that the feminine is excluded from the cultural unconscious by the cultural repression studied by Lacan's psychoanalysis and by the metaphysical repression that is the focus of Derrida's deconstruction. She has developed a feminist philosophy of sexual difference and proposes a liberation of both men and women from the distortions of their gender roles. Her main works include *Speculum of the Other Woman* (1974) and *Je, Tu, Nous: Towards a Culture of Difference* (1990).

irony
PHILOSOPHICAL METHOD [from Greek *eironeia*, dissembling] In simple cases, irony is the use of an expression to imply the opposite of its literal **meaning**, for example by calling a stupid answer a smart reply. In

some cases, not all auditors are intended to grasp the irony. Irony can also involve distancing oneself from what one is saying. In dramatic irony, some characters do not understand what the audience or other characters understand. In historical irony, events reverse expectations, sometimes in a way that seems morally appropriate. Socratic irony also involves a tension or contrast, based on the actual or affected ignorance of Socrates in the early dialogues of Plato. Socrates found flaws in the arguments of his interlocutors and pushed the argument forward, but he claimed that he himself did not know or did not have an answer for the question under discussion. In Greek culture, this sort of irony was regarded as negative. In modern philosophy, various kinds of irony have been important in the works of **Hegel**, the romantics, and **Kierkegaard**. Irony has also been discussed in the philosophy of language.

> "Here we have the well-known Socratic irony, and I knew it and predicted that when it came to replying you would refuse and dissemble and do anything rather than answer any question that anyone asked you." **Plato,** *Republic*

irrationalism
EPISTEMOLOGY, METAPHYSICS [Latin *ir*, not] Irrationalism in philosophy does not reject the role of **reason** entirely, but it rejects the claim that the function of reason is unlimited or supreme. In many areas, such as the first principles of a study, the ultimate ground of human existence, and the profoundest religious truths, reason cannot grasp the **truth**. Hence, according to different versions of irrationalism, we must appeal to non-logical and unmediated modes of **cognition**, such as **intuition**, immediate **experience**, and **faith**, to gain the truth, and must also take **culture** and **tradition** into account. Many philosophers who are the chief proponents of reason, such as **Plato**, **Aquinas**, and **Kant**, realized the limits of rational activity. Much religious philosophy, especially **fideism**, claims that reason plays at most a subordinate role in **understanding**. **Nietzsche** and the **existentialists** criticized the **Enlightenment** claim of the superiority of reason, a view taken up in a different context by contemporary **postmodernists**.

> "The issue about irrationalism can be sharpened by noting that when the pragmatist says: 'All that

can be done to explicate "truth", "knowledge", "morality", "virtue" is to refer us back to the concrete details of the culture in which these terms grew up and developed', the defender of the Enlightenment takes him to be saying 'truth and virtue are simply what a community agrees that they are'." **Rorty, "Pragmatism, Relativism, Irrationalism,"** *Proceedings and Address of the American Philosophical Association* **53**

irrationality

EPISTEMOLOGY, ETHICS, PHILOSOPHY OF MIND, PHILOSOPHY OF ACTION The incorrect use of information for attaining **truth** or achieving practical goals. An irrational **action** violates normal and standard processes of **deliberation** without any justification in terms of **reason**. The discussion of how practical or theoretical irrationality is possible is often focused on the issues of **self-deception** and **weakness of will**. In addition to philosophical discussion of how irrationality is possible, there are psychological or sociological attempts to characterize and explain the processes of irrationality. Irrational thought and action may be overtly deranged and obsessive, but need not be so, and we have varying insight into our own irrationality. Irrationality has been seen positively as a source of creativity as well as negatively as a danger to reason.

"Irrationality is a failure to make proper use of material already in the mind." **Pears,** *Motivated Irrationality*

irrealism

METAPHYSICS, ETHICS A word coined in the 1980s in both metaphysics and moral theory, but the idea can be traced to **Hume**'s **skepticism**, which denies the possibility of **knowledge** of a physical **reality** beyond our **senses**. Irrealism declares that there is no objective reality and hence **realism** is not right. But in the meantime irrealism does not commit itself to any existing forms of **anti-realism**. It holds that it is impossible for us even to form the idea of a body that has a continued existence independent of our minds, let alone any idea of the inner structure and invisible constitution of such a body. It does not accept that realism and anti-realism exhaust all the possible views. It questions whether we can establish a **discourse** that conforms to

the somewhat minimal constraints of **syntax** and the discipline called for by the applicability of truth-predicates.

"Irrealism does not hold that everything or even anything is irreal, but sees the world melting into versions making worlds, finds ontology evanescent, and inquires into what makes a version right and a world well-built." **Goodman,** *Of Mind and Other Matters*

irreflexive, see reflexive

is

LOGIC, METAPHYSICS The third-person singular form of the verb "to be," generally held to have three distinct senses: (1) the copulative sense with the **syntactical** function of joining subjects to **predicates** in **sentences**, for example, "This house *is* white"; (2) the sense expressing **identity**, for example, "The Morning Star *is* the Evening Star"; and (3) the **existential** sense, for example, "There *is* a house." There are also other attempts to classify the meaning of "is." There have been disputes over whether these senses are connected, whether some of them can be reduced to others or are really irreducibly different. Many contemporary analytical philosophers, especially **Wittgenstein** and the **logical positivists**, argue that traditional **metaphysics** is wrong to take **being** (the participle of to be) as a subject-matter, because doing so confuses the copulative sense and the existential sense of "is."

"Thus the word 'is' figures as the copula, as a sign for identity, and as an expression for existence." **Wittgenstein,** *Tractatus*

is/ought gap

LOGIC, METAPHYSICS, ETHICS Also called the fact/value gap or Hume's law, initially drawn by David **Hume** as a logical distinction between factual **statements**, which describe how the world *is*, and value judgments, which prescribe how the world *ought* to be. Factual statements are seen as value-free, and value judgments are seen as evaluative or normative. **Description** and evaluation are thought to be different activities. Hence we cannot deduce a moral judgment from a non-moral one. *Ought* cannot be inferred from *is*. There is no logical bridge between fact and **value**. It is further inferred that ethical terms or properties cannot be defined by non-ethical or natural terms or properties. Otherwise, to use Moore's terminology, we commit a **naturalistic fallacy**. This dichotomy has been held by many moral philosophers, including **Mill, Kant, Moore**, and **Hare**, to be a datum, but its validity has been challenged by others who claim that the recognition of fact is itself a value-laden activity, and that a moral judgment also has **descriptive meaning**. The soundness of this distinction has been the focus of the debates between **naturalism** and anti-naturalism and between **cognitivism** and **non-cognitivism**. John **Searle** and others have tried to show how we can derive an ought statement from is statements.

> "I have always remarked, that the author proceeds for some time in the ordinary way of reasoning, and establishes the being of God, or makes observations concerning human affairs; when of a sudden I am surprised to find, that instead of the usual copulations of propositions, is, and is not, I meet with no proposition that is not connected with an ought, or an ought not." **Hume,** *A Treatise of Human Nature*

isomorphism

LOGIC, METAPHYSICS, PHILOSOPHY OF LANGUAGE [from Greek *isos*, equal + *morph*, form or shape] The structural **identity** or one-to-one correspondence of **properties** between two **propositions** or two systems. In **Wittgenstein**'s *Tractatus*, a proposition is a picture that is isomorphic with a corresponding possible **state of affairs**. This is the core point in his **picture theory**. In its stronger version, it suggests that not only the **names** but also the significant **relations** between the names will stand in a relation of **reference** to the world. In its weaker version, it suggests that only relational **facts** will be symbolized by relational **sentences**, with no requirement that the significant relation in such a sentence will have reference to a relation in the world. It is sometimes argued that Wittgenstein's thought develops from the stronger version to a weaker one. **Carnap** claims that if two sentences are **logically equivalent**, and have the same number of corresponding components, they are intensionally isomorphic. They not only have the same **intension**, but also are equivalent in analytical **meaning**.

> "Isomorphism, or that structural identity, is a relation between interpreted languages . . . To say of two systems that they are isomorphic is to say that they have the same structure (logical form)." **Pap,** *Elements of Analytic Philosophy*

isotheneia

ANCIENT GREEK PHILOSOPHY, EPISTEMOLOGY [Greek equipollence] Greek **skeptics** use it to refer to the phenomenon where two arguments which express opposite views about the same problem possess the same strength and credibility. It thus results in a state of mental suspense existing in order not to disturb the balance between pro or contra arguments. Skeptics set up many incompatible but equally valid arguments in order to show that **dogmatism** is not adequate. There is no sufficient ground for holding that either the pro or contra argument justifies a decision about what is **true**, or even about what is more **probable**. In terms of *isotheneia*, a skeptic retains his general suspension of mind and attains peace of mind.

> "The sceptic is inclined to try to preserve isothenia, that is, to look for counterarguments and counter counterarguments." **Naess,** *Scepticism*

I–Thou

METAPHYSICS, MODERN EUROPEAN PHILOSOPHY For Martin **Buber**, one of the two main relationships exists between oneself and another **person** or **thing**. I–Thou (or I–You) stands in contrast to **I–It**. Thou may be either human or not human. I–Thou is a mutual and reciprocal relation, involving personal engagement and dialogue. I is for Thou, and Thou is for I. In this relationship, Thou is not an object to be manipulated, but something responding to the I in its **individuality**, something which the I must address with all that is most intimate and personal in oneself. The I becomes I by virtue of having a relationship to a Thou. Different I–Thou relationships generate different Is. An I–Thou relationship is always present.

> "The basic word I–You can be spoken only with one's whole being. The concentration and fusion into a whole being can never be accomplished by me, can never be accomplished without me. I require a You to become, becoming I, I say You." **Buber,** *I and Thou*

J

Jackson, Frank (1943–)
Australian philosopher of mind, logic, and meta-physics, born in Melbourne, Professor of Philosophy, Australian National University. Jackson argued for a representative theory of perception and introduced the influential knowledge argument in support of qualia. He follows Grice in distinguishing between the truth-conditions and the assertability conditions of material conditionals to explain why we do not always assert material conditionals when their truth-conditions are fulfilled. His major works include *Perception: A Representative Theory* (1977) and *Conditionals* (1987).

Jacobi, Friedrich Heinrich (1743–1819)
German philosopher of feeling, born in Düsseldorf, President of the Academy of Sciences in Munich. Jacobi rejected the use of pure reason in philosophy as leading to Spinozistic pantheism, and argued from his reading of Hume for the necessity of irrational belief and faith. He accepted Kant's practical philosophy but argued against Kant's conception of reason. His main works include *Edward Allwill's Collected Letters* (1776) and *David Hume on Belief* (1787).

James, William (1842–1910)
American pragmatist philosopher and psychologist, born in New York City and taught mainly at Harvard. James developed pragmatism from Peirce's theory of meaning to become a metaphysics of truth and meaning. He sought to determine what it means

to believe and what it means for an idea to be meaningful and true. His account of the "will to believe" held that where we lack a rational basis to choose between alternatives, our belief can legitimately be decided by emotional consequences. An idea is true if the results of accepting the idea are good. Truth is made rather than discovered, although the invention of truth is conventional rather than arbitrary. Philosophy involves temperament and personal attitudes toward the world and is not merely a logic for seeking solutions to a set of problems. He saw the history of philosophy as a battle between tough-minded philosophers (who reject everything aside from facts as false) and the tender-minded ones (who value certain principles more than facts), although James sought to reconcile these approaches in his own work. His accounts of the "stream of consciousness" and of emotion have had great influence. His major works include *The Principles of Psychology* (1890), *The Will to Believe and Other Essays in Popular Philosophy* (1897), *The Varieties of Religious Experience* (1902), *Pragmatism* (1907), *A Pluralistic Universe* (1909), *The Meaning of Truth* (1909), and *Essays in Radical Empiricism* (1912).

James–Lange view
PHILOSOPHY OF MIND The view that **emotions** are feelings generated by characteristic bodily changes in response to external stimuli. Hence emotion follows bodily changes rather than, as the traditional position holds, causes them. We are afraid because

we tremble, and we feel sorry because we cry, rather than the contrary. This view was proposed independently by the American philosopher William **James** in 1884 and the Danish anatomist Carl G. Lange in 1895. Psychologically, this claim helped to put the study of emotion on the basis of a naturalist inquiry rather than on the traditional basis of **introspection**. Philosophically, this thesis opened a new era for the discussion of the relationship between **reason** and emotion.

> "The famous James–Lange theory – developed by the American psychologist William James and the Danish physician C. G. Lange – asserted, that one did not feel the inner cause of emotion, but simply some part of the emotional behaviour itself."
> **Skinner, *Science and Human Behaviour***

Jansenism

PHILOSOPHY OF RELIGION A philosophical and religious movement named after the Dutch Theologian Cornelius Otto Jansen (1585–1638). The movement was inspired by **Augustine**'s anti-Pelagian teachings and theology of **grace**. Its other major defenders included Antoine **Arnauld** and Abbé de Saint-Cyran. The movement had its center in the Convent of Port-Royal. Jansenism flourished in the seventeenth and eighteenth centuries in Western Europe, especially in France. Characteristic features included extreme predestinarianism and moral austerity. Jansenist **determinism** held that we cannot fulfill **God**'s commands without divine grace, but cannot resist grace if it is offered. **Sin** is possible even for the righteous without interior **freedom** of choice through insufficient grace. The **virtues** of pagans are only vices. The Jansenist doctrine was condemned as heretical by Pope Innocent X, and the Jansenist community was dissolved in 1709. The influence of the movement, which influenced the thinking of **Pascal**, continued into the nineteenth century. Jansenism is also remembered because of the *Port-Royal Logic* that was developed by its followers.

> "Jansenism . . . was an authentic catholic belief: it based itself on St. Augustine and would not quit the City of God, the universal church. None the less it was a subjective religion, which stresses 'grace' above 'works'." **Brailsford, *Voltaire***

Jaspers, Karl (1883–1969)

German existentialist philosopher, born in Oldenburg, worked mainly in Heidelberg and Basle. Jaspers's magnum opus is *Philosophie*, 3 vols. (1932). Other works include *Psychology of World Views* (1919), *Man in the Modern Age* (1932), *Reason and Existence* (1935), *The Question of German Guilt* (1946), *On Truth* (1947), *On the Conditions and Possibilities of a New Humanism* (1957), and numerous monographs on various intellectual figures in history. His philosophy was influenced by his early training in psychology. Jaspers criticized what he saw as the excessive prominence of science and technology in contemporary life and argued that genuine philosophical problems, arising directly from personal existence, should aim to explicate human existence. His philosophy sought the nature of one's authentic inner self or *Existenz*. *Existenz* is not an external object, but is unique and subjective. It is the experience of the infinity of possibilities and a striving to transcend one's ordinary existence. Freedom of choice is central to man, and man is always more than he can ever be said to be. The ultimate and indefinite limits of being that we experience in all its fullness and richness is "the encompassing." Jaspers was also a major historian of philosophy.

Jevons, William Stanley (1835–82)

English economist and logician, born in Liverpool, Professor at University of Manchester and University College, London. Jevons was an intellectual pioneer in many fields. He developed a mathematical economics and theory of utility, adapted a simplified Boolean logic, and produced a logical machine that foreshadowed the modern computer. He challenges Mill's account of induction with a hypothetico-deductive method in science and a subjective theory of probability. His main works include *Pure Logic* (1864) and *Principles of Science* (1874).

Johnson, W(illiam) E(rnest) (1858–1931)

English logician, born in Cambridge, taught in Cambridge. Johnson was a philosophical logician concerned with the normative study of thought. His work focused on the proposition and discussed differences between formal implication and inference, between formal constitutive syntactic and semantic conditions and informal epistemic pragmatic conditions in logical theory, and between logical premises and logical principles. His account of inductive inference led to a discussion of space, time, and causality, and he introduced discussions of determinants and determinables and ostensive definition. His main work is *Logic*, 3 vols. (1921–4).

joint method of agreement and difference

LOGIC The third of **Mill**'s five **inductive** methods, after the **method of agreement** and the **method of difference**. A phenomenon, P, occurs both in circumstances A and B. These two circumstances differ in every aspect except the factor E. Furthermore, P does not occur in the circumstances C and D, and C and D differ in every aspect except that they both do not have E. Thus, we may conclude that E stands in a causal relationship with the phenomenon P. The method proceeds by ascertaining the difference between the cases in which the phenomenon is present and those in which it is absent. What we uncover through this method is both a **sufficient** and a **necessary condition** for the phenomenon under investigation.

"This method may be called the indirect method of difference, or the joint method of agreement and difference, and consists in a double employment of the method of agreement, each proof being independent of the other, and corroborating it." *The Collected Works of John Stuart Mill*, **vol. VII**

judgeable content

LOGIC **Frege**'s term for what is thought and asserted when we make an **assertion**. It is prefixed by the **content-stroke**: ⊢. The judgeable content merges the **thought** expressed and its **truth-value**. It contrasts to the unjudgeable content, which is its constituent. Together they form the conceptual content. For Frege, judgeable content is a **state of affairs**, an entity rather than an act of making a **judgment** or assertion. It is an **abstract entity** existing independently of our judging it and is the **object** of judgment. If different **sentences** have the same assertions, they express the same judgeable content and conceptual content. Logic is the science of the relations among conceptual contents.

". . . the content of what follows the content-stroke must always be a possible content of judgement." **Frege,** *Philosophical Writings of Gottlob Frege*

judgment

LOGIC, PHILOSOPHY OF MIND A **sentence** by which something is affirmed or denied. Different sentences can express the same judgment, and the same sentence can also express different judgments. Certainly, not all sentences are judgments. A judgment, like a **proposition**, is characteristically used to make a **true** or false claim, and judgments are verbally expressed in propositions. Judgments and propositions are often used interchangeably, although judgment has a psychological or metaphysical tone, while proposition has a symbolic and material tone. To judge is to have a **mental state**, which is a **propositional attitude**. It has been a matter of debate how to understand the capacity of the mind to form judgments. For **Frege**, to judge is to acknowledge a **thought** as true. Judgment is made manifest by a sentence uttered with assertive **force**, but one can grasp and express a thought without acknowledging it as true, that is, without judging it.

"A judgement expressed in language is precisely what is meant by a proposition." **Keynes,** *Formal Logic*

judgment of obligation

ETHICS A **judgment** that tells us what is **right** to do or what we **ought** to do, such as "It is not right to cheat" or "you ought to follow your teacher's advice". These judgments are directly related to our conduct and they are also called **deontic judgments**. Judgments of obligation contrast to judgments of **value**, which are not directly relevant to our behavior or **action** but concern **persons** and **motives**. Judgments of value tell us what is **good** or what has value, for example, "Freedom is a valuable thing." They also tell us who is responsible or blameworthy. They are also called "aretaic judgments." In teleological ethics such as **utilitarianism**, since the right thing to do is the action that has the best consequences, a judgment of obligation depends upon a judgment of value. But in non-teleological ethics, which is not concerned with the consequences of actions, there is no such a connection.

"In some of our moral judgements, we say that a certain action or kind of action is morally right, wrong, obligatory or a duty, or ought or ought not to be done. In others we talk . . . about persons,

judgment of taste, see aesthetic judgment

judgment of value, see judgment of obligation

judgment stroke, see assertion-sign

Jung, Carl Gustav (1875–1961)
Swiss psychoanalyst, born in Kesswil. Jung was
influenced by Sigmund Freud, with whom he col-
laborated from 1907 to 1912, before splitting with
Freud and founding his own school of "analytic
psychology." Jung's psychoanalysis focused on the
conflicts and tensions in the individual's personality
rather than on repressed sexuality. Personalities
can be classified as introvert, tending to withdraw
from the external world, and extrovert, tending to
outgoing sociable engagement. The unconscious
is both individual, based on one's own life history,
and collective, based on inherited tendencies of
human experience. He applied his theory of the
collective unconscious to the study of mythology
and religion and to exploring relations between
archetypal patterns of the unconscious and symbols in human culture. Major works include *The
Psychology of the Unconscious* (1911–12), *Symbols of
Transformation* (1912), *Psychic Energy* (1928), *Archetypes of the Collective Unconscious* (1934), *Psychology
and Religion* (1937), *The Undiscovered Self* (1957), and
his autobiography, *The Memories, Dreams, Reflections*
(1962).

jurisprudence, see philosophy of law

jus ad bellum, see just war

jus in bello, see just war

jus talionis, see *lex talionis*

just war
ETHICS, POLITICAL PHILOSOPHY Originally, a Catholic
notion involving the claim that the use of force is

legitimate for punishing external evil-doers, and now
a major topic in political philosophy regarding the
morality of the use of force for political purposes.
Traditionally, a theory of just war involved two
conditions: a just cause for a war (Latin *jus ad bellum*)
and a just means of war (Latin *jus in bello*).
With respect to the first condition, contemporary
theorists claim that a war can only be justified if it
is a response to aggression, either to defend the
borders of one's own country or to rescue another
country from aggression. The use of force must be
the last resort, and the war must be undertaken with
the goal of establishing peace. The right of national
self-defense is derived analogically from an **individual**'s right of self-defense. But the extent to
which this **analogy** may be sustained is a matter of
controversy. It is not clear whether it is permissible
to take thousands of lives for the sake of defending
a piece of land. With regard to the second condition, the main requirement is that war should be
proportionate to the wrong suffered. All the means
that cause gratuitous or otherwise unnecessary
destruction should be avoided. More important, non-
combatants, especially innocent civilians, must be
immune from attack. They should be protected as
far as possible from the ravages of war and should
enjoy protection from direct and intentional **harm**.
The problem is that in the practice of modern war
it is difficult to distinguish between combatants and
non-combatants. Furthermore, many combatants
are also innocent. The theory of what makes a war
just changes and adapts to the particular needs of
time and place and the changing character of war.
New technologies of mass destruction, such as
atomic, biological, and chemical weapons, would
inevitably kill a great many innocent civilians if used
in a war. For this reason, they are widely regarded
as morally unacceptable in a just war. Similarly,
genocide is universally condemned as an aim or
consequence of war.

justice

POLITICAL PHILOSOPHY, PHILOSOPHY OF LAW, ETHICS [Greek *dikaion*, from *dike*, a suit in law; the Latin equivalent is *justum*, from *jussum*, that which has been ordered. Etymologically, justice is the pre-scribed manner of doing things, which should be enforced by authority] From its origin, justice has concerned both fair dealing and righteousness. In law, justice is the sum of **principles** and **rules** that ought to be followed. Hence, a system of law is also called a system of justice. In moral and political philosophy, justice is roughly equivalent to **fairness** or **equity**. It is just to treat people in proportion to their relevant differences, and justice is a **virtue** concerning relationships among **individuals** and between individuals and societies. As a principle of social order giving individuals their due, justice demands that the **rights** of individuals are not violated by other members of society or by the **state**. **Plato** in his *Republic* defined justice as the harmoni-ous order between different elements of the **soul**, or between different classes of society. **Aristotle**'s distinction between distributive justice (the correct allocation of scarce resources) and rectificatory justice (the rectification of injustice by punishing offences) is still of fundamental importance. Since seeking justice involves seeking social order and stability, justice has been a central topic in moral and political philosophy. **Hume**'s **conventionalism**, **social contract** theory, **utilitarianism**, and **Rawls**'s rational choice of principles in an **original position** are some of the significant attempts to justify the principles of justice. When the established pattern of social norms is basically fair, justice serves as a principle to protect this order. When the existing order is not fair, justice becomes a principle of reform calling for social revision.

Contemporary discussions of justice surround Rawls's theory of justice. On this account, the essence of justice is fairness. Inequality in the dis-tribution of **primary goods** or social values can be accepted only if it improves the situation of every-one, especially of the least advantaged. Otherwise **inequality** is simply unjust. This general concep-tion of justice leads to Rawls's fully articulated conception, which comprises **two principles of justice**. The first principle gives priority to equal **liberty** and the second principle deals with equality of opportunity and the just distribution of goods.

The general notion summarizes the common point in the two principles and shares their orientation. Since Rawls focuses on the two principles rather than on this general notion, there has been a dispute about whether this general notion is a substantive notion of justice or merely a pattern of reasoning leading to a determinate concept. Many aspects of this account of justice have led to important methodological and substantive discussion and the development of rival positions.

> "It will be recalled that the general conception of justice as fairness requires that all primary social goods be distributed equally unless an unequal distribution would be to everyone's advantage." **Rawls,** *A Theory of Justice*

justification

EPISTEMOLOGY, ETHICS, PHILOSOPHY OF SCIENCE Whatever is provided as grounds to prove or defend one's claim or conduct. If a **principle** or a position is deduced from relevant premises, it is said to be justifiably inferred. To seek justification for a **statement** or **action** is the fundamental charac-teristic of a rational being, although there is con-troversy over what counts as reliable justification. Justification is especially required in epistemology and science in order to meet the challenge of **skepticism**. Epistemological justification has two senses. One is called objective justification and is concerned with what we should believe given what is in fact true, and is thus identified with **truth**. The other is the subjective sense, which is to determine what we should or should not believe given what we actually do believe, regardless of whether or not it is objectively correct. The latter is the ordinary sense of the term. It requires that we specify the norms under which we may hold a **belief**. To determine what to believe is a funda-mental problem for epistemology, and justifica-tion is a necessary condition for **knowledge**. For a long time, historically, philosophers agreed that knowledge is justified true belief. But this analysis has been challenged by E. **Gettier** in his famous **Gettier's problem**.

> "Justification, on most views, aims at producing something else: rational or justified belief." **Nozick,** *Philosophical Explanations*

justificationism

PHILOSOPHY OF SCIENCE **Popper** divided philosophy into two main groups. One proposes justificationism, which holds that science is the quest for **justification**, **certainty**, or **probability**. These philosophers also support **verificationism**, which identifies knowledge with verified or proven knowledge. A belief is acceptable only if it can be confirmed or verified by positive observation and **experience** and past **evidence** renders future happenings probable. Popper criticized this position as unscientific and proposed a rival program of **falsificationism**, which claims that the rationality of science does not seek justification or verification, but seeks to test theories through attempted **refutation**. We can never establish certainty for a theory, and only theories which are falsifiable are scientific.

> "The members of the first group – the verificationists or justificationists – hold, roughly speaking, that whatever cannot be supported by positive reasons is unworthy of being believed, or even of being taken into consideration." **Popper,** *Conjectures and Refutations*

K

kalon, the Greek word for beauty

Kant, Immanuel (1724–1804)

German philosopher, born in Königsberg (now Kaliningrad), educated and taught at the University of Königsberg. Kant's monumental position in the history of philosophy was established through his "critical philosophy," a system that profoundly shaped later work in almost every field of philosophy. The nature of knowledge and the nature of morality were two major concerns of his philosophical thinking.

Kant's masterpiece, Critique of Pure Reason (1781; 2nd edn. 1787), examined the cognitive powers of the mind in order to answer the question of how experience is possible. Kant launched what he called his "Copernican Revolution" in philosophy, which replaces the traditional assumption that all our knowledge must conform to objects with the claim that objects must conform to our knowledge. Theoretical knowledge must involve both sensibility and understanding and is possible solely through a fundamental role for synthetic a priori judgments. To explain how synthetic a priori knowledge is possible, Kant argued for the existence of a priori intuitions (space and time) in sensibility and a priori concepts (categories) in understanding. These intuitions and concepts, rather than being empirically discovered, constitute the basic forms necessary for having any experience. This account sought to reconcile and overcome the limited doctrines of Leibniz's or Wolff's rationalism and Hume's empiricism. Kant argued that the conflicting views of traditional metaphysics were inevitably generated by the tendency of pure reason to go beyond the limits of sensory experience, where it cannot provide knowledge. Kant sought to replace traditional metaphysics by a transcendental metaphysics based on the justification of the categories. Although this metaphysics denied traditional knowledge claims, it allowed for faith in the existence of God and room for human freedom. The Prolegomena to Every Future Metaphysics (1783) outlines the main argument of the Critique of Pure Reason.

Kant's duty-based moral philosophy, with its vision of the rational self-legislation of free and autonomous agents, has been the major rival of utilitarian consequentialism and Aristotelian virtue ethics in modern ethical thinking. The supreme principle of his moral system is the "Categorical Imperative," which in various formulations requires the universality of moral judgments, respect for humanity in oneself and others as ends-in-themselves, and action as autonomous members of a moral community or "kingdom of ends." Kant's moral theory is delineated in the Foundations of the Metaphysics of Morals (1785), the Critique of Practical Reason (1788), and the Metaphysics of Morals (1797).

In his Critique of Judgement (1790), Kant claimed that aesthetical judgments (judgment of taste), although lacking the objectivity of theoretical judgments and ethical judgments, have subjective universal validity. This third *Critique* also deals with natural teleology and shows the unity of his system. Other works from his critical period include *Metaphysical Foundations of Natural Law* (1786), *Religion within the Limits of Reason Alone* (1793), and *Opus Postumum*. Kant's pre-critical writings and lectures on a variety of philosophical subjects also repay attention.

Kantian ethics

ETHICS **Kant**'s ethics and other ethical systems which follow it in at least some fundamental aspects. Contemporary Kantian moral philosophers include John **Rawls**, Alan **Donagan**, Alan **Gewirth**, and, to some degree, R. M. **Hare**. The general characteristics of a Kantian ethics are as follows: (1) Universalism and **formalism**. The search for a single or a few supreme moral **principles** or laws, which are **abstract** and universal, to govern all rational beings regardless of their particular and historical circumstances. (2) **Rationalism**. These principles and laws are formed from **reason** alone, independent of our **desires** and emotions. (3) **Autonomy**. These principles express the rational agency or **freedom** of human beings. (4) The emphasis on **obligation** or duty. The moral value of our behavior is determined in terms of its conformity with the universal moral principles. (5) A realm of ends. Human beings must be respected as **ends** rather than as mere **means**, and the creation of a **kingdom of ends** is the priority of human activity. Kantian ethics is a target of the contemporary **anti-theory** movement and is criticized for ignoring differences in social and historical situation, for excluding human emotion and desire, for ignoring **moral luck**, underestimating the value of **virtue**, and rejecting practical **intuition**.

> "Whatever may be true of Kant, it would seem that, at least among the present-day linguistic analysts who have tried to adapt certain features of Kantian ethics to their purposes, the effect has been made to recognise the purely formal features of moral laws, without attempting to explain and account for such features in terms of the peculiar nature and constitution of rational, moral beings." **Veatch**, *For an Ontology of Morals*

Kantianism

PHILOSOPHICAL METHOD All philosophical thought that developed out of the spirit and themes of **Kant**'s critical philosophy. Although such developments moved in different directions, they all originated from aspects of Kant's philosophy or dealt with the same topics in different interpretations. Some followers demanded that we go back to Kant, but many others tried to go beyond Kant. **Fichte** elaborated the Kantian notion of the transcendental subject and led German idealism toward **Schelling** and **Hegel**, on the one hand, and **Schopenhauer**, on the other. The **neo-Kantian** movement dominated German philosophy for several decades from the late nineteenth to the early twentieth century. Kant's account of the **self**, including the central notion of the **transcendental unity of apperception**, not only inspired the **phenomenology** of **Husserl** and **Heidegger**, but also figured prominently in discussions of **personal identity** and **consciousness** in **analytical philosophy**. **Kantian ethics** and **utilitarianism** have been the two major trends of moral thinking. Kant's theory of **experience**, the limitations he placed on **reason**, his account of **space**, **time**, and mathematics, his notion of **things-in-themselves**, his account of **synthetic *a priori* judgments**, his theory of **categories**, his conception of the **categorical imperative**, his distinction between **theoretical** and **practical reason**, and his account of **judgment** were significantly discussed by major successors in diverse schools. **Strawson**'s **descriptive metaphysics** is essentially a Kantian project. There has been much recent sympathetic interpretation of Kantian moral theory. In other ways as well, Kant's philosophy has been a principal source of modern and contemporary philosophy. The neo-Kantian Liebmann described the situation in this way: "You can philosophize with Kant, or you can philosophize against Kant, but you cannot philosophize without Kant".

> "Kantianism would still maintain that in the long run observed variations are to be conceived of as modifications in something absolutely constant, and that science advances precisely by seeking out this enduring or constant something." **Schlick**, *General Theory of Knowledge*

Kaplan, David (1933–)

American logician and philosopher of language, born in Los Angeles, Professor of Philosophy at University of California at Los Angeles. Kaplan has moved from a Fregean position to criticism of Frege in developing important insights into the theory of reference and singular propositions in the context of intensional and modal logic, with implications for metaphysics, philosophy of language, and philosophy of mind. He has also produced influential discussions of referential opacity, naming and describing, quantifiers, demonstratives, and indexical terms. His main papers include "Quantifying in" (1968) and " 'Demonstratives' and 'Afterthoughts' " (1989).

katalepsis, Greek term for apprehension

Kelsen, Hans (1881–1973)
Austrian-American legal positivist philosopher of law, born in Prague, Professor at Universities of Vienna, Cologne, and Prague, Harvard University and University of California, Berkeley. Kelsen proposed a pure theory of law that is independent of ethics, politics, and the social sciences. He conceived law as a hierarchical system of norms in which each norm is validated by others, with the whole system resting on a *Grundnorm* or basic norm that is presupposed by legal thinking. His major works include *General Theory of Law and State* (1949), *Principles of International Law* (1967), *Pure Theory of Law* (1967), and *General Theory of Norms* (1991).

Kenny, Sir Anthony (1931–)
British philosopher of mind and religion and historian of philosophy, born in Liverpool, Fellow and Master of Balliol College, Oxford. Kenny's training in scholastic philosophy and theology and in analytic philosophy provides a breadth of reference and historical sense that is lacking in the work of many analytic philosophers. He has used analysis to expound and criticize the thought of Aristotle and Aquinas and ancient and medieval philosophy to explore contemporary questions, especially in the philosophy of mind. His major works include *Action, Emotion and Will* (1963), *The Anatomy of the Soul* (1973), and *Will, Freedom and Power* (1975).

Keynes, John Maynard, Baron Keynes of Tilton
(1883–1946)
British economist, probability theorist and moral philosopher, born in Cambridge, Fellow of King's College, Cambridge and many official posts. Keynes is famous for his economic theory and its justification

for the intervention of the state in economic affairs. His most important philosophical work offers an objective theory of probability as a relation among propositions. His main works include *A Treatise on Probability* (1921) and *The General Theory of Employment, Money and Interest* (1936).

Kierkegaard, Søren (1813–55)
Danish philosopher, born in Copenhagen, a founder of existentialism. Kierkegaard attacked Hegelian rationalism on the grounds that it dissolves concrete individual existence into abstraction. He sought to develop an alternative "either/or" philosophy of free choice and subjectivity. Philosophy is to understand the existence of the individual. To exist is to choose one's own way to live and to constitute one's self. A choice is not a matter of rational reflection, but is generated by passion and without criterion. Human life faces choice at three stages: the hedonism-centered aesthetic life, the duty-centered ethical life, and the religious life. To move from the ethical life to the religious life, one needs a leap of faith. Kierkegaard extensively analyzed religious concepts, such as faith, choice, love, despair, and dread. His major books include *On the Concept of Irony* (1841), *Either/Or* (1843), *Fear and Trembling* (1843), *Philosophical Fragments* (1844), *Stages on Life's Way* (1845), *Concluding Unscientific Postscript* (1846), and *The Sickness unto Death* (1849).

killing
ETHICS **Action** which ends a life. Killing a human being has always been regarded as the greatest moral **evil**, and the right to life has been regarded as the most fundamental human **right**. The injunction not to kill an innocent person is the oldest and most universal moral maxim. In ancient societies, this maxim applied only to one's own **community**. Under Christianity, it was extended to all human beings, because all humans were regarded as having an immortal **soul**. Modern moral theory justifies the inviolability of human life in terms of our human **dignity** as **rational** beings. Traditionally, killing has been justified only in **a just war** and as **capital punishment**, although both of these grounds have been challenged. The principle that forbids killing provides fundamental support for the anti-**abortion** and anti-**euthanasia** movements. Disputes in this area have led to controversies about the

scope and limits of this principle. Contemporary **animal rights** campaigners attempt to extend the principle to protect sentient non-human animals and claim, controversially, that killing animals is morally wrong.

> "Killing in self-defence is an exception to a general rule making killing punishable." **Hart, *Punishment and Responsibility***

kinesis

METAPHYSICS, ANCIENT GREEK PHILOSOPHY [Greek, change, movement or motion] **Aristotle** sometimes restricted *kinesis* to non-substantial changes in a continuing thing, including change of place, qualitative change, or quantitative change, while using *gignesthai* for substantial **change** and *metabole* for **change** which includes both *kinesis* and *gignesthai*. But these distinctions were not always observed, and on many occasions the words were used interchangeably. Aristotle also contrasted *kinesis* with *energeia* (activity). According to this distinction, *kinesis* is movement having an **end** outside itself and incomplete until its end is achieved. In contrast, *energeia* is movement containing its end within itself and complete throughout the movement. Writing a book is *kinesis* because it is not complete until the end it achieved, while writing is *energeia* because without a definite endpoint it is complete throughout. For this reason, as soon as I can say that I am writing I can also say that I have written, but I cannot say that I have written the book as soon as I can say that I am writing the book. However, Aristotle sometimes treated *kinesis* as a species of *energeia*.

> "For every kinesis (motion) is incomplete – making thin, learning, walking, building; these are kineses, and incomplete at that." **Aristotle, *Metaphysics***

kingdom of darkness

PHILOSOPHY OF RELIGION In the New Testament, the kingdom of darkness was believed to be led by Satan, and is also called the kingdom of Satan. In **Hobbes**'s philosophy, it refers to all errors or obstacles that interfere with a person's **salvation**. In *Leviathan*, IV, Hobbes lists the following categories of errors: misinterpreting the Bible (particularly in the doctrines of Catholic Papists and Presbyterians);

the influence of pagan mythology (demonology, the belief in demons) upon Christianity (such as the imported ideas of Greek philosophy in Christianity); and misinterpreting the history and traditions of Christianity. The kingdom of darkness stands in contrast to the kingdom of **God**, which includes a natural kingdom in which the laws are promulgated by human **reason**, although commanded by God, and a prophetic kingdom in which the laws are promulgated through prophets.

> "The kingdom of darkness . . . is nothing else but a confederacy of deceivers, that to obtain dominion over men in his present world, endeavour by dark, and erroneous doctrines, to extinguish in them the light, both of nature, and of the Gospell; and so to dis-prepare them for the kingdom of God to come." **Hobbes, *Leviathan***

kingdom of ends

ETHICS For **Kant**, a kingdom is a systematic conjunction of rational beings under common laws, and the kingdom of ends is an ideal union or world in which each rational being is treated as an **end** rather than merely as a **means** to an end, and each pursues his ends in conformity to the requirements of the universal law, which he has freely made. According to one version of Kant's **categorical imperative**, a rational being must always regard himself as a legislator in a kingdom of ends. Such a kingdom abstracts from the personal differences between rational beings and also from the content of their private ends, for in this world each pursues his own interests in ways that not only do not conflict with the purposes of others, but also assist their purposes. It is actually nothing other than the highest good (***summum bonum***) and is therefore an ideal or intelligible world (*mundus intelligibilis*), which serves as a regulation for testing practical **maxims**. This notion also enabled Kant to take **God** as the sovereign head legislating in this moral kingdom of ends. It thus provided the basis for a moral proof of the existence of God, in the sense that the concept of God is alleged to be necessary to make our moral life intelligible.

> "For all rational beings stand under the law that each of them should treat himself and all others never merely as means but always at the same

time as an end in himself. Hereby arises a systematic union of rational beings through common objective laws, i.e., a kingdom that may be called a kingdom of ends (certainly only as an ideal)." **Kant,** *Groundwork for the Metaphysics of Morals*

kingdom of God, see kingdom of darkness

KK-thesis

LOGIC, EPISTEMOLOGY The thesis that knowing that p entails that the subject knows that he knows that p. Taking K to represent knowing, the thesis can be symbolized as "Kp→KKp". The thesis is **internalist** and can be traced to **Plato** and **Aristotle**. **Schopenhauer** explicitly emphasized that my knowing and my knowing that I know are inseparable. Jaakko **Hintikka** introduced this claim into contemporary epistemology and argues for its truth. The thesis holds that knowledge cannot be implicit. What counts as proper **knowledge** must be evident to the subject itself. Accordingly, if an agent does not know the process that gives rise to a belief, the belief is unjustified. But some philosophers deny the validity of this thesis on the grounds that it leads to regress. For if I know only when I know that I know, then I know that I know only when I know that I know that I know, and so on. It is also claimed that knowing is first-order knowledge, while knowing that one knows is second-order knowledge. These are different things. If the KK-thesis is false, a proposition may be known without it being known that it is known.

"What is sometimes called 'the KK thesis' . . . holds that in order to know something, you must at the same time know that you know it." **Carruthers,** *Human Knowledge and Human Nature*

Kneale, William (1906–90)

English logician, born in Liverpool, Fellow of Exeter College, Oxford and Professor of Moral Philosophy at University of Oxford. Kneale is best known for the scholarly knowledge and clear exposition of the history of logic that he produced with his wife. Although Aristotle and Frege are the most important figures in this history, the work drew attention to other important developments in Greek, medieval, and modern logic. Kneale's examination of probability and induction develops his own theories, especially that laws of nature are modal propositions

about natural necessities. His main works are *Probability and Induction* (1949) and *The Development of Logic* (with Martha Kneale) (1962).

knower paradox

LOGIC A self-referential **paradox**, first formulated by **Kaplan** and Montague, similar to the **liar paradox**. There is a sentence S, which says that "the negation of this sentence is known to be true". If S is true, its negation should be true; but if its negation is true, S cannot be true and must be false. On the other hand, if its negation is true, since this is what S says, S must be true. Hence S is both true and false. There are various solutions to this paradox, although none is free from difficulty. Among the solutions, the most influential one appeals to a distinction between different classes of knowing, that is, between knowing in the **metalanguage** and knowing in the **object language**. Another influential proposal is that sentences of this kind do not have **truth-values**. The existence of this paradox sets certain constraints upon any formalized theory of language.

"In view of certain obvious analogies with the well-known paradox of the liar, we call the paradox . . . [the paradox of] the knower." **Montague,** *Formal Philosophy*

knowing how

PHILOSOPHY OF MIND, PHILOSOPHY OF ACTION **Ryle** distinguishes between knowing how and knowing that, with the aim of demolishing the **Cartesian** account of intelligence. Knowing how is to know how to do something correctly and concerns the ability to organize and exploit truths when discovered. It is basically a way of behaving or performing, a **disposition** to do something efficiently. Knowing that, on the other hand, is knowledge that such and such is the case, knowledge of this or that truth, the state of being in possession of information. Knowing that is factual knowledge that comprises the stock of truths that the mind can acquire and retain. In the Cartesian tradition, intellectual operations are thought to be the core of mental conduct, and they are thought to be mainly the acts of **cognition**, that is, of knowing that. The tradition assimilates knowing how to knowing that by arguing that intelligent performance involves the observance of rules and the application of these rules. Ryle argues in contrast that intellectual activities are chiefly cases of know-ing how, and that knowing how is logically prior to knowing that. In many intelligent performances the rules or criteria are unformulated. Furthermore, if intellectual operations must refer to a rule and if the formulation of the rule itself involves intellectual operations, an infinite regress will arise. Thus, factual knowledge and theorizing on the basis of such knowledge is not the core of intelligence and not the fundamental form of mental life. To say that people have **minds** is to say that they are able and prone to do certain things. Thus Ryle substitutes for the Cartesian concept of intelligence, a disposi-tional analysis of intellectual activities.

"'Intelligent' cannot be defined in terms of 'intel-lectual'; or 'knowing how' in terms of 'knowing that'; 'thinking what I am doing' does not connote 'both thinking what to do and doing it'." **Ryle,** *The Concept of Mind*

knowing that, see knowing how

knowledge

EPISTEMOLOGY Epistemology is the systematic inquiry into knowledge, its nature, possibility, kinds, and scope. Knowledge has been distinguished into vari-ous species on different grounds, such as proposi-tional and non-propositional knowledge, knowledge by **acquaintance** and by **description**, *a priori* and *a posteriori* knowledge, and **knowing how** and knowing that, among others. What is the common definition for all these kinds of knowledge? Starting from **Plato**'s dialogue *Theaetetus*, knowledge has been thought to consist in three necessary conditions: **belief, truth,** and **justification**. Traditionally, the focus is on the nature of justification. Epistemolo-gists are divided into advocates of **foundationalism**, **coherentism**, and **contextualism**, each of which has various versions. In 1963 **Gettier** showed that these three conditions do not really explain what know-ledge is. For I may hold a justified belief which is true but which I believe to be true only as a matter of luck. Such a belief cannot count as knowledge. Epistemology since then has been debating whether the original conditions need to be modified, or whether further conditions must be introduced. The causal **theory of knowledge** claims that knowledge should be analyzed as true belief where there is a

causal connection between that belief and the state or event represented by that belief. **Reliabilism** suggests that knowledge should be analyzed as true belief acquired by a reliable method or procedure. The position which proposes that the conditions that distinguish knowledge from non-knowledge must be available to the subject is **internalism**, while the position which does not insist such an awareness is **externalism**.

"To know is to have a belief that tracks the truth. Knowledge is a particular way of being con-nected to the world, having a specific real factual connection to the world: tracking it." **Nozick,** *Philosophical Explanations*

knowledge argument

PHILOSOPHY OF MIND, EPISTEMOLOGY An argument introduced by the Australian philosopher Frank **Jackson** against the thesis of **physicalism**. Physic-alism states that to know a **mental state** and event is to know the information about the relevant nervous system. A colorblind person, however, does not know what it is like to see a red thing until he is cured and can see the thing himself. The informa-tion about his brain remains unchanged, yet his **qualia** become different when he gains color vision. The same point can extend to other senses, such as tasting or hearing, and can apply to the sensations and experiences of a physically normal person in varying circumstances. This indicates that physic-alism leaves something out. Certain **sensations** and perceptual **experiences** cannot be reduced to states of the brain because complete physical knowledge does not provide knowledge of qualia.

"The polemical strength of the knowledge argu-ment is that it is so hard to deny the central claim that one can have all the physical information without having all the information there is to have." **Jackson, "Epiphenomenal Qualia,"** *Philo-sophical Quarterly* 32

knowledge by acquaintance, see knowledge by description

knowledge by description

EPISTEMOLOGY Russell distinguished between know-ledge by description and knowledge by **acquaintance**.

The latter, sometimes simply called acquaintance, is a dyadic **relation** between a knowing subject and an **object** of direct **awareness** (that is, awareness without the mediation of any process of inference or any knowledge of truth). The objects of acquaintance include **particulars** like **sense-data**, **memories**, and our own awareness of objects. They also include **universals** like redness and roundness, the awareness of which Russell called conceiving. Physical **objects** and **other minds**, on the contrary, are known by **description**. Description is of two kinds: ambiguous description, which is conveyed by any phrase of the form "a so-and-so," and definite description, which is conveyed by any phrase of the form "the so-and-so." Acquaintance is knowledge of things, while description is knowledge of truths. Russell's theory of definite descriptions analyzes such descriptions to avoid the apparent need to posit special **entities** as their objects when they do not succeed in picking out actual objects.

"We have acquaintance with sense-data, with many universals and possibly with ourselves, but not with physical objects or other minds . . . Our knowledge of physical objects and of other minds is only knowledge by description." **Russell,** *Mysticism and Logic*

knowledge *de dicto*, see knowledge *de re*

knowledge *de re*

LOGIC, EPISTEMOLOGY Of a specific **object**, **knowledge** that it has a certain **property** or stands in certain **relation**, such as "Beijing is the capital city of China." If this object is oneself, and the subject knows it, then the knowledge is knowledge *de se*, which is usually expressed in the form of "I am . . ." or "I have . . ." In contrast is "knowledge *de dicto*," which is about a **fact** or **proposition** rather than about a specific object. For example, "There is a capital city in China." A person who knows this fact does not necessarily know that this capital is Beijing.

"The definition of the concept of de re knowledge is comparatively simple: X is known by S to be F = def There is a proposition which is known by S and which implies X to be F." **Chisholm,** *Person and Object*

knowledge *de se*, see knowledge *de re*

knowledge of matters of fact, see knowledge of relations of ideas

knowledge of relations of ideas

LOGIC, EPISTEMOLOGY **Hume** distinguished between **knowledge** of matters of fact and knowledge of the **relations** of **ideas**. Some knowledge depends upon the relations of ideas, and a **statement** that expresses such knowledge will not fall into **contradiction**. Knowledge of relations of ideas can be discovered either by **intuition** or through **deduction**. On the other hand, for statements expressing knowledge of matters of fact, the **contraries** are possible, and this kind of knowledge is based on **experience** and the relation of **cause** and effect. Hume sometimes also characterized the difference between these two kinds of knowledge as a distinction between knowledge and **probability**. Hume's distinction was foreshadowed by **Leibniz**'s distinction between truths of **reason** and truths of fact, or between **necessary** and **contingent** truths. Hume, in turn, provided the precursor of **Kant**'s distinction between **analytic** and **synthetic** judgments. Because Kant held that some synthetic judgments can be known *a priori*, Hume's distinction is more directly comparable to the **logical positivists**' distinction between analytic and synthetic judgments.

"All the objects of human reason or enquiry may naturally be divided into two kinds, to relations of ideas, and matter of fact." **Hume,** *Enquiries*

kosmos

ANCIENT GREEK PHILOSOPHY, METAPHYSICS, PHILOSOPHY OF SCIENCE [Greek, cosmos] Etymologically *kosmos* means good order, but its meaning is extended to refer to the ordered universe, for the Greeks observed that the major cosmic events are marked by their regular order. For them, order meant arrangement, structural perfection, and **beauty**. In contrast to *apeiron* (unbounded), *kosmos* is finite both in **space** and in **time**, having an origin and an **end**; a limited *kosmos* must have *telos* (end) and be *teleion* (complete) and living. Greek philosophy started by thinking about how a *kosmos* is generated and how all the changes maintain their orders.

> "We must say that this kosmos is a living, intelligent animal." **Plato,** *Timaeus*

Kotarbinski, Tadeusz (1886–1981)

Polish nominalist philosopher and logician, Professor at the Universites of Warsaw and Lodz and President of the Polish Academy of Sciences. Kotarbinski developed a radical nominalism that he called "reism" to distinguish between genuine names that designate bodies and apparent names that appear to refer to things such as properties, numbers, mental states, and events, but can be eliminated from discourse. His praxiology systematized ethical prescriptions under general principles aiming to protect others from suffering. His major works include *Gnosiology* (1929) and *Praxiology: The Science of Efficient Action* (1955).

Kripke, Saul (1940–)

American logician and philosopher of language and metaphysics, born in New York, Professor of Philosophy at Rockefeller and Princeton Universities. Kripke provided a possible-world semantics for modal logic and drew a range of conclusions from this framework concerning identity, reference, logical and natural necessity, *a posteriori* necessary propositions, meaning, names, descriptions, essences, natural kinds, and the mind–body problem. He has made important contributions to the understanding of intuitionist logic, the theory of quantification and the theory of truth, and a skeptical reading of Wittgenstein on meaning and following a rule. His major works include *Naming and Necessity* (1980) and *Wittgenstein on Rules and Private Language* (1982).

Kuhn, Thomas (1922–97)

American philosopher of science, born in Cincinnati, Ohio. In *The Structure of Scientific Revolutions* (1962; 2nd edn. 1970), Kuhn developed a theory of paradigms and paradigm shifts to explain scientific change. A paradigm is a set of related beliefs, values, and practices shared by a scientific community, which is used in periods of normal science as a model to solve problems. Scientific revolutions occur when unsolved problems accumulate within an old paradigm, leading to its replacement by an incommensurable new paradigm. This theory challenged the traditional claim that the progress of science is cumulative and unidirectional within a stable framework and has had immense influence in contemporary philosophy of science.

L

Lacan, Jacques (1901–81)

French psychoanalyst, philosopher of mind and language, born in Paris, President of the Champ Freudien, University of Paris VIII (Vincennes). Lacan integrated Freudian theory with Saussurian theory of language, philosophy of mind, and language and literary theory. Language forms the world and a person's self-identity through a public rule-governed structure that is the source of objectification and deception, but also has a capacity for free association that is driven by the unconscious to undermine fixed meanings and a false conception of oneself. His major writings include *Écrits I and II* (1966) and *The Ego in Freud's Theory* (1978).

Langer, Suzanne K. (1895–1985)

American philosopher of aesthetics, mind, and language, born in New York, Professor of Philosophy, Connecticut College. Langer developed a systematic theory of art as creative symbolic expression of human feeling. Her conception of symbol in ritual, myth, and art was based on a Kantian conception of experience and explored what could not be expressed discursively in language. Her major works include *Philosophy in a New Key* (1942), *Feeling and Form* (1953), and *Mind: An Essay on Human Feeling*, 3 vols. (1967–82).

laissez-faire

POLITICAL PHILOSOPHY, PHILOSOPHY OF SOCIAL SCIENCE
[French *laisser*, to allow or to let + *faire*, to do, hence to leave things alone and let them go their own way] A social and economic theory fashioned in nineteenth-century France. The theory advocates economic **liberalism**, claiming that free exchanges between individuals and the operation of market forces without intervention will produce a more efficient economic order. It also claims that society has its own order as well and that it should be governed by nature instead of the intervention of policy. Individual **actions** will naturally lead to an optimal state, and the government should be strictly limited to those activities that cannot be accomplished by individual actions. With its **individualistic** methodology, *laissez-faire* is the basis of **libertarianism**, and the term has become a motto for those opposed to government intervention in economic activity. Those who see flaws or gaps in the market question the adequacy of *laissez-faire* as an approach to the economy and society.

> "*Laissez-faire* is the theory that everyone will gain relatively to any other economic policy if everyone pursues his own interests within a certain framework of laws." **Barry, *Political Argument***

Lakatos, Imre (1922–74)

Hungarian-born British philosopher of science and philosopher of mathematics, born in Debrecen and taught at the London School of Economics. Lakatos is known for his "methodology of scientific research programs," which explains the continuity in the growth of science by the replacement of degenerate research programs by progressive research programs, that is, by programs that both generate and solve scientific problems. He held that all theories are born falsified and, hence, that the rejection of falsified theories cannot constitute scientific rationality. The theory is an influential alternative to Karl Popper's falsificationism and Thomas Kuhn's theory of scientific paradigms. Lakatos also applied his methodology to the growth of mathematical knowledge. His most important works are: *Proofs and Refutations* (1976) and *Philosophical Papers* (1978, vol. I: *The Methodology of Scientific Research Programmes*; vol. II: *Mathematics, Science and Epistemology*).

La Mettrie, Julien Offray de (1709–51)

French philosopher and physician, born in St Malo, Brittany. La Mettrie developed the mechanistic theory that man is a living or organic machine in *Man the Machine* (1747). He attempted to explain all mental functions and processes in terms of changes in the brain and the central nervous system, and held that all human conduct is determined by natural causes. Through this theory, La Mettrie became a representative of eighteenth-century French materialism. He denied the significance of faith, the immortality of the soul, and the existence of free will. In ethics, he was an Epicurean hedonist, holding that the goal of life is happiness and that virtue is enlightened self-love. Other works include the *Natural History of the Soul* (1745), the *Discourse on Happiness* (1748), and the *Art of Enjoying Pleasures* (1751).

land ethics

ETHICS An approach to environmental ethics initiated by Aldo Leopold and elaborated by J. Baird Callicott and others. Informed by ecology, which reveals that all **individuals**, including human beings, are internally related to one another and are in an ecological web of interdependence, it claims that the land should be included in the community of moral consideration and that we have **obligations** toward the land in itself for it has the **right** to exist. Distinct from animal-centered ethics and life-centered ethics, it proposes that the central concern of environmental ethics should be the ecological system or the biotic community itself and its sub-systems, rather than the individual members it

contains. It is therefore also called ecocentrism. As a **holistic** or totalitarian approach, land ethics is in contrast to traditional individualistic ethics. Its moral slogan is described by Leopold as "A thing is right when it tends to preserve the integrity, stability, and beauty of the biotic community; it is wrong when it tends otherwise." The strength of land ethics is its concern for the environment as a whole and its ability to deal with many environmental crises with which other approaches fail to cope. Its critics claim that since land is not the subject of experience, it cannot be included in the moral community. It is also criticized as being environmental **fascism** because of its holistic characteristics.

> "The land ethic simply enlarges the boundaries of the community to include soils, waters, plants, and animals, or collectively: the land." **Leopold,** *A Sand County Almanac*

language of thought

PHILOSOPHY OF MIND, PHILOSOPHY OF LANGUAGE A term from the title of a book (1975) by the American philosopher Jerry **Fodor**, also called mentalese. Inspired by the notion of a **Turing machine**, Fodor believes that just as a computer employs a machine language as a medium of computation, so might human thinking employ a human machine language, that is, a language-like system of contentful representations. His **hypothesis** is plausible because there are parallels between the structures of thought and language and because the sounds and marks in natural languages are meaningless in themselves but can be used to express meaning. If thinking can be understood as talking to oneself, a **thought** as a mental **representation** can be seen as a linguistic expression within a language of thought. The language of thought is the hypothetical formalized-language analogue in the brain, which has, like a computational system of **symbols**, its own representational elements and combinatorial rules. Such a structure is realized in the neural structure of the brain and determines the significance of spoken words. The central tenet of the language of thought hypothesis is to explain the origin of mental representation and the source of linguistic **meaning**. It seeks to reverse **Frege**'s priority of language over thought. For Fodor, this hypothesis is a precondition for any sort of serious theory construction in cognitive psychology. But his critics point out that this hypothesis is regressive, for if spoken words derive their meanings from meaningful interior speech, then what is the source of meaning of the language of thought? The language of thought is close to what **Dennett** calls brain writing.

> "It will have occurred to the reader that what I am proposing to do is resurrect the traditional notion that there is a 'language of thought' and that characterizing that language is a good part of what a theory of the mind needs to do." **Fodor, *The Language of Thought***

language-games

PHILOSOPHY OF LANGUAGE [German *Sprachspiel*] A response developed by **Wittgenstein** in his later philosophy to claims about the essence of language. The **formalists** once compared arithmetic to a game played with mathematical symbols. Wittgenstein extends this game analogy to language as a whole. Like a game, language is an indefinite set of ruled-governed operations carried out by different groups of people for different purposes. The rules constitute **grammars**. Just as there is no common feature in all games but a family likeness, there are various overlaps, but no common feature, in the wide variety of ways in which words and **sentences** are employed. Using language is like playing a game. Language is an autonomous activity and needs no external goal. The **meaning** of a word does not lie in what it stands for, but is determined by its employment in grammar. To learn the meaning of a word is to learn how to use it. Hence the idea of language as game is closely connected with the theory of meaning as use. Wittgenstein claims that many persisting philosophical problems result from confusing the different rules or conventions, so the clarification of rules of language-games should be the main business of philosophy. The account of language-games opposes Wittgenstein's earlier view of language in the *Tractatus* and sees the correlation between names and the named objects as only one feature of language.

> "We can also think of the whole process of using words ... as one of those games by means of which children learn their native language. I will call these games 'language-games'." **Wittgenstein, *Philosophical Investigations***

language/speech, see langue/parole

langue/parole

PHILOSOPHY OF LANGUAGE, PHILOSOPHY OF SOCIAL SCIENCE A distinction drawn by **Saussure** in his linguistics and translated as the language/speech distinction. According to Saussure, language as a whole can be divided into institutional and innovational elements. The institutional element is called *langue*, and the innovational element is called *parole*. *Langue* comprises language rules, which exist as social **conventions**. It contains the traditional stock of knowledge held by members of a society that make communication possible. *Langue* is a social phenomenon and cannot be created or modified by the individual. *Parole*, in contrast, is language in use whereby new definitions of situations are created day by day. It is individual, and the source of linguistic change. The *langue/parole* distinction has had great influence in linguistics, philosophy, and other social scientific and humane disciplines. It is the precursor of **Chomsky**'s **competence/performance** distinction.

> "For language itself can be analysed into things which are at the same time similar and yet different. This is precisely what is expressed in Saussure's distinction between langue and parole, one being the structural side of language, and the other the statistical aspect of it, langue belonging to a reversible time, parole being non-reversible." **Lévi-Strauss, *Structural Anthropology***

laughter, see humor

law of contradiction

LOGIC Also called the law of non-contradiction. The law of contradiction, the **law of the excluded middle**, and the **law of identity** form the basic **laws of thought** in classical logic. The law of contradiction states that for any proposition p, p and not p cannot both be true at the same time and in the same respect. The law forbids the joint affirmation of a proposition and its **negation** or contradictory. According to this law, we judge that any proposition involving a **contradiction** is false, and that any proposition negating a contradiction is true. **Aristotle** in *Metaphysics*, 1006a2–3 defined it as the view that "it is impossible for anything at the same time to be and not to be," and claimed that "this is the most indisputable of all principles." A strong motive for maintaining the law is that in classical logic the possibility of any meaningful discourse is undermined by accepting contradictions because every proposition is implied by a contradiction. In recent times, logical systems have been developed in which some contradictions are tolerated.

> "By means of these propositional variables we can state the general logical law, 'Not both p and not-p'. This is called the Law of Non-Contradiction and is one of three so called Laws of Thought which traditionally were regarded as, in some special but ill-defined way, basic." **D. Mitchell,** *An Introduction to Logic*

law of identity, see identity, law of

law of nature

ETHICS, POLITICAL PHILOSOPHY, PHILOSOPHY OF LAW, PHILOSOPHY OF SCIENCE [Latin *lex naturalis*] Also called natural law. In a moral and political sense, the natural rules of conduct or the general **commands** of morality, such as "do harm to no man," "seek peace," "do not steal," or "use self-defense." These laws are claimed to be **universal**, eternal, and independent of the will of any human legislator. They are discovered by **reason** and are the basis of **natural rights** and **duties**. As dictates of reason, they contrast with human law, which is legislated by the will of the holder of state sovereignty. In **Hobbes**'s political philosophy, there are two fundamental laws of nature for men in the natural state. One is to seek peace and the other is to do all one possibly can to defend oneself. According to **natural law** theory, human law or positive law gains its binding force only from natural law. Christian authority maintains that the existence of natural law authored by **God** is the basis of the universal moral order. Other theories ground natural law in some aspect of human nature or universal human interests. A critical response is given by **legal positivism**, whose founder Jeremy **Bentham** rejected the possibility of natural law.

In science, natural laws are objective orders or regularities in the natural world, which are independent of human minds and discovered by scientific investigation. They are the basis for sound human prediction. The existence and character of natural law in this sense has been a major focus of debate in the philosophy of science. Until the eighteenth century, scientific laws were sometimes backed metaphysically and theologically by appeal to God as their author, but more recently their justification has been sought within the enterprise of science itself.

> "We ought to distinguish between a two-fold signification of the term of law of nature; which words do, either denote a rule or precept for the direction of the voluntary actions of reasonable agents, and in that sense they imply a duty; or else they are used to signify any general rule which we observe to obtain in the works of nature, independently of the wills of men, in which sense no duty is implied." **Berkeley,** *Passive Obedience*

law of non-contradiction, another term for the law of contradiction

law of the excluded middle

LOGIC, METAPHYSICS One of the basic **laws of thought** that underlie all demonstrations in classical logic. The law says that a thing is either P or not-P and that it is not possible for it to be neither P nor not-P at the same time and in the same respect. Semantically it can be expressed that for any **predicate** p and any **object** x, either p or its **negation** is true of x. **Aristotle** defined the law in *Metaphysics* 1011b23: "there cannot be an intermediate between contradictions, but of one subject we must either affirm or deny any one predicate." When we say that a **proposition** or **statement** must be either true or false, the law of the excluded middle becomes the principle of **bivalence**. It serves as the basis for the **truth-table** method, but is rejected in **many-valued logic** and **intuitionistic logic**. The question of whether to adhere to this law or the principle of bivalence has been a watershed that distinguishes **realism** and **anti-realism** in contemporary logic and philosophy.

> "$(\varphi \lor \sim\varphi)$ illustrates the law of the excluded middle, which is commonly phrased as saying that every statement is true or false." **Quine,** *Mathematical Logic*

laws of thought

LOGIC Sometimes any **truth** of logic is called a law of thought, but generally the term is confined to three laws that have long been regarded as the most fundamental rules of reasoning, that is, the **law of identity** (P = P), the **law of contradiction** or non-contradiction (not both P and not-P), and the **law of excluded middle** (either P or not-P). In traditional logic, these laws are viewed as true and irrefutable. They are held to underlie all forms of reasoning and to be the fundamental principles that guide reasoning and justify valid **inference**. Contemporary logic usually contends that there is no reason to think that these laws are more fundamental than other truths of logic, and logical systems have been developed which reject one or more of their claims.

> "Theorem . . . ('If p then p'), forms part of the 'law of identity', which is one of the three traditional 'laws of thought', the other being the law of the excluded middle and the law of contradiction." **Prior,** *Formal Logic*

Le Doeuff, Michèle (1948–)

French feminist philosopher, teaches at the École Normale Supérieure de Fontenay. Le Doeuff argues that philosophy relies on an underlying "imaginary" of metaphors in pursuing its conceptual aims and that uncovering these metaphors in the language of philosophy reveals elitist exclusions affecting women and others. Her main work is *Hipparchia's Choice: Essays Concerning Women and Philosophy* (1990).

legal gap

PHILOSOPHY OF LAW The situation in which existing legal **rules** lack sufficient grounds for providing a conclusive answer in a legal case, for example, when there is no legal reason determining that a defendant is guilty or innocent. No available correct answer guides the decision. A gap can occur because the law is **open-textured** or because there are conflicting rules. A situation in which rules conflict creates a legal gap because conflicting legal rules block the capacity of one or another to apply throughout an appropriate domain. Rules do not have truth-values, but legal gaps can be compared to truth-value gaps. It is generally held that legal gaps should be filled by discretionary decisions, but this is rejected in **Dworkin**'s **rights thesis**, which rejects discretion in favor of the claim that individuals must be accorded basic **rights** that cannot be easily overridden by considerations of community welfare.

> "When an action is neither legally prohibited nor legally permitted there is a legal gap." **Raz,** *The Authority of Law*

legal philosophy, another expression for philosophy of law

legal positivism

PHILOSOPHY OF LAW A tradition in legal philosophy, opposed to the **natural law** theory, founded by Jeremy **Bentham**. Although there are different versions, the basic position can be summarized by the following two claims. First, there is no internal and necessary relation between law and **morality**; the definition of law does not contain a moral element, and is hence morally neutral. Secondly, the validity of law is determined exclusively by reference to factual sources such as legislation, judicial precedents, and custom, without regard to whether it is just or reasonable. The existence of law is a fact, that which is, rather than an ideal, that which ought to be. Accordingly, the law must be positive, and so-called natural law does not exist. For **Austin**, "The existence of law is one thing; its merit or demerit another." Most legal positivists deny the possibility of an objective knowledge of moral right or wrong. Other major proponents of legal positivism include John **Austin**, Hans **Kelsen**, and H. L. A. **Hart**. They differ from each other by invoking different factual sources for legal validity, and by holding different views about the normative character of law.

> "Here we shall take Legal Positivism to mean the simple contention that it is in no sense a necessary truth that laws reproduce or satisfy certain demands of morality, though in fact they have often done so." **Hart,** *The Concept of Law*

legal realism

PHILOSOPHY OF LAW Also called rule skepticism, a school of legal philosophy that flourished in the early part of the twentieth century. It maintains that the traditional theories of law are mythological in that they take legal **rules** to be **abstract entities** and legal concepts to have metaphysical essences. In contrast to legal formalism, legal realism is skeptical of the notion of legal rules. Rules by their nature cannot control decisions in court, and the function of law is to solve actual disputes. Law must be understood by reference to the reality of actual legal systems. Legal realism has two traditions. American legal realism, represented by O. W. Holmes, Jr. and Karl Llewellyn, was influenced by **pragmatism**. It claims that the law is constituted by how legislation is enacted and by what courts actually decide. Scandinavian legal realism, represented by Axel Hagerstrom, Karl Olivercrona, and Alf **Ross**, was influenced by **Comte**'s **positivism**. It claims that the **normativity** of law must be explained in terms of the psychological reactions of judges, citizens, or both. Legal realism is an attempt to understand laws in terms of what they are and how they operate. Its strength is that it is deeply rooted in the practices, insights, and practical arts of lawyers, but its weakness is that it can neither account for the **legal reasoning** of judges nor explain the necessity of legal reform.

> "Legal realism is, in large measure, the lawyer's perspective, and though it is unlikely that this perspective is the whole story, it is almost certain that it is such an important part of the story that any legal theory that leaves it out will be essentially flawed." **Murphy and Colman,** *The Philosophy of Law*

legal reasoning

PHILOSOPHY OF LAW The rationality manifested in matters of law, especially in the public process of litigation and adjudication. It is used to seek legal justification for conduct and decisions, that is, to show that they have a sufficient legal warrant and in consequence to persuade the court to reach a favorable conclusion. Legal reasoning is also employed by lawyers to predict what the other side is likely do or what a judge is likely to decide within the limits of the law. Like other justificatory argumentation, it can be either inductive or deductive, but its chief characteristics include appeal to the plain meaning of terms in legal rules and the conceivable consequences of a decision. Legal philosophers vary in their opinions about the suitable criteria of legal reasoning.

> "Any study of legal reasoning is therefore an attempt to explicate and explain the criteria as to what constitutes a good or a bad, an acceptable or unacceptable type of argument in law." **MacCormick,** *Legal Reasoning and Legal Theory*

Legal rights, see rights, legal

legitimacy

POLITICAL PHILOSOPHY A basic question in political philosophy concerns the grounds of legitimacy for a government or authority. The question can also be asked in terms of political **obligation**, that is, the basis of one's obligation to obey the coercive power of a government or authority. Answering these questions requires a rationale for the right of an authority to make decisions and its justification for having them obeyed. A major attempt to justify authority, initiated by **Hobbes**, is provided by a variety of **social contract** theories. The ruled consent to the transformation of political power into political authority in exchange for benefits such as justice, security, happiness, and liberty. In contemporary political theory, the test for this ground for legitimacy is whether a government upholds certain basic human **rights**. Max **Weber** suggested three sources of legitimacy: traditions or customs, rational-legal procedures, and individual charisma.

> "A state is legitimate if its constitutional structure and practices are such that its citizens have a general obligation to obey political decisions that purport to impose duties on them. An argument for legitimacy need only provide reasons for that general situation." **Dworkin,** *Law's Empire*

Lehrer, Keith (1936–)

American epistemologist, born in Minneapolis, Professor of Philosophy, University of Arizona. Lehrer provides a contemporary version of Thomas Reid's philosophy of common sense. His theory of knowledge explores the justification of belief in terms of defeasibility and criticizes foundationalist programs in epistemology in favor of subjective and objective justification involving a sophisticated account of coherence. His main works include *Knowledge* (1974) and *Theory of Knowledge* (1990).

Leibniz, Gottfried Wilhelm (1646–1716)

German philosopher, logician, mathematician, and scientist, born in Leipzig and a founder of Academy of Berlin. Along with Descartes and Spinoza, Leibniz is a major figure of early modern rationalism. His principal writings include *Discourse of Metaphysics* (1685), *Theodicy* (1710), and *Monadology* (1714). *New Essays on Human Understanding* (completed 1704, published 1765) systematically responded to Locke's *Essay on Human Understanding*. He also maintained a vast learned correspondence with intellectuals in many fields. Leibniz held that the world is a compound, ultimately comprising an infinity of indivisible and mutually isolated simple substances or "monads." Monads are soul-like and each is a mirror of the universe. There is no causal interaction among monads. Each individual substance is created to evolve according to its own determinate nature, but is nevertheless in complete harmony with other monads. The world as created by God is the best of all possible worlds and has a pre-established harmony, in contrast to Malebranche's occasionalism, which requires the order of the world to be maintained by repeated divine interventions. Leibniz contributed many seminal ideas, such as the distinction between contingent truths and necessary truths, the principle of the identity of indiscernibles, the principle of sufficient reason, the idea of a universal language, the development of the first logical calculi, mereology, the relational account of space and time, and the idea of possible worlds. Leibniz and Newton were the two founders of mathematical calculus.

Leibniz's law, see indiscernibility of identicals

lemma

LOGIC [Greek, something assumed or premise; plural, lemmata or lemmas] A **proposition** that is assumed or proved as a **theorem** in the course of argument in order to proceed to a different main conclusion. If an assumed lemma is false, the conclusion is unreliable. In ancient commentaries on **Plato**, lemmata were portions of text selected to be commented on.

> "I think in this connection of the characterisation of the lemma Y which can be 'interpolated' in an attempt to derive a certain conclusion Z from a certain premise set K." **Beth,** *Aspects of Modern Logic*

lesbian ethics

ETHICS A lesbian is a woman who loves and has sexual relations with another woman. Lesbian ethics tends to address the lesbian experience and the nature of lesbian **identity** with the purpose of seeking the **well-being** of lesbians. It joins **feminist ethics** in charging traditional Western ethics with promoting male dominance and female subordination

through social control. Sometimes it is considered as a branch of feminist ethics. Lesbian ethics claims that while both heterosexuality and male homosexuality imply the superiority of men over women, lesbians, traditionally viewed as manhaters, suffer the worst oppression. Hence, lesbian love forms a special challenge to sexism, and is a revolutionary act against the dominant political and social system. The ethics rejects the values of dominance and subordination, and promotes the value of choice and self-understanding. It encourages intimacy, engagement, and cooperation and develops lesbian **integrity** and moral agency. Although it functions only for those who choose its values, lesbian ethics claims to be applicable also for heterosexual women. The term "lesbian ethics" was coined by S. Hoagland in 1978. Currently there are two professional journals in this field: *Lesbian Ethics* and *Gossip: A Journal of Lesbian Feminist Ethics*.

> "This book is my attempt, with much stimulation and input from a number of lesbian communities, to describe at least one way we might continue to move toward lesbian connection and create a means by which we spin out of oppressions. I call this attempt Lesbian Ethics." **Hoagland,** *Lesbian Ethics*

Lesniewski, Stanislaw (1886–1939)

Polish nominalist logician and philosopher of mathematics, born in Serpukhov, Russia, Professor of Philosophy, University of Warsaw. In addition to important work on prepositional and predicate calculus, Lesniewski developed a mereology of wholes and parts based on his account of classes and an ontological interpretation of logic as yielding truths about the general structure of the world. His works appear in *Collected Papers* (1988).

Lessing, Gotthold (1729–81)

German philosopher and dramatist, born in Kamenz. Lessing was an Enlightenment figure, but anticipated Romantic concerns with expressiveness and freedom and hostility to formal constraints. He distinguished painting, which deals with the spatial array of color and form, from poetry, which is temporally organized to express passion and action. His main works include *Laocoön: On the Limits of Painting and Poetry* (1766).

Leviathan

POLITICAL PHILOSOPHY *Leviathan* is a mythical sea monster with terrifying power, which is described in several places in the Old Testament. Many authors associate it with evil, but Shakespeare took it to symbolize strength. The British philosopher **Hobbes** took this name, with a reference to Job 41, for the title of his most important book and used it as a metaphor for the state and its sovereign. He argued that such an artificial Leviathan should have absolute and undivided **power**. Leviathan is the authority in civil government that keeps human society in order and enables people to live in peace. The book's full title is *Leviathan or the Matter, Form, and Power of a Commonwealth Ecclesiastical and Civil*, published in English in 1651, and in a revised Latin version in 1668. It is divided into four parts: Of Man, Of Commonwealth, Of a Christian Commonwealth, and Of the **Kingdom of Darkness**. It is the main *locus* of Hobbes's moral and political philosophy.

"Leviathan [is] . . . that mortal God, to which we owe under the immortal God, our peace and defence." **Hobbes**, *Leviathan*

Levinas, Emmanuel (1905–95)

French Jewish phenomenologist, ethical philosopher and philosopher of religion, born in Kaunas, Lithuania, Professor of Philosophy, University of Paris (X, IV), Director of the École Normale Israélite Orientale. Levinas employed phenomenology in the study of an individual's ethical relation with another person. He held that this relation has priority to a person's relation to himself or his relation to the world of objects and can not be understood through concepts introduced through these other relations. Face-to-face encounters involve love, desire, and ultimately responsibility, but the absolute otherness of the other person is infinite, beyond conceptualization and language. His major works include *Totality and Infinity* (1961), *Otherwise than Being or Beyond Essence* (1974), and *Ethics and Infinity* (1982).

Lévi-Strauss, Claude (1908–)

French social anthropologist and structuralist philosopher, born in Brussels. Lévi-Strauss turned to anthropology when lecturing at São Paulo University, Brazil, and conducted extensive anthropological studies in central Brazil. He is regarded as a founder of structuralism, holding that structured codes are the source of meaning and that the elements of a structure should be understood through their mutual relations. Social structures are independent of human consciousness and are found in myth and ritual. He rejected Lévy-Bruhl's theory of primitive mentality, but followed Saussure in developing a structural approach to linguistics that he applied to the analysis of phenomena such as kinship and myth. His main works include *The Elementary Structures of Kinship* (1949), *Structural Anthropology* (1958), *The Savage Mind* (1962), and the *Mythologics*, 4 vols. (1964–72).

Lewis, C(larence) I(rving) (1883–1964)

American logician and epistemologist, born at Stoneham, Massachusetts. Lewis's principal writings are the *Mind and the World-Order* (1929), *Symbolic Logic* (with C. H. Langford, 1932), and *An Analysis of Knowledge and Valuation* (1946). As a logician, he developed the calculus of strict implication as an attempt to avoid the paradoxes arising from Russell and Whitehead's theory of material implication, and laid down the basis for modern modal logic. He called his epistemology "conceptual pragmatism" and sought to revise Kantian views through pragmatism. The judgments that are completely verifiable are about appearance. Human conceptual systems or categories are pragmatically justified on convenience and the long-term satisfaction of our needs rather than on Kantian transcendental arguments.

Lewis, David (1941–2001)

American analytical philosopher, born in Oberlin, Ohio, taught mainly in Princeton. Lewis made original and important contributions to many areas of philosophy. His modal realism about possible worlds argues that the world we inhabit is just one of a plurality of self-contained real worlds that can be ordered in terms of their likeness to one another. He developed influential theories of convention and counterfactuals and a mereological approach to set theory. He was a structural realist in the philosophy of science, a probabilist and contextualist in epistemology, and a materialist and reductionist in the philosophy of mind. His books include *Convention: A Philosophical Study* (1969), *Counterfactuals* (1973), *On the Plurality of Worlds* (1986), and *Parts of Classes* (1991). In addition, he published five volumes of collected papers (1983, 1986, 1998, 1999, 2000).

lexeme

PHILOSOPHY OF LANGUAGE A word may have different inflections and may be presented in different forms depending on its position in a **sentence**. But there must be a basic core that determines that all the various forms are the forms of the same word. This basic core is called a lexeme. For instance, "builds," "building," "built" are all particular inflectional variants of the verb "to build." "To build" is the lexeme. Precisely speaking, meaning is ascribed to a lexeme rather than to a word. Hence, it is more proper to speak of lexical meaning than of word meaning.

"Within semantics, the notion of word that is most useful is that of the lexeme which is an abstract grammatical construct that underlies a set of word forms which are recognised as representatives of 'the same word' in different syntactic environments." **Cann, Formal Semantics**

lexical ambiguity, an alternative expression for semantic ambiguity

lexical order, see two principles of justice

lex talionis

PHILOSOPHY OF LAW [Latin, law of retaliation] A law of retaliation, which proposes to maintain a correspondence or equivalence between crime and punishment. It is stated in Exodus (21:22–5): "life for life, eye for eye, tooth for tooth, . . . wound for wound." It is also called *jus talionis* (the right of retaliation). In contemporary theory of **punishment**, this law is quoted to justify the view that a man must be punished if his action has violated some **rule** for which he deserves a penalty. Furthermore, the penalty he receives must be proportionate to the wrong he committed.

"We are to observe (as we are elsewhere told explicitly) the *lex talionis*: an eye for an eye, a tooth for a tooth." **Honderich, Punishment**

liar paradox

LOGIC, PHILOSOPHY OF LANGUAGE A **semantic paradox**, dealing with matters of **reference** and **truth**.

There are many versions, but it was initially proposed by the Magarian **Eubulides** in ancient Greece, although another tradition takes **Epimenides** as the author. The original version is: "A man says that he is lying. Is what he says true or false?" If he is speaking truly, then he is not lying, so what he says is not true; if what he says is not true, then he is indeed lying, and what he says is true. In another version, ascribed to Epimenides, a Cretan says that all Cretans are always liars. If what he says is true, then it is false. The **paradox** arises because the **statement** says something **self-referentially** about its own truth or falsity. The need to avoid the liar paradox was partly responsible for the development of **Tarski**'s **semantic theory of truth**, and more generally the paradox is a key constraint on attempts to devise consistent semantic theories.

"Any version of the [liar] paradox involves the assertion that all propositions satisfying a certain condition are false, where the assertion itself is a proposition which satisfies that condition." **Copi, Symbolic Logic**

liberalism

POLITICAL PHILOSOPHY A political and social theory fundamentally emphasizing the priority of the **liberty** and **equality** of **individuals**. It begins with the priority of the individual rather than the **community**. According to liberalism, individuals have innate human **rights** regardless of any particular political system. They have interests that they seek to advance both publicly and in private life. Society and government should protect and promote individual **freedom** rather than imposing constraints. It is the mandate of government to respect individual rights. The plurality and diversity of society should be encouraged, and a society should be equal and just in the distribution of opportunities and resources. The political process should provide a fair procedure for resolving disputes when the interests of individuals clash.

Because liberty and equality come into conflict, various kinds of liberalism have been formulated, depending on whether the theory emphasizes liberty or equality, or on how one seeks to reconcile them. Classical market liberalism tends to insist that civil rights are fundamental to human beings, while contemporary egalitarian liberalism focuses more on equality and argues that government or society should increase its scope of intervention in areas such as health care, education, social welfare, and discrimination. On this version, civil rights can legitimately be qualified in such areas to secure justice.

Liberalism provided justification for capitalism, although it was also associated with the appeal for religious **toleration** in the sixteenth and seventeenth centuries. Some notable liberal theorists in England include John **Locke**, John Stuart **Mill**, T. H. **Green**, Isaiah **Berlin**, H. L. A. **Hart**, and Ronald **Dworkin**; in France they include **Montesquieu**, **Voltaire**, and Benjamin Constant; in Germany they include **Kant** and W. H. von **Humboldt**, and in America John **Rawls** and Robert **Nozick**. Persons who believe in liberalism are called liberals. Liberalism is the theoretical basis of the democratic system and has dominated political and social thought in the modern Western world. Critics of liberalism are suspicious of its association with the free market. **Communitarians** argue that liberalism overemphasizes the autonomy of the individual and ignores the ways in which individuals are embedded in social customs and **traditions**. The latter is also a long-standing theme of conservative opposition to liberalism.

"Liberalism was once, not very long ago, almost a consensus political theory in Britain and the United States, at least among political and legal philosophers. They disagree about it a great deal, but they all seem to accept, as close to axiomatic, a kind of egalitarian individualism." **Dworkin**, *A Matter of Principle*

libertarianism

POLITICAL PHILOSOPHY, ETHICS, METAPHYSICS A twentieth-century political and moral movement. It is a radical form of **liberalism** and argues that no intervention from state and government is necessary or justified. Free choice is supreme and all conflicts can be settled through the mechanism of the market. Its strong **anarchist** form insists that all government is illegitimate, and that all coercive political universalism is unacceptable. In its moderate anarchist form, it concedes that government may appropriately engage in police protection, enforcement of contracts, and national defense, but no more than that. Libertarianism emphasizes in particular the **rights** of individuals to acquire and hold **property**

and questions the legitimacy of the tax system. It proposes to develop rational egoism or Aristotelian **eudaimonism**. The most influential advocate of libertarianism is Robert **Nozick** in his *Anarchy, State and Utopia*.

Libertarianism is also a metaphysical term. In this sense, it is opposed to **determinism** and holds that the past does not determine a single future. We can act, on the basis of **rationality** or the self we possess, independent of necessitating causal laws, no matter what happened in the past. This theory is now often supported by appealing to quantum mechanics, which asserts that there are uncaused **events** in the universe, but it is not clear that quantum **indeterminism** is the right way to allow for rationality and **choice**.

"Libertarians are against what they describe as an 'interventionist' policy in which the state engages in 'interference'." **G. Cohen,** *Self-Ownership, Freedom and Equality*

libertinism

PHILOSOPHY OF RELIGION, ETHICS A movement that flourished in the sixteenth and seventeenth centuries, which demands freedom of conscience in religious affairs and moral issues. It is regarded as an anti-theoretical position. Theories that are based not on **reason** but on divine **revelation**, such as **immortality** of the soul and punishment in the afterlife, should be rejected. Libertinism is associated with **deism**, **materialism**, and **Epicureanism**. Its major proponents were P. Charron, **Montaigne**, P. Gassendi, Pietro Pomponazzi, and **Campanella**.

"[L]ibertinism – the belief that by grace, by the new life in Christ and salvation by faith, law or rules no longer applied to Christians." **Fletcher,** *Situation Ethics*

liberty, a synonym for freedom

libido

PHILOSOPHY OF MIND **Freud**'s term for the psycho-physical energy or motive force produced by sexual instinct. It is the energy of the **id**, and can be directed either toward the self or an **object**. The direction of the libido toward the self produces narcissism. Freud viewed the libido as a motive force for progress, with the intellectual evolution of society explicable in terms of a theory of the libidinous development. The libido is not anatomically located, but its existence is assumed in the development of biology. Freud later replaced the concept of the libido with the concept of *eros*.

"Libido is a term used in the theory of the instincts for describing the dynamic manifestation of sexuality." Freud, *Standard Edition of the Complete Psychological Works of Sigmund Freud*, vol. 18

life instinct, another term for *eros* (Freud)

lifeboat case
ETHICS Tom Regan's hypothetical case against his claim that animals have **rights** and hence are entitled to the same moral consideration as humans. There are five survivors on a lifeboat, each with approximately the same weight. Four of the five are human beings and the fifth is a dog. Because the boat can only support four of the survivors without being overturned, one survivor must be thrown overboard or else all will die. Which one should go? Common sense suggests that the dog should be sacrificed, but if the dog has an equal right to be respected or not to be harmed, as advocates of animal rights claim, what should the survivors do? Regan argues that this objection does not undermine the claim that animals have equal rights, because animal rights theorists can safely answer that the dog should be cast overboard. For the rights are *prima facie* and can be overridden in such circumstances depending on the loss of whose life will cause more harm. Since the loss of a human life will bring about greater harm than that of a dog's life, it is justifiable to override the dog's right to life in this case. Only some moral philosophers would allow the same considerations to determine which human life should be lost if all the survivors were human.

"The lifeboat case would not be morally any different if we supposed that the choice had to be made, not between a single dog and the four humans, but between humans and any numbers of dogs." Regan, *The Case for Animal Rights*

life-world
METAPHYSICS, MODERN EUROPEAN PHILOSOPHY [from German *Lebenswelt*] **Husserl**'s term for the historical world in which we live as historical beings and the culturally and historically determined **horizon**. The life-world forms the framework of processes of reaching **understanding**, in which participants agree or discuss something in their communal social world. The life-world is given to us prior to all acts of **consciousness** and is not consciously intended. Our objective **knowledge** of the natural sciences springs from the life-world. This knowledge reflects the concerns of specific **communities** and serves as one means of accomplishing their needs. Hence, the scientific world is rooted in the life-world, and the sciences are characteristic of being historically and culturally situated. The conception of the life-world is further developed in **Heidegger**'s account of "**Being-in-the-world**," in **Gadamer**'s notion of historical understanding, and in **Habermas**'s theory of **communicative action**. However, Husserl believed that various cultural life-worlds are themselves derived from an *eidos* or formal non-historical life-world, which is the product of transcendental subjectivity. In his view, one of the main tasks of **phenomenology** is to describe the structure of this *eidos* life-world.

"The life-world, for us who wakingly live in it, is always already there, existing in advance for us, the ground of all praxis whether theoretical or extratheoretical." **Husserl**, *The Crisis of European Sciences*

light of reason, an alternative expression for natural light

like to like
ANCIENT GREEK PHILOSOPHY, PHILOSOPHY OF SCIENCE The principle of the mutual attraction of similars in the philosophy of the Greek philosopher **Empedocles**, independent of his two cosmic agents of **Strife** and **Love**. While Love is the principle of unifying different elements, and Strife of separating different elements, the principle of like to like means that any portion of any element has a natural tendency to seek out and gather with other portions of the same element. It is the basis of Strife. Empedocles also employed this principle to explain **sensation**, which arises because one element in the body of the subject meets with the same element outside. All generating things are incessantly giving off

effluences, and when these effluences are of the right size to fit into the pores of the sense organ, the meeting happens and we have sensation.

> "For by earth, Empedocles says, we see earth, by water, by air bright air, by fire consuming fire, Love by love, and Strife by gloomy strife." **Aristotle**, *Metaphysics*

limited variety, principle of

LOGIC A principle in the theory of **probability** introduced by J. M. **Keynes** in *A Treatise on Probability*. It proposes that the domain from which a generalization is inferred and to which it can be applied should contain a limited or finite number of independent characteristics. This principle is held to increase the reliability of the conclusions derived in terms of **Mill's methods** and of **eliminative induction**. If the extent of possible independent variation is infinite in the objects of our generalization, **induction** cannot be meaningful. The principle is close to the principle of the **uniformity** of nature. Both are regarded as basic assumptions for the validity of induction.

> "As a logical foundation for Analogy, therefore, we seem to need some such assumption as that the amount of variety in the universe is limited in such a way that there is no one object so complex that its qualities fall into an infinite number of independent groups." **Keynes**, *A Treatise on Probability*

line, simile of the

ANCIENT GREEK PHILOSOPHY, EPISTEMOLOGY, META- PHYSICS A simile employed by **Plato** in the *Republic* to help in explicating the difference between the perceptible world and the intelligible world. Take a line AB, and divide it into two unequal parts, AC and CB, with AC representing the perceptible world and CB representing the intelligible world. Then divide each of these two parts in the same ratio. Thus we have: A—D——C———E————B, with AD:DC = AC:CB = CE:EB.

Plato distinguished the portions of the perceptible world AC, by assigning different objects and corresponding mental states to them. AD stands for **images** (*eikones*) such as shadows and reflections of objects, and the corresponding mental state is **illusion** or **imagination** (*eikasia*); DC stands for

the originals of these images, such as natural and artificial things, and the corresponding mental state is **belief** (*pistis*).

In the intelligible world CB, Plato distinguished the two sections by the different methods of inquiry the mind uses in each of them. In CE, the mind uses the sensible objects of DC as illustrations, starting from **hypotheses** and proceeding not to a first principle but to a conclusion. This is the method of the mathematical sciences, and the state of mind is *dianoia* (intelligence, mind, thinking, reasoning). In EB, the mind makes no use of illustrations, conducts the inquiry solely by means of **Forms**, and proceeds to an unhypothetical **first principle**. This is the method of philosophy or **dialectic**, and the state of mind is *noesis* (intellect or understanding). Sometimes CE is understood to be concerned with mathematical entities and EB to be concerned with moral Forms, but this interpretation is disputable.

These four sections provide a classification of cognitive states and their objects, and from AD to EB the line constitutes a continuous scale of increasing degrees of clarity and reality. The Simile is closely related to the Simile of the **Sun**, and the Simile of the **Cave**. Plato's text is difficult, but the simile provides a basis for exploring a number of important metaphysical and epistemological issues.

> "There are four such processes in the soul, corresponding to the four sections of our line: *noesis* for the highest, *dianoia* for the second; give the name of *pistis* to the third, and *eikinos* to the last." **Plato**, *Republic*

linguistic act, see speech act

linguistic analysis

PHILOSOPHICAL METHOD In its broad sense linguistic analysis is the major characteristic of **analytic philosophy**, which regards it as the real function of philosophy. Linguistic analysis aims to clarify and reveal the proper structure of **ordinary language**. It tries to show how certain uses of ordinary language have provoked metaphysical problems and how language has been misused in many alleged solutions. It is claimed that this approach might eliminate or solve the traditional philosophical problems that arise because of the misuse of language. Linguistic analysis is in the tradition of British **empiricism**.

"Linguistic analysis distinguished it [metaphysics] sharply from science, regarding it either as a diseased intellectual condition to be cured by the therapy of the linguistic analyst, or as a group of problems that inevitably arise from the use of natural languages, and that are to be solved by linguistic elucidation." **Owens,** *An Elementary Christian Metaphysics*

linguistic determinism, another expression for the Sapir–Whorf hypothesis

linguistic framework

PHILOSOPHY OF LANGUAGE, METAPHYSICS, PHILOSOPHY OF SCIENCE A chosen language or a set of analytical principles that provides the method and criterion for the formulation of any significant assertion and its solution within this framework. A body of significant **knowledge** can only be justified by reference to the principles or rules that make up the framework. Different frameworks reflect different ways of talking about the world. But once we adopt a framework according to the principle of tolerance we must obey all of its principles. The framework is a basis for reaching agreement about any disputed problem. It follows that any answer to a question about kinds of **entities** recognized by a language is relative to a framework. **Carnap** divided internal and external questions in terms of the notion of a linguistic framework. **Internal questions** are formulated according to the rules of the framework, while external questions are outside the context of any particular framework and concern the existence of the systems of entities as a whole. These latter questions are therefore metaphysical and lack theoretical significance. This conception not only played a central role in **logical positivism**, but also greatly influenced the development of the philosophy of science.

"If someone wishes to speak in his language about a new kind of entities, he has to introduce a system of new ways of speaking, subject to new rules; we shall call this procedure the construction of a linguistic framework for the new entities in question." **Carnap,** *Meaning and Necessity*

linguistic meaning

PHILOSOPHY OF LANGUAGE The meaning possessed by a linguistic expression, which is inseparable from

the linguistic form, that is, the fixed combination of signaling-units or phonemes. It is the **semantic** feature of an expression (a word, a phrase, or a sentence) and is the common element whenever the expression is uttered, regardless of the circumstances in which it is used. Linguistic meaning contrasts to the pragmatic meaning of an expression determined by the situation in which it is employed. When the philosophy of language talks about the nature of meaning, it is generally concerned with the linguistic meaning.

"By uttering a linguistic form, a speaker prompts his hearers to respond to a situation; this situation and the response to it are the linguistic meaning of the form." **Bloomfield,** *Language*

linguistic phenomenalism, see phenomenalism

linguistic phenomenology

PHILOSOPHICAL METHOD **Austin's** term characterizing his own philosophical approach, which is generally called **linguistic philosophy** or **ordinary language** philosophy. He probably used the term as a methodological corrective to the phenomenological philosophy of **Husserl** and his followers. Austin claimed that discussing the functions of certain words and sentences and inventing new ways of describing phenomena is not merely linguistic, but improves our perception of reality or phenomena on the basis of a sharpened awareness of words. Hence it should be considered to be a sort of phenomenology. Austin's philosophy itself sharpens our perception of English grammar, although appreciation of its philosophical value has declined.

"When we examine what we should say when, what words we should use in what situations, we are looking again not merely at words (or 'meanings', whatever they may be) but also at the realities we use the words to talk about . . . For this reason I think it might be better to use, for this way of doing philosophy, some less misunderstanding name than those given above – for instance, 'linguistic phenomenology', only that is rather a mouthful." **Austin,** *Philosophical Papers*

linguistic philosophy

PHILOSOPHICAL METHOD In a narrow and technical sense linguistic philosophy is a synonym for **ordinary**

language philosophy, an approach that seeks to illuminate and solve traditional philosophical problems through the investigation of everyday language use. It was characteristic of the Oxford style of analytic philosophy and flourished mainly in the 1950s and 1960s, led by figures such as Gilbert **Ryle** and J. L. **Austin** and showing the strong influence of the later **Wittgenstein**.

In a broad sense it is the philosophical method that takes language as a fundamental issue in discussions of philosophy. We must first come to understand the role of language before we understand our ideas and the subjects of the ideas. Starting from **Plato** and **Aristotle**, such a linguistic approach has been important, and it became dominant in the twentieth century. The whole of **analytic philosophy** is linguistic philosophy in this sense, and ordinary language philosophy or linguistic philosophy in the narrow sense is one of its many schools. Linguistic philosophy, which deals with a broad range of philosophical problems in many areas of the subject, can be distinguished from the philosophy of language.

> "The term 'linguistic philosophy' . . . is tied to that quite special version of analytical philosophy which flourished at Oxford in the 1950s and 60s." **Dummett**, *The Interpretation of Frege's Philosophy*

linguistic rule

PHILOSOPHY OF LANGUAGE The conventionally accepted rules that constitute or regulate the correct use of the constituent words and grammatical forms of sentences. These rules do not describe empirical facts, but determine **necessary truths**. Violations of the rules are classically said to result in **meaninglessness**, although we can often understand ungrammatical and even logically malformed utterances. I understand the **meanings** of the expressions of my language when I know the system of rules that determine the meanings of the sentences that contain its expressions. Misunderstandings follow from ignorance or misapplication of the rules. The notion of a linguistic rule was emphasized by **Carnap** and other **logical positivists** in their discussion of language. Their account opposed the referential theory of language, according to which each word must **refer** to something external in order to have a meaning. They had specific objections to this account for

the **logical constants**, whose meaning can better be understood as constituted by the laws of logic as linguistic rules. They argued that a referential theory of language requires the existence of unnecessary metaphysical entities and misconstrues the nature of logic and language. Logical positivists argued that discussing meaning in terms of linguistic rules can lead not only to a satisfactory understanding of meaning, but also to an understanding of **rationality**, because science, which is the model of rationality, is essentially a set of rules governing scientific language. Accordingly, philosophy should be concerned mainly with describing the rules that govern linguistic behavior and uncovering the rule-governed relations between language and experience. Criticisms by **Wittgenstein** on rule-governed behavior and **Quine** on analyticity have questioned this account of linguistic rules.

> "In order to understand this conception of laws of logic as linguistic rules, we should reflect on the method of specifying the meanings of logical constants." **Pap**, *An Introduction to the Philosophy of Science*

linguistic turn

PHILOSOPHICAL METHOD In a broad sense, a movement claiming that the **analysis** of thought and knowledge must be conducted through the analysis of language and, hence, that language should be the central concern of philosophy. Traditional philosophical problems can be solved by reducing them to issues in the philosophy of language. This movement was initiated by **Frege**, **Russell**, and **Wittgenstein** and characterizes twentieth-century **analytic philosophy**. More narrowly, it is a general tendency, particularly associated with Oxford, which suggests that we should deal with philosophical problems by appealing to language as it is actually used. Philosophy must find the **logical form** of ordinary language, and expose those natural imperfections that have given rise to so many philosophical questions. This trend was influenced by Wittgenstein, and its leaders were figures such as **Ryle**, **Austin**, **Strawson**, and **Grice**.

> "Once the linguistic turn had been taken, the fundamental axioms of analytical philosophy – that the only route to the analysis of thought goes through the analysis of language – naturally

appeared compelling." **Dummett,** *Origins of Analytical Philosophy*

linguistic universals

PHILOSOPHY OF LANGUAGE, PHILOSOPHY OF MIND **Chomsky**'s term, also called universals of language, for the basic similarities contained in all known languages. They are further divided into substantive universals and formal universals. Substantive universals are common abstract **syntactic** features which can be found in the analysis of any natural language, for example, nouns, verbs, words, sentences, particles, morphemes, and phonemes. Formal universals are the common formal properties of grammatical structures, that is, the general characteristics of the rules that appear in grammar and the ways in which they are interconnected. Linguistic universals are closely connected with the problem of **innateness**. Chomsky and his followers claim that a child must possess tacit and innate knowledge of these universals and unconsciously apply them to the data of the language he or she is learning in order to grasp that language efficiently.

"The study of linguistic universals is the study of the properties of any generative grammar for a natural language." **Chomsky,** *Aspects of the Theory of Syntax*

lived experience

MODERN EUROPEAN PHILOSOPHY, PHILOSOPHY OF MIND, PHILOSOPHY OF SOCIAL SCIENCE [German *Erlebnis*, from the verb *erleben*, to live through] **Dilthey**'s term for what is immediately given to individual consciousness regarding one's own thought and feeling. It can also be used for the experience which orients a person's self-conception and around which an individual life organizes itself. Through lived experience, the **meaning** of a particular life history unfolds. We can understand society as our world on the basis of our lived experience of the forces that move society. Lived experience is distinguished from *Erfahrung* [German, scientific experience], the data of experiment and measurement, which can be gathered indirectly. The distinction between lived experience and scientific experience serves as a basis for the distinction between natural sciences and human sciences in Dilthey's philosophy. He held that the human sciences are grounded in lived experience and are thus a distinct domain from the natural sciences, which are based on scientific experiences.

"A more thoroughgoing grounding of the independent status of the human sciences vis-à-vis the natural sciences . . . will be developed step by step in this work through the analysis of our total lived experience of the human world and its incommensurability with all sensory experiences of nature." **Dilthey,** *Selected Works*, vol. I

Locke, John (1632–1704)

British empiricist philosopher, born in Wrington, Somerset, studied and worked in Oxford, a political associate of the Earl of Shaftesbury. Locke's *Essay Concerning Human Understanding* (1690) is one of the most important works regarding knowledge and mind. He rejected the doctrine that we have innate ideas and claimed that our mind was like a blank sheet of paper (*tabula rasa*) at birth. All ideas and all knowledge are ultimately derived from experience, through sensation and reflection. Locke believed in the real existence of an external world, but distinguished between the primary qualities (such as extension and solidity) and secondary qualities (such as color and sound), holding that secondary qualities are not in the objects themselves but that our ideas of them are produced by powers grounded in primary qualities.

Locke's *Two Treatises of Government*, which appeared anonymously in 1689, is a classic of political liberalism. The first treatise attacked Robert Filmer's *Patriarchia*, which advocated the divine right of absolute monarchy, and the second developed a theory of social contract to explain and justify civil government. He argued that the authority of government is justified by the tacit consent of its subjects. For Locke, civil government, in addition to preserving peace, must protect the individual's right to property. Locke's *Letter on Toleration* (1689) provided classic arguments on behalf of religious toleration.

locutionary act

PHILOSOPHY OF LANGUAGE [from Latin *loqui*, speak, utter] **Austin**'s first level of analysis of **speech acts**. To perform a locutionary act is to perform the basic linguistic action of uttering sounds that have meaning or definite reference. In doing so, one says something in the central and basic sense of "to say." Compared with Austin's two other kinds of speech act, **illocutionary acts** and **perlocutionary acts**, locutionary acts are concerned mainly with **meaning**. Locutionary acts are further divided into three kinds: phonetic acts, which are merely the act of uttering certain noises; phatic acts, which utter a grammatical sentence; and rhetic acts, which utter something with a certain sense and with a certain reference.

"The act of 'saying something' in this full normal sense I call, i.e. dub, the performance of a locutionary act, and the study of utterances thus far and in these respects the study of locutions, or of the full units of speech." **Austin, How to Do Things with Words**

logic

LOGIC [from Greek *logos*, reason, speech, measure] Logic is the study concerned with the conditions of valid **reasoning** or the structure and principles of correct **inference**. It is mainly thought to deal with the form of **argument**, independent of content, although the distinction between form and content is sometimes questioned. **Aristotle**, who made logic a special discipline, established the first logical system, which dominated Western conceptions of logic until the twentieth century, when **Frege** and others developed powerful modern systems of logic. Aristotle referred to his own logical works as analytic, and the technical sense of logic did not appear until the commentaries of Alexander of Aphrodisias. Logic is now divided into two branches: formal or symbolic logic and **philosophical logic**. Within **formal logic**, classical modern logic is based on the development of the **propositional calculus** and the predicate **calculus**, although important formal systems that supplement or rival these basic systems have been developed. In philosophical logic, philosophers examine logical terms such as **proposition**, **meaning**, **truth**, falsity, proof, **implication**, **entailment**, **reference**, **predication**, **constant**, **variable**, **quantifier**, **function**, **necessity**, possibility, and tense. Sometimes, especially in the nineteenth century, logic has meant the study of epistemology and scientific methodology, as exemplified in German idealism.

"If we use 'proposition' as a general name for what, when these forms are exemplified, we introduce or specify by such 'that'-, 'whether'- or 'if-'clauses, then logic is the general theory of the propositions. It has a formal part and a philosophical part." **Strawson (ed.), Philosophical Logic**

logic (Hegel)

PHILOSOPHICAL METHOD **Hegel** called his own philosophy the science of logic, but for him logic is not a static formal system of valid deduction. Rather, it concerns the process of thought according to which one **category** is implied by another, from which it develops as its **contradictory**. These categories move to unity in a higher whole, which opens the way for further stages of development. For Hegel, this is the fundamental logical process from thesis to antithesis and then to **synthesis**. This dynamic process, which relates concepts to each other in a systematic way, is the subject-matter of Hegel's logic. Each concept is one moment, or inseparable part, in the self-reflection of thought. Logic is the examination of this process by which thinking itself works. This logic is thus contrasted to traditional formal logic in the sense that it involves the development of the thinking process rather than the abstract form of deduction. It also involves the contents rather than merely the forms of thinking. Furthermore, Hegel's logic is also intended to be true of the objective world because the thinking process is the essential structure of all that actually happens in the world. Logic in this sense is also metaphysics. Hegel also called his logic a **dialectic** of being and dialectic logic. It was further developed by **Marx** and Engels as a reflection of the ever-changing processes of things based on their immanent contradictions. Critics have asked searching questions about the program of Hegel's logic and about its details, including the notions of dialectic and contradiction, the thesis-antithesis-synthesis formula, the dynamic aspect of the logic, the relation between logic and metaphysics, the relation between logic and thought, and the ability of Hegelian method to deliver truth.

"Logic is the science of the pure idea; pure, that is, because the idea is in the abstract medium of thought." **Hegel, Logic**

logic of change, another name for tense logic

logic of scientific discovery, see demarcation, criterion of

logic of terms, another name for predicate logic

logica docens, see *logica utens*

logica modernorum, see *logica vetus*

logica nova, see *logica vetus*

logica utens

Logic The distinction between *logica utens* and *logica docens* was drawn by medieval logicians and borrowed by **Peirce**. *Logica utens* is one's unreflective judgment of the validity of informal arguments. It is a general idea of what good reasoning is. In contrast, *logical docens* is the reflective and precise rules of reasoning in formal systems.

"Such a classification of arguments, antecedent to any systematic study of the subject, is called the reasoner's logic utens, in contradistinction to the result of the scientific study, which is called logic docens." **Peirce,** *Collected Papers,* **vol. II**

logica vetus

Logic [Latin, old logic] Medieval logicians called **Porphyry**'s *Isagoge,* **Aristotle**'s *Categories* and *De Interpretatione,* and **Boethius**' commentaries on them the old logic because these were the logic texts available until the middle of the twelfth century. Aristotle's other logical books in the *Organon,* namely *Topics, Prior Analytics, Posterior Analytics,* and *Sophistici Elenchi,* were then introduced into the Latin world and were called *logica nova* (new logic). Medieval logicians called their own development of logic *logica modernorum* (contemporary logic). *Logica modernorum* was mainly concerned with the analysis of linguistic **fallacies** and **syncategoremata** and its connection with more general topics in logic. This work was stimulated by Aristotle's discussion of fallacies.

"These very short and very difficult books [*Categories* and *De interpretatione*], along with a handful of associated treatises stemming from late antiquity, constituted the secular philosophical library of the early Middle Ages, and became known as the Old Logic [*Logica vetus*] by contrast with the New Logic – the rest of Aristotle's *Organon* – as it became available during the second half of the twelfth century." **Kretzmann et al. (eds.),** *The Cambridge History of Later Medieval Philosophy*

logical analysis

PHILOSOPHICAL METHOD Logical analysis aims to discover the **logical forms** of **propositions**, which are often concealed in philosophically crucial cases by the overt structure of language, and to show the philosophical significance of providing correct accounts of different logical forms. It is concerned to show how propositions relate to one another and to provide insight into the underlying structures of language. In a broad sense, logical analysis, as the logical articulation of concepts and statements to gain philosophical understanding, has been a central feature of philosophical method throughout the history of Western philosophy. In a more technical sense, however, logical analysis is a program inspired by **Frege**'s logic and exemplified in the writings of **Russell** and **Wittgenstein**. On the assumption that for philosophical purposes **ordinary language** is too vague, ambiguous, and misleading in its apparent structure, one approach to analysis sought to replace ordinary discourse by propositions that can be understood in terms of their clear and perspicuous logical form, while another approach claimed that ordinary language needed clarification rather than replacement. Some analysts sought to reduce complex propositions into **atomic or elementary propositions,** and eventually to terminate their analysis by identifying the constituents of these elementary propositions, while others sought to clarify the logical structure of propositions through paraphrase without subscribing to a reductionist program. Many contemporary analytical philosophers consider logical analysis to be the main activity of philosophy and see their work as inspired by earlier forms of analysis, but they now have important disagreements over what analysis should be.

"Logical analysis is, indeed, linguistic in the sense that it begins with an examination of the ways certain expressions are used." **Pap,** *Elements of Analytic Philosophy*

logical calculus

LOGIC Also called formal language, or by Leibniz *calculus ratiocinatur* (Latin, a calculus of reasoning). Distinguished from mathematical calculus, which is used for calculation, logical calculus is a **syntax** of logic or a system used to construct valid **arguments**. Its basic idea originated with **Leibniz**, but was developed as a branch of mathematics by **Frege** and **Russell**. Any logical calculus must have a list of **symbols**, a set of **axioms**, and a set of **rules** of **inference**. It can determine the construction of a logical formula and whether a sequence of logical formulae forms a proof. Different calculi are concerned with different kinds of valid forms of argument. The most influential logical calculi in modern logic are the **propositional calculus** and the predicate **calculus**.

> "The logical calculus, therefore, is, in all other parts of mathematics, of quite fundamental importance. It supplies, together with arithmetic, the type of all possible judgements concerning manifolds as such." **Russell**, *The Collected Papers of Bertrand Russell*, vol. II

logical consequence

LOGIC If a statement B can be validly inferred or deduced from the premises A_1, A_2, . . . A_n, in such a way that it is impossible that all the premises A_1, A_2, . . . A_n can be true while B is false, then B is a logical consequence of these premises. Every consequence of true propositions must be **true**. The deductive relation that holds between premises and the conclusion is independent of the subject-matter of the words contained in premises and conclusion. Logical consequence is generally symbolized by a double turnstile ⊨. That B is the logical consequence of A_1, A_2, . . . A_n, can be written "A_1, A_2, . . . A_n ⊨ B." Logical consequence is a synonym of logical implication. It indicates that there is a necessary relationship between premises and conclusion. The inference is necessary, leading invariably to true conclusions from true premises.

> "We can define the concept of logical consequence as follows: The sentence X follows logically from the sentences of the class K if and only if every model of the class K is also a model of the sentence X." **Tarski**, *Logic, Semantics and Metamathematics*

logical constant

LOGIC The structural components of a **sentence** that indicate its **logical form**. Their significance does not depend upon their subject-matter, rather they serve as **operators** of inference. Any word in a formula can be a constant, but not necessarily a logical constant; for example bachelor is a constant, but not a logical constant. The choice of expressions that can count as logical constants varies among logicians. We can follow **Quine** by enumerating logical constants as basic particles, such as the **truth-functions** not, and, or, and implies; the **identity** relation, **equivalence**, and the **quantifiers** some and all. We can also include necessarily and possibly for **modal logic**, past, present, and future for **tense logic** and similarly basic terms for other kinds of logic. It is not clear whether we can go beyond enumeration to provide a principle justifying a choice of terms as logical constants. Each logical constant has a symbolic counterpart in symbolic logic. A formula that contains logical constants as its only constants is called a **logical formula**.

> "Expressions dignified by selection by formal logicians to figure as constants in their representative verbal patterns or formulae are sometimes called 'logical (formal) constants'." **Strawson**, *Introduction to Logical Theory*

logical construction

PHILOSOPHY OF LANGUAGE, METAPHYSICS, EPISTEMOLOGY Reductive analytical procedure seeking to show that a **symbol** purporting to **refer** to an inferred **entity** can be replaced by a symbol whose denotation is given in sense-experience. On this view, any sentence containing a term denoting an inferred entity can be analyzed or translated into some sentence that does not contain such terms, but consists only of terms for items which are available to experience. In this sense, logical constructions provide analyses of sentences containing terms such as Russellian **incomplete symbols**, but are not identical with the sentences that they analyze. **Russell** extends this method from mathematics to the physical world, and reconstructs physical **objects** in terms of sets of **sense-data** or sensations. Epistemologically he brings physical objects closer in their nature to the experiential foundations of our knowledge, and metaphysically he eliminates inferred entities such as **matter**, the self, and **other minds**. Logical construction as a method has been widely adopted in many areas of analytical philosophy.

In another sense Russell also applies the term "logical construction" to symbols or entities constructed out of other entities, and thus makes logical constructions identical with incomplete symbols and **logical fictions**.

> "The supreme maxim in scientific philosophising is this: wherever possible, logical constructions are to be substituted for inferred entities." **Russell,** *Collected Papers of Bertrand Russell,* **vol. VII**

logical construction theory, Broad's term for the bundle theory of mind

logical determinism

METAPHYSICS Since ancient Greece, some philosophers have believed that logic supports the thesis that a person's fate is predetermined and that there is nothing we can do to alter it or to avoid what will happen. Any statement about the future must be either true or false now. Correspondingly, the future event it represents may either happen or not happen. Hence a statement about the future is either true before the event takes place or false before the event fails to occur. There is nothing that anyone can do to alter the truth or falsity of the statement or the occurrence or non-occurrence of the event. Stoics and **scholastics** advocated this doctrine to prove fatalism or **God**'s **omniscience**. The issue was first discussed by **Aristotle** in *De Interpretatione*, with the example of the **sea-battle** tomorrow. Aristotle's implicit solution is that we should deny the universal validity of the principle of **bivalence**. The future statement is neither true nor false before the event actually occurs. This is developed in contemporary logic into **three-valued** or **many-valued logic**. Others suggest that we can deal with the problem by distinguishing different modal conceptions. Only a necessary statement entails that the event will necessarily happen. The issue is still a matter of controversy.

> "Logical determinism maintains that the future is already fixed as unalterably as the past." **Lucas,** *The Freedom of the Will*

logical empiricism

EPISTEMOLOGY, METAPHYSICS Another term for the philosophy of the **Vienna Circle** and broadly equivalent to **logical positivism**. Some members of the circle, including **Schlick**, preferred to call their philosophy "logical empiricism." This title indicates their affinity with the British empiricist tradition and their development of that tradition through the methodology of empirical science and, more important, the **logical analysis** of language. This analysis sought to characterize **elementary propositions** and to test them against experience (according to the verification principle), as empiricism requires. For the main philosophical content of logical empiricism, see logical positivism.

> "The positivist theory of meaning has found its most precise formulation in contemporary logical positivism (or 'logical empiricism') . . . : it is postulated that concepts be formed in such a way that it is empirically decidable whether the concept does or does not apply in a given sense." **Pap,** *Elements of Analytic Philosophy*

logical equivalence

LOGIC The relationship of logical equivalence between two **propositions** is one of mutual **inference**. If p is logically equivalent to q, then we can derive p from q and q from p in accordance with logical rules. The denial of such a deduction is self-contradictory. We may also define p in terms of q, or q in terms of p. If two **sentences** are logically equivalent, they **denote** the same proposition. Logical equivalence should be distinguished from **material equivalence**, according to which two propositions have the same **truth-value** (either both true or both false), without necessarily being mutually deducible.

> "'p' and 'q' . . . are logically equivalent if they are mutually deducible such that it would be self-contradictory to affirm p and to deny q, or to affirm q and to deny p." **Pap,** *Elements of Analytic Philosophy*

logical falsity, see logical truth

logical fiction

PHILOSOPHY OF LANGUAGE, METAPHYSICS Also called pseudo-object. A type of **logical construction** according to which **symbols** are constructed from the characteristics of **entities** they do not **denote**. They are fictions because these symbols at first glance appear to denote some entities, but upon analysis this turns out to be false. Symbols that are logical fictions are symbolic devices only and do not denote any constituent of the world. The objects they appear to denote do not have their own being and are not constituents of reality. In logic and mathematics, **Russell** considered such crucial conceptions as **classes**, the class of classes, and **numbers** as logical fictions. As non-referring descriptions they are all **incomplete symbols**, that is, they do not have meaning in themselves but have meaning only as used in the context of a **proposition**.

> "There may be no entity named by the eliminable symbol at all; if this is the case, the object seemingly referred to by the symbol under analysis may be called a 'logical fiction' (Russell) or a 'pseudo-object' (Carnap)." **Pap,** *Elements of Analytic Philosophy*

logical form

LOGIC The pattern or structure of a **statement** or **proposition** that is shared with other propositions of the same type. To discover the hidden logical form from natural language is precisely the task of logic starting from **Aristotle**, from whom the term "formal logic" derives. Logical form is topic-neutral, for it is independent of the content of the proposition. An **inference** is valid or invalid in virtue of the logical form of argument. Arguments that share the same logical form have the same validity. The logical form of a proposition is determined by its constituents. A fully general proposition is a logical form closed by universal **quantification**. According to the doctrine of logical atomism, philosophy as **logical analysis** is a matter purely concerned with logical form. On this view, logical form corresponds to the basic structure of reality, for which it provides a logical picture.

Some analytical philosophers tend to distinguish logical form from grammatical form, which is the surface grammatical structure of a sentence. The fact that two sentences share the same grammatical form does not entail that they share the same logical form. On the contrary, grammatical form can cover a difference of logical form and give rise to

philosophical trouble. In **Ayer**'s illustration, "Martyre exists" and "Martyre suffers" have the same grammatical form, for each sentence consists of a noun following an intransitive verb. From this people infer that "to exist" is an attributive verb like "to suffer," but the logical form of existential sentences is very different from the logical form of sentences ascribing a feature to a subject.

> "What any picture, of whatever form, must have in common with reality, in order to be able to depict it – correctly or incorrectly – in any way at all, is logical form, i.e. the form of reality." **Wittgenstein,** *Tractatus*

logical formula, see logical constant

logical grammar, another term for logical syntax

logical implication, another term for logical consequence

logical modality, see modality

logical necessity

LOGIC The necessity of what is logically true and guaranteed by the laws of logic. The nature and standard of logically necessary propositions has been a major concern from **Leibniz** to **Wittgenstein**, **Carnap**, C. I. **Lewis**, **Kripke**, and **Hintikka**. Logical necessity has a set of different but connected senses. It is a property attributable to a proposition P, which according to Kripke's modal **semantics** means that P is true in all **possible worlds**. Denying such truths would conflict with the laws of logic and render all thinking chaotic. Logical necessity is equivalent to conceptual necessity or being non-contingent. It is ascribed to **analytical truths**, originally understood as subject-predicate sentences in which the predicate term is contained in the subject, but now understood as sentences that are true in virtue of their **logical form** alone. In another sense, all consequences deduced from the laws of logic are truths having logical necessity. It is a matter of debate whether logical necessity is the sole valid form of **necessity** and whether necessity is confined to the sphere of ideas rather than the sphere of facts. Logical truths and, according to standard accounts, mathematical truths are logically necessary, and there are different views whether we can specify acceptable independent notions of metaphysical, transcendental, physical, nomic, or theoretical necessity. There is also debate about whether logical necessity is conventional and varies according to different logical systems. If so, there are questions about what gives the "hardness" to logical necessity and whether logical necessity is a matter of **convention**, discovery, **construction**, or choice.

> "A logical necessity . . . is nothing but the necessity of holding-to-be-true according to logical laws of the understanding and of reason." **Kant,** *Lectures on Logic*

logical oddness

LOGIC, PHILOSOPHY OF LANGUAGE Nowell-Smith's term, referring to the denial of contextual **implications**. If P contextually implies Q, then to assert P we would naturally assert Q. But if one asserts P, but denies Q, or asks whether Q, one acts in a way that is logically odd. In the former case, the person denying Q is in a self-contradiction. In the latter case, the answer to the person's question has already been implied, and no further or better answer can be expected to be given.

> "I shall say that a question is 'logically odd' if there appears to be no further room for it in its context because it has already been answered." **Nowell-Smith,** *Ethics*

logical paradox

LOGIC **Russell** believed that his ramified **set theory** provides a unified solution for all **paradoxes**, but **Ramsey** claims that there are two kinds of paradoxes: logical or set-theoretical paradoxes and **semantic paradoxes**. Logical paradoxes occur in a logical or mathematical system and are synonymous with **antinomies**. They are represented by **Russell's paradox, Burali-Forti's paradox**, and **Cantor's paradox**. They arise because of the peculiar nature of some set-theoretical concepts or due to faulty logic and mathematics. Semantic paradoxes such as the **liar paradox** arise, on the other hand, because of ambiguities with respect to certain of the terms or notions employed. The general solution to logical paradoxes is to restrict the principles governing the existence of **sets**.

> "A number of paradoxes known variously as the Antinomies or the logical paradoxes are often said to share the common feature of self-reference." **Champlin,** *Reflective Paradoxes*

logical picture, another term for logical form

logical positivism

EPISTEMOLOGY, PHILOSOPHY OF SCIENCE, METAPHYSICS A general philosophical position, also called **logical empiricism**, developed from the 1920s by members of the **Vienna Circle**, such as **Schlick, Neurath**, and **Carnap**, on the basis of traditional empirical thought and the development of modern logic. Logical positivism confines **knowledge** to science. It divides all meaningful propositions into two categories: **analytic propositions**, which are necessarily true and can be known *a priori*; and **synthetic propositions**, which are **contingent** and can be known empirically or *a posteriori*. On the one hand, logical positivism pays special attention to mathematics and logic and develops logical **syntax** and **semantics** in order to reveal the logical structure of the world. On the other hand, it insists on **verificationism**, that is, that the **meaning** of a **proposition** consists in its method of verification. A purportedly empirical or factual proposition is meaningless if it proves incapable of being verified in experience. All justified **beliefs** can be reduced ultimately to protocol statements, which can be shown to be true directly without inference from other statements. On this basis, logical positivism claims that traditional metaphysical problems are not false but meaningless, for they cannot be shown to be true by *a priori* analysis and cannot be verified in experience. With these two approaches exhausted, they have no truth-value and are meaningless. Logical positivism greatly promoted the development of **analytical philosophy** in the first half of the twentieth century, but after the Second World War, all of its major tenets were criticized respectively by **Quine** and Oxford **ordinary language philosophy**.

> "'Logical positivism' is a name for a method, not for a certain kind of result. A philosopher is a logical positivist if he holds that there is no special way of knowing that is peculiar to philosophy, but that questions of fact can only be decided by the empirical methods of science, while questions that

can be decided without appeal to experience are either mathematical or linguistic." **Russell,** *Logic and Knowledge*

logical product, see logical sum

logical proposition, see fully generalized proposition

logical/real opposition

EPISTEMOLOGY, METAPHYSICS A dichotomy that **Kant** introduced in his *Attempt to Introduce the Concept of Negative Quantities into Philosophy*. A logical opposition is an abstract relation between a **proposition** and its negation, namely logical **contradiction**, which can be discerned through conceptual analysis. A real opposition involves opposing forces or tendencies that exist in the qualities of external things and can be discovered through empirical methods rather than through logical analysis. The distinction undermines the claim of **rationalism** that reason alone is the guarantee of **knowledge**, because we cannot understand real oppositions through reason alone. This distinction developed into the distinction between **reason** and **sensibility** in Kant's *Critique of Pure Reason*.

"Two things are opposed to each other if one thing cancels that which is posited by the other. This opposition is two-fold: it is either logical through contradiction, or it is real, that is to say, without contradiction." **Kant,** *Theoretical Philosophy, 1755–1770*

logical sentence

LOGIC A sentence that consists solely of logical **symbols**. It is either **analytical** and, hence, a **logical truth** or **contradictory** and, hence, a logical falsehood. Such a sentence is the same as a logical formula.

"A logical sentence is one that contains only logical signs." **Bergmann,** *Meaning and Existence*

logical space

LOGIC, METAPHYSICS The possible ways in which **objects** can combine into **states of affairs**. The term is used by analogy to physical space, which presents us with a set of locations, positions, or places that can be occupied by objects in relation to other objects. Logical space is thus the ensemble of logical **possibilities**,

a universe composed of all possible-and-existing states of affairs and all possible-and-non-existing states of affairs. For **Russell**, it is a system of proper logical **relations**. **Wittgenstein** makes use of this conception to show that **facts** do not compose the world as a heap and that there is a structure of **logical relations** amongst them. The world is the totality of facts in logical space.

"The logician is led to give the name 'space' to any system of relations having the same or similar logical properties." **Russell,** *Collected Papers of Bertrand Russell,* **vol. VI**

logical sum

LOGIC A logical sum results from the **disjunction** of two **propositions** ($p \vee q$), or from the union of two **sets**. It is the inclusive sense of the connective "or," that is, "p or q or both" (rather than the exclusive sense of "or," that is, "p or q, but not both"). The logical sum is contrasted to the logical product, which results from the **conjunction** of two propositions ($p \wedge q$), or from the intersection of two sets. The logical product is the truth-functional compound of p and q, that is, its truth-value is determined by the truth-value of p, the truth-value of q, and the logical connective "and."

"Frege and Russell introduced generality in association with logical product or logical sum." **Wittgenstein,** *Tractatus*

logical syntax

LOGIC, PHILOSOPHY OF LANGUAGE, METAPHYSICS Also called logical **grammar**. A system of rules governing the use of **signs**, which determines whether a combination of signs can be a **proposition**, that is, whether it can represent a logically possible **state of affairs**. Logical syntax belongs to the purely formal part of a logical system and is discovered through **logical analysis**. It aims to display the hidden **logical forms** of propositions. In contrast to the surface syntax or grammar of ordinary language, it is the syntax of logical or **ideal language**. Aside from avoiding the use of the same sign for different significations, it is not concerned with the meaning of the signs. It excludes some combinations of signs as **nonsense**. To say that traditional metaphysical problems are nonsensical means that they violate logical syntax. The term was used in **Wittgenstein**'s *Tractatus*, but is abandoned in his later works. **Carnap** attempts to establish such a system in his *Logical Syntax of Language* (1934).

> "In order to avoid such errors we must make use of a sign-language that excludes them by not using the same sign for different symbols and by not using in a superficially similar way signs that have different modes of signification: that is to say, a sign-language that is governed by logical grammar – by logical syntax." **Wittgenstein,** *Tractatus*

logical truth

LOGIC, EPISTEMOLOGY A logical symbol or logical formula can be a logical truth because it is true under all **interpretations**. A **statement** or **proposition** is logically true if it is validly deduced in a logical system. In this sense, a logical truth is generally a **theorem** of a logical system. More often, we say that a statement is a logical truth because it is an instance of a valid **logical form**. For example, "A house cannot be both warm and not warm." The logical form of this sentence is "not both p and non-p," and it is thus in accord with the principle of non-contradiction. If a statement is logically true, then it is **analytic** and is necessarily true. On the contrary, if a statement violates a logically valid form, that is, if its logical form conflicts with some logical principle, it is logically false or a logical falsity. If a statement is logically false, it is necessarily false. Accounts of the kind of logical truth that depends upon the meaning of the expressions contained in a proposition have come under pressure from **Quine**'s rejection of the **analytic-synthetic distinction** and the notions of **synonymy** and **meaning**. Without reliance on meaning, a logical truth becomes any truth which can be obtained from a valid logical scheme.

> "A logical schema is valid if every sentence obtainable from it by substituting sentences for simple sentence is true. A logical truth, finally, is a truth obtainable from a valid logical schema." **Quine,** *Philosophy of Logic*

logical type

LOGIC Words or expressions can be classified into a hierarchy of **classes**, such as individuals, classes, class of classes, and so on. The logical type of a word or

an expression is the class it is in. When two words *a* and *b* are of the same logical type, for any sentential function F*x*, F*a* and F*b* are either both meaningful or both meaningless. In "Socrates is a philosopher" and "Aristotle is a philosopher," "Socrates" and "Aristotle" are of the same logical type, for both of them are individuals. Yet this does not extend to "A man is a philosopher." For "man" is a class, and hence is of a different type.

> "The definition of a logical type is as follows: A and B are of the same logical type if, and only if, given any fact of which A is a constituent, there is a corresponding fact which has B as a constituent, which either results by substituting B for A, or is the negation of what so results." **Russell,** *Collected Papers of Bertrand Russell*, **vol. IX**

logical words

LOGIC, PHILOSOPHY OF LANGUAGE **Russell** divides words into two kinds: factual words, which contribute to indicating facts, and logical words, which contribute to indicating the structures of sentences and inferences. He further divides logical words into two kinds: general words such as "all" and "some," and conjunctions such as "not," "or," "and," and "if-then," by means of which we combine atomic sentences into molecular sentences and make various inferences. Logical words are also called **logical constants**. Although there is broad agreement in the enumeration of the logical constants, it is much more difficult to determine why certain words have this status.

> "There are logical words such as 'or', 'not', 'some', and 'all'." **Russell,** *Human Knowledge*

logically impossible

LOGIC A purported **state of affairs** or **fact** that violates the laws of logic, and is therefore inconsistent or **self-contradictory**, is logically impossible. For instance, "God is a skeptic" is logically impossible because it would be self-contradictory to ascribe skepticism to a being defined as having perfect knowledge. The logically impossible should be distinguished at least from metaphysical, epistemic, and scientific impossibility, each with its own grounds. A proposition is scientifically impossible, for example, if it violates the laws of nature. Propositions are logically possible if they do not violate the laws of logic. We do not necessarily know of every proposition whether it is logically possible or logically impossible. Nor do we have a clear understanding of how different kinds of impossibility and different kinds of possibility are related.

> "When we hold a proposition to be logically impossible, we are claiming that it is incompatible with some general proposition which is itself logically true." **Ayer,** *Probability and Evidence*

logically perfect language

LOGIC, PHILOSOPHY OF LANGUAGE Also called an artificial language or ideal language. Because they were dissatisfied with the ambiguities and bewildering **syntax** of ordinary language and because they believed that these difficulties formed the main obstacles to progress in philosophy, **Frege**, **Russell**, and **Wittgenstein** followed **Leibniz** in advancing the project of an ideal or logically perfect language. Such a language would have both perfect syntax and perfect vocabulary. Perfect syntax would be provided by classical predicate **calculus** with **identity**, and the perfect vocabulary would include only unanalyzable words holding of simple **objects**. A perfect language would immediately show the logical structure of its **propositions** and the logical structure of the **facts** asserted or denied, and in a perfect language the **logical form** and the grammatical form would entirely coincide, so conforming to the logical requirement that language should avoid **contradiction**. A sample of perfect language is the language of mathematical logic. Russell sometimes thinks that such a language will afford insight into the nature of language in general and that in this way its significance is to make graphic some metaphysical and epistemological doctrines. Because this language would be entirely free from the philosophical defects of ordinary language that Russell and Wittgenstein claim to discover, such as **ambiguity**, **vagueness**, and singular terms without **reference**, it is also called an ideal language. A logically perfect language is supposed to represent our thought perfectly, but having a language that expresses any one thought in only one way is generally regarded as an unattainable ideal. Furthermore, many philosophers follow the later Wittgenstein in rejecting a logically perfect language as a proper ideal to guide philosophical work. Nevertheless,

a narrow notion of a logically perfect language, incorporating only the logical symbolism of Frege and Russell (predicate calculus and **propositional calculus**) supplemented by later logical developments, is regarded as providing a reliable instrument for carrying out deductive **inferences** without the risk of **fallacy**. This goal has been achieved to a great extent, but without fulfilling earlier promises of fundamental consequences for the whole of philosophy.

> "In a logically perfect language, there will be one word and no more for every simple object, and everything that is not simple will be expressed by a combination of words, by a combination derived, of course, from the words for the simple things that center in one word for each simple component." **Russell,** *Logic and Knowledge*

logically possible, see logically impossible

logically proper name

LOGIC, PHILOSOPHY OF LANGUAGE A proper **name** is a simple **symbol** designating a **particular**. **Russell** distinguishes ordinary proper names from logically proper names. An ordinary proper name, such as "Socrates" or "The Golden Mountain" has a **sense**, but it has its sense because it is, in fact, a **description** in disguise. It is not always the case that there is a bearer that satisfies the description. Logically proper names are **egocentric** words or indexical words, such as "I," "this," "that," and "here." They are names for items available in current experiences, and have their **meaning** solely in terms of the **objects** they stand for. If such an object does not exist, a logically proper name is meaningless. Its meaning changes if the object it designates changes. Hence, a logically proper name refers to an object, and it refers directly without any implicit description. It denotes, but it does not connote anything. This distinction between ordinary proper names and logically proper names is crucial to Russell's theory of **definite descriptions**. Whether any term can function as a logically proper name is discussed within the general context of the theory of names.

> "The mark of a logically proper name being that its significant use entailed the existence of the object which it was supposed to denote." **Ayer,** *Metaphysics and Common Sense*

logicism

PHILOSOPHY OF MATHEMATICS An approach to philosophy of mathematics developed by **Frege**, **Russell**, and **Carnap**, which claims that logic provides the foundations of mathematics, such that the two are continuous and even identical. According to Russell, logic has two parts: one is philosophical and deals with forms of reality and formal analysis; the other is mathematical and deals with the foundations of mathematics and the theorems deduced from these foundations. This mathematical part, which justifies the term "logicism," is also called symbolic logic, logistic, or mathematical logic. In contrast to two other major forms of philosophy of mathematics, namely **intuitionism** and **formalism**, logicism believes that every mathematical truth – or at least the most significant ones – can be expressed as a true logical proposition which is a **logical truth**, and that all such truths can be deduced from a small number of logical **axioms** and **rules**. Logicism is thus a program to translate the basic mathematical ideas and theorems into logic in order to ensure that mathematical truth has the same epistemological status as logical truth. The classical presentations of logicism can be found in Frege's *Foundation of Arithmetic* and Russell and Whitehead's *Principia Mathematica*. However, to avoid **paradoxes** Russell introduced **set theory** into his program and extended the basis of logicism beyond the purely logical. **Quine** argues that logicism succeeds in reducing mathematics not to logic but to logic plus set theory. However, the current close relationship between the study of mathematics and the study of logic is inspired by logicism.

> "Logicism, represented by Frege, Russell, Whitehead, Church, and Carnap, condones the use of bound variables to refer to abstract entities known or unknown, specifiable and unspecifiable, indiscriminately." **Quine,** *From a Logical Point of View*

logistic, another term for logicism

logistic method

LOGIC The method of constructing a formal deduction system. It starts with a specification of the primitive **symbols**. A sequence of symbols acceptable in a system is called a **sentence** or a **well-formed formula**. Certain well-formed formulae are singled out as **axioms**, and a set of **rules** of inference are laid down, according to which some well-formed formulae can be inferred from other well-formed formulae, which serve as premises. The method establishes a **decision procedure** that determines in accordance with rules of inference whether an arbitrary formula is a **theorem** of the system. The aim of this method is to make deductive reasoning mathematically precise and to deal with the major features of a theory, such as **implication**, compatibility, and interdependence, in a formal way. The formalized system of logic built by this method is called a logistic system.

> "By the logistic method, the principles of logic are not antecedently presumed as rules of demonstration." **Lewis and Langford,** *Symbolic Logic*

logistic system, see logistic method

logocentrism

MODERN EUROPEAN PHILOSOPHY A **postmodernist** characterization of the Western metaphysical tradition, taking *logos* (**reason**) as the locus of **truth** and **meaning** and believing that truth can be known by the subject via the inner light of reason. This tradition takes **being** as subject-matter and is excessively concerned to establish a hierarchical ordering of various conceptual oppositions and to maintain the stability of **meaning** and the validity of reason. According to this criticism, Western metaphysics neglects the complexity of reason in the **life-world** and restricts it to its cognitive-instrumental dimension. The dominant concern of traditional metaphysics with the articulation of the source of order and structure of things is based on its **cosmological** and **ontological** assumption that the world has an ordered ground. Logocentrism is the target of **Derrida's** **deconstruction**. In his view, philosophy should be concerned with the condition of the possibility of *logos*, rather than viewing *logos* as the condition of the possibility of truth. For Derrida, logocentrism presents itself chiefly in history as phonologism, or the emphasis of speech over writing. "Phonologism" is always used by Derrida as a synonym for "logocentrism."

"Logocentrism would thus support the determination of the being of the entity as presence. To the extent that such a logocentrism is not totally absent from Heidegger's thought, perhaps it still holds that thought within the epoch of onto-theology, within the philosophy of presence, that is to say, within philosophy itself." **Derrida,** *Of Grammatology*

logos

METAPHYSICS [Greek, from the verb *legein*, to say, to speak] From its basic meaning of anything said, a term with a wide range of derivative meanings, including speech, reputation, thought, cause, reason, argument, measure, structure, proportion, ratio, relation, principle, formula, and definition. Its exact meaning must be decided in context, but three meanings had greatest prominence in Greek philosophy: (1) in the philosophy of **Heraclitus**, who first uses *logos* as a technical term, an objective universal principle which is equally true and equally accessible for all; Stoicism also took *logos* to be a cosmic force, the principle both of **knowledge** and of **causation**; (2) the rational part of the **soul**; (3) an account or, more precisely, an account expressing the essential nature of anything, that is, a **definition**. The second and third meanings played a great role in the philosophy of **Plato** and **Aristotle**.

"Listen not to me but to the Logos." **Heraclitus, in Diels and Kranze,** *Die Fregmente Der Vorsokratiker*

lottery paradox

LOGIC A **paradox** formulated by Henry Kyburg in *Probability of the Logic of Rational Belief* (1961). I believe rationally that of a million lottery tickets there is one that will win. But I do not believe rationally that Ticket 1 will win, nor do I believe that Ticket 2 will win, and so on through all the tickets. Eventually there is no reason to believe that any single ticket will win. A paradox then arises, for I certainly believe that there is one ticket that will win. The paradox involves the relation between partial belief and full belief.

"All the lottery paradox shows in any case is that in some circumstances a claim to knowledge is not adequately supported by the reasonableness of any particular partial belief however strong." **Mellor,** *The Matter of Chance*

Lotze, Rudolf Hermann (1817–81)

German idealist philosopher. Lotze accepted mechanistic explanation for nature, but argued against the possibility of explaining consciousness in this way. He held that causally interacting entities must be conceived of on the model of consciousness as finite spirits that are grounded in an infinite spirit aiming to realize moral goodness. His major works include *Microcosmos* (1856–64), *Logic* (1874), and *Metaphysics* (1879).

love

ETHICS, PHILOSOPHY OF MIND As commonly understood, love is closely related to sexual affection. Some philosophers, such as **Schopenhauer** and **Nietzsche**, regard it as a natural impulse. But in the history of Western philosophy, love has been treated in various ways under different names, such as *eros*, *philia*, *agape* (universal benevolence), Romantic love, Sacred love (the love of God), comradeship, **sympathy**, **care**, and concern. **Plato** in his *Symposium* and *Phaedrus* argued that love (*eros*) begins with a desire for personal beauty, but its spiritual ascent culminates in a desire for **beauty** in itself, that is, the love of **wisdom**, which is philosophy in its original sense. Spiritual and divine love, which has been a major philosophical theme from the **Neoplatonists** to **Augustine** and **Dante**, still inspires many writers. **Aristotle** held that true love (*philia*, friendship) between virtuous people enables one to look after another for the other person's sake. In the final analysis, however, he considered true love to be a form of self-love that is obedient to one's rational voice. Aristotle is highly praised in contemporary **virtue ethics** for taking love or personal attachment into the sphere of ethical consideration. **Feminism** tends to develop a related ethics of care. However, since love involves partiality in personal relationships and emotions, an issue has arisen about the possibility of reconciling love with the impartial requirements of morality.

"In spite of all the misuses to which the word love is subjected, in literature and daily life, it has not lost its emotional power. It elicits a feeling of warmth, of passion, of happiness, or fulfilment, whenever it is used." **Tillich,** *Love, Power and Justice*

Löwenheim–Skolem theorem, see Skolem's paradox

loyalty

ETHICS, POLITICAL PHILOSOPHY A trait of character marked by faithfulness and devotion to a person, a group, a country, a cause, or a principle. Such a feeling is not easily altered either by external forces or by the discovery that the object of loyalty lacks its supposed merits. Loyalty is related to compassion and **gratitude**. It is classed as a **virtue** because it involves selfless commitment. The stability of any political society requires at least some loyalty on the part of its citizens. In contrast to measured loyalty, loyalty can be blind and unreflective, even to the extent of taking the object of loyalty to be sacred. Because loyalty is always partial and emotional, it is difficult to reconcile with the impartial requirements of morality.

> "The feeling of allegiance, or loyalty . . . may vary in its objects . . . but whether in a democracy or in a monarchy, its essence is always the same; viz. that there be in the constitution of state something which is settled, something permanent, and not to be called in question; something which, by general agreement, has a right to be what it is, and to be secure against disturbance, whatever else may change." *The Collected Works of John Stuart Mill*, vol. X

Lucretius (c.95–c.54 BC)

Roman Epicurean philosopher, little is known about his life and character. Lucretius wrote the long philosophical poem *De Rerum Natura (On the Nature of Things)*. This work systematically expounded the Epicurean philosophy of atomism and is the main source for our knowledge of its doctrines. The book, published by Cicero, is also one of the greatest Latin literary works.

Lukács, Gyorgy (1885–1971)

Hungarian Marxist philosopher and literary theorist, born in Budapest. In his most influential book, *History and Class Consciousness* (1923), Lukács developed a Hegelian interpretation of Marxist thought by focusing on the notions of reification and alienation, and sought to overcome the duality of subject and object in terms of Marxist dialectics. The interpretation, which diverged from orthodox Marxist analysis of culture as superstructural phenomena related to an economic base, was worked out before the discovery of the more Hegelian doctrines of Marx's early *Economic and Philosophical Manuscripts*. Lukács also made great contributions to the reconstruction of the philosophy of the young Marx and to aesthetics, especially in his theory of the novel. His other major books include *The Soul and its Forms* (1911), *The Theory of the Novel* (1920), *The Young Hegel* (1948), *The Destruction of Reason* (1954), and *Problems of Aesthetics* (1969).

Lukasiewicz, Jan (1878–1956)

Polish logician, born in Lvov, Professor and Rector at University of Warsaw, Professor, Royal Irish Academy. Lukasiewicz founded three-valued logic that denied the principle of bivalence in order to deal with Aristotle's questions about the truth of future-tense statements in a way that would allow for human freedom. He used his system to deal with modal logic, and his work led to a wider range of multi-valued logics. He also introduced Polish notation in logic, reinterpreted Aristotelian syllogistic, and revived interest in Stoic logic. His major works include *Aristotle's Syllogistic from the Standpoint of Modern Formal Logic* (1957) and *Selected Works* (1970).

Luther, Martin (1483–1546)

German theologian, Professor of Philosophy and Professor of Theology at University of Wittenberg. Luther was the leader of the Protestant Reformation. He argued for the priority of grace and revelation over reason in religion and for justification and, hence, salvation, through faith alone. His works are collected in *Luther's Works*.

lying

ETHICS Deliberately saying what one knows or believes to be false in order to deceive one or more other persons. Liars have one thing in their mind and state another conflicting claim with the **intention** to deceive, or at least with a lack of care about the possibility of deceiving. There is disagreement whether there should be a universal moral prohibition against lying. Both **Aquinas** and **Kant** denounced lying as a moral vice. For Kant, truthfulness constitutes a basic moral relationship between rational beings. Because it violates this relationship, lying is wrong in itself, whether or not it produces good consequences. J. S. **Mill**, on the other hand, argued that lying to avoid a greater evil could be justified. This is also the position implied by **Plato**'s concept of the noble lie. According to the utilitarian principle that an act is morally permissible if it maximizes the good, lying is not simply an evil, but must be judged according to its good or bad consequences. Accordingly, the treatment of lying is an area in which the difference between **deontology** and **utilitarianism** is clearly indicated.

"I shall define as a lie any intentionally deceptive message which is stated." **Bok,** *Lying*

Lyotard, Jean-François (1924–98)

French postmodernist, Professor of Philosophy, University of Paris VIII (Vincennes) and University of California, Irvine. Lyotard rejected his early Marxism and other modernist grand narratives promising truth and justice on the grounds of their implausibility and authoritarianism. He favored little narratives of individuals that pragmatically aim at freedom from specific abuses and held that the discourses of these little narratives are incommensurable. He argued that differends, capturing the incommensurability between the language-games of conflicting narratives, are intractable and frustrate Habermas's proposal to reconcile differences through communication in ideal speech situations. His main works include *The Post-modern Condition* (1979) and *The Differend* (1983).

M

Mach, Ernst (1838–1916)
Austrian physicist and empiricist philosopher of science, born in Turas, Moravia. Mach held that science rests on sense-experience and that all branches of sciences can be unified because they are all studies of sensations. A scientific theory does not represent reality, but is an aid to predicting how things will occur. As a radical empiricist, he was deeply suspicious of any metaphysical speculation about unobservable entities and focused on the logical analysis of the structure of scientific theory. Mach's philosophy was a precursor of logical positivism and also exerted great influence on Einstein. His views were bitterly criticized by Lenin in *Materialism and Empiriocriticism* (1908). Mach made important scientific discoveries in various fields of physics, especially in aeronautical design and the science of projectiles. His major works include *The Science of Mechanics* (1883) and *The Analysis of Sensations* (1906).

Machiavelli, Niccoló (1496–1527)
Italian political theorist and statesman, born in Florence. Machiavelli's masterpiece, *The Prince* (completed 1513, published posthumously 1532), was a handbook for rulers about how to acquire and maintain power. He held that men are dominated by self-interest and contended that effective rulers should be indifferent to conventional moral standards and other constraints. Immoral means are justified if they are necessary to promote the order and stability of the state. The state should be an organic political entity independent of the Church. His other works include *Discourses* (1516), *Art of War* (1520), and *Florentine Histories* (1525).

machine functionalism
PHILOSOPHY OF MIND A type of **functionalism** proposed by **Putnam**, also called Turing machine functionalism, which understands the mind's function as the operation of the computational states of a **Turing machine**. It claims that each **mental state** is identical to a machine-table state and can be defined simply in terms of the latter. A difficulty facing this version of functionalism is that while a Turing machine can only be in one computational state at a time, a mind can have several psychological states at the same time.

> "Putnam envisioned a theory of mind whose explications of individual mental state-types would take the form 'to be in a mental state M is to realize or instantiate machine program P and be in functional state S relative to P'. Let us call the view that some such set of explications is correct machine functionalism." **Lycan, *Consciousness***

MacIntyre, Alasdair (1929–)
British moral philosopher and historian of philosophy, born in Glasgow, Fellow of University College, Oxford and Professor at Universities of Essex,

Boston, Vanderbilt, and Notre Dame. MacIntyre argues that moral concepts make sense only within the context of historically alterable institutions and practices and that modern liberal moral theory, rather than an advance on Greek and medieval morality, is a symptom of the collapse of meaningful social patterns. Practices also shape conceptions of rationality that can be used to judge among moral orders and to seek to overcome the disarray of modern moral life. His major works include *A Short History of Ethics* (1966), *After Virtue* (1981), *Whose Justice? Which Rationality?* (1988), and *Three Rival Versions of Moral Enquiry* (1990).

Mackie, J(ohn) L(eslie) (1917–81)

Australian philosopher, born in Sydney, Professor of Philosophy, Universities of Otago, Sydney, and York and Fellow of University College, Oxford. In his important study of causation, Mackie argues that a cause is an insufficient but necessary part of an unnecessary but sufficient condition of an effect. He claims that singular causal statements have priority over causal laws and as counterfactual statements incorporate notions of natural necessity. Mackie argues that our moral thought depends on the objectivity of ethical values, but that claims for this objectivity are groundless. Instead, we must reinvent our moral vocabulary without commitment to moral objectivity as a means of regulating our communal life. His major works include *The Cement of the Universe: A Study of Causation* (1974) and *Ethics: Inventing Right and Wrong* (1977).

McDowell, John (1942–)

British Philosopher of mind, language and ethics, Fellow of University College, Oxford and Professor of Philosophy at University of Pittsburgh. McDowell has published important papers over a wide range of topics, including meaning and truth, sense and reference, intentionality, practical reason and virtue. He has written on Plato and Aristotle, Kant, Frege, Wittgenstein and many contemporary analytic philosophers, but his own systematic philosophy also shows the influence of Hegel and Heidegger. He has developed a naturalist account of human knowledge, thought, value and action, but his naturalism allows a realist view of mental states and an externalist view of meaning. His main works include

Mind and World (1994), *Mind, Value, and Reality* (1998) and *Meaning, Knowledge, and Reality* (1998).

McTaggart, John (1866–1925)

British metaphysical philosopher of time and scholar of Hegel, born in London, Fellow of Trinity College, Cambridge. McTaggart was a clear and rigorous ontological idealist who was indebted to Spinoza and a major expositor of Hegelian method. He is remembered chiefly for his arguments for the unreality of time. His main works are *A Commentary on Hegel's Logic* (1910) and *Nature of Existence*, 2 vols. (1921–7).

macrocosm

ANCIENT GREEK PHILOSOPHY, METAPHYSICS Macrocosm means large world-system, in contrast to microcosm, which means little world-system; the former refers to the universe which was, in the mind of the ancient Greeks, an organic living being, and the latter refers to man. Thus, the universe is a large creature and man is the small universe. It is said that **Democritus** was the first to use the term microcosm to refer to man. This analogy reflects the intimate relationship between the universe and the human body, the natural bounty and human goodness. This analogy pervades almost all Greek philosophy. In **Leibniz**, **monads** are microcosms of the world, since each in itself mirrors the entire universe.

> "If it can occur in microcosm it can also occur in macrocosm." **Aristotle,** *Physics*

magnanimity, another expression for great-soulness

maieutic method, another term for midwifery

Maimonides, Moses (1135–1204)

The leading medieval Jewish philosopher, born in Córdoba, Spain and lived mainly in Cairo. In his major philosophy work, *The Guide to the Perplexed* (1190), Maimonides sought to explain scriptural terms through the study of Aristotle's philosophy and to resolve the perplexities arising from tensions between Greek philosophy and the teachings of Judaism. His studies contributed to the rediscovery of Aristotle in the West. Maimonides developed a negative theology, holding that we can know what

God is not, but cannot ascribe any positive attribute to God. He also held that only just souls can be immortal. Maimonides greatly influenced Aquinas and Spinoza.

Maine de Biran, François-Pierre (1766–1824)

French empiricist philosopher. Maine de Biran focused on the inner experience of our belief and will to justify our claims to know our own existence, the existence of a necessary connection between cause and effect, the existence of other persons, and the existence of the external world. His main work is *Essay on the Foundation of Psychology* (1812).

major premise

LOGIC In a standard categorical **syllogism**, which consists of two premises and one conclusion, the **predicate** of the conclusion is called the major term, and its subject, the minor term. The term that appears twice in the premises but not in the conclusion is called the middle term. The premise that contains the major term is called the major premise, while the premise that contains the minor term is called the minor premise.

"The major premise, by definition, is the one that contains the major term." **Hurley**, *A Concise Introduction to Logic*

make-believe

PHILOSOPHY OF MIND, EPISTEMOLOGY, AESTHETICS A state of mind that is close to pretending and to the exercise of **aesthetic imagination**. A person knows that an object is not genuine or does not even exist, but ignores the distinction between the real and the not real and accepts being affected by the object as if it were real or had a different character. In a well-lit room a child plays that the fur rug is a bear. He knows that it is not really a bear. When the light is off, however, the child might lose a sense of safety because of the make-believe and fear that there really is a bear in the room. In some cases, make-believe carries the possibility of taking the imagined as real; in other cases, this possibility does not arise or exists only at the margins of awareness and interpretation.

"It will be noticed that in some varieties of make-believe, the pretender is deliberately simulating and

dissimulating, in some varieties he may not be quite sure to what extent, if any, he is simulating or dissimulating, and in other varieties he is completely taken by his own acting." **Ryle**, *The Concept of Mind*

Malebranche, Nicolas (1638–1715)

French philosopher and theologian, born in Paris. Malebranche sought to overcome difficulties in Descartes's dualism by advancing a doctrine of occasionalism to explain the interaction between mind and body. There is no true causation between mind and body or among bodily or physical movements. God causes every event and acts on the proper occasion to make things harmonious. To explain how our knowledge of eternal and necessary truths is possible, Malebranche argued that "we see all things in God" because ideas are not produced by external objects. Ideas exist in the divine understanding and are independent of us. Our knowledge participates in God's knowledge. Malebranche's philosophy influenced both Berkeley and Hume. His most important work is *The Search after Truth* (1674–5), and other works include the *Treatise on Nature and Grace* (1680), *A Treatise of Morality* (1684), and *Dialogues on Metaphysics and Religion* (1688).

malicious demon

EPISTEMOLOGY [Latin *malignus genius*] **Descartes's** fiction that there might be some omnipotent evil demon who deliberately, constantly, and systematically deceives me. Consequently, the universe and its parts may be such that they never can be clearly understood, and we can never be certain of our **knowledge**. The argument is introduced after Descartes's other three main arguments for subjecting our beliefs to **doubt** (that is, unreliability, the possibility of **dreaming**, and the possible error in the reasoning of mathematics) and pushes methodological doubt to its limit. It expresses in all its rigor the radical decision "to doubt whatever can be doubted." For Descartes, the only **belief** that can survive the challenge of the malicious demon argument is my awareness of my present existence, that is, *cogito ergo sum*, which is therefore the starting-point for establishing the **certainty** of knowledge.

"I shall then suppose, not that God who is supremely good and the fountain of truth, but some
malicious demon not less powerful than deceitful, has employed his energies in deceiving me."
Descartes, *Meditations on First Philosophy*

Manichaeism

PHILOSOPHY OF RELIGION A religion founded by the
Persian Mani (*c.*216–77), which claimed that there
is no single supreme being. Instead, the world is
governed by two balanced and antagonistic cosmic
forces: Light and Darkness. They dwell in different
realms and are co-eternal but independent. Their
strife is the cosmic background of the moral conflict in human history and in every human life. Light
is associated with **God**, **goodness**, and spirit, and
Darkness with Satan, **evil**, and matter. Humanity is
also a mixture of these two forces, with the **soul**
representing Light, and the **body** representing Darkness. They are in a constant struggle, although eventually victory is assured for the Good. Manichaeism
advocated the pursuit of an ascetic life in order to
free the soul by releasing the Light that is trapped in
the body. **Augustine** was briefly an adherent of this
religion before he became a Christian. Manichaeism
was derived from Zoroastrianism and flourished
between the third and fifth centuries AD. It was
condemned by orthodox Christianity, but many
philosophers, such as **Bayle**, **Hume**, and **Voltaire**,
believed that it provided a better account of the
origin of evil than orthodox Christian doctrine.

"Positively, Manichaeism offered a comprehensive system of truth, a cosmology, a soteriology and
an Eschatology. Its cosmology was based on the
old Zoroastrian dualism of Good and Evil, Light
and Darkness." **Burleigh,** *The City of God*

manifest image

EPISTEMOLOGY, METAPHYSICS, PHILOSOPHY OF SCIENCE
A term introduced by the American philosopher
Wilfried **Sellars** for a conception or framework in
terms of which we understand that we are in the
world, with **beliefs**, **desires**, and **intentions**. This
contrasts with what he calls the scientific image,
which postulates **theoretical entities** to explain the
relations of perceptible things. Sellars held that the
contrast between these two images is not between
pre-scientific and scientific images, or between

uncritical and critical images, for one's manifest
image also employs correlational techniques to explain one's **behavior**. However, he did believe that
the scientific image is the only real image and that
theoretical sciences determine what really is and
what really is not. Traditional philosophy has tried
to understcand the structure of the manifest image,
but Sellars claims that the aim of philosophy is the
unification of these images of man-in-the-world.

"Our contrast then, is between two ideal constructs: (a) the correlational and categorical refinement of the 'original image', which refinement
I am calling the manifest image; (b) the image
derived from the fruits of postulational theory
construction which I am calling the scientific
image." **Sellars,** *Science, Perception and Reality*

manifold

EPISTEMOLOGY **Kant**'s term for the material of
experience acquired through **sensation**. Its elements are given either empirically or through pure
a priori intuition in **space** and **time**, and it is unified
or held together pre-cognitively by the synthetic
activity of the **imagination**. The **synthesis** of the
manifold is the first step toward **knowledge**. According to Kant, the manifold is indispensable, because
without it the concepts of pure understanding are
without content and are entirely empty.

"Synthesis of a manifold (be it given empirically
or *a priori*) is what first gives rise to knowledge."
Kant, *Critique of Pure Reason*

many-valued logic

LOGIC A part of logic for which **truth-values** other
than true and false are conceivable for **propositions**.
It thus abandons certain theorems or inferences in
traditional two-valued logic, such as the **law of the
excluded middle** (the principle of **bivalence**) and
the law of **non-contradiction**. Although it may be
traced to Hugh MacColl and **Peirce**, it was inaugur-
ated by the Polish logician **Lukasiewicz**'s development of three-valued logic, and independently by
the American philosopher Post's elaboration of an
n-valued **calculus**. Three-valued logic is one of the
chief forms of many-valued logic and is the model
for higher-valued logics. There are various ways to
designate and interpret the truth-value or truth-

values other than true or false, usually in terms of the degrees of truth or the degrees of falsity. In three-valued logic developed by Lukasiewicz, truth is represented by "1," false by "0," and the third value, interpreted as half-true, is represented by "1/2." An infinite-valued logic means that for propositions an infinite degree ranging from completely true to completely false can be designated. Unlike **modal logic**, the truth-value of a complex proposition in many-valued logic is still determined by the truth values of its constituents. Lukasiewicz was motivated by the problem of **future contingents**, and others have applied many-valued logics to deal with **vagueness**, **logical paradoxes**, and **quantum** mechanics.

> "The mainstream of the development of many-valued logic proceeded on the basis of elaborations of Lukasiewicz's ideas – especially in their formulation in his widely read paper of 1930, where the 3-valued logic was generalised to the many-valued logic, indeed even infinite-valued logic." **Rescher,** *Topics in Philosophic Logic*

Marcel, Gabriel (1889–1973)

French Christian existentialist philosopher and dramatist, born in Paris. Marcel focused on the phenomenology of our being-in-the world as a participant in life and personal relationships. Our being is a condition for our life and is constantly in jeopardy. He used a distinction between reflection that distances oneself from relationships and reflection that returns oneself to relationships with an awareness of being in order to discuss religious conceptions of incarnation, survival, faith, hope, and charity. His main works are *Being and Having* (1935) and *The Mystery of Being*, 2 vols. (1949–50).

Marcus Aurelius (121–180)

Roman Stoic philosopher, born in Rome, Emperor from 161 to his death. Marcus Aurelius endowed chairs of philosophy in the four schools in Athens. His major writing, *The Meditations*, was a collection of essays that developed moral philosophy within the framework of early Stoicism. He held that the universe has a rational order directed by divine Providence. We should be guided by reason because it is placed in man by Providence. The end of life, peace of mind, can be acquired by living in accordance with nature. Death is a natural occurrence that we have no reason to fear. Because all men have the same nature, we have a duty of love toward our fellow man.

Marcus, Ruth Barcan (1921–)

American logician, born in New York, Professor of Philosophy, Yale University. Marcus was a major pioneer in the development of modal logic. She established a system of modal predicate logic, employed substitutional quantification to deal with problems of mixing quantification, modality, and intentional contexts, held that true identity statements are necessarily true, and explored questions of reference and modal essentialism. Her main works include *Modalities* (1993).

Marcuse, Herbert (1898–1979)

German-American social philosopher, born in Berlin and moved to the United States in 1933, an important member of the Frankfurt School. Marcuse believed that the task of philosophy is to achieve emancipation from oppressive political and social reality. In his most influential book, *One Dimensional Man* (1964), he condemned the repressive conditions of modern industrial society, which he held destroyed freedom of the individual and reduced people to the status of tools. His theory inspired student movements in 1960s. Although his major target of criticism was Western capitalist societies, he was equally hostile to communist dictatorships. His other important works include *Reason and Revolution* (1941), *Eros and Civilization* (1955), *Soviet Marxism* (1958), *A Critique of Pure Tolerance* (with Robert Paul Wolff and Barrington Moore, Jr., 1965), and *The Aesthetic Dimension* (1978).

Maritain, Jacques (1882–1973)

French philosopher, born in Paris. Maritain converted to Catholicism in 1906 and became the leading exponent of neo-Thomism. In his major work, *The Degree of Knowledge* (1932), he developed an innovative interpretation of Thomas Aquinas that he applied to contemporary epistemology. He sought to justify and reconcile different sources of knowing and argued that scientific, metaphysical, and mystical knowledge are different in kind but equally legitimate and significant. His discussions of mystical union and metaphysical intuition have been influential. He added a sixth argument for the existence of God to Aquinas's five ways: "I" must be eternal, yet any particular person is finite; hence "I" must be in the act of thinking of the infinite being. Other works include *Art and Scholasticism* (1920), *Integral Humanism* (1936), and *The Person and the Common Good* (1947).

Marx, Karl (1818–83)

German political economist, philosopher of history, and social philosopher, born in Trier. In his early *Economic and Philosophical Manuscripts* (written in 1844, but not published until 1932), Marx used the concept of alienation to describe the relation of workers to their products under capitalism. *The Communist Manifesto* (with Engels, 1848) has had worldwide influence upon subsequent radical thought and political action. *Grundrisse* (1857–8) and Preface to *A Critique of Political Economy* (1859) led to Marx's monumental *Capital* (3 vols., 1867, 1885, and 1894), in which he employed a materialist transformation of Hegel's dialectic to examine and criticize the theory and practice of capitalism. Marx developed his theory of surplus value to show the exploitation of the working class. He held that the economic base of society, involving the forces and relations of production, determines its ideological and cultural superstructure, and that contradictions between base and superstructure would, as a matter of historical inevitability, lead to social revolution and socialism. Changing emphases and theoretical formulations in different periods of Marx's work leave room for differing interpretations and schools of Marxism.

Marxism

PHILOSOPHICAL METHOD, METAPHYSICS, PHILOSOPHY OF SOCIAL SCIENCE, PHILOSOPHY OF HISTORY A term for ideas developed in the works of Karl **Marx** and Friedrich Engels, and later developments based on their thinking. The attempt to work out a coherent Marxist system starts with Engels himself. Later Marxists have different versions, and each believes his own to be orthodox and condemns the other versions as revisionist. In the communist countries, orthodox Marxism has been developed by Lenin and Stalin in the Soviet Union and by Mao Zedong in China. The central doctrines of Marxist philosophy are called **dialectical materialism** and **historical materialism**.

The essential claims of Marxism are that society consists of an economic base containing **forces and relations of production**, a political and legal **superstructure** determined by the economic base, and **ideology** that corresponds to the superstructure. The superstructure has partial autonomy, but the development of the forces of production are the ultimate ground for historical progress through stages, from primitive society to slave society, feudalism, capitalism, and eventually socialism and communism. **Persons** are members of different classes according to their respective positions in the social economy. However it is seen by members of a society, history is a history of class-struggle. All existing institutions and agencies represent, consciously and unconsciously, the interest of one or another class. Even morality, which most theorists regard as an historical and cultural matter that allows room to criticize authority, is said to reflect the interests of the ruling class. In Marxist thought, class-divisions will not disappear until the ultimate stage of social development: communism. Engels held that Marxism is the science of the general laws of motion and development of nature, human society, and thought. Marxism is not merely a theory, but a social project as well, as expressed in Marx's claim: "The philosophers have only interpreted the world . . . the point, however, is to change it." The publication of Marx's early *Economic and Philosophical Manuscripts* around 1930, and the end of the Second World War, led Marxism to became an area of flourishing academic research in the West, especially in Europe. Various interpretations of Marxism emerged to form different schools under the general title of Western Marxism. Major schools were initiated by Gyorgy **Lukács**, Antonio **Gramsci**, the Frankfort School's **critical theory**, represented by Max **Horkheimer**, Theodor **Adorno**, Herbert **Marcuse**, and Jürgen **Habermas**, existential Marxism, represented by Maurice **Merleau-Ponty** and Jean-Paul **Sartre**, and **Althusser**'s structuralist Marxism. Analytic Marxism, which uses the methods of analytical philosophy to examine Marxist thought, is represented by G. A. **Cohen**, John **Elster**, John Roemer, and Alan Wood.

"We have today a galaxy of different Marxisms, within which the place of Marx's own thought is ambiguous." **Thomas, in Carver (ed.),** *The Cambridge Companion to Marx*

masculinism

ETHICS, POLITICAL PHILOSOPHY, EPISTEMOLOGY From a feminist point of view, masculinism is an attitude which ignores the existence of women and is concerned exclusively with male opinions and interests. It tries to justify the claim that only male views have value and the further claim that anything that cannot be reduced or translated into men's experience should be excluded from the subject-matter of philosophy. In another sense, masculinism advocates the elimination of all discrimination against men because they are male. The goal of this sort of masculinism is the equality between men and women, and it is a reaction against extreme feminist claims for the superiority of women over men.

"By masculinism in general I mean the assertion of masculine dominance over the feminine and also the practice of taking this first 'superiority' as a point of reference to assert other forms of supremacy which apparently have nothing to do with the duality of the sexes." **Le Doeuff,** *Hipparchia's Choice*

masked man fallacy

LOGIC A fallacious argument of the following form: you say that you know your father, but that you do not know this masked man and conclude that this masked man is not your father; however, this masked man is indeed your father. The recognition of this fallacy can be traced to **Eubulides** of Megara (third century BC) and was discussed by the Stoics. However formulated, this fallacy occurs because it treats a **referentially opaque context** as if it were **referentially transparent**. It is sometimes argued that **Descartes** committed this fallacy when he said that he knows certain things about his mind, but does not know anything about the nature of his body, so mind and body are really distinct. Descartes's argument, however, is more sophisticated than this fallacy.

"[A] fallacy recognized by Stoic logicians, which came to be known as the *larvatus* or 'masked man' fallacy: I do not know the identity of this masked man; I do know the identity of my father; therefore this masked man is not my father." **B. Williams,** *Descartes*

masochism

ETHICS, METAPHYSICS, MODERN EUROPEAN PHILOSOPHY Generally, the practice of obtaining sexual **pleasure** by means of one's own **pain** and humiliation. In **Sartre**'s use, a person is a masochist by becoming a mere **object** for a loved person, in a state of complete dependence. This kind of human relation leads to frustration and to a failure of love. For Sartre, a person cannot be a mere object and must make free **choices**. A person cannot be lost completely in being-for-the-other.

"Masochism is thus in principle a failure. There is nothing surprising in this when we think that masochism is a 'vice' and that vice is, in principle, love of failure." **Sartre,** *Being and Nothingness*

mass term

METAPHYSICS, PHILOSOPHY OF LANGUAGE In contrast to count nouns or **sortals**, mass terms or nouns cannot occur with a definite or indefinite article. They do not refer distributively and provide no principle of countability. While a count noun is associated with **quantifiers** such as many and few, a mass noun is associated with quantifiers such as much and little. Examples of mass nouns are water, gold, music, intelligence, and information. Many abstract mass nouns are closely related to adjectives, for instance intelligence–intelligent or virtue–virtuous. There are various alternative terms for mass nouns. **Strawson** calls them characterizing terms; **Goodman** refers to them as collective predicates, and **Quine** calls them partitive terms or bulk terms.

"So-called mass terms like 'water', 'footwear', and 'red' have the semantic property of referring cumulatively: any sum of parts which are water is water." **Quine,** *Word and Object*

master argument

METAPHYSICS An argument about possibility introduced by Diodorus Cronus (*c*.284 BC), a member of the Greek Megarian School. The argument turns on three propositions: (1) Everything that is **past** is **necessary**; (2) nothing impossible follows from the **possible**; (3) what neither is nor will be is possible. According to Diodorus, (1) and (2) are evidently true, but (3) cannot be supported by (1) and (2) and must be wrong. On his account, therefore, only what is true or will be true is possible. This is also his response to **Aristotle**'s discussion of **future contingents**. But the Stoics argued that (3) is correct, and either (1) or (2) might be wrong.

> "According to Alexander, Diodorus constructed the Master Argument in order to establish his own definition of possibility, but a modern scholar has suggested that the title refers to the overmastering power of fate." **Kneale and Kneale, *The Development of Logic***

master morality

ETHICS, MODERN EUROPEAN PHILOSOPHY **Nietzsche** held that two fundamental types of morality, arising out of different traditions, have engaged in struggle throughout history. The first, master morality, is rooted in the self-affirmation by the strong man and the ruling group and calls **good** everything that is noble and powerful and calls bad everything that is mediocre, undistinguished, ugly, and weak. According to Nietzsche, master morality is vigorous and desires to train man for heights. In contrast, slave morality is associated with the resentment of the weak man and the ruled group. Slave morality talks of good and evil rather than good and bad. It calls **evil** whatever is threatening and harmful and calls good whatever is benefiting and advantageous. Slave morality is shaped in direct and insidious reaction to master morality and emphasizes preservation from destruction. Each morality develops into a kind of value-schema rather than into a morality of a segment of the population. Nietzsche claimed that any higher complex **culture**, including the bourgeois, is a mixture of these two types of morality, and he attempts to find a reconciliation between them. The two moralities even exist within the **soul** of the same **person**. Nietzsche himself preferred master morality, but did not accept it as a whole, for he admitted that this type of morality contains an aspect of inhumanity. His master corresponds to **Aristotle**'s **great-souled man**. Master morality, for Nietzsche, was also called noble morality, and slave morality was also called herd morality.

> "According to slave morality, therefore, the 'evil person' arouses fear; according to master morality, it is precisely the 'good person' who arouses and wishes to arouse fear, whilst the 'bad man' is felt to be contemptible." **Nietzsche, *On the Genealogy of Morals***

master/slave

ETHICS, POLITICAL PHILOSOPHY, PHILOSOPHY OF HISTORY **Hegel**'s metaphor to describe the evolution of moral and political consciousness. Initially, each man is a particular individual who strives to impose himself upon **others** and to achieve external recognition. On this basis, one man enslaves another. The master, through his command over things, orders the slave to work for the sake of satisfying the master's own **desire**. The slave, in order to survive and to retain his life, must repress his own instinct and his **essence** by **negating** himself. In a second stage, the slave **transcends** himself by working and becomes the master of **nature**. Because work raises him from slavery to **freedom**, the slave changes himself by changing the world. The future belongs to the working slave rather than the consuming master. History is simply the progressive negation of his own slavery by the slave. Eventually, **consciousness** reaches a third stage, in which men recognize themselves as **universal** and respect each other as **ends**. This mutual recognition achieves the integrity of life and essence. The thesis of mastery and the antithesis of slavery are **dialectically** overcome. The opposition between master and slave becomes the motive principle of the historical process. Hegel's rich metaphor has been borrowed by a wide range of later moral and social theorists and philosophers.

> "While the one combatant prefers life, retains his single self-consciousness, but surrenders his claim for recognition, the other holds fast to his self-assertion and is recognised by the former as his superior. Thus arises the status of master and slave." **Hegel, *Phenomenology of Mind***

material adequacy

LOGIC, PHILOSOPHY OF LANGUAGE According to **Tarski**, any acceptable definition of **truth** should meet two conditions: material adequacy and formal correctness. The condition of material adequacy sets limits on possible contents, requiring that any acceptable definition of truth has as consequences all instances of the (T) schema ('p' is true if and only if p). This determines what the **extension** of the truth-predicate should be. The condition of formal correctness sets limits on the possible structural form of a language of any acceptable definition, requiring that a definition of truth should not be **semantically**

closed. A definition that meets these two conditions will be able to answer our pre-theoretical intuitions about what it means for a sentence to be true.

> "The present article is almost wholly devoted to a single problem – the definition of truth. Its task is to construct – with reference to any given language – a materially adequate and formally correct definition of the term 'true predicate'." **Tarski, "The Concept of Truth in Formalised Languages," in** *Logic, Semantics, Metamathematics*

material analysis, see analysis

material conditional, another term for material implication

material equivalence, see logical equivalence

material implication

LOGIC A term used by **Russell** and **Whitehead**, representing the **truth-function** of two propositions P and Q in the form of the **statement** "If P then Q." The relation is symbolized by a horseshoe ⊃, written as "P ⊃ Q," or alternatively by an arrow →, written as "P → Q." It is true that P materially implies Q in each of the following three cases: (1) both P and Q are true; (2) P is false, and Q is true; (3) both P and Q are false. It is false only if P is true and Q is false. This is called material implication because what is expressed by the sign '⊃' is different from our ordinary notion of **implication**. A statement such as "If Rome is in Italy, then London is beautiful" is true by material implication, but does not seem to be an implication at all in the ordinary sense, for there is no relation between antecedent and consequent. It is due to this difference that material implication leads to many **paradoxes**. Some philosophers claim therefore that we should say that it is a material conditional relation instead of a relation of material implication.

> "The relation in virtue of which it is possible for us validly to infer is what I call material implication . . . The relation holds, in fact, when it does hold, without any reference to the truth or falsehood of the proposition involved." **Russell,** *The Principles of Mathematics*

material implication, paradoxes of

LOGIC The unpalatable consequences arising from the definition of material implication: a false proposition, merely because it is false, implies every proposition; and a true proposition, merely because it is true, is implied by every proposition. Put it in another way, whenever P is false, P ⊃ Q is true; whenever Q is true, P ⊃ Q is true. The problem arises because **implication** is ordinarily used for a relation between two **propositions**, while a statement of material implication can be true even if there is no relation at all between its component propositions. Material implication does not concern the subject-matter or content of its components. To avoid these consequences, it is suggested that we speak of the material conditional instead of material implication.

> "Russell's definition of 'p implies q' as synonymous with 'either not p or q' solicited the justified objection that according to it a true proposition is implied by any proposition and a false proposition implies any proposition (paradoxes of material implication)." **Pap,** *Elements of Analytic Philosophy*

material mode of speech

PHILOSOPHY OF LANGUAGE **Carnap** draws a distinction between the material mode of speech and the formal mode of speech. The material mode of speech uses **propositions** in an **object language** to describe **facts**, **objects**, or phenomena. The formal mode of speech uses propositions in a **metalanguage** to talk about words or linguistic forms (syntactical sentences). An example of the material mode of speech is "Red is a quality," and an example of the formal mode of speech is "'Red' is a quality-word." For Carnap, many traditional problems arise because we treat claims about words as claims as objects. On this basis, we then speak in the material mode, producing many **pseudo-object** sentences. Philosophy should translate these sentences into the formal mode, that is, replace talk about **meaning** by the talk about the formal relations of words.

> "The true situation is revealed by the translation of the sentences of the material mode of speech, which are quasi-syntactical sentences, into the correlated syntactical sentences and thus into the formal mode." **Carnap,** *The Logical Syntax of Language*

material objects

METAPHYSICS, EPISTEMOLOGY Also called physical objects, the objects which possess physical characteristics such as position, size, shape, and solidity. Such objects include physical entities such as rocks, trees, houses, and living organisms such as plants, animals, and human beings. The existence of material objects is independent of our **perception**, but they are the objects of perception. In this sense material objects stand in contrast to another kind of alleged object of perception, **sense-data**. The perception of material objects is public and durable, but it is indirect because it involves **inference** and **interpretation**, and is therefore also less certain than perception of sense-data seems to be. This contrast leads to major disputes about the nature of material objects. How can we prove the existence of material objects and combat **skepticism** and **idealism**? What is the relation between material objects and sense-data?

> "Nothing can be a material object except what has position in space." **Moore,** *Some Main Problems in Philosophy*

materialism

METAPHYSICS, EPISTEMOLOGY, PHILOSOPHY OF MIND The doctrine that all items in the world are composed of **matter** and that the **properties** of matter determine all other things, including **mental phenomena**. Every explicable thing can be explained on the grounds of **natural laws**. Materialism has a long history, starting from the Ionian natural philosophers and ancient **atomists**. It was developed by **Gassendi** and **Hobbes** in the seventeenth century, the French materialists in the eighteenth century, and **Marx**'s **dialectical materialism** and **historical materialism** in the nineteenth century. There has been some dispute about the nature of matter. **Physicalism**, which claims that all items in the world are physical entities, is a popular contemporary version of materialism, because not all physical entities are material. Both materialism and physicalism reject **abstract entities** and embrace the reality of **particulars**. Materialism claims to be an ally of **common sense** and it is generally **deterministic**. Contemporary materialism has become less **ontological** and is not so much concerned with the composition of things. Accordingly, the traditional contrast between

materialism and idealism does not always apply. The physicalism of **logical positivism** was essentially epistemic and logical, claiming that all **predicates** can be reduced to physical predicates. **Central-state materialism** in the philosophy of mind proposes that all mental phenomena can be explained by appeal to neuro-physical items with which they are identical. **Eliminative materialism** seeks to get rid of what it claims to be scientifically inadequate folk psychological terms, like **belief** and **desire**, in favor of neuro-scientific notions.

> "Materialism was taken to be a logical analysis of statements about the mind and not a very general contingent or empirical theory about the nature of mental entities." **Quinton,** *The Nature of Things*

materialist theory of mind

PHILOSOPHY OF MIND A theory developed as a result of the criticisms of the dualist theory of the relationship between **body** and **mind**. While **dualism** claims that mind and body are two independent **entities**, varieties of materialism claim that mental phenomena are determined by, **identical** with, or supervenient on physical phenomena. Materialism holds that human beings are distinguished from other physical objects only because of the special complexity of their physical organizations. This theory has two main versions: **behaviorism** claims that to have a mind is to have tendencies to behave physically in a certain way, and **central-state materialism** or **identity theory** claims that mental events are identical with certain physical events in the brain. **Supervenience** can allow a person to have mental states in virtue of having certain brain states without the mental states being reduced to the brain states.

> "In sharp opposition to any form of dualism we have materialist or physicalist theory of mind. For a materialist, man is nothing but a physical object, and so he is committed to giving a purely physical theory of mind." **D. Armstrong,** *A Materialist Theory of Mind*

mathematical cyclist

LOGIC, METAPHYSICS A **paradox** devised by **Quine** to criticize the division between **essence** and **accidents** that is fundamental to **essentialism**. For Quine there is no absolute way to distinguish between the **necessary** or essential attributes and the **contingent** or accidental attributes of an object X, for our decisions in this regard are always related to our interests. In relation to some interests, some properties are essential; and in relation to others, they are accidental. Thus, essentialism is faced with a paradox that a given individual will be both essentially and accidentally so and so. A mathematician is necessarily rational and not necessarily two-legged; a cyclist is necessarily two-legged and not necessarily rational; then what of an individual who is both a mathematician and a cyclist?

"Mathematicians are conceivably said to be necessarily rational, and not necessarily two-legged; and cyclists necessarily two-legged and not necessarily rational. But what of an individual who counts among his eccentricities both mathematics and cycling?" **Quine,** *Word and Object*

mathematical logic

LOGIC, PHILOSOPHY OF MATHEMATICS Also called symbolic logic or modern logic. The modern embodiment of **formal logic**, mainly consisting of **propositional** and **predicate logic**, with **quantifiers**, **variables**, and **functions** as its central notions. It can be traced to **Leibniz**, **Boole**, and Peano, but in its modern form began in 1879, with the publication of Gottlob **Frege**'s *Begriffsschrift*. It was further developed by **Russell** and **Whitehead** in their *Principia Mathematica*. Frege, Russell, and Whitehead sought to deduce mathematics from logic. Mathematical logic is a branch of mathematical study and relies heavily on symbolic techniques and mathematical methods. It is also a logical theory of mathematical analysis and is applicable to other more traditional branches of mathematics Many philosophical problems have arisen from the development of modern logic, but advanced modern logic has become a technical field for mathematicians and the philosophy of mathematics.

"By the name 'mathematical logic', then, I will denote any logical theory whose object is the analysis and deduction of arithmetic and geometry by means of concepts which belong evidently to logic." **Russell,** *Collected Papers of Bertrand Russell,* vol. VI

matrix method, another name for truth-table method

matter

METAPHYSICS, PHILOSOPHY OF SCIENCE [from Greek *hule,* wood] **Aristotle** considered matter and **form** to be relative terms, with matter as the material of a thing (the basic stuff) as opposed to form as its structure. Matter is a factor within the **category** of **substance**, but is not primary substance. Matter and form together are the two major components of reality. Matter, as the subject or **substratum** of **change**, can accept **contraries** and so make change possible. At the beginning of change, there are remote matter-like elements, which would be **prime matter** in a general discussion of change. At the end of generation there is proximate matter, which is the matter appropriate to the product. A material substance is a composite of matter and form. Matter is usually, but not always, associated with **potentiality**. Aristotle also occasionally mentioned spatial extension as intelligible matter. The characteristics of Aristotle's notion of matter were retained in the later development of metaphysics.

In the seventeenth and eighteenth centuries, matter was thought to be something in a spatio-temporal location and to have the properties of extension and movability. **Descartes** called it **extended substance** in contrast to **mind** or **soul** as **thinking substance**. This led to the problems raised by matter–mind **dualism**. In modern science, matter is characterized in terms of mass and extension, and is distinguished from energy on the grounds that each has its own law of conservation. This distinction no longer holds in contemporary physics. Matter is now mainly a subject for the philosophy of physics.

"For my definition of matter is just this – the primary substratum of each thing, from which it comes to be without qualification, and which persists in the result." **Aristotle,** *Physics*

matter of fact, see knowledge of relation of ideas

maxim

ETHICS, PHILOSOPHY OF ACTION Generally, any simple rule or guide in our life, but in **Kant**'s moral theory a practical proposition that connects one's subjective conditions, that is, one's reason or motive, to one's decision to act. Such maxims have the form "I will do A if that will make me happy." Hence a maxim is a principle upon which one acts. For Kant, there are maxims of action, which express a determination to act in a certain way when a certain condition is met, and maxims of ends, which express a determination to form an intention when a certain condition is met. A maxim is distinguished from a practical law. For a maxim, the conditions (the reason or motives) are **subjective** and differ among persons because each person has different **desires** or purposes. For a practical law the conditions are **objective**, that is, universally valid. Therefore, Kant called a maxim the subjective principle of volition and the practical law the objective principle of volition, that is, the **categorical imperative**. All maxims have form or universality, matter or plurality, and totality in the complete determination. Maxims must be tested by the categorical imperative. Accordingly, a morally commendable action requires a person to act on a maxim, which can at the same time make itself a universal law so that the subjective principle of volition coincides with the objective principle of volition.

"A maxim contains the practical rule which reason determines in accordance with the conditions of the subject (often his ignorance or his inclinations) and is thus the principle according to which the subject does act. But the law is the objective principle valid for every rational being, and it is the principle according to which he ought to act, i.e. an imperative." **Kant, Groundwork for the Metaphysics of Morals**

maximin rule

ETHICS, POLITICAL PHILOSOPHY, PHILOSOPHY OF ACTION, PHILOSOPHY OF SOCIAL SCIENCE A strategy for choosing under uncertainty, according to which we should consider the worst possible outcome for each **choice** and adopt the one that has the least bad consequences. According to **Rawls**, because the rational **agents** in the **original position** are ignorant of their own initial positions in the society they are devising, they will reasonably employ the maximin rule for choosing principles of **justice**. The rationality of this strategy under conditions of ignorance is the basis for Rawls's **difference principle**, according to which a just society would make the situation of its worst-

off group as good as possible. While the maximin rule seeks to maximize the minimum gain, a related strategy governed by the minimax rule enjoins rational agents to minimize their maximum loss. The two rules are generally taken to be equivalent.

"The maximin rule tells us to rank alternatives by their worst possible outcomes: we are to adopt the alternatives the worst outcome of which is superior to the worst outcome of the others." **Rawls, A Theory of Justice**

Mead, George Herbert (1863–1931)

American social philosopher and philosopher of mind, born in South Hadley, Massachusetts. The main concern of Mead's social behaviorism was to explain the genesis of the mind and the self in terms of social language. He argued that the self develops through communication with others. His views gave rise to the school of symbolic interactionism in sociology. In metaphysics, he claimed that all reality is an active process. His major works include *Mind, Self and Society from the Standpoint of a Social Behaviourist* (1934), *Philosophy of the Act* (1938), and *The Individual and the Social Self* (1982).

mean

ETHICS [Greek *mesotes*, a noun derived from *mesos*, middle, intermediate] **Aristotle** claimed that **virtue** of character is a mean. Unlike an arithmetic mean, virtue as a mean is not a middle point between two extremes, which is one and the same for all. Instead, it is in relation to **passions** and **actions** and is a state in which passions are neither indulged without restraint (excess) nor suppressed entirely (defect). The right amount of passion is relative to us, and is different in different situations. However, that does not entail that different persons measure it in different ways. Rather, virtue is determined by **practical reason**.

Aristotle employs the mean to analyze not only virtue in general, but also particular virtues. The doctrine of the mean in Aristotle's ethics is famous, although it is not clear how much it tells us about virtue and vice. In addition, he uses it in his theory of perception, saying that a sense organ must be in a mean state (e.g. less hot and less cold) if it is to perceive the extreme qualities (e.g. hot or cold).

meaning

PHILOSOPHY OF LANGUAGE, LOGIC, PHILOSOPHY OF MIND, EPISTEMOLOGY, METAPHYSICS Generally, what is expressed, said, or referred to in an expression. Literal meaning is what one can directly tell or draw from the words used in an expression themselves. If two or more expressions have the same meaning, they are said to be **synonymous**. Meaning is used in the same way as **sense**, **connotation**, and **intension** in contrast to **reference**, **denotation**, and **extension**. Determining the way the meaning of an expression is generated involves determining the way language relates to reality, the relation between meaning and psychological states, and the relation between meaning and other key **semantic** notions such as **truth** and **reference**. All these make the notion of meaning a central and difficult concept, not only in the philosophy of language, but also in the philosophy of mind, epistemology, and metaphysics. Various theories about meaning have been developed in the twentieth century. This dictionary has a single entry for each of the major influential theories. They include the **behavioral theory of meaning**, the **ideational theory of meaning**, the **image theory of meaning**, the **picture theory of meaning**, the **referential theory of meaning**, the truth-conditional theory of meaning, the **use theory of meaning**, and the **verificationist theory of meaning**.

meaning of a sentence

PHILOSOPHY OF LANGUAGE, LOGIC In contrast to the meaning of a word, which is a potential meaning that is realized when the word is used in a sentence, the meaning of a sentence is claimed to be a certain extra-linguistic **fact**. Even philosophers who reject an **ontology** of facts can retain the priority sentence meaning over word meaning. Philosophers who accept the notion of a **propositional attitude** see the meaning of a sentence as the object of propositional attitudes.

meaning of life

ETHICS An ancient and central philosophical question asks what is the meaning of life. Some philosophers argue that nothing outside of life could give it meaning. For others, there is nothing but life, and it is **meaningless**. Another view is that an overall plan or ultimate goal, preferably chosen by us, gives life its meaning. In some versions, the plan and goal must be part of a larger project or derived from a source, where the project or source extends beyond the life and gives place to the commitments of the life. There are different views about the projects or sources that could give meaning to life, with candidates including **God**, **immortality**, **tradition**, and **rationality**. There are also debates over the **objectivity** or **subjectivity** of the meaning of life. If the meaning of life is an objective matter, a life can seem to have a meaning through passionate intensity, coherence, and satisfaction, without really having meaning. Accepting that there is a meaning in life leads to consideration of how one should live.

meaning postulate

PHILOSOPHY OF LANGUAGE, LOGIC A term introduced by **Carnap** in 1953 and originally intended to explicate but not strictly define an **analytical statement** that is not logically true. It was later extended to any statement or rule that specifies or clarifies the **meaning** of a **predicate** and hence determines the **entailments** that derive from that predicate in the non-logical vocabulary of a **natural language**. Examples of this kind of meaning postulate include **recursive definitions** and **definitions in use**. The advantage of this device is that it avoids a sharp distinction between the logical and non-logical vocabulary of the **object language**.

"We draw an analytic-synthetic distinction formally only in connection with formalised languages whose inventors list some statements and rules as 'meaning postulates'. That is, it is stipulated that to qualify as correctly using the language one must accept those statements and rules." **Putnam, "The Analytic and the Synthetic," in *Minnesota Studies in the Philosophy of Science*, vol. III**

meaningless

PHILOSOPHY OF LANGUAGE, LOGIC Loosely, what is obviously false, absurd, or pointless. In a stricter sense, questions and answers which are devoid of **meaning** or **sense**. In **logical positivism**, metaphysical statements are examined by logical **analysis** and claimed to be meaningless. One cannot say that metaphysical statements are true or false, because we lack any **criterion** to determine whether they are true or false. Only statements allowing such a criterion are meaningful. According to logical positivism, there are two kinds of meaningful statements: first, the formulae of logic and mathematics and second, empirical or factual statements. Any other statements that do not fall in these categories are rejected from serious philosophy as meaningless, metaphysical statements or **pseudo-statements**.

"In the strict sense, however, a sequence of words is meaningless if it does not, within a specified language, constitute a statement." **Carnap, "The Elimination of Metaphysics through Logical Analysis," in Ayer (ed.), *Logical Positivism***

means/end

ETHICS, PHILOSOPHY OF ACTION, PHILOSOPHY OF RELIGION Some things are done to achieve a further goal or purpose and are means to ends. If a thing is done not for some purpose outside itself but for its own sake, it is an end in itself, but an end can also be a means to a higher end. In line with this reasoning, many philosophers infer that there is an ultimate or **final end**, which is an end in an absolute sense. Such means–end reasoning, called a teleological approach or analysis [from Greek *telos*, end], is applied in both theology and ethics. Some philosophers hold that **rationality** is restricted to selecting means as instruments to achieve ends that are given non-rationally, while others hold

that the selection of ends is also a matter for reason. Modern teleological ethics, represented by **utilitarianism**, claims that acts should be judged by their consequences, including the ends they realize. **Deontology**, which holds that acts should be judged according to their **motive** or **duty** rather than by their consequences, also uses the distinction between means and ends, with **Kant**'s **categorical imperative** requiring that we treat rational beings as ends rather than merely as means. **Aristotle** had another conception of the means–ends relation. Rather than being merely instrumental, a means can be constitutive of an end or be a major component of the end. This later conception is important for understanding Aristotle's notion of happiness. There has been much controversy whether good ends can justify evil means.

"A means is the object of an interest which is asymmetrically dependable on an ulterior interest whose object is the end." **Perry, *Realms of Value***

means of production, see productive force

mechanism

METAPHYSICS, PHILOSOPHY OF SCIENCE A paradigm of **explanation** modeled on mechanics and holding that everything can be explained by the mechanistic principle, that is, by the interaction and combination of material particles. On this view, both animals and human beings are machines, and **mental phenomena** are nothing more than the sophisticated arrangement of different minute parts. In general, mechanism reduces all differences of quality into the differences of quantity. The world as a whole is an aggregate rather than an organic unity. All **relations** among particles are external relations. This paradigm was developed by **Descartes** and **Hobbes** and was supported by **Newton**'s mechanics. It denies both **action at a distance** and Aristotelian **final causes** or **teleology**. It therefore opposes **vitalism** and organicism.

"Mechanism represents the tendency opposed to teleology because its adherents think that the course of all phenomena in the world occurs as if in a mechanism and is not directed by purpose in the way that human conduct is." **Ajdukiewicz, *Problems and Theories of Philosophy***

mechanistic materialism

METAPHYSICS, PHILOSOPHY OF SCIENCE The type of materialism prevalent in the seventeenth and eighteenth centuries, represented by **Hobbes, Gassendi,** and French materialists such as **La Mettrie, Diderot, Holbach, Helvétius,** and **Condillac**. The theory was influenced by mechanics, which was the most highly developed natural science at that time. On this view, all phenomena, including those involving life and the mind, can be explained in terms of the interactions of forces and the simple or complex arrangement of material particles. Both universe and man are viewed as machines, with La Mettrie calling his major work *L'Homme Machine*. Things can affect one another only by direct mechanical contact. Because the mind lacks an independent status and is explained in mechanical terms, this theory has difficulty in accounting for **free will**. **Marx** and Engels took this kind of materialism to represent outmoded metaphysical thought and claimed that it must be superseded by **dialectical materialism**.

"Mechanical materialism not only denies that spiritual substance exists, it also considers even mental phenomena (thought, feelings, etc) to be physical processes." **Ajdukiewicz,** *Problem and Theories of Philosophy*

mediate inference, see immediate inference

mediate perception, see immediate perception

medical ethics, see bioethics

medieval philosophy

PHILOSOPHY OF RELIGION, METAPHYSICS, LOGIC, ETHICS, PHILOSOPHY OF LANGUAGE The central theme of medieval philosophy was the attempt to join **faith** and **reason**. Philosophers sought to make Christian faith intelligible and to prove the compatibility of Christianity and reason. Historical accounts of medieval philosophy normally start with **Augustine**, who applied **Plato**'s thinking to Christianity. The translation and commentary of **Aristotle**'s logical works by **Boethius** shaped much Latin technical philosophical vocabulary. **Anselm** of Canterbury, in virtue of his **ontological argument**, is known as the father of **Scholasticism**, a tradition that debated questions such as the **ontological** status

of **universals, free will** and **determinism,** and the problem of **evil**. In the twelfth and thirteenth centuries, the whole body of Aristotle's work became available to Europe through transmission from the Islamic world, together with the commentaries of Arabic scholars such as al-Farabi, **Avicenna** (Ibn Sina), and **Averroes** (Ibn Rushd). The greatest medieval thinker, Thomas **Aquinas**, attempted to reconcile Christianity in an Aristotelian framework. Later major thinkers included **Duns Scotus, William of Ockham,** and **Francisco Suárez**. The divorce of philosophy and theology and the influence of modern science in the work of later philosophers, such as F. **Bacon, Hobbes,** and **Descartes,** marked the end of medieval philosophy. Many issues of medieval logic, ethics, and philosophy of language still excite interest among contemporary philosophers.

"The assertion that the most important philosophical event in medieval philosophy was the discovery by the Christian West of the more or less complete works of Aristotle is an assertion which could, I think, be defended." **Copleston,** *A History of Philosophy*, **vol. III**

meditation

PHILOSOPHY OF RELIGION, PHILOSOPHICAL METHOD Usually used in religion as a synonym for contemplation, by which one beholds some spiritual object or obtains spiritual insight. **Descartes** chose this word for the title of his metaphysical masterpiece: *Meditations on First Philosophy* (1664). Meditation here is the reflection of a solitary thinker or meditator, who retreats from the sensible world and frees himself from the influence of preconceived opinions. The purpose of meditation is to discover the indubitable first **principles** that can serve as the secure **foundation** of the system of knowledge. The *Meditations on First Philosophy* purports to describe the **soul**'s solitary quest for **truth** and its discovery.

"I shall first of all set forth in these Meditations the very considerations by which I persuade myself that I have reached a certain and evident knowledge of the truth, in order to see if, by the same reasons which persuaded me, I can also persuade others." **Descartes,** *Meditations on First Philosophy*

Meinong, Alexius von (1853–1920)

Austrian philosopher and psychologist, born in Lemberg, Galicia, a disciple of Brentano. Meinong distinguished the objects of mental acts from the contents of those acts. His philosophy was mainly devoted to the investigation of various objects of thought. In contrast to traditional metaphysics, Meinong claimed that objects should not be confined to the actual. He separated the being of an object (*Sein*) from its character or nature (*Sosein*) and held that objects that do not actually exist, such as "the round square" or "the golden mountain," can still be the subjects of true predications. The objects of judgment and assumption, which he called "objectives," contain objects as constituents. Russell's theory of descriptions rejected Meinong's account of non-existent objects. In his theory of value, Meinong classified and analyzed various kinds of feeling. His main works include *Human Studies*, 2 vols. (1877, 1882), *On Assumptions* (1902), *On Object Theory* (1904), *On Possibility and Probability* (1915), and *Ground-work of the General Theory of Value* (1923).

memory

EPISTEMOLOGY, PHILOSOPHY OF MIND The capacity to recall past **experience** and to retain in the present the **knowledge** acquired in the past. Although some **skeptics** reject **belief** based on memory as knowledge on the grounds that there is always a gap between the present remembering and the past, many philosophers consider memory to be a source of knowledge. In most cases memory gives us knowledge of the past. There has been some debate as to what counts as memory, how it is possible to have knowledge of that which is no longer present, and how past knowledge can be retained in the present. Because it is generally taken that there is an **analogy** between memory and **perception**, all theories of perception have their counterparts in theories of memory. While **indirect realism**, or the **representative theory** of memory developed by **Aristotle** and **Hume**, claims that what we remember is an **image** that represents the past, **direct realism** argues that our awareness of the past is direct without an intermediary image. For **phenomenalism** the existence of the past is nothing more than the availability of memory experience.

"Memory demands (a) an image, (b) a belief in past existence. The belief may be expressed in the words 'This existed'." **Russell,** *The Analysis of Mind*

Mendelssohn, Moses (1729–86)

German Jewish philosopher, born in Dessau. Mendelssohn initiated the integration of Jewish culture and Enlightenment values. He argued for the immortality of the soul and sought to show the incoherence of moral authority. In his writing on art, he distinguished aesthetic perfection, which is a subjectively appreciated artificial unity of objects that humans take to be wholes, from metaphysical perfection, which is real unity in multiplicity known to God. Beauty, as aesthetic perfection, is the human representation of metaphysical perfection. His main works include *Phädon* (1776) and *Jerusalem* (1783).

mens rea

PHILOSOPHY OF LAW [Latin guilty mind or guilty mental state] The **mental state** that a defendant has when he commits a crime. In order to secure a conviction, the prosecution must prove that the defendant has a guilty mind. The malice aforethought of such a mind and the defendant's *actus reus* (Latin, guilty activity) constitute sufficient grounds for the defendant to be liable to **punishment**. Accordingly, a person is punishable if and only if he or she had a choice whether or not to break the law and exercised that choice in favor of breaking it. *Mens rea* varies from crime to crime, and the common feature is that the defendant has knowledge of the bad consequence of the action but still recklessly intends to bring it about. The *mens rea* requirement is contained in the definition of almost all crimes, with the exception of strict liability, which does not depend upon the mental state of the agent. If *mens rea* can be negated, for example by insanity or negligence, the same act will be treated rather differently. *Mens rea* is viewed as a restraint upon the **utilitarian** theory of punishment, according to which a punishment is justified if it promotes generally good consequences.

"In order to prove murder, the state has the burden of proving, among other things, that the accused acted with the appropriate mental states. Such mental states requirements are usually called *mens rea* (very loosely, 'guilty mind') requirements." **Murphy and Coleman,** *The Philosophy of Law*

mental act

PHILOSOPHY OF MIND Activities or processes such as seeing, hearing, smelling, feeling pains, calculating, or deliberating in one's own mind. Starting with **Brentano,** there has been a tradition that separates the occurrence of a mental act from its **content.** All mental acts are **mental events,** but not *vice versa.* Mental events such as suddenly noticing something are not regarded as mental acts. But how precisely to distinguish between mental acts and other mental events has been an intensively debated problem. Other philosophers such as **Russell** claim that it is unnecessary to establish a special category of mental acts.

> "To begin with, then, I see, I hear, I smell, I taste, etc. . . . And because, in a wide sense, they are all of them things which I do, I propose to call them all 'mental acts'. By calling them 'acts' I do not wish to imply that I am always particularly active when I do them." **G. Moore, "The Subjectivity of Psychology," in Vesey (ed.),** *Body and Mind*

mental causation

PHILOSOPHY OF MIND A term for the phenomenon of a **mental event** causing another **event,** whether physical or mental. As **causation** involving mental phenomena, it contrasts with physical causation. It is, however, uncertain whether there can be an intelligible notion of non-physical causation. Some believe that mental causation can be understood in purely mental terms. Some argue that mental events have both physical and mental **properties** and that mental properties are not **epiphenomenal** and have a significant causal role. A satisfactory explanation of **behavior** or mental events is implausible without referring to the mental properties of other mental events. Such a claim is sometimes called mental indispensability. **Davidson's anomalous monism** claims that there are no psychophysical laws. Following this line, many philosophers believe that mental events, if they can produce any physical effects, must be themselves physical and that mental causation is due to the physical properties of mental events. They claim that mental causation is intelligible only when mental events or states are related

to physical phenomena and to physical causality by being determined by physical causality or **supervenient** upon it.

> "The mental causation must be realized or constituted by the physical process." **Child,** *Causality, Interpretation and the Mind*

mental event

PHILOSOPHY OF MIND An event that has mental **properties,** such as thinking, feeling, or willing. Either mental events exist independently or they have more fundamental physical properties. If a mental event causes some effect, must this **causation** be explained in terms of its physical properties, or is it because its mental properties themselves are causally potent? This question is related to the problem of the relationship between mental events and physical events, which is one of the central issues in the current debate of philosophy of mind. **Davidson's anomalous monism** claims that while every mental event is a physical event, there are no strict psychophysical laws that connect the mental and physical realms.

> "Mental events (by which I mean events described in the mental vocabulary, whatever exactly that may be) are like many other sorts of events, and like material objects, in that we give their locations with no more accuracy than easy individuation (within the relevant vocabulary) demands." **Davidson,** *Essays on Actions and Events*

mental indispensability, see mental causation

mental phenomenon

PHILOSOPHY OF MIND **Brentano's** term, also called a psychical phenomenon, in contrast to a physical phenomenon. He argued that mental phenomena are characterized by their **reference** to something as an **object,** but that their objects, using the **scholastic** term, have **intentional inexistence** and need not **exist.** Mental phenomena have immanent contents of **consciousness** and intentional objects, in contrast to physical phenomena, which contain external objects that transcend the mind. Brentano's distinction between mental and physical phenomena in terms of **intentionality** has had great influence. He classified mental phenomena into presentation (I see, I hear), **judgment** (I affirm, I reject), and emotional acts (I feel, I wish). Mental phenomena are not merely static, but are characteristically active and directed upon some object. Mental phenomena are the objects of inner **perception** and the subject-matter of psychology. The terms "mental phenomenon" and "intentional inexistence" have been closely examined by R. **Chisholm** and have been the subject of vigorous debate.

"Every mental phenomenon is characterized by what the Scholastics of the Middle Ages called the intentional (or mental) inexistence of an object and what we might call, though not wholly unambiguously, reference to a content, direction toward an object (which is not to be understood here as meaning a thing), or immanent objectivity." **Brentano,** *Psychology from an Empirical Standpoint*

mental representation

EPISTEMOLOGY, PHILOSOPHY OF MIND, PHILOSOPHY OF LANGUAGE Representation in the mind. It is commonly believed that to think about something is to have that thing represented in one's mind. Etymologically, "meaning" is associated with the "mind." To mean something is to have it in one's mind. It is claimed that to think about the White House is to have an **image** of the White House in one's mind. A word or a **concept** is associated with a certain image in the mind of the language user. If two concepts are synonymous, they are associated with the same mental representation. But the problem of clarifying the nature of mental representation is a vexed issue. Some believe that to represent the world is to have a model of it in your mind; some believe that a representation is an image that represents things in virtue of **resembling** them; some suggest that a mental representation is a language-like symbol that does not have to be similar to what is symbolized; and still others think that mental representation is simply a neurophysiological state. According to **Fodor**, mental representations are linguistic expressions within the **language of thought**, and mental representations have **syntactic** and **semantic** properties comparable to those of a natural or an artificial language. There are various types of representation. Which kind counts precisely as a mental representation? Does mental representation constitute the **content** of thought? Does mental representation serve merely

as an image or have a **causal** role in the brain? How can representations get to be about things in the world? These and other problems have been matters of dispute.

"The central question about mental representation is this: what is it for a mental state to have a semantic property? Equivalently what makes a state (or an object) in a cognitive system a representation?" **Cummins,** *Meaning and Mental Representation*

mental state

PHILOSOPHY OF MIND Mental phenomena such as **beliefs, desires, intentions,** and **sensations**. The nature of these phenomena has been a central question in the philosophy of mind. Different theories of mind are distinguished largely according to their respective answers to this problem. According to **Cartesian dualism,** mental states are inner, non-material states of a mental **substance**. According to **Hume,** the **self** or mind is a succession of mental states. According to **behaviorism,** mental states consist simply in dispositions to behave in various ways. According to the **identity theory,** mental states are identical with states of the brain. According to **functionalism,** mental states are defined in terms of their causal relations to input stimuli, other mental states, and external behavior. All mental events are mental states, but not all mental states are mental events.

"Let us describe a mental state as a state which can be directly observed only through introspection and cannot be directly observed by more than one individual, viz. the individual who is in that mental state." **Pap,** *Elements of Analytic Philosophy*

mentalese, another term for language of thought

mentalism

METAPHYSICS Synonymous with **idealism** and **panpsychism**. The position that physical or bodily things can be explained in terms of mental things, and that the latter exist in a real sense. On this view, everything is mental in character. Mentalism is thus opposed to the materialist claim that all mental things are explained in terms of physical things and that the latter exist in a real sense. **Berkeley** and other mentalists claim that physical objects are nothing but **sensations** or **perceptions**. **Leibniz** said that the **monads** that compose the world are ultimately spiritual. **Hegel** and other **absolute idealists** consider the whole material world to be mental in nature. These philosophers hold different versions of mentalism.

> "Some theories of mind and body try to reduce body to mind or some property of mind. Such theories may be called mentalist theories." **D. Armstrong,** *A Materialist Theory of Mind*

mentalistic linguistics

PHILOSOPHY OF LANGUAGE **Chomsky**'s characterization for his own approach to linguistics. On the basis of the distinction between **competence and performance**, he claims that linguistics should study competence, that is, the speaker's internalized transformational-generative rules of language. **Introspection** is one excellent source of data for the study of language. Linguistics is a branch of cognitive psychology that deals with structure and process in human **minds** and can be connected with observed **behavior** only in an indirect way. Such a mentalistic approach is opposed to behaviorist approaches, which reject introspection, **consciousness**, and other mentalistic terms for the purpose of explaining behavior. The contrast between mentalism and behaviorism in the philosophy of language is essentially a contrast between **rationalism** and **empiricism**.

> "Mentalistic linguistics is simply theoretical linguistics that uses performance as data (along with other data, for example the data provided by introspection) for the determination of competence, the latter being taken as the primary object of its investigation." **Chomsky,** *Aspects of the Theory of Syntax*

mentality

PHILOSOPHY OF MIND The possession of a **mind**. The features that enable a human being to think, feel, imagine, and act. Different philosophies have different explanations of mentality. According to **Cartesian dualism**, mentality consists of inner states independent of physical states. According to some versions of **physicalism**, all facts about mentality can be reduced to facts about the states of central nervous systems. Mentality in this sense becomes the subject-matter of brain science. Non-reductive physicalism identifies mental states with brain states, but retains the mental for discussion at an autonomous level of **theory**. Mentality can also refer to what is going on in an individual's mind that makes him a distinct **person**. In this broad sense, mentality is synonymous with style of thought or way of thinking and is formed partly as a result of one's social and cultural setting.

> "[H]is own mentality . . . is his own assumptions, values, expectations, and perceptions of what is possible." **Tiles and Tiles,** *An Introduction to Historical Epistemology*

mercy

ETHICS Also called nonmaleficence, an ethical demand that one should do one's best to relieve the **pain** or suffering of another person where this is possible and to the extent that the relief is in the suffering person's interest. In contemporary ethics, this moral demand is closely linked with the issue of **euthanasia** or mercy killing, that is, whether it is morally justified to end the life of a terminally ill and gravely suffering patient who is of sound mind and wants to die. Mercy is a major reason for supporting the permissibility of voluntary euthanasia, but some consider such deaths as murder. There are also problems about patients who make choices under the influence of others, about the presentation of cases of involuntary euthanasia as voluntary cases, and about euthanasia for those who are not of sound mind or who cannot express a view. In all of these cases, considerations of mercy might support euthanasia, but respect for life and free **consent** might oppose it.

> "This principle of mercy establishes two component duties: 1. the duty not to cause further pain or suffering, and 2. the duty to act to end pain or suffering already occurring." **Battin,** *The Least Worst Death*

mercy killing, another term for euthanasia

mereological essentialism

METAPHYSICS A theory developed by Roderick **Chisholm**, which claims that if anything is ever a part of a whole, then it is a part of that whole as long as the whole exists. The whole possesses that part in every **possible world** in which the whole exists. The theory is **mereological** because it deals with the relationship between wholes and parts, and it is **essentialist** because it holds that the parts of an object are essential to that object. At first glance, this claim conflicts with common sense, for we usually deny that having a part is essential for an ordinary thing to persist. But Chisholm argues that we must distinguish between a proper part in a strict philosophical sense and an improper part in a looser ordinary sense. The loss of a proper part will cause an object to change its **identity**, whilst the identity of an object will be maintained with the loss of an improper part. Chisholm's theory deals with parts which a whole has **necessarily** and which are essential to that whole. This theory is useful in dealing with puzzles such as that of the ship of **Theseus'** ship, in which we ask whether an object maintains its identity after each of its parts is successively replaced.

"The principle of mereological essentialism that I have advocated may be put this way: For every X and Y, if X is ever part of Y, then Y is necessarily such that X is part of Y at any time that Y exists." **Chisholm**, *Person and Object*

mereology

LOGIC, METAPHYSICS, PHILOSOPHY OF MATHEMATICS [from Greek *meros*, part] The formal theory of logical relationships between wholes and parts, derived from **Aristotle** and developed in the twentieth century by figures such as **Lesniewski**, **Tarski**, and Nelson **Goodman**. It claims that any individual whole is a mereological sum, that is, the least inclusive thing that includes all of its parts. It is composed of these parts and of nothing else. Consequently, two individuals, X and Y, if identical, must have the same proper parts. David **Lewis** claims that a world is the mereological sum of all the **possible** individuals that are parts of it. Mereology was intended to provide an alternative foundation of mathematics, but its claims are controversial. Many counterexamples exist to its theorems, especially with regard to organic wholes. Nevertheless, the applications of this important formalism are still being explored. Because mereology applies to **individuals**, it is called the **calculus** of individuals, in contrast to **set theory**, which is called the calculus of **classes**.

"Mereology is the theory of the relation of parts to wholes, and kindred notions. One of these kindred relations is that of a mereological fusion, or sum: the whole composed of some given parts." **D. Lewis**, *Parts of Classes*

merit

ETHICS, POLITICAL PHILOSOPHY Excellence or worth which deserves reward. We can distinguish between moral merits, such as virtues, and non-moral merits, such as skills and abilities. All merits are qualities that are or should be respected and admired in society. Whether or not a quality is a merit is determined in relation to the social purpose it serves. In contrast to **egalitarianism** and **utilitarianism**, a **meritocratic** political philosophy would distribute benefits and responsibilities in proportion to the merit of those who receive them, and a society would be just if it conformed to this distribution. Since merit is not allotted equally, distribution according to merit demands that unlike cases should be treated unequally. On this view, those possessing special merit deserve special and discriminatory treatment. Merit is closely related to the idea of **desert**, **equity**, **fairness**, and **justice**. A distribution based on merit is not an equal one, but it aims to promote fairness and justice. A difficulty facing this position is the ease with which power, influence, and the pretence of merit can displace real merit as a basis for enhanced reward.

"I distinguish desert, which is concerned with what an agent has done, from merit, which is concerned with what he is." **Lucas**, *Responsibility*

meritocracy

POLITICAL PHILOSOPHY A society in which all institutional positions are filled according to selection procedures based on relevant qualifications, skills, abilities, achievements, and promise. It judges and promotes people on the grounds of the quality of their existing service. Meritocracy is a type of **aristocracy**, for it creates an elite group of people with special powers, but it is also **democratic**, for it is based on the equality of opportunities, according to which the distribution of opportunities is in accordance with capacities and achievements. However, meritocracy might lead to many types of inequalities, and it is controversial whether talent is a suitable fundamental ground for justifying these inequalities. In contrast to traditional inegalitarian meritocracy, two new forms of meritocracies have recently been proposed. In egalitarian meritocracy, inequalities would not be based on the social functions of the job but on the **needs** or other **deserts** of the job-holders. In maximin meritocracy, inequalities would be allowed, but under certain conditions that are favorable to those whose abilities are unlikely to gain high-reward jobs. Rawls raises the question of whether the talents that are used in a meritocracy as a basis of assigning positions should be seen as straightforwardly belonging to the individual in a just society.

"Meritocracy: a social order built around a particular notion of merit." **Daniels,** *Justice and Justification*

Merleau-Ponty, Maurice (1908–61)

French phenomenological philosopher, born in Rochefort-sur-Mer. Merleau-Ponty rejected the Cartesian dualism of body and soul. The role of the body in the human subject's experiential relationship with the world is a central theme of his philosophy. He rejected both realist and subjectivist accounts of consciousness. He held that the objects of experience are neither wholly given to us in sense-perception nor wholly constructed by us, but are by nature ambiguous. He stressed the primacy of perception and claimed that all perspectives are local. His most important book is *The Phenomenology of Perception* (1945). Other works include *The Structure of Behaviour* (1942), *Sense and Nonsense* (1948), and *The Visible and the Invisible* (1964).

meshing problem

POLITICAL PHILOSOPHY According to classical **utilitarianism**, we should choose a society containing the maximum total good over societies containing less good. We also believe that we should choose a society with the most nearly equal distribution of good over other societies in which the good is distributed more unequally. The ideal, of course, is to combine the greatest possible total good with the most nearly equal distribution. But the world is not perfect, and we cannot necessarily realize this ideal. The meshing problem asks how we can mesh or harmonize the desire to maximize good and the desire to distribute good relatively equally. If one

society possesses more good but distributes it less equally and another society possesses less good but distributes it more equally, which one should we choose? How can we assess the **merits** of each society, and how can we strike a balance between them? The meshing problem indicates that the **principle of utility** has the severe limitation of ignoring distributive **justice**.

"This 'meshing problem' of balancing the total amount of good at issue in a given putative distribution against the fairness of the distribution in cases where these two desiderata cut against one another is one which utilitarians (and non-utilitarians, for that matter) have never resolved satisfactorily." **Rescher,** *Distributive Justice*

meta-epistemology

EPISTEMOLOGY Meta-epistemology is the epistemology of epistemology. Normal epistemology can be called "substantive epistemology" and concerns relations between **knowledge** and **belief**, between knowledge and **truth**, and between knowledge and **justification**, and deals with inquires about the origin of knowledge, while meta-epistemology compares and evaluates all kinds of epistemology. It analyzes basic epistemic concepts, determining their limits and the conditions of their application.

"Meta-epistemology is concerned with the basic concepts we employ in epistemology, concepts of knowledge, truth, belief, justification, rationality, and so on, and with the methods, procedures, and criteria to be employed in determining how to apply these concepts." **Alston,** *Epistemic Justification*

meta-ethics

ETHICS Meta-ethics is usually said to deal with ethics itself, in contrast to **normative** ethics, which deals with substantive ethical questions. The major components of meta-ethics include the study of the nature of ethics, the conceptual analysis of key moral terms, and inquiry into the method for answering moral questions. The purpose of the study of the nature of ethics is to discuss what ethics is and does and to discuss the **objectivity** and validity of ethical claims themselves. The purpose of **conceptual analysis** is to state the necessary and sufficient conditions of the application of major moral concepts.

The purpose of the inquiry into method is to specify the ways to answer moral questions from a moral point of view. Meta-ethics is, then, a logical and epistemological inquiry concerning the nature of normative ethical statements.

The distinction between meta-ethics and normative ethics appeared with the development of **linguistic philosophy** in the twentieth century and was deeply influenced by **Moore**'s distinction between saying what goodness is and saying what things are good. **Ayer** and **Stevenson** explicitly drew upon this distinction. Many analytical philosophers believed that meta-ethics should be the main concern of ethics, and this claim became one of the main characteristics of the development of ethics in English-speaking countries in the twentieth century. However, this distinction itself has become more and more problematic. Recent moral philosophers view meta-ethical judgments and normative judgments as interdependent and many judgments are hard to classify according to this distinction.

> "Twenty or thirty years ago, it was standard practice to distinguish 'ethical' from 'meta-ethical' theories. The first made substantive claims about what one should do, how one should live, what was worthwhile, and so on. The second concerned itself with the status of those claims: whether they could be knowledge, how they could be validated, whether they were (and in what sense) objective, and so on." **B. Williams,** *Ethics and the Limits of Philosophy*

metalanguage

PHILOSOPHY OF LANGUAGE, LOGIC **Tarski** drew a distinction between **object language** and metalanguage. The object language is that with which we talk about extra-linguistic things and objects (the language in which we speak), while the metalanguage is the language in which we talk about the object language (the language about which we speak). An example of an object language statement is "New York is a large city" and an example of a metalanguage statement is "'That New York is a large city' is true." Tarski argued that the definition of **truth** must be relative to a language, for the one and the same **sentence** may be true in one language but false in another. The object language is the language for which truth is defined, and the meta-

language is the language in which we construct the definition of truth in the object language. Truth is in this way viewed as a semantic property of object language sentences and a **predicate** of a metalanguage applicable to sentences of its object language. A metalanguage contains either the object sentence itself or a translation of it. The appeal to metalanguage can avoid the danger of **semantic paradoxes**, for in a metalanguage the object sentences are not used but only mentioned and discussed. This distinction is significant for formal **semantics**.

> "The names of the expressions of the first language, and of the relations between them, belong to the second language, called metalanguage." **Tarski,** *Logic, Semantics, Metamathematics*

metalogic

LOGIC Motivated by **Hilbert**'s distinction in mathematics between meaningful **inference** and formalized **calculus**, metalogic takes the systems of formal logic as its subject-matter. It is therefore the theory of logic. It is the result of the combination of **Boole**'s **formalism** and **Frege**'s theory of proof. The first system of metalogic was developed by **Tarski**. It differs from formal logic in that it is not concerned with meaningful inference, but only with purely formal questions arising from formal logical systems, that is, formal properties of formal logic systems such as **consistency**; consequence, **completeness**, **decision procedure**, **deduction**, categoricalness, and **satisfaction**. It differs from the philosophy of logic because it deals with the conditions under which various formal theories possess these properties, rather than with the philosophical issues raised by logic systems.

> "Metalogic is the study of formal properties of formal logical systems." **Haack,** *Philosophy of Logics*

metaphilosophy

PHILOSOPHICAL METHOD A term introduced by Lazerowitz for the philosophical discussion of philosophy itself, including, for example, its nature, method, goals, autonomy, and objectivity. Hence it is second-order philosophy. According to the first-order branch of philosophy under discussion, such as metaphysics, epistemology, or ethics, we can also divide metaphilosophy into metametaphysics (meta-ontology), **meta-epistemology**, and **meta-ethics**. The division between first-order and second-order studies has lost some of its popularity, and philosophers now find it more difficult to draw a sharp distinction between metaphilosophy and philosophy. For those who believe that philosophy comes to an end, metaphilosophy refers to the theoretical activities after the death of philosophy.

> "We must recognize the distinction between the philosophic and meta-philosophic perspectives: there is a difference between the one who develops and defends a philosophical position and the one who examines that position critically." **Yolton,** *Metaphysical Analysis*

metaphor

PHILOSOPHY OF LANGUAGE, AESTHETICS, CONTEMPORARY EUROPEAN PHILOSOPHY [from Greek *metaphora*, a transfer, a change] A figure of speech or a verbal composition in which an expression is used to **denote** a thing to which its literal sense does not apply. For example, "A baby is a flower" is a metaphor because "flower," taken literally, does not describe a "baby." If there were only literal meaning, all metaphors would be false. The best metaphors evoke a complex and productive mental response through indicating certain likenesses between what an expression literally denotes and the thing it metaphorically describes. The power of metaphors can also involve dissimilarities as well as likenesses. Starting from **Aristotle**, the nature and scope of metaphor has been of interest to philosophers. This interest has intensified in contemporary philosophy of mind and philosophy of language. Major issues concerning metaphor include: can a metaphor itself be literally paraphrased? How clear-cut is the distinction between literal meaning and metaphorical meaning? Traditionally metaphor is regarded as a decoration of speech that does not contribute to the cognitive meaning of **discourse**. Others argue that metaphor contributes indispensably to the cognitive meaning of discourse, but there is no agreement over the kind of contribution it makes. **Davidson** claims that what is crucial to a metaphor is not a matter of meaning, but of use. In his view, a metaphor lacks meaning peculiar to itself other than literal meaning. But **Nietzsche** claimed that the nature of language itself is metaphorical, for it works by means of transference from one kind of reality to another. This view has been widely adopted by continental philosophers, who regard metaphor not merely as a rhetorical device or an aspect of the expressive function of language, but as one of the essential conditions of speech. They claim that as the way in which many kinds of discourse are structured, metaphor powerfully influences how we conceive things.

> "The study of metaphor is becoming important as it is being realised that language does not simply reflect but helps to constitute it." **Sarup,** *An Introductory Guide to Post-Structuralism and Post-Modernism*

metaphysica generalis

METAPHYSICS General metaphysics, in contrast to *metaphysica specialis*, special or particular metaphysics. The distinction can be traced back to **Aristotle**'s metaphysics. Aristotle himself referred to metaphysics as **first philosophy** or *sophia* (wisdom), that is, the science of ultimate **causes** and **principles**. Sometimes he said that metaphysics is the science of **being** *qua* **being** and that such an enquiry provides a starting-point for all other sciences. Elsewhere he held that metaphysics is concerned with a special kind of being that is beyond the sensible substances, namely **God**, and that it is therefore theology. The medieval philosophers called these two accounts of metaphysics respectively *metaphysica generalis* and *metaphysica specialis*. Aristotle believed that these two accounts of metaphysics are reconcilable, but did not offer any convincing argument for that conclusion. The problem of dealing with these two accounts has given rise to major debate in Aristotelian scholarship and greatly affects our understanding of his metaphysics. The distinction was retained in the later development of metaphysics, but the meaning varied. In the seventeenth and eighteenth centuries, general metaphysics was identified with **ontology**, which was concerned with general concepts, while special metaphysics was identified with **natural theology**. For Wolff, general metaphysics concerned *ens qua ens* (being *qua* being), and special metaphysics concerned **substance** and its **attributes**. Brentano distinguished between broad ontology and narrow ontology. The former amounts to general metaphysics, discussing the general nature of things, and the latter amounts to special metaphysics, with theology as its subject-matter.

> "What is important . . . is the conception of an inquiry into being in general – general ontology, or what medieval philosophers called metaphysica generalis, as opposed to metaphysica specialis." **Hamlyn,** *Metaphysics*

metaphysica specialis, see *metaphysica generalis*

metaphysical deduction

METAPHYSICS, EPISTEMOLOGY, LOGIC, PHILOSOPHY OF MIND, PHILOSOPHY OF LANGUAGE Part of the **transcendental analytic** in **Kant**'s *Critique of Pure Reason*, although its official title is "the clue to the discovery of all pure concepts of the understanding." The metaphysical deduction is concerned with uncovering the origin of the **categories** and identifying them systematically, in contrast to the **transcendental deduction**, which is concerned with establishing the legitimacy of these categories. **Knowledge** must be derived from what is given in sensible **intuition** and the **judgments** we make on that basis. Taken together, these two determinations indicate that our intuition of things must conform to the logical functions of judgment. The categories are – or stem from – these logical functions of judgment. Kant therefore derived twelve categories or pure concepts of the **understanding** from what he regarded as the complete classification of the kinds of judgments. Only by applying one of these categories to **experience** can we make a judgment. This derivation is his metaphysical deduction of the categories. It shows that there is a fundamental structure of **thought** in judgment that gives unity to the **synthesis** of the **manifold** of intuition. Critics might accept the relation of categories to the logical functions of judgment, but seek to revise his classification of kinds of judgment in line with modern developments of logic.

> "In the metaphysical deduction the a priori origin of the categories has been proved through their complete agreement with the general logical functions of thought." **Kant,** *Critique of Pure Reason*

metaphysical entity

METAPHYSICS, EPISTEMOLOGY Also called inferred entities. The term that **Russell** uses to refer to such items as **material objects**, **space**, and **time**, which are initially postulated as the ultimate constituents of reality, but which cannot be directly experienced and are instead known by inference. He also calls them unknown entities or inferred entities. In Russell's logical atomism, these entities can be eliminated and replaced by **logical constructions**, and we therefore need not include them among the real constituents of the world. In contrast, the class of entities which comprise the logical constructions are called known entities.

> "By metaphysical entities I mean those things which are supposed to be part of the ultimate constituents of the world, but not to be the kind of thing that is ever empirically given." **Russell,** *Collected Papers of Bertrand Russell*

metaphysical exposition

METAPHYSICS Part of the **transcendental aesthetic** in **Kant**'s *Critique of Pure Reason*. The metaphysical exposition of the concept of **space** contains four arguments: (1) "space is not an empirical concept which has been derived from outer experiences"; (2) "space is a necessary *a priori* representation, which underlies all outer intuitions"; (3) "space is not a discursive . . . but a pure intuition"; and (4) "space is represented as an infinite given magnitude." The first two claim that space is *a priori*, and the latter two claim that space is an **intuition**. The metaphysical exposition of the concept of **time** makes similar points about time.

> "The exposition is metaphysical when it contains that which exhibits the concept as given a priori." **Kant,** *Critique of Pure Reason*

metaphysical subject

METAPHYSICS, PHILOSOPHY OF MIND The **Cartesian** self and related versions of the "philosophical 'I'," classically a separate, **simple** thinking **substance**, tracing a **subjective** path through the world and capable of surviving bodily death. **Hume**'s discussion of **personal identity** and **Kant**'s rejection of the main aspects of the rational theory of the **soul** do much to undermine such positions. Kant's **transcendental unity of apperception**, the "**I think**" which accompanies all of my **representations**, provides more austere grounds for an account of the metaphysical subject. Contemporary philosophers have also raised questions about the metaphysical self. **Heidegger**'s *Dasein* is an attempt to replace the traditional notion of the self as part of his rejection of metaphysics. **Wittgenstein**, like Kant, rejects the view that the metaphysical subject is one **object** among others in the world and links his discussion of the self to his assessment of **solipsism** and the claim that the world is my world.

> "The philosophical I is not the human being, not the human body or the human soul with the psychological properties, but the metaphysical subject, the boundary (not a part) of the world."
> **Wittgenstein**, *Notebooks, 1914–1916*

metaphysics

METAPHYSICS A term originally used as the title of a compilation of **Aristotle**'s writings, according to tradition by Andronicus of Rhodes in the first century AD. The title *Ta meta ta phusika* was used because the compilation came after (*meta*) the physical writings in the classification of Aristotle's works. This position, however, had a philosophical basis in its subject-matter, because Aristotle intended it to be an inquiry into objects that are prior to or higher than physical objects, giving reasons for what we instinctively believe. Hence this title can be applied to a whole branch of philosophy. Metaphysics now generally refers to the study of the most basic items or features of reality (**ontology**) or to the study of the most basic **concepts** used in an account of reality. On some accounts, metaphysics deals primarily with non-sensible entities or with things outside the scope of **scientific method**, but other metaphysical views reject these claims.

Aristotle himself referred to this kind of investigation as **first philosophy** or *sophia* (wisdom), that is, the science of ultimate **causes** and **principles**. He sometimes said that it is the science of **being qua being**, or what it is simply to be. Sometimes, he identified it with **theology** because it is concerned with a special kind of being, namely God, which is beyond the sensible **substances**. Medieval philosophers called these aspects of metaphysics respectively *metaphysica generalis* (general metaphysics) and *metaphysica specialis* (special or particular metaphysics).

In the rationalist tradition, metaphysics was seen to be an inquiry conducted by pure **reason** into the nature of an underlying reality that is beyond **perception**, although major metaphysicians, such as **Plato, Descartes, Spinoza, Leibniz**, and **Hegel**, disagreed sharply over what the underlying reality might be. Christian **Wolff** divided metaphysics into four parts: ontology (a general theory of being or existence), rational theory (about God), rational psychology (about the soul), and rational cosmology (about the world).

Kant labeled all attempts to use pure reason to account for a **transcendent** reality beyond human **understanding** as speculative metaphysics. Kant thought that metaphysics is a necessary propensity of the human mind toward total explanation and that its transcendent subject-matter (**God, Freedom of the Will**, and **Immortality**) can be the grounds for the right way to act (metaphysics of morals), even though speculative metaphysics cannot yield knowledge. Kant's critical philosophy is a metaphysics in another sense, which deals with the conditions for the possibility of experience and the presuppositions of science.

Carnap and other **logical positivists** defined metaphysics as the field of alleged knowledge of the **essence** of things that transcends the realm of empirical sciences, and believed that this field should be eliminated as **nonsensical**. On the other hand, they considered that their own work was restricted to logic and experience and should be called scientific philosophy.

For different motives, **Heidegger** and **Derrida** also sought to exclude metaphysics from their thought, although they did not satisfy themselves that they succeeded.

Strawson drew a famous distinction between revisionary metaphysics and descriptive metaphysics. He called speculative metaphysicians revisionary, in contrast to descriptive metaphysics, which is concerned with the conceptual scheme according to which we think and talk about the world. Accordingly, logical positivism and other anti-metaphysical philosophies are themselves a kind of metaphysics insofar as they deal with the conceptual structure of human language and thought.

In a special use associated with **Marxism**, metaphysics is considered to be a partial, stationary, and isolated way of thinking opposed to Hegelian **dialectics**.

> "Metaphysics is for us the name of a science, and has been for many centuries, because for many centuries it has been found necessary, and still is found necessary, to think in a systematic or

orderly fashion about the subjects that Aristotle discussed in the group of treatises collectively known by that science." **Collingwood,** *An Essay on Metaphysics*

metaphysics (Kant)

METAPHYSICS In a positive sense, metaphysics for **Kant** is the system of knowledge arising out of pure **reason**, that is, knowledge which is attained *a priori* and involves only *a priori* **concepts**. It is divided into a speculative part, the metaphysics of nature, and a practical part, the metaphysics of morals. In a strict sense, metaphysics is confined to the metaphysics of nature, but in a wider sense, metaphysics also includes the metaphysics of morals and criticism, that is, the investigation of the faculty of **reason** in respect of all its pure *a priori* knowledge, and is propaedeutic. Metaphysics in this wide sense is the same as the philosophy of pure reason.

The metaphysics of nature discusses the principles of pure reason that are derived from mere **concepts** and employed in the theoretical knowledge of all things. It is further divided into **transcendental philosophy**, which deals with **understanding** and reason without taking into account the objects given, and the physiology of pure reason, that is, the rational physiology of objects that can be given in **experience**. The latter is divided into transcendent and immanent parts. The metaphysics of morals, also called morals proper, deals with the *a priori* principles of morality, that is, the principles that determine and make necessary all of our **actions**.

In both the metaphysics of nature and the metaphysics of morals, there is a **transcendental analytic**, which concerns the legitimate application of their *a priori* principles within the limits of experience, and a **transcendental dialectic**, which exposes the **fallacies** in traditional metaphysics arising when pure reason applies these principles to **things in themselves** beyond experience. The *Critique of Pure Reason* reveals in detail the **illusions** or errors of traditional metaphysics, especially of rational cosmology, rational psychology, and rational theology. The analytic and dialectic represent both sides of Kant's attitude toward metaphysics. He scorns the claim of traditional metaphysics to be the queen of the sciences, but believes that the metaphysics of his critical philosophy can inquire into the properties of

things and show the limits of human reason. Hence, rather than being totally demolished, metaphysics needed redefinition or reconstruction.

"The title 'metaphysics' may also, however, be given to the whole of pure philosophy, inclusive of criticism, and so as comprehending the investigation of all that can ever be known a priori as well as the exposition of that which constitutes a system of the pure philosophical modes of knowledge of this type – in distinction, therefore, from all empirical and from all mathematical employment of reason." **Kant,** *Critique of Pure Reason*

metaphysics of difference, see presence

metaphysics of morals, see metaphysics (Kant)

metaphysics of nature, see metaphysics (Kant)

metaphysics of presence, see presence

metempsychosis, see transmigration of the soul; reincarnation

methexis, Greek term for participation

method

PHILOSOPHICAL METHOD A combination of rules, assumptions, procedures, and examples determining the scope and limits of a subject and establishing acceptable ways of working within those limits to achieve **truth**. The question of philosophical method is itself a matter for philosophy and constitutes a major example of the **reflective** nature of the subject. Philosophers disagree about the appropriate philosophical method. The identifying mark of a philosophical school or movement lies mainly in the method it adopts. Ancient philosophy was developed according to various interpretations of **dialectic method**, and modern philosophy was initiated by **Descartes's method** of doubt. **Analytic philosophy** is characterized by linguistic method, while nonanalytic European philosophy is characterized by **phenomenological**, historical, and textual methods. Historically, philosophers have tried to model their work on the methods of successful sciences, such as mathematics, physics, biology, psychology, and computer science, but the appropriate relationship between philosophical and **scientific method** is a matter of dispute. Some philosophers draw methodological implications from the claim that philosophy is a part of science or ancillary to science, while others derive their account of philosophical method from the claim that philosophy is prior to science and other disciplines and presupposed by them.

"By a 'method' I mean reliable rules which are easy to apply, and such that if one follows them exactly, one will never take what is false to be true or fruitlessly expend one's mental efforts, but will gradually and constantly increase one's knowledge till one arrives at a true understanding of everything within one's capacity." **Descartes**, *Philosophical Writings*

method of agreement

LOGIC, PHILOSOPHY OF SCIENCE The first of **Mill's** five inductive **canons**. Take two instances, A and B, of a given phenomenon. If we observe that the possible **causes** of A include c, d, and e, and the possible causes for B include f, g, and e, we eliminate c and d, which are peculiar to A, and f and g, which are peculiar to B. There remains a common factor e for both A and B, and we may conclude that e is the cause or part of the cause of the phenomenon. The principle underlying this method is that whatever can be excluded without doing injustice to the phenomenon has no causation with it. What we uncover through this method is a **sufficient condition** for the phenomenon under investigation.

"As this method proceeds by comparing different instances to ascertain in what they agree, I have termed it the method of agreement." *The Collected Works of John Stuart Mill*, **vol. VII**

method of concomitant variations

LOGIC, PHILOSOPHY OF SCIENCE The fifth of **Mill's** five inductive **canons** states that if it is the case that when the phenomenon P changes, another phenomenon Q changes concomitantly, this sort of functional dependence between these two phenomena suggests that P must be a **cause** of Q, or Q of P, or both of them are the **effect** of the same cause. However, we need further methods to determine the exact relationship between P and Q.

"Method of concomitant variations . . . is regulated by the following canon: whatever phenomenon varies in any manner whenever another phenomenon varies in some particular manner, is either a cause or an effect of that phenomenon, or is connected with it through some fact of causation." *The Collected Works of John Stuart Mill*, **vol. VII**

method of difference

LOGIC, PHILOSOPHY OF SCIENCE The second of **Mill's** five **canons** or inductive methods. Suppose a phenomenon P happens in circumstances A, but not in the circumstances B. A contains conditions c, d, e, and f, and B contains conditions c, d, and e. Since A and B differ only in condition f, and P occurs in A, but not B, we may conclude that f is the **cause** of the phenomenon P. The principle underlying this method is that whatever cannot be excluded without preventing the phenomenon is the cause of the phenomenon. What we uncover through the method of difference is a **necessary condition** for a phenomenon.

"The canon which is the regulating principle of the method of difference may be expressed as follows: If an instance in which the phenomenon under investigation occurs, and an instance in which it does not occur, have every circumstance in common save one, that one occurring only in the former; the circumstance in which alone the two instances differ is the effect, or the cause or an indispensable part of the cause, of the phenomenon." *The Collected Works of John Stuart Mill*, **vol. VII**

method of elimination, another expression for induction by elimination

method of residues

LOGIC, PHILOSOPHY OF SCIENCE The fourth of **Mill's** five **canons** applies to cases in which a phenomenon P can be caused by any one of the conditions e, f, or g, and we wish to determine which condition is the **cause**. We already know through previous **induction** that neither e nor f is the cause of P. Then, the remaining condition g, which is the residue, might be the **sufficient condition** of P. Such a conclusion is inferred and needs to be proved by further observations.

"The canon of the method of residues is as follows: subtract from any phenomenon such part as is known by previous induction to be the effect of certain antecedents, and the residue of the phenomenon is the effect of the remaining antecedent." *The Collected Works of John Stuart Mill, vol. VII*

methodological collectivism

PHILOSOPHY OF SOCIAL SCIENCE Also called methodological holism, a collective or **holistic** approach to social phenomena. In contrast to the assertion of **methodological individualism** that all **explanations** of social phenomena must be reduced to facts about **individuals**, methodological collectivism holds that collective phenomena are explanatorily prior to facts about individuals. Social wholes are much better known and more immediately accessible than the individuals that constitute them. Whilst we can learn much from the study of aspects of individual humans and their actions, the social whole has its own sophisticated and complex **laws** that cannot be defined by appeal to the features of its component individuals. Facts about society cannot be reduced to the decisions, attitudes, and dispositions of the individuals. The social whole is a real entity and is the basis for making sense of the description of individuals, for in most of their activities individuals behave in culturally sanctioned ways. Methodological collectivism was developed by **Comte** and **Durkheim**. **Hegelians** and **Marxists** are also generally regarded as methodological collectivists.

"[M]ethodological collectivism [is the] tendency to treat 'wholes' like 'society' or the 'economy', 'capitalism' (as a given historical 'phase') or a particular 'industry' or 'class' or 'country', as definitely given objects about which we can discover laws by observing their behaviours as wholes." **Hayek, in O'Neill,** *Modes of Individualism and Collectivism*

methodological holism, another expression for methodological collectivism

methodological individualism

PHILOSOPHY OF SOCIAL SCIENCE A kind of **reductionism** which believes that a social whole or structure is merely a **logical construction** out of its individual components or parts, and hence that statements about the social whole can be explained in terms of statements about the features or properties of the individuals. An explanation is sound only if it is couched wholly in terms of facts about **individuals**. No explanations that appeal to social structures, institutional factors, and so on are legitimate. The position can be traced back to **Hobbes**, who claimed that it is necessary to understand the constitutive parts out of which a compound is built before we can properly understand the compound itself. This methodology was further maintained by J. S. **Mill**, Max **Weber**, and Karl **Popper**. All of them held that the basic elements in the explanation of historical and social progress are individual human beings. The beliefs, dispositions, and situations of the individuals are essential for understanding social phenomena. The theory is opposed to **methodological holism**, which holds that a social whole has its own sophisticated and complex laws that cannot be reduced to **laws** about its component individuals. On the contrary, a social whole is a real entity and is the basis for making sense of statements about its constituent individuals. The debate between methodological individualism and holism is prominent in sociology and the philosophy of social sciences.

"The doctrine of methodological individualism may therefore be viewed as implying the reducibility of the specific concepts and laws of the social sciences (in a broad sense, including group psychology, the theory of economic behaviour, and the like) to those of individual psychology, biology, chemistry, and physics." **Hempel,** *Philosophy of Natural Science*

methodological socialism, another expression for methodological collectivism

methodological solipsism

PHILOSOPHY OF MIND A term introduced by **Putnam** in 1975 in relation to his claim that there are two types of **mental state**, wide and narrow. **Narrow** mental states, such as **pain**, do not presuppose the existence of any individual other than the subject to whom that state is ascribed. **Wide** mental states, such as being jealous of somebody, carry reference to the world outside the subject. Narrow mental content is intrinsic, while wide content refers to one's physical or social environment. Methodological solipsism is the doctrine that psychology ought to be concerned exclusively with narrow mental or psychological states and that mental states should be individuated by reference to items internal to the individual whose mental states they are. We should explain the **content** of a **propositional attitude** solely by identifying it with events occurring inside the mind. There is no need to investigate the environmental causes or behavioral effects of the mental states or processes. The doctrine likens a mental process to the computing of a machine that is fully determined by its physical elements. In a sense, both **physicalism** and **functionalism** carry the restriction of methodological solipsism forward to their physical account of the mental. **Fodor** takes it as a research strategy in cognitive psychology that psychological states are individuated without respect to their **semantic** evaluation. And he contrasts this strategy with his rendering of **methodological individualism**, which tries to individuate psychological states by reference to their causal powers. But Putnam objects to the restrictive program of methodological solipsism on the grounds that it is incompatible with the existence of ordinary mental states such as belief, jealousy, and regret.

> "When traditional philosophers talked about psychological states (or 'mental states'), they made an assumption which we may call the assumption of methodological solipsism. This assumption is the assumption that no psychological state, properly so called, presupposes the existence of any individual other than the subject to whom that state is ascribed." **Putnam**, *Mind, Language and Reality*

middle knowledge

EPISTEMOLOGY, PHILOSOPHY OF RELIGION [Latin *scientia media*] A kind of knowledge that was first ascribed to **God** by the Spanish theologian Luis de Molina, with the aim of reconciling the tension between God's **foreknowledge** and human **free will**. According to this doctrine, God knows what free action a person would perform were a counterfactual condition actualized. He knows that P would freely do A were he in condition F. It is true that it is up to God to decide whether to instantiate the condition F, but before he makes his decision, the statement of what P would do in condition F has a **truth-value**. Since this kind of knowledge falls between God's knowledge of what is actual (*scientia visionis*, knowledge by intuition) and his knowledge of what is possible (*scientia simplicis intelligentia*, knowledge of simple understanding), it is called middle knowledge. This term was recently revived by A. **Plantinga** in his approach to solving the problem of **evil**. It is also called counterfactuals of freedom.

> "What they call middle knowledge is nothing but the knowledge of contingent possibles." **Leibniz**, *Philosophical Essays*

midwifery

PHILOSOPHICAL METHOD, ANCIENT GREEK PHILOSOPHY In the **Platonic** dialogues, **Socrates'** art of eliciting from others what was in their minds. In *Theaetetus*, Socrates said that his mother was a midwife, a job that was normally taken by women who were too old to conceive or bear children themselves. He then claimed that he himself virtually practiced the art of midwifery in philosophy. He did not produce philosophical wisdom himself, but could elicit ideas from others and test these ideas for correctness. The characteristic of his midwifery was to be concerned with the **soul** rather the body, and the offspring were not real children but **ideas** that could be checked for **truth** and falsehood. The description of this method fits with Socrates' practice in the earlier Platonic dialogues and has deeply influenced Western philosophy of education. Because the Greek term for midwifery is *maieutikos*, this method is also called the *maieutic* method.

> "Heaven constrains me to serve as a midwife, but has debarred me from giving birth." **Plato**, *Theaetetus*

Mill, James (1773–1836)

Scottish utilitarian philosopher and economist, born in Forfar, assistant to Jeremy Bentham and father of John Stuart Mill. Mill developed an associationist psychology and proposed radical utilitarian educational and political reforms, arguing especially for democratic rule to ensure the greatest happiness for the greatest number. His main works include *The Analysis of the Phenomena of the Human Mind* (1829).

Mill, John Stuart (1806–73)

British logician, utilitarian moral and political philosopher, and economist, born in London, educated by his father James Mill (1773–1836) who was also a philosopher, and served as an administrator in the East India Company. Mill's *Utilitarianism* (1861) developed and systematized the utilitarianism founded by Jeremy Bentham. A morally right action is the one that brings about the greatest happiness for everyone affected by the action, with happiness understood in terms of pleasure and the absence of pain. Mill altered Bentham's position by distinguishing qualities as well as quantities of different kinds of pleasures and claimed that "it is better to be a human being dissatisfied than a pig satisfied; better to be Socrates dissatisfied than a fool satisfied." *On Liberty* (1859), a classic statement of political liberalism, defined and defended individual freedom and argued that restrictions on liberty are acceptable only to avoid harm to others. His *System of Logic* (1843) made significant contributions to the theory of inductive reasoning. *The Subjection of Women* (1869), which was radical when published, has now become a classic of liberal feminism. Mill's main work as an economist was *Principles of Political Economy* (1848).

Mill's canons

LOGIC, PHILOSOPHY OF SCIENCE Also called Mill's methods, the five **inductive** laws formulated and generalized by **Mill** for discovering the causal relations among phenomena. (1) The Canon or **Method of Agreement**: "If two or more instances of the phenomenon under investigation have only one circumstance in common, the circumstance in which alone all the instances appear is the cause (or effect) of the given phenomenon." (2) The Canon or **Method of Difference**: "If an instance in which the phenomenon under investigation occurs, and an instance in which it does not occur, have every circumstance in common save one, that one occurring in the former; the circumstance in which alone the two instances differ, is the effect, or the cause, or an indispensable part of the cause, of the phenomenon." (3) The Joint Canon or Method of Agreement and Difference: "If two or more instances in which the phenomenon occurs have only one circumstance in common, while two or more instances in which it does not occur have nothing in common save the absence of that circumstance, the circumstance in which alone the two sets of instances differ, is the effect, or the cause, or an indispensable part of the cause." (4) The Canon or **Method of Concomitant Variations**: "Whatever phenomenon varies in any manner whenever another phenomenon varies in some particular manner, is either a cause or an effect of that phenomenon, or is connected with it through some fact of causation." (5) The Canon or **Method of Residues**: "Subduct from any phenomenon such part as is known by previous induction to be the effect of certain antecedents, and the residue of the phenomenon is the effect of the remaining antecedents."

"The classical exposition of the inductive method is as Mill's Canons." **Harré,** *The Philosophies of Science*

Mill's methods, another expression for Mill's canons

mimesis, Greek term for imitation

mimetic theory, another expression for imitation theory

mind

PHILOSOPHY OF MIND **Descartes** used the terms mind and **soul** interchangeably. For him, the mind is identical to **self**, **person**, the **substance** that thinks, believes, doubts, desires, and acts. For others, like **Hume**, the mind is a set of psychological states, and in this sense it is close to **consciousness** but contrasts to physical states. Different understandings of mind lead to different understandings of the **mind–body problem**. If one believes in a Cartesian mental substance, the mind–body problem involves the relationship between one's mind as a mental substance and one's body as a physical substance. If, on the other hand, one holds that minds are collections of psychological states, the problem is to explain the relation between one's psychological properties and one's physical properties. There has been renewed interest in the **Aristotelian** account of the mind that Descartes displaced. On this view, the mind or soul is the **form** of the body, although this position might have theoretical presuppositions that cannot be revived.

"The substance in which thought immediately resides is called mind. I use the term 'mind' rather than 'soul', since the word 'soul' is ambiguous and is often applied to something corporeal." **Descartes,** *The Philosophical Writings of Descartes*

mind–body problem

PHILOSOPHY OF MIND Problems concerning the relationship between **soul** and body can be traced to **Plato** and **Aristotle**, but it is **Descartes** who gave the issue a central position in modern philosophy. He believed that mind has thinking as its **essence** and is a totally distinct entity from body or extended **substance**. This view is an expression of mind–body **dualism**. How, then, can a spatial body interact with a non-spatial mind? How can mental phenomena be both irreducibly psychological and somehow dependent on a mechanistic causal base, such as the brain or nervous system? Descartes's failure to provide a satisfactory account to the problem has led to many objections to his dualism and various alternative accounts of the relationship between mind and body or between mental phenomena and physical phenomena. This has become the central topic of the philosophy of mind. Of various theories developed, the most influential ones include: **occasionalism**, **epiphenomenalism**, psychophysical parallelism, **idealism**, **monism**, **dual-aspect theory**, **panpsychism**, **behaviorism**, **identity theory** or **central-state materialism**, **functionalism**, and **anomalous monism**, all of which are discussed in separate dictionary entries. The mind–body problem continues to provoke important debate in current philosophy. Until recently, the discussion of this problem has been from the standpoint of mind, but some philosophers are taking our new scientific understanding of the workings of the brain and nervous system as a starting-point for dealing with the question. If there is an adequate solution to the mind–body problem, it could lead to an integrated science of human nature. Other philosophers argue that there cannot be an adequate solution because raising the problem is a mistake based on misleading Cartesian assumptions. Some holding this position seek to return to an **Aristotelian** account of the mind or soul as the **form** of the body.

"The question as to the relation between mental phenomenal world and physical states of the body, specifically the brain, is generally referred to as 'the mind–body problem'." **McGinn,** *The Character of Mind*

minimal theory of truth

LOGIC, PHILOSOPHY OF LANGUAGE One form of the deflationary theory of truth, proposed by Horwich. It holds that truth, like **existence**, is a logical property rather than a natural property. The truth **predicate** does not invoke **meaning**-like entities. Instead, it provides a device that enables us to formulate **propositions** that can be the objects of **belief**, desire, and so on, in cases where the proposition of primary concern is inaccessible. The simplest way of introducing this device is to introduce a new predicate of being true.

"Because it contains no more than what is expressed by uncontroversial instances of the equivalence schema '(E) It is true that p if and only if p', I shall call my theory of truth 'the minimal theory'." **Horwich,** *Truth*

minimax rule, see maximin rule

minimum sensible

EPISTEMOLOGY A term introduced by **Berkeley** for the least number of our **sense-impressions** of extension required in order to reject the idea that extension is infinitely divisible. This is similar to what **Locke** calls the sensible point, that is, the smallest particle of matter or space we can discern. Berkeley's argument is that all the objects of immediate perceptions are sense-impressions. There is nothing in a sense-impression but what is actually perceived in it, and I cannot be mistaken about my immediate sensations. The capacities of our senses are finite. Hence, sense-impressions are not infinitely divisible, but must be composed of a finite number of minimum sensibilia. There must be a minimum tangible or a minimum visible, beyond which sense cannot perceive. A minimum visible should be the same for all beings endowed with the faculty of vision. It does not include any parts and the ultimate component of any sensation is extension. Furthermore, since **to be is to be perceived**, the immediate objects of perceptions must also be composed of minimum sensibilia. Hence, the idea of the minimum sensible is closely related to Berkeley's **immaterialism**. For Berkeley, a minimum visible has no existence without the mind of the perceiver. The position encounters difficulties in meeting **Zeno's paradoxes**. It is also difficult to determine what we actually perceive.

"Upon a thorough examination it will not be found, that in any instance it is necessary to make use of or conceive infinitesimal parts of finite lines, or even quantities less than the minimum sensible; nay, it will be evident that this is never done, it being impossible." **Berkeley,** *The Principles of Human Knowledge*

minimum vocabulary

PHILOSOPHY OF LANGUAGE, EPISTEMOLOGY, METAPHYSICS For **Russell**, the words contained in a minimum vocabulary allow us to express every **proposition** in a given body of **knowledge**. No word in this vocabulary can be defined in terms of other words in it, but can only be mastered by **acquaintance** with the things. These words represent the hard core of **experience** by which our **sentences** are connected to the extra-linguistic world. For Russell, such a vocabulary will reduce the number of **entities** one's language forces us to assume and so lessen the possibility of an unwarranted metaphysics of **substance**. The minimum vocabulary required for a given subject-matter diminishes with the development of the inquiry into that subject-matter.

"I call a vocabulary a 'minimum' one if it contains no word which is capable of a verbal definition in terms of the other words of the vocabulary." **Russell,** *Human Knowledge*

miracle

PHILOSOPHY OF RELIGION [from Latin *miror*, wonder at] An extraordinary event whose occurrence does not conform with **natural law**, and which is deemed to have a supernatural cause, such as **God**. The Bible records many miracles, such as the waters of the Red Sea dividing for Moses and Jesus raising Lazarus from the dead. The miracles are used as signs of God's **omnipotence**. However, the nature and possibility of miracles have been subject to debate. It is difficult to ascertain whether events of this kind occur. Even if extraordinary events do occur, we may provide a scientific **explanation** for them. Even if science cannot explain such events, we still do not need to posit a supernatural cause for them, for the explanatory gap might be due to the limitation of our present knowledge. Since miracles are sharply in conflict with science, their possibility has been rejected by many religious thinkers.

"A miracle may be accurately defined, a transgression of a law of nature by a particular volition of the Deity, or by the interposition of some invisible agent." **Hume,** *An Enquiry Concerning Human Understanding*

Mises, Richard von (1883–1953)

German philosopher of probabilty, born in Lemberg, Professor of Mathematics at University of Strasbourg, Dresden Technical University, University of Berlin, University of Istanbul, and Harvard University. Von Mises was an applied mathematician, pioneer of aerodynamics, philosopher of science, theorist of probability and statistics, and a member of the Vienna Circle. In seeking to develop a unified theory of probability and statistics, he proposed a frequency theory of probability. His major works include *Probability Statistics and Truth* (1928).

mitigating circumstance, see excuse

mitigation

PHILOSOPHY OF LAW The procedure for determining a less severe penalty than usual for a crime. In a criminal trial, before sentence is passed on someone convicted of a crime, a plea in mitigation can normally be presented by or on behalf of the accused, suggesting why the **punishment** should be moderated. This is usually done by citing evidence such as the abnormality of the criminal's mentality when he conducted the crime or by debating the effect of minimizing the importance of other evidence or facts. Mitigation is different from justification, which proves that an action is in accordance with law, and excuse, which seeks to acquit the accused of responsibility for the action.

"Mitigation . . . presupposes that someone is convicted and liable to be punished and the question of the severity of his punishment is to be decided." **Hart,** *Punishment and Responsibility*

mixed hypothetical syllogism

LOGIC A **syllogism** that has a conditional proposition as one premise, and a categorical proposition as another. Its conclusion is a categorical proposition. It has two correct forms of inference: the constructive hypothetical syllogism (also called *modus ponens*):

"If p then q; p; therefore q," and the destructive hypothetical syllogism (also called *modus tollens*): "If p then q; not q, therefore, not p." It also has two incorrect forms of inference. In contrast to the constructive hypothetical syllogism is the fallacy of **affirming the consequent**: "If p then q; q; then p." In contrast to the destructive hypothetical syllogism is the fallacy of **denying the antecedent**: "If p then q; not p; therefore not q." A mixed hypothetical syllogism contrasts with a pure hypothetical syllogism, which has conditional propositions as both of its premises and also has a conditional proposition as its conclusion.

"A syllogism having one conditional premise and one categorical premise is called a mixed hypothetical syllogism." **Copi, *Introduction to Logic***

mixed modes, see mode (Locke)

mnemic causation

PHILOSOPHY OF MIND, EPISTEMOLOGY [from Greek *mneme*, memory] A term employed by **Russell**, inspired by the psychologist Richard Semon, to express the relationship between a past event and the subsequent remembering of it. An animal's response to present impulse is determined not only by the present value of a stimulus but also by **memories** of past rewards and frustration. It is a kind of action at a distance by which **experience** produces subsequent memory-images, but it is argued that such a relation does not have to be causal.

"We find sometimes that, in mnemic causation, an image or word, as stimulus, has the same effect (or very nearly the same effect) as belongs to some object." **Russell, *An Analysis of Mind***

modal epistemic logic, see epistemic modality

modal logic

LOGIC A branch of logic which deals with the logical relationships between **propositions** containing modal terms such as **necessarily** or **possibly**. Its study originated with **Aristotle** and flourished in the medieval period. In the last century it was revived by C. I. **Lewis** out of dissatisfaction with the account of **material implication** given by **Frege** and **Russell**. Lewis introduced two new operators to proposi-

tional and predicate **calculus** and used them to construct modal **axiom** systems. The operator L is symbolized as □ and read as "It is necessary that . . . ," and the operator M is symbolized as ◊ and read as "It is possible that . . ." Important additional modal systems have been constructed, but the validity of the principles of **inference** in modal logic has been a matter of debate. **Quine** has been especially critical of **modality**. However, through the work of **Kripke**, D. **Lewis**, and others, modal logic has been closely associated with **possible world semantics** and has become a central focus of work in contemporary logic.

"Modal logic is intended to represent arguments involving essentially the concepts of necessity and possibility." **Haack, *Philosophy of Logics***

modal realism

LOGIC, METAPHYSICS, PHILOSOPHY OF LANGUAGE A theory associated with the American philosopher David **Lewis**, claiming that different **possible worlds** exist and are as real as the actual world. These other worlds are unactualized possibilities. The inhabitants of possible worlds have their respective **counterparts** in our world. The only significant difference between the actual world and other possible worlds is that the actual world is the world that we inhabit and that is spatially and temporally related to us. Hence, to think in terms of logical possibilities is to think of different real worlds. Every way that a world could be is a way that some world is. Whenever such-and-such might be the case, there is some world in which such-and-such is the case.

This theory has been under attack. One criticism is that if possible worlds and the actual world have the same **ontological** status, then a possible world would be actual rather than possible. If this were true, we could not account for the difference between an **event** happening in our world and merely being a logical possibility. But Lewis argues that his theory can provide the most satisfactory interpretation of modal **propositions**. On his account, "it is possible that p" is true if and only if in some possible worlds, p; and "it is necessary that p" is true if and only if in every possible world, p. He also believes that modal realism can be used to explain phenomena such as **causation**, **conditionals**, the **content** of **propositional attitudes**, and **existential** quantification.

modality

LOGIC, METAPHYSICS, PHILOSOPHY OF LANGUAGE The ways or modes in which a **proposition** or **statement** is judged to be **true** or false. There are various classifications of modalities, such as epistemic modality [it is known (or unknown) that p]; deontic modality [it is obligatory (or permissible) that p]; temporal modality [it was (or is now or will be) p]. Of central concern to logic is logical or alethic modality [necessarily (or possibly) p]. **Modal logic** studies the logical relationships between statements of alethic modality. The doctrine of **possible worlds** has been developed to provide a **semantics** for modal logic and has stirred much recent debate in logic and metaphysics.

Modality can be distinguished into **modality** *de re* (in which a modal term modifies a **predicate** ascribed to a subject, such as "a is necessarily f") and **modality** *de dicto* (in which a modal term modifies a whole proposition, such as "it is necessary that fa").

modality *de dicto*

LOGIC, PHILOSOPHY OF LANGUAGE, METAPHYSICS Modality *de dicto* attributes modal terms (necessary, possible) to describe a **proposition** (Latin *dictum*), such as "it is necessary that p." This contrasts with modality *de re*, which attributes modal terms to modify an object (Latin *res*), such as "a is necessarily f." The distinction can be traced to **Aristotle**'s *Prior Analytic*, I.9, and is widely discussed together with **essentialism** because necessity *de re* asserts of some object that it has some property essentially. This seems to support the recent revival of essentialism, but anti-essentialists or **nominalists** reject the claim that an object can necessarily possess a property and argue that all necessity is *de dicto*.

modality *de re,* see modality *de dicto*

mode

METAPHYSICS, EPISTEMOLOGY [from Latin *modus*, measure, form, or manner] The determinations a thing possesses, the way a **quality** presents itself, or the form in which a thing can be understood. In medieval philosophy, a mode is a characteristic of a thing that marks it out from other things. In both **Descartes** and **Spinoza**, there is a system of **substance-attribute**-mode. **Thinking** and **extension** are the two principal attributes of substance, and modes are various ways or forms of thinking or extension. **Locke** took modes as one kind of **complex idea**. He divided them into simple modes, which are different combinations of the same idea, and mixed modes, which are the combinations of several different simple modes.

mode (Locke)

METAPHYSICS, EPISTEMOLOGY Both **Descartes** and **Spinoza** defined a mode as the affection of **substance**, but **Locke** used the word for one sort of **complex idea** that depends on **substances**. Modes are further divided into two kinds: simple and mixed. Simple modes are complex ideas that are combinations of the same simple ideas or ideas of the same kind. They are the result of the mental operations of compounding or enlarging the simple ideas given in experience. **Space**, **time**, number, and infinity, for example, are all classified as simple modes. Mixed modes are complex ideas that are combinations of different kinds of simple ideas. They can be gained through **experience** and observation, by invention, and by explaining the **names** of **actions**. Mixed modes differ from ideas of substance because ideas of substance must have a prototype in nature, but the mind in framing mixed modes need not determine whether they designate what exists in nature.

The majority of examples of mixed modes lie in the sphere of morals and law. Mixed modes can be said to be the names of specific qualities and actions that are important for social life, especially for moral judgments.

> "First, modes I call such complex *ideas* which, however compounded, contain not in them the supposition of subsisting by themselves, but are considered as dependences on, or affections of substances; . . . And if in this I use the word mode in somewhat a different sense from its ordinary signification, I beg pardon." **Locke, *An Essay Concerning Human Understanding***

mode of production

PHILOSOPHY OF SOCIAL SCIENCE The way of producing goods. **Marx** used this term in various senses. The material mode of production contains the productive forces. The social mode of production comprises the social characteristics of the productive process, including the purpose of production, the form of surplus labor presented by production, and the mode of exploitation in the production. In some uses, the mode of production includes both material and social modes and combines the productive forces and the relations of production. For Marx, modes of production vary historically.

> "The mode of production of material life conditions the social, political and intellectual life-process generally." **Marx, Preface to *A Contribution to the Critique of Political Economy***

modern logic, another name for symbolic logic

modernity

PHILOSOPHICAL METHOD An ambiguous term that generally refers to the central characteristic of the modern period as established in the **Enlightenment**. Postmodernists contrast modernity with postmodernity. In philosophy, modernity is normally taken to begin with **Descartes**'s work in the seventeenth century and to be concerned with the issues, problems, and standards of relevance that have since occupied Western philosophers. Authors and critics vary in their accounts of the main strands of modernity. In general, modernity is associated with the supremacy of pure **rationality** and with the self-assertiveness of the modern **self**. Equipped with

rationality, modern persons seek consensus over a unified metaphysical framework to view the world. They seek their own subjective **autonomy** and ignore the constraints of history, **tradition**, and **culture**. They aggressively attempt to organize and control the natural environment, with science as their guiding discipline. Aesthetic objects and their appreciation are measured in terms of economic benefit. Modernity was effective in the rise of industrial capitalism. The critique of modernity has been the chief topic of **critical theory**, **postmodernism**, **post-structuralism**, and **communitarianism**. Each criticism is from a separate standpoint and from a different understanding of modernity.

> "The project of modernity formulated in the 18th century by the philosophers of the Enlightenment consisted in their efforts to develop objective science, universal morality and law, and autonomous art according to their own logic." **Habermas, in Foster (ed.), *Postmodern Culture***

modes of skepticism

ANCIENT GREEK PHILOSOPHY, EPISTEMOLOGY [from Greek *tropos*, way, manner + *skepsis*, investigation, enquiry] As a technical term in ancient skepticism, a pattern of **argument**, something like **Aristotle**'s *topos*. Ancient skepticism established many modes aiming to show the oppositions or **contradictions** of **appearance** and to conclude that **suspension of judgment** is necessary. The most famous and important are the Ten Modes, which form the methodology of skepticism. They are recorded by **Sextus Empiricus** and ascribed to the Pyrrhonist philosopher Aenesidemus: (1) the mode depending on the variations among animals; (2) that depending on the differences among animals; (3) that depending on the variable constitutions of the sense-organs; (4) that depending on circumstances; (5) that depending on positions; (6) that depending on admixtures; (7) that depending on the quantities of things; (8) that depending on relativity; (9) that depending on the frequency of encounters; (10) that depending on customs and laws.

> "In order for us to get a more accurate impression of these oppositions, I shall append the modes through which suspension of judgment is inferred." **Empiricus, *Outline of Pyrrhonism***

modularity

PHILOSOPHY OF MIND A theory of the cognitive processes in the philosophy of mind that originated largely with Jerry **Fodor**'s book *The Modularity of Mind* (1983). The traditional theory of mind considers it to be a general **faculty** that is exercised in various domains. But theorists of modularity claim that mind is composed mainly of modules. Modules are cognitive systems (input systems) which are relatively independent of each other, each performing its own information-processing autonomously. Fodor lists eight characteristics of being a module: domain specificity, mandatoriness, information encapsulation, speed, shallow output, lack of access of other processes to intermediate representations, natural localization, and susceptibility to characteristic breakdown. According to the modularity hypothesis, the human mind should have unique physical structures for acquiring language and for parsing sensations. Although this hypothesis has been disputed, it has led to much fruitful debate.

"Roughly, modular cognitive systems are domain specific, innately specified, hardwired, autonomous, and not assembled. Since modular systems are domain-specific computational mechanisms, it follows that they are species of veridical faculties. I shall assume, hopefully, that this gives us a notion of modularity that is good enough to work with." **Fodor**, *The Modularity of Mind*

modus ponens

LOGIC [Latin, affirming mood, also called *modus ponendo ponens*] A form of hypothetical **syllogism** named by medieval logicians and providing a rule of inference of the form: "If p then q; p; therefore q." By this rule we infer from the antecedent of a true **implication** to its consequent. It is the principle that whatever a true proposition implies is itself true. It is also called the affirming mood. In contrast, *modus tollens* has the form: "If p then q, not q; not p." In *modus ponens*, if the categorical premise affirms the consequent rather than the antecedent of the conditional premise, that is, "If p then q; q; therefore p," the argument commits a **fallacy** called **affirming the consequent**.

"In the *modus ponens* (also called the constructive hypothetical syllogism) the categorical premise affirms the antecedent of the hypothetical premise, thereby justifying as a conclusion the affirmation of its consequent." **Keynes**, *Studies and Exercises in Formal Logic*

modus tollens

LOGIC [Latin denying mood, also called *modus tollendo tollen*] A form of hypothetical **syllogism** providing a rule of inference of the form: "If p then q; not q; therefore not p." By *modus tollens*, we infer from the denial of the consequent of an **implication** to the denial of its antecedent. It is the principle that whatever implies a false proposition is itself false. It contrasts with *modus ponens*: "If p then q; p; therefore q." In *modus tollens*, if the categorical premise denies the antecedent rather than the consequent of the conditional premises, the argument commits a **fallacy** called **denying the antecedent**.

"In the *modus tollens* (also called the destructive hypothetical syllogism) the categorical premise denies the consequent of the hypothetical premise, thereby justifying as a conclusion the denial of its antecedent." **Keynes**, *Studies and Exercises in Formal Logic*

molecular facts, see atomic fact

molecular propositions

LOGIC **Propositions** that are built from the conjunction of **atomic propositions** related by words such as "and," "or," and "if-then." For example, "*p* or *q*" is a molecular proposition made from the atomic propositions "*p*" and "*q*" and the logical connective "or." While atomic propositions represent "**atomic facts**," molecular propositions represent "molecular facts" composed of atomic facts. A molecular proposition is a **truth-functional** compound of atomic propositions. That is, its truth-value is decided by the **truth-values** of the atomic propositions composing it and by the logical terms conjoining those atomic propositions.

"'Molecular' propositions are such as contain conjunctions – if, or, and, unless, etc. – and such words are the marks of molecular proposition." **Russell**, *Our Knowledge of the External World*

Molyneux's problem

EPISTEMOLOGY A problem about the correlation between sight and touch, proposed by the Irish politician and scientist William Molyneux (1656–98) in a letter addressed to **Locke**, and which is included by Locke in the second edition of *Essay Concerning Human Understanding* (ii, ix, 8). Suppose a blind person has learned to distinguish a cube from a sphere of the same metal by the sense of touch. If the person is suddenly made to see, can he immediately distinguish the two objects by sight before touching them? Both Molyneux and Locke answered this question in the negative. They believed that our ordinary **perceptions** depend on **judgments** based on **experience**. A perceiver must learn to build perceptual knowledge by correlating the contents from different channels. **Berkeley** agreed with this solution but claimed that it proved his own thesis that the data of touch and the data of sight are heterogeneous. **Leibniz** also discussed this problem, but derived a different answer. He suggested that the two sets of experience have one element in common, that is, **extension**. Hence it is possible to infer from one type of idea to another. Empirical testing seems to favor Locke's solution.

> "A farther confirmation of our tenet may be drawn from the solution of Mr. Molyneux's problem, published by Mr. Locke in his Essay . . . that the blind man at first sight would not be able with certainty to say which was the globe which the cube, whilst he only saw them." **Berkeley, *An Essay Towards a New Theory of Vision***

monadic relation, Russell's term for quality

monadology, see monads

monads

METAPHYSICS [from Greek *monas*, unit] **Leibniz**'s mature term for his conception of **substance**. In his early period he used terms such as **substantial form**, substantial unity, atom of substance, or **entelechy**. Monads are the ultimate constituents of reality. They are **simple**, without parts, **extension**, or shape, and are indivisible. They do not affect each other. So each monad is windowless, like a world of its own. It is self-sufficient and a true atom of nature. The simplicity of a monad, however, is compatible with its internal complexity. Leibniz identified monads with **perception** and appetition. Thus each monad changes, but its change comes from an internal principle and not from an external cause. To be active is the main

characteristic of monad. Based on the contents of their perceptions, Leibniz distinguishes three grades of monads. The first grade possesses only basic properties of perception and appetition, with no **self-consciousness**. The second grade is animal **soul**, whose perceptions are more distinct and accompanied by **memory**. The third grade is spirits or rational **minds**, which are completely self-conscious. Within any monad's perceptual states there is a **representation** of the relatedness of that monad to all other monads. This provides the foundation for intermonadic **relations**. Each monad is a mirror of the whole universe. Although each of them is self-enclosed, there is a perfect harmonious relation among them that is **pre-established** by **God**. Leibniz's theory of monads is called monadology. Many of the puzzling features of Leibniz's doctrine of monads can be understood in the context of his logic and science.

> "A simple substance is that which has no parts. A composite substance is a collection of simple substances, or monads. Monad is a Greek word signifying unity, or what is one." **Leibniz, *Philosophical Essays***

monarchy

POLITICAL PHILOSOPHY [from Greek *mon*, one + *arche*, rule, rule by one] A type of government in which supreme **power** and **sovereignty** are held by one person: the monarch, king, or emperor. In many cases, especially where succession to the monarchy is determined by a long-standing hereditary principle, the monarch is viewed as an incarnation of the historical national identity. In some cases, monarchs are elected or emerge through victory in war. The power of monarchical government does not arise from **consent** or a **social contract**. The traditional absolute monarchy was inherited and supported by the theory of the divine right of kings. Monarchy contrasts with **aristocracy**, in which sovereignty lies in the hands of a class of persons, and with **democracy**, in which sovereignty is in the hands of the majority of people. European monarchies were threatened by the French Revolution. Britain developed a compromise between absolute monarchy and **liberalism**, called constitutional monarchy, in which the monarch mainly plays a ceremonial role, with sovereignty formally held by the monarch and parliament.

> "The sovereign may concentrate the entire government in the hands of one single magistrate, from whom all the others will derive their power. This . . . form of government is the most common, and is called monarchy or royal government." **Rousseau,** *The Social Contract*

mongrel categorical statements

PHILOSOPHY OF LANGUAGE, PHILOSOPHY OF MIND **Ryle**'s term for a statement that falls between categorical statements, which are statements of **fact**, and hypothetical statements, which are statements of **inference** or **conditionals**. They are semi-dispositional claims that explain something as being an occurrence but at the same time a **disposition**, for example, "The bird is migrating" and "John drives carefully." They are employed to refer to an activity which is the actual display of a disposition and thus to explain something in terms of both occurrence and disposition. These kinds of statements can make sense of some mental concepts such as heeding and minding, which seem always to include an element of the actual or the here and now.

> "I shall call statements like 'you would do the thing you did' 'semi-hypothetical' or 'mongrel categorical statements'." **Ryle,** *The Concept of Mind*

monism

METAPHYSICS A term coined by Christian **Wolff** for any metaphysical theory claiming that only one kind of entity really exists. What really exists may be **matter** (as **materialism** holds) or **mind** (as **idealism** holds). **Neutral monism** holds that mind and matter are both derived from some neutral primary reality. **Spinoza**'s monism argued that God-Nature was the single ultimate reality. The argument for monism can be traced to **Parmenides** in ancient Greece. Monism is opposed both to **dualism**, which claims that there are two fundamental realities in the world, and to **pluralism**, which claims that there are many ultimate non-reducible principles in reality. A special case of monism was put forward by the British neo-Hegelians, especially **Bradley**. According to this claim, all **relations** are internal to their terms and form part of the **identity** of the related terms. In saying that any one object exists, we are therefore implicitly affirming the existence of all other objects

and reality forms a single unity. Monism has a wider application, referring to any attempt to account for phenomena by a single principle.

> "In its extreme form monism sees it as a matter of logic that everything is unified." **Ayer,** *Philosophy in the Twentieth Century*

Montaigne, Michel de (1533–92)

French humanist and essayist, born in Périgord. Montaigne's chief work is *Essays* (3 vols.), including the philosophically influential *Apology for Raymond Sebond* (1580). Montaigne revived the Greek Pyrrhonist skepticism presented in Sextus Empiricus and combined it with Christian theology during the Renaissance. His motto was "What do I know?" (French, "Que sais-je?"). He held that the grasp of true principles is through divine revelation and that history has demonstrated the fallibility of rationality in achieving knowledge in theology, philosophy, or science. Since man does not really know moral truth, there is much to recommend following the simple and innocent life of the animal.

Montesquieu, Charles-Louis de Secondat (1689–1755)

French Enlightenment political philosopher, born at the Château de la Brède. *The Spirit of the Laws* (1748), a monumental work of modern political science, compared the legal and political systems of different countries and argued that the laws of a country are related to its social customs, commerce, and geographic situations. Influenced by Locke, Montesquieu held that the best and most durable form of government is a constitutional monarchy in which executive, legislative, and judicial powers are separated. This type of government can safeguard against despotism and protect individual liberty. The love of law is the principal political virtue. His other important works include *The Persian Letters* (1721) and *Considerations on the Romans* (1734).

mood

LOGIC, PHILOSOPHY OF MIND, PHILOSOPHY OF LANGUAGE In syllogistic logic, mood is every valid form within each of the four figures of categorical **syllogism**. For instance, the first mood of the first figure is called "Barbara," with the form: "If all S are Q, and all P are S, then all P are Q."

In the philosophy of mind, mood is a temporary emotional state of the mind that colors a person's reactions.

In the philosophy of language, different moods, such as indicative, imperative, optative, and subjunctive, indicate different **forces** of the same utterance.

> "Given any signal σ of the system, L is to assign it an interpretation <μ,τ>. The component, μ, called a mood, indicates whether σ is indicative or imperative. The component τ of an interpretation, called a truth condition, indicates the state of affairs in which σ is true." **D. Lewis, *Convention***

Moore, G(eorge) E(dward) (1873–1958)

British philosopher, born in London, a founder of twentieth-century analytical philosophy. Moore believed that the principal task of philosophy is to analyze ordinary concepts and arguments. His influential *Principia Ethica* (1903) argued that goodness is a fundamental and indefinable value that can be grasped only by intuition. Any attempt to define values in terms of facts or non-ethical concepts commits the "naturalistic fallacy." He advocated an "ideal utilitarianism," according to which we should act in order to maximize goodness, found especially in the experience of friendship and aesthetic enjoyment. In metaphysics, Moore broke from the neo-Hegelian Idealism that dominated English philosophy at the end of the nineteenth century and defended a common sense view of the world against skepticism. Moore's paradox (the absurdity of saying "It is raining, but I do not believe that it is raining") raises important questions in the philosophy of mind and the philosophy of language. His other works include *Philosophical Studies* (1922) and *Some Main Problems of Philosophy* (1953).

moral

ETHICS [from Latin *moralis*, manner, custom, conduct, corresponding to Greek *êthos*. Latin *moralis* places greater emphasis on the sense of social expectation, while Greek *êthos* gives heavier weight to individual character] Being moral concerns human **actions** that can be evaluated as **good** or bad and **right** or wrong. These actions are in our power and we can be held responsible for them. If a person's actions conform to **rules** of what is morally right, he is said to be moral. If he violates them, he is

immoral or morally wrong. A moral action is also opposed to an amoral action, which is morally value-free, that is, neither right nor wrong. Conflicts can arise between socially accepted rules of morality and rules determined by reason and individual conscience.

> "The word 'moral' when it is used as a term of praise is contrasted with 'immoral', or sometimes 'amoral', but is contrasted with 'non-moral' when used as a universe-of-discourse word." **Cooper, *The Diversity of Moral Thinking***

moral absolutism

ETHICS The view that there are certain objective moral **principles** which are eternally and universally **true**, no matter what consequences they bring about. These principles can never justifiably be violated or given up. Paradigms of such principles include "don't lie," "keep your promises," and "don't kill innocent people." Moral absolutism is generally represented by various religious moral systems. **Kantian deontology** is closely associated with moral absolutism, since it claims that some actions are right or wrong intrinsically or in themselves and that they may never be used as means to ends. However, contemporary deontology tends to distance itself from absolutism by admitting the principle of **double effect**, although the extent to which this stance is successful is disputed. Generally, moral absolutism is contrasted to **consequentialism**, which believes that the rightness or wrongness of an action is determined by the consequences it promotes, and hence any moral principle can be overridden. It is also contrasted to **ethical relativism**, which claims that all concepts of right and wrong are culturally relative and provincial.

> "By 'moral absolutism' is meant the theory according to which there are certain kinds of actions that are absolutely wrong; actions that could never be right whatever the consequences." **Haber (ed.), *Absolutism and its Consequentialist Critics***

moral agent

ETHICS Any **individual** who is capable of formulating or following general **moral principles** and rules, and who has an autonomous **will** so that he can decide ultimately what acts he should perform and not perform. Moral agents can react to the acts of other moral agents. Accordingly they are responsible for their acts and are the subject of blame or praise. Adult human beings are paradigmatic moral agents. Moral agents are contrasted to **moral patients**: beings that lack rationality and cannot be held morally accountable for their acts.

"Moral agents are individuals who have a variety of sophisticated abilities, including in particular the ability to bring impartial moral principles to bear on the determination of what, all considered, morally ought to be done and having made this determination, to freely choose or fail to choose to act as morality, as he conceives it, requires." **Regan, *The Case for Animal Rights***

moral argument for the existence of God

PHILOSOPHY OF RELIGION An argument credited to **Kant** for the existence of **God** based upon human moral experience. Kant derived morality from **reason** alone and not from divine authority, but believed that being moral is not sufficient to secure happiness. Happiness must be added to morality, although only a moral person is worthy of being happy. Being happy means that everything proceeds according to my **will** and **desire**. A happy moral person has the highest good that can be acquired in the world. But to guarantee that everything will go according to a person's will and desire and thus to ensure the moral person's ultimate happiness, it is inevitable that we postulate the existence of God. The moral argument has been very popular since **Hume** and Kant attacked the **ontological** and **cosmological arguments** and the **argument from design**, although later versions depart from Kant's formulation. In later versions the argument proceeds from the existence of moral **commands** to the existence of God as moral commander, from the existence of moral authority to the existence of God as the authorizer, and from the existence of moral laws to the existence of God as law-giver. Thus, morality itself is claimed to be determined by divine will. This argument is criticized by **naturalistic ethics**, which sees no need to postulate God in order to explain the existence of human moral institutions.

"The Moral Argument is a transcendental argument in the sense that it endeavours to show the existence of God is a necessary condition of morality." **McPherson, *The Philosophy of Religion***

moral atomism

ETHICS A variety of ethical theories which take **individuals**, their **rights**, **values** or interests, as the basis for our thinking about moral right and wrong. It contrasts with moral holism, which places ultimate value on the system rather than on the individuals that compose the system. Most Western ethical theories belong to moral atomism, while **Plato**'s ethics in the *Republic* is an example of moral holism. The contrast between moral atomism and holism is striking in environmental ethics. While one position extends human-centered ethics to consider the rights or interests of animals, the other position, represented by land ethics, claims that the ecosystem rather than the various individuals in it should be the focus of our moral consideration. This version of moral holism is also called ecological holism.

"Despite their many differences, all of the normative ethical theories discussed so far are in a certain sense atomistic; that is, each demands that individuals be considered equitably." **Regan (ed.), *Matters of Life and Death***

moral certainty

EPISTEMOLOGY, PHILOSOPHY OF SOCIAL SCIENCE The certainty that the natural sciences possess is regarded to be **universal** or **demonstrative**, while the social sciences cannot achieve such a degree of certainty, for it involves human affairs. Accordingly, social science is said to possess only moral certainty, because it is generally but not universally true. The word "moral" here is not associated with good or bad, but means pertaining to human affairs or practical concerns. This distinction can be traced to **Aristotle**'s *Nicomachean Ethics*, and has been widely endorsed in the history of philosophy.

"Moral certainty is sufficient to regulate the conduct of one's life even if it is in principle possible that we can be mistaken." **Descartes, *Principles of Philosophy***

moral community

ETHICS Those within the scope of moral consideration. In traditional ethics, only human beings were held to have membership of the moral community. They are the only objects of moral concern because only human beings have **reason** and hence know what they are doing. Furthermore, only human beings can be in reciprocal relationships involving the recognition of oneself and others as being in a moral relationship. This implies that the moral community consists exclusively of **moral agents**. Some contemporary moral philosophers, especially those working in environmental ethics, claim that only prejudice restricts the moral community to human beings. If cognitive conditions are necessary for moral concern, some humans, such as infants and brain-damaged persons, should be excluded, and some kinds of animals should be included. They claim that rationality should not be the grounds for belonging to the moral community. But the question of what the criterion should be is a matter of dispute. Some philosophers suggest that all **subjects-of-a-life** should have the same right to be respected as a member and that the moral community should extend to many kinds of animals. Others believe that **sentience** should be the criterion and that the moral community should include any being that is capable of suffering. Some argue that plants as well as animals should be included, while others believe that the whole ecosystem and its members belong to the moral community. Some philosophers claim that even if we encountered fully rational non-human beings, our basic moral concern would be restricted to humans on the basis of a recognition of ourselves as members of a species.

> "Let us define the notion of the moral community as comprising all those individuals who are of direct moral concern or alternatively, as consisting of all those individuals toward whom moral agents have direct duties." **Regan,** *The Case for Animal Rights*

moral compromise, see compromise

moral conservatism
ETHICS A contemporary ethical position emerging out of the **anti-theory** movement, represented by **Williams, Nussbaum,** and **MacIntyre.** It attempts to establish ethics without appealing to universal principles, but through examination of particular social **conventions, traditions,** and practices. Its central characteristics include an emphasis on the plurality and diversity of the **values** and practices of a **community** and an objection to any impersonal or universal point of view that places **moral judgments** above local context. It believes that moral claims can only be assessed from within the historical

tradition in which they are embedded and objects to the universal application of prescriptions. It denies the dichotomy of **reason** and **emotion**, and emphasizes the formation of **virtue**. Moral conservatism is associated with **virtue ethics, moral particularism,** and **communitarianism.** However, though it tries to distance itself from **ethical relativism** and advocates the practice of critical **reflection,** it still faces the major difficulty of explaining how it is possible to criticize a culture if the ethical life of the community is primary. The theory is still being developed.

> "The second group of writings, *moral conservatism,* offers positive accounts of morality in terms of custom and practice." **Clarke and Simpson,** *Anti-Theory in Ethics and Moral Conservatism*

moral dilemma
ETHICS A situation in which one person is morally pulled in opposite directions. In these situations, different apparently sound reasons support different courses of **action** that cannot be jointly undertaken. The moral agent has reason to do A and has reason to do B, but he cannot do both A and B. Although it is not this person's fault for getting into the **dilemma,** whatever direction is chosen will inevitably be morally wrong in some respect and result in a sense of **guilt** or remorse. For example, a case may arise in which telling the **truth** (which is required as a moral principle) will involve moral wrongdoing by breaking a promise to someone else to remain silent. In another case, returning a weapon one has borrowed may predictably lead to serious injuries to some innocent person. In such cases one cannot do all that is morally required. Moral dilemmas are the stuff of tragedies. Since to hold that there is one sovereign **moral principle,** for example **utilitarianism,** leads to moral dilemmas in many circumstances, this phenomenon represents a challenge to such theories. However, it is a test of every moral theory that it provides some reasonable way to deal with moral dilemmas, although the fact that no way is completely effective might tell us something about the nature of morality.

> "The standard definition of moral dilemmas seems to include all and only situations when (at the same time) an agent ought to adopt each of two alternatives separately but cannot adopt both together." **Sinnott-Armstrong,** *Moral Dilemmas*

moral epistemology, see moral knowledge

moral expert

ETHICS Moral philosophers are often regarded as being able to offer advice about how one should live or about whether an action is **right** or wrong, just as an art-historian can advise whether an art-work is real or a forgery. This attitude takes moral philosophers to be moral experts. The notion of a moral expert is strongly objected to by moral **non-cognitivism**. Non-cognitivism denies the existence of objective ethical value and accordingly rejects the view that there is any authority who can tell us how to live our lives. According to this theory, morality is nothing but an expression of one's own preferences or emotions. What I need to know when I am making a moral judgment is what I feel in the situation in question. The position of non-cognitivism is not widely shared. Nowadays many philosophers sit on government commissions of enquiry and corporate and institutional ethics committees. The need for advice on a variety of morally complicated issues has greatly promoted the development of **applied ethics**. However, it is not clear whether moral advice is a matter of good judgment that can be detached from any moral theory, an ability to articulate and clarify moral issues without drawing moral conclusions, or a combined capacity to provide moral theory leading to moral conclusions. Although they accept the notion of moral advice, some philosophers object to moral experts making moral decisions for us on the grounds that this would compromise our **autonomy** as **moral agents**. They claim that leading a life on someone else's plan is not to lead a good life, however good the plan might be. In any case, they argue that morality cannot be taught like other subjects. On this view, the nature of moral expertise becomes problematic.

> "The notion of a moral expert makes no sense on the non-cognitivist view, (for) there are no moral facts about which he or she might have special knowledge." **McNaughton,** *Moral Vision*

moral holism, see moral atomism

moral judgment

ETHICS The content of a **proposition** that typically discriminates between **good** or bad or between **right** and wrong and determines what should be done in a moral context. Also, moral judgment is the capacity to make such judgments or to make them well. Moral judgments are practical in that they provide direct guidance for **action**. Different ethical theories have different views about the nature of moral judgments and their relation to action. Moral **objectivism** claims that a true moral judgment corresponds to objective moral properties, but leaves open the question of why knowledge of such **facts** would guide action. **Deontology** holds that a moral judgment is a type of **command**, used to tell people, including ourselves, what we should or should not do. **Emotivism** claims that a moral judgment is an expression of a purely personal preference. A view derived from **Aristotle** holds that a moral judgment is an application of universal **moral principles** to a particular situation within the scope of the principles. This view recognizes that **practical reason** might need to reach an equilibrium between universal **rules** and particular circumstances when the rules cannot be straightforwardly applied to the circumstance. On this view, a moral judgment has cognitive and rational elements and is more than a mere response of feeling. It can be **universalized** and publicly advocated rather than merely privately preferred.

> "To make a moral judgement of an action, person, etc. is to judge the action by relating it to either a moral rule or a moral ideal." **Gert,** *The Moral Rules*

moral knowledge, another term for ethical knowledge

moral law

ETHICS For **Kant**, all moral laws are **principles** or **maxims**, but not all principles or maxims are moral laws. A moral law is a maxim on which a rational being acts, and which he would will to be a maxim for all rational beings. A moral law must have objective **necessity** and be recognized by **reason**. It must give rise to **imperatives** that are definite and specific, yet **universal** in application. In Kant's ethics, a moral law applies only to rational beings and determines how a rational being as such would necessarily act. It lays down a **rule** that does not admit of exceptions and which commands rather than counsels. A moral law is a **categorical imperative**.

It is not derived from empirical fact, but is prescribed by reason itself as the ground of its own action. Since Kant believed that a person obeys a categorical imperative only if his **will** is free, the notion of a moral law leads to an assertion of the existence of freedom.

Kant's notion of a moral law is the culmination of a tradition in Western ethics that views ethics as a network of moral laws which are recognized *a priori* and applied universally. This tradition is opposed to the tradition of **Aristotelian virtue ethics**, which holds that the application of universal principles should be adjusted according to the salient features of the circumstances in which the principles are applied. Kant's notion of a moral law has become the main target of the current revival of virtue ethics.

"In contrast to laws of nature, these laws of freedom are called moral laws." **Kant,** *Metaphysics of Morals*

moral luck

ETHICS Traditional ethics claims that one's moral status is not subject to luck, that is, to matters of **chance** or factors beyond one's control. **Kant** states at the outset of his *Foundation of the Metaphysics of Morals* that good **will**, which is the source of moral worth, is independent of the contingencies of the world. Hence he distinguishes between a moral area that is immune to luck and an amoral area that is inevitably vulnerable to luck, and confines his ethics to rational agency and universal principles. This luck-free morality is challenged by **Williams** and **Nagel**. They argue that the estimation of moral worth, and notions such as **responsibility**, **justification**, and blame, are indeed subject to luck, and hence morality is also threatened by luck. Williams maintains that luck will influence one's **motives**, **intentions**, and personality, and is hence closely related to one's moral decisions and moral justifications. Nagel distinguishes different kinds of luck that deeply affect morality: constitutive luck, that is, the factors that influence one's constitution as an agent (for example, different family background, different environment or education); circumstantial luck, for example, the problems and situations one faces; the luck which affects the cause of an **action**; and the luck which affects the result of an action. **Moral dilemmas** can

also be viewed as a kind of circumstantial luck. Different luck will result in different levels of **responsibility** for the agent and different **moral judgments** by others. If I drive a car carelessly, my action will not mean much if no serious consequence occurs, but it means something entirely different if I happen to crash and kill a child. The problem of moral luck is an indispensable part of the **anti-theory movement** and leads to the creation of moral stances that recognize the contingencies of luck, such as **virtue ethics** and moral **contextualism**.

"If moral luck is thinkable, possibly even acceptable, in regard to the character of particular acts, then perhaps the status of certain virtues as virtues can depend on a kind of cosmic (moral) luck." **Slote,** *Goods and Virtues*

moral patient

ETHICS A moral status, in contrast to that of **moral agent**. Traditionally, only rational human beings can be moral agents, for they must hold **responsibility** for their **actions**. Marginal human beings, such as children and brain-damaged people, are not regarded as having moral responsibility for their behavior, and hence are not moral agents. However, they are still the objects of moral consideration and are protected from suffering by moral laws. Accordingly they are referred to as moral patients. Moral patients cannot formulate or follow moral **principles** and **rules**. They can bring about great pain and even disasters to others, but we cannot say that they are morally wrong for doing that. Equally, their acts may bring about good consequences, but we do not say that they are morally right for performing them. Moral agents can act wrongly or rightly in ways that affect moral patients, but moral patients cannot act reciprocally toward moral agents. Contemporary environmental ethics claims that the scope of moral patients should not only include marginal human beings, but also sentient animals, and even the whole biocommunity. A difference in moral status requires different moral considerations and can involve the appeal to different moral principles. This results in a variety of moral tensions in practice. For instance, a fetus is a moral patient. To consider its interest might make abortion immoral. On the other hand, if we appeal to the **autonomy** of the mother, abortion might be permissible.

> "In contrast to moral agents, moral patients lack the prerequisites that would enable them to control their own behaviours in ways that would make them morally accountable for what they do." **Regan,** *The Case for Animal Rights*

moral philosophy, see ethics and morality

moral point of view
ETHICS To consider or judge behavior from the perspective of moral **rules** or **principles**, rather than from the viewpoint of one's **self-interest**. The main question of moral philosophy is "Why ought I to be moral?" Thus we must justify why human beings should consider their acts from a moral point of view. Different moralists provide and argue for different points of view, and they are always in conflict. A central tradition of modern moral philosophy claims that from a moral point of view morality is the only important thing in one's life, but contemporary **virtue ethics** believes that morality, in itself, is at most a part of what is valuable and that human lives should have other commitments. On this basis, the main question of moral philosophy would be Socrates' question "How should I live?"

> "In order to consider the relation between individual rationality and what is sometimes called 'the moral point of view' one has to decide on criteria of rationality, and this is a semi-conceptual investigation." **Cooper,** *The Diversity of Moral Thinking*

moral principle, see moral rule

moral psychology
ETHICS, PHILOSOPHY OF LAW An essential part of ethics, especially contemporary **virtue ethics**, concerned with the structure and phenomenological analysis of those psychological phenomena that have great bearing on moral behavior or **action**. These phenomena include cognitive states such as deliberation and choice; emotional states such as **love**, mercy, satisfaction, **guilt**, remorse, and **shame**; and **desires**, character, and personality. Moral psychology aims to improve understanding of human motivation and also has a role in the philosophy of law.

> "The problem of the origin of moral judgements and moral sentiments, which is often discussed in 'ethical' writings . . . but nonetheless belongs to the province of moral psychology." **Pap,** *Elements of Analytic Philosophy*

moral realism
ETHICS Any moral theory which holds that moral **facts** or ethical **properties**, such as being **good** or bad or being virtuous or evil, exist independent of our **beliefs** and **will**, and that ethics should find out truths about them. It is realism applied to moral affairs and moral statements. It is related to moral **objectivism**, but contrasts to moral subjectivism and **ethical relativism**. Corresponding to **Dummett**'s characterization of realism, moral realism is also defined as the claim that **moral judgments** obey the **law of excluded middle** and must be either true or false. The truth of moral judgments is independent of the evaluator's moral beliefs.

Jean Piaget used the term 'moral realism' for an essential early stage of moral belief in which moral **rules** are viewed as external and independent of social function and in which the degree of praise and blame depends on the consequences of actions rather than intent. According to Piaget, this view may be found in the moral development of children in our societies and among adults in primitive societies.

> "Moral realism can now be defined as the claim that some moral judgments are true and every moral judgement is true if and only if certain conditions obtain that are independent of the actual and ideal moral beliefs and choices of the people who judge and are judged." **Sinnott-Armstrong,** *Moral Dilemmas*

moral reason
ETHICS The representative form of **practical reason**, the sort of thinking that leads one to make **moral judgments** and that guides one's moral acts. Moral reason brings general **moral principles** to bear on the particular situations of the **agent** and judges whether one's **action** and the way it is performed conform to the requirements of moral principles. It enables an agent to decide whether he should act and what he should do. The characteristic feature of moral reason is that it employs ethical terms and makes moral judgments that issue commands and advice. It has been disputed whether the procedure of moral reasoning can be formalized into practical **syllogism** and whether it deals with **ends** as well as **means**.

> "Moral reasons are ordinary considerations such as the pain I will cause here if I don't tell her soon. This is a moral reason because it is a salient feature of a situation which generates a demand – the demand that I tell her soon, perhaps." **Dancy,** *Moral Reasons*

moral rights, see rights, moral

moral rule

ETHICS A general statement guiding **action** and feeling by characterizing certain kinds of action, such as telling the truth or stealing, as generally right or generally wrong. Moral rules are distinguished from **moral principles**, which underlie moral rules, justify their validity, and clarify their scope of application. While moral rules are specific and **concrete**, moral principles are general and **abstract**. While moral rules are variable, moral principles hold in all circumstances. Moral principles are used to justify rules and to generate new rules to cope with unforeseen circumstances. Rules are more directly involved than principles in determining the morality of behavior. The elaboration of a consistent and intelligible body of moral principles and rules is the central task of an ethical theory.

> "A moral rule states that a certain kind of action is generally right (or obligatory), and leaves open the possibility that an act (or omission) of that kind may be justifiable." **M. Singer,** *Generalization in Ethics*

moral sense

ETHICS Analogous to the sense of **beauty**, moral sense is supposed to be an intuitive, disinterested **faculty** which enables us to recognize moral qualities, such as being good and bad, virtuous and vicious, from what we feel. If the observation of an action is painful and disquieting, the action must be bad or evil. If the observation of an action results in a pleasant feeling, the action is good and virtuous. On such a basis, moral sense further motivates us toward morally right and virtuous behavior. Moral sense conflicts with the theological position that **God**'s will is the basis of morality and is also opposed to **rationalism**, since it insists that reason cannot account for our motivation and claims that morality is felt rather than reasoned. The theory that argues for the existence of moral sense is called moral sense theory, and is particularly associated with the eighteenth-century British philosophers **Shaftesbury**, Francis **Hutcheson**, and David **Hume**. Moral sense theory tries to base itself on **Locke**'s theory of knowledge, and it is a version of moral **intuitionism**. It is also called sentimentalism. Its major contribution is to emphasize the role of feeling in morality. Criticism of this theory generally alludes to the fact that there is no justification for positing an extra faculty of moral sense and that such a theory cannot avoid moral relativism.

> "One man (Lord Shaftesbury, Hutcheson, Hume, etc) says, he has a thing made on purpose to tell him what is right and what is wrong; and that it is called 'moral sense'." **Bentham,** *An Introduction to the Principles of Morals and Legislation*

moral sense theory, see moral sense

moral theory, see ethics and morality

moral virtue, an alternative expression for ethical virtue

morality, see ethics and morality

morals, another term for ethics or moral philosophy

morals proper, see metaphysics (Kant)

More, Henry (1614–87)
British philosopher, a leading Cambridge Platonist, born in Lincolnshire, educated and worked at Cambridge. More denied the Cartesian dichotomy between mind and matter and the mechanistic view of the world. He believed in the pre-existence of the soul and claimed that the universe is alive with souls. Spirit causes motion or action. More sought to reconcile reason and faith and maintained that man can be unified with God through right reason and moral ascent. His works include *Philosophical Poems* (1647) and *Divine Dialogues* (1668).

More, Thomas (1478–1535)
English Renaissance humanist, born in London. More was executed for refusing to recognize Henry VIII as head of the English Church. In *On the Best Government and on New Island Utopia* (1516, usually called *Utopia*), More invented an ideal society characterized by communism, the equality of men and women, and the provision of communal education.

Utopian thought, which can be traced to Plato's *Republic* and Christian Epicureanism, was further developed by Campanella's *City of the Sun* and Bacon's *New Atlantis*.

Morris, Charles (1901–79)

American philosopher of language and theorist of signs. Research Professor, University of Chicago. Morris, a pragmatist who studied with George Herbert Mead, followed Peirce in developing a general semiotics or theory of signs in *Foundations of the Theory of Signs* (1938) and *Writings on the General Theory of Signs* (1971). Morris divided semiotics into three branches: syntactics, dealing with the relations among signs; semantics, dealing with the relations of signs to what they signify; and pragmatics, dealing with the relations between signs and their users and uses. Morris's attempt to place semiotics within Mead's framework of social behaviorism is less widely accepted.

motion, see change

motive

PHILOSOPHY OF ACTION, ETHICS The moving force which leads a person to behave or act in this way rather than in another way. A motive is closely related to our **desire** for the objects for which we act. **Reasons** and **causes** are generally appealed to for explaining **behavior**. While many philosophers believe that a reason is also a motive, **Hume** denied that reason has a moving force. It is a continuing matter of controversy whether motivational **explanation** is also a type of causal explanation, and there is also some disagreement whether a motivational explanation is an explanation in terms of pattern.

> "A motive is a want that leads to action, that is, a goal appraised as good for action without further deliberation; it includes effective and deliberate action tendencies." **Arnold, in Mischel (ed.),** *Human Action*

motive-consequentialism, see consequentialism

motive utilitarianism

ETHICS A version of utilitarianism that applies the principle of **utility** directly to behavioral **dispositions** and indirectly to **actions**. It claims that concern for the maximization of human happiness is good, but tries to shift ethical consideration from the traditional utilitarian focus on the moral assessment of actions to the assessment of motives that give rise to actions.

> "The theory that will be my principal subject here is that one pattern of motivation is morally better than another to the extent that the former has more utility than the latter . . . Let us call this doctrine motive utilitarianism." **Adams, "Motive Utilitarianism,"** *Journal of Philosophy* **73**

moving rows, paradox of

LOGIC, METAPHYSICS One of **Zeno's paradoxes** designed to show the impossibility of **motion**. Suppose that there are three equally sized rows A, B, and C. Each member of each row occupies a minimal unit of **time** and a minimal part of **space**. The row A is at rest, but rows C and B move in opposite directions with equal velocities. When the first member of B passes two members of A (taking two units of time), it will at the same time pass four members of C (taking four units of time), leading to the conclusion that "double the time is equal to half the time." The arguments of this paradox are complicated, and there are various other versions.

> "The fourth argument is that concerning the two rows of bodies, . . . This, he thinks, involves the conclusion that half a given time is equal to double that time." **Aristotle,** *Physics*

M-predicate, see P-predicate

mundus intelligibilis, see intelligible world

mundus sensibilis, see intelligible world

Murdoch, Iris (1919–99)

Irish-born philosopher and novelist. Fellow of St Anne's College, Oxford. Murdoch's philosophical works include *Sartre: Romantic Rationalist* (1953), *The Sovereignty of the Good* (1970), *The Fire and the Sun* (1977), *Acastos* (1986), and *Metaphysics as a Guide to Morals* (1992). Murdoch was drawn to the unity of metaphysics, morality, and religion in Plato's philosophy and was also influenced by Wittgenstein in exploring her major themes of truth, reality, the good, God, the soul, language, and the nature of art. Complex individual selves, whose memory and imaginative moral reflection allow them to be imperfect bearers of virtue, were crucial to her philosophical thought.

mysticism

EPISTEMOLOGY, PHILOSOPHY OF LANGUAGE, META-PHYSICS, PHILOSOPHY OF RELIGION The view that there exists a **transcendent** or ultimate reality that cannot be experienced or rationally conceived. That domain is beyond the description of ordinary language, and knowledge of it can only be achieved through mysterious **intuition** resulting from long-term spiritual cultivation. By gaining a vision of this **ineffable** ultimate reality, one reaches a joyous and ecstatic union with it, and this union constitutes the ultimate meaning of human life. Mysticism is associated with religious experience and doctrines. Many properties of the Christian **God** are ineffable and can only be divinely revealed. Mysticism is also associated with traditional metaphysics or speculative philosophy, which seeks after **first principles** that cannot be rationally discussed. Since the existence of mystical entities is not provable, and mystical experience is untestable, mysticism is always under suspicion. **Wittgenstein** was also concerned with mysticism. For him, the mystical is a realm of ultimate importance that can be shown, but cannot be said. This view of the mystical is aesthetic and ethical and is distinguished from logic.

"The term mysticism is at present used, as a rule, to designate what is mysterious and incomprehensible; and in proportion as their general culture and way of thinking vary, the epithet is applied by one class to denote the real and the true, by another to name everything connected with superstition and deception." **Hegel,** *Logic*

myth of passage

METAPHYSICS A term introduced by D. C. Williams in his paper "The Myth of Passage" (1951). It is very common to believe that **time** flows and is a passage. Some philosophers even believe that time as a rolling stream is the feature that distinguishes time from other instances of one-dimensional order, such as the order of points on a line. Williams argued that if time flows past us or if we advance through time, this would be a motion with respect to a hypertime, because we could not say that the motion of time is a motion with respect to time itself. Furthermore, if it is of the essence of time that time passes, then hypertime will pass as well, requiring a hyper-hypertime and so on *ad infinitum*. Williams concluded that the passage of time is a myth and should be abandoned.

"[There is a proposition] that over and above the sheer spread of events, with their several qualities, along the time axis ... there is something extra, something active and dynamic, which is often and perhaps best described as passage. This something extra, I am going to plead, is a myth." **D. Williams,** *Principles of Empirical Realism*

myth of the given

EPISTEMOLOGY A term introduced by the American philosopher W. **Sellars** in his essay "Empiricism and the Philosophy of Mind." Many **empiricists** claim that there is a sort of knowledge that is directly presented to our **consciousness** and call this knowledge the given. The given, to which each of us has **privileged access**, presupposes no learning and no forming of associations, but provides the **foundation** for empirical knowledge. It offers the ultimate court of appeal for all our knowledge claims about the world. All other forms of knowledge are derived from the given according to certain rules.

Sellars labels the alleged existence of such knowledge as "the myth of the given." To call something a myth means that it does not exist at all. Sellars rejects all the central arguments that have been put forward to support the existence of the given and claims that empirical knowledge, which is a rational and self-correcting enterprise, has no need for the given. His position has had much influence in questioning the need for foundations in epistemology and other areas of philosophy.

"The idea that observation, strictly and properly so-called, is constituted by certain self-authenticating non-verbal episodes, the authority of which is transmitted to verbal and quasi-verbal performances when these performances are made 'in conformity with the semantic rules of the language', is, of course, the heart of the myth of the given." **Sellars,** *Science, Perception and Reality*

N

Nagel, Ernest (1901–85)

Czech-born American philosopher of science. As a naturalist, Nagel maintained that the world must be understood in terms of efficient causation. He rejected the view that logic was ontologically determined and held instead that logical principles must be understood contextually or operationally. He also claimed that theories of knowledge should be based on the examination of the methods and results of sciences. Nagel's principal writings are *An Introduction to Logic and Scientific Method* (with Morris R. Cohen, 1934), *Logic Without Metaphysics* (1956), and *The Structure of Science* (1961).

Nagel, Thomas (1937–)

American philosopher of mind and moral philosopher, born in Belgrade, Yugoslavia, Professor of Philosophy at Princeton University and New York University. Nagel shows great ingenuity in exploring relations between the philosophy of mind and ethics. He argues from the prudence of adopting a stance of temporal neutrality regarding the satisfaction of desire over the span of one's life to the rationality of neutrality over whose desires are to be satisfied that characterizes altruism. Our inability to eliminate consciousness and subjective mental states from the metaphysics of the self leads to two ways of seeing oneself and the world – subjectively, as the center of experience of the world, and objectively, as part of the world along with other persons and things. He uses the interplay between these two views to discuss questions of morality and political philosophy. His main works include *The Possibility of Altruism* (1970), *Mortal Questions* (1979), and *The View from Nowhere* (1986).

naive realism

EPISTEMOLOGY The **common sense** view of the world held by most ordinary people. According to this view, the external world consists of **objects** such as rocks and trees and the qualities they possess. The world exists and develops independently of our **sensations** and **thought**. Our sensations, like mirrors, reflect this world as it is. Such a view also believes uncritically that we have the ability to know the world. However, upon reflection, philosophers find that the nature of the world and our knowledge about it are both much more complicated and puzzling than naive realism suggests. Many so-called **secondary qualities** such as color, taste, and smell are inseparable from our senses rather than properties of things independent of us. Our **perceptions** sometimes deceive us. From here we may derive many fundamental philosophical questions, such as "What is real?" "What is **appearance**?" "How is **illusion** possible?" "Is our experience a reliable source of **knowledge**?" One of the major tasks of philosophy is to uncover the difficulties hidden in the common assumptions of views such as naive realism in order to understand the world better.

"Naive realism leads to physics, and physics, if true, shows that naive realism is false. Therefore naive realism, if true, is false; therefore it is false." **Russell,** *An Inquiry into Meaning and Truth*

name

LOGIC, PHILOSOPHY OF LANGUAGE A name is traditionally believed to be a mark, sign, or expression referring to things in the world. Names are generally divided into general or common names (referring to kinds of individuals) and single or **proper names** (referring to particular **individuals**). Names help people to communicate **ideas** or to remember ideas. **Frege** distinguished between the **sense** (*Sinn*) and **reference** (*Bedeutung*) of a name. He held that the fact that two names for the same thing cannot always be used interchangeably indicates that names are not merely referential devices but also have sense in terms of which they refer to objects. **Russell** rejected Frege's distinction between sense and reference and claimed that only **logically proper names** such as "this" or "that" refer to objects. Ordinary proper names are actually **definite descriptions** in disguise. **Kripke** rejects the view that names are descriptions in part on the grounds that the user of a name does not require identifying information about the object in question. He has proposed a theory of names according to which a name is a **rigid designator** that refers to the same individual in all worlds in which that individual exists. On his account, the connection between a name and its object is established and maintained causally rather than through descriptive content.

"The name itself is merely a means of pointing to the thing." **Russell,** *Logic and Knowledge*

narcissism

PHILOSOPHY OF MIND [from the Greek myth, *narkissos*, the youth at the riverside who fell in love with his own reflection in water] Narcissism is self-love or an erotic interest in oneself. Freud believed that narcissism exists when the **libido** is directed toward the **self**. Narcissism as a psychological phenomenon normally occurs in childhood, when individuals believe that they possess every valued perfection and that they are their own ideal. When people grow up, the response of others and their own critical judgment will lead to the realization that they are

not perfect and they will seek to replace childhood narcissism with a new form of ego ideal.

"Clinical experience had made us familiar with people who behaved in a striking fashion as though they were in love with themselves and this perversion had been given the name of narcissism." **Freud,** *Standard Edition of the Complete Psychological Works of Sigmund Freud,* **vol. 18**

narrative

PHILOSOPHY OF HISTORY, AESTHETICS A mode of **discourse** that establishes orders or logical relations among various events and places them in a sequence. Such a sequence is not merely a chronology of events, but provides a configurational **understanding** by which each occurrence introduced in the narrative forms part of a meaningful whole. In this way a narrative forms a story. A narrative can be oral or written, about what has happened or about the present, in the first person, third person, or in a mixture of the two. Narrative differs from **analysis** and dialogue. We also need to distinguish between the narrative and its narration, as we distinguish between the story and its telling. Any narrative is open to infinite possibilities of re-narration. Narrative is merely a form of language and is neutral regarding the **truth** of its contents. However, narrative has its own discoverable structure rather than being a purely subjective projection. Narrative is the characteristic way of presenting **historical knowledge** and literature. Its **epistemological** status and **ontological** implications have been major topics in contemporary analytic philosophy of history and philosophy of literature. Narrative seems to have important cognitive functions, but it is difficult to settle what these functions might be.

"Narrative is a major organising device. It is as important to literature as representation to painting and sculpture; that is to say, it is not the essence of literature, for (like representation in plastic art) it is not indispensable, but it is the structural basic on which most works are designed." **Langer,** *Feeling and Form*

narrative sentence

PHILOSOPHY OF HISTORY A sentence employed by historians in ascribing historical significance to events or persons by connecting them to something that came afterwards, such as "When Petrarch climbed Mount Ventoux he opened the Renaissance." The problem of assessing the **truth-value** of narrative sentences reflects a distinctive feature of **historical knowledge**. A person who saw Petrarch climb Mount Ventoux did not know that Petrarch opened the Renaissance because no one at that time knew that there would be a Renaissance. As a consequence, a contemporary witness could not know the truth of that narrative sentence. However, historians know that it is true through knowing what happened later. In general, the truth-value of a narrative sentence can be known only by those who have access to a temporal whole including all of the relevant time periods.

> "I shall designate them as 'narrative sentences'. Their most general characteristic is that they refer to at least two time-separated events though they only *describe* (are only *about*) the earliest event to which they refer." **Danto, *Analytical Philosophy of History***

narrow content

PHILOSOPHY OF MIND The kind of **content** of a **mental state** that is purely in the mind of the subject. It is not related to words and is taxonomized according to its causal power. It is not subject to **existential generalization** and is not freely substitutable by co-extensive terms. Narrow content contrasts with the ordinary attributes of occurring **thoughts** and **propositional attitudes**, which is called **wide content** or broad content. Wide content is not wholly in the mind and has a set of **truth conditions**. The notion of narrow content is based on **Putnam**'s distinction between **narrow states** and wide states. It is useful for providing psychological **explanations** of **behavior** and explaining the **privileged access** we seem to have to our own mental states.

> "The narrow content of a mental state is supposed to be a kind of content that is wholly internal to the mind of the person in the mental state." **Stalnaker, "Narrow Content," in Anderson and Owen (eds.), *Propositional Attitudes***

narrow state

PHILOSOPHY OF MIND A term introduced by **Putnam** for the **mental states** that do not presuppose the

existence of any **individual** other than the subject to whom that state is ascribed. This is in contrast to **wide states**, such as being jealous of somebody, which have wide content that refers to the world outside the subject. Methodological **solipsism** is a doctrine that holds that psychology ought to be concerned exclusively with narrow mental or psychological states. What is characteristic of narrow states is **narrow content**, which is constituted simply by what is in the **mind**. **Fodor** uses the notion of a narrow state for those mental states that can be **individuated** by **content** without regard to **truth** or **reference**. These states are determined solely by the intrinsic **properties** of an individual, without presupposing that anything other than that individual exists. Other philosophers use the term for mental states shared by molecule-for-molecule duplicates. Different thinkers use different criteria for narrowness, but all agree that a narrow state cannot be a belief that is individuated by particular objects in the believer's environment.

> "We shall . . . refer to the states which are permitted by methodological solipsism as 'psychological states in the narrow sense'." **Putnam, *Mind, Language and Reality*.**

Nash equilibrium, see game theory

national character

PHILOSOPHY OF SOCIAL SCIENCE, PHILOSOPHY OF HISTORY, POLITICAL PHILOSOPHY The pattern of thought, feeling, and action that is peculiar to a society and its people and forms their particular **identity**. A national character is cultivated from historical and cultural **traditions**. Although the explanatory role of national character is disputed, society is claimed to inherit its character from its earlier states, and its character is claimed to form its subsequent states. National character is embodied in public sentiment and social custom, and it greatly influences a society's **laws** and form of government. J. S. **Mill** claimed that by analogy to political economy, the social sciences should have a branch, which he called political ethology, to study national character. Some advocates of the importance of national character, represented by **Vico** and **Herder**, emphasize that there is no common measurement of worth for different **cultures** or characters. This position is echoed by contemporary **communitarians**. Major problems facing this view are how to avoid relativism and how to make intercultural criticism possible. This approach to national character contrasts with **liberal** universalism, which holds that a set of universal **values** and **rights** applies to human beings irrespective of the national **communities** to which they belong.

> "The laws of national (or collective) character are by far the most important class of sociological laws."
> *The Collected Works of John Stuart Mill*, **vol. VII**

nationalism

POLITICAL PHILOSOPHY In its positive aspect, adherence to a national **identity** formed by the distinctive characteristics typically derived from one's national history, **culture**, language, and religion. Nationalism emphasizes the nation's **rights** to **self-determination** and **sovereignty** and demands the preservation of its culture. Nationalists often claim that the nation's **values** and interests, at least in times of danger or crisis, override the individual rights of its citizens. Citizens are required to display patriotism by being loyal to the nation and by serving its collective aims.

Negatively, nationalism attaches unreasonable importance to one's national moral, cultural, and political values. An exclusive concern for the interests of one's own nation leads to blindness and belligerence in assessing the values and interests of other nations or minorities within one's own nation. In this sense, nationalism is nearly indistinguishable from chauvinism.

> "Nationalism, if we extended the sense of the word 'nation' somewhat, could include the self-centred pursuit of the interest of any individual group."
> Hare, *Essays on Political Morality*

Natorp, Paul (1854–1924)

German neo-Kantian philosopher, born in Dusseldorf, a member of the Marburg school. Influenced by Plato and Kant, he developed methodological transcendentalism to examine culture, history, and the logical foundation of science. He interpreted Plato's Ideas as laws and principles that form the basis of sciences. Natorp's major works include *Plato's Theory of Ideas: An Introduction to Idealism* (1903) and *The Logical Foundations of the Exact Sciences* (1910).

natura naturans

PHILOSOPHY OF RELIGION, METAPHYSICS [Latin, literally nature naturing, that is, generating or active nature, in contrast to *natura naturata*, literally nature natured, that is, generated or passive nature] These two terms derive from **scholastic** philosophy, in which *natura naturans* refers to **God** and *natura naturata* refers to the created world. **Spinoza** employed them in his *Ethics*, where *natura naturans* is used for **substance** and **attributes**, because they are self-explanatory. *Natura naturata* is used for **modes**, which follow from substances and attributes and must be explained by them. Accordingly, God and the world are one, but are not absolutely **identical**.

> "From what has gone before, I think it is plain that by *natura naturans* we are to understand that which is in itself and is conceived through itself, or those attributes of substance which express eternal and infinite essence." **Spinoza, *Ethics***

natura naturata, see *natura naturans*

natura non facit saltum, see contiguity

natural deduction

LOGIC The method that constructs a logical system merely on the basis of a set of rules of **inference** without employing any **logical truths** as **axioms**. It contrasts with the standard axiomatic method of forming a logical system that requires both a set of axiom-like logical truths and a set of rules of inference. The method of natural deduction was developed independently in 1934 by the Polish logician S. Jaskowski and the German logician G. **Gentzen**. While standard axiomatic formalization makes logic concentrate on the choice and **justification** of logical truths, the axiomless formalization of natural deduction focuses on **logical consequence**, that is, on the move from premises to conclusions. For example, from a pair of sentences as premises one infers their **conjunction**, and from a conjunction one infers either conjunct. With natural deduction, a premise can be introduced at any stage of deduction without need of justification, and a **hypothesis** can also serve as a premise. In this way, logic not only gets rid of the most troublesome task of justifying its choice of logical truths, but also conforms more properly to its original task, that is, the study of inference.

> "The methods of proof so far assembled (techniques for 'natural deduction', as they are sometimes called) permits the demonstration of all logically true propositions constructed out of truth-functional connectives and the quantification of individual variable." **Copi,** *Symbolic Logic*

natural kinds

METAPHYSICS, PHILOSOPHY OF SCIENCE Things which are naturally distinguished, including the **species** of things such as whales and apples and elements or mass items such as water and gold. These things occur naturally, in contrast to things such as televisions and tables, which are invented by human beings. Traditionally, terms naming natural kinds, that is, natural kind terms, are taken to be general **names** that should be defined by giving a **connotation** or by specifying the necessary and sufficient conditions of their application.

In the 1970s, **Kripke** and **Putnam**, arguing against the traditional theory, suggested that natural kind terms, like **proper names**, are not connotative. While proper names are **rigid designators** of an **individual**, natural kind terms are rigid designators of a kind. They have an **essential property**, namely, the underlying structure discovered through empirical investigation. Water is H_2O in all **possible worlds**, so anything that is not H_2O is not water, even if it satisfies some list of superficial features that we think characterize water. Accordingly, it is a **necessary truth** that water is H_2O, although this truth is *a posteriori*, that is, empirically known. A natural kind term is ascribed historically, and the justification for its use is passed on through a causal chain.

> "What really distinguishes the classes we count as natural kinds is itself a matter of (high level and very abstract) scientific investigation and not just meaning analysis." **Putnam, in Schwartz (ed.),** *Names, Necessity and Natural Kinds*

natural language, see ordinary language

natural law, another expression for law of nature

natural law theory

PHILOSOPHY OF LAW, POLITICAL PHILOSOPHY A position holding that there is a system of natural laws that guides political and legal **authority** and sets the moral standards for human conduct. It argues that law is essentially **normative** and that an unjust law is not a law. Natural law theory has two major forms. Classical natural law theory is based on the distinction between **nature** and **convention** and considers natural law to be a conception of **justice**. It is **universal** and everlasting, grounded either in **God**'s **will** or in **human nature** and discovered by human **reason**. This form can be traced to **Aristotle**'s teleological **ethics** and Stoicism and was developed by medieval philosophers in combination with Christian thought. It was revived in the twentieth century, especially by John **Finnis** and Robert **Nozick**. Modern natural law theory claims that natural laws grant **natural rights** to each **individual**. These include rights to freedom, life, and equality. Political rights and **obligations** are derived through a **social contract** among individuals who hold these natural rights. This theory was developed by **Grotius, Locke,** and **Rousseau** and was revived in the twentieth century, especially by John **Rawls**. Natural law theory forms a major tradition in legal philosophy in virtue of its claim that law is necessarily connected with morality. Human law derives its binding force from natural law and is null if it does not conform to natural law. The chief motive for developing **legal positivism** was to reject natural law theory.

> "A 'natural law' theorist . . . would insist that all valid moral standards are tacitly incorporated by the Constitution, so that any interpretation that ascribes to it moral standards of an inferior or defective kind must be mistaken." **Feinberg,** *Offense to Others,* **1985**

natural light

EPISTEMOLOGY [Latin *lumen naturale*, also called *lux rationis*, the light of reason] Generally regarded by seventeenth-century philosophers as a universal **faculty** shared by all human beings that could be expected to reach the same view about certain basic issues. **Descartes** in particular favored this term, using it to refer to the transparent clarity of **cognition**. Truths that are presented to the intellect by the natural light allow no room for denial and are not open to **doubt**. Descartes used it as an authority whenever he wished to introduce some fundamental premises as a basis for further argument. He associated this notion with **intuition** by defining intuition as what the mind clearly and indubitably conceives from the natural light. According to this view, the natural light could be developed through the study of sciences, but could also be obscured if we are not capable of heeding **reason**.

> "The light of nature or faculty of knowledge which God gave us never encompass any object which is not true in so far as it is indeed encompassed by this faculty; that is, in so far as it is clearly and distinctly perceived." **Descartes**, *The Philosophical Writings*

natural philosophers

ANCIENT GREEK PHILOSOPHY, PHILOSOPHY OF SCIENCE [Greek *phusikoi* or *phusiologi*, literally the men who talk about nature; also translated as physicists, referring to the pre-Socratic philosophers, who attempted to explain the world by appeal to natural causes, in contrast to the *theologi*, who explained the generation and structure of the world in terms of myth and supernatural forces] **Aristotle** claimed that the founder of natural philosophy was **Thales**. Natural philosophy is concerned with the question "What is the world made of?" and natural philosophers usually answer the question by appeal to a single material **substratum**, something equivalent to Aristotle's material cause. Historians of philosophy, however, generally believe that Aristotle's account is not very accurate, for natural philosophers did not have the concept of **matter**, and their keyword was "nature," the **principle** of a thing's growth and present organization. Most of them wrote books entitled "On Nature."

> "Natural philosophers have two modes of explanation. The first set make the underlying body one . . . The second set assert that the contrarieties are contained in the one and emerge from it by segregation." **Aristotle**, *Physics*

natural philosophy, another name for philosophy of nature

natural religion, another expression for natural theology

natural rights

POLITICAL PHILOSOPHY, PHILOSOPHY OF LAW Rights which belong to us simply because of our humanity and not because of any special legal, political, or social institutions. According to many writers of the **Enlightenment**, natural rights, which are held in the **state of nature** in virtue of **natural law**, can not be transferred to the government through a **social contract**. According to **Hobbes**, with no government in the state of nature, an **individual** has a right to take everything necessary to preserve his life or to promote his survival. The supreme natural right to defend and preserve oneself also establishes one of the basic natural laws. But because everyone has natural rights that can conflict with the natural rights of everyone else, Hobbes depicted the state of nature as a state of war of all against all. According to John **Locke**, natural rights include the rights to life, **liberty**, and **property**. **Bentham** notoriously rejected the possibility of natural rights on the grounds that nature does not provide rights and that rights can be created only by law. In spite of his objections, the notion of natural rights remains influential in moral, social, and political thought. Natural rights are considered to be basic rights at the core of human **rights**. Writers are divided over the need to associate natural rights with natural law.

> "The right of nature, which writers commonly call *jus naturale*, is the liberty each man hath, to use his own power, as he will himselfe, for the preservation of his own nature; that is to say, of his own life; and consequently, of doing anything, which in his own judgment, and reason, hee shall conceive to be the aptest means thereunto." **Hobbes**, *Leviathan*

natural selection

PHILOSOPHY OF SCIENCE A central term of Charles **Darwin**'s theory of **evolution**. Organisms have features with **functions** that are adapted to the natural world and that help them survive and reproduce. Christianity claims that this is due to God's design, but Darwin showed that this functional adaptation for survival can be explained by a causal mechanism, natural selection. Adaptations are selected because they aid the survival of **individuals** or **species** and are transmitted to succeeding generations. Natural selection gives rise not only to the often striking forms and functions of living creatures but also to their enormous diversity. Those organisms that fail to develop suitable features lose in the struggle for survival and reproduction. The basic spirit of natural selection is summarized in **Spencer's** phrase **"survival of the fittest."** Natural selection is still at the center of evolutionary theory, although whether it operates at the level of species, individual, or gene is a matter of controversy.

> "Drawing on the analogy of the animal and plant breeders' skill at transforming through picking desired forms, Darwin christened his new mechanism 'natural selection'." **Ruse,** *Taking Darwin Seriously*

natural theology

PHILOSOPHY OF RELIGION, METAPHYSICS Also called natural religion or rational theology, a theological discipline which tries to prove **truths** about the existence and attributes of **God** through the employment of natural human **reason**. From this viewpoint, reason unaided by **revelation** can provide a firm basis for religion and shows that there exists an **omnipotent**, **omniscient**, and perfectly **good** God who created the world. It does not propose a supernatural communication with God through revelation and **grace**, because such revelation is not rationally justifiable. Rather, it makes use of data available to all rational beings. It intends to prove that theistic beliefs are not only true to believers, but to all rational human beings. It also tries to understand the action of divine **providence** regarding human beings and to deal with the **problem of evil**. Natural theology is thus contrasted with supernatural theology, which locates the source of truths about God in revelation. In this sense, natural religion is rational, while supernatural theology is not based on reason. This contrast is associated with the contrast between rational and revealed theology. For this reason, natural theology is a branch of **metaphysics** dealing with divine being. Many traditional arguments for God's existence, such as the **ontological argument**, **cosmological argument**, teleological argument, **moral argument**, and **argument from design**, are examples of natural theology. **Aquinas' five ways** are its paradigm. Natural theology was criticized by **Hume** and **Kant**. Hume provided especially important criticism of the argument from design. For Kant, natural theology cannot be right because the object whose existence it aims to prove is outside possible human experience where reason inevitably falls into conflict with itself, although he claimed that **belief** can be maintained not as knowledge but as a matter of **faith** and hope. Much of natural theology has been assimilated into contemporary philosophical theology.

> "The fourth branch of metaphysics is natural or rational theology. The notion of God, or God as a possible being, the proofs of his existence, and his properties, formed the study of this branch." **Hegel,** *Logic*

natural virtue

ETHICS For **Hume**, **virtue** is the moral quality in ourselves or others that is approved of by our moral sentiments. He distinguished between natural virtue and artificial virtue. Natural virtues are virtuous tendencies and characteristics that arise from the fundamental propensities of human nature itself and are not cultivated deliberately. These characteristics include **charity**, **benevolence**, **generosity**, **love** of ones' children, clemency, and so on. Artificial virtues, such as **justice**, allegiance, and **fidelity**, in contrast, are effects of artifice and education and are obtained over a long period of time. They are artificial and invented, but not arbitrary. Hume claimed that natural virtues provide the basis for family life and intimate friendship, while artificial virtue is required for our broader social life.

> "When I deny justice to be a natural virtue, I make use of the word, natural, only as opposed to artificial." **Hume,** *A Treatise of Human Nature*

naturalism

METAPHYSICS, EPISTEMOLOGY, ETHICS, AESTHETICS, PHILOSOPHY OF MIND, PHILOSOPHY OF SCIENCE The claim that everything is a part of the world of **nature** and can be explained using the methodology of the natural sciences. Naturalism accepts explanatory **monism** rather than **dualism** or **pluralism**, is committed to **science**, and is opposed to **mysticism**. In different areas, naturalism has different forms. In metaphysics, it rejects the postulation of any unnatural **theoretical entities**, **faculties**, or **causes**, and it rejects supernatural beings and processes that are inaccessible to scientific inquiry. It also contests the claim that **first philosophy** is prior to natural science.

In epistemology, naturalism holds that epistemological **justification** and **explanation** are continuous with natural science and argues that **scientific method** is the only way to secure our **knowledge**. According to nineteenth-century **psychologism** and twentieth-century **naturalistic epistemology**, epistemology should be assimilated to empirical psychology. Ethical naturalism rejects the **is–ought** or **fact–value distinction** and explains ethical terms in terms of natural **properties**. This position was characterized by **Moore** as the "naturalistic fallacy," but it is uncertain whether it is a real **fallacy**. In aesthetics, naturalism holds that an artwork should represent the world as it is. In philosophy of mind, naturalism holds that **mental phenomena** are, or are **caused** by, brain processes. Recent naturalistic interpretations of **Hume**, **Kant**, and **Wittgenstein** place emphasis on unavoidable natural human tendencies rather than on the priority of science. For any form of naturalism, there is a corresponding form of anti-naturalism.

"Naturalism has a representative already in 1830 in the antimetaphysician Auguste Comte, who declared that positive philosophy does not differ in method from the special sciences." **Quine, *Theories and Things***

naturalistic epistemology

EPISTEMOLOGY A term from **Quine**'s paper, "Epistemology Naturalised," although Quine himself does not offer an explicit definition of it. Quine takes it as an epistemological project, which suggests that in order to discover the grounds for construing knowledge and its acquisition, we must appeal to **behavioral** psychology and to the historical study of science. The proper questions about knowledge are not about the **justification** of claims to knowledge, but about how the formation of knowledge is to be explained. We need to reconstruct the notion of **evidence** so that it refers to the sensory stimulations that cause us to have the scientific **beliefs** that we possess. The main question that epistemology asks is how one's output of a theory of nature, which transcends one's input of evidence, is generated in a human subject. Naturalized epistemology was established partly by criticizing traditional epistemology, which was initiated by **Descartes**, and asks how we ought to arrive at our

beliefs prior to any scientific reasoning. **Quine** argues that epistemology should be a branch of natural science, especially a chapter of psychology. Epistemology is contained in the natural sciences and the natural sciences are contained in epistemology. Quine believes that the approach of naturalized epistemology can diminish **skepticism** and free epistemology from the labor of refuting skepticism.

Quine's controversial project has been followed by many other philosophers, who explicitly consider themselves to be pursuing normative epistemology. They see human beings and their cognitive **faculties** are entities in nature and hold that the results of natural sciences, particularly biology and empirical psychology, are crucial to epistemology.

"The systematic assessment of claims to knowledge is the central task of epistemology. According to naturalistic epistemologists, this task can not be well performed unless proper attention is paid to the place of the knowing subject in nature." **Shimony and Nails (eds.), *Naturalistic Epistemology***

naturalistic ethics

ETHICS Also called ethical naturalism. In a broad sense, the view that ethical **statements** are empirical or positive and must be understood in terms of natural propensities of human beings, without mysterious **intuitions** or divine help. As attacked by **Moore**, it is the view held, for example, by **utilitarianism** and **evolutionary ethics**, according to which there is no sharp demarcation between statements of **fact** and statements of **value**. As a consequence, ethical properties are natural properties and we may derive "**ought**" from "**is**." Moore accuses this view of committing the **naturalistic fallacy**, but proponents of naturalistic ethics have tried to show that this is not a **fallacy** at all.

"Theories which owe their prevalence to the supposition that good can be defined by reference to a natural object . . . are what I mean by the name . . . 'Naturalistic Ethics'." **G. E. Moore, *Principia Ethica***

naturalistic fallacy

ETHICS **Moore** claims that philosophers traditionally define the conception of **good** in terms of natural properties or attributes, such as pleasure, the desirable, progress in evolution; in so doing they confuse the ethical conception of "good" with a natural object, and ignore the distinction between what good means and what things are good. This, according to Moore, is the "naturalistic fallacy." Instead of seeking a naturalistic definition, Moore argued that we should see "good" as a simple indefinable non-natural quality to which we have access through a kind of intuition. Moore argues that all philosophers who derive ethics from metaphysics committed this fallacy. Consequently, he claims that ethics could not be based on metaphysics and could not be reduced to any natural or social science. This idea echoes Hume's view that "ought" is different from and can not be derived from "is." But it is disputable whether this is really a genuine fallacy. In particular, there have been recent attempts to justify the derivation of "ought" statements from "is" statements. Moore's influential *Principia Ethica* attempted to dispose of the naturalistic fallacy, but his arguments both against naturalism and for his own account have been challenged.

"That [naturalistic] fallacy, I explained, consists in the contention that good means nothing but some simple or complex notion, that can be defined in terms of natural qualities." **Moore, *Principia Ethica***

nature

METAPHYSICS, ETHICS, PHILOSOPHY OF SCIENCE [Greek *phusis*, from the verb *phuein*, to grow or to give birth to; Aristotle's book *Physics* is "On Nature"] Nature stands in contrast to things made by men, such as conventional things or artifacts. **Aristotle** defines nature as the inner origin of the **change** or stability of a thing. Such a source comprises (1) the material from which a thing is made, and (2) the structure of the thing. Both **matter** and **form** are thus nature, although Aristotle held that form is more a nature than matter. Pre-Socratic philosophy is generally called the philosophy of nature because it seeks for the ultimate material stuff out of which the world is constructed. For Aristotle, a discussion of matter as nature leads to a discussion of **necessity**. His discussion of form as nature leads to **teleology**, and eventually to the theory of the

unmoved mover as the **final cause** of nature, for Aristotle claims that a formal cause coincides with an efficient cause and a final cause. Aristotle requires those who study nature to know both matter and form, but the latter is more important. In Aristotle's ethics, nature means (1) the original constitution or tendency that a man has without involving human intervention, in contrast to what results in him from law and education, and (2) a man's **function** or the **end** to which he tends. The task of ethics is to develop this natural tendency in order to achieve the appropriate natural end.

Nature is also used to refer to the totality of things in the universe. Our knowledge of this natural world changes with the development of sciences. Nature in this sense is sometimes contrasted with man, with nature seen as exploitable by human rationality, but this attitude has been recently challenged by some aspects of environmental philosophy, according to which humans must be seen only as part of nature.

"The word nature has two principal meanings: it either denotes the entire system of things, with the aggregate of all their properties, or it denotes things as they would be, apart from human intervention." ***Collected Works of John Stuart Mill*, vol. X**

Naturphilosophie

PHILOSOPHY OF SCIENCE [German, nature-philosophy] A view of nature that flourished in the Romantic criticism of science in Germany at the beginning of nineteenth century and was fully elaborated by the German philosopher **Schelling**. It criticized the **Newtonian** scientific view of nature that treated nature as **mechanistic** and meaningless and suggested that nature undergoes a process of self-development culminating in a state of self-presentation. It emphasized unities between the subjective and objective and between the **ideal** and **real**. In opposition to the **scientific method** of exploring nature through external observation and experiment, it sought to understand nature's own language through **intuition** and contemplation on the grounds that natural phenomena are expressions of life. It also rejected the **dichotomy** of subject and **object**, according to which the thinking subject is simply opposed to nature as a world of objects. Instead it claimed that the subject is itself part of nature.

"If you recall what was said about the *Natur-philosophie*, what in humankind is conscious of itself and has come to itself is what has gone through the whole of nature, which has, as it were, carried everything, experienced everything, it is that which has brought everything back into itself, into its essence, from self-alienation." **Schelling,** *On the History of Modern Philosophy*

nausea

MODERN EUROPEAN PHILOSOPHY For **Sartre,** an **existentialist** feeling of disgust for the **facticity** and contingency of our bodies in **analogy** to our physical disgust at our bodies. According to Sartre, awareness of my own body is the basic means by which I have contact with the **external world**, and nausea becomes my primitive and original feeling about the world and my pure apprehension of myself as factual experience. This basic nausea produces vomiting and provides the ground for various concrete and empirical nauseas, such as those caused by spoiled meat or fresh blood. Nausea is an inescapable concomitant of physical existence and is a disclosure that one's existence is contingent. Nausea is **nihilated** by active **transcendence**. The title of one of Sartre's novels is *Nausea*.

"This perpetual apprehension on the part of my for-itself of an *insipid* taste which I cannot place, which accompanies me even in my efforts to get away from it, and which is *my* taste – this is what we have described elsewhere under the name of *Nausea*. A dull and inescapable nausea perpetually reveals my body to my consciousness." **Sartre,** *Being and Nothingness*

necessarily false, see logical truth

necessarily true, see logical truth

necessary condition

LOGIC Suppose the **statements** P and Q are related so that Q only if P. Consequently, if P is not the case, then Q is not the case, and if P is the case, then Q is not necessarily the case. P is then a necessary condition of Q.

In contrast, suppose P and Q are related so that if P then Q. Consequently, if P is the case, then Q is the case, but if P is not the case, then Q is not necessarily the case. P is then a **sufficient condition** of Q. If P is a necessary condition of Q, then Q is a sufficient condition of P, and if P is a sufficient condition of Q, then Q is a necessary condition of P.

If P and Q are related so that P if and only if Q and Q if and only if P, then P is both a necessary and sufficient condition of Q. If P is a necessary and sufficient condition of Q, then Q is a necessary and sufficient condition of P. P and Q are then **logically equivalent** statements. Logicians use "iff" as shorthand for "if and only if."

"When one statement entails another, the truth of the first is a sufficient condition of the truth of the second, and the truth of the second is a necessary condition of the truth of the first." **Strawson,** *Introduction to Logical Theory*

necessary/contingent, see contingent/necessary

necessary truth

LOGIC, EPISTEMOLOGY, METAPHYSICS, PHILOSOPHY OF SCIENCE The distinction between necessary truth and contingent truth is a version of **Leibniz**'s distinction between truths of reason and truths of fact. A necessary truth must be true and could not be false, whatever way the world is. It is true in itself. A contingent truth, on the other hand, depends upon the empirical world and might have been false had the world been different. Logically necessary truths are based on the principle of **contradiction**, having **negations** that are **logically impossible**. Necessary truths are not established on the basis of **sense-experience**. They are either intuitively **analytic** or deduced from intuitively acceptable premises. Logical and mathematical truths are generally regarded as the paradigms of necessary truths. For **rationalism**, necessary truth is truth of reason and is based on the insight into real connections between **facts**. For **empiricism**, knowledge of the world must be based on **perception**. Hence either there are no necessary truths, or there are necessary truths, but they have no direct reference to the factual world. The **necessary/contingent** distinction is closely related to the *a priori/a posteriori* distinction and the **analytic/synthetic** distinction. It is difficult to get an adequate grasp of any one of these without understanding the others. A crucial question is whether **Kant** was justified in claiming that some fundamental necessary truths are **synthetic** and *a priori*. Kripke has argued that some necessary truths are *a posteriori*.

If there are other kinds of **necessity** and possibility, such as metaphysical or natural necessity and possibility, they could also be used to distinguish between necessary and contingent truths, and necessary truth would become relative to the sort of necessity in question. We could then ask about the relations among the various kinds of necessary truths. In this sense, the term "necessary truth" becomes ambiguous and varies with different accounts of necessity.

"It appears that necessary truths, such as we find in pure mathematics and particularly in arithmetic and geometry, must have principles whose proof does not depend on instances nor, consequently, on the testimony of the senses, even though without the senses it would never occur to us to think of them." **Leibniz,** *New Essays on Human Understanding*

necessitarianism

METAPHYSICS, PHILOSOPHY OF SCIENCE The doctrine that what happens in the world is determined or necessitated by the **essence** of things or by general **laws**, and hence that **necessity** and possibility are objective notions. The world has different modes of necessity, such as logical, nomic, and metaphysical necessity. Objectively necessary relations in the natural world are the subject-matter of scientific inquiry. The clearest expression of necessitarianism is physical **determinism**, which claims that nature is determined by universal laws. Necessitarianism is opposed by philosophers who reject all necessity, reject non-logical necessity, or consider necessity to be a matter of expectation, a degree of epistemic commitment, or a verbal feature, rather than as an objective **property**. This opposing view can be termed anti-necessitarianism. Another contrasting theory is **contingentism**, which holds that **nature** and **mind** are not completely predetermined and that the world contains irreducible elements of the unpredictable. As necessitarianism is associated with determinism, contingentism is related to **indeterminism** and accepts the existence of **free will**.

"Peirce gave the name 'necessitarianism' to the belief in the principle of universal lawfulness." **Bunge,** *Causality*

necessity

LOGIC, METAPHYSICS, EPISTEMOLOGY, PHILOSOPHY OF SCIENCE Necessity is ascribed to a state that must occur or is always the same, irrespective of changing circumstances or of our interventions. Necessity is distinguished from contingency or possibility, which is ascribed to a state that may or may not occur and that varies with circumstances. If necessity is unconditional, it is absolute necessity, but if it is based on certain premises, it is relative necessity. Logical necessity is ascribed to a **statement** or **proposition** that could not have been false and is guaranteed to be true by the laws of logic. In contrast, a contingent statement is one whose **contradiction** is possible. Necessity attached to a whole proposition (in the form "it is necessarily true that . . .") is necessity *de dicto*, in contrast to necessity *de re*, in which necessity belongs to an object. Necessary knowledge is true under all circumstances and is hence **universal**. Traditionally, a **necessary truth** is thought to be **analytical** and to be known *a priori*, although **Kant** introduced **synthetic** *a priori* **judgments** and the notion of transcendental necessity to characterize judgments giving the conditions for the possibility of **experience**. **Kripke** introduced the notion of necessary *a posteriori* truth for truths concerning the **essence** of a thing that are known through empirical inquiry. This is also called metaphysical necessity. Some philosophers hold that nature is governed by **laws** of natural necessity, but **Hume** argued that what appear to be necessary connections in the world are **associations of ideas** in **mind** and involve psychological necessity rather than objective necessity.

"A thing is called necessary either in reference to its essence or its cause. For the existence of a thing necessarily follows either from the essence and definition of the thing itself or from a given efficient cause." **Spinoza,** *Ethics*

necessity, absolute

LOGIC, METAPHYSICS, PHILOSOPHY OF MATHEMATICS For **Leibniz**, the contrast between absolute necessity and hypothetical necessity is basic. Absolute necessity, also called logical, metaphysical, or mathematical necessity, is necessary in itself. It is the necessity possessed by a truth whose denial would involve a **contradiction**, as in the case of the truths of arithmetic and geometry. Absolute necessity is universally and unconditionally the case. The truth of such necessity is the truth of **reason**. Hypothetical necessity, also called moral, consequential, or physical necessity, is necessary, given that such and such antecedents occur. The term "hypothetical necessity" is derived from **Aristotle**'s *Physics* 200a13–14. According to Leibniz, the present state of the world is not absolutely necessary, but is only hypothetically necessary. All **laws of nature** are only hypothetical, for they depend on **God**'s **will** to create the best possible world. The distinction between absolute and hypothetical necessity is an attempt to avoid **Spinozistic** rigid **determinism** and to establish the possibility of **freedom of the will**. It also plays an important role in Leibniz's metaphysics of **possible worlds**. For other philosophers, hypothetical necessity is also called relative necessity because it is relative to underlying premises.

> "There are necessities, which ought to be admitted. For we must distinguish between an absolute and a hypothetical necessity." **Leibniz,** *The Leibniz– Clarke Correspondence: Fifth Paper to Clarke*

necessity, hypothetical, see necessity, absolute

necessity, natural

PHILOSOPHY OF SCIENCE Also called physical necessity. The necessary connection existing between distinct **events** in the natural world. This sort of necessity is not logical, for it is not guaranteed by the laws of logic, but is based on the **laws of nature**. It exists, according to some philosophers, because objects are endowed with a force that compels, under certain circumstances, the occurrence of such and such effects. **Rationalism** generally holds that such a natural necessity serves as the basis of **induction** and scientific **knowledge**. But **Hume** and his followers object to its existence, for no such force is **observable**. For them, the necessity between matters of fact is psychological, arising from the **constant conjunction** of **states of affairs** of given kinds.

> "Some necessity is itself necessary; other necessity is contingent. It is, moreover, feasible to think that logical necessity is of the formal type, but that natural or physical necessity is of the latter." **von Wright,** *Truth, Knowledge and Modality*

necessity, physical, another name for natural necessity

necessity, psychological

PHILOSOPHY OF MIND A form of necessity first discussed by **Hume**. According to **rationalists**, **logical necessity** was the sole valid form of necessity and was confined to the sphere of **ideas**. Hume claimed that in our knowledge of the natural world, we connect one idea with another through the relations of **resemblance**, **contiguity**, and **causality**. There is a sort of necessary connection between the idea of a cause and the idea of its effect, but that is not logical necessity. The causal relation is simply a relation of regularity. This sort of necessity is brought about by the **constant conjunction** of the two ideas in our minds. Hence it is subjective and psychological rather than objective and logical.

> "Psychological necessity, in Hume's view, marks some of our knowledge of matter of fact." **Walsh,** *Reason and Experience*

necessity, relative, see necessity, absolute

needs

ETHICS, POLITICAL PHILOSOPHY Anything required to lead a normal human life. It is widely claimed that fundamental and universal needs for a rational **agent** include the physical conditions for survival and **freedom**. Further, it is held that a central task of any government is to arrange for the satisfaction of the basic needs of its members, either by itself or through non-governmental institutions. There are various other kinds of human needs, some of which are culturally relative. Philosophers dispute the weight that should be given to the claims of needs in considering how to treat the members of society and how to distribute resources. These disputes are important in discussing **justice** and in determining the relation between **equality** and **equity**.

> "The thought we have now arrived at is that a person needs X [absolutely] if and only if, whatever morally and socially acceptable variation it is (economically, technologically, politically, historically, etc.) possible to envisage occurring within the relevant time-span, he will be harmed if he goes without X." **Wiggins,** *Needs, Values, Truth*

negation

LOGIC, METAPHYSICS [from Latin *negare*, to say no] As a logical term, negation is contrasted to affirmation and the positive and denies either a **proposition** as a whole or a **predicate** within a proposition. The standard sign of negation is ¬. In standard logic, a proposition and its negation form a **contradiction**: both can not be true and both can not be false. The truth of one implies the falsehood of the other. If a proposition is true, its negation must be false, and *vice versa*. A predicate and its negation are also contradictory. Negation is thus a **truth-functional operator**, so that we can know the **truth-value** of a proposition formed by the negation of an initial proposition if we know the truth-value of the initial proposition.

In Hegel's philosophy, negation is mainly a feature of **concepts** or things. Following **Spinoza**'s idea that all **determination** is negation, Hegel claimed that negation is also a way of determining what it negates and hence has a positive result.

"Negation is no longer an abstract nothing, but as a determinate being and somewhat, is only a form of such being – it is as otherness." **Hegel,** *Logic*

negation of the negation

LOGIC, METAPHYSICS, PHILOSOPHY OF HISTORY Also called double negation. In **formal logic**, the negation of the negation of a **proposition** returns to the starting-point of the original and unnegated proposition. The negation of "this is red" is "this is not red," but the negation of "this is not red" once again becomes "this is red."

Hegel supposed that a negation of the negation does not return to its original affirmative state, but reaches a higher degree of affirmation than the initial state and represents a greater development of the thing itself. Any finite affirmative contains its contrary or its negation and, according to Hegel, will develop into the latter. This is the first negation. The negation of the negation overcomes the opposition between the original affirmation and its negation. The negation of the negation will itself be negated as the process of negation proceeds. The process of "affirmation–negation–negation of the negation" is equivalent to the process of "thesis–antithesis–synthesis." It provides the **architectonic** of Hegel's philosophy and is omnipresent in his system. In this process, the first stage is a simple or

natural unity; the second stage is one of separation; and the third stage, the negation of the negation, repairs the separation and restores unity on the higher level of a harmonious whole. Hegel also took this pattern of development to characterize the process of **cognition**. The first stage of cognition is abstract and corresponds to **understanding**; the second stage corresponds to negative **reason**; and the third stage, the negation of the negation, corresponds to positive reason.

The negation of the negation was later adopted to become a basic feature of **dialectical materialism**, especially by Engels in *Anti-Dühring*. He claimed that the negation of the negation is also a **law** of the natural world and a law in the history of philosophy. Critics have questioned the alleged ubiquity of the dialectic pattern and its capacity to explain the development of **consciousness**, **nature**, cognition, or history. They question Hegel's understanding of negation and logic.

"The second negative, the negative of the negative, at which we have arrived, is this sublating of the contradiction." **Hegel,** *Science of Logic*

negative facts

METAPHYSICS, PHILOSOPHY OF LANGUAGE A negative fact is the non-existence of a **state of affairs**, that is, "something is not the case," in contrast to a positive fact, the existence of a state of affairs, that is, "something is the case." There has been a debate about the nature of negative facts. **Russell** believes that negative facts exist and are represented by negative **propositions**. **Wittgenstein** claims that all **elementary propositions** depict positive facts and that negative facts, rather than really existing, merely indicate that there is no such combination between **objects** or things. Hence, what corresponds to a negative fact is a false elementary proposition.

"I think you will find that it is simpler to take negative facts as facts, to assume that 'Socrates is not alive' is really an objective fact in the same sense in which 'Socrates is human' is a fact." **Russell,** *Logic and Knowledge*

negative freedom

PHILOSOPHY OF ACTION, ETHICS The ability to act independent of constraint, coercion, or compulsion external to the one's own **will**. Negative freedom (freedom from . . .) is contrasted with positive freedom (freedom to . . .) or the power of a subject to choose his own goals and course of conduct among alternatives. Negative freedom is freedom from **determination** by external **causes**, while positive freedom is the capacity of **pure reason** to determine itself as a will. Isaiah **Berlin** used a related distinction between positive and **negative** conceptions of **liberty** to argue that too much emphasis on the positive conception of liberty has led to tyranny.

> "Freedom of choice is this independence from being determined by sensible impulses; this is the negative concept of freedom. The positive concept of freedom is that of the capacity of pure reason to be of itself practical." **Kant, *Metaphysics of Morals***

negative liberty

POLITICAL PHILOSOPHY The Oxford philosopher Isaiah **Berlin** distinguished between positive and negative liberty. Positive liberty is the "liberty or freedom to," while negative liberty is the "liberty or freedom from." Negative liberty is characterized by an absence of coercive force. With negative liberty, one is protected from the constraints of moral, legal, political, and social requirements, but such constraints seem needed to achieve any sort of positive freedom. Different political philosophies give different priorities to these two kinds of freedom, with proponents of each seeing the rival conception as frustrating its own notion of liberty. Berlin, himself, supports the **liberalism** associated with negative liberty, while others from a **Hegelian** or **idealist** perspective emphasize positive liberty. The soundness of this distinction has been contested, but rich debate has contributed much to contemporary discussions of liberty.

> "The first of these senses of freedom or liberty (I shall use both words to mean the same), which (following much precedent) I shall call the 'negative' sense, is involved in the answer to the question 'What is the area within which the subject – a person or group of persons – is or should be left to do or be what he is able to do or be, without interference by other persons." **Berlin, *Four Essays on Liberty***

negative responsibility

PHILOSOPHY OF ACTION, ETHICS The responsibility for something which is not caused directly by the **agent** but which the agent fails to prevent from happening. The notion is derived from the distinction between **action** and omission or between intervening and letting things take their own course. Moral agents must bear positive responsibility for their actions or interventions, but should they be responsible for their omissions or for letting things happen? It is a matter of dispute whether we can have negative responsibility. **Utilitarianism** claims that we should bring about the best consequences, and this implies that we all have negative responsibility. But its critics point out that by accepting this claim we would have boundless responsibilities.

> "[T]he notion of negative responsibility: that if I am ever responsible for anything, then I must be just as much responsible for things that I allow or fail to prevent, as I am for things that I myself, in the more everyday restricted sense, bring about." **B. Williams, in Smart and Williams (eds.), *Utilitarianism: For and Against***

negative theology

PHILOSOPHY OF RELIGION Also called apophatic theology, **theism** based on the method of the *via negativa*. It describes **God** by saying what he is not, rather than what he is, because as finite beings we can not recognize God's **attributes** in any real and full sense and because God is beyond what our language can positively describe. Negative theology claims that religious language is **non-cognitive** and equivocal. The ultimate thing is beyond all human **concepts**, and so what is affirmed of it must also be denied. Hence, all **predicates** – not only the negative ones such as evil and false, but also the positive ones such as good and true – should be subtracted from God. Such a negation of **description** does not lead to **skepticism** or unbelief, but leads instead to the truth that God is beyond all such words. It is only by removing from God all the imperfections of his creatures that his **transcendence** and otherness can be safeguarded. Negative theology enables us to maintain the radical distinction between God and his creatures. The Scriptures are full of **paradoxical** descriptions of God because they try to show something inexpressible that can not be stated positively. This type of theology is rooted in **Platonic** thought as developed in **Neoplatonism**. **Clement of Alexandria** is thought to be its founder, and its main proponents were the Jewish philosopher Moses **Maimonides** and the German theologian Eckhart.

"When the negative theology says that no conceptions apply to God, it is, in a perhaps still subtler way, making a comparable mistake. For where there are no definite common aspects there are no definite contrasts either." **Hartshorne,** *Creative Synthesis and Philosophical Method*

neo-Darwinism, see Darwinism

neo-Hegelianism
PHILOSOPHICAL METHOD, METAPHYSICS Also called British idealism. A Hegelian school developed in the latter part of the nineteenth century by the British philosophers F. H. **Bradley**, Bernard **Bosanquet**, John **McTaggart**, and the American philosopher Josiah **Royce**. This school sought to build an idealistic metaphysical system in which all internally connected **particulars** are absorbed into a single reality. It ignored the dialectical and historical dimension of Hegel's thought and instead emphasized the relations between **time** and **eternity**, between **matter** and **mind**, and between the many and the one. It claimed that "what is" is the manifestation of **spirit** and in principle can be known by the human spirit. Subject and **object** are correlative because they are both rooted in one ultimate spiritual principle. Neo-Hegelianism was a form of **absolute idealism** that opposed the British empirical tradition and dominated British philosophy for nearly half a century. The interpretation of Hegel in the English-speaking world has been greatly influenced by this school. The **analytic philosophy** of **Russell** and **Moore** grew out of their criticisms of neo-Hegelianism.

"It is not altogether unreasonable to describe British idealism, as is often done, as a Neo-Hegelian movement, provided at least that it is understood that it was a question of receiving stimulus from Hegel rather than of following him in the relation of pupil to master." **Copleston,** *A History of Philosophy,* **vol. VII**

neo-Kantianism
PHILOSOPHICAL METHOD, EPISTEMOLOGY, METAPHYSICS, PHILOSOPHY OF SCIENCE A philosophical movement prevailing in late nineteenth- and early twentieth-century German philosophy, with a motto "back to Kant" from Liebman's manifesto, *Kant and the Epigoni*. Precursors of the movement included H. von Helmholtz, Liebman, A. Lange, E. Zeller, and Kuno Fischer. Common features of the movement were the repudiation of speculative naturalism and materialism, irrationalism, and the authority of natural science and its emphasis on the central status of **Kant**'s epistemology in philosophy. More loosely, neo-Kantianism comprised a variety of schools which had different directions and which debated with one another. Among these, the Marburg and Heidelberg schools were the most influential. The logico-methodological Marburg school emphasized Kant's theoretical philosophy, especially his **idealism** in relation to natural science. Its major representatives were H. Cohen, P. Natorp, and E. Cassirer. The axiological Heidelberg school, also called the Baden or Southeast German school, was more interested in applying Kant's **transcendental** method to specifying universal cultural value. Its major representatives were W. Windelband and H. Rickert. Outside these schools, A. Riehl's realistic neo-Kantianism argued for the reality of Kant's **thing-in-itself**. In Göttingen, L. Nelson developed a psychological neo-Kantianism, which holds that **introspection** plays a central role in discovering *a priori* **principles**.

"Neo-Kantians . . . announced that they had had enough of the airy metaphysical speculations of the idealists and that it was time to return to the spirit of Kant himself." **Copleston,** *A History of Philosophy,* **vol. VII**

Neoplatonism
ANCIENT GREEK PHILOSOPHY, METAPHYSICS, PHILOSOPHY OF RELIGION The philosophical tradition founded by **Plotinus**, developed through his disciple **Porphyry**, the Syrian School of Iamblichus, the school of Athens, represented by Plutarch, **Proclus**, and Simplicius, and the Alexandrian school until the fall of Alexandria in 642. Plotinus' *Enneads* (edited by Porphyry) was the source of this tradition, and Proclus' *Elements of Theology* was the systematic exposition of its doctrines. Neoplatonism, which

was the last philosophical system of the classical world, explained the origin of the world in terms of Plotinus' three *hypostases* (the **one**, **nous**, and the **soul**) and the process of **emanation**. Neoplatonism attempted to reconcile the two supposedly incompatible systems of **Plato** and **Aristotle**, by considering Aristotle's philosophy as an introduction to Plato's higher **wisdom**. This attitude led many Neoplatonists to comment extensively on both Plato and Aristotle and thus contributed greatly to the history of philosophy. Neoplatonism advocated **polytheism** and **mysticism** and had a favorable attitude toward theology. Hence it became the main opposition of early Christianity, which it directly attacked. The school of Athens, which was based on Plato's academy, was closed by the emperor Justinian in 529 precisely because of its conflict with Christianity. This event is usually regarded as marking the end of **Hellenistic philosophy**. However, Neoplatonism exerted great influence upon the development of Christian philosophy because it sought to explain the world by appeal to one ultimate **principle**. Neoplatonism was revived in the Renaissance by **Ficino** in Florence, and there was another resurgence by the **Cambridge Platonists** in the seventeenth century.

"Neo-platonism emphasised that aspect of Plato's thought that stressed the transcendence of the One (or the Good), and the way the One is beyond all categorical language or thought." **Stiver,** *The Philosophy of Religious Language*

neo-pragmatism

PHILOSOPHY OF LANGUAGE, METAPHYSICS, PHILOSOPHY OF SOCIAL SCIENCE A **postmodern** version of **pragmatism** developed by the American philosopher Richard **Rorty** and drawing inspiration from authors such as **Dewey**, **Heidegger**, **Sellars**, **Quine**, and **Derrida**. It repudiates the notion of universal **truth**, epistemological **foundationalism**, **representationalism**, and the notion of epistemic **objectivity**. It is a **nominalist** approach that denies that **natural kinds** and linguistic entities have substantive **ontological** implications. While traditional pragmatism focuses on **experience**, Rorty centers on language. Language is contingent on use, and **meaning** is produced by using words in familiar manners. The **self** is seen as a "centerless web of beliefs and desires," and Rorty

denies that the subject-matter of the human sciences can be studied in the same ways as we study the subject-matter of the natural sciences. Neo-pragmatism, which focuses on social practice and political experimentation, claims that there is no objective and **transcendental** standpoint from which to pass judgment and that truth must be relative to specific social contexts and **practices**.

"The senses in which the new pragmatism differs from the old are, first, with regard to the shift from experience to language and, second, with regard to an acquired suspicion of 'scientific method' deriving from the historicizing of science in the works of thinkers such as Thomas Kuhn and P. F. Feyerabend." **D. Hall,** *Richard Rorty*

neo-Pythagoreanism

ANCIENT GREEK PHILOSOPHY, PHILOSOPHY OF RELIGION A philosophical and religious tendency that flourished from the first century BC to the third century AD. It regarded **Pythagoras** as the revealer of religious truth, but it actually mixed early Pythagorean material, **Plato**'s doctrines, and the views of the **Peripatetics** and Stoicism. It stressed the necessity of purification and represented the change of **soul** according to moral progress. It advocated abandoning all theoretical research and living in union with both superior and inferior gods. It popularized the notion of moral retribution in a future life. Major proponents of neo-Pythagoreanism include Figulus, Apollonius of Tyana, and **Philo of Alexandria**. Neo-Pythagoranism deeply influenced **Neoplatonism** and early Christianity.

"For the neo-Pythagorians, philosophy became the art of curing, or a devotional guide. Men were no longer seeking to understand." **Sheen,** *Philosophy of Religion*

neo-realism

EPISTEMOLOGY, METAPHYSICS Also called new realism. An American philosophical movement of the early twentieth century, which originated with a common manifesto published in the *Journal of Philosophy* (1910), entitled "A Program and First Platform of Six Realists." The six philosophers were Ralph Barton **Perry**, William P. Montague, E. B. Holt, Walter Pitkin, Edward Spaulding, and Walter Marvin. In

1912 they published a cooperative volume, *The New Realism*, that gave the movement its name. New realism rejected **idealism**, in particular that of **Royce**. It claimed that idealism argues fallaciously from the premise that everything known is known to the conclusion that for everything to be is to be known. It rejected the **egocentric predicament**, which moves from our being at the center of what we know to the claim that this placement affects the nature of what we know. The nature of reality can not be inferred merely from the nature of knowledge. The entities that are the objects of scientific studies are not conditioned by their being known, although they are presented to **consciousness** and have cognitive relations. As a version of **direct realism**, neo-realism emphasized a direct **acquaintance** with physical **objects** and claimed that what is known is independent of the knowing relation. Reality is a datum, given independently of whatever **ideas** may be formed about it. The perceived object is identical in **substance** with a part or aspect of the physical object. The movement was replaced by critical realism as a result of its failure to provide a satisfactory account of error, **illusion**, **doubt**, **hypothesis**, and the progress of knowledge. Occasionally, the term new realism is also used to refer to the rejection of idealism by **Russell** and **Moore**, and to their attempt to establish a logical method by which legitimate conclusions can be derived from any body of data.

"Neo-realism arose as a protest against Roycean absolutism in particular, and idealism in general." **Werkmeister**, *A History of Philosophical Ideas in America*

neo-scholasticism

PHILOSOPHY OF RELIGION, METAPHYSICS, PHILOSOPHY OF SCIENCE Also called neo-Thomism, a Roman Catholic philosophical and theological movement of the nineteenth and twentieth centuries. It is a revival of Thomism and seeks to demonstrate that medieval scholasticism, especially the philosophy of Thomas **Aquinas**, is consistent with the development of modern science. The movement assumes that Aquinas' doctrines can be re-appropriated to solve modern philosophical problems such as those arising from **Cartesian dualism**. Neo-scholasticism attempts to bring

Aristotelian and Thomistic metaphysics into a modern intellectual setting in order to deal with contemporary issues. In 1879 Pope Leo XIII sent his letter *Aeterni Patris* to all bishops of the Church, making Thomas Aquinas the leading Doctor of the Church, and thus sanctioning Thomism as the authoritative and orthodox Catholic theology. It proposed to consider Thomism as the exclusive response in Catholic philosophy and theology to modern philosophical systems. This greatly stimulated the development of neo-scholasticism, first in Catholic educated circles and then for a wider public. Scholars produced intensive examinations and interpretations of Aquinas' works and established a variety of Thomistic systems. There is not a unified set of doctrines in neo-Thomism, because different philosophers have adopted different versions of Thomism. Some have even resisted the description neo-Thomist, although Aquinas' **five ways** for demonstrating **God**'s existence were regarded as vital for all neo-Thomist thinkers. The Institute Supérieur de Philosophie at Louvain founded by Cardinal Mercier has been an influential center for neo-Thomism. The French philosopher Etienne **Gilson** established an Institute of Medieval Studies in Toronto, where the influential scholar Joseph Owens applied Thomism to reconstruct Aristotle's metaphysics. Another important representative was Jacques **Maritain**, whose work has had wide public influence.

"Neo-Scholasticism, a new-realism once more, a doctrine that refuses to fall in with the method foreshadowed by Descartes, or at least if it does so tries hard to avoid its conclusion." **Gilson**, *The Spirit of Medieval Philosophy*

network theory of meaning, an alternative term for conceptual role theory

Neumann, John von (1903–57)
American mathematician, economist, and philosopher of quantum mechanics and game theory, born in Budapest, Hungary. Von Neumann developed the theory of linear operators and made fundamental contributions to set theory, mathematic logic, Hilbert's proof theory, econometrics, and the theory and design of computers. He founded game theory and demonstrated how the theory

could be applied to economics. His main works include *Mathematical Foundations of Quantum Mechanics* (1955), *The Theory of Games and Economic Behavior* (with Morgenstern) (1944), and *The Computer and the Brain* (1958).

neural network modeling, see connectionism

Neurath, Otto (1882–1945)

Austrian sociologist and philosopher, a founding member of the Vienna Circle. Neurath tried to eliminate all terminology with multiple meanings and all metaphysical presuppositions in sociology. He was a major advocate of physicalism in logical positivism, claiming that all scientific statements should be translated into statements that are descriptive of the observable world. His anti-foundationalist remark that "we are like sailors who have to build their ship on the open sea . . ." influenced Quine. Neurath's major works include the *Empirical Sociology* (1931) and the *Foundations of the Social Sciences* (1944). He planned and co-edited (with Rudolf Carnap and Charles Morris) the uncompleted *International Encyclopedia of Unified Science*.

Neurath's ship

EPISTEMOLOGY, PHILOSOPHY OF SCIENCE A metaphor invented by the Austrian sociologist and philosopher Otto **Neurath**. Neurath was a leading member of the **Vienna Circle**, but disagreed with the epistemological **foundationalism** of another important member, Rudolf **Carnap**. Carnap believed that there is a set of **incorrigible** protocol statements that directly report sense-**experience**. All other valid complex statements are constructed out of these protocol statements. In criticizing this picture, Neurath compared our body of **knowledge** to a ship, and said: "We are like sailors who have to rebuild their ship on the open sea, without ever being able to dismount it in dry-dock and reconstruct it from the best components." Accordingly, knowledge is historically conditioned and is maintained if a sufficient range of its claims is acceptable at any given time. Nevertheless, any piece of knowledge can be replaced to keep the whole project of knowledge going. Nothing can claim to be the foundation of knowledge. This metaphor was adopted by **Quine** and is widely cited as a powerful image of anti-foundationalism.

> "The philosopher's task was well-compared by Neurath to that of a mariner who must rebuild his ship on the open sea." **Quine, *From a Logical Point of View***

neuro-philosophy, see connectionism

neustic/phrastic

PHILOSOPHY OF LANGUAGE Different **sentences** may have the same **content** but different **moods**. For example, "Shut the door!" and "You will shut the door." The content of these two sentences – your shutting the door in the immediate future – is the same, but the sentences differ because one is a **command** and the other is a **statement**. In *The Language of Morals*, R. M. **Hare** called the common content of such sentences the phrastic [from Greek *phrazein*, literally what is said, to indicate or to show] and called their different moods the neustic [from Greek *neuein*, to nod, to assent]. With this distinction, he claims that phrastics allow **imperatives** to stand in logical relations.

> "I shall call the part of the sentence that is common to both moods (your shutting the door in the immediate future) the phrastic, and the part that is different in the case of commands and statements (yes or please), the neustic." **Hare, *The Language of Morals***

neutral monism

METAPHYSICS A theory formulated by the American Pragmatist William **James** and developed by American **realism**, but propounded independently by the Austrian philosopher Ernst **Mach**. In contrast both to idealistic monism (that **mind** is the real existent) and materialistic monism (that **matter** is the real existent), the theory holds that both mental things and physical things are **constructed** out of the same primary stuff, which is neither mental nor physical but neutral between them. Both mind and matter are logical **functions** of the same stuff. Thus there is no real distinction between mind and matter. **Russell** in one period accepted this view by claiming that the world is composed of neutral **events**. This position proposed a solution to the mind–body problem, but there are difficulties with the neutral status of that which constitutes minds and bodies and with how arrangements of what is neutral can issue in minds and bodies. If **experiences** are pro-posed as the neutral entities, it is not clear whether neutral monism clarifies or obscures the nature of experience.

> "'Neutral monism' . . . is the theory that the things commonly regarded as mental and the things commonly regarded as physical don't differ in respect of any intrinsic property possessed by the one set and not by the other, but differ only in respect of arrangement and context." **Russell,** *Collected Papers of Bertrand Russell,* **vol. VII**

new criticism

AESTHETICS A school of literary criticism developed by J. C. Ransome, A. Tate, C. Brooks, among others, in the United States during the 1930s and 1940s. It rejected the historical method in literary study that emphasized the influence of history upon literature. Instead it suggested that a literary work is not an historical object, but should be treated merely as a text. It embraced the idea of art for art's sake and emphasized the autonomy of art. The central task of literary criticism should be to focus on the literary devices present in a work, such as harmony, structure of **discourse**, imagery, figurative use of language and rhythm. Facts external to the work itself were claimed to be irrelevant to the appreciation or criticism of that work. The movement has affinities with **Derrida**'s more recent theory of **deconstruction**.

> "This doctrine (of the new criticism) holds that in trying to understand a work of art we cannot make use of facts external to the work itself – facts of biography, convention and (perhaps) intention." **Casey, "The Autonomy of Art," in Vesey (ed.),** *Philosophy and the Arts*

New England transcendentalism, see trans-cendentalism

new organon

PHILOSOPHY OF SCIENCE, LOGIC The title of Francis **Bacon**'s major book and also a technical term in his philosophy. The book, titled *Novum Organum* in Latin, was published in 1620, as the second part of an uncompleted project called the Great Instauration. The subtitle of *Novum Organum* is "true directions concerning the interpretation of nature." It was intended as a guide to the correct use of human **understanding** in the investigation of nature. The central idea is that we should interpret rather than anticipate nature. We can only know on the basis of what has been **observed** in fact or in thought. Hence, the traditional **syllogistic** deductive logic that starts from abstract notions and **principles** is not adequate. Bacon called his own logic new in order to distin-guish it from Aristotle's *Organon*, in which syllogistic logic is systematically elaborated. The correct logic should be inductive, although it is not the method of **induction** in general that he favors, but **induction by elimination**. What, then, does Bacon mean by a new organon? He claims that there are three basic differences between the old logic and his new logic. (1) While the old logic is aimed at inventing arguments and overcoming an opponent's argu-ment, the new logic aimed to discover the principles of nature itself and to command nature in action. (2) While the old logic focuses mainly on syllogism, new logic rejects it and claims that induction is the form of demonstration that upholds sense and mirrors nature. (3) While in the old logic the starting-point of inquiry is principle, new logic requires that we start with a judgment about the information obtained through the **senses**.

> "As for the legitimate form [of induction] I refer it to the new organon." **Bacon,** *The Philosophical Works*

new realism, another name for neo-realism

new riddle of induction

LOGIC, PHILOSOPHY OF LANGUAGE A problem which has provoked heated debate about the nature of **induction**. Induction is normally characterized in terms of inference to the continuation of previously observed regularities on the assumption of the **uniformity of nature**. But Nelson **Goodman** argued that this analysis itself depends on an unjustifi-able assumption. Suppose that so far all observed emeralds have been green. The classical analysis of induction will lead us to believe that future emer-alds will be green. But suppose there is another **predicate** grue, such that x is grue if and only if it is green when observed before time T (in the future) and blue thereafter. Given this, all our evidence for the **hypothesis** that emeralds are green equally supports the hypothesis that emeralds are grue. The evidence that we naturally take as **confirming** a given hypothesis always confirms some contrary hypothesis to an equal degree. Thus correct induction can not be defined in terms of **inferences** to events similar to those observed. There are no language-independent similarities in nature. Induction can only apply to properties that have **projectibility**, but the **paradox** shows that it is unclear what these properties are. This new riddle of induction is also called Goodman's paradox or the grue paradox.

> "We have so far neither any answer nor any promising clue to an answer to the question what distinguishes lawlike or confirmable hypotheses from accidental or non-confirmable ones; and what may at first have seemed a minor technical difficulty has taken on the stature of a major obstacle to the development of a satisfactory theory of confirmation. It is this problem that I call the new riddle of induction." **Goodman, *Problems and Projects***

Newcomb's problem

LOGIC, PHILOSOPHY OF ACTION A **paradox** about choice formulated by the American physicist William Newcomb in the early 1960s and published by Robert **Nozick** in his paper "Newcomb's Problem and Two Principles of Choice" (1969). Suppose that a Supreme Being who has a successful record of **prediction** offers you two boxes A and B. You can choose to have either both boxes or box B alone. He puts a thousand pounds in Box A, and puts either a million pounds in B if he has predicted that you will choose B alone, or nothing if he has predicted that you will choose both boxes. Now which alternative should you choose? One line of reasoning suggests that you should trust the demonstrated predictive capacity of the Supreme Being and choose B alone; so you will end up rich. The other reasoning suggests that you should take both, for you can get at least one thousand pounds in this way. If you choose B alone and the Supreme Being has predicted that you would take both boxes, you will end up with nothing. Both ways of reasoning are sound, but they are incompatible. If the Supreme Being's prediction were based on the assumption of your **rationality** and one option were more rational than the other, you would know what to choose, but

any attempt to predict your choice on the basis of rationality will not produce a determinate result.

> "Newcomb's problem presents a conflict between dominance reasoning and expected utility reasoning, both of which seem to have great intuitive appeal." **Campbell and Sowden (eds.), *Paradoxes of Rationality and Co-operation***

Newman, John Henry (1801–90)

English philosopher of religion, born in London, the founder of the Birmingham Oratory, made a cardinal in 1879. Newman's main philosophical work, *Essay in Aid of a Grammar of Assent* (1870), developed a concrete mode of reasoning that operated in the middle ground between formal and informal reasoning. Newman held that the mental activity that engaged in concrete reasoning, which he called the "illative sense," involves personal experience and insight and yields certitude in our assent to informal judgments. He argued that his theory of mind explained our certitude in religious faith.

Newton, Isaac (1642–1727)

English scientist and mathematician, born in Woolsthorpe, Lincolnshire. Newton's *Philosophiae Naturalis Principia Mathematica* ("The Mathematical Principles of Natural Philosophy," 1687) was a revolutionary work in modern physics and mathematics that established the three laws of motion and a general law of gravitation to explain the system of the world. The laws of motion presuppose the existence of an absolute space and time. He rejected speculative hypotheses and maintained that scientific knowledge should be based on experimental observation and induction. Newton's achievement led to the development of the view that the universe is a rational and orderly system available to mathematic reason. His work led to the development of explanations of all kinds of phenomena in terms of the concepts and theorems of the Newtonian system. Newton and Leibniz were the two founders of mathematical calculus.

Nicholas of Cusa (1401–64)

German theologian, philosopher, and mathematician, made a cardinal in 1448. Nicholas revived Neoplatonism and was influential in the Renaissance. In *De docta ignorantia* ("Of Learned Ignorance," 1440), he claimed that knowledge was learned ignorance and argued for the limitation of rational inquiry. He held that rational enquiry can bring human beings closer to the infinite God, but that such enquiry can not comprehend God. Whilst the law of non-contradiction applies to finite things, all oppositions are united in God. Intuitive intellect enables us to grasp the coincidence of opposites.

Nicod's criterion

LOGIC A test of the relevance of **evidence** for **confirmation** put forward by the French philosopher Jean Nicod, saying that for a generalization "All As are Bs," an instance A is B provides confirming evidence; an instance A is not B disconfirms the generalization and justifies its rejection, and evidence of something which is neither A nor B is irrelevant, that is, it neither confirms nor disconfirms. This criterion is plausible in its own right, but when it is put together with other principles of confirmation, **Hempel's paradox** of confirmation arises.

"Nicod's criterion . . . states that 'φa.φa' always confirms, 'φa.~φa' always disconfirms, while '~φa.φa' and '~φa.~φa' are always irrelevant to, 'of physical necessity all φ's are φ's'." **Swinburne,** *An Introduction to Confirmation Theory*

Nietzsche, Friedrich (1844–1900)

German philosopher, born in Rocken, Prussia. As a founder of modern irrationalism, Nietzsche claimed that the will to power worked in all living things as a fundamental motive to attain a higher and more perfect state. He held that the will to power is characterized by self-overcoming and is life-affirming. All purposes, aims, and means are only different modes expressing the will to power, which attained its zenith in the Superman (*Übermensch*) and its most spiritual expression in philosophy. The Superman, as the realization of profound human potentialities, is the ideal of life for human beings when God, as a non-human source of value, is dead. Nietzsche sought to reassess all values in ethics and held that the two basic types of morality are engaged in struggle throughout history. Slave morality was derived from the resentment of the weak man and the ruled group, whereas master morality was rooted in the self-affirmation of the strong man and the ruling group. Nietzsche suffered a mental and physical collapse in 1889 and remained insane until his death.

He has had great influence as a cultural critic and philosopher, although every interpretation of his philosophy has been controversial. His main works include *The Birth of Tragedy* (1872), *Thus Spoke Zarathustra* (1883–5), *Beyond Good and Evil* (1886), *Toward a Genealogy of Morals* (1887), and *The Will to Power* (1889).

nihil ex nihilo, see *ex nihilo nihil fit*

nihilism

METAPHYSICS, EPISTEMOLOGY, ETHICS, POLITICAL PHILOSOPHY [from Latin *nihil*, nothing] A theory that advocates that nothing is believable and that no distinction is significant. Metaphysical nihilism claims that the world and human life do not have the **value** and **meaning** we suppose them to have. Epistemological nihilism holds that no **knowledge** is possible. Ethical nihilism supposes that there is no ground to justify any absolute moral value. Political nihilism suggests that any political organization must be corrupt and unworthy of support. **Nietzsche** claimed that he is a nihilist, but his nihilism holds that the world lacks value and meaning if value and meaning are conceived in a traditional way. His nihilism is the devaluation of all values and provides a motive to seek new values.

"Right here is where the destiny of Europe lies – in losing our fear of man we have also lost our love for him, our respect for him, our hope in him and even our will to be man. The sight of man now makes us tired – what is nihilism today if it is not that?" **Nietzsche,** *On the Genealogy of Morals*

no-ownership theory

PHILOSOPHY OF MIND A theory which maintains that states of **consciousness** do not belong to anything, although they may be causally dependent on the **body** in a contingent way. If something is owned, its **ownership** is logically transferable, but this is not the case with experience. **Strawson** ascribed this theory to **Wittgenstein** at one period and to **Schlick**, and criticizes it in his own discussion of **persons**. He accepts that the theory correctly claims that the unique role of a single body in one's **experience** is not sufficient for ascribing experience to it, but argues that the theory itself is incoherent. For the experience of consciousness to be causally dependent on states of the body, it must be owned by something. We could not refer to an independent particular experience. We refer to **mental states** by way of their owners, and therefore experience must be owned.

> "The [no-ownership] theorist could maintain his position only by denying that we could ever refer to particular states or experiences at all; and his position is ridiculous." **Strawson, *Individuals***

noble lie

ANCIENT GREEK PHILOSOPHY, POLITICAL PHILOSOPHY, PHILOSOPHY OF SOCIAL SCIENCE A falsehood uttered for the interest of the state. The term was introduced by **Plato** in *Republic* 414–415 for a myth used to safeguard social harmony by persuading a population to accept class distinctions. According to the myth, God made human beings from the earth. For the rulers, he added gold to the composition; for the **auxiliaries**, he added silver; and for the farmers and other workers, he added iron and bronze. For this reason, rulers should enjoy the greatest prestige. The distinction is not firmly fixed, for a golden child might be born of silver parents. It is the duty of the rulers to ensure that only a golden person can become a ruler. Plato believed that the myth can make the citizens happy with their current status and can thus promote social stability. Other Western political thinkers have accepted the legitimacy of political lies for the sake of public or party interest, and some theorists have examined related questions about the role of myth, **ideology**, or false consciousness in political life.

> "How then . . . might we contrive one of those opportune falsehoods of which we were just now speaking, so as by one noble lie to persuade if possible the rulers themselves, but failing that the rest of the city." **Plato, *Republic***

noble savage

POLITICAL PHILOSOPHY, ETHICS A term associated with J. J. **Rousseau**'s conception of human beings before the appearance of **civilization** and government. In contrast to **Hobbes**'s view that men in the **state of nature** are savage, Rousseau claims that if they are savages, they are noble savages. He held that human beings in the state of nature are free, peaceful, innocent, independent, and happy. They are faithful to **human nature** and are free from the disease of our civilization. It is the establishment of society that deforms human nature and makes humans subject to the conditions of domestic slavery. But it is argued that Rousseau held this view only in the early stage of his thought and that in general he did not think that men in the natural state are capable of **virtue** and moral relationships.

> "Except possibly in the Discourse on the Arts and Sciences, written before his theories had been properly thought out, Rousseau was no believer in the 'noble savage', though that expression is often wrongly associated with his name." **J. Hall, *Rousseau***

noema

MODERN EUROPEAN PHILOSOPHY, PHILOSOPHY OF MIND [from Greek *noema*, what is thought about; in contrast to a correlative term, *noesis*, the act of thinking. The terms are related to *nous*, reason] **Husserl** distinguished two aspects of intentional **experience**, the **material** and the **formal**. While the material aspect comprises the diverse sensory stuff passively received by **consciousness**, the formal aspect, or *noesis*, bestows sense on the material stuff and generates unity among multiplicity by means of its **synthetic** activities. This account is deeply influenced by **Kant**'s discussion of **apperception**. *Noema*, in contrast, is what is unified and synthesized by *noetic* activity. For Husserl, a major task for **phenomenology** is to reveal the *noetic-noematic* structure of intentional experience. The interpretation of *noema* is difficult and has been subject to dispute. Generally, it is neither an **object** nor a part of an object, but is an entity corresponding to **Frege**'s sense (in his distinction between **sense** and **reference**). *Noema* is a complex that includes every factor determining the meaning of *noetic* activity. It is the crucial notion for Husserl's theory of **intentionality**, for he claims that mental acts are directed upon *noema* rather than objects.

> "Corresponding at all points to the manifold data of the real noetic content, there is a variety of data displayable in really pure intuition, and is a correlative 'noematic content', or briefly, 'noema' – terms which we shall henceforth be continually using." **Husserl, *Ideas***

noesis

ANCIENT GREEK PHILOSOPHY, MODERN EUROPEAN PHILOSOPHY, PHILOSOPHY OF MIND [Greek, variously translated as intellection, intelligence, and understanding; it is cognate with the verb *noein* and its object *to noeton*] In a wider sense *noesis* is **thought**, in contrast to **perception** (Greek *aisthesis*). In its narrow sense, *noesis* is identified with *nous* (immediate or intuitive thinking) and contrasted to *dianoia* (discursive thinking). It is the thought that constitutes the being of the **Unmoved Mover** in **Aristotle**'s *Metaphysics* and is pure intuitive **apprehension** in **Neoplatonism**. In **Plato**'s simile of the **line**, *noesis* is beyond *dianoia*, and while *dianoia* is concerned with mathematical entities, *noesis* is the highest state of the mind, which reasons from **Forms** to Forms, reaches **first principles**, and then deduces from them. It is **dialectical** or philosophical **reason**. In modern times, the contrast between *noesis* and *noema* is fundamental to Husserl's **phenomenological** account of **intentional experience**.

> "Life is defined in the case of animals by the power of perception, in that of man by the power of perception or noesis." **Aristotle,** *Nicomachean Ethics*

nomic necessity

METAPHYSICS, PHILOSOPHY OF SCIENCE The regularity and uniformity existing amongst contingent natural phenomena. "Spring follows winter" and "Ice melts at a certain temperature" are statements that express **empirical laws**. They are not logically or mathematically necessary, but appear to be necessary in some sense. This sort of **necessity** is often called nomic or law-like necessity. Such a necessity reveals that things will at least generally happen in that way or, in a stronger form, that they must happen in that way or that it is inevitable that they will so happen. Law-like necessity is often expressed in a hypothetical supposition: if anything had the characteristics $c_1 \ldots c_n$, then it would have the characteristic x. Different philosophers have offered various interpretations of this sort of necessity. **Hume** denied its **objectivity** by claiming that it is nothing more than our habitual expectation. Among those who have admitted it, medieval thinkers considered it to be due to **God**'s force, while **Kant** suggested that it results from the imposition of our **categories** of **understanding** upon **experience**.

> "The nomic necessity – anything characterised by p q r would be characterised by x – implies the factual universal that 'everything that is p q r is actually x'." **Johnson,** *Logic*

nominal definition, see real definition

nominal essence

METAPHYSICS The distinction between **real essence** and nominal essence, drawn by **Locke**, roughly corresponds to the traditional metaphysical division between **substance** and **quality** or between **essence** and **appearance**. A nominal essence is the quality or qualities by which we recognize an item and which justifies on any given occasion applying the item's **name** to it. For Locke, it is the **abstract ideas** for which a general or **sortal** name stands. For example, according to its nominal essence gold is a metal that is malleable, heavy, and yellow. Because gold has these **properties**, we can recognize it as such and can apply the name "gold" to it. A thing's real essence is its internal but unknown constitution. While the qualities that constitute the nominal essence depend on the real essence, only the nominal essence serves to distinguish one thing from another. Traditional metaphysics emphasized real essences, but Locke's philosophy shifted the emphasis to nominal essences. This distinction made essence *qua* unknown real essence superfluous. **Berkeley** and his followers therefore rejected the notion of real essence, and this leads to **phenomenalism**.

> "[Real essence] is the real constitution of its insensible parts, on which depend all those properties of colour, weight, fusibility, fixedness, &c, which makes it to be gold, or gives it a right to name, which is therefore its nominal essence." **Locke,** *An Essay Concerning Human Understanding*

nominalism

METAPHYSICS, EPISTEMOLOGY, PHILOSOPHY OF LANGUAGE [from Latin *nomen*, name] The view that the only feature that **particulars** falling under the same general term have in common is that they are covered by the same term. Hence, **universals** are only **names** rather than **entities** in their own right, although there are universal elements in knowledge. Nominalism is opposed to **realism**, according to which universals are real entities that are required to explain how general terms apply to different particulars. For nominalism, language, rather than independent reality, underlies perceived similarity. Everything that exists is particular, and universals are terms invented by the mind to talk about similarities. Talk about **properties** and **abstract entities** is legitimate only if it can be reduced to talk about particulars. Nominalism follows the spirit of **Ockham's razor**, that is, by avoiding positing the existence of unnecessary entities. Nominalism is the traditional **empiricist** theory of universals, and its major advocates include **William of Ockham**, **Hobbes**, **Locke**, **Berkeley**, and in the twentieth century **Carnap** and **Quine**, although different philosophers in the tradition have different reasons for rejecting universals and ways of eliminating them. Many philosophers are attracted to the ontological austerity of nominalism, but problems remain concerning how language, especially **predication**, works on nominalist principles.

> "Nominalism maintains that universals are names only, corresponding to no reality." **Walsh, *Reason and Experience***

nomological, see nomic

nomological dangler

PHILOSOPHY OF SCIENCE, PHILOSOPHY OF MIND A term introduced by **Feigl** in his 1958 article "The Mental and the Physical," referring to the law-like relations which connect intersubjectively confirmable events with events that are in principle not intersubjectively and independently confirmable. It means in particular the laws that relate non-physical conscious **experience** to their associated brain processes. We accept these relations or **laws** but they can not be accounted for in scientific formulations. They are quite outside normal scientific conceptions, that is, they dangle from the nomological net of science. The **identity theory of mind** attempts to rule out these danglers.

In his 1960 paper "Sensations and Brain Processes," **Smart** used this term for the physical entity that is supposed to dangle from the psychological law rather than to the psychophysical law itself. But he later reverted to Feigl's use, although he viewed such laws with great suspicion.

> "At best a nomological dangler would merely subsume a lot of As that are associated with Bs under the generalization 'All As are Bs'. The reason for this is that the nomological danglers would be laws purporting to connect physical events, in fact, neurophysiological ones, with allegedly non-physical ones, conscious experiences." **J. Smart, *Essays Metaphysical and Moral***

nomos

ANCIENT GREEK PHILOSOPHY, METAPHYSICS, ETHICS **Law** or **convention**, and used to refer to written or customary laws and **rules**, customs, habits, and conventions. Because all of these are men-made and can be changed and modified by men, in Greek philosophy *nomos* is contrasted to *phusis* (nature). **Democritus** claims that such things as color and taste are conventions, while only **atoms** and the **void** are real (natural). In the fourth and fifth centuries BC, philosophers disputed whether **human nature** or human **morality** is *nomos* or *phusis*. The defenders of *nomos*, e.g. **Protagoras**, insist that human nature or morality is affected by the beliefs of different societies. **Socrates**, **Plato**, and **Aristotle** all attack this **ethical relativism**, and attempt to base human morality on objective grounds.

> "What is fine and what is just, the topics of inquiry in political science, differ and vary so much that they seem to rest on nomos only, not on nature." **Aristotle, *Nicomachean Ethics***

non-cognitivism

ETHICS Also called non-descriptivism, a type of **meta-ethical** theory that denies that we can have **moral knowledge** by **intuition**, and also denies that ethical statements can be construed as **scientific statements**, confirmable by observation or **inductive reasoning**. It claims that ethical terms do not refer to **properties** and that **ethical judgments** are neither true nor false and are not used to convey what is the case. Thus, it is opposed to the many traditional ethical theories that hold that there is ethical knowledge and that normative ethical judgments can be said to be true or false. These rival theories are therefore termed **cognitivism** and include both **naturalist** and **non-naturalist** varieties.

The positive thesis of non-cognitivism is that in ethical thinking we should concentrate on the non-fact-stating functions of ethical expressions. Exactly what these functions are is an issue dividing many forms of non-cognitivism. For some, ethical expressions express **attitude**; for some, they issue **commands**; for some, they express exclamations; for some, they are prescriptions; and so on. The most influential non-cognitive theories are **emotivism**, developed by **Stevenson**, and **prescriptivism**, developed by **Hare**.

"Noncognitivism: the job of ethical sentences is not to state facts." **Brandt,** *Ethical Theory*

non-consequentialism, see consequentialism

non-descriptivism, see non-cognitivism, descriptivism

non-doxastic theory, see doxastic theory

non-Euclidean geometry

PHILOSOPHY OF MATHEMATICS, PHILOSOPHY OF SCIENCE We can informally render Euclid's fifth 'parallels' postulate (or Axiom XI) as follows: "through a given point P not on a line L, there is one and only one line in the plane of P and L that does not meet L." This **axiom** turns out to be independent of the other axioms of Euclid. The exploration of the consequences of this fact led to the development of various non-Euclidean geometries. They develop systems in which two different denials of this postulate are used: Lobachevskian geometry contains an infinite number of parallels through P; Reimannian geometry contains no parallels through P. Reimannian geometry has played a crucial role in the development of the general **relativity** theory.

"If the parallel axiom is independent of the other axioms of Euclid, then a statement incompatible with the parallels axiom can be substituted for it without logically contradicting the other axioms. By trying different alternatives, new axiom systems, called non-Euclidean geometries, were created." **Carnap,** *Philosophical Foundations of Physics*

non-monotonic logics

LOGIC In logic, an **inference** is monotonic if a conclusion C, which can be inferred validly from a set of premises, can also be inferred validly no matter what further premises are added to the originally valid argument. It is non-monotonic if the addition of further information leads to a different conclusion. Non-monotonic logics, used in **artificial intelligence** research, explore logical systems in which monotonicity does not hold.

"Non-monotonic inferences are inferences of the form: *a*; there is no reason to suppose otherwise; so *b*." **Priest,** *Beyond the Limits of Thought*

non-natural property

ETHICS According to G. E. **Moore**, ethical terms such as "good" refer to objective properties that are the basis of **truth-values** of ethical statements. However, these ethical properties are not natural, that is, they are not observable or subject to scientific **explanation**. Instead they can only be known through **moral intuition**. According to Moore, any attempt to define ethical terms by appeal to natural terms commits the **naturalistic fallacy**. However, critics deny the existence of such properties or qualities, and claim that the appeal to a special kind of intuition is not convincing. In addition, it is hard to say how non-natural moral properties could guide our **actions**.

"The alleged concept of a nonnatural property is not connected with experience, does not function to guide expectations, is not part of a theoretical system with consequences predicative of observation, in the way in which this is true of the concepts of empirical science." **Brandt,** *Ethical Theory*

non-naturalism, ethical

ETHICS In opposition to ethical **naturalism**, ethical non-naturalism claims that ethical terms can not be defined by appeal to natural terms. Ethical **properties** are presented as non-natural properties that are not observable and not subject to scientific explanation. There is a firm distinction between **ought** and **is**, or between **value** and **fact**, so that ethical statements (value statements or "ought" statements) can not be derived from statements of facts. To attempt to do so is to commit the so-called **naturalistic fallacy**. In contrast to **non-cognitivism**, non-naturalism argues that ethical statements have objective **meanings** and **truth-values** because they refer to **non-natural ethical**

properties, but they can only be known by **intuition**, rather than by observation or experiment, as naturalism holds. In the twentieth century, the main proponent of non-naturalism is G. E. **Moore**.

"The most vulnerable point of nonnaturalist doctrine, however, is the epistemology, the theory of how we know or are justified in believing ethical statements." **Brandt,** *Ethical Theory*

non-reflexive, see irreflexive

nonsense

METAPHYSICS, PHILOSOPHY OF LANGUAGE In line with **Kant**'s description of **reason**'s inevitably failed attempt to extend beyond the limits of knowledge, **Wittgenstein** draws a demarcation between meaningful **propositions** and **meaningless** propositions. While meaningful propositions are bipolar, that is, either true or false, meaningless propositions are not bipolar and are hence nonsensical. Such propositions are not obviously false or pointless, but simply lack sense. Most questions asked in philosophy and the propositions with which we attempt to answer them are nonsense (German *Unsinn*), and one can not say that they are true or false. These propositions fail in their attempt to say something about the world, due to our failure to understand the **logical syntax** of language that is obscured by **grammar**. Nonsense can be divided into overt nonsense and covert nonsense. Overt nonsense can be seen intuitively to be nonsense, such as the question "Is the good more or less identical than the beautiful?" but covert nonsense has to be discovered by **analysis**. For Wittgenstein, the task of proper philosophy is to clarify good sense. What is nonsensical cannot be said, but can be shown. In this respect, even Wittgenstein's own theory of logical syntax is nonsensical, for it tries to say what can only be shown. Nonsense should be distinguished from what is **senseless**.

In the **Vienna Circle**, all statements that are not capable of scientific treatment or are not verifiable are nonsense, and "nonsense" accordingly becomes a label for metaphysical statements.

"It will therefore only be in language that the limit can be shown, and what lies on the other side of the limit will simply be nonsense." **Wittgenstein,** *Tractatus*

non-teleological ethics, see consequentialism

non-tuism

PHILOSOPHY OF SOCIAL SCIENCE, ETHICS A term coined by the economist Wicksteed in *The Common Sense of Political Economy and Selected Papers and Reviews on Economic Theory* (1933), originally referring to the specific character of economic relations. Non-tuists are not interested in the interests of those with whom they interact. This sort of motivation is neither **egoistic** nor **altruistic**. Some philosophers extend this term to the moral area to offer a rationale for morality, suggesting that people are neither egoists nor altruists. We need moral constraints, but morality is merely a device rather than a fundamental concern for others.

"The market requires only that persons be conceived as not taking an interest in the interests of those with whom they exchange. This is Wicksteed's requirement of non-tuism." **Gauthier,** *Morals by Agreement*

normative

ETHICS, PHILOSOPHY OF SOCIAL SCIENCE From norm, which means standard or **rule**, and it is associated with evaluation. A theory is normative if it involves norm-prescription and is descriptive if it simply describes the facts but does not prescribe what one ought to do. Normative ethics is the subject of inquiring about the **principles** or **rules** of correct moral behavior and is contrasted to **meta-ethics**, which analyzes the meaning and logical relations of evaluative terms. To define a normative term in terms of non-moral properties is called by **Moore** the **definist fallacy**. Sociologists as well as moral philosophers have pictured our lives as governed by complex hierarchies of norms.

"Theories that prescribe standards are normative." **Glymour,** *Thinking Things Through*

normative egoism, see egoism, ethical

notation

AESTHETICS The abbreviation for a notational system or notational scheme, which consists of certain characters or symbols. Notation is the mark of identification distinguishing one type of art from another and determining whether two works belong to the same form of art. It also determines whether two performances are instances of the same work or whether different inscriptions are copies of the same score. Notation indicates the constitutive **properties** of a work and distinguishes them from its **contingent properties**. Establishing this distinction generally relies on boundaries drawn in the antecedent **practices**. Some forms of art, such as music, have traditional notation, while others, like painting, do not. For other forms of art, like dance, attempts to provide a notation have lacked total success. Since notation is a system of characters, it should be **syntactically** disjoint so that all marks belonging to the same character are interchangeable without syntactic effects. It should also be finitely differentiated, that is to say, by using the notation we can tell whether or not two marks belong to the same character. Moreover, a notation should also be **semantically** unambiguous, so that, for example, performances of different works can not conform to the same score.

> "In sum, the properties required of a notational system are unambiguity and syntactic and semantic disjointness and differentiation. These are in no sense merely recommended for a good and useful notation but are features that distinguish notational systems – good or bad – from non-notational systems." **Goodman,** *The Languages of Art*

notational scheme, see notation

not-being

METAPHYSICS, ANCIENT GREEK PHILOSOPHY That which is not. **Parmenides** claimed that not-being can be neither spoken nor thought, for everything that can be spoken or thought is **being**. He also believed that **Heraclitus**' position, that everything is always in **change**, amounts to saying that a thing is both being and not-being, and this is an account which can only lead to opinion rather than **truth**. **Plato** argues that **Forms** or **Ideas** are truly beings and that the sensible world as **appearance** is both being and not-being. According to Plato's analysis in the *Sophist*, not-being is neither absolutely nothing nor a kind of thing. Instead it is the absence of being, and is "other than" or "being different from" a positive determination or being. In **Plotinus**,

"not being" refers to **matter**, which is at the bottom of the hierarchy of reality, and is identified with pure passivity, evil, and darkness. Modern discussion tends to follow Plato and characterize not-being in negative terms and claim that it can be expressed by negative propositions. But there has been debate concerning how to avoid a commitment to non-existents through negative propositions. If not-being is a negative property, then we must find a way to distinguish negative properties from positive properties. Non-being is generally taken to be identical with **nothingness**.

> "When we speak of 'not being', it seems that we do not mean something contrary to what exists but only something that is different." **Plato,** *Sophist*

nothingness

METAPHYSICS, MODERN EUROPEAN PHILOSOPHY, PHILOSOPHY OF LANGUAGE Also called **negation, not-being,** or nihilation. Nothing is an abbreviated form of "not-anything." The nature of negation has been a difficult puzzle since the pre-Socratic philosophers. Through nominalization, negation seems to become an **entity**, "the not," and the ontological status of nothing becomes a problem. **Parmenides** claimed that not-being is unsayable. **Plato** suggested that not-being exists and means "other-than-being." **Aristotle** believed that not-being is what lacks any and every property. The dispute continued through medieval philosophy, which tried to connect nothingness, privation, and evil. At the beginning of his *Logic*, **Hegel** proposed a **dialectic** of Being and Nothingness.

In contemporary philosophy, there are two quite different usages. **Heidegger** took "nothingness" (German *das Nichts*) as a **referring expression**, denoting a special kind of subject-matter. We can experience nothingness in experiencing that human existence has no ground and is meaningless. This experience is revealed in **anxiety** and culminates in the experience of death. **Sartre** distinguished between **being-for-itself** and **being-in-itself**. The former is conscious being, especially human being, and the latter is the being of things in the world that are causally determined. **Consciousness** as being-for-itself is directed upon some object, but is also aware of itself as conscious of some object. Hence it presents a vacancy or gap between itself and its object, by which consciousness detaches itself from the rest of the world or being-in-itself and identifies itself by reference to the things that are other than itself. For Sartre, this gap is precisely what nothingness is, as an awareness of he-is-not-what-he-is or he-is-what-he-is-not. Hence, nothingness is the separation between itself and its object and is an implicit awareness of not-being-the-object. Sartre holds that this separation is the source of human **freedom** by causing human beings to choose what they will be rather than simply being. Consciousness is negation in itself because it can not exist without a separation from its object. Human being, as the agent of consciousness, is the only being that can bring nothingness into the world. It takes a different view of being-in-the-world and modifies it. The awareness of nothingness results in feeling **anguish**, and an escape from anguish leads one to fall into **bad faith**. The conception of nothingness lies at the foundation of Sartre's *Being and Nothingness*.

On the other hand, **Carnap** rejects Heidegger's use of "nothing" as typical metaphysical nonsense. Nothing does not refer to anything, but simply marks the absence of an expected existent. For Carnap, Heidegger's question about nothing is a violation of **logical syntax**. It is generally held in analytic philosophy that nothingness is a pseudo-object that is invoked to fill the gap produced by insisting that every **mental state** is **intentional** in form. In modern logic, "nothing" is interpreted in terms of **quantified** sentences rather than as a designator of an object.

> "We perceived then that Nothingness can be conceived neither outside of being, nor as a complementary, abstract notion, nor as an infinite milieu where being is suspended. Nothingness must be given at the heart of Being, in order for us to be able to apprehend that particular type of realities which we have called *négatités*." **Sartre, *Being and Nothingness***

noumenon

METAPHYSICS, EPISTEMOLOGY [from Greek *noein* to think, hence the thing thought or the intelligible thing; plural, *noumena*] A thing as **intelligible object** or ultimate reality, in contrast to a *phenomenon*, which is a thing as it appears or is sensed. This ancient distinction was carefully explored in **Plato**'s theory of **ideas**, But the term *noumenon* is especially associated with **Kant**. In his philosophy, *noumenon* is mainly used in a negative sense, as something that is beyond the limits of **sensibility**, **intuition**, or **experience**, that is, beyond the world of **appearance**. Hence, a *noumenon* is an unknown thing, employed to show the limits of possible knowledge, which is postulated by **pure reason** as a starting-point for all scientific inquiries. Kant held that such a postulation is necessary as a condition of a human **freedom**. Also, if we attribute **objectivity** to the *noumenon*, we proceed from a logical **form** without **content** to an object necessarily existing in itself as an object of positive knowledge. For Kant, this is a **dialectical** error that leads inevitably to the errors of traditional metaphysics. *Noumenon* is sometimes used interchangeably with **thing-in-itself**, although each term has its own emphasis.

> "The concept of a noumenon – that is, of a thing which is not to be thought as object of the senses but as a thing in itself, solely through a pure understanding – is not in any way contradictory." **Kant, *Critique of Pure Reason***

nous

ANCIENT GREEK PHILOSOPHY, PHILOSOPHY OF MIND [Greek intellect in general or in some aspect] **Anaxagoras** took *nous* to be a cosmic force separating elements from the primitive mixture and setting up the order of the world. Although not satisfied with the detailed explanation given by Anaxagoras, **Socrates** was inspired by this account. In his simile of the **line**, **Plato** took *nous* to be the highest level of intellect. In contrast to *dianoia* (discursive reasoning), which is concerned with mathematical reality and proceeds from hypotheses to a conclusion, *nous* is concerned with **Forms** and proceeds from hypotheses to the **first principle** from which everything else is deduced. **Aristotle** used *nous* in various senses: (1) general rational **thought** and **understanding** which is not distinguished from *dianoia*; (2) intuitive **reasoning** which grasps the first principles of demonstrative sciences, principles that are necessary and admit of no further justification; (3) practical *nous* which grasps the relevant features of particular cases, and is an element of **practical reason**; (4) **active reason**, which immediately grasps pure forms and is an eternal, divine intellect altogether separable from body, an account that conflicts with Aristotle's other views about **soul**.

> "No other kind of thought except nous is more accurate than scientific knowledge." **Aristotle,** *Posterior Analytics*

Nozick, Robert (1938–2002)

American political, moral, and epistemological philosopher, born in Brooklyn, New York, Professor of Philosophy at Harvard University. Nozick is best known for his libertarian political philosophy, which argues for the fundamental importance of rights, the entitlement to legally acquired property unconstrained by demands for an allegedly just pattern of distribution, and the limitation of the state to a minimal role. His epistemology introduces a notion of tracking truth in an analysis of knowledge that leads on to a more extensive theory of rational action and rational belief. His major works include *Anarchy, State and Utopia* (1974), *Philosophical Explanations* (1981), *The Nature of Rationality* (1993), and *Invariances: The Structure of the Objective World* (2001).

nuclear deterrence, see deterrence

null class

LOGIC A **class** or set of which nothing is a member. It is often symbolized by "ø" and is also called the null set or empty class. This is the smallest set possible. Logically, since sets are distinguished from one another by the number of members, only one null class is possible. Since we tend to think of a set or class as a heap, the existence of the null class seems puzzling, but if we think of classes more abstractly the puzzle disappears.

> "One of these concerns the null-class, i.e. the class consisting of no members, which is difficult to deal with on a purely extensional basis." **Russell,** *Logic and Knowledge*

nulla poena sine lege

PHILOSOPHY OF LAW [Latin, no punishment without law making it so] A principle that requires any determination of offense to be justified by appeal to clearly defined and pre-announced laws. The grounds for imposing **punishment** on wrongdoers can not be a discretionary matter, but must be according to expressed or expressible legal forms. Statutes must be clear in what they enjoin and forbid, so that the citizens have clear knowledge about how they should behave. An associate principle is *nullum crimen sine lege* (Latin, no crime without law making it so).

> "*Nulla poena sine lege* is the battlecry (and translated with strict accuracy, let us not forget, it means 'No punishment without a statute')." **MacCormick,** *H. L. A. Hart*

nullum crimen sine lege

PHILOSOPHY OF LAW [Latin, no crime without law making it so] A principle that conduct does not constitute a crime unless it has previously been declared to be criminal by the law. Anything that is not forbidden by a certain normative rule or system is permitted by that rule or system. Whatever is not prohibited is thereby *ipso facto* permitted. It is a rule about people's **freedom** to act, which is also called the principle of legality. If a judge creates new offenses in order to punish morally objectionable or harmful acts, he violates this principle. The principle is associated with the rule *nulla poena sine lege* (Latin, no punishment without law making it so).

> "A *nullum crimen* [*sine lege*] rule permitting all not-forbidden acts and forbearances may or may not occur within a given normative order." **von Wright,** *Norm and Action*

number

PHILOSOPHY OF MATHEMATICS Philosophical issues arise over the ontological status of numbers. The Greek Pythagoreans discovered relationships of ratio and proportion among natural numbers and even considered number to be the first principle that determines the structure of the world. The tendency of contemporary philosophy of mathematics to identify numbers with **sets** has led to the revival of **Platonism** in mathematics. The traditional position holds that numbers are used to answer questions of the form "How many X's are there?" and, hence, that a number is a **property** ascribed to an object or group of objects. This view was rejected by **Frege,** who argued that a number-statement ascribes a property to **concepts** rather than to **objects**. Hence a number is a **second-level predicate** rather than a first-level predicate. On this basis, Frege inferred that **existence**, like number, is a property of concepts rather than of objects.

> "The content of a statement of number is an assertion about a concept." **Frege, *The Foundations of Arithmetic***

numinous

PHILOSOPHY OF RELIGION, AESTHETICS [from Latin *numin*, a spirit inhabiting a natural object or phenomenon, filling it with a sense of divine presence] A term introduced by the German philosopher of religion Rudolf **Otto**. Otto claimed that the term **holy** is used both in a religious and in an ethical sense and suggested that we need a term simply for the part of the meaning of holy that is distinct from absolute moral goodness. He put forward the numinous as a term to designate the awe-inspiring and overpowering object of human **religious experience**. The numinous has been understood as a distinguishing feature of religion. Although the experience of the numinous is meant to characterize religion in isolation from moral sense, it is a matter of dispute whether a distinction between the numinous and other aspects of

the holy is tenable. In a related secular sense, the numinous appeals to the high emotions or aesthetic sense.

> "For this purpose I adopt a word coined from the Latin numen. Omen has given us 'ominous', and there is no reason why from numen we should not similarly form a word 'numinous'." **Otto, *The Idea of the Holy***

Nussbaum, Martha (1947–)

American philosopher of ancient Greek philosophy, ethics, literature, and law, born in New York, Professor at Harvard University, Brown University, and University of Chicago. Nussbaum brings together scholarly understanding of Plato, Aristotle, and Hellenistic philosophy, critical intelligence in her response to literature, and a concern for practical reason in the complex circumstances of moral life. Her conception of reason encompasses imagination and emotion to give unity to her philosophical examinations of ethics and the self. Her main works include *The Fragility of Goodness: Luck and Ethics in Greek Tragedy and Philosophy* (1986), *Love's Knowledge: Essays on Philosophy and Literature* (1990), *The Therapy of Desire: Theory and Practice in Hellenistic Ethics* (1994), and *Upheavals of Thought: The Intelligence of Emotion* (2001).

O

Oakeshott, Michael (1901–90)

English idealist philosopher and political theorist, born in Harpenden, Hertfordshire. Oakeshott believed that various distinct modes of human experience constitute the world and that philosophy involves the perception of experience as a whole. Thus, he sought a comprehensive understanding of experience from history, science, practice, and art. He considered himself to be a liberal, although conservatives have been drawn to his rejection of the primacy of rationalist abstract theory in politics. His major works are *Experience and Its Modes* (1933), *Rationalism in Politics* (1962), *On Human Conduct* (1975), and *On History* (1983).

obiter dictum, see *ratio decidendi*

object

METAPHYSICS, PHILOSOPHY OF MIND [German *Gegenstand*] A generic term for whatever is the bearer of a **proper name**, or whatever can be referred to or designated, approximately identical with "thing." Objects can be distinguished from their **properties** and **relations** and also from subjects. Physical objects are real, but there are also unreal objects such as phantoms or **images**. Unlike physical objects, abstract objects are not spatio-temporal. Intentional objects are objects of **mental states**, like **desire** or **hope**, and need not exist. Objects are often recognized in **ontology** as the most **basic particulars**,

although some recent arguments have rejected the priority of objects in favor of **events**.

For early **Wittgenstein** objects are the constituents of **states of affairs** or **atomic facts**, and thus form the **substance** of the world. Every object contains in its nature all the possibilities of combining with other objects. In themselves, objects are simple and unchanging. What changes is the combination or separation of objects (the complex objects). In this way objects are related to the **atoms** of ancient atomism. Objects are correlated to the simple **names** that constitute **propositions**. The simple names are discovered through **logical analysis** and are the terminus of such analysis.

> "A name means an object. The object is its meaning." **Wittgenstein**, *Tractatus*

object language

LOGIC, PHILOSOPHY OF LANGUAGE **Russell** developed the notion of a hierarchy of languages. The language of the lowest order, in which symbol and vocabulary are not determined by the logical conditions, is called the object language or primary language. This is the language with which we talk about extra-linguistic things and **objects**. It applies object words and studying it involves the relation between **sentences** and non-linguistic occurrences. Any given ordinary language is an object language, in contrast to higher-order languages, which deal not with objects, but with the lower-order languages. **Tarski** takes the notion of an object language and contrasts it with **metalanguage**, in which we talk about an object language.

> "I call this the 'object language', or the 'primary language'. In this language, every word 'denotes' or 'means' a sensible object or set of such objects; and when used alone, asserts the sensible presence of the object, or of one of the set of objects, which it denotes or means." **Russell,** *An Inquiry into Meaning and Truth*

object sentence, see pseudo-object sentence

object words
LOGIC, PHILOSOPHY OF LANGUAGE Object words indicate the presence of what they mean through indicating something that one can point to, such as "cat," "France," and so on. In contrast, **syntax words** are words such as "or," "not," "than," "but," which do not indicate anything one can point to, but can only be defined verbally in terms of other syntax words.

> "Some words denote objects, others express characteristics of our belief-attitude; the former are object-words, the latter syntax-words." **Russell,** *Human Knowledge*

objective knowledge
EPISTEMOLOGY **Popper**'s term for linguistically formulated **theories** that form the constituents of his "World 3." Knowledge in this sense is man-made but transcends its origins and has various **properties** and **relationships** independent of any subject's awareness of them. In Popper's view, it contrasts with subjective knowledge, which is a **dispositional** expectation or anticipation of relevant impending events and is a kind of adaptation to the environment. The study of subjective knowledge belongs to psychology. Popper claimed that this distinction between objective and subjective knowledge is ignored in traditional epistemology. Traditional epistemology views **knowledge** as justified true belief or as **perception**, and hence limits knowledge to the utterances or expressions of the knowing subject. This is the source of many difficulties in traditional epistemology, especially its **justificationism**.

> "The traditional theories of knowledge (from Plato's *Theaetetus* to Wittgenstein's *On Certainty*) fail to make a clear distinction between objective and subjective knowledge." **Popper,** *The Philosophy of Karl Popper*

objective particulars
METAPHYSICS **Strawson**'s term for **particulars** that are not the private occurrences or states or conditions of oneself or anyone else, but rather are the actual or possible public **objects** of **experience** or states of **consciousness**. These particulars are reidentifiable in speaker-hearer identification. Objective particulars, which Strawson also calls public particulars, contrast to private particulars, that is, **sensations**, **mental events**, or **sense-data** in general.

> "I shall henceforth use the phrase, 'objective particulars' as an abbreviation of the entire phrase, 'particulars distinguished by the thinker, etc.'." **Strawson,** *Individuals*

objectivism
METAPHYSICS, EPISTEMOLOGY, ETHICS, AESTHETICS The contrast between objectivism and **subjectivism** is a central and recurring feature of philosophy. Objectivist theories claim that **truth** and falsity are determined by external **objects** and their **relations** independent of our **minds**, while subjectivist theories claim that truth and falsity are relative to our minds. The contrast between these two positions is presented differently in different areas of philosophy. Objectivist metaphysics claims that the **external world** exists without regard to our minds, while subjectivist metaphysics claims that the world exists only insofar as it exists for us. Objectivist epistemology holds that the source and validity of **knowledge** are derived from external objects, while subjectivist epistemology claims that the source and validity of knowledge are derived primarily from our **sensibility** and our ability to form **conceptions**. Both **naturalist** and anti-naturalist varieties of objectivist ethics suggest that ethical properties and **values** exist independent of our **belief** and **desires**, while subjectivist ethics proposes that **moral judgments** cannot be judged true or false according to an objective standard, but are rather the expression of our emotions or feelings. Objectivist aesthetics

484 objectivity

holds that **aesthetic properties** are inherent in things, while subjectivist aesthetics claims that they are projected by us upon the objects. Subjectivism is associated with **anti-realism** and **idealism**, while objectivism is associated with **realism**. However, objectivism is not identical with **materialism**, for it can be held in either materialist or idealist form.

> "[T]he objectivism of the natural sciences tries to view them [social complexes] from the outside; it treats social phenomena not as something of which the human mind is a part and the principles of whose organisation we can reconstruct from the familiar parts, but as if they were objects directly perceived by us as a whole." **Hayek, in O'Neill,** *Modes of Individualism and Collectivism*

objectivity

METAPHYSICS, EPISTEMOLOGY, PHILOSOPHY OF SCIENCE, PHILOSOPHY OF HISTORY, ETHICS Belonging to **objects** and not to ourselves as subjects; also, **beliefs** or **perceptions** that are not limited or distorted by the bias or partiality. Objectivity can be contrasted with **subjectivity** and with a lack of objectivity. We can be objective in determining beliefs, and our **judgments** themselves can be objective. In spite of the dangers, we often use our assessment of the person judging to guide our determination of the objectivity of the judgment. A commitment to objectivity is a general mark of intellectual **integrity**, according to which one respects the virtue of **truth** and seeks valid and unbiased **theories**, **explanations**, and judgments. A theory or judgment is objective if it corresponds to external **facts** or can be determined to be true or false by rational means. Sometimes these two senses are related because a theory can be rationally judged as conforming or not conforming to facts, but more often a theory is **abstract** and **idealized** and does not correspond directly or sensibly to any facts. In this case, a theory is regarded as objective if it can be justified rationally, with agreement available or expected from all reasonable persons. The primary task of a theory should be to explain the sort of objectivity that is possible for it and to state the conditions that would justify its rational acceptance. Moreover, a sound account of **rationality** is required to enable us to achieve the objectivity of theories and judgments through overcoming partiality, arbitrariness, relativity, and bias, and to assess the objectivity of

people. Because personal and social intention and prejudice are indispensably involved in many fields, the possibility of objectivity in history and ethics, for example, has been an issue of dispute.

> "We might explain the objectivity of a judgement that p as follows. There exists knowledge k such that everyone with this knowledge agrees that p is true (and expects that anyone else with this knowledge would agree that p is true and would have this very same expectation), while there is no further knowledge which, when added to k, undercuts the agreement that p." **Nozick,** *Philosophical Explanations*

objectual quantifier

LOGIC **Quine** distinguishes two interpretations of the **quantifier**, the objectual quantifier and the **substitutional quantifier**. He, along with **Davidson**, endorses the objectual quantifier interpretation, according to which one should interpret **a quantifier in terms the values of a variable as the objects over which the variable ranges**. For example, (x)Fx is interpreted as "For all objects x in the domain D, Fx." According to the substitutional quantifier interpretation one should interpret a quantifier by appealing to substituends rather than values of the variable, that is, the expressions that can be substituted for the variable. On this view, (x)Fx is interpreted to be "All substitution instances of F . . . are true." These two interpretations involve some different consequences. For example, the substitutional interpretation of the quantifier says that the truth of quantified formulae can be directly defined by the truth of their substituted atomic formulae, but this is not admitted by the objectual interpretation. Also, the substitutional interpretation allows quantifiers to replace terms, such as **predicates** and **relations**, which do not designate objects.

> "The Q-quantifiers are called 'objectual'. The reason is that whether or not a quantification is true upon an interpretation depends on how things are with the objects in the domain of interpretation." **Sainsbury,** *Logical Form*

obligation

ETHICS [from Latin *obligare*, to bind one to something] Generally, something we are required to do arising from some circumstance, such as having signed a contract or having made a promise. **Duty** is also something we are required to do, but generally because of some social or other role that we occupy. In **Kant**'s ethics, an obligation is the general dependence of the human **will** upon the **moral law**, while duty is the necessity of acting from obligation. Obligation informs not only duty but also **rights**. Many philosophers, however, use obligation and duty interchangeably as a determination of what ought to be done.

> "The connexion between duties and the demands of others comes out clearly in the fact that we use the word 'obligation' as a synonym for 'duty'." **Nowell-Smith**, *Ethics*

obligationes

LOGIC, MEDIEVAL PHILOSOPHY [Latin, the conditions under which the parties to a dispute agree to proceed] A form of disputation adopted in medieval universities from the early thirteenth century. It involved a respondent and an opponent. The opponent was obliged to make the respondent concede or deny his initial **propositions**. On the basis of **Aristotle**'s discussion of the form of debate in *Topics* and *De Sophistic Elenchus*, medieval logicians engaged in various studies concerning the rules of *obligationes*. Normally, the rules were characterized in terms of the feature of constructive **counterfactual** reasoning.

> "Obligationes are obligations assumed by a party to a disputation, or conditions within which such a discussion must be conducted." **Kneale and Kneale**, *The Development of Logic*

oblique intention, see direct intention

observation language

EPISTEMOLOGY, PHILOSOPHY OF LANGUAGE, PHILOSOPHY OF SCIENCE Many philosophers divide the language of each branch of the sciences into observation language and **theoretical language**. Observation language is directly related to **sense-impressions** and can be analyzed in the standard empirical way. It is characterized by observability, explicit definability, and **extensionality**. Theoretical language, on the other hand, is not directly related to sense-**experience**, but talks about unobservable properties

and **events** (for example, atoms, electrons) that are also called **theoretical constructs** or hypothetical constructs. The terms an observation language employs are called **observational terms**, and those employed by theoretical language are called **theoretical terms**. One major issue in the methodology of science is about the relationship between the two kinds of languages. Should theoretical language be translated and replaced by observation language? How can it be done? How can we know that theoretical language is meaningful? What is the ontological status of an item to which a theoretical expression refers? Further discussion of these issues can be found in entries on **double language model**, **Craig's theorem**, **Ramsey sentence**, and **correspondence rules**.

> "The observation language uses terms designating observable properties and relations for the description of observable things or events." **Carnap,** **"The Methodological Character of Theoretical Concepts,"** in *Minnesota Studies of the Philosophy of Science*, **vol. I**

observation proposition, see basic proposition or protocol sentence

observation sentence

EPISTEMOLOGY, PHILOSOPHY OF LANGUAGE Observation sentences are a subset of **occasion sentences**. An occasion sentence is a report about observation, **sense-data**, or stimulations, but its acceptance relies on the circumstances of its utterance. If an occasion sentence is assented to or dissented from consistently in response to the same stimulation, it is an observation sentence. The verdict of its **truth** and falsity depends only on present sensory stimulation, although certain stored information that is implied in the expression of the sentence itself is inevitably relevant to determining whether it is true. Hence, an observational sentence is not **private**, but must be acceptable by the speech community. All speakers of a language give the same verdict when given the same concurrent stimulation. Observation sentences correspond to the **protocol sentences** of **logical positivism**, which offered an influential account of the foundations of empirical knowledge. Critics deny that protocol sentences are the basis of empirical knowledge, either because they lack the possibility of being true or false or because empirical knowledge does not need foundations.

> "A sentence ... is an observation sentence if all verdicts on it depend on present sensory stimulation and on no stored information beyond what goes into understanding the sentence." **Quine,** *Ontological Relativity and Other Essays*

observation term

PHILOSOPHY OF SCIENCE, EPISTEMOLOGY **Empiricist** philosophy of science has commonly divided the language of science into **theoretical language**, concerning unobservable entities, **properties**, and **relations**, and **observation language**, concerning items, like **sense-impressions**, that are claimed to be observable, although "observation" in this sense covers **perception, sensation,** and even **introspection**. Observation terms are employed in this observation language to refer to observable items. Each observation term has an explicit and determinate **extension** and can be displayed in a limited model. According to proponents of this view, observation terms are learned mostly by ostension, with their meaning reinforced by the presence of their objects, with any questions of **context** or **definition** irrelevant to **understanding** them. Observation terms are widely applied to publicly observable bodies as well as to private sensory states. Observation terms can be directly analyzed empirically. In contrast to observation terms, theoretical terms are employed by theoretical language to refer to unobservable or **theoretical entities** and their features. Philosophers of science disagree whether all theoretical terms can be eliminated from a theory, that is, whether they can be translated into or replaced by observation terms. Some philosophers claim that the distinction between observation terms and theoretical terms can not be maintained because all terms are **theory-laden**.

> "In regard to an observational term it is possible, under suitable circumstances, to decide by means of direct observation whether the term does or does not apply to a given situation." **Hempel, "The Theoretician's Dilemma," in** *Minnesota Studies in the Philosophy of Science,* **vol. II**

obversion

LOGIC In traditional logic, an immediate **inference** that derives a conclusion from another **proposition** by negating its **predicate term** and changing its **quality** either from affirmative to negative or from negative to affirmative. The conclusion, called the obverse, is a logical equivalent of the premise, called the obvertend. All four forms of proposition in traditional logic can be validly obversed: "All s are p" is obversed into "No s are non-p"; "No s are p" into "All s are non-p"; "Some s are p" into "Some s are not non-p"; and "Some s are not p" into "Some s are non-p."

> "Obversion is a process of immediate inference in which the inferred proposition (or obverse), while retaining the original subject, has for its predicate the contradictory of the predicate of the original proposition (or obvertend)." **Keynes,** *Studies and Exercises in Formal Logic*

occasion sentence

PHILOSOPHY OF LANGUAGE, EPISTEMOLOGY **Quine's** term for **sentences** whose **meanings** are relative to their **context** and which contain indexical words, for example, "It is snowing" or "It is Thursday." They are true on some occasions of utterance, and false on others. Whether such a sentence is acceptable depends on the background. We should only assent to these sentences when it is indeed snowing or Thursday. The sentence "It is snowing" is more observational than "It is Thursday." Observation sentences are a subset of occasion sentences. If all speakers assent to an occasion sentence in response to the same stimulations, then it is an observation sentence. Occasion sentences are directly connected with sensory stimulations and are contrasted to **standing sentences**, which are not relative to context and which have assent by all speakers all the time. Standing sentences are either analytic or statements of a common-sense truism, for example, "Snow is white."

> "We must concentrate on occasion sentences. These, as opposed to standing sentences, are sentences whose truth value changes from occasion to occasion, so that a fresh verdict has to be promoted each time." **Quine,** *Theories and Things*

occasionalism

METAPHYSICS, PHILOSOPHY OF MIND A doctrine developed by **Descartes's** disciple **Malebranche** as a solution to the Cartesian **mind–body problem**. He claimed that the two completely distinct **substances**, *res cogitans* and *res extensa*, can causally interact with each other because of the miraculous intervention of **God**. God regulates the world so that our **volitions** are followed by bodily movements, and conversely that certain patterns of bodily movements give rise to appropriate **emotions** and **sensations** in the mind. The so-called natural **causes** are actually occasions on which God acts to produce the **effects** that usually accompany the natural causes. There is no real **causation** in the finite created world, no real efficacy of finite causes. Only an infinite **substance** can be a genuine cause of anything at all. Occasionalism maintained mechanical explanation by grounding it outside the limits of physics proper. This provided a new metaphysical framework. This theory was criticized by **Leibniz**, who replaced it with his own theory of **pre-established harmony**.

"The occasionalists were a group of 17th century philosophers who maintained that human volitions never really cause bodily movements but are only the occasions for divine intervention in the physical world." **Pap**, *Elements of Analytical Philosophy*

Ockham's razor

METAPHYSICS A methodological principle in **theory** construction associated with the medieval philosopher **William of Ockham**, although **Aristotle** suggested it in his criticism of **Plato**'s Theory of Ideas. The principle states that one should not posit the existence of more entities than are absolutely necessary for adequate philosophical explanation. Accordingly, if two or more theories have the same explanatory force, the one that makes use of the fewest assumptions and explanatory **principles** should be chosen, other things being equal. Common formulations of this principle are "Entities are not to be multiplied beyond necessity" or "Plurality is never to be posited without need" (Latin *Entia non sunt multiplicanda prater necessitate*). But this is the invention of the seventeenth century rather than Ockham's own formulation, which was "It is pointless to do with more what can be done with fewer." **Simplicity** is the spirit of this principle. The term Ockham's razor was introduced by Sir William Hamilton, who identified it with the so-called principle of parsimony: nature never works by more

complex instruments than are necessary. Ockham's razor is also called the principle of simplicity or the principle of economy, and has wide application in metaphysical debates.

"Ockham's razor counsels us against an unnecessary luxuriance of principles or laws or statements of existence." **J. Smart**, *Essays Metaphysical and Moral*

Oedipus complex

PHILOSOPHY OF MIND In Greek myth, Oedipus, acting according to his destiny, killed his father and married his mother. **Freud** claimed that in the mental life of a male child there is desire for his mother as a sexual object and hatred for his father as a rival. He calls this pattern the "Oedipus complex" and claims that it is a central factor in the child's experience of his relations to his parents and in his later sexual development. Because the Oedipus complex can lead to later neuroses, Freud sought access to the feelings, images, and relations characterizing the complex in dealing with later problems. The complex itself presents a fundamental tension between sexual drive and the submission to parental authority. It is also claimed to be a source of religion, society, morals, and arts. In girls, the complex is allegedly manifested as a wish to take the mother's place. Moving beyond the complex in a child is meant to allow acceptance of the values of one's parents. The dissolution of the complex in society provides defense of authority.

"In the very earliest years of childhood (approximately between the ages of two and five) a convergence of the sexual impulses occurs of which, in the case of boys, the object is the mother. This choice of an object, in conjunction with a corresponding attitude of rivalry and hostility towards the father, provides the content of what is known as the Oedipus Complex, which is of the greatest importance in determining the final shape of his erotic life." **Freud**, *Standard Edition of the Complete Psychological Works of Sigmund Freud*, **vol. 18**

offense, see harm

oligarchy

ANCIENT GREEK PHILOSOPHY, POLITICAL PHILOSOPHY, PHILOSOPHY OF SOCIAL SCIENCE [from Greek *oligos*, few or small] Literally, rule by the few, but for **Plato** a **state** ruled by the rich, maybe because the rich are the few most likely to dominate a state. In the *Republic*, oligarchy is the second stage in the degeneration of the Ideal State, the first stage being **timocracy**, or rule by the spirited rather than the rational element. Oligarchy is dominated by the appetite for moneymaking, and the unity of the state is fragile because of conflict between the poor and the rich. Parallel to this state, the oligarchic man also lacks internal **harmony**. He is dominated by the desire for money, and his **reason** and spirits are forced to work only in the interests of money. Oligarchy is more unjust and more miserable than timocracy and will further degenerate into **democracy** and tyranny.

"Oligarchy is of necessity not one city but two, one of the poor and the other of the rich, living in the same place and always plotting against each other." **Plato, *Republic***

omnipotence

PHILOSOPHY OF RELIGION [from Latin *omnis*, all + *potens*, powerful] One of the chief **divine attributes**. By being all powerful, **God** has infinite or maximal power and is the ruler of everything. The notion of an all-powerful being has given rise to many logical impossibilities, called the **paradoxes** of omnipotence. Can God create a rock so large that he cannot move it? If he cannot, he is not omnipotent because there are limits on what he can create. If he can, he is not omnipotent, because there are limits on what he can move. Other questions leading to paradox include "Can God deny God's essence?" "Can God lie?" "Can God sin?" Some philosophers try to redefine the notion of omnipotence in order to avoid such problems. A deeper philosophical problem emerges from combining divine omnipotence, **omniscience**, and goodness. How are the claims that God is all-powerful, all-knowing, and perfectly good compatible with the existence of **evil**? None of the many responses to this question, such as the claim that evil is due to the fall of the first man or the claim that God permits evil as a means of purifying the soul, has won general approval, but belief in God is often enhanced rather than diminished through experience of evil in the world.

"Theists have often wished to claim that God is omnipotent, that is, literally, can do anything." **Swinburne, *The Coherence of Theism***

omniscience

PHILOSOPHY OF RELIGION [from Latin *omnis*, all + *sciens*, present participle of *scire*, to know] One of the chief **divine attributes**, according to which **God** is all-knowing or has unlimited knowledge. This attribute gives rise to the **paradox** of God's **omniscience**, a perennial problem concerning **freedom of the will**. This paradox has two versions. The first concerns God's omniscience and human freedom. If every future thing happens exactly as God knows it will happen, how is there room for human freedom of the will? This version of the paradox has led philosophers to examine whether God's **foreknowledge** of a future human act implies that the human agent lacks control over the act or is not responsible for it. Another version of the paradox concerns God's omniscience and his own free will. If everything occurs according to complete divine foreknowledge, how can God exercise his own free will? Another problem concerning the scope of divine foreknowledge arises if God is held to have no sensory organs and to exist outside time. It is difficult to understand how God in these circumstances could have knowledge of material and temporal things.

"Traditionally, God is said to be omniscient, to know all things." **Swinburne, *The Coherence of Theism***

on [Greek, the participle of being], see *ousia*

one

METAPHYSICS, ANCIENT GREEK PHILOSOPHY [Greek *hen*] Many Greek philosophers argued that their **first principles**, no matter whether they are one or many, must be at one with themselves and form a unity. **Aristotle** discussed various meanings of the term one in *Metaphysics*, book 5. Things might be called one because of **accidental** features or by their own **nature**. Of things that are called one in terms of their nature, they might be continuous, have the same **substratum**, have the same **genus**, or share the same **definition**. Things can also be one in number, in **species**, or in genus. **Plotinus** called his absolute transcendent first principle the One, and identified it with the **Good** or **God**. It is the power behind everything, the source of the Divine **Mind** and **Souls** (**Forms**), although the One itself is neither Mind nor Soul. It is beyond **being**, for if it is a being, it must be describable by a **predicate**, and that would involve duality and compromise its unity. Therefore, the One can only be understood negatively and is beyond the reach of our **thought** or language. It is the simple object of **intuitive knowledge**. Plotinus' One is based on the **Good** in **Plato**'s *Republic*, and prepared the way for the development of **negative theology**.

> "Everywhere the one is indivisible either in quantity or in kind." **Aristotle**, *Metaphysics*

one–many problem, see one over many

one over many
METAPHYSICS, ANCIENT GREEK PHILOSOPHY We can apply one **predicate** to many different things. How can they be related in this way? According to **Plato**, a common **description** suggests that there is a common intrinsic feature or **nature** shared by these different things that determines their real existence. This common nature is one and the same and stands over many particular things. This is Plato's "one over many principle." He called the one common nature **Form** or **Idea** and declared that Ideas are **objects** independent of our **minds** and that each of the many **particulars** imitates or **participates** in their Idea. Ideas are objects of **knowledge**, while particulars are objects of opinion. The central aim of Plato's **Theory of Ideas** is to argue for this principle and to deal with various difficulties arising from it. These difficulties have become the problem of the relation between **universals** and particulars. The discussion of this problem forms one of the chief issues in Western metaphysics, although it is closely linked to logical questions about **meaning** and **predication**. The one over many problem is also called the one–many problem, but this latter expression is also used to ask whether the **substance** of the world is one or many in the debate between **monism** and **pluralism**.

> "Those who say that the Forms exist, in one respect are right, in giving the Forms separate existence, if they are substances; but in another respect they are not right, because they say the one over many is a Form." **Aristotle**, *Metaphysics*

O'Neill, Onora (1941–)
British Kantian moral and political philosopher, born in Aughafatten, Northern Ireland, Professor of Philosophy at the University of Essex and Principal of Newnham College, Cambridge. O'Neill offers a subtle and complex interpretation of Kant's moral and political philosophy, which she employs to deal with questions in applied ethics that are often considered only from a utilitarian standpoint. Her understanding of Kant leaves room for communitarian values and for the individual and social cultivation of virtues. Her main works include *Acting on Principle* (1975), *Faces of Hunger* (1986), and *Constructions of Reason* (1989).

ontico-ontological distinction
MODERN EUROPEAN PHILOSOPHY, METAPHYSICS **Heidegger**'s distinction, two levels of analysis of *Dasein*. The ontic level is concerned with the concrete, specific, and local matter of *Dasein*, that is, the factual matter open to observation, which Heidegger calls **existentiell**. The ontological level is, on the other hand, concerned with the deep **structure** that underlies and instantializes the ontical or existentiell matter and provides a **phenomenological description**. This deep structure is called by Heidegger existentiale. *Dasein* has three main existentiales, namely **existentiality**, **facticity**, and **fallingness**. The problem of traditional metaphysics is to confuse these two levels by taking **being** as **entity**. Heidegger's own **fundamental ontology** is both ontical, that is, the analysis of the actual existence of *Dasein*, and ontological, that is, the analysis of the general conditions of possibility for existence. This is because *Dasein* itself is both ontical (as an entity), and ontological (the only entity that can ask the question of Being). In these terms, his thought contrasts with **Husserl**'s phenomenology, which **brackets** the **phenomenon**.

> "By indicating *Dasein*'s ontico-ontological priority in this provisional manner, we have grounded our demonstration that the question of Being is ontico-ontologically distinctive." **Heidegger**, *Being and Time*

ontological argument
PHILOSOPHY OF RELIGION, METAPHYSICS, LOGIC One of the most celebrated arguments attempting to prove the **existence** of **God**. It was first formulated in the

eleventh century by **Anselm** of Canterbury in *Proslogion*. The argument assumes that God is a being than which nothing greater can be conceived. If he is thus, God must exist in our **understanding**. But if he exists in the understanding only and does not exist in **reality**, a being that is greater than God is conceivable, namely a being that exists both in our understanding and in reality. Since it is a premise of the argument that God is a being than which nothing greater can be conceived, it is **contradictory** and logically impossible for us to conceive a being that is greater than God. Therefore, God must exist not only in the understanding, but also in reality.

Gaunilo, a contemporary of Anselm, and later figures such as **Descartes** sought to reject the ontological argument by asserting that similar arguments could prove the existence of absurd things, such as the greatest possible island. Anselm replied that in talking about a thing so great that nothing greater could be conceived, he was making a logical point about greatness rather than a factual point about different kinds of things.

Kant proposed the most important objection to the ontological argument with his claim that existence is not a **predicate**. His view is a major topic of discussion in contemporary philosophical logic.

Few philosophers are convinced by the ontological argument, but many find it difficult to overcome. Today there are both opponents and defenders of the argument, and many new versions have been elaborated, with some relying on recent developments in **modal logic**. The American philosopher Alvin **Plantinga** argues in this way. It is possible for there to be a being that has maximal greatness. Therefore, a possible being in some world *w* has maximal greatness. A being has maximal greatness in a given world only if it has maximal excellence in every world. A being has maximal excellence in a given world only if it has omniscience, omnipotence, and moral perfection in that world. If a being has maximal excellence in every world, it has maximal excellence in this world. If a being has maximal excellence in this world, then it has omniscience, omnipotence, and moral perfection in this world. But these are the attributes of God, and if a being has these attributes in this world, then that being is God.

The ontological argument is so fascinating because it leads into many significant philosophical questions, such as "Is existence a property?," "Can there be existential propositions that are necessarily true?," and "What sense of 'is' is involved in saying that something does not exist?" The modern versions are more plausible if entities retain their **identity** across worlds, but are less persuasive if terms designate **counterparts** from one world to another or if **possible worlds** and their contents are understood as **descriptions** rather than as real **objects** of reference. If these and many other problems are not solved, a proper analysis of the ontological argument will continue to elude us.

> "Because of the crucial role which the concept of existence or being plays in this argument it has been called the Ontological Argument."
> **C. Williams**, *What is Existence?*

ontological commitment

METAPHYSICS, LOGIC, PHILOSOPHY OF LANGUAGE The use of language commits us to the **existence** of **objects**. A person's **ontology** comprises the set of objects that he takes to exist and thereby to make up the furniture of the world. Theories differ according to the objects they posit to exist. Ontology is the answer to the question "What is there?" Determining which answer is right amounts to determining what ontological commitments are acceptable. We are thus faced with the problem of finding a **criterion** for ontological commitment. The famous criterion put forward by **Quine** concerns the ontological commitments of a theory: a **theory** is committed to those objects that must exist if it is true and is committed to the existence of entities of a certain kind if and only if they must be counted among the **values** of its bound **variables** of **quantification** in order for the theory to be true. This criterion is a development of **Russell's theory of descriptions**, which shows that the occurrence of a **singular term** in a true **statement** does not automatically warrant an assertion that the term refers to something real or existent, but that the **analysis** of the statement into its correct **logical form** reveals the objects that must exist if the statement is true.

> "If what we want is a standard for our own guidance in appraising the ontological commitments of one or another of our theories, and in altering those commitments by revision of our theory, then the criterion at hand well suits our purpose."
> **Quine**, *From a Logical Point of View*

ontological guilt, another expression for anguish

ontological relativity

METAPHYSICS, PHILOSOPHY OF LANGUAGE One of **Quine**'s main doctrines, which holds that there are no absolute **facts** according to which we may determine the **ontological commitments** of a **theory**. There is no determinate answer either to the question "What is there?" or to the question "What objects is one really talking about?" The ontological import of a theory can only make sense relative to a **translation** or an **interpretation** of some background theory or language; and this background theory is itself relative to some further translation into another theory. An ontological question, if taken absolutely, is meaningless. To answer "What is F?" we have to say "An F is a G." But then we can ask: "What is G?" We always need further terms in relation to which we can again ask or answer questions. The regress can only be stopped when we ultimately accept some background theory at face value. Hence, a full interpretation of a theory is nothing more than a complete translation of the theory into another theory, using a manual of translation that is essentially inscrutable and indeterminate. This relativity thesis is a radical departure from a basic assumption held by many analytic philosophers, including **Carnap** and the early **Wittgenstein**, that we can start with absolute talk about the **structure, meaning**, or **content** of linguistic expressions. Ontological relativity implies not only that **reality** itself is indeterminate, but also that the conceptual import of our language in talking about reality is similarly incomplete and indeterminate. Carnap's distinction between **external questions** that deal with linguistic structures and **internal questions** that deal with facts collapses if this thesis is accepted, because external questions themselves become relative and factual.

"Paraphrase in some antecedently familiar vocabulary, then, is our only recourse; and such is ontological relativity." **Quine, *Ontological Relativity and Other Essays***

ontology

METAPHYSICS [from Greek *logos*, theory + *ont*, being] The Latin term *ontologia* was introduced in the seventeenth century for a branch of metaphysics to be distinguished from other branches, namely **rational theology**, **rational cosmology**, and **rational psychology**. Christian **Wolff** did much to gain acceptance for the term. As the theoretical or general part of metaphysics and as the general theory of **being**, ontology is often used for metaphysics as a whole. Ontology deals with the essential characteristics of being itself (of **Aristotle**'s **being** *qua* **being**), and asks questions such as "What is or what exists?," "What kind of thing exists primarily?" and "How are different kinds of being related to one another?" The investigation of the meaning of being began with **Parmenides** and received a systematic discussion in Aristotle. In this century, **Heidegger** and **Quine** have taken completely different approaches to ontology. Heidegger asks what character being must have if human consciousness is to be what it is. Quine proposes his maxim "To be is to be the value of a bound variable" to determine what things a theory claims to exist. His doctrine of **ontological relativity** suggests that what we can take to exist is relative to the theory and language that we bring to the situation.

"The use of the term 'ontology' to refer to metaphysics appears in early modern philosophy and is still with us. Indeed, many contemporary metaphysicians speak of their discipline as ontology." **Gracia, *Metaphysics and Its Task***

open concept, see open texture

open-question argument

ETHICS **Moore**'s argument against **naturalism** in *Principia Ethica*. Naturalism, in his understanding, defines "**good**" or other ethical terms by reference to natural or non-ethical qualities. If such a procedure were right, he argues, then the statement "Whatever is F (some natural property) is good" would be identical with the statement "Whatever is F is F." But this is not the case. For "Whatever is F is F" is a **tautology** and its denial involves **self-contradiction**, while "Whatever is F is good" remains open to question. Whatever natural properties a naturalist uses to define "good," we can still ask, "Are these natural properties good?" A negative answer to such a question will not involve self-contradiction. Hence this kind of statement is not really a definition of "good," and naturalism is wrong. Moore claims that "good" is indefinable. This argument is a subject of controversy, for it is not generally accepted that the **definition** of an ethical term must be analytic. Further, not all forms of naturalism require that "good" is definable by the natural properties that turn out to be good. Also, if the meaning of an ethical term does not require definition, then ruling out a definition does not render the term indefinable. The nature and philosophical role of definition more generally can be called into question in assessing the argument.

> "Moore's most important suggestion was the proposal of what has been called the 'open question' test or criterion for sameness of meaning." **Brandt,** *Ethical Theory*

open sentence

LOGIC, PHILOSOPHY OF LANGUAGE A **formula** that has one or more free **variables**, in contrast to a **closed sentence**, which is a formula that has no free variable. When the variables in an open sentence are replaced by ordinary expressions or attached to **quantifiers**, it becomes a genuine or closed sentence. For instance, "X is mortal" is an open sentence. If we replace "X" with "Socrates," we have a closed sentence, "Socrates is mortal." If we attach "X" to an existential quantifier, we have a closed sentence "∃X, X is mortal." Open sentences are sentential or **propositional functions** rather than **sentences** or **propositions** themselves, and hence are neither **true** nor false. An open sentence is true or false according to the **values** of its variables. The **extension** of an open sentence is the **class** of all the **objects** of which the open sentence is true. A closed sentence, on the other hand, has a **truth-value** and is, or can be, used to make a **statement**.

> "Expressions such as 'X is a book', 'X = X', 'X is a man ⊃ x is mortal', which are like statements except for containing 'X' without a quantifier, are called 'open sentences'." **Quine,** *Methods of Logic*

open society

POLITICAL PHILOSOPHY, PHILOSOPHY OF SOCIAL SCIENCE The distinction between an open society and a closed society was first proposed by **Bergson**, but **Popper** gave the term its current importance. Members of an open society are autonomous individuals who can decide on the basis of their own intelligence what to do. Members compete fairly for social positions. In contrast, a closed society is **authoritarian** or **totalitarian**, and its members do not have a free **choice** over what to do. A closed society is supported by an **ideology** that functions like a magical taboo, while an open society is **rational** and **critical**. **Liberal democratic** society is an example of an open society, while the **Platonic** ideal state is a typical closed society.

> "The magical or tribal or collectivist society will also be called the closed society; the society in which individuals are confronted with personal decisions, the open society." **Popper,** *The Open Society and Its Enemies*

open texture

PHILOSOPHY OF LANGUAGE, PHILOSOPHY OF LAW A term introduced by Friedrich Waismann in his paper "Verifiability" (1945) for an unavoidable feature of empirical **terms** or **statements**. An empirical term, no matter how precise its core meaning, faces unlimited uncertainties of meaning when its dominant **reference** is extended or when it is employed in different **contexts**. The number of possible conditions in which it may be used is infinite. In the face of such open texture, Waismann concluded that no final verifiability is available for empirical statements. Open texture is the possibility of **vagueness**, because vagueness arises when a word is actually used in a fluctuating way while open texture exists because there are always possible gaps in determining the **meaning** of a term. The term is used widely in legal philosophy for the particular cases in which a legal rule, although having a core of settled meaning, is unclear regarding what it prescribes or prohibits. No clean-cut conceptual boundary is provided in these cases, and consequently general legal rules are limited in their capacity to determine decisions and must be supplemented by judicial discretion. H. L. A. **Hart** took this feature of legal rules as an instrument for the criticism of legal **formalism**.

The notion of an open concept, which is derived from open texture, is a concept that has an incomplete **intension** and needs to be modified in order to deal with unforeseen situations. It does not admit of a precise **definition**. The necessary and sufficient conditions of its application are not fixed. An open concept is not a vague concept but is the basis of the possibility of vagueness. Such concepts can be extended or modified, but they cannot be replaced by concepts that are not open. All concepts displaying what **Wittgenstein** called **family resemblance** are open concepts.

> "Open texture, then, is something like possibility of vagueness." **Waismann, in Flew (ed.),** *Logic and Language* **(first series)**

operational definition

PHILOSOPHY OF SCIENCE A **definition** of a **theoretical term** formed by constructing a set of performable operations or activities. A conception of an **object** is the sum of our ideas of the observable consequences of this object disclosed by operations. This idea can be traced back to Peirce's **pragmatic maxim** and is a type of definition articulated by **Bridgman** as the central doctrine of **operationism**. A scientific term can be meaningful only when it can be defined operationally. The claim, to a certain extent, is a generalization of the working practice of scientists.

> "[O]perational definitions [are] statements specifying the meanings of theoretical terms with the help of observational ones." **Hempel, "The Theoretician's Dilemma," in** *Minnesota Studies in the Philosophy of Science,* **vol. II**

operationalism, another term for operationism

operationism

PHILOSOPHY OF SCIENCE, PHILOSOPHY OF MIND [from Latin *operari*, work] Also called operationalism, a theory first proposed in physics by P. W. **Bridgman**, and then applied to other fields. It holds that things and their **properties**, **powers**, and interactions, as the subject-matter of science, should be understood in terms of operations that scientists perform. Scientific knowledge is knowledge of operations, and the **meaning** of scientific terms is established in terms of a description of a set of operations, that is, in terms of operational definitions. To be operationally meaningful, a statement must be confirmable at least in principle. This theory denies the distinction between **theory** and **evidence**. In the final analysis, a scientific theory is connected to operations that are empirically rooted. As a movement within the philosophy of science, it is closely linked with **logical positivism**. The application of this theory to the field of psychology led to the emergence of **behaviorism**. A major difficulty is that it cannot

guarantee that the experiments or selected operations are scientifically valuable or that the meaning of a term remains the same if it is approached from more than one experimental direction.

> "The principle of operationism says that a term is empirically meaningful only if an operational definition can be given for it." **Carnap, "The Methodological Character of Theoretical Concepts," in** *Minnesota Studies in the Philosophy of Science,* **vol. I**

operator, see logical constant

O-proposition, see A-proposition

optimism

PHILOSOPHY OF RELIGION, ETHICS, PHILOSOPHY OF HISTORY [from Latin *optimus*, the best] A French term (*optimisme*) referring to **Leibniz**'s claim in *Theodicy* that the actual world is the best of all possible worlds because **God** who created it is the most perfect being. More generally, optimism is a positive and hopeful attitude toward things and the future, involving the claim that in the long run things are getting better. Optimism is contrasted to **pessimism**, which holds that this world is radically imperfect or that the future will be worse than the present. **Schopenhauer**'s thought is the most important example of pessimism in philosophy.

> "I cannot here withhold the statement that optimism, whether it is not merely the thoughtless talk of those who harbour nothing but words under their absurd, but also a really wicked, way of thinking, is a bitter mockery of the unspeakable sufferings of mankind." **Schopenhauer,** *The World as Will and Representation*

ordinary language

PHILOSOPHY OF LANGUAGE Everyday and nontechnical language as an object of philosophical investigation. It can be distinguished from **natural language**, a term for actual human languages as studied in the philosophy of language and linguistics. Language has been a central concern of twentieth-century philosophy. Some philosophers believe that ordinary language is defective and must be replaced by a rigorously reconstructed language or grammatical system (an **ideal language**), while others argue that we should rather seek to understand the logical diversity and complexity of ordinary language and its correct use to deal with philosophical problems. It holds that a replacement for ordinary language is unnecessary and impossible. This difference in attitude has led to a major division in **analytical philosophy** between ideal language philosophy, represented by **Russell** and **Carnap**, and ordinary language philosophy, represented by **Moore**, the later **Wittgenstein**, **Ryle**, and **Austin**.

"Certainly, then, ordinary language is not the last word: in principle it can everywhere be supplemented and improved and superseded. Only remember, it is the first word." **Austin, Philosophical Papers**

ordinary language philosophy

PHILOSOPHICAL METHOD A kind of **linguistic philosophy**, originating with criticism of the **ideal language** philosophy of **Russell**, certain interpretations of **Wittgenstein**'s early philosophy, and **logical positivism**. Ideal language philosophy claims that we need an artificial language to be a suitable vehicle for philosophical reasoning, with a view to solving the philosophical perplexities caused by the unsystematic, irregular, and imperfect nature of ordinary language. Ordinary language philosophy believes that the creation of an ideal language to replace ordinary language is unnecessary or impossible. Rather, we must pay close attention to the **meanings**, **categories**, **implications**, grammatical or **logical forms**, functions, uses, and distinctions of ordinary language. This approach to philosophy was pioneered by **Moore** and practiced in varying ways by the later Wittgenstein, **Ryle**, **Hare**, **Austin**, and **Strawson**. Because this approach to philosophy was fully developed in Oxford, it also became known as **Oxford philosophy**. According to Strawson, we must uncover the nature of linguistic structure as it has traditionally been presented. Ordinary language presupposes a structure of **reality**, and hence an investigation of that language is a fruitful means of understanding what the extra-linguistic world may really be like. This is the essence of his **descriptive metaphysics**. Ordinary language philosophy emphasizes in particular the problems that have arisen from the use of linguistic expressions. This dimension was developed in Austin's **speech act** theory.

"Ordinary language philosophers saw the task of linguistic philosophy to lie in the clarification of the ordinary concepts that give rise to philosophical puzzles." **Katz, Linguistic Philosophy**

Organon

LOGIC [Greek, instrument or tool] The title given to the collection of **Aristotle**'s logical works by sixth-century commentators rather than by Aristotle himself. These logical works include the *Categories*, *De Interpretatione*, *Prior Analytics*, *Posterior Analytics*, *Topics*, and *Sophistic Elenchi*. These works do not form an organic whole and were composed at different dates. The reason for naming them collectively derived from Aristotle's view that logic is not a part of science, but is rather an instrument of thought.

"Logical matters have the place of a tool (Organon) in philosophy." **Alexander of Aphrodisias, Topics**

original apperception, see transcendental apperception

original choice, an alternative expression for fundamental project

original position

POLITICAL PHILOSOPHY, ETHICS A hypothetical bargaining situation postulated by **Rawls** in *A Theory of Justice*, in which the basic structure of just society can be rationally chosen. Each participant in the original position acts under two conditions. The first condition limits their **knowledge** through a **veil of ignorance**. Participants are ignorant of the circumstances of their society and their position in them, their particular talents, and their special interests. The second condition is motivational – participants are **rational** and mutually **self-interested**. They are not **altruistic** and do not have substantive moral **sentiments**. In addition, there are some formal constraints upon the **principles** to be chosen. They must be formulated in general terms that avoid proper names and hold for a well-ordered society in perpetuity; they must be **universal** and hold for everyone in the society throughout their lives; they must be open to public knowledge; they must be capable of ordering competing claims; and they must provide the highest and final court of appeal for claims.

According to Rawls, the principles chosen in the original position will be the principles of **justice**, partly because the original position is intended to achieve ideal **impartiality** and partly because the principles selected will cohere with our intuitive notion of justice. The original position can be viewed as a procedural interpretation of **Kant**'s conception of **autonomy** and the **categorical imperative**. All **agents** in that position are free, equal, and rational beings who are **autonomous** because they choose the **law** themselves. The original position differs from the **state of nature** in classical **social contract** theory because it is a device to give us insight into our moral and political thinking rather than an exercise in historical speculation. If an agreement on principles is not reached in the original position, we remain in our imperfect and imperfectly understood society. In classical social contract theory, the participants would return to the state of nature.

> "The idea of the original position is to set up a fair procedure so that any principle agreed to will be just." **Rawls**, *A Theory of Justice*

original sin

PHILOSOPHY OF RELIGION A Judeo-Christian doctrine. According to the Bible, the common ancestors of all human beings, Adam and Eve, could not resist the temptation of the devil and broke the divine injunction not to eat the fruit of the tree of knowledge. Hence they committed original sin and lost the favor of God. Psalms 51:5 says: "I was brought forth in inequity, and in sin did my mother conceive me" (cf. Genesis 3, Romans 5:21). This sin has been transmitted to all the descendants of Adam and Eve and is therefore shared by them all, although the precise method of this transmission has been a subject of dispute among theologians. This official doctrine of original sin is essential for the Catholic Church, for it justifies the need to have **grace** for redemption, the need for the sacrament of baptism, and the justification of eternal punishment for those who are not saved. It is, however, unclear whether this is a personal **guilt** on the part of each individual or each individual's share of a defective **human nature**. The doctrine is criticized as being inconsistent with **God**'s **omnipotence**, **omniscience**, and his absolute **goodness**, for it must be God who created the Devil, and God must have had **foreknowledge** that Adam

would be tempted. Critics ask why God did not help Adam to overcome this temptation. It is also cruel for God to multiply Adam's sin throughout humanity. Philosophically, the doctrine might be regarded as a confession of the natural inadequacy of human beings and our inability to lead perfectly **virtuous** lives. The enduring power of the account of original sin lies more in the biblical narrative and in our recognition of our own imperfection than with the philosophical argument.

> "Original sin consists in human nature being left to itself by the withdrawal of the supernatural gift which God has bestowed on men's creation." **Aquinas**, *Summa Theologiae*

Ortega y Gasset, José (1883–1955)

Spanish existentialist philosopher, born in Madrid, Professor of Metaphysics at the University of Madrid. The conception of vital reason at the center of Ortega's attempt to reconcile idealism and realism places us in contact with reality, including the ever-present danger of catastrophe. He distinguished between oneself and one's life and enjoined us to live an authentic life as a drama in which we recognize that we lack a fixed identity. His politics were aristocratic, and he claimed that the masses lacked the creativity and vision to make a success of revolution. His major works include *Meditations on Quixote* (1912) and *The Rebellion of the Masses* (1930).

ostensive definition

LOGIC, PHILOSOPHY OF LANGUAGE The term, introduced by W. E. **Johnson** in his *Logic* in 1921, was discussed in detail by **Russell**, **Wittgenstein**, and the **logical positivists**. An ostensive definition proceeds by simply pointing to something or showing actual examples of the thing being defined, as we usually do when we teach a child. For example, we point to a house and say, "The word 'house' means this." There are three factors in this kind of definition: a demonstrative term, a deictic (pointing) gesture, and a sample of what the word designates. For Wittgenstein, an ostensive definition only answers the question "What is that called?" and does not settle how a term will be used in the future. It therefore does not fix the **meaning** of a term at all. For a private ostensive definition, I seemingly could concentrate my attention on a particular sensation and associate it with a particular sign. The problem is that the sign must be defined in terms of our public language, but in a private ostensive definition it can only be used to name the sensation for myself alone. Wittgenstein denied the possibility of a private ostensive definition as part of his rejection of the possibility of a **private language**.

> "It is obvious that an ostensive definition must depend upon experience." **Russell**, *An Inquiry into Meaning and Truth*

ostensive proposition

EPISTEMOLOGY **Ayer**'s term for a kind of **proposition** that other **logical positivists** held to be the direct record of an immediate **experience** and therefore to have **self-evident** validity. These propositions are taken to be purely demonstrative in character and cannot be refuted by further evidence. Instead, they are the ultimate foundation for determining the validity of other empirical propositions. Ayer himself denies the existence of ostensive propositions, for if a proposition is ostensive, it must consist of purely demonstrative symbols. As a consequence, it would merely **name** a situation without **describing** anything about it. Such a sentence cannot be a genuine proposition and cannot even be expressed.

> "But a proposition would be ostensive only if it recorded what was immediately experienced, without referring in any way beyond." **Ayer**, *Language, Truth and Logic*

Other, the

MODERN EUROPEAN PHILOSOPHY, ONTOLOGY, ETHICS, POLITICAL PHILOSOPHY In **phenomenological** philosophy since **Husserl**, humans other than the subject, self, or **ego**. The self's relation to the Other gives rise to the problem of one's knowledge of **other minds** that is also discussed in analytical philosophy, but issues concerning the Other in ontology, ethics, and political philosophy have come to be considered more fundamental. Emmanuel **Levinas** argued that the possibility of ethics rests on respecting the absolute alterity or otherness of the Other rather than reducing the Other to an object of consciousness. Our ability to satisfy this radical demand depends on our understanding of how we can think an alterity that transcends our **categories** of **thought**. The Other presents problems of

separation, opposition, and **alienation**. In broader cultural terms, **death**, madness, and the **unconscious** have been called the Other because they fall outside the model of rational self-consciousness. The notion of the Other has been embraced in anthropology, post-colonial philosophy, and feminism in an attempt to undermine the entrenched conceptual priority of the metropolitan culture and the male.

> "The absolutely other is the Other. He and I do not form a number. The collectivity in which I say 'you' or 'we' is not a plural of the 'I'." **Levinas**, *Totality and Infinity*

other minds

PHILOSOPHY OF MIND If one can have direct **knowledge** only of one's own **mental states**, it is a serious philosophical question how and what we can know about other minds, that is, whether other persons have minds and what other persons are thinking and feeling. **Descartes** saw free and intelligent **action**, especially in the use of language, inexplicable without the actor having a **mind**. A prominent traditional account relies on an argument by **analogy**. We may find correlations between our own physical behavior and our own psychological or mental states. The knowledge of these correlations can be used as inductive evidence, so that if we observe similar physical behavior exhibited by another person, we can infer ultimately by appeal to our own experience, that he has a certain kind of mental state. The conclusion thus inferred is not secure, for physical resemblance does not logically entail mental resemblance, the inductive base is very small, and we can never check to see if our inference is sound. This argument is criticized for example by **behaviorists**, who argue that if psychophysical relationships are **contingent**, then one cannot even establish a correlation between bodily states and mental states. **Wittgenstein**'s rejection of the possibility of a **private language** has challenged the basis of the argument by analogy, and for some philosophers it has undermined the problem of other minds itself.

> "Let us begin with the problem of other minds. How can we know another person is in pain, or thrilled, or overcome with emotion, or thinking about philosophy?" **Nozick**, *Philosophical Explanations*

other-regarding, see self-regarding

Otto, Rudolf (1869–1937)
German neo-Kantian philosopher of religion, born in Peine, Hanover. In his most influential work, *The Idea of the Holy* (1917), Otto examined "the numinous" as the awe-inspiring and overpowering object of human religious experience. He classified religious feeling as numinous feeling and claimed that it has two aspects: a feeling of religious dread and a feeling of religious fascination. He provided a variety of phenomenological descriptions of numinous feeling and distinguished these from descriptions of aesthetic and moral feelings. His other important books include *Naturalism and Religion* (1904) and *Mysticism East and West* (1926).

ought
ETHICS [related to owe, suggesting that something that is not being done should be done] A general word used in moral discourse as the principal expression of **obligation** and **duty**. Many moral philosophers consider "I ought to . . ." to be identical in meaning to "I am obligated to . . . " Major issues surround the notion of ought. Is there a kind of "ought" which is specifically moral and, if so, how does it relate to other kinds of "ought"? What is the relation between ought and is? In particular, can evaluative claims about what we ought to do be derived solely from factual claims? Does ought imply can or are there things which we ought to attempt to do even if we know that we shall fail? Is the moral "ought" independent of other motives to action, such as sympathy or self-interest, and is the moral worth of what we do spoiled if we act on these other motives rather than through a recognition of the authority of this "ought"? The analysis of ought-statement is one of the main topics of **prescriptivism**.

"If the analysis of 'ought' which I have just sketched bears any close relation to the use of 'ought' in ordinary language, it shows how it is that moral judgements provide reasons for acting in one way rather than another." **Hare,** *The Language of Morals*

ought implies can
ETHICS A formula in **Kant**'s ethics, meaning that correctly judging that a given agent is morally obliged to perform a certain action logically presupposes that the agent can perform it. He can perform it not just if he wants, prefers, or **wills** to, but in some absolute sense. This capacity is a categorical **freedom** in contrast to the hypothetical freedom defended by **Hume** and others, for it is freedom both to do and to forbear doing a certain action under the same set of conditions.

"Perhaps all that the formula 'ought implies can' means is that it would be pointless to issue an imperative if it were impossible that the imperative should be obeyed." **Pap,** *Elements of Analytic Philosophy*

ousia
ANCIENT GREEK PHILOSOPHY, METAPHYSICS [Greek, substance, essence, entity, reality, from *ousa*, the singular feminine participle of *einai*, to be; the term is closely linked to *on*, the neutral participle of *einai*] Although **Plato** used *on* and *ousia* synonymously, **Aristotle** classified different kinds of being and used *ousia* for *on* (being) in its first sense, namely, ultimate **reality**. In the *Categories*, Aristotle defined *ousia* as the ultimate subject that underlies everything else. According to this test, a sensible individual is primary *ousia*, while **species** and **genus** are secondary *ousiai*. In the *Metaphysics*, *ousia* is **the focal meaning** of being, but it is divided into **form**, **matter**, and the composite of matter and form. If *ousia* were still determined by the subject **criterion**, matter would be the primary subject and hence primary *ousia*. But Aristotle held this to be impossible, and presented the separation (independent existence) of substance and its status as a this (*tode ti*) as more important criteria for deciding what is *ousia*. According to these new criteria, form is *ousia* in the primary sense, with composites of form and matter being *ousia* in a derivative sense. Species and genus, which are secondary *ousia* in the *Categories*, are rejected as *ousiai* in the *Metaphysics*. This has given rise to the problem of explaining the relation between form and the **universal**.

To search for primary *ousia* is tantamount to searching for primary being. Aristotle emphasized the central position of *ousia* in the network of **categories**. All other categories depend on *ousia* for their existence, and *ousia* is prior to them in time, knowledge, and definition. Thus, Aristotle claimed in the *Metaphysics* Z that the study of being can be reduced to the study of *ousia* (ousiology). Ousiology has come to be used for describing Aristotle's mature view of ontology.

Ousia is generally translated as **substance** as a consequence of **Boethius**' influential medieval commentary on the *Categories*, in which *ousia* and subject coincide. But this translation is unsatisfactory because substance has no etymological connection with *ousia*. Moreover, the translation does not really fit with the doctrine of *ousia* in the *Metaphysics*. Alternative English translations of *ousia* include **essence**, **entity**, and **reality**.

> "It follows, then, that 'ousia' has two senses, (a) the ultimate substratum, which is no longer predicated of anything else, and (b) that which, being a 'this', is also separated – and of this nature is the shape or form of each thing." **Aristotle,** *Metaphysics*

ousiology, see *ousia*

outer sense, see inner sense

overman, an English translation of *Übermensch*

Owen, G(wilym) E(llis) L(ane) (1922–82)

British philosopher of ancient Greek philosophy, born in Portsmouth, Professor at University of Oxford, Harvard University, and University of Cambridge. Owen exerted great influenced in the modern study of ancient Greek philosophy by combining scholarly acumen with a philosophical appreciation of method and argument that extended to contemporary controversies. His discussions of Plato's *Timaeus*, Aristotle's Platonism, and Aristotle's conception of dialectic are central to an appreciation of the importance of his work. His major works include *Logic, Science and Dialectic* (1986).

owl of Minerva

PHILOSOPHICAL METHOD, PHILOSOPHY OF HISTORY Minerva was the Roman goddess of wisdom, and her companion the owl was traditionally regarded as being wise. In his preface to the *Philosophy of Right*, **Hegel** used the owl of Minerva, which flies only at dusk, as a metaphor for the nature of philosophy. It implies that philosophy is essentially retrospective and can provide understanding of a stage of reality only after it has occurred. This claim challenges the view that we have a universal capacity to know, independent of our **context** as subjects of knowledge.

> "When philosophy paints its grey in grey, then has a shape of life grown old. By philosophy's grey in grey it cannot be rejuvenated but only understood. The owl of Minerva spreads its wings only within the falling of the dusk." **Hegel,** *Philosophy of Right*

ownership

POLITICAL PHILOSOPHY, PHILOSOPHY OF LAW, PHILOSOPHY OF MIND In political and legal philosophy, a relationship of absolute or limited control between **persons** and **property**. We can ask about the origin of ownership and about its **legitimacy**. We can argue that ownership should be governed by **rules** of licit acquisition and transmission or by rules of fair **distribution**. As part of a general exploration of **rights**, we can examine whether ownership rights are absolute or relative to other social concerns. We can explore the claim that some things should not be owned or the claim that persons, if they may be owned at all, should be the subject of **self-ownership**. We can examine whether other social relations, including relations between parents and children or between persons and social or political institutions, can be understood in terms of ownership. We can ask whether we own our **actions** and the actions of those whom we authorize to represent us in institutions.

Ownership has been extended to examine our relations, as persons or bodies, to our **mental states** and to explore the claim that our bodies are our own. An investigation of ownership in this domain leads to questions about the nature of persons and about the **mind–body** relationship. Different accounts of causal relations between mental events and bodily events carry different justifications for our ownership of our mental states. Although in the following views ownership of our mental states is ascribed to ourselves as bodies, the mind–body relations that are discussed can also offer a necessary basis for ascribing ownership to ourselves as persons.

According to **interactionism**, a body owns mental states if there is a particular sort of interaction between them. For **epiphenomenalism**, a body owns mental states if events in the body are the main or only cause of events in the mind. For **double-aspect theory**, mental states are owned by a body because a mind and a body are different aspects of the same basic entity and are not causally distinct from one another. For **parallelism**, there is a parallel relationship between mental and bodily states, with ownership related to this association rather than to causal priority. According to the **identity theory of mind**, mental states are owned by the body that has brain states that are identical to those mental states.

All of these theories, which link mental states to bodies, conflict with a **no-ownership theory**, which denies that mental phenomena must belong to a certain person or to a certain body. **Hume's bundle theory of mind** implies that mental items are not necessarily owned by the mind to which they belong because the mind is an accidental collection or bundle of such items, but other philosophers reject the possibility of mental states that do not belong to a subject or person.

The questions of what makes my body mine and how I know that my body is mine require an understanding of the place of our bodies in our being subjects and agents.

> "Let us name the relation which everybody speaks of in this way by calling a certain body his own, the relation of ownership." **Wisdom**, *Problems of Mind and Matter*

Oxford philosophy

PHILOSOPHICAL METHOD Philosophy has been studied and taught at Oxford since the thirteenth century, and, from as early as the fourteenth century, Oxford has contributed eminent philosophers such as **Duns Scotus** and **William of Ockham**. **Hobbes**, **Locke**, and **Bentham** were students of Oxford. From the nineteenth century to the first part of the twentieth century, Oxford has contributed John Henry **Newman**, Joseph **Butler**, John **Cook Wilson**, H. A. **Prichard**, and R. G. **Collingwood**, among others. However, "Oxford philosophy" as a technical term refers to a distinct approach to analytical philosophy that flourished at Oxford after the Second World War. It places emphasis on clarifying perennial philosophical problems in terms of the analysis of ordinary language, and is in contrast to **logical positivism** and the Russellian strand of philosophy in Cambridge. This approach started with H. H. **Price** and Gilbert **Ryle**, although it is related to the work of G. E. **Moore** and **Wittgenstein**'s later work in Cambridge. It was further articulated in distinctive ways by J. L. **Austin** and P. F. **Strawson**. It made Oxford the dominant center of analytical philosophy from the 1940s to the 1960s, and is also called **ordinary language philosophy**. Other contemporary Oxford philosophers include H. L. A. **Hart**, A. J. **Ayer**, Elizabeth **Anscombe**, Philippa **Foot**, H. P. **Grice**, G. E. L. **Owen**, Michael **Dummett**, Bernard **Williams**, David **Pears**, R. M. **Hare**, Charles **Taylor**, and Ronald **Dworkin**. But these philosophers have different approaches, and some would vigorously reject being classed as Oxford philosophers in the above sense. Oxford is still a major center of philosophy today and is the birthplace of this dictionary.

> "During the last quarter of a century Oxford has occupied, or reoccupied, a position it last held, perhaps, six hundred years ago: that of a great centre of philosophy in the Western world." **Strawson**, *Logico-Linguistic Papers*

P

pacifism

POLITICAL PHILOSOPHY [from Latin *pacificare*, to make or be at peace] A position that objects to war as a means to achieve national aims or to solve disputes. More broadly, it objects to any sort of killing and violence. It claims that even the use of force to meet force is wrong and that nobody may use force without specific overriding justification. Pacifism advocates cooperation and negotiation and actively encourages activities promoting peace. Absolute pacifism holds that war and violence are intrinsically wrong and cannot possibly be justified. Critics argue that pacifists fail to distinguish between aggression and legitimate national defense in a **just war**, and fail to distinguish between intentional harming or killing and legitimate individual self-defense. Many forms of pacifism are conditional, in that they claim that war and violence are *prima facie* wrong, but allow that wrong to be overridden. In this respect, they approach their rival theory of a just war.

"A. J. P. Taylor coined the word pacifism as a general descriptive term designed to cover all the different attempts made (for any reason) to abolish war, and we can contrast this idea with that of pacifism proper, which involves being against a war on more than merely pragmatic grounds. Pacifism proper involves a moral judgement and a personal commitment." **Teichman,** *Pacifism and the Just War*

paideia

ANCIENT GREEK PHILOSOPHY, ETHICS [Greek, education, from *pais*, child] In ancient Greece, *paideia* included *mousike* (mainly literature and song) and gymnastics. Moral education trained a youth by habituation until he acquired the right habits, that is, the right patterns of **action**. Education was not confined to children and youth, for adults were held to need it as well to become as **virtuous** as possible.

"What will this *paideia* be? . . . It is in part physical training for the body and training in the arts for the soul." **Plato,** *Republic*

pain

PHILOSOPHY OF MIND Either physical or mental suffering that is generally regarded to be a negative feeling. The main tenet of **hedonism** is that it is **human nature** to pursue **pleasure** and to avoid pain. However, philosophers have been puzzled by the nature of this feeling. **Wittgenstein** sought to show that pain is not a private sensation expressed by a **private language** that can be understood only by oneself. In order to be used in a public language, expressions for pain must have **meanings** for which there are public criteria given in the outward expression of pain. Other philosophers reject the criterial account in favor of reducing pain to pain behavior. This **behaviorist** move is rejected by the **identity theory**, which identifies pain with neurological processes. On the basis of his account of meaning and identity, **Kripke** argues that because we can describe a world in which pain states and accompanying physical states are not identical, they are not identical in the actual world. Some philosophers ask why we would wish to avoid pain on accounts that do not give central consideration to its raw qualitative feel. Scholars also debate over whether there is a common and intrinsic quality shared by all token feelings of pain.

> "The truth is: it makes sense to say about other people that they doubt whether I am in pain, but not to say it about myself." **Wittgenstein, *Philosophical Investigations***

Paine, Thomas (1737–1809)

English revolutionary and political thinker, born in Thetford. Paine supported the American Revolution and offered an intellectual defense of the French Revolution against Edmund Burke's powerful attack. He also opposed clerical authority with an enlightened deism and proposed a radical agenda of social and economic reform, including proposals for the eradication of poverty. His main works include *The Rights of Man* (1791–2) and *The Age of Reason* (1794–5).

panentheism

PHILOSOPHY OF RELIGION [from Greek *pan*, all + *en*, in + *theos*, god] The view that all things are imbued with God's being through being parts of **God** or **Absolute Being**. Because on this view God extends beyond all that there is in the world, panentheism rejects the **pantheist** claim that God is identical with the totality of things. Rather, God is **consciousness** and the highest possible unity. This position was developed by the German philosopher Karl Christian Krause by combining **Spinoza**'s notion of **substance** and **Fichte**'s notion of **self-consciousness**. **Whitehead** also used this term in his **process theology**.

> "Pantheism is the view that all is God, while panentheism occupies a position midway between theism and pantheism. For panentheists, while it is not strictly true that everything is God, everything is lodged or embedded within God, making the two interdependent." **Taliaferro, in Bunnin and Tsui-James (eds.), *Blackwell Companion to Philosophy***

panosomatism, another term for reism

panpsychism

METAPHYSICS, PHILOSOPHY OF RELIGION [from Greek *pan*, all + *psyche*, soul] The view that everything in the universe, including things that we ordinarily regard as not living, possesses a mental aspect or level of **consciousness**, although this does not imply that each thing has a **mind** or **soul** like our own. The universe as a whole is considered to be alive, with the character of an animated organism. **God** is described as being completely immanent in all things as a psychic force or spirit. Panpsychism is also called **animism**, **hylozoism** (from Greek *hule*, matter + *zoe*, life), or **mentalism**.

In spite of the difficulty of accepting panpsychism's explanation of mental aspects, the theory has been endorsed by some thinkers who find greater difficulty in alternative explanations of how mental phenomena can be caused by non-mental things. **Leibniz**, **Schopenhauer**, **Schelling**, and **Whitehead** offer different forms of panpsychism.

> "By panpsychism I mean the view that the basic physical constituents of the universe have mental properties, whether or not they are parts of living organisms." **T. Nagel, *Mortal Questions***

pantheism

PHILOSOPHY OF RELIGION [from Greek *pan*, all + *theos*, god] A term originated by John Toland for the belief that **God** is identical with the universe, that is, with the totality of all there is, rather than being a supernatural power above or alongside the universe. Because God is the universe taken as a whole, no divine act of **creation** is required and the distinction between God and his creatures, sharply drawn in Christianity, is denied. All is God, and God is all. Everything in the universe is a **mode** or element of God. The claim that the divine is all-inclusive distinguishes pantheism from **panentheism**, which holds that God includes all things but is greater than their totality. The most important pantheist was **Spinoza**, who offered sophisticated arguments to support the claim that there is only one **substance** and that this substance can be understood as God or **nature**. **Hegel** was also a pantheist in virtue of his identification of God with the whole of **Being**.

"Pantheism applies the term 'God' in such a way that nothing positive can be distinct from him. God is considered wholly immanent within the universe, and the universe – in so far as it has being – is identical with God." **Ferré**, *Basic Modern Philosophy of Religion*

paradigm

ANCIENT GREEK PHILOSOPHY, METAPHYSICS, PHILOSOPHY OF SCIENCE [from Greek *paradeigma*, model, pattern] **Plato** describes **Forms** as paradigms to which particular **objects** have a likeness or **resemblance**, and to which we must look in order to acquire **knowledge**. In the *Republic* it is said that the ideal state might be a paradigm laid up in the heaven; in another dialogue, the *Timaeus*, Forms are paradigms by reference to which the divine craftsman constructs the sensible world.

In the twentieth century, the American philosopher Thomas **Kuhn** in his classic *The Structure of Scientific Revolutions* (1962), employs the word "paradigm" to refer to a framework of **concepts**, assumptions, and approaches within which members of a scientific community conduct their research. When a paradigm has to be changed or shifted, there comes a **scientific** revolution.

"Close historical investigation of a given speciality at a given time discloses a set of recurrent and quasi-standard illustrations of various theories in their conceptual, observational, and instrumental applications. These are the community's paradigms, revealed in its textbooks, lectures, and laboratory exercises." **Kuhn,** *The Structure of Scientific Revolutions*

paradigm case argument

EPISTEMOLOGY A challenge to **skepticism** regarding the existence of such things as the **external world**, **free will**, valid inductive arguments, **certainty**, or **time**. The paradigm case argument claims that if we have learned to use a **referring expression** for which typical or paradigmatic referents have become the **meaning** of that expression, then such an expression refers in standard cases to genuine existents. Our ability to employ a certain type of expression in ordinary speech is proof that it has application. Accordingly, if words such as "table" and "chair" are in common use, there must be physical objects. Similarly, the fact that words such as "choose" and "decide" are in common use shows the existence of free will. This argument, influenced by **Wittgenstein**'s account of **language games**, had wide appeal in the 1950s and 1960s. The argument was criticized because different ways of teaching an expression might involve different, and perhaps conflicting, paradigms. Many philosophers are dissatisfied with conformity to linguistic norms as the mark of **truth**. Accordingly, the argument is currently little used.

"The argument which we have been discussing has come to be known as the argument from paradigm cases. It is used as a weapon against philosophical scepticism in the interest of common sense." **Ayer,** *The Concept of a Person and Other Essays*

paradigm shift

PHILOSOPHY OF SCIENCE In contrast to the traditional view that science is cumulative in the gradual increase of its empirical content within a stable framework, **Kuhn** explained scientific change in terms of revolutionary shifts in scientific **paradigms**, as well as in terms of work carried out within a paradigm in periods of normal science. A paradigm, in Kuhn's sense, has two dimensions. First, it is a set of **beliefs**, **values**, techniques, practices, and examples of explanatory success shared by a scientific community within a social and institutional context. Secondly, a paradigm is the model or explanatory framework that normal sciences apply to solve problems. However, the scope of any given paradigm is limited. Once there is an accumulation of outstanding problems that cannot be solved within a paradigm, a scientific community goes into crisis. In response to the crisis, a new paradigm will emerge. The new paradigm is better than its predecessor because it can formulate new problems and set procedures for solving the existing accumulation of outstanding problems. Scientific revolutions happen when scientists reject an old paradigm and replace it with a new one. Because a new paradigm involves fundamental shifts in concepts, theoretical structures, and scientific practices, the old and new paradigms are **incommensurable**. Hence scientific revolution is equivalent to paradigm shift. The replacement of a paradigm by another is also informed by political and social development.

paradox

LOGIC [from Greek *para*, beyond + *doxa*, belief] Literally, something which is against the generally accepted view or something which looks implausible but implies a philosophical challenge. In logic, a paradox is a **contradictory** position arising from sound premises or sound proof. In this sense, it is a synonym for an **antinomy**. Medieval logicians called paradoxes *insolubilia*. In ancient Greece, **Zeno of Elea** and the Megarians invented a number of interesting paradoxes, but paradoxes became the focus of modern philosophical concern after the discovery of **Russell's paradox**, which posed fundamental issues of philosophical **method** and principles. Russell's paradox gave rise to a crisis in **Frege**'s **logicist** program, and the intellectual advance of the program depended upon overcoming this paradox.

Generally, following Peano and **Ramsey**, paradoxes are divided into two main types: **semantic paradoxes** and **logical paradoxes** (or **set-theoretical paradoxes**). Semantic paradoxes, such as the **liar paradox**, **Berry's paradox**, Richard's paradox, and **Grelling's paradox**, arise because of some peculiarity of semantic **concepts**, such as **truth**, falsity, and definability. Logical paradoxes, such as Russell's paradox, **Burali-Forti's paradox**, and **Cantor's paradox**, arise because of some peculiarity of set-theoretical concepts and due to faulty logic and mathematics. Such a distinction is not without controversy. Russell, for instance, claimed that all paradoxes arise because of violations of the **vicious circle principle**. The general solution of semantic paradoxes involves replacing ordinary language with artificially constructed language. The general procedure for solving logical paradoxes involves restricting set-existence principles. But both of these types of solutions have been contested. Recent work in paraconsistent logic seeks to tolerate some paradoxes while preventing ruinous consequences for the systems in which they are embedded. Various paradoxes are recorded in this dictionary under their particular names.

paradox of confirmation, another expression for Hempel's paradox

paradox of God's omniscience, see omniscience

paradox of self-deception, see self-deception

paradox of size, see Cantor's paradox

paradox of the heap, see sorites paradox

parallel distributed processing, see connectionism

parallelism

PHILOSOPHY OF MIND Also called psycho-physical parallelism, a theory which is particularly associated with **Spinoza**. It claims that the mental realm and the physical realm, or **thought** and **extension**, do not affect each other in any way. Instead, they are independent of each other, although there is a precise correspondence between them. "The order and connection of ideas is the same as the order and connection of things" (Spinoza, *Ethics*, II, 7). If two items in the physical realm are similar, their counterparts in the mental realm are similar; and vice versa. If two items in thought are related as **cause** and **effect**, their corresponding items in extension are also related as cause and effect. However, mental events never cause bodily events, and bodily events never cause mental events. There are physical causal laws and there are psychological laws, but there can not be any psycho-physical causal laws. Parallelism is a classical response to the Cartesian **mind–body problem**. Sometimes Spinoza claimed that such a parallelism is a relation of **identity** on the grounds that each mental mode is a physical mode. This view, together with his claim that thought and extension are different **attributes** of one and the same **substance**, has led many scholars to argue that Spinoza's philosophy of mind should be termed a **dual-aspect theory**.

> "Parallelism, in the mild sense, is the proposition that for every mental event there is a bodily event which always accompanies it." **Wisdom,** *Problem of Mind and Matter*

paralogism

LOGIC, PHILOSOPHY OF MIND [from Greek *para*, beyond + *logizesthai*, to reason] Generally, a formally invalid **inference**. **Aristotle** in *Poetics* defined a paralogism as the **fallacy** of inferring from the truth of the consequence to the truth of the premise. For **Kant**, a paralogism is the inevitable erroneous outcome of reason in rational psychology when it extends beyond the limits of experience. Reason leads from the **transcendental** ground of the **"I think"** to four kinds of paralogism: (1) the **soul** is a **substance**; (2) the soul is **simple**; (3) the soul is **identical** over time; and (4) the soul is **conscious** only of itself. Kant also called these claims transcendental paralogisms. He held that all of these inferences are invalid because they infer from the formal conditions of thought to a substance of thought. Kant's target in exposing the paralogism is the rational psychology of **Descartes** and his **rationalist** successors and the alleged misinterpretation of the *Cogito* that infers existence from thinking.

> "In the first kind of syllogism I conclude from the transcendental concept of the subject, which contains nothing manifold, the absolute unity of this subject itself . . . This dialectical inference I shall entitle the transcendental paralogism." **Kant,** *Critique of Pure Reason*

paraphrasis, another term for contextual definition

Pareto improvement, see Pareto optimality

Pareto optimality

PHILOSOPHY OF SOCIAL SCIENCE, POLITICAL PHILO-SOPHY A principle, also called Pareto efficiency, named after the Italian economist and sociologist Vilfredo Pareto, referring to a state whereby no one can be better off without making someone else worse off. A change that makes at least one person better off and no one worse off is called a Pareto

improvement. In this case, at least one individual prefers X to Y, and no one else regards Y as better than X. To change from Y to X certainly improves the welfare of the whole society. Pareto optimality and Pareto improvement are widely accepted as criteria for justifying or criticizing changes in economic policy. They are also used to evaluate the **utilitarian** summing of welfare across individuals without the need to compare interpersonal **utility**. Since each policy change in a social context generates a loser, a Pareto improvement is hard to achieve.

> "The familiar economist's concept of Pareto efficiency (or Pareto optimality) is a very different matter. A distribution of resources is Pareto efficient if no change in that distribution can be made that leaves no one worse off and at least one person better off." **Dworkin,** *A Matter of Principle*

Parfit, Derek (1942–)

British moral philosopher and philosopher of mind, born in Chengdu, China, Fellow of All Souls College, Oxford. Parfit argues that we can deal with the problem of personal identity by seeing that it is rational to be concerned with degrees of continuity and connectedness in life rather than with the all-or-nothing identity relationship. His metaphysics of the self underlies a wealth of engaging utilitarian arguments that endorse the rationality, in some cases, of acting to achieve the ends of others before one's own ends. His major works include *Reasons and Persons* (1984).

Parmenides (flourished c.480 BC)

Greek philosopher, born in the City of Elea. The main extant work of Parmenides, *On Truth*, was written in hexameter verses. He is regarded as the originator of ontology, although there is scholarly disagreement about the details of his theory. He introduced the conception of being, on which he centered his philosophical speculation. His claim that what-is-there-to-be-thought-of and what-is-there-to-be are the same deeply influenced metaphysics in **Plato** and **Aristotle**. Parmenides rejected the reliability of sense-perception and argued that change is unreal. His successors in natural philosophy were challenged to overcome this reasoned denial of change.

parsimony, the principle of, another term for Ockham's razor

partial concept

LOGIC, PHILOSOPHY OF LANGUAGE For **Kant**, each **concept** typically contains other concepts, namely, various **predicates** that can jointly apply to the **object** or instance of this concept. A predicate contained in this concept is a partial concept, for it can identify its object only in virtue of being conjoined with other predicates contained in the same concept. All partial concepts are related, either coordinately, such as being a man and being rational, or subordinately, such as being a man and being an animal. The process of clarifying all partial concepts and their relationships is **conceptual analysis**, and the result of this process is an analytic judgment.

> "For when I make a distinct concept, I begin with parts and proceed from these to the whole." **Kant, Logic**

participation

ANCIENT GREEK PHILOSOPHY, METAPHYSICS [Greek, *methexis*, from the verb *metechein*, to participate, to share in and to partake] In **Plato**'s **theory of Forms**, particular things possess some characteristic because they participate in the relevant Forms; for example, beautiful things are beautiful because they participate the Form "beauty." So particular things are only the less complete realization of the Form. However, the Form is one, and particular things are many. How can one single Form be in many things at the same time? In what way do things participate in a Form? This is the problem of how **universals** can be in particulars. Plato formulates this problem in his self-criticism in the *Parmenides*, and the problem remains today. In his later dialogues Plato talks more about the participation of one Form in other Forms, rather than the participation of particular things in the Forms. **Neoplatonism** also uses this concept in the sense that the lower orders of beings participate in the higher.

> "It seems to me that whatever else is beautiful apart from absolute beauty is beautiful because it participates in that absolute beauty, and for no other reason." **Plato, *Phaedo***

particular

METAPHYSICS [from Latin *pars*, *partis*, part] For **Aristotle**, particulars cannot be **predicated** of things, in contrast to a **universal**, which can be predicated of many things. "Particular" is used as an adjective for things that are partial, limited, or some, rather than whole, unlimited, or all. As a noun, "particular" has various applications, some of which lead to philosophical dispute. As a single **entity** of a **class** or kind, a particular has a unique path through **space** and **time** and unlike universals cannot be instantiated by other entities, however similar they are to the initial particular. A particular is a unity, in contrast to an aggregation of things. If we maintain the notion of **substance**, a particular is a substance that bears **attributes**, qualities, or **properties**, whilst attributes are universals. Particulars include historical **events**, **material objects**, people and their shadows, but do not include qualities and properties, **numbers** and **species**. Particulars should be distinguished from **individuals**, for while all particulars are individuals, many individuals, instead of being particulars, are **abstract** and **general**. Philosophers have different opinions about the ontological status of particulars, depending on their account of universals.

> "A particular is defined as an entity which can only enter into complexes as the subject of a predication or as one of the terms of a relation, never as itself a predicate or a relation." **Russell, *Collected Papers of Bertrand Russell*, vol. VII**

particular proposition

LOGIC In traditional syllogistic logic, propositions of the form "some s are p" or "some s are not p" are called particular propositions. Propositions of the first form, particular affirmative propositions, are symbolized as "I" (SIP), and propositions of the second form, particular negative propositions, are symbolized as "O" (SOP). In modern predicate **calculus**, a particular affirmative proposition is analyzed as "there is at least one x such that x is s and x is p." Particular propositions are generally held to contain **referring expressions** and therefore to have **existential import**. Particular propositions are contrasted to **universal propositions**, that is, propositions of the form "all s are p" and "all s are not p." Together, these are the four basic types of propositions in traditional logic.

> "The proposition 'Some x's are y's' makes an assertion about part of the class x and is, therefore, called a particular proposition." **Stebbing,** *A Modern Introduction to Logic*

particularized quality, another term for abstract particular

partition

LOGIC The division of a **class** into sub-classes (each of which is called a partition class, and all of which jointly form an exclusive class), or a process of dividing a whole into its parts, as long as the parts are homogeneous with each other and with the whole. For instance, the property "having the same weight as" can divide a class in terms of weight into a sub-class that includes all objects with that weight. An object with that weight belongs to only one sub-class. Partition is closely related to the notion of equivalent class within which each member bears an equivalent relation to every other member. A related concept is resolution, which is a process of exhibiting a whole in terms of its components. Both partition and resolution are forms of **analysis**.

> "By partition is meant transforming what is first presented as a mere unit by exhibiting it in the form of a whole consisting of parts." **Johnson,** *Logic*

partitive term, Quine's expression for mass term

Pascal, Blaise (1623–62)

French philosopher and mathematician, born in Clermont-Ferrand. His most important philosophical work *Pensées* was posthumously published in 1670. Pascal maintained that our knowledge of first principles is based on faith rather than on reason. Because reason is unable to establish first principles, the foundations of science and mathematics are fundamentally uncertain. This same skeptical argument led him to conclude that it is impossible to achieve a demonstrative proof of God's existence. However, he proposed "Pascal's wager," the argument that it would be wiser to choose to believe in God's existence, because if there is no God, we have no significant loss, but if God does exist, we gain eternal happiness. Pascal was also a pioneer of **decision theory**.

Pascal's wager

PHILOSOPHY OF RELIGION A practical argument to suggest that it is **rational** to believe in **God**, formulated by the French thinker Blaise **Pascal** in his *Pensées* (1670). Pascal initiated the use of practical argumentation as a new line of thought in support of Christian faith. If we can not use metaphysics to prove decisively whether or not God exists, what then should we do? On the basis of his work on **probability**, Pascal claimed that belief in God is the soundest bet in the face of the uncertainty of an afterlife. If we believe, then God either exists or does not exist. If he does not exist, we lose little. If he exists, we will be awarded eternal bliss and avoid the possibility of going to hell. Hence, the choice to be a believer carries with it the possibility of immense gain, while the choice not to believe carries with it the possibility of a vastly greater loss. This argument has been treated scornfully by critics, but it has been accepted by some as a legitimate theological use of **practical reason**. It can be placed in a context of examples from rational choice theory, although Pascal's wager concerns the choice of belief rather than action. For this reason, it is related to problems about the **will** and **belief** that arise in William **James**'s **pragmatism**.

> "Notwithstanding its methodological modernity as a course of argumentation cast in the mold of decision theory, the spirit of Pascal's Wager is thus profoundly conservative in its substantive message." **Rescher,** *Pascal's Wager*

passion, see feeling

passive intellect, see active intellect

past

METAPHYSICS, PHILOSOPHY OF HISTORY The past is meant in some sense to contain what happened at an earlier time, but it is not clear that the past is **real**. **Objectivists** argue that the past exists independent of human **minds** and **knowledge** and provides a basis for historical statements. For **skeptics**, the past can hardly exist. What actually exists must be present, but if the past were present, it would not be the past. Because it is the past, it can not exist. For **subjectivists** and **relativists**, the past exists merely as a **construction** of historians.

How, then, would it be possible to establish the **truth** of a statement about the past? For skeptics, the past does not exist and knowledge of the past is impossible. According to relativists, because the intentions and prejudices of historians are indispensable to historical inquiry, historical knowledge need not be rejected, but it is not objective. For objectivists, historical knowledge represents what really took place, but because historical statements are made on the basis of **memory**, testimony, and **evidence** rather than on direct observation, we can still ask how it is possible to secure the reliability of statements about the past. Some claim that such statements are about the present rather than about the past, and others claim that they are rules for the **prediction** of future historical experiences. The existence and intelligibility of the past have been important topics in contemporary **analytic philosophy**.

"From my own part, I do not find anything excessively paradoxical in the view that propositions about the past are rules for the prediction of those 'historical' experiences which are commonly said to verify them, and I do not see how else 'pure knowledge of the past' is to be analysed." **Ayer,** *Language, Truth and Logic*

past-referring term

PHILOSOPHY OF HISTORY In our **conceptual scheme**, all expressions or terms describing present objects can be classified into three kinds: past-referring terms, temporally neutral terms, and future-referring terms. Past-referring terms apply to present events or objects in a way that entails the existence of an event or object at an earlier time logically related to the present object. For example, to call a woman a mother entails that she gave a birth to a child. Temporally neutral terms apply to present events or objects, but do not imply any reference to past or future items. For example, to call somebody a man does not imply anything about the past or future. Future-referring terms apply to present items in a way that is conditioned by their reference to some future objects or events. For example, to call a woman a mother-to-be entails that she will give birth at some future time. Historical language is rich in past-referring terms, but philosophers and logicians argue over the possibility of determining

the **truth-value** of historical statements that contain past-referring terms.

"By a past-referring term, I shall mean a term, whose correct application to a present object or event, logically involves a reference to some earlier object or event which may or may not be causally related to the object to which the term is applied." **Danto,** *Analytical Philosophy of History*

paternalism

ETHICS, POLITICAL PHILOSOPHY [from Latin *pater,* father] Paternalism is derived from parental caring towards one's children. In ethics it means interfering with another person's **liberty** or **freedom** in the belief that one is promoting the **good** of that person, or preventing **harm** from occurring to that person, even if one's action provokes that person's disagreement or protest. Paternalism is challenged by **liberalism** and is now often viewed as a violation of liberty, **autonomy**, and individual **rights**. It can be justified toward **moral patients**, who do not have a sufficient degree of rationality to choose and act.

"Paternalistic intervention must be justified by the evident failure or absence of reason and will." **Rawls,** *A Theory of Justice*

pathetic fallacy

AESTHETICS The term was introduced by John Ruskin in *Modern Painters,* vol. 3 (1856), referring to the alleged fallacy of projecting or ascribing human emotions, intentions, dispositions, and thoughts to inanimate things as if they were really capable of these qualities. For instance, one has committed this fallacy if one says that weather is friendly or that the sea is angry. In general, it means the human tendency to project our subjective feeling caused by an external thing onto the external thing itself.

"Pathetic fallacy . . . is the fallacy of treating a psychological relation as an independently existing property." **Sorensen,** *Thought Experiments*

pathos

ANCIENT GREEK PHILOSOPHY, PHILOSOPHY OF MIND [Greek, suffering, feeling or what happens to affect a person; plural, *pathe*; from *paschein,* to suffer, to undergo, to experience] For **Aristotle,** *paschein* and the contrasting *poiein* (to make, to do) are both categories. *Pathos* has a passive tone. In Greek, *pathos* is a changeable **quality**, but especially concerns extreme grief, misfortune, or distress. As the feeling of an individual, it is also contrasted with *éthos* (communal feeling).

> "By *pathe*, I mean appetite, anger, fear, confidence, envy, joy, love, hate, longing, jealousy, pity, in general whatever implies pleasure or pain." **Aristotle**, *Nicomachean Ethics*

patriarchy

POLITICAL PHILOSOPHY, PHILOSOPHY OF SOCIAL SCIENCE, ETHICS [from Greek *pater*, father + *arche*, rule] Originally, a social system centered around an extended family with a male as its leader (patriarch). For many **feminists**, patriarchy is the universally perpetuated male **power** over women and male aggression toward women. They claim that a patriarchal attitude or prejudice runs through all economic and social institutions. Societies are often patriarchal in the sense that the male half of the population uses various deeply embedded means to control the female half. A main concern of radical feminism is to uncover the roots of patriarchy and to reveal its various representative forms.

> "A name that was coined to denote the universal domination of women by men." **Nyre**, *Feminist Theory and the Philosophy of Man*

Pears, David (1921–)

English philosopher of language and mind, born in Bedfont, Professor of Philosophy at University of Oxford. Pears's subtle and stimulating works on Hume, Russell, and Wittgenstein contributed to the development of his own naturalistic empiricism. His accounts of action, personal identity, self-deception, weakness of will, solipsism, and rule-following have all been widely influential. His major works include *Questions in the Philosophy of Mind* (1975), *Motivated Irrationality* (1984), and *The False Prison: A Study of the Development of Wittgenstein's Philosophy*, 2 vols. (1987–8).

Peirce, Charles Sanders (1839–1914)

The founder of American pragmatism, born in Cambridge, Massachusetts. Peirce wrote extensively in many fields of philosophy and his thought altered and developed in the different stages of his life. He formulated pragmatism as a theory of meaning, claiming that the meaning of a proposition is the sum of practical consequences that might conceivably result from the truth of that proposition. In his later writings, he called his theory "pragmaticism," to distinguish it from the pragmatism of James and other philosophers. Peirce initiated many major developments in modern logic and philosophy of science through his theory of signs, his logic of relations, his theory of abduction, and his discovery of quantification. He rejected traditional metaphysics and, as a fallibilist, claimed that all theories and categories are answerable to further scientific investigation, although he saw truth determined by the ultimate convergence of such investigations. He developed his own metaphysics, assigning everything there is to the categories of Firstness, Secondness, and Thirdness, and held that the world contains real continuous phenomena. Peirce published no book in his lifetime, but his many papers were gathered in *The Collected Papers of Charles Sanders Peirce* (eight volumes).

Peirce's thesis

PHILOSOPHY OF LANGUAGE The claim that the **meaning** of a **sentence** is determined by the **evidence** for its **truth**. In other words, the conditions of semantic evaluation **supervene** upon confirmation relations or confirmation relations are semantic relations. This is a form of **verificationism** that equates meaning with evidence. According to this theory, if two **theories** have different **entailments**, they differ with respect to what observation statements are true.

> "Peirce's thesis just is the claim that confirmation relations constitute semantic relations and are therefore not contingent." **Fodor and Lepore**, *Holism*

per accidens

METAPHYSICS [Latin, by accident] A **scholastic** term for the **accidents** possessed by a **substance** or for the non-essential **properties** which a thing has but which it may lose without changing its **nature**. A *per accidens* **predication** is a predication in which an accident is predicated of a substance. A *per accidens* thing is either an accident or a composite of a substance and an accident. *Per accidens* contrasts with *per se* (Latin, by itself), which is a substance itself or is the **essential property** that a thing possesses and cannot lose without changing its nature. In scholastic philosophy, **God** alone is a being *per se* in the absolute sense, for anything else will have to depend on God for existence. Sometimes, *per se* means what is directly intended in an action, while *per accidens* is a result that is not directly intended.

> "All that exists of another (*quod est per accidens*) comes back to what exists of itself (*quod est per se*)." **Aquinas, *Summa Theologiae***

per se, see *per accidens*

percepta

EPISTEMOLOGY The term for the **properties** that an **observer** actually perceives or observes. Percepta contrast with **percipienda**, the properties that we think that an **object** should appear to have, according to our **knowledge** of its **nature** and its position. When I look at a round tower from a distance, it is round according to percipienda, but might be square according to percepta. There are various forms of discrepancy between the percepta and percipienda of a given object. One may change while the other does not change. This distinction is useful in discussing the nature of perceptual **consciousness**.

> "I shall use the term 'percepta' or 'actually perceived properties' to refer to how the object actually appears to an observer." **Hirst, *The Problem of Perception***

perception

EPISTEMOLOGY The **faculty** of being aware of the world, the contents of sensory **experience** and what is perceived. Perception involves both our capacity to be sensorily affected by external objects and our ability to bring these objects under **concepts**, although other capacities might also have a role to play. The analysis of perception and the attempt to deal with skeptical arguments about perceptual knowledge are central philosophical topics, in particular in epistemology. A major problem is whether we directly perceive **sense-data** or the external physical world. This is related to problems about the nature of the external world and our knowledge of it. Perception is the area where **skepticism**

functions actively and where the distinction between **phenomenalism** and **realism** is sharply drawn. There are various positions about how to understand perception, such as the **causal theory of perception**, the **representative theory of perception**, and various forms of perceptual realism. There are also competing accounts of the relations between perception and **belief** and between perceptual knowledge and inferential knowledge.

> "'Perception' is a generic term which may be defined disjunctively as either seeing or hearing or touching or ... etc. Perception, in short, is awareness of the external world through the senses." **Pap, *Elements of Analytic Philosophy***

percepts

EPISTEMOLOGY Sometimes identified with **sense-data**. Whereas sense-data directly represent **particulars** and concrete items, percepts are closer to subjective states in an act of perception. Percepts are contrasted with **concepts**, which are the **abstractions** in thinking.

> "The immediate object of all knowledge and all thought is, in the last analysis, the percept." ***Collected Papers of Charles Sanders Peirce*, vol. 4**

perceptual consciousness

EPISTEMOLOGY The **consciousness** that is presented in the same way in normal **perception**, **illusion**, and **hallucination**. The term is introduced by H. H. **Price** in order to deal with the relation in perception between **sense-data** and **material objects** and to uncover the nature of perceiving. However, the nature of perceptual consciousness itself is disputed. Some philosophers believe that it consists in seeing a datum and **judging** or **inferring** that the datum belongs to a material object. For others, including Price, perceptual consciousness senses a datum and takes it for granted that it belongs to a material object. The dispute between "judging" and "taking for granted" in an account of perceiving is characteristic of many philosophical arguments in which slight verbal differences signal important theoretical conflicts.

> "We must find some name for the non-sensuous mode of consciousness of which we have spoken. For the present we shall simply call it 'perceptual consciousness'." **Price, *Perception***

perceptual knowledge

EPISTEMOLOGY Knowledge about the world around us acquired through the activation of our sense organs, especially our eyes. We know that we can cross the street when we see that the traffic light is green. Perceptual knowledge is concerned with perceptual **facts**, and so must be distinguished from the perception of simple **objects**. It is not **sensation**, pure **perception**, or mere **acquaintance**. Perceptual knowledge is associated with previously acquired **ideas**. A **proposition** of the form "S knows that P" reports perceptual knowledge if P is a perceptual proposition. It is controversial whether sense perception itself can lead to justified **beliefs**. While **direct realism** insists that **experience** itself can provide the **justification** required for this kind of knowledge, many other philosophers believe that such knowledge must involve some background knowledge or assumptions about connecting regularities that might be gained by inductive inference from past observations.

"Perceptual knowledge is knowledge that one sees or hears or smells or tastes or feels some specific sort of non-mental thing(s) or state(s) of affairs or event(s)." **Ginet, *Knowledge, Perception and Memory***

percipienda, see percepta

perennial philosophy, English expression for *philosophia perennis*

perfect duty, see imperfect duty

perfection, the principle of, another expression for the principle of the best

perfectionism

ETHICS, POLITICAL PHILOSOPHY The ethical position which claims that the **good** of human **actions** consists in their promotion of the maximal realization of human **excellence**, measured by the ideal standards of perfection in fields such as art, science, and culture. This theory presupposes that there are certain kinds of **activities** or **experiences** that possess the highest **values** and the deepest significance and encourages people to pursue these activities and experiences. It supposes that some human beings are intrinsically inferior to other human beings and that some forms of human life are intrinsically inferior to other forms of human life. Hence it endorses an **aristocratic** view of human society and is opposed to **egalitarianism**. It argues that a society should be so arranged as to maximize the achievement of human excellence. John **Rawls** employed this term to refer to the position held by **Aristotle** and **Nietzsche**. Rawls argues that since the notion of intrinsic value is controversial, perfectionism should be bypassed as a political **principle**.

"Teleological doctrines differ, pretty clearly, according to how the conception of the good is specified. If it is taken as the realisation of human excellence in the various forms of culture, we have what may be called perfectionism." **Rawls, *A Theory of Justice***

performance and competence, see competence and performance

performative

PHILOSOPHY OF LANGUAGE **Austin**'s term for utterances that are contrasted with ordinary **statements**, or **constatives**. The distinction mainly consists in two aspects. First, while a constative merely states an independently existing **fact**, a performative utterance, such as "I name this ship the Queen Elizabeth," or "I bet you sixpence it will rain tomorrow," does not describe anything, but constitutes an **action**. Such **sentences** actually do something in the appropriate circumstances, for example, naming or betting. Secondly, while the **truth** or falsity of a constative is determined by the distinct fact or **state of affairs** it describes, a performative is open to assessment according to whether it is a happy or unhappy act, not in terms of truth and falsity. Austin made a great effort to establish a clear-cut distinction between constatives and performatives, believing that many philosophical problems have arisen because people do not understand the nature of performatives. But Austin was unable to find a satisfactory **criterion** for performatives, and he gave up this distinction in favor of his theory of **speech acts**, involving **locutionary**, **illocutionary**, and **perlocutionary acts**, in *How to Do Things With Words*.

"The name [performative] is derived, of course, from 'perform', the usual verb with the noun 'action': it indicates that the issuing of the utterances is the performing of an action – it is not normally thought of as just saying something." **Austin, How to Do Things with Words**

performative theory of truth

LOGIC, PHILOSOPHY OF LANGUAGE A form of **deflationary theory of truth**, ascribed to Peter **Strawson**. It claims that the truth predicate is used not to describe things, but to perform certain **speech acts** such as agreeing, conceding, or endorsing. By saying, "That is true," we agree or endorse another speaker's utterance. The primary characteristic of **truth** is to perform this endorsing or confirmatory speech function. The theory is also called "the amen theory of truth."

"A less familiar case is Strawson's performative account of truth. This turns on . . . the fact that by saying 'That is true' we can endorse an utterance made by another speaker." **Price, Facts and the Functions of Truth**

Peripatetics

ANCIENT GREEK PHILOSOPHY A term applied to **Aristotle** and his pupils. According to tradition, the term was derived from *peripatein* (to walk about) because Aristotle and his pupils were said to spend long periods every day walking up and down discussing advanced philosophical questions in the garden of the Lyceum, the school Aristotle founded in 335 BC. But according to another account, the term was derived from *peripatos* (covered walking hall), which was a part of the Lyceum. The Peripatetics whose names are known include Theophrastus of Eresus, Strato of Lampsacus, and Eudemus of Rhodes. If the chief characteristic of **Plato's Academy** was its mathematical achievement, the Peripatetics contributed greatly to various natural sciences, in particular to botany, biology, and medicine. In the **Hellenistic** period, the Peripatetics, Academics, Stoics, and **Epicureans** were the four major schools in Athens.

"The Peripatetic school, as an institution comparable to the Academy, was probably not founded until after [Aristotle's] death. But with some distinguished students and associates he collected a natural history museum and library of maps and manuscripts . . . and organised a program of research which inter alia laid the foundation for

all histories of Greek natural philosophy, mathematics and astronomy, and medicine." **G. Owen, Logic, Science and Dialectic**

perlocutionary act

PHILOSOPHY OF LANGUAGE **Austin**'s term for his third kind of **speech act**. While **locutionary acts** are concerned with **meaning**, and **illocutionary acts** are concerned with the way an utterance is taken, perlocutionary acts are linguistic acts which, by saying something with design or **intention**, bring about specific effects on the feelings, thoughts, or behavior of the hearers, for example, persuading or convincing someone to do something. It is essentially a consequential act.

"Saying something will often, or even normally, produce certain consequential effects upon the feelings, thoughts or actions of the audience, or of the speaker, or of other persons . . . We shall call the performance of an act of this kind the performance of a perlocutionary act or perlocution." **Austin, How to Do Things with Words**

Perry, Ralph Barton (1876–1957)

American philosopher, born in Poultney, Vermont. As a founding member of American New Realism, Perry maintained that the independent and real world is directly present to the mind and that nothing stands between the knower and the independent world. He formulated the "Ego-centric Predicament." He defined value as that which makes something an object of interest and characterized interest in terms of expectancy. He held that moral value lies in the harmony of interests. Perry's principal works include *General Theory of Value* (1926) and *Realms of Value* (1954).

perseity, see aseity

person

METAPHYSICS, PHILOSOPHY OF MIND, ETHICS, PHILOSOPHY OF LAW [from Latin *persona*, mask or actor, a man's role or dignity in relation to other men] In theological usage, *persona* is the equivalent of the Greek *hypostasis* (standing under) and is closely related to the notion of *ousia* (**substance**). For **Boethius**, a person is an individual substance of a rational nature.

Locke, in his discussion of **personal identity**, argued that **consciousness** provides the criterion of being the same person over time, although being a person presupposes having a body. Locke in turn identified consciousness with **memory**. He also held that person is a forensic notion that is related to **responsibility** and to reward and **punishment**. Hence, in a legal sense, there can be artificial persons, like companies, as well as natural persons, so long as persons have legal responsibility and status. For **Descartes** and later dualists, a person is a combination of a **mind** and a **body** that are essentially distinct. In contrast, **Strawson** held that "person" is a logically primitive technical term. A person owns both states of consciousness and bodily characteristics, but cannot be reduced either to something mental or to something physical. The concept of a person is presupposed by both physical states and state of consciousness. Strawson's arguments have led to much discussion and have helped to place the nature of a person as a central topic in contemporary metaphysics.

Metaphysics usually discusses persons rather than human beings, partly to leave conceptual room for non-human persons and partly to avoid giving too much emphasis to biological classification in forming the concept of a person. Some forms of species-based **naturalism** would challenge both of these motives. The notion of a person implies that the central phenomena of personhood, such as thinking, experiencing, acting, and having moral worth, are related to one another, although many philosophers would defend the status of severely brain-damaged human beings as persons.

> "What I mean by the concept of a person is the concept of a type of entity such that both predicates ascribing states of consciousness and predicates ascribing corporeal characteristics, a physical situation, &c. are equally applicable to a single individual of that single type." **Strawson, Individuals**

person-affecting restriction

ETHICS A position that claims that the evaluation of moral **choices** should appeal to the outcome produced by the choices for the **persons** affected. If choice A brings a worse outcome than choice B to at least some specific individuals and if choice B does not bring a worse outcome than choice A to

any specific individuals, then choice A is worse than choice B. According to Derek **Parfit**, such a restriction can be applied universally in moral areas. Many choices, particularly those involving the interests of **future generations**, cannot be judged by their effects on future individuals because we have no way of telling what individuals there will be.

> "The Person-affecting Restriction: This part of morality, the part concerned with human well-being, should be explained entirely in terms of what would be good or bad for those people whom our acts affect." **Parfit, Reasons and Persons**

personal identity

METAPHYSICS, PHILOSOPHY OF MIND, ETHICS In a popular sense, personal identity is determined by the fundamental values, loyalties, associations, and aims of a person's life. In contrast, the philosophical investigation of personal identity seeks to explain the criteria by which an individual is identified as the same person at different times, in spite of having changed characteristics. The problem of personal identity (also called the problem of the self or the problem of self-identity or the problem of self-knowledge) arises from the difficulties in accounting for how the ascription of personal identity is justified. Since the discussion of personal identity concentrates on the necessary and sufficient conditions under which we recognize or re-identify a person, the problem is also called the problem of the criteria of personal identity, although criterial relations can be looser than those set out by necessary and sufficient conditions.

Locke and **Hume** provided two classic discussions of personal identity. Locke claimed that the criterion of personal identity is **consciousness**, in particular **memory**. His position has been attacked as not providing sufficient conditions for personal identity by those who argue that personal identity is impossible without bodily continuity. Moreover, Locke's view seems circular if we distinguish between genuine memory and apparent memory. The memory test of personal identity seems to fail because genuine memory presupposes identity rather than providing an independent test for identity.

According to Hume, we perceive nothing but **impressions** and **ideas** and do not have an impression or idea of a unique and simple self.

He therefore maintains that the notion of personal identity is a fiction. What we really have is a bundle or collection of particular **perceptions**, which we ascribe without **justification** (and perhaps without need of justification) to a continuing self.

Contemporary discussion is characterized by sophisticated testing of the arguments for the bodily criterion and the memory criterion of personal identity. Discussion has been shaped by considerations of the logic of **identity**, which is an all-or-nothing relationship and a relationship that blocks two distinct **entities** at the same time from being identical with one another. In particular, **thought experiments** about split brains indicate that an apparent advantage for the bodily criterion is illusory. The English philosopher Derek **Parfit** argues that attempts to cope with the problem of personal identity fail, but that what is really important to us is continuity and connectedness in our lives and our **survival** as a person. He claims that these matters can be understood while avoiding the rigidities of personal identity. Other philosophers hold that the discussion of personal identity should be closer to science than to the science fiction of the examples introduced in many recent discussions. **Quine** has argued that the problem of personal identity adds nothing important to the more general problem of identity.

Personal identity is intensively discussed in contemporary philosophy for its own sake, but also because it is related to other major issues, such as **dualism**, survival and **immortality**, self-knowledge, **responsibility**, **morality**, and the self.

> "Philosophers are continuing the long-standing debate as to whether personal identity should be analysed in terms of the identity of the relevant bodies or in terms of some sort of continuity of memory and character." **Brody,** *Identity and Essence*

personalism

METAPHYSICS, PHILOSOPHY OF RELIGION, LOGIC Also called personism, a philosophical movement that flourished in the early part of the twentieth century in the United States, with G. H. Howison, B. P. Bowne, and E. S. Brightman as its leading proponents. According to its central doctrines, persons are ontologically ultimate and personality has the highest **value**. **Experience**, which discovers **meaning**, belongs to some self. All hypothetical and inferred **entities** must be reduced to the experience of a self, with their **truth** tested by their coherence with the total **data** of experience. **Reality** as a whole is an expression of a universal personal **consciousness**, and characteristics possessed by persons and their personality are the fundamental elements in the explanation of reality. For personalists, **God** is the external person who constitutes the most coherent value of all interactions.

Personalism, which has developed over the last two centuries, can be traced back to the theological use of the notion of person. The Greeks associated person and *hypostasis* (standing under) with the notion of *ousia* (substance). As a consequence, personalism has been integrally connected with **theism**, holding that God is the transcendent person and the creator of all other persons. Personalism has had realistic, absolutist, idealistic, pantheistic, and other forms, many of which can be viewed as varieties of **idealism**. The exploration of human existence in **existentialism** and **phenomenology** has been influenced by personalism.

In a related use, personalism concerns ideas developed by the French philosophers and theologians E. Mounier, J. **Maritain**, and E. **Gilson**, who claimed that God is an infinite person in contrast to finite persons like ourselves and that the **autonomy** and value of the person is of supreme importance.

The term personalism also designates the philosophy of **probability**, initiated by **Ramsey** and **de Finetti** and developed by L. J. Savage, according to which probability is a personal expression of a degree of confidence in the **truth** of a **proposition** and not something objective to be discovered.

> "Personalism or personism is the philosophical theory that a person is (or many persons are) the supreme reality, i.e. highest in value and dominant in power." **Werkmeister,** *A History of Philosophical Ideas in America*

personality

PHILOSOPHY OF MIND, PHILOSOPHY OF SOCIAL SCIENCE, ETHICS, POLITICAL PHILOSOPHY The general character of being a **person** or the distinctive features of **mind** and character of an individual person. As a biological concept, personality is related to species membership. Philosophers of mind and philosophers of psychology are interested in personality as a psychological concept dealing with psychological functions, abilities, and capacities. Moral philosophers are interested in ethical personality. Political and social philosophers are concerned with persons in relation to political or social entities. The conception of personality thus has different levels.

> "Personality is the totality of human potentialities, activities, and habits organized by the person in the active pursuit of his self ideal." **Arnold, in Mischel (ed.), _Human Action_**

perspective

MODERN EUROPEAN PHILOSOPHY, METAPHYSICS, EPISTEMOLOGY **Nietzsche** held that all knowing is perspectival and involves **interpretations** from one or another point of view. There is no neutral universal point of view from which we can obtain **objective** knowledge. Nevertheless, one point of view can be preferred to another according to its value for life rather than through objective correspondence with facts.

For **Russell**, a perspective is all the momentary sets of data, both perceived and unperceived, which present the universe from a certain point of view. In doing so he uses the subjective data of psychologists in their classification of particulars that correspond to the "things" used by physicists to classify objects. An actually perceived perspective is called by Russell a "private world," that is, the view of the world that a percipient has at any given moment. The totality of perspectives in an individual's life is that person's "biography."

> "The assemblage of all my present objects of sense, which is what I call a 'perspective'." **Russell, _Mysticism and Logic_**

persuasive definition

PHILOSOPHY OF LANGUAGE A term introduced by **Stevenson**. In defining terms that have both **descriptive meaning** (referring to qualities in things), and strongly **emotive meaning** (expressing or arousing affective or emotional states), we alter the descriptive meaning but keep the emotive meaning unchanged in the term's application. The purpose of persuasive definition is, consciously or unconsciously, to secure a change in people's attitudes and interests. The speaker introduces a new **sense** that the hearer accepts without being aware that

he is being influenced. For example, when Hitler claimed that "national socialism is true democracy," he was employing a persuasive definition.

> "A persuasive definition, tacitly employed, is at work in redirecting attitudes." **Stevenson, _Ethics and Language_**

pessimism

PHILOSOPHY OF RELIGION, ETHICS, PHILOSOPHY OF HISTORY [from Latin _pessimus_, the worst] A term originally used for **Schopenhauer**'s world view in _The World as Will and Representation_ (1844). He believed that this world is the worst of all **possible worlds** because it is determined by blind and irrational **will**. Hence hope is unreasonable, and life is nothing, empty, meaningless, and painful. The term also applies to philosophies that emphasize **nihilism, nothingness, anxiety, absurdity,** and **death**, for example those of **Nietzsche, Heidegger,** and **Sartre**. In common use, pessimism is a negative and despondent attitude that focuses on the least hopeful side of situations. In contrast, **optimism** is a hopeful attitude that sees the world as meaningful. In a form proposed by **Leibniz**, optimism claims that this world is the best of all possible worlds.

> "There are unhappy men who think the salvation of the world impossible. Theirs is the doctrine known as pessimism." **W. James, _Pragmatism_**

Peter of Spain (_c._1215–77)

Spanish scholastic philosopher and theologian, born in Lisbon, made a cardinal in 1273 and elected pope (John XXI) in 1273. Peter's _Summulae Logicales_ provided an admirable presentation of the essentials of Aristotelian logic and was a fundamental logic text until the seventeenth century. His distinction between signification and supposition corresponds to the distinction between connotation and denotation. In _Scientia Libri de Anima_, he developed a Platonist theory of soul.

petitio principii, Latin term for begging the question

Petrarch, Francesco (1304–74)

Italian humanist and poet, born at Arezzo. Petrarch was the major representative of Renaissance Humanism. He attacked Scholastic learning and claimed that man and the problems of man should be the central concern of philosophy. His enthusiasm for Plato led to later humanist translations of Plato and the development of the Florentine Academy. Petrarch's important treatises include *On the Remedies of Good and Bad Fortune* (1366) and *On His Own Ignorance and Many Others* (1367).

phantom limb

EPISTEMOLOGY, PHILOSOPHY OF MIND A phenomenon which was first described and investigated by **Descartes**. If one's arm is amputated, one may afterwards feel that it is still there and feel **pain** in the non-existent fingers, wrist, and forearm. This is because the nerves that previously connected the arm to the brain, and that remain in the untouched part of the limb, continue to send impulses like those normally caused by external stimulations. This phenomenon has importance for the philosophy of perception. First, it seems to indicate that **sensations** occur only in the brain and that the **mind** is not immediately affected by all parts of body, but only by the brain. Secondly, the **mental states** of phantom limb patients can be explained by **psycho-physical laws**. The pain this patient feels is akin to an **hallucination**. This last point suggests problems for the **representative theory of perception** because there is a **representation** without a thing being represented.

> "The brain – or some part of it – inadvertently played a mechanical trick on the mind. That was Descartes' explanation of phantom-limb hallucinations." **Dennett,** *Consciousness Explained*

phenomenal property, see qualia

phenomenalism

EPISTEMOLOGY Acceptance of the **sense-datum theory**, according to which what we are directly aware of in **perception** is not the **material object** itself but rather sensa, renders problematic the nature and status of material objects as the **cause** of perception. Phenomenalism is one attempt to elucidate the nature of material objects by reducing them to sense-data. It is derived from **Berkeley's immaterialism**, which holds only phenomena or **sense impressions** can be known. There is no underlying **substratum** behind **appearance**. Reality is the totality of all actual and possible conscious **experience**, and can not be said to exist independent of these experiences. Berkeley, unlike later phenomenalists, holds that material objects are combinations of actual sense-impressions. As a consequence, he has to introduce **God** to preserve the continuity of objects and the existence of unobserved objects. **Hume**'s claim that what we know to exist is nothing more than sensa occurring in various patterns or sequences raises the problem of what fills the gaps between actual sensa. J. S. **Mill**'s position, which is called factual phenomenalism, is that material objects are permanent possibilities of sensation. Hence a material thing consists of a family of actual and possible sense-data. However, it sounds odd to say that possible sense-data are constituents of material things. Another way of filling the gap between actual sensa, called sensibilism, was developed by **Russell** (although he later abandoned it) and **Price**. On this view, **sensibilia** are unsensed sense-data, while sense-data amount to sensed sensibilia. Hence a material thing is described as a family of items with a similar status, except that sense-data are sensed and sensibilia are unsensed. The dominant version of phenomenalism to appear in the twentieth century was developed by the **logical positivists** and **operationalists** and is called linguistic phenomenalism or analytical phenomenalism. This theory attempts to explain the notion of material objects by reducing or translating all **statements** about material objects into statements about perceptual experience or sensa. The main difficulty with linguistic phenomenalism is that the equivalence between statements about sensa and statements about physical objects is hard to find. Phenomenalism is generally considered to be unsuccessful, for to specify the meaning of sensa and to distinguish one sense-datum from another always seems to involve reference to material things. Phenomenalism gives priority to experience and constructs the world out of it, but experience itself needs to be constructed out of the actual way of the world. Even **Ayer**, a chief proponent of linguistic phenomenalism, disavowed it in his later works.

> "The phenomenalist is bound to hold that the identity of any physical body is subject to analysis in terms of sense-data." **Ayer,** *The Problem of Knowledge*

phenomenological epoche, see phenomenological reduction

phenomenological reduction

MODERN EUROPEAN PHILOSOPHY, EPISTEMOLOGY, PHILOSOPHY OF MIND The characteristic methodological procedure of **Husserl's phenomenology**. Phenomenological reduction is a means of detecting the **intentional** or essential structure of **experience**. By turning away from the sense-contents of my own stream of experiences, I can concentrate on what is essential, basic, and irreducible in experience. The reduction moves from the empirical to the **transcendental** level and provides access to the intentional structure or *noematic* content of experience, which is the source of our **knowledge** of the world. The reduction contrasts to the reduction of all knowledge into certain **basic** or protocol sensory experiences or **statements** in **phenomenalism** or logical **positivism**.

The basic instrument of phenomenological reduction is phenomenological *epoche* (Greek, holding back, hence suspension of judgment). In our cognitive relationship with the world, our natural attitude assumes the existence of the external spatio-temporal world and assumes the existence of ourselves as psycho-physical individuals. Husserl's phenomenological *epoche* "**brackets**" this natural attitude or puts it out of play. This bracketing does not deny the existence of the fact-world, but refrains from any **judgment** regarding the world and our own physical being within it. For Husserl, we can thus regard our experience in a different manner and enter the region of transcendentally purified experiences. We can consider **consciousness** strictly as intentional agency, also called "transcendental consciousness," "pure consciousness," or "absolute consciousness." We are in a position to have *eidetic* or essential **intuition** toward the intentional structures of experience.

Phenomenological *epoche* is also called transcendental reduction. This is what phenomenological reduction normally means, but sometimes Husserl broadens its reference to include *eidetic* intuition as well. The whole program is influenced by the Cartesian **method** of doubt and is intended to provide absolutely certain grounds for knowledge.

"On grounds of method this operation will split up into different steps of 'disconnexion' or 'bracketing', and thus our method will assume the character of a graded reduction. For this reason we propose to speak, and even preponderate, of phenomenological reductions (though, in respect of their unity as a whole, we would speak in unitary form of the phenomenological reduction)."
Husserl, *Ideas*

phenomenology

MODERN EUROPEAN PHILOSOPHY, PHILOSOPHICAL METHOD [from Greek *phainomenon*, to appear + *logos*, theory, literally, a theory of appearance] The idea of phenomenology can be traced to **Aristotle's** "saving the phainomena," but the word was first used by J. H. Lambert, a follower of Christian **Wolff**, in his *Neues Organon* (1764), meaning the study of the forms of **appearances** and **illusions**. **Kant** took over this word, claiming that phenomenology determined the principles of **sensibility** and **understanding** that can be applied only to the world of **appearance** and not to **things-in-themselves**. **Hegel's** *Phenomenology of the Spirit* brought this word into prominence. However, for Hegel, phenomena are not illusions or appearances. They are stages in the development of **knowledge**, in the manifestations of which **Spirit** itself appears, and are the expressions of a self-developing **absolute idea**. Phenomenology is therefore the study of the evolutionary process of **consciousness** from its simplest to its most sophisticated forms. The American pragmatist C. S. **Peirce** developed in his early work a kind of phenomenology, also called "phaneroscopy," as a system of **categories** to classify the main types of phenomena that make up the world.

Phenomenology in its most popular sense refers to an influential philosophical movement, founded by Edmund **Husserl** and developed in Germany by Max **Scheler**, Nicolai **Hartmann**, and Martin **Heidegger** and in France by Gabriel **Marcel**, Jean-Paul **Sartre**, and Maurice **Merleau-Ponty**. It has gradually fused with **existentialism** and **hermeneutics**. In this sense, phenomenology is a philosophy of consciousness concerned with the truth or rationale of immediate **experience**. Originally, Husserl conceived phenomenology as a philosophical method to reveal and elucidate the internal structures and essential features of various types of experience. Through **analysis** of this sort, one could discover the ultimate sources of our knowledge, especially the fundamental logical and epistemological categories. In his later stage, Husserl considered phenomenology to be **first philosophy**, which could describe the region of pure experience in which all sciences are rooted and provide a unified theory of **science** and knowledge. Husserl's phenomenology was deeply influenced by **Descartes**'s demand that knowledge be **clear and distinct** and opposed relying on any *a priori* assumption that has to be justified elsewhere. Phenomenology in this sense differs from studies that seek to explain things, for example, from their causal relations or **evolutionary** origins. Its slogan is "to the things (phenomena) themselves." Husserl emphasized the function of **intuition** in achieving insights into the essential structures of experience. Phenomenology characteristically emphasizes the **intentionality** of consciousness. Its philosophical novelty is the demonstration that intentional objects of every sort, existing and non-existing, can and should be described in their own right. Phenomenology can be contrasted with **analytical philosophy**, which is concerned with the analysis of **propositions**, although J. L. **Austin** sometimes called his work linguistic phenomenology.

Heidegger analyzed the two components of the word "phenomenology." On his analysis, *phenomenon* means that which shows itself in itself and *logos* is derived from *legomenon*, that which is exhibited. He concludes that phenomenology means "to let that which shows itself in itself be seen from itself." Accordingly, phenomenology is merely a method, which prescribes how a study should be conducted rather than what should be studied. The method indicates that any subject-matter must be treated by exhibiting it directly and demonstrating it directly. Heidegger called his own approach to *Dasein* and **Being** "hermeneutic phenomenology." Here "hermeneutic" does not refer to a method for uncovering the **meaning** embodied in an expression, but to the constitution of *Dasein*. The whole expression refers to a method by which Being can be approached or brought to self-showing.

"Phenomenology is accordingly the theory of experience in general, inclusive of all matters, whether real or intentional, given in experiences, and evidently discoverable in them." **Husserl**, *Logical Investigations*

phenomenon

EPISTEMOLOGY, ANCIENT GREEK PHILOSOPHY [from Greek *phainomenon*, what appears by itself, hence appearance] Perceptual **appearance** in general, that is, what may be observed and how things look. For **Aristotle**, all widely accepted **beliefs** about a certain matter, either those commonly held or held by the wise, are also phenomena. In this latter sense, phenomenon means the same as *legomenon* (what is said) and *endoxa* (common belief). Phenomena of this kind were taken by Aristotle to be the starting-point of **dialectical** argument. He claimed that a good theory should start from the phenomena and insofar as possible should be consistent with the phenomena and explain the phenomena. This is what he called **saving the phenomena**. A scientific **theory** should enable us to understand the empirical phenomena, and a philosophical theory should enable us to understand the phenomena in the sense of common beliefs.

"This view [that there is no weakness of will] plainly contradicts the phenomena." **Aristotle**, *Nicomachean Ethics*

philanthropy

ETHICS, POLITICAL PHILOSOPHY [from Greek *philos*, love + *anthropos*, man, loving one's fellow men] A synonym for **love, benevolence, altruism**, and **charity**. Philanthropy is regarded as a **virtue**, especially in Christian ethics. In modern times, the term is used for large-scale actions to help those who are poor and in need. Sometimes, governmental agencies offering social support, such as the social welfare or health systems, are regarded as socially philanthropic institutions. Some occupations in the areas of health, education, welfare, or social work are associated with a philanthropic vocation.

"If social work is to exist at all, there have to be either private philanthropists or a system of imposing philanthropy on the general public by means of taxes." **Downie and Telfer**, *Caring and Curing*

philia

ETHICS, ANCIENT GREEK PHILOSOPHY [Greek, friendship, derived from *philein*, love, but without sexual implications. Empedocles uses a slightly different term *philotes* (also love or friendship) which, in opposition to *neikos* (strife), is the unifying principle of elements.] *Philia* is an affectionate personal relationship, requiring some degree of mutual goodwill, mutual recognition, and shared activities. *Philia*, which is much broader than our current notion of **friendship**, includes the **love** of members of families for each other, the favorable attitudes of business partners and of fellow citizens for each other, and the mutual admiration between virtuous men for virtuous character. *Philia* is a major topic in Greek ethics, for it is taken as a kind of **virtue** and as a necessary condition for happiness. **Aristotle** chiefly distinguishes three types of friendship: for **pleasure**, for usefulness, and for **goodness**. While the first two kinds are incidental, the last kind is complete and perfect, especially between virtuous men. Each virtuous person wishes the **other** to be good for the good of the other party itself. The root of the perfect friendship is to take the friend as another self, with friendship being a kind of self-love of a good man. Aristotle's discussion of friendship seems to offer an approach for breaking the antithesis between **egoism** and **altruism** and therefore attracts much current attention. Friendship is also a major topic in **contextualist** and **feminist** approaches to moral philosophy.

> "The defining features of *philia* (friendship) that are found in friendship to one's neighbours would seem to be derived from features of friendship towards oneself." **Aristotle, *Nicomachean Ethics***

Philo of Alexandria (*c*.20 BC–*c*.50 AD)

Hellenistic Jewish philosopher, born in Alexandria. Philo used Greek philosophy, especially the works of Plato, to interpret scripture. He held that God created the world by will and governed it directly. God has the power to infringe upon the laws of nature that he implanted in the world with its creation. There is individual providence as well as universal providence. Between God and the lower world there is an intermediate being that he called "Logos." Although human knowledge of God is limited to God's existence and not God's essence, we can achieve contact with God through Logos. Philo's synthesis of Greek philosophy and Jewish thought exerted great influence upon Neoplatonism and on medieval Jewish and Latin Christian philosophy. Philo's major works include *Concerning the Artisan of the World, On the Contemplative Life,* and *On the Eternity of the World.*

philosophe

EPISTEMOLOGY, METAPHYSICS, PHILOSOPHY OF RELIGION, POLITICAL PHILOSOPHY [French, philosopher] The eighteenth-century French thinkers of the **Enlightenment**, such as **Voltaire, Rousseau, Diderot, Montesquieu, Helvétius, Condillac, d'Holbach,** and other Encyclopedists. These philosophers are generally **materialists, atheists,** and **liberals**. They believed in the strength of **reason** and scientific knowledge and intended to judge everything in accordance with the measure of reason.

> "The French philosophes of the eighteenth century were the examples we sought to imitate, and we hope to accomplish no less results." **Mill, *The Collected Works of John Stuart Mill*, vol. I**

philosopher-king, see guardians

philosophia perennis

METAPHYSICS, PHILOSOPHY OF RELIGION [Latin, perennial philosophy] A metaphysical thesis that there is a single Divine reality as an impersonal **Absolute** is common to all great Western and Eastern religions. The **soul** is the divine spark of light in our body, and by means of its contemplative practice we can have mystical access to this divine reality. The term and the basic idea can be traced to **Leibniz**, but the thesis was fully explicated by Aldous Huxley in *The Perennial Philosophy* (1946). According to Huxley, perennial philosophy unifies all religions, with the consequence that there is only one sort of **mysticism** or fundamental metaphysics. Opponents who argue against the thesis say it wrongly amalgamates different strands of mysticism.

> "Philosophia perennis – the phrase was coined by Leibniz, but the thing – the metaphysic that recognises a divine reality substantial to the world of things and lives and minds; the psychology that finds in the soul something similar to, or even identical with, divine reality; the ethic that places

man's final end in the knowledge of the imman-ent and transcendent ground of all being – the thing is immemorial and universal." **Huxley,** *The Perennial Philosophy*

philosophical anthropology

PHILOSOPHY OF SOCIAL SCIENCE, PHILOSOPHY OF MIND [from Greek *anthropos*, man] The comprehensive study of **human nature**, which considers each human being as a biological, psychological, cultural, social, and religious complex, in contrast to the simplicity of **God** and to the traditional **rational-ist** view of man as an exclusively rational being. All discussions about man as such belong to philo-sophical anthropology, and in this broad sense it is as old as philosophy itself. **Kant** considered anthropology to be a pragmatic branch of philo-sophy concerning "what man as a freely acting entity makes of himself or can and should make of himself." **Feuerbach** took anthropology as a synonym for philosophy. Based on the German philosophical tradition, Max **Scheler** introduced philosophical anthropology in *Man's Place in Nature* (1928) as a special discipline. This discipline was a synthesis of **Dilthey**'s life philosophy and **Husserl**'s phenomenology, but also embraced most of the social sciences. Scheler attempted to discover the basic structure of human nature and accordingly to explain human **existence**, **experiences**, **potentialit-ies**, and various other aspects of human activities. He also sought to establish philosophical anthropo-logy as the foundation of other social sciences in virtue of its central aim of achieving human self-understanding. Consistent with this aim, Scheler used philosophical anthropology to criticize his contemporary bourgeois society in terms of the theory of **alienation** of **Hegel** and **Marx**. Other major figures of philosophical anthropology include Plessner, Gehlen, **Cassirer**, and **Sartre**. As an inter-disciplinary study, philosophical anthropology has practitioners in many areas and has developed various approaches to the study of man.

"The theorists disagree, often very strongly, over the wants and desires that people have (their 'philo-sophical anthropology', as it is often termed), but neither side doubts that if only people's wants and beliefs could be identified their action would be intelligible." **Yearley,** *Science and Sociological Practice*

philosophical behaviorism, see behaviorism

philosophical logic

LOGIC **Russell**'s term for the study of philosophical problems arising from applying **formal logic** to nat-ural language. It does not contain formal logical sys-tems themselves, and it is not confined to arguments that formal logic has codified. In British philosophy, philosophical logic is considered to be a basic philo-sophical discipline, concerned with the **analysis** of key notions indispensable to rational thinking such as analyticity, **necessity**, **definition**, **description**, **entailment**, **existence**, **identity**, **reference**, **predica-tion**, **proposition**, quantification, **truth**, **meaning**, **negation**, and **existential statements**. Many of the problems in philosophical logic are intertwined with other branches of philosophy, especially with **epistemology** and **ontology**.

Some scholars suggest that philosophical logic can also be called "philosophy of logic." But others try to distinguish them on the grounds that philo-sophical logic is a philosophy interested in language, **thought**, and the world structure, while philosophy of logic is the study of the scope and nature of logic systems, especially philosophical issues arising from **deviant logic**.

"The contrast between philosophical logic and philosophy of logic can accordingly be put like this: when one does philosophy of logic, one is philosophising about logic; but when one does philosophical logic, one is philosophising." **Grayling,** *An Introduction to Philosophical Logic*

philosophical psychology, see philosophy of psychology

philosophical radicals

POLITICAL PHILOSOPHY, PHILOSOPHY OF SOCIAL SCIENCE A group of political and economic **liberals** deeply influenced by Jeremy **Bentham** and active in London in the first half of the nineteenth century, including the philosopher James **Mill** and later his son John Stuart **Mill**, legal philosopher John **Austin**, economist David Ricardo, lawyer E. Chadwick, and classical historian George Grote. They criticized the evils existing in the government and social policies of Britain at that time and believed that the source of all evils lay in the aristocratic principle adopted by the government, economic monopolies, and the established church. The group embraced Bentham's utilitarianism, Adam **Smith**'s economics, Austin's rational jurisprudence, and J. S. Mill's rationale for **democracy**. They tried to provide a justification for radically transforming the traditional aristocratic regime into a modern, secular, democratic market society. This group exerted great influence upon British philosophy and political life.

> "Those whom ... we call philosophic radicals are those who in politics observe the common practice of philosophers – that is, who, when they are discussing means, begin by considering the end, and when they desire to produce effects, think of cause." **Mill,** *The Collected Works of John Stuart Mill,* **vol. VI**

philosophical theology

PHILOSOPHY OF RELIGION A contemporary discipline largely derived from the methods and subject-matter of natural theology. It employs standard techniques of reasoning and makes use of every possible consideration to justify **theistic** belief and to examine the coherence and implications of various traditional theistic doctrines. It aims to clarify the content of the central concepts, presuppositions, and tenets of theological commitment. Its main questions include the concept of **God**, the nature of **divine attributes**, the source of our ideas of God, proofs of the existence of God, the nature of divine knowledge, the essence of divine **creation**, God's relation to **time**, and God's relation to human beings. It differs from the philosophy of religion in that it is not a neutral discussion about theism, but presupposes the existence of God. It is essentially a way of using philosophy to do theology rather than an independent philosophical enterprise.

> "Philosophical theology is a species contained within the theological genus. Insofar as its specific difference is that it makes use of philosophical methods and techniques to explicate the meaning or to discover the implications of theological doctrines, it continues to stand within [the] 'theological circle'." **Ferré,** *Basic Modern Philosophy of Religion*

philosophy (Kant)

PHILOSOPHICAL METHOD **Kant** held that philosophy is a mere idea of a possible **science** which nowhere

exists concretely, but which we can endeavor to approximate by many different routes. What we learn is not philosophy itself, but how to philosophize by exercising our talent to reason on certain actually existing philosophical attempts. Since human **reason** is always active, it is impossible to offer an ultimate and dogmatic answer to the question of what philosophy is and who possesses it. That would mean the end of philosophizing and hence the death of philosophy.

Accordingly, for Kant philosophy is an activity of reason rather than a static body of **knowledge**. He thought that the **scholastic** tradition took philosophy to be the logical perfection of knowledge, but another conception that forms the real basis of philosophy takes it as a science for relating all knowledge to the essential ends of human reason. The so-called philosopher is the lawgiver of human reason. Philosophical knowledge can arise either out of **pure reason** or empirical inquiry. Kant's own philosophy is systematic, attempting to answer all the questions of philosophy in a single scheme, and **critical**, determining the limits as well as the extent of our knowledge through an examination of reason by itself.

Kant divided the philosophy of pure reason into propaedeutic, which deals with the *a priori* knowledge of the faculty of reason, and **metaphysics**, as the system of pure reason. The latter is divided into the metaphysics of **nature**, which is concerned with what is, and the metaphysics of **morals**, which is concerned with what ought to be. They are respectively the **theoretical** and **practical** employment of pure reason.

> "The legislation of human reason (philosophy) has two objects, nature and freedom ... the philosophy of nature deals with all that is, the philosophy of morals that which ought to be." **Kant,** *Critique of Pure Reason*

philosophy (logical positivism)

PHILOSOPHICAL METHOD On the basis of a strong conviction that **science** serves as a **paradigm** for all knowledge, logical positivism requires philosophy to have scientific standards of precision and **objectivity**. There are only two kinds of **statements** that meet the strict standards of science, that is, *a priori* statements of **logic** and pure mathematics, and empirical statements. Thus, most of the statements in traditional **metaphysics** and **moral philosophy** cannot constitute **knowledge** and should be eliminated. The positive role of philosophy is concerned with the logical **analysis** of the rules and frameworks of scientific theory and language and is a department of logic. Philosophy must employ **scientific method** to provide **knowledge**, and **epistemology** is nothing more than the **philosophy of science**.

> "Once philosophy is purified of all scientific elements, only the logic of science remains."
> **Carnap**, *The Logical Syntax of Language*

philosophy (Ryle)

PHILOSOPHICAL METHOD To clarify the nature of philosophy was one of **Ryle**'s major concerns. Logical positivism had dethroned philosophy from its position of priority regarding the sciences, and Ryle tried to show what is left for philosophy to do. He held that philosophy does not have its own domain and is not concerned with the problem of **entities**. It is a meta-occupation and an activity with the role of laying bare the logical **categories** that underlie the surface **grammar** of our ordinary or scientific language. This is necessary because these logical structures are often hidden or distorted by surface grammar. Philosophy has the function of mapping and comparing the logical geography of **concepts** and clarifying the connections between concepts. In brief, the task of philosophy is not to discover **truth** about the world but to rearrange and analyze language in order to reveal its correct **logical form** or real **meaning**. It is not an empirical science, but is closely associated with the **logic** of diverse categories or forms. Ryle's work was a major example of the linguistic turn taken by English-speaking philosophy in the twentieth century.

> "Science talks about the world, while philosophy talks about talk about the world." **Ryle**, *Collected Papers*

philosophy (Wittgenstein)

PHILOSOPHICAL METHOD Philosophy does not present any picture of reality, and it can neither explain nor deduce anything. In trying to do so, philosophy becomes traditional **metaphysics**, which can give no **meaning** to its expressions. Proper philosophy should stop this misleading way of working. Philosophy is different from the natural sciences and shares no method with them. It can neither confirm nor refute scientific investigations. Since the whole of natural science is constituted by the totality of true **propositions**, philosophical propositions are not **truths**.

Philosophy is an activity rather than a **theory** and aims to cure us of the misuse of **ordinary language** by means of clarifying propositions. Most traditional philosophical questions are generated through the misuse of language, and hence we should not seek to answer them (the solutions for them do not exist). We should rather treat the questions as we treat illness. We should make the questions disappear by showing how they violate **logical syntax**. In the *Tractatus* Wittgenstein proposes that the way to clarify language is to reveal its hidden structure, but in *Philosophical Investigations* he turns to the study of **language-games** to clarify language.

> "All philosophy is a 'critique of language'."
> **Wittgenstein**, *Tractatus*

philosophy of art, see aesthetics

philosophy of biology

PHILOSOPHY OF SCIENCE A relatively independent area of the philosophy of science, dealing with philosophical issues arising from biological studies. Because of certain characteristics of biological inquiry, philosophy of biology is more than the mere application of general principles of scientific explanation. Biology explains a trait of an organism in terms of its **function** to promote the well-being, development, or **survival** of that organism, its genes, or its **species**. This functional explanation seems to explain a **cause** by its **effect** and hence to differ from a standard causal explanation, which explains an effect by its cause and it also differs from the **covering law model** of explanation. The nature of functional or teleological explanation and its rationality therefore become major topics in the field. Many philosophers argue that we should understand biological traits in terms of the past evolutionary history of the organism rather than in terms of their future consequences. On this view, functional explanation can be assimilated to a causal account. Other philosophers of biology argue for an autonomous level of functional explanation that can not be reduced to ordinary causality.

Darwin's theory of **evolution** led to the formulation of various philosophical problems concerning,

522 philosophy of education

for example, the logic of **natural selection** and the implications of the concepts of adaptation and fitness. In a sense, philosophy of biology is the discussion of the philosophical problems raised by the theory of evolution. The biological classification of species had been a **paradigm** of philosophical classification of reality. Darwin suggested that species themselves evolve. The features of a species are not eternal, and the distinctions between species are not fixed. This evolutionary perspective has seriously transformed our understanding of the structure of the world. From the theory of evolution, philosophers have developed **evolutionary epistemology**, which attempts to explain cognitive faculties, knowledge acquisition, and the progress of **knowledge** in terms of the process of natural selection. Philosophers have also proposed an **evolutionary ethics**, which claims that what we ought to do should be determined on an evolutionary basis according the principle of the **survival of the fittest**. Evolutionary ethics can also have a less controversial role in explaining the pattern of our ethical thinking in terms of our being members of a particular naturally evolved species. Some philosophers also attempt to explain social, cultural, and psychological phenomena in terms of biological structure in a reductionist approach called **sociobiology**.

"Evolutionary biology is the centre of gravity for both the science of biology and for the philosophy of the science. The philosophy of biology does not end with evolutionary issues, but that is where I think it begins." **Sober**, *Philosophy of Biology*

philosophy of education
PHILOSOPHY OF SOCIAL SCIENCE, ETHICS, POLITICAL PHILOSOPHY A branch of applied philosophy dealing with philosophical issues in education. Although philosophy of education can be traced to **Plato**'s *Republic*, it did not become a specific branch of philosophy until the beginning of the twentieth century. Interacting with **political philosophy**, the philosophy of education attempts to work out a conception of education that is suitable for contemporary **liberal** society. In contrast to both Plato and **Rousseau**, who believed that education aims at a **just** society with strongly shared values, contemporary liberal education theorists, such as John **Dewey**, Michael **Oakeshott**, Paul Hirst, and R. S. Peters,

hold that education is **individualistic**, existing simply for the sake of developing one's rational **mind**, exploring with our natural inquisitiveness, acquiring **knowledge** for the sake of knowledge, or cultivating personal **autonomy**. The philosophy of education is concerned with a series of problems arising from this picture of education, such as the relation between education and moral development, education and **censorship**, education and the role of art, the education of personal **emotion** and feeling, and the **equality** of education opportunity. It also provides a critical evaluation of educational theory. Different theories of **human nature** result in different theories of education. In the twentieth century, the development of psychology, such as **Freud**'s psychoanalysis and Piaget's theory of the stages of psychological development in the child, has deeply affected the discussion of education, although in Freud's case not always to its benefit. In radically incompatible ways, **Chomsky**'s linguistics and Skinner's **behaviorism** altered notions of learning. Philosophy of education is less developed than other branches of the philosophy of the social sciences.

"Philosophy of education focuses on the language of educational theory and practice." **T. Moore**, *Philosophy of Education*

philosophy of history
PHILOSOPHY OF HISTORY History is the actual human past, but it is also a branch of knowledge about the human past. Correspondingly, there are two major types of philosophy of history. **Speculative philosophy of history** is concerned with actual history and seeks to provide a philosophical history of the world. **Analytic** philosophy of history, in contrast, is concerned with historical thinking and **knowledge** and with other philosophical issues arising out of the practice of historians. The distinction between these two kinds of philosophy of history is widely characterized as also being a distinction between substantive and critical philosophy of history and between **material** and **formal** philosophy of history.

Speculative philosophy of history can be traced to its origin in **Augustine**'s *City of God*. It assumes that history is not a sequential aggregate of random past **events** and argues that an underlying factor or structure renders the whole historical process **rational** and **intelligible**. The claim that temporal succession itself has logical implications was first derived from a theology and teleological world-view that viewed human history as controlled by some divine force. In the **Enlightenment**, some philosophers, such as the eighteenth-century French **Encyclopedists**, were inspired by the development of physics to explore the uniformity of history on the basis of the assumption of the uniformity of **human nature**. Others, such as Giambattista **Vico** and J. G. **Herder**, endorsed a more empirical approach in connecting the **meaning** of history with its cultural milieu. **Hegel** claimed that history has a plot and that the development of history is a **dialectical** movement governed by the **absolute spirit**. **Marx** substituted an economic foundation for Hegel's absolute spirit as the engine for historical development. In the twentieth century, authors such as Arnold Toynbee and Oswald Spengler continued to believe in the overall meaning of human history, but substantive philosophy of history is, in general, out of favor.

Analytic philosophy of history emerged in the twentieth century. Rather than dealing with the underlying structure of actual history, its subject-matter is the underlying structure of **historical explanation** and the nature of historical understanding. It is concerned with the conceptual framework of historical thinking and the nature of historical **objectivity**. Analytic philosophy of history has two general tendencies. The first, represented by **Hempel**, attempts to assimilate historical explanation to scientific explanation and to offer a model of universal **laws** for historical knowledge. The second, influenced by the works of Rickert, **Dilthey**, **Croce**, **Collingwood**, Walsh, and **Dray**, is the mainstream of analytic philosophy of history. It distinguishes historical study from the natural sciences and argues for the autonomy of history. It does not take a historical **event** as an instance of a covering law, but attempts to **understand** the **reasons** behind each **action**. In the work of **Lyotard**, **Foucault**, and others, it is concerned with the **epistemological** status of **narrative**, which is the characteristic form of presenting historical knowledge.

"Unlike their speculative predecessors, most present-day contributors to the philosophy of history take it to be a second order form of inquiry with the aim, not of trying to seek and assess the human past itself, but rather of seeking to elucidate and assess the ways in which historians typically describe or comprehend that past." **Gardiner (ed.), The Philosophy of History**

philosophy of language

PHILOSOPHY OF LANGUAGE Contemporary philosophy of language resulted from the linguistic turn in philosophy and is based on the assumption that all philosophical **analysis** can be reduced to the analysis of language. In a broad sense, philosophy of language is nearly synonymous with analytic philosophy. Hence, **logical positivism**, **ordinary language philosophy**, and the early and later **Wittgenstein** all exemplified different philosophical approaches to language in dealing with philosophical problems.

In a narrow sense, philosophy of language is related to linguistics or the science of language and is concerned with the underlying reality of language and its philosophical import. Traditionally **semiotics** is divided into **syntax**, **semantics**, and **pragmatics**. The philosophy of language deals with the problem of the distinction between syntax and semantics, and some pragmatic problems, for example in the theory of **speech acts** and Grice's theory of **conversational implicature**. There are different conceptions of what the philosophy of language should be, but its central concern is with semantic questions, such as **meaning**, **truth**, **reference**, **predication**, quantification, and the nature of **propositions**. Other major issues in this field of philosophy are the universal features of language and the relationships between language and world and between language and **thought**. Because of the inseparable relations between **logic** and language and among **intentionality**, **understanding**, **thinking**, and language, the philosophy of language shares many common topics with **philosophical logic** and the **philosophy of mind**. It is sometimes regarded as a part of the philosophy of mind and sometimes even as a part of the philosophy of **action**. An influential type of philosophy of language developed out of **Chomsky**'s **generative grammar**, which tries to uncover the structure of conceptual knowledge by revealing the linguistic structure underlying surface irregularities and variations.

"Though the philosophy of language might reasonably be thought of as comprising anything that philosophers do when they think, qua philosophers, about language . . . I have presented the philosophy of language in one of its guises, as an attempt to get clear about the basic concepts we use in thinking about language." **Alston,** *Philosophy of Language*

"The philosophy of law studies philosophical problems raised by the existence and practice of law." **Dworkin (ed.),** *The Philosophy of Law*

philosophy of logic, see philosophical logic

philosophy of law

PHILOSOPHY OF LAW Also called legal philosophy, a branch of philosophy that deals with philosophical problems or issues concerning the law and legal systems and that applies philosophical method to legal problems. The major topics of this field are: the nature and the **definition** of law, properties and identity conditions of legal systems, the ends to be attained by law, legal **responsibility**, legal **reasoning**, the nature and justification of **punishment**, the nature and justification of the **state**'s coercive **power**, and the relationships between moral **right** and legal right, between moral **obligation** and legal obligation, and between law and **justice**.

Philosophy of law is often used as a synonym for **jurisprudence** (from Latin *juris prudentia*, knowledge of or skill in law). Jurisprudence, however, has a wider reference. Some of its divisions, such as analytical jurisprudence (the logical analysis of law and of legal concepts) and normative or critical jurisprudence (the evaluation of law and legal obligations) fall into the domain of philosophy of law. Other divisions such as historical jurisprudence (dealing with the origin and development of law), sociological jurisprudence (dealing with the relationship between legal rules and legal behavior), and functional jurisprudence (dealing with legal norms and social needs), are not the concerns of philosophy of law.

Philosophy of law can be traced to **Plato**'s *Laws*, and **Aristotle**'s distinction between distributive justice and corrective justice. Major philosophical approaches to law include **natural law theory**, represented by Thomas **Aquinas**, which holds that law is essentially connected with moral right and **good**; **legal positivism**, represented by Jeremy **Bentham**, John **Austin**, and H. L. A. **Hart**, which argues for the moral neutrality of law and separates law from morality; and **legal realism**, represented by Oliver Wendell Holmes, Jr. and Alf Ross, which claims that the law should be understood in terms of how it operates in courts.

philosophy of mathematics

PHILOSOPHY OF MATHEMATICS Starting with **Plato**, mathematics has been viewed by philosophers as the model of **necessary truth** and *a priori* **knowledge**. Hence, the ontological status of mathematical **objects**, the foundation of mathematics, the nature of mathematical **knowledge** and **truth**, and the structure and function of mathematical **theories** have been of central interest for many philosophers. Modern philosophy of mathematics started with **Frege**'s **logicism** and the establishment of **set theory** in mathematics. In opposition to the traditional claim that there is a kind of mathematical **intuition** that guarantees the necessity of mathematical truth, logicism argues that mathematics can be reduced to logic, and this idea was classically presented in **Russell** and **Whitehead**'s *Principia Mathematica*. The approach inspired **logical positivism**, but was attacked by **Quine** with his criticism of the notion of analyticity. The **paradox** Russell discovered in set theory led to a foundational crisis of mathematics. To cope with the crisis, philosophers of mathematics have adopted different approaches. Some philosophers, following Plato, believe that mathematical objects are **abstract entities** independent of our **minds**, and this **realistic** position is called mathematical Platonism. Others, like **Quine** and **Putnam**, suggest that mathematics does not have objects proper to itself. **Hilbert**'s **formalist** program saw the **meaning** of mathematical expressions in terms of the formal mathematical system to which they belong rather than in terms of objects. Hilbert's attempt to prove the **consistency** and **completeness** of formal systems expressing arithmetic was undermined by **Gödel**'s **incompleteness theorems**. In the **Kantian** tradition, others claim that mathematical objects are mental constructions or creations, a view best represented by **constructivism**. **Brouwer**'s **intuitionism**, which attempted to explain mathematical reasoning in terms of the construction of proofs, led to the denial of the **law of excluded middle** that is at the heart of classical mathematics.

Philosophy of mathematics is closely connected with contemporary issues in **ontology** and **epistemology** and with current debates between **realism** and **anti-realism**.

> "The central problem in the philosophy of mathematics is the definition of mathematical truth." **Curry,** *Outline of a Formalist Philosophy of Mathematics*

philosophy of mind

PHILOSOPHY OF MIND The philosophical examination of the nature of the mind and its relationship with body. **Plato** and **Aristotle** provided theories of mind, and so have many modern philosophers, in particular **Descartes, Locke, Hume,** and **Kant**. But only with the emergence of psychology as a distinct discipline at the end of the nineteenth century did the philosophy of mind become an independent sub-discipline within philosophy. Since then, theories of mind have aimed at deepening our understanding of the mind itself, rather than at placing an account of the mind within a traditional metaphysical or epistemological framework. Franz **Brentano** and his successors played a major role in this process.

Contemporary philosophy of mind established a new focus with the publication of Gilbert **Ryle**'s *The Concept of Mind* (1949). Ryle tried to understand our **mental states** by analyzing the logical structures and relations of our mental **concepts**. This work is distinguished from psychology, which studies the actual operations of mind through experimental methods, and from philosophy of psychology, which investigates the philosophical implications of the results and methods of psychology. Major topics in the philosophy of mind include the **mind–body problem**; the nature of the mind; **consciousness; mental causation; intentionality, propositional attitudes,** and mental **content; knowledge** and **belief; representation; perception; feelings; sensations; thought** and language; **will;** and the **emotions**. Various approaches to the mind have been explored, such as **dualism, phenomenalism, epiphenomenalism, behaviorism, parallelism, materialism, functionalism,** and **eliminativism**. The philosophy of mind has been an extremely active discipline in recent decades. In the most recent years, some philosophers have sought to soften the distinction between philosophical and empirical studies of the mind and have linked philosophy of mind with such fields as computational modeling and cognitive psychology.

> "The aim of the philosophy of mind is to conduct an a priori investigation into the essential nature of mental phenomena, by elucidating the latent content of mental concepts." **McGinn,** *The Character of Mind*

philosophy of nature

PHILOSOPHY OF SCIENCE In one sense, the **analysis** and clarification of the **concepts** used by natural scientists, particularly those concepts that cut across the frontiers of the various scientific disciplines. In a traditional sense, philosophy of nature employs the philosophical contemplation of nature to work out general principles to explain the constituent stuff, basic structure, and movement of the natural world. This study was the main preoccupation of the **pre-Socratic** philosophers who originated Western philosophy. Philosophy of nature is also called "physics" [from Greek *phusis*, nature], and one of **Aristotle**'s major philosophical works is entitled *Physics*. Philosophy of nature has been a standard part of Western **metaphysical** systems, although it has been increasingly superseded by the empirical study of nature. **Kant**, however, held that philosophy of nature should seek to determine the basic concepts and **principles** on which scientists could build the whole structure of their **knowledge** of the world by establishing the *a priori* presuppositions of natural science. For **Hegel**, philosophy of nature stood above the empirical natural sciences by providing its own insights into the structure of **facts** and by going beyond scientific investigation. Philosophy of nature is also called "natural philosophy," but it should not be confused with the nature-philosophy (*Naturphilosophie*) of the German romantic movement.

> "The philosophy of nature takes up the material which physics has prepared for it empirically, at the point to which physics has brought it, and reconstitutes it, so that experience is not its final warranted base." **Hegel,** *Philosophy of Nature*

philosophy of organism

METAPHYSICS A term used by Alfred North **Whitehead** for his own metaphysical outlook, although his metaphysics is also called process philosophy. Influenced by field theory in physics, he believed that the ultimate basis of the natural world is **force** rather than **matter**. Nature is analyzed into units called actual occasions. An actual occasion is a process of **becoming** with its own orientation. It is like the **Leibnizian monad**, although, rather than being windowless, each actual occasion actively interrelates with other actual occasions in its immediate past. This process is called *concrescere* (Latin, to grow together) and generates an actual entity. Whitehead claimed that this picture explains the organic structure of the world. Physics studies smaller units, while biology studies larger units. Each unit has its own inner structure and is an organism. Larger units are systems of smaller units.

> "In all philosophic theory there is an ultimate which is actual in virtue of its accidents. It is only then capable of characterization through its accidental embodiments, and apart from these accidents is devoid of actuality. In the philosophy of organism this ultimate is termed 'creativity'."
> **Whitehead,** *Process and Reality*

philosophy of physics

PHILOSOPHY OF SCIENCE A discipline of philosophy of science dealing with the philosophical impact of the development of modern physics, in particular philosophical issues arising in the theory of **relativity**, **quantum** mechanics, modern thermodynamics, and contemporary **cosmology**. The major topics of philosophy of physics **include space**, **time**, **motion**, **probability**, **causation**, and **objectivity** in the quantum world. The discipline also investigates the foundations of physical theory, the aim of a physical theory, the interrelation of physical theories, and scientific methodology in physics and the logical systems suitable for modern physics. By exploring ideas and methods developed in physics, philosophy of physics contributes to our understanding of physics as a science. It tests the implications of new metaphysical claims arising within physics and shapes our insight into both human knowledge and the nature of things.

> "The philosophy of physics performs at least four useful functions, which may be called philosophical assimilation, research planning, quality control, and home cleaning." **Bunge,** *Philosophy of Physics*

philosophy of psychology

PHILOSOPHY OF SCIENCE, PHILOSOPHY OF MIND The study of psychological concepts and theories, philosophical presuppositions of approaches to psychology, and implications of psychological discoveries. It is part of a general development in the philosophy of science toward the integration of empirical and philosophical aspects of study, but in some respects philosophy of psychology overlaps with **philosophy of mind**. For many contemporary philosophers, philosophy of psychology has replaced philosophical psychology, which sought to analyze psychological concepts without attending to major developments in scientific psychology.

Philosophy of psychology is concerned with empirical or experimental psychology. Empirical psychology as an independent discipline began with the establishment of the first psychology laboratory at University of Leipzig in 1879 by the German psychologist Wilhelm Wundt, although empirical psychology was also based initially on the **associationist** theory developed by **Hume** and J. S. **Mill**. Philosophy of psychology explores complex relations among different theories of mind, empirical data, and experiment in seeking a general account of the nature of mind. Psychological theories contributing to philosophical discussions about the mind have included *Gestalt* **theory**, **Freudian** theory, and **behaviorism**, but the source of much recent influence is **cognitive science**, in which the boundary between philosophy and psychology remains undetermined. This boundary is also challenged within philosophy, with **Quine**'s **naturalistic epistemology** tending to reduce **epistemology** to psychology.

> "[P]hilosophy of psychology, that is, the philosophical study of the nature and significance of the results and methods of scientific psychology."
> **McGinn,** *The Character of Mind*

philosophy of pure reason, see metaphysics (Kant)

philosophy of religion

PHILOSOPHY OF RELIGION A branch of philosophy dealing with the meaning, nature, and philosophical implications of religious **beliefs** and claims and of religious practices. Theoretically, all religions constitute its subject-matter, but since the philosophy of religion is a specialty developed in Western countries, it naturally focuses on the claims of Western religions, especially the doctrines of Christianity but also including the doctrines of Judaism and Islam. Its main topics include: the conception of **God**; the conceptual analysis of **divine attributes** such as **omnipotence, omniscience, goodness, eternity**, and the **paradoxes** resulting from these attributes; the logical characteristics of religious language; the examination of the logical structure of arguments for and against the existence of God, in particular of the most influential arguments such as the **ontological argument**, the **argument from design**, the **cosmological argument**, and the **problem of evil**; the relation between **faith** and **reason**; the relations between religion and **morality**, art and science; the philosophical comparison of different forms of religion; the **phenomenology** of religious experience and its role, if any, in **justifying** religious belief; the methods of religious argument; the **afterlife** or **immortality**; the discussions of particular Christian doctrines such as the Trinity, Incarnation, and Atonement. Many of these themes are also included in **metaphysics** and were the central topics in **medieval philosophy**.

"What are the distinctive features of religious ideas? Do they here and there contain contradictions? On what possible basis can they be considered true or false? How do they mesh in, if at all, with the other concepts which we use? Such are the questions which typically fall within the ambit of the philosophy of religion." **N. Smart**, *The Philosophy of Religion*

philosophy of science

PHILOSOPHY OF SCIENCE The study of **logical, epistemological**, and **metaphysical** problems arising from reflections on the sciences and scientific activities. It is a philosophical critique of science. This area is new as a specific discipline and has emerged in conjunction with the intellectual achievements of modern science, but in a wider sense has been a part of epistemology and metaphysics in the philosophical tradition. The exact bound of its research domain is hard to define, for science itself comprises a wide range of activities, modes of thought, and **discourses**. In general, the most important issues it investigates include the aims of science; the relations between scientific **concepts** and between scientific **propositions**; the **principles** assumed

in science; the nature and structure of scientific **rationality** and methodology; scientific **knowledge** and its **confirmation**; rationality and scientific progress; **explanation**; scientific laws; natural **necessity**; **probability**; the unity or diversity of science; **reduction** and relations among the sciences; **objectivity** in science; **certainty** and fallibility in science; **theory**, observation, experiment in science; models in science; the ontological implications of science and the nature of **theoretical entities**; scientific **creativity**, invention, and discovery; science and other knowledge; science and religion; the social effects of scientific ideas; the relation of philosophy of science to history and sociology of science; the **ethics** of science. Major figures in this field include the **logical positivists** (logical **analysis** of the structure of science, **verificationism**), **Hempel** (scientific **explanation**), **Popper** (**falsificationism**), **Lakatos** (progressive and degenerating **research programs**), and **Kuhn** (**paradigm shift** and scientific revolutions). Before the Second World War, philosophy of science mainly focused on the logic of science. Since then, philosophers have been more interested in the developmental paradigms of sciences and the epistemology of science.

Aside from general issues regarding the enterprise of science, there are specific problems arising in particular fields of science leading to discipline-specific studies, such as **philosophy of mathematics, philosophy of physics, philosophy of biology**, and **philosophy of psychology**.

"In any event, much is gained in the way of clarifying the aims of philosophical analysis by limiting the philosophy of science to a group of related questions that arise in attempting to understand the intellectual products of scientific inquiry as embodied in explicitly formulated statements." **E. Nagel**, in Danto and Morgenbesser (eds.), *Philosophy of Science*

philosophy of social science

PHILOSOPHY OF SOCIAL SCIENCE In the eighteenth-century **Enlightenment**, social sciences aimed to achieve the ideal of scientific **objectivity** and universality. But are **natural sciences** and social sciences similar? Philosophers who emphasize the **meaning** of human **action** or the role of **ideology** in social scientific inquiry believe that social sciences explain the social world in a distinct way. The tension between scientific **explanation** and interpretative **understanding** led to the emergence of the philosophy of social sciences. This discipline is concerned with the methodology and **knowledge** claims of the social sciences, especially with the logic of **theory** construction in the social sciences, with the nature, validity, and adequacy of social theory, and with **causation** or **laws** among social phenomena. It is also concerned with **explanation** without universal laws and the role of meaning and **interpretation** in the social sciences. It aims to elucidate the forms of **reasoning** and explanatory frameworks practiced in social sciences. A central question concerns the relation between social institutions and **individuals** with regard to explanatory priority, leading to a long-standing controversy concerning **methodological collectivism** and **methodological individualism**. Major approaches in the philosophy of social science include those initiated by Émile **Durkheim**, Karl **Marx**, and Max **Weber**. The **hermeneutics** of Wilhelm **Dilthey** and Hans-Georg **Gadamer** have challenged the unity of science model of the social sciences proposed by the **logical positivists**. The later work of **Wittgenstein** influenced Peter **Winch**'s attack on an account of the social sciences on the model of the natural sciences. Martin Hollis, who emphasizes the importance of **rationality** in understanding society, has argued for a possible accommodation between the rival traditions in the philosophy of social sciences. On this view, we must take care to determine the sort of questions we are asking and the sort of answers that would be appropriate. The philosophy of social sciences should be distinguished from social philosophy, for while social philosophy is the philosophical discussion of the features of human society, the philosophy of social science deals with philosophical, in particular epistemological and methodological, issues arising out of the practice of social scientists. Nevertheless, the work of Alasdair **MacIntyre** is a recent example of how these two philosophical enterprises can influence one another and in some instances merge.

"To what extent can society be studied in the same way as nature? Without exaggerating, I think one could call this question the primal problem of the philosophy of the social sciences." **Bhaskar,** *The Possibility of Naturalism*

philosophy of thought

PHILOSOPHY OF MIND, PHILOSOPHY OF LANGUAGE A new philosophical approach to thought represented by Christopher Peacocke and the late Gareth Evans. Its roots can be traced to **Frege**'s criticism of **psychologism** and his assertion that thought is the third realm (the others being the physical and the psychological). In contrast to the central tenet of traditional **analytical philosophy**, that an analysis of thought must depend on the analysis of language and that language is prior to thought, advocates of the philosophy of thought believe that the order of priority of this analysis should be reversed. Language can only be explained in terms of antecedently given notions that are thought-laden. Hence, the central consideration of philosophy is no longer language, but thought. It is thought that determines language, and not vice versa. Thought can be explained independently of language. Of course, traditional Cartesian epistemology also focuses on the question of the nature of thought, but the philosophy of thought considers thought as the **content** of **propositions** and deals with questions such as what it is to be a thought, how a thought can be grasped, how a thought is structured, how a thought can be about something, how we can judge a thought to be true, and how **concepts** that we grasp are related to thoughts. This type of philosophy is distinct from the philosophy of language and philosophy of mind, although it is related to them.

"The philosophy of thought concerns itself with the question what it is to be a thought, and with the structure of thoughts and their components: what it is for a thought to be about an object of one or another kind, what it is to grasp a concept and how a concept can be a component of a thought." **Dummett,** *Origins of Analytical Philosophy*

phonologism

MODERN EUROPEAN PHILOSOPHY **Derrida**'s term for the feature of traditional metaphysics that establishes an opposition between speech and writing and then prefers speech or voice to writing. Voice [Greek *phono*] is traditionally considered to be the locus of **truth**, the real sign of **essence** and truth and the **presence** of **consciousness** to itself. One "hears" the voice of "reason" when one seeks the truth. Writing is considered to be a parasitic, supplementary, inferior, and derivative form of communication. Such a philosophical tradition is fully presented in **Plato**'s *Phaedrus*, and even **Lévi-Strauss** accepts this view. Derrida's notion of phonologism is closely associated with, or even used interchangeably with, his notions of **logocentrism** and metaphysics of presence. The speech/writing opposition is one of the main objects of Derrida's **deconstruction**.

> "This notion remains therefore within the heritage of that logocentrism which is also phonocentrism: absolute proximity of voice and being, of voice and the meaning of being, of voice and the ideality of meaning." **Derrida, *Of Grammatology***

phrase-marker

PHILOSOPHY OF LANGUAGE **Chomsky**'s term for the components of the structural skeleton of a **sentence**. It is generated by starting with a **rule** for rewriting the sentence and further expanding its components using phrase-structure rules, eventually reaching a categorial structure. This structure will mark items such as noun phrases, prepositional phrases, and clauses. Phrase-markers are the elementary units from which deep structures are constituted. When we insert words into phrase markers and tidy them up, for example to ensure that the words have the right endings, we will have an actual sentence.

> "The base of the syntactic component is a system of rules that generate a highly restricted (perhaps finite) set of basic strings, each with an associated structural description called a base phrase-marker." **Chomsky, *Aspects of the Theory of Syntax***

phrase-structure grammar

PHILOSOPHY OF LANGUAGE One of the three models **Chomsky** uses in order to characterize our understanding of language and **grammar** (the other models are **finite-state grammar** and **transformational grammar**). It is a form of grammar associated with the theory of linguistic structure based upon immediate constituent analysis or parsing (from Latin *pars*, part). This analysis parses a sentence into various components and then assigns these components to categories such as Noun, Verb, Adverb, and so on. A language that can be thus derived is called a phrase-structure language. This analysis is characterized by the use of diagrams and the introduction of rewriting rules for turning symbols into other symbols. For example, we can rewrite "Sentence" as "Noun Phrase + Verb Phrase" and then rewrite "Noun Phrase" as "Article + Noun," and so on. The different aspects of an utterance are successively disclosed in such an analysis. However, it can only be applied when we know what sentence we want to derive, and it fails to exhibit the intuited interrelationships that hold between different sentences. For instance, this grammar cannot incorporate "to be" into the class of verbs. Hence, Chomsky takes this grammar to be inadequate for linguistic description, and holds that it should be replaced by transformational grammar.

> "A phrase-structure grammar consists of an unordered set of rewriting rules, and assigns a structural description that can be represented as a tree-diagram with nodes labelled by symbols of the vocabulary." **Chomsky, *Aspects of the Theory of Syntax***

phrase-structure language, see phrase-structure grammar

phrastic, see neustic/phrastic

phronesis, Greek term for practical wisdom

physical determinism

METAPHYSICS, PHILOSOPHY OF SCIENCE, ETHICS The belief that everything in the world, including human **action**, is governed by universal **laws of nature**. This position was presented in ancient **atomism**, and was fully articulated by **Hobbes**. The development of modern science, especially physics, led many to think that physical determinism must be true. Science claims that its aim is to discover these objective laws. If we can provide a complete physical explanation at this time for one thing, we will be able to predict its future on the grounds of natural laws. Human **freedom** should be understood as the lack of constraints, rather than as freedom from such causation. If all that we do is explicable in terms of physical laws, the **immortality** of soul must be denied.

> "Physical determinism is based on there being physical laws of nature, many of which have actually been discovered, and of whose truth we

> can reasonably hope to be quite certain, together with the claim that all other features of the world are dependent on physical factors." **Lucas,** *The Freedom of the Will*

physical objects, another term for material objects

physical phenomenon, see mental phenomenon

physicalism

PHILOSOPHY OF SCIENCE, PHILOSOPHY OF MIND A refinement of **materialism** introduced because not all physical phenomena are material. Physicalism assumes that physical science can encompass everything in the world, and that ultimately everything in the world can be explained through physics. It is possible to reduce any scientific predicate to a physical predicate. The word was introduced by the **logical positivists** for the claim that all scientific statements could be translated into statements about physical or observable objects. In this sense, physicalism is close to **scientism**, which claims that any language that can not be reduced to scientific language is defective. **Carnap** took physicalism as a synonym for **behaviorism**. However, the Australian philosopher J. J. C. **Smart** contrasted physicalism with behaviorism, taking the former to be a scientific approach and the latter a linguistic approach. Smart's physicalism is also called the **identity theory of mind** or **central-state materialism**, because its main thesis is that **mental events** are identical to brain events. On this view, **propositions** about mental states turn out to be propositions about brain states that belong to the science of neurophysiology. Neuro-physiology, in turn, is reducible to physics. However, the physicalist view that the identity between mental states and brain states is **contingent identity** has been challenged by **Kripke**'s claim that all identity is necessary identity. The issues raised by this criticism include the nature of **reference**, **description**, **meaning**, **identity**, **modality**, and **theory**.

> "The thesis of physicalism maintains that the physical language is a universal language of science – that is to say, that every language of any subdomain of science can be equipollently translated into the physical language." **Carnap,** *The Logical Syntax of Language*

physico-theological argument

PHILOSOPHY OF RELIGION **Kant**'s term for his version of the **argument from design**. The physico-theological argument is one of the three main theistic proofs for the existence of God, the other two being the **ontological argument** and the **cosmological argument**. It argues from observations that the world is **purposive** and teleologically arranged to the conclusion that there must be an intelligent designer who created it. For Kant, this argument is not sufficient to prove the existence of God because it relies upon the presupposition that there is a supreme being and is thus ultimately based on the ontological argument. Kant argued in detail for the impossibility of the ontological argument and held that its rejection showed that both the cosmological and physico-theological arguments are impossible as well.

> "Thus the physico-theological proof of the existence of an original or supreme being rests upon the cosmological proof, and the cosmological upon the ontological." **Kant,** *Critique of Pure Reason*

pictorial form

METAPHYSICS, PHILOSOPHY OF LANGUAGE **Wittgenstein** claimed that a **proposition** is a logical picture of reality. The elements in a picture are connected with one another in a certain way, and this is the structure of a picture. But how is such a structure possible? The possibility of the structure is called its pictorial form, which is the common element shared by a picture and the reality it represents. Pictorial form is the way a picture represents how **objects** are related to one another, allowing a picture to depict any reality whose form it has. The conception of pictorial form generalizes the notion of picture beyond its primitive base. The distinction between form and structure enables Wittgenstein to solve the ancient puzzle of the possibility of false judgment.

> "Pictorial form is the possibility that things are related to one another in the same way as the elements of the picture." **Wittgenstein,** *Tractatus*

picture theory

METAPHYSICS, PHILOSOPHY OF LANGUAGE **Wittgenstein**'s theory of the **proposition** in the *Tractatus*, according to which a proposition is a picture of reality. To understand a proposition is to know the situation that it represents. The term "picture" (German *Bild*) is derived both from a drawn picture and from the mathematical sense of an abstract model. All propositions are **truth-functions** of **elementary propositions**. Each elementary proposition is composed of unanalyzable **names** that designate simple **objects**. The **sense** of a proposition is the **state of affairs** it depicts. The way that elements are related in a proposition represents the same way in which objects are related to each other. Hence, a proposition has a pictorial nature. However, it is a logical picture that shares a **pictorial form** with what it depicts, rather than resembling what it depicts spatially. Although all propositions are pictures, not all pictures are propositions. It is a matter of dispute whether the picture theory of propositions collapses with Wittgenstein's rejection of the metaphysics of logical atomism of the *Tractatus*.

"It is commonly said that Wittgenstein after the *Tractatus* abandoned the picture theory of propositions." **Kenny, *The Legacy of Wittgenstein***

piecemeal engineering

POLITICAL PHILOSOPHY, PHILOSOPHY OF SOCIAL SCIENCE **Popper**'s proposal for an approach to social change. Piecemeal social engineering contrasts with the **utopian engineering** of rapid, large-scale **reform** or **revolution**. Instead of setting up a positive blueprint for society and then seeking the means to realize it, piecemeal engineering confronts the ills of society through a succession of limited reforms. Social life is so complicated that we can not tell in advance the unintended consequences of any policy, and these consequences might be harmful. If reform is too complex, rapid, or wide-ranging, we can not trace harmful consequences to their source and correct them. Popper argued that reforming society by piecemeal social engineering would improve institutions and maintain social stability more effectively that utopian strategies. Some critics argue that a policy of piecemeal social engineering would succeed only if there were social agreement, but on such matters there are often deep divisions.

"The piecemeal engineer will, accordingly, adopt the method of searching for, and fighting against, the greatest and most urgent evils of society, rather than searching for, and fighting for, its greatest ultimate good." **Popper, *Open Society and Its Enemies***

pietism

PHILOSOPHY OF RELIGION A devotional religious movement within Protestantism, springing from Lutheranism and flourishing in Germany in the seventeenth and early eighteenth centuries. It was founded by a German Lutheran pastor, Philipp Jakob Spener. The name of the movement was derived from the twice-weekly Bible study meetings for devout lay-people (called *collegia pietatis*) under Spener's organization. The movement aimed at being free from the influence of Church and tradition. It stressed **autonomous subjectivity** and claimed that the real purpose of redemption is to bring the religious subjectivity of man into lively play. The real interest of theology should be to promote the exercise of godliness. The individual should determine the shape of his own religious life by confronting the Bible. The movement emphasized individual experience and practicality rather than **evidence** and **reason**. It was concerned with particular problems and situations rather than with the establishment of universal **principles**. Pietism was the religion of **Kant**, and the movement also produced figures such as Friedrich **Schleiermacher** and Gotfried Arnold.

"Pietism represented a turning towards a more inward, emotional, and enthusiastic form of Christianity." **Pinson, *Pietism as a Factor in the Role of German Nationalism***

pineal gland

PHILOSOPHY OF MIND **Descartes** held that mind and body are two **entities** that are completely different in **nature**. How, then, can the **soul** have a unified relationship with the entire body? How can mind and body mutually affect one another? Descartes's answer is that the soul does not exercise its functions directly on the body, but affects the body through the pineal gland. The pineal gland is an organ that is situated in the middle of the brain and is unique to humans. For Descartes, the pineal gland is the seat of the soul. He claimed that the mind generates movements in the pineal gland, which in turn generates movements in the nerves and hence the body. Giving a location to mind–body interaction is not a satisfactory solution to the problem of **psycho-physical causation**. The rejection of this appeal to the pineal gland led to the **parallelism** of **Spinoza**, the **occasionalism** of **Malebranche**, and the **pre-established harmony** of **Leibniz**.

> "There is no other place in the body where they can be thus united unless they are so in this gland."
> **Descartes, *The Passions of the Soul***

plagiarism, see forgery

Plantinga, Alvin (1932–)

American logician and philosopher of religion, born in Ann Arbor, Michigan, Professor at Calvin College and University of Notre Dame. Plantinga has used the techniques of modern logic and philosophy to discuss classical questions in the philosophy of religion. He argues that belief in the existence of God can be justified in the same way as belief in the existence of other minds. An account of modal logic in terms of possible worlds is the basis of his treatment of the problem of evil and of his version of Anselm's ontological argument. His major works include *God and Other Minds* (1967) and *The Nature of Necessity* (1974).

Plato (427–347 BC)

Greek philosopher, born in Athens, founder of a school, the Academy, in Athens in 387 BC. Plato's writings are in the form of dialogues in which the main speaker is **Socrates**. Hence, there are problems in distinguishing between the philosophy of the historical Socrates and Plato's own philosophy. There are also controversies about the chronological order of his dialogues. The orthodox division recognizes three stages: the early, middle, and late dialogues. The early dialogues include *Apology*, *Crito*, *Laches*, *Charmides*, *Euthyphro*, *Hippias Minor*, *Ion*, *Protagoras*, and *Gorgias*. These dialogues are generally short (except the last two), aporetic, and ethical in content. They are considered to be closely related to the thought and practice of the historical Socrates and are also called the "Socratic dialogues." The middle dialogues, including *Meno*, *Phaedo*, *Symposium*, *Republic*, and *Phaedrus*, contain Plato's mature thought. In them Plato established his influential theory of Ideas (or Forms). Beyond the sensible world there is a world of Ideas that is the real object

of knowledge. The existence of sensible things is due to their participation in Ideas. In the *Republic*, the centerpiece of Plato's philosophy, he developed various metaphors to illustrate the relation between two worlds, such as the allegories of the Sun, the Line, and the Cave. He also established theories of the tripartite soul, the ideal state, and the philosopher-king. All these were aimed to answer the question of why one should be moral. The late dialogues include *Parmenides*, *Theaetetus*, *Cratyus*, *Timaeus*, *Critias*, *Sophist*, *Statement*, *Philebus*, and *Laws*. The first part of the *Parmenides* introduced the Third Man argument to criticize the theory of forms established in the middle dialogues, but scholars disagree about the implications of this self-criticism. Other late dialogues mainly developed different themes of the *Republic*. There are various approaches in reading Plato's dialogues. Some claim that Plato's philosophy undergoes a development of several different stages. Others believe that we should treat his thought as a unified whole. Still others suggest that we should read each dialogue separately.

Plato's beard

LOGIC **Quine**'s term for a classical puzzle, which can be traced to **Plato**'s *Sophist* and concerns the existence of non-being. We can formulate the true sentence, "The Queen of China does not exist," but it seems plausible to claim that the non-existent Queen must in some sense be for us to make sense of denying her existence. Yet it seems **self-contradictory** to say that we can infer the **being** of something from its non-being. This puzzle has led philosophers to examine both the nature of **reference** and the **logical form** of **existential propositions**.

> "This is the old Platonic riddle of nonbeing. Nonbeing must in some sense be, otherwise what is it that there is not? This tangled doctrine might be nicknamed Plato's beard." **Quine, *From a Logical Point of View***

Platonism

METAPHYSICS Philosophy derived from the spirit of the philosophy of **Plato**, in particular from his **Theory of Forms**, which contrasts **reality** with phenomena; **soul** with **body**; **knowledge** with opinion; **reason** with **sensation**; and **rationality** with **emotion**. It then claims that the first member of each contrasting pair is superior or more real than the second member. Such contrasts form an essential ingredient of Western philosophy and have inspired many philosophers since Plato. In this sense, **Whitehead** reasonably claimed that all subsequent philosophies are footnotes to Plato. Those who claim explicitly to be the heirs of Plato include the Academy tradition (the Old, Middle, and New Academy), **Neoplatonism**, the Renaissance Platonism of Marsilio **Ficino**, and the **Cambridge Platonism** of the seventeenth century.

In contemporary philosophy, all positions that suggest the independent existence of abstract objects are called Platonism. According to these accounts, **abstracta** can be grasped by the **mind**, but can not be created by it. Platonism in this sense is virtually synonymous with **realism** and is opposed to **nominalism**.

> "Empiricism may properly be contrasted with platonism. For the platonist believes . . . that the propositions of logic and mathematics concern an abstract (non-physical and changeless) but genuinely mind-independent realm of objects, including universals such as beauty and wisdom, as well as mathematical entities such as the natural numbers." **Carruthers**, *Human Knowledge and Human Nature*

plausibility

EPISTEMOLOGY A claim is plausible if it **subjectively** seems worthy of **belief** even if we have not necessarily studied its **objective** ground. Plausibility is thus acceptable credibility, and its degree of credibility can depend in part on the **authority** that advocates it. A plausible claim can turn out to be **false**, and an implausible claim can turn out to be true. People can disagree on what they find plausible. Plausibility is distinct from **probability**, which is related to alternatives. A belief is probable if its degree of likelihood is greater than that of its alternatives. On most accounts, probability is more objective than plausibility, although the **personalism** of **de Finetti** and **Ramsey** understands probability as a subjective degree of belief.

> "All holding-to-be-true based on grounds concerning which we do not investigate whether they contain a large or a small degree of truth is plausibility." **Kant**, *Lectures on Logic*

pleasure

PHILOSOPHY OF MIND, ETHICS, PHILOSOPHY OF ACTION [Greek *hedone*, from which hedonism is derived] Pleasure is taken to be contrary to **pain** but related to enjoyment and liking. **Plato** in the *Philebus* argues that pleasure is an indeterminate state and can not be measured, a position challenged by social **choice** and other theories that depend on some way of measuring pleasure. **Aristotle** holds that pleasure, in contrast to movement, is an activity having its own end and is the natural accompaniment of successful **activity**, whether of the **mind** or the **senses**. Pleasure is not identical to happiness, but is an important part of it. This position opposes traditional **hedonism**, which claims that pleasure is the only **good** or the highest good. According to **Utilitarianism** an **action** is justified to the extent that it tends to produce pleasure and to reduce pain. Pleasure is often viewed as an agreeable feeling, but there is much debate regarding its nature, classification, and relation to **desire**, in part because of its central role in the discussion of human motivation and **value**.

> "Appetite's concern is pleasure and pain." **Aristotle**, *Nicomachean Ethics*

Plekhanov, Georgii Valentinovich (1856–1918)

Russian Marxist philosopher, born in Lijseck. He sought to develop the thought of Marx and Engels into a system, which he called dialectical materialism. Plekhanov criticized economic determinism and maintained that historical development was also partly influenced by psychological and other noneconomic factors. He also extended his version of Marxism to aesthetics and ethics. Plekhanov was once a collaborator of Lenin, but later supported the Mensheviks against the Bolsheviks. Plekhanov's major writings include *In Defense of Materialism* (1895) and *The Development of the Monist View of History* (1895).

Plotinus (c.204–270)

Greco-Roman philosopher, born in Egypt, founder of Neoplatonism. Plotinus' masterpiece is the *Enneads*, a collection of 54 essays, which his student Porphyry, who edited the volume, arranged into six groups, each containing nine treatises. Plotinus claimed that the world had three hypostases or realities: (1) the One, which, as the highest principle, is above Being and is ineffable; (2) Intelligence, which is the realm of true being; and (3) the Soul. The relationship among these realities was described as a process of "emanation": Intelligence emanates from the One, and the Soul emanates from Intelligence. Further, matter emanates from the Soul. Man can grasp the One by contemplating it and by becoming one with it. In that state, the Soul experiences ecstasy.

pluralism

METAPHYSICS, ETHICS [from Latin *pluris*, more than one] A doctrine, opposed to **monism** and **dualism**, holding that **reality** consists of many things and that none of its constituents is more fundamental than any of the others. It is therefore impossible to reduce everything in reality to one or two ultimate **principles**. For pluralism there are many worlds that we are able to construct through the use of different systems of **concepts** and different standards of measurement. **Leibniz**'s theory of **monads**, **Russell**'s logical atomism, and later **Wittgenstein**'s theory of **language-games** are different forms of pluralism. Sometimes pluralism means that reality has no basic unity or **continuity**, but is essentially fragmented or indeterminate. In ethics, pluralism means that there are various competing ethical interests or **values** that can not be reduced to one single overriding interest or value.

> "The extreme form of pluralism is the assumption that all relations are external, with the consequence that the existence of any one object is logically independent of the existence of any other." **Ayer, *Philosophy in the Twentieth Century***

pneuma

ANCIENT GREEK PHILOSOPHY, PHILOSOPHY OF SCIENCE [Greek, breath] A key term in Stoic **philosophy of nature**. *Pneuma* was held to be a compound of fire and air, although not a simple chemical compound, and was also called artistic or intelligent *pneuma*. Through having two components, *pneuma* was held to have a peculiar tensional movement making it continuously active. It was described as a material **substance** with fine and tenuous structure, but also as a cohesive **force** or energy that pervades the universe to account for its **change** and persistence. As **nature**, **God**, or the universal *logos*, it acted on **matter**, that is, the elements of earth and water,

to hold them together. *Pneuma* worked in the **macrocosm** and also in every individual body. The concept of *pneuma* was influenced by the **pre-Socratics** and in turn influenced the postulation of *aether* in the science of the seventeenth to nineteenth centuries. It is also comparable to a **field** of force in contemporary physics.

> "This pneuma possesses two parts, elements or conditions, which are blended with one another through and through, the cold and hot, or if one wished to describe them by different names taken from their substances: air and fire." **Chrysippus, in Gelen, *On Hippocrates and Plato's Doctrines***

pneumatology, another expression for rational psychology

poiesis

ANCIENT GREEK PHILOSOPHY, PHILOSOPHY OF ACTION [Greek from *poiein*, to act, to do, or to make] For **Aristotle**, *poiesis* is restricted to making or producing that has as its aim something beyond itself, for example shipbuilding, which has the aim of producing a vessel. It is distinguished from *praxis* (**action**, conduct), which has aims and value in itself. *Poiesis* belongs to *techne* (craft), while *praxis* belongs to *phronesis* (**practical reason**). In another sense, *poiesis* is used specifically for poetry and its composition.

> "The state involving reason and concerned with action is different from the state involving reason and concerned with *poiesis*." **Aristotle, *Nicomachean Ethics***

Poincaré, Jules Henri (1854–1912)

French scientist and philosopher of science, born in Nancy. As a conventionalist, he maintained that the fundamental geometrical axioms were established as a matter of convention, according to the criteria of simplicity and economy. Hence, these axioms are neither verifiable nor non-verifiable. However, he also accepted the order of the external world and claimed that the aim of physics is to discover this universal order. In mathematics, he was an intuitionist and rejected Russell's philosophy of mathematics. Poincaré's major books in philosophy of science include *Science and Hypothesis* (1902), *The Value of Science* (1905), and *Science and Method* (1908).

political obligation   535

polar-related concept pair

PHILOSOPHY OF LANGUAGE, METAPHYSICS A pair of **concepts** that are opposite in **meaning**, where each of them can be understood or identified only in terms of its contrast with the other. The notion is also called conceptual polarity. Neither member of the pair has an autonomous existence as a concept apart from the other, and neither member can logically be reduced to the other. In many cases, one concept of the polar pair is formed in association with the other from which it is distinguished. Examples of polar pairs include up and down, unity and **plurality**, **physical** and **mental**, and error and **truth**. The application of each entails the possibility of applying the other. In the history of Western philosophy, various polarities have been established, and usually one member is thought to be superior to the other. **Derrida**'s **deconstructionism** is intended to reject dichotomous conceptual structures and their relations of unequal **power** and **value**, but it is difficult to determine whether we can do without such concept pairs or whether objectionable implications of value can be detached from them.

> "A particularly important type of discrimination is that where one concept, so to speak, includes by exclusion. Concepts related in this way constitute the most important concepts of our thinking, we denoted as 'polar-related concept pairs'." **Reiss, *The Basis of Scientific Thinking***

Polish notation

LOGIC The notation employed in contemporary logic is generally Russellian symbolism. Yet there is an important kind of notation that was originated by the Polish logician **Lukasiewicz** and was widely employed by Polish logicians between the two world wars. It was also preferred by the logician Arthur **Prior**. The chief characteristic of Polish notation is that it places all its operators immediately before their **arguments**, and thus gets rid of parentheses. This helps avoid **ambiguity** and better serves automatic processing. The following is the list of this set of notation, with an English explanation in bracket:

Np (not p)
Apq (either p or q)
Kpq (both p and q)
Cpq (if p then q)
Epq (p if and only if q)

Mp (possibly p)
Lp (necessarily p)
Ixy (x is the same as y)
Sxfx (for some x, fx)
Pxfx (for every x, fx)

> "Polish notation shows which expressions are arguments and which expressions are functions by always writing all arguments to the right of their functions." **Williams, *What is Existence***

political liberty

POLITICAL PHILOSOPHY According to **liberalism**, the basic **rights** or **liberties** that citizens of a **just** society hold equally. It is the liberty held in virtue of **citizenship**. Political liberty includes **negative liberties**, such as freedom from arbitrary arrest and the freedom to pursue one's own interest and plan without obstruction, and **positive liberties**, such as freedom of thought, **freedom of speech**, freedom of assembly, and the right to possess **property**. Political liberties provide the main content of human **rights**.

> "I am normally said to be free to the degree to which no man or body of men interferes with my activity. Political liberty in this sense is simply the area within which a man can act unobstructed by others." **Berlin, *Four Essays on Liberty***

political obligation

POLITICAL PHILOSOPHY The **duty** to obey the **laws** and rules of the **state**. A fundamental problem for political philosophy concerns the grounds for accepting the **authority** of the state, given that state jurisdiction has the character of universality and compulsion. Under what conditions is obedience required or disobedience justified? These issues are closely associated with attempts to determine the basis of the authority of the state, the distinction between **legitimate** and illegitimate governments, and the problem of **civil disobedience**. Political obligation can not be understood merely in terms of **prudence** and the fear of coercive **power**. Various theories of political obligation have been put forward over the centuries, such as those focusing on divine right, the **social contract**, **consent**, the **general will**, **justice**, **rationality**, or membership in an historically determined **community**.

"[H]aving a political obligation ordinarily presupposes the existence of a rule (whether a legal rule or some other type) which forbids or requires a specified form of conduct." **Flathman,** *Political Obligation*

political philosophy

POLITICAL PHILOSOPHY Political philosophy is distinguished from political science on the grounds that political science is empirical and descriptive, explaining how government in fact works, while political philosophy is **normative**, establishing the norms or ideal standards that prescribe how governments ought to work. In fact, the boundary between the two fields is not clear. Political theory includes both empirical and normative investigations. Contemporary political philosophers bring analytic skill and ethical commitment to their work. They seek theoretical insight into basic political concepts, such as **justice**, **equality**, **liberty**, **democracy**, **nationalism**, the **state**, **power**, **authority**, **citizenship**, **rights**, and **obligations**, and look for **rational** grounds to accept or reject particular political institutions. Political philosophers assess existing political institutions and **ideologies** and in some cases seek to justify alternative political and social systems if existing arrangements are unacceptable. **Plato**'s *Republic* remains the major classic. Other prominent political philosophers include **Aristotle**, **Machiavelli**, **Hobbes**, **Locke**, **Hume**, **Rousseau**, **Kant**, **Burke**, **Hegel**, **Mill**, and **Marx**. Much recent discussion in political philosophy has responded to the work of John **Rawls** and Robert **Nozick**.

A rigid demarcation between political and social philosophy is impossible, and social philosophers, such as Jürgen **Habermas**, have influenced recent political philosophy. Social philosophy also deals with philosophical issues relating to institutions such as the family, religion, and education. Critiques of culture and **modernity** derived from **Nietzsche** and his successors have also influenced political philosophy.

"Politics is the exercise of the power of the state, or the attempt to influence that exercise. Political philosophy is therefore, strictly speaking, the philosophy of the state." **Wolff,** *In Defense of Anarchism*

political theory

POLITICAL PHILOSOPHY, PHILOSOPHY OF SOCIAL SCIENCE An academic discipline aiming to provide a systematic understanding of the nature and purpose of government and to provide certain views about how political institutions ought to be improved. It is distinct from **political philosophy**, which seeks to explicate and give theoretical insight into normative political concepts, such as **justice**, **liberty**, **equality**, the **state**, **democracy**, **authority**, **citizenship**, and **rights**, and from political science, which seeks to provide explanatory **theories** and classifications in relation to the empirical data of politics. Nevertheless, political theory is closely related to these other disciplines and is often regarded as the theoretical aspect of political science. Traditionally, its main preoccupation has been to analyze the work of the classical political thinkers, from **Plato** to **Marx**, and to apply their insights to current political affairs. Recently, political theorists have become interested in constructing formal models of political processes. With the contemporary questioning of the **analytic-synthetic** and **fact-value** distinctions, political philosophy, political theory, and political science have drawn more closely together.

"Political theory is . . . an essentially mixed mode of thought. It not only embraces deductive argument and empirical theory, but combines these with normative concerns . . . so acquiring a practical, action-guiding character." **Miller and Siedentop (eds.),** *The Nature of Political Theory*

polyadic, see dyadic

polysyllogism

LOGIC An **inference** composed of a series of **syllogisms** in which the conclusion of an earlier syllogism becomes a premise of a later syllogism in the series. The earlier syllogism is called a prosyllogism, and the later syllogism is called an episyllogism. For example, take (1) all *rs* are *ps*; (2) all *ps* are *qs*; (3) all *rs* are *qs*; (4) all *qs* are *ds*; (5) all *rs* are *ds*. Not only is (3) a conclusion derived from (1) and (2), but it is also a premise of the syllogism composed of (3), (4), and (5). A syllogism with more than two premises is generally analyzed as two or more syllogisms.

"A series of syllogisms, one providing a premise of another, is called a polysyllogism." **Joseph,** *An Introduction to Logic*

polytheism

PHILOSOPHY OF RELIGION [from Greek *poly*, many + *theos*, god] A belief that there are many gods, instead of one. Religions that accept and worship many gods are called polytheistic religions. This view is opposed to monotheism (from Greek *mono*, one, single + *theos*, god), the belief that there is only one **God**. The religion of the ancient Greeks was polytheistic, and Judaism, Christianity, and Islam are monotheistic. It is often held that polytheism is inconsistent with true religious **belief**, because its gods, who are pictured as quarrelling, lying, and cheating, are far from moral perfection. Based on the observation that polytheism characterizes the religions of early societies, monotheists argue that polytheism is a stage of human religious development that culminates in monotheism.

"Polytheism: more than one god exists." **Sorensen,** *Thought Experiment*

Pomponazzi, Pietro (1462–1525)

Italian Renaissance Aristotelian philosopher, born in Mantua. Pomponazzi distinguished between what we know through natural reason and what we accept through faith, and said that, in view of conflicting arguments about mortality and immortality, we can accept the immortality of the human soul as a matter of faith. He maintained that divine predestination and human free will are compatible and argued that natural causes can explain apparent miracles. His main books are *On the Immortality of the Soul* (1516) and *On Fate, Free Will, and Predestination* (1520).

pons asinorum

LOGIC [Latin, the bridge of asses, because asses were traditionally thought to have difficulty in crossing bridges] This term has several uses. It refers to proofs from Euclid's *Elements* of two theorems: first, if two sides of a triangle are equal, then the angles opposite those sides are also equal; and secondly, the **Pythagorean** theorem, the square of the hypotenuse of a right triangle is equal to the sum of the squares of the other two sides. Those who fail to follow these proofs are considered to be as stupid as asses. In another sense, a *pons asinorum* is a bridge-like diagram proposed by Alexander of Aphrodisias in his commentary on **Aristotle**'s *Prior Analytics*. It was used as a study aid to show how to proceed from premises to a given conclusion.

"In the later Middle Ages this diagram (with accompanying mnemonic verses to distinguish good connexions from bad) was used extensively for the teaching of syllogistim and came to be known as the *pons asinorum*." **Kneale and Kneale,** *The Development of Logic*

Popper, Sir Karl Raimund (1902–94)

Austrian–British philosopher, born in Vienna, knighted in 1965. In philosophy of science, Popper's important books include *The Logic of Scientific Discovery* (1935, 1959), *Conjectures and Refutations* (1963), and *Objective Knowledge* (1972). In contrast to the verifiability criterion of meaning put forward by logical positivists, Popper proposed a criterion of falsifiability to demarcate empirical science from metaphysics and pseudo-sciences. He held that science advances by proposing daring conjectures and then testing them by seeking falsifying instances, in contrast to the traditional empiricist view that science grows by finding inductive support for hypotheses. In this way, he sought to circumvent the traditional problem of induction and saw science to be provisional rather than dogmatic. His propensity theory of probability understood probability as the propensity or disposition of an individual situation to produce a given result. His epistemology involved the evolution of a world of things objectively known as well as physical things and subjective states. In social and political philosophy, his major books include *The Open Society and Its Enemies*, 2 vols. (1945) and *The Poverty of Historicism* (1957). He defended the ideal of an open society against authoritarianism in Plato, Hegel, and Marx and rejected claims that laws of history lead to inevitable outcomes. He argued that social reform by piecemeal social engineering, which allows the intended and unintended consequences of change to be rationally assessed, is preferable to revolution and utopian planning.

popular art

AESTHETICS Art is often distinguished into serious, higher, or esoteric art and popular art. Popular art has dominated modern mass-media culture and has great social influence. Critics of popular art claim that it is inferior to the higher forms of art and fear that it corrupts higher culture. They allege that popular art lacks creativity in both **form** and **content** and does no more than please its audience. They see it as intellectually shallow and emotionally disruptive and argue that its appreciation requires neither effort nor training, but only passive response. Popular art is alleged to produce spurious gratification rather than real aesthetic satisfaction. In all, these critics see popular art as intrinsically worthless in aesthetic terms. Cultural elitists claim that popular art is a lower taste that reduces the quality of our culture. Perhaps led by aesthetic attention to film, many recent critics and cultural theorists have adopted a more favorable attitude toward popular arts. They have challenged much of the hostile assessment given above and have argued that fastidious higher arts have benefited greatly from the exuberant strength of popular arts. We should at least distinguish among different forms of popular art. Intelligent appreciation might improve them without destroying their character or their legitimate function.

> "The distinction between esoteric and popular arts almost coincides in our civilisation with that between art and entertainment, but need not do so; the former distinction, unlike the latter, does not impute insincerity and the will to manipulate." **Sparshott,** *The Structure of Aesthetics*

pornography
AESTHETICS, ETHICS A genre of fiction, initially associated with brothels, focusing on the representation of obscene – often perverse – sexual activities, with the intention of sexually arousing its readers, mainly men. The term now extends to cover any work in any medium with the same content and intention. Although the boundaries are difficult to draw, hardcore pornography, which depicts cruelty, violence, and explicit arousal can be distinguished from soft-core, which does not. Pornography, as distinct from erotic art, is generally considered to have little redeeming aesthetic interest, for its dominant aim is the gratification of sexual fantasy. Because pornography is thought to be morally harmful and degrading to individuals and society, many consider that

any material found to be pornographic should be restricted or prohibited. Others argue that pornography should be eliminated because it supports in fantasy real and objectionable patterns of **patriarchal** domination in society. Opponents argue that pornography has a positive function of dealing with sexual desire without involving unwelcome sexual advances. The issue of **censorship** of pornography is debated in terms of the **freedom** of thought and the press, on the one hand, and the need to avoid degrading creators and users of pornography, women and society, on the other.

> "If we assume that the majority is correct, and that people who publish and consume pornography do the wrong thing, or at least display the wrong sort of character, should they nevertheless have the legal right to do so?" **Dworkin,** *A Matter of Principle*

Porphyrian tree
ANCIENT GREEK PHILOSOPHY, PHILOSOPHICAL METHOD The Greek **Neoplatonist Porphyry**, the editor of **Plotinus'** *Enneads*, wrote an introduction (Greek *Isagoge*) to **Aristotle's** *Categories*. It was translated into Latin by **Boethius** and became the standard philosophical textbook in the Middle Ages. In his introduction, Porphyry presented the basis of Aristotle's thought as a tree-like scheme of **dichotomous** divisions, which indicates that a species (subgenera) is **defined** by *genus* et *differentia* and that the process continues until the lowest species (**infima species**) is reached. In the category of substance, the tree is:

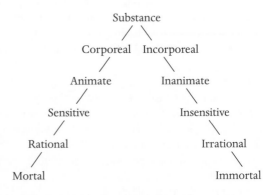

Thus, to define a **human being** (for example, Socrates), we shall say that he is a mortal, rational, sensitive, animate, corporeal substance. The tree is the standard device by which medieval metaphysics classified natural kinds.

> "A Porphyrian Tree begins with an Aristotelian category . . . and moves via a series of dichotomies from the most general genus through at least some of its species." **Kretzmann, *The Metaphysics of Theism***

Porphyry (c.232–c.305)

Neoplatonist philosopher, born in Tyre, the editor of Plotinus' *Enneads*. Porphyry helped to popularize and spread Neoplatonism throughout the Roman Empire. In his commentary on Aristotle's *Categories, Isagoge* (Introduction), he introduced "species" as the fifth predicable and presented the "Tree of Porphyry" as a way of relating genus, species, and individuals. This work was translated into Latin by Boethius and exerted a great influence on medieval logic and discussion of the problem of universals.

Port-Royal Logic

LOGIC In 1662, French theologians and philosophers Antoine **Arnauld** and Pierre Nicole published *La Logique; Ou, l'Art de Penser* (*Logic; Or the Art of Thinking*). Both of them were teachers at Port Royal, a monastery in the southwest of Paris and the intellectual center of **Jansenism**. Hence the book is generally called the *Port-Royal Logic*. The book defines logic as the art of managing one's **reason** in the **knowledge** of things for the instruction of others and one-self. It claims that the **mind** has four principal operations: conceiving, judging, reasoning, and ordering, and the book is divided into four corresponding parts. The *Port-Royal Logic* is established on the basis of Cartesian epistemology and rejects the subtleties of medieval logic. It introduced into logic modern **scientific methods** and contributed to **propositional logic**. The book became the standard logic textbook until the nineteenth century and had a wide impact on the development of modern logic. It is also regarded as the precursor of modern **linguistic analysis**.

> "Port Royal Logic . . . both contains an argument against probabilism and is the first occasion on which 'probability' is actually used in what is identifiably our modern sense, susceptible of numerical measurement." **Hacking, *The Emergence of Probability***

posit

EPISTEMOLOGY, METAPHYSICS The assumption or **hypothesis** that is given as the starting-point of a **theory** or an **explanation**. The question of its **truth** is often left to a later stage of dealing with the theory or explanation, or is not dealt with separately at all. For **Quine**, all the **entities** we use to explain and organize sense experience are posits. Hence, they are everything that we claim to exist aside from sense **experience**, including abstract objects as well as **physical objects**.

> "Everything to which we conclude existence is a posit from the standpoint of a description of the theory-building process and simultaneously real from the standpoint of the theory that is being built." **Quine, *Word and Object***

positive fact, see negative fact

positive freedom, an alternative expression for positive liberty

positive law

PHILOSOPHY OF LAW [from Latin *jus*, law + *positivum*, to lay down, hence laws established by human society and institutions] In contrast to **natural law**, which holds that laws were authored by **God** or are based on **human nature**, positive law relies on the will of legislators and applies only to the members of the **community** for which the legislators legislate. In the philosophy of law, natural law theory claims that the authority of positive law is derived from its compliance with natural law, while **legal positivism** argues that there is no necessary connection between positive law and **morality**. In **Austin**'s **command theory of law**, the conception of positive law is narrowed to the laws laid down by the **sovereign** of a political society or its subordinates.

> "As contradistinguished to natural law, or to the law of nature (meaning, by these expressions, the law of God), the aggregate of the rules, established by political superiors, is frequently styled positive law, or law existing by position." **Austin, *Lectures on Jurisprudence***

positive liberty

ETHICS, POLITICAL PHILOSOPHY Positive liberty or positive freedom is concerned with enabling one to be the self-determining master of one's own life and action. With positive liberty, one is **autonomous** and can freely exercise one's own **will**. On this view, one's life and decisions do not depend on external forces, but are limited solely by one's capabilities, resources, and opportunities. According to Isaiah **Berlin**, positive liberty contrasts with **negative liberty**, which is **freedom** from external interference. Unlike negative liberty, positive liberty has a specific content, so that a person is not deemed to be free unless living according to that content. Berlin argued that such a notion of positive liberty carried with it the danger of despotism and he preferred the more open political systems incorporating negative liberty.

"The positive sense of the word 'liberty' derives from the wish on the part of the individual to be his own master." **Berlin,** *Four Essays on Liberty*

positivism

PHILOSOPHY OF SCIENCE, EPISTEMOLOGY, PHILOSOPHY OF SOCIAL SCIENCE, PHILOSOPHY OF RELIGION A philosophical tradition founded by the French philosopher Auguste **Comte**, although its ancestry may be traced to Francis **Bacon**. The general spirit of positivism is that philosophy should only be concerned with what is positively **given** (this is also the meaning of the word "positive") and should avoid any **speculative** thinking that goes beyond given **experience**. Accordingly, positivism takes the study of **scientific** methodology as its major task and presents itself as a kind of **philosophy of science**. Comte's positivism has a famous Law of the Three Stages, which claims that the human **mind** has developed historically through stages. An initial theological stage was characterized by attempts to explain the inner **nature** of things in terms of supernatural beings. In a subsequent metaphysical stage, earlier deities were depersonalized and became explanatory abstractions such as **essence** or **force**. Finally, in the positivist stage, the human mind realizes that all genuine **knowledge** is based on sense **experience** and can only be advanced by means of observation and therefore understands that **metaphysics** should be abandoned. Comte also initiated a positive sociology, which studied human **societies** in terms of positive methods, and a positive religion, which sought to replace the worship of **God** with

the worship of Humanity. Herbert **Spencer** linked positivism with the theory of **evolution** to make the study of the all-embracing evolutionary process the major task of philosophy. The descendants of positivism include the **empirio-criticism** of **Mach** and Avenarius, which held that science describes sense-experience and has no need to postulate any hidden entities such as the atom; the **logical positivism** of the **Vienna Circle**, which developed the principle of verification, incorporated the new logical developments of **Frege**, **Russell**, and **Wittgenstein**, and held an extremely hostile attitude to metaphysics; and **legal positivism**, which emphasizes that law should be as it is (**positive law**) rather than as we might believe it should be (**natural law**).

"Apart from Kantianism, there is no contemporary philosophical movement so closely associated with exact science as positivism." **Schlick,** *Philosophical Papers*

possibilism, see actualism

possible world

LOGIC, PHILOSOPHY OF LANGUAGE, METAPHYSICS Although philosophers had been talking about what is possible long before, the origin of a possible world discourse is generally credited to **Leibniz**, who claimed that although our world contains much that is **evil**, it is nonetheless the best of all possible worlds. In contemporary philosophy, discussion of possible worlds developed into a **semantic** interpretation for **modal logic** and a proposal to solve the **truth-value** problem of counterfactual conditionals. The idea is to construe a counterfactual as stating some possible **states of affairs** in which things are other than the way they actually are. There are two views about how to understand possible worlds. One is the extreme possibilism held by David **Lewis**, which claims that the actual world we inhabit is only one of many real worlds, each of which exemplifies ways that things could have been besides the ways that they are. Such an objective interpretation gives rise to the problem of **transworld identity**, which in turn motivated Lewis to develop his **counterpart theory**. The other account of possible worlds, represented by **Kripke**, is in terms of one or more **intensional** items such as **properties**, **propositions**, or states of affairs and of some modal notions such as instantiability or possible truth. On this view, a possible world is a world whose properties are not actually instantiated or a world that has obtainable but not actually obtaining states of affairs. According to this latter interpretation, a possible world is not another world, but is given by the **descriptive** conditions we associate with it. In order to distinguish this account from Lewis's account, Kripke sometimes suggests that we use terms such as a possible state or history of the world or a counterfactual situation to replace the notion of a possible world. There is much debate about the theory of possible worlds, regarding problems such as **essentialism**, possible but non-actual **entities**, transworld identity, **reference** and **meaning**. Currently, modal concepts are often interpreted in terms of possible worlds. "Necessarily p" is equivalent to "P is true in every possible world," and "Possibly p" is equivalent to "P is true in some possible world."

> "Possible worlds are total 'ways the world might have been', or states or histories of the entire world." **Kripke, *Naming and Necessity***

post-historical art, see death of art

post hoc ergo propter hoc, see fallacy of false cause

postmodernism

AESTHETICS, MODERN EUROPEAN PHILOSOPHY A fashionable but elusive term used originally among New York artists and critics in the 1960s to reject any dominant framework dictating artistic style. Postmodernism in art was a reaction to modernism, which has provided such a framework throughout the twentieth century. Modernism emphasizes **experimentation**, an inner **truth** behind surface **appearances**, and the presence of **paradoxical ambiguities** and uncertainties in our life experience. In art and literature, postmodernism seeks to cancel the boundary between art and daily life and the distinction between elite and popular taste. It emphasizes surface instead of depth and stylistic **form** rather than **content**.

In the 1970s, postmodernism was taken up by some influential continental philosophers. Modernity is normally taken to have begun with the work of **Descartes** in the seventeenth century and

has shaped the issues, problems, and standards of relevance that have occupied Western philosophers since then. If Descartes is seen as the father of modernism, then postmodernism comprises a variety of cultural positions that reject major features of Cartesian (or allegedly Cartesian) modern thought. A major characteristic of Cartesian modernism is to insist on the supremacy of pure rationality. The pursuit of knowledge should be independent of practical concerns, traditional beliefs, and any social, political, and economic interests of those seeking knowledge. Views that stress the priority of the **social** to the **individual**; that reject the universalizing tendencies of philosophy; that prize irony over knowledge; and that give the irrational and the rational equal claims to roles in our procedures for acquiring knowledge all fall under the postmodernist umbrella. Postmodernism tries to replace **logic** with **narrative** because it disputes the claim that meaning can be determined by logical and **semantic analysis**. It denies univocality and linearity and rejects any theoretical grounds for culture.

The major exponents of postmodernism include Jacques **Derrida**, Richard **Rorty**, Jean-François **Lyotard**, Emmanuel **Levinas**, Michel **Foucault**, Jean Baudrillard, and Gilles **Deleuze**. Postmodernism has also greatly influenced the contemporary **feminist** movement, represented by Julia Kristeva and Luce **Irigaray**. Postmodernist criticism of modernist concerns with **meaning**, **truth**, **objectivity**, **rationality**, and universality has not led a constructive alternative, but not having a constructive alternative is perhaps part of the point of postmodernism.

> "Postmodernism is of great interest to a wide range of people because it directs our attention to changes, the major transformations, taking place in contemporary society and culture." **Sarup,** *An Introductory Guide to Post-structuralism and Post-modernism*

***post res* universals,** see *universalia, ante rem*

post-structuralism

MODERN EUROPEAN PHILOSOPHY The Saussurian model of linguistics is the basis of **structuralism**. Post-structuralism originated with the rejection of that model. While **Saussure** emphasized that each signifier acquires its **semantic** value only by virtue of its differential position within the structure of language, post-structuralists augmented their account of the **relations** among signifiers through, for example, **Nietzschean** concerns with **power** and **Freudian** concerns with **unconscious** origin. They reject the existence of the unity of the stable **sign** and question the possibility of any descriptive and **analytical** language. They do not believe that authors are the authority for the **meaning** and **truth** of what they write, but claim instead that reading is an active performance creating **interpretations** rather than a passive consumption of a product. Post-structuralism rejects a static notion of meaning and is hostile to any system or attempt at system-construction. A truth-claim for what we say or write is not a matter of course, and meaning is not tightly bound up with truth. **Thought** is constituted through and through by the codes, **conventions**, **language-games**, and **discourses** that make up a given cultural order. In a sense, post-structuralism seeks to subvert the traditional understanding of the structures of language. The movement is influenced by Nietzsche, and its major representatives include Gilles **Deleuze**, Felix Guattari, Jean-François **Lyotard**, Michel **Foucault**, and Jacques **Derrida**. Post-structuralism shares many common features with postmodernism.

> "While structuralism sees truth as being 'behind' or 'within' a text, post-structuralism stresses the interaction of reader and text as a productivity." **Sarup, *An Introductory Guide to Post-Structuralism and Post-modernism***

postulates of empirical knowledge

EPISTEMOLOGY, METAPHYSICS For each of his four groups of **categories**, **Kant** introduced **principles** to show the objective validity of the employment of categories of that kind. For the categories of quantity, **quality**, and **relation**, the principles are respectively the axioms of intuition, **anticipations of perception**, and **analogies of experience**. For the categories of **modality**, the principles are the postulates of empirical knowledge. While the other principles determine the ways in which **appearances** are related to each other, the postulates determine the modes in which the subject of experience is related to its experiences. The postulates include the principle of the **possible**, which requires that the

concepts of things should agree with the formal conditions of experience; the principle of the actual, which requires that the concept is connected to the material conditions of experience; and the principle of the **necessary**, which requires that the actual experience conforms to both the formal and material conditions of experience. These principles are called postulates, not in the mathematical sense of being immediately certain without justification, but in the sense that they are procedural specifications of **relations** between the **understanding** and the synthesis of appearances.

> "The same can be asserted of the postulates of empirical thought in general, which concern the synthesis of mere intuition (that is, of the form of appearance), of perception (that is, of the matter of perception), and of experience (that is, of the relation of these perceptions)." **Kant, *Critique of Pure Reason***

potentiality

METAPHYSICS, ANCIENT GREEK PHILOSOPHY [Greek *dunamis*, the power or capacity of one subject to effect change in another subject or the power or capacity of one subject to be affected by another thing] We can distinguish non-rational capacities (the capacity of eyes to see) from rational capacities (the capacity of a person to build). The realization of these capacities is their exercise. For **Aristotle**, however, this sense is not important philosophically. Potentiality was important for him through connection with substantial **change**, in which potentiality is associated with **matter**. In this sense, potentiality was the possible but unrealized state of a thing. See also the entry on **potentiality/actuality**.

> "For in the course of our analysis it will also become clear, with regard to potentiality, that we not only ascribe potentiality to that whose nature is to move something else, or to be moved by anything else . . . but also use the word in another sense." **Aristotle, *Metaphysics***

potentiality/actuality

METAPHYSICS, ANCIENT GREEK PHILOSOPHY When **Aristotle** moved from a static discussion of the structure of **reality** to a dynamic discussion, he introduced a distinction between potentiality and actuality in association with a distinction between **matter** and **form**. He even used these two distinctions interchangeably. Aristotle divided relationships between actuality and potentiality into two major kinds. The first kind likened the relationship to that between **motion** and **power**. It conformed to the etymological senses of potentiality and actuality and concerned **relations** such as that between the capacity to build and the exercise of that capacity. The second kind likened the relationship to that between generated **substance** and matter. With regard to Aristotle's discussion of substance, it can also be divided into two types. In the first type, matter (potentiality) develops into some form (actuality) to generate a thing, with potentiality and actuality thus belonging to two different stages. In the second type, form (actuality) and proximate matter (potentiality) in a sense exist together as two aspects of the same thing. In various ways, Aristotle held that actuality is prior to potentiality. In Aristotle's **theology**, **God**, having an eternal **nature**, is pure actuality, without involving any potentiality.

"To all such potentialities, then actuality is prior both in formula and in substantiality; and in time it is prior in one sense, and in another not." **Aristotle,** *Metaphysics*

pour-soi/en-soi, see being-for-itself

power
POLITICAL PHILOSOPHY, PHILOSOPHY OF SOCIAL SCIENCE
The ability or capacity to compel others to act according to one's aims so that they will do what they would not otherwise have done. Power can also affect how such **actions** are performed. Political power is the ability to get people to obey explicit or tacit commands in virtue of what they anticipate to be the consequences of obeying or disobeying them. The consequences can range from crude threats and promises to subtle patterns of social control. Political power is not only power to do something, but is also power over others through coercion, domination, or **hegemony**. Understanding the relationship between political power and political **authority** is central to understanding the relationship between political science and political philosophy. Unlike authority, power does not involve **rights**, but it is related both to responsibility

and force. Relations of political power may be shaped by culture, history, or tradition as well as by brute force.

"Power is the probability that one actor in a social relationship will be in a position to carry out his own will despite resistance, regardless of the basis on which this probability rests." **Weber,** *The Theory of Social and Economic Organisation*

P-predicate
METAPHYSICS, PHILOSOPHY OF LANGUAGE, PHILOSOPHY OF MIND **Strawson**'s term for any **predicate** ascribed to **persons** and only persons. To apply a P-predicate to something at least implies the possession of **consciousness** by that individual. Examples of this kind of predicate include "is smiling," "is in pain," "believes that you will meet on Tuesday." Philosophical problems arise concerning the possibility of delimiting the class of P-predicates and concerning the closely related possibility of formulating the concept of a person. The logical criteria for the ascription of P-predicates to others closely involves the question of **personal identity**. P-predicates are contrasted to M-predicates, which can be ascribed to material **bodies** without consciousness as well as to persons.

"The second kind consists of all the other predicates we apply to persons. These I shall call P-predicates." **Strawson,** *Individuals*

practical ethics, see applied ethics

practical law, see maxim, categorical imperative

practical reason (Kant)
ETHICS, PHILOSOPHY OF MIND, PHILOSOPHY OF ACTION
The practical application of **reason**, which concerns what one **ought** to do, in contrast to the theoretical application of reason (theoretical or speculative reason), which concerns what is. Although Kant held that theoretical and practical reason are fundamentally the same, he recognized their different functions and claimed that practical reason has primacy over theoretical reason, in line with the primacy of our being rational **agents** over our being rational knowers. While theoretical reason is limited by the bounds of **experience**, practical reason is inseparable

from **freedom**. Kant identified practical reason with the **will**, which initiates action. Like theoretical reason, practical reason determines and applies its own **principles**, but in the case of practical reason the application of its principles commands **action**. Its supreme principle is the **categorical imperative**. Hence it is the home of the **moral law** and is the fundamental basis of our **autonomy**. In Kant's critical philosophy, three works, *The Groundwork for the Metaphysics of Morals*, *The Critique of Practical Reason*, and *The Metaphysics of Morals* examine the operation of practical reason.

> "Pure practical reason is a capacity for ends generally." **Kant,** *Metaphysics of Morals*

practical reasoning

PHILOSOPHY OF ACTION, ETHICS, PHILOSOPHY OF SOCIAL SCIENCE A kind of argumentation that is directed toward a certain goal and is based on **knowledge** of an **agent**'s situation and knowledge that a certain sort of action is a means to reach that goal. Its conclusion is an **imperative** to pursue a course of **action** for a particular agent. Its sequence of **inference** is called practical inference because it aims at a practical conclusion. Practical reasoning gives reasons for actions or **desires** and it is essentially pragmatic. In contrast, **theoretical** reasoning aims to derive **truth** from premises and concentrates on the formal **validity** of arguments. Practical reasoning was first discussed in **Aristotle**'s theory of **practical wisdom**, where the action itself was seen as the conclusion. In the twentieth century, practical reasoning became a special field of philosophical inquiry, partly due to the works of **Anscombe** and **von Wright**. It is characterized as a form of argument appropriate to the humanities, rather than as merely a vehicle of means–end **deliberation**. Although there is much debate about the elements, scope, and procedure of practical reasoning, it is widely agreed that it is significant for explaining human action, establishing ranking and priority in one's life plan, understanding personal **responsibility** for action, and evaluating the actions of others. Some theorists have employed a wider notion of practical reasoning to extend rational choice theory in seeking to understand institutions as well as individual behavior. **Moral** reasoning is one of the main forms of practical reasoning.

> "What then, is practical reasoning? It is the transition (not necessarily conscious) from belief in the premises to acceptance of the putative conclusions of a practical inference." **Raz (ed.),** *Practical Reason*

practical syllogism

ANCIENT GREEK PHILOSOPHY, ETHICS, PHILOSOPHY OF ACTION **Aristotle**'s concept, although he instead used the term *sullogismos ton prakton* (syllogism about action). An inference of **practical reason** starting from a universal ethical premise and concluding with an **action**. It has a major premise, such as "since the end is such and such," and a minor premise, such as "this is such and such," and a conclusion. In contrast to modern thinking, Aristotle insisted that the conclusion is not an **imperative** to do something, but the action itself. According to him, if a man gets an order but does not proceed to act, it is not a practical reason. Of the two premises, one provides the **good end**, and the other gives a possible way to achieve the end. Aristotle offers many examples in his writings, but he does not formalize this reasoning. There is much controversy whether such a formalization is possible.

> "For the syllogism about actions have an origin, viz. 'since the end, i.e. what is best, is of such and such a nature', whatever it may be." **Aristotle,** *Nicomachean Ethics*

practical wisdom

ANCIENT GREEK PHILOSOPHY, ETHICS, PHILOSOPHY OF ACTION [Greek *phronesis*, thought or understanding, also translated as intelligence, practical reason or prudence] **Aristotle**'s technical term for the reasoning that leads to practical activity. In contrast, contemplation, or theoretical wisdom, is concerned with invariable things, although both theoretical and practical wisdom are **intellectual virtues**. Like theoretical wisdom, practical wisdom operates at a general level, concerned with the **truth** of practical judgment and formulating general **rules** of **action**. But practical wisdom also works at a particular level, applying general rules to concrete situations of life and finding the **right** actions to do. It contains a practical **intuition**, which grasps the features of the particular action, and a **practical syllogism**, which infers ways and means of achieving the end.

Practical wisdom is inseparable from the **virtues** of character, for the latter decides the right **end**. Without a right end, a man can only be said to have cleverness rather than practical wisdom. A person of practical wisdom is a *phronimos*.

Aristotle's theory of practical wisdom is ambiguous and unsystematic. It was criticized by **Hume**, who claimed that **emotion** rather than **reason** determines action. It has nevertheless attracted much attention in contemporary moral theory, especially in **virtue ethics**. If there really is a kind of reason peculiar to moral actions, it may give a new foundation to ethics and solve many traditional difficulties, such as the tension between **objectivity** and the practical application of **moral judgment**.

> "[P]ractical wisdom is a state grasping the truth, involving reason, concerned with action about what is good or bad for human beings." **Aristotle,** *Nicomachean Ethics*

practicalism, another expression for experimentalism

pragmatic maxim, see pragmaticism

pragmatic theory of truth

LOGIC, EPISTEMOLOGY, PHILOSOPHY OF LANGUAGE A theory of truth held in different forms by the American **pragmatists Peirce**, **James**, and **Dewey**. Their common ground was the claim that truth should be approached by enquiring about the difference made by a **belief** being true, namely to examine the idea of truth at work in its context of use. But their views are somewhat different. Peirce held that truth is the eventual consensus of those who use **scientific method** and go on long enough in their exploration. James believed that true beliefs are those that are **confirmed** or **verified** by **experience** in the long run. For Dewey, truth is a property attaching to ideas that we are warranted in asserting. He preferred the term **warranted assertibility** to truth.

In addition to his attempt to connect **utility** with verifiability, according to which truth is useful belief in the sense that it is belief that is secure in the long run, James held that truth is that which is **good**, useful, or expedient to believe. Truth is the expedient in our way of thinking just as the right is the expedient in our way of behaving. This account of truth connects truth with utility and was bitterly criticized by **Moore**, **Russell**, and **Carnap** on the grounds that false ideas can have utility and still be false and that we should seek truth for itself rather than for its consequences. This later version of James's theory is generally taken to be the standard pragmatic theory of truth, although the accounts of Peirce and Dewey might prove more fruitful.

> "It is the cardinal feature of pragmatic theories of truth that true propositions are characterised as those that we accept." **Ayer,** *The Concept of a Person*

pragmaticism

LOGIC, PHILOSOPHY OF LANGUAGE, EPISTEMOLOGY, PHILOSOPHY OF SCIENCE Although **Peirce** introduced the word **pragmatism**, he later invented the term pragmaticism for his own version of pragmatism, in order to distance himself from other versions, in particular from the anti-intellectualism he saw in **James**'s more popular pragmatism. Pragmaticism was originally a method of logic based on Peirce's pragmatic maxim: "Consider what effects, that might conceivably have practical bearings, we conceive the **object** of our conception to have. Our conception of these effects is the whole of our conception of the object." This is a **criterion** of the clarity of **meaning** that connects the meaning of general terms with expectations of consequences. To attain a clear meaning of an abstract formula, we need only consider what conceivable practical effects it may involve. The conception of these effects is for us the whole positive significance of that formula. Peirce then tried to use this criterion to clarify traditional problems of philosophy and to dismiss traditional **metaphysical** problems, although he developed his own robust metaphysical doctrines. Peirce emphasized that pragmaticism is a theory of logic rather than a speculative philosophy.

> "So then, the writer, finding his bantling 'pragmatism' so promoted, feels that it is time to kiss his child good-by and relinquish it to its higher destiny; while to serve the precise purpose of expressing the original definition, he begs to announce the birth of the word 'pragmaticism', which is ugly enough to be safe from kidnappers." **Peirce,** *Collected Papers,* **vol. V**

pragmatics

PHILOSOPHY OF LANGUAGE [from Greek *pragma*, action] The analysis of the relations between **signs** or languages and their users. It is a branch of **semiotics**, the other two branches being syntactics or **syntax**, which deals with **grammar**, and **semantics**, which deals with **reference** and **truth**. General pragmatics is concerned with the general principles of utterance, and applied pragmatics is concerned with special kinds of linguistic interaction. Pragmatics focuses on the context of the actual use of language by speakers such as its purposes, effects, implications, and the relations between speakers and listeners. Many philosophers are concerned with its relations to semantics. Pragmatics classifies a wide variety of interesting types of **speech acts**, and studies the use and implications of indexical **expressions**, such as I, you, this, here, and now. Pragmatics is an important aspect of contemporary philosophy of language.

"Pragmatics is the study of linguistic acts and the contexts in which they are performed." **Stalnaker, "Pragmatics," in Davidson and Harman (eds.), *Semantics of Natural Language***

pragmatism

LOGIC, PHILOSOPHY OF LANGUAGE, EPISTEMOLOGY, PHILOSOPHY OF SCIENCE [from Greek *pragma*, things done, action] When **Peirce** introduced this term in his article "How to Make Our Ideas Clear" (1878), he called it his pragmatic maxim, a **criterion** of **meaning** according to which the meaning of a **theory** is equivalent to the practical effects of adopting it. The term was borrowed by William **James**, who extended pragmatism from a criterion of meaning to a theory of **truth**, such that an idea is respectable or true if the results of accepting it are **good** or satisfactory. This theory was further developed by John **Dewey** and F. C. S. **Schiller**. **Russell** and **Moore** accused James of confusing the theory of truth with the theory of **utility**. Pragmatism claims that **knowledge** must relate to practical human purposes and to our adaptation to our environment. Intellectual **beliefs** should be justified in terms of their social, moral, and biological utilities. Truth and theory are tools or instruments, and they are not for solving abstract enigmas. Any idea that proves to have a value for concrete life is true. Pragmatism rejects **abstraction**

and absolute **principles** and turns toward **concreteness**, **facts**, and **action**. This philosophy tries to assimilate modern science, especially the theory of **evolution** and new statistical modes of reasoning, within a **fallibilist** philosophy and criticizes traditional **metaphysical** speculations. This theory also became an attitude toward life and a movement emphasizing actions and practices. But Peirce himself disliked the anti-intellectual tone of this later development and introduced the word **pragmaticism** for his own version of pragmatism. Pragmatism has been regarded as a typically American approach to philosophy and has exerted great influence upon contemporary American philosophers such as **Quine**, **Putnam**, and **Rorty**.

"Pragmatism represents a perfectly familiar attitude in philosophy, the empiricist attitude, but it represents it, as it seems to me, both in a more radical and in a less objectionable form than it has ever yet assumed." **W. James, *Pragmatism***

praxis, Greek term for action

preconceived opinions

EPISTEMOLOGY [Latin *praejudicia*, prejudices] **Descartes** adopted this term for the **beliefs** that everyone forms in childhood. These beliefs are derived from a reliance on tradition and **authority** and are also generated from the mere use of **senses** without consulting the **light of reason**. These opinions are always so deeply rooted in one's **mind** that they are generally regarded as implanted by **nature** and are accepted as utterly true and **evident**. According to Descartes, these preconceived opinions are the chief source of **error** and when we begin to philosophize seriously, the first step should be to **doubt** the **certainty** of these preconceived opinions and replace them with ideas which are consistent with the standards of **reason**.

"We must first of all lay aside all our preconceived opinions, or at least we must take the greatest care not to put our trust in any of the opinions accepted by us in the past until we have first scrutinised them afresh and confirmed their truth." **Descartes, *Principles of Philosophy***

preconception

ANCIENT GREEK PHILOSOPHY, EPISTEMOLOGY [Greek *prolepseis*, also translated as anticipation] A term in the epistemology of **Epicurus** and Stoicism, a general **concept** or mental picture generated by repeated similar **impressions** and **experience**. Preconceptions record and classify our experience of the world and are foundations of **judgments**. For example, when we hear "table," we anticipate the kind of thing to which this term **refers**. Preconceptions are also viewed as the criteria of true **perceptual statements**. They can be combined together as a basis for **inference**, and can be used to form new concepts of things not encountered in experience.

> "Preconception, they say, is as it were a perception, or correct opinion or conception, or universal 'stored notion' (i.e. memory) of that which has frequently become evident externally."
> **Diogenes Laertius**, *Lives of Eminent Philosophers*

preconscious

PHILOSOPHY OF MIND **Freud**'s term for the latent elements of mind waiting to be discovered. These elements, though not in **consciousness**, can be brought to consciousness by ordinary introspective methods. Freud distinguishes explicitly between the **unconsciousness** and the preconscious. The unconscious is **repressed** and cannot become conscious in an ordinary way. Furthermore, the unconscious is dynamic in that it is active in the determination of **behavior**. The preconscious does not have this function.

> "The latent, which is unconscious only descriptively, not in the dynamic sense, we call 'preconscious'." **Freud**, *Standard Edition of the Complete Psychological Works of Sigmund Freud*, vol. 9

predestination

PHILOSOPHY OF RELIGION, METAPHYSICS, LOGIC [from Latin *praedestinare*, a synonym of predetermination] A theological doctrine that means that all events in someone's life, no matter whether they have happened, are happening, or will happen, have been determined to happen in advance by **God**. Whether a **person**'s soul will go to heaven or hell has also been decreed by the sovereign **will** of God when

that person was born, no matter how the person behaves in life. According to the doctrine of predestination, God not only has **foreknowledge** of all that will happen, but also has foreordained that it will happen. This claim arises from the view that God is the **cause** of everything and is also associated with the view that human beings can be saved only by God's **grace**. The position had scriptural support in Romans 8 and 9 and Ephesians 1 and was held by **Augustine** and **Calvin**, among others. The notion of predestination or predetermination provides the basis for **fatalism**.

Problems arise for the notion of predestination. If God plans everything and we do not have **free will**, then God seems to be **responsible** for our **evil** deeds. But this can not be true if God is perfectly **good**. It is difficult to understand the relation between God's foreknowing and God's foreordaining. In this domain, his **omniscience** and **omnipotence** seem hard to distinguish.

In logic, the **law of excluded middle** has been thought by **Lukasiewicz** and others to force us into logical predestination when applied to **statements** about the **future**. On this view, the truth or falsity of such statements has always been fixed independent of any questions concerning divine knowledge or power. This thought provided a major motive for giving up the law of excluded middle and for developing **many-valued logic** in contemporary non-classical logic, but others – including many who admire the achievements of many-valued logic – attempt to overcome logical predestination within classical logic.

> "If it is held that everything that happens . . . is planned in every detail, then I do not see how it can be denied that if the responsibility for what we do can be assigned to anyone at all, it must ultimately fall upon the planner rather than ourselves . . . For someone who takes this view, the doctrine of predestination does seem irresistible."
> **Ayer**, *The Concept of a Person and Other Essays*

predetermination, another term for predestination

predicables

LOGIC, METAPHYSICS The different relations in which a **predicate** might stand to a subject in a **proposition**. In the *Topics*, **Aristotle** distinguished various predicables: (1) **definition**, in which the predicate states the **essence** of the subject; (2) **property**, in which the predicate expresses something which is not a constitutive part of the essence, but is inseparably bound up with the subject, for example, as 'is capable of learning' is bound up with man; (3) **genus**, in which the predicate defines the subject together with a **differentia**; (4) **accident**, in which the predicate expresses a feature that is neither a constitutive part of the essence nor inseparably bound up with the subject. In the first two of these predicables, the subject and predicate are **convertible** (we can argue from "X is Y" to "Y is X"), but the latter two are not convertible. According to Aristotle, all problems can be brought under one or other of the predicables, so these predicables are the framework for his whole treatment of the *topoi* (commonplaces). The medieval logician **Porphyry** added species as a fifth kind of predicable. Because species is a subject rather than a predicate for Aristotle, Porphyry's classification produced much confusion.

In addition to this historical sense of predicable, there is an additional sense introduced by the contemporary British philosopher Peter **Geach**. He noticed that in modern logic the term predicate might refer both to a role that a particular word or phrase is playing in a particular proposition and to a syntactical category to which expressions belong in virtue of their ability to play this role. To avoid this ambiguity, he uses predicable for membership of the syntactical category and reserves predicate for the actual performance of the predicative role.

"I use 'predicables' as a term for the verbal expressions called 'predicates' by other logicians; I reserve the term 'predicate' for a predicable actually being used as the main function in a given proposition." **Geach, *Logic Matters***

predicament, the medieval scholastic equivalent of an Aristotelian category

predicate

LOGIC, PHILOSOPHY OF LANGUAGE [from Latin *pare*, in front + *dicere*, to say, literally that which is said in front of] A basic **sentence** expresses a **proposition** that some **object** has a certain **attribute** ("The dog is running" or "This flower is red") or that there is

certain **relation** between two or more objects ("The horse is larger than the sheep"). The expressions standing for an object (for example "the dog," "this flower," or "the horse" and "the sheep") are called subjects, and the expressions standing for an attribute (for example "is running," "is red") or relation (for example "is larger than") are **predicates**. A predicate is what is said of a subject in a sentence. A predicate can be a verb, adjective phrase, or noun phrase. Predicates are also called predicate expressions or predicate terms. If a given sentence has one subject, its predicate is a one-place predicate; if there are two subjects, its predicate is a two-place predicate, and so on. One-place predicates are connected with intransitive verbs, and two-place predicates are connected with transitive verbs or relations. There is also a distinction between logical (first-order) and grammatical (second-order) predicates. A logical or first-order predicate applies to some object, and a grammatical or second-order predicate is predicated of a first-order predicate. According to this distinction, words such as "exist" are grammatical predicates rather than logical predicates.

"The subject is that term about which affirmation or denial is made. The predicate is that term which is affirmed or denied of the subject." **Keynes, *Studies and Exercises in Formal Logic***

predicate logic, another name for predicative calculus

predicate nominalism

PHILOSOPHY OF LANGUAGE, METAPHYSICS A term introduced by the Australian philosopher David **Armstrong** for the theory that what **universals** there are is simply a matter of what **predicates** there are. In other words, universals are parasitic upon predicate expressions. Although a predicate-like "tree" can apply in principle to more than one object, we need not posit some common **property** by which a common predicate or general term applies to objects. On the contrary, the applicability of a common predicate needs no further explanation and determines the existence of a universal. **Strawson**'s characterization of universals in *Individuals* is sometimes said to express this theory. Predicate nominalism is one attempt to solve the fundamental difficulty of **nominalism**, namely, if only **particulars** exist, how can we bring numerically different particulars under the same general terms? The difficulty for predicate nominalism is that it does not explain how predicates can determine properties or universals.

"According to Predicate Nominalism, an object's possession of (say) the property, being white, is completely determined by the fact that the predicate 'white' applies to this object." **D. Armstrong,** *Universals and Scientific Realism,* **vol. 1:** *Nominalism and Realism*

predicate term, another name for predicate

predication

LOGIC, PHILOSOPHY OF LANGUAGE The attribution of a **predicate** to a subject, or the combination between them. Predication expresses the **relation** between a **thing** and its **attributes**, which is the basic combination in logical thinking. Much of logic depends on understanding the different logical roles of subject and predicate. Predication can be symbolized as Fa (a is F) or Rab (a has relation R with b). **Frege** held that predicates are unsaturated, that is, they contain logical holes that can be filled by subject terms or be held open by **variables**. If a predication contains a one-place predicate, it is a one-place predication. If it contains a two-place predicate, it is a two-place predication, and so on. Frege suggested that we distinguish predication from **assertion**, for assertion involves an assent to the **truth** or falsity of the **sentence**. While every assertion must be expressed by a predication, not every predication is necessarily an assertion.

"Predication: in logic, the joining of a predicate to a subject of a proposition so as to increase the logical breadth without dismissing the logical depth." **Peirce,** *Collected Papers,* **vol. II**

predication, metaphysical

METAPHYSICS A kind of predication related to **Aristotle**'s theory of **matter** and **form**, particularly his view that form is predicated of matter, also called form predication. Metaphysical or form predication differs from linguistic predication, which picks out a logical subject and states what that subject is or has. In metaphysical predication, such as "these bones and flesh are Socrates," **matter** as subject is not a

logical subject, but indicates the kind of material stuff (bones and flesh) from which the predicate (Socrates) is **constituted** or generated by substantial **change**.

"Let's say that a predicate (a linguistic term) is linguistically predicated of its subject, but that a predicable (a metaphysical term) is metaphysically predicated of its subject." **F. Lewis,** *Substance and Prediction in Aristotle*

predicative adjective, see attributive adjective

predicative calculus

LOGIC Also called the logic of terms, predicate logic, or the calculus of predicates. A logic that analyzes subject-predicate sentences, including sentences involving "not" and the **quantifiers** "all" and "some." It deals with the inner structure of **propositions**, and the **arguments** whose **validity** depends on the arrangement of the terms within the premises and conclusion. Predicative calculus is thus distinguished from **propositional calculus**, which is concerned with propositional structures and has propositions as its units. Predicative calculus is sometimes characterized as the logic of terms, while propositional logic is the logic of propositions. Predicative logic introduces "x, y, z" as **variables** ranging over individual **objects** and "F, G, H" as signs for predicates. At its core is quantification theory, which was developed by **Frege** to analyze the logical **properties** of **quantifiers**. First-order predicate logic, which is elementary logic and a modern replacement of Aristotelian **syllogism**, deals only with individual variables and their quantifications, while second-order or other higher-order predicate logic is also concerned with predicates and other predicate variables.

"The laws of the predicative calculus are of two kinds; 1. those that are peculiar to itself (that is to the logic of terms) and 2. those that are analogous or specifications of the laws of the propositional calculus. The propositional calculus and the predicative calculus belong to one system." **D. Mitchell,** *An Introduction to Logic*

prediction

EPISTEMOLOGY, PHILOSOPHY OF SCIENCE To forecast that something will happen in advance of its actual happening. This capacity is essential for the human species to survive and is also a central feature of human intelligence. Predicting and controlling the future is a major reason that we pursue **knowledge**. The problem of how to predict rationally has been of central interest in epistemology and the philosophy of science. Predictability is the main measure by which we may test the efficiency of a scientific theory. The notion of prediction has been associated with the discussion of topics such as **free will** and **determinism**, chaos and **chance** and **induction**. Problems concerning the **truth-value** of predictions led to the development of **three-valued logic**.

> "The chain of reasoning which leads from given observational findings to the 'prediction' of new ones actually involves, besides deductive inferences, certain quasi-inductive steps each of which consists in the acceptance of an intermediate statement on the basis of confirming, but usually not logically conclusive, evidence." **Hempel,** *Aspects of Scientific Explanation*

prediction paradox, another term for surprise examination paradox

pre-established harmony

METAPHYSICS, PHILOSOPHY OF MIND **Leibniz**'s proposed solution to the Cartesian **mind–body problem**. The world, including minds and bodies, is ultimately composed of independent **substances** or **monads**. Each monad is isolated and self-enclosed, and develops in accordance with its own internal **nature**. There is no **interaction** between finite minds and bodies. No state of a substance has as a real **cause** some state of another substance, for a substance that is properly so called, must have a kind of self-sufficiency that is incompatible with causal dependence. Yet **God**, in creating the universe, has pre-established a perfect non-causal harmony of activity among all possible monads. Each monad is like a mirror that reflects the whole universe. A change in one will correspond to a change in all others. This harmony is analogous to the non-causal harmony of activity existing between two clocks whose ticking is synchronized perfectly. The doctrine of pre-established harmony is at the center of Leibniz's metaphysics. It is, in a sense, an incorporation of **occasionalism** and the view that each substance has its own internal activity.

> "There remains only my hypothesis, that is the way of pre-established harmony, through a prior divine artifice, which has formed each of these substances from the beginning in such a way that by following only its own laws, laws which it received with its being, it nevertheless agrees with the other, as if there were a mutual influence, or as if God always meddled with it, over and above his general concourse." **Leibniz,** *Philosophical Essays*

preface paradox

LOGIC, EPISTEMOLOGY An author, based on the experience that all her previous works contain some mistakes, reasonably acknowledges in the preface of her new book that it also contains mistakes, in spite of her best efforts. This acknowledgment creates a contradiction. On the one hand, she holds that propositions P1, P2, P3, . . . Pn (which are the views she argues for in this book) are true; on the other hand, she also believes that at least one of them is **false**. This amounts to saying that at one and the same time she believes that all these propositions are true and believes that some of them are false. This reveals an imperfection in what we take ourselves to know.

> "We occupy the posture of the so-called 'preface paradox' – standing in the shoes of the author who apologises in his preface for those errors that have doubtless made their way into his work, and yet blithely remains committed to all those assertions in the body of the work itself." **Rescher,** *Empirical Inquiry*

prejudice

EPISTEMOLOGY, MODERN EUROPEAN PHILOSOPHY Prejudice is a target of Cartesian **doubt** and other rationally based philosophy because it is thought to obstruct **reason** and philosophy in the pursuit of **truth**. Prejudice is rehabilitated in **Gadamer**'s **hermeneutics**, where it is viewed as an essential element in our **understanding**, on the basis of **Heidegger**'s notion of a fore-structure of **understanding**. All understanding involves the projection of **meanings** arising out of one's own situation and obtained from a certain **perspective**. Because this fore-structure of understanding is prejudice, understanding is inevitably rooted in prejudice. There is no neutral point of view from which we may get the "real" meaning of a text. According to Gadamer, this does not mean that understanding and **interpretation** are purely **subjective**. Prejudice is not a matter of subjective opinion, nor is it personal property. Instead, he holds that it is part of **tradition** and is developed within the historical tradition to which we belong. Prejudice is the historically and culturally determined **horizon** and the **effectivity** of history. Furthermore, Gadamer claims that prejudice is not an obstacle or limit to understanding, but by serving as our orientation to meaning, it is the basis for the possibility of understanding.

> "What is necessary is a fundamental rehabilitation of the concept of prejudice and a recognition of the fact that there are legitimate prejudices, if we want to do justice to man's finite, historical mode of being." **Gadamer,** *Truth and Method*

pre-reflective cogito

PHILOSOPHY OF MIND, MODERN EUROPEAN PHILOSOPHY Sartre's term for a crucial kind of human **consciousness**. Our consciousness is always directed upon some **object** of which we are aware. This is the Cartesian or reflective **cogito**. But this consciousness is itself accompanied by a consciousness that we are aware. Sartre called this second-order awareness, which is consciousness directed upon consciousness, pre-reflective cogito. This consciousness, which always passes without being reflected upon, makes **reflection** possible. The pre-reflective cogito is the condition of the reflective cogito. On Sartre's view of **intentionality**, therefore, consciousness operates on two levels at once. Sartre's account of consciousness led to his rejection of **Freud**'s notion of the **unconscious**. A major task of Sartre's philosophy was to give a descriptive account of the pre-reflective cogito.

> "I believe that I have demonstrated that the first condition of all reflection is a pre-reflective cogito. This cogito, to be sure, does not posit an object; it remains within consciousness. But it is nonetheless homologous with the reflective cogito since it appears as the first necessity for non-reflective consciousness to be seen by itself." **Sartre,** *Being and Nothingness*

prescriptivism

ETHICS A moral theory developed by R. M. **Hare** in *The Languages of Morals* (1952) and *Freedom and*

Reason (1963). According to this theory, the main concern of moral philosophy is to clarify the nature of moral terms and moral statements. Distinct from fact-stating statements that tell us what is the case, ethical statements tell us to do something and are used to guide **choices**. Such statements must have irreducibly prescriptive elements. To express agreement to a prescription or to accept it is to express one's resolve or decision to carry it out. Prescriptivism emphasizes the typically prescriptive use of moral judgments. It also claims that moral prescription is universal, and is directed to everyone at all times. This principle of **universalizability** is the reason that Hare calls his theory "universal prescriptivism." Both prescriptivism and **emotivism** are types of **non-cognitivism**, but they have significant differences. While emotivism emphasizes the emotional impact of a moral judgment, and its influence on the hearer's attitude, prescriptivism thinks that this result is not necessary for the success of prescription. Emotivism, in distinguishing between factual statements and ethical statements, claims that only factual statements are the objects of reasoning. Prescriptivism, on the other hand, claims that one can also reason about moral questions. It thus avoids the charge of **irrationality**.

> "For the sake of a name, let me refer to the type of doctrine which I put forward in *The Language of Morals*, and still hold, as 'universal prescriptivism' – a combination, that is to say, of universalism (the view that moral judgements are universalizable) and prescriptivism (the view that they are, at any rate typically, prescriptive)." **Hare,** *Freedom and Reason*

presence

MODERN EUROPEAN PHILOSOPHY, METAPHYSICS According to **Derrida**, Western metaphysics from **Parmenides** to **Husserl** held the prejudice that the locus of **truth** is in the pure presence of things themselves to **consciousness**. Hence he calls traditional Western metaphysics the metaphysics of presence. Because presence gives priority to the spoken over the written, he also considers Western metaphysics to be a tradition of phonocentrism. "To return to the things themselves" has been a central philosophical slogan of the tradition. For **Plato**, truth lay in the **idea** or *eidos* (**form**) that is present to reason, the soul's sight. Plato thus united the notions of presence and **evidence** with those of **objectivity**, ideality, and the **Good**. He established the **dichotomy** of **sensibility** and **rationality** as an ultimate pair of opposing concepts. Plato authorized philosophy as the philosophy of presence or philosophy of **logos**. Derrida calls reason-centered philosophy **logocentrism**. **Aristotle** set up a notion of temporal presence through a **continuity** of **time** and history. He developed a position of taking the presence of a thing to be its **substance**, **essence**, and **existence**. **Descartes** claimed that the condition of the possibility of **knowledge** and truth is the **clarity and distinctness** of **ideas** immediately present to consciousness. **Hegel** systematically demonstrated the self-presence of the subject. For most people, presence is the province of **certainty**. By denying presence, Derrida seems to deny the importance of actual **experience**. The implications of the complex displacement of presence, speech, and reason require careful assessment.

> "We already have a foreboding that phonocentrism merges with the historical determination of the meaning of being in general as presence, with all the subdeterminations which depend on this general form and which organise within it their system and their historical sequence." **Derrida, *Of Grammatology***

presence-at-hand, see ready-to-hand

pre-Socratics

ANCIENT GREEK PHILOSOPHY A term invented by historians of philosophy to group together the Greek thinkers living between approximately the first half of the sixth century BC and **Socrates'** lifetime. These include mainly the Milesian school (**Thales**, **Anaximander**, and **Anaximenes**), the **Pythagoreans**, the **Eleatic** school (**Parmenides**, **Zeno**, and Milissus), **Empedocles**, **Anaxagoras**, and the atomists (Leucippus and **Democritus**). The name is sometimes misleading because some philosophers in this period were actually contemporaries of Socrates. The unity consists rather in the fact that none of them was influenced by Socrates and **Plato**. They were also called **natural philosophers**, for many of them concentrated on finding principles to explain the world of nature, although this is not true of Parmenides' way of truth or of Zeno.

The pre-Socratics took part in the first period of the history of Western philosophy, which began the tradition of free and rational inquiry. None of these philosophers left us a single complete work, so the study of them relies on the scanty and disconnected fragments preserved in the quotations and discussions of the later philosophers, in particular in **Aristotle**'s works and those of his commentators. There was no separation of science and philosophy in this period, but the road leading to this separation was prepared by them. Many contemporary philosophers admire the intellectual freedom and speculative brilliance of the pre-Socratics and are inspired by their views of man and universe.

> "In saying that the Pre-Socratics were rational men I mean no more than this: that the broad and bold theories which they advanced were presented not as ex cathedra pronouncements for the faithful to believe, and the godless to ignore, but as the conclusions of arguments, as reasoned propositions for reasonable men to contemplate and debate." **Barnes, *The Presocratic Philosophers***

presumption

EPISTEMOLOGY A **statement** that has some grounds to be considered a candidate for **truth**, but whose truth is not yet established. It is provisionally acceptable, but falls short of being conclusively acceptable. A presumption possesses a positive but low-level cognitive status and is the raw material for the production of **knowledge**. A presumption has some similarity to **Epicurus'** notion of *prolepsis*, the anticipation of the application of a term.

> "A presumption is a thesis that is avowedly not known (i.e. known to be true), but having some claim – however tentative or imperfect – to be regarded as a truth." **Rescher, *Methodological Pragmatism***

presupposition

LOGIC In general, what is taken to be true without question as a premise for some conclusion. In this sense, if A presupposes B, B is derivable from A. As a **semantic** notion, presupposition is a relation between two **statements** A and B such that A presupposes B if the truth of B is a **necessary condition** of A of being either true or false. The relation of presupposition differs from the relation of **entailment**, for if A entails B, the truth of B is a necessary condition of the truth of A, rather than a necessary condition of A possessing a truth-value at all. This distinction between presupposition and entailment was employed by **Strawson** in his attack on **Russell**'s theory of **descriptions**. For Russell, the statement "The present king of France is bald" entails "There is a present king of France." But Strawson claimed that the former presupposes the latter, but does not entail it. The notion of presupposition is important in the debate about whether "exists" is a **predicate** and in challenges to the principle of **bivalence** in **three-valued logic**.

> "For if a statement S presupposes a statement S′ in the sense that the truth of S′ is a precondition of the truth-or-falsity of S, then of course there will be a kind of logical absurdity in conjoining S with the denials of S′." **Strawson, *Introduction to Logical Theory***

Price, H(enry) H(abberlay) (1899–1984)

English philosopher of mind, belief, and perception, Professor of Logic at University of Oxford. Price developed a non-phenomenalist account of the place of sense-data in perception and a dispositional account of conceptual thought. His examination of theories of belief in the philosophy of mind is important in its own right and also led to a defense of the rationality of belief in the immortality of the soul and in the existence of God. His works include *Perception* (1932), *Thinking and Experience* (1953), and *Belief* (1969).

Price, Richard (1723–91)

Welsh moral philosopher, born in Tynton, Glamorgan. In *Review of the Principal Questions and Difficulties in Morals* (1758), Price criticized the moral sense theory of Hutcheson and Hume and argued that right and wrong are objective characteristics of actions that can be perceived by the understanding. His book on the French revolution, *Discourse on the Love of Our Country* (1789), provoked Edmund Burke's *Reflections on the Revolution in France*.

Prichard, H(arold) A(rthur) (1871–1947)

British philosopher, born in London, a leading Oxford moral intuitionist. Prichard is best known for his paper "Does Moral Philosophy Rest on a Mistake?" (*Mind*, 1912), in which he criticized Kant

from the perspective of moral intuitionism. He argued that a general theory of obligation or duty is impossible and that an attempt to formulate such a theory is a mistake. Instead, he claimed, we saw what we ought to do by direct perception in particular situations.

prima facie duties

ETHICS [Latin *prima facie*, so far as it appears on the surface, or on first appearance] A notion elaborated by W. D. **Ross** in his ethics, for duties relative to occasions, in contrast to absolute duties or duties proper, which we ought to perform in any situation without exception. *Prima facie* duties are also called conditional duties. We have many sorts of self-evident duties, such as keeping a promise, **beneficence**, **justice**, and self-improvement. In a particular moral situation, more than one of these duties may matter. In such a situation, we have no way of knowing for certain which duty is fundamental. The only thing we can do is to rank all **obligations** involved in this particular situation and attempt to decide which one is most important on this occasion or to determine where the balance lies. The duty on which we act and which we take to be the most important on this occasion could be less important on another occasion. Thus, all such duties that we perform are *prima facie*, rather than absolute. Ross's theory rejects the moral monism of **Kantian** or **utilitarian** theories, which hold that there is an ultimate **moral principle** to guide our **choices** or **actions**. It faces the problem of accounting for the possibility of measuring the importance of different kinds of duties.

> "I suggest 'Prima facie duty' or 'conditional duty' as a brief way of referring to the characteristic (quite distinct from that of being a duty proper) which an act has, in virtue of being of a certain kind (e.g. the keeping of a promise), of being an act which would be a duty proper if it were not at the same time of another kind which is morally significant." **Ross, *The Right and the Good***

prima facie **justification,** see defeasibility

prima facie **rights,** see rights, *prima facie*

primary and secondary qualities

METAPHYSICS, EPISTEMOLOGY The distinction between primary and secondary qualities can be traced to the ancient **atomist Democritus** and was also suggested by **Galileo**, **Descartes**, and the seventeenth-century **corpuscularian** philosophers such as Robert **Boyle**. But it is **Locke** who provided philosophical argument for this distinction and made it a significant topic in modern philosophy. For Locke, primary qualities are those that are not separable from the **body**, such as size, shape, texture, and bulk, while secondary qualities are those that are not in the objects themselves but are the **powers** of primary qualities to produce in us various **sensations** such as colors, sounds, and tastes. In an even broader sense, a secondary quality is also a thing's power to change another thing's operation. The **ideas** produced by primary qualities resemble the qualities themselves, that is, these ideas are qualitatively identical with the qualities in the body that initiated the whole **causal** process of **perception**. In contrast, the ideas of secondary qualities do not resemble anything in the bodies at all, for although we habitually think of these qualities as existing in the objects themselves, they are actually only powers to produce ideas in us rather than actual **attributes** which these ideas resemble. Primary qualities, because they really exist in the bodies, are called **real qualities**. The ideas of primary qualities, unlike the ideas of secondary qualities, were taken to offer something that could be measured and were thus considered a suitable basis for scientific **explanation**. Further, it was claimed that all secondary qualities could be **reduced** to primary qualities.

While Locke claimed that secondary qualities have their physical basis in the bodies that are causally responsible for the ideas of them, **Berkeley** interpreted secondary qualities as those qualities that do not exist independently of the perception of them. Berkeley took Locke's distinction between perceptible qualities and powers as a distinction between mind-independent and mind-dependent qualities. Because he rejected the possibility of the former, he saw all qualities to be on the same footing.

> "These I call original or primary qualities of body, which I think we may observe to produce simple *ideas* in us, viz., solidity, extension, figure, motion or rest, and number." **Locke,** *An Essay Concerning Human Understanding*

primary goods

ETHICS, POLITICAL PHILOSOPHY For **Rawls**, the things that every **rational person** would want, whatever his plan of life or **value** orientation might be. Primary goods are basic to the life plans of all rational beings. They are divided into two categories: natural primary goods, including health, vigor, intelligence, and imagination, and social primary goods, including wealth, **power**, opportunities, **civil rights**, such as **freedom of thought and speech**, and the right to participate in political decision making, and, as Rawls particularly emphasizes, self-respect. The distribution of social primary goods is of basic concern to the participants who choose the **principles of justice** in the **original position**. Primary goods are the subject-matter of the single **thin theory of good** and provides the motivation for the unanimous selection of principles of justice behind the **veil of ignorance**. Critics argue that consideration of primary goods can not lead to a decision about the principles of justice, either because too little is known for any **choice** or because too much is known for a unanimous choice. Others argue for a different array of primary goods with different consequences for justice or claim that different values and life plans will affect the weighting of the goods even if the agents are temporarily ignorant of them.

> "Now primary goods, as I have already remarked, are things which it is supposed a rational man wants whatever else he wants." **Rawls,** *A Theory of Justice*

primary language, another term for object language

primary matter

METAPHYSICS **Leibniz** distinguished between primary matter and secondary matter. Primary matter is **matter** in itself, or bulk. It is not a complete **substance**, for it is separated from **soul** or **substantial form**, and needs the latter to be an organic unity. Primary matter is what is **passive** in any complete substance, but it serves as the foundation of **continuity**. Secondary matter, on the other hand, as an aggregate or mass, is a collection of substances.

> "I understand matter as either secondary or primary. Secondary matter is, indeed, a complete substance, but it is not merely passive; primary

matter is merely passive, but it is not a complete substance." **Leibniz,** *Philosophical Essays*

primary reason

PHILOSOPHY OF ACTION Traditionally, **reason** has been held to **explain action**. What, then, is the exact relation between a reason and the action it explains? **Davidson** claims that when **agents** perform actions, they have a pro-attitude toward an action under a certain kind, because reason has led them to see or think they see in an action under the description of that kind some feature or consequence which they want or **value**. Furthermore, agents need to have a **belief** that acting in a certain way promotes that which they want or value. Such a pro-attitude and belief form the primary reason for agents to act as they do. On Davidson's view, this is how reasons rationalize an action. Their logical relationship can be expressed by a **practical syllogism** involving the **propositional contents** of the belief and the pro-attitude. The doctrine of primary reason is the central element of Davidson's **causal theory of action**, because a primary reason for acting in a certain way can cause an agent to act in that way.

"R is a primary reason why an agent performed the action A under the description D only if R consists of a pro-attitude of the agent towards action with a certain property, and a belief of the agent that A, under the description, has that property." **Davidson,** *Essays on Actions and Events*

primary rules, see rule of recognition

prime matter

METAPHYSICS, ANCIENT GREEK PHILOSOPHY **Aristotle**'s concept of what exists at the absolute beginning of generation. While elements are basic matter for all things, prime matter serves as the subject when elements change into each other. It is therefore more basic than the elements. Prime matter lacks characteristics in itself, but is what remains after even the three dimensions are stripped away, with nothing left to be removed. In itself, prime matter is in none of the **categories**, but can **potentially** be everything.

"And not only is nature the prime matter (and this in two senses, either the first, counting from the thing, or the first in general; . . .), but also the form and essence." **Aristotle,** *Metaphysics*

prime mover, an alternative expression for unmoved mover

primitive belief, see primitive knowledge

primitive force

METAPHYSICS **Leibniz** claimed that active force is either primitive or derivative. Primitive force is inherent in every corporeal **substance** and stands in contrast to primary matter. It provides the principle of unity for primary matter and forms an organic unity with it. It is what Leibniz also called **substantial form** or the first **entelechy**. Derivative force, on the other hand, arises from a limitation of primitive force through the collision of **bodies** with one another.

"Primitive force (which is nothing but the first entelechy) corresponds to the soul or substantial form." **Leibniz,** *Philosophical Essays*

primitive ideas

LOGIC, PHILOSOPHY OF MATHEMATICS, EPISTEMOLOGY The ideas which serve as the grounds for explaining other ideas in a system, but which are not themselves **defined** by any other ideas within the system. These terms can only be explained by pointing to what is meant. Primitive ideas are associated with primitive propositions, which are the propositions within a given system that are undemonstrable by any other propositions but which form the basis for **demonstrating** other propositions. Each **axiomatic system** contains certain primitive ideas and primitive propositions. It is **methodologically** preferable that any such system should contain the least possible number of primitive ideas and primitive propositions.

"Following Peano, we shall call the undefined ideas and undemonstrated propositions primitive ideas and primitive propositions respectively." **Whitehead and Russell,** *Principia Mathematica*

primitive knowledge

EPISTEMOLOGY **Russell** draws a distinction between primitive knowledge and derivative knowledge. Since **knowledge** is used here in the sense of **belief**, the distinction is also drawn between primitive belief and derivative belief. Primitive knowledge or belief is immediate **self-evident experience**, which does not need the support of any outside **evidence**.

Derivative knowledge or belief is the belief **caused** by other beliefs and is something that we believe as a result of **inference**, although the inference might not be strictly logical. For instance, we judge somebody's feelings from the expression on his face. This distinction between primitive and derivative knowledge is similar to that between hard **data** and soft data.

> "The first thing that appears when we begin to analyse our common knowledge is that some of it is derivative, while some is primitive." **Russell,** *Our Knowledge of the External World*

principle

ETHICS [from Latin *principium*, composed of *primus*, first, chief + *cipium*, a termination, corresponding to Greek *arche*, starting-point, beginning] A general **reason** for doing or omitting to do something or for believing or not believing something. A principle is a foundation or starting-point for any physical or mental operation that applies in a wide range of situations. The most general principles are normally not proven by appeal to subordinate principles derived on their basis.

> "All unprovable judgements, in so far as they are the ground of all judgements, are called principles, and they are either theoretical or practical." **Kant,** *Lectures on Logic*

principle of charity

PHILOSOPHY OF LANGUAGE A **methodological principle** for **translation** or **interpretation**. A favored **truth** theory for a language L should assign **truth conditions** to most of its **sentences** held true by a speaker of L, in accord with our own view of what is true. In interpreting or translating a system of thought, we must assume that most of the **propositions** in it are true, that is, we must maximize the extent of rationality of the subjects from our point of view. For **Quine**, this principle is a pre-condition for the possibility of **radical translation**, and for **Davidson** it is a pre-condition for **radical interpretation**. A good theory of interpretation, according to Davidson, should maximize agreement. The principle is based on the claim that only against a background of massive agreement can we intelligibly agree and disagree. It is a charitable assumption about human **rationality**. It might be false, but

if there is no better alternative in interpretation, the principle can help us to **understand** what we want to interpret and can thus make communication possible.

> "Charity is forced on us; whether we like it or not, if we want to understand others, we must count them right in most matters." **Davidson,** *Inquiries into Truth and Interpretation*

principle of fractional prudence

PHILOSOPHY OF ACTION A term introduced by C. I. **Lewis** for the human tendency to choose a good thing which is available now rather than a better thing in the future, even though it is equally likely that one will be able to obtain the latter. It is an expression of the preference that humans have for satisfying present **desires** and the immediate future. Other authors call such a tendency time-preference. On some interpretations, humans are biologically determined to care less about our remote desires and about the distant future. Lewis claimed that this kind of concern is irrational, and Derek **Parfit** calls it a bias because a sound **rationality** should be concerned with the good of our whole life and should not sacrifice distant goods to near ones. Others, including **Bentham**, argue that a preference for the near future is a requirement of **practical rationality**.

> "This anomalous conception, that although we should rationally be concerned with the future, we should be less concerned about it according as it is more remote . . . This might be called the principle of fractional prudence or of prudence mitigated by impulse." **C. I. Lewis,** *An Analysis of Knowledge and Valuation*

principle of humanity

PHILOSOPHY OF LANGUAGE A principle put forward by Richard Grandy with the intention of improving the **principle of charity**. The principle of charity claims that when we **translate** a different language, we should suppose that most of its **assertions** and **inferences** are true and **rational**. However, granted that, if the translation turns out to be unintelligible for us, it is still useless for our purpose. Hence, in interpreting or translating a system of thought, we must impute to this system patterns of relations among **beliefs** and **desires** that are similar to our own. We should suppose that the speaker of that language is a person and has certain basic similarities to ourselves. In this way, we can make the best possible **predictions** and **explanation** of the speaker's **behavior**.

> "We have, as a pragmatic constraint on translation, the condition that the imputed patterns of relations among beliefs, desires and the world be as similar to our own as possible. This principle I shall call the principle of humanity." **Grandy, "Reference, Meaning and Belief," *Journal of Philosophy* 70**

principle of indeterminacy

PHILOSOPHY OF SCIENCE, EPISTEMOLOGY, METAPHYSICS
Also called the principle of uncertainty. A principle established by the German physicist Werner Heisenberg in 1927, claiming that in the subatomic world it is in principle impossible to determine simultaneously to an arbitrary degree of accuracy both the position of certain particles, such as electrons, and the momentum (velocity or direction) of their movement. If the position is known, the determination of their motion is uncertain, and vice versa. Hence full predictive **knowledge** is permanently impossible concerning the future behavior of these particles. It has been a major issue whether this uncertainty is a matter of epistemology or **ontology**. A corollary of this principle is that observed phenomena in the subatomic world do not give an accurate picture of reality, for the process of discovery affects what is discovered in the world at this level. On this basis, **determinism** can not apply to the subatomic world and is therefore seriously limited. Some philosophers believe that these limits on determinism make room for **freedom of the will**, while others argue that indeterminacy provides an inappropriate ground for the **rationality** and intelligence required for the notion of freedom.

> "If this principle [of indeterminacy] is true, and physicists seem to have little doubt that it is, it follows that some events are strictly unpredictable even in theory. We simply cannot know enough to make a valid prediction." **Baylis, *Ethics***

principle of indifference

LOGIC, PHILOSOPHY OF SCIENCE If we do not have positive reason to favor either one of a pair of mutually exclusive and competing **theories**, we must be indifferent or **impartial**, and ascribe to them the same degree of **probability**, since there is no positive ground for assigning unequal degrees. This principle was proposed by Bernoulli, who called it the principle of non-sufficient reason, Laplace, and J. M. **Keynes**, who also criticized it. The principle is useful in the theory of **choice**, but faces difficulties with **inductive** theories. Its application leads to **Bertrand's paradox**.

> "The principle of indifference asserts that if there is no known reason for predicting of our subject one rather than another of several alternatives, then relatively to such knowledge the assertions of each of these alternatives have an equal probability." **Keynes, *A Treatise on Probability***

principle of individuation

METAPHYSICS To individuate is to specify a character possessed solely by a thing and thus to distinguish it from other things within the same **class** or **species**. The principle of individuation explains how such distinctions can be drawn. The problem is associated by medieval philosophers with **Aristotle**. In *Metaphysics* Z8 he said that when **form** is **universal**, matter becomes the principle to distinguish **individuals** within the same form. However, Aristotle's view of individuation varied, for he also argued that matter itself is indeterminate and must be individuated by form.

Leibniz proposed the **identity of indiscernibles** as a principle of individuation. He argued that if two entities possess exactly the same characteristics, then these two entities are numerically identical. This principle implies that entities are different because each possesses a unique set of characteristics and is described by a unique set of **predicates**. But it is highly disputed whether Leibniz's principle is a **necessary truth**, with some philosophers arguing that it is logically possible for two numerically distinct entities to have precisely the same set of characteristics.

In *Individuals*, **Strawson** argues that **space** and **time** lie at the basis of all **identification** and that we can pick out an individual by making reference to the spatio-temporal path it follows and its current position. There are problems with his view, although they can perhaps be overcome. If space and time are relative to entities, then we can determine the spatio-temporal location of any one entity only against the background of an established system of individuated **objects** in space and time. It is not clear whether our inability to individuate all entities within an absolute space and time is a crucial flaw in a Strawsonian program of individuating within a relativist setting.

Some philosophers argue that individuation is determined by the bundle of all the characteristics possessed by an individual, and others argue that it is determined by the **essential properties** of an individual. The essentialist view has different versions, according to whether **individual essences** as well as essences of kinds are admitted.

The principle of individuation has an **ontological** dimension, dealing with the process or circumstances whereby something becomes an individual.

> "Given that there are substances, the question that next arises is what marks off any one substance from any other. The mediaeval philosophers called this the problem of the principle of individuation."
> **Hamlyn,** *Metaphysics*

principle of induction

LOGIC, PHILOSOPHY OF SCIENCE The ground for the **validity** of inductive reasoning. It assumes that if a certain type of thing A has been found to be associated with a certain type of thing B, if no As are observed that are not associated with Bs, and if the number of observed associations between As and Bs is sufficiently great, then when we observe on a new occasion the presence of an A, a B will probably appear as well. Sometimes this is regarded as equivalent to the principle of the **uniformity of nature**, which assumes that the future will resemble the past. Because the principle of induction seems to be justified only on the basis of induction, the proof of the principle, if one is needed, presupposes itself.

> "The principle [of induction] itself is constantly used in our reasoning, sometimes consciously, and sometimes unconsciously; but there is no reasoning which, starting from some simpler self-evident principle, leads us to the principle of induction as its conclusion." **Russell,** *The Problems of Philosophy*

principle of non-sufficient reason, another term for the principle of indifference

principle of parsimony, another name for Ockham's razor

principle of perfection, see principle of plenitude

principle of plenitude

METAPHYSICS [from Greek *pleroma*, fullness, completeness] A principle that anything that is **possible** is realized. A temporalized version of the principle, ascribed to **Aristotle**, claims that if p is genuinely possible, p will be actualized or realized at some time. The American philosopher Arthur Lovejoy introduced this term and connected the principle with the doctrine of the **great chain of being**. On his formulation, "no genuine possibility of being can remain unfulfilled." The principle of plenitude is a negative version of the principle of **sufficient reason**: unless there is sufficient reason for something not to be, then that thing exists. According to Lovejoy, the principle has been widely held in the history of philosophy and is identical with what **Russell** called the **principle of perfection** in his discussion of **Leibniz**'s philosophy. The principle implies that nature makes no leaps and that there are no sudden transitions of level in the hierarchy of **beings** in the universe. If an apparent possibility cannot be realized, then it is not genuine, and there are no non-actualized possibilities. These intriguing claims have given rise to much debate.

> "I shall call it the principle of plenitude, but shall use the term to cover a wider range of inference from premises identical with Plato's than he himself draws; that is, not only the thesis that the universe is a plenum formarum in which the range of conceivable diversity of kinds of living things is exhaustively exemplified, but also any other deductions from the assumption that no genuine potentiality of being can remain unfulfilled."
> **Lovejoy,** *The Great Chain of Being*

principle of substitutivity, another name for indiscernibility of the identicals

principle of the best

PHILOSOPHY OF RELIGION, METAPHYSICS, ETHICS **Leibniz** claimed that when **God** created this world, he did not exercise his **will** at random but acted according to the principle of the best. God intended to choose to create among an infinite number of **possible worlds** the best possible world and had the **power** and **knowledge** necessary to work out what that best world would be. Thus, any part of the world, any particular **contingent** thing, has the nature that it has because it is a part of the best possible world. This principle, also called the principle of fitness, or the principle of perfection, offers a **reason** why this world rather than any other was created and explains the **cause** of **events** and **existence** of things. Leibniz also used this principle to distinguish contingent truths from **necessary truths** by saying that while necessary truths are based on the principle of non-contradiction, a contingent truth is that "which is or appears to be the best among several things which are equally possible." Sometimes Leibniz called this principle the principle of **sufficient reason**, although the precise meaning of the latter is that every truth has a reason.

> "The contingent which exists owes its existence to the principle of what is best, the sufficient reason for things." **Leibniz,** *The Leibniz–Clarke Correspondence*

principle of tolerance

LOGIC, PHILOSOPHY OF LANGUAGE, PHILOSOPHY OF SCIENCE At one stage **Carnap** claimed that an **objective** answer to questions can be reached so long as all researchers share the same **linguistic framework**. A linguistic framework embodies a system of logical principles, and sets up logical relations that connect **experience** to non-**protocol sentences**. Because linguistic frameworks are various, a problem arises about how we decide to employ one framework rather than another, for we adopt a framework only if we believe that it is true – but this seems to be circular. Carnap replied that in choosing a framework, we are not concerned with truth, but with **pragmatic** considerations of **simplicity** and usefulness. Thus we are at liberty to build up our own form of language or our own logic as we wish. Such an attitude concerning the choice of framework is called by Carnap the principle of tolerance, and it is also called the principle of the conventionality of language forms. For Carnap, there are no morals in logic. What is required of a logician

is that he state his **method** clearly. We should be cautious in making **assertions** and be critical in examining them, but should be tolerant in permitting linguistic forms.

> "The Principle of Tolerance: It is not our business to set up prohibitions, but to arrive at conventions." **Carnap,** *The Logical Syntax of Language*

principle of uncertainty, another term for the principle of indeterminacy

principle of utility

ETHICS, POLITICAL PHILOSOPHY, PHILOSOPHY OF LAW Also called the greatest happiness principle or the greatest felicity principle, the principle of utility is central idea of **utilitarianism** and was first formulated by Jeremy **Bentham**. It claims that we should judge the **moral value** of an **action** according to the consequence it produces. An action is **right** in proportion to its tendency to promote utility or happiness and wrong according to its tendency to produce **pain** for the parties concerned. Utility is proposed not only as the sole **criterion** of **morality**, but also as the basis for assessing institutions and for justifying **political obligation** to the **state**. Bentham claimed that the principle is the secular foundation of any legal system, with utility as the test for what laws there ought to be. The principle of utility has been challenged on many grounds, including its emphasis on consequence rather than **intention** in evaluation of actions, the priority it gives to the theory of **good** over the theory of right, its indifference to the distribution of happiness, and the difficulty in measuring and aggregating happiness. Versions of the principle have replaced happiness with other goods, such as the **satisfaction** of wants.

> "By the principle of utility is meant that principle which approves or disapproves of every action whatsoever according to the tendency which it appears to have to augment or diminish the happiness of the party whose interest is in question." **Bentham,** *An Introduction to the Principles of Morals and Legislation*

Prior, Arthur (1914–69)

New Zealander logician, born in Masterton, Professor of Philosophy at Universities of Canterbury and Manchester and Fellow of Balliol College, Oxford.

Prior employed deontic logic in his study of ethics, invented tense logic on the model of modal logic to deal with the philosophy of time, and explained the logic of belief statements and statements involving propositional attitudes in terms of a special kind of connective between individuals and propositions. More generally, his formal inventiveness has extended the application of logic in many areas of philosophy. His major works include *Logic and the Basis of Ethics* (1949), *Formal Logic* (1955), *Time and Modality* (1957), *Objects of Thought* (1971), and *Worlds, Times, and Selves* (with Kit Fine) (1977).

prisoner's dilemma

PHILOSOPHY OF ACTION, POLITICAL PHILOSOPHY, ETHICS A classical problem in the theory of **choice** and the theory of **self-interest**. Two prisoners charged with some joint crime are questioned by the prosecutors separately. Both of them know the following options: (1) if neither of them confesses, each will serve one year in prison; (2) if each confesses, everyone will serve two years; (3) if one confesses and the other does not, then the one who confesses will be released, and the other will serve three years. Neither knows the other's choice. What is the rational choice for each?

If every prisoner pursues his own best interest, the reasonable choice for him is to confess. But then neither gets the best result, and there is the worst overall outcome (four person-prison years). The case shows that furthering one's own interest does not entail that one gets the best consequence or that the **public good** will be furthered efficiently. On the contrary, only if both **cooperate** and neither confesses will the best overall result be obtained. The prisoner's dilemma is widely discussed in modern social, political, and moral philosophy, for it challenges fundamentally the theory of self-interest. Many political situations, such as an arms race between powers, can be modeled as prisoner's dilemmas.

> "The hazards of the generalised prisoner's dilemma are removed by the match between the right and the good." **Rawls,** *A Theory of Justice*

privacy

PHILOSOPHY OF MIND In traditional **dualism**, one assumes that whatever is **mental**, such as **experiences**, **sense-data**, **representations**, or **ideas**, is private. This can be meant in two senses. In the first sense, my mental phenomena are inalienably owned by me. Only I have them. In the second sense, only I have access to my mental phenomena. They are incommunicable. For example, only I am in a position to know or to feel that I am in pain. This idea leads to **skepticism** about **other minds**, for it implies that one can never know whether another person is in pain. It also leads to **solipsism**, for if all experiences must be interpreted through my private experience, the world can only be my world. The idea of privacy is attacked in detail by later **Wittgenstein**.

> "In what sense are my sensations private? – Well, only I can know whether I am really in pain; another person can only surmise it. – In one way this is wrong, and in another nonsense."
> **Wittgenstein,** *Philosophical Investigations*

private good, see common good

private language

PHILOSOPHY OF LANGUAGE, PHILOSOPHY OF MIND A term introduced by **Wittgenstein** in his later philosophy. A private language is a language the words of which **refer** to the speaker's immediate private **sensations** and can not be **understood** by another person. Modern philosophy generally starts by claiming that our **knowledge** is based on our own immediate experience and this experience can be expressed by language, at least to oneself. The possibility of such a private language seems to be supported by the apparent capacity of a person to record the occurrence of a particular kind of sensation in his diary and to propose calling it by some **name**. Wittgenstein, in the *Philosophical Investigations*, sections 243–315, argues against the possibility of a private language and the capacity to name occurrences of a kind of private sensation. He held that any use of language presupposes a **community** in which there is agreement in the **rules** of applying words and signs in **judgments**. If a language is private, there is no way to distinguish between thinking that one is obeying a rule and actually obeying it. So a private language is not a language, and the notion of a private language is not coherent. Philosophy based on the possibility of a private language is misguided because it misunderstands both the nature of **experience** and the nature of language. The so-called "private language argument" of Wittgenstein is complicated and is subject to various interpretations. It has stimulated much discussion in contemporary philosophy.

> "And sounds which no one else understands but which I 'appear to understand' might be called a 'private language'." **Wittgenstein,** *Philosophical Investigations*

private morality, see public morality

private ostensive definition

PHILOSOPHY OF LANGUAGE In a private ostensive definition, I concentrate my attention on a particular **sensation** that can be **named** only by myself **privately** rather than in terms of a public language. I associate the sensation with a **sign**, for example the sign "S." I alone can know the **meaning** of this private sign, and another person can not understand it. For this to be the case, a private ostensive definition requires that there be a private **object** that only I can recognize. This view is rejected, along with the possibility of a **private language**, by Wittgenstein in *Philosophical Investigations* I, 243–311. If a private object exists as the object of a private ostensive definition, there must be private **thought**, expressible only in terms of a private language. However, a private language is impossible. Any means of communication must involve criteria of meaning available to others. It is true that sensations have an aspect of **subjectivity**, but their subjectivity is not of the radical sort that would support a private language and private ostensive definitions.

> "You keep on steering towards the idea of the private ostensive definition." **Wittgenstein,** *Philosophical Investigations*

private particular

METAPHYSICS, PHILOSOPHY OF MIND **Strawson**'s term covering **sensations**, **mental events**, or **sense-data**, in contrast to public or objective particulars. To identify private particulars in our common language we need to identify another class of particulars, that is, **persons** who have them. For instance, to identify a private impression of red one must assign the impression to the person who has it. Because of the dependence of their identification upon the identification of persons, Strawson denies that private particulars

can be **basic particulars**, in contrast to the **empiricist** tradition of constructing persons and external **objects** from allegedly basic mental entities.

> "Identifying reference to 'private particulars' depends on identifying reference to particulars of another type altogether, namely persons." **Strawson,** *Individuals*

private/public dichotomy, see public/private dichotomy

private world, another expression for perspective

privation

ANCIENT GREEK PHILOSOPHY, METAPHYSICS [Greek *steresis*, from *steresthai*, to lack or to be deprived of] Normally, something suffers privation when it lacks an **attribute** that, according to its nature, it should possess. According to **Aristotle**'s analysis, privation, **substratum**, and **form** are the three basic elements in the process of **change**. Privation at the beginning of change is the absence of a character which the change will provide at its completion and which the substratum is capable of receiving. For example, if a man changes from being unmusical to being musical, the man is the substratum, unmusical is the privation, and musical is the form the man will gain when the change is finished.

> "For a thing comes to be from the privation, which in its own nature is not-being – this not surviving as a constituent of the result." **Aristotle,** *Physics*

privileged access

EPISTEMOLOGY The special position that apparently gives one awareness of what is presently going on in one's own **mind**, such as one's **thoughts**, **beliefs**, **intentions**, and **emotions**. Privileged access is contrasted with the lack of special access in one's **knowledge** of the **external world** and **other minds**. For while one's knowledge of the world and other minds is mediated through certain **causal** factors and is subject to being checked by **experience**, one's awareness of one's mind is claimed to be immediate, **infallible**, and **incorrigible**. On this view, either these states are detectable by oneself alone or one is the final authority concerning their existence and their character. On either version, the accuracy of the reports of these mental states is **verified** by oneself. Since **Descartes**, many philosophers have believed that this special position exists. One's mental states are **private** and the **first-person** account has authority. But **Ryle**, **W. Sellars**, **Wittgenstein**, and others denied that one has special access to one's own mind that differs from one's access to other minds, in part because the **meaning** of expressions used from a first-person **perspective** needs the support of a **third-person** use in a single language. It is still difficult to understand how to avoid a collapse of mental terms into first-person **solipsism** or third-person **behaviorism**.

> "I have also tried to show that from the fact that I do have privileged access to my present thoughts and feelings, in the sense that my testimony concerning them cannot be overridden, it does not follow that they are exclusively mine." **Ayer, The Concept of a Person and Other Essays**

pro-attitude

ETHICS, PHILOSOPHY OF ACTION A term borrowed by **Davidson** from ethical theory for his **causal** theory of action. A pro-attitude is an **agent**'s mental attitude directed toward an action under a certain **description**. Such attitudes include wants, **desires**, urges, moral views, aesthetic principles, and economic prejudices. Such a set of mental attitudes, together with the agent's **belief** that acting in a certain way promotes what the agent wants or **values**, form the **primary reason** for an agent to act in that way.

> "Reference to other attitudes besides wanting, or thinking he ought, may help specify the agent's reasons, but it seems that some positive, or pro-attitude must be involved." **Davidson, Essays on Actions and Events**

probabilism

ETHICS, EPISTEMOLOGY, LOGIC, PHILOSOPHY OF SCIENCE Initially, a doctrine developed by the Jesuits in the sixteenth century to determine what one should do when different authorities are found to disagree. The theory claims that if one is willing to perform an action, and that action has some **probability** in its favor, one has reason to perform that action without being condemned. Here, probable means supported by authority rather than supported by **evidence**. One may follow a course of action if it is authorized by some authority of the Church. It does

not matter how much weight the authority has. The theory has difficulty in making sense of **responsibility** and was criticized by the **Port-Royal Logic**. The appearance of probabilism suggests a sense of loss of the **certainty** that characterized the Renaissance.

In another sense, probabilism is any position that requires one to be content with probability because certainty does not obtain or because it is difficult to know whether certainty could obtain.

Probabilism is also used for the claim that, all things being equal, the simplest theory is the most probable. When two theories seem to be equally supported by the evidence, the simpler one is in general more likely to be true.

> "The first contact of theories of probability with modern ethics appears in the Jesuit doctrine of probabilism. According to this doctrine, one is justified in doing an action for which there is any probability, however small, of its results being the best possible." **Keynes, A Treatise on Probability**

probability

LOGIC, EPISTEMOLOGY The different degrees of truth that a **rational belief** has when such a belief is more or less inconclusive. Probability can apply the occurrence of **events**, the existence of **states**, or the **truth** of **propositions**.

There are various conceptions of probability corresponding to different theories of probability. Relative frequency theory, associated with J. **Venn** and R. **von Mises**, identifies probability with the frequency of occurrence of events of a given kind. Such an understanding of probability is addressed mainly to physical probability, that is, probability as an objective factor in the world and as the subject-matter of statistics. Physical probability is indefinite in that it attaches to **states of affairs** or **attributes** rather than to **propositions**. **Propensity** theory argues that physical probability can pertain to specific **individuals** as propensities. **Subjectivism** or **personalism**, associated with **de Finetti** and **Ramsey**, takes probability as the **degree of belief** in an event. On this understanding probability is epistemic and is concerned with **knowledge** and opinion rather than with the physical structure of the world. This kind of probability is definite in the sense that it attaches to propositions rather than to attributes. **Confirmation** theory and **range** theory hold that probability is a connection between our **judgment** and the objective world. On this understanding probability has physical and epistemic aspects. All theories of probability attempt to establish that their notion of probability satisfies the formal requirement of the **probability calculus**.

> "In metaphysics, in science, and in conduct, most of the arguments, upon which we habitually base our rational beliefs, are admitted to be inconclusive in a greater or less degree. Thus, for a philosophical treatment of these branches of knowledge, the study of probability is required." **Keynes, A Treatise on Probability**

probability, *a priori* theory of
another expression for probability, logical relation theory of

probability, classical theory of

LOGIC The earliest interpretation of probability, developed during the eighteenth century by Bernoulli, **Bayes**, and Laplace. Laplace defined probability as the ratio of the number of favorable cases to the total number of relevant and equally likely cases. This came to be known as the classical definition of probability. This theory takes probability as a ratio among equipossible alternatives and has received comprehensive mathematical elaboration. According to the **principle of indifference**, it assumes that prior to having any evidence, the same degree of probability (equipossibility) should be assigned to each alternative. This account involves a vicious circle because it defines probability in terms of equipossible alternatives, but equipossibility presupposes an understanding of probability. Various attempts have arisen to emend the principle of indifference to avoid this consequence.

> "The classical interpretation [of probability] is one of the oldest and best known; it defines probability as the ratio of favourable to equally possible cases." **Salmon, The Foundations of Scientific Inference**

probability, logical relation theory of

LOGIC Also called the logical theory of probability or the *a priori* theory of probability, an interpretation of probability which proposes that probability is related to **propositions** rather than to the occurrence of **events**. Unlike the relative frequency theory, it holds that probability does not concern frequency but is a logical relation between propositions that have been formulated in accordance with **evidence**, and other **propositions** that are **hypotheses**, whose **truth** or falsity has not yet been determined by evidence. The probability of a proposition is thus relative to the given evidence and varies with it. It is a measure of the logical support for a proposition on the basis of evidence. The theory was developed by J. M. **Keynes**, W. E. **Johnson**, Harold Jeffreys, and **Carnap**, among others. While Keynes and Jeffreys rejected the frequency interpretation of probability, Carnap believed that logical probability differs in nature from empirical or statistical probability, which is the subject-matter of frequency theory. Logical relation theory is a more sophisticated version of the classical theory of probability. It defines probability as the degree of certainty that our **beliefs** about future events can have as rationally **justified** by the available evidence. A problem for the theory is that it can not **verify** the ways of constructing the required logical relation. Also, as Carnap saw, not all probability claims can be dealt with by the theory.

> "The whole logical relation theory is vitiated, I believe, because it makes out probability to attach to the relations between evidence and conclusions rather than to propositions, or propositional functions, by themselves." **Lucas, The Concept of Probability**

probability, propensity theory of

LOGIC, PHILOSOPHY OF SCIENCE An interpretation of probability, associated with **Popper**, that developed out of the relative frequency theory of probability. Both theories agree that probability is an **objective** feature of **reality**. While the relative frequency theory considers probability to be an attribute of an infinite sequence of **events** that we can represent with a finite sample, the **propensity** theory considers probability primarily to be a primitive undefined attribute of single events, although it can also account for the probability of **sequences**. Probability should be understood as the propensity or disposition of a situation to produce a given result. The main difficulty with this theory lies in the primitiveness of the notion of propensity, which seems to introduce a mysterious **theoretical entity**. Also, it is unclear whether the propensity of a single case is necessary to understand probability over a sequence.

"All versions of the propensity theory have two important features that no relative frequency account can have. They apply just as well to indefinite populations as to finite ones. And they all allow probabilities to be assigned to superficial individual events." **L. Cohen,** *An Introduction to the Philosophy of Induction and Probability*

probability, relative frequency theory of

LOGIC, PHILOSOPHY OF SCIENCE An interpretation of probability that holds that probability is the relative or statistical frequency of occurrence within a reference class. It applies primarily to infinite **sequences**, of which we must take finite samples. It is an **objective** theory for, as observed frequency, probability is an attribute of the real world. A probability **statement** is taken as an **assertion** about the world. Probability concerns a group or a series. That one **event** is more likely to happen than another means that, for an infinite sequence or a large finite sample, events of the first kind will occur more frequently than events of the other kind. The theory can be traced to **Aristotle**, who claimed that the probable is that which happens for the most part. Its modern expositors include John **Venn**, Hans **Reichenbach**, and Richard **von Mises**. This theory fits well with common sense and has great appeal for the **empiricists**, but its understanding of probability in terms of hypothetical infinite sequences is rejected by some as being unnecessarily abstract. The theory invites other objections, including those related to the possibility of ascertaining the values of the limit to which the relative frequency will tend over an infinite sequence. There are also problems in applying a frequency to the probability of a single event. A given event may be seen as belonging to different reference classes yielding different probabilities.

"Relative frequency theory [of probability] . . . defines probability as the (limiting) relative frequency of some characteristic in some (infinite) sequence." **Logue,** *Projective Probability*

probability, subjective theory of

LOGIC, EPISTEMOLOGY, PHILOSOPHY OF MIND Also called **personalism**, an interpretation of probability which claims that the probability of a **proposition** is the measure of the subject's degree of reasonable **belief** or confidence in it. Reasonable belief is constrained by **coherence** rather than by empirical **evidence**. Since the intensity of confidence varies from one person to another, it follows that probability varies between subjects. Probability is the degree of belief that a given person has in a given **statement** on the basis of given evidence. If I believe with perfect **certainty** that it will rain tomorrow, then my **subjective** probability is 1. This theory differs from the logical relation theory of probability in that it does not take the relation between a statement and a body of evidence as a purely logical relation. This position has been defended by **Ramsey**, B. **de Finetti**, and L. J. Savage. Its major difficulty is to justify the notion of reasonable belief, which seems to require a conception of probability. It also has difficulty in explicating the **intersubjective** assessment of probabilities. Hence, a subjective theory of probability can not fully account for the concept of probability.

"The subjective theory . . . defines probability as the degree of belief of a given person in a given proposition at a specific time." **Weatherford,** *Philosophical Foundations of Probability Theory*

probability calculus

LOGIC Of the conclusions inferred from probable **inferences**, some are more **reliable** than others. Logicians and probabilists have developed a branch of mathematics to determine degrees of probability, and this is called the probability calculus. This is a deductive meta-logical system, which is neutral about the material meanings of probability and studies only the mathematical laws involving probability or the logical structure of probability. There are many versions of this calculus. The basic **axioms** these different systems share include: (1) If P and Q are disjoint, their probability is the sum of the probability of each disjunct minus the probability of their conjunction: Prob (P ∨ Q) = Prob (P) + Prob (Q) − Prob (P ∧ Q); (2) If P is a tautology, then Prob (P) = 1; (3) 0 ≤ Prob (P) ≤ 1.

"We have then a calculus of probability, which, when given its customary interpretation in terms of scientific statements, allows us to calculate relative probabilities of alternative hypotheses in the light of changing evidence." **Caws,** *The Philosophy of Science*

problem of evil, see evil

problem of other minds, see other minds

problem of the self, see personal identity

problem of the speckled hen, an alternative expression for the dilemma of attention

process–product ambiguity
METAPHYSICS An expression is **ambiguous** if it has more than one **meaning** and it is uncertain which meaning should be used in a given context. Some expressions can be used both to stand for a process and to stand for the product resulting from that process. The word "see" might mean either "I am seeing" or "I have seen." The failure to distinguish between a process and a product in the same context can lead to confusion.

"As a source of confusion, the process–product ambiguity is over-rated. Most processes are easily distinguished from their corresponding product." **Dretske,** *Explaining Behaviour*

process theology
PHILOSOPHY OF RELIGION An approach to **God** within the conceptual framework of **Whitehead**'s process philosophy, also employed by the American philosopher and theologian Charles **Hartshorne**. While in traditional theology God is pure **actuality** and stands above the world of **change**, process theology explains God and his relation to the world in terms of change. It emphasizes the **temporality** of God and believes that to be unchanging is to be **abstract** and dead. For Whitehead, God's **being** has two aspects: a primordial **nature**, which is his nature in himself, and a consequential nature, which is constituted by his response to the temporal world and is characterized by process or **becoming**. The former aspect is **formal**, conceptual, and unconscious, while the latter aspect is **material**, determined, and conscious. Hartshorne also adopts a similar distinction between the necessary existence of God and his **contingent actuality**. He claims that God can be understood as a temporal process of experiential events.

"The term 'process theology' is applied to the theological speculations produced by a group of twentieth century thinkers. . . . They believe that

the idea of 'process' or 'becoming' must be taken as the chief category for interpreting the nature of both the world and God." **H. Owen,** *Concepts of Deity*

Proclus (c.410–485)
Greek Neoplatonist, born in Constantinople, the last head of Plato's Academy. In works including *Elements of Theology, Platonic Theology,* and *Concerning Providence and Fate,* Proclus maintained that reality as universal consciousness is mental but objective. The world comprises a hierarchy of One, Power, Mind, Soul and/or Nature, and the world of appearances. The One, which is God, is the ultimate cause and contains all diversity within its identity, whereas the world of appearance is the effect of this cause.

productive force
PHILOSOPHY OF SOCIAL SCIENCE, PHILOSOPHY OF HISTORY [German *Productivkräfte,* also translated as force of production or productive power] The key **category** in **Marx**'s **historical materialism**, covering the sum of the elements or factors in the process of producing material use-value, including both the subjective factor of human labor power and the objective factors of the means of production. The means of production are further divided into the object of labor (natural resources including both raw materials and non-raw materials) and the means of labor, such as instruments. For historical materialism, the forces of production are fundamental in explanatory terms. They determine the character of the **relations of production**, that is, the economic structure, and inform the legal/political and ideological **superstructure** with content. Productive forces set humans above animals and actualize human capacity. According to Marx, the forces of production always advance throughout history. When they develop to a certain stage, the existing relations of production will no longer correspond to them and will constrain further development. At such times, Marx claimed, social **revolutions** will take place because the forces of production will break through the fetters of existing relations of production and establish new relations of production that are suitable for further progress. Productive forces are the ultimate determinant of human history.

All of the main claims for the role of productive forces in Marx's explanatory structure have been challenged and defended within Marxism and by other theorists.

> "A social formation never comes to an end before all the forces of production which it can accommodate are developed and new, higher relations of production never come into place before the material conditions of their existence have gestated in the womb of the old society."
> **Marx, *Preface to the Critique of Political Economy***

prohairesis, Greek term for decision

projectibility

LOGIC, EPISTEMOLOGY, PHILOSOPHY OF SCIENCE A term introduced by **Goodman** in his discussion of the problem of **confirmation**. A projection is an **inference** from the known to the unknown on the grounds of **induction** from past **experience**. Projectibility is the degree of **entrenchment** of this inference. If all observed emeralds are green, we may reasonably infer that future emeralds are green, but not that they are **grue** (green before some future time T and blue thereafter), for "green" is a projectible predicate and is well entrenched, having a high frequency of projection, while "grue" is not well entrenched. This is true even though the claims that all emeralds are grue and that all emeralds are green have equal inductive support. Grounding projectibility involves distinguishing between valid projections and invalid projections. Inductive reasoning can apply only to projectible **properties** or **hypotheses** rather than to all properties or hypotheses. Hence, to decide which property is projectible becomes an important issue in **epistemology**. According to Goodman, a hypothesis is projectible if all conflicting hypotheses are overridden. By introducing the notion of projectibility, and by defining it in terms of the historical record of entrenchment through actual projections, Goodman rejects the traditional discussion of confirmation that allows green and grue to be equally confirmed and aims to construct a purely **syntactical definition** of confirmation.

> "If we start with past projections as well as evidence and hypotheses, our task becomes that of defining valid projection – or projectibility – on the basis of actual projections." **Goodman, *Fact, Fiction and Forecast***

proof theory

PHILOSOPHY OF MATHEMATICS, LOGIC A **theory** dealing with **axiomatic** systems, founded by **Hilbert** in the 1920s as a tool for carrying out his program in the foundations of mathematics. In rejecting the claim that the foundations of mathematical analysis were built on sand, Hilbert introduces proof theory to show the **consistency** of both analysis and **set theory**, and to establish the **decidability** of each mathematical question. Although Hilbert's program was undermined by **Gödel's incompleteness theorem**, Gerhard **Gentzen** proved the consistency of elementary mathematics by using **natural deduction** and sequent calculi. Gentzen extended proof theory into a general theory that examines how proofs in formal logical systems, that is, systems determined by their **axioms** and rules of **inference**, can be investigated by mathematical techniques. Proof theory is now a branch of mathematical logic.

> "Hilbert introduced his proof theory. This theory treated the axiom systems of mathematics as pure syntax, distinguishing them from what he called mathematics, where meaning was permitted."
> **Moore, in *Minnesota Studies in the Philosophy of Sciences*, vol. XI**

propensity

METAPHYSICS, LOGIC, PHILOSOPHY OF MIND Generally conceived as the inner and probabilistic **disposition** or **state** in virtue of which a thing or a **person** will act in a certain way under normal circumstances, unless it is blocked by some external force. That I have a propensity to reduce my weight means that I do so if no counter-measures are taken. That I have the propensity to have a certain **belief** means that I will maintain this belief unless it is strongly refuted by some concluding **evidence**. The term propensity is closely related to the acquisition of belief and to the theory of **probability**. Popper developed a propensity interpretation of probability according to which the probability of a single case is its propensity.

> "Let us say that someone has a propensity to be j if he is in such a state that he will be j unless some special blocking factors intervene." **Smith and Jones, *The Philosophy of Mind***

proper name

Logic, philosophy of language A **simple symbol** for a **particular**, which does not have further symbols as its parts, in contrast to a **description**, which is a complex symbol. Whether a proper name has **sense** in itself has been a puzzling question since **Plato**'s *Theaetetus*. **Frege** points out that proper names can occur in informative identity statements, for example "The Morning Star is the Evening Star," and uses his distinction between sense and **reference** to account for this phenomenon. The claim that proper names have descriptive content gains support from the fact that proper names can appear in **existential statements**, such as "The Morning Star exists." **Wittgenstein** in the *Tractatus* claims that a proper name designates a particular directly and has that particular as its **meaning**. As a consequence, the proper name has no sense in itself. **Russell**, in a defense of Wittgenstein's view, distinguishes between ordinary proper names and logically proper names. An ordinary proper name has sense, but is in fact a **disguised description**. For example, "Socrates" is an abbreviation of something like "the philosopher who drank hemlock." On the other hand, logically proper names, for example names for the items in one's current experience, have their meaning in the **objects** they stand for. **Kripke** and **Putnam** criticize Frege's and Russell's accounts of proper names. Descriptions can be useful in fixing the reference of a proper name, but the meaning of the name is determined by the **essential** features (for example, of inner structure or origin) that make the item what it is. These features need not be immediately available to **experience** but, like water being H$_2$O, can be discovered.

> "The only kind of word that is theoretically capable of standing for a particular is a proper name, and the whole matter of proper names is rather curious." **Russell,** *Logic and Knowledge*

proper name theory

Metaphysics, epistemology, philosophy of mind A theory about the meaning of the word "**I**," holding that the word "I" is a logically **proper name**, that is, a word that directly designates an **object** with which the speaker is **acquainted**. I can know that I am aware of something or that I am having a certain experience only because I have **perceived** that there

is a subject of **experience** that has this awareness or experience. "I" is a proper name for this particular subject. A difficulty for this position is that even if we accept that I perceive a self as a subject of experience, it is not clear how I would establish that this self is myself.

> "According to proper name theory the person who knows an ego-centric fact is prehending, not only a certain particular as an experience of a certain kind, but also another particular." **Broad,** *Examination of McTaggart's Philosophy*

property

Metaphysics A property is a feature or aspect by which a thing can be **described** or characterized. It is a characteristic that a thing is said to possess and is synonymous with "**attribute**." An **Aristotelian** or medieval *proprium*, a characteristic which is unique to the **essence** of a thing but which is not in its **definition**, is also a property. Properties are often divided into **essential** and **accidental properties**, which are also called internal and external properties. An essential or internal property belongs to the essence of a thing, such that the thing can not lose an essential property without losing its **identity**. On the other hand, the possession or non-possession of an accidental or external property by a thing does not affect its identity. Interest in essential properties has been revived by recent work in **modal logic**, the logic of necessity and possibility.

> "A property is simply an aspect of a thing as described or characterized – a predicable." **Hamlyn,** *Metaphysics*

property (political and legal philosophy), see ownership

property dualism, see dualism

property instance, another term for abstract particular

proposition

Logic, philosophy of language The basic unit of **logical analysis**, characteristically stated by a declarative sentence and the bearer of the **truth-value true** or false. There is controversy over the relationships between propositions, **statements**, and **sentences**. Many theorists identify propositions with statements. Both are distinguished from sentences, but some philosophers wish to eliminate propositions as **abstract entities** in favor of sentences. If both kinds of entity are accepted, all propositions are sentences or are expressed by sentences. Only declarative sentences generally express propositions, although sentences of interrogative, imperative, and other forms have **propositional content**. A proposition can usually be represented by a "that" clause. Understanding the nature and structure of propositions is often seen as the central task of **philosophical logic**. Philosophers consider the functions of components of propositions, such as **names**, **predicates**, and **logical constants**, and consider how the components are unified into something having a truth-value. They examine how the **form**, **meaning**, and use of propositions are related and how different propositions can enter into logical relations. There has been much recent discussion of how linguistic or psychological states can have **propositional content**.

> "Let us . . . define a proposition as any complete sentence capable of expressing a statement."
> **Russell,** *Collected Papers,* **vol. VII**

proposition/sentence

LOGIC, PHILOSOPHY OF LANGUAGE A sentence is a group of words (**symbols**, **signs**) ordered according to some grammatical rule in any natural or artificial language. Sentences of various grammatical forms are best suited to indicate, plead, request, order, interrogate and so on, although such sentences can also be used outside their primary functions. A sentence is not necessarily meaningful, and the same sentence may have different meanings and may be used in different ways. All these characteristics make it difficult to determine in the abstract whether a given sentence is true or false or even whether in principle it is verifiable.

Philosophers therefore introduce the term "proposition" for abstract objects that are expressed by sentences and which bear **truth-values**. A proposition can in principle be expressed by a sentence, but not all sentences express propositions. Once sentences and propositions are distinguished, philosophers ask how features of **meaning** and **truth** should be divided between the two, which is

the vehicle for **asserting** or denying, for **stating** that some **predicate** holds of some subject or that certain items are **related** in a certain way. A proposition can be expressed by grammatically different sentences or by sentences in different languages, so long as the sentences have the same **content**. For instance, "A conquered B" and "B was conquered by A" are two sentences that express the same proposition. Propositions seem at first glance to be most closely related to indicative sentences, but sentences of other kinds can also be understood as having **propositional content**.

Ayer takes propositions to be **logical constructions** out of **synonymous** sentences rather than as **Platonic entities** existing in their own right. A proposition, not a sentence, is generally recognized as the truth-bearer, whilst meaning is often ascribed to sentences or statements. We can say that truth or falsity are not merely for one particular sentence S, but for all sentences that are **logically equivalent** to S. However, there are widely disputed problems in **philosophical logic** about the existence, nature, and individuation of propositions. Philosophers hostile to abstract entities try to do without propositions or to see them as a mere device for dealing with sentences. **Realists** and **reductionists** of various sorts must all provide accounts of how propositions and sentences are related.

> "The word 'proposition' . . . will be reserved for what is expressed by sentences which are literally meaningful." **Ayer,** *Language, Truth and Logic*

propositional attitude

PHILOSOPHY OF MIND **Russell**'s term for **mental activities** signified by verbs, such as think, hope, fear, want, wish, believe, guess, and consider. These verbs are propositional verbs, in contrast to the cognitive verbs such as know, see, smell, or feel. Both kinds of verb demand a grammatical accusative. However, propositional verbs, unlike cognitive verbs, do not necessarily have to have something in reality that answers to their grammatical accusatives. If I see X, there is an X, and if I see that p, then p is true. However, if I hope for X, it is open whether there is an X or not, and if I hope that p, it remains open whether p is true. A propositional attitude expresses an attitude to a **proposition**. Thus, the contexts of all propositional attitudes are **intentional**.

There are many philosophical problems associated with the notion of propositional attitudes. These include the question of whether co-referential designators can be substituted *salva veritate* in the context of propositional attitudes. If not, these contexts are **referentially opaque**. There are also problems with related notions such as **belief**, **intentionality**, and **content**.

> "We pass next to the analysis of propositional attitudes, that is believing, desiring, doubting, etc. that so-and-so is the case." **Russell**, *An Inquiry into Meaning and Truth*

propositional belief, see belief in and belief that

propositional calculus

LOGIC One main branch of modern **formal logic**, also called propositional logic, sentential calculus, sentential logic, the logic of propositions, and the theory of **truth-functions**. Anticipated partially by the Stoics, the prepositional calculus was systematically developed in the works of **Frege**, **Peirce**, **Russell**, and **Wittgenstein**. It formulates the principles of **inference** in terms of the truth-functional **constants** of **arguments**. These constants include **negation** (not), **conjunction** (and), **disjunction** (or), **implication** (if . . . then), and **equivalence** (if and only if). Each of them is symbolized by logical notation. There are various schemes of logical notation, but one widely used notation contains "~" (negation), "∧" (conjunction), "∨" (disjunction), "⊃" (implication), and "≡" (equivalence). The basic constituents of an argument are **propositions** (symbolized as p, q, r . . .). The **validity** of an argument is determined through the **truth-table** method by the **truth-values** of its components and the logical constants connecting them. Since **propositional logic** requires that all the propositions are either true or **false** and can not be both, it is also called two-valued logic. Because of its importance for any systematic development of thought, it was also called by **Whitehead** and Russell, the theory of deduction, or by **Kneale** primary logic.

> "The propositional calculus is characterised by the fact that all its propositions have as hypothesis and as consequent the assertion of a material implication." **Russell**, *The Principles of Mathematics*

propositional content, see content

propositional form, another term for form of proposition

propositional function

LOGIC An expression or schema, such as "x is mortal," which can be converted into a **proposition**, such as "Socrates is mortal," by replacing "x" with a determinate value, in this case "Socrates." The term originates in **Frege**'s investigation into the possibility of deriving mathematics from logical **axioms**. **Russell**, who applies the notion of propositional functions in the **analysis** of propositions, argues that general propositions state connections between propositional functions. For instance, "all men are mortal" can be analyzed into "whatever x may be, if x is a man, x is mortal." The appeal to propositional functions enables Russell to dispose of the grammatical subjects of universal propositions that we wrongly suppose to refer to existing **objects**. This maneuver is a major factor in his theory of **descriptions**. A propositional function is necessary if it always true. It is possible if it is sometimes true and sometimes false. It is impossible if it is never true.

> "A form of words containing an undetermined variable – for instance, 'x is a man' – is called a 'propositional function' if when a value is assigned to the variable, the form of words becomes a proposition." **Russell**, *Human Knowledge*

propositional knowledge

EPISTEMOLOGY **Knowledge** that something is the case, instances of which are expressed in the form S knows that p, where "S" stands for a person and "p" can be replaced by a proposition. As **knowing-that** or **knowledge by description**, propositional knowledge contrasts with **knowledge by acquaintance** (perceptual knowledge of a simple object), *a priori* knowledge, and **knowing-how**. The traditional or standard **analysis** of propositional knowledge is that it must satisfy three conditions: A knows p requires that (1) A **believes** that p, (2) p is true, and (3) A is **justified** in believing p. Historically, the majority of epistemological theories have analyzed each of these conditions and their interrelationships. Since **Gettier** posed his counterexamples to this **definition**, epistemologists have discussed whether we need to add a fourth condition to propositional knowledge and, if so, what it should be.

"The general definition of propositional knowledge that I propose to defend is along traditional lines and can be expressed as follows: S knows that P if and only if (1) P, (2) S is confident that P, and (3) S's being so is supported by a disinterested justification for being so, (4) that is externally conclusive." **Ginet,** *Knowledge, Perception, Memory*

propositional logic, another term for propositional calculus

propositional object, another expression for proposition

propositional sign
LOGIC A **sign** that expresses a **thought** or a **proposition**. In medieval Latin *propositio* has this meaning, although in modern English "proposition" refers rather to **propositional content**. According to **Wittgenstein**, if a sign is a propositional sign, all of its elements must be coordinated with one another in a determinate way. A proposition is not a different **entity** from a propositional sign, but is just a propositional sign taken together with its **pictorial** relation to its **objects**.

"A proposition is a propositional sign in its projective relation to the world." **Wittgenstein,** *Tractatus*

propositional verb, see propositional attitude

prosentential theory of truth
LOGIC The term "prosentence" was formed on analogy with "pronoun," in line with the claim that **sentences** containing **truth** predicates such as "That is true" relate to sentences in the way that pronouns relate to nouns. An anaphoric pronoun acquires its **references** from antecedent expressions and can be replaced by its antecedent. For instance, in "John is a student, and he is intelligent," the pronoun "he" acquires its reference through its relation to the earlier expression "John" and can be replaced by "John." The prosentential theory of truth claims that a sentence with the truth predicate "is true" has a similar anaphoric function. The only difference is that its reference is acquired from an antecedent sentence rather than an antecedent noun. "That is

true," can be replaced by an antecedent sentence. Accordingly, the truth predicate responds to and comments upon the **assertion** expressed by that sentence. In particular, the truth predicate does not introduce a **property** or common characteristic shared by true **propositions**. It is content-redundant and can be used to provide emphasis. The theory resembles the **disquotational theory of truth**.

"Briefly, a principal claim of the prosentential theory is that 'That is true' and 'It is true' are 'prosentences'. Prosentences function much as pronouns do, expect that prosentences occupy the positions in sentences that declarative sentences occupy, while pronouns occupy the positions names occupy." **Grover,** *A Prosentential Theory of Truth*

Protagoras (490–420 BC)
Greek philosopher, a leading sophist, born in Abdera. All of Protagoras' works were lost, with only a few fragments surviving. His claim that "man is the measure of all things" shows optimism about human strength and creativity, but has also been interpreted to imply epistemological relativism. Protagoras maintained that all customs are equally arbitrary and, hence, equally valid. He was agnostic about the existence or features of the gods and was an influential teacher of the rhetorical art. He claimed that there are two contradictory *logoi* or accounts about everything. He was portrayed in Plato's dialogue *Protagoras*.

protocol sentences
EPISTEMOLOGY, PHILOSOPHY OF SCIENCE [from German *Protokollsatze*, sometimes translated as protocol statements] For **Carnap** and **Neurath**, **statements** which others call **basic propositions**, basic sentences, or basic statements. They are also similar to the **atomic proposition** of **Russell** and **Wittgenstein**. Carnap, in the **material** mode of speech, defines protocol sentences in terms of our simplest state of **knowledge** and holds that they refer to directly given **experience** or phenomena. More satisfactorily, in the **formal** mode of speech he characterizes these sentences by their logical place in science, saying that they are the statements that need no further **justification** and that all other statements of science are **verified** by reference to them. The notion of

protocol statement is significant for **logical positivism**, which held that science is a system of statements based on and verified by experiment and observation and that protocol statements are the basis of verification.

It is a characteristic of protocol sentences that they can be verified only **solipsistically** and that they therefore provide a poor basis for publicly shared scientific knowledge. Given their peculiar nature, problems arise about the **meaning** and **truth** of protocol sentences. There are difficulties in deciding how to identify sentences as protocol sentences and to explain why their truth should be immune from further tests. The **private language argument** deepens these problems. These difficulties about protocol sentences made the views of logical positivism about the foundations of **science** untenable. As a result, Carnap and Neurath were driven to rely upon the logical relations between statements rather than ascribing a privileged epistemological position to some. Protocol sentences are also called "observation sentences," but **Schlick** claimed that observation statements, unlike protocol statements, can not be written down or memorized.

"Regardless of this diversity of opinion it is certain that a sequence of words has a meaning only if its relations of deductibility to the protocol sentences are fixed, whatever the characteristics of the protocol sentences may be." **Carnap, "The Elimination of Metaphysics Through Logical Analysis of Language," in Ayer (ed.),** *Logical Positivism*

providence

PHILOSOPHY OF RELIGION [from Greek *pronoia*, foresight, foreknowledge and the Latin equivalent, *providentia*] A crucial religious term for the relation between **God** and the world, although the extent and meaning of providence has been a topic of dispute. In Stoicism, providence is a non-personal divine order pervading the world. In Christianity, it concerns God's prior **knowledge** or his plan that guides the path of the world and man. In a broad sense, it covers all of the activities by which God directly controls **nature**, man, and history, including creating and sustaining the world. Theologians usually distinguish between general providence, which is God's working through **natural laws**, and special providence, which is God's working through

some specific action such as delivering a message through a prophet. Some argue that special providence includes **miracles** as well, but this view was rejected by **Aquinas**. No matter how providence is understood, the relationship between providence and human **free will** has been a central problem for theology.

"In taking care of things, there is a distinction between the two, namely the reason in their planned disposition, and this is termed providence, and the disposing and execution, and this is termed government. The first is eternal, the second temporal." **Aquinas,** *Summa Theologiae*

prudence

ETHICS The exercise of intelligence or **rationality** to safeguard one's own interests. According to prudence, the calculation of individual loss and gain **motivates** an **action**. It judges what one ought to do with respect to one's **desires**, inclinations, and interests. Prudence differs from morality, which judges what one **ought** to by reference to the **rights** of others and one's **obligations** to others, as well as by reference to one's moral concerns with oneself. To act prudently is in itself neither moral nor immoral, but is simply to act **wisely** and rationally within the scope of one's aims and interests. Acting prudently does not entail that one will satisfy one's own desire at the expense of others. Prudence is opposed not to morality, but to imprudence, that is, to acting unwisely, irrationally, or foolishly. An immoral person does not necessarily act prudently, and an imprudent person does not necessarily act immorally. Prudence often coincides with common-sense morality.

"The word 'prudence' is used in a double sense: firstly, it can mean worldly wisdom, and secondly, private wisdom. The former is the skill of someone in influencing others so as to use them for his own purposes. The latter is the sagacity to combine all these purposes for his own lasting advantage. The value of the former is properly reduced to the latter, and it might better be said of one who is prudent in the former sense but not in the latter that he is clever and cunning, but on the whole imprudent." **Kant,** *Groundwork for the Metaphysics of Morals*

pseudo-concepts

PHILOSOPHY OF LANGUAGE, METAPHYSICS A **logical positivist** term for **concepts** that appear to be meaningful but which are actually **meaningless**. Any word or concept should have a **meaning** that allows it to pick out **objects** or other entities. According to logical positivists, however, many words are deprived of any meaning through their **metaphysical** use. Terms such as **Principle**, **God**, the **Absolute**, the **Infinite**, **Being** as Being and **Essence** are all pseudo-concepts. Although metaphysicians think that they have meaning, these words can not be used in **sentences** to assert anything. They are merely allusions to associated **images** and feelings that do not bestow a meaning on the expressions. They fail to satisfy empirical criteria of meaningfulness, and the **definitions** given to them in metaphysics are pseudo-definitions. The sentences that contain a pseudo-concept are pseudo-sentences.

"If it only seems to have a meaning while it really does not, we speak of a 'pseudo-concept'." **Carnap, "The Elimination of Metaphysics through Logical Analysis," in Ayer (ed.), *Logical Positivism***

pseudo-definitions, see pseudo-concepts

pseudo-object, another term for logical fiction

pseudo-object sentence

PHILOSOPHY OF LANGUAGE, METAPHYSICS **Carnap** distinguishes among three kinds of sentences: (1) An "object sentence," which speaks of an **object**, for instance, "Babylon was a big town"; (2) a "syntactical sentence," which speaks of a word, for instance, "The word 'Babylon' occurred in yesterday's lecture"; (3) a "pseudo-object sentence," which is formulated as though it refers to objects in the world while in reality it is a **syntactical** sentence that concerns expressions of the **object-language**, for instance, "Babylon was treated of in yesterday's lecture." Such a sentence has a misleading resemblance to a sentence that speaks about the object Babylon, but it is actually about the word "Babylon." The sentence "Roundness is a universal" is a pseudo-object sentence, and should be replaced with the syntactical sentence "'round' is a predicate." Carnap also calls this kind of sentence a quasi-syntactical sentence. According to him, philosophical statements are syntactical, but in the history of philosophy they have been treated as object sentences or statements. In this mistake lies the root of many traditional problems. We should translate pseudo-object sentences from the **material mode** of speech into the **formal mode** of speech by replacing them by their syntactical equivalents, that is, we should treat pseudo-object sentences as claims about words, a practice which would avoid much confusion and endless controversy.

"Thus, these sentences are syntactical sentences in virtue of their content, though they are disguised as object sentences. We will call them pseudo-object sentences." **Carnap, *The Logical Syntax of Language***

pseudo-paradox, see barber paradox

pseudo-predicate

PHILOSOPHY OF LANGUAGE, METAPHYSICS Also called metaphysical predicate. A term introduced by **Carnap** for predicates such as "individual," "universal," "number," and "necessary," which are employed frequently in metaphysics. Sentences in which these **predicates** function appear to convey certain **ontological** information, but they do not actually introduce any **properties** of the **objects** designated by these sentences. A sentence containing a pseudo-predicate is either **analytically true** or **meaningless**. The real role of these predicates concerns **syntactical** classification. The sentence "2 is a number" does not express anything about a property of 2, but rather classifies "2" as a numerical expression. A pseudo-predicate is eliminated when one converts a **material mode** of speech into a **formal mode of speech**.

"'P' is a pseudo-predicate if any sentence obtained from the sentential function 'Px' by substituting a value for 'x' is either analytically true or meaningless on account of resulting from the substitution of an inadmissible value." **Pap, *Elements of Analytic Philosophy***

pseudo-problem

PHILOSOPHY OF LANGUAGE, METAPHYSICS Early **analytical** philosophy, especially **logical positivism**, claimed that the majority of traditional and perennial **metaphysical** problems are not genuine questions, although they appear to be. Logical **analysis** reveals that although these problems have the same grammatical form as genuine questions, they in fact arise from a misuse of language. For example, the question "Does God exist?" arises because metaphysicians confuse the copulative use and the existential use of the verb "to be." Accordingly, pseudo-problems can be dismissed through **semantic** analysis.

"Grammatical similarities foster the illusion, which proves a source of immortal metaphysical pseudo-problems, as though 'real' and 'unreal' referred to opposite properties of things, just like 'kind-unkind', 'living-dead', 'stable-unstable'." **Pap,** *Elements of Analytic Philosophy*

pseudo-proposition

PHILOSOPHY OF LANGUAGE A term introduced by **Wittgenstein** in the *Tractatus*, referring to any **judgment** that attempts to **say** that which can only be **shown**. Unlike other **propositions**, pseudo-propositions can not be analyzed into atomic **pictures** and their combinations and therefore they are not pictures of the world. Wittgenstein thinks that in different ways the propositions of logic, mathematics, the *a priori* parts of natural science, ethics, and philosophy – including the propositions of his own *Tractatus* – are all pseudo-propositions. **Logical positivists** develop this idea in their attack on metaphysics by saying that all propositions and statements that purport to make a **factual** claim but which can not be **verified** by experience are pseudo-propositions. They have emotional significance, but lack cognitive meaning. There are many attempts to retrieve at least some of the fields discarded in this way by logical positivism.

"The propositions of mathematics are equations, and therefore pseudo-propositions." **Wittgenstein,** *Tractatus*

pseudo-science

PHILOSOPHY OF SCIENCE [from Greek *pseudo*, false or unreal] A doctrine or set of views that falsely claims the status of science or **knowledge**. In unhealthy academic circumstances, especially where an enforced orthodoxy exists, all other schools can be condemned without justification as pseudo-sciences. Determining whether a doctrine is a pseudo-science

is an issue in the philosophy of science and requires that one first determine what counts as scientific knowledge. For **logical positivism**, if a thesis satisfies the verifiability **criterion**, it is scientific; otherwise it is pseudo-scientific. Accordingly, traditional **metaphysics** is pseudo-scientific and **meaningless** because none of its claims can be verified. **Popper** claimed that the criterion for **demarcating** science from pseudo-science is that of **falsifiability**. To be scientific, a **theory** must be falsifiable, that is, in principle there must be some observation statements that would contradict the theory. Popper does not deny that the statements of a pseudo-science are meaningful. Some critics of Popper claim that pseudo-sciences are typically both falsifiable and falsified, but are still retained by their supporters. From this perspective, the **integrity** of individual investigators and of the institutions of the scientific community is a more important consideration in distinguishing science from pseudo-science.

"Social scientists use the epithets 'scientific' and 'pseudo-scientific' as a major part of the ritual language of denunciation." **Yearley,** *Science and Sociological Practice*

pseudo-statement

PHILOSOPHY OF LANGUAGE, METAPHYSICS A statement-like word sequence which can not be reduced to **protocol sentences** or statements and which can not pass the test of the verification **principle**, either because it contains **meaningless** words (**pseudo-concepts**) or because it puts together meaningful words in a way violating **syntax**. Such a word-sequence appears to be a **statement** but it is not. It fails to **assert** anything and expresses neither a true proposition nor a false proposition. Pseudo-statements are of major concern to **logical positivism**, which labels all metaphysical statements as pseudo-statements. They claim that the origin of metaphysical pseudo-statements lies in the logical defects of **ordinary language**. The notion of pseudo-statements is the target of much criticism that has been directed at logical positivism.

"Our thesis, now, is that logical analysis reveals the alleged statements of metaphysics to be pseudo-statements." **Carnap, "The Elimination of Metaphysics through Logical Analysis of Language," in Ayer (ed.),** *Logical Positivism*

psyche, Greek term for soul

psychoanalysis

PHILOSOPHY OF MIND, PHILOSOPHY OF SOCIAL SCIENCE
A therapeutic practice and associated **theory** of
mind founded by **Freud**. As a theory, it postulates
the existence of an **unconscious** mind, comprising
painful thoughts that through **repression** are
excluded from **consciousness**, except as disguised
through symbolic transformation in such phenomena as dreams, puns, and slips of the tongue.
The unconscious has a dynamic role in determining **behavior**. Psychoanalytic theory places great
emphasis on the origin of neurosis in the sexual
drives and fantasies of early childhood, especially
in the relations of a child to his parents through
the **Oedipus complex**. The theory claims to reveal
and explain a variety of affective disturbances and
intellectual blindnesses in people not suffering
from a psychic disorder. The theory has a **causal**
physical side in Freud's early concern with the workings of the nervous system, but also an interpretative side, based on interpreting back to their origin
the repressed thoughts that surface consciously in
symbolically distorted ways. For analysts, anything
important in an analytic session is likely to be below
the surface of overt meaning.

As a therapy, classical psychoanalysis is ideally
conducted as a kind of talking cure. In regular conversations between analyst and patient, the analyst's
neutrality allows the patient to project the repressed
early relations and **emotions** allegedly at the root
of the disorder. The analyst may employ various
techniques, including dream interpretation or free
association, to reach what is repressed. The analyst
analyzes what the patient says, trying to reveal from
the recovered material the repressed unconscious
thoughts considered to be at the root of the
patient's illness. The main aim of psychoanalysis is
to bring repressed thoughts to consciousness, and
this kind of discovery, when accepted by the patient,
is meant to lead to a cure.

Freud claimed that psychoanalysis, after the
Copernican and **Darwinian** revolutions, was the
third blow to human claims to uniqueness. He
believed that it provided a key to the theory of
human nature and suggested that philosophy
should correct its long-term prejudice in favor of
the conscious. The discovery of the processes of

the unconscious mind would enlarge our conception of the self and greatly enhance human
self-knowledge. Freud also used a psychoanalytic
approach to interpret art and **culture**.

In spite of a suggestive richness that placed
psychoanalysis near the center of many developments of twentieth-century culture, virtually all of
its major claims as a theory and its major practices
as a therapy have been attacked by outside critics
and through schisms and expulsions among those
within the psychoanalytic movement. The promise
of therapeutic success remains broadly unfulfilled.
Psychoanalysis has been attacked as bad **science**,
as **pseudo-science**, and as a bad humane discipline,
and the best way to characterize and assess the
enterprise remains in dispute. Some philosophy
of mind and almost all major schools of modern
European philosophy have been influenced by
psychoanalysis.

> "Psycho-analysis is the name (1) of a procedure
> for the investigation of material processes which
> are almost inaccessible in any other way; (2) of a
> method (based on that investigation) for the treat-
> ment of neurotic disorders and (3) of a collection
> of psychological information obtained along those
> lines, which is gradually being accumulated into a
> new scientific discipline." **Freud,** *Standard Edition*
> *of the Complete Psychological Works of Sigmund Freud,*
> **vol. 18**

psycholinguistics

PHILOSOPHY OF SOCIAL SCIENCE, PHILOSOPHY OF MIND,
PHILOSOPHY OF LANGUAGE An interdisciplinary science
of psychology and linguistics, dealing mainly with
individual psychological reality and the processes
which determine the production, acquisition, and
learning of language. Although the name of this
discipline appeared in 1895 in a book by the German
scholar Meringer, the discipline did not flourish
until the 1950s, marked by the publication of C. E.
Osgood and T. A. Sebeok (eds.), *Psycholinguistics:
A Survey of Theory and Research Problems* (1954). The
development of psycholinguistics is stipulated by
Chomsky's work in linguistics and psychological
cognitivism. Scholars disagree widely about the
characterization of this discipline and its main problems. But its basic tenet is to oppose the **behavioral**
theory of language, to discover the psychological

entities behind linguistic structures and to determine the **competence** beneath the **performances** of language speakers. Recently its focus has been on the devices of language acquisition.

> "Psycholinguistics is the study of the mental mechanisms that make it possible for people to use language. It is a scientific discipline whose goal is a coherent theory of the way in which language is produced and understood." **Garnham,** *Psycholinguistics*

psychological determinism

PHILOSOPHY OF MIND, PHILOSOPHY OF ACTION The view that human **behavior** or **action** is determined by psychological **events** within the agent's **mind,** rather than by objective **natural laws,** as physical **determinism** claims. What underlies this position is the **dualist** view of the relation between body and soul that was dominant in ancient Greek philosophy and was fully articulated by **Descartes.** On this view, the body and soul are two distinct **entities,** with the soul governing the body. Psychological determinism denies that there is a problem of **free will. Freedom** is freedom from coercion and **constraints,** and an act is free if the agent performs it in accordance with the determination of the mind.

> "Psychological determinism maintains that there are certain psychological laws, which we are beginning to discover, enabling us to predict, usually on the basis of his experiences in early infancy, how a man will respond to different situations throughout his later life." **Lucas,** *The Freedom of the Will*

psychological egoism

PHILOSOPHY OF MIND, PHILOSOPHY OF ACTION The position that by **nature** people pursue what they **believe** to be in their **self-interest** and are by nature **egoistic.** Certainly, people may sacrifice their immediate and obvious self-interests but only if doing so is a means to a longer-term self-interested goal. This is a psychological theory about the **dispositions** and motivations of human nature, rather than an **ethical** position about the moral **virtue** of these motivations and consequent **behavior.** For this reason, ethical egoism is also called **normative egoism.** Psychological egoism provides a basis for ethical egoism, and, if it is true, all versions of ethical **altruism** are psychologically

groundless. Yet it is hard to prove that psychological egoism is true, and critics maintain that we are also motivated by non-egoistic **desires.**

> "Psychological egoism . . . can be formulated as follows: A person can perform an act only if that act has at least as much agent utility as any alternative." **Feldman,** *Introductory Ethics*

psychologism

LOGIC, PHILOSOPHY OF MIND, PHILOSOPHY OF SOCIAL SCIENCE A **theory** that became popular in the nineteenth century and was initiated by the German philosophers J. F. Fries and F. E. Beneke. According to its **neo-Kantian** position, psychology is the basis of philosophy and **introspection** is the primary method of philosophical enquiry. Every discipline in philosophy is nothing more than applied psychology. The view was especially associated with **logic.** In that area it rejected **Kant**'s **transcendental** psychology as unscientific and claimed that logic is based upon **laws of thought** that can be explained in terms of empirical psychological **principles.** It attempted to explain logical connections in terms of psychological **causes** and therefore tended to confuse logical issues and psychological issues. It had some connection with both British **empiricism** and **naturalism.** J. S. **Mill** and R. H. **Lotze** defended psychologism in their logic by claiming that introspection provides the only basis for the **axioms** of mathematics and the principles of logic. The position was severely criticized by **Frege** and **Carnap,** but has been revived in **naturalized epistemology.**

> "Psychologism, that is, the explanation of sense in terms of some inner psychological mechanism possessed by the speaker." **Dummett,** *The Seas of Language*

psychologist's fallacy

PHILOSOPHY OF SOCIAL SCIENCE William **James**'s term for the confusion of a psychologist's own characterizations of a **mental state** with the actual features of the original mental state that he is studying. It has different formulations, and can refer either to a psychologist's relation to the **experience** of others or to a person's comments on his own experience. The fallacy also arises from the psychologist's failure to recognize the hierarchy of relations of an original mental state. A person who possesses such a mental state may report at a higher level, and the psychologist will comment in turn on the report. He will believe that the original mental state may only have the characteristics he defines within his **theory** and will take his own **knowledge** as the whole sphere of knowledge about the **object**. With the formulation of this fallacy, James claimed that there is a gap between **theoretical constructs** and the experience on which they are based.

"Another variety of the psychologist's fallacy is the assumption that the mental state studied must be conscious of itself as the psychologist is conscious of it." **W. James,** *The Principles of Psychology*

psycho-physical parallelism, see parallelism

public choice
POLITICAL PHILOSOPHY, PHILOSOPHY OF ACTION, PHILOSOPHY OF SOCIAL SCIENCE Also called social choice, an area of political philosophy that is heavily influenced by economic theory and concerns the establishment of a logic of rational social action, such as voting procedures, lobbying, or electoral reform. Each **individual** is **motivated** to act by **self-interest**, and a rational choice is necessary for an **action** to achieve greatest advantage. However, under many circumstances, action has to be social, and the rationality of individual choice has to depend on the rationality of the choices of other **agents**. Otherwise, a choice seeking the best consequence can turn out to obtain the worst outcome, as the **prisoner's dilemma** powerfully indicates. A major concern of public choice theory is to establish how rational agents might coordinate their choices to achieve their mutual advantage. Since the public good is not the simple aggregate of individual goods, another aspect of public choice theory is to work out the strategy by which a society can generate a single rational and impartial choice to maximize public goods from the various rational preferences of individuals, although Kenneth **Arrow** has shown that on certain plausible assumptions this is not possible. Since **democracy** is based on such an ideal, public choice theory becomes important for virtually every operation of democracy.

"Public choice applies economists' method to politics, and in particular, to two central problems: the collective action problem and the problem of aggregating preferences." **McLean,** *Public Choice*

public goods
POLITICAL PHILOSOPHY Goods that anyone may enjoy whether or not they pay for them, for instance police protection or traffic lights. They are not subjected to crowding, that is, one person's enjoyment of a public good does not entail that other people will enjoy the good less. The problem of public goods is associated with that of the **free rider**, for if no one pays for enjoying them, the public goods will be difficult to maintain. As a result, either the quality of the goods will be reduced or these goods might be entirely withdrawn. Understanding the possibility of maintaining public goods is also a central concern of **public choice theory**.

"A pure public good is defined as a good requiring indivisibility of production and consumption, non-rivalness and non-excludability." **McLean,** *Public Choice*

public morality
ETHICS, POLITICAL PHILOSOPHY, PHILOSOPHY OF LAW The sphere in which standards of human **behavior** are enforced by the law and violations of this moral legislation are subject to **punishment** according to the criminal law. Murder and stealing, for instance, are matters for public morality. It is generally held that public morality is essential to the maintenance of communal existence. In contrast, private morality and law are different spheres, and violations of private moral principles are condemned but are not subject to the law. Sometimes the demarcation between public and private morality is not easy to draw, for example in the cases of prostitution and **pornography**. It is a matter of controversy on what grounds and to what extent a society has the right to enforce its prevailing morality.

"The public morality of a state consists partly of those central tenets of morality which no reasonable man, we think, can reasonably dissent from; and partly of those collective aspirations and ideals which the community, either implicitly in the course of its history, or explicitly by deliberate avowals, has collectively adopted or affirmed." **Lucas,** *The Principles of Politics*

public particulars see objective particulars

public/private dichotomy

ETHICS, POLITICAL PHILOSOPHY, PHILOSOPHY OF LAW
The distinction between the public and private
spheres amounts to a distinction between the political and the personal and between what falls under
the **law** and what falls outside the law. The **state**
and social power should not apply to the private
sphere, which is the limit of the public institutions
of law. Traditionally, the family, home, and personal
taste and preference are private or domestic matters.
Religion sometimes joins these other concerns
and is a sign that the distinction is not absolute.
Whatever the boundaries, the invasion of the private sphere is considered shameful. In contrast, the
public sphere is the domain of relationships that
are subject to the regulations of law and **political**
authority. The distinction between the public and
the private is essential for **liberal** theory to maintain the privacy-based **rights** and freedom of the
individual (although other rights are based in the
public sphere) and to **indicate** the legitimate extent
of political authority. The distinction is not respected
in fascist and **totalitarian** systems.

The distinction is challenged by many **feminists**,
who describe the public sphere as one of **justice**,
autonomy, and **independence** and the private
sphere as one of **care**, nurturing, and bonding. Feminists claim that the distinction is gender-based,
that it legitimates the exclusion of women from
the public sphere, that it ignores domestic violence
and male domination over women and children in
the private sphere. Hence, feminism attempts to
demolish this **dichotomy** or to remove it from
patterns of domination.

> "A clear dichotomy between the public (political
> and economic) and the private (domestic and
> personal) has been taken for granted, and only the
> former has been regarded as the appropriate sphere
> for developmental studies and theories of justice,
> respectively, to attach to." **Okin, in Nussbaum and
> Glover (eds.), Women, Culture and Development**

punctuate property

METAPHYSICS, PHILOSOPHY OF LANGUAGE Also called
atomistic property, a **property** that is unique to the
thing that possesses it and is not shared by any
other things. In contrast, an **anatomic property** or

holistic property is a property possessed by at least
two things. A major question in contemporary
philosophy of language asks whether a **semantic**
property can be punctuate.

> "An atomistic or punctuate property is one which
> might, in principle, be instantiated by only one
> thing." **Fodor and Lepore, Holism**

punishment

ETHICS, PHILOSOPHY OF LAW Punishment contains
three factors: (1) It is the infliction of **harm** to the
wrongdoer; (2) this infliction is imposed by **authority**; (3) the authority imposes the infliction **intentionally**. Since punishment itself looks like a kind
of harm, it requires a theoretical **justification**.
Historically, there are two rival theories of the justification of punishment. The first is retributivism,
which claims that a wrongdoer deserves a punishment
because it is in proportion to his **offense**. Through
punishment, a society indicates its intolerance of
certain types of **behavior** committed by **rational**
beings. Accordingly, punishment in itself is an
intrinsic **good**. The second position is **utilitarianism**
or **consequentialism**, which claims that punishment
itself is an evil, but it can be justified if this evil is
outweighed by the good consequences of its results.
These consequences include deterring the same
offender from committing crime again, preventing
others from doing the same wrong, and rehabilit-
ating the offender. There is much debate among
consequentialists about which of these consequences
should have priority in justifying punishment.
These two positions have vied with one another
for acceptance. According to retributivism, a utilitarian position could justify punishment of the
innocent provided that it can produce better consequences. Utilitarianism, on the other hand, charges
retributivism with cruelty, for it favors harm
and suffering even if it does not produce any good.
Various proposals have been advanced to reconcile
the conflict between retributivism and utilitarianism concerning punishment, but they are generally
unconvincing. One influential suggestion is that
utilitarianism should be appealed to when we justify
the need for a society to have a system of punishment, and retributivism should be appealed to if
we need to justify the punishment of a particular
person in a particular way.

"Let us describe punishment as simply an authority's infliction of a penalty on an offender, and now allow an offender to be a man who has broken a rule out of intention or negligence, or a man who has broken certain rules out of neither, or a man who occupies a certain position of authority with respect to a rule-breaker in either of the preceding sense." **Honderich,** *Punishment*

pure
METAPHYSICS, EPISTEMOLOGY In **Kant**'s philosophy, something that is independent of experience. For Kant, "pure" is associated with terms such as **transcendental**, **form**, **spontaneity**, **autonomy**, **original**, *a priori*, and **rational** and is contrasted with terms such as empirical, **matter**, receptivity, **heteronomy**, **derived**, *a posteriori*, and **sensational**. Kant always used pure as an adjective to qualify terms such as **apperception**, **concept**, **intuition**, **principle**, **reason**, and **representation**.

"A priori modes of knowledge are entitled pure when there is no admixture of anything empirical." **Kant,** *Critique of Pure Reason*

pure apperception, see transcendental apperception

pure concepts of reason, see ideas (Kant)

pure ego theory
EPISTEMOLOGY, METAPHYSICS, PHILOSOPHY OF MIND **Locke** claimed that we do not know the **substance** that is the bearer of all **attributes** and only recognize its **existence** through its various attributes. The pure ego theory of the self is the application of this epistemological and metaphysical claim to the problem of the self. The theory holds that the self itself is unknown, for it is outside **experience**, yet we know of its existence through its manifestations. A pure ego is the substance of all psychological attributes, and is the grammatical subject of all psychological statements. It is a peculiar constituent that supports the unity of the various **events** in one **temporal** slice of the history of a self, and it is the unity of the successive slices of the total history of a self. Such a pure ego is an **inferred entity**, which is posited because there must be something that underlies and supports various modes of experience. We may call it the I, the self, the **ego**, or the

subject. The totality of states of the same **mind** belong to this pure ego, and it persists as long as the mind persists. This theory can be contrasted to **Hume**'s **bundle theory**. A major difficulty faced by pure ego theory is how to account for the **knowledge** of one's own self. **Kant**'s claim that the "**I think**" which accompanies all our **representations** is not an **object** and **Wittgenstein**'s critical assessment of the **metaphysical** subject might help us to retain the self without requiring that it is a pure substantial basis for our experiences.

"The pure ego theory preserves the unity and the endurance of the self, but it does so at the cost of making the self non-experiential, and that is at odds with our native knowledge of ourselves." **Evans,** *The Subject of Consciousness*

pure hypothetical syllogism, see mixed hypothetical syllogism

pure reason, see *Critique of Pure Reason*

pure theory of law
PHILOSOPHY OF LAW A theory developed by the Austrian legal philosopher Hans **Kelsen** and philosophically based on **neo-Kantianism**. The theory is **pure** in the sense that the law should be a **universally** valid system that is free of all that is changeable and yet able to give ideals that guide lawyers in the search for **justice**. All moral, political, and sociological contents must be purged from the science of law. According to Kelsen, law is a system of norms, a hierarchy of normative relations that measures human conduct by the use of sanction. The legal norms constitute a relation of condition and sequence rather than a **command**: "If A is done, B ought to happen." The validity of legal norms is not based on conflicting **authorities**, but is ultimately derived from a **basic norm** (*Grundnorm*) that is **postulated** in the historically first constitution. The validity of the basic norm is not derived, but must be assumed as an initial **hypothesis**. Legal theory is concerned with the conceptual tools for **analyzing** the relations between the fundamental norms and all lower norms within a legal system. It is not concerned with its moral content, which should be the subject-matter of politics or **moral theory**. On this basis, Kelsen

attacked **natural law theory**, which insists on a **necessary** connection between law and **morality**. He drew a sharp distinction between **"is" and "ought,"** and denied the possibility of obtaining **objective knowledge** of legal norms. The science of law is **descriptive** rather than **prescriptive**. Kelsen's pure theory of law is one of the most influential twentieth-century legal theories. His approach is similar to **Austin**'s **analytical jurisprudence**, and was further developed by H. L. A. **Hart**.

> "A pure theory of law must be uncontaminated by politics, ethics, sociology, history. Its task is knowledge of all that is essential and necessary to law, and therefore freed from all that is changing and accidental in it." **Friedmann, *Legal Theory***

purely referential, see referentially opaque

Putnam, Hilary (1926–)

American philosopher of mathematics, science, mind, language, metaphysics, epistemology, and social sciences, born in Chicago, Illinois, Professor of Philosophy at Massachusetts Institute of Technology and Harvard University. Putnam not only has a broad range of interest, but also has rejected important positions that he previously advocated, including realism in the philosophy of science and functionalism in the philosophy of mind. His famous twin earth argument opposes the claim that meaning is in the mind and leads to influential views about meaning and reference. His major works include *Mathematics, Matter and Method* (1975), *Mind, Language and Reality* (1975), *Realism and Reason* (1983), and *Representation and Reality* (1988).

Pyrrho (c.360–c.271 BC)

Hellenistic philosopher, born in Elis, founder of Pyrrhonic skepticism. Pyrrho wrote nothing, and his views were reported by his disciple Timon. Pyrrho questioned the basis for claims to knowledge and truth in other philosophical schools and held that it is impossible to know the real nature of the entities that we assume to exist independently of our perceptual experiences. Contradictory accounts of all matters cause much confusion in our minds. Since each account can be countered by its contradictory, none is more valid than any other. The wise should

suspend judgment in order to achieve peace of mind or tranquility.

Pyrrhonism, see skepticism

Pythagoras (c.570–495 BC)

Pre-Socratic Greek philosopher, born on Samos in the eastern Aegean and moved to Croton (in southern Italy) around 525. Pythagoras was reported to have founded a religious and political community, but little is known about his own views. Pythagorean philosophy is a mixture of the views of Pythagoras and his followers. From their study of mathematics and music, the Pythagoreans believed that **number** is the principle of the cosmos and that the entire universe is a harmonious arrangement (in Greek, *kosmos*) ordered by number. This theory provides a mathematical or formal interpretation of the universe, in contrast to the materialist interpretation of the Milesians. Pythagoreans also held the doctrine of the **transmigration of souls**.

Pythagoreanism

ANCIENT GREEK PHILOSOPHY Philosophy of the Greek philosopher **Pythagoras** and his followers. Little literature exists to enable us to present a systematic picture of this philosophy or even to distinguish Pythagoras' own view from those of his followers. Generally, Pythagoreanism is a mixture of religion and science. It accepted the **transmigration of the soul** and enjoined the practice of an **ascetic** way of life. The aim of philosophy was to purify the soul. Through its study in mathematics, music, and astronomy, Pythagoreanism derived the doctrine that **number** is the **first principle** of all things and that the whole universe is a **harmony**. Accordingly, it held that everything could be explained in mathematical terms. All this deeply influenced Euclid, **Empedocles**, and especially **Plato**. In the first century BC there was a revival of Pythagoreanism, usually called **neo-Pythagoreanism**, which concentrated on the **mystical** and superstitious side of Pythagoeanism and its reverence for number. This revival had great impact on **Neoplatonism**.

> "With Pythagoreanism begins the transformation of the Greek mode of thought by a foreign element which originated in the Orphic mysticism." **Zeller, *Outlines of the History of Greek Philosophy***

Q

quadrivium

LOGIC, PHILOSOPHY OF LANGUAGE, PHILOSOPHY OF SCIENCE The liberal arts curriculum in the medieval university consisted of seven disciplines, which were divided into a lower division of *trivium*, including grammar, rhetoric, and logic, and a higher division of *quadrivium*, including geometry, arithmetic, astronomy, and music. The former is concerned with the art of discussion, and the latter is concerned with the physical world and its **principles**. The *quadrivium* was studied after the study of the *trivium* was completed. Virtually every graduate of a medieval university received training in these seven subjects.

"The *quadrivium* – geometry, arithmetic, astronomy and music – constituted a 'scientific' syllabus, summarising the principles of order in the physical world." **Haren, *Medieval Thought***

quale, singular of qualia

qualia

EPISTEMOLOGY, METAPHYSICS [the plural of quale, from Latin *qualis*, of such a kind or qualities] The immediately **experienced contents** or **objects** of sense-awareness, giving what it feels like to have a **sensation** or to be in a perceptual state. Qualia, which include things such as the smell of coffee or the taste of sugar, are also called **phenomenal properties**. Qualia are neither **intentional** nor **representational**.

How to understand the nature of qualia has been a matter of debate. Different accounts have been developed on the basis of different analyses of **sense-data**. The term was introduced by C. I. **Lewis** and **Goodman** for the simplest qualitative elements in the contents of sense-experience. **Ayer** claims that a quale should be distinguished from a sensory **particular** that is confined to a momentary episode of **awareness**. Instead a quale is a sensory **universal**, **intersubjective** and repeatable. It can be empirically realized in different **minds** and at different times.

"My qualia, then, are visual or other sensory patterns. I conceive of their range as being very wide. Anything counts as a quale that a person is able to pick out as a recurrent or potentially recurrent feature of his sense-experiences, from a two-dimensional colour expanse to a complex three-dimensional gestalt." **Ayer, *The Origins of Pragmatism***

qualified good

ETHICS **Kant**'s distinction between qualified good and unqualified good contrasts with the distinction between instrumental goods and intrinsic goods drawn by **utilitarianism**. For Kant, many goods are intrinsic, such as **pleasure**, the absence of **pain**, and happiness in general, because they are not for further **ends**. But they are still goods with qualification, rather than goods that are absolute or unqualified. Even happiness is good only when it is **deserved** and is not good if enjoyed by a bad person who does not deserve it. Many other traditional goods, such as moderation or **courage**, can be put to bad use under some circumstances. Kant held that the only unqualified good that is good whatever the circumstances is a good **will**, and that other goods always presuppose a good will.

> "Moderation in emotions and passions, self-control, and calm deliberation are not only good in many respects but even seem to constitute part of the intrinsic worth of a person. But they are far from being rightly called good without qualification ... For without the principles of a good will, they can become extremely bad." **Kant, Groundwork for the Metaphysics of Morals**

quality of life

ETHICS, POLITICAL PHILOSOPHY, PHILOSOPHY OF SOCIAL SCIENCE The degree of **well-being**, **satisfaction**, or happiness in one's life. A traditional version of **utilitarianism** claims that the quality of life should be assessed according to an **objective** measure of **utility**, such as per capita GNP. But even if we assign a central role to utility, there are problems about its distribution and bearing on people's lives. Other **indicators** might be needed to judge quality of life, such as health care, education, social and natural environments, life expectancy, the legal privileges one enjoys, and the freedom one has. Furthermore, some philosophers consider quality of life to be a **subjective** assessment of how one feels about one's life, without regard to external conditions. A person could be very happy in situations that others judge to be miserable. We can ask whether there is a unique standard, such that we have a better quality of life the more completely it is satisfied. In discussions of **euthanasia** and **suicide**, some philosophers ask whether it is morally permissible to terminate a life that is not worth living judged according to quality of life.

> "When we inquire about the prosperity of a nation or a region of the world, and about the quality of life of its inhabitants, Sissy Jupe's problem still arises: how do we determine this? What information do we require? Which criteria are truly relevant to human 'thriving'?" **Nussbaum and Sen (eds.), The Quality of Life**

quantifier

LOGIC In **categorical propositions** of standard form, "some" is a quantifier for **particular propositions** and "all" or "no" are quantifiers for **universal propositions**. Modern **predicate logic** calls "some" the **existential quantifier** and "all" the **universal quantifier**. The existential quantifier is symbolized as $(\exists x)$, which reads "there is at least one x that ..." or "for some x ...". The universal quantifier is symbolized as (x) or $(\forall x)$, which reads "for any x ..." or "for all x ...". Quantifiers are employed in **sentences** with **variables** (x, y, ...), **predicates** (F, G, ...), **relations** (R, ...), the identity sign (=), and the **logical constants** (and, or, not, if-then ...). $(\exists x)(\exists y)$ (if Fx and Gy, then x = y) reads "For some x and for some y, if x is F and y is G, then x is identical with y." The individual or multiple use of the universal quantifier "all" and the existential quantifier "there exists" to bind variables in sentences has been seen as the key to the development of a powerful and flexible system of modern predicate logic. Quantifiers can occur more than once in a **statement**, for example "All human beings have some ancestors." The application of the quantifier, called quantification, turns an **open sentence** with unbound variables into a **closed sentence** in which the variables are bound with quantifiers. There is debate whether quantifiers can bind items other than individual variables, such as predicate, relational, or sentential variables, and a related debate over a **referential** interpretation of quantification, focusing on the objects in the domain of the quantifier, and the **substitutional** interpretation of quantification, focusing on the expressions that can be suitably substituted for the quantifier.

> "Usual notations for these respective purposes are '(x)' and '($\exists$x)', conveniently read 'everything x is such that' and 'something x is such that'. These prefixes are known, for unobvious but traceable reasons, as quantifiers, universal or existential." **Quine, Word and Object**

quantum theory

PHILOSOPHY OF SCIENCE A modern physical theory, developed by Planck, Bohr, Heisenberg, and Schrödinger to deal with the structure and behavior of subatomic particles. According to quantum theory, in the subatomic world the position and velocity of an electron at any moment can be known only with mutually related uncertainty. **Newton**'s theory of **causality** does not apply in the microworld. For subatomic particles, we can specify neither the energy at a particular time nor the momentum at a particular position with precision. We can, however, calculate the energy over a period of time or the momentum over a range of positions. This lack of certainty at a fundamental physical level establishes a new picture of reality and seriously undermines the classical conceptions of particle and thing. The principle "every event has a cause" is no longer true *a priori*. If the theory of **relativity** challenges the traditional concepts of **time** and **space**, quantum mechanics challenges the traditional conceptions of physical causality and **determinism**. Although the theory has had great empirical success, interpreting the theory and explaining why it succeeds have been matters of fierce debate. The Copenhagen interpretation, developed on the basis of the views of Bohr and Heisenberg, offers an **anti-realist** interpretation, which claims that quantum theory reflects **indeterminacy** in the world. The rival realist interpretation, developed from Einstein's criticism of Bohr and defended by **Popper** and **Putnam**, argues that a quantum system is really fully determinate like classical systems, even though our **knowledge** of the system is indeterminate.

> "Quantum theory gives us a highly workable algorithm for making prediction about the results of measurements, but philosophers and physicists are in total disagreement about what . . . quantum theory tells us about the way the quantum world is." **Gibbins**, *Particles and Paradoxes*

quasi-syntactical sentence, see pseudo-object sentence

quaterno terminorum, the Latin name for the four-term fallacy

quidditas

METAPHYSICS [from Latin *quid*, what, and *quidditas*, whatness, quiddity] The essential characteristic or **nature** of a thing, the nature that makes a thing the kind of thing it is. *Quidditas* serves as the content of **definition** and as the **object** of *intellectus*. It is a synonym of *essentia* (**essence**). To discover *quidditas* is to answer the question *Quad est?* (What is it?). **Duns Scotus** contrasted *quidditas* to *haecceitas*, that is, a unique essence or **individual essence** that determines a thing's **individuality**.

> "The proper object of the intellect is the whatness of things (quidditas)." **Aquinas**, *Summa Theologiae*

quid facti, see deduction (Kant)

quid juris, see deduction (Kant)

Quine, Willard Van Orman (1908–2000)

American philosopher and logician, born in Akron, Ohio, taught at Harvard. Quine was influenced by Russell, the empiricism of the Vienna Circle, and pragmatism. He made numerous original contributions to logic, philosophy of mathematics, philosophy of science, philosophy of language, and philosophy of mind. He modified Russell and Whitehead's logicist program of reducing mathematic to logic, rejected the possibility of a formalized intensional logic, and resisted Kripke's turn to modality. Quine is most famous for seeking to undermine the traditional analytic/synthetic distinction as a dogma of empiricism. The Quine–Duhem thesis argued that empirical tests can be applied only to the whole web or network of hypotheses and not to single theoretical sentences. His theory of radical translation and principle of the indeterminacy of translation attempted to account for language without invoking abstract or mental entities. His claim that "to be is to be the value of a variable" determines our ontological commitments according to our choices about logic and language. His books include *From A Logical Point of View* (1953), *Word and Object* (1960), *Set Theory and Its Logic* (1963), *The Ways of Paradox* (1966), *Ontological Relativity* (1969), *The Roots of Reference* (1974), and *Theories and Things* (1981).

Quine–Duhem thesis, see Duhem–Quine thesis

R

racism

POLITICAL PHILOSOPHY The claim that there is a biologically determined hierarchy of capacity or **value** among different races and that allegedly inferior races should be ruled by allegedly superior races. Racism is generally driven by fear and hatred and has led to major genocidal violence. Modern European racism can be traced to the eighteenth century, along with the emergence of anthropology, a discipline that compares and evaluates racial differences. This development, however, was preceded by similar patterns in the period of discovery and conquest of non-European peoples that began at the end of the fifteenth century. Racism has often been presented as a scientific enterprise, but its notion of race and its empirical claims about different peoples have repeatedly been shown to be unjustified and it is best understood as a pseudo-science. Racism has been particularly identified with the **ideology** and practice of slavery and other repressive control of African, Asian, and indigenous American and Australian peoples. Historically, racism was employed to justify colonialism and **imperialism** and to destroy indigenous people and their **culture**. Racism is related to anti-Semitism and in Germany was the intellectual foundation of Nazism. Theories attending to economic, cultural, historical, social, or universal human factors have sought to explain the conditions under which racism arises and why it provides such deep and powerful motives for destructive action. Colonial studies and post-colonial studies place these questions in historical context. All forms of racism are dangerous in practice, for they tend to create the inequalities between people that they claim to discover. Some philosophers try to determine whether oppression based on class, race, or gender is most fundamental to understanding modern society and culture.

"Most definitions of racism tend to be based on the concept of biologically determined superiority of one human population, group or race over another." **Castles,** *Here for Good*

radical empiricism

EPISTEMOLOGY, METAPHYSICS, PHILOSOPHY OF SCIENCE William **James**'s characterization of his empirical doctrine, which has three basic facets: a postulate that only things definable in terms drawn from **experience** are debatable; a statement of fact that the **relations** between things are as much matters of direct particular experience as the things themselves; and a generalized conclusion that the parts of experience hold together from next to next by relations that are themselves parts of experience. Experience is pure and needs no trans-empirical support. The radical nature of this empiricism is in its conclusion, which takes experience to be something neither **mental** nor **physical**. Instead, experience becomes the ultimate constituent of the universe out of which material and mental things are constructed. This is a position developed later by **Russell** in his *Analysis of Mind* as **neutral monism**. Radical empiricism is distinguished from traditional empiricism through denying the distinction between our **sensations** and external **objects**. James tried to provide a new account of **knowledge** and a solution to the **mind–body problem**. He called his position "radical," not because it was extreme, but because it attempts to remedy the defects he saw in traditional empiricism, namely its failure to include the relations of experience within the basic contents of experience. He also tried to reconcile empiricism and **rationalism**, using his distinction between tough-minded and tender-minded temperaments. James claimed that his radical empiricism and his **pragmatism** do not entail one another. However, commentators usually conclude that at least some features of pragmatism lend support to radical empiricism.

Feyerabend used the term radical empiricism for the position that science should employ a single set of mutually consistent **theories** and reject theoretical pluralism.

"I am interested in another doctrine in philosophy to which I give the name of radical empiricism, and it seems to me that the establishment of the pragmatist theory of truth is a step of first-rate importance in making radical empiricism prevail." **W. James,** *The Meaning of Truth*

radical feminism

POLITICAL PHILOSOPHY, PHILOSOPHY OF SOCIAL SCIENCE [from Latin *radicalis*, having a root] The belief that dominant political and social systems are characterized by oppression and that male oppression of women has provided the model for all other forms of oppression, such as racial or class oppression. The material condition of the subjection of women lies in their role in reproduction. Women are always slaves or objects, and men are always masters or subjects. Radical feminists argue that rape, pornography, prostitution, marriage, and heterosexuality are all imposed by male power over women, either directly or through a range of indirect stratagems. They claim that the relationship between male and female must always be conflictual. Radical feminism seeks to analyze the roots of the oppression of

women by men and to uncover the various ways in which male power is exercised, with the desire that such understanding will lead to drastic political and social reforms. This position was initiated by de **Beauvoir**'s *The Second Sex* (1949), which was influenced by **Sartre**'s existentialism. Other influential works include Figes' *Patriarchal Attitude* (1978), Firestone's *The Dialectic of Sex* (1971), Greer's *The Female Eunuch* (1970), and Millett's *Sexual Politics* (1985).

"The breadth of subjects treated in *The Second Sex* prepared the way for radical feminist claims that: Patriarchy is the universal constant in all political and economic systems, that sexism dates from the beginning of history, that society is a repertoire of manoeuvres in which male subjects establish power over female objects." **Nye,** *Feminist Theory and the Philosophy of Man*

radical interpretation

PHILOSOPHY OF LANGUAGE A process of **interpreting** a language unknown to the interpreter without relying upon existing linguistic knowledge. It tries to answer the question how we can **understand** a particular utterance that is not antecedently given and can not be helped by a translation manual. The theory is developed by **Davidson**, patterned on **Quine**'s radical translation. While radical translation intends to establish a linking of synonyms, radical interpretation requires that we establish the **truth conditions** of the sentences of a foreign language. Quine's radical translation avoids the use of psychological terms like **belief** and **desire**, whereas radical interpretation requires the interpreter to specify the beliefs and desires of the speakers. This interpretation relies heavily on the **principle of charity**, that is, the assumption that most of the utterances in the language express true beliefs.

"The term 'radical interpretation' is meant to suggest strong kinship with Quine's 'radical translation'. Kinship is not identity, and 'interpretation' in place of 'translation' marks one of the differences: a greater emphasis on the explicitly semantical in the former." **Davidson,** *Inquiries into Truth and Interpretation*

radical philosophy

POLITICAL PHILOSOPHY, PHILOSOPHY OF HISTORY, PHILOSOPHY OF SOCIAL SCIENCE, MODERN EUROPEAN

PHILOSOPHY, FEMINISM A British philosophical movement that arose in the 1970s, with the journal *Radical Philosophy* (1972–) as its main forum. Its aim has been to contest the philosophical predominance of **analytical philosophy** in British universities and intellectual life. In its early phase, it rejected **Oxford philosophy**, although many members of the radical philosophy group were educated in Oxford. It complained that analytical philosophy was narrow and complacent and that it ignored many crucial issues that require a philosophical response, including specific questions of **culture**, **tradition**, history, and politics. It held that the dominant British philosophy was a specialized subject that had little to offer anyone outside a small circle of professional philosophers. Radical philosophy has attempted to change this situation by challenging and subverting **linguistic philosophy**. The journal did not lay down a philosophical line, although it paid a great deal of attention to traditions ignored by analytical philosophy, especially to European philosophical movements such as **phenomenology** and **existentialism**, contemporary **Hegelian** and **Marxist** philosophy, **structuralism**, **post-structuralism**, and **deconstructionism**. Recently, it has been more associated with **feminism** and **postmodernism**. It has been hostile to the constraints of university institutions and has criticized the academic and social environments in which orthodox philosophy is maintained. Radical philosophy should not be confused with philosophical radicals.

"What radical philosophy objects to is not the investigation of language and concepts but rather the assumption that for philosophers such study means professional isolation from the world of material reality and acceptance of the ordinary language criterion of meaningfulness." **Edgley and Osborne (eds.),** *Radical Philosophy Reader*

radical translation

PHILOSOPHY OF LANGUAGE The translation of an alien language that has no links to familiar ones, where the translator can not appeal to any dictionary, compare other translations, or consult any studies of that language. The only place he can begin is with the **sentences** that seem to be directed immediately on to **stimulus** conditions. A rabbit runs by and the speaker says "gavagai." The translator guesses

from observation that this might refer to the rabbit, and then he subjects his guess to tests relating to further cases. He tries to ascertain whether the native speaker assents, dissents, or does neither. What he gets from this process is at best a working **hypothesis**, and he can never be sure that his translation is the only correct one. Radical translation is a device designed by **Quine** for his discussion of the **indeterminacy of translation** and is a model for all attempts to understand the language of another.

"What is relevant to our purposes is radical translation, i.e. translation of the language of a hitherto untouched people." **Quine,** *Word and Object*

Ramsey, Frank Plumpton (1903–30)

English logician and philosopher. In his brief academic career, Ramsey made a number of original contributions, including improvements to the program of Whitehead and Russell's *Principia Mathematica*, the development of the redundancy theory of truth, the articulation of a subjectivist or personalist theory of probability, and papers on philosophy of science and economics. He held that what came to be called a "Ramsey sentence" could cast a whole scientific theory in the form of one sentence by conjoining all the sentences of the theory and replacing all of its theoretical terms with existentially bound variables. Ramsey is also remembered because his critical philosophical appreciation of the *Tractatus* and later conversations were important factors in Wittgenstein's philosophical development. Ramsey's major philosophical papers were posthumously published in *The Foundations of Mathematics and Other Logical Essays* (1931).

Ramsey sentence

PHILOSOPHY OF SCIENCE Also called a Ramsey sentence of a theory. The Cambridge philosopher Frank Ramsey claimed that the whole empirical content of a **theory** can be cast in the form of one **sentence** by conjoining sentences expressing the content of the theory and by replacing all **theoretical terms** in the sentence by existentially **bound variables**. By replacing theoretical terms with bound variables, theories cease to be committed to specific kinds of **entities** and are rendered neutral concerning what entities will turn out to satisfy them. This approach to theories can support an **instrumentalist** view about what a scientific theory should be. It suggests that only **observational terms** are **cognitive**, while theoretical terms, as formal and non-descriptive symbols, should be eliminated. This account of theory is close to **Craig's theorem** and drew much attention in the 1950s and 1960s, when the distinction between theoretical terms and observation terms and their relationship became a major topic in the philosophy of science.

"In general, the Ramsey sentence of a theory is formed as follows: Form the conjunction of a set of statements sufficient to express the content of the theory, and then replace each theoretical term by an existentially quantified variable of appropriate type, making the scope of each quantifier the entire conjunction." **Maxwell, "Structural Realism and the Meaning of Theoretical Terms," in** *Minnesota Studies in the Philosophy of Science,* **vol. IV**

range

LOGIC The **set** of a **formula**, such that the members of the set are the **values** of the formula. The range of a **quantifier** is the collection of things from which values of the quantified **variable** can be drawn. In this case, range is synonymous with **domain**. The domain of a **relation** is a collection of things that stand in the relation to something else. The set of these related things constitutes the range or counterdomain of this relation. The domain and the range together constitute the field of the relation. A range of a **function** is the set of things that define the function, that is, that serve as possible **arguments** for this function. A range or universe of discourse is the collection of things talked about during the discourse.

"We take the range of the formula E_i to be the class of those value-assignments at which E_i comes to be true; the class of all possible value-assignments for E_i (i.e. for the value-bearing signs that occurs in E_i) we call the total range of E_i; the empty class of such value-assignments we call the null range." **Carnap,** *Introduction to Symbolic Logic and Its Applications*

ratio

METAPHYSICS, EPISTEMOLOGY, PHILOSOPHY OF MIND, LOGIC, PHILOSOPHY OF ACTION [Latin, corresponding to the Greek *logos*, and sharing the complicated and wide usage of the latter] *Ratio* can be used for the objective **meaning** of a thing (in a sense close to **form**), to the **power** to discern such meanings (in a sense close to **mind**), to the capacity to draw what is true from the premises when we pursue truth, and to the capacity to determine what to do when we plan **action**. In English, *ratio* can be translated by terms such as **reason, argument,** or **description**. Generally, *ratio* is contrasted with **emotion** and appetite, which it is normally supposed to control in us. In the philosophy of **Spinoza**, *ratio* is the second way of **knowing**, in contrast to **imagination** (**perception**) and scientific **intuition**. *Ratio* is exemplified in the thinking of scientists, who begin with common and evident truths and proceed to draw general conclusions from them. The model of this type of thinking is Euclidean geometry.

"The Ratio expressed in a word is something the intellect [*intellectus*] conceives from things and expresses in speech." **Aquinas,** *Summa Theologiae*

ratio decidendi

PHILOSOPHY OF LAW [Latin, the reason for deciding, a principle of judicial decision] A ruling on a point of law that a judge provides because he conceives it to be necessary to the **justification** of his particular decision. Such a ruling is the *ratio* of the case. It can be the **rule of law** laid down in a precedent or the rule of law that others regard as having binding **authority**. It can also be a material evidential **fact**. In contrast, an *obiter dictum* is any statement about the law made by the court that was not necessary to the decision. How to identify a *ratio decidendi* in a case is a fundamental issue. There is much debate about what the *ratio* is and about how to find it. Different judges in different courts are likely to hold different views so that a *ratio decidendi* in an original court will be considered as an *obiter dictum* in an appeal court or vice versa.

"The ratio decidendi of a case is any rule of law expressly or implicitly treated by the judge as a necessary step in reaching his conclusion, having regard to the line of reasoning adopted by him, or as a necessary part of his direction to the jury." **Cross,** *Precedent in English Law*

rational cosmology, see cosmology

rational egoism, see egoism, ethical

rational explanation
PHILOSOPHY OF HISTORY, PHILOSOPHY OF ACTION
Also called rational reconstruction. Developed by
Collingwood and William **Dray** as an alternative
mode of **historical explanation** to the **covering law
model**. It claims that historical explanation does not
consist in bringing an **event** under a covering general causal law, but rather explains by establishing a
relation between an **action** and the **rationality** of
its **agent**. We should explain an action by reference
to the reasons presented as contained in it. A historian should rethink and reconstruct the rationality
of the agent when the agent decided to act. Among
others, these factors include the agent's **knowledge**
of the actual situation, the agent's **purpose**, and the
agent's **deliberation** concerning the **means** appropriate to his **end**. If we discover an agent's reason
for performing an action, we achieve an **understanding** of that action. Certainly, if an agent is rational,
the considerations issuing in action must have conformed to some general standards of rationality, but
it does not follow that the action is **caused** or determined by those standards. Some critics argue that
irrational and non-rational behavior, in which actors
misunderstand their actions, are more important
than rational action in understanding history.

> "When the historian can see that the agent's
> beliefs, purposes, principles, etc., give him a reason
> for doing what he did, then he can claim to under-
> stand the action. The kind of understanding thus
> achieved, it might be argued, is different in *concept*
> from that sought on the scientific model . . . The
> former – which we might perhaps call 'rational' ex-
> planation – tries to make clear its *point* or *rationale*."
> **William Dray,** *Philosophy of History*

rational number
PHILOSOPHY OF MATHEMATICS A **real number** is any
number that can be expressed as an infinite decimal.
It can be either rational or irrational. A rational
number is any number that can be expressed as a
ratio x/y, where x is a positive or negative integer
or 0 and y is a positive integer, although the same
rational number can often be represented by more
than one ratio of integers. An irrational number

is any real number that is not rational, such as π or
the square root of 2.

> "The irrational numbers, such as the square root
> of 2, were supposed to find their place among
> rational fractions, as being greater than some of
> them and less than the others, so that rational and
> irrational numbers could be taken together as one
> class, called 'real number'." **Russell,** *Introduction to
> Mathematical Philosophy*

rational psychology
METAPHYSICS, PHILOSOPHY OF MIND In Christian
Wolff's division of metaphysics, one branch of
special metaphysics (along with **cosmology** and
rational **theology**). Its subject-matter is the **soul** or
mind, and its major task to prove the **immortality**
of the soul. In contrast to modern empirical psychology, which is based on observation and experiment,
rational psychology is purely **speculative**. Rational
theology is also called pneumatology (from Greek
pneuma, spirit), a study of the spirit or soul.

> "The second branch of the metaphysical system
> was rational psychology or pneumatology. It dealt
> with the metaphysical nature of the soul – that is,
> of the Mind regarded as a thing. It expected to
> find immortality in a sphere dominated by the
> law of composition, time, qualitative change, and
> qualitative increase or decrease." **Hegel,** *Logic*

rational reconstruction, another expression for
rational explanation

rational self-interest, see self-interest

rational theology, another expression for natural
theology

rationalism
PHILOSOPHICAL METHOD, EPISTEMOLOGY, METAPHYSICS
In an **epistemological** sense, rationalism is a philosophical tradition developed during the seventeenth
and eighteenth centuries in Europe, represented
mainly by **Descartes**, **Spinoza**, and **Leibniz**. Epistemological rationalism claimed that **knowledge**
is due to the exercise of the faculty of **reason** or
intellect and that **sensory experience** cannot establish **certainty**. The way of reason is the road to true
knowledge. Rationalism took mathematics as the

model of knowledge and admired the **axiomatic method**. It proposed that the method of philosophy should be the same as the method of mathematics. It held that all knowledge is connected and can be deduced from certain **self-evident first principles**. It also accepted the existence of *a priori* **knowledge** or **truths of reason**. Rationalism tried to construct a rational science of **nature** and attempted to solve certain metaphysical problems such as the general structure of the world, the relation of **mind** to **body** and **immortality**. As a tradition, it stood in contrast to the empiricism represented by the British philosophers Francis **Bacon, Hobbes, Locke, Berkeley**, and **Hume**, which claimed that all knowledge is derived ultimately from **experience**. **Kant** synthesized the rational and empirical traditions by giving both reason and experience crucial roles in the acquisition and **justification** of **knowledge**. Nevertheless, the tension between these two epistemological approaches can still be perceived in the contemporary **philosophy of language** and other areas. In the post-Kantian period, the continental rationalist tradition, while holding that reason is the supreme cognitive **faculty**, has held that its exercise should go beyond the scope of natural science. It has extended the exercise of reason to politics, history, art, religion, and in general to the *Geisteswissenschaften* (human sciences), and has tried to establish universal knowledge in these areas.

In its general sense, rationalism refers to all theories and practices that appeal to human rationality and rational principle, and is in contrast to positions that emphasize religious **faith**, moral **sentiment**, **emotion**, and other irrational elements. In this sense, empiricism is a form of rationalism, and rationalism contrasts with **irrationalism**.

> "Traditional rationalism, observing that any principles which should serve as ultimate criteria or determine categorical interpretation must be prior to and independent of the experience to which it applies, has supposed that such principles must be innate and so discoverable by some sort of direct inspection." **C. Lewis**, *Mind and the World-Order*

rationality

PHILOSOPHY OF MIND, PHILOSOPHY OF ACTION, ETHICS, LOGIC The exercise of human **reason**, the ability exhibited in **deduction**, **induction**, calculation, and other less formal intellectual processes. According to **Plato**'s tripartite analysis of the human **soul**, rationality contrasts with **emotion** (**passion**) and the appetites. He held that persons must subject their emotions and appetites to the rule of reason in order to find **truth** and to have a **happy** and harmonious life. **Aristotle** put forward a function-based argument, claiming that reason is the peculiar **function** that distinguishes human beings from other kinds of animals. Human **virtue** rests in the performance of this function. He even suggested on this basis that pure rational activity, that is, contemplation, is the happiest life. Aristotle made **practical reason** and moral virtue interdependent, but also acknowledged the possibility of **weakness of the will**, that is, knowing what is right but doing the contrary. To be rational in this sense is opposed to being emotional or acting according to appetite and intuition, which he described as irrational. Both **rationalism** and **empiricism** support the values of rationality, although rationalism emphasizes the role of the **faculty** of reason, while empiricism places emphasis on observation and experiment.

Hume claimed that only deductive and mathematical reasoning is rationally sound and that induction is not rationally justified. This has given rise to the long-standing dispute about the nature of inductive reasoning and the problem of induction. Hume also denied that reason plays a fundamental role in moral life and hence denied the existence of practical reason except as reasoning about **means** to obtain **ends** given by the passions. This position is also controversial, and some philosophers consider ends and passions to be within the scope of rationality.

In another sense, to call something rational or reasonable means that it conforms to general **rules**, **laws**, and acknowledged aims and also adheres to certain qualities of thinking such as **consistency**, **coherence**, and **completeness**. Being rational in this sense means, for example, being appropriate, making sense, or being understandable. This sense is concerned with the correct exercise of human reason, as opposed to its invalid exercise. **Creative** thought and activity that does not fall within the scope of formal systems can also be assessed for rationality.

"Rationality is a matter of seeking to do the very best we can (realistically) manage to do in the circumstances." **Rescher,** *Rationality*

rationes seminales

ANCIENT GREEK PHILOSOPHY, PHILOSOPHY OF RELIGION, PHILOSOPHY OF SCIENCE [Latin, from the Greek *logoi spermatikoi*, germinal principles or original factors] A notion employed by the Stoics, **Neoplatonists**, and **Augustine**. It is usually translated as seminal **reason** or seminal **virtue**. By this term Augustine meant the seeds, potential **powers**, or **causes** of the subsequent developments in the physical order after **God**'s **creation**. Change is simply the realization of what already exists virtually. These seeds were themselves created by God when he created the world. The view was intended to reconcile the tension between the belief that God created all things and the evident fact that new things are constantly developing, for according to this view, the development of every new thing is simply the unfolding of what has been in the world from the beginning. It is a metaphor, derived from the growth of a plant, which is the realization of the seed's latencies. The concept was possibly influenced by **Plato**'s theory of **recollection**, according to which **knowledge** involves remembering what one already knew. This term was later developed by the Franciscans to oppose Aristotelian naturalism.

"Augustine aptly termed *rationes seminales* all those active and passive powers that are the originative sources of the coming into being of natural things and of their changing." **Aquinas,** *Summa Theologiae*

ravens paradox, another expression for Hempel's paradox

Rawls, John (1921–2002)

American political philosopher, born in Baltimore, Maryland, educated at Princeton, and taught at Princeton, Cornell, MIT, but mainly Harvard. Rawls is widely considered to be the most important political philosopher of the twentieth century. His book *A Theory of Justice* (1971) reshaped the field of political philosophy and revived a Kantian version of political liberalism and the social contract tradition. In exploring his central theme of justice as fairness,

Rawls developed two principles of justice to govern the basic structure of society. First, "Each person is to have an equal right to the most extensive basic liberty compatible with a similar liberty for others"; second, "social and economic inequalities are to be arranged so that they are both (a) reasonably expected to be to everyone's advantage, and (b) attached to positions and offices open to all." Rawls's work exerted a profound influence on the understanding of justice in a pluralistic society, and both his methodology and his substantive views have been the object of much subsequent debate. His other books include *Political Liberalism* (1993), *The Law of Peoples* (1999), *Collected Papers* (1999), *Lectures on the History of Moral Philosophy* (2000), and *Justice as Fairness: A Restatement* (2001).

ready-to-hand

MODERN EUROPEAN PHILOSOPHY **Heidegger**'s term for **entities** within-the-world which we make use of as equipment or as **instruments**. The **Being** possessed by this kind of entity is called readiness-to-hand, which Heidegger contrasts to **presence-at-hand**, that is, the Being of the determinate and isolable entities investigated by science. The same entity can be ready-to-hand or present-at-hand, depending upon our attitude or relationship to it. The attitude that determines an entity as ready-at-hand is **concern** (German *Besorgen*). Concern leads us to emphasize practical meaning and the use of an entity instead of focusing on the entity itself. Presence-at-hand is the object of a theoretical attitude, for which an entity is encountered in its own right, independent of its **relations** with other entities and with their **purposes**. Taking an entity as ready-to-hand is a pre-theoretical attitude; taking an entity as present-at-hand is a theoretical attitude. In contrast to both, the **ontological** attitude rejects taking *Dasein* as another object in the world.

"When we make use of the clock-equipment, which is proximally and inconspicuously ready-to-hand, the environing Nature is ready-to-hand along with it." **Heidegger,** *Being and Time*

real definition

PHILOSOPHY OF LANGUAGE, METAPHYSICS A **definition** that reveals the **meaning** of a **concept** or the **essence** of the thing being defined, a definition based on the real **property** of the **definiendum**. A real definition involves some sort of a discovery. It is contrasted to **nominal definition**, which determines what a word means on the basis of arbitrary **convention** and which is popular when a new term or word is introduced. In this context, the word "real" (Latin *reale*) means "to apply to a thing," while "nominal" (Latin *nominales*) means "to apply to a word." Real definition is also called essentialist definition. All definitions *per genus et differentium* are real definitions.

> "All definitions are either *nominales* or *reale* definitions. *Nominales* definitions are ones that contain everything that is equal to the whole concept that we make for ourselves of the thing. *Reale* definitions, however, are ones that contain everything that belongs to the thing in itself." **Kant,** *Lectures on Logic*

real distinction

METAPHYSICS For **Descartes**, a distinction between two things where each thing can exist without the other and we can conceive of one without being logically compelled to conceive of the other. Descartes claimed that such a distinction occurs between **mind and body**, for **doubt** reveals that I have, on the one hand, a **clear and distinct idea** of myself as a **thinking thing** that is not extended, and, on the other hand, a clear and distinct idea of my body as a thing that is extended and does not think. Hence my mind is truly distinct for my body, and each can exist without the other. Such a real distinction is, besides the existence of **God**, the major claim that *Meditations* purports to prove. Real distinctions contrast with modal distinctions between a **substance** and its **modes**, for example between a body and its size. The size can not exist apart from the relevant body.

> "Two substances are said to be really distinct when each of them can exist apart from the other." **Descartes,** *The Philosophical Writings*

real essence

METAPHYSICS **Locke** distinguished between real essence and **nominal essence**. The real essence is the real but unknown constitution of each thing, upon which depend all the **properties** of the **particulars** that make up the world. The real essence perishes when the **object** ceases to exist or undergoes radical **change**. The nominal essence, on the other hand, is the set of qualities that we construct out of observed existing qualities, or collect under one **idea** or **name** and is, in effect, a **nominal definition** provided by a **description** of the common properties of a thing. Nominal essence depends on real essence. Real essence individuates particulars, while nominal essence groups those particulars into a **class** for our use. For example, the nominal essence of gold is a **complex idea** that the word "gold" stands for, including features such as being a body, yellow in color, of a certain weight, and malleable. The real essence is the constitution of the insensible parts of that body upon which those qualities and all other qualities of gold depend. Locke believed that this distinction avoids **Aristotle**'s mistake of confusing the **meaning** of an expression with the **nature** of the object that the expression characterizes. This distinction is influential in modern philosophy, for it leads to **phenomenalism**, which drops the unknown **essence**, and also leads to the characteristic emphasis on the study of meaning in contemporary philosophy.

> "This, though it be all the essence of natural substances that we know, or by which we distinguish them into sorts, yet I call it by a peculiar name, the nominal essence, to distinguish it from that real constitution of substances, upon which depends this nominal essence, and all the properties of that sort; which, therefore, as has been said, may be called the real essence." **Locke,** *An Essay Concerning Human Understanding*

real/logical opposition, see logical/real opposition

real number, see rational number

real variable, another term for free variable

realism

METAPHYSICS Realism of various sorts ascribes **objective existence** to various **objects** and **properties**, such as the **external world**, mathematical objects, **universals**, **theoretical entities**, causal relations, **moral** and **aesthetic properties**, and **other minds**. The central idea of realism is that things of a certain problematic sort exist independent of our **minds**, whether or not we **know** or **believe** them to exist.

In general terms, realism is opposed by various sorts of **anti-realism**, which are expressed, for example, as **nominalism**, subjective **idealism**, or **semantic** anti-realism. Hence, in different areas the opposition between realism and anti-realism is presented in different forms. It must be noted that the distinction between realism and anti-realism does not correspond to the distinction between **materialism** and **idealism**, for **Platonic** objective **idealism** and **Hegelian absolute idealism** are also forms of realism.

One of the most common forms of realism concerns the ontological status of **universals** and claims that universals have real existence and are **objects of knowledge**. There are two major versions of this form of realism. First, **Platonic** realism argues that universals exist in a realm of their own and are more real than sensible objects, which are never fully instantiated in everyday **experience**. Secondly, **Aristotelian** realism argues that a universal has no separate existence of its own, but is a structure embedded in things (a **universal *in re***). Realism regarding universals contrasts both with **nominalism**, which claims that a universal is only a common **name**, and with **conceptualism**, which claims that a universal is **concept** produced by the mind.

See entries for different kinds of realism, such as **naive realism**, **direct realism**, **critical realism**, **moral realism**, **legal realism**, mathematical realism, and quasi-realism.

> "Realism is most compelling when we are forced to recognize the existence of something which we cannot describe or know fully, because it lies beyond the reach of language, proof, evidence, or empirical understanding." **T. Nagel**, *The View from Nowhere*

reality

METAPHYSICS A term that is frequently used, but is ambiguous. Sometimes it means what there is in contrast to **appearance**. One aspect of the **realism** and **anti-realism** debate concerns how much we can count as reality. Reality is a synonym for the world or the sum total of all that there is. In this sense, **Wittgenstein**'s claim that the world is a world of **facts**, not of things, concerns the logical structure of reality. Some philosophers distinguish between **objective reality**, to which our language and **perception** refer, and formal reality, which is the mode

of our language or thought. Sometimes reality is used for objective existence that is independent of our **consciousness** and **will**. The question of reality arises also in a wide variety of **realist** doctrines.

> "It will be enough, for our purposes, to define 'reality' as a quality appertaining to phenomena that we recognise as having a being independent of our own volition (we cannot 'wish them away')." **Berger and Luckmann**, *The Social Construction of Reality*

reason

EPISTEMOLOGY, LOGIC An ability to move from the **truth** of some **beliefs** to the truth of others. Some philosophers consider this capacity to be more or less sufficient to determine a single correct and systematic account of **reality**, while others argue that such an account, if possible at all, must be based primarily upon **experience**. **Kant**, following **Aristotle**, saw reason divided into two parts, **theoretical** and **practical** – the latter issuing in **actions** rather than beliefs – but held that at a deep level the two capacities were the same. **Hegel** saw reason and much else altering at different stages of historical development. **Hume** restricted practical reason to finding **means** to obtain the **ends** set out by the **passions**, but others have rejected the means–ends account. Reason enters the account of institutions through models of the interaction of the **choices** of **individuals** and through the direct assessment of practices and **societies**.

> "Reason is the faculty of the derivation of the particular from the universal or cognition a priori." **Kant**, *Lectures on Logic*

reason and understanding

EPISTEMOLOGY, METAPHYSICS [German *vernunft*, reason; *verstand*, understanding, associated with to stand] The distinction between reason and understanding was first discussed in **Kant**'s philosophy. Kant claimed that **understanding** applies its own **categories** to **experience** and generates scientific **knowledge**, while **reason** moves from **judgment** to judgment and seeks to go beyond the limits of experience. Reason tries to apprehend the unconditional, but ends with **antinomies**, in which reason falls into conflict with itself. **Hegel** offered a different account of the distinction. He considered understanding to be a fixed or mechanical way of thinking, which produces clear **analysis** and is in general the first stage of **logic** and **science**. But understanding isolates things from one another and is partial, finite, and without fluidity. Reason stands in contrast to the absolute fixation of the understanding. It is associated with **inference** and **argument** and tries to discover connections among **truths**. Reason has two forms. Negative reason uncovers and collapses the **contradictions** implicit in the **abstractions** of understanding. Positive reason draws positive conclusions from the work of negative reason. The final purpose of reason is to resolve all conflicts and to grasp totality. For Hegel, reason and understanding are immanent in the **absolute idea** and govern its processes and hierarchies. Human reason and understanding can be genuine only by conforming to this inherent and objective reason and understanding.

"The abstract thinking of understanding is so far from being either ultimate or stable, that it shows a perpetual tendency to work its own dissolution and swing round into its opposite. Reasonableness, on the contrary, just consists in embracing within itself these opposites as unsubstantial elements." **Hegel,** *Logic*

reason/cause

PHILOSOPHY OF ACTION When a person performs an **act**, it is appropriate to seek an **explanation** or **justification** for it in terms of some reason. In the philosophy of action, this raises questions of continuing dispute whether a reason is a cause and whether an explanation by reason is a causal explanation. Some philosophers do not believe that a reason is a cause, on the grounds that a reason bears an **internal relation** to the action it explains, and that the **logical relation** between reason and action differs from the external **contingent** relation between **events** or other items that are causally related. Others, represented by **Davidson**, reject the argument from internal relation: the descriptions "the cause of x" and "x" are also internally related without destroying the possibility of external contingent relations under different **descriptions**. Davidson also claims that many reasons are actually **dispositional** states such as wanting, believing, and intending. Such states are causally connected with the actions they

explain. Accordingly, they provide grounds to reject a clear-cut distinction between reasons and causes.

"Two ideas are built into the concept of acting on a reason (and hence, the concept of behaviour generally): the idea of cause and the idea of rationality. A reason is a rational cause." **Davidson,** *Essays on Actions and Events*

reasoning

LOGIC, PHILOSOPHY OF MIND, PHILOSOPHY OF ACTION The cognitive **process**, close to **inferring**, of **arguing** and giving reasons for or against a **judgment** or an **act**. It contrasts to a direct appeal to **experience** or **authority**. Discursive reasoning proceeds from premises to a conclusion. It is either **deductive** (reasoning from the universal to the particular) or **inductive** (reasoning from the particular to the universal). **Analogical** reasoning argues by comparing similarities and dissimilarities of different things. If the conclusion of a piece of reasoning is about how things are, it is **theoretical** reasoning. If the conclusion is about what we **ought** to do, it is **practical reasoning**. Logic is the study of the **rules** of reasoning. If a piece of reasoning follows logical rules, it is good. Otherwise, it is bad or invalid in that the conclusion is not supported by the premises. Consistent reasoning is an essential feature of philosophizing.

"Reasoning is a process in which the reasoner is conscious that a judgement, the conclusion, is determined by another judgement or judgements, the premises, according to a general habit of thought, which he may not be able precisely to formulate, but which he approaches as conclusive to true knowledge." **Peirce,** *Collected Papers,* **vol. 2**

recognition statement

PHILOSOPHY OF LANGUAGE **Dummett**'s term for a **statement** of the form "this is a," which identifies some concrete or ostensible **object** as the bearer of a **proper name**. Issuing such a statement depends on the recognition of the relevant **criterion** of **identity**.

"In general, the sense of any proper name 'a' of an ostensible object (an object that can be pointed to) will consist in the criterion for the truth of what we may call 'recognition statements' of the form "that is a." **Dummett,** *Frege: Philosophy of Language*

recollection

ANCIENT GREEK PHILOSOPHY, EPISTEMOLOGY [Greek *anamnesis*] **Plato** separated the **Forms** from the **particulars**. How can we acquire **knowledge** of the Forms if they are outside the particulars? The theory of recollection is one of Plato's answers to this question. The **soul** is eternal, and has seen the realm of Forms in heaven. But when the soul comes into a body, this knowledge is forgotten and needs to be recollected. Recollection is the process of learning, and because the particulars are imperfect copies of the Forms, they can only act as reminders. Since this doctrine depends on **hypotheses** about the **immortality** and **transmigration** of the soul that can not be proven, Plato adopted it only in a few earlier middle dialogues (*Meno, Phaedo, Phaedrus*) and later quietly dispensed with it. However, he continued to hold that universal knowledge can not come directly from **experience** and that there must be some inner functions that make knowledge possible. This belief was inherited and developed by the **rationalists** such as **Descartes** and **Leibniz**, as well as by **Kant** and **Chomsky**.

"Seeking and learning are in fact nothing but recollection." **Plato**, *Meno*

rectificatory justice

POLITICAL PHILOSOPHY, PHILOSOPHY OF LAW Also called corrective justice or remedial justification. A kind of justice that **Aristotle** contrasted to distributive justice. Injustice can arise in transactions between persons if one party gains at the expense of another. Such transactions include both those that are **voluntary**, such as buying, selling, or lending, and those that are **involuntary**, such as stealing, bearing false witness, or assaulting. In rectificatory justice, a judge redresses or rectifies this injustice by awarding compensation to the injured party. The compensation is not a **punishment**, although in modern times injuries caused by involuntary transactions might be subject to criminal prosecution. According to Aristotle, a judge must establish an arithmetic proportion to achieve justice through rectification. The two parties, A and B, are originally equal. If A unjustly takes a part C from B, they become A+C and B−C respectively. The judge restores the balance by taking C from A and giving it back to B.

"Rectificatory justice is what is intermediate between loss and profit." **Aristotle**, *Nicomachean Ethics*

recursive definition

LOGIC, PHILOSOPHY OF MATHEMATICS [from Latin *recurrere*, run back] Recursion is a procedure applied to a first instance and then applied to the result of the first application and so on for each successive application. Recursive definition, or **definition** by **induction**, defines the result of an operation for 0 and then defines the result of the operation for any number n+1 in terms of the result of the operation for n. For **classes**, a recursive definition first defines one sub-class of a term and then defines other sub-classes in accordance with their relations to the first sub-class. A typical example defines "Smith's ancestors" as follows: (1) Smith's parents are Smith's ancestors and (2) any parents of Smith's ancestors are Smith's ancestors. In a recursive definition, the *definiendum* appears in a sense in the *definiens*, but this does not entail circularity. Recursive function theory, also called computability theory, is a branch of mathematical logic that studies **functions** in terms of recursive procedures. Recursive functions depend on recursive definitions. A recursively enumerable set has a recursive function that enumerates its members. This is equivalent to **decidability** or **completeness**. Hence, if a set of theorems, like those of predicate **calculus**, is not recursively enumerable it is not decidable.

"The recursive definition comprises two sentential formulas; the first formula specifies the value at zero of the functor being defined (or the truth-value at zero of the predicate being defined), and the second formula specifies the value at x+1 in terms of the value at x." **Carnap**, *Introduction to Symbolic Logic and Its Applications*

red herring fallacy

LOGIC A **fallacy** in which one ignores the original topic of an argument and subtly changes the subject, but still claims that the conclusion concerning the original subject is reached although the argument actually has little to do to the conclusion. The fallacy gets its name by analogy to the procedure of training hunting dogs to follow a scent. In this procedure a red herring with a particular scent is used to mislead the dog. This fallacy is similar to *ignoratio elenchi* and occurs when a reasoner is led off the track.

> "The red herring fallacy is committed when the arguer diverts the attention of the reader or listener by addressing a number of extraneous issues and ends by presuming that some conclusion has been established." **Hurley,** *Logic*

reductio ad absurdum

LOGIC [Latin, reduction to absurdity, also called *reductio ad impossible*, reduction to the impossible] A form of argument which draws out conclusions or **entailments** from some **statement** or **theory** to show that these conclusions are absurd because, for example, they clash with unshakeable beliefs, involve an **infinite regress**, or are **self-contradictory**. Since the conclusions are absurd, the premises from which they are derived are to be rejected. According to **Ryle**, this argument is the paradigm of philosophical **analysis**, for philosophy does not test a theory or statement by observation or experiment, but by showing whether it creates **paradoxes** or gives rise to other logically intolerable results. A *reductio ad absurdum* can reveal that there is a misunderstanding about the **logical form** of the relevant **propositions**, and the theory or statement in question must be rejected or revised. Philosophers should work back from these paradoxes to locate their sources, and find the true logical form of the statement or theory underlying the paradox. This argument can also be used to prove that a theory is true by arguing that its denial or negation will involve absurd consequences.

> "A pattern of argument which is proper and even proprietary to philosophy is the *reductio ad absurdum*. This argument moves by extracting contradictions or logical paradoxes from its material." **Ryle,** *Collected Papers*

reductio ad impossible, see *reductio ad absurdum*

reductionism

PHILOSOPHY OF MIND, PHILOSOPHY OF LANGUAGE, METAPHYSICS, PHILOSOPHY OF SCIENCE Also called reductivism. A position based on the assumption that apparently different kinds of **entities** or **properties** are **identical** and claiming that items of some **types** can be explained in terms of more fundamental types of entities or properties with which they are identical. Reductionism has different forms in different areas. In the philosophy of mind, **behaviorism** is reductionist through accounting for all mental phenomena in terms of behavior. The **identity theory of mind** explains mental phenomena in terms of **type-type** or **token-token identities** with states of the central nervous system. Reductionism can have linguistic versions, according to which **predicates** or **sentences** of different sorts are shown to be **equivalent**. In metaphysics, **phenomenalism** reduces sentences about physical **objects** to basic sentences about actual or possible immediate **experiences**. In philosophy of science, the program to establish the unity of science is based on the reductionist premise that the **theories** of one science can be systematically explained by the theories of another more basic science, or that the laws of complexes can be reduced to the laws of the parts of the complexes.

> "Modern empiricism has been conditioned in large part by two dogmas. One is a belief in some fundamental cleavage between truths which are *analytic* . . . and truths which are *synthetic* . . . The other dogma is *reductionism*: the belief that each meaningful statement is equivalent to some logical construct upon terms which refer to immediate experience." **Quine,** *From a Logical Point of View*

reductivism, see reductionism

redundancy theory of truth

PHILOSOPHY OF LANGUAGE A theory claiming that the **predicate** "true" is redundant, for to say that it is true that P is equivalent to saying that P. The **assertion** that a **sentence** is true is precisely the same as the assertion of that sentence. For instance, "It is true that grass is green" amounts to: "Grass is green." Hence, "is true" or "is false" are predicates that matter only stylistically and rhetorically, and can be eliminated without **semantic** loss. The concept of truth is useless in giving a theory of **meaning**. Truth is essentially a shallow concept. The problem of truth is nothing but a linguistic muddle. This theory was developed by philosophers such as **Frege, Ramsey, Wittgenstein, Prior, Ayer, Mackie,** and **Grover.** However, although the truth-predicate is redundant, there are still many philosophical problems about the nature of truth. Asking what makes "It is true that grass is green" true will lead to admitting an extra-linguistic **reality**. The truth-predicate enables us to move from talk about language to talk about the world. Hence, the redundancy theory does not cover all meanings of truth. Nevertheless, this theory of truth is also a starting-point for **Tarski**'s **semantic theory of truth**.

> "The forms 'p' and 'It is true that p' yield the same sense no matter what English sentence is substituted for 'p'. This is appropriately referred to as 'the redundancy theory of truth'." **Horwich,** *Truth*

re-embodiment, see disembodiment

reference

PHILOSOPHY OF LANGUAGE, METAPHYSICS The **relation** between a **name** or other **referring expression** and its referent, although sometimes the term is used for the referent itself. Philosophical problems arise over how expressions can point beyond themselves to their referents or be about something. Traditionally, a term is a referring expression if it picks out a **particular object** and thereby enables the **sentence** in which it occurs to be true or false.

Frege's distinction between **sense** and reference initiated the modern examination of reference. According to Frege, two terms having the same reference or **extension** can differ in sense or **intension**. Sense and reference are related for Frege because the reference of an expression is determined by its sense. A name picks out a referent that the rest of a sentence **describes** to provide a claim to knowledge.

Russell rejected Frege's distinction between sense and reference and replaced it by a single notion of "standing for" to explain reference. He distinguished sharply between **logically proper names**, which pick out objects of immediate **experience**, and **definite descriptions**. Definite descriptions are **quantified** expressions that can be intelligible even if they fail to pick out anything.

Strawson argued that Russell's account of definite descriptions wrongly conflates reference and **assertion**, leading to the mistaken claim that a sentence like "The present King of France is bald" upon analysis asserts that there is a present King of France and is therefore false. Strawson's positive account

depends on distinguishing sentences or expression, their use and their utterance.

Donnellan criticizes both Russell and Strawson for ignoring a crucial distinction between **referential and attributive** uses of definite descriptions. A referential use picks out a particular **individual** even if the description is mistaken, whilst an attributive use fits whatever satisfies the description.

The Fregean tradition regarding names and referents has been challenged by **Kripke** in *Naming and Necessity*. Krikpe accounts for names as **rigid designators**, that is, designators that apply to the same individual in every **possible world** in which that individual exists. He argues against the use of descriptions as the way to determine a relation between names and their referents. Our current descriptions might be mistaken and other things might satisfy correct descriptions. There are similar problems with **natural kind** terms, such as water or gold. Kripke ties reference to the **essence** of individuals or kinds, even if these essences are unknown to us, and to a causal account that fixes reference by providing a chain from an initial use to the present. This is sometimes called the **causal theory of reference**.

> "The reference of a proper name is the object itself which we designate by its means ..."
> **Frege,** *Translations from the Philosophical Writings of Gottlob Frege*

referent, see reference

referential contradiction, see referential tautology

referential tautology

PHILOSOPHY OF LANGUAGE David **Pears**'s term in relation to the problem of whether "exists" is a **predicate**. If the subject term of a singular **existential statement** implies **existence**, then if the verb **asserts** existence, the resulting statement will be a referential **tautology**. If the statement denies existence, it is a referential contradiction. For example, in the statement "This room exists," the subject "this room" implies that there is a room and adding "exists" re-asserts the existence of the room. This is a tautology. The statement "This room does not exist" denies the existence of the room that is implied by the subject. This is a referential contradiction. Accordingly, "exists," although it says something about the subject, is not a genuine predicate, because it adds nothing new, especially nothing that has not been implied by the subject.

> "So perhaps we could say that the thesis that existence is not a predicate at least means that the verb "to exist" produces referential tautologies and referential contradictions in this way." **Pears, in Strawson (ed.),** *Philosophical Logic*

referential theory of meaning

PHILOSOPHY OF LANGUAGE, METAPHYSICS A theory that is based on the assumption that language is used to talk about things outside language and claims that the **meaning** of a word (except a **syncategorematic** word) is the **object** it denotes, and the meaning of a **sentence** is the **proposition** it expresses. Every meaningful expression has meaning because there is something that it **refers** to, **designates**, **signifies**, or **denotes**. It is a **symbol** that stands for something other than itself. The theory is also called the denotative theory of meaning. A naive version of this theory claims simply that the meaning of an expression is that to which the expression refers. But a sense-reference distinction shows that two expressions can have different meaning but the same referent. A more sophisticated version of this theory, such as that developed by **Russell**, claims that meaning is a referring or denoting relation between a term and the object it picks out. This theory is the most influential one in the modern discussion of meaning and reference, but it has been challenged because of its metaphysical requirement that there is something or other to which a word refers. Such a metaphysics is controversial, and furthermore not all meaningful expressions refer to something.

> "The referential theory [of meaning] identifies the meaning of an expression with that to which it refers or with the referential connection." **Alston,** *Philosophy of Language*

referentially opaque

PHILOSOPHY OF LANGUAGE, LOGIC **Quine**'s term, in contrast to referentially transparent. If a context conforms to the principle of intersubstitutivity *salva veritate*, that is, if two terms that have the same **reference**, like "Shanghai" and "the largest city of China," are interchangeable without changing the **truth-value** of the **sentences** formed by the terms

and their context, then the context is referentially transparent or purely referential. For example, given the context "—is beautiful," "Shanghai" and "The largest city of China" can be substituted for one another without changing the truth-value of the sentences. Hence "—is beautiful" is a referentially transparent context.

However, if substituting co-referential terms for one another within a context can change the truth-value, the context is referentially opaque. Such opacity occurs in the contexts of quotation and propositional attitudes such as belief and modality. For example, "Tony believes that Shanghai is beautiful" need not have the same truth-value as "Tony believes that the largest city of China is beautiful" because Tony might not know that Shanghai is the largest city in China.

> "What is important is to appreciate that the contexts 'Necessarily . . .' and 'Possibly . . .' are, like quotation and 'is unaware that . . .' and 'believe that . . .', referentially opaque." **Quine,** *From a Logical Point of View*

referentially transparent, see referentially opaque

referring expression, see reference

reflection (Hegel)

EPISTEMOLOGY, PHILOSOPHY OF MIND [German *Nachdenken*, literally after-think] An important term in **Hegel**'s philosophy for thinking over what is immediately present to one's **mind** and producing **thought** about it. Hegel's notion differs from the notion of reflection used by **empiricist** philosophers such as **Locke**, for whom reflection is limited to what is present to the mind. For Hegel, reflection starts from the immediately **given**, such as a **perception** or **feeling**, but proceeds to find behind the given what is **essential** and what is significant. Hence, to reflect involves thinking of the thinking. The main principles by which a mind can reflect what is essential include the principles of **identity**, **difference**, non-contradiction, and **sufficient reason**. However, reflection is partial and provides knowledge of the opposite, but not knowledge of origins. Reflection, for Hegel, is distinguished from speculation, which is **holistic** and can uncover the underlying unity of opposites.

> "Those who insist on this separation of religion from thinking usually have before their minds the sort of thought that may be styled after-thought. They mean 'reflective' thinking, which has to deal with thoughts as thoughts." **Hegel**, *Logic*

reflection (Locke)

EPISTEMOLOGY, PHILOSOPHY OF MIND For **Locke**, the source, along with **sensation**, of material for **ideas** and **knowledge**. Analogous to the **perception** of sensible **objects**, reflection is the perception of our own **mental operations**, the operations perceived and reflected on by our selves. Hence, Locke also called reflection **inner sense**. In today's terminology, it is **introspection**. The difference between reflection and sensation arises mainly because reflection is not directly stimulated by objects external to us. Ideas provided by reflection include perceiving, thinking, doubting, believing, reasoning, knowing, willing, and all the various other actions of our own **minds**. Locke's account of reflection has been criticized for misunderstanding the structure of mental acts and what it means for them to be available to **consciousness**.

> "By 'reflection' then, in the following part of this discourse, I would be understood to mean that notice which the mind takes of its own operations, and the manner of them, by reason whereof there come to be IDEAS of these operations in the understanding." **Locke**, *An Essay Concerning Human Understanding*

reflective equilibrium

ETHICS A method of reconciling **judgments** and **principles** in moral philosophy through a two-way accommodation between them. There is always the possibility of a discrepancy between general principles and judgments about particular cases. A rational response to these differences requires a process of mutual adjustment of principles and judgments. We revise principles to adjust to judgments or alter judgments to conform to principles until an equilibrium is reached with principles and judgments fitting together or coinciding. The equilibrium is reflective because it yields insight into the relations between our judgments and principles and into their rational grounds. The equilibrium is temporary and can be upset by further reflection or by new cases, but this difficulty also arises, although less transparently, if one tries to determine principles by other procedures. The term gained its currency from **Rawls**, who traced its origin to **Goodman**.

> "This state of affairs I refer to as reflective equilibrium. It is an equilibrium because at last our principles and judgements coincide; and it is reflective since we know to what principles our judgements conform and the premises of their derivation." **Rawls**, *A Theory of Justice*

reflective judgment, see *Critique of Judgement*

reflexive

LOGIC A **relation** is reflexive if and only if for all **objects** X, X can have the relation to itself ($\forall$x) Rxx. For example, because X must be the same age as himself, ". . . the same age as . . ." is a reflexive relation. A relation is irreflexive if and only if for all objects X, it is not the case that X can have the relation to itself. For example, X can not be a father of himself. Hence ". . . is the father of . . ." is an irreflexive relation. A relation is non-reflexive if it is neither reflexive nor irreflexive. For example, regarding ". . . loves . . .," we have no idea from the relation whether B loves B. Hence ". . . loves . . ." is a non-reflexive relation.

> "A relation is said to be reflexive if any individual a has that relation to itself if there is something b such that either Rab or Rba." **Copi**, *Symbolic Logic*

reformer's paradox

ETHICS A **paradox** raised by moral **conventionalism** concerning reform. Imagine that a reformer sees that his fellow citizens are lazy, selfish, and leading meaningless lives. Because he believes that they are this way because of the **morality** they accept, he advocates the need to reform the existing morality. His motive is to elevate the moral consciousness of his fellow citizens. However, the reformer must begin his reforms in a world that he did not create, but which has shaped him. He is bound by the customs and conventions of the society in which he grew up. According to moral conventionalism, an act is morally right if and only if it conforms to the conventions of the society. Hence, if the reformer wants to change the conventions, he becomes immoral, yet if he keeps the conventions his fellows remain morally inadequate. The same problem applies to the reformer of the system of distribution.

"Justice limits utility at exactly the point of the 'reformer's paradox': Given an imperfect existing initial distribution, any redistribution in the interests of arriving, from the standpoint of justice, at a superior distribution runs headlong into the pattern of existing claims that cannot – in the interests of the very justice that provides the rationale for the entire enterprise – be brushed aside as an irrelevant obstacle." **Rescher,** *Distributive Justice*

refutation, see conjecture

regularity theory of causation

METAPHYSICS, EPISTEMOLOGY The **causal** theory generally held by **phenomenalism** in order to reject common sense **realism** about the existence of material things with causal properties. The theory is a **sense-data** version of **Hume**'s theory of **causation**. It claims that when we say "A causes B," the statement can be analyzed into sequences or correlations of sense-data. Since we observe that whenever A occurs, B occurs, and this succession is regular, we assert that this is a **law**. Beyond these sequences of sense-data, we have no reason to believe that the causes exert a compelling power or that there is a necessary but unobservable relation between **cause** and **effect**. The main difficulty is that it is hard to account for the fact that the causal regularity exists when unobserved by us without relying on a theoretical apparatus involving **necessity**. In order to account for this, phenomenalists usually appeal to the notion of possible sense-data.

"Above all, the suggested analysis of unobserved causes, even granted the Regularity Theory of Causation, makes actual effects depend on cause whose existence is only possible." **Hirst,** *The Problem of Perception*

regulative principles, see constitutive principles

Reichenbach, Hans (1891–1953)

German-American philosopher of science, born in Hamburg, a leading logical positivist, taught at UCLA. Reichenbach developed the relative-frequency interpretation of probability and proposed a probability theory of meaning that holds that a proposition is meaningful if it is possible to determine its degree of probability. In the context of his probabilistic approach, he contributed important views to the justification of inductive inference, the theory of space and time, and the interpretation of quantum theory. Reichenbach's major books include *The Philosophy of Space and Time* (1928), *Theory of Probability* (1935), *Experience and Prediction* (1938), and *The Rise of Scientific Philosophy* (1951).

Reid, Thomas (1710–96)

Scottish philosopher, born in Strachan, Kincardineshire, taught at Aberdeen and Glasgow, a critic of Hume and the leading figure of the Scottish school of common sense. Reid argued that common sense, which prevailed in daily life, should be the first principle of philosophy and the authority in matters of philosophical dispute. His account of perception argued for the role of innate principles in the transformation of sensations into beliefs about external objects. He held that the only things that exist are individuals and that Humean "impressions" and "ideas" are not our primary data. In ethics, he maintained that we can know objective moral truths through moral intuition, and his account of human freedom centered on an analysis of agent causation. In several respects, it is worth comparing Reid's and Kant's responses to Hume. Reid's major books include *An Inquiry into the Human Mind on the Principles of Common Sense* (1764), *Essays on the Intellectual Powers of Man* (1785), and *Essays on the Active Power of Man* (1788).

reification, an alternative term for hypostatization

reincarnation

PHILOSOPHY OF RELIGION, PHILOSOPHY OF MIND The belief that the **soul** is **immortal** and that after the **death** of one body a person's life is reborn in another body. Death is thus merely the death of the body, and the soul can take residence in different bodies, either human or animal. In contemporary philosophy, reincarnation is not merely a topic of theology, but also an issue regarding **personal identity**. The problem concerns the conditions under which the reincarnated self would retain its former identity. If it does retain its identity, then according to what **criterion** of personal identity does it do so? If it does not, reincarnation does not seem to be a rebirth of the same life. Reincarnation is synonymous with **transmigration** or **metempsychosis** (from Greek *meta*, beyond + *en*, in + *psyche*, soul), the term used by **Pythagoras**.

> "The affirmation that there is life after death in another world or reincarnation on earth is widespread." **Swinburne,** *The Coherence of Theism*

reism

METAPHYSICS A term introduced by the Polish philosopher Tadeusz **Kotarbinski** in 1929 for the position that only things exist. All **statements** about abstract objects can be reduced to the statements about things. The term "things" covers both organic and inorganic things. There are no **objects** other than things. **Propositions** which appear to imply the existence of abstract entities of one kind or another either can be rephrased without any loss of relevant content or must be rejected as false. Since the term "reism" is easily confused with "realism," Kotarbinski proposed that it be replaced by "concretism."

Brentano was an earlier reist, for he claimed that only individuals (*entia realia*) exist and can be thought of, and that non-individuals (*entia irrealia*) such as **possibilities**, **concepts**, and **propositions** do not exist. Kotarbinski held an even more radical view. He proposed that an entity can be a thing if and only if it is extended in **time** and **space**. Accordingly, nothing other than material things exists. This position is in sharp contrast to **Platonism**, which allows the existence of abstract objects. To distinguish his position from that of Brentano, Kotarbinski calls his own doctrine **somatism** or **pantosomatism** (from Greek *pantos*, all + *soma*, body).

> "So much for the reduction of categories of objects to the category of things. The stand taken in favour of such a reduction might be called reism." **Kotarbinski, in McAlister (ed.),** *The Philosophy of Brentano*

relation

METAPHYSICS, LOGIC Although **Aristotle** classifies relation as one of his ten basic **categories** of **being**, it is not until **Leibniz** that relations become a major focus of **metaphysics**. Leibniz puzzles over the nature and location of relations, since they can be identified with neither one of the related terms nor with the void between them. In addition, **propositions** of a relational form can not be reduced to those of single **subject-predicate** form. He claims that relations, in contrast to one-place properties, are unreal and hence declares that his basic entities, the **monads**, are windowless, with none of the features of one monad requiring a **reference** to other monads and their features. His view gives rise to many debates, one of which is whether relations are **internal** or **external**. **Absolute idealism** believes that all relations are internal, that is, part of the **essential nature** of the related terms. **Russell** rejects this thesis and claims that all relations are external, that is, **accidental** to the related terms. Modern formal **semantics** considers relations to be **predicates** of n-tuple individuals. A two-place predicate is a relation between two individuals, a three-place predicate is a relation among three individuals, and so on. The main kinds of relation include **reflexive**, **symmetric**, transitive, **ordering**, and **equivalent** relations. Modern mathematics takes relations as **classes** of ordered pairs.

> "Any entity which can occur in a complex, as 'precedes' occurs in 'A precedes B' will be called a relation." **Russell,** *Collected Papers of Bertrand Russell,* **vol. VII**

relation of ideas, see knowledge of relations of ideas

relations of production

PHILOSOPHY OF SOCIAL SCIENCE, PHILOSOPHY OF HISTORY In Marxist philosophy, relations between productive forces and their owners, in which the owner has **power** to use the productive forces, and between owners and others in the society. The power of the owners implies the exclusion or **alienation** of others from employing the same productive forces. Hence, relations of production are basically ownership relations. According to **Marx**, **property** relations are a legal expression of relations of production. He did not give a formal definition of this term, and there is controversy about how to use his various remarks to formulate a coherent account by which relations of production are explained as a social factor distinct from any item of the **superstructure**. For Stalin, relations of production defined ownership relations, relations of **persons** in production, and relations of distribution. In Marxism, relations of production are called the **form** or base of all historical human society. They involve power rather then **rights** and hence are more basic than political and legal relations. Relations of production are related to the division of labor and are independent of the **will** of individuals. The totality of relations of production in a society forms its economic structure, also called its economic base, which is determined by productive forces but in turn determines the superstructure. The essential principle of the economic structure in a class society is the pattern of the ruling class, by which a small ruling class owns most of society's means of production, while the majority owns few or none of the means of production. According to Marx, relations of production vary from age to age, and their development corresponds to the development of the productive forces from primitive communism to a slave-owning system, feudalism, and capitalism, and will proceed to **communism**. Communism, it is claimed, will abolish private ownership and eliminate the alienated nature implied in capitalist relations of production. To assess Marx's concept of the relations of production it is necessary to assess the theoretical structure in which the concept plays a fundamental role.

> "In the social production of their lives men enter into relations that are specific, necessary and independent of their will, relations of production which correspond to a specific stage of development of their material productive forces." **Marx,** *Preface to the Critique of Political Economy*

relative identity

LOGIC, PHILOSOPHY OF LANGUAGE, METAPHYSICS The sentence "a is identical with b" is traditionally understood as equivalent to "a is the same as b." Peter **Geach** calls this notion **absolute identity**, but claims that it is incomplete. He argues that "a is identical with b" means "a is the same *x* as b," with "*x*" being an unstated kind term that is understood from the context of utterance. He calls this notion relative identity and believes that it fits into our ordinary use of natural language. On his view, all

identity is relative to a kind, and two things can not be identical if there is not some kind term under which they both fall. Geach's position is disputed by others, including David **Wiggins**, who in *Sameness and Substance* defends absolute identity based on **Leibniz's law**. Some philosophers suggest that relative identity is a qualitative notion, while absolute identity is numerical identity.

> "Identity statements in natural language come in two syntactic varieties. Some are of the form 'a is the same as b' or 'a is identical with b'. These are absolute identity statements. Others have the form 'a is the same so-and-so as b'. These are relative identity statements." **N. Griffin,** *Relative Identity*

relative product

LOGIC The combination of two **relations**. Suppose there is a relation R such that xRy, and a relation S such that ySz, then we can combine these two relations R and S (called relative multiplication) and get a relation between x and z. The obtained relation is called the relation product of R and S. **Russell** symbolizes it as R/S.

> "By the relative product of the relation R by the Relation S is meant that relation which exists between x and y if and only if there is a u such that x bears the relation R to u and u bears the relation S to y." **Carnap,** *Introduction to Symbolic Logic and its Applications*

relativity theory

PHILOSOPHY OF SCIENCE, METAPHYSICS, EPISTEMOLOGY The special theory of relativity is a modern physical theory proposed by **Einstein** in 1905, according to which neither **space** nor **time** has an independent absolute value or **existence** but is each relative to the other. Thus, the classical view of space and time is replaced by a theory in which the two are aspects of the same underlying reality: **space-time**. The general theory of relativity extended the special theory from considering frameworks in uniform relative motion to one another to considering frameworks in arbitrary relative motion to one another. The general theory resulted from combining the principle of relativity, that all **laws of nature** must have the same form in any relatively moving frame of

reference, with Mach's principle, that the fundamental description of any realistic physical system
must be closed. It replaced **Newton**'s theory of universal gravitation and is currently the accepted basis
for the theory of gravitation. Relativity theory introduced a revolution in twentieth-century physics and
greatly advanced our understanding of the structure
of the universe. Its space-time theory gives rise to a
variety of important methodological, metaphysical,
and epistemological problems.

> "The theory of relativity takes the view that
> there are purely objective (non-relative) features of
> the world that are independent of any individual
> who might look in." **Sachs, *Ideas of the Theory of
> Relativity***

relevance logic

LOGIC, PHILOSOPHY OF LANGUAGE A non-classical
formal logic that proposes that the premises and
conclusion of a **valid argument** must be relevant
to one another. The notion of relevance is defined
as the sharing of a **variable** (that is content) and
dependency. This suggests a new conception of
entailment or **deducibility**, according to which q
is deducible from p only if p is used in the derivation of q. If q is deducible from p in this sense, p
relevantly implies q. This puts a restriction upon
classical logic, in which a **contradiction** entails any
statement whatsoever, so that (p ∧ ~p) implies q,
no matter whether or not q has anything to do with
p. The classical notion of **implication** leads to the
paradoxes of **material implication** and of **strict
implication**. The avoidance of these paradoxes of
implication is one of the most important reasons for
the development of relevance logic. Relevance logic
was first established by Wilhelm Ackermann in a
paper of 1956, and was developed by A. Anderson
and N. Belnap. It has not been widely accepted or
applied.

> "Someone who rejects the table as an account of
> the meaning of 'if . . . then' therefore owes us a
> new account of 'if . . . then' introduction, presum-
> ably involving a requirement that the antecedent
> be non-redundantly used in deriving the con-
> sequent. There is a branch of logic known as
> relevance logic which develops this approach."
> **Forbes, *Modern Logic***

relevant implication, see relevance logic

reliabilism

EPISTEMOLOGY An **externalist** approach to epistemic
justification with various forms. David **Armstrong**
proposes that the **truth** of a justified **belief** is guaranteed by **law-like** connections in nature. The most
influential version of reliabilism is called process
reliabilism, claiming that a belief is justified if and
only if it is produced by a reliable psychological
process. In other words, a justified belief is one produced by an appropriate **cognitive** process, while an
unjustified belief is produced by an inappropriate
process. Such things as standard **perception** and
good **reasoning** are reliable, while wishful thinking,
emotional reaction, and guesswork are unreliable.
The reliability of a cognitive process is linked to
whether what is believed is true in the actual world.
Hence knowledge is identified with true belief
obtained as a result of law-like connection between
us and the world. This form of reliabilism is associated with Alvin **Goldman**, and it has the advantage
of connecting cognitive psychology with epistemology. It is open to counterexamples, for in some
cases, such as the **brain-in-a-vat** case, beliefs thus
formed are unjustified, but according to reliabilism
they must be justified.

> "The theory of epistemic justification that has
> received the most attention recently is reliabilism.
> Roughly speaking, this is the view that epistemo-
> logically justified beliefs are the ones that result
> from belief-forming processes that reliably lead to
> true beliefs." **Feldman and Conee, "Evidentialism,"
> *Philosophical Studies* 48**

religious experience

PHILOSOPHY OF RELIGION The feeling of the power
of mystery, awe, wonder, and fascination, generally
occurring in a context of religious expectation, which
is beyond ordinary rational **explanation**. Religious
experience is claimed to be an inner self-attestation
of supernatural reality. Theology claims that this
sort of feeling is produced by the agency of **God**,
and it generally describes this sort of experience
as a sharing in eternal life or being in touch with
the **Holy**, with a consequent sense of joyfulness.
Various kinds of religious experience are recorded
in the Bible. Many theologians and metaphysicians

try to prove the existence of God by appeal to religious experience, although the changes brought about in us by such experience should perhaps be understood in terms of **conversion** rather than of rational persuasion.

> "We may now lay it down as certain that in the distinctively religious sphere of experience, many persons . . . possess the objects of their belief, not in the form of mere conceptions which their intellect accepts as true but rather in the form of quasi-realities directly apprehended." **W. James,** *The Varieties of Religious Experience*

Religiousness A

PHILOSOPHY OF RELIGION **Kierkegaard** distinguished three stages of **existence**: **aesthetic**, **ethical**, and religious. He further subdivided the religious stage into Religiousness A and Religiousness B. In Religiousness A, **God** is thought to be immanent, and the eternal **truth** to be rationally accessible. The transition from the ethical level to Religiousness A is marked by resignation, suffering, guilt, and humor. In this stage, conventional morality no longer appears as an adequate means of bringing the **individual** into **harmony** with the whole of existence. In seeking this harmony, the individual must have recourse to the Deity. Hence, a finite individual retains an essential relationship to the eternal. In Religiousness B, this relationship no longer holds. The individual ceases to believe that by virtue of some specific exercise of thought or action he is capable of realizing some latent kinship with the eternal. The individual tries to relate himself in time to the eternal in time, that is, to become the eternal itself. Religiousness B is Christianity, in which God is incarnated as a human being as an ethical example. This stage is to account for how to become a Christian. According to Kierkegaard, one can progress from overcoming **objectivity**, to achieving **subjectivity** (or **truth**) and on that basis to become a Christian through a leap of faith.

> "Religiousness A is the dialectic of inward deepening; it is the relation to an eternal happiness that is not conditioned by a something but is the dialectical inward deepening of the relation, consequently conditioned only by the inward deepening, which is dialectical." **Kierkegaard,** *Concluding Unscientific Postscript to Philosophical Fragments*

Religiousness B, see Religiousness A

reluctant desire, see embraced desire

Renaissance

PHILOSOPHICAL METHOD [from French, rebirth] Historians dispute the distinctive characteristics and limits of the period of the Renaissance. A narrow sense was formulated by the Swiss art historian Jacob Burckhardt, who used the term for the revival or rebirth of learning and arts initiated in Italian culture. In a wider sense, it concerns European history from the early fourteenth to the early seventeenth century, involving a disparagement of the Middle Ages, yet the chronological term is closely related to the development of **culture** and art. This period is also called the age of adventure, represented by voyages of exploration and the discovery of new lands. It witnessed the religious Reformation, sparked by Martin **Luther** and John **Calvin**. This period is admired because of the huge progress of science and technology, represented by the **Copernican** heliocentric theory.

This period was also notable for its achievements in classical learning, the arts, and literature, which were products of its **humanism**. The humanist movement was stimulated by the discovery of large amounts of previously unknown literature from ancient Greece and Rome. **Aristotelianism** was still influential, but people read his work in Greek rather than in Latin translation. **Platonism** underwent a resurgence, especially in the Florentine school directed by **Ficino**, and Plato's complete works were translated into Latin for the first time. Stoicism, **Epicureanism**, and **Skepticism** all exerted great influence. The revival of different schools of ancient philosophy created different schools in the humanist movement and became the major contents of Renaissance philosophy. The **philosophy of nature** also developed greatly in this period, and indeed philosophy at that time also covered many subjects that now belong to different areas of natural science. The major thinkers include Ficino, Pico, **Nicholas of Cusa**, Lorenzo Valla, **Erasmus**, **More**, **Machiavelli**, and Giordano **Bruno**.

> "By the 'Renaissance' I understand that period of Western European History which extends approximately from 1300 to 1600, without any

presupposition as to the characteristics or merits of that period, or of those periods preceding and following it." **Kristeller**, *Renaissance Thought and Its Sources*

representation

EPISTEMOLOGY, PHILOSOPHY OF MIND In general, an item in the mind, picture, model, copy, or other thing which stands for something else because of a likeness or on some other grounds. **Kant** distinguished between representation with **consciousness** and representation without consciousness. Under the heading of conscious representation, he placed all the elements of **experience** and **knowledge**. For Kant, representation is crucially involved in **perception**, which is divided into subjective perception or **sensation** and objective perception or **cognition**. The representations of cognition are further divided into **intuitions** and **concepts**, a duality that is fundamental to Kant's philosophy through his claim that knowledge requires both kinds of representation through the application of concepts to intuitions.

With the development of **cognitive science**, representation has become a prominent term in the philosophy of mind, but many philosophical problems relating to the notion of representation remain.

"We have representations in us, and can become conscious of them. But however far this consciousness may extend, and however careful and accurate it may be, they still remain mere representations, that is, inner determinations of our mind in this or that relation of time." **Kant**, *Critique of Pure Reason*

representational form

LOGIC, PHILOSOPHY OF LANGUAGE [German *Form der Darstellung*] **Wittgenstein**'s term, also called **form** of **representation**. These forms enable us to describe or represent reality and are a necessary condition for **understanding** and **truth**. For Wittgenstein, representational forms are determined by **grammar**, which lays down **rules** or norms of **description** and guides us in making intelligible **statements** about the world. The **necessity** involved in using these forms is logically or grammatically based and can not be **justified** by the **reality** it represents.

"A picture represents its subject from a position outside it. (Its standpoint is its representational form)." **Wittgenstein**, *Tractatus*

representational theory, another expression for imitation theory

representationalism

EPISTEMOLOGY Also called the **causal** theory of perception, the representative theory of perception, or the two-world theory. A major theory of **perception** that contrasts with **direct** or **naive realism** and **phenomenalism**. While direct realism takes what we immediately perceive to be physical **objects**, representationalism claims that perception is the result of the operation of nerves and brain and that we are directly aware of subjective **private sensations**, that is, **sense-data** or **ideas**, which can not exist independent of perception. While phenomenalism holds that physical objects are **constructions** out of sense-data and can not exist independently, representationalism claims that sense-data are representations or symbolizations of the physical objects, which are **inferred** as the **causes** of the sense-data. Thus, physical objects exist in their own right, and we may indirectly know them through sense-data. Such a theory is scientifically inspired and is widely held by neurophysiologists. The main difficulty faced by the theory is that if private sensations are the only things to which we can have direct access, it is not clear how we can compare them with the features of the physical world that they are supposed to represent. This problem gives rise to **skepticism** about the **external world** and leads to phenomenalism. Nevertheless, the representative theory is perhaps the best available explanation of the uniformity of sequences of sensations.

"Representationalism is the view that a percept is veridical only when it is caused by its correspondent object." **Danto**, *Analytical Philosophy of Action*

representative theory of mind

PHILOSOPHY OF MIND A theory holding that **propositional attitudes** can be understood in terms of token **mental representations**. Although there are no general **type** correlations between **propositional attitudes** and physical **properties**, there are token correlations. An organism's propositional attitude bears a **functional relation** to a mental representation that is a real and physically realized entity. **Mental** processes are **causal** sequences of token mental representations. The properties of a **belief** are explained in terms of the properties of its associated representations. The only properties of a representation that could influence its causal behavior are its **syntactical** properties. Hence, a representation's syntactic properties must mirror its **semantic** properties in order to preserve the match between the semantic content of a belief and its causal role. For **Fodor**, the representational theory is the same thing as the **language of thought** hypothesis, but others argue that one can believe in the representational theory of mind without believing in the language of thought hypothesis.

"What I am selling is the representational theory of mind . . . At the heart of the theory is the postulation of a language of thought: an infinite set of 'mental representations' which function both as the immediate objects of propositional attitudes and as the domains of mental processes." **Fodor,** *Psychosemantics*

representative theory of perception, another term for representationalism

repression

PHILOSOPHY OF MIND The term **Freud** used for the force or forces in the mind that are the causal factors of unconscious processes. Repression turns unacceptable or painful parts of reality or impulses away from **consciousness** and confines them to the unconscious system through a variety of mechanisms. According to Freud, the process of repression does not annihilate these **ideas**, but prevents them from becoming conscious. Repression is a species of psychic defense, and we can be aware of the repressive forces in the form of resistance, that is, the patient's rejection of allegedly correct psychoanalytic **interpretations**. Sometimes "repression" is employed interchangeably with "suppression." However, repression is claimed to be an instinctual and unconscious denial, rather than a voluntary or conscious restraint upon unwanted **desires**. Freud claims that repressed instincts can turn to creative forces in **sublimation**. The basic goal of psychoanalysis is

to make those repressed impulses conscious both for therapeutic benefit and for intellectual insight.

"The neuroses are the expressions of conflicts between the ego and such of the sexual impulses as seem to the ego incompatible with its integrity or with its ethical standards. Since these impulses are not ego-syntonic, the ego has repressed them: this is to say, it has withdrawn its interests from them and has shut them off from becoming conscious as well as from obtaining satisfaction by motor discharge." **Freud,** *Standard Edition of the Complete Psychological Works of Sigmund Freud,* **vol. 18**

Republic

ANCIENT GREEK PHILOSOPHY, POLITICAL PHILOSOPHY, METAPHYSICS, EPISTEMOLOGY [Greek *politeia*, the public and political life of a community, Latin *res publica*, public business] The English translation of the title of **Plato**'s most important dialogue. The translation comes from the Latin *res publica*, which originally had the same meaning as *politeia* and only later came to be used for a particular form of constitution. For Plato, *politeia* was simply any constitution of a Greek *polis* (city-state), and Plato's book is about the **state** and society. *Politeia* might better be translated as political system. In the *Republic*, Plato set up an ideal state and within that context examined many topics such as the theory of **Forms**, the role of art, the structure of society, the parts of the **soul**, the best sort of education, the nature of morality and religion, and the place of women in society. The *Republic* is one of the great books in human history and has inspired and perplexed generations of its readers. Many Western students began their philosophical education with the *Republic*.

In its modern sense, a republic is a form a society governed by the people, protecting **rights** and promoting civic **virtue**. By allowing change of rulers within the constitution, a republic contrasts with both a hereditary **monarchy** and a dictatorship.

"The Republic is the centre around which the other dialogues may be grouped; here philosophy reaches the highest point to which ancient thinkers ever attained." **Jowett,** *The Dialogues of Plato*

republicanism

POLITICAL PHILOSOPHY [from Latin *res publica*, public business] The theory of the institutionally organized realm of public affairs in a commonwealth or **state** in which the people or citizens have a decisive say in its organization and conduct. Republican theory and practice can be traced to the Roman republic and **Renaissance** Italian city-states. Traditionally, republics have linked citizenship to **property**, and citizens have tried to arrange government to avoid domination by one individual or group and to provide institutions that would protect **liberty**. Contemporary republicanism criticizes **liberal democratic** theory and society on the grounds of their juridical formalism, their emphasis on **rights** rather than on **virtue** and civic **duty**, and their failure to provide the protections that a commonwealth should offer its citizens. As part of its attack on liberal democracy, it controversially reinterpets modern political history as developing initially from republican thought before being subverted by a democratic revolution.

> "The opposition between liberalism and republicanism, which is a source of inspiration for the recent revival of the latter, is more an invention of this revival than ascertainable historical fact." **Haakonssen, "Republicanism," in Goodin and Pettit (eds.), *A Companion to Contemporary Political Philosophy***

res cogitans

METAPHYSICS, PHILOSOPHY OF MIND [Latin *res*, thing + *cogitan*, to think, thinking thing] **Descartes**'s term for thinking **substance**, in contrast to *res extensa* (Latin, extended thing), Descartes's term for extended or corporeal substance. According to Descartes, I can **doubt** anything. But when I doubt, I am thinking, and as long as I am thinking, I exist. Thinking is inseparable from me. Thus I have a **clear and distinct idea** that I am a mind, or intelligence, and my nature is a thinking thing. On the other hand, I have also a clear idea of **body** as an extended and non-thinking thing. He concludes that *res cogitans* and *res extensa* are two independent **entities**. This dichotomy is the foundation of Descartes's **dualism**.

> "For all that I am a thing that is real and which truly exists. But what kind of a thing? . . . A thinking thing (*res cogitans*)." **Descartes, *The Philosophical Writings***

res extensa, see *res cogitans*

Rescher, Nicholas (1928–)
American pragmatic idealist epistemologist, logician, and philosopher of science, born in Hagen, Germany, Professor of Philosophy at University of Pittsburgh. Rescher argues for an idealism that is based on a coherence theory of truth and an objective pragmatism that is grounded in considerations of methodology and the long-term survival of theories. He has made strikingly original contributions over a wide range of topics. In some cases, such as the development of logics that tolerate inconsistency, he has opened up important new fields of enquiry. His major works include *The Coherence Theory of Truth* (1973), *A Theory of Probability* (1975), *Induction* (1980), *Rationality* (1988), and *A System of Pragmatic Idealism* (1992–3).

research program
PHILOSOPHY OF SCIENCE **Lakatos**'s term in the philosophy of science for a set of **methodological rules** for the conduct of research. These can be divided into two kinds: rules that prohibit certain kinds or methods of research, which are called the negative heuristic; and rules that advocate certain kinds of research, which are called the positive heuristic. Each research program has a hard core that is surrounded by a protective belt of auxiliary **hypotheses**. When the research program encounters problems or needs to be revised, scientists characteristically change some part of the protective belt rather than its core. This explains the continuity in the growth of science. This account of science is related to **Popper**'s **falsificationism**. Testing leads to the falsification of hard-core and auxiliary hypotheses, but we alter the auxiliary hypotheses in order to protect the hard core. A research program is the unit by which the nature and direction of scientific growth is analyzed. If a program can continue to anticipate and solve new problems and to determine new **facts**, it is progressive; and if it ceases to do this, it is degenerating. We can account for scientific progress in terms of the replacement of a degenerating program with a progressive one, although these are relative notions and some degenerating programs can become progressive. Such progress is not linear, but a complex process involving a proliferation of different **theories** at the same time. According to Lakatos, **Newton**'s

gravitational theory serves as a classic example of a research program.

> "A research programme is successful if all this leads to a progressive problem shift; unsuccessful it is leads to a degenerating problem shift." **Lakatos, in Lakatos and Musgrave (eds.),** *Criticism and the Growth of Knowledge*

resemblance, theory of, see resemblance nominalism

resemblance nominalism

METAPHYSICS All things that fall under the same **predicate** resemble one another. **Realists** claim that they resemble one another because they are all instances of the same **universal**. According to resemblance nominalism or the theory of resemblance, however, the resemblance, instead of being derived from a universal, is itself ultimate or fundamental. The features by which things resemble one another have different degrees of intensity in different individuals. The common character of things falling under the same predicate can be analyzed simply in virtue of a resemblance among **particulars**. We might say that A has some **property** P if and only if A suitably resembles a **paradigm** case of F. But the paradigm F is another particular, and for F and A both to have P does not require the introduction of a universal. There need not be a universal "redness" for things to be red; all that is needed is a resemblance to, for example, a certain tomato. Resemblance nominalism can be traced back to **Hume**, and is articulated in detail by H. H. **Price**, *Thinking and Experience* and R. **Carnap**, *The Logical Structure of the World*. **Wittgenstein**'s notion of "**family resemblance**" can be seen as a variant of resemblance nominalism. Resemblance nominalism faces some major difficulties. First, resemblance itself might be a universal. Secondly, two things might need an element in common in order to resemble each other. Both criticisms attempt to introduce items of a sort which resemblance nominalism tried to banish.

> "Despite the many difficulties which can be raised against Resemblance Nominalism it is by far the most satisfactory version of Nominalism." **Armstrong,** *Nominalism and Realism*

resentment

ETHICS A frustrated emotion or attitude in which one, for example, feels offended, injured, oppressed, humiliated, or ignored in reaction to others or their actions. It is the emotion of victims toward their offenders. According to **Nietzsche**, resentment is related to revenge; as a mark of slave morality it is an essential feature of Judaeo-Christian morality. **Rawls** believes that resentment, in contrast to envy, is based on a sense of inequality and injustice. In "Freedom and Resentment," **Strawson** examined situations in which we do or do not feel resentment toward others, to provide a new perspective on **freedom** and **determinism**.

> "Resentment, or what I have called resentment, is a reaction to injury or indifference." **Strawson,** *Freedom and Resentment*

resolution, see partition

responsibility

ETHICS, POLITICAL PHILOSOPHY, PHILOSOPHY OF LAW [from Latin *respondo*, I answer] The accountability of **persons**, primarily for **actions** and their consequences but sometimes for other items as well. A person who is held responsible or answerable for an action is subject to responses such as blame, praise, **punishment**, or reward on account of the action. One is legally responsible if one is subject to a legal **obligation** and is morally responsible if one is subject to a moral obligation. Because of the difference between law and morality, moral responsibility and legal responsibility do not always coincide. Normally, a person is responsible for an action because he does the action or brings it about either directly or indirectly. We are responsible for some, but not all, of the consequences of our actions. Not all responsibilities presuppose a **causal** link. We are responsible for some of our omissions, and moral luck also plays a role in ascribing responsibility to an **agent**. With important exceptions, the conditions of responsibility require that persons know what they are doing and that they have at least a certain degree of freedom to control the acts that they perform. Accordingly, freedom and responsibility are closely related, and responsibility is central to the question of **freedom** and **determinism**. The discussion of responsibility can be traced to **Aristotle**'s consideration of **voluntary** and involuntary actions in the *Nicomachean Ethics*. It was carried forward through medieval discussions of human **evil** to investigations of action, **deliberation**, motivation, **choice**, **intention**, **weakness of will**, and **diminished responsibility** in contemporary ethics, political philosophy, and legal philosophy.

> "The central core of the concept of responsibility is that I can be asked the question, 'why did you do it?' and be obliged to give an answer." **Lucas,** *Responsibility*

retributive justice, see justice

retroduction, another name for abduction

retrospection

PHILOSOPHY OF MIND, EPISTEMOLOGY The mental process of looking back or recalling one's own past items of **consciousness** or past **actions**, for example, for the purpose of finding patterns amongst them. Such a process need not be **private**. It is more or less the same process as discerning such patterns in the behavior of others. Retrospection is thus not as mysterious as **introspection**. **Ryle**, when attacking introspection, argues that since the operation of retrospection can provide whatever information we do have about our own **mental states**, we do not need to posit the existence of mysterious processes such as introspection and **self-consciousness**.

> "Part, then, of what people have in mind, when they speak familiarly of introspecting, is this authentic process of retrospection." **Ryle,** *The Concept of Mind*

revealed theology

PHILOSOPHY OF RELIGION The positive justification of theistic **beliefs** from contents of some supernatural **revelation** accepted by **faith**. A revelation is mediated through a sacred book, through the words of a prophet, or through the authoritative teachings of a church. Revealed theology is also called supernatural theology. It contrasts with **natural theology**, which employs the standard norms of **reasoning** and empirical **data** in attempting to prove the existence of **God**. Revealed theology claims that to reason we need to have premises on the ground of which the reasoning proceeds. But the premises of reasoning

can not be obtained through reasoning and can only be found through revelation.

> "In revealed theology . . . reason is confined to systematising and drawing conclusions from premises which natural reason cannot discover . . . They have to be learned through revelation alone and held on faith." **Penelhum,** *Problems of Religious Knowledge*

revelation

PHILOSOPHY OF RELIGION In theology, the disclosure through the agency of **God** of fundamental **truths** that would be otherwise inaccessible to human beings. God is the agent who reveals, and human beings receive the revelation. While **natural theology** claims that human reason unaided by revelation can know God's **nature**, revealed theology insists that the eternal **knowledge** about God can only be acquired through revelation. It is through revelation that human beings learn about the existence, **attributes**, and purposes of God, and about the moral and other directives that humans have to follow. The revelation can be through nature, visions, dreams, in God's words and activity. Sometimes it needs to be communicated through prophets. It is claimed that in revelation the human being enters into a self-manifesting encounter with God.

> "We speak of revelation wherever the unconditional import of meaning breaks through the form of meaning. Faith is always based on revelation." **Tillich,** *What is Religion?*

revenge

ETHICS The deliberate infliction of a wrong in return for a wrong suffered by oneself, one's family, or one's friends. In ancient Greek, **justice** and revenge were closely associated, with *dikaiosunê* (justice) also meaning a fair deal. The Old Testament suggested that we should exact an eye for an eye. But **Socrates** argued that returning evil for evil is morally wrong, and the New Testament also advocates forgiveness. Mainstream Western philosophers generally argue that while retribution is rational and **justified**, revenge should be rejected as an emotional indulgence in which an individual usurps the role of the **law**. However, it is unclear that we can draw a clear-cut distinction between retribution and revenge.

"A man who has been injured by another and then revenges himself upon him is not authorised to act as he does. That is, he is not empowered by generally accepted rules, as a judge is empowered by the law to fix and enforce penalties." **Honderich,** *Punishment*

reverse discrimination

POLITICAL PHILOSOPHY A proposal or an actual policy in many Western countries that holds that members of oppressed social groups that have suffered from systematic discrimination in the past should receive preferential treatment to correct the consequences of that discrimination. On this view, we should deliberately make policies to grant such groups privileges in areas such as employment, education, health care, and housing. The policy aims to restore a fair balance in society and involves compensatory **justice**. However, opponents argue that this practice is unjust because reverse discrimination is still discriminatory. It does not conform to the **principle** of equal competition, but still treats people differently according to certain external features such as race or gender. Further, they reject the claim that injustice regarding an earlier generation justifies preferential treatment of a later generation.

"We may begin by defining reverse discrimination as preferential treatment for minority-group members or women in job hiring, school admissions or training-program policies." **Goldman,** *Justice and Reverse Discrimination*

revisionary   metaphysics,   see   descriptive metaphysics

revisionism, see Marxism

rhetoric

ANCIENT GREEK PHILOSOPHY, LOGIC, POLITICAL PHILOSOPHY [from Greek *rhein*, to flow and *rhetor*, orator] The art of making elegant speeches in order effectively to persuade or influence an audience. In contrast, grammar is the art of using language correctly. Rhetoric was one of the main subjects taught in ancient Athens to the youth who were enthusiastic about politics. **Plato** attacked rhetoric as an art that is interested in victory in debate by appeal to emotion rather than being interested in

truth. **Aristotle**'s *Rhetoric* is a systematic examination of the argumentative form of rhetoric. This rendered rhetoric a part of logic in relation to **dialectic** and a suitable subject of philosophy. Rhetoric was one of the seven liberal arts in medieval universities. In the twentieth century, **hermeneutics** and **postmodernism** have led to a revival of interest in rhetoric.

"Rhetoric may be defined as the faculty of observing in any given case the available means of persuasion." **Aristotle,** *Rhetoric*

Ricoeur, Paul (1913–2005)

French hermeneutic philosopher, born in Valence, Professor of Metaphysics, University of Paris IV and X and Professor, University of Chicago. Ricoeur developed his philosophical hermeneutics, dealing with structures of meaning and interpretation, after early existentialist and phenomenological studies. The displacement of meaning from the acts of Husserl's Cartesian ego to diverse sources of meaning leads Ricoeur to relinquish the ideal of a single authoritative narrative interpretation or discourse. His major works include *History and Truth* (1955), *The Symbolism of Evil* (1960), *The Conflict of Interpretations* (1969), and *Time and Narrative* (1983–4).

right

ETHICS [from Latin *rectus*, straight, in contrast to Latin *tortuos*, twisted, wrong] As an adjective, "right," like "good," has a wide application. We may say "right road" or "right answer." When it is applied to moral **acts** (the moral "right"), different moral theories, according to their understanding of morality, vary in their account of what a right act is. What is morally right is equivalent to what is moral, and a main aim of ethics is to find the right thing to do. The relation between the **good** and the right is complicated. **Utilitarianism** defines "good" in terms of **utility**, and then defines "right" as being that which maximizes the good. **Deontology** argues that the good consequences of an action do not guarantee that it is the right thing to do and holds that an action is right if one **ought** to do it or if it is a **duty**. According to **virtue ethics**, right action proceeds from the **virtue** of the **agent**. **Intuitionism** holds that the right, like the good, is a primitive unanalyzable concept.

"Most of the words in any language have a certain amount of ambiguity; and there is special danger of ambiguity in the case of a word like 'right', which does not stand for anything we can point out to one another or apprehend by one of the senses." **Ross,** *The Right and the Good*

right (Kant)

ETHICS, POLITICAL PHILOSOPHY, PHILOSOPHY OF LAW
For **Kant**, right concerns the limitation of each person's **action** so that it is compatible with the **freedom** of everyone else. Although he distinguished various kinds of rights, his primary distinction is between innate rights and acquired rights, roughly corresponding to the distinction between natural and statutory rights. Innate rights, also called internal **properties**, belong to everyone by **nature**, independent of any juridical acts. Acquired rights, also called external properties, are established by legal acts. The notion of innate right is the ultimate basis of moral rights. Kant held that there is only one innate right, namely the right to lawful freedom, which is based on the harmony of one's freedom with the freedom of everyone else in accordance with universal law. Accordingly, human freedom is the supreme moral value. An action is right insofar as its freedom can subsist with the freedom of everyone.

"Rights, considered as (moral) capacities to bind others, provide the lawful ground for binding others." **Kant,** *Metaphysics of Morals*

rights

ETHICS, POLITICAL PHILOSOPHY, PHILOSOPHY OF LAW
The idea that a person can have certain natural, inalienable, and indefeasible rights emerged in the seventeenth century and played a crucial role in modern bourgeois revolutions and in the production of such documents as the French *Declaration of the Rights of Man*, and the American *Bill of Rights*. Rights are also a central ethical notion in contemporary moral theory. Many major arguments, especially those in **applied ethics**, are conducted in terms of rights and their violations. The chief characteristic of the rights approach to ethics is that it views questions from the point of view of victims or the oppressed, rather than from the perspective of those with **power**.

The notion of rights has been subjected to much subtle analysis. The most influential framework of analysis is provided by the jurist W. N. Hohfeld, who classifies a fourfold distinction of rights: (1) as claim-rights, which are enforceable claims to someone's action or inaction. If one has a right to X, then one can demand X as one's due; (2) as privileges or **liberties**, which do not involve claims against others, but are simply an absence of an **obligation** on one's part; (3) as normative **power**, that is, as a legal capacity for altering the juridical relations of another person; i.e. the power to make a will; (4) as immunities, which enable a person to be protected from the actions of another.

Of these (1) is the dominant sense. This sense of rights pairs with the notion of **obligation** or of **duty**. If one has a right to have or to do X, then another person, or group of persons, has a correlative duty or obligation to respect this entitlement. Claim-rights can be sub-classed in many ways. One way is to divide them into personal rights, which one holds against determinate or special persons (for example, the right of the landlord to collect rent from his tenants), and *in rem* rights, which one holds against people generally (for example, the right not to be killed). Another way is to divide claim-rights into positive rights, which demand other persons' positive actions, and negative rights, which merely require other persons' non-action or forbearance. Negative rights can further be divided into active rights to be free from the interference of others and passive rights which are claims not to have certain things done to us.

Rights are also categorized into **natural rights**, legal rights, moral rights, and human rights, all of which have separate entries.

"We can locate the place of rights within the ethics of responsiveness to value, by noticing that (generally) a right is something for which one can demand or enforce compliance." **Nozick,** *Philosophical Explanations*

rights, absolute

ETHICS, POLITICAL PHILOSOPHY, PHILOSOPHY OF LAW
Absolute rights are those rights that are **universal** and inherent. They can not be overridden under any conceivable circumstances. They are imprescriptible, inalienable, and are not subject to any

rational constraint. Persons possessing such a right are justified in demanding and exercising it no matter what kind of situation they are in, while other moral **agents** must respect it. **Human rights** are generally regarded as absolute rights. Absolute rights are contrasted to *prima facie* **rights**, which a person possesses with respect to a given circumstance.

> "For an absolute right is a right that human beings have qua human beings and not, as in the case of special rights, rights that they have only if certain conditions, which pertain to their social relations and the transactions in which they engage with one another, are satisfied." **Melden,** *Rights and Persons*

rights, animal

ETHICS A conception appearing in the **animal liberation** movement, and articulated by Tom Regan in *The Case for Animal Rights*. Animals are, according to him, **subjects-of-a-life** that have inherent **value** independent of their usefulness to others. They therefore have **rights** related to the protection of this value. These rights are not **legal rights**, such as the right to vote, but **moral rights**, to be respected as **ends in themselves**. However, Regan explains that when the rights to life of humans and animals conflict, **human rights** have a heavier claim than animal rights, for animals rights are *prima facie* rather than **absolute rights** and can be justifiably overridden under certain circumstances. The notion of animal rights is part of an attempt to base animal ethics on an objective ground rather than merely as an expression of human decency. If the extension of rights to animals is justified, hunting, trapping, indifference toward endangered animals, the use of animals in scientific experiments, and other human activities that treat animals merely as **means** for some human interests are all morally wrong. Yet it is much disputed whether animals have rights in a proper sense. Many philosophers argue that rights involve reciprocal relationships and moral **autonomy**, and that there is no reason to ascribe rights to animals. But this argument is challenged on the grounds that although infants and some afflicted adults lack these features, we generally accept that they have rights.

> "[A]nimals have certain basic moral rights including in particular the fundamental right to be treated with the respect that, as possessors of inherent value, they are due as a matter of strict justice." **Regan,** *The Case for Animal Rights*

rights, human

ETHICS, POLITICAL PHILOSOPHY, PHILOSOPHY OF LAW A conception of the necessary conditions that constitute the full **dignity** of a human being and that societies have **obligations** to accord to persons. People possess these rights simply because they are people, regardless of characteristics such as their race, gender, social position, culture, or customs. All people everywhere have these rights. Hence, human rights are generally regarded as **universal**. According to **Kant**, the fundamental right of a human being is to be treated as an end in oneself, not merely as a **means**. An extensive list of the basic rights that a human being should have is proposed by the United Nation's *Universal Declaration of Human Rights* (1948), and its core includes the recognized **natural rights** proposed by the eighteenth-century political philosophers, such as the right to life, to freedom of expression, and to **property**, and the four freedoms asserted in 1941 by F. D. Roosevelt as the war aims of the Allied nations: **freedom of speech** and expression, freedom of every person to worship God in his own way, freedom from want, and freedom from fear. The conception of human rights presupposes a standard below which human beings lose their dignity, rendering their life intolerable.

There are various theoretical debates surrounding this notion. The central point is to **justify** the universal and absolute existence of rights of this kind. For philosophers who accept the notion of **absolute rights**, human rights are a conception related to the notion of an inner person independent of social context. But cultural relativists claim that it is improper to apply a fixed set of rights to diverse **cultures** and traditions. Another issue is whether human rights may ever be violated. While many philosophers insist that these rights are supreme and can not be violated under any circumstances, others propose that they are *prima facie* **rights** and that sometimes a basic human right has to be sacrificed in a given context.

> "They are 'human rights' in that they are rights that all humans have as human agents . . . It is these rights that directly enter into the supreme principle of morality." **Gewirth,** *Reason and Morality*

rights, inalienable

ETHICS, POLITICAL PHILOSOPHY, PHILOSOPHY OF LAW
The natural, innate rights, which can not be relin-
quished, forfeited, or waived under any circumstances and which can not be handed over or
transferred to another **person**. Fundamental inalienable rights include the right to life and the right
to **liberty**. These rights are essential for a human
being as a human being. Inalienable rights in some
cases can conflict with **freedom** and hence render
many practical moral problems difficult to solve. For
instance, if the right to life is inalienable, it must be
immoral to permit voluntary **euthanasia**, although
it should be permitted if we have an **obligation** to
respect the **will** of the patient.

"These rights are inalienable because, being
necessary to all action, no agent could waive them
or be deprived of them and still remain an agent."
Gewirth, *Reason and Morality*

rights, legal

PHILOSOPHY OF LAW The rights that are ascribed by
the laws of a society and that vary from society to
society. Within the limit of legal rights, **persons** are
free to do as they please. Correspondingly, the same
legal system imposes a legal **duty** on others to act
or to refrain from acting in some way regarding the
things about which a person has legal rights. Those
violating this duty are legally open to **punishment**.

"To say that I have a legal right to do something is
not to say I must do it. I am merely given a liberty
to do so, if I wish." **Brandt**, *Ethical Theory*

rights, moral

ETHICS A moral right entitles a **person** to perform
certain actions, especially those that are supported
by sound or conclusive moral arguments. Although
there can be substantial overlap, **legal rights** and
moral rights are distinct. This difference allows moral
rights to be a platform for criticizing the legal system.
Generally, but not always, possession of a moral
right entails that somebody else has a corresponding
moral **obligation** or **duty**. Many **legal positivists**
define moral rights as rights conforming to the standard regulations of society that are sanctioned by
public opinion rather than by law. But this is problematic, for slavery in Rome was a standard practice,
but we can at least argue that slaves have a moral
right to **freedom**.

"We can say, roughly, that to have a moral right
to something is for someone else to be morally
obligated (in the objective sense) to act or to
refrain from acting in some way in respect to the
thing to which I am said to have the right, if I
want him to." **Brandt**, *Ethical Theory*

rights, *prima facie*

ETHICS A *prima facie* right is a right that a **person**
has in given circumstances, in contrast to an **absolute right**, which is **universal** and inherent and
can not be overridden in any situation. If there is
no conflicting right, a *prima facie* right becomes an
absolute right. However, it can be overridden in
circumstances in which other moral rights have a
stronger claim. An absolute right entails a correlative
absolute **obligation** or **duty** on others to respect it,
while a *prima facie* right entails only a correlative
prima facie obligation or duty. Some philosophers
argue that all rights are *prima facie* and that there
are no absolute rights.

"As in the case of duties one might wish to
employ the expression 'prima facie rights' in order
to speak about the rights a person may be said to
have in the case in which it may not be right to
exercise them or for others to accord them."
Melden, *Rights and Persons*

rights thesis

PHILOSOPHY OF LAW, ETHICS, POLITICAL PHILOSOPHY A
theory about the nature of law developed by Ronald
Dworkin. He argues that law is not merely a body
of **rules** laid down by statute, for there are many
hard cases that can not be solved by the application
of valid rules. In these cases, judges must be guided
to their decisions by non-rule standards such as policies and **principles**. Dworkin distinguishes between
an argument of principle, which seeks to solve
hard cases by appeal to the **rights** an individual
possesses, and an argument of policy, which seeks
to settle hard cases by taking into consideration the
good of the community. It is generally believed that
arguments of policy dictate the solutions to hard
cases, but in his rights thesis Dworkin argues that
arguments of principle should govern these judicial
decisions. Each person has an equal right to equal

concern and respect. These rights originate from the need of members of society to protect certain interests that they collectively regard as valuable. These rights are political trumps that restrict society from interfering with individuals for the purpose of advancing social goods and should have a certain threshold weight against the consideration of the welfare of the community. The specification and guarantee of these rights is a fundamental requirement for **justice** in society. Dworkin thus rejects the basic assumption of **legal positivism** that there is a sharp distinction between law and **morality**. He also claims that judges are not lawmakers, for they need to find deeper moral principles embedded in written laws to solve hard cases. But Dworkin also concedes that the operation of certain rights may be restricted in situations where they conflict with certain major benefits that can be acquired for all the members of the society. It is highly controversial whether judges should ignore completely social or community goods.

"The rights thesis . . . provides a more satisfactory explanation of how judges use precedent in hard cases than the explanation provided by any theory that gives a more prominent place to policy." **Dworkin,** *Taking Rights Seriously*

rigid designator

LOGIC, PHILOSOPHY OF LANGUAGE, METAPHYSICS According to **Kripke**, **proper names** are rigid designators because they **refer** to the same **individual** in every **possible world** in which that individual exists. **Natural kind** terms, like "water" or "gold," are rigid designators because they designate items with the same **essential** features across possible worlds. In contrast, accidental or non-rigid designators designate different things according to what satisfies their associated descriptions. A proper name, such as "Socrates," simply designates a specific individual, and since it does not describe that individual, its designation is not in virtue of the individual satisfying a certain description, but simply because it is that individual. Whether or not the individual satisfies some list of commonly associated descriptions, the proper name will always designate that individual. The conception is devised to challenge the traditional theory of proper names, such as **Russell**'s view that a name

designates a thing by describing **properties** usually attributed to it.

"Let's call something a rigid designator if in every possible world it designates the same object, a nonrigid or accidental designator if this is not the case." **Kripke,** *Name and Necessity*

role

PHILOSOPHY OF SOCIAL SCIENCE A basic term in the theory of social **behavior** and society. As a theatrical term, a role was originally related to persona, mask, and character, and was the prescribed pattern of behavior for an actor in a given part in a play. Later, the notion of a role was extended by analogy to a social position that carries with it a repertoire of expected behavioral regularities. These regularities are **normative** and reflect the demands of the society, and hence any person occupying a given role is required to conform to them. Sanctions may be used to discipline a person who fails to satisfy the **rules** or norms constituting or regulating his role. Roles typically belong to patterns of role relations that determine the structure of society or its component groups. Roles govern human interactions in social relations and can be conceived without reference to particular **persons**. Roles can be described in relation to things such as family, occupation, nationality, class-membership, gender, age, or religion. Since a person may assume a multitude of roles, it is inevitable that sometimes his different roles will conflict with one another. Such conflicts may pose serious moral problems, especially for theories that have no moral standpoint beyond the fulfillment of the **duties** attached to one's roles. Roles must be flexible or **open-textured** to allow a society to cope with unexpected circumstances and to leave room for individuality. For these reasons, some theorists hold that however important roles are for understanding social action, the **explanations** offered by roles have limits.

"Social roles . . . are bundles of expectations directed at the incumbents of positions in a given society." **Dahrendorf,** *Essays in the Theory of Society*

role-reversal test

ETHICS A **thought experiment**, involving an imaginative or hypothetical identification of oneself with others in making ethical decisions. It requires that one thinks oneself into someone else's position and imagine how one would be affected if one were that **person**. Such a test is the basis for the **universalizability** of **moral judgments**, not only in the ethical positions of **Kant** and **Hare**, which give special emphasis to moral universality, but also generally.

> "In doing this, I apply a 'role-reversal', and think what I would want or prefer if I were in their positions." **B. Williams**, *Ethics and the Limits of Philosophy*

Rorty, Richard (1931–2007)

American neo-pragmatist philosopher, born in New York, Professor of Philosophy at Princeton University and University of Virginia, Professor of Comparative Literature at Stanford University. Rorty seeks to replace a conception of philosophy that accords a privileged status to mind or language in formulating and solving timeless problems with a conception of philosophy as creative conversation that is nearer to the hermeneutics that emerged from the work of Nietzsche, Heidegger, and Derrida and the pragmatism of James and Dewey. His major works include *The Linguistic Turn* (1967), *Philosophy and the Mirror of Nature* (1979), *Consequences of Pragmatism* (1982), *Contingency, Irony, and Solidarity* (1989), and *Objectivity, Relativism, and Truth* (1991).

Ross, Sir W(illiam) D(avid) (1877–1971)

British moral philosopher and Aristotelian scholar, born in Thurso, Scotland, knighted in 1938. As a moral philosopher, Ross published *The Right and the Good* (1930) and *Foundations of Ethics* (1939). He developed the influential *prima facie* duty theory, according to which absolute duty does not exist and all duties are conditional. A *prima facie* duty becomes an actual duty only if there is not a stronger *prima facie* duty in the circumstance. Ross distinguished the right from the good by ascribing the right to acts and the good to motives. He claimed that the right and the good are objective qualities that are known intuitively. As an Aristotelian scholar, he was the editor and main translator of the *Oxford Translations of Aristotle* and contributed highly valuable commentaries to Aristotle's major works.

Rousseau, Jean-Jacques (1712–78)

French political and social philosopher, born in Geneva. Rousseau used a version of social contract theory to explain the origin and formation of both human society and human individual self-understanding within society. He held that the original goodness of human beings in the state of nature has been both elevated and corrupted by society, with the cause of inequality traced to the establishment of private property. Yet humanity requires justice, morality, and reason. He maintained that political obligation is justified solely on the basis of the general will. He also held that the aim of education is to make children grow in accordance with nature by cultivating their heart rather than their reason. Rousseau's political thought and subtle psychological insights profoundly influenced the French Revolution, and his *Social Contract* is a major source of both democratic thought and some strands of totalitarian thought. Rousseau's major works include *Discourse on the Origin and Foundation of Inequality Among Humans* (1755), *Émile* (1762), *The Social Contract* (1762), *Confessions* (1782–9) and the novel *Julie, ou la Nouvelle Héloïse*.

Royce, Josiah (1855–1916)

American philosopher, born in Grass Valley, California. Royce's philosophy, which he called "absolute pragmatism," was a version of neo-Hegelian absolute idealism. He maintained that we should approach the problem of being by examining the process of knowing. The Absolute as the ultimate reality is an infinite and ordered fullness of experience for which all facts are subject to universal law. Royce also developed a theory of loyalty in ethics, according to which loyalty is the essence of all human virtue. Royce's numerous works include *The Religious Aspect of Philosophy* (1885), *The World and the Individual*, 2 vols. (1899–1900), and *The Philosophy of Loyalty* (1908).

rule-consequentialism, see act-consequentialism

rule-following

PHILOSOPHY OF LANGUAGE An important notion in later **Wittgenstein**, rule-following is subject to different interpretations. Wittgenstein claims that language comprises **language-games** governed by sets of **rules**. Though we do not commonly think of rules when talking and can not usually specify rules governing our usage, rules exist which determine the conditions for the correct application of what we say. Wittgenstein does not offer a linguistic definition of what a rule is, but illustrates rules through many examples. Following a rule is not a matter of **interpretation**. The ability to **understand** existing rules rests upon a brute reaction to training, that is, on repetition. By this view, Wittgenstein is suggesting that the **meaning** of a term is its use. To mean something is to follow a definite rule, otherwise using words to say something would be to string words together aimlessly. On the other hand, rules do not carry their own interpretation, and "going on in the same way" is settled practically by the context in which rules are followed rather than by the rules themselves. Understanding is reacting correctly, on the basis of training, to the rule-following application of words. The notion of rule-following is also a major point in Wittgenstein's **private language** argument. Since in a private language there is no way to distinguish between thinking that one is following a rule and actually following it, there is no language at all.

"Following a rule is analogous to an order. We are trained to do so." **Wittgenstein,** *Philosophical Investigation*

rule of generalization, see generalization

rule of law

PHILOSOPHY OF LAW, POLITICAL PHILOSOPHY A technical term, credited to A. V. Dicey's *An Introduction to the Study of the Law of the Constitution* (1885), for a system in which the **powers** of government and of state officials are limited by law. The rule of law contrasts with despotic or arbitrary rule. Under the rule of law, political **power** is generally divided into several branches, such as the legislative, executive, and judicial, and its exercise in each branch is restrained in order to prevent it from being abused. The law lays down general standards of conduct, which are clear and are made known to all those to whom the law applies. The legislators themselves are subject to the law, which is reasonable and relatively stable. Civil **liberty** is guaranteed, and violations of legal rules are punished. The transference of political power is through fair elections. According to its proponents, the rule of law is a

political ideal of **liberalism** and is an essential aspect of various forms of **democracy**.

"In a purely formal sense, the ideal of the rule of law is none other than what I have just described: the ideal of laws clearly delimiting citizens' duties and officials' powers, under which every abusive exercise of public or private power against the legal liberty of any person is suppressed or penalised, and with no one going in peril of coercion for anything other than breach of a pre-announced law." **MacCormick,** *Legal Right and Social Democracy*

rule of quality

LOGIC Two rules for **categorical syllogisms** that determine the valid **inference** of qualitative connections between premises and conclusion: (1) From two negative premises nothing can be inferred; (2) if one premise is negative, the conclusion must be negative; and to prove a negative conclusion, one of the premises must be negative. The first rule is sound because in the case where there are two negative premises, the middle term does not establish any connection between the major term and the minor term. Violation of this rule will lead to the **fallacy** of exclusive premises. The second rule is sound because one negative premise determines that the relation between the major term and the minor term must be exclusive. Violation of this rule will lead to the fallacy of drawing an affirmative conclusion from a negative premise. Only from two affirmative premises can one infer an affirmative conclusion.

"[They] are called rules of quality because they refer to the ways in which the negative quality of one or both premises restricts the kinds of conclusions that validly may be inferred." **Copi,** *Introduction to Logic*

rule of recognition

PHILOSOPHY OF LAW **Hart** claimed that a developed legal system is a union of primary rules and secondary rules. Primary rules are rules of **obligation** which regulate conduct and impose **duties**, while secondary rules are power-conferring rules to regulate the identification, modification, and adjudication of primary rules. If a law had only primary rules, it would have three major defects: (1) uncertainty, because all rules are merely a set of separate standards with no common identification; (2) inflexibility in rule-changing; (3) inefficiency in the face of the complex social situations. Hence, a set of secondary rules must be introduced to remedy these defects, and this is the step from the pre-legal to the legal world. For improving the defect of uncertainty, we need to introduce a set of rules that stipulate some identifying marks and criteria of the **validity** of primary rules and that decide their scopes. These are called rules of recognition. For improving the defect of inflexibility, we need to introduce rules of change that allow individuals or groups to introduce new primary rules and to eliminate old ones. Finally, for improving the defect of inefficiency, we need to introduce rules of adjudication that enable individuals to determine when a primary rule has been broken. This conception of law has provoked vigorous discussion in the philosophy of law. In particular, rules of recognition have provided a focus for debate, for they provide a new ground for legal validity in place of **Austin**'s **command** of the sovereign.

> "The simplest form of remedy for the uncertainty of the regime of primary rules is the introduction of what we shall call a 'rule of recognition'. This will specify some feature or features possession of which by a suggested rule is taken as a conclusive affirmative indication that it is a rule of the group to be supported by the social pressure it exerts." **Hart,** *The Concept of Law*

rule-skepticism, another expression for legal realism

rule-utilitarianism

ETHICS, POLITICAL PHILOSOPHY In contrast with act-utilitarianism, a version of **utilitarianism** in which general rules rather than acts are assessed for **utility**, thus shifting concern from **individuals** to practices and institutions. Acts are endorsed not in their own right, but because they accord with practices or institutions which meet the test of maximizing utility. The rules of rule-utilitarianism can be understood as possible (ideal) rules or actual (existing) rules. The rule-utilitarianism that considers possible rules is a position not far from **deontology**. According to this version, a moral action should follow

a rule which, if generally followed, would have the maximum utility. The rule-utilitarianism that deals with actual and existing rules is developed by Toulmin and many others. According to this version, a moral action should be in accord with the existing moral code. This moral code yields greatest utility if it has general acceptance or universal compliance. The basic difficulty of rule-utilitarianism is that in many cases the rule it prescribes is not the most beneficial to obey on every given individual occasion. Rule-utilitarianism is thus inconsistent with the basic moral motivation of utilitarianism, namely, beneficence.

> "For rule-utilitarianism rules are morally binding because general adherence to them maximises, or would maximise, welfare, individual acts being right or wrong in virtue of their conformity to such rules." **Sprigge,** *The Rational Foundations of Ethics*

Russell, Bertrand (1872–1970)

British logician and philosopher, born in Ravenscroft, England, succeeded to an earldom in 1931, a founder of twentieth-century analytic philosophy. He contributed various significant theories to logic, philosophy of mathematics, epistemology, metaphysics, and philosophy of mind, although he often changed his views in his long philosophical career. He sought to derive pure mathematics from logical principles and was instrumental in developing symbolic logic. His discovery of "**Russell's paradox**" undermined Frege's logicist program, and his effort to solve this paradox led to the formulation of his theory of types. Russell's logical atomism aimed to determine an ideal language with which reality would have an isomorphic structure, and claimed that all knowledge could be stated in terms of atomic sentences and their truth-functional compounds. His theory of definite descriptions showed how we could speak meaningfully of non-existent objects without committing ourselves to their existence. He drew the distinction between knowledge by acquaintance and knowledge by description. Politically, Russell was a pacifist, and he received the Nobel Prize in Literature in 1952. Among Russell's extensive writings are *Principles of Mathematics* (1903), *Principia Mathematica* (with Whitehead) (1910–13), *Problems of Philosophy* (1912), *The Theory of Knowledge* (1913), *Our Knowledge of the External World* (1914), *The Philosophy of*

Logical Atomism (1918), *Introduction to Mathematical Philosophy* (1919), *The Analysis of Mind* (1921), *The Analysis of Matter* (1927), *An Inquiry into Meaning and Truth* (1940), and *Human Knowledge* (1948). His intellectual autobiography, *My Philosophical Development*, was published in 1959.

Russell's paradox

LOGIC A **paradox** regarding the membership of **classes**, formulated by **Russell** in *The Principles of Mathematics* (1903). Some classes or **sets** (for example the set of abstract objects) are members of themselves, while others (for example the set of cows) are not. Now consider the set that consists of all sets that are not members of themselves. Is this set a member of itself or not? If it is a member of itself, then it has the property that is shared by its members and is not a member of itself. If it is not a member of itself, then it qualifies for membership in the set and is a member of itself. Either way involves **self-contradiction**. This paradox is considered as a prime example of the **set-theoretical paradoxes** like **Cantor's paradox**. **Frege** took Russell's paradox as a serious check on the development of any arithmetic system. It undermined many **axioms** of **set theory**, especially the axiom of comprehension,

that for every **property** expressible in the notation of set theory, there is a set consisting of all and only those things that possess that property. Russell offered a formal solution for this paradox in his theory of **types**, and a philosophical solution in his **vicious circle principle**.

> "Russell's paradox about classes, which he discovered in 1901, led to an enormous amount of work in the foundations of mathematics."
> **Sainsbury,** *Paradoxes*

Ryle, Gilbert (1900–76)

British philosopher, born in Brighton, a leading figure of Oxford ordinary language philosophy. Ryle's most influential book was *The Concept of Mind* (1949), in which he rejected Cartesian dualism as the dogma of "the ghost in the machine." He argued that mental phenomena could be explained in terms of dispositions to certain characteristic performances. In his view, Cartesian dualism committed a category mistake, by describing the mind as belonging to the category of substance, rather than understanding the mental in terms of dispositions. Ryle also wrote many articles illustrating ways in which philosophical problems arise from conceptual confusions.

S

sacred, see holy

St Petersburg paradox

LOGIC A paradox of **probability** theory. Imagine gambling on the toss of a coin. If heads appears first time, you win $1. If it does not appear until your second toss, you win $2. Your potential winnings double each time tails turns up and you do not win. Your gamble will stop only when heads appears. How much should you expect to win by gambling according to these simple rules and how much should you be willing to pay for a chance to play? The surprising answer, an **infinite** amount, is derived from the series of $(1/2) + (2 \times 1/4) + (4 \times 1/8) \ldots$, which has an infinite sum. But this expected return seems unreasonable and has been used to argue against using infinite **utilities** in **decision theory**. The paradox is so called because it first appeared in a memoir by Daniel Bernouilli in the Commentarii of the St Petersburg Academy.

> "The St. Petersburg paradox arises out of a game in which Peter engages to pay Paul one shilling if a head appears at the first toss of a coin, two shillings if it does not appear until the second, and, in general, a r-1 shillings if no head appears until the rth toss." **Keynes,** *A Treatise of Probability*

salva veritate

LOGIC [Latin, saving the truth] A term in logic that means "preserving without losing the truth-value,"

in relation to the intersubstitutivity of co-referring expressions, that is, expressions having the same **reference**. For a wide range of contexts, if two expressions A and B have the same reference, then A can be substituted for B in a **sentence** in which B occurs without changing the **truth-value** of the sentence. **Frege** was concerned to develop an **extensional logic**. Accordingly atomic co-referring sentences can be substituted for one another in molecular sentences truth-functionally compounded out of them without changing the truth-values of the molecular sentences. This feature is related to the principle of substitutivity. However, intersubstitution *salva veritate* is not possible in other contexts, such as those involving **propositional attitudes** or **modal** terms, contexts which **Quine** calls **referentially opaque**.

> "A natural suggestion, deserving close examination, is that the synonymy of two linguistic forms consists simply in their interchangeability in all contexts without change of truth value – interchangeability, in Leibniz's phrase, *salva veritate*." **Quine,** *From a Logical Point of View*

salvation

PHILOSOPHY OF RELIGION In the New Testament, Jesus is regarded as the lord and savior Jesus Christ, and the purpose of the incarnation is claimed to be for our purpose. It is one of the basic teachings of Christianity that human beings are sinful, and hence something must be done to heal or put right our sinful lives. Jesus was sent by **God** as the savior of the world, to save people from their **sins** and to make the **soul** participate in all the glory of God. Christians believe that salvation can not be won merely by human efforts and requires **grace**. It is the essential object of hope.

> "For practical life at any rate, the chance of salvation is enough." **W. James**, *The Varieties of Religious Experience*

sanctity of human life

ETHICS A claim originating in the Old Testament, Genesis 1:27: "God created man in his own image," and claiming that human life is **sacred** and has a natural, inestimable, and **transcendent** worth or **value**. This value is equal for all of us and is independent of any other values that can be ascribed to individual **persons** in virtue of features such as their efforts, accomplishments or talents. It implies that we have an absolute **duty** to preserve and protect human life and that it is morally wrong to take human life as having merely **instrumental** value. The idea of the sanctity of life provides grounds for the right to life and, according to some philosophers and social theorists, renders practices such as **capital punishment**, **euthanasia**, and **abortion** indefensible, although it is debatable whether this principle has paramount validity. We can also ask whether the sanctity of human life implies that human life is superior to the lives of other species.

> "... the view that it is always wrong to take an innocent human life. We may call this the 'sanctity of life' view." **P. Singer**, *Animal Liberation*

Sandel, Michael (1953–)

American communtarian political philosopher, Professor of Government, Harvard University. Sandel helped to initiate the liberalism–communitarian debate with a rejection of the abstract individualism of liberal theory in favor of a conception of personal identity that is constituted by relations to a community. His work has led to discussion of the role of community in political theory and of the nature of the self in philosophy of mind and ethics. His main work is *Liberalism and the Limits of Justice* (1982).

Santayana, George (1863–1952)

Spanish-born American philosopher, poet, and novelist, born in Madrid, taught at Harvard. Santayana's first important philosophical writings were *The Sense of Beauty* (1896) and *The Life of Reason*, 5 vols. (1905–6). He viewed aesthetics and philosophy in general as a psychological inquiry, and defined beauty as objectified pleasure. He also sought to trace the role of reason in the progress of human creativity. *Scepticism and Animal Faith* (1923) and *Realms of Being*, 4 vols. (1927–40) mainly focused on ontology. He claimed that we have positive knowledge of essences, but maintained that the existence of objects could not be proved. Thus, he was both a Platonist and a skeptic. He held that through "animal faith" we believe what is necessary for survival.

Sapir–Whorf hypothesis

PHILOSOPHY OF LANGUAGE, METAPHYSICS Also called linguistic determinism, a principle of linguistic relativity developed by the linguists Edward Sapir and Benjamin Lee Whorf. It claims that, in addition to being a technique of communication, language is even more significantly a device that gives its speakers habitual modes of analyzing **experience** into significant **categories**. Language functions more to define the speaker's experiences than to report experience. The grammatical structure of the language we speak determines our way of **understanding** or thinking about the world. Consequently, metaphysics or **ontology** relies on **grammar**. Whorf attempted to prove this principle empirically by comparing modern European languages with the native languages of the American Indians. For example, he claimed that Hopi Indians do not have a notion of **time**, because their language lacks means of marking temporal distinctions. The thesis can be traced to **Aristotle**'s *Categories*, **Vico**'s *New Science*, and the philosophy of W. V. **Humboldt**. The thesis is controversial, and there are methodological disputes about what would count as evidence for or against it.

> "Sapir–Whorf hypothesis . . . claims that the form of our languages in some way determines the fundamental beliefs that we hold." **Bird**, *Philosophical Tasks*

Sartre, Jean-Paul (1905–80)

French existentialist philosopher, novelist, playwright, and biographer, born in Paris. Sartre's primary concern was the existential situation of human individuals in a world of necessity. He maintained that tensions between facticity and freedom and between freedom and responsibility define our humanity. His claim that "existence precedes essence" implies that individual and particular human existence is given, but that human beings are always free to choose and invent their own natures. Consciousness, as what is not or nothing, is the source of activity in choosing and negating. In the end, one is radically responsible for what one chooses, including the background against which one makes one's choice. If one regards oneself as merely a passive subject of outside influences and as a thing with a fixed nature instead of a being-for-itself, one falls into "bad faith." Sartre developed a detailed phenomenological psychology and sought to defend Marxism in term of existential anthropology and psychoanalysis. His novels and plays earned him the 1964 Nobel Prize in literature, but he declined to accept it. Sartre's principal philosophical writings include *Sketch for a Theory of the Emotions* (1939), *The Psychology of Imagination* (1940), *Being and Nothingness* (1943), *Existentialism and Humanism* (1946), and *Critique of Dialectical Reason*, 2 vols. (1960, 1985).

satisfaction

LOGIC In a technical sense first used by **Tarski** in defining "truth," a relation between an **open sentence** and ordered N-tuples of **objects**. Open sentences like Fx or Gx are neither true nor false. They are sentential **functions** rather than sentences because they contain free **variables** marking gaps into which suitable terms or expressions have to be substituted. If an open sentence is true of the objects that are designated by the expressions that are substituted for its variables, the objects satisfy the open sentence. "X taught Y who taught Z" is satisfied by (Socrates, Plato, and Aristotle), for it is true that Socrates is the teacher of Plato, and that Plato is the teacher of Aristotle. An interpretation satisfies a **formula** if and only if that formula is true under that interpretation. On this basis, Tarski defined a sentence as true just in case it is satisfied by all members in an infinite sequence, and as false just in case it is satisfied by none. For this reason his **semantic theory of truth** is regarded as being a version of the **correspondence theory of truth**.

"A function satisfies an unstructured n-place predicate with variables in its n places if the predicate is true of the entities (in order) that the function assigns to those variables." **Davidson,** *Inquiries into Truth and Interpretation*

satisficing

PHILOSOPHY OF SOCIAL SCIENCE, PHILOSOPHY OF ACTION, ETHICS A term introduced by the economist Herbert A. Simon for a model of rational choice that seeks to find a satisfactory solution rather than best solution to a problem. The model can also be conceived in terms of seeking a good enough outcome rather than the best outcome. In contrast, the **maximizing**/optimizing model of rationality seeks to achieve one's greatest **good**. The notion has been borrowed by ethics and rational choice theory, especially to formulate versions of **consequentialism**. Accordingly, one should seek to achieve morally satisficing behavior because under many circumstances an optimal moral choice or action is too difficult to determine or to achieve. The actor is constrained not only by the external environment, but also by a limited access to information and by uncertainty about the **value** and **probability** of each of the alternative courses of **action**. Hence, each human actor is subject to the limits of his cognitive capacities. Positively, a satisficing choice represents a reasonable sense of when one has enough. It corresponds to the idea of moderation in Greek ethics.

"Defenders of satisficing claim that it sometimes makes sense not to pursue one's own greatest good or desire-fulfilment, but I think it can also be shown that it sometimes makes sense deliberately to reject which is better for oneself in favour of what is good and sufficient for one's purposes." **Slote,** *Beyond Optimising*

saturated, see unsaturated

Saussure, Ferdinand de (1857–1913)

Swiss linguist, born in Geneva, founder of structural linguistics. In his main work, the posthumously published *Course in General Linguistics* (1916), Saussure distinguished between *langue* (language) and *parole* (speech) and claimed that language is a synchronic or static system. He maintained that linguists should determine the nature of language and analyze the relations between elements that compose the structure of a given language. His work in linguistics exerted great influence upon French structuralist philosophy and modern semiology.

saving the phenomena

ANCIENT GREEK PHILOSOPHY, PHILOSOPHICAL METHOD, METAPHYSICS A type of empirical methodology initiated by **Aristotle**. It requires that a scientific discipline should start from phenomena and then develop **hypotheses** to explain the ground of the phenomena, rather than being satisfied solely with discovering the **nature** of things. The term "phenomena" should be understood to include both observed **facts** and common and learned assumptions about a certain subject matter. The methodology may apply to both natural and social sciences.

In Greek philosophy, the term also concerns the ground of the world of **appearance** in discussion developing from **Parmenides**' metaphysical claim that only the **One** is real **being** and that there is no real **motion**.

"Originally in Aristotle and his immediate successors the task is to give an account of phenomena in terms of basic physics which in turn must be constructed in such a way that the phenomena can be accounted for. Later on basic physics is taken for granted and phenomena must be explained in its terms. This is how the idea of saving the phenomena (rather than giving an account of them) arises." **Feyerabend**, *Problems of Empiricism*

saying and showing

PHILOSOPHY OF LANGUAGE, LOGIC, METAPHYSICS, ETHICS, PHILOSOPHY OF RELIGION **Wittgenstein**'s distinction, also presented as a contrast between what can be said and what can be shown. Something can be said only if it could be passed on to somebody as a piece of information. To say something without knowing its **truth conditions** is not really saying in this sense. Anything that can be said at all can be said in a **proposition**. All factual propositions say something about the world, but all **pseudo-propositions**, including logical, metaphysical, ethical, and religious propositions, attempt to say what can only be shown and are not really saying anything. Instead of specifying the precise meaning

of "showing," Wittgenstein makes a list of what can be shown but not said. The only common point linking them is negative, namely that they are things that can not be expressed in factual language. In his *Tractatus* Wittgenstein examines them one by one to see why they are excluded from factual language.

"What *can* be shown, *cannot* be said." **Wittgenstein, *Tractatus***

Scheler, Max (1874–1928)

German philosopher, born in Munich, a leading phenomenologist, taught at Jena, Munich, and Cologne. Scheler's major works include *Formalism in Ethics and the Non-Formal Ethics of Value* (1913–6) and *Problems of a Sociology of Knowledge* (1926). Scheler extended the phenomenological method to areas of ethics, axiology, religion, and anthropology. He claimed that values are objective and that the experience of a value is an intentional act. He defined a person as the concrete unity of acts. His works provided extensive analysis of moral feelings, such as sympathy, repentance, resentment, love, and joy.

Schelling, Friedrich (1775–1854)

German idealist philosopher, born in Leonberg. Schelling was the link between Fichte's subjective idealism and Hegel's absolute idealism and was regarded as the leading philosopher of romanticism. Schelling argued that the world of nature existed objectively rather than as a construction of the ego. Nature is an infinite process of unconscious self-development and is a system of opposed forces. The Absolute is an undifferentiated unity of subject and object. Art is the perfect union of freedom and necessity and of history and nature. Only in art can mind become fully aware of itself. Schelling later called his philosophy the system of identity, which contained his transcendental idealism and philosophy of nature. His major works include *Ideas for a Philosophy of Nature* (1797), *The System of Transcendental Idealism* (1800), and *Philosophical Investigations concerning the Nature of Human Freedom* (1809).

schema (Kant), see schematism

schematism

EPISTEMOLOGY, METAPHYSICS An important section of **Kant**'s ***Critique of Pure Reason***, dealing with a procedure of **judgment** that adapts the **categories** or pure concepts of **understanding** to **experience**. Kant held that schematism is necessary because the categories do not have their origin in experience. He argued that an application of the categories in experience is possible because each category has an empirical counterpart or schema. It is not an **image**, but a **rule** for production of images. Each schema is a **transcendental** determination in **time**. For example, the schema of **substance** is permanence of the **real** in time, and the schema of **necessity** is the existence of an **object** at all time. In a sense, a schema is just the category itself with the condition of temporality added. As **universal** and *a priori*, the schema is homogeneous with the category, but it is also homogeneous with **appearance** because it involves **imagination**, time, and the empirical **representation** of the **manifold** contained in time. With these characteristics, the schema can mediate between the **concept** and **intuition**, which are otherwise heterogeneous, and enable judgments to take place. Without the schema, the concepts are insignificant because only with the aid of schema can they be applied to phenomena. Some critics argue that the schematism restates rather than solves the problem of applying concepts, especially the categories.

> "This schematism of our understanding, in its application to appearances and their mere form, is an art concealed in the depths of the human soul, whose real modes of activity nature is hardly likely ever to allow us to discover, and to have open to our gaze." **Kant,** *Critique of Pure Reason*.

Schiller, F(erdinand) C(anning) S(cott) (1864–1937)

British pragmatist, born in Schleswig-Holstein, taught in Oxford. Schiller opposed the prevailing neo-Hegelian absolute idealism of his day. In virtue of his concern for the intentions, needs, and activities of individual human beings, he called his philosophy "humanism" or "voluntarism." He was influenced by Protagoras' maxim that man is the measure of all things, and denied the existence of an independent reality that is irrelevant to human experience and claimed that reality is of our own making. He also denied the existence of absolute truth and claimed that truth is merely the best

solution available. Truth is useful, although not everything useful is true. He applied his humanism to logic and sought to replace formal logic with his "logic of application." Schiller's principal works are *Humanism: Philosophical Essays* (1903), *Studies in Humanism* (1907), and *Formal Logic: A Scientific and Social Problem* (1912).

Schiller, Johann Christoph Friedrich (1759–1805)

German philosopher of aesthetics, poet, and playwright, born in Marbach. Schiller maintained that art or beauty is an intermediary realm between the spheres of nature and freedom. Beauty is characterized as "freedom in appearance." In human nature, there is an "aesthetic impulse," which can reconcile and harmonize material and formal impulses. Aesthetic education should acknowledge the interests of the aesthetic impulse in order to achieve harmony and unity in an individual's life and in society. Schiller's most important philosophical books were the *Letters on the Aesthetic Education of Mankind* (1794–5) and *On the Sublime* (1793–1801).

Schleiermacher, Friedrich (1768–1834)

German philosopher theologian and Platonic scholar, born in Breslau, founder of modern hermeneutics and modern Protestant theology. He claimed that religion is a feeling of absolute dependence upon the infinite that man experiences as a finite being. He held that Christianity should be understood in historical tradition and that in interpreting a written text, we should seek a psychological understanding of the mind of the author. Schleiermacher's major works include *On Religion* (1799), *Monologen* (1800), *Brief Outline of the Study of Religion* (1811), and *The Christian Faith* (1821–2).

Schlick, Moritz (1882–1936)

German-Austrian physicist and logical positivist philosopher, born in Berlin, taught at University of Vienna, the founder of the Vienna Circle. Schlick's main concern was to determine the criteria for scientific knowledge. He held that the task of philosophy is to analyze concepts, propositions, and methods of the special sciences and to clarify meanings. Traditional metaphysics is meaningless and must be demarcated from exact scientific knowledge. The propositions of logic and mathematics are analytic instead of synthetic *a priori*. In ethics

Schlick rejected the idea of absolute value. In 1936, he was shot by a deranged student while on the way to a lecture. Schlick's important works include *Space and Time in Contemporary Physics* (1917), *General Theory of Knowledge* (1918), and *Problems of Ethics* (1930).

scholastic philosophy, see scholasticism

scholasticism

PHILOSOPHICAL METHOD, LOGIC, METAPHYSICS, PHILOSOPHY OF RELIGION Also called scholastic philosophy, the dominant philosophy in the medieval intellectual world. It started in the fifth century with the influential commentary of **Aristotle**'s logical works by **Boethius**, and lasted until the middle of the seventeenth century. The heyday of scholasticism was from the eleventh to the thirteenth century, when the universities of Paris and Oxford were founded and the Western philosophical tradition reproduced itself through reading and commenting upon the works of ancient authors, particularly Aristotle, whose works were translated into Latin in this period. The most celebrated exponent of scholastic philosophy, who was also the greatest commentator on Aristotle, was Thomas **Aquinas**. Other prominent scholastics included **Abelard**, **Buridan**, **Duns Scotus**, **William of Ockham**, and **Suárez**. The major characteristic of scholasticism is the attempt to reconcile the conflict between **reason** and **faith** by rendering Greek thought, especially Aristotle's doctrines, consistent with Christian theology, and so to employ philosophy in support of theology. The conjunction of faith and **knowledge** started with Boethius, and Ockham argued that the prospects of a marriage between them were not hopeful. For this reason, Ockham is said to be the last of the scholastics. Scholasticism was characterized by its disputation of contested points of detail. These formal disputes were conducted according to well-recognized rules derived from Aristotle's logic. In this way it contributed greatly to logic.

Scholasticism is so called because it was philosophy done in the universities (Greek *schola*, leisure, also the origin of the terms school and scholar), for only when one has leisure time can one learn and contemplate. Scholasticism has had a bad reputation since the **Renaissance**, and was the major target of attack for early modern philosophers, such as **Descartes**, **Bacon**, **Hobbes**, and **Locke**, in their initiation of the modern study of philosophy and science. However, over the last century philosophers have renewed their appreciation of the contributions of scholasticism to logic, linguistics, and metaphysics.

"What defined the great age of scholasticism? The fact that its leading minds, Thomas and Bonaventura, say, carried out that co-ordination between believing acceptance of revealed and traditional truth on the one hand and rational argumentation on the other hand with unfailing resoluteness – although they knew just where to draw the line between the claims of reason and the claims of faith." **Pieper,** *Scholasticism*

Schopenhauer, Arthur (1788–1860)

German philosopher, born in Danzig. Schopenhauer's masterpiece was *The World as Will and Idea* (1818). Against Hegelian rationalism, he stressed the importance of unconscious rather than conscious mental processes and took the will to be the central concept of his philosophy. Creative will is the blind and non-rational force in both the world and human nature. Man might separate himself from the dominance of the will only in free aesthetic contemplation. Influenced by Indian Buddhism, Schopenhauer was pessimistic regarding human life. His voluntarism deeply influenced Kierkegaard, Nietzsche, and Freud. His other books include *On the Fourfold Root of the Principle of Sufficient Reason* (1813), *On the Will of Nature* (1836), *The Two Basic Problems of Ethics* (1841), and *Parega and Paralipomena* (1851).

Schrödinger's cat

PHILOSOPHY OF SCIENCE, LOGIC, METAPHYSICS Suppose that a cat is locked in a box with a bottle of poisonous gas that will break if a device connected to it registers that an atom in a radioactive substance in the box decays. The chance of decaying in the next hour is fifty-fifty. If the bottle breaks, the cat will be killed. According to **quantum** mechanics, the cat, gas, and device form a superposition of states that is **indeterminate** until a measurement or an observation is made. For this reason, the issue of the cat's being alive or being dead in the box is indeterminate until we look inside the box. Although it sounds **paradoxical**, before we look it is not true that the cat is alive and it is not true that the cat is dead. This thought experiment, introduced in 1935 by the Austrian physicist Erwin Schrödinger, indicates the difficulty in conceiving quantum indeterminacy in terms of daily language.

> "Schrödinger's cat thought experiment did not show that quantum mechanics is logically false, but it did show that it is wildly counter-intuitive, perhaps to the point of being absurd." **Brown,** *The Laboratory of the Mind*

Schutz, Alfred (1899–1959)

Austrian phenomenological philosopher of social science, born in Vienna, Professor at the New School for Social Research. Schutz provided a phenomenological theoretical basis for his acceptance of Weber's ideal types in sociological theory, but replaced the mental acts of Husserl's transcendental subject as a source of meaning with an account involving the transcendental intersubjectivity of Husserl's later philosophy. His main work is *The Phenomenology of the Social World* (1932).

scientia media, see middle knowledge

scientific determinism

PHILOSOPHY OF SCIENCE The success of **Newtonian** physics led many scientists and philosophers to believe that there is a natural order governed by the **laws of nature**. Given the initial state of a system, we can determine any future state by applying the laws of nature and the information about the initial state. Phenomena are necessary outcomes of the operation of laws in the situations that produce them. The future occurrence of an event is **predictable**. **Chance** is a name for our ignorance of the laws of nature or of the antecedent conditions of the **event**. The association of determinism and scientific predictability was established by Laplace. Determinism was widely accepted as a fundamental **principle** of science and as the very essence of scientific understanding. The truth of science seemed to prove that the whole universe must indeed be a vast and intricate **mechanism**. In spite of its great prestige, scientific determinism was challenged by the theory of **relativity**, chaos theory, and **quantum** mechanics. As a result, the debate between determinism and indeterminism has generated major

tensions in the philosophy of science. Traditionally, this debate has occurred mainly in physics, although biological determinists have gained support for the claim that the development of a **person** is determined by his genetic inheritance.

> "Science is inconceivable without determinism, but the latter is taken in a purely phenomenalist sense: in order to formulate any laws at all, we have to assume that identical conditions produce identical phenomena." **Kolakowski,** *The Alienation of Reason*

scientific experience, see lived experience

scientific image, see manifest image

scientific method

PHILOSOPHY OF SCIENCE A central concern of the philosophy of science. Various positions regarding method may be distinguished in terms of answers to the following questions: (1) How are scientific **hypotheses** formulated and how is scientific **truth** discovered? These questions focus on the nature of scientific reasoning, including the method of **induction** initiated by F. **Bacon** and elaborated by J. S. **Mill**. (2) How is **knowledge** accepted as being scientific? This problem has been the subject of intensive debate, especially since **Popper**'s criticism of verifiability and his proposal to use **falsifiability** as the **criterion** of **demarcation** between science and non-science. (3) How does science develop? **Logical positivists** attempted to establish a unified method for all sciences, but their program has not been universally accepted. Traditionally, the method of physics has been accepted as the paradigm of scientific method, although the development of biology has produced a rival paradigm. Thomas **Kuhn**'s theory of scientific revolutions challenged the picture of science as developing smoothly within the framework of a single methodology in which all theories are **commensurable** and scientific change is **rational**. Imre **Lakatos** understood the progress of science in terms of the relative success of progressive **research programs** in generating problems and their solutions. Some philosophers see science as a patchwork of different methods in which local successes do not depend on a coherent integrated system.

"The practice of scientific method is the persistent critique of arguments, in the light of canons for judging the reliability of the procedures by which evidential data are obtained, and for assessing the probative force of the evidence on which conclusions are based." **E. Nagel,** *The Structure of Science*

scientific realism

PHILOSOPHY OF SCIENCE, EPISTEMOLOGY, METAPHYSICS A position claiming that scientific **postulates** or **theoretical entities**, such as electrons and quarks, have real existence independent of our **minds** and that scientific **universals** are abstractions of the facts. Scientific realism represents the commonsensical view that there is a world that exists independent of our **experiences**, and holds that any scientific theory has **ontological** implications. Correct scientific theories describe and explain real features and objective structures of the external world. There is an intrinsic connection between how a theory depicts nature and its other features, including its power to **explain**. Scientific realism contrasts with many other positions in the philosophy of science, such as **operationism** or **instrumentalism**, which commonly claim that theoretical entities are merely fictions.

"Scientific realism says that the entities, states and processes described by correct theories really do exist." **Hacking,** *Representing and Intervening*

scientism

EPISTEMOLOGY The view that science is the only **knowledge** and that scientific methodology is the only proper method for obtaining knowledge. Everything should be **understood** and **explained** by the employment of scientific **theories**. Other fields of inquiry, including philosophy, art, history, religion, morality, and the social sciences, either are assimilated to science or are excluded as a source of knowledge. Scientism denies that any of these fields has a distinct methodology and in many versions rejects claims that there is aesthetic, moral, or religious knowledge. Philosophers who maintain that there is an autonomous field of humanistic knowledge to which scientific methodology is inapplicable reject scientism and often use the term pejoratively.

"Scientism is actually a special form of idealism, for it puts one type of human understanding in charge of the universe and what can be said about it." **T. Nagel,** *The View from Nowhere*

scope

LOGIC Scope is attributed to **syntactical operators** and affects the part of a sentence upon which the operator has immediate effect. An operator is an **expression** that alters the logical properties of another expression to which it is attached. In the expression "$(A \land B) \supset C$," the scope of $\land$ comprises "A" and "B." In ordinary language, scope is often not clearly demarcated. Hence the same sentence might be interpreted in alternative ways, depending on how one understands the context in which the sentence occurs. This gives rise to structural **ambiguities**, such as *de re/de dicto* ambiguities. For example, "I shall go to London and race if the weather is good" means either "I shall go to London anyway, but race only when the weather is good" or "If the weather is not good, I will not go to London and race." Arguments proceeding on the basis of this sort of ambiguity are said to commit the **fallacy of scope**. Artificial languages have been invented with the aim of preventing scope ambiguity. The scope of the **quantifier** is generally the whole **formula**. An operator attached to a **sentence** to produce a new sentence is a sentential operator and has the original sentence as its scope. Brackets are conventionally used to indicate the scope of the various operators. **Russell**'s theory of descriptions explicitly specifies the scope of a definite description.

"The sentence to which an operator is attached is called a scope of the operator." **Quine,** *Word and Object*

Scotism

METAPHYSICS, PHILOSOPHY OF RELIGION, ETHICS A form of **scholastic philosophy** and theology developed by **Duns Scotus** and his followers, especially among the Franciscans. Scotism was accepted by the Catholic Church as authoritative in 1633, and was taught widely in the universities around the world from the sixteenth century to the eighteenth century. Scotism and **Thomism** are two main trends in scholasticism. Other famous Scotists include Francis Mayron, John de Bassolis, Peter of Aquila, and Luke

Wadding, who in 1639 edited the first edition of the complete works of Scotus.

Scotism accepted the **Aristotelian** view that metaphysics is concerned with **being** *qua* **being** and with various connected **transcendental** conceptions, rather than with the **essence** of material things, as **Aquinas** maintained. The purpose of metaphysics is to demonstrate **God** as **infinite** and as the First Being. In demonstrating the existence of God, Duns Scotus developed several arguments of Thomas Aquinas. God created the world *ex nihilo*, and all created things are finite and contingent. Other than the common nature shared by particular things, there is also an individual form (*haecceitas*) that is peculiar to each **particular**. This doctrine differs from the doctrine of Aristotle and Aquinas, who believed that in a composite of **matter** and **form**, matter is the principle of **individuation** and that among distinct entities, which can not be separated from one other, there is a formal distinction. Scotism opposed the **Augustinian** theory of **divine illumination** and claimed that being is the primary object of intellect. It also appealed to intellectual intuition in explaining our **experience** of **God**. In ethics, Duns Scotus attempted to reconcile the divine **will** with the **rationality** of **moral law** and claimed that human **freedom** lies in our ability to move from **desire** to **justice**. Scotism presented the most sophisticated metaphysics in later medieval philosophy and has been admired by **Peirce** and **Heidegger**.

> "If one looks on Scotism in its position as a stage in the development of medieval thought, it would be idle to deny that de facto it helped to stimulate the critical movement of the fourteenth century." **Copleston, *A History of Philosophy*, vol. II**

Scottish philosophy

EPISTEMOLOGY, METAPHYSICS, ETHICS, POLITICAL PHILOSOPHY, PHILOSOPHY OF SOCIAL SCIENCE Education in Scotland has long placed great emphasis on the importance of philosophy. The earliest important Scottish philosophers were **Duns Scotus** and John Mair. The golden age of Scottish philosophy was the eighteenth century, which contained major figures such as Francis **Hutcheson**, David **Hume**, Adam **Smith**, Thomas **Reid**, Adam **Ferguson**, and Dugald Stewart. These philosophers of the Scottish **Enlightenment** were commonly opposed to the orthodox Calvinism that dominated Scottish church and society at that time. Their work helped to shape the European Enlightenment as a whole. Hutcheson's account of moral **sentiments**, Hume's **skepticism**, and Reid's philosophy of **common sense** have all influenced the later development of philosophy. Smith's philosophical work is valued as well as his foundation of modern economics in *Wealth of Nations*. Scottish philosophy has generally been empirical, anti-rationalistic, and closely connected with psychology, as it reflected the fact that in Scottish universities the study of philosophy traditionally included logic (or general philosophy), moral philosophy, psychology, and natural philosophy (or physics).

> "The philosophy of common sense became 'the Scottish philosophy' and schooled several generations of Scotsmen." **Grave, *The Scottish Philosophy of Common Sense***

sea-battle

LOGIC, METAPHYSICS **Aristotle**'s example to illustrate the problem of **future contingents** in *De Interpretatione* ix. Either there will be or there will not be a sea-battle tomorrow; so the statement "There will be a sea-battle" is either true (and its negation false), or false (and its negation true). However, if the sea-battle has not yet happened, how can we claim that a statement about it is true or false? If it is already true or already false, what will happen happens of **necessity**. Aristotle concluded that statements in the future tense, though **potentially** either true or false, are actually neither. There has been much discussion about whether Aristotle's argument is sound and whether he pointed to a need to modify logic. **Lukasiewicz** developed Aristotle's thoughts on the sea-battle as the basis for **three-valued logic**.

> "For example, it would be necessary that a sea-battle should neither take place nor fail to take place tomorrow." **Aristotle, *De Interpretatione***

Searle, John (1932–)

American philosopher of mind and language, born in Denver, Colorado, Professor of Philosophy, University of California, Berkeley. Searle has developed J. L. Austin's theory of speech acts to provide an integrated theory of language and mind. His non-reductivist naturalism regarding the mind resists accounting for the mind in computational terms. In his influential Chinese room argument, he distinguishes between the syntactic capacities of computer programs and the syntactic and semantic capacities of human language users. His early discussion of deriving "ought" from "is" remains influential. His major works include *Speech Acts* (1969), *Intentionality* (1983), *The Rediscovery of the Mind* (1992), and *The Construction of Social Reality* (1995).

secession

POLITICAL PHILOSOPHY The dismemberment of a **state** into two or more new sovereign states, typically in response to problems of national, religious, ethnic, or cultural conflict within the state. There are several different reasons for secessionist movements. For example, some attempt to restore a nation that was forcibly and unjustifiably annexed by a larger state, as in the case of some of the republics in the former Soviet Union. Some attempt to escape the consequences of **discrimination** and genocide, as in the formation of Israel. Although there are significant objections, many commentators argue that secession can be justified in these two cases. There have been attempts to justify other secessionist movements by distinct ethnic groups asserting a **right** to **self-determination** to protect their language, traditions, religion, culture, or nationality, or to avoid losing their majority in their own area through imposed population redistribution. It is unclear whether these reasons are morally conclusive in favor of secession. Self-determination is possible without full political independence and can not justify secessionist claims to territory or sovereignty. Secession on this basis would undermine the existence of any state containing groups distinguished in terms of ethnicity, language, religion, culture, or nationality and would lead to political fragmentation. As an alternative to secession, some political philosophers are exploring the possibilities of satisfying the legitimate demands of different groups within an altered conception of a sovereign state.

"The problem of secession arises only in cases where an established state houses two or more groups with distinct and irreconcilable national identities." **Miller,** *On Nationality*

secondary matter, see primary matter

secondary qualities, see primary and secondary qualities

secondary rules, see rule of recognition

second-level concept, see first-level concept

second-level predicate, see first-level concept

Secondness, see Firstness

second-order logic, see first-order language

second-order predicate, see predicate

seeing in

AESTHETICS, EPISTEMOLOGY A term introduced by the British philosopher Richard **Wollheim** with regard to the nature of **representation** in art. There have been various attempts to understand the relation of representation. Different philosophers have claimed respectively that representation is an **illusion**; that it is the arousal of **sensation**; that it is a character of a **symbol** system satisfying certain formal requirements; that it is **resemblance**; or that it delivers the information found in what is represented. Wollheim finds that none of these accounts is satisfactory and instead argues that pictorial representation, at least, is best understood in terms of seeing in, according to which a representation of x is a configuration in which x could be seen. As one and the same simultaneous perceptual experience, seeing in contains two aspects in virtue of our psychological capacity both to attend to the marks on painted surface present to the eyes and to see in the figurative effects of those marks.

"I shall simply offer, in a necessarily crude version, what seems to me the best available theory of representation . . . The theory is stated in terms of 'seeing-in'. For at least central cases of representation, a necessary condition of R representing x is that R is a configuration in which something or other can be seen and furthermore one in which x can be seen." **Wollheim,** *The Mind and its Depths*

self

METAPHYSICS, ETHICS, PHILOSOPHY OF MIND The subject or bearer of mental attributes such as **experience**, **consciousness, thoughts, beliefs, emotions, intentions**, and **sensations**. The self is the human **agent** who **deliberates** and initiates **actions**, and who bears **responsibility** for its action. It is the referent of the first-person pronoun. The self is sometimes considered to be the equivalent of the person, although a **person** is associated with the body and with public or social **roles**, while the self is more related to the inner part or aspect of a person. Sometimes, the self is identified as the pure I, **ego**, **unity of consciousness**, **metaphysical** subject, **soul**, or **mind**. The self is a unity that integrates all experiences, beliefs, and feelings of an **individual** and enables an individual to have **identity** as the same person at different times.

The self is often taken to be the subject of **self-consciousness**, which includes itself or its states among the **objects**. The nature of the self has been a contentious issue in the history of philosophy, starting with the Greek injunction to know oneself. Many philosophers consider the self as an inner entity, but **Hume** objected to this, claiming that the self is nothing but a **bundle of perceptions**. **Kant** agreed that the self is not an object of experience, but offered a complex doctrine, with the self as unity of **apperception** grounding the possibility of experience and the **noumenal** self grounding **freedom** and **morality**.

> "It must be some one impression, that gives rise to every real idea. But self or person is not any one impression, but that to which our several impressions and ideas are supposed to have a reference. If any impression gives rise to the idea of self, that impression must continue invariably the same, throughout the whole course of our lives; since self is supposed to exist after that manner. But there is no impression constant and invariable." **Hume, *A Treatise on Human Nature***

self-alienation, see alienation

self-awareness, another expression for self-consciousness

self-consciousness

EPISTEMOLOGY, PHILOSOPHY OF MIND Also called self-awareness, including the distinctive properties of the self: first, the subject's awareness of itself as a subject, expressed by the pronoun "I"; secondly, the awareness that one has **consciousness**, through experiencing the contents of one's consciousness, such as **sensations, thoughts**, or **feelings**; and thirdly, the **reflexivity** of consciousness, which allows consciousness to be an object of **knowledge**. Different senses of self-consciousness raise various philosophical problems concerning the certainty and logical structure of our awareness of ourselves as an "I," **introspection**, and the nature and character of self-knowledge.

> "The expression 'self-consciousness' can be respectably explained as 'consciousness that such-and-such holds of oneself'." **Anscombe, in Guttenplan (ed.), *Mind and Language***

self-contradiction

LOGIC A **proposition** that has the form P and not P or implies a proposition that form. A proposition is self-contradictory if it contains or implies its own **negation** and effectively **asserts** and denies the same **thought**. Such a proposition can not be true and must be false, because it involves self-refutation. Some self-refutation can be **pragmatic**, with the use of the proposition conflicting with its **semantic content**. **Descartes** claimed that the proposition "I am not a thinking being" is self-contradictory because saying "I am not a thinking being" shows that one is a thinking being. In this case, the content of the utterance does not imply its negation, but asserting the content ensures that the content is false. Self-contradiction is a crucial objection to any mathematical or logical **principle** or **axiom**, and an axiomatic system that lacks self-contradiction meets the test of **consistency**. **Paradoxes** arise where apparently legitimate lines of reasoning end in self-contradiction. Philosophers are sometimes puzzled how one and the same proposition can contradict itself. The discussion of self-contradiction is related to the problem of **self-deception**, in which a person **believes** what he **knows** or believes to be false.

> "The philosophical critic does not always restrict himself to pointing out inconsistencies or to showing that a certain theory leads to contradictions; he frequently alleges that certain propositions – propositions, often enough, which have been put

forward by his fellow philosophers – are self-contradictory in themselves." **Passmore, *Philosophical Reasoning***

self-control

ETHICS [from Greek *enkratia*, controlling or mastering oneself over irrational desires, as opposed to *akrasia*, incontinence or weakness of will, the lack of control] An ability enabling oneself to pursue what one **believes** to be **right** whilst resisting temptations to do something else. It is strength of **will**. In **Plato**'s tripartite division of **soul**, self-control means the mastery of **reason** over **emotion** and appetite. A self-controlled person can pursue greater and longer-term goals without being corrupted by immediate gratification, and can adhere to the **principles** he endorses in the face of temptation to deviate from them. Such a person, according to Plato, is a free man rather than a slave of his **desires**. Self-control is the capacity to overcome the influences of desires and differs from **temperance**, which involves not having excessive desires.

"This is so when we describe it as calling for a kind of self-mastery, which consists in reason ruling over desires, a self-control which contrasts to being dominated by one's appetites and passions." **Taylor, *Sources of the Self***

self-deception

PHILOSOPHY OF MIND, EPISTEMOLOGY, ETHICS Deliberate blindness to what is true or believing what one knows or believes to be false on the basis of a certain motivation. **Sartre**'s account of self-deception as **bad faith** (French *mauvaise foi*) is closely focused on his **existentialist** claim that we seek to evade our **freedom** by attempting to take on the character of a thing. He analyzes self-deception in terms of **lying to oneself** on the model of deceiving others, but this gives rise to the so-called **paradox** of self-deception. In deceiving another, the deceiver knows the truth and conceals it from the one to be deceived. But how can deception occur if the deceiver and the one to be deceived are the same? A person deceiving himself must already know the truth. Hence a self-deceiver knows that he is deceiving and this seems to rule him out as a victim of his deception. A successful self-deceiver would believe both p and not-p, but this seems to be impossible.

Various proposals concerning the structure of the mind, the scope of the **will**, the nature of **knowledge** and **belief** and their logic have been made to avoid the paradox, but each proposed solution is open to dispute. The analysis of self-deception is closely connected with attempts to understand the problem of incontinence (Greek *akrasia*, lack of self-control) or **weakness of will**. The incontinent person does what he knows or believes to be wrong or fails to do what he knows or believes to be the best.

"The paradox of self-deception was formulated in the following way: 'how can the self-deceiver believe that something is not so and yet persuade himself that it is so'." **Pears, *Motivated Irrationality***

self-determination

ETHICS, PHILOSOPHY OF ACTION, POLITICAL PHILOSOPHY A moral characteristic by which a moral **agent** is the source or **cause** of his own **actions**. A self-determining agent can exercise rational **will** without being determined by anything else. Self-determination is viewed as synonymous with **autonomy** and opposed to the **fatalism** of **determinism**. In modern ethics, especially in **Kant**, **Nietzsche**, **Sartre**, and **Hare**, self-determining agency is the **principle** that is basic to our respect for **persons**. Self-determination has been viewed as a basic moral right of persons and as the basis for human **freedom**.

In political theory, a right to self-determination allows a people to form and live under autonomous political institutions without undue outside interference.

"The balance or see-saw between self-determination and external determination is the form in which moral experience presents itself." **Hampshire, *Morality and Conflict***

self-evident

LOGIC, PHILOSOPHY OF MATHEMATICS, EPISTEMOLOGY That which is intuitively true, generally referring to the **principles** of logic and **axioms** of mathematics, whose truth can not be **doubted** and which do not require a proof. A proposition is self-evident if its truth can be derived from the **meaning** of the terms it includes, so that anyone who knows the meaning of the words knows that the proposition is true. Such a proposition must be **analytic**. Being self-evident is generally used as a synonym for *a priori*.

But the discovery of logical **paradoxes** shows that faith in self-evidence of logical and mathematical axioms is not secure. Self-evidence is not the same as being obvious, for a thing might be obvious, but not true. On the other hand, a truth can be self-evident without being immediately obvious. Reasoning might still be required in order to grasp it.

> "In calling anything self-evident we mean not that it is evident without need for understanding, but that we need consider nothing but the terms of the judgement, to see its necessity." **Joseph, *An Introduction to Logic***

self-fulfillment

ETHICS Also called self-realization, fulfillment or actualization of one's best capacities or potentialities. The **capacity** or **potentiality** must be defined to be **good** for a person as a rational being, and the fulfillment concerned must be linked with achievement. Self-fulfillment has been taken by many ethical systems to be the highest good, although these systems might differ over what is the best potentiality to realize. For **Aristotle**, the potentiality to realize is the human faculty of **rationality**, and in some texts he saw contemplation of eternal **truth** as the greatest happiness. Generally, the fulfillment or actualization of one's best capacity is held to lead to a successful life and the achievement of a true or real self.

> "The goal of self-management is often called self-fulfilment or self-actualisation." **Skinner, *About Behaviourism***

self-identity, see personal identity

self-interest

ETHICS, PHILOSOPHY OF ACTION Interest in one's own **well-being** or in the advantages that one can gain for oneself. According to psychological egoism, everyone's **actions** are consciously or unconsciously **motivated** by the pursuit of self-interest. Even seemingly altruistic actions are held to be egoistic at their roots. Ethical egoism allows that actions can be motivated by factors other than self-interest, but advocates the pursuit of self-interest as morally leading to the best outcome. Because morality often seems to require sacrifice of one's own interests, moralists advocating the pursuit of self-interest

try to harmonize moral considerations with self-interest. According to Adam **Smith**, the individual pursuit of self-interest promotes the common **good** through the mechanism of the invisible hand, which balances and reconciles interests in a more effective way than the commands of the **state**. Although extreme ethical egoism is widely rejected, many moral philosophers propose that we should pursue enlightened or rational self-interest, according to which **morality**, **altruism**, and **benevolence** are compatible with one's deeper self-interest over a longer term. They claim that people will satisfy their own interests through seeking the best interest of others.

> "Since the time of Glaucon's challenge to Socrates, moral philosophers have attempted to show it is in our rational self-interest to act morally." **Nozick, *Philosophical Explanations***

self-intimation

EPISTEMOLOGY The **truth** of a self-intimating **statement** entails that it is known by someone. If there are any true self-intimating statements, they could exist either without further **implications** or as the foundation of a more extensive system of **knowledge**. Some philosophers hold that statements about some of my own **mental states**, such as my **pain**, are self-intimating because their truth entails that I know them to be true. Self-intimation is therefore offered as one major ground for our alleged first-person authority.

> "Philosophers have not distinguished carefully between incorrigibility and another supposed property of statements of a closely similar and related kind: self-intimation. By this I mean a statement's truth entailing its being known." **Quinton, *The Nature of Things***

self-love

ETHICS The desire to maximize one's own **well-being**. **Aristotle** distinguished two types of self-love. The noble type seeks to satisfy the **rational** part of one's **soul** by pursuing **virtue**. The base type seeks to satisfy the **appetitive** part of one's soul. The British philosopher Joseph **Butler** also drew a distinction between two kinds of self-love. Cool self-love, which is long-term, deep-seated, and compatible with **benevolent actions** is contrasted with self-love as sensual selfishness. **Rousseau** distinguished between *amour de soi* and *amour-propre*, but both can be translated as self-love. *Amour de soi* is the desire of a **person** in the **state of nature** to preserve himself, while *amour-propre* presupposes a comparison between oneself and others in **civil society**. It aims to achieve superiority over others and is the source of our **desires** and motivations.

> "Conscience and self-love, if we understand our true happiness, always lead us the same way."
> **Butler,** *Fifteen Sermons*

self-ownership

ETHICS, POLITICAL PHILOSOPHY The central **libertarian** principle that each **person** is the rightful owner of his own person and **powers**. Each person is therefore free to use these powers as he wishes, as long as he does not direct them to harm others. Other **individuals** and groups can not restrict one's **freedom** without one's **consent**, and one may not use one's powers to force anyone else to supply products or services. Self-ownership is moral **sovereignty**, similar to human **autonomy**. This idea is proposed by **Nozick** in his influential book, *Anarchy, State and Utopia.* It prohibits treating a person as a mere **means** rather than as a being of ultimate **value**, and also prohibits reducing a person, in any particular circumstance, to the condition of a **slave**. A consequence of this view is that the action of the **state** to redistribute wealth in favor of badly off people violates the **rights** of individuals over themselves and represents a form of partial enslavement. These views are controversial, and other philosophers seek to reject the notion of self-ownership or to show that it is compatible with policies excluded by Nozick's argument.

> "The libertarian principle of self-ownership says that each person enjoys, over herself and her powers, full and exclusive rights of control and use, and therefore owes no service or product to anyone else that she has not contracted to supply."
> **G. Cohen,** *Self-Ownership, Freedom and Equality*

self-predication, see Third Man argument

self-presenting

PHILOSOPHY OF MIND A term introduced by **Meinong** for the capacity of **mental states** to present themselves directly to **thought**. **Chisholm** used this notion as a source of **certainty**. For him, a self-presenting state is self-justifying. A **proposition** is self-presenting if it constitutes its own **justification**. Belief that one has certain first-person **intentional** mental states, such as **believing**, **thinking**, and **feeling**, is justified by the fact that to be in these states is to be aware of being in them. Hence these mental states are self-presenting. When a proposition such as "I am thinking" is true for a person S at time t, S is justified in believing it at t. This proposition is self-presenting because it is evident to S even though the only things that make the proposition evident to S are things that entail it. But it is a matter of controversy whether self-presenting or **evidence** is either **necessary** or **sufficient** for justification.

> "H is self-presenting for S at t = def h is true at t; and necessarily, if h is true at t, then h is evident for S at t." **Chisholm,** *Theory of Knowledge*

self-realization, another expression for self-fulfillment

self-reference

LOGIC The character of a **sentence** that is about itself, in crucial cases leading to **paradox**. For example, a person says, "I am lying." If what he says is true, then he is lying and it is false. If what he says is false, then he is not lying and it is true. **Russell** devised the theory of **types** in order to rule out this kind of paradox. According to Russell's theory, we can avoid such paradoxes if we distinguish between first-order sentences that are about **objects** and second-order sentences that are about first-order sentences. There have been other attempts to deal with this and other paradoxes of self-reference.

> "It is true that self-reference is a general feature of logically paradoxical utterances and if it is ruled out as senseless they cannot be formulated."
> **Quinton,** *The Nature of Things*

self-regarding

ETHICS J. S. Mill drew a distinction between self-regarding **actions**, which involve only one's own interests, and other-regarding actions, which affect the interests of other people or of the **community**. Self-regarding actions are private and should be immune to interference by society. Other-regarding actions, on the other hand, are the stuff of **morality** and of social regulation. There is also a distinction between self-regarding **virtues**, such as prudence, fortitude, elegance, and other-regarding virtues, such as generosity and consideration. Contemporary **virtue ethics** has criticized modern ethical theories for limiting their concern to other-regarding actions or virtues while ignoring self-regarding actions and virtues. The distinction between self-regarding and other-regarding actions or virtues is not always clear-cut, and some actions or virtues can be both self-regarding and other-regarding from different perspectives.

"I am the last person to undervalue the self-regarding virtues; they are only second in importance, if even second, to the social." **Mill, *On Liberty*, in Robson (ed.), *Collected Works*, vol. XVIII**

Sellars, Wilfrid (1912–89)

American philosopher, born in Ann Arbor, Michigan, taught at Minnesota, Yale, and Pittsburgh. Sellars's papers, "Empiricism and the Philosophy of Mind" (1956) and "Philosophy and the Scientific Image of Man" (1960), are classics of contemporary philosophy. He rejected the fundamental empiricist claim that there is a sort of knowledge that is directly available to our consciousness as "the myth of the given." He sought to give due weight philosophically to both the "manifest image" and the "scientific image" of ourselves and the world and brought Kantian, naturalist, and nominalist insights to bear on metaphysics, epistemology, philosophy of science, philosophy of language, and philosophy of mind. His books include *Science, Perception and Reality* (1963), *Philosophical Perspectives* (1967), *Science and Metaphysics: Variations on Kantian Themes* (1968), *Essays in Philosophy and Its History* (1974), and *Naturalism and Ontology* (1980). His father Roy Wood Sellars (1880–1973) was a leading American realist philosopher.

semantic ambiguity

PHILOSOPHY OF LANGUAGE If different **senses** or **references** are associated with a single word, it can be unclear in a given context which is meant. If **ambiguity** of this sort arises from the multiplicity of senses of a word, it is called lexical or semantic ambiguity. For example, the statement "I will wait

for you at the bank in an hour," is ambiguous because the word "bank" can be understood either as a financial institution or as a place at the riverside.

"A constituent C is semantically ambiguous just in case the set of readings assigned to C contains two or more members." **Katz, *Semantic Theory***

semantic anti-realism, see anti-realism

semantic ascent

PHILOSOPHY OF LANGUAGE A term introduced by **Quine** for the shift in which the language we use to **refer** to the world becomes something we talk about in its own right. It is a shift from questions about **objects** to questions about words. For example, we can move from the proposition "Shanghai is a city" to the proposition " 'Shanghai' is a name ascribed to a city," or from the proposition "Socrates is wise" to the proposition " 'Socrates is wise' is true." This is a change from what **Carnap** called the **material mode** of speech to the **formal mode**. The shift is an ascent because at the new level expressions deal with the **semantic properties** of words or **sentences** in a language and thus it becomes a higher **metalanguage**. This strategy tends to reduce questions of philosophy to questions about language.

"The strategy of semantic ascent is that it carries the discussion into a domain where both parties are better agreed on the objects (viz. words) and on the main terms concerning them." **Quine, *Word and Object***

semantic holism

PHILOSOPHY OF LANGUAGE, METAPHYSICS, EPISTEMOLOGY Also called meaning holism, the view that **meaning** is holistic rather than **atomistic**. The unit of meaning is not the word or the **sentence**, but rather the **theory** or language of which the word or sentence is a component. The meaning of an **expression** lies in its **relations** with other expressions of the language in which it is embedded. It is **nonsense** to speak of a linguistic component abstracted from the linguistic whole to which it belongs. Semantic holism might be divided into content holism, in which the meaning or **content** of a sentence is determined by the meanings of all the other sentences in the language, and translation holism, which claims that a translation of a sentence can preserve its meaning only if its associative or inferential relations with other sentences in the home language are preserved in the targeted language. The position is derived from **epistemic** holism, which claims that whole theories are units of **confirmation**. The leading advocates of semantic holism include **Quine**, **Davidson**, and **Putnam**. The view is highly controversial, in part because we use sentences not theories to say things. Semantic holism does not say much about the meaning of any particular sentence.

> "Semantic holism is a doctrine about the metaphysically necessary conditions for something to have meaning or content." **Fodor and Lepore,** *Holism*

semantic meaning, another term for descriptive meaning

semantic paradox

LOGIC, PHILOSOPHY OF LANGUAGE Semantic paradoxes are represented by the **liar paradox**, **Berry's paradox**, Richard's paradox, and **Grelling's paradox**. These paradoxes can not be explained in logical terms alone. They contain some empirical reference to **thought**, language, or **symbolism** and arise as a result of some peculiarity of **semantic** concepts such as **truth**, falsity, and definability. Their occurrence shows that there must be flaws in our thought and language. Hence, semantic paradoxes are distinguished from **logical paradoxes**, which indicate that there must be something wrong with our logic and mathematics. **Ramsey** introduced the distinction between semantic and logical paradoxes, although he himself calls semantic paradoxes "epistemic paradoxes." The general approach to avoiding semantic paradoxes requires the distinction between **object language** and **metalanguage** rather than appealing to **Russell**'s ramified theory of **types**.

> "It is our choice whether to keep our old familiar semantic concepts, and continue to live with the semantic paradoxes; or whether to search for a brave new world of stability, from which the savagery of contradiction is banished." **Read,** *Thinking about Logic*

semantic theory of truth

LOGIC, PHILOSOPHY OF LANGUAGE A theory developed by **Tarski** and originally intended to solve **semantic paradoxes**, especially the **liar paradox**. It suggests that a **definition** of **truth** cannot be adequately provided in the **object language**, that is, in the language that describes the world and does not contain the truth-predicate. It has to be formulated in a **metalanguage**, that is, the language that talks about the object language. According to this theory, "'P' is true if and only if P," where 'P' is the **name** of the **sentence** and P is the sentence itself. For example, "Snow is white" is true if and only if snow is white. A sentence is true in a given language if its elements are so combined as to state what is the case. The theory has two parts: **adequacy conditions** on definitions of truth and a definition of truth in terms of **satisfaction**. Tarski thought that this theory is suitable only for certain **artificial** and **formal languages** but not for **natural languages**. Donald **Davidson** has developed a **truth-conditional** approach to **meaning** on the basis of this theory by relating sentences in a particular language with their truth conditions. This theory has become very influential in contemporary philosophy.

> "Tarski's so-called semantic theory of truth is essentially the view that 'S is true' assigns a property – truth – to the sentence named by 'S'." **Danto,** *Analytical Philosophy of Knowledge*

semantically closed language

PHILOSOPHY OF LANGUAGE A language containing not only its expected stock of **expressions**, but also the **names** of these expressions and **semantic** terms like "true" that refer to the sentences of the language. According to **Tarski**, the source of the **semantic paradoxes** lies in the **self-reference** of the sentences expressing the paradoxes. He held that the possibility of such self-reference belongs to semantically closed languages. Such a language has a tacit assumption that all sentences that determine the use of "true" can be **asserted** in the language itself. To avoid this fault, Tarski distinguished between an **object language** and a **metalanguage**.

> "We have implicitly assumed that the language in which antinomy is constructed contains, in addition to its expressions, also the names of these expressions, as well as semantic terms such as the term 'true' referring to sentences of this language. A language with these properties will be called 'semantically closed'." **Tarski,** *Logic, Semantics, and Metamathematics*

semantics

PHILOSOPHY OF LANGUAGE [from Greek *sema*, sign] A term that pertains to the **meaning** of a **sign** or set of **symbols**. Semantics is a discipline dealing with the meaning of linguistics signs or symbols, that is, the words, **expressions**, and **sentences** of a language. It belongs to **semiotics**, the study of signs, and contrasts with the other two branches of semiotics, that is, **syntax** or syntactics (the study of logical or grammatical form) and **pragmatics** (the study of the contribution of contextual factors to the meaning of what is said). In semantics, the language whose meaning is discussed is called the **object language**, while the language that is used to talk about the object language is the **metalanguage**. For example, in the sentence, "'Snow is white' is true," "Snow is white" is in the object language, while the whole sentence is in the metalanguage.

Formal semantics discusses the meaning of linguistic signs by appeal to formal and logic method. Its main representative is truth-conditional **semantics**, developed by **Tarski** and **Davidson** on the basis of **Frege**'s logic, which ascribes semantic values to the basic symbols of the language, takes them as elements of structure, and then derives the semantic values of complex expressions from these elements in accordance with formation rules. In truth-conditional semantics, the meaning of every sentence is determined by the truth-conditions of its component sentences.

Semantics is closely related to the philosophy of language, for both employ the same central notions such as **reference**, **predication**, **meaning**, **synonymy**, and **truth**. These key notions and their relations form the subject-matter of meta-semantics, which can be treated as a part of the philosophy of language.

"Semantics is concerned with linguistic expressions in two respects: reference and meaning." **Quine,** *From Stimulus to Science*

seminal reason, English translation of *rationes seminales*

semiology, an alternative name for semiotics

semiotics

PHILOSOPHY OF ACTION [from Greek *seme*, sign] The general study of **signs**, also called theory of signs or, by the Swiss linguist **Saussure**, semiology. Charles **Morris** takes semiotics as a study of linguistic signs, that is, words, **expressions**, and **sentences**. In his *Foundations of the Theory of Signs*, he distinguishes three sub-disciplines: **syntax**, which deals with relations between linguistic signs or sentential structures; **semantics**, which deals with relations between linguistic signs and the **objects** they are talking about; and **pragmatics**, which deals with relations between linguistic signs and the ways they are used. More broadly, semiology can be viewed as a general inquiry into every sign, both verbal and non-verbal, both human and natural. The extension of "sign" is not confined to linguistic symbols. **Peirce** defined "sign" as "something that stands for something in some respect or capacity." This broad sense is preferred by French **structuralists**.

"The entire theory of an object language is called the semiotic of that language; this semiotic is formulated in the mental language." **Carnap,** *Introduction to Symbolic Logic and Its Applications*

Sen, Amartya (1933–)

Indian economist and theorist of social choice, Professor at Harvard University and Master of Trinity College, Cambridge. Sen's theory of social choice has been influential in economics, ethics, and political philosophy. He rejects an account of welfare in terms of the satisfaction of individual preferences and employs his capability theory of well-being in the theory of economic and social development. His consequentialism in ethics and political philosophy is combined with a conception of rights and an empirically supported account of the good. His theories of poverty and famine have won widespread acclaim. His major works include *Choice, Welfare and Measurement* (1982).

Seneca, Lucius Annaeus (*c.*2 BC–65 AD)

Roman Stoic moral philosopher, orator, and tragic playwright, also called Seneca the Young, born in Cordoba, Spain. Seneca was the tutor and advisor of the Emperor Nero, who forced him to commit suicide. His major philosophical works are *Letters to Lucilius* and *Physical Problems*. Because Seneca considered true philosophy to be a means to improve the soul, his main works were focused on conduct and moral exhortation. According to his account of the will, everyone has the power to take the path of virtue if he wills to do so. He also applied Stoic individualism to questions of government.

sensa

EPISTEMOLOGY A term (singular, *sensum*) introduced by **Broad** to refer to things that are directly perceived, such as color patches, sounds, shapes, smells, and tactile feelings As **objects** of **perception**, they are contrasted to material or **physical objects**. Sensa are usually taken to be **private** and known directly with a special **certainty**. Material objects are public and known indirectly with less certainty. The existence of sensa is mind-dependent. For Broad, they can not exist independent of acts of sensing. They are objective constituents of **sensations** and are a part of a sensible field. Many names have been given to what Broad calls sensa, the commonest being sensations and **sense-data**. Others terms include **ideas** of sense (**Locke**), sensible qualities (**Berkeley**), **impressions** (**Hume**) and **sense-contents** (**Ayer**).

"Whenever I truly judge that X appears to me to have the sensible quality Q, what happens is that I am directly aware of a certain object Y, which (a) really does have the quality Q, and (b) stands in some particularly intimate relation, yet to be determined, to X. Such objects as Y I am going to call sensa." **Broad, *Scientific Thought***

sensation

EPISTEMOLOGY [From Latin *sensatus*, gifted with sense] The **mental state** aroused in a subject in perceiving, a primitive level of mental existence. When we see something, visual sensations are produced in us; when we hear something, auditory sensations are produced. There are also sensations of taste, smell, and touch. Sensations arise not only through senses, but also through the body, such as the bodily sensations of cold, pain, and hunger. Sensations are generally distinguished from **experiences** and **perceptions**, but are part of these more complex states, which involve such additional capacities as **judgment** and **inference** and are subject to error. Sensations must be owned by some subject. However, it is generally believed that sensations are independent of the conceptual capacities of the subject and hence can also be possessed by animals and young children. A major question is whether sensa-tions are purely **private** or can be known by others. This is related to the problem of **private language** and the problem of alleged **first-person** authority concerning accounts of what we experience. Another major problem concerns the relation between sensations and **sense-data**. Some philosophers identify them, leading to the question of whether what we perceive directly are sensations or external **objects**. Others distinguish them by claiming that while sensations are the **subjective** aspect of perception as the experience itself, sense-data are the objects of experience or perception.

"Our senses, conversant about particular sensible objects, do convey into the mind several distinct perceptions of things, according to those various ways wherein those objects do affect them; . . . This great source of most of the *Ideas* we have, depending wholly upon our senses, and derived by them to the understanding, I call sensation." **Locke, *An Essay Concerning Human Understanding***

sensationalism

EPISTEMOLOGY, PHILOSOPHY OF MIND A view which claims that **sensations** are the only sources of **knowledge**; that all **ideas** can be traced to an origin in sensation; that all **statements** can be reduced to statements concerning the relations between sensations and that nothing can be said beyond sensations; and that sensations are also the ultimate criteria of verification of all knowledge. In all, sensationalism can be summarized into one sentence: "the world is my sensations." This view may be traced to the ancient Greek philosopher **Protagoras**, and is classically derived from the British **empiricist** tradition from the seventeenth to the nineteenth centuries. In the twentieth century, its major representative is Ernst **Mach**. Sensationalism is opposed to **rationalism** and the theory of **innate ideas**. A sensationalist theory of mind claims that all **mental events** can be analyzed in terms of having of sensa-tions Sensationalism also draws a distinction between **perception** and sensation, according to which perception, unlike sensation, involves **judgment** and is open to error. However, its notion of sensation is very ambiguous, including not only sensible qualities, bodily affections, but also **desires**, **emotions**, and **feelings** such as anger and jealousy. There are problems in considering these various items as belonging to the same kind, and it is difficult to see how our full range of empirical knowledge can be derived from the austere basis of sensation.

"Sensationalism is the theory that all ideas or concepts are derived from sense-perception." **Pap, *Elements of Analytic Philosophy***

sense and reference

LOGIC, PHILOSOPHY OF LANGUAGE For **Frege**, every complete **sign** expresses a **sense** (German *Sinn*) and designates something we call its **reference** (German *Bedeutung*). Frege introduced this distinction by consideration of the **statement** "The morning star is identical with the evening star." While the two phrases "the morning star" and "the evening star" designate the same **object**, the planet Venus, they have different senses. Hence, the sentence "the morning star is the morning star" provides nothing new, while the sentence "the morning star is the evening star" is informative.

This distinction is closely related to the distinction between **connotation** and **denotation** and between **intension** and **extension**. It shows that the **meaning** or sense of an expression and its reference do not always vary together, a point having considerably influenced the subsequent development of **analytic philosophy**. For Frege, a basic **sentence** consists of a **referring expression** as subject and a **predicate** as **function** or **concept**. Frege called the sense or meaning of a sentence, which is composed of the senses of the components of the sentence, a **thought** and said that the reference of a sentence is its **truth-value**.

Russell rejected Frege's two basic notions of sense and reference and proposed to deal with meaning using a single basic notion of standing for.

"A proper name (word, sign, sign combination, expression) expresses its sense, stands for or designates its reference. By means of a sign we express its sense and designate its reference." **Frege, "On Sense and Reference,"** *Philosophical Writings*

sense-contents

EPISTEMOLOGY **Ayer**'s term, which he introduces to replace the notion of **idea** used by **Locke** and **Berkeley**. For Locke, ideas are related to a single unobservable underlying **substratum**, and Berkeley insists that they are necessarily mental. Arguing that

both Locke and Berkeley were mistaken, Ayer considers that sense-contents are neutral, that is, neither physical nor mental, and are the **sense-data** provided by both outer and **introspective sensations**. According to Ayer's **phenomenalism**, **material things** are constituted out of actual and possible occurrences of sense-contents and can be defined in terms of them. He also suggests that it is misleading to say that sense-contents **exist**, because this carries the danger of treating them as if they were material things. Instead, we should say that they occur.

"We define sense-contents not as the object, but as a part of a sense-experience." **Ayer,** *Language, Truth and Logic*

sense-data, another term for sensa

sense field, see visual field

sense/force

PHILOSOPHY OF LANGUAGE An influential distinction in modern philosophical **semantics**. Each **sentence** can be divided into a descriptive **content** and a force-indicator. The **sense** or descriptive content is the **state of affairs** that the sentence describes and its **meaning**. It is the bearer of a **truth-value**. The force is the assertive, interrogative, or imperative or other way in which the content is conveyed. Force has nothing to do with the truth or falsity of a sentence. Sentences with the same sense can occur with different forces, and a force can be attached to any given sense. This distinction is generally believed to be based on Frege's distinction between **assertion** (**judgment**) and **thought** (content). On this basis, **Austin** developed his **speech act** theory, for it is the force that determines what speech act is performed by an utterance of a sentence. It is also the basis for the **emotivist** distinction between **descriptive meaning** and **evaluative meaning**. R. M. **Hare**'s distinction between **phrastics** and **neustics** corresponds to it as well. **Dummett** makes use of this distinction to criticize **Wittgenstein**'s claim that philosophy of language is an investigation of how language is used in particular **language-games**. The same linguistic expression certainly has different forces in different games, but that does not mean that the expression does not have a persistent sense. It is because of that sense that we can learn language.

"Adopting Frege's terminology, we may call this ingredient of meaning the sense of the expression; . . . Force, or, more properly, the indication of force, is the significance possessed by a linguistic element which serves to indicate which type of linguistic act is being performed." **Dummett,** *The Logical Basis of Metaphysics*

sense-impression, another term for sense-datum

sense qualia

EPISTEMOLOGY, METAPHYSICS [from Latin *qualia*, singular *quale*, quality, nature, state] Both the qualities of **sensations** considered in abstraction, such as redness or sweetness, and the qualities sensed in association with specific objects, such as the redness of a red car or the sweetness of a sweet fruit. For many **empiricists**, the **physical object** is an idealization of sense **qualia**, from which the object directly derives its perceptual **properties**. In this latter sense, the concept of sense qualia is similar to that of **sense-data**. Attempts to explain relations between qualia and objects quickly become complex.

"It is of course possible to designate a sense-quale and ask how it is related to the physical object to which it corresponds." **Ayer,** *Philosophy in the Twentieth Century*

senseless

LOGIC, METAPHYSICS, PHILOSOPHY OF LANGUAGE [German *sinnlos*] Senseless **propositions** are **tautologies** and **contradictions**. A tautology is unconditionally true (true whatever way the world is), and a contradiction is unconditionally false (false whatever way the world is). Senseless propositions should be distinguished from **nonsense** (German *Unsinn*). Like nonsensical propositions, senseless propositions say nothing about the world and can be neither confirmed nor rejected by how things are in the world. They do not give pictures of reality. But, unlike nonsensical propositions, they show the logical or structural properties of their components. Since they do not say truly or falsely that the world is such-and-such, as genuine **contingent** propositions do, they are senseless, but are not nonsense because they show the logical structure of language and the world and do not violate any principles of **logical syntax**.

"Tautologies and contradictions are senseless." **Wittgenstein,** *Tractatus*

sensibilia

EPISTEMOLOGY, METAPHYSICS **Russell**'s term for entities which are exactly like **sense-data**, but with which one is not acquainted. Once sensibilia enter into the relation of **acquaintance**, they become sense-data. Russell uses the notion of sensibilia to replace the notion of **matter** or **physical objects**, which he construes as **logical constructions** out of sensibilia, although the existence of sensibilia themselves is a mere metaphysical **hypothesis**.

"I shall give the name sensibilia to those objects which have the same metaphysical and physical status as sense-data, without necessarily being data to any mind." **Russell,** *Mysticism and Logic*

sensibilism, see sensibilia, phenomenalism

sensibility

EPISTEMOLOGY, PHILOSOPHY OF MIND, METAPHYSICS **Kant** took sensibility and **understanding** to be two fundamental and related capacities of the human **mind**. **Objects** are given to us through sensibility but **thought** by understanding. Sensibility is the capacity to have **representations** through being affected by objects, and operates in two ways. As **outer sense**, sensibility produces sensory states of things outside us; as **inner sense**, sensibility produces sensory states of our own representations. For Kant, sensibility is receptive but not passive, for there is a **formal** aspect as well as a **material** aspect. The forms of sensibility are **space** and **time**, which are *a priori* intuitions, not derived from the independent **properties** of objects as they are in themselves. Space and time set the order for **matter**, and hence matter received in sensibility is spatially and temporally organized. Kant intended to reconcile **rationalism** and **empiricism** by emphasizing both the rational character and the receptive character of sensibility. Sensibility must be supplemented by understanding if **experience** is to be possible. Traditional metaphysics is wrong because it used the concepts of understanding without any corresponding evidence of sensibility.

"Sensibility is the faculty of intuition: (a) sense, faculty of intuition in the present; (b) imagination, faculty of intuition in the absence of the object." **Kant,** *Lectures on Logic*

sensory illusion

EPISTEMOLOGY The **perception** of external **objects** that leads to a false **belief** about the world. Different persons perceiving the same object will sometimes see it differently. In some cases this will result from different **perspectives** or conditions of perception but not produce false beliefs. The perceptions are sensory illusions if they produce or tend to produce false beliefs. The existence of sensory illusion is cited as a proof of the existence of **sense-data** that are different from physical objects. Illusions present a challenge for **naive** or **direct realism**, which holds that we perceive nothing but the physical object itself.

"To suffer sensory illusion is to acquire a false belief or inclination to a false belief in particular propositions about the physical world by means of our senses." **D. Armstrong,** *Perception and the Physical World*

sentence

LOGIC, PHILOSOPHY OF LANGUAGE A grouping of words (**symbols**, **signs**) that normally can be used to say something in a **natural** or artificial language. A sentence must be **well-formed** grammatically, but not all sentences are **meaningful**. A sentence may have different **meanings**, and the same sentence may be used in a variety of ways. Thus, a sentence is distinguished in modern logic from a **proposition** or **statement**. A proposition or a statement is what is expressed by a sentence that **asserts** or denies something, for example, a sentence that states that some **predicate** holds of some subject or that certain items are **related** in a certain way. A proposition rather than a sentence is ordinarily recognized as the bearer of **truth-value**. Logical relations exist among propositions or statements, but not among sentences.

"So it will not do to identify the statement either with the sentence or with the meaning of the sentence." **Strawson,** *Introduction to Logical Theory*

sentence token

PHILOSOPHY OF LANGUAGE We can apply the **token/ type** distinction to sentences to distinguish between sentence tokens and sentence types. A sentence type is grammatically complete, while a sentence token is a concrete occurrence, that is, an actual inscription or utterance. "I am thirsty" is a sentence type. However, this sentence can be uttered by particular people on particular occasions. These particular utterances of the same sentence type are sentence tokens. This distinction is philosophically useful because it is believed that only sentence tokens can be either true or false.

"A sentence token is just the physical sentence resulting from someone's speaking or writing at a particular time; a sentence type, in contrast, is the abstract class of all such sentence utterances or inscriptions that, roughly speaking, have the same form." **Moser and Nat,** *Human Knowledge*

sentence type, see sentence token

sentential calculus, another term for propositional logic

sentential function

LOGIC An expression containing one or more **free variables**, such as "X is wise." This is also called an **open sentence**. Once the free variable is replaced by a constant, an actual or **closed sentence** is formed. For instance, if we substitute "Socrates" for X in the above sentential function, we get the closed sentence "Socrates is wise." Obviously, various sentences of the same type can be formed from such a function. A sentential function can be quantified both **existentially** ("There is at least one X such that X is wise") and universally ("For every X, X is wise"). A sentential function is sometimes distinguished from a **propositional function**, which is what a sentential function denotes, but more often these two expressions are treated as synonymous.

"A sentential function, as this technical term is used by logicians, is an expression containing a variable such that a sentence which is either true or false results when a constant is substituted for the variable." **Pap,** *Elements of Analytic Philosophy*

sentience

ETHICS, PHILOSOPHY OF MIND The capacity to **experience pleasure** and **pain**. Since the basic moral **principle** of **utilitarianism** is to maximize pleasure and minimize pain, **Bentham** suggests that the basis for moral consideration should be sentience rather than **reason** or language. In our moral considerations, we should ask whether a living entity has the ability to suffer. Since not only human beings but also animals are sentient, that is, have the ability to suffer, Peter **Singer** argues in his **animal ethics** that we should extend moral consideration to animals. The suffering of animals should be a matter of ethical concern no less than that of our fellow human beings. Pain is an evil. If an animal feels pain, it has its own interests, and its treatment deserves moral consideration. Hence, sentience becomes the passport to the moral community.

> "The humane moralists, for their part, insist upon sentience as the only relevant capacity a being need possess to enjoy full moral standing." **Callicott, In Defence of the Land Ethic**

sentiment

ETHICS, PHILOSOPHY OF MIND The immediate reactive **feeling** and **sense** about other people and their actions. According to **Hutcheson**, **Hume**, and Adam **Smith**, human sentiment is the ground of moral attitudes and moral **actions**. The rules of morality are formed because in a variety of instances one type of conduct constantly pleases in a certain manner, and because in a variety of instances another type of conduct constantly displeases in a certain manner. Sentiment is the basis of moral approval and disapproval. This is the notion that Hutcheson called moral sense, Hume called approbation or sympathy, and Adam Smith called sympathy. In holding this position they opposed the view that morality is a matter of **reason** or that moral action is determined by rational **deliberation**. Since their position grounds ethics on sentiment, it is also called sentimentalism. This is a type of **non-cognitivism**. While for Hutcheson moral sense is a single moral **faculty**, Smith held that there are a plurality of moral feelings. Accordingly Smith referred to this type of moral theory as the theory of sentiments.

> "All morality depends upon our sentiments; and when any action, or quality of the mind, pleases us *after a certain manner*, we say it is virtuous; and when the neglect, or non-performance of it, displeases us *after a like manner*, we say that we lie under an obligation to perform it." **Hume, A Treatise of Human Nature**

sentimentalism, see sentiment

separation

ANCIENT GREEK PHILOSOPHY, METAPHYSICS [Greek *chorismos*; *choristos*, separable] For **Plato**, separation was a mark of division, severance, or disjunction. He held that **Ideas** or **Forms** are separated from the **individuals participating** in them. This separation is a symmetrical relationship: If Ideas are separated from individuals, individuals are separated from Ideas. **Aristotle** claimed that **Socrates** sought the **definition** of the **universal** but did not separate it from the individuals, while Plato did separate the universal from the individuals and as a consequence committed many errors in his Theory of Ideas, especially relating to the **Third Man argument**.

In Aristotle's own doctrine of **substance** in the *Metaphysics*, separation became a **criterion** for primary substance. Here, separation means independent existence and is an asymmetrical relationship. Separation applies to the relation between the **category** of substance and other categories. According to this relation, substance can exist separately from other categories, but other categories can not exist independent of substance. Separation also applies to the **relations** among **form**, **matter**, and the composite of form and matter, in which form satisfies the criterion of separation in the strongest sense and is therefore primary substance.

> "The separation is the cause of the objections that arise with regard to the ideas." **Aristotle, Metaphysics**

serial theory of the mind, see bundle theory of mind

set

LOGIC, PHILOSOPHY OF MATHEMATICS A collection of distinct **entities**, classically determined by means of a **property** or **principle** that sharply distinguishes members from non-members. For many purposes, sets and **classes** are the same, but restrictions were introduced on what is allowed to be a class in order to avoid **logical paradoxes**. Classes with **infinite** members may not be treated as completed totalities. Not all classes are capable of being members of sets. There are ultimate classes that can not be members of a further class. However, set theory ignores these distinctions and covers all types of classes and sets. A fuzzy set does not have sharp boundaries between members and non-members and can allow different degrees of belonging to the set. There is disagreement between an account of classes and sets as real entities and the view that they are devices that lack **ontological** implications.

> "Basically, 'set' is simply a synonym of 'class' that happens to have more currency than 'class' in mathematical contexts." **Quine,** *Set Theory and its Logic*

set-theoretical paradox, another term for logical paradox

set theory

LOGIC, PHILOSOPHY OF MATHEMATICS Classically, a **set** or **class** is a collection of things taken as a whole, with a determining **property** that distinguishes the collection from things in other sets, although this condition is relaxed in the theory of fuzzy sets. A set can be divided into subsets as well as into members. Set theory is the study of relationships within a set and among sets and the nature of sets themselves. Its pioneer is **Cantor**, and other major contributors include Zermelo, **Russell**, Fraenkel, **Gödel**, Skolem, and **von Neumann**. Set theory is essential for mathematics, and many kinds of pure mathematics can be formulated within set theory. It is crucial for logical **deduction**. However, naive set theory often leads to **paradoxes**, such as **Burali-Forti's paradox**, **Cantor's paradox** and, most famously, **Russell's paradox**. Russell sought to avoid these paradoxes by formulating an **axiomatic** set system in which sets are arranged in a hierarchy of **types**. Various axiomatic set systems have been proposed, but each has some difficulties.

> "Set theory is the mathematics of classes. Sets are classes." **Quine,** *Set Theory and its Logic*

seven deadly sins, see sin

sex, see gender

sexism

ETHICS, POLITICAL PHILOSOPHY The attitude holding that one's own sex is superior to the other and leading in practice to limited respect for the **rights**, **needs**, and **values** of the other sex. The term is analogical to **racism**, which regards one's own race as superior to others. Both sexism and racism are thought to be major social evils. In contemporary **environmental ethics**, **speciesism**, the claim that the human species should dominate other species, is controversially held to be a third evil of this sort. Men are more likely than women to be called sexist because historically women have generally been dominated by men. A main aim of **feminism** is to criticize sexism by revealing its roots, showing the forms it takes in various areas, and suggesting ways of correcting its practices and **ideology**. Some feminist theorists claim that overcoming sexism will change both women and men and establish social practices that are free from male-dominated gender relations.

> "The choice can only be whether animals benefit from our practices or are harmed by them. This is why speciesism is falsely modelled on racism and sexism, which really are prejudices. To suppose that there is an ineliminable white or male understanding of the world, and to think that the only choice is whether blacks or women should benefit from 'our' (white, male) practices or be harmed by them: this is already to be prejudiced." **B. Williams,** *Ethics and the Limits of Philosophy*

Sextus Empiricus (c.150–c.225)

Greek skeptic and physician, active in Alexandria and Rome. Sextus Empiricus' books, *Outlines of Pyrrhonism* and *Against the Dogmatists*, are the principal sources for our knowledge of Greek skepticism and the doctrines of many other Greek philosophical schools. In his own philosophy, he claimed that the only thing that we really aim at in life is the absence of pain and frustration. Since all ethical beliefs are dogmatic and diminish our happiness by disturbing inner tranquility, we should relinquish them. In epistemology, he argued that it is impossible to determine whether perceptual experience is accurate.

Shaftesbury, 3rd Earl of (1671–1713)

English moral philosopher, born in London, privately educated and studied with John Locke. Shaftesbury is regarded to be the first to use the term "moral sense" in British moral philosophy. He rejected Hobbes's view of the selfishness of human nature and maintained that man has a natural affection for virtue and for the good of the species. He also argued that morality is self-determining and can exist independent of religion. Shaftesbury's numerous essays are collected in *Characteristics of Men, Manners, Opinions, Times*, 3 vols. (1711).

shame, see guilt

shared name, another expression for sortal

Sheffer function

LOGIC Also called a Sheffer stroke or stroke function. There are five primitive **logical constants** or functions, namely **negation** (∼), **conjunction** (∧), **disjunction** (∨), **implication** (⊃), and **equivalence** (≡). Logicians showed that they can be reduced to negation and disjunction. In 1913, the American logician H. M. **Sheffer** proposed obtaining all of them from a single binary **truth-function**, which he symbolized by a vertical stroke (|). With this notation, p|q is read as not both p and q. Accordingly, negation (∼p) can be defined as p|p; disjunction (p ∨ q) can be defined as (p|p)|(q|q), and so on. The truth-table for the Sheffer stroke function is:

p	q	p|q
T	T	F
T	F	T
F	T	T
F	F	T

"A function from which all others may be obtained is called a Sheffer function, after the discoverer of the stroke function." **Goodstein,** *Development of Mathematical Logic*

Shoemaker, Sydney (1931–)

American philosopher of metaphysics and mind, born in Boise, Idaho, Professor of Philosophy at Cornell University. Shoemaker has explored arguments for physical and mental criteria of personal identity and self-knowledge without criteria. He introduced a notion of quasi-remembering, which is remembering without the implication that the experience quasi-remembered is that of the person, and discussed thought experiments involving personal fission and fusion. His functionalism in the philosophy of mind differs from standard versions in accepting the existence of qualia. His major works include *Self-Knowledge and Self-Identity* (1963) and *Identity, Cause, and Mind* (1984).

Sidgwick, Henry (1838–1900)

British moral philosopher, born in Skipton, Yorkshire, Professor of Philosophy at Cambridge, a main advocate of utilitarianism. In his main work, *The Methods of Ethics* (1874, with subsequent revised editions), Sidgwick examined three main approaches to ethics: intuitionism, egoism, and utilitarianism. His sophisticated discussion of these methods and their relations led to the conclusion that utilitarianism and intuitionism reinforce each other and should be combined, with utilitarianism based on our moral intuition that we ought to aim at pleasure. Sidgwick's philosophical rigor has been influential as well as the contents of his views.

sign and symbol

LOGIC, PHILOSOPHY OF LANGUAGE Both **Peirce** and **Wittgenstein** drew a distinction between **sign** and **symbol**. A sign is an **expression** perceptible by senses, while a symbol is an expression's meaningful use and the **rules** for its application. A sign is what can be perceived of a symbol, while a symbol is a mode of signification of a sign. The same sign may be used in different symbols, or, in other words, different symbols may have their sign in common. For example, the sign "bear" in English can be used either as a verb (to carry) or as a noun (a mammal). Wittgenstein makes use of this distinction to criticize **Russell's** theory of **types**. Other than this, the distinction is not always observed. Signs are widely taken to include their symbols.

"In order to recognise a symbol by its sign we must observe how it is used with a sense." **Wittgenstein,** *Tractatus*

significant form

AESTHETICS An elusive and abstract term introduced by the British art critic Clive Bell, referring to the formal structure or unity common and peculiar to all visual works of art. This formal structure is the source that provokes aesthetic emotion. For Bell, the existence of this form and its capacity to arouse aesthetic emotion are the only criteria for being a work of art. The artist sees **objects** as pure forms, distinct from any associations they may have or **ends** that they may serve. This form is independent of any everyday human significance of objects in the world and is an end in itself. We can not recognize significant form in cognitive terms, and it is not open to empirical **confirmation** or **falsification**. But it can be felt, and it is refined and intensified by artists in their work. In seeing the significant form of things, the artist somehow glimpses "ultimate reality." The essence of artistic **creation** is to express the aesthetic emotion that the artist feels before such forms by re-creating them in a work of art. Correspondingly, to appreciate a work of art is to contemplate and feel this form.

"Line and colours combined in a particular way, certain forms and relations of form stir our aesthetic emotions. These relations are combinations of line and colours, these aesthetically moving forms, I call 'significant form'; and 'significant form' is the one quality common to all works of visual art." **Bell**, *Art*

simple nature

EPISTEMOLOGY, METAPHYSICS [Latin *naturae simplices*] For Francis **Bacon**, the ultimate qualities, such as red, white, and hard, out of which the whole natural world is constituted. For **Descartes**, simple natures were the starting-point for the constitution of knowable **objects** and also for human knowledge of these objects. Simple natures are all **self-evident**, never contain any falsity, and are grasped by **intuition** or the **natural light**. These things are **simple** because they are known so **clearly and distinctly** that they can not be divided by the **mind** into further items that can be known more clearly and distinctly. Descartes distinguished three kinds of simple nature: (1) pure **material** natures that are recognized to be present only in bodies, such as shape, extension, and movement; (2) pure intellectual natures, such as knowing and doubting, which the intellect recognizes by means of a sort of innate light and which do not involve any corporeal **substance**; (3) common simple natures, including common **concepts** that can be ascribed both to the physical and to the mental, such as **existence**,

duration, and the fundamental laws of **logic** that are called common notions. The first two kinds of simple natures are the building blocks of human knowledge and can be combined again and again into various complex natures. The common simple natures, applicable to both the physical and the mental, are the cement that binds them together.

"These simple natures are all self-evident and never contain any falsity." **Descartes**, *The Philosophical Writings*

simplicity, principle of

PHILOSOPHICAL METHOD, PHILOSOPHY OF SCIENCE One **theory** is simpler than another if it postulates fewer **entities** and explanatory **principles**. The principle of simplicity generally means the same thing as the principle of parsimony or **Ockham's razor**. Simplicity is generally taken as one, although not the only, **criterion** for determining the acceptability of rival theories. The competing theories might be chosen in terms of **consistency**, **scope**, **precision**, and **predictive** power. However, everything else being equal, a simpler theory, that is, the theory that makes the fewest assumptions, is more acceptable than its complex rivals. The philosophical problem is whether it is possible to justify this preference for simplicity as something beyond a mere consideration of convenience. The traditional belief is that **nature** itself is simple. "Nature does nothing in vain." But the principle of the uniformity of nature itself is a problematic notion. Contemporary philosophy of science takes simplicity as a part of methodology. **Quine** connects it with high **probability**. **Popper** connects it with his criterion of **falsifiability** by claiming that simple statements are highly desirable because they have richer empirical content and because they are more testable. The dispute about the validity of the principle of simplicity as a sign of truth has yet to be resolved.

"The principle of simplicity (also referred to as the principle of parsimony) . . . affirms that other things being equal, the simpler theory should be chosen." **Regan**, *The Case for Animal Rights*

simulation theory

PHILOSOPHY OF MIND An account of how we know about the **propositional attitudes** of others. It claims that our **knowledge** of other people's **beliefs** comes not from the application of a **theory**, but as a result of using our own psychological processes to simulate those of others. It is an extension of our capacity to know our own beliefs. We **imagine** that we are in someone else's position and then imagine what we would think or do in that situation. Simulation is used in explaining the meaning of **intentional** concepts such as **belief** and **desire**. The proponents of this theory include Gordon, **Goldman**, **Stich**, and Nichols.

> "Simulation theory suggests an account of the mechanisms underlying our capacity to predict and explain people's behaviour, and that explanation makes no appeal to an internalised theory or knowledge structure." **Stich,** *Deconstructing the Mind*

sin

PHILOSOPHY OF RELIGION, ETHICS A theological term for the severe wrongdoing or faults of moral character due to disobedience of a divine command or a violation of **natural law**. A person's sense of sin is one paradigm of **religious experience**. According to the New Testament, all men are sinful, because we inherited original sin from Adam, the common father of humankind. Christians believe that the death of Jesus was a sacrifice for human sins. A person after death will be sent to hell if judged by **God** to be an unrepentant sinner. In a loose sense, sin is synonymous with **evil**, but strictly speaking, sin is an evil committed toward God, rather than to other persons. Only God may be asked to pardon sins. On some interpretations, sin results from following our sensory nature against our rational nature. It is committed when we do not do the **good** we know that God requires of us. Persons who believe that they have sinned often feel that they are cut off from God, the vision of God, or God's **grace**. The origin of sin is generally ascribed to human **free will**, but this point is controversial. In medieval philosophy and theology, pride, covetousness, envy, gluttony, anger, sloth, and lust are listed as the seven deadly sins.

> "By his sin a sinner cannot really injure God, and yet, for his own part, he acts contrary to God in two ways. First, he despises God and his commandments and secondly, he does in fact harm someone, either himself or someone else." **Aquinas,** *Summa Theologiae*

sincerity

ETHICS Frankly and plainly presenting oneself to oneself and others, rather than hiding or adding something in order to present oneself as different from what one actually is. Sincere people say and do what they really believe. Insincerity to oneself is a form of **self-deception**, while insincerity to others is lying or **hypocrisy**. Sincerity has been regarded as a **virtue**, but it is controversial whether any form of insincerity counts an **evil**. Those who modify their views to avoid serious political consequences are only sometimes judged to have acted immorally. The sincerity of skeptics has been a matter of debate because such a person has difficulties in carrying out his belief in his daily life.

> "Real sincerity implies that all the contradictory facets of the self are given free expression." **Elster,** *Ulysses and the Sirens*

sine qua non

PHILOSOPHY OF LAW, PHILOSOPHY OF ACTION [Latin, without which not, also written *conditio sine qua non*, a condition without which not, in law a necessary condition] If an event B would not have happened if a prior event A had not happened, then A is a *conditio sine qua non* of B. This is generally viewed as a factual cause independent of policy or rule. A detailed examination of the relationship between this kind of condition and causally relevant factors in human **action** can be found in Hart and Honoré, *Causation in the Law*.

> "When a negative answer is forthcoming to the question 'Would Y have occurred if X had not?' X is referred to not merely as a 'necessary condition' or *sine qua non* of Y but as its 'cause in fact' or 'material cause'." **Hart and Honoré,** *Causation in the Law*

Singer, Peter (1946–)

Australian utilitarian moral philosopher, born in Melbourne, Professor of Philosophy, Monash University, and Princeton University. Singer has contributed to a reorientation of moral philosophy, from meta-ethics to questions in practical and applied ethics, especially questions of human and animal suffering, life, and death. He proposes utilitarian arguments to reject the species prejudice that gives priority to human over animal well-being and to allow infanticide and euthanasia in cases where there is no prospect of a life worth living. His major works include *Animal Liberation* (1975) and *Practical Ethics* (1979).

singular term

LOGIC The distinction between singular terms and **general terms** has been drawn since **Mill**, and receives much discussion in contemporary **analytic philosophy**. A singular term is a term that **denotes** or ostensively **refers**, under a given circumstance, to an individual **object**. Terms that belong to the categories of **proper names**, indexicals, **definite descriptions**, and so on are all singular terms. A singular term can replace, or be replaced by, an individual **variable** in an **open sentence**. It can only be the grammatical subject of a subject-predicate sentence and can never be a **predicate**. In contrast, a general term introduces a kind or a type of individual thing. While a singular term can only be a subject, a general term can serve either as a subject or as a predicate. The distinction between singular and general terms is widely supported, but it has been criticized by Peter **Strawson** in *Individuals*.

"Semantically the distinction between singular and general term is vaguely that a single term names or purports to name just one object, though as complex or diffuse an object as you please; while a general term is true of each, severally, of any number of objects." **Quine,** *Word and Object*

Sittlichkeit, see ethical life

situation ethics

ETHICS An anti-theoretical position that flourished among Christian religious moralists after the Second World War, influenced by American **pragmatism**, and operated with the slogan: be loving and do as you please. It claims that ethics is essentially a matter of reacting to the contexts or situations one confronts and that moral choice must be situational, particular, and determined by case-to-case analysis. It proposes that there is only one moral **principle**, that is, *agape* or love. Other than this, there should be no packaged moral **judgments** for Christians. To build an ethical system is meaningless, and the rigid application of the universal moral principles and **rules** should be rejected. The ethical maxims of

the **community** in which one lives can serve as illuminators, but we should always be prepared to compromise in the situation where love seems better served by doing something else. The systematic exponent of this ethics is Joseph Fletcher, who claims that situation ethics is not **relativistic**, for it holds that love is the ultimate judge of the **norm** of **action**. Hence situation ethics is a middle approach between legalism, which emphasizes systematic rules and regulations, and **antinominism**, which rejects all principles whatever. This position has similarities with act-utilitarianism and **casuistry**.

"Situation ethics goes part of the way with natural law, by accepting reason as the instrument of moral judgements, while rejecting the notion that the good is 'given' in the nature of things, objectively. It goes part of way with Scriptural law by accepting revelation as the source of the norm while rejecting all 'revealed' norms or laws but the one command – to love God and thy neighbour." **Fletcher,** *Situation Ethics*

situational semantics

PHILOSOPHY OF LANGUAGE Developed in the late 1970s by J. Barwise and J. Parry and intended as an alternative to **Tarski**'s formal truth-conditional **semantics**. A situation in this account is the part of reality that **agents** find themselves in and about which they exchange information. Situational semantics claims that the **meaning** of a **sentence** is not given merely through its truth-conditions, but should also be determined by the relations of the sentence to the situation in which it is uttered and information about its speaker. The meaning of an **expression** can not be described independently of the use of the expression. It involves a relation between the circumstance that the expression describes and the circumstance in which it is uttered, because rational speakers or agents must use information extracted from their situation in order to reason and communicate effectively.

"In this book I have been urging the development of a theory of meaning and information content, one rich enough to give a semantics for English that can account for the way language users handle information, and suggesting a shape for this general theory. We call this situation theory, and the applications to natural language situational semantics." **Barwise,** *The Situation in Logic*

skepticism

EPISTEMOLOGY, ETHICS, ANCIENT GREEK PHILOSOPHY [from Greek *skepsis*, investigation, enquiry] Also written "scepticism," a critical philosophical attitude, questioning by systematic arguments the reliability of **knowledge** claims and our ability to establish objective **truth**. When ancient Greek philosophers called themselves skeptics, they probably meant that they were undogmatic investigators. The founder of Greek skepticism was **Pyrrho** of Elis, and skepticism is also called Pyrrhonism. Pyrrhonism claimed to set up many modes of **argument** to show that the world of **appearance** is full of **contradictions** and that there is no guarantee that we apprehend things as they really are. Thus it is better to adopt an attitude of **suspension of judgment** and to achieve a state of tranquility. Most arguments of Pyrrhonism are recorded in the writings of **Sextus Empiricus**. Various versions of modern skepticism can be found in figures such as **Montaigne, Gassendi, Descartes, Hume**, and the **logical positivists**. While ancient skepticism attacked both knowledge and **belief** and was a philosophy of life, modern skepticism is a challenge to knowledge only. This is why some philosophers hold that ancient skepticism is more serious. There is also a distinction of subject-matter between ethics and science in modern skepticism, and ethical or moral skepticism, which claims that there are no objective **values**, has become a separate concern. Skepticism is a negative but dynamic force in the history of philosophy. In attempting to attack and overcome skepticism, philosophers sharpen the formulation of philosophical problems and their attempts to solve them.

"Scepticism is an ability which sets up antitheses among appearances and judgements in any way whatever." **Empiricus,** *Outline of Pyrrhonism*

Skolem's paradox, see Skolem–Löwenheim theorem

Skolem–Löwenheim theorem

LOGIC Skolem and Löwenheim established that in **set theory** for any class of **formulas** of predicate **calculus**, if there is an **interpretation** that suits all of them, there is also an interpretation whose **domain** consists of natural numbers that suits all of them. This Skolem–Löwenheim theorem implies that if first-order set theory is **consistent** and has a model, it must also have a denumerable infinite model whose **continuum** is a countable set and is thus apparently non-standard. This result is called Skolem's **paradox** because it conflicts with **Cantor's theorem**, according to which within set theory we can establish that there is a set of real numbers that is not denumerable. To avoid Skolem's paradox, we should suppose that the distinction between denumerable and non-denumerable models is relative to an **axiom system** rather than absolute. Others believe that the paradox indicates that standard first-order predicate calculus is not sufficient to reveal the structure of the continuum.

"There is a remarkable theorem in classical logic, the Skolem–Löwenheim theorem, which says that any consistent set of sentences (whether a finite or infinite set of sentences) has a model in the natural numbers." **J. Smart,** *Our Place in the Universe*

slave/master, see master/slave

slave morality, see master morality

slave of the passions

PHILOSOPHY OF ACTION, ETHICS **Hume**'s term for the role of **reason** in **action**. The traditional ethical belief was that morality is a matter of **rationality** and that we act according to the dictates of reason. Hume claimed that this is wrong. Reason is useful and can direct our **judgment** concerning **good** and **evil**, but it is impotent with respect to **motivating** action. Reason is not a **causal** factor in promoting moral actions. What directly impels us to act is **passion** or **emotion**. In contrast to the traditional view that emotion should be subjected to reason, Hume believed that reason is the slave of the passions in the genesis of action. This does not mean that there is a conflict between reason and passion. For Hume, that which is opposed to reason can only be reason itself rather than passion.

"Reason is, and ought only to be the slave of the passions, and can never pretend to any other office than to serve and obey them." **Hume,** *A Treatise of Human Nature*

slippery slope argument

LOGIC, ETHICS An argument seeking to persuade an audience not to take the first step on the grounds that it will lead to further steps having disastrous consequences. The argument can be formulated in many ways, but its central version is the one that is also called the **wedge argument**. According to the argument, some **actions** are like the first step on a slippery slope. Although they can be **justified**, their performance will inevitably lead to further actions with bad consequences. Hence, it is better not to permit the first action. This argument has a wide application in moral discussions. For example, some argue that if active **euthanasia** is legalized, terrible consequences will follow. For once societies openly allow deliberate killing under some circumstances (for example, when dying persons are suffering intolerable pain), we will move to allow involuntary euthanasia and even the killing of old people who become a burden to society. Thus, we move from mercy killing to non-merciful killing and from justified killing to unjustified killing. Life, which should be valued, will become cheap. Slippery slope arguments are generally taken to be unconvincing, for there is no rational ground for claiming that we can not firmly draw the line between justified and unjustified acts, although initial steps might alter the context in which subsequent steps are judged.

"A slippery slope argument is a kind of argument that warns you if you take the first step you will find yourself involved in a sticky sequence of consequences from which you will be unable to extricate yourself, and eventually you will wind up speeding faster and faster towards some disastrous outcome." **Walton, *Slippery Slope Arguments***

Smart, J(ohn) J(amieson) C(arswell) (1920–)
Australian materialist utilitarian philosopher, born in Cambridge, England, Professor of Philosophy at Australian National University. Smart was an early proponent of a materialist theory of the mind in response to his dissatisfaction with philosophical behaviorism. His materialism is part of his more general integration of the concerns of science and philosophy. In ethics, he has argued for an act-utilitarianism. His major works include *Philosophy and Scientific Realism* (1963), *Essays Metaphysical and Moral* (1987), and *Our Place in the Universe* (1989).

Smith, Adam (1723–90)
Scottish economist and moral philosopher, born in Kirkcaldy, taught at Glasgow. In *The Theory of Moral Sentiments* (1759), Smith explained moral goodness

in terms of the pleasure taken by an impartial spectator in observing virtue, and this idea was later developed in the "ideal observer theory." In contrast to Hutcheson's moral sense theory, he argued that the essence of moral sentiments was sympathy. In *An Inquiry into the Nature and Causes of the Wealth of Nations* (1776), Smith established the basis of modern economic thought. His notion of an "invisible hand" that coordinates the workings of a free market has retained its importance in the philosophy of social science and in the theory of rational social action.

social action
PHILOSOPHY OF ACTION, PHILOSOPHY OF SOCIAL SCIENCE **Actions** of social groups, such as a rebellion, and actions conducted within a framework of social relations, such as marriage or holding a conversation. Social actions can be ritualized, with fixed sequences of correct behavior, or flexible and diverse, so long as the action of one individual takes account of the behavior of others. For **methodological individualists**, social action can be reduced to the actions of individuals, but this account is rejected by **methodological holists**, who claim that social actions have collectively determined **meanings** and **intentions** that can not be analyzed in terms of individual action. While all actions are contingent on the external world, social action is also contingent on the interdependence of **choices** and orientations among rational **agents**. This double contingency is a characteristic feature of social action. Any social action must follow **rules** represented, for example, by cultural frameworks, communication systems, or value systems. A main task of sociology is to understand social actions by understanding the social practices and the institutions that embody them.

"Action is 'social' insofar as its subjective meaning takes account of the behaviour of others and is thereby oriented in its course." **Weber, *Economy and Society*, vol. 1**

social choice, another expression for public choice

social contract
POLITICAL PHILOSOPHY A contract providing the legitimate basis of **sovereignty** and **civil society** and of the **rights** and **duties** constituting the **role** of **citizen**. According to the social contract theory that flourished in the seventeenth and eighteenth centuries, a

social contract based on individual **consent** permits men to enter civil society from the **state of nature**, whether from the brutal world of **Hobbes** or the relatively self-sufficient world of **Locke**. The move to civil society was accomplished by giving up certain **natural rights** in return for the protection, rights, and advantages offered by the state. For Hobbes, the contract is agreed between people and a proposed sovereign, who received absolute **authority**. For Locke and **Rousseau**, the contract is agreed among the people themselves to vest **power** in a government. For Locke, **persons** in the state of nature are very much like ourselves, but for Rousseau they become persons by entry into civil society. In Rousseau's view, the social contract is the condition through which the **will** of all, the aggregation of individual wills, becomes the **general will** that wills the **common good**. It has been a matter of controversy whether classical accounts of the social contract are meant to present an actual or hypothetical contract. Some critics hold that before employing this theory to justify the **legitimacy** of political authority and the grounds of **political obligation**, we must provide independent justification for the theory itself. Social contract theory has been employed in the theory of **justice** of the contemporary political philosopher John **Rawls**. For Rawls, a contract between **rational self-interested** actors who are ignorant of their own positions in society determines **principles** of justice, but this hypothetical contract offers only one aspect of Rawls's justification of his theory.

"What man loses by the social contract . . . is his natural liberty and the absolute right to anything that tempts him and that he can take; what he gains by the social contracts is civil liberty and the legal right of property of what he possesses." **Rousseau,** *The Social Contract*

social Darwinism

ETHICS, POLITICAL PHILOSOPHY, PHILOSOPHY OF SOCIAL SCIENCE A theory resulting from the application of **Darwinism** to human society. By deducing norms of human conduct directly from evolutionary biology, it attempted to deal with ethical, economic, and political problems on the assumption that society is a competitive arena and that the **evolution** of society fits the Darwinian paradigm in its most individualistic form. According to social Darwinism,

the fittest climb to dominant social positions as a consequence of social selection, just as **natural selection** determines the **survival of the fittest**. Because on this view human possession of **consciousness** does not have any moral implications, social Darwinism held that social inequality and the exploitation of lower classes, suppressed races, and conquered nations by the stronger were morally acceptable. It opposed any plan of social reform or welfare system to protect the weak or poor by claiming that such measures disturbed the natural order and hindered the progress of the human species. **Altruism** was held to be nothing more than hypocrisy. Social Darwinism flourished at the end of the nineteenth century and in the early twentieth century, with Herbert **Spencer**'s political theory as its most important theoretical expression. It is now mainly of historic interest, with its science and its ethics both seen to be deeply flawed.

"A purely biological perspective will give no grounding to individual rights, and might tend to a sort of social Darwinism, in which individuals would be seen in terms of their contribution to the survival and improvement of the species or society." **O'Hear,** *Experience, Explanation and Faith*

social democracy

POLITICAL PHILOSOPHY A term originally used for the **Marxist** approach to socialism, in contrast to revisionist forms of socialism. Since the Russian revolution, Marxist socialism has been called communism. The term social democracy has lost its relationship with Marxist socialism, and has been employed in revisionist and **liberal** thought. In contrast to classical market liberalism, which emphasizes the primacy of classical civil **rights** such as **freedom of speech**, freedom of association, freedom of religious and ideological belief, and freedom to pursue one's own happiness, social democracy holds that these fundamental rights can be qualified to secure a fair and **just** distribution of resources and opportunities. Consequently, it allows or requires state agencies to play an active role in many areas of life in order to maintain a just society.

"After 1920, and up to the present, the term social democracy has had its strongest links with the related reformist socialism and social liberal tradition." **Vincent,** *Modern Political Ideologies*

social fact

PHILOSOPHY OF SOCIAL SCIENCE A **fact** about a social institution or group, such as a family, school, class, or community. In contrast, individual facts concern individual **agents** and their psychological states. A social fact is unobservable, but can be determined through statistical generalizations about certain kinds of social interaction within a given society. **Durkheim** claimed that the existence of social facts enables the social sciences to conduct studies as **objective** as those of the natural sciences, which deals with things. For **methodological holists**, the existence of social facts must be presupposed in interpreting individual behavior, whereas for **methodological individualists**, social fact can be reduced to individual facts or individual behavior.

"A social fact is every way of acting, fixed or not, capable of exercising on the individual an external constraint; or again, every way of acting which is general throughout a given society, while at the same time existing in its own rights independent of its individual manifestations." **Durkheim,** *The Rules of Sociological Method*

social philosophy

POLITICAL PHILOSOPHY, PHILOSOPHY OF SOCIAL SCIENCE The philosophical examination of substantive social issues, such as the relations between society and the **state**; the relations between society and its members; social equality; morality and law; and issues of health care and child protection. Social philosophy critically assesses political **ideologies** and societal arrangements and tries to discern clearly what a good society would be like, and how it might be achieved. **Plato**'s *Republic*, **Hobbes**'s *Leviathan*, and **Rousseau**'s *Social Contract* can be regarded as classical works in the area of social philosophy. Social philosophy is **normative** in character and overlaps with political philosophy concerning many issues. It is distinguished from the neutral, methodologically oriented versions of the philosophy of social science, which are mainly concerned with the logic of **justification** of social scientific **theories**. It is closer to those versions of philosophy of social science that allow room for **value** and social criticism within social science.

"Social philosophy . . . is concerned with the varying view about the nature of desirable social systems or societies, and sometimes it puts forward its own proposals about what constitutes a good or desirable society." **Rudner,** *Philosophy of Social Science*

sociobiology

PHILOSOPHY OF SOCIAL SCIENCE, ETHICS, POLITICAL PHILOSOPHY A study inspired by **Darwin**'s theory of **natural selection** and attempting to explain human social **behavior** by human biological features, particularly genes. Sociobiology focuses on the shared features of genetic design among human beings rather than on cultural and historical dimensions of human life. It claims that genes play a fundamental role in determining human behavior and that, like the social behavior of animals, human social behavior is informed by its **evolutionary** purposes. The field emerged as a separate discipline with Edward O. Wilson's *Sociobiology: The New Synthesis* in 1975. Many of its claims provoke heated debates. Some critics reject sociobiology as a modernized version of **social Darwinism**, while others reject its genetic **determinism** and claim that much human behavior is culturally formed and open to modification. Nevertheless, sociobiology has raised important questions with its emphasis on the evolutionarily determined genes and their role in human **consciousness**, behavior, and institutions. Sociobiologists believe that humans might recognize that cooperation is a better strategy than purely egoistic pursuits in the search for survival. Accordingly, biological evolution might lead to a type of **altruism** and form a biological basis for a **social contract**. Because biological altruism suggests that we will more willingly cooperate with our close kin rather than with strangers, however, even this version of sociobiology denies that our obligations extend to others equally. Sociobiology suggests that biology and morality are closely related, although many of these claims are both speculative and contested.

"Sociobiology is the evolutionary theory of the origin and stability of social behaviour. When fully developed, it may account for the evolution of ethics." **von Schilcher and Tennant,** *Philosophy, Evolution and Human Nature*

sociology of knowledge

EPISTEMOLOGY, PHILOSOPHY OF SOCIAL SCIENCE On the assumption that **knowledge** is not merely the result

of the meeting of the individual **mind** with the physical world, but is socially and historically conditioned,
sociology of knowledge studies the **social facts** or
elements that shape and condition the acquisition,
justification, change and growth of knowledge. This
discipline claims to have enriched traditional epistemology by adding a social dimension to it. It claims
that in every society there is a fabric of **meaning**
that is conveyed to us in childhood as a set of lores.
The social elements considered include such things
as the social status and the interests of the subject
(either as a group or as an individual), tradition,
and convention and the process of socialization.
Although sociology of knowledge appeared as a separate discipline only in the twentieth century, through
Karl Mannheim's *Ideology and Utopia*, many of its
ideas can be traced to **Plato**. Max **Scheler** and Karl
Marx also advocated similar positions. In its early
stage, sociology of knowledge was confined to
investigating the general conditions surrounding the
emergence and modification of bodies of institutionalized collective beliefs and the social sources of
prejudices and distortions. This program presupposes
that knowledge is historically relative and can not
be **objectively** valid, but is, rather, a reflection
of the interests of a certain social class. A rival
program explores the possibility that social factors
can be adequate grounds for objective knowledge.

"We have witnessed the rebirth of the notion
of the 'sociology of knowledge', which suggests
that not only our methods but our conclusions
and our reasons for believing them, in the entire
realm of knowledge, can be shown to be wholly
or largely determined by the stage reached in the
development of our class or group, or nation or
culture, or whatever other unit may be chosen."
Berlin, *Four Essays on Liberty*

Socrates (469–399 BC)

Greek philosopher, born in Athens, teacher of Plato.
Socrates' claim that "an unexamined life is not worth
living" and his unconditional commitment to
philosophy at the expense of his own life, have
inspired Western philosophical thought for over
two thousand years. Socrates' philosophical journey
began with his attempt to understand the meaning
of the Delphic oracle in saying that he was the wisest person. Having examined various people who

were thought to have wisdom, Socrates concluded
that he was said to be the wisest because he knew
that he knew nothing. He continued to examine
others in the belief that he served God by revealing
the limits of human wisdom.

Socrates did not write anything. We know his
thought through Aristophanes' play *The Clouds*,
Xenophon's writings, Aristotle's reports and, most
importantly, Plato's dialogues, in which Socrates is
always the major speaker. As a result, we have the
enduring problem of distinguishing Plato's Socrates
from the historical Socrates. A conventional view
holds that the position expressed by the character
Socrates in Plato's early dialogues is close to that
of the historical Socrates. These dialogues are characterized by the irony of Socrates' claim to have
no knowledge, by the Socratic method of cross-
examining interlocutors to find flaws and incon-
sistencies in their views, and by the failure to
overcome *aporia* to reach acceptable answers to the
questions raised. On this reading, Socrates, despite
his disavowal of knowledge, held the following
doctrines: happiness is our final end; to be happy a
person must look after soul, which is the only thing
in us worth saving; to care about soul is to care
about virtue; virtue is knowledge; no evil thing can
happen to a good man; and because no one does
evil willingly, weakness of will is impossible. Socrates
was tried and sentenced to death by the Athenians
in 399 BC on the charges of impiety and the corruption of youth. A major concern of Plato's philosophy
was to defend Socrates against these charges.

Socrates' question

ANCIENT GREEK PHILOSOPHY, ETHICS, METAPHYSICS,
PHILOSOPHY OF LANGUAGE A term that is used in two
ways. First, it is a question about how one ought to
live or about what is a life worth living. **Socrates**
raised this question several times in the Platonic
dialogues. Its classical expression is at *Gorgias*, 500b:
"Do not either take what I say as if I were merely
playing, for you see the subject of our discussion –
and on what subject should even a man of slight
intelligence be more serious? – namely, what kind
of life one should live." It is a general question about
what to do for one's whole life, not a question about
whether to do this or that action. The question
invites one to reflect about one's own life, and
Socrates himself held that an unexamined life is not

worth living. It provides an adequate starting-point for moral theories, and any serious **moral theory** must answer the question in some way.

The term is also used for various questions posed by Socrates in the earlier Platonic dialogues in the form: "What is . . . ?," such as "What is piety?" "What is justice?" "What is courage?" and "What is temperance?" These questions sought to examine general conceptions that determine what is the same in many different particulars. Socrates did not offer conclusive answers to these questions, but they led philosophers to deal with the problem of **universals**, the relation between the general and the particular, and the nature of **predication**. The methodology implied by these questions, which was essential for the later development of Western philosophy, led directly to the birth of Plato's Theory of **Forms**.

"In Socrates' question the general as such is discovered." **G. Martin,** *An Introduction to General Metaphysics*

Socratic elenchus

ANCIENT GREEK PHILOSOPHY, ETHICS, PHILOSOPHICAL METHOD [from Greek *elenchein*, to refute, to examine, to test] Although **Socrates** himself did not use this term, it is widely used for his characteristic **method** of inquiry and his central daily activity. Also called the Socratic method, *elenchus* involved Socrates in a cross-examination of an interlocutor through a sequence of questions by which Socrates sought to expose conflicts in the views held by the interlocutor. He then tried to reconstruct these beliefs as a result of reflections on the conflicts and on their possible resolution. The earlier Platonic dialogues, in which Socrates showed various *elenchi*, are called elenctic dialogues. Since this kind of cross-examination always ended without reaching any definite conclusion, these dialogues are also called **aporetic** dialogues. Socratic *elenchus* is neither purely negative nor merely for the purpose of exposing confusions in his interlocutors. It was thus distinguished both from **Zeno of Elea**'s method and from **sophistry**, although it was similar in form to them. Socrates employed his *elenchus* in an attempt to get people to see things themselves. The questions by which he conducted his *elenchus* were not trivial, but rather had to do with the concepts and principles by which the

Athenians lived. By this method Socrates questioned the morality of his time. Influenced by **Vlastos**'s work, scholars have recently examined the logical form of elenchus and its implication for understanding **Plato**'s earlier dialogues.

"Socratic elenchus is a search for moral truth by adversary argument in which a thesis is debated only if asserted as the answerer's own belief, who is regarded as refuted if and only if the negation of his thesis is deduced from his own beliefs." **Vlastos, "The Socratic Elenchus," in** *Oxford Studies in Ancient Philosophy,* **vol.** 1

Socratic method, another term for Socratic elenchus

soft data, see data

solipsism

PHILOSOPHY OF MIND, METAPHYSICS, EPISTEMOLOGY [from Latin *solus*, alone + *ipse*, self] A metaphysical theory which claims that only I and my **experience** exist. The argument for solipsism asserts that every claim about what exists and what I know is grounded in experience and can not transcend it, but that experience is immediate and **private** to me; therefore nothing exists beyond myself and my experience. The world is my presentation. Solipsism is closely associated with the claim of traditional British **empiricism** that immediate **perception** is the source of all knowledge, and also with **Descartes**'s *cogito ergo sum*. Like **skepticism**, solipsism is criticized as logically incoherent and unintelligible, but a complete refutation is difficult to find. **Russell** believes that there is something true in it, though he himself chooses not to accept it. **Wittgenstein** in the *Tractatus* thinks that since the limits of my language show the limits of my world, there is something correct about solipsism, although it can not be expressed in factual language. He sees the temptation to solipsism as related to the **metaphysical subject**.

"Here it can be seen that solipsism, when its implications are followed out strictly, coincides with pure realism. The self of solipsism shrinks to a point without extension, and there remains the reality co-ordinated with it." **Wittgenstein,** *Tractatus*

somatism, see reism

sophia, Greek term for wisdom

sophism, see fallacy of ambiguity

sophist

ANCIENT GREEK PHILOSOPHY [Greek *sophistes*, from *sophos*, wise and *sophia*, wisdom] Initially, any wise man like a poet, seer, or sage, but in the fifth century BC, a special term for a professional teacher who wandered from city to city to teach many non-traditional courses, including rhetoric and linguistics, which young Greeks needed to pursue political careers. Sophists charged their students for this service. At that time the term did not have a derogatory sense. The sophists did not form a sect or school, and many of them were not philosophers at all. Among the most famous sophists were **Protagoras**, Gorgias, Thrasymachus, Prodicus, and Hippias. Only in the next generation did "sophist" acquire the unfavorable sense that it still bears today. This change largely resulted from the hostile propaganda of **Plato** and **Aristotle**, who accused the sophists of making money for their teaching and of neglecting higher values by teaching techniques aimed merely at winning debates. Many sophists are targets of **irony** in Plato's dialogues, where they are distinguished from the practitioners of serious intellectual pursuits. However, from the scant information we possess, it seems that the sophists together formed a loose movement that was **skeptical** in tradition and having some features of an enlightenment. They made important contributions to the history of thought in fields such as grammar and linguistic theory, moral and political doctrine, and the theory of the nature and origin of man and society. Because no writings survive from any of the sophists, it is difficult to correct the traditional prejudice against them.

"A sophistes writes or teaches because he has a special skill or knowledge to impart. His sophia is practical, whether in the fields of conduct and politics or in the technical arts." **Guthrie,** *The Sophists*

sorites paradox

LOGIC, PHILOSOPHY OF LANGUAGE [from Greek *soros*, a heap and *sorites*, a heaper] Also the **paradox** of the heap, a paradox that concerns how a series of small changes does not affect the possession of a **property** when taken individually but does affect the possession of the property when the changes are taken together. One grain of sand does not make a heap. Adding a further grain does not make a heap. We can go on adding grains without making a heap, and there is no particular number of grains that will make a heap. Yet many grains of sand certainly do make a heap. If no addition of a single grain can turn a non-heap into a heap, it is difficult to understand how a heap can emerge. The problem can be stated conversely. Removing one grain of sand from a heap does not make the heap disappear. Nor does removing a second grain make the heap disappear, and so on. There seems no point at which the heap disappears, yet it does disappear. A variant of the sorites paradox is the bald man paradox. A man with a full head of hair will not become bald if he loses one hair. Nor will the loss of a second hair make him bald, and so on. There appears to be no point at which the removal of an additional hair will make him bald, but the man does become bald.

The problem for all versions of the sorites paradox is the same: how can a series of changes, each of which does not make a difference, make a difference eventually when taken together? Attempted solutions deny the claim that if the first change does not make a difference in the possession of the property, then no subsequent change makes a difference; use the notion of degrees of truth regarding the possession of the property; or deal with the property using fuzzy logic, which recognizes degrees of applicability of **predicates**.

". . . the sorites paradox, the ancient paradox of the heap: If removal of a single grain from a heap always leaves a heap, then, by mathematical induction, removal of all the grains leaves a heap." **Quine,** *Theories and Things*

sortal

EPISTEMOLOGY, METAPHYSICS, PHILOSOPHY OF LANGUAGE Although the idea can be traced to **Aristotle**'s notion of secondary **substance**, the word "sortal" was introduced by John **Locke** from sort, on analogy with the derivation of "general" from genus. For Locke, a sortal was a type of **abstract idea** that denotes the **essence** of a sort or a kind. **Frege** introduced sortals into contemporary discussion for a type of **predicate** by which we know the sort of **object** to which it applies; sortals delimit that object from other objects. Terms such as "cat" and "person" are sortals. A sortal predicate contains a **criterion** of identification and distinction. It provides a principle of countability and can be used with a definite or indefinite article. A sortal predicate applies to an object but does not apply to the parts of that object because the object it applies to does not permit arbitrary division. The term "cat" does not apply to a part of a cat, because the part is not itself a cat. On the other hand, a general but non-sortal predicate such as "a red thing" may apply to both the object itself and its parts. For a part of a red thing might itself be red. The use of sortals in considering various topics of contemporary philosophy owes much to Peter **Strawson**'s discussion in *Individuals* and to the views that all scientific **laws** require sortal predicates and that **identity** claims are sortal-relative. If a **particular** is an instance of a **universal**, it is said to be sortally tied to the universal. There are alternative expressions for "sortal." Strawson used the expression "individuate term" but later reverted to the standard term in his *Individuals*. **Geach** used the term "count noun," and **Quine** used the expression "divided reference." Sortals are also called shared names.

"A sortal universal supplies a principle for distinguishing and counting individual particulars which it collects." **Strawson**, *Individuals*

sortal predicate, see sortal

soul

METAPHYSICS, PHILOSOPHY OF MIND, PHILOSOPHY OF RELIGION [Greek *psyche* and Latin *anima*, originally the breath of life] An **entity**, the presence of which in a body causes the body to possess life and in the absence of which the body is dead. The soul gives the body the faculty of **cognition** and, in the case of man, **thought**. The soul gives body the power of self-motion. By analogy, the changing world is sometimes claimed to be a living thing and to have a **world soul**. **Pythagoras** introduced the notion that the soul is **immortal** and **transmigrates** between many bodies. This idea was reinforced by **Plato** and led to a perennial topic in philosophy covering

identity, **survival**, resurrection, and **disembodiment**. **Materialists** claim that the soul can not exist independently of the body. **Aristotle** said that the soul is the **form** or actuality of any organic body and in this sense can not be separate from body, but he also claimed that humans have an imperishable and separate active soul or **reason**.

Plato made a tripartite division of the soul into rational, emotional, and appetitive, and believed that only human beings have the rational part. He believed that these three parts are in a state of constant conflict, and that a **just** person should make use of his reason to control the appetitive part, with the aid of emotion. This tripartite division has framed much later discussion in the history of Western philosophy. Psychology, which studies the operations and relations of these three parts, is derived from *psyche*, the Greek term for soul.

Descartes preferred to use the term **mind** (from Latin *mens*) rather than soul. The mind is the **consciousness** or the thinking part of the soul, although there are difficulties in giving a conceptually unified account of all that might belong to thinking and the mind. Other philosophers, such as **Locke**, used mind as a synonym for **understanding**. Descartes argued that the mind is an independent and incorporeal **substance**. This thesis gives rise to the **mind–body problem**, which is the most fundamental problem of the philosophy of mind. Soul is also taken as a synonym of spirit.

"It is the soul by or with which primarily we live, perceive and think." **Aristotle**, *De Anima*

sovereign

POLITICAL PHILOSOPHY, PHILOSOPHY OF LAW The **agent** with supreme **power** who is habitually obeyed in a political society, but who does not habitually obey others. In a monarchy, the sovereign is an individual person; in an aristocracy, the sovereign is a group of people; and in a democracy, the sovereign is the populace or its majority. The sovereign has the power to inflict **punishment**. For **Hobbes**, a sovereign should have absolute power and be able to control all areas of life and behavior. Its power is a unity and is irrevocable. John **Austin** maintained that the sovereign is a pre-legal political fact and must be assumed as a basis for explaining and defining all other legal concepts. In his legal philosophy, the command of the sovereign, like **Kelsen**'s **basic norm** or **Hart**'s **rule of recognition**, is the ground of legal validity.

"If, following Austin, we call such a supreme and independent person or body of persons the sovereign, the laws of any country will be the general orders backed by threats which are issued either by the sovereign or subordinates in obedience to the sovereign." **Hart,** *The Concept of Law*

sovereignty

POLITICAL PHILOSOPHY, PHILOSOPHY OF LAW Supreme legal **authority**. A concept originating in the medieval conflicts between church and **state** and now a feature of independent states, their people or their rulers. External sovereignty is the supreme authority of the state regarding its relations with other states or international authorities. It is a state's **right** to the integrity of its territory and its right to join or withdraw from any international treaty or organization as an independent party. External sovereignty is a major factor in modern international relations and can be limited or augmented by international law. Internal sovereignty concerns the body of laws and **rules** by which a state conducts its affairs. Within its territory, a sovereign state has final legal authority, with which external forces may not legitimately interfere. Because law and morality differ, there can be tension between internal sovereignty and recognized individual **rights**. External sovereignty is threatened by foreign invasion and interference, while internal sovereignty is threatened by usurpation and **secession**.

"To say that the State is sovereign is to say that the State has supreme or final authority in a community, that its rules override the rule of any other association." **Raphael,** *Problems of Political Philosophy*

space

METAPHYSICS, PHILOSOPHY OF SCIENCE The nature of space, along with the nature of **time**, is a fundamental question in philosophy. Space is viewed as a continuant that gives form to the possible **relations** in which things and **events** stand in the world. It is constituted by all spatially related **places**. In ancient Greece, the **Eleatics** denied the possibility of empty space. They also denied that space is material, for otherwise space itself would have to be in another kind of space. **Atomists** argued that a **void** exists which separates **atoms**. **Zeno's paradoxes** show the puzzling nature of space and time, especially with regard to the problem of infinity. **Kant**, echoing Zeno, claimed that **antinomies** result if we think of space and time as objectively real, and argued that space and time are forms of intuition by which **sensibility** organizes sensibly given materials into **experience**. Space is not a **concept**, because unlike the different instantiations of concepts, all spaces are parts of one space.

A major dispute about space concerns whether it is substantial or relational. **Plato** defined space as a receptacle that does not have any characteristic itself. **Aristotle** did not distinguish space from place, which he defined as the adjacent boundary of a containing body. Both seem to take space as an **objective** container. A standard version of the account of space as substantial is offered by **Descartes**, who claimed that the **essence** of **matter** is **extension** and thus identified space with matter. In his account of absolute space, **Newton** insisted that space would remain similar and immovable even if it lacked relations to anything else. Radically opposed to Newton's account is **Leibniz**'s relational view of space. Leibniz argued that, rather than being a substance, space is a system of relations in which indivisible **monads** stand next to one another. The power and attraction of the positions in the dispute are captured in the famous Leibniz–Clarke correspondence, in which Samuel **Clarke** defended Newton. The dispute still goes on today, especially in light of the concept of **space-time** in **general theory of relativity** and **quantum** mechanics.

"A space, in the literal sense of the term, is that in which material objects are situated, and move or remain still. They change their place by moving through space." **Swinburne,** *Space and Time*

space, absolute

METAPHYSICS, PHILOSOPHY OF SCIENCE **Newton** maintained that space has its own **nature**, without dependence on anything else. The three-dimensionality of space is an intrinsic, **essential property** of space. Mathematicians can describe spaces having other dimensions, but these are not our space. If one part of space is different from another part, this is not because of differences in space itself, but because of the things that occupy space. Absolute space is also separate from **time**. In contrast to absolute space, relative space depends for its character upon the nature of the things it relates. It would vanish were there no spatially related **entities**, and in principle it is subject to change.

> "Absolute space, in its own nature, without relation to anything external, remains always similar and immovable." **Newton,** *Mathematical Principles of Natural Philosophy*

space-time

METAPHYSICS, PHILOSOPHY OF SCIENCE The theory of **relativity** uses a unified notion of space-time to replace the separate notion of **space** and **time**. Within its framework, space and time can be traded, like mass and energy. As a result, it has become common practice in physics to view the world as a manifold of four dimensions: length, width, height, and interval. Space-time can also be considered a four-dimensional **tenseless** space, in contrast to our ordinary conception of space as something which endures through time. Many issues, such as infinity, **continuity**, and their absolute or relational nature, are common to space and time and can be dealt with in a unified theory. On the other hand, it is not clear in what contexts space-time replaces space and time in other aspects of our thought. Some philosophers argue that we could not have spatio-temporal **experience** of the world in terms of space-time rather than in terms of space and time. Others reply that our experience is in terms of space-time or of any theory that proves to be true.

> "We must not forget that space-time is a space in the mathematical sense of the word." **J. Smart (ed.),** *Problems of Space and Time*

species, see genus

species chauvinism, another term for speciesism

speciesism

ETHICS A term invented by the English writer Richard Ryder in *Victims of Science* (1975), but popularized by the Australian philosopher, Peter **Singer**. It refers to the discrimination which human beings exercise over non-human animals. Racism is a preju-

dice on the basis of race. Sexism is a prejudice on the basis of sex. Speciesism, then, is a prejudice on the basis of species. Human beings have been using animals as means, and exploiting them ruthlessly on the assumption that human beings as **rational** beings are morally more valuable than animals. However, many members of the human species such as children and mentally retarded persons, although not rational, are still entitled to moral consideration, simply because of their membership of the human species. Singer contends that if racism and sexism are wrong, speciesism must also be wrong. The **animal liberation** movement that he helped to initiate has as its main goal the removal of speciesism. Speciesism is called by other authors, species chauvinism or human chauvinism.

> "Speciesism – the word is not an attractive one, but I can think of no better term – is a prejudice or attitude of bias in favour of the interests of members of one's own species and against those of members of other species." **P. Singer,** *Animal Liberation*

specious present

EPISTEMOLOGY, METAPHYSICS Our awareness of now or the present as a momentary time interval between **past** and future. E. R. Clay believed that this experience of a present is not real and is actually a period of time ending at the present. The concrete individual time that we perceive is not strictly instantaneous and is never co-present with our **consciousness**. It is rather a recent past instead of a real present. Clay called what we perceive the specious present. **James** borrowed this term and used it extensively to express his view that consciousness of time is indeed a stream or a continuant. Earlier **events** are temporally extended and are still present in our experience of later events. The specious present includes the recent past and even a bit of future. Past, present, and future are nothing but our conceptual ascription. The term specious present is also employed by **Russell** and **Broad**, but is criticized by H. J. Paton.

> "The time-series, then, of which any part is perceived by me, is a time-series in which the future and the past are separated by a present which is a specious present." **McTaggart,** *The Nature of Existence*

speculative philosophy

METAPHYSICS [from Latin *speculatio*, contemplation, in turn derived from *specere*, to see, to look; equivalent to Greek *theoria*, contemplation, derived from the verb to see] Etymologically, what is speculative is **theoretical**, in contrast to the **practical** and empirical. **Kant** connected speculative philosophy with metaphysics and believed that it resulted from mistakenly applying **concepts** to **things-in-themselves** rather than to empirical **objects**. For Kant, speculative philosophy has a pejorative sense through being concerned with the **transcendent** and with reality as a whole, in spite of lacking the proper support of sense-**experience**. **Hegel** described speculative philosophy in this sense as **dogmatism**, but called his own system speculative in another sense because it dealt with conceptual process and not because it dealt with the supersensible. It is a **dialectical** process in which the opposition between **objectivity** and **subjectivity** is **sublated**, and in which all branches of human **knowledge** are systematically unified to reveal the true meaning of reality and of humankind. In general, speculative philosophy employs the results of various sciences and religious and ethical experiences to derive general conclusions regarding the nature of the universe and our position in it. Although its **holism** and sense of system have attractions, most **analytic philosophers** regard speculative philosophy as purely conjectural and as being close to poetry and **mysticism**.

"Speculative philosophy is the endeavour to frame a coherent, logical, necessary system of general ideas in terms of which every element of our experience can be interpreted." **Whitehead, *Process and Reality***

speculative philosophy of history, see philosophy of history

speech act

PHILOSOPHY OF LANGUAGE A central concept of the use theory of **meaning** elaborated by **Austin** in *How to Do Things with Words*. In an account of the meaning of an **expression**, one main factor is what the expression is used to do, and this is the speech act aspect of language use. A speech act involves actually saying in contrast to merely thinking, and in this sense to say something is to do something, to perform a linguistic act. A speech act is hence also

called a linguistic act. Austin divided speech acts into three kinds. First, a **locutionary act** is an act of saying something, which is further divided into three kinds: the phonetic act, which is merely the act of uttering certain noises, the phatic act, which makes a grammatical sentence, and the rhetic act, which utters something with a certain **sense** and with a certain **reference**. Secondly, an **illocutionary act** is an act performed in saying something, for example promising, questioning, suggesting, or ordering. Thirdly, a perlocutionary act is an act performed by saying something that will produce certain consequential effects upon the feelings, thoughts, or actions of the audience. Austin claimed that by clearly distinguishing these acts we are able to get rid of many traditional philosophical problems. **Searle** has examined and developed this doctrine on the hypothesis that speaking a language is engaging in a rule-governed form of behavior. Most studies of speech acts focus on illocutionary acts. Speech act theory characterizes the nature of communicative intentions. It opposes accounts of meaning based exclusively on **semantics** and can be seen to be a branch of **pragmatics**.

"The form that this hypothesis will take is that speaking a language is performing speech acts, acts such as making statements, giving commands, asking questions, making promises, and so on." **Searle, *Speech Acts***

speech act fallacy

PHILOSOPHY OF LANGUAGE An **analysis** that reduces the basic **meaning** of a **statement** to what a speaker does in using it. For instance, it uses the **speech act** of prescribing or commending to explain moral terms, the speech act of re-asserting to explain the meaning of the word "true," and the speech act of expressing belief or giving guidance or partial assurance to explain the meaning of "probable." According to John **Searle**, this is a **fallacy** because it ignores the **locutionary** speech act that must precede the **illocutionary act**. Many words have a literal occurrence in some sentences, and understanding their meaning need not require us to consider the performance of speech acts beyond locutionary acts. This fallacy, which is similar to what Peter **Geach** calls **ascriptivism**, is linked by some philosophers to the **use theory of meaning**.

"The general nature of the speech act fallacy can be stated as follows, using 'good' as our example. Calling something good is characteristically praising or commending or recommending it, etc. But it is a fallacy to infer from this that the meaning of good is explained by saying it is used to perform the act of commendation." **Searle, *Speech Acts***

Spencer, Herbert (1820–1903)

English philosopher, born at Derby, a leading social Darwinist. Spencer created a system of synthetic philosophy by applying the principle of evolution to explain not only organisms, but also every phenomenon and entity, including feeling, society, ethical principle, and education. Influenced by Darwin's *The Origin of Species*, he developed a social philosophy based on "the survival of the fittest." Spencer denied that the process of evolution has a final goal and denied that the principle of evolution can be applied to an unknowable God or to ultimate reality. Spencer's major works include *First Principles* (1862), *Principles of Sociology*, 3 vols. (1876–96), and *Principles of Ethics* (1879–93).

sphere of existence, an alternative expression for stage of existence

Spinoza, Benedict (Baruch) (1632–77)

Dutch Jewish philosopher, born in Amsterdam. In *Ethics* (1677), Spinoza used a Euclidean geometric method to present one of the great rationalist metaphysical systems of the seventeenth century. His other major books include *Treatise on the Improvement of the Intellect* and *Tractatus Theologico-Politicus* (1670). He developed a system of substance, attributes, and modes and argued that there could be only one substance: God or Nature (*Deus sive Natura*). He rejected Descartes's mind–body dualism and replaced it with a mind–body parallelism grounded in underlying substance. He distinguished three levels in the hierarchy of knowledge (opinion or imagination, adequate ideas, and intuitive knowledge) and held that intuitive knowledge is the highest grade. He believed that the goal of philosophy is to achieve freedom by knowing causes and by controlling the passions. His conceptions of liberty and tolerance were important features of his political philosophy. In 1656, Spinoza was excommunicated by the Jewish Community in Amsterdam for heresy. In order to preserve his intellectual freedom and independence, he supported himself by lens grinding, an occupation that led to consumption and his premature death.

spirit, see soul

spirit of seriousness

MODERN EUROPEAN PHILOSOPHY **Sartre**'s term for the belief that there is something intrinsically **good** in itself, which is inherent in the world as **absolute value** and is discoverable by men. Such a belief leads to **bad faith**. According to Sartre, people fall into the spirit of seriousness because they forget that values are **contingent** and are chosen and assigned by our own **subjectivity**.

"The spirit of seriousness has two characteristics: it considers values as transcendent givens independent of human subjectivity, and it transfers the quality of 'desirable' from the ontological structure of things to their simple material constitution." **Sartre, *Being and Nothingness***

spiritualism

METAPHYSICS Spiritualism claims that spirit or **soul**, rather than **matter**, is the ultimate **substance** of the world. Body has only a **phenomenal** existence and, as an expression of the reality of spirit, has spirit or **mind** as its sole ground. In this sense, spiritualism is a synonym for **idealism** and is opposed to **materialism**. Various versions of spiritualism differ regarding how they characterize the fundamental role of spirit in the world.

"Spiritualism says that mind not only witnesses and records things, but also runs and operates them." **W. James, *Pragmatism and Selections from the Meaning of Truth***

spontaneity

EPISTEMOLOGY, METAPHYSICS In **Kant**'s philosophy, the **theoretical** aspect of **freedom**, corresponding to **autonomy**, which is the **practical** aspect of freedom. Spontaneity is **reason's** active capacity, in contrast to passive receptivity. It is the absence of external **determination** and legislates **rules** for itself to **synthesize appearances**. **Pure** forms of **intuition** and pure concepts of **understanding** are all produced by the spontaneity of human reason. Kant held that spontaneity and receptivity must be combined for **knowledge** to be possible. The development of Kant's idea of spontaneity into a conception of an absolute spontaneous subject by **Fichte** and **Schelling** was criticized by Hegel.

> "Our knowledge springs from two fundamental sources of the mind; the first is the capacity of receiving representations (receptivity of impressions), the second is the power of knowing an object through these representations (spontaneity (in the production) of concepts)." **Kant, *Critique of Pure Reason***

spontaneity/indifference

METAPHYSICS, PHILOSOPHY OF ACTION, ETHICS A **Scholastic** dichotomy involving two kinds of **liberty** that was also employed by **Locke** and **Hume** in discussing the problem of **free will**. Liberty of spontaneity is doing what one wants or chooses to do while free from the constraints and violence of others. Liberty of indifference is having the power to do A and the **power** not to do A, given that the **necessary conditions** of each are satisfied. It is generally believed that the **contradictory** of spontaneity is compulsion, while the contradictory of indifference is being **determined**. Spontaneity is therefore compatible with determinism and, according to some philosophers, is not real **freedom**. Indifference, on the other hand, can choose between alternative courses of **action** and is seen by critics of spontaneity as the basis for moral **responsibility**. Other philosophers, however, reject liberty of indifference and argue for the compatibility of the liberty of spontaneity with freedom and responsibility.

> "There are traditional names for these two contrasting concepts of freedom: freedom defined in terms of wanting is liberty of spontaneity; liberty defined in terms of power is liberty of indifference." **Kenny, *Will, Freedom and Power***

square of opposition

LOGIC In traditional logic there are four basic **propositions**: A (universal affirmative, "All X are Y"), E (universal negative, "All X are not Y"), I (particular affirmative, "Some X are Y"), and O (particular negative, "Some X are not Y"). There are various logical relationships among these propositions. (1) A and E

are **contraries**: they can not both be true, but can both be false. (2) I and O are **subcontraries**: they can not both be false, but can both be true. (3) A and O are **contradictories**, and so are E and I: of each pair, if one is true, the other must be false. (4) A implies I: if A is true, I must be true. Also, E implies O. The relationship of **implication** is also called **subalternation**. All these logical relationships can be presented in terms of the following diagram which is called the "square of opposition":

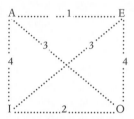

1. contraries
2. subcontraries
3. contradiction
4. implication

> "The formal relations of propositions with identical terms of four forms, A, E, I, O, were represented by traditional logicians by a diagram called the square of opposition." **D. Mitchell, *An Introduction to Logic***

stage of existence

PHILOSOPHY OF RELIGION, ETHICS, MODERN EUROPEAN PHILOSOPHY Also called sphere of existence. A stage is generally a phase of development or a moment in an evolutionary process. But for **Kierkegaard**, a stage is a view about the possibility of life or of a way of life. He mainly distinguishes three stages: the **aesthetic** stage, in which one is self-centered and considers life to be a matter of sensuous **pleasure**; the ethical stage, in which one becomes conscious of being a part of a **community**; and the religious stage, in which one recognizes that one's life has a relation to the **Absolute**. The religious stage is in turn divided into **Religiousness A** and **Religiousness B**. Each stage is an enclosed world, an independent sphere of life. An aesthetic individual concentrates on enjoying life. An individual in the ethical stage takes a sense of **responsibility** and **duty** as the **meaning** of life. In Religiousness A, an individual assumes an essential relationship to the eternal, and in Religiousness B, the individual becomes eternal. Kierkegaard believed that in moving from the aesthetic stage to the ethical stage and from the ethical stage to the religious stage, there is an ascent. Each stage in turn aims at something higher in humanity. However, he did not think that one stage will inevitably develop into another stage, although it is possible for one to leap from one to another. The relationship between the aesthetic and ethical stages is discussed in *Either/Or*, while the relationship between the ethical and religious stages is most clearly explicated in *Fear and Trembling*.

"The different existence-stages rank according to their relation to the cosmic in proportion to their having the cosmic inside or outside themselves, yet not in the sense that the cosmic should be the highest." **Kierkegaard,** *Concluding Unscientific Postscript to Philosophical Fragments*

Stalnaker, Robert Culp (1940–)

American philosopher of logic, language, and mind, born in Princeton, New Jersey, Professor of Philosophy at Cornell University and Massachusetts Institute of Technology. Stalnaker has used a possible-world semantics to develop an influential theory of counterfactual conditionals. He has also worked on the semantics and pragmatics of natural languages, the ontology of possible worlds, belief, and mental content. His major works include *Inquiry* (1984).

standing sentence, see occasion sentence

state

POLITICAL PHILOSOPHY, PHILOSOPHY OF LAW A set of organized institutions operating in a territory with a substantial population composed of its citizens or subjects. It has a legal system to regulate the activities of society and to reconcile conflicting claims of **individuals** and groups belonging to it. The legal system is backed by a monopoly of legitimate coercion. In its positive functions, a state promotes welfare and **justice** for its citizens. In its negative functions, a state defends the integrity of its territory from foreign invasion, keeps order, and maintains the security of its citizens. A state recognizes the equal **sovereignty** of other states and enters inter-state relations subject to international law. There are various theories about the origin and nature of the state. **Anarchism** denies the need for the coercive power of the state and argues for the limitation of the state's functions. **Social contract**

theorists justify the state in terms of the benefits of security and **freedom** offered by **civil society**, in contrast to the impotence and misery of an actual or hypothetical **state of nature**. **Communitarians** claim that individuals are molded by the state. **Individualists** and **holists** disagree whether the existence, nature, and actions of the state can be reduced to those of its individual members.

"We should say that a state is a group of persons who have supreme authority within a given territory or over a certain population." **Wolff,** *In Defense of Anarchism*

state of affairs

METAPHYSICS, PHILOSOPHY OF LANGUAGE [German *Sachverhalt*] **Wittgenstein**'s term for the combination of **objects** or things in a determinate way. Its structure is determined by the possible ways in which the objects can be combined. States of affairs are independent of one another, and **facts** comprise their existence or non-existence. The totality of states of affairs constitutes the world. States of affairs are on the side of the world rather than on the side of language. They are the fundamental picturable items corresponding to **elementary propositions** in language.

"In a state of affairs objects fit into one another like the links of a chain." **Wittgenstein,** *Tractatus*

state of nature

POLITICAL PHILOSOPHY In **social contract** theory, the actual or hypothetical natural human condition prior to entry into organized **civil society**. The concept has been a powerful analytical tool in modern political philosophy in justifying political **authority** and in explaining human **rights**. Different philosophers make different use of the state of nature. For **Hobbes**, it is a brutal state of continual of war of all against all. There is neither peace nor any reasonable way of solving conflicts. To escape, human beings contract with an all-powerful **sovereign** to give up their **natural right** to whatever they want in return for stability and protection. For **Locke**, the state of nature is governed by the law of nature and is more inconvenient than brutal. It lacks established law and has neither impartial judges nor the use of legitimate force in enforcing the law. Our rational desire to seek better protection and impartial enforcement of natural rights leads human beings to form a political or civil society through a unanimous contract and to entrust a government with legislative, executive, and judicial powers. **Rousseau** claimed that human beings in the state of nature are noble savages, whose nature is perfected, and possibly corrupted, by the formation of civic society. For **Hegel**, society constitutes the **nature** of human beings rather than human beings constituting the nature of society.

> "The state of nature has a law of nature to govern it, which obliges everyone. And reason, which is the law, teaches all mankind who will but consult it, that being all equal and independent, no one ought to harm another in his life, health, liberty, or permission." **Locke, *Two Treatises on Government***

statement/proposition

LOGIC, PHILOSOPHY OF LANGUAGE Statements are usually defined as **sentences** that state (that is, **assert** or deny) something. "Statement" and "proposition" are widely treated as synonyms, with both distinguished from "sentence." But **logical positivists** draw a distinction between statements and propositions. Suppose that a proposition must be both meaningful and the bearer of **truth** and falsity, and that the **verification principle** can only used to test propositions (not sentences which are neither true nor false). There would be no point in employing the principle to distinguish meaningful from meaningless propositions because propositions are by definition verifiable and meaningful. To cope with this, logical positivists claim that although all indicative sentences are statements, not all of them propositions. Unlike propositions, indicative sentences might be meaningful or not meaningful. All indicative sentences are statements, but only those that are meaningful according to the verificationist theory of meaning are proposition. Thus, propositions become a sub-class of statements, namely, those statements that are meaningful. The principle of verification is a **criterion** for determining whether an indicative sentence expresses a propositional or a non-propositional statement.

> "To say that indicative sentences mean propositions is indeed legitimate, just as it is legitimate to say that they express statements." **Ayer, *Language, Truth and Logic***

Stevenson, C(harles) L(eslie) (1908–79)

American moral philosopher, taught at Michigan and Bennington College. In *Ethics and Language* (1944), Stevenson contributed to analytic moral philosophy by presenting a systematic account of ethical **emotivism**. He distinguished between the descriptive meaning and emotive meaning of expressions and argued that the meaning of ethical terms is primarily emotive. An ethical statement expresses one's emotion or attitude, and to say that something is good is to express approval of it. He held that ethical argument is often a matter of "persuasive definition" between those who agree on ethical meaning but disagree on descriptive meaning.

stimulus meaning

PHILOSOPHY OF LANGUAGE For **Quine**, the stimulus meaning of a **sentence** is given when we describe the kind of stimulus that would prompt assent to it. If all speakers assent to a sentence in any circumstance in which it arises, that sentence is stimulus **analytic**; if two sentences are assented to in just the same circumstances, they are stimulus **synonymous**. Generally, the stimuli that prompt people's assent to an **occasion sentence** are the same, but they vary from person to person in the case of **standing sentences**. This is one major argument by which Quine claims that the facts about stimulus meaning do not determine a unique correct translation manual, and hence that translation is indeterminate.

> "The stimulus meaning of a sentence for a subject sums up his disposition to assent to or dissent from the sentence in response to present stimulation." **Quine, *Word and Object***

stipulative definition

PHILOSOPHY OF LANGUAGE A definition which gives a particular **meaning** to a new expression, or a new meaning to an established term. It is provided to indicate how one intends to use the term in order to improve clarity and precision of communication or discussion. It is generally expressed in something like the following form: "By the term X what I mean here is . . ." or "I shall use this word to mean so-and-so." It does not imply that the word has been used by anyone else to mean this, in contrast to lexical definition, which reports what people in general mean by the word. Sometimes it is necessary for scholars and scientists to characterize the meanings of words to suit to the task at hand.

> "By 'stipulative definition' I mean establishing or announcing or choosing one's own meaning for a word." **Robinson, *Definition***

Stirner, Max (1806–56)

German egoist philosopher. Stirner was a left Hegelian who argued for an extreme individualism. He held that reality is limited to the individual ego and that value depends on serving the interests of the ego. He rejected the authority of institutionally entrenched ideas that could not be controlled by the individual. His main work is *The Ego and Its Own* (1845).

strategic action

PHILOSOPHY OF ACTION, PHILOSOPHY OF SOCIAL SCIENCE For **Habermas**, a model of **action**, in contrast to **communicative action**, in which the participants direct their actions through egocentric calculation of **utility**. Each **agent** seeks appropriate **means** to achieve an **end** with a favorable outcome for himself. Strategic action is not reciprocal and is not performed on the basis of mutual **understanding**. In communicative action, participants harmonize their respective plans on the basis of having a common understanding of the situation, and make claims that all concerned can accept as valid. The distinction between strategic action and communicative action provides the framework by reference to which Habermas seeks to explain a wide range of social phenomena.

> "*Strategic action* is distinguished from *communicative actions* under common conditions by the characteristic that deciding between possible alternative choices can in principle be made monologically – that means, *ad hoc* without reaching agreement, and indeed must be made so, because the rules of preference and the maxims binding on each individual partner have been brought into prior harmony." **Habermas, *Theory and Practice***

Strauss, Leo (1899–1973)

American political philosopher, born in Germany, Professor at the University of Chicago. Strauss argued for the importance of normative political theory not in general terms, but in order to overcome the mediocrity of democratic mass culture and to restore anti-egalitarian moral concerns to politics. As an intellectual historian, he has reinterpreted important works by looking for textual clues to doctrines that had to be hidden by their authors because of censorship and other forms of persecution. His main works include *Natural Right and History* (1953) and *Persecution and the Art of Writing* (1952).

straw man fallacy

LOGIC An argument against a position that substitutes another view for the opponent's actual stance and gives the impression that the actual position has been refuted. The position that is misleadingly ascribed generally sounds more unlikely than the actual position and is hence more easily exposed to criticism. Because the alleged position is not what the opponent holds and is weaker than the actual position, it is like a straw man that can be far more easily overcome than a real man.

> "The best and purest cases of the straw man fallacy . . . go like this. I argue for a certain position, . . . you then try to refute me, not by arguing against my conclusion, but against an exaggeration." **T. Richards, *The Language of Reasons***

Strawson, Sir Peter Frederick (1919–2006)

British philosopher of logic, language, and metaphysics, born in London, Professor of Metaphysical Philosophy, University of Oxford. Strawson has made major contributions to philosophical logic, philosophy of language, metaphysics, and the history of philosophy. His early work on truth and on Russell's theory of descriptions preceded a general account of the relations between formal logic and ordinary language. He is best known for introducing descriptive metaphysics into analytic philosophy, arguing that material objects are basic particulars, for the priority of persons as entities to which we can ascribe both conscious states and physical properties and for the importance of relating the subject-predicate distinction in logic to the particular-universal distinction in metaphysics. His work on Kant and its exposition of Kant's transcendental arguments led to the revival of Kantian projects in contemporary British and American philosophy, and his work on skepticism and naturalism has contributed to renewed interest in non-reductionist naturalism. His major works include *Introduction to Logical Theory* (1952), *Individuals* (1959), *The Bounds of Sense* (1966), *Logico-Linguistic Papers* (1971), *Freedom and Resentment* (1974), *Subject and Predicate in Logic and Grammar* (1974), *Skepticism and Naturalism: Some Varieties* (1985), and *Analysis and Metaphysics* (1992).

stream of consciousness

PHILOSOPHY OF MIND A metaphor introduced by William **James** to describe the character of **consciousness**. Consciousness is not made out of units, but is a stream-like **process**. Past, present, and future are our conceptual ascription. Because any awareness of "present" is seen as an awareness of a recent past, the stream of consciousness is associated with the notion of a **specious present**.

> "Consciousness . . . does not appear to itself chopped up in bits . . . a 'river' or 'stream' are the metaphors by which it is most naturally described."
> **W. James,** *Principles of Psychology*

strict conditional, see strict implication

strict identity

LOGIC **Butler** initiated a distinction between two meanings of **identity**, that is, identity in the strict sense, and identity in a loose and popular sense. That A is strictly identical with B means that whatever can be said of one can be said of the other. That is, A and B are identical in all **possible worlds**. Identity or sameness in our daily conversation only requires that two things are identical in certain parts or aspects. A man yesterday is identical with this man today. But this is not a strict identity, for the man today has some characteristics that were not possessed by the same **person** yesterday. For instance, yesterday the person was sick, while today he is well; yesterday he was single, but today he is married.

> "Strict identity is governed by a principle that is called the Indiscernibility of Identicals. This says that if a is strictly identical with b, then a and b have exactly the same properties." **D. Armstrong,** *Universals*

strict implication

LOGIC In order to avoid the paradoxes of **material implication**, C. I. **Lewis** introduced the notion of strict implication. One **proposition** implies another

(If P then Q) in the strict sense of the word if and only if it is impossible that P should be true and Q false, that is, if the statement "P is true and Q is false" is inconsistent. Lewis claimed that strict implication was the relation that justified inference from the premises to a conclusion in a deductive argument. Hence it can avoid the paradoxes of material implication and does justice to our ordinary notion of **implication**. He therefore developed a **propositional calculus** on the basis of strict implication in order to replace **Russell**'s propositional calculus, which was established on the basis of material implication. However, his definition of strict implication also implies a paradox: an impossible proposition implies every proposition; and a necessary proposition is implied by every proposition. Hence, just as the term **material conditional** was proposed to replace the term material implication, it has been suggested that strict conditional should replace strict implication.

> "If p implies q, then it is not the case that p is true and q false . . . this is the main distinction between strict implication and material implication." **Lewis and Langford,** *Symbolic Logic*

strife and love

ANCIENT GREEK PHILOSOPHY, METAPHYSICS [Greek *neikos*, strife; *philia*, love or friendship] Two **principles** of movement in the cosmology of the Greek philosopher **Empedocles**. By analogy with human emotions, Strife is the power to dissolve or separate the four basic elements: fire, air, water, and earth, and Love is the power to form and maintain their union. Both principles are eternal. They have no perceptible qualities of their own, but are detectable by their effects. They alternately dominate the cosmos as a whole, making the cosmic system a never-ending cycle. When Love is in control, all elements are fused uniformly, but when Strife rules, the elements are at war with each other. These two principles were meant not only to account for process and **change** in the natural world, but also to work in social relationships.

> "These things never cease from continual shifting, at one time all coming together, through Love, at another each borne apart from the others through Strife." **Simplicius,** *Physics*

structural ambiguity

PHILOSOPHY OF LANGUAGE Also called syntactical ambiguity. The **ambiguity** arises from the grammatical structure of a language, that is, from the different ways in which words in a sentence of that language can be related meaningfully to each other. This sort of ambiguity is ascribed to a **sentence** or **statement**, and is in contrast to semantic or **lexical ambiguity**, which is ascribed to a word and arises from the multiplicity of **senses** associated with a single word. The grammatical relations that most often produce structural or syntactical ambiguity include misplaced modifiers, loosely applied adverbs, elliptical constructions, and omitted punctuation. For instance, the statement that "The fat businessman's son is nice" is structurally ambiguous, for the adjective "fat" can be taken either to modify "businessman" or "the businessman's son."

"A denoting expression is called structurally ambiguous if there is a model with respect to which it is ambiguous." **Montague, *Formal Philosophy***

structural linguistics

PHILOSOPHY OF LANGUAGE, PHILOSOPHY OF SOCIAL SCIENCE The school of modern linguistics which holds that language is a system or structure of elements that happen to occur in a single speech community at a particular time. Each language is a unique system without any presumption about other languages. The job of linguists is to describe the structure of a given language, namely, to analyze the relations between elements that compose the structure, such as phonemes, morphemes, and phrases. The founder of structural linguistics was Ferdinard de **Saussure**, who had great influence through his posthumously published *Cours de Linguistique Generale*, although he used the word "system" rather than "structure." In criticizing the diachronic perspective of nineteenth-century comparative grammar, Saussure claimed that language has a systematic aspect. It embodies laws of equilibrium that operate on its elements and yield a synchronic system. Structural linguistics separates linguistics from other disciplines and renders it a special science. Other major expositors of structural linguistics include Bloomfield (*Language*, 1931) and Zellig Harris (*Methods in Structural Linguistics*, 1952). Through criticism of structural linguistics,

Chomsky developed his transformational-generative linguistics. Chomsky believes that the wholeness of linguistic structures is based on the laws of transformation. Hence, linguistics should study the creative aspect of language, together with its synchronic aspect.

"It is extremely interesting that, despite the very strong arguments for keeping linguistic structuralism within synchronic confines, present-day linguistic structuralism, as represented by the work of Zellig S. Harris, and above all, his pupil Noam Chomsky, has, as regards syntax, a clearly 'generative' orientation." **Piaget, *Structuralism***

structural property

METAPHYSICS A **property** of a thing that results from the structure of the thing or a system. If a **relation** R is symmetric, then every relation having the same structure as R will also be symmetric. This property of being symmetric is a structural property because it relies only on the structure of the relation and is not affected by a change in the items within the structure. The structure itself is a structural property.

"In general we say a property of n-place relation is a (n-place) structural property provided it depends simply on the structure, i.e. provided it is preserved under isomorphism." **Carnap, *Introduction to Symbolic Logic and Its Applications***

structural violence

POLITICAL PHILOSOPHY A term for social and institutional injustice, such as apartheid, rather than conflict and injury caused by force. Structural violence is exemplified by unfair laws or entrenched customs that deny certain groups in the **community** fair access to the available social, economic, political, or cultural opportunities. Structural violence does not necessarily involve physical force. It is called violence, which ordinarily means the use of physical force, to justify rebellion against unjust institutions by appeal to the right to self-defense. Structural violence and institutional violence are sometimes used interchangeably, but the latter is more properly restricted to legally sanctioned violence. Institutional violence has often been used to maintain structural violence.

"Structural violence is a name for what would more correctly be called social injustice." Teichman, *Pacifism and the Just War*

intellectual obligations of honesty, views progress in terms of gradual approximation." **Piaget,** *Structuralism*

structuralism

PHILOSOPHY OF SOCIAL SCIENCE, MODERN EUROPEAN PHILOSOPHY The basic claim of structuralism is that all social phenomena, no matter how diverse their superficial appearance, are internally connected and organized according to some unconscious patterns. These internal **relations** and patterns constitute structures, and uncovering these structures is the object of human studies. Generally, a structure is characteristically whole, transformational, and self-regulatory. Structuralism is a methodology that emphasizes structure rather than **substance** and relations rather than things. It holds that things exist only as elements of a signifying system. Structural methodology originated in **Saussure**'s structural linguistics, which describes language as a rule-governed social system of **signs**. In the 1960s, the French anthropologist Claude **Lévi-Strauss** extended this methodology not only to anthropology (anthropological structuralism) but, indeed, to all signifying systems. Lévi-Strauss is generally regarded to be the founder of modern structuralism. Through his work, structuralism became a major intellectual trend in Western Europe, especially France, and greatly influenced the study of the human sciences. **Foucault** was influenced by this methodology in his radical reconstruction of intellectual history. **Lacan** relied on both Saussure and **Freud** in his development of **psychoanalysis** (psycho-structuralism). **Althusser** applied the methodology to the analysis of Marxism (structural Marxism). The structuralist method is also applied to mathematics. In contrast to the compartmentalization characteristic of other approaches to mathematics, structuralism claims to recover unity through isomorphisms in different branches of mathematics. Structuralism became a major methodological movement, although its doctrines and interpretations of its crucial term "structure" varied in different fields. In many areas, structuralism has been superseded by **post-structuralism**.

"Structuralism is essentially a method, with all this term implies – it is technical, involves certain

structured violence

POLITICAL PHILOSOPHY, ETHICS, PHILOSOPHY OF LAW Bernard **Williams** drew a distinction between structured violence and unstructured violence among official violent acts in his paper, "Politics and Moral Character." Only the **state** can be justified in performing acts of structured violence, such as judicial execution, regular military operations, and the application of legal force by the police. No private citizen is lawfully allowed to do them, and it would not even make sense to say that a private person performed some of them. Acts of unstructured violence may be performed by a political leader, but in accordance with law and for the sake of defending the national interest. Acts of this sort especially appear in international relations, which generally are less structured than relationships within a society. Unstructured violence is the topic of public morality.

"It may be said that structured violence constitutes acts which none but the state could even logically perform." **Williams, in Hampshire (ed.),** *Public and Private Morality*

style

AESTHETICS The manner in which a thing is made or done. Style is generally ascribed only to artifacts rather than to nature. The style of a work of art is a complex consisting of ways of creating, modifying, selecting, and interpreting the material. Style manifests the peculiarity and personality of an artist, and directs the audience to the salient features of the work they are appreciating. The same **content** can be presented with different styles, and different artists are identified by their different styles. Styles can characterize works of a period, **tradition**, or school as well as those of an individual artist. Some philosophers are puzzled why in some cases critics can articulate the complex character of a style only in retrospect.

"A style is a way of doing things; but what we have in nature is just the way things happen. The arts are means of expression, and style in art plays the part in expression that is played in communication by language." **Sparshott,** *The Structure of Aesthetics*

"Two propositions are said to be subcontraries if they cannot both be false, although they might both be true." **Copi,** *Introduction to Logic*

Suárez, Francisco (1548–1617)

Spanish scholastic philosopher and theologian, born in Granada. In *Disputationes Metaphysicae* (1597), Suárez provided a comprehensive and systematic discussion of all the major metaphysical problems of late scholasticism. The work greatly influenced modern metaphysics. In *De Legibus ac Deo Legislatore* (1612), he characterized law as an act of will and divided law into eternal law, divine law, natural law, and human law. This work influenced Grotius.

subaltern

LOGIC In traditional logic, a **universal proposition** implies a **particular proposition** of the same quality. Hence A (All S are P) implies I (Some S are P), and E (All S are not P) implies O (Some S are not P). Logicians call I the subaltern of A, and O the subaltern of E. Correspondingly, A is called the superaltern of I, and E the superaltern of O. The whole relationship between a universal proposition and its corresponding particular proposition (which has the same subject and **predicate** terms and the same quality as the universal) is subalternation and is represented in the **square of opposition**. A subaltern is also termed a subimplicit, while a superaltern is also termed a superimplicit. If the universal proposition is true, so is its corresponding particular proposition, but not vice versa.

"Subaltern . . . is a particular proposition which follows by an immediate inference from its corresponding universal to which it is said to be subaltern." **Peirce,** *Collected Papers,* **vol. II**

subcontraries

LOGIC If two **propositions** can not both be false but may both be true, they are subcontraries. Hence we may infer from the falsity of one that the other is true, but can not infer the truth-value of the other from the truth of one of them. In traditional logic, this logical relationship occurs between the particular affirmative proposition I (Some S are P) and the particular negative proposition O (Some S are not P).

subjective knowledge, see objective knowledge

subjective-objective distinction

EPISTEMOLOGY, METAPHYSICS, ETHICS, AESTHETICS The subject contributes what is subjective to such things as perceptual, moral, and aesthetic **judgment** and **experience**; the **objects** of such judgments and experience contribute what is objective. The subjective seems prone to variation among subjects, while the objective appears to provide a basis for **universal** agreement. There is disagreement over the contribution of the subject and the object to such judgments. The subjective view is also called the internal view, and is that in which the situation of the **agent** itself is involved. The objective view is also called the external view, and is that in which agent-related factors are abstracted or surpassed. The subjective is not always **private**, and the objective is not identical with what can be touched or sensed. Different notions of **objectivity** might be suitable in different domains. Historical judgments, for example, might be objective if the historian making them is unbiased and has not come to his conclusions as a result of having a favored relation to the relevant objects.

"The distinction between subjective and objective is relative. A general human point of view is more objective than the view from what you happen to be, but less objective than the view point of physical science." **T. Nagel,** *Mortal Questions*

subjectivism, see objectivism

subjectivity

METAPHYSICS, EPISTEMOLOGY A term correlated with **objectivity**. **Ontologically,** subjectivity is a mode of **existence,** in which a thing exists in virtue of being sensed or experienced by a subject. Epistemologically, a **knowledge** claim is subjective if determining its **truth-value** requires offering priority to someone having a **first-person** standpoint regarding the claim. Such priority, however, is unjustifiably claimed on behalf of personal opinions, biases, and arbitrary preferences that are not related to objective **facts**. If a **theory** or a **judgment** is subjective in this sense, it obstructs the achievement of **truth** and **validity** and should be rejected along with other forms of partiality, arbitrariness, and bias. On the other hand, the priority of the subjective need not be restricted to individual **experience**, and perhaps can be justified by the **perspectives** carried by a person as an historical and cultural being or as a result of special education and training, but it is difficult to determine how to treat the subjectivity of personal and social cultural **horizons**, social presuppositions, and moral, religious, and aesthetic attitudes. Too great an emphasis on these factors will lead to relativism or extreme subjectivism, but eliminating them is impossible, for they are basic conditions for inquiry. Admitting a place for subjectivity allows that there are alternative and reasonable views, perhaps by using subjective claims as a starting-point that can then be incorporated into a structure of objective knowledge. Executing such a plan has been a central concern for many philosophers.

"We often speak of judgements as being 'subjective' when we mean that their truth or falsity cannot be settled 'objectively', because the truth or falsity is not a simple matter of fact but depends on certain attitudes, feelings, and points of views of the makers and the hearers of the judgements." **Searle, *The Construction of Social Reality***

subject-of-a-life

ETHICS A term introduced by Tom Regan for **individuals** who are more than merely alive and **conscious**. Subjects-of-a-life are characterized by a set of features including having **beliefs**, **desires**, **memory**, **feelings**, **self-consciousness**, an emotional life, a sense of their own **future**, an ability to initiate **action** to pursue their goals, and an existence that is logically independent of being **useful** to anyone else's interests. Such an individual has inherent **value** independent of its **utility** for others. Because of this inherent value, a subject-of-a-life has **rights** to protect this value and not to be harmed. Other subjects have a **duty** to respect these rights. Regan then argues that all mature normal mammals fit the conditions for a subject-of-a-life; so they have inherent value and have rights. We have natural duties toward these animals, and should treat them equally and not interfere with their normal life course.

Being a subject-of-a-life is his **criterion** for inclusion of an individual in the moral community.

"Those who satisfy the subject-of-a-life criterion themselves have a distinctive kind of value – inherent value – and are not to be viewed or treated as mere receptacles." **Regan, *The Case for Animal Rights***

sublation

METAPHYSICS, EPISTEMOLOGY [from Latin *sublatus*, past participle of *tollere*, (1) to raise, to lift up or (2) to remove, to destroy. German *aufheben* has an additional meaning: (3) to keep, to preserve] In **Hegel**'s philosophy, the three senses of sublation are used together, rather than as three separate meanings. Sublation is the **negation** of the negation, a negation that has a positive consequence. What is sublated is not reduced to **nothing**, but has a result that originated in what has been negated. For Hegel, a thing is negated by its opposite, and both are removed from their immediacy but also preserved as items by a higher whole. This higher whole is an improvement over the original thing and its negation, and is an elevation of them, although the higher whole is itself open to further sublation. For Hegel both **concepts** and things can be sublated. The term is also translated as supersede, supersession, and **sublimation**.

"To sublate has a twofold meaning in the language: on the one hand it means to preserve, to maintain, and equally it also means to cause to cease, to put an end to . . . Thus, what is sublated is at the same time preserved; it has only lost its immediacy but is not on that account annihilated." **Hegel, *Science of Logic***

sublimation

PHILOSOPHY OF MIND [from Latin *sublimare*, to elevate] For **Freud**, a process of adapting the libidinal instinct, directing it away from its sexual aim and discharging it in areas other than sexuality. Through sublimation, the claims of the **ego** can be met without **repression** and libidinal energy can fuel social and creative efforts. On Freud's account, sublimation is thus contrasted with repression.

"The most important vicissitude which an instinct can undergo seems to be sublimation; here both object and aim are changed, so that what was

substance (Descartes)

665

originally a sexual instinct finds satisfaction in some achievement which is no longer sexual but has a higher social or ethical valuation." **Freud, *Standard Edition of the Complete Psychological Works of Sigmund Freud*, vol. 18**

sublime

AESTHETICS The feeling of awe, respect, majesty, astonishment and even horror aroused by vastly great and overwhelmingly powerful objects, such as the starry sky at night, huge mountains, towering cliffs, volcanoes, or raging seas. The concept can be traced to the Greek rhetorician Longinus. The Latin translation *De Sublimitate* (1674) of his book *Peri Hupsos* (*On the Impressiveness of Style*) made the sublime a central notion for eighteenth-century aesthetics. J. Addison, E. **Burke**, and **Kant** all distinguish sublimity from **beauty** as a basic species of artistic excellence. While the beautiful arouses **pleasure** and inspires love, the sublime commands respect and inspires the elevation of the **soul**. How, then, can we enjoy what causes us to feel horror and fear? Kant claimed that the sentiment of the sublime shows us that we are rational beings who transcend nature and legislate over sense. The sublime is the triumph of **reason** and is the bridge that enables us to turn from the vulgar and common to our real moral **freedom**. But others suggest that the feeling engendered by the vast spectacle of **nature** makes us feel that we are insignificant parts of nature. Postmodern aesthetics revives the distinction between the beautiful and the sublime and claims that while the beautiful is associated with the apprehension of **form** and rule, the sublime is associated with the formless and the resistance to rule.

"The sublime moves, the beautiful charms . . . The sublime must always be great; the beautiful can also be small. The sublime must be simple; the beautiful can be adorned and ornamented." **Kant, *Observations on the Feelings of the Beautiful and Sublime***

substance (Aristotle)

METAPHYSICS, ANCIENT GREEK PHILOSOPHY [The usual translation of the Greek *ousia*. Like *on* (being), *ousia* comes from *ousa*, the singular feminine normative participle of *einai*, to be] **Plato** used *on* and *ousia* synonymously. **Aristotle** classifies different kinds of

being, and substance is being in its first sense, namely, the ultimate **reality**. In the *Categories*, Aristotle defined substance as the ultimate subject that underlies everything else, and he also distinguished between primary substance (the sensible **individual**) and secondary substance (**species** and **genus**). In the *Metaphysics*, substance is the focal **meaning** of being. However, the **category** of substance is divided into **form**, **matter**, and the composite of matter and form. If substance is still subject, matter will be primary substance. But Aristotle held this to be impossible, with **separation** and *tode ti* (a this) presented as more important criteria to decide what is substance. According to these new criteria, form is substance in its primary sense, and the composite is substance in a derivative sense. Species and genus, which are secondary substances in the *Categories*, are rejected as substances. This has given rise to the problem explaining the relation between form and the **universal**.

Substance as a translation of *ousia* gained its currency historically because of the medieval philosopher **Boethius**' influential commentary on the *Categories* in which substance and subject coincide, but the word 'substance' has no etymological connection with *ousia*, and is not a precise translation of the notion of *ousia* in the *Metaphysics*. Alternative English translations of *ousia* include **essence**, **entity**, and **reality**.

"It follows, then, that 'substance' has two senses, (a) the ultimate substratum, which is no longer predicated of anything else, and (b) that which, being a 'this', is also separated – and of this nature is the shape or form of each thing." **Aristotle, *Metaphysics***

substance (Descartes)

METAPHYSICS **Descartes**'s **criterion** for substance is virtually the same as **Aristotle**'s subject criterion. He defined substance as that whose **existence** does not depend on other things and claimed that there is, strictly speaking, only one substance, namely **God**. However, although God is the only uncreated substance, created substances may be recognized because, although they need the concurrence of God in order to exist, they are independent of any other created things, such as **accidents** or **modes**. Instead, created substances are the bearers of **properties**, modes, and accidents.

A created substance for Descartes can be a thinking thing (*res cogitans*) or mind, or it can be an extended thing (*res extensa*) or body. All other modes are reducible to these two orders of existence. For thinking substance, thought is its principal attribute, because a thinking substance without thought is unintelligible. For corporeal substance, extension is its principal attribute, because a corporeal substance without extension is unintelligible. Thought and extension are the only two principal attributes that constitute, respectively, the **essence** of thinking and corporeal substances. Where there are two principal attributes there are two substances. This is to say, no existent substance can be a substance of more than one kind of attribute. This is the **dualism** of Descartes.

> "By substance, we can understand nothing else than a thing which so exists that it needs no other thing in order to exist." **Descartes, *Principles of Philosophy***

substance (Hegel)

METAPHYSICS Influenced by **Spinoza**, Hegel claimed that there is only one substance, that is, the **absolute**. In contrast to Spinoza, Hegel's absolute as substance is also subject. For **Descartes**, individual subjects are thinking substances, and for **Leibniz**, **monads** as substances have **self-consciousness**. Hegel developed these ideas and held that substance as subject is the movement of positing itself and of developing into its contrary, and is further unified by the movement to a higher unity. By repeating such a movement, substance generates and dissolves its **attributes**, that is, its **appearance**. Substance and attributes are mutually inclusive, for substance can be substance only through revealing itself in its attributes. The development of substance is the reflection into self of the subject, and the subject makes itself what it becomes.

> "Substance is accordingly the totality of the accidents, revealing itself in them as their absolute negativity (that is to say, as absolute power) and at the same time as the wealth of all content." **Hegel, *Logic***

substance (Leibniz)

METAPHYSICS Starting with the traditional **Aristotelian** claim that substance is the ultimate subject of **predicates**, Leibniz claimed that all the predicates of a given subject are contained within the **concept** of that subject, including every **past** and **future** state of that subject. He then asked what it is for a substance to have an **attribute**, that is, what is the foundation of and reason for all the predicates that can truly be asserted of that substance. In answering this question, he reverted in some sense to the pre-Cartesian view of **hylomorphism**, arguing that because a substance is a being that subsists in itself, it has a principle of **action** within itself. It has a **substantial form** analogous to the **soul** that organizes and systematizes all the functions and activities of the substance. The **essence** of a substance is its primitive force of action. Later Leibniz called his substances **monads**. Since a substance as a subject contains all its predicates, changes in monads are not due to the effect of external **causes** but rather to the unfolding of their own internal **natures**. Each monad is completely self-contained and perfect, although there is a **pre-established harmony** among monads giving the impression of **interaction**.

> "This being promised, we can say it is the nature of an individual substance or complete being to have a concept so complete that it is sufficient to make us understand and deduce from it all the predicates of the subject to which the concept is attributed." **Leibniz, *Discourse on Metaphysics***

substance (Locke)

METAPHYSICS The notion of substance that Locke inherited was the **Aristotelian** notion, from the *Categories*, of an underlying subject (substratum). Locke believed in the real existence of substance in the world. For the perceived qualities and **properties** carry the supposition of a **substratum** and can not be thought to exist by themselves. Hence, as a matter of necessity of thought we must infer a substance as the ground of the qualities. We find in nature certain groups of simple ideas in constant and uniform conjunction and tend to believe that there is a substratum behind them. As long as there is any sensible quality, substance can not be dismissed. However, the **real essence** of such a substance is unclear. Our ideas are limited to **sensation** and **reflection**, and do not reach sufficiently far to provide **knowledge** of the **nature** of substance. The ideas we have of substance are **complex ideas**; they are nothing but the collection of simple ideas of qualities, products of our mental operations. In all, substance has no positive content but only a supposition that it supports qualities. We know nothing about this supposition itself. Locke's criticism of the concept of substance paves the way for **Berkeley** and **Hume** to deny the existence of material substance and was a crucial step in the development of **empiricism**.

> "Because, as I have said, not imagining how these simple ideas can subsist by themselves, we accustom ourselves to suppose some substratum wherein they do exist, and from which they do result, which therefore we call substance." **Locke, *An Essay Concerning Human Understanding***

substance (Spinoza)

METAPHYSICS The standard definition Spinoza offered for substance is something which is "in itself" and "conceived through itself." The former part of this definition is similar to **Aristotle**'s definition of substance as subject, and the determination of the later part means that the **concept** of substance is formed without need to think about anything else. For otherwise the **knowledge** of substance would have to be dependent on the knowledge of something else, which would be another substance. Unlike **Descartes**, Spinoza did not refer to created things as substances. For him, substance was *causa sui*, its own cause. **Extension** and **thought** are **attributes** that constitute the **essence** of substance. But two attributes do not constitute two beings or two different substances. One substance can instantiate more than one attribute. There cannot be two distinct substances of the same nature. Substance is necessary, **infinite**, eternal, unique, and all-inclusive. Spinoza called substance **God** or **nature**. Substance for Spinoza was therefore identical with a wholly self-sufficient, all-embracing **reality**. This **pantheistic** notion of substance allowed Spinoza to challenge Descartes's **dualism**, although the relation between substance and attributes in Spinoza is much disputed.

> "By substance I understand that which is in itself and is conceived through itself." **Spinoza, *Ethics***

substantial chain, see *vinculum substantiale*

substantial form

METAPHYSICS A notion originating in **Aristotle**'s metaphysics and fully developed by the **scholastics**. It is the internal **principle** of a thing that accounts for it being a substance of a certain kind. The substantial form of a thing is the goal of its behavior and its explanatory principle. Early modern scientists and philosophers rejected the notion of substantial form, preferring to explain natural phenomena in terms of size, figure, and motion alone. However, Albinos held that this mechanistic philosophy was insufficient, for it failed to account for the inner **action** and the organic unity of a thing. **Leibniz** rehabilitated substantial forms and took them to be a **principle** of **change** and unity. He held them to be true unities or real entities. A corporeal **substance** is composed of indeterminate and passive **matter** and determining **form** that acts as the **cause** and **explanation** of its **properties**. This determining form is its substantial form and corresponds to the **soul** in human beings. Leibniz differed from the scholastics in his use of the term, for he claimed that this form is a general explanatory principle that supplies **nature** with organic activity, and did not use substantial forms to account for particular natural phenomena. For Leibniz, a form is an activity or **entelechy**, and a substantial form is a primitive force and first entelechy.

> "In order to find these real entities I was forced to have recourse to a formal atom, since a material thing cannot be both material and, at the same time, perfectly indivisible, that is, endowed with a true unity. Hence, it was necessary to restore, and, as it were, to rehabilitate the substantial forms which are in such disrepute today." **Leibniz, *Philosophical Essays***

substantive universal

PHILOSOPHY OF LANGUAGE A sort of linguistic **universal** that belongs to the **description** of the substantive universal **properties** of a language, in contrast to a formal universal, which gives the abstract universal properties of language. Accordingly, substantive universals contribute to determining the vocabulary for the description of language. According to this notion, all languages must have certain substantive phonetic elements for phonetic representation, certain specific central features of **syntax**, and certain **semantic** features to provide a universal framework for semantic description.

> "A study of substantive universals claims that items of a particular kind in any language must be drawn from a fixed class of items." **Chomsky, *Aspects of the Theory of Syntax***

substitutional quantifier, see objectual quantifier

substratum

METAPHYSICS, ANCIENT GREEK PHILOSOPHY [Greek *hupokeimenon*, that which underlies, hence the subject or bearer of properties] In the *Categories*, **Aristotle** defined **substance** as the substratum because it underlies the other **categories**, and he used substance and substratum virtually interchangeably. In the *Metaphysics*, he divided the category of substance into **form**, **matter**, and the composite of form and matter. While the composite is the substratum of **properties**, matter is the substratum of **form**. If substance still meant mainly "that which underlies," matter would be the ultimate subject and therefore primary substance. But Aristotle now claimed that instead of being a substratum, (primary) substance is that which is **separate** and **a this** (*tode ti*). Thus, although matter is the subject of form, this does not give matter a better claim than form to being substance.

> "The substratum is that of which everything else is predicated, while it is itself not predicated of anything else." **Aristotle,** *Metaphysics*

subsumption theory of explanation, another expression for covering law model

success verb, see achievement verb

such

METAPHYSICS, ANCIENT GREEK PHILOSOPHY [Greek *toionde*] For **Aristotle**, a kind, common **nature** or common **predicate**. **Form**, as *toionde*, is a **universal** form. Such, which is general, contrasts with **a this** (*tode ti*), which is **individual**. Aristotle claimed that by separating an **idea** (*toionde*) from the things exemplifying it and by thus making the idea a this, **Plato** made many mistakes in his Theory of **Forms** or Ideas. Aristotle tried to keep a clear distinction between a this and such by claiming that **substance** is a this and that an idea, as a universal, is not a substance.

> "...no common predicate indicates a 'this', but rather a 'such'. If not, many difficulties follow and especially the 'third man'." **Aristotle,** *Metaphysics*

sufficient and necessary condition, see necessary condition

sufficient condition

LOGIC A **condition** in the presence of which a specific thing must **exist** or a specific **event** must occur: if A, then B. The condition can also be stated at a **formal** level: if A is true, then B is true. If one is seriously ill, then one will be weak. Hence, being ill is a sufficient condition for being weak. In contrast, a **necessary condition** must be present for a thing to exist or for an event to occur, but does not guarantee that the thing will exist or the event occur. If A is a sufficient condition of B, then B is a necessary condition for A. A condition can be necessary and sufficient, unnecessary and sufficient, or necessary and insufficient. If it is unnecessary and insufficient, it is not a condition. Conditions can be parts of other conditions, so that, as in **Mackie**'s account of **causation**, we can have an insufficient but necessary part of an unnecessary but sufficient condition.

> "A sufficient condition for the occurrence of an event is a circumstance in whose presence the event must occur." **Copi,** *Introduction to Logic*

sufficient reason, the principle of

METAPHYSICS A law that can be traced to the medieval philosopher **Abelard**, but is usually associated with **Leibniz**. In its most common formulation, it is the claim that there is nothing without a **reason** for being thus and not otherwise. Leibniz formulated the principle in a number of ways, and applied it freely, depending on how he defined sufficient reason at a given time. Sometimes he took it, together with the principle of non-contradiction, as one of the two great principles used in reasoning. Sometimes sufficient reason was a form of *a priori* proof founded on the nature of the subject and **predicate** terms in every true **proposition**, no matter whether it is **necessary** or **contingent**. Sometimes sufficient reason meant efficient cause and, in particular, **final cause**. In this case, the principle is not concerned with the logical relation between subject and predicate, but with the **cause** of **events** and the existence of things. It is the basis of Leibniz's rejection of **Newtonian** absolute **space** and **time**. Sometimes the principle of the best or **perfection** is also said to be a version of the principle of sufficient reason.

"The principle of sufficient reason, namely, that nothing happens without a reason why it should be so rather than otherwise." **Leibniz**, *Philosophical Essays*

suicide

ETHICS Deliberately and **voluntarily** ending one's life with the aim of self-destruction. Suicide is distinguished from sacrificing one's life as a means to achieve another end and from engaging in actions or a way of life that risks one's life. From **Plato** and **Aristotle** onward, there has been controversy whether suicide is morally justified. On one view, suicide should be morally prohibited on the grounds that life is divine, that suicide causes harm to one's family and community, and that suicide is an offense to **God** who created life. In contrast, suicide is claimed to be a self-regarding act that lies outside the prohibition on harming others. It is claimed that without stronger objections, the right should be recognized to determine when to terminate one's own life. **Aquinas** and **Kant** argued against suicide, while **Hume** argued in favor of tolerating it. These different attitudes lead to controversy whether we should intervene if somebody has the intention of committing suicide. If suicide is immoral, then we are obliged to prevent it. If suicide is morally justifiable, the intervention beyond advice will be **paternalistic** interference that violates the **agent**'s **rights**. Suicide has been frequently discussed in contemporary **applied ethics** through its relations with the issues of **euthanasia** and assisted suicide.

"Let us here endeavour to restore men to their native liberty, by examining all the common arguments against suicide, and showing that that action may be free from every imputation of guilt or blame, according to the sentiments of all the ancient philosophers." **Hume**, *On Suicide*

summum bonum

ETHICS, METAPHYSICS [Latin, the highest or supreme good] A **good** without any qualification and an absolute end in itself. All other goods are pursued for its sake, for they are good because of this supreme good. Hence, the concept of a supreme **end** unites all other ends and is the crown for any system of ends. Ethically, the *summum bonum* is the moral ideal of a possible state of affairs in which a morally perfect being is supremely happy and also worthy of being supremely happy. Different moral theories offer different accounts of what constitutes the *summun bonum*, such as **pleasure**, happiness, self-actualization, contemplation, a good **will**, fulfillment of **duty**, or obedience to **God**. Metaphysically it is regarded as the ultimate **principle** and the source of **value** and **being**. Critics question whether a system of ends requires a highest good to be intelligible.

"And I wish to point out certain conclusions which appear to follow, with regard to the nature of the Summum Bonum, or the state of things which would be the most perfect we can conceive." **G. E. Moore**, *Principia Ethica*

Sun, simile of the

ANCIENT GREEK PHILOSOPHY, METAPHYSICS, ETHICS, EPISTEMOLOGY A device used by **Plato** in the *Republic* to illuminate the nature of the **Form** of the **Good**, **knowledge** of which the **guardians** must attain. The simile is based on the distinction between the visible world and the world of the Forms. As the source of light in the visible world, the sun enables both the eye to see and the object of sight to be seen. Furthermore, it causes the process of generation and growth. The roles played by the Good in relation to the world of the Forms correspond to the roles played by the sun in relation to the visible world. The Good enables both the **mind** to know and the Forms to be known. Furthermore, it is the **cause** of **being** and reality of the Forms. As the Sun is beyond sight, light, and process in its power, the Good is beyond **truth**, knowledge, and being in its power and dignity. The sovereignty of the Good illustrated in this simile is obscure and its interpretation remains a subject of dispute, but as a metaphysical attempt to establish a fundamental **principle** for any **explanation**, the simile has exerted a great influence on many subsequent metaphysical systems. In the *Republic*, the simile of Sun is complemented by the simile of **Line** and the simile of the **Cave**.

"What the Good itself is in the world of thought in relation to the intelligence and things known, the sun is in the visible world, in relation to sight and things seen." **Plato**, *Republic*

superego, see ego

supererogation
ETHICS [from Latin *super*, beyond + *erogare*, to pay out] The category of good **actions** that go beyond the requirements of common morality, such as risking one's own life to save another. Supererogatory deeds are often arduous and costly. They are encouraged by morality as meritorious and are worthy of praise or honor. Nevertheless, one has no **obligation** to do them, and their omission is neither morally wrong nor subject to moral blame. Supererogation aims at a moral ideal rather than the standard of common morality. **Chisholm** classifies supererogation as one of five kinds of morally appraised actions, along with actions that are morally obligatory, indifferent, forbidden, and offensive. Some versions of **utilitarianism** eliminate the possibility of supererogatory acts, because the need to maximize happiness leaves no room to distinguish between the requirements of ordinary morality and acts that go beyond them. Some claim that such positions demand too much from ordinary moral agents, who do not aspire to the moral lives of saints or heroes.

"Supererogatory virtue is shown by acts of exceptional sacrifice for the benefit of others. Such acts are praiseworthy and not regarded as irrational, but they are not thought either morally or rationally required." **T. Nagel,** *The View from Nowhere*

Superman, see *Übermensch*

supernatural theology, another name for revealed theology

superstructure
PHILOSOPHY OF SOCIAL SCIENCE The metaphor of base and superstructure, or foundation and superstructure, is of fundamental importance to the methodology of **historical materialism**. The economic structure is said to be the foundation on which the **state**, including the police, army, courts and bureaucracy, and **ideology** are built. The state is called legal/political superstructure, while the ideology is called the ideological superstructure. The superstructure arises because of the conflict of interests of different classes inherent in the economical base and is thus **determined** by the base. The **function** of the superstructure is to keep the base intact by keeping the collective interests of the ruling class intact. This is accomplished by the sanctioned and coercive regulation of the legal/political superstructure and by the persuasive force of the ideological superstructure. When the development of the productive forces brings changes in the **relations of production**, **Marx** claims that the superstructure will consequentially be transformed. The distinction between base and superstructure depends on there being an explanatory priority given to the base in its relations with the superstructure, but this priority need not be absolute. Writers disagree concerning the autonomy of the superstructure in its own affairs and the power it has in shaping the base.

"The totality of these relations of production forms the economic structure of society, the real basis from which rises a legal and political superstructure, and to which correspond specific forms of social consciousness." **Marx,** *Preface to the Critique of Political Economy*

supervenience
ETHICS, PHILOSOPHY OF MIND, METAPHYSICS, EPISTEMOLOGY, PHILOSOPHY OF SCIENCE, AESTHETICS A term which can be traced to G. E. **Moore**, but which gained wider use through the work of R. M. **Hare**. Hare used it for the claim that moral or evaluative **properties** such as goodness must supervene upon natural properties such as intelligence, health, and kindness. If something has the moral property in virtue of having the natural property and if anything having the natural property would in virtue of having it also have the moral property, then the moral property supervenes upon the natural property. If two things are alike in all descriptive respects, the same evaluative properties must be applied to both of them. On this view, good is supervenient upon underlying natural properties, although it is not reducible to them. **Davidson** extended this notion to the philosophy of mind, and claims that mental properties are supervenient upon physical properties. If two things are alike in all physical properties, they can not differ in mental properties, but the mental can not be reduced to the physical. Supervenient **physicalism** offers

an alternative to **reductionist identity theory**. Supervenience is an irreducible relation of dependence upon base properties by supervenient properties. The term has a wide application. In **ontology**, **mereological** supervenience can be used to describe the relation between part and whole. In **epistemology**, properties such as being justifiable or reasonable are said to be supervenient properties. Recently, weak, strong, and global supervenience have been introduced by J. Kim. For the actual world or a given possible world, property A weakly supervenes on property B, if anything in that world having B also has A. Across different **possible worlds**, A strongly supervenes on B if any individual having B will also have A across all of those worlds. For global supervenience, if the histories of two worlds agree in all of their subvening respects, the worlds will also be indiscernible in their supervening respects. Supervenient properties are also called consequential characteristics or tertiary qualities. The latter notion was introduced by **Bosanquet** for the aspects of beauty and sublimity which we recognize in nature but which are not features of nature.

> "Entity Q supervenes on entity P if and only if every possible world that contains P contains Q."
> **D. Armstrong,** *Universals*

supposition

LOGIC [from Latin *suppositio* and the verb *supponere*, to put something under] The signification of a term in a **proposition**. The doctrine of *suppositio*, one of the most significant parts of medieval logic, was developed in the thirteenth and fourteenth centuries. Through recognition of the **ambiguity** of a term, medieval logicians devoted themselves to classifying the various types of *suppositio* a term may have in the context of a proposition. A distinction between simple supposition (*suppositio simplex*) and personal supposition (*suppositio personalis*) was drawn. The former signifies a common **nature**, and the latter signifies an **individual**. This corresponds somewhat to the distinction between *suppositio discreta*, which directly **refers** to an individual, and *suppositio communis*, which refers to many. *Suppositio personalis* was further divided by **William of Ockham** into *suppositio determinata*, which can be explained by reference to one individual, and *suppositio confusa*, which involves all or many individuals

of the species. *Suppositio confusa* has two main types: *mobile* and *distributiva*. There is also a kind of material supposition, *suppositio materialis*, by which a word refers to itself. Logicians differed about the types of supposition and the relations among the types. This difficult doctrine is of contemporary interest through its relevance to issues of **meaning** and **reference**.

> "Supposition is the signification that a certain kind of term has in the context of a proposition."
> **Broadie,** *Introduction to Medieval Logic*

surface structure, see deep structure

surprise examination paradox

LOGIC A semantic **paradox**, also called the examination paradox or prediction paradox. A teacher announces that there will be a surprise examination next week. Then a student claims that such an examination can not occur. The examination can not be on Friday (the last working day of the week), for at that time it would not be a surprise. It can not be on Thursday. For if there is no examination given on Wednesday, we will know that it will come either on Thursday or Friday, but since Friday has been ruled out, Thursday will be the only day left, and then the examination will not be a surprise. The other days can be eliminated in the same manner. Hence there can be no surprise examination next week. Some critics argue that if the student calculates that the surprise examination can not take place on Friday (or any other given day), it would be a surprise if it were to take place then and that it therefore could take place on any day of the week. The paradox was originally observed by a mathematics teacher in Stockholm during the Second World War, when he heard a declaration from the authorities that, as an exercise, there would be a surprise air-raid alarm some day during the next week, during which people should go to an air-raid shelter.

> "The class's argument falls into two parts: one applies to whether there can be an unexpected examination on the last day, Friday; the other takes forward the negative conclusion on this issue, and purports to extend it to the other days." **Sainsbury,** *Paradoxes*

survival, problem of

METAPHYSICS, PHILOSOPHY OF RELIGION, PHILOSOPHY OF MIND, ETHICS Traditionally the problem of **immortality**, concerning whether the self or **soul** can survive bodily **death** and also concerning the form that survival might take. Some philosophers argue that the soul could exist on its own after death, with a continuation of its earthly **identity** and with mental capacities very much like those of its embodied state. Others argue that preserving one's identity and capacities would require either the resurrection of one's earthly **body** or its replacement by a special body. Others argue that survival is unintelligible without a continuing relationship with a living body and that survival of bodily death is therefore impossible.

A different problem of survival is extensively discussed by Derek **Parfit**, and distinguished by him from the problem of **personal identity**. Imagine that my brain is divided into two halves and that each half is transplanted into the skull of a new body. If character and memories were related to both sides of the brain, the result of successful transplantation would be that two persons would have my character and my apparent memories. To which of them am I identical? Not to one of them alone, because the other would have equally good claim to be me. Not to both of them, because then two distinct individuals existing at the same time would be identical to each another, and our notion of identity makes this impossible. Nevertheless I do survive. On this basis, Parfit argues that the problem of survival and the problem of identity should be distinguished. While identity can not be settled in this case, we can answer the question of survival. Identity is a one–one relation, while survival can be a one–many relation. While identity is an all-or-nothing relation, that is, either X and Y are identical or X and Y are completely distinct, most of the relations which matter in survival are relations of degree. I can survive as two persons who share a common past in me without being either or both of them. If survival is what matters to me, I can give up my concern for identity. Parfit's separation of these two problems attempts to end the long-standing debate about personal identity, and it also has moral consequences regarding how I conceive of myself and how I value my future happiness as compared to the happiness of others. Since what matters in our continued existence is constituted mainly by relations of degree, Parfit believes that we have reason to diminish our self-absorption and our self-concern.

> " 'Will I survive?' seems ... equivalent to 'Will there be some person alive who is the same person as me?" Parfit, **"Personal Identity," in** *Philosophical Review* **80**

survival of the fittest

PHILOSOPHY OF SCIENCE, PHILOSOPHY OF SOCIAL SCIENCE, ETHICS, POLITICAL PHILOSOPHY The central idea of **social Darwinism**. A trait is fitting if it helps its **species** to survive. Fitness is a key concept in **Darwin**'s **explanation** of differential reproduction. According to his theory of **evolution**, the various species evolved as the result of the action of an environment that favored the survival of some organisms while destroying others. Social Darwinism applies this idea to the explanation of the development of society and claims that economic competition produces human progress. The idea is fully expressed by Herbert **Spencer**, who claimed in *Social Statistics* that just as competition in the natural world ensures that only the fittest survive, so free competition in the economic world ensures that only the most capable individuals survive and rise to the top. Society favors those who both understand the conditions of existence and are able to meet their requirements. He thought that competition and its outcome are necessary for the development of the human race. Social Darwinism and the notion of the survival of the fittest are now widely rejected in science and morality.

> "The phrase 'survival of the fittest' has been used, ever since Herbert Spencer first coined it, to describe an individualistic law showing such ... as co-operation, love and altruism to be unreal, a law which (somewhat mysteriously) both demands and predicts that they should always give way to self-interest." **Midgley,** *Evolution as a Religion*

suspension of judgment

ANCIENT GREEK PHILOSOPHY, EPISTEMOLOGY [Greek *epoche*, also translated as suspension of belief] A key term in ancient **skepticism** for the epistemological stance, which does not deny or affirm anything. It is an attitude of indifference to the nature of a thing, arising from the modes of skepticism. Since our sensations tell us neither **truth** nor falsehood, we should be uncommitted and resist any temptation to hazard opinions. According to the skeptics, suspension of judgment may lead to **tranquility** and therefore to happiness.

> "Broadly speaking, suspension of judgement comes about because of the setting of things in opposition." **Empiricus,** *Outline of Pyrrhonism*

syllogism

LOGIC [from Greek *sullogismos*, argument] **Aristotle**'s famous logical achievement, described in his *Prior Analytics* and *Posterior Analytics*. A syllogism is a formally valid **inference** to a conclusion from two premises (a major premise and a minor premise). The premises and the conclusion all have **subject-predicate** forms. The premise containing the predicate of the conclusion is the major premise, and the premise containing the subject of the conclusion is the minor premise. The term that appears in both premises but does not appear in the conclusion is the middle term. The subject-predicate relation is either affirmative or negative and is either **universal** or **particular**, yielding four kinds of propositions in syllogism: all x is y, no x is y, some x is y, and some x is not y, symbolized in traditional logic by the letters A, E, I, O respectively. Syllogisms can be divided into four figures according to the different positions of the middle term in the premises, although Aristotle only describes the first three, with the fourth figure added by medieval logicians. In each figure the different possible combinations of forms of premise result in different moods, but not all moods are valid. An example of the first mood of the first figure (called Barbara) is: All men are mortal, Socrates is a man; therefore, Socrates is mortal. Syllogism was the core of the first abstract and rigorous system of logic, and dominated logic until the nineteenth century. However, since it only deals with subject-predicate relations, its scope of application is limited, and even as an account of predication it has been superseded by modern predicate **calculus**.

> "A syllogism is discourse in which, certain things being stated, something other than what is stated follows of necessity from their being so." **Aristotle,** *Prior Analytics*

symbol, see sign/symbol

symbolic logic, another term for mathematical logic

symmetric relation

LOGIC A **relation** R between two terms, X and Y, is symmetric if and only if XRY **entails** YRX and YRX entails XRY. For example, from "Smith is the brother of John," we can infer that "John is the brother of Smith." A relation R is asymmetric if XRY entails not YRX. For example, from "Smith is the father of Peter," we can infer that "Peter is not the father of Smith." A relation R between two terms can also be non-symmetric, that is, neither symmetric nor asymmetric. For example, from "John likes Jane," we can not tell whether or not Jane likes John.

> "What all cases of equivalence have in common, is mainly the mark of a symmetrical relation, namely, the two axioms: If A = B, then B = A; If A = B, and B = C, then A = C." **Russell,** *The Collected Papers of Bertrand Russell*, **vol. II**

sympathy

ETHICS [from Greek *sym*, together + *pathos*, passion] A general **disposition** or propensity to feel what others around us are feeling and to be affected or moved by this feeling. We are delighted if we observe others who are delighted, and feel sorrow if we observe others in pain. For **Hume**, sympathy is a part of human nature. In contrast to **reason**, it is the basis for forming what we regard to be **virtues** and vices. In a further development of Hume's view, Adam **Smith** held, in *The Theory of Moral Sentiments*, that sympathy is an analogous emotion that arises in spectators from imaginatively putting themselves in the situation that **causes** the feeling in the agent. Sympathy is what **Hutcheson** called **moral sense** and what Hume called approbation. All of these are different expressions for **sentiment**. For British theorists of moral sentiments, sympathy is our ground for making **moral judgments** and moral rules.

> "Pity and compassion are words appropriated to signify our fellow feeling with the sorrow of others. Sympathy, though its meaning was, perhaps originally the same, may now, however, without much impropriety, be made use of to denote

our fellow-feeling with any passion whatever."
Smith, *The Theory of Moral Sentiments*

syncategorematic

LOGIC [from Greek *syn*, with + *kategoria*, category]
A term introduced by medieval logicians. Categorematic terms were originally those falling under
Aristotle's ten **categories** to denote **entities** of
ten different kinds, with each forming an independent meaningful unit as an expression. Later, any
term that stands for something and can serve as a
subject or **predicate** in a categorical **proposition**
was considered to be categorematic. In contrast,
syncategorematic terms are those terms that can not
function to **refer** to anything but have to be used
together with categorematic terms. They are terms
such as "and," "or," "not," "if," "every," "some,"
"only," and "except." Because they do not stand for
anything, they do not have **meaning** in isolation.
Although they need other terms to make a meaningful unit of language, they have special logical
importance because they show the **form** of a **statement**. The notion of a syncategorematic term has
now been replaced in modern logic by the notion of
a **logical constant** or topic-neutral expression.

"Such words are called syncategorematic because
they are only capable of being used along with others
in predication." **Joseph,** *An Introduction to Logic*

syndicalism

POLITICAL PHILOSOPHY [from French *syndicat*, trade
union] A socialist theory based on the experiences
of the French trade union movement. Syndicalism
claimed that the working class should adopt direct
action against capitalism through trade unions or
other working-class organizations. The general strike
was regarded as the most important weapon. Militant
syndicalism advocated class war and the destruction
of capitalism by armed violence. Classical syndicalism distrusted political and state activity and rejected
all state-oriented politics. It envisaged the reconstruction of society according to a federal formation of
local workers' units after the abolition of the **state**.

"The term 'syndicalism' has two meanings. It can
denote simply trade unionism in a neutral sense.
On the other hand, it signifies revolutionary or
militant trade unionism, devoted to the overthrow
of capitalism and the state. The usual mechanism of
overthrow was the general strike." **Plant,** *Modern
Political Thought*

synonym

LOGIC, PHILOSOPHY OF LANGUAGE A **relation** between
things or expressions. Two things are synonymous
if they share the same expression, and the expression
applies to them for the same reason. For instance,
both a man and a horse are called "'animal," in the
sense that both of them are living things that can
move themselves. Thus both a man and a horse are
synonymous with regard to the expression "animal."
Synonymity today is more likely to be ascribed
to **expressions** than to things. Two expressions
are synonymous if they have the same **meaning**.
Usually, an expression can be replaced with its
synonym without affecting the **truth-value** of the
proposition in which it occurs, although this does
not apply to **propositional attitudes** or other
opaque or non-extensional contexts.

"A word is synonymous to a word or phrase if
the substitution of the one for the other in a
sentence always yields an equivalent sentence."
Quine, *Theories and Things*

syntactical ambiguity, an alternative expression
for structural ambiguity

syntactical sentence, see pseudo-object sentence

syntax

LOGIC, PHILOSOPHY OF LANGUAGE [from Greek *syn*,
together + *taxis*, order or arrangement] The rules of
sentence construction that indicate how **sentences**
may be formed out of diverse kinds of words. The
syntactic **rules** for each language distinguish those
combinations of words that are acceptable from
those that are unacceptable. Syntactics is the study
concerned with the formal aspects of sentence formation, that is, the structural relationships among
symbols in a language, in contrast to **semantics**,
which studies questions of **meaning** or **truth** in a
language. According to **Russell**, early **Wittgenstein**,
and the **logical positivists**, the syntax or **grammar**
of ordinary languages like English is ambiguous and
allows the same grammatical form to be used for
both meaningful and meaningless utterances. For

instance, "Caesar is a prime number" is grammatically correct but logically meaningless. On this view, the grammar of ordinary language becomes a central source of **metaphysical nonsense** masquerading as intelligible discourse. Consequently, these philosophers suggest that a major task of philosophy is to construct a logical syntax in which grammatical and logical structures coincide.

Syntax is also discussed in recent philosophy as a result of the work of N. **Chomsky**. He argues for the existence of an **innate universal grammar**, in part from the impossibility of children acquiring the complex syntax of **natural language** on **empiricist** principles.

> "If grammatical syntax corresponds exactly to logical syntax, pseudo-statements could not arise." **Carnap, "The Elimination of Metaphysics through Logical Analysis of Language," in Ayer (ed.),** *Logical Positivism*

syntax words, see object words

synthesis

EPISTEMOLOGY, METAPHYSICS, PHILOSOPHY OF MIND [from Greek *syn*, with, together + *tithenai*, put, place, literally, putting together] A mental process of drawing together separate items or **ideas** and combining them in some way as a whole. Synthesis also means the outcome of such a mental process. In general, synthesis moves from the **simple** to the complex, in contrast to **analysis**, which breaks up a whole into its constituents and its manner of combination. **Kant** made sophisticated use of the notions of synthesis and analysis in *The Critique of Pure Reason*. In **Hegel's dialectics**, synthesis is the third stage of a triadic process, involving both thought and reality, of thesis, antithesis, and synthesis. It reconciles both thesis and antithesis by preserving what is **rational** in them and rejecting what is irrational through what Hegel calls **sublation**.

> "Synthesis may be defined as the discovery of a complex consisting of given constituents combined in a given manner." **Russell,** *Collected Papers of Bertrand Russell*, **vol. VII**

synthesis (Kant)

METAPHYSICS, EPISTEMOLOGY The act of unifying or combining the **manifold representations** in intuition into one **consciousness** or one **cognition**. It is the act of combining **intuitions** and **concepts**. The **forms** of sensible intuition, **space** and **time**, organize **appearances** in **experience** to a certain extent, but this is not enough. The intuited manifold still needs to be connected and put together. This is the job of synthesis, which is the main act of the **understanding** or the unity of **apperception**. Since this act is logical, not physical, Kant calls it **intellectual** synthesis. Since acts of synthesis take place *a priori*, not in the empirical time-series but rather added to experience, Kant also calls it **transcendental** synthesis. Synthesis plays an essential role in **knowledge** by allowing intuition to enter into concepts and providing them with **contents** that they would otherwise lack. Without synthesis, nothing can be thought or known. Some critics argue that Kant's elaborate account of synthesis provides an unnecessary transcendental psychology to deal with important logical or metaphysical problems.

> "By synthesis, in its most general sense, I understand the act of putting together different representations, and of grasping what is manifold in them in one knowledge." **Kant,** *Critique of Pure Reason*

synthetic *a priori* judgment

EPISTEMOLOGY, METAPHYSICS **Judgments** may be divided into **analytic** judgments, in which the **predicate** adds nothing new to the subject, and **synthetic** judgments, in which the predicate can not be extracted from the **analysis** of the subject. *A priori* judgments are independent of **experience** and are hence **universal**, **necessary**, and immune to rejection by experience, while *a posteriori* judgments require empirical **justification**. **Kant** claimed that there is a kind of judgment that is at once synthetic and *a priori*. Such judgments do not derive their **truth** solely from the meanings of the words in the **sentences** expressing them, but express something that can not be refuted by experience. They are universally agreed by **reason** and **apodictically certain**. Kant argued that not all *a priori* truths are analytical and that certain fundamental truths of mathematics, science, and philosophy are synthetic *a priori*. He then asked how synthetic *a priori* judgments are possible and, through their possibility, how metaphysics is possible. He saw this question as setting the central task of the *Critique of Pure Reason*. In order to answer this question, he established the existence of *a priori* **intuitions** (**space** and **time**) and *a priori* concepts (the **categories**) and related them to possible empirical knowledge.

The notion of synthetic *a priori* judgment was held to be **self-contradictory** by **logical positivists**, who argued that the **analytic–synthetic distinction** and the *a priori–a posteriori* **distinction** are identical. **Quine** has also rejected this notion on the grounds that we can not draw the analytic–synthetic distinction without circularity. **Kripke** has accepted Kant's distinctions, but has introduced the notion of the necessary *a posteriori* in his **essentialism**. Some critics argue that the achievements of the first *Critique* can be detached from Kant's account of synthetic *a priori* judgments.

> "We can confidently say that certain pure synthetic knowledge a priori is real and given, namely, pure mathematics and pure natural science; for both contain propositions which are everywhere recognised, partly as apodictically certain by mere reason, partly by universal agreement from experience, and yet as independent of experience." **Kant,** *Prolegomena*

systematic ambiguity

LOGIC A term introduced in **Russell**'s theory of **types**. An **expression** is systematically ambiguous if it seems to be applicable to **objects** of different types. Systematic ambiguity is similar to the way that a common noun may be used to label either a thing of a given kind or a picture of such a thing or the way that a word may be used to refer to itself. Such an expression has to be differently interpreted according to the order of the **propositions** in which it occurs. But without the theory of types, the different **meanings** would not have been noticed. The word "class" is systematically ambiguous because it has different meanings when used at different levels in the hierarchy of types. This is the case for all **existential propositions** with the expression "there are." Systematic ambiguity has come to refer to a property that a term has if it means different things in different applications. We need special signs, such as particular modifying words or quotation marks, to remove this sort of ambiguity.

> "The word 'there is' is a word having 'systematic ambiguity', i.e., having a strictly infinite number of different meanings which it is important to distinguish." **Russell,** *Logic and Knowledge*

T

tabula rasa

EPISTEMOLOGY [Latin, blank tablet] A metaphor for the **soul** or **mind** as a blank or empty tablet at birth. The phrase comes from the Latin translation of **Aristotle**'s *De Anima* 429b30–430a3, where Aristotle said that the soul is like a writing tablet that is **potentially** whatever is thinkable, though **actually** it is nothing until it has thought. The phrase was widely used in **scholasticism** to express the idea that there is nothing in intellect that was not first in the **senses**. The phrase has been especially associated with **Locke**, although he adopted this expression not in his *Essay*, but in other works. Instead, Locke used some associated metaphors: mind is a white paper, a dark room, or an empty cabinet. His point is that there are no **innate** moral and logical **principles** inscribed on the mind before birth and that at the beginning of **cognition** the mind is a void and **passive** entity, a receptacle awaiting **ideas** from **experience**. The mind, however, has the potential to acquire ideas and **knowledge**. This is the cornerstone of his **empiricism**.

"There is the question whether the soul in itself is completely blank like a writing tablet on which nothing has as yet been written – a tabula rasa – as Aristotle and the author of the Essay maintain." **Leibniz**, *New Essays on Human Understanding*

tacit belief

PHILOSOPHY OF MIND, PHILOSOPHY OF ACTION A person may have an unlimited number of **beliefs** at any time. Those that he explicitly asserts or that figure in his internal soliloquy can be called his explicit beliefs. But many others are implied by these explicit beliefs but are not themselves explicit because, for example, he has not drawn the necessary **inferences** at that moment. These are called tacit beliefs. Some tacit beliefs play a **causal** role in **behavior**, but it is difficult to distinguish tacit beliefs that have a causal role from tacit beliefs that do not have a causal role.

"Call 'tacit' any belief that one really has but has not explicitly entertained." **Churchland**, *Neurophilosophy*

tacit knowledge

EPISTEMOLOGY, PHILOSOPHY OF MIND, PHILOSOPHY OF LANGUAGE In addition to explicit **knowledge-how** and **knowledge-that**, **Chomsky** introduced another sort of **knowledge**, that is, the speaker's **unconscious** knowledge of the grammatical rules of his language. This tacit knowledge is the basis for linguistic **competence**. Chomsky argues that a child does not know that these are the rules, but can easily master the intricate set of specific rules that distinguish what is grammatical from what is not grammatical. This suggests that the child already has knowledge of the language, but that this knowledge is not learned and can not be explained in **empiricist** terms such as stimulus control, conditioning, or analogy. He claims that tacit knowledge must belong to an **innate** faculty and that the study of language should provide insight into human psychology. The idea of tacit knowledge is the core of Chomsky's Cartesian linguistics.

> "Chomsky suggested that we might have tacit knowledge – propositional knowledge which we are unaware of having and cannot report having, which nevertheless guides out behaviours."
> **D'Agostino,** *Chomsky's System of Ideas*

Tarski, Alfred (1902–83)

Polish-born American logician and mathematician, born in Warsaw, a member of the Institute for Advanced Study, Princeton and taught at University of California, Berkeley. Tarski is best known for his semantic theory of truth, according to which a theory of truth for a language is adequate if we can derive within it every instance of the schema " 'P' is true if and only if P," where 'P' is the name of the sentence in a metalanguage and P is the sentence itself. This theory is the basis of truth-conditional semantics, and Tarski also developed an axiomatic theory of formal systems, a theory of logical consequence, and a theory of definability. Tarski's most important papers are collected in *Logic, Semantics, and Metamathematics* (1956), and other works include *Introduction to Logic and to the Methodology of the Deductive Sciences* (1941) and *Logic, Methodology, and Philosophy of Science* (1962).

taste

AESTHETICS Sensitivity to the **aesthetic properties** of **objects** and the aesthetic **intuition** and response that enable one to tell, for example, what is **beautiful** or elegant. Taste is a major conception of eighteenth-century aesthetics. **Shaftesbury** and **Hutcheson** regarded taste as a quasi-perceptual **inner sense**, akin to **moral sense**, but for **Kant** it is simply a special operation of our normal **cognitive faculties**. There exist vast differences of taste among different **cultures** and different individuals. This makes taste appear to be purely **subjective** and a matter of personal preference. However, for some aesthetic objects there seems to be widespread – even cross-

cultural and timeless – agreement in taste. Hence, **Hume** sought to ascertain the grounds of this intersubjective agreement. For Kant, the **judgment of taste** is subjective, but since it addresses the formal features of an object rather than its content, it is **universally** valid. Others believe that taste is a product of cultivation, demanding training and upbringing. People with the same social and educational background are more likely than people with diverse backgrounds to have the same taste regarding the same objects.

> "Taste is the ability to judge an object, or a way of presenting it, by means of a liking or a disliking devoid of all interest. The Object of such a liking is called beautiful." **Kant,** *Critique of Judgement*

tautology

LOGIC [from Greek *tauto*, the selfsame + *logos*, word or expression, literally, repetition of what has been said] A logical **formula** which is true whatever the truth-possibilities of its constituent **propositional variables**. Thus, a tautology takes the **truth-value** "true" for every truth-combination in a **truth-table**. Its truth can not be established by **experience** and need not be so established. The denial of a tautology is a **contradiction**. A tautology is not concerned with any subject-matter, and says nothing about the world, but exhibits the logical properties of genuine **propositions** or restates the same idea in different words. The study of tautology is of great importance in logic.

> "In one of these cases the proposition is true for all the truth-possibilities of the elementary propositions. We say that the truth-conditions are tautological." **Wittgenstein,** *Tractatus*

Taylor, Charles (1931–)

Canadian moral and political philosopher, Professor at University of Oxford and McGill University. Taylor argues against a mechanistic scientific account of man in favor of a philosophical anthropology that situates the self and language within a context of history, morality, culture, and society. His study of Hegel and his own developing thought have contributed to communitarian views of politics, ethics, and the self. His sense of historical diversity in the formation of the self has enriched his discussion of a multicultural politics of recognition. His major works include *The Explanation of Behaviour* (1964), *Hegel* (1975), *Philosophical Papers*, 2 vols. (1985), *Sources of the Self* (1989), *The Ethics of Authenticity* (1991), and *Multiculturalism and the Politics of Recognition* (1992).

techne

ANCIENT GREEK PHILOSOPHY [Greek, craft or art, normally meaning skill] A skill in contrast to a natural capacity. **Plato** regularly asked whether **virtue** is *techne* and so teachable. **Aristotle** took *techne* to be a rational discipline concerned with production (***poiesis***). He held that as productive science it contrasts both to demonstrative science (*theoretikos*) and to **practical reason** (*phronesis*), which is concerned with **action**. In this sense, *techne* is skill in producing plus knowledge of the nature of relevant things. Despite Aristotle's distinction between practical reason and *techne*, his examples of practical reason often turn out to be illustrations of *techne*.

"A techne is the same as a state involving true reason concerned with production." **Aristotle,** *Nicomachean Ethics*

teleological argument for the existence of God

PHILOSOPHY OF RELIGION [from Greek *telos*, end] Also called the **argument from design**, an argument seeking to derive the existence of **God** from the teleological order of the world, resting on an analogy with the relation between an intelligent craftsman and human artifacts. **Aquinas**' fifth way of proving God's existence is a teleological argument. According to this argument, since everything in the world shows some order, regularity, or purpose in its behavior, there must be a supreme **intelligence**, namely God, outside the universe and directing natural things toward their ends. A classical version of the argument from design was formulated by William Paley. The various parts of a watch cooperate in complex ways to produce the result of keeping time because the watch is designed by a watchmaker. The universe resembles a watch in the sense that it is a system of adaptations of **means** to **ends**. The only way to explain the complex and pervasive adaptation to ends in the universe is to postulate a supernatural designer. For the teleological argument, what is at stake is not merely that the universe displays order or regularity, but also that the order and

regularity is directed toward ends. In *Dialogues Concerning Natural Religion*, **Hume** formulated a similar version of the argument by comparing the world to a machine. However, Hume devoted much of this work to criticizing this argument, on the grounds that what the argument from design seeks to explain can be explained in alternative ways and that the teleological argument can not conclusively show the existence of God. **Kant** held that adaptation of things to the needs of other things in nature can suggest but can not prove the existence of a designer. Hume's view is supported by the development of the Darwinian **theory of evolution**, which provides natural explanations of **functional** adaptation in the world.

"Linked with the notion of design and order is that of purpose (hence the name Teleological Argument – from *telos*, 'end')." **McPherson,** *The Philosophy of Religion*

teleological ethics, see consequentialism

teleological explanation

PHILOSOPHY OF SCIENCE, PHILOSOPHY OF SOCIAL SCIENCE, ANCIENT GREEK PHILOSOPHY To explain a **property** or **behavior** in terms of purpose (Greek *telos*). This sort of explanation was initiated by **Socrates**, and fully developed by **Aristotle** with his notion of **final cause** (Greek *to hou heneka*, for the sake of which a thing comes about). In medieval philosophy, teleological explanation presupposed a Divine and omniscient designer. Everything operates for a goal, and the goal is predetermined by **God**. Teleological explanation was vehemently criticized by early modern science and philosophy. However, Aristotle mainly applied his final-cause interpretation to living or organic things, and accounts for the **function** of each part of an organism by appeal to its contribution to the perfect state of the organism as a whole. This sort of teleological **functionalism** is still applicable in contemporary biology and social science, although some philosophers try to reduce such explanations to efficient causality.

"The teleological form of explanation [is] an explanation in terms of reason rather than in terms of causes." **Ayer,** *The Concept of a Person and Other Essays*

teleological functionalism, see functionalism

teleology

ANCIENT GREEK PHILOSOPHY, PHILOSOPHY OF SCIENCE, PHILOSOPHY OF RELIGION [from Greek *telos*, the end or aim of a thing + *logos*, study] **Aristotle** assumed that everything that happens in the universe must be understood as the striving of something toward an **end** promoting its well-being or helping it to survive. He ascribes *telos* to plants and animals, believing that their behavior serves their needs and preserves their life. In view of the regularity in the natural world, he claims that nature itself must have an internal end or purpose.

Aristotle did not admit a **conscious**, rational **agent** in his teleological explanation, but in the teleological argument or argument from design, the Christian tradition infers from the regularity in nature that there is a supernatural designer, **God**, who designed everything in the world to be of service to man. The theory of **evolution** denies the need to posit a purposive designer, but confirms that **functional** adaptation serves a purpose of survival in **natural selection**. Since purposive and functional activities are observed universally, teleology is much discussed in the philosophy of science. Whether functional or teleological explanation is a distinctive kind of explanation or can be reduced to causal explanation is a matter of controversy.

> "Questions about teleology are, broadly, to do with whether a thing has a purpose or is acting for the sake of a purpose, and if so, what that purpose is." **Woodfield,** *Teleology*

telishment

ETHICS A term proposed by John **Rawls** to indicate a crucial problem of the **utilitarian** view of **punishment**. Utilitarianism claims that punishment is **justifiable** only by reference to its probable consequences with regard to promoting public **good** or preventing crime, rather than because the wrongdoing itself merits punishment. Rawls suggests that we can imagine a situation in which the authority knows that a suspected criminal is innocent, but still imposes a harsh punishment on him because such an action can produce better social consequences. This practice should not be termed punishment, because the subject of suffer-

ing is not a wrongdoer. Rawls names it telishment. Telishment is intuitively wrong but seems to be justifiable according to the utilitarian view of punishment.

> "Try to imagine, then, an institution (which we may call 'telishment') which is such that the officials set up by it have authority to arrange a trial for the condemnation of an innocent man whenever they are of the opinion that doing so would be in the best interests of society." **Rawls, "Two Concepts of Rules," in Acton (ed.),** *Philosophy of Punishment*

telos

ANCIENT GREEK PHILOSOPHY, PHILOSOPHY OF SCIENCE, ETHICS [Greek, end, aim, or goal] For **Aristotle**, one of the four **causes**: the **final cause** for the sake of which a process occurs or something is done. According to Aristotle's distinction between activity (*energeia*) and motion (*kinesis*), every **action** has an **end**, either an internal end in itself or an external end outside itself. By appealing to the *telos*, which is associated with the formal cause or even identical to it, Aristotle explained the generation of things and natural movement. He also called the characteristic **function** of a thing its end, because the benefit brought about by this function accounts for the existence of the thing and its aim. Thus cutting is the end of a knife. In his ethics, Aristotle connected *telos* with the **good**, happiness, and **virtue**. Every action is for an end, but happiness is the complete end (*teleis*). *Telos* as function and the associated notion of teleology are major, if controversial, concepts in contemporary science, especially biology and social science.

> "It is for the sake of the end (*telos*) that everyone does the other things." **Aristotle,** *Nicomachean Ethics*

temperance

ETHICS, ANCIENT GREEK PHILOSOPHY [Greek *sophrosune*, self-control or moderation in the satisfaction of bodily desire, from *phronein*, sound mind] A **virtue** discussed by both **Plato** and **Aristotle**. A temperate man has a **mind** sufficiently sound to control **desires**. He knows his own limitations and practices restraint in **action**. Plato's dialogue *Charmides* sought a definition of temperance. In the *Republic*, temperance was described as a **harmony** between different classes in the ideal city and between different parts of the **soul**. In this harmony, the higher part controls the inferior part, with the consent of the latter. Aristotle understood temperance to be a **mean** state with regard to such desires such as eating, drinking, and sex.

> "Temperance is understood not to be carried away by the desires, but preserving a decent indifference toward them." **Plato,** *Phaedo*

temporal logic, another term for tense logic

temporality

MODERN EUROPEAN PHILOSOPHY For **Heidegger,** *Dasein* exists in relation to three temporal dimensions at once. Its **Being** is constituted by taking the past with it, by being concerned with the present, and by being the projection of the future. Hence, its Being is necessarily temporal. Temporality makes up the primordial meaning of *Dasein*'s being. The fundamental structures of *Dasein*, **existentiality**, **facticity**, and **fallingness**, are modes of the temporalizing of temporality. They respectively correspond to three ecstasis of temporality: the past, the present, and the future. Ecstacy literally means standing out, indicating that at each ecstacy *Dasein* stands out from the general flow of time and existence. Philosophers traditionally focus on the present and conceive time as a series of happenings or the occurrence of actual facts. In contrast, Heidegger claimed that temporality is an ecstatic unity that is independent of any chronological relations. Among the three ecstasis, the future is the primary phenomenon of the primordial **authenticity** of temporality. This ecastic unity is also called the **transcendence** of **time** or the transcendence of *Dasein*.

> "This phenomenon has the unity of a future which makes present in the process of having been; we designate it as 'temporality'." **Heidegger,** *Being and Time*

temporally neutral term, see past-referring term

tender-mindedness, see tough-mindedness

tense logic

LOGIC A **formal logic** about tense and temporality, concerned with the systematization of **inference** involving **propositions** containing tensed verbs or notions of **change**, process, and **time**. This area is not covered by standard logic, which presupposes that the relations of **predicate** expressions to their subjects is timeless and static. Tense logic holds that the world changes and that it is possible that the same thing has and has not a given property at different times. The **truth-values** of tensed statements about the past, present, and future vary at different times. This part of logic holds that terms such as before, after, now, next, always, and sometimes should match the formal patterns of **modal logic**. It introduces the operators P to stand for the past tense ("it was the case that"), T for the present tense ("it is now the case") and F for the future tense ("it will be the case that"). It can also be presented as a many-valued system. The logic is said to have been heralded by J. N. Findley, but the first system was provided by A. N. **Prior** in *Time and Modalities* (1957) and was conceived as an alternative solution to the problem of **future contingents**. **Rescher** and **von Wright** are also important contributors to the development of tense logic. The logic is also called temporal logic, chronological logic, and the logic of change.

> "The object of chronological logic – 'tense logic', or 'change logic', as it has also been called by various logicians – is to systematise reasoning with propositions that have a temporal copula." **Rescher,** *Topics in Philosophic Logic*

term

LOGIC, PHILOSOPHY OF LANGUAGE Any word or phrase that **denotes** an **individual** or a **class** and functions as a single unit in expressing **meaning**. In **Russell**'s theory of **meaning**, a term is also an object that is referred to by a word or expression. He divides terms into two kinds: terms as things indicated by **proper names** and terms as **concepts** indicated by all other words. Hence, a man, a moment, a number, a class, a relation, a chimera, and anything else that can be mentioned are all terms. In a broad sense, a word that does not have its own meaning but determines the meaning of the **proposition** containing it is also a term, and hence we have the concept of a **syncategorematic** term.

> "Let us say that anything which is introduced, or can be introduced, into a remark by an expression is a term." **Strawson,** *Individuals*

tertiary quality, see supervenience

tertium non datur

LOGIC [Latin, there is no third] A way of expressing the **law of excluded middle**, that is, the law that every **proposition** is either true or false and that there is no third possibility. In contrast, *tertium quid* means that there is some third possibility.

"Either one might, or one might not, have been otherwise. *Tertium non datur.*" **Hartshorne,** *Creative Synthesis and Philosophical Method*

tertium quid, see *tertium non datur*

Thales of Miletus (6th century BC)

Born in Miletus, Ionia, flourished around 585 BC. Thales is regarded as the first philosopher in the history of Western Philosophy because he was the first to seek an explanation of nature in terms of reason rather than in terms of a supreme power. He claimed that a single element, water, underlies cosmic development. This conclusion was probably based on his observation that nourishment and living organisms come from moist things.

thanatos, another expression for death instinct

theism

PHILOSOPHY OF RELIGION [from Greek *theos*, god] In opposition to **atheism**, the belief in the existence of **God** (monotheism) or gods (**polytheism**) as a personal being or beings. In contrast to **deism**, the belief that God **transcends** the world but is also immanent within it or within us; that God is **perfect** and is therefore **omnipotent**, **omniscient**, and perfectly **good**; and that God is the loving creator of the world who manifests himself to human beings through caring for us and communicating with us. In contrast to pantheism, theism claims that God exists independent of the world. Theism is the central feature in the monotheistic religious tradition of Judaism, Christianity, and Islam. Various arguments concerning the existence of God seek to establish theism, although critical responses are raised against each of its major claims.

"Theism, common to traditional Judaism, Christianity, and Islam, is the view that the cosmos is created and kept in existence by an omnipresent, omniscient, omnipotent, supremely good being. It preserves some distinction between God and the creation, according to which the two are not identical however interwoven." **Taliaferro, in Bunnin and Tsui-James (eds.),** *Blackwell Companion to Philosophy*

theistic voluntarism, see voluntarism

theodicy

PHILOSOPHY OF RELIGION [from Greek *theos*, god + *dike*, justice, right, the justification of God] A term introduced by **Leibniz** in *Theodicy: Essays on God's Goodness, Man's Freedom and the Origin of Evil* (1710), but the basic problem was formulated by **Boethius**: *Si Deus Justus – unde malum?* (If God is righteous, why evil)? It is the part of theology that focuses on the reconciliation of the existence of **God**, as an **omnipotent**, **omniscient**, perfectly **good** and loving **absolute being**, with the existence of **evil** in the world. The human experience of suffering and guilt makes faith in God's justice a problem. Either God is able to stop evil but he does not want to, in which case he is omnipotent but not good or just; or he wishes to prevent evil but fails to achieve this, in which case he is good but not omnipotent. The main task of theodicy is to provide positive reasons to justify God's permission of the existence of moral and natural evil and to seek to prove that our world is the **best of all possible worlds**.

"A response must explain God's action, or lack of action, by presenting a suitable reason for the existence of the evil. This kind of response is traditionally called a theodicy, a vindication of God's goodness." **Prevost,** *Probability and Theistic Explanation*

theological determinism

PHILOSOPHY OF RELIGION A position initiated by **St Augustine**, holding that **God** is **omnipotent** and has determined everything that will occur. As a consequence, everything in this world depends on God for existence. In addition, God is **omniscient** and knows all **truths** from the beginning of **time**. All **actions** that men are going to perform are known by him in advance. One version also claims that because of God's absolute **goodness**, this world is the **best possible world**. Theological determinism faces major difficulties in reconciling God's **foreknowledge** with human **self-determination** and in reconciling God's goodness with the existence of **evil**.

> "Theological determinism argues that since God is omniscient, he knows everything, the future included." **Lucas, *The Freedom of the Will***

theological virtues, see charity

theology

PHILOSOPHY OF RELIGION [from Greek *theos*, god + *logos*, theory, study] For **Aristotle, first philosophy** as the contemplation of the fundamental **principle** or ultimate **substance**. In general, theology is a discipline that deals with the **explanation** and **justification** of the teachings, doctrines, and practices that constitute a religion. Each religion has its own theology, but in European thought, Christian theology has the greatest historical prominence as the rational account of Christian faith, although Jewish and Islamic theological writings have also had great influence. Christian theology is divided into many sub-disciplines, such as biblical theology, which tries to provide the precise ideas contained in the various biblical documents; historical theology, which traces the historical development of Christianity and the Christian Church; systematic theology, which aims at integrating into a coherent whole a wide array of fundamental religious beliefs; practical theology, which deals with the interaction of belief and behavior; and philosophical theology, which applies philosophical methods in order to clarify religious **concepts** and **presuppositions**. While the philosophy of religion exists to criticize these doctrines and to assess their philosophical implications, theology assesses a religion from within and acts as a spokesman rather than as a critic. There are nevertheless various debates among theologians about how to explain certain religious elements. Theology presupposes **faith** and tries to acquire **knowledge** of God by employing scholarly methods. It is faith seeking to understand itself. In Christianity, its goal is to serve **salvation**.

> "Theology is 'the science of God'." **McPherson, *The Philosophy of Religion***

Theophrastus (*c*.371–*c*.287 BC)

Greek philosopher, born in Lesbos, Aristotle's disciple and successor as head of the Lyceum. Theophrastus preserved Aristotle's works, but of his own writings, only two books on botany and some fragments are extant. *On the Opinions of the Physical Philosophers*, now lost, is believed to be the main source of later historians of the pre-Socratics. *Characters* is a typology of human ways of falling short of virtue.

theoretical construct

EPISTEMOLOGY, PHILOSOPHY OF SCIENCE Also theoretical term, a term for something that is unobservable and **postulated**, such as force, atoms, field, or electrons. According to **logical positivism**, these postulated items do not really exist, and these **concepts** are merely economical devices or constructs that are used to explain observable phenomena. It has been a matter of dispute in the philosophy of science whether theoretical terms can be eliminated or replaced by **observational terms**. Scientific **realists** reject the notion of a theoretical construct as an interpretation of theoretical terms and accept that **theoretical entities** in true theories really exist.

> "... 'theoretical constructs' ... cannot be mentioned in observation statements." **Pap, *An Introduction to the Philosophy of Science***

theoretical entity, see theoretical term

theoretical language, see observation language

theoretical pluralism, see anarchism (scientific)

theoretical sentence

EPISTEMOLOGY, PHILOSOPHY OF SCIENCE In contrast to an **observation sentence**, a theoretical sentence is one whose meaning can not be determined by itself as a single sentence. It has meaning only within a theory to which it belongs. It makes sense only together with its theoretical context. Most sentences, apart from observation sentences, are theoretical. This term is central for **Quine's epistemic holism**.

> "Theoretical sentences in general are defensible only pragmatically: we can but assess the structural merits of the theory which embraces them along with sentences directly conditioned to multifarious stimulations." **Quine, *Word and Object***

theoretical term

EPISTEMOLOGY, PHILOSOPHY OF SCIENCE Carl **Hempel** divided the vocabulary of empirical sciences into two classes: **observational terms**, which **denote** an observable **entity** or **property**, and theoretical terms, which denote an unobservable entity or property. Observational terms are terms such as long and red, whose applicability to a given situation can be determined through direct **observation**. Theoretical terms are terms such as electron and quark, which are intended to establish an explanatory connection among observables and to construct a scientific system. Theoretical terms denote **theoretical entities**, which are **postulated** hypothetically by a theory. It is not clear where to draw the distinction between the theoretical and observational, for the term "observable" can refer either to what can be observed merely by the unaided **senses** or to what can be observed by using sophisticated scientific instruments, the operation of which is understood in terms of a theory. In addition, there have been challenges to the **empiricist** account of theory and observation underpinning Hempel's distinction and his claim that the principal role of theories is to **explain** empirical **generalizations**. There are important disputes concerning the real existence of theoretical entities.

"Theoretical terms . . . usually purport to refer to not directly observable entities and their characteristics; they function . . . in scientific theories intended to explain empirical generalisations." **Hempel,** *Aspects of Scientific Explanation*

theoretician's dilemma

PHILOSOPHY OF SCIENCE, METAPHYSICS A **dilemma** formulated by **Hempel**, involving the ontological status of **theoretical terms**. It reflects the empirical tradition that the theoretical terms of modern sciences such as atom, field, and force are merely "convenient myths." Theoretical terms either serve their purpose or do not. If they serve their purpose, they are unnecessary, because that purpose is to organize experiential data, and that can be done by **laws** that link observational antecedents to observational consequents without theoretical terms. If they do not serve their purpose, they are obviously unnecessary. Therefore theoretical terms are unnecessary. To escape this dilemma and avoid eliminating theoretical terms, philosophers normally reject or modify the first branch of the dilemma. Theoretical terms can have other functions that can not be reduced to those of **observational terms**. These proposed functions include **explanation**, observation of results, and economical summary. It is claimed that theoretical terms are a prerequisite of scientific growth and of certain forms of inductive reasoning.

"If the terms and principles of a theory serve their purpose they are unnecessary, as just pointed out, and if they don't serve their purpose, they are surely unnecessary. But given any theory, its terms and principles either serve their purpose or they don't. Hence, the terms and principles of any theory are not necessary. This argument . . . will be called the theoretician's dilemma." **Hempel, "The Theoretician's Dilemma,"** in *Minnesota Studies in the Philosophy of Science,* **vol. II**

theoria

ANCIENT GREEK PHILOSOPHY, EPISTEMOLOGY, ETHICS, METAPHYSICS, PHILOSOPHY OF RELIGION [Greek, vision of the real in the mind, hence contemplation or speculation, from *theorein*, to contemplate and *theasthai*, to gaze on, giving contemplation visual associations] In **Aristotle**'s *Metaphysics, theoria* is the activity that involves no change. It can provide the eternally and supremely happy life which is ascribed to the **unmoved mover** or **God** and is available only occasionally to men.

In Aristotle's ethics, *theoria* is distinguished from practical activities. This is the origin of the contrast between theory and practice, though *theoria* does not actually mean theory. *Theoria* is about eternal and unchanging **objects** and is the highest and best activity of which a human being is capable. A man engages in contemplation not *qua* man but in virtue of the divine intellect (*nous*) in him. Contemplation is higher than **practical reason** and is the supremely valuable life, providing complete human happiness. A tension between Aristotle's claim that contemplation is the **highest good** and his commendation of practical **virtue** has been the subject of much dispute.

Aristotle also distinguished theoretical or contemplative sciences, including theology, physics, and mathematics, from practical and productive sciences. Theoretical sciences have their end in themselves and are not pursued for practical purposes or **utility**.

All of these senses of *theoria* are connected, but they are not in complete harmony with one another.

> "Complete happiness will be its activity expressing its proper virtue; and we have said that this activity is activity of contemplation." **Aristotle, *Nicomachean Ethics***

theory of knowledge, another name for epistemology

theory of sentiments, see sentiment

theory of value, see axiology

theory-laden

PHILOSOPHY OF SCIENCE A term introduced by Hanson in 1959. A **concept**, **term**, or **statement** that is theory-laden makes sense only in the light of a particular theory or set of **principles**. Even **experience** is always shaped by theoretical traditions and expectations. Every observational term and sentence is alleged to carry a theoretical load. This position challenges the view of **logical positivism** that a protocol statement is a theoretically neutral report of experience, and denies **reducibility** of theory-laden terms to a purely observational level of **knowledge**. The term implies a rejection of the influential dichotomy of **theoretical terms** and **observational terms**.

> "There is a sense, then, in which seeing is a 'theory-laden' undertaking. Observation of x is shaped by a priori knowledge of x." **Hanson, *The Patterns of Discovery***

theory-theory

PHILOSOPHY OF MIND, PHILOSOPHY OF ACTION A theory of mind concerning how we come to know about the **propositional attitudes** of others. It tries to explain the nature of ascribing certain **thoughts**, **beliefs**, or **intentions** to other **persons** in order to explain their **actions**. The theory-theory holds that in ascribing beliefs to others we are tacitly applying a theory that enables us to make **inferences** about the beliefs behind the actions of others. The theory that is applied is a set of **rules** embedded in **folk psychology**. Hence, to anticipate and **predict** the **behavior** of others, one engages in an intellectual

process moving by inference from one set of beliefs to another. This position contrasts with another theory of mind, the **simulation theory**, which holds that we need to make use of our own motivational and emotional resources and capacities for **practical reasoning** in explaining actions of others.

> "So called 'theory-theorists' maintain that the ability to explain and predict behaviour is underpinned by a folk-psychological theory of the structure and functioning of the mind – where the theory in question may be innate and modularised, learned individually, or acquired through a process of enculturation." **Carruthers and Smith (eds.), *Theories of Theories of Mind***

theosophy

PHILOSOPHY OF RELIGION, METAPHYSICS [from Greek *theo*, god + *sophia*, wisdom, wisdom about God] A term first employed by the **Neoplatonists** for their own doctrine, which emphasizes the unity of religion and philosophy, and for one's **mystical** acquaintance with the nature of **God**. The term was later used for several trends in German religious thought after the **Renaissance**, in particular the thinking of the Swedish natural philosopher Emanuel Swedenborg, which tended to blend the natural and the spiritual world and to combine rationalistic **cosmology** and biblical revelation. The term was also associated with the Theosophical Society, a movement initiated in 1875 by Helena Blavatsky, which aimed to introduce Eastern religions and metaphysics into Western thought.

> "[Theosophy] is the appropriate term for a theoretical cognition of divine nature and (God's) existence that would suffice to explain both the character of the world and the vocation of the moral laws." **Kant, *Critique of Judgement***

Theseus' ship

METAPHYSICS After the hero Theseus accomplished his mission to sail to Crete to kill the Minotaur, his ship (Ship 1) was put on display in Athens. As the time went by, its original planks and other parts were replaced one by one with new materials until one day all of its parts were new, with none of its original parts remaining. Do we want to say that the completely rebuilt ship (Ship 2) is the same as the original or that it is a different ship? The case is further complicated. If all the original materials were kept and eventually used to construct a ship (Ship 3), would this ship be the same as the original? This example has inspired much discussion concerning the problems of **identity** and individuation.

> "To be something later is to be its closest continuer. Let us apply this view to one traditional puzzle about identity over time: the puzzle of the ship of Theseus." **Nozick, *Philosophical Explanation***

thin theory of the good

ETHICS, POLITICAL PHILOSOPHY For **Rawls, primary goods** are essential for pursuing any rational plan of life and are used to determine a thin conception of the **good**. A thin theory of the good explains why these primary goods are what any rational person would **desire** and it also gives insight into the notion of **rationality** that leads from these goods to the **choice** of principles of **justice**. Such an account is necessary to understand the **motives** and choices of participants in the **original position**. Once principles of justice are derived from the original position, we may develop a full conception of the good and therefore a full theory of the good.

> "We need what I have called the thin theory of the good to explain the rational preference for primary goods and to explicate the notion of rationality underlying the choice of principles in the original position." **Rawls, *A Theory of Justice***

thing

METAPHYSICS In a general sense, a thing is any item that can be referred to or named. It can be any constituent of a metaphysical world, including **substances** and **properties**, **essences** and **accidents**, **particulars** and **universals**, **concrete** and abstract objects. A material body is a thing, and so is a **number**, a **relation**, and an **illusion**. In this sense, "thing" is synonymous with "**being**" or "**entity**." Along with other questions about things, metaphysicians have asked why there are things ("Why is there something rather than nothing?") and what kinds of thing are fundamental.

In a narrower and more technical sense, things have their own **identity** and possess qualities and relations. This **concept** of a thing is close to the concept of a substance or of an **object**. In sentences, things are designated by subjects rather than by **predicates**, which in turn introduce properties ascribed to things. In different theoretical contexts, a thing is what **Frege** calls an object of a **proper name**, what **Quine** calls the **value** of a **bound variable**, and what **Strawson** calls an **individual**. It is the nature of things in this latter sense that is a focus of contemporary metaphysics.

> "In its widest sense 'thing' can be applied to any object of reference whatever, to any possible subject of discourse . . . The kind of thing we are concerned with here is much more narrowly circumscribed. It is, essentially, an observable, spatiotemporal entity, a concrete object of perception." **Quinton, *The Nature of Things***

thing-in-itself

METAPHYSICS [German *Ding an sich*] **Kant**'s term, used interchangeably with *noumenon*, for things as they are independent of the conditions of possible **experience** and outside the legitimate application of the **categories**. A thing-in-itself contrasts with an **appearance** or *phenomenon*, which is a thing as it appears to us. Since the world of appearance is the only possible **object** of **knowledge**, the thing-in-itself is thinkable, but unknown. In using this term, Kant emphasized his claim that the thing-in-itself is the true correlate of **sensibility**. The central thesis of **transcendental idealism** holds that the **objects** given to us in experience are only appearances of things in themselves. Although things in themselves can not be known through the **representations** of our sensibility, we must **postulate** them because there can not be an appearance without anything that appears. This is a dogmatic point in Kant's philosophy that has been criticized by later philosophers. Other philosophers have asked whether appearances and things in themselves are meant to be the same objects taken differently or different objects. There are problems with both answers.

> "The transcendental concept of appearances in space, on the other hand, is a critical reminder that nothing in space is a thing in itself, that space is not a form inhering in things in themselves as their intrinsic property, that objects in themselves are unknown to us." **Kant, *Critique of Pure Reason***

thing-language

EPISTEMOLOGY, PHILOSOPHY OF SCIENCE **Carnap**'s term for the language that we use in speaking about the **properties** of observable things, such as "hot," "cold," "small," "large," "red," and "blue." It is the language to which all psychological **statements** and scientific statements are reducible. By introducing this term, Carnap intends to distinguish between the language of scientific theory and the language of ordinary things, and between a language requiring the use of instruments and a language not requiring it. He also claims that all statements in the thing-language about material **objects** can be reduced to statements about sense-experience.

"Terms like 'hot' and 'cold' may be regarded as belonging to the thing-language, but not 'temperature' because its determination requires the application of a technical instrument." **Carnap, in Hanfling (ed.), *Essential Readings in Logical Positivism***

thinking

PHILOSOPHY OF MIND A **mental act** displaying a **person's rationality**, including theoretical contemplation and **reasoning** and practical **deliberation**. Traditionally, thinking is conceived to be an **inner** and conscious activity that is closely related to speech. For **Plato** and **Aristotle**, thinking (Greek *noesis* or *dianoia*) inherently involves cognitive **consciousness** of a universal **object** and the application of the **universal** to the **particular**. For **Descartes**, thinking (Latin *cogitatio*) comprises mental phenomena in general, and is the main attribute of the **substance** of **mind**. Along with many later **rationalists** and **empiricists**, Descartes considered that thinking is a process that brings **concepts** or **ideas** before the mind. For **Hobbes**, it is a dialogue in the **soul** involving the use of verbal **images**. For **Berkeley** and **Hume**, thinking is a sequential series of ideas or images in the mind. For **Kant**, thinking (German *Denken*) is **cognition** by means of concepts, although it is empty if it does not also involve sensory **intuition**. **Ryle** initiated a new approach to the notion of thinking. He argued that thinking is a **disposition** rather than something that must be done silently in the soul. In his later period, Ryle puts forward an **adverbial** account of thinking, claiming that it is an adverbial modification of activities and not itself an activity. Ryle's approach has given rise to much

debate. Some critics claim that developing an adequate account of thinking requires a richer body of theory about the mind, such as **Fodor**'s **language of thought** hypothesis. Price suggested that cognition in absence is another distinguishing feature of thinking. Thinking is usually distinguished from **perception**, **imagination**, and **emotion**.

"We can all agree that thinking is rightly described as conceptual cognition." **Price, *Thinking and Experience***

thinking substance

METAPHYSICS, PHILOSOPHY OF MIND The **mind**. **Descartes**'s term, in contrast to **extended substance** or corporeal substance, that is, **body**. This division is the main characteristic of Descartes's **dualism**. While the principal **attribute** of extended substance is **extension**, the principal attribute of thinking substance is thinking. Descartes further divided thinking substances into those that possess and use a body and those that do not possess or use bodies. The former include human minds, while the latter include God and angels. Thinking substance is also called thinking thing (*res cogitans*), while extended substance is also called extended thing (*res extensa*).

"A thinking substance is one which understands or wills or doubts or dreams or imagines or has sensory perceptions." **Descartes, *The Philosophical Writings***

thinking thing, the English translation of *res cogitans*

Third Man argument

METAPHYSICS **Plato**'s argument in *Parmenides* 132a–b to show that his own Theory of **Forms** involves an infinite regress. Plato's own example concerns largeness, but following **Aristotle** scholars generally state the problem in terms of man. The basic principle to establish a **Form** is that when one sees a number of similar particulars, one will think that there must be something common to them all, and that thing is a Form. If, however, we consider the Form of man along with other particular men, there must also be something common to all of them, and that thing would be a third man in addition to particular men and the Form of man. But the process of adding something in common, begun with particular men, the Form of man and the third man, would go on indefinitely, leading to an **infinite regress**.

There has been much debate whether this is a valid argument, whether it is a valid objection to the Theory of Forms, and whether Plato himself believed it to be valid. Gregory **Vlastos** has argued that two implicit premises are needed for the Third Man argument to succeed. The first premise, concerning **self-predication**, requires that what is predicated is itself a subject of that same predicate. The other premise, concerning non-identity, requires that what is predicated is something different from the subject of which it is predicated. The discussion that arose out of this interpretation has contributed greatly to our understanding of Plato and his relation to contemporary philosophy. It has also helped our understanding of Aristotle, who diagnosed the root of the problem of the Third Man as the **separation** of the Form from the particulars and Plato's confusion of *toionde* (**such**) and *tode ti* (**a this**), that is, his confusion of the **universal** and the **particular**.

> "No common predicate indicates a this, but rather a such. If not, many difficulties follow and especially the 'Third Man'." **Aristotle,** *Metaphysics*

Thirdness, see Firstness

third-person perspective, see first-person perspective

third realm

LOGIC, PHILOSOPHY OF LANGUAGE, METAPHYSICS **Frege**'s term. Traditionally, philosophers contrast the realm of **ideas** or **mental entities** with the realm of **material objects**. Frege called mental entities the first realm and material objects the second realm. Based on his distinction between **sense** and **reference**, he claimed that there is a third realm of sense or **thought**. It is different from the realm of ideas because any idea needs a bearer (they are yours or mine), but the senses of words we use in communication exist independently of us. A true **proposition** is true no matter whether anyone takes it to be true or even entertains it. It is accessible to all in common, but its **contents** are immutable and

immaterial. The third realm is also different from the realm of objective things we talk about or the realm of reference, for many **names** may have sense but lack reference. Thus senses or thoughts form a third realm between us and objects, and this realm leads us from the inner world of **sense-impressions** to the outer world of perceptible things.

> "So the result seems to be: thoughts are neither things of the outer world nor ideas. A third realm must be recognised. What belongs to this corresponds with ideas, in that it cannot be perceived by the senses, but with things, in that it needs no bearer to the contents of whose consciousness to belong." **Frege, "The Thought: A Logical Inquiry," in Strawson (ed.),** *Philosophical Logic*

thisness, another expression for a this

Thomism

METAPHYSICS, PHILOSOPHY OF RELIGION The philosophical tradition founded by Thomas **Aquinas** and developed by his followers in the Catholic tradition. It tried to combine **Aristotle**'s philosophy with Christian teaching and claimed that all created things are a composition of **existence** and **essence**. It extensively applied the Aristotelian distinctions between **form** and **matter** and between **actuality** and **potentiality** to explain various relationships. Form is necessary being and matter is **contingent** being. **God** contains both essential being and contingent being. The **soul** is viewed as the **substantial form** of the body whilst also being regarded as **immortal**. Thomism represents a valuable contribution to the analyses of the relationship between **reason** and **faith** and the relationship between **free will** and **determinism**. We are free not in spite of God's **power**, but because of it. Aquinas' doctrine was condemned after his death, but was soon rehabilitated and he was canonized in 1323. Since the thirteenth century, Aquinas has been the Common Doctor for all Catholic schools of thought. Hence, it is not merely a partial school in **scholasticism**. It is often used as a synonym of scholasticism. In the neo-Thomist movement of the nineteenth century, the Catholic authorities declared again that the philosophy of Aquinas must be studied by all Catholic clergy. Thomism is recommended as the norm for theological teaching. More recently, philosophers such as Peter **Geach** and Anthony **Kenny** have applied the methods of **analytical philosophy** to the issues and concepts of Thomism, including **intentionality**, **action**, **freedom**, **being and essence**, **causation**, and **virtue**. This is sometimes called analytical Thomism.

"The foundation of Thomism was that reason supplemented faith, not denied it." **Leff,** *Medieval Thought*

Thoreau, Henry David (1817–62)

American philosopher, born in Concord, Massachusetts, a major figure of New England transcendentalism. In his most important work, *Walden, or Life in the Woods* (1854), Thoreau compared nature and society, claiming that in contrast to the evil of any state, nature offers absolute freedom and the basis for a life of spontaneity. He pursued natural simplicity and practiced self-reliance in life. Thoreau provided a theory of civil disobedience that has had great practical influence.

thought

LOGIC, PHILOSOPHY OF LANGUAGE, PHILOSOPHY OF MIND Normally, what we are aware of within our **mind**. For **Frege**, a thought is the **sense** of a **sentence** that can be used to make an **assertion** or to ask a question that is answerable "Yes" or "No." The **contents** of thoughts can be true or false. Thoughts in this sense are logical or conceptual rather than a matter of individual psychology. Different individuals may share the same thought, although they can not share the same act of **thinking**. Thus, Frege called thought the **third realm** (the others being the physical and the psychological). If we take thought psychologically, the central tenet of traditional **analytical philosophy** is that the **analysis** of thought presupposes the analysis of language, and that language is prior to thought. In contrast, **philosophy of thought** argues that this priority in the order of analysis should be reversed. **Fodor**'s **language of thought** hypothesis holds that thought is a form of symbol manipulation with its own **syntax** and **semantic** properties.

"The thought, in itself immaterial, clothes itself in the material garment of a sentence and thereby becomes comprehensible to us. We say a sentence expresses a thought." **Frege, "The Thought: A Logical Inquiry," in Strawson (ed.),** *Philosophical Logic*

thought experiment

PHILOSOPHICAL METHOD, PHILOSOPHY OF SCIENCE An attempt to test a **hypothesis** through an imagined situation when an actual experiment is impossible in practice or perhaps even in theory. It conceives of the consequences of an intervention in the world without actually intervening. This device is employed widely by philosophers and theoretical scientists. It exercises the **imagination** in order to show what is possible or impossible. Thought experiments can be used either destructively or constructively. A destructive use is directed against a theory, typically through a *reductio ad absurdum* argument, to show that a theory is internally inconsistent or conflicts with some well-entrenched belief. Constructive thought experiments proceed either from some unproblematic phenomena to a well-articulated theory or from a given background theory to a new conclusion.

"A thought experiment is an experiment that purports to achieve its aim without the benefit of execution." **Sorenson,** *Thought Experiment*

three-valued logic

LOGIC The earliest presentation of a three-valued system was elaborated by **Lukasiewicz** in the 1920s, motivated by his desire to provide a solution to the problem of **future contingents**. This problem was put forward by **Aristotle** in his example of the **sea-battle** tomorrow. Lukasiewicz reasoned: my presence in Warsaw at a certain time in the future is not settled at the present moment either positively nor negatively; it is therefore possible but not **necessary** that I shall be present in Warsaw at the stated future time; according to this presupposition, that I shall be present in Warsaw at that future time is neither true nor false at the present time; to say either that this is true or that this is false will be contradictory to the presupposition; so we need to deny the principle of **bivalence**, that is, that every **statement** is either true or false. He then argued that the possible should be an additional truth-value. If 1 is used to represent truth, 0 to represent falsity, the third value possible can be represented by $1/2$.

Hence we have more possible combinations of truth-values from two component **propositions**. For instance, the truth-table of "not p" in three-valued logic is:

P	~P
1	0
1/2	1/2
0	1

Some logicians argue that bivalence does not necessarily entail **determinism** and that three-valued logic should have another basis, but this part of logic has been adopted and developed by **Reichenbach**, **Putnam**, Bochvar, and others. It has been a model for **many-valued logic** in general.

> "With a view to the future-contingency proposition of the third truth-value, Lukasiewicz introduced a modal operator of possibilities into his three-valued logic." **Rescher,** *Topics in Philosophic Logic*

ti esti, Greek term for what-it-is

Tillich, Paul (1886–1965)

German existentialist philosopher of religion, born in Brandenburg, taught at Frankfurt, Union Theological Seminary, Harvard, and Chicago. Tillich held that religious questions arise from human existential situations and that Christian faith is grounded in our ultimate concern. Because philosophy and theology address the same ontological question, although in different ways, Christianity can be used to provide solutions to human practical and existential problems. Tillich's most important works include *Systematic Theology,* 3 vols. (1951–63), *The Courage to Be* (1952), and *Dynamics of Faith* (1957).

time

METAPHYSICS One of the most mysterious philosophical topics, but also one of the most richly discussed. Time concerns the progression and ordering of **events** in terms of before and after or in terms of **past**, present, and future. Time is commonly conceived to be a passage or a flowing stream, but this gives rise to the criticism of the **myth of passage**. Time is generally thought to have one dimension and an irreversible direction, but it is unclear what gives time its direction, whether there can be a backward temporal order, or how to account for the asymmetry between the past and the future. **Zeno's paradoxes** raise fundamental questions about time as an infinite **continuum** and similar problems arise concerning **space**. Even with contemporary developments in mathematics, it remains disputable whether time is infinitely divisible. **Plato** claimed that time is created and is the moving image of **eternity**. Philosophers continue to debate whether time has a beginning and whether we can make sense of a timeless existence. **Aristotle** in *Physics* expressed many puzzles about the existence of time. **Kant** argued that time, like space, is a form of intuition and understood mathematical knowledge to be determined in relation to these forms. Kant gave time a crucial role in his account of the **categories** and their application to **experience**. **Bergson** distinguished between intellectualized physical time and **duration**, which as the time of **consciousness** is the real essence of time. The validity of **McTaggart**'s attack on the reality of time is still under debate. Another enduring dispute concerns whether time is **absolute** or **relational**. **Heidegger**'s account of **temporality** is fundamental to his account of human being. In **existentialism**, time is more subjectively conceived through its connection with the problem of human experience.

> "What then is time? If no one asks me, I know. If I wish to explain it to one that asks, I do not know." **Augustine,** *Confessions*

time, absolute

METAPHYSICS, PHILOSOPHY OF SCIENCE **Newton** maintained that time is absolute in virtue of being independent of physical **events** and having its own nature, flowing uniformly without regard and without **relation** to any external thing. Absolute time is mathematical time, in contrast to the relative or external clock time in common use. Absolute time is **real**, and relative time is only apparent. Newton represents one radical position in a lasting dispute whether time and space are absolute or **relational**.

> "Absolute, true, and mathematical time, of itself, and from its own nature, flows equably without relation to anything external, and by another term

> is called duration." **Newton,** *Mathematical Principles of Natural Philosophy*

time-gap argument,

another term for time-lag argument

time-lag argument

EPISTEMOLOGY Also called the time-gap argument, an argument, put forward by **Russell** in *Human Knowledge*, against the **naive realist** assumption that **perception**, such as seeing or hearing, is a matter of direct awareness. Science proves that light travels at a finite speed, with a time-gap between the transmission of light from an external **object** and the perception of the object. The light of the sun that strikes our eyes has taken a long time to reach us, so the sun that we see now is actually the sun that existed some time ago and that may have ceased to exist. Although its current non-existence would not affect the fact that we see it now, the immediate object of our visual experience is not actually identical with the sun that is being seen. The same case is applied to the hearing. If a gun is fired some distance from us, we first see the flash with a small time-lag and then hear the sound with a greater time-lag. Because there is time-lag in all perceptions, perception is not a direct confrontation, but a **process**. The object of experience is always internal. This denial of the immediacy of perception poses a threat to direct or naive realism, which claims that perception is concerned only with immediate objects in the present, and raises many problems about the nature of perception.

> "I have in mind the famous 'time-lag' argument. Some philosophers . . . claim that the connection between experiential and temporal presence is only apparent. The case of stellar explosions . . . shows that things (events) can be present in experience, after they cease to exist." **Valberg,** *The Puzzle of Experience*

time-preference,

another expression for principle of fractional prudence

time travel

METAPHYSICS Time is normally thought to be directed from the past toward the future, but we can raise the question whether it is logically possible to travel backward in time or to ascribe more than one direction to time. Travel into the past would necessarily involve **backward causation**, with some later **events** causally affecting earlier events. Some claim that if this were true a traveler could travel back to murder his ancestors and prevent his own birth, but David **Lewis** argues that backward travel does not imply that the traveler could change the past.

We are normally thought to move at the same rate with everything else through time. The time elapsed from a traveler's departure to his arrival is the same as the duration of the journey. But it might be logically possible for a traveler to move from his departure to his arrival with the time spent on his journey not equal to the clock time from departure to arrival. Would there, then, be two unequal lengths of time depending upon how we measure the same journey? Would this allow us to travel into the future in the way that backward time travel would allow us to move into the past? In general, time travel is a **thought experiment** for inquiring into the nature of time.

> "What is time travel? Inevitably, it involves a discrepancy between time and time." **D. Lewis,** *Philosophical Papers*, **vol. 1**

timocracy

ANCIENT GREEK PHILOSOPHY, POLITICAL PHILOSOPHY, ETHICS [from Greek *time*, honor + *kratos*, strength, power, rule by those valuing honor] A type of **state** that **Plato** described in the *Republic*, in contrast to the Ideal State. Because the rulers of a timocratic state value honor, the state is ruled by the spirited element instead of the **rational** element that governs the Ideal State. Consequently the unity of the state is undermined by timocratic rule. Parallel to the city, the timocratic man is also dominated by the spirited element in the **soul**. **Self-interest** diverts him from impartial ideals and causes inner instability. According to Plato, timocracy is the first stage in the degeneration of the Ideal State.

> "There is only one thing which appears in timocracy most clearly under the rule of the spirited part, namely the love of victory and of honours." **Plato,** *Republic*

to be, see is or being

to be is to be perceived, see *esse est percipi*

to ti en einai, Greek term for essence

tode ti, Greek term for a this

toionde, Greek term for such

token

PHILOSOPHY OF LANGUAGE, METAPHYSICS, PHILOSOPHY OF MIND Together with **type**, a pair of terms that was introduced by C. S. Peirce to classify different **signs**. A token is "an actual existent thing or event which is a sign," and type is "a law that is a sign" or "a definitely significant form." A token shares the feature that identifies a type but is an **instance** or example of that type. A type is instantiated by different tokens. Different tokens resemble one another if they belong to the same type. In a sense, a token of a type is an instance of the type. Walking is a type, and this particular act of walking is a token. **Strawson**'s book *Individuals* is a type, while this copy of *Individuals* is a token. In a sense, this distinction is close to the distinction between the **particular** and the **general**. It has gained a wide currency in the philosophy of language, especially in the discussion of the relationship between a linguistic expression and an actual use of that expression, and also in the philosophy of mind. The **identity theory of mind** has been developed in two versions, respectively called **type-type identity theory** and **token-token identity theory**.

> "A single event which happens once and whose identity is limited to that one happening or a single place at any one instant of time. Such event or thing being significant only as occurring just when and where it does . . . I will venture to call a token." **Peirce, *Collected Papers of Charles Sanders Peirce***

token-reflexive

PHILOSOPHY OF LANGUAGE Also called indexical expressions, Hans **Reichenbach**'s term for expressions involving a **reference** back, reflexively, to their own **token** utterance, that is, to the speaker, place, time, or context of utterance. For example, to say that A is past amounts to saying that A is earlier than this

utterance. An understanding of such an expression involves understanding all the features of an utterance mentioned above and an ability to identify the utterance itself. The **truth-value** of a sentence containing a token-reflexive expression is liable to change as the relevant circumstances of the utterance change.

> "A token-reflexive expression is one like 'I', 'here', 'now', whose essential occurrence in a sentence renders that sentence capable of bearing different truth-values according to the circumstances of its utterance – by whom, when, and where it is uttered, to whom it is addressed, with what gestures it is accompanied, and so forth." **Dummett, *Truth and Other Enigmas***

token-token identity theory

PHILOSOPHY OF MIND One version of the **identity theory of mind** or **central-state materialism**, according to which there is a token-token identity between mental and physical states or events. Each **token** instance of a **mental event** is as a matter of fact the same as some token instance of a physical event. The mental event is simply the physical event seen from the inside. This theory contrasts with another version of the identity theory, the **type-type identity theory**, which suggests that there is a type-type identity between mental states or events and bodily states or events. It is difficult to specify and prove this token-token identity, and the importance of the theory can be questioned because it seems to exclude the provision of a theoretical basis of mental-physical identity promised by the type-type theory.

> "The thesis that for every token instance of a mental state, there will be some token neurophysiological event with which that token instance is identical. Such views were called 'token-token identity theory'." **Searle, *The Rediscovery of the Mind***

toleration

ETHICS, POLITICAL PHILOSOPHY, PHILOSOPHY OF RELIGION Refraining from acting against persons or practices that one disapproves of for religious or political reasons, on the grounds that all persons have the right to their own religious beliefs and other opinions. Toleration has been a touchstone of a **democratic state** and society. **Locke**'s *A Letter on*

Toleration is the classic text on questions of toleration, especially with regard to religious toleration.
Locke advocated extending to all things lawful in
the constitution, although his own tolerance did not
extend to **atheists**. Locke's arguments for toleration
included his view that a church has no right to per-
secute people and, more importantly, that human
knowledge is so limited and open to error that we
can never be sure that one religious opinion is right
and another is wrong. Toleration supports a notion
of **liberty** that is equal and impartial. It has, however, its own dilemma concerning tolerating the
intolerant: if we tolerate an individual or group that
lacks the spirit of tolerance, toleration can lead to
our own destruction; if we refuse to tolerate the
intolerant, we will sacrifice the principle of tolerance to expediency.

> "The toleration of those that differ from others
> in matters of religion, is so agreeable to the gospel
> of Jesus Christ, and to the genuine reason of
> mankind, that it seems monstrous for men to
> be so blind, as not to perceive the necessity and
> advantage of it, in so clear a light." **Locke**, *A Letter
> Concerning Toleration*

topic-neutral

PHILOSOPHY OF LANGUAGE, PHILOSOPHY OF MIND
Originally, **Ryle**'s term for **logical constants**, such
as "of" "not," "every." They are not endowed with
special **meanings**, and are applicable to discourse
about any subject-matter. They do not **refer** to any
external **object** but function to organize meaningful
discourse. J. J. C. **Smart** calls a term topic-neutral
if it is noncommittal about designating something
mental or something physical. Instead, it simply
describes an **event** without judging the question
of its intrinsic **nature**. In his central-state theory of
mind, Smart develops a topic-neutral analysis of
mental expressions and argues that it is possible to
account for the situations described by mental concepts in purely physical and topic-neutral terms.

> "In this respect, statements like 'I am thinking
> now' are, as J. J. C. Smart puts it, topic-neutral.
> They say that something is going on within us,
> something apt for the causing of certain sorts of
> behaviour, but they say nothing of the nature of
> this process." **D. Armstrong**, *A Materialist Theory of
> the Mind*

topos

ANCIENT GREEK PHILOSOPHY, LOGIC [Greek, place]
For **Aristotle**, "a place in which arguments are to
be found." A *topos* is a standard procedure, pattern,
or strategy for an argument, whatever its subject-
matter. The logical work in which Aristotle deals
with various *topoi* is accordingly called the *Topics*.
This is a handbook for conducting arguments in
disputes.

> "One *topos* is to look and see if a man has
> described as an accident what belongs in another
> way." **Aristotle**, *Topics*

totalitarianism

POLITICAL PHILOSOPHY [from Italian *totalitario*, absolute, complete, all-embracing] A form of rule, originally associated with Italian fascism, that places every
politically significant element under the control of a
highly centralized government. A totalitarian **state**
generally has an official **ideology** and suppresses
the plurality of thought and opinion. It has one
dominant party, typically under a single leader, and
co-opts or destroys any opposition. Competitive
interest groups and other previously independent
organizations are either suppressed or brought into
a corporativist structure to express populist support.
The whole society is hierarchically and cohesively
organized. The economy, military, and mass media
are tightly controlled, with a focus on alleged enemies used to maintain discipline and enthusiasm.
There is no strict distinction between public and
private or between party and state. Totalitarian
rulers appear to organize their population into a dis-
ciplinary unity and can mobilize their resources to
achieve one goal over a short time, but unacknow-
ledged political conflicts beneath the surface and
repression of public debate can have heavy costs, with
some achievements more a matter of propaganda
than efficiency. In the West, especially after the out-
break of the Second World War, totalitarianism
became a pejorative term. Unlike **authoritarian**
rule, a totalitarian regime not only denies individual
freedom and human **rights** and requires order and
stability, but also seeks to realize a specific ideology.
As a doctrine, totalitarianism derives from older patterns of tyranny and despotism, but transforms them
under the conditions of **modernity**. It is unclear to
what extent a single theory of totalitarian rule can

694 tough-mindedness

apply to regimes with different origins, formations, and ideologies.

> "Totalitarianism is a new form of dictatorship . . . It was characterised by the predominance of the leader of the victorious movement, who, with the aid of his subordinate elite and a manipulated ideology, aimed at total control over state, society and the individual." **Schapiro,** *Totalitarianism*

tough-mindedness

PHILOSOPHICAL METHOD William **James** claimed that philosophy is first of all a kind of aesthetics for expressing some temperament or attitude toward the world rather than a kind of logic for seeking solutions to a set of problems. Philosophy is decided by the temperament of the philosopher. He further suggested that the history of philosophy is to a great extent a clash of two kinds of human temperaments, namely tough-minded and tender-minded temperaments. Tough-minded philosophers hold on to **facts** and declare that everything else is false, while tender-minded philosophers value certain **principles** rather than concentrate on facts. This distinction can be seen in the conflict of **empiricists** like **Hume** and **rationalists** like **Hegel**. The tension between tender-minded and tough-minded philosophers is further represented through tensions between **intellectualistic** and **sensationalistic** views, **idealistic** and **materialistic** views, **optimistic** and **pessimistic** views, religious and irreligious views, belief in **free will** and **fatalism**, **monism** and **pluralism**, and **dogmatism** and **skepticism**. James himself attempts to reconcile both temperaments in his **radical empiricism**.

> "The tough-minded are the men whose alpha and omega are facts." **W. James,** *Pragmatism*

tradition

POLITICAL PHILOSOPHY, ETHICS, PHILOSOPHY OF SOCIAL SCIENCE The existing social customs, institutions, patterns of **belief**, and codes of **behavior** that are accepted by a **community** and form its **culture**. Every person belongs to at least one tradition and grows up through emulating or rebelling against what his traditions indicate. Tradition is inherited from previous generations and is transmitted, perhaps in an altered form, to future generations. It

is the bond and continuity of a nationality, culture, or religion. In political philosophy, liberal **individualism** stresses **rationality** and personal rights and rejects tradition as a force that hampers social progress and personal **freedom**. **Conservatism**, on the other hand, believes that we should respect tradition, and that large-scale change, especially violent revolution, can only lead to calamity. This conservative view is shared by contemporary **communitarian** theory. In **ethics**, modern **utilitarianism** and **deontology** focus on interests, **rights**, and **duties**, but **virtue ethics** respects the role of tradition in the cultivation of **virtues**. A general criticism of modern morality is that it isolates rationality from tradition.

> "Self-contained traditions rarely raise questions of existence and reality. A member of such a tradition may ask whether a particular event has occurred and he may doubt a particular tale, but hardly anybody considers the 'ontological implications' of all terms, statements, and stories in a certain domain." **Feyerabend,** *Problems of Empiricism*

traditional logic

LOGIC The logic in **Aristotle**'s works, especially his syllogistic logic, including also contributions made by the Stoics to what would now be called **propositional calculus**, and the contributions by medieval logicians to problems such as **reference** and **modality**. It is also called Aristotelian logic. Traditional logic has been superseded by modern **symbolic** or **mathematical logic**, initiated in **Frege**'s work, and is retained as a part of **predicate logic**. Modern logic holds that several basic assumptions in traditional logic, such as the claims that propositions are restricted to the **subject-predicate** form and that we must accept the principle of **bivalence**, are problematic. The core of traditional logic is the syllogism.

> "The doctrine of the syllogism is the main achievement of traditional logic." **Strawson,** *Introduction to Logical Theory*

tranquility

ANCIENT GREEK PHILOSOPHY, ETHICS, EPISTEMOLOGY [Greek *ataraxia*, non-disturbance] A key term in ancient **skepticism** for a state that is free from disturbance and remains untroubled, both intellectually and in ordinary life. Tranquility is both the outcome and reward of **suspension of judgment**. It emerges from a negative response to claims concerning the **objectivity** of **values** and accessibility of **truth**. Tranquility is what skepticism calls happiness.

> "As end the Sceptics name suspension of judgement, upon which tranquillity follows like a shadow." **Diogenes Laertius, *Lives of the Eminent Philosophers***

transcendent

PHILOSOPHY OF RELIGION, METAPHYSICS, EPISTEMOLOGY, MODERN EUROPEAN PHILOSOPHY [from Latin *trans*, over, beyond + *scandere*, climb, being superior to, surpassing or separated from certain limits, in contrast to immanent] That which lies beyond certain crucial limits. In medieval philosophy, **God** was said to be transcendent because he goes beyond all the finite limits of this world and even beyond the scope of conceptual thinking. The **scholastics** also employed the term *transcendentia* for ontological **predicates**, such as thing, one, true, and good, that go beyond **Aristotle**'s classification of ten **categories** and are coextensive with the whole world of **being**.

In **Kant**'s philosophy, transcendence has two different senses. First, there are **principles** that go beyond the limits of possible **experience**, including the psychological, cosmological, and theological **ideas** discussed in the **transcendental dialectic**. Secondly, **things-in-themselves**, which exist beyond the limits of possible experience are transcendent. Kant also called this transcendent reality. When transcendental ideas are thought to be transcendent realities, we have what Kant calls transcendental **illusions**. However, the use of transcendental in these contexts is confusing, because the transcendent is carefully distinguished by Kant from the **transcendental**, which concerns the conditions for the possibility of experience.

Husserl claimed that intentional acts have an immanent transcendence, by which they are related to **objects** of our **awareness** that are not parts of consciousness. **Heidegger** employed the notion of transcendence for man's experience of the whole as a whole, in contrast to the experience of oneself and parts of the whole.

> "We shall entitle the principles whose application is confined entirely within the limits of possible experience, immanent; and those, on the other hand, which profess to pass beyond these limits, transcendent." **Kant, *Critique of Pure Reason***

transcendental

METAPHYSICS, EPISTEMOLOGY **Kant** contrasted the transcendental with the **transcendent**. Something transcendent goes beyond the limits of **experience**, while the transcendental is related to the conditions of the possibility of experience. It is the form of **knowledge** that is concerned not with **objects** themselves, but with the modes in which we are able to know these objects, namely, with the conditions of possible experience. Generally, the transcendental is distinguished from the empirical and is associated with the *a priori*. Thus a system of *a priori* concepts might be called transcendental philosophy. Kant used the term **transcendental** to qualify many other terms, such as **logic**, **aesthetic**, **analytic**, **dialectic**, and **deduction**, in order to show that these topics are considered in terms of their role in establishing the conditions of the possibility of experience. These discussions use a type of reasoning called **transcendental argument**, the prime example of which is Kant's **transcendental deduction** of the **pure** concepts of the **understanding**.

> "I entitle *transcendental* all knowledge which is occupied not so much with objects as with the modes of our knowledge of objects in so far as this mode of knowledge is to be possible a priori." **Kant, *Critique of Pure Reason***

transcendental aesthetic

EPISTEMOLOGY, METAPHYSICS, PHILOSOPHY OF MATHEMATICS [from Greek *aisthesis*, sensibility] The first part of **Kant**'s *Critique of Pure Reason*. Aesthetics is now associated with problems of art, but Kant used the term in its root meaning concerning **sensibility**. The transcendental aesthetic is Kant's view of sensory **knowledge** and deals chiefly with **space**, **time**, and mathematics. In contrast, the **transcendental logic** is concerned with the intellect. According to the traditional aesthetic, sensibility is passive receptivity, but Kant held that sensible **perception** has its own **form** and **matter**. In terms of his metaphysical exposition and transcendental exposition, he argued that space and time are *a priori* **intuitions** by which we structure the sensory. As *a priori* forms of sensible intuition, they are the forms of our sensibility and are not determinations that attach to the **objects** themselves. In other words, they are **subjective** conditions of sensibility. Through its account of the *a priori* construction of mathematical **concepts** in space and time, the transcendental aesthetic gives a preliminary answer to Kant's central question of how **synthetic** *a priori* **judgment** is possible. It has been the basis for many later accounts of its central topics.

"The science of all principles of a priori sensibility I call transcendental aesthetic." **Kant,** *Critique of Pure Reason*

transcendental analytic

METAPHYSICS, EPISTEMOLOGY, LOGIC A division of the **transcendental logic** of Kant's *Critique of Pure Reason*, the other division being the **transcendental dialectic**. In the analytic, Kant sought to discover by **analysis** the **concepts** and **principles** of **pure reason**. The transcendental analytic contains the central arguments of the *Critique*. It is divided into the analytic of concepts and the analytic of principles. The analytic of concepts includes the **metaphysical deduction**, which shows the number and character of the **categories**, and the **transcendental deduction**, which seeks to **justify** the **objective** validity of the categories. The analytic of principles presents the principles under which the categories may legitimately be related to **sensibility** in general, and includes discussions of the **schematism** of the **pure concepts** of the **understanding**, the system of all principles of pure understanding and the distinction of all **objects** into phenomena and **noumena**. The transcendental analytic is the central part of Kant's critical philosophy and the core of his **Copernican revolution**.

"Transcendental analytic consists in the dissection of all our a priori knowledge into the elements that pure understanding by itself yields." **Kant,** *Critique of Pure Reason*

transcendental apperception

EPISTEMOLOGY, METAPHYSICS, PHILOSOPHY OF MIND The term **apperception** was introduced by **Leibniz** for

consciousness or reflective knowledge of an **inner** state that represents external things, but **Kant** argued that Leibniz's understanding of apperception was empirical and diverse, without relation to the **identity** of the subject. In contrast, Kant called his own version transcendental apperception, pure apperception, or original apperception and used this notion as a crucial factor in the **transcendental deduction**. Transcendental apperception is the **power** to combine **concept** and **intuition** in **knowledge**, that is, to introduce order and regularity in **appearances** and thus to achieve a synthetic unity in accordance with the **categories**. This involves the transcendental unity of apperception or unity of consciousness as a purely formal notion of the unity of the subject of experience. Apperception is different from intuition, for while intuition is receptive, transcendental apperception is a **spontaneous** act that brings intuitions to a subject and enables them to be combined into a **judgment**. The transcendental unity of apperception has the form of "**I think**," which can accompany all of one's **representations**, and has **synthesis** as its main function. In unifying appearances, it must act in accord with the categories, but it is prior to the categories and is indeed their source. Transcendental apperception can not be further determined and is the highest principle in the sphere of human knowledge. This notion is the direct source of **Fichte**'s philosophy and exerted great influence on the later development of German idealism. There are many important problems in expounding and justifying Kant's use of this difficult notion.

"This pure original unchangeable consciousness I shall name *transcendental apperception* . . . The numerical unity of this apperception is thus the a priori ground of all concepts, just as the manifoldness of space and time is the a priori ground of the intuitions of sensibility." **Kant,** *Critique of Pure Reason*

transcendental argument

METAPHYSICS, EPISTEMOLOGY An argument that starts from some accepted **experience** or **fact** to prove that there must be something which is beyond experience but which is a **necessary condition** for making the accepted experience or fact possible. The goal of a transcendental argument is to establish the truth of this **precondition**. If there is something X of which Y is a necessary condition, then Y must be true. This form of argument became prominent in **Kant**'s *Critique of Pure Reason*, where he argued that the existence of some fundamental *a priori* concepts, namely the **categories**, and of **space** and **time** as **pure** forms of **sensibility**, are necessary to make experience possible. In contemporary philosophy, transcendental arguments are widely proposed as a way of refuting **skepticism**. **Wittgenstein** used this form of argument to reject the possibility of a **private language** that only the speaker could understand. Peter **Strawson** employs a transcendental argument to prove the perception-independent existence of material **particulars** and to reject a skeptical attitude toward the existence of **other minds**. There is disagreement about the kind of **necessity** involved in transcendental arguments, and Barry Stroud has raised important questions about the possibility of transcendental arguments succeeding.

"A transcendental argument attempts to prove q by proving it is part of any correct explanation of p, by proving it a precondition of p's possibility." **Nozick** *Philosophical Explanations*

transcendental deduction

METAPHYSICS, EPISTEMOLOGY, ETHICS, AESTHETICS For **Kant**, the argument to prove that certain *a priori* concepts are legitimately, universally, necessarily, and exclusively applicable to **objects** of **experience**. Kant employed this form of argument to establish the legitimacy of **space** and **time** as the **forms** of **intuition**, of the claims of the **moral law** in the *Critique of Practical Reason*, and of the claims of the **aesthetic judgment** of **taste** in the *Critique of Judgement*. However, the most influential example of this form of argument appeared in the *Critique of Pure Reason* as the transcendental deduction of the **categories**. The **metaphysical deduction** set out the origin and character of the categories, and the task of the transcendental deduction was to demonstrate that these *a priori* concepts do apply to objects of experience and hence to prove the objective validity of the categories. The strategy of the proof is to show that objects can be thought of only by means of the categories. In **sensibility**, objects are subject to the forms of space and time. In **understanding**,

experienced objects must stand under the conditions of the **transcendental unity of apperception**. Because these conditions require the determination of objects by the **pure concepts** of the **understanding**, there can be no experience that is not subject to the categories. The categories, therefore, are justified in their application to **appearances** as conditions of the possibility of experience.

In the second edition of the *Critique of Pure Reason* (1787), Kant extensively rewrote the transcendental deduction, although he held that the result remained the same. The first version emphasized the **subjective** unity of **consciousness**, while the second version stressed the **objective** character of the unity, and it is therefore possible to distinguish between a subjective and objective deduction. The second version was meant to clarify the argument, but remained extremely difficult to interpret and assess. The presence of the two versions of this fundamental argument makes interpretation even more demanding. Generally speaking, European philosophers prefer the subjective version, while Anglo-American philosophers prefer the objective version.

The transcendental deduction of the categories was a revolutionary development in modern philosophy. It was the main device by which Kant sought to overcome the errors and limitations of both **rationalism** and **empiricism** and propelled philosophy into a new phase.

"The explanation of the manner in which concepts can thus relate a priori to objects I entitle their transcendental deduction." **Kant,** *Critique of Pure Reason*

transcendental dialectic

EPISTEMOLOGY, METAPHYSICS In **Kant**'s *Critique of Pure Reason*, the part of the **transcendental logic** that is concerned with **reason**, especially with certain kinds of malfunction of reason. In contrast, the other part of transcendental logic, the **transcendental analytic**, is concerned with **understanding**. For Kant, **dialectic** means "pertaining to error or illusion" or "uncovering judgements which bear a semblance of truth but are in fact illusory." These errors of human reason are natural, inevitable, and incurable, for they are rooted in the human demand for **completeness** and unity. **Pure reason** commits these errors when it mistakenly applies the **categories** to **things-in-themselves**, that is, things beyond the limits of **experience**, and mistakenly takes the **Ideas** of Reason to characterize something that is given in experience. These errors are the source of traditional metaphysics. The transcendental dialectic is Kant's criticism of traditional **ontology**, especially as discussed by **Wolff**. It chiefly addresses three metaphysical disciplines: rational psychology, which discusses the **soul** or thinking subject as an empirical entity and leads to **paralogisms**; rational **cosmology**, which discusses **appearance** as a whole and leads to **antinomies**; and rational **theology**, which attempts to prove the existence of **God** and leads to the **ideal** of pure reason.

"The transcendental dialectic will therefore content itself with exposing the illusion of transcendental judgements, and at the same time taking precautions that we be not deceived by it." **Kant**, *Critique of Pure Reason*

transcendental ego

MODERN EUROPEAN PHILOSOPHY, METAPHYSICS, PHILOSOPHY OF MIND For **Husserl**, the **phenomenological reduction** leads to the discovery that whatever is in the world is only as **object** of our **pure consciousness**, that is, an object of the transcendental ego. This **ego** is the unity of the empirical ego's **stream of consciousness**. It can not be **bracketed** because it is essentially **entailed** by the *cogito*. It is **transcendental** because it precedes the **being** of the world. This ego constitutes itself through its **acts**. It is **self-aware** and announces itself in its conscious acts. The transcendental ego, according to Husserl, is also one's "ultimately constitutive subjectivity," "ego in its full concreteness," a "monad" and "the active subject of consciousness." It is the source of all mental operations and plays crucial roles in the organization of **experience** and in the production of **intentionality**. This notion is intended to provide a starting-point for phenomenological **reflection** and to distinguish **phenomenology** from empirical sciences.

"As transcendental ego I am thus the absolutely responsible subject of whatever has existential validity for me. Aware of myself as this ego, thanks to the transcendental reduction, I stand now above all worldly existence, above my own human life and existence as man." **Husserl**, *Shorter Works*

transcendental exposition

EPISTEMOLOGY, METAPHYSICS, PHILOSOPHY OF MATHEMATICS, PHILOSOPHY OF SCIENCE An argument in the **transcendental aesthetic** of Kant's *Critique of Pure Reason*. According to the transcendental exposition of the **concept** of space, it is necessary for space to be an *a priori* **intuition** if **synthetic** *a priori* knowledge in geometry is possible. Although there is no mathematical discipline that is related to **time** as geometry is related to space, Kant claimed that it is necessary for time to be an *a priori* intuition if the body of *a priori* synthetic knowledge exhibited in the general doctrine of **motion** is possible.

"I understand by a transcendental exposition the explanation of a concept, as a principle from which the possibility of other a priori synthetic knowledge can be understood." **Kant**, *Critique of Pure Reason*.

transcendental ideal, see ideal (Kant)

transcendental ideas, see idea (Kant)

transcendental illusion

EPISTEMOLOGY, METAPHYSICS Traditional metaphysics usually started from empirical or sensory **illusions** in order to show that the **senses** sometimes deceive us and that **appearance** is illusory. **Kant** claimed that traditional metaphysics was itself permeated by illusions, which arise from the deceptive extension of the **concepts of pure understanding** beyond the limits of **experience** or **appearance** to **things-in-themselves**. It takes **regulative principles** as **knowledge** of **objects**. These transcendental illusions are not generated by appearance, but are in contrast with it. They cheat us not by the senses, but by **reason**. Kant claimed that these illusions are natural and inevitable and result from the natural quest of reason for the absolute condition. The task of his critical philosophy was to determine the limits of human reason and to guard against the illegitimate transgression of these limits. His *Critique of Pure Reason* is divided into two parts: the **transcendental analytic** seeks to determine the legitimate sphere of **pure reason**; and the **transcendental dialectic** seeks to show how transcendental illusions result once reason does not observe its proper limits.

"Transcendental illusion, on the other hand, does not cease even after it has been detected and its invalidity clearly revealed by transcendental criticism." **Kant,** *Critique of Pure Reason*

transcendental logic

METAPHYSICS, EPISTEMOLOGY The main part of **Kant**'s *Critique of Pure Reason*, including both the **transcendental analytic** and the **transcendental dialectic**. Breaking from the pattern of general or **traditional logic**, which dealt strictly with the **form** of **thoughts**, transcendental logic not only excluded modes of **knowledge** which have empirical roots, but also sought to trace the origin of *a priori* **knowledge**. Transcendental logic used the table of **judgments** of traditional logic as a clue to determine the **pure concepts of the understanding** or **categories** and proceeded to determine how these *a priori* concepts have **objective** reference. Transcendental logic also sought to explain the inevitable **illusions** of reason by its tendency to employ the categories beyond the limits of **experience**.

"Such a science, which should determine the origin, the scope, and the objective validity of such knowledge, would have to be called transcendental logic." **Kant,** *Critique of Pure Reason*

transcendental object

METAPHYSICS, EPISTEMOLOGY A **concept** which, like *noumenon* or **thing-in-itself**, seems to designate an unknown object outside the limits of **experience**. The concept is adopted to show that there is something that lies at the basis of **appearances** and is the **intelligible cause** of the latter. The transcendental object is the intelligible correlate of **sensible** appearances. The **postulation** of its existence is the theoretical consequence of **Kant**'s belief that there can be no appearance without anything that appears. Although the transcendental object can be confused with the thing-in-itself, the two concepts have different functions.

"This transcendental object cannot be separated from the sensible data, for nothing is then left through which it might be thought." **Kant,** *Critique of Pure Reason*

transcendental paralogism, see paralogism

transcendental philosophy

PHILOSOPHICAL METHOD, METAPHYSICS, EPISTEMOLOGY **Kant**'s term for an exhaustive and systematic **analysis** of the whole of *a priori* **knowledge**. In this philosophy, he sought to answer the question of how **synthetic** *a priori* **judgments** are possible and, more specifically, how the **sciences** are possible. Transcendental philosophy is distinguished from **ontology** because it is concerned only with the **concepts** and **principles** of **understanding** and **reason** and takes **objects** as something **given** and not in need of a philosophical account, although his actual discussion of objects is complex and puzzling. According to Kant, the *Critique of Pure Reason* was to lay down the fundamentals for the whole system of transcendental philosophy, but because the *Critique* was an essential but incomplete examination of synthetic *a priori* knowledge, it was not the whole system itself.

"The critique of pure reason therefore will contain all that is essential in transcendental philosophy." **Kant,** *Critique of Pure Reason*

transcendental place, see transcendental reflection

transcendental reflection

EPISTEMOLOGY, METAPHYSICS An operation of **mind** prior to the construction of any **objective judgment** that **synthesizes concepts** and **intuitions**. This operation has the purpose of reflecting on or comparing the character of **representations** in order to decide whether they belong to **understanding** or to **sensible intuitions**. The act of comparison employs a list of so-called concepts of reflection or concepts of comparison, which have no reference to an **object** but are merely means for orienting judgment. These concepts include **identity** and **difference**, agreement and **opposition**, **inner** and **outer**, **matter** and **form**. These concepts are prone to **amphiboly** because they are applied both to concepts and intuitions. If we take them to be **properties** of objects, then **ontological** errors occur. These concepts of reflection are also called transcendental topics. According to the employment of these concepts in **sensibility** or in **understanding**, transcendental reflection assigns a place to a representation. This place is called the transcendental place.

"The act by which I confront the comparison of representations with the cognitive faculty to which it belongs, and by means of which I distinguish whether it is as belonging to the pure understanding or to sensible intuition that they are to be compared with each other, I call transcendental reflection." **Kant,** *Critique of Pure Reason*

transcendental synthesis, see synthesis

transcendental topic, see transcendental reflection

transcendental unity of apperception, see transcendental apperception

transcendentalism

METAPHYSICS, PHILOSOPHY OF RELIGION, ETHICS Also called New England transcendentalism, an early nineteenth-century spiritual and philosophical movement in the United States, represented by Ralph Waldo **Emerson** and Henry David **Thoreau**. It was centered in the so-called Transcendental Club in Boston, and published a quarterly journal *The Dial*. Influenced by **German idealism** and **Romanticism**, it claimed that there is a **spirit** of the whole, the over-soul, which is beyond the **space** and **time** of the everyday world but at the same time immanent in it, and which forms a higher spiritual reality. It advocated an **ascetic** lifestyle, emphasized self-reliance and communal living, and rejected contemporary civilization. The eventual goal of life is to achieve a mystical unity with this spiritual reality, that is, with **nature**. Transcendentalism is viewed as a mixture of **speculative** philosophy and semi-religious **faith**. This philosophical movement had a deep influence upon **existentialism**, **James**'s **pragmatism**, and contemporary environmental philosophy.

In a broad sense, transcendentalism is any doctrine that emphasizes the **transcendental**, and is taken as a synonym of transcendental philosophy. In this sense, all types of **absolute** philosophy, especially those idealist systems that emphasize the **transcendence** of the **Absolute** over the finite world, are considered examples of transcendentalism. Thus, transcendentalists had aims differing from those of **Kant**'s transcendental philosophy, which criticized those who wished to extend **knowledge** beyond

experience and instead sought to use a **transcendental argument** to establish the **conditions** for the possibility of **experience**.

"The transcendentalists believed in man's ability to apprehend absolute Truth, absolute Justice, absolute Rectitude, absolute goodness. They spoke of the Right, the True, the Beautiful as eternal realities which man can discover in the world and which he can incorporate into his life. And they were convinced of the unlimited perfectibility of man." **Werkmeister,** *A History of Philosophical Ideas in America*

transformational grammar

PHILOSOPHY OF LANGUAGE The most powerful of the three kinds of grammar distinguished by **Chomsky**. The other two are **finite-state grammar** and **phrase-structure grammar**. Transformational grammar is a replacement for phrase-structure grammar that (1) **analyzes** only the constituents in the structure of a **sentence**; (2) provides a set of phrase-structure **rules** that generate **abstract** phrase-structure **representations**; (and 3) holds that the simplest sentences are produced according to these rules. Transformational grammar provides a further set of transformational rules to show that all complex sentences are formed from simple elements. These rules manipulate elements and otherwise rearrange structures to give the surface structures of sentences. Whereas phrase-structure rules only change one symbol to another in a sentence, transformational rules show that items of a given grammatical form can be transformed into items of a different grammatical form. For example, they can show the transformation of negative sentences into positive ones, question sentences into affirmative ones and passive sentences into active ones. Transformational grammar is presented as an improvement over other forms of grammar and provides a model to account for the ability of a speaker to generate new sentences on the basis of limited data.

"The central idea of transformational grammar is determined by repeated application of certain formal operations called 'grammatical transformations' to objects of a more elementary sort." **Chomsky,** *Aspects of the Theory of Syntax*

translation holism

PHILOSOPHY OF LANGUAGE A type of **semantic holism** that claims that the **meaning** of an expression is determined by its relations to many other expressions in its language. Translating the expression into another language can preserve its meaning only if its associative or inferential relations with other expressions in the home language are preserved in the expressions of the target language. To translate one **sentence** in isolation into another language will result in the distortion of its meaning. The thesis of translation holism seeks to recognize constraints on the expressive power of a language.

> "What we will call translation holism is the claim that properties like meaning the same as some formula or another of L are holistic in the sense that nothing can translate a formula of L unless it belongs to a language containing many (non-synonymous) formulas that translate formulas of L." **Fodor and Lepore,** *Holism*

transmigration of the soul

ANCIENT GREEK PHILOSOPHY, PHILOSOPHY OF MIND, PHILOSOPHY OF RELIGION A doctrine introduced into the Western tradition by **Pythagoras**, who might have been influenced by oriental mysticism. It claims that **soul**, which has an essential kinship with the divine and **immortal**, is a temporary sojourner in the **body** and may live through successive incarnations in various animal and human bodies. If it keeps itself pure, not being polluted by bodily **passions**, it may eventually return to its true or godlike state. If it sins, it will be punished by prolonged suffering in more miserable incarnations. A soul must therefore do its best to keep apart from body. **Plato**'s famous doctrine of **recollection** is based on the transmigration of the soul. The transmigration of the soul is also called **metempsychosis** [Greek *meta*, among, in company with + *en*, in + *psyche*, soul].

> "First, that he [Pythagoras] maintains that the soul is immortal; next, that it changes into other kinds of living things, . . . Pythagoras seems to have been the first to bring these beliefs into Greece." **Diels and Kranz,** *Die Fregmente Der Vorsokratiker*

trans-world identity

METAPHYSICS Since **Leibniz**, it has been believed that each **object** exists in just one world. This is supported by the **idealist** doctrine of **internal relations**. Contemporary discussion of **possible worlds** is divided over this issue. Some philosophers insist that any object is confined to only one world and can not exist in more than one possible world. Thus, each **individual** is a world-bound individual. Other philosophers claim that the same individual can exist in a plurality of possible worlds. Accordingly, each individual, instead of being world-bound, becomes a trans-world individual. A problem arises about how to **identify** such an individual. A thing X is thought to exist in more than one world, W_n and W_m. Since only when W_n differs in at least one respect from W_m are they two worlds, X-in-W_n has at least some properties distinct from X-in-W_m. If this is so, X-in-W_n and X-in-W_m are discernible, and according to the principle of the **indiscernibility of identicals**, they are not identical. Some philosophers reject this claim, on the ground that each individual is identifiable in terms of its **essence** whatever world it is in. Other philosophers hold that trans-world identity is unintelligible. David **Lewis** developed a **counterpart theory** that claims that no individual inhabits more than one world, but any individual might have counterparts in other worlds that resemble it more or less closely in important respects of intrinsic **quality** and extrinsic **relations**. He thus replaces trans-world identity of individuals with the trans-world **resemblance** of counterparts.

> "What comes from trans-world resemblance is not trans-world identity, but a substitute for trans-world identity: the counterpart relation." **D. Lewis,** *Counterfactuals*

trial and error

EPISTEMOLOGY, PHILOSOPHY OF SCIENCE, PHILOSOPHICAL METHOD A **method** of scientific invention and thought. A scientist formulates a **hypothesis** or a theory and then uses it to attempt to solve some definite problem. This is the step of testing or trial. If the hypothesis fails the trial and is confronted by counterexamples, it is generally rejected as erroneous. All theories are tentative hypotheses and trials. All experiments are performed in order to see whether theories work and to find where they go wrong. If a theory goes wrong, we formulate a new theory and test it by new observations and experiments. **Popper** viewed the development of empirical science as a continuous process of trial and error, which he calls **conjecture** and **refutation**. In using this method, we learn from our mistakes and achieve progress. He believed that conjecture and refutation is also the basic method of philosophy.

> "We must have a question before we can hope that observation or experiment may help us in any way to provide an answer or put in terms of the method of trial and error, the trial must come before the error." **Popper,** *The Poverty of Historicism*

trinity

PHILOSOPHY OF RELIGION A Christian theological doctrine that **God** is one **substance** (Latin *substantia*, Greek *ousia*) consisting of three **persons** (Latin *personae*, Greek *hypostaseis*): Father, Son (Jesus Christ), and Holy Spirit. Each of them is God, but there are not three Gods but one. The doctrine is based on remarks in the New Testament at 1 Epistles 5:7: "There be three that bear witnesses in heaven, the father, the word, and the Holy Spirit; and these Three are one." Such an idea was influenced by **Plotinus'** three **hypostases**. Our knowledge of the existence of three persons is through **revelation**. In the Christian tradition, each person is ascribed one peculiar **attribute**: paternity to the Father, filiation to the Son, and procession to the Holy Spirit. Procession is explained in two ways: either the Holy Spirit proceeds from the Father through the Son, or it proceeds from the Father and from the Son. This difference of interpretation leads to the division between Eastern Orthodox Christianity and Western Christianity.

The are puzzles concerning the different persons of the Trinity. For example, the early Church also divided over the question of the **nature** of Jesus Christ. The monophysites held that there was one nature, which was both human and divine, and the dyphysites held that there were two separate natures. The monophysite doctrine, supported by some Eastern Churches, was criticized for being unintelligible. The dyphysite doctrine, adopted by the Roman Church, was criticized because it allowed only the human Jesus to suffer. Without divine suffering, Christian narrative about salvation becomes incoherent.

> "God, who has been represented (that is, personated) thrice, may properly enough be said to be three persons; though neither the word person, nor Trinity be ascribed to him in the Bible." **Hobbes,** *Leviathan*

tripartite definition of knowledge

ANCIENT GREEK PHILOSOPHY, EPISTEMOLOGY The traditional standard analysis of propositional knowledge, initiated by **Plato'**s claim in *Theaetetus* (201c–202d), that knowledge is true **belief** plus a **logos**. It holds that knowledge is justified true belief and obtains when the following three conditions apply: A knows P if and only if (1) P is true, (2) A believes P, and (3) A is justified in believing P. This definition is seriously challenged by **Gettier's problem**.

> "Because there are three parts to this definition it is called the tripartite definition or the tripartite account." **Dancy,** *Introduction to Contemporary Epistemology*

trivium, see *quadrivium*

trolley problem

ETHICS An ethical problem put forward by Philippa **Foot** in her 1967 paper "The Problem of Abortion and the Doctrine of the Double Effect." Suppose that the only possible way to steer a runaway trolley is to move it from one track to another. One man is working on the first track, and five men are working on the other. Anyone working on the track the trolley enters will be killed. Most people would accept that the driver should steer the trolley to the track on which only one person is working because the death of five persons is worse than the death of one person. Now suppose that the trolley, left to itself, will enter the track on which five men are working and kill them. If you are a bystander who can change the course of the trolley, would it be morally required or morally permissible to interfere to switch the trolley to the other track, on which only one person would be killed? According to **utilitarianism**, you should switch the trolley. However, if you do not interfere, you have not done anything to make you **responsible** for the five deaths, while if you do interfere your act does make you responsible for one death. Your own **integrity** or **moral rules** about how to act might lead you to reject the utilitarian conclusion. The trolley problem touches on both the nature of morality and concrete moral perplexity. If the driver is right to steer the trolley onto the track with one person in order to save the lives of five persons, why is it wrong to execute an innocent man to stop a riot in which five innocent people will be killed? Or why is it morally wrong to save five patients who would die without transplants at the cost of killing one healthy man for his organs? In dealing with the trolley problem and these related questions, some philosophers turn to the principle of **double effect**, according to which a moral distinction between the intended and unintended consequences of an action can help to decide when bad consequences of an action are acceptable.

> "If what people who say 'killing is worse than letting die' mean by it is true, how is it that [the driver] may choose to turn that trolley? . . . I like to call this the trolley problem, in honour of Mrs Foot's example." **Thomson and Parent, *Rights, Restitution and Risk***

truth

LOGIC, EPISTEMOLOGY, PHILOSOPHY OF LANGUAGE While science seeks to determine what is true, philosophy asks what is the nature of truth. Traditionally, truth is contrasted with falsity. It is viewed as a **property** that has a bearer, although it is disputed what the bearer is. Some ascribe truth to **sentences**, others to **propositions**, **statements**, **judgments**, or **utterances**. Consequently, some ask what renders a proposition true, while others ask what renders a sentence or an utterance of a sentence true.

What then does truth consist in? Since truth involves a **relation** to features of **reality**, a natural answer is that if a **belief** corresponds to reality it is true. This **correspondence theory** is the most widely held account of truth. However, this theory has many difficulties and the attempts to remove them have led to many alternative theories of truth, including the **coherence theory of truth** and the **pragmatic theory of truth**.

Many contemporary philosophers challenge the traditional assumption that truth is a property of something and hold that truth neither has a bearer nor describes a proposition. This **deflationary theory** of truth has various versions. The best known is the **redundancy theory of truth**, but there are other versions. The **disquotational theory of truth** claims that "p is true" means the same as "p." The **performative theory of truth** suggests that to say "p is true" amounts to performing a **speech act** of agreeing or repeating. Because it is like saying "ditto" after someone says that p, it is also called the ditto theory of truth. The **minimalist theory of truth** argues that saying "it is true that p" is necessarily equivalent to saying "p." The **semantic theory of truth** also belongs to this group, although it tends to defend the traditional notion of correspondence. Nowadays, a theory of truth can have various orientations. It can be a theory of truth itself, a theory of the **meaning** of the word "true," or a theory of the **function** of the truth **predicate**. Some theories might deal with all of these aspects.

> "Truth is the concern of all honest men: they try to espouse only true assertions, claims, theories, and so on. This is truth in extension. Philosophers worry also about truth in intension – that is about the concept of truth or the meaning of the term 'truth'." **Pitcher (ed.), *Truth***

truth (Heidegger)

MODERN EUROPEAN PHILOSOPHY Truth is traditionally conceived to be an agreement between **understanding** and **things**. It is seen as a **correspondence** between **objects** and **judgments** and to be located in judgments. However, the etymological sense of the Greek word for truth, *aletheia*, is unconcealment or unhiddenness. On this ground, **Heidegger** claims that truth in its most primordial sense is *Dasein*'s disclosedness or uncoveredness, that is, *Dasein*'s openness to its **possibilities**. Being true means being uncovered. At this primordial level, untruth is the **fallingness** of *Dasein* being closed off. Truth is the basic constitution of *Dasein* and its *existentiale*. Truth in this sense is prior to language and judgment and is the ground of truth in the traditional sense. Heidegger held that it is possible to compare whether there is an agreement between understanding and things only after *Dasein* has shown itself.

> "The Being-true (truth) of the assertion must be understood as Being-uncovering." **Heidegger, *Being and Time***

truth conditions

LOGIC, PHILOSOPHY OF LANGUAGE More fully expressed as truth and falsity conditions, the conditions under which a **statement** is true or false. In standard logic, the truth conditions of a composite **formula** are determined by the truth conditions of its components and by the **truth-functional connectives** linking its components. This can be shown in a **truth-table**.

Truth-conditional **semantics** holds that we know the **meaning** of a statement if we know its truth conditions and that a theory of **meaning** for a language assigns truth conditions for all the statements of that language.

For extensional contexts, if a statement in an argument is replaced by another statement with the same truth conditions, the validity of the original argument will not be altered.

> "The truth conditions of a truth-functional formula are the ways in which the truth-value of any statement of the form of that formula is determined by the truth-values of its constituent statements." **Strawson, *Introduction to Logical Theory***

truth-function

LOGIC A relationship that holds if the **truth** or falsity of a compound depends on the truth or falsity of its components. A compound of this sort, composed of **propositional variables** and **truth-functional connectives**, is a truth-functional **formula**. If **propositions** are substituted for the propositional variables in a truth-functional formula, we obtain a truth-functional **statement**, and its truth and falsity is determined entirely by the truth or falsity of its constituent statements and by the way in which the constituent statements are combined by truth-functional connectives. If all of its constants are truth-functional, a system of logic is truth-functional.

> "The whole meaning of a truth-function is exhausted by the statement of the circumstances under which it is true or false." **Russell, *Introduction to Mathematical Philosophy***

truth-functional connective

LOGIC Also called a truth-functional operator or truth-functional **constant**. These connectives are special **signs** for the various **relations** between sentences, **propositions**, or **statements** in a truth-functional system. They can not be used in isolation. Truth-functional connectives include: ~ (**negation**), ∧ (**conjunction**), ∨ (**disjunction**), ⊃ or → (**implication**), and ≡ or ↔ (**equivalence**). The role of these connectives is to determine the **truth-value** (the truth or falsity) of a truth-functional **statement** by the truth or falsity of its constituent statements. In daily language ~ is expressed by "not," ∧ by "and," ∨ by "either . . . or," ⊃ or → by "if . . . then," and ≡ or ↔ by "if and only if." However, the logical connectives and their ordinary language counterparts can differ in **implicature** or even in **meaning**.

> "Any sentential connective whose meaning can be captured in a truth-table is called a truth-functional connective and is said to express a truth-function." **Forbes, *Modern Logic***

truth-functional constant, another term for truth-functional connective

truth-functional operator, another term for truth-functional connective

truth of fact, see truth of reason

truth of reason

EPISTEMOLOGY **Leibniz** established a contrast between truths of reason and truths of **fact**. Truths of reason, which he used interchangeably with **necessary truths**, are primary **principles** that themselves require no proof and propositions that can be established by **analysis** from primary principles. Truths of reason are not established on the basis of empirical investigations, but are necessary and true in all actual and **possible worlds**, so that not even **God** can change them. Truths of fact, in contrast, are **propositions** that are established through **experience**. They are not necessarily and **universally** true, but just happen to be true of something. They are capable of change, and their **contradictories** are possible. According to Leibniz, truths of reason are **innate** and need only reason to be discovered, while truths of fact or **contingent** truths are gained through the **senses**.

> "Truths of reason are necessary, and those of fact are contingent. The primary truths of reason are the ones to which I give the general names

truth-table

LOGIC In the **propositional calculus**, the **truth-value** of a **formula** as a whole is determined by the truth-values of its components. This can be shown by a **truth-table**. The application of a truth-table to a logical problem is called the truth-table or matrix method. If p and q are **propositional variables** representing two constituent **statements**, the truth-tables of the formulae, $\sim$ p (not p), p $\vee$ q (p or q), p $\wedge$ q (p and q), p $\supset$ q (if p then q) and p $\equiv$ q (p if and only if q) can be shown in the following matrix:

p	q	~p	p∨q	p∧q	p⊃q	p≡q
T	T	F	T	T	T	T
T	F	F	T	F	F	F
F	T	T	T	F	T	F
F	F	T	F	F	T	T

These are the basic formulae, and the truth-conditions of the more complicated truth-functional propositions can be decided by the systematic applications of these. The truth-table lays down the truth-conditions of a truth-functional formula, and states the rule for the use of truth-functional **constants**. The truth-table method is an easy way of establishing whether formulae are **tautologies** (logically **necessary**), **self-contradictory** (logically impossible), or **contingent**.

> "[T]ruth table . . . determines the truth or falsity of the function for each combination of the truth-values of the elements." **Lewis and Langford, *Symbolic Logic***

truth-table method, see truth-table

truth-value

LOGIC Classical logic assumes that every **statement** must be either true or false, and its **truth** or falsity is its truth-value. If the statement is true, its truth-value is truth; if it is false, its truth-value is falsity. That "Coal is white" is false, so we say that the **sentence** has the truth-value falsity. That "Snow is white" is true, so we say that the sentence has the truth-value

truth. If two statements are **identical**, they have the same truth-value. The truth-value of a statement formed by using **truth-functional connectives** to combine component statements is calculated through the use of a **truth-table**. While the principle of **bivalence** in classical logic admits only two truth-values, some forms of modern logic deny this assumption and introduce **three-valued** or **many-valued logic**. **Strawson** argues that there can be **statements** that lack truth-value, that is, statements that are neither true nor false and for which there is a **truth-value gap**.

> "The truth-value of a proposition is its truth if it is true, and its falsehood if it is false." **Russell, *Collected Papers of Bertrand Russell*, vol. VI**

truth-value gap

LOGIC The lack of **truth-value** of a **statement** containing an expression that lacks **reference**. On some views, such a statement is neither true nor false. This phenomenon arises because the truth-value of a statement relies on the success or failure of the application to **objects** of the **general terms** it contains. But these general terms would be deprived of success or failure if a **singular term** in the statement failed to have reference. Other reasons for truth-value gaps include **category mistakes**, unsatisfied **presuppositions**, **ambiguity**, and **vagueness**. The existence of truth-value gaps makes **deductive reasoning** unreliable. There is controversy whether truth-value gaps are a defect of **natural language** or an inevitable consequence of the circumstances in which any language is used.

> "The claim that the radical failure of a definite singular term results in a truth-gap is in some cases more intuitively satisfactory, and in others less intuitively satisfactory, than the claim that it results in falsity." **Strawson, in Davidson and Hintikka (eds.), *Words and Objections***

T-sentence

PHILOSOPHY OF LANGUAGE The basis of **Tarski**'s proposal for an **adequacy condition** on **definitions** of **truth**. A theory of truth for a language is adequate if every instance of the schema "X is true if and only if P" can be derived within it. In this schema, "P" can be replaced by any sentence of the **object** language and "X" is replaced by a **name** of the sentence that replaces "P." "X" is in a **metalanguage**, that is, a language for talking about the object language. The general form of the schema is "(T) X is true if and only if P." An instance of (T) would be "'Snow is white' is true in English if and only if snow is white," where the object language sentence on the right-hand side is referred to by its quotation-marked name in the metalanguage on the left-hand side. According to Tarski, the T-sentence fixes the **extension** of the term "true" rather than its **intension** or **meaning**. The T-sentence is not a definition of truth, but any instance of it is a partial truth. Truth in general for a language will be a logical **conjunction** of all these partial definitions.

> "A theory of truth entails a T-truth for each sentence of the object language, and a T-sentence gives truth conditions." **Davidson**, *Inquiries into Truth and Interpretation*

Tugendhat, Ernst (1930–)

German analytic philosopher, born in Büenn, Czechoslovakia, Professor of Philosophy at University of Heidelberg and Free University of Berlin. Tugendhat has drawn on Frege and Heidegger to bring the rigor and clarity of analytic philosophy to bear on fundamental philosophical questions. His work on self-consciousness and self-determination brings together philosophy of mind and language and social philosophy. His major works include *Tradition and Analytical Philosophy* (1976) and *Self-Consciousness and Self-Determination* (1979).

tu quoque fallacy

LOGIC [from Latin, you are another or you too] An argument of the form "if I face this charge, you face it equally." In logic textbooks this is considered a variant of the *ad hominem* fallacy, for it does not establish its conclusion according to relevant facts or rational arguments, but instead attacks one's opponent. This sort of argument is especially popular in political debates. For instance, A says to B, who accuses him of accepting illegal contributions in his election campaign: "If I used illegal contributions in my campaign, how about you? You took illegal contributions as well."

> "The *tu quoque* fallacy is committed when one tries to reply to a charge made by an opponent by making the same or a similar against him." **Carney and Scheer,** *Fundamentals of Logic*

Turing, Alan (1912–54)

British mathematician, born in London, Fellow of King's College, Cambridge. Turing is famous for his fundamental development of computer theory and his practical development of the computer, as well as for his crucial code-breaking work in the Second World War. His conception of a machine that can perform any operation that a human mind can perform (a Turing machine) led him to ask whether there were criteria by which a person could distinguish the communications of the machine from the communications of a person. If not, he held that we would have no reason to reject a computational model of the mind. His major works include "Computing Machinery and Intelligence," in *Mind* 59 (1950), and *Collected Works of A. M. Turing* (1990).

Turing machine

PHILOSOPHY OF MIND, PHILOSOPHY OF LANGUAGE An imagined computer described by the British logician and mathematician Alan **Turing**. This computer would have a finite number of states S_1, S_2, $S_3 \ldots S_n$, and would operate by changing periodically from one state to another. In doing this it would interact with a paper tape of infinite length marked off into small squares. The machine would scan one square at a time and could "read" or "write" something. It could also erase what had been written. Furthermore, it could move the tape one square at a time to the left or right. When it reached a certain point and completed its task, it would stop itself. It would therefore be possible to give a complete description of each step of the machine. This is called a machine table. This result shows that the machine could do whatever other automata can do. If a machine of this sort could fool us into believing that it was a human being in a test in which we could not say whether the machine or a human was responding to our questions (**a Turing test**), there would be no grounds for distinguishing between the **mental attributes** we ascribe to the machine and those we ascribe to ourselves. This idea has had a great influence on the philosophy of mind, especially on **artificial intelligence**, and in the philosophy of language.

> "According to Turing, a Turing machine can carry out certain elementary operations . . . It is controlled by a program of instructions and each instruction specifies a condition and an action to be carried out if the condition is satisfied." **Searle,** *The Rediscovery of the Mind*

Turing test

PHILOSOPHY OF MIND, PHILOSOPHY OF LANGUAGE A **thought experiment** proposed by the British logician and mathematician Alan **Turing**, who called it the imitation game, for showing that the abilities of digital computers are in principle indistinguishable from human intellectual capacities. In this test, a Turing machine and a human being are in a closed room but able to communicate with a human questioner outside the room via a teleprinter. Both the Turing machine and the human being answer the questions sent in by the questioner, who attempts to judge which answer is from the machine and which is from the man. Turing claimed that given a limited time for questioning the questioners would experience difficulty in distinguishing between the computer answers and the human answers. He predicted that at some point we would accept that machines could think, but critics argue that passing a Turing test is not a sufficient proof of intelligence.

> "Consider how a zimbo might perform in the Turing test, Alan Turing's famous proposal (1950) of an operational test for thinking in a computer." **Dennett,** *Consciousness Explained*

Twardowski, Kazimierz (1866–1938)

Polish analytic philosopher, born in Vienna, Austria, Professor of Philosophy, University of Lvov. Twardowski developed a rigorous philosophical method on the basis of Brentano's descriptive psychology. He distinguished the unity of a mental act and its content from its external object and used this distinction to develop a general theory of objects. He used the distinction between a mental act and

its product to develop a non-psychologistic account of logic. Twardowski's work led to a flowering of Polish philosophy in the interwar period. His major works include *On the Content and Object of Presentations* (1894).

twin earth

PHILOSOPHY OF LANGUAGE, PHILOSOPHY OF MIND, METAPHYSICS A **thought experiment** concerning **meaning** and **mental content**, introduced by **Putnam** in his paper "The Meaning of 'Meaning'" (1975). Imagine that elsewhere in space there is a duplicate of our planet that is exactly like it, except that the chemical composition of what we call water is H_2O, but the chemical composition of what people on twin-earth call water is XYZ. Hence, although the **minds** and **mental states** of the inhabitants of twin-earth are like ours, when they utter the word "water," they are **referring** to a substance composed of XYZ, while when we utter the word "water," we are referring to a substance composed of H_2O. Accordingly, if meaning were determined by mental states, our word "water" and their word "water" would have the same meaning. But the two words do not have the same meaning because our word applies to H_2O and their word applies to XYZ. The meanings of words in a language are not merely in our minds but at least partly depend upon causal relations with external things. This is to reject the traditional conception of meaning according to which meanings are mental states and the **intension** of a word determines its **extension**.

> "One might hold that water is H_2O in all worlds (the stuff called 'water' in W2 is not water) but 'water' does not have the same meaning in W1 and W2. If what was said before about the Twin Earth case was correct, then [this] is clearly the correct theory." **Putnam,** *Mind, Language and Reality*

two-factor theory

PHILOSOPHY OF MIND A theory of **meaning** based on **Putnam**'s distinction between **narrow content**, which is entirely in the **mind** of a subject, and **wide content**, which is at least partly **individuated** by the subject's environment. On this theory, the two kinds of content are components or aspects of meaning. The narrow contents or internal states of the subject contribute to the meanings of psychological states and remain constant across changes in the environment. Hence, we may develop a theory of **cognition** that focuses on the same cognitive system amidst radically different environments.

"This suggests a 'two-factor' semantic theory of psychological states: one factor, narrow content, is to be determined solely by nonrelational properties of the subject; the other factor, the truth condition, is to be determined in part by the subject's environment." **Baker,** *Saving Belief*

two-place predicate, see predicate

two principles of justice

POLITICAL PHILOSOPHY **Rawls** argues that the participants in the **original position** behind the **veil of ignorance** would choose two principles of **justice** to determine the permanent basic structure of their society, whatever their position in society turns out to be. The two principles assign **rights** and **duties** and regulate the distribution of social and economical goods. The first principle calls for **equal** systems of basic **liberties** for all. The second principle applies to the distribution of social and economic goods. Unlike the first principle, it allows inequality, but this inequality is constrained by fair equality of opportunity and must benefit the least well off. Together these two principles form one conception of justice.

The two principles, according to Rawls, have a **lexical order**, in which the first principle has an absolute priority over the second in a just or nearly just society. If one situation P is better than another situation S according to the first principle, then P must be preferred even if S would be better than P according to the second principle. In a just society, it would be irrational to trade basic liberties for social and economical gains. However, this priority applies only to societies with a highly developed civilization and economy. Within the second principle, fair equality of opportunity has lexical priority over the **difference principle** concerning benefit to the least advantaged.

Critics claim that the rational actors of the original position would choose other principles of justice or that they could not choose any principles

in the conditions specified. They also argue that Rawls's principles would come into conflict with one another, for example because the inequality of the second principle would undermine the worth of the equal liberty of the first principle for the least advantaged. Much useful debate has emerged from such criticism.

"I now wish to give the final statement of the two principles of justice for institutions . . . First principle: Each person is to have an equal right to the most extensive total system of equal basic liberties compatible with a similar system of liberty for all. Second principle: Social and economical inequalities are to be arranged so that they are both: (a) to the greatest benefit of the least advantaged, consistent with the just saving principle, and (b) attached to offices and positions open to all under conditions of fair equalities of opportunity." **Rawls,** *A Theory of Justice*

two-space myth

EPISTEMOLOGY **Space** is ordinarily seen to be a unique individual. All real things are contained in one and the same space, and all spaces are part of the one space. In principle, every place can be reached from every other place by traveling through intermediate places. The spatial **relation** is **symmetrical**. Anthony Quinton devised a **thought experiment** to challenge this picture. Suppose that we have richly coherent and connected **experience** in our dreams just as we have in waking life, so that it becomes arbitrary to claim that our dream experience is not of an **objectively** existing world like the world of our waking experience. If the space of my waking world and my dream world are not mutually accessible, it is unlikely that we are justified in claiming to be living in a single spatially isolated world. Hence, space is not essentially singular. In assessing this account, we might distinguish between systematic and public physical space and fragmentary and private experiential space. The two-space myth raises questions about how we can justify moving from experiential space to objective space in the world as it is.

"We can at least conceive circumstances in which we should have good reason to say that we know of real things located in two distinct spaces." **Quinton, "Spaces and Times,"** *Philosophy 37*

two-valued logic, another term for traditional logic

two-world theory, see representative theory of perception

type and token

PHILOSOPHY OF LANGUAGE, METAPHYSICS A distinction drawn by **Peirce**, corresponding to the distinction between a **species** and an **individual** that is a member of this species. A token is a **particular** and **individual sign** or a single **object** or **event**. A type is a pattern that **similar** tokens exemplify or a **class** of similar tokens. A type is not a single thing or event and can only exist through the tokens by which it is embodied. A sentence token is a series of marks on paper or sound waves constituting an inscribed or spoken **sentence**, occurring at a definite space or existing for a definite period. A sentence type is a class to which different sentence tokens belong or the class of the many sayings of the same sentence. For example if one writes or utters "Socrates is a snub-nosed philosopher," and again "Socrates is a snub-nosed philosopher," these are two sentence tokens, but one sentence type. However, the criteria of identity for a sentence type are a matter of dispute. Some philosophers require typographical or auditory similarity, while others require sameness of **meaning**.

"In order that a Type may be used, it has to be embodied in a Token which shall be a sign of the Type, and thereby of the object the Type signifies. I propose to call such a Token of a Type an instance of the Type." **Peirce,** *Collected Papers*, **vol. IV**

type-type identity theory

PHILOSOPHY OF MIND One version of the **identity theory of mind**, according to which every **type** of **mental state** or **event** is identical with some type of physical state or event. There are many views about what exactly is the correlation between the mental and the **physical**. The theory contrasts with another version of the identity theory, the token-token identity theory, which claims that each token mental event is identical with a token physical event. A problem for the type-type identity theory is that different people might have the same **beliefs**, but lack the same neural states. In addition, it is conceivable that non-humans have the same mental states as humans, but have different neural states.

In spite of these difficulties, type-type identity might be needed if theoretical insight into the identity is to be achieved.

"Most advocators of a dual aspect theory assert a type-type identity between the mental and the physical: that the identity of mental events and physical events is associated with systematic correlations between types of mental events and types of physical events." **Hodgson,** *The Mind Matters*

types, theory of

LOGIC **Russell**'s influential solution to the problem of **logical paradoxes**. The theory was developed in particular to overcome **Russell's paradox**, which seemed to destroy the possibility of **Frege**'s **logicist** program of deriving mathematics from logic. Suppose we ask whether the **set** of all sets which are not members of themselves is a member of itself. If it is, then it is not, but if it is not, then it is.

The theory of types suggests classifying **objects**, **properties**, **relations**, and sets into a hierarchy of types. For example, a class of type 0 has members that are ordinary objects; type 1 has members that are **properties** of objects of type 0; type 2 has members that are properties of the properties in type 1; and so on. What can be true or false of items of one type can not significantly be said about those of another type and is simply **nonsense**. If we observe the prohibitions against **classes** containing members of different types, Russell's paradox and similar paradoxes can be avoided.

The theory of types has two variants. The simple theory of types classifies different objects and properties, while the ramified theory of types further sorts types into levels and adds a hierarchy of levels to that of types. By restricting **predicates** to those that relate to items of lower types or lower levels within their own type, predicates giving rise to paradox are excluded. The simple theory of types is sufficient for solving logical paradoxes, while the ramified theory of type is introduced to solve **semantic paradoxes**, that is, paradoxes depending on notions such as **reference** and **truth**.

"Any expression containing an apparent variable is of higher type than that variable. This is the fundamental principles of the doctrines of types." **Russell,** *Logic and Knowledge*

U

Übermensch

MODERN EUROPEAN PHILOSOPHY, ETHICS **Nietzsche**'s superman or overman, the **perfectionist** ideal of life he offers as a goal to human beings when their former ideal, namely **God**, is dead. *Übermensch* is a worldly antithesis of God, a union of the strongest mind and strongest body. For Nietzsche, it is the realization of the profoundest human potentialities and gifts, the overcoming or negation of the mediocrities of the merely human. *Übermensch* involves no bifurcation of humanity. It is the creator of **meaning** of life and the full affirmation of life. It affirms the **eternal recurrence**, and in it the **will to power** attains its zenith. Human beings should transcend themselves and become supermen. They would thus be saved not by a divine Savior, but by the glorification of the human species. The aim of **culture** should be to produce supermen. For Nietzsche, any culture that generates a multitude of mediocrities must be sick and should be condemned. Human life, which has **value** only as a means of producing supermen, stands between beast and superman. Superman is the ideal man. Nietzsche does not mention any single example, but denies that either he or Zarathustra is a superman.

"Behold, I teach you the Übermensch, the Übermensch is the meaning of earth. Let your will say: the Übermensch shall be the meaning of the earth." **Nietzsche, *Thus Spoke Zarathustra***

ugliness

AESTHETICS As **beauty** is a general term representing positive aesthetic value, ugliness is a general term representing negative aesthetic value or aesthetic disvalue. Ugliness is the **property** of an **object** eliciting distaste and unappealing feelings. Corresponding to different modes of beauty, there are various modes of ugliness, such as the deformed, ill-placed, or disharmonious. Aesthetic evaluation of an object assesses its beauty and ugliness. Artists, however, can make beautiful depictions of ugly objects, thus using ugliness to reinforce the aesthetic value of the whole.

"Beauty, or ugliness, was defined as the character of an object which is such that, in aesthetic contemplation, it yields to the contemplation feelings that are pleasant, or, respectively, unpleasant." **Ducasse, *The Philosophy of Art***

Unamuno y Jugo, Miguel de (1865–1935)

Spanish existentialist philosopher and writer, born in Bilbao, Professor of Greek and Rector, University of Salamanca. Unamuno argued for a conception of human nature and the human predicament that focuses on our concrete embodiment and pervasive anxiety and the irrationality of our needs and our surrounding world. Our main task is to lead a life of authenticity in the face of a world that does not grant us immortality. His major works include *The Tragic Sense of Life* (1913).

unconscious

PHILOSOPHY OF MIND For **Leibniz**, the unconscious comprises the appetitive **intentions** of a **transcendent nature** in the self, which subsequent German idealists called the blind **will** or the **desire** of which the **mind** is ignorant. **Freud** took over this term for a fundamental concept of his psychology. The unconscious comprises **mental** items or processes of which we are unaware, but which we can posit through **interpretation** of their indirect determination of phenomena such as dreams, slips of the tongue, humor, and neurotic behavior. A wide range of **experience** influences what we think and do although we are not conscious of it. According to Freud, the **contents** of the unconscious that are most important for his theory of the mind are **repressed** and unavailable to **consciousness**. The unconscious, however, is dynamic in the sense that it is active in the determination of **behavior**. The unconscious contrasts with the preconscious, which comprises latent elements of mind waiting to be discovered. The preconscious is sometimes loosely equated with the unconscious.

According to Freud, what is conscious is only a small part of the **mind**, with most mental contents in the unconscious. The unconscious is a wider concept than the repressed, for while everything that is repressed is unconscious, not everything unconscious is repressed. In his early writings, Freud considered the opposition between the unconscious and the conscious to be a mental conflict. The unconscious has no organization, lacks differentiation, has no sense of **morality**, and is impersonal, yet it is the fertile source of **culture** and civilization. The dynamic unconscious is the defining preoccupation of **psychoanalysis**. In Freud's later writings, the **id** takes over the attributes of the unconscious, although the **ego** also has an unconscious part. The theory of the unconscious was further developed by **Jung** and **Lacan**.

"For the time being we possess no better name for psychical processes which behave actively but nevertheless do not reach the consciousness of the person concerned and that is all we mean by our 'unconsciousness'." **Freud, Standard Edition of the Complete Psychological Works of Sigmund Freud, vol. 9**

understanding (Heidegger)

MODERN EUROPEAN PHILOSOPHY [German *Verstehen*] Traditional philosophy takes understanding to be one of the major **cognitive** abilities of the subject or **mind** and subordinates the question of the understanding to the problem of **knowledge**. Heidegger breaks with this tradition by claiming that understanding is a basic mode of *Dasein's* **being**. Rather than discovering or making **assertions** about the particular **facts** of the world, understanding is the **awareness** of **possibilities**, that is, the disclosedness (*Erschlossenheit*) of the for-the-sake-of-which of *Dasein's* **being-in-the-world**. Understanding operates in terms of projecting those possibilities that are tied to *Dasein's* worldly situation. It has a threefold "fore" structure, that is fore-having, foresight, and fore-conception. In this way, understanding is *Dasein's* self-understanding. While the state of mind, another mode of *Dasein's* being, discloses **facticity**, that is, *Dasein's* thrownness into this world, understanding becomes aware of its inevitable **freedom**. For Heidegger, the traditional conception of the understanding is derived from the understanding as the **existential** awareness of possibilities. Working out the possibilities projected in understanding is **interpretation**. Heidegger's theory of understanding establishes the basis for the hermeneutic turn.

"With the term 'understanding' we have in mind a fundamental existentiale, which is neither a definite species of cognition distinguished, let us say, from explaining and conceiving, nor any cognition at all in the sense of grasping something thematically." **Heidegger, Being and Time**

understanding (Kant)

EPISTEMOLOGY, METAPHYSICS, PHILOSOPHY OF MIND [German *Verstand*, corresponding to Greek *dianoia* and Latin *intellectio*] **Kant** distinguished understanding from **sensibility** and **reason**. While sensibility is receptive, understanding is **spontaneous**. While understanding is concerned with the range of **phenomena** and is empty without **intuition**, reason, which moves from judgment to judgment concerning phenomena, is tempted to extend beyond the limits of **experience** to generate **fallacious** inferences. Kant claimed that the main **act** of understanding is judgment and called it a **faculty** of judgment. He claimed that there is an *a priori* **concept** or **category** corresponding to each kind of judgment as its logical function and that understanding is constituted by twelve categories. Hence understanding is also a faculty of concepts. Understanding gives the **synthetic unity** of **appearance** through the categories. It thus brings together intuitions and concepts and makes experience possible. It is a lawgiver of **nature**. **Herder** criticized Kant for separating sensibility and understanding. **Fichte** and **Hegel** criticized him for separating understanding and reason. Some **neo-Kantians** criticized him for deriving the structure of understanding from the act of judgment.

> "Now we can reduce all acts of the understanding to judgements, and the understanding may therefore be represented as a faculty of judgement."
> **Kant, *Critique of Pure Reason***

understanding (Locke)

EPISTEMOLOGY, PHILOSOPHY OF MIND One of **Locke**'s two main works is entitled *An Essay Concerning Human Understanding*. He took understanding to be a **faculty** of the **mind** and called it the most elevated faculty of the **soul** and a faculty that searches after **truth**. Understanding has a more fundamental importance than other faculties, such as **sensation**, **reasoning**, or **memory**. Locke divided the **actions** of the mind into two main parts: the power of **thinking**, which is called understanding, and the power of **volition**, which is called the **will**. He often used understanding interchangeably with the cognitive mind, rather than as just one of its faculties. The purpose of his *Essay* on human understanding is to "inquire into the original, certainty, and extent of human knowledge, together with the grounds and degrees of belief, opinion, and assent."

> "Since it is the *understanding* that sets man above the rest of sensible beings, and gives him all the advantage and dominion which he has over them, it is certainly a subject, even for its nobleness, worth our labour to inquire into." **Locke, *An Essay Concerning Human Understanding***

understanding/explanation

PHILOSOPHY OF HISTORY, PHILOSOPHY OF SOCIAL SCIENCE, MODERN EUROPEAN PHILOSOPHY [German *Verstehen*, understanding and *Erklarung*, explanation] Ordinarily, the distinction between explanation and understanding is blurred, in part because explanation furthers our understanding. Yet in German philosophy of history, philosophy of social science, and **hermeneutics**, the two terms are sharply distinguished. Explanation is the subsumption of individual cases under hypothetically assumed general **laws of nature** and is the method characteristic of the natural sciences. In contrast, understanding is a **cognitive** mode peculiar to the social sciences. It is an empathic or participatory understanding of a given subject's point of view by imaginatively putting oneself into the place of the **subject**. It is the reconstruction of the subject's purposes, **values**, and **meaning**. The distinction was first drawn by Droysen, although he actually put forward a trichotomy: philosophical method (knowledge), physical method (explanation), and historical method (understanding). **Dilthey** fully elaborated the distinction between *Verstehen* and *Erklarung*, claiming that it forms the fundamental difference between the social sciences (*Geisteswissenschaften*) and the natural sciences (*Naturwissenschaften*) and that the distinction is the basis for the claim that the social sciences have a distinctive methodology. Max Weber believed that both *Verstehen* and *Erklarung* are necessary in the social sciences.

> "The German historian-philosopher Droysen appears to have been the first to introduce a methodological dichotomy which has had great influence. He coined for it the names explanation and understanding, in German *Erklaren* and *Verstehen*."
> **von Wright, *Explanation and Understanding***

undistributed middle

LOGIC A logical fallacy in traditional syllogistic logic, resulting from the violation of the rule that the middle term (the term that appears twice in premises) must be **distributed** at least once in the premises. Any **syllogism** that commits this error is invalid. Consider "All philosophers are persons," and "Some persons are bad." No conclusion follows from these two premises because "persons" in the first premise is the predicate of an affirmative proposition, and in the second is the subject of a particular proposition. Neither of them is distributed.

> "If in a syllogism the middle term is distributed in neither premise, we are said to have a fallacy of undistributed middle." **Keynes, *Formal Logic***

unexpected examination paradox, another name for surprise examination paradox

unhappy consciousness

EPISTEMOLOGY, PHILOSOPHY OF HISTORY, PHILOSOPHY OF MIND Hegel's term for a **consciousness** that desires complete **knowledge** of itself but cannot obtain it. Hegel believed that **self-consciousness** proceeded in history from pre-history (the struggle for recognition) to Greece and Rome (Stoicism and **skepticism**) and medieval Christianity (unhappy consciousness). At the stage of skepticism, consciousness claims that all knowledge is **relative** to the subjective point of view. However, to make this claim meaningful, it must be assured that there is a universal point of view to see that all knowledge is thus relative. As a result, a skeptic has to admit that he is unable to justify these **beliefs** outside of his own contingently held point of view. He has a divided form of consciousness, with a tension between its **subjective** and **objective** points of view. Here skepticism gave way to the stage of unhappy consciousness. Such a consciousness is internally divided, for it has to assume both points of view. It is the consciousness of separation between man and **nature** and between man and man. Christianity's message is a call to men to restore the lost unity of consciousness by bringing their subjective points of view into line with the impersonal eye of **God**. In general, the unhappy consciousness describes a **form of life** in which people's conceptions of themselves and of what they claim to know involves an enduring state of crisis. Such a mental state is later called by **Kierkegaard** "despair."

> "Hence the unhappy consciousness, the Alienated Soul which is the consciousness of self as a divided nature, a doubled and merely contradictory being." **Hegel, *Phenomenology of Spirit***

unified science

PHILOSOPHY OF SCIENCE, PHILOSOPHY OF SOCIAL SCIENCE [German *Einheitswissenschaft*] Logical positivists held that no essential differences in aim and **method** exist between the various branches of science. The scientists of all disciplines should collaborate closely with each other and should unify the vocabulary of sciences by **logical analysis**. According to this view, there is no sharp demarcation between natural sciences and social sciences. In particular, to establish **universal laws** in the social sciences may be difficult in practice, but it is not impossible in principle. Through Otto **Neurath**, this ideal of scientific unity became a program for logical positivists, who published a series of books in Vienna under the heading *Unified Science*. After the dissolution of the **Vienna Circle**, Neurath renamed the official journal *Erkenntnis* as *The Journal of Unified Science*, and planned to continue publication of a series of works in the United States under the general title *The International Encyclopedia of Unified Science*. He thought that the work would be similar in historical importance to the eighteenth-century French *Encyclopédie* under the direction of **Diderot**. Unfortunately, this work was never completed, although **Carnap** and **Morris** published some volumes originally prepared for it under the title *Foundations of the Unity of Science*.

> "We have repeatedly pointed out that the formation of the constructional system as a whole is the task of unified science." **Carnap, *The Logical Structure of the World***

uniformity of nature

METAPHYSICS, EPISTEMOLOGY, PHILOSOPHY OF SCIENCE A **principle** claiming that nature is uniform and that consequently the future will resemble the **past** and that **generalizations** holding for observed cases will apply to unobserved cases so long as the background conditions remain sufficiently similar. In traditional **epistemology**, Francis **Bacon** and J. S. **Mill** assumed the principle to be the ground for the validity of inductive reasoning and scientific **predictions**. The aim of science is to find uniformity. But **Hume** argued that the principle can only be justified by **induction** and thus that justifying induction by appeal to the principle involves **vicious circularity** or question-begging. **Popper**, in his rejection of inductive method, claimed that the uniformity of nature is a matter of faith.

> "The belief in the uniformity of nature is the belief that everything that has happened or will happen is an instance of some general law to which there are no exceptions." **Russell, *The Problems of Philosophy***

unity of consciousness, see transcendental apperception

universal

LOGIC, METAPHYSICS, PHILOSOPHY OF LANGUAGE, PHILOSOPHY OF MIND Something is universal if it pertains to all members of a **class** or is unlimited, such as a universal **law**. In logic, universal **statements** (A and E statements in traditional logic) are contrasted with particular statements (I and O statements). A universal expresses abstract features, such as justice, beauty, wisdom, and goodness, and such universals give rise to many major and persisting problems in the history of philosophy.

The concept of a universal can be traced to **Plato**'s conception of **idea** or **form** (*eidos*) and **Aristotle**'s *katholou*. Ideas or forms are the common characteristics which many **particulars** share and which are the object of **knowledge**. *Katholou* [Greek *kata*, belonging to + *holou*, the whole] is defined as being **predicated** of many, while a particular is predicated of nothing else. Both Plato and Aristotle contrasted universals with particulars. Plato's theory of **ideas** is regarded as the first and most penetrating discussion of the problems of universals, although Aristotle's treatment of the problem from the point of view of predication is currently widely followed.

Since Plato and Aristotle, the debate about the nature and status of universals has run through the whole history of philosophy. Many rival theories have been proposed, the most important of which include **realism**, **nominalism**, and **conceptualism**. Realism claims that universals are mind-independent **objective entities**, which can in principle be exemplified or instantiated by a number of different things. On the basis of this objective entity, predicate-expressions can be applied to many **subjects**. Nominalism holds that a universal is not an objective entity but is only a **general** name or word. Our ability to apply these general words is based on their linguistic function established by **convention**. The major representatives of nominalism include **William of Ockham** and Thomas **Hobbes**. Conceptualism, usually associated with the British **empiricists**, suggests that universals are mind-dependent **concepts** or **thoughts**, constructed by the mind after experiencing particular things. Each position has its strengths as well as famous weaknesses. There are many further versions under each general heading. Plato and

Aristotle, for instance, are realists, but their doctrines have striking differences. **Wittgenstein** in his later philosophy proposed an account of **family resemblance** as complicated networks of overlapping similarities to replace our mistaken demand for **properties** that are common to all members of a class.

> "By the term 'universal' I mean that which is of such a nature as to be predicated of many subjects, by 'individual' that which is not thus predicated. Thus, 'man' is a universal, 'Callias' an individual." **Aristotle,** *De Interpretatione*

universal characteristic, another expression for universal symbolistic

universal grammar

PHILOSOPHY OF LANGUAGE Also called general grammar or philosophical grammar. In contrast to particular grammar, which is the grammar peculiar to a particular language, universal grammar refers to the deep-seated regularities in linguistic **categories**, **rules**, and processes that underlie the diversity of natural languages. It consists of a set of genetically determined rules and **principles** common to all natural languages. Universal grammar is rooted in human linguistic capacity and is the necessary and sufficient natural condition for any language to be possible. It is a basic biological endowment of the initial state of the human **mind**. Because of universal grammar, a child can effortlessly acquire language. According to **Chomsky**, the idea of a universal grammar was common for eighteenth-century linguists such as Beattie and Du Marsa, but was ignored by modern linguistics. He revived the notion and believes that without being supplemented by a universal grammar, a grammar of a particular language cannot provide a full account of the speaker-hearer's **competence**. The natural **necessity** of universal grammar as a condition of the possibility of language can be compared with the *a priori* **intuitions** and categories that were held by **Kant** to be the **transcendentally necessary** conditions for the possibility of **experience**.

> "Such a 'universal grammar' (to modify slightly a traditional usage) prescribes a schema that defines implicitly the indefinite class of 'attainable grammars'; it formulates principles that determines how each such system relates sound and meaning;

it provides a procedure of evaluation for grammars of the appropriate form." **Chomsky, *Studies on Semantics in Generative Grammar***

universal proposition

LOGIC In traditional logic, propositions of the form "all s are p" or "all s are not p" are called universal propositions, in contrast to **particular propositions**, which have the form "some s are p" or "some s are not p." The form "all s are p," which is equivalent to "every s is p," is the form of a universal affirmative proposition and is symbolized as "A." The form "all s are not p," which is equivalent to "no s is p," is the form of a universal negative proposition and is symbolized as "E."

In modern predicate **calculus**, a universal affirmative proposition "all s are p" is analyzed as "for all x, if x is s and x is p." Unlike particular propositions, universal propositions do not contain **referring expressions** and therefore lack **existential import**.

"The grammatical subjects of universal propositions, however expressed, are not referring expressions." **D. Mitchell, *An Introduction to Logic***

universal quantifier

LOGIC **Frege** suggests that the universal categorical **statements** of traditional logic, that is, "All s are p," and "All s are not p," can be read respectively as "For all x, if x is s, then x is p," and "For all x, if x is s, then x is not p." The former can be symbolized as "(x) (sx → px), and the latter as "(x) (sx → ~px)." (x) is called the "universal quantifier" and means that "For all x . . ." or "For every x . . ." The universal quantifier and the existential quantifier (There exists an x . . .) have been crucial in the development of modern predicate logic and the philosophy dependent upon it. The universal quantifier is also symbolized as "∀(x)."

"The universal quantifier (x) may be read 'each object x is such that . . .'." **Quine, *Theories and Things***

universal symbolistic

LOGIC, PHILOSOPHY OF LANGUAGE Also called universal characteristic, **Leibniz**'s project for providing a system of **symbols** or an artificial language for overcoming the deficiencies of **natural language** and for representing rational **thought** more accurately and effectively. For Leibniz it is a universal system of writing and an "alphabet of human thought." Through the combination of the letters of this alphabet and through the analysis of the words produced from them, we can discover and judge everything. To establish a universal language for communication among different languages was not a new idea, but Leibniz attempted to extend the notion of such a language to form an art of discovery and an art of **judgment**. He believed that it would be one of the greatest inventions if it succeeded. There is much dispute among scholars about the scope, nature, and significance of this project. On one reading, the universal symbolistic is intended to be a type of **ideal language**, a language composed of real characters capable of expressing symbolically the **contents** of thought. On this reading, it is the predecessor of the ideal language proposed by some modern **analytical** philosophers. On another reading, this project is concerned only with the form, not the content, of rational thought. It is a plan for a general science of form and for expressing the logical relations among **concepts** and **propositions**. On this reading, the universal characteristic is a precursor of modern **symbolic logic**. On a further reading, Leibniz's thought developed from the ambitious project of constructing a system representing content to a less ambitious project that was concerned solely with the form of logical **reasoning**.

"I should still hope to create a kind of universal symbolistic in which all truths of reason would be reduced to a kind of calculus." **Leibniz, *Philosophical Papers and Letters***

universalia, ante rem see *universalia, in rebus*

universalia, in rebus

METAPHYSICS [Latin, universals existing within particular things, also called *in rebus universalia*] A position held by the **Aristotelians** about the **ontological** status of **universals**. It contrasts with the **Platonist** position *universalia, ante rem* [Latin, universals existing prior to or independently of the particular things that instantiate them, also called *ante res universalia*]. It is also contrasted with *post rem universalia* [Latin, universals existing after or derived from particular things, also called *post res universalia*], a view held by both **nominalism** and **conceptualism**.

"We can adopt the view whose Latin tag is universalia in rebus, 'universals in things'. We can think of a thing's properties as constituents of the thing and think of the properties as universals. This may have been the position of Aristotle."
D. Armstrong, *Universals and Scientific Realism*

universalia, post rem, see *universalia, in rebus*

universalizability

ETHICS The idea that **moral judgments** should be universalizable can be traced to the **Golden Rule** and **Kant**'s ethics. In the twentieth century it was elaborated by **Hare** and became a major thesis of his **prescriptivism**. The principle states that all moral judgments are universalizable in the sense that if it is **right** for a particular person A to do an action X, then it must likewise be right to do X for any person exactly like A, or like A in the relevant respects. Furthermore, if A is right in doing X in this situation, then it must be right for A to do X in other relevantly similar situations. Hare takes this feature to be an essential feature of moral judgments. An **ethical statement** is the issuance of a universal prescription. Universalizability is not the same as **generality**, for a moral judgment can be highly specific and detailed and need not be general or simple. The universalizability principle enables Hare to avoid the charge of irrationality that is usually lodged against **non-cognitivism**, to which his pre-scriptivism belongs, and his theory is thus a great improvement on **emotivism**.

"I have been maintaining that the meaning of the word 'ought' and other moral words is such that a person who uses them commits himself thereby to a universal rule. This is the thesis of universalizability." **Hare,** *Freedom and Reason*

universals of language, another expression for linguistic universals

unknown entities, another term for metaphysical entities

unmoved mover

ANCIENT GREEK PHILOSOPHY, METAPHYSICS, PHILO-SOPHY OF RELIGION The **substance** that initiates movement without itself being moved, also called the prime mover. In the later part of the *Physics* and *Metaphysics* XII, **Aristotle** developed a **cosmological argument** attempting to show that there must be an unmoved mover. Because **time** is eternal, without beginning and end, **change**, which is a con-comitant of time, must also be eternal. The eternal and continuous change is the circular movement of the outer heavenly sphere. What produces this eternal motion? On analogy with the objects of our **desires** and **thoughts** and the **intentional** bodily movements for which they account, Aristotle inferred that there must be some ultimate object of desire and thought in the universe, a substance which acts on the outer sphere and then indirectly on the order of the whole universe. This substance moves not because it intends, but because it is loved and thought. Thus it is an unmoved mover that is immune to change and thus has no **matter** or **potentiality**. It is pure **actuality** and pure **self-reflective** thought, with pure contemplation of itself as its object. The unmoved mover is also called **God**. But the Aristotelian God itself does not care or think about changes in the world, although the **harmony** and order of the world are due to the imitation of the unmoved mover. While Aristotle's God is a passive object of admiration, medieval philosophers, especially Thomas **Aquinas**, attempted to transform it into a **conscious agent**.

"And since that which is moved and moves is intermediate, there is something, which moves without being moved, being eternal, substance and actuality." **Aristotle,** *Metaphysics*

unqualified good, see qualified good

unsaturated

LOGIC, PHILOSOPHY OF LANGUAGE **Frege**'s distinction between saturated expressions and unsaturated expressions corresponds to the distinction between **objects** and **concepts**. A saturated expression refers to an object or **argument** and has a complete **sense** in itself, while an unsaturated expression refers to a concept or **function** and does not have a complete sense. For example, in the sentence "Socrates is the teacher of Plato," "Socrates" and "Plato" are **proper names** and are saturated, while ". . . is the teacher of . . ." is unsaturated, for it has empty spaces that must be filled with saturated expressions before it gains a complete sense.

> "Statements in general . . . can be imagined to be split up into two parts; one complete in itself, and the other in need of supplementation, or 'unsaturated'." **Frege, "Function and Concept,"** *Philosophical Writings of Gottlob Frege*

unwritten doctrines

ANCIENT GREEK PHILOSOPHY Doctrines ascribed to **Plato**, which he is said not to have written down but only to have taught to his pupils orally. Remarks by **Aristotle** are our chief source for these doctrines. The ideas are difficult and even impossible to reconstruct, but they are roughly like this. There are two ultimate **principles**, **the One** and the indefinite **dyad**, which generate the **Forms**, and through the Forms become the **causes** of everything. Forms are **numbers**, and between Forms and particulars there are indeterminate mathematical entities. While most Platonic scholars do not pay much attention to these ideas, the Tübingen school, headed by K. Gaiser and H. Kramer, claim that the unwritten doctrines represent the real essence of Plato's philosophy and the dialogues are only a preliminary stage toward this serious philosophy.

> "It is true, indeed, that the account he gives in the *Timaeus* of the participant is different from what he says in his so-called 'unwritten doctrines'." **Aristotle,** *Physics*

use theory of meaning

PHILOSOPHY OF LANGUAGE The later **Wittgenstein** criticized the view that language has a single function that explains **meaning** and observed that language has a variety of uses. He claimed that the meaning of a word has to be understood in terms of its employment in the context of different **language-games**. To give the meaning of an expression is to show how that expression enters into the language-games in which it functions. He held that the meaning of a word is its use in a language. Instead of asking what a word means, we should ask how the word is used. An expression's role in language determines its **sense**, and the sense of a **sentence** is its employment. Accordingly, to determine the meaning of an expression one must invoke the

conditions under which it is appropriate to use it, including the states of mind of speakers or hearers in a given context. This account, which contrasts with Wittgenstein's earlier **picture theory of meaning**, has been widely influential and has developed into many versions after Wittgenstein. Critics suggest that while a use account of meaning helps our understanding of the various roles of linguistic expressions, it is preliminary to a theory of meaning rather than a theory in its own right.

> "As a tool of analysis, the use theory of meaning can provide us only with certain data, i.e. raw material for philosophical analysis." **Searle,** *Speech Acts*

utilitarianism

ETHICS, POLITICAL PHILOSOPHY, PHILOSOPHY OF SOCIAL SCIENCE A major modern ethical theory, advanced by **Bentham**, J. S. **Mill**, **Sidgwick**, and many others, which suggests, broadly speaking, that the **rightness** or wrongness of an **action** is determined by its **utility**, that is, the good (pleasant or happy) or bad (painful or evil) consequences it produces. The morally right **action** that one should choose is the one that will provide the greatest **pleasure** and least **pain** of all the alternatives. Because utilitarianism judges actions in terms of their consequences, it is a major representative of **consequentialism**.

There are many species of utilitarianism, based on different understandings of action and consequences. There is a distinction between **act-utilitarianism** and **rule-utilitarianism**; the former judges in terms of the consequences of particular actions, and the latter in terms of the consequence of adopting some general **rules** for sorts of actions. There is a distinction between egoistic and universalistic utilitarianism; the former considers the goodness or badness of the consequences for the **agent** himself, and the latter for all individuals involved. There is also a distinction between **hedonistic** and ideal utilitarianism; the former takes the goodness or badness of a consequence to depend only on its pleasure or pain, and the latter (represented by G. E. **Moore**) takes into account things other than pleasure, such as intellectual and aesthetic qualities. There is also a distinction between **normative** and **descriptive** utilitarianism, distinguishing how agents should act and how they actually do act. These various distinctions cut across one another. A recent version, called motive utilitarianism, defines the morality of actions in terms of the motives that give rise to them.

Utilitarianism has played a great role in modern English and American society as the basic principle of morality and legislation. However, it has also been a subject of criticism in moral and political philosophy. The various versions of utilitarianism have weaknesses. Concentrating on its consequentialism, the main objections are: First, it is difficult to determine what consequences various possible actions would have; secondly, the action that will produce the greatest happiness is often not the morally right action; thirdly, utilitarianism focuses on the consequences of actions, but ignores the **integrity** of moral agents; finally, utilitarianism seeks to maximize the utility of consequences without regard to the distribution of utility among persons or among different periods in one person's life. All these and other criticisms suggest that utilitarianism should be employed together with other moral principles, although its fundamental viewpoint is unlikely to be completely removed.

"The chief reason for adopting the name 'Utilitarianism' was, indeed, merely to emphasise the fact that right and wrong conduct must be judged by its results." **G. E. Moore,** *Principia Ethica*

utilitarianism, act

ETHICS Act-utilitarianism judges the rightness of an **action** in terms of the good or bad consequences that the action itself can produce. We should pursue the action that will produce the greatest happiness in every circumstance. It contrasts with **rule-utilitarianism**, which judges the rightness of an action in terms of the good or bad consequences that ensue from following general moral rules of conduct, such as "keep promises" and "never lie," rather than from performing a particular action. According to rule-utilitarianism, we should pursue the action that conforms to a set of moral **rules** whose general observance would maximize **utility**. Classical utilitarians such as **Bentham**, **Mill**, and **Sidgwick** are generally considered as act-utilitarians, though they themselves were not aware of this distinction. Act-utilitarianism can also be defined in terms of expected utility rather than the utility

of actual consequences. The basic difficulty for act-utilitarianism is how to assess with certainty the consequences of an action considered in itself. It is also criticized for ignoring the agent's **integrity** or **desires**. Sometimes it is disputed whether the distinction between act-utilitarianism and rule-utilitarianism is sound. Moral theorists such as **Hare** believe that if a certain action is right, it must be the case that any action just like it in relevant aspects will also be right.

"Assuming that the objections to act-utilitarianism are conclusive, the choice of a general theory of obligation seems to lie between some kind of formalism and at least something like rule-utilitarianism." **Brandt,** *Ethical Theory*

utilitarianism, ideal

ETHICS W. D. **Ross**'s term, for the type of **utilitarianism** initiated by **Moore**. In contrast to classical or **hedonistic** utilitarianism, which claims that consequences are good or bad depending only on pleasure or pain, Moore claims that things other than pleasure, such as knowledge and the enjoyment of beautiful objects, also determine the goodness of consequences.

"In fact the theory of 'Ideal Utilitarianism', if I may for brevity refer so to the theory of Professor Moore, seems to simplify unduly our relations to our fellows." **Ross,** *The Right and the Good*

utility

ETHICS What is useful or **good** and leads to **pleasure** or happiness. Utility is the property that generates happiness or felicity, but more often it is directly identified with happiness. Utility has been an important consideration in ethics since the ancient Greeks. **Hume** believed that it is the measure of all **virtues**. Since **Bentham** advanced the principle of utility, there has been a specific ethical theory called **utilitarianism**. For utilitarianism, utility is the sole criterion for judging whether an act is **right** or wrong. If an act produces utility, it is right; otherwise, it is wrong. Bentham also proposed a calculus of **felicity** to determine the amount of utility or happiness produced by an **action** and to allow comparisons between actions. In many circumstances, however, an act that brings about the greatest utility is not the act that we morally approve. Furthermore, there are many problems in measuring and comparing different kinds of utilities. Attempts to identify happiness and utility might involve a misunderstanding of happiness. Problems also arise because utilitarians seek to maximize utility without regard to its distribution among people or among different periods in an individual life.

> "By utility is meant that property in any object whereby it tends to produce benefit, advantage, pleasure, good, or happiness . . . or . . . to prevent the happening of mischief, pain, evil, or unhappiness to the party whose interest is considered." **Bentham,** *An Introduction to the Principles of Morals and Legislation*

utility calculus, see hedonistic calculus

utopia

POLITICAL PHILOSOPHY [from Greek *ou*, not + *topos*, place, literally, a place that does not exist] A word first used in Sir Thomas **More**'s book *Utopia*, in which he depicts an ideal **state** that has perfect economic, social, political, legal, and religious structures. Similar descriptions of an imaginary ideal state can be found in such works as **Plato**'s *Republic*, Tommaso **Campanella**'s *The City of the Sun* (1612), Francis **Bacon**'s *New Atlantis* (1627), Edward Bellamy's *Looking Backward* (1888), William Morris's *News from Nowhere* (1890), and H. G. Wells's *A Modern Utopia* (1905). Utopia is generally conceived to be an unrealizable, impractical, and purely imaginary ideal state. Unrealistic political and social theories are described as utopian, especially those proposing fanciful schemes of education to change **human nature** or placing the hope of realizing the ideal state upon the character of great rulers. Utopian theories are often criticized for not being based on human experience. Nevertheless, they represent human aspirations and have always served as an instrument for political criticism. **Marx** called

the work of his predecessors utopian socialism, in contrast to his own scientific socialism, which he argued was grounded on the analysis of existing class conflicts in capitalism.

> "The ideal of utopia, the perfect society, has long exerted a powerful influence upon the thinking, feeling, and action of human beings." **Richter (ed.),** *Utopias*

utopian engineering

POLITICAL PHILOSOPHY **Popper**'s term for a **methodological** approach to bringing about social and political change. Utopian engineers draw up an initial blueprint of **society** as a whole and then attempt to realize this ideal state by deciding the best means to achieve the predetermined ends. This approach entails large-scale social revolution and is represented by the program for society in **Plato**'s *Republic*. In contrast, **piecemeal engineering** focuses on existing social problems and practices to propose a series of relatively modest individual changes. According to Popper, piecemeal engineering is a rational means of pursuing change, while utopian engineering, because it aims at a perfect state, will demand centralized rule and lead to dictatorship. Although utopian engineering starts with an apparently good plan, it can lead to disaster because of the complex realities of **human nature** and of social life. All change produces unintended as well as intended consequences. With piecemeal engineering it is easier to recognize when unintended consequences are negative and to trace these consequences to their origins in order to eliminate or to control them.

> "The Platonic approach I have in mind can be described as that of utopian engineering, as opposed to another kind of social engineering which I consider as the only rational one, and which may be described by the name of piecemeal engineering." **Popper,** *The Open Society and Its Enemies*

V

vacuous occurrence

LOGIC If replacing a descriptive term t in a **proposition** p by other grammatically appropriate **constants** does not affect the truth-value of p, then t occurs vacuously in p. If a change of **meaning** of a term in an **argument** a does not affect the **validity** of the argument, then the term occurs vacuously in a. In a **tautology** or a **self-contradictory** proposition, all descriptive terms occur vacuously. Vacuous occurrence contrasts with essential occurrence. With essential occurrence, the replacement of a term t will affect the truth-value of the proposition in which it occurs, and a change of meaning of a term in an argument will affect the validity of the argument.

"By vacuous occurrence of a descriptive constant (i.e. either individual constant or predicate constant) is meant that the truth-value of the sentence does not change if any other admissible descriptive constant is substituted." **Pap**, *Elements of Analytic Philosophy*

vagueness

LOGIC, PHILOSOPHY OF LANGUAGE, METAPHYSICS The indeterminacy of the field of application of an expression, in contrast to precision. For instance, the expression "young man" is vague since the point at which its appropriate application to a person begins and ends cannot be precisely defined. Vagueness should be distinguished from **ambiguity**, by which a term has more than one **meaning**. The vagueness of an expression is due to a **semantic** feature of the term itself, rather than to the subjective condition of its user. Vagueness gives rise to **borderline cases**, and **propositions** with vague terms lack a definite **truth-value**. For this reason, **Frege** rejected the possibility of vague **concepts**, although they are tolerated in recent work in vague or fuzzy logic. Various **paradoxes** arise due to the vagueness of words, including the ancient **sorites paradox**. It is because of its intrinsic vagueness that some philosophers seek to replace **ordinary language** with an **ideal language**. But ordinary language philosophers hold that this proposal creates a false promise of eliminating vagueness. **Wittgenstein**'s notion of **family resemblance** in part is a model of meaning that tolerates vagueness. As a property of expressions, vagueness extends to all sorts of cognitive representations. Some philosophers hold that there can be vagueness in things as well as in the representation of things.

"A representation is vague when the relation of the representing system to the represented system is not one–one, but one–many." **Russell**, *Collected Papers of Bertrand Russell*, vol. IX

validity

LOGIC A **property** attributed to an **inference** or an **argument**, which can be defined both **syntactically**, in terms of the **axioms** or **rules** of a logical system, and **semantically**, in terms of **interpretations** or models. Suppose that $A_1, A_2, A_3, \ldots$ are premises, and A_0 is a conclusion. Syntactic validity means that A_0 is derivable from $A_1, A_2, A_3, \ldots$ If all the premises are true and the inference complies with the rules of logic, then the inference or argument is valid. Semantic validity means that A_0 is true if according to interpretations or models in non-logical language $A_1, A_2, A_3, \ldots$ are true. The task of traditional logic is to establish the rules of syntactic validity. Validity is not the same as **truth**, for truth is a property ascribed to **propositions** or **statements** rather than to inferences or arguments.

"An argument is valid if and only if it is logically impossible for all the premises to be true yet the conclusion false." **Sainsbury, *Logical Form***

value

PHILOSOPHY OF SOCIAL SCIENCE, ETHICS, AESTHETICS [from Latin *valere*, to have worth, to be strong] Its original sense, the worth of a thing, appears in economics. In the nineteenth century German philosophers such as the **neo-Kantians**, **Schopenhauer** and **Nietzsche** expanded the sense of value and used it as a major technical notion in their philosophy. **Marx**'s distinction between use-value and exchange-value was a basic feature of his account of economy and society. The conception of value can be traced to the idea of the **Good** in **Socrates** and **Plato**. Its use is associated with distinctions between **fact and value** and between **is and ought** in modern philosophy. The general study of value, including ethical and aesthetic value, is called **axiology**.

In ethics, something has value if it is good or worthwhile, although negative values are also possible. Generally speaking, value means the quality of a thing that makes it **desirable**, useful, or an object of interest. Value has been understood in terms of the **subjective** appreciation or as something projected onto **objects** by a subject. In this sense "valuable" amounts to "being judged to have value." On this view, objects can have different values for different individuals, groups, or nations. A contrasting claim is that there can be **objective** value independent of subjective appreciation, although philosophers disagree over the sense in which value is meant to be objective.

There are various classifications of value. Most commonly, there are distinctions among extrinsic or instrumental **value** (good as a means for some end), intrinsic **value** (good as an end in itself), and inherent value (the basis for our seeing something as desirable).

In logic, value is the result of applying a **function** to an **argument**. For instance, "7" is the value of applying the function "x + y" to the arguments "3" and "4."

"Values express the objective will. Ethical values in particular result from the combination of many lives and sets of interests in a single set of judgements." **T. Nagel, *The View from Nowhere***

value, intrinsic

ETHICS In its ordinary sense, intrinsic value is the value a thing has to most people in normal circumstances, in contrast to the **value** that the same thing has for special persons in special circumstances. This latter might be called sentimental value. For instance, a lover's gift might have little intrinsic value, but great sentimental value to the loved one.

In another sense, intrinsic value is objective value, that is, the value a thing has independent of anything else, so that it would have its value even if it were the only thing that existed. This sense seems to be proposed by **Moore**.

In its standard wider use, which can be traced to **Aristotle**'s notion of final **good**, intrinsic value is synonymous with what is intrinsically **desirable** or intrinsically **good**. This value is desirable for its own sake and worth pursuing in itself without reference to any other objects. In this sense, intrinsic value contrasts to extrinsic or instrumental value, which is not pursued for itself.

"To say that a kind of value is 'intrinsic' means merely that the question whether a thing possesses it, and in what degree it possesses it, depends solely on the intrinsic nature of the thing in question." **G. E. Moore, *Philosophical Studies***

value, theory of, see axiology

value of a variable

LOGIC A variable ranges over the members of a **set**. Any entity that falls within the range of the variable is a value of the variable. An expression designating a value of a variable can be substituted for the variable. In the sentential function "x is wise," x is a variable, and Socrates is a member of its range and hence one of its values. Substituting "Socrates" for x yields the **closed sentence** or **proposition** "Socrates is wise." On a substitutional rather than referential view, we can consider the expressions that can be substituted for a variable to be its values.

> "Specific terms within the range of meaning of a variable in a function are called 'values' of that variable." **Quine,** *Set Theory and Its Logic*

value words

PHILOSOPHY OF LANGUAGE, ETHICS The words that are used to express **taste** and **preferences**, to express **decisions** and **choices**, to criticize and evaluate, to advise, warn, persuade, praise, and encourage. Their function is to guide our own choices and those of other people by commending or **prescribing**. Typical examples are "good," "right," and "ought," but any word, if used **evaluatively**, might count as a value word. Value words can be negative or positive. **Judgments** that contain value words are value judgments. Value words form the web of moral discourse, and the analysis of their **implications** and connections is one of the main jobs of moral philosophers, especially those concerned with **meta-ethics**.

> "The words with which moral philosophers have especially to do, which are usually called 'value-words', play many important parts." **Nowell-Smith,** *Ethics*

Van Fraassen, Bastiaan (1941–)

American philosopher of science, logic, and semantics, born in Goes, The Netherlands, Professor of Philosophy at the University of Toronto, University of Southern California, and Princeton University. Van Fraassen rejects realism in the philosophy of science in favor of an anti-realist constructive empiricism. Scientific theories tell us what the world would be like if they were true, but we hold them for their empirical adequacy rather than for their truth. His work on quantum theory involves discussion of the interpretation of theories and the rejection of laws of nature in favor of symmetry.

His discussions of space and time, scientific explanation, the logic of questions, a model semantics of scientific theories and free logic have all been influential. His major works include *An Introduction to the Philosophy of Time and Space* (1969), *The Scientific Image* (1980), *Laws and Symmetry* (1989), and *Quantum Mechanics: An Empiricist View* (1991).

variable

LOGIC In **predicate logic**, x is called a variable in a general **statement** like "x is white" because it ranges over a **domain** of **objects** and can be replaced by any expression designating any object to which the predicate is applied. Generally, "x, y, z, . . ." are used in predicate logic as individual variables representing **individuals**. The domain of objects a variable ranges over is called the range of the variable. A term designating any object within this range can replace or substitute for the variable to produce a sentence. Variables can be divided into **bound variables** and **free variables** (Russell and Whitehead called them respectively real and apparent variables). A variable inside the **scope** of a **quantifier** is said to be bound, for example "x" in (∃x)Fx is bound by the quantifier "∃" (some). A variable not bound by any quantifier is free, for example "x" in Fx. In **propositional logic**, "p, q, r . . ." are used as propositional variables, representing **propositions**.

> "Those expressions in formulae, the replacement of which by a word or phrase would result in a sentence, are called free variables, or simply, variables." **Strawson,** *Introduction to Logical Theory*

veganism, see vegetarianism

vegetarianism

ETHICS The moral **attitude** that we should not eat the meat of animals. Vegetarianism has existed for a long time in some religious traditions, but the term "vegetarian" did not become popular until the foundation of the Vegetarian Society in England in 1847. The issue of vegetarianism became more prominent with the rise of the **animal liberation** movement. Vegetarians argue that eating meat takes animals as a **means to an end**, and thus fails to respect them as beings with inherent **value** or with a right to respect. Different theorists provide different sorts of a moral basis for vegetarianism. Some argue that animals have interests, others argue that they have **rights**. All of these are controversial views. Vegetarian arguments depend on the criterion one takes as the basis of moral consideration. Tom **Regan** claims that an animal is a **subject-of-a-life** and that one is not permitted to eat anything that is a subject-of-a-life. Peter **Singer** considers that **sentience** is the crucial grounds for moral treatment and that no sentient being can be used as food. For the animal liberation movement, the vegetarian lifestyle is fundamental as a personal means of shifting our moral consciousness toward animals. Generally, vegetarianism prohibits meat eating, but not animal products such as milk and eggs. An extreme form of vegetarianism that advocates the avoidance of all animal products is called veganism.

> "Killing animals for food normally means not only that the animals die but that they must be exploited throughout their lives in order to reduce the costs of production. Thus, the case for vegetarianism is strong whatever view we take of the value of animal life." **Singer, in Regan (ed.), *Matters of Life and Death***

veil of appearance, see veil of perception

veil of ignorance

POLITICAL PHILOSOPHY The major condition that Rawls imposes in his **original position** on participants who are to determine by rational choice the principles of **justice** governing the basic structure of society. All participants are situated behind a veil of ignorance, where they have no **knowledge** of their particular characteristics, abilities, religious beliefs, and personal histories. They do not know the economic condition or political situation of their society or their own social status or class position. They have general theoretical knowledge about society and know that they are **rational** and will pursue **primary goods** whatever their circumstances and plan of life. The veil of ignorance is meant to guarantee that the choice made by the participants will not be biased by their specific interests or advantages, and to oblige them to determine principles **impartially** and **objectively**. It is not clear that persons behind the veil of ignorance would have enough knowledge to choose any conception of justice. If they know more about themselves and

their society, the demand that they are unanimous in their conception of justice is at risk. It is also possible that individuals can be biased by their history even if they are ignorant of that history.

> "The principles of justice are chosen behind a veil of ignorance. This ensures that no one is advantaged or disadvantaged in the choice of principles by the outcome of natural chance or the contingency of social circumstances." **Rawls, *A Theory of Justice***

veil of perception

EPISTEMOLOGY Also called the veil of appearance. **Locke** and many later **empiricists** have claimed that what we perceive are not external objects themselves, but are sensory **ideas** or **sense-data** that are produced in our **minds** by external things. These ideas, like a veil, stand as intermediaries between the conscious subjects and external objects. Our **senses** can only show us sense-data or **appearances**. Such a theory is different from **Platonism**, which claims that **perception** and appearance are unreliable and that **reality** can be known only through the intellect. The view also differs from **naive realism**, which holds that what we sense is the object itself rather than its appearance, and from **phenomenalism**, which holds that external objects are constructed out of actual and possible sense-data. Because appearances can hide the real nature of things and prevent us from knowing reality as it is, the theory of the veil of perception has led to **skeptical** challenges to our knowledge of the external world.

> "We are restricted to the passing show on the veil of perception, with no possibility of extending our knowledge to the world beyond." **Stroud, *The Significance of Philosophical Scepticism***

Venn, John (1834–1923)

British logician, born in Hull. Venn's major works include *The Logic of Chance* (1866), *Symbolic Logic* (1881), and *The Principles of Empirical or Inductive Logic* (1889). In the first book, he established the frequency theory of probability according to which probability is identified with the statistic frequency of occurrence within a reference class. He invented the "Venn diagram," which uses overlapping circles to check the validity of syllogistic deductions.

verification theory of meaning

PHILOSOPHY OF LANGUAGE, EPISTEMOLOGY The theory of meaning advocated by the **logical positivists** and associated with the criterion of verifiability. The latter provides a **criterion** of meaningfulness for **sentences**, while the verification theory of meaning specifies the nature of meaning. According to the criterion, a sentence is cognitively meaningful if and only if it is logically possible for it to be verified. The meaning of a sentence is its method of verification, that is, the way in which it can be verified or falsified, particularly by **experience**. The theory has been challenged because the best formulations still exclude meaningful sentences and allow meaningless sentences. Critics also claim that the theory is a test for meaningfulness rather than a theory of meaning proper. Further, they claim that it fails to recognize that the interconnectedness of language might allow a sentence that cannot itself be verified to be meaningful.

"The verification theory of meaning, which dominated the Vienna Circle, was concerned with the meaning and meaningfulness of sentences rather than words." **Quine,** *Theories and Things*

verificationism

PHILOSOPHICAL METHOD, PHILOSOPHY OF SCIENCE, PHILOSOPHY OF LANGUAGE A position fundamental to **logical positivism**, claiming that the **meaning** of a **statement** is its method of verification. Accordingly, apparent statements lacking a method of verification, such as those of religion and **metaphysics**, are **meaningless**. **Theoretical expressions** can be defined in terms of the experiences by means of which assertions employing them can be verified. In the **philosophy of mind**, **behaviorism**, which tries to reduce unobserved inner states to patterns of behavior, turns out to be a version of verificationism. Some philosophers require conclusive verification for a statement to be meaningful, while others allow any positive evidence to confer meaning. There are disputes whether every statement must be verified separately or theories can be verified as a whole even if some of their statements cannot be individually verified. Attempts to offer a rigorous account of verification have run into difficulties because statements that should be excluded as meaningless nevertheless pass the test of verification and statements that should be allowed as meaningful are excluded.

"For over a hundred years, one of the dominant tendencies in the philosophy of science has been verificationism, that is, the doctrine that to know the meaning of a scientific proposition . . . is to know what would be evidence for that proposition." **Putnam,** *Mind, Language and Reality*

verisimilitude

PHILOSOPHY OF SCIENCE [from Latin *verisimilar*, like the truth] The degree of approximation or closeness to **truth** of a **statement** or a theory. **Popper** defined it in terms of the difference resulting from truth-content minus falsity-content. The truth-content of a statement is all of its true consequences, while the falsity-content of a statement is all of its false consequences. The aim of **science** is to find better verisimilitude. One theory has a better verisimilitude than competing theories if it can explain the success of competing theories and can also explain cases where the other theories fail. Popper emphasized that verisimilitude is different from **probability**. Probability is the degree of logical **certainty** abstracted from content, while verisimilitude is degree of likeness to truth and combines truth and content.

"This suggests that we combine here the ideas of truth and content into one – the idea of a degree of better (or worse) correspondence to truth or of greater (or less) likeness or similarity to truth; or to use a term already mentioned above (in contradistinction to probability) the idea of (degrees of) verisimilitude." **Popper,** *Conjectures and Refutations*

Verstehen

PHILOSOPHY OF HISTORY, PHILOSOPHY OF SOCIAL SCIENCE [German, understanding] Because **understanding** is a general notion, many English translations and philosophers leave the theoretical term *Verstehen* untranslated. In German philosophy of history and philosophy of social science, *Verstehen* is used for a cognitive mode peculiar to the study of human life and society. It is an empathic or participatory understanding of a subject's point of view by imaginatively putting oneself into the place of the subject. Through **hermeneutics** or **interpretation**, it reconstructs the subject's purposes, **values**, and **meaning**.

In contrast, **explanation** (German *Erklaren*), which seeks causal relations and appeals to general **laws**, is the method characteristic of the natural sciences. Proponents of classical *Verstehen* theory rejected the claim that the social sciences should follow the natural sciences by searching for the **objective** meaning of the social world. The claims of *Verstehen* are opposed to **scientism** and **positivism**, although Max **Weber** argued that both *Verstehen* and *Erklaren* belong to the methodology of social science. The notion of *Verstehen* can be traced to Giambattista **Vico** and J. G. von **Herder**, but it was fully elaborated by **Dilthey** in order to demonstrate that the human sciences have a distinct methodology. **Heidegger** and **Gadamer**, however, view *Verstehen* not as a cognitive mode but as the essential feature of human beings situated in a world that projects infinite possibilities.

"A *Verstehen* approach to the study of human beings is any which assumes that the inquiry cannot be modelled on natural sciences: any 'humanistic' or 'non-scientist' approach, to use other terms in common employment; an *Erklaren* approach is one which makes the contrary assumption." **Macdonald and Pettit,** *Semantic and Social Science*

via antiqua, see *via moderna*

via eminentiae, see *via positiva*

via moderna
PHILOSOPHY OF LANGUAGE, METAPHYSICS, PHILOSOPHY OF SCIENCE [Latin, the modern way] A term for the **nominalist** movement that arose in the fourteenth century, influenced by the writings of **William of Ockham**. It was opposed to the *via antiqua* (the old way), that is, the **realist** schools that were dominant in the twelfth and thirteenth centuries, including **Thomism**, **Scotism**, and **Augustinianism**. The movement emphasized logic and direct **experience** and rejected empty speculation and **abstraction**. **Ockham's razor**, the principle that plurality is never to be posited without need, was the basic spirit of the movement. The advocates of the *via moderna* believed in the principle of the **uniformity of nature** and engaged actively in scientific research. The *via moderna* exerted a great impact on the later development of modern physics.

"Ockham's teachings had, rather, a stimulating effect. They awakened many somewhat independent thinkers who were united at least against the realism of the older scholastics. These 'nominales' (in the medieval sense) constituted the via moderna, which was not so much a school as a trend of thought." **Boehner (ed.),** *Ockham: Philosophic Writing*

via negativa
PHILOSOPHY OF RELIGION, PHILOSOPHY OF LANGUAGE A way of describing **God** who transcends human **experience** by denying limited qualities to God by the use of such adjectives as incorporeal and uncreated. It is claimed that we can come to know God by knowing what he is not. *Via negativa* is contrasted to *via positiva*, which ascribes to God positive **attributes**, such as **omnipotence, omniscience**, and absolute **goodness**.

"The idea of God can be approached through the use of imagination (the *via imaginative*) and varies to the extent that it employs positive attributions (the *via positiva*) or negative (the *via negativa*)." **Taliaferro, in Bunnin and Tsui-James (eds.),** *The Blackwell Companion to Philosophy*

via positiva, see *via negativa*

vicious circle
LOGIC, PHILOSOPHY OF MATHEMATICS Circular reasoning, also called **begging the question** or *petitio principii*, makes use of the conclusion to be proved as a premise, and hence renders the **argument** invalid. A circular **definition** explains the *definiens* in terms of the *definiedum* and renders the **definition** empty. Circularity in these cases is vicious. According to **Russell, paradoxes** in the foundations of mathematics are due to vicious circularity, for they violate the vicious circle principle that "whatever involves all of a collection must not be one of the collection." His theory of **types** is established on the basis of this principle and attempts to avoid all paradoxes of this sort.

Not all circularities in argument or definition, however, are vicious. All **deductions** mean to derive the conclusion from the premises and hence the conclusion must have been implied in the premises. If the circle is large enough, and the argument or definition can still provide new **knowledge**, it is considered to be a virtuous circle.

> "The vicious circles in question all arise from supposing that a collection of objects may contain members which can only be defined by means of the collection as a whole." **Russell,** *Collected Papers of Bertrand Russell,* **vol. VI**

vicious circle principle

LOGIC, PHILOSOPHY OF MATHEMATICS Before **Russell**, **Poincaré** noticed that many **paradoxes** stem from viciously circular definitions, which he called **impredicative definitions**. Russell formulates a vicious circle principle to solve the various paradoxes at the foundation of mathematics. It has several versions, including "whatever involves all of a collection must not be one of the collection"; "if, provided a certain collection had a total, it would have a member only definable in terms of that total, then the said collection is not total"; or "whatever contains an apparent variable must not be a possible value of that variable." For Russell, all **set theories** that violate this principle are unintelligible and unsound. Corresponding to this principle, Russell established his theory of the hierarchy of **types**, according to which, whatever contains an apparent **variable** belongs to a different type from the possible values of that variable. Hence no paradox will arise.

> "These fallacies . . . are to be avoided by what may be called the 'vicious-circle principle'; that is 'no totality can contain members defined in terms of itself'." **Russell,** *Logic and Knowledge*

Vico, Giambattista (1668–1744)

Italian philosopher, born in Naples, taught at University of Naples. In his major work *The New Science* (1725, with revised editions 1730 and 1744), Vico developed a speculative philosophy of history. He argued that because what is true and what is made are convertible, we can only know what we have made. As a consequence, man must be understood historically, and language is significant for historical understanding. He held that the history of each nation develops in determined recurring cycles of the divine, the heroic, and the rational, and that at any given stage a society presents a coherent structure. He also claimed that the study

of history and other humane disciplines is methodologically distinct from the study of natural science.

Vienna Circle

EPISTEMOLOGY, LOGIC, PHILOSOPHY OF LANGUAGE, PHILOSOPHY OF SCIENCE A philosophical and scientific movement originated in the 1920s under the leadership of Professor Moritz **Schlick** of the University of Vienna by a group of philosophers and scientists who shared many basic ideas. The name derived from the manifesto of the movement "The Scientific Conception of the World: The Vienna Circle," published in 1929. Leading members of the circle included M. Schlick, R. **Carnap**, O. **Neurath**, F. Waismann, H. **Feigl**, and K. **Gödel**. Its philosophy, which is called "Logical Positivism" or "Logical Empiricism," was introduced to English readers by A. J. **Ayer**'s book *Language, Truth and Logic* (1936). The Vienna Circle's journal *Erkenntnis* was its main medium of publicity, but it also published a series of monographs under the general title "Unified Science" (*Einheitswissenschaft*, German), and organized many international congresses. The Vienna Circle disintegrated after the death in 1936 of Schlick, who was shot by an insane student, and with the German invasion of Austria. Many members emigrated to United States, England, and the Scandinavian countries, and exerted great influence in their new countries. Neurath made great effort to keep the movement going. He changed the title of *Erkenntnis* into *The Journal of Unified Science*. Together with Carnap he initiated publication of a series of works at the University of Chicago under the general title *The Encyclopedia of Unified Science*. In spite of these efforts, the Vienna Circle was no longer a school.

> "The philosophers with whom I am in the closest agreement are those who compose the 'Viennese circle', under the leadership of Moritz Schlick, and are commonly known as logical positivists." **Ayer,** *Logic, Truth and Language*

vinculum substantiale

METAPHYSICS [Latin, substantial bond or chain] A controversial doctrine in **Leibniz**'s later thought. Only **monads** are **real** in **nature**, and everything else is composed of them. A plurality of monads constitutes a corporeal substance if and only if they are united by a *vinculum substantiale* (a substantial chain); otherwise, things would be mere phenomena. Thus, *vinculum substantiale* is necessary for the substantiality and unity of corporeal substance. It is itself a substantial thing, but not a monad or an **accident**. Leibniz introduced this doctrine in order to account for the miracle of transubstantiation, but it was criticized by **Russell** and others as being inconsistent with the general tenet of his theory of monads, within which monads themselves are responsible for the unity of corporeal substances.

"If that substantial chain (vinculum substantiale) for monads did not exist, all bodies, together with all of their qualities, would be nothing but well-founded phenomena." **Leibniz,** *Philosophical Essays*

virtue

ANCIENT GREEK PHILOSOPHY, ETHICS, PHILOSOPHY OF MIND, PHILOSOPHY OF ACTION, POLITICAL PHILOSOPHY [Greek *arete*, also translated as excellence. In English, virtue is a transliteration from Latin *virtus*, manliness] In Greece, virtue was not only human excellence or moral virtue, but also the excellence of anything in performing its essential **function**. Excellence at cutting is the virtue of a knife; excellence at seeing is the virtue of eyes. The traditional Greek human virtues are generally thought to include **courage**, **temperance**, piety, **justice**, and **wisdom**, but there were conflicting beliefs about them. **Socrates** devoted all of his life to clarifying the **meaning** of these virtues, claiming crucially that virtue is **knowledge**. One main aspect of **Plato's theory of ideas** was to establish the metaphysical foundation for moral virtues and to determine how a man should live.

Aristotle inferred on the basis of its original meaning that virtue is a thing's good performance of its functions and that human virtue is the excellence of man in performing his rational function. A good man performs well activities involving thought. Since a man not only has the ability to think, but also has the ability to control his **desire** and conduct by **reason**, Aristotle divides virtue into intellectual virtue, including, among others, **practical wisdom** (*phronesis*) and theoretical wisdom (*theoria* or contemplation), and moral or ethical virtues (excellence of character). These latter are internalized **dispositions** of **action**, **desire**, and

feeling closely connected with practical wisdom. Aristotle's ethics is essentially a theory of virtue.

For **Epicurus**, virtue is necessary for happiness not because it is an essential ingredient, but because it is a **means** to its attainment. For Stoicism, virtue is a pattern of **behavior** that follows from a disposition perfectly in tune with the rationality of **nature**, and it is the only good worthy of **choice**. In its later development, moral virtue is understood differently in different cultures. The seven Christian **cardinal virtues** include Plato's four virtues in the *Republic* (courage, temperance, wisdom, and justice), plus **faith**, hope, and **love**.

In addition to the nature of virtues, philosophers have explored relations among the virtues themselves, relations between virtues and non-virtuous states, the place of virtues in our psychology and their role in achieving happiness. Virtues offer a basis for ethical life rivaling those provided by **Kantian principles** or **utilitarian** calculation of happiness, although an account of ethics might reasonably include principles, consequences, and virtues. A recent revival of **virtue ethics** has been motivated in part by dissatisfaction with the abstract **universal** nature of the main alternative views, and is intended to correct this through the emphasis on cultivating virtues in concrete human individuals.

"Virtue, then, is a state that decides, (consisting) in a mean, the mean relative to us, which is defined by reference to reason, i.e., to the reason by reference to which the intelligent person could define it. It is a mean between two vices, one of excess and one of deficiency." **Aristotle,** *Nicomachean Ethics*

virtue (Kant)

ETHICS In contrast to the Aristotelian tradition, which defined virtue as a settled habit or **disposition**, **Kant** defined virtue as a struggle and as a moral strength of **will** in overcoming temptation to transgress the **law**, that is, in resisting urges and **inclinations** opposed to the demands of **duty**. A virtuous person has a strong sense of duty or a strong reverence for the moral law. Kant claimed that the traditional virtues are valuable only as a means to the ends of a **good** will, but he also ascribed to virtue an important place in his moral theory. He divided his *Metaphysics of Morals* into two parts: the doctrine of rights, which is a doctrine of morality in general, and the doctrine of virtue, which concerns duties that do not come under external laws. The doctrine of virtue is also divided into two parts. The first deals with duties of virtues to oneself as both an animal being and as a moral being, and the second deals with the duties of virtues to others.

> "The capacity and considered resolve to withstand a strong but unjust opponent is fortitude, and with respect to what opposes the moral disposition within us, virtue (moral fortitude)." **Kant,** *Metaphysics of Morals*

virtue ethics

ETHICS, PHILOSOPHY OF ACTION, ANCIENT GREEK PHILOSOPHY An ethical theory that takes virtue as primary and asserts that the central question of ethics, "How should I live?," can be construed as "What kind of person should I be?" Its goal is to describe types of character that are admired within a certain **culture** or society. For the ancient Greeks, ethics was something concerned with character (*êthos*), and hence ethics was understood as virtue ethics. Most **Socratic** dialogues examine the common beliefs about what virtue is. **Plato** in his *Republic* discussed four cardinal virtues and then connected them to different parts of the **soul**. **Aristotle**'s *Nicomachean Ethics* is the most celebrated system of virtue ethics. He connected virtue with human **function** and *telos*, divided virtue into intellectual and moral virtues, and argued that a full virtue is a **disposition** to choose and **act** and is the **mean** state between deficiency and excess relative to a person that is prescribed by **practical reason**. For the Stoics, virtue lay in conformity to **nature**, and the virtuous life was **self-sufficient**. Virtue ethics continued to develop in the medieval era, especially in **Aquinas**, but declined with the rise of modern ethical theories, in particular **utilitarianism** and **deontology**, which take it that morality must be determined by the calculation of **utility** of the consequences of action or by the **rules** and **principles** governing moral actions. Since the mid-twentieth century there has been a revival of virtue ethics, represented by **Anscombe**, **MacIntyre**, **Williams**, **Foot**, **von Wright**, and Annette **Baier**. It claims that modern ethical theories cannot help us to deal with many moral problems and that the focus

of ethical consideration must shift from the **agent**'s **action** to the agents themselves and to their ambitions and projects. Virtue ethics is essentially a neo-Aristotelian position. However, while some virtue theorists tend to give up all modern principle-based ethics, others argue that Aristotelian ethics fails to deal with the moral problems regarding the relationship among human beings and must be revised.

The major issues discussed in virtue ethics include the formation of character, **practical reason**, moral **education**, connections between character and **friendship**, and the analysis of specific traits such as **courage**, **loyalty**, **shame**, **guilt**, and many traditional vices. This is a newly exploited area and much discussion is still going on. Although such an approach cannot do all the work of ethics, it is valuable for uncovering the character-forming area of life that has long been ignored by other moral theories.

> "'Virtue ethics' is a term of art, initially introduced to distinguish an approach in normative ethics which emphasizes the virtue, or moral character, in contrast to an approach which emphasizes duties or rules (deontology) or one which emphasizes the consequences of actions (utilitarianism)." **Hursthouse,** *On Virtue Ethics*

virtuous circle, see vicious circle

visual field

EPISTEMOLOGY The totality of a person's visual **sense-impressions** or immediate **perceptions** at a given time. This field includes all true or false visual **data** immediately acquired without any element of **inference**. It is a **mental** field of vision, rather than the range of external spatial things that are available to a person's eye. Parallel notions include other sensory fields connected with touch, hearing, taste, and smell. All these together form the notion of a sense-field.

> "Whenever I open my eyes I am aware of a coloured field of view, which I will call a 'visual field'." **Broad,** *Scientific Thought*

vitalism

PHILOSOPHY OF SCIENCE The doctrine that holds that living organisms owe their characteristics to some special vital principle, which is subject to different **laws** from those governing physical **matter**, so the **behavior** of living things cannot be sufficiently explained in **mechanistic** or **materialistic** terms. Thus this doctrine, in opposition to mechanistic **explanations** of life, insists on a fundamental distinction between organic and inorganic phenomena. **Aristotle**, as the ancestor of vitalism, claims that the life of an animal consists in a *psyche* (Greek, soul), which by **teleological** causation accounts for the morphological development of the organism. In modern times, the French philosopher **Bergson** forcefully argued for vitalism, using the concept of *élan vital* (life force). Vitalism is challenged by the development of molecular genetics, which tends to support the view that physiological processes also follow the laws of physics and chemistry.

> "Aristotle thought that there was a vegetable soul in every plant or animal, and something similar has been widely believed by vitalists." **Russell, *Human Knowledge***

Vlastos, Gregory (1907–91)

American historian of ancient Greek philosophy, born in Istanbul, Professor of philosophy at Queen's University, Ontario, Cornell University, Princeton University, and University of California, Berkeley. Vlastos used the methods of analytic philosophy to identify and examine philosophical questions arising in the works of Plato. His discussion of the Third Man argument in the *Parmenides* and his attempt to distinguish the philosophical method of Socrates from Plato's later philosophical development have had great influence. His major works include *Platonic Studies* (1973) and *Socrates: Ironist and Moral Philosopher* (1991).

void

ANCIENT GREEK PHILOSOPHY, METAPHYSICS, PHILO-SOPHY OF SCIENCE A term introduced by the Greek **atomists** Leucippus and **Democritus** for empty space. Earlier Greek thinkers held that what is must have a bodily form, but the atomists argued that what has no bodily form also really exists, and that is the void. On **Aristotle**'s interpretation, the void is not a continuous space, but is rather what occurs in between bodies, while **Epicurus** described the void simply as the space that bodies may and may not occupy. The conception of the void enabled atomism to explain how **plurality** and movement

are possible and in this way reacted to the **Eleatic** challenge that denied the possibility of plurality and movement. It was also the first abstract conception of passive and empty space, which was indispensable to classical physics, although discarded by quantum mechanics.

> "Democritus . . . calls space by these names – 'the void', 'nothing' and 'the infinite', while each individual atom he calls 'hing' ('nothing' without 'not'), the compact and being." **Aristotle, *On Democritus***

volition

PHILOSOPHY OF MIND, PHILOSOPHY OF ACTION The act of **will** which precedes a bodily movement, sometimes used as a synonym for **choosing**, determining, or preferring. Volition is presented as the ground of the distinction between **intentional** or voluntary action and mere **behavior**. On this basis, we infer that many actions are voluntary, willed, or **caused** by volition. According to the **Cartesian** tradition, the will is an **entity** that acts to translate our **ideas** into voluntary actions. This doctrine came under fire from **Ryle**, who claimed that there is neither direct nor indirect **evidence** to prove the existence of volitions. Furthermore, if volitions are said to be **mental acts** and to be the basis of voluntary actions, we may ask whether volitions are **voluntary** or **involuntary**. If they are voluntary, then the voluntary acts are themselves preceded by a voluntary act, and we enter an **infinite regress**; if they are involuntary, there will be an absurd result that voluntary acts are based on involuntary mental acts. There are various attempts to solve this dilemma, but none has gained general approval. The later **Wittgenstein** also claimed that if we view volitions as acts of willing, we will be confronted with the consequence that one could will willing. It is uncertain whether new theoretical approaches to the mind and mental states will revive interest in volitions and the will.

> "Volitions have been postulated as special acts, or operations, 'in the mind', by means of which a mind gets its ideas translated into facts." **Ryle, *The Concept of Mind***

Voltaire, François-Marie (1694–1778)

French philosopher, playwright, and novelist, born in Paris, a leading Encyclopedist. In the spirit of empiricism and humanism, Voltaire wrote extensively on various topics in metaphysics, religion, ethics, and political philosophy. He introduced John Locke's empiricism and Newton's scientific methods to France and fought for individual rights and religious tolerance. In his satirical novel *Candide* (1759), he attacked the optimism of Leibniz's claim that this is the best of all possible worlds. Voltaire's major philosophical writings include *Philosophical Letters* (1733), *Treatise on Tolerance* (1763), *Philosophical Dictionary* (1764), and *The Philosophy of History* (1766).

voluntarism

EPISTEMOLOGY, METAPHYSICS, ETHICS, PHILOSOPHY OF RELIGION [from Latin *voluntas*, will] Any philosophical position that holds the concept of **will** as the central explanatory principle. Will is the origin of all order, of **essence** and **moral laws**. To be **meaningful** is to be willed. In contrast, **reason** is subordinate to will and is even rejected as idle. Will is a higher faculty than the intellect. The tradition of voluntarism in Western philosophy is associated with the tradition of **irrationalism**. It was a predominant aspect of fourteenth-century and fifteenth-century medieval thought and has been a trend in modern and contemporary philosophy. In different fields, it is presented in different forms, including doxastic voluntarism, which claims that **believing** is willing; ethical voluntarism, which proposes that the will is the ultimate source of **moral value**; metaphysical voluntarism, which claims that the will is the ultimate principle of **reality** and rejects **determinism** and **intellectualism**; and theological or theistic voluntarism, which holds that religious beliefs are not determined by reason and claims that **God**'s will is the moral law.

"This term [of voluntarism], classical but in need of clarification, was applied to both man and God. We know it in its application to man – that is, in terms of the problem of beatitude, one asks by what power of the intellect or the will the soul enters into the possession of the absolute good, into the enjoyment of the divine trinity." **Vignaux,** *Philosophy in the Middle Ages*

voluntary-involuntary

ANCIENT GREEK PHILOSOPHY, ETHICS, PHILOSOPHY OF ACTION [Greek *hekousia-akousia*, although these terms, employed by Aristotle, are more comprehensive

than their English counterparts] A voluntary **action** is performed by an **agent** who has the initiative in himself and involves neither compulsion nor reluctance. The agent knows the important circumstances that will affect the result of his action. An involuntary action is done under threat of force or owing to **ignorance**. Sometimes Aristotle ascribes voluntary actions also to animals and children, although generally he confines them to those agents he believes to be capable of rational **desire**. The voluntary-involuntary distinction is used to determine the conditions for ascribing **responsibility**. A man is responsible only for what he has done voluntarily.

"These receive praise or blame when they are voluntary, but pardon, sometimes even pity, when they are involuntary." **Aristotle,** *Nicomachean Ethics*

Vorstellung

EPISTEMOLOGY, METAPHYSICS [German, literally, putting forward; normally translated as representation] In addition to being a term for representation, *Vorstellung* is employed as a counterpart of the British **empiricist** terms "idea" or "sense-datum" and is used in a variety of ways by different philosophers. For these reasons, many authors prefer not to translate it into English. For **Kant**, representations include **sensations**, **intuitions**, **concepts**, and **ideas** and thus appear in **sensibility**, **understanding**, and **reason**. Representations provide the elements that are combined in **judgment**. The **categories** are representations, and the "**I think**" that must be able to accompany all my representations is a representation. Representations can be as ephemeral and **subjective** as sensations and as robust and objective as spatio-temporal **objects**, that is, Kantian **appearances**. Ideas, for Kant, differing radically from empiricist ideas, are representations that go beyond the possibility of **experience**. **Hegel** contrasted *Vorstellung* with "**concept**." **Schopenhauer** claimed that "the **world** is my *Vorstellung* (representation)."

"Kant in effect makes his philosophical starting-point a notion of Vorstellung or an 'idea'. This 'idea' or experience can be thought of as the interface between the experiencing mind, the subject, and something in the world, an object." **Podro,** *The Manifold in Perception*

voting paradox

POLITICAL PHILOSOPHY, PHILOSOPHY OF SOCIAL SCIENCE
A **paradox** relating to **social choice** discovered by **Condorcet** in 1785. It is a special case of "**Arrow's paradox**." Suppose that three voters, John, Sam, and David, vote to choose one among three candidates A, B, C. John's sequential ordering of preference is A>B>C; Sam's ordering is B>C>A; and David's ordering is C>A>B. The consequence of voting according to these preferences will be that a majority prefers A to B, a majority prefers B to C, and a majority prefers C to A. Hence, although each **individual** has an ordering of **choice**, no ranking in society that is consistent with that ordering will emerge. This indicates the difficulty of transmitting the aggregation of individual preferences into a social choice. It also shows that the majority rule principle, which is supposed to be the essence of **democracy**, is less clear than is supposed to be the case. For if election is sequential, the social choice would change cyclically without a change in individual preferences.

"The best known example of a voting procedure's producing an irrational result is given in the so-called 'paradox of voting' which had already been fully characterised in the nineteenth century."
Pettit, *Judging Justice*

W

Ward, James (1843–1925)

English philosopher and psychologist, born in Hull, Professor of Mental Philosophy, Cambridge. According to Ward's analysis of mind, mental experience has three modes: cognitive, affective, and conative. Cognition determines feeling, and feeling determines conation. He replaced the prevailing associationist psychology with a type of genetic psychology. His major works include *Naturalism and Agnosticism* (1899), *The Realm of Ends* (1911), and *Psychological Principles* (1918).

warranted assertibility

EPISTEMOLOGY, PHILOSOPHY OF SCIENCE A term introduced by John **Dewey** as a substitute for **knowledge** or **truth** in order to indicate that knowledge is gained as a result of an ongoing, self-correcting process of inquiry, rather than as a result of internal mental activity. An **assertion** is a **judgment** arrived at after determining the significance of the related **data**. If this assertion does the work that it is supposed to do, it is warranted. Any warranted assertion must be refined and **justified** by being subjected to continuous **testing** through public **experience**. From the viewpoint of warranted assertibility, there is no absolute truth known by rational insight with **certainty**, and knowledge is not a system of truths.

"If inquiry begins in doubt, it terminates in the institution of conditions which remove need for doubt. The latter state of affairs may be designated by the words belief and knowledge. For reasons that I shall state later I prefer the words 'warranted assertibility'." **Dewey, *Logic***

wayward causal chain

PHILOSOPHY OF ACTION, PHILOSOPHY OF MIND Also called a deviant causal chain or causal deviance. In normal **causation**, if a person performs an action because he intends to do it, then his **intention** is the cause of his doing it. But sometimes causation can go astray and deviate from the normal route in intentional **action**, **perception**, **meaning**, or **memory**. For example, because Smith is angry with Jones, Smith decides to go to Jones's home to injure him. On the way, he drives recklessly and hurts somebody. The injured person happens to be Jones. In such a case, Smith realizes his intention to hurt Jones, but that occurs only as an accidental consequence. Does this mean that Smith does the hurting intentionally in this case? The existence of wayward causal chains creates problems for the analysis of normal causal chains.

"Since there may be wayward causal chains, we cannot say that if attitudes that would rationalise x cause an agent to do x, then he does x intentionally." **Davidson, *Essays on Actions and Events***

weakness of will, see incontinence

Weber, Max (1864–1920)
German sociologist and philosopher of social science, born in Erfurt. While accepting the distinction between natural and human sciences, Weber maintained that sociology needs *Verstehen*, but does not exclude causal explanation. He argued that social science must employ "ideal types" as heuristc devices in the analysis of concrete social events. His account of authority distinguished three types: traditional authority, charismatic authority, and the rational-legal authority that is characteristic of modern bureaucratic society. He sought to understand the rationality of social processes in terms of a theory of social action, in which the rational deliberation of each actor takes account of the likely deliberation of other actors. His interest in the relations between religion and social and economic conditions led to his influential theory that the development of European capitalism can be explained in terms of the ascetic secular consequences of Protestant theology. Weber's most influential works are *The Protestant Ethic and the Spirit of Capitalism* (1904–5) and *Economy and Society* (1922).

wedge argument
ETHICS A species of the **slippery slope argument**, elaborated by Bishop Sullivan against legalizing active **euthanasia**. Once a single instance of direct killing is approved of by society, we have admitted the thin edge of a wedge. We will then inevitably concede more cases by pressing the wedge forward and eventually put all life at risk. To avoid this terrible consequence, we should outlaw from the very beginning any mercy killing. But many philosophers reject this argument on the grounds that we are reasonable enough to distinguish between justifiable killing and unjustifiable killing.

> "[T]o permit in a single instance the direct killing of an innocent person would be to admit a most dangerous wedge that might eventually put all life in a precarious condition." **Sullivan, in Kohl (ed.),** *Beneficent Euthanasia*

Weil, Simone (1909–43)
French social and religious philosopher, born in Paris. Weil claimed that a crucial conflict between the mechanical necessity of the universe and the human expectation of good gives rise to human frustration, a state that can be overcome by relinquishing individuality in contemplative mystic experience. She applied her Christian Platonism in developing an egalitarian social and political philosophy. Weil's major works include *Gravity and Grace* (1946), *Waiting for God* (1950), *The Notebooks of Simone Weil*, 3 vols. (1951–6), and *Oppression and Liberty* (1955).

welfare
POLITICAL PHILOSOPHY, ETHICS Welfare and its relations to **rights**, **needs**, and **equality** are familiar topics in contemporary political philosophy. Welfare can be discussed regarding **individuals** and regarding society. Individual welfare concerns **good** for the individual, but there is debate concerning whether individual good should be understood in terms of the **satisfaction** of actual **preferences**, of **needs**, or of well-informed, long-term interests. Social welfare concerns the overall good for society. Some believe that all social goods can be reduced to individual goods and that every aspect of social goods can be derived from individual goods. It follows from this view, which is called **welfarism**, that a **state** should focus on individual goods. Others argue that some types of social goods are irreducible. This debate leads to a further difference. Unlike traditional political thinking, for which the primary goal of a state is the security of its citizens, contemporary political philosophy considers that the main function of a modern state is to promote welfare and **justice**. According to some, however, the state should promote individual goods, while others believe that the state should maximize social welfare. A welfare state takes a basic minimum of material welfare for its citizens to be a primary concern of policy making.

> "'Welfare' is a vague term. It may refer only to means to physical well being, such as food, housing, and medical care. Or it may include also some means to mental or spiritual well being, such as education, art galleries, museums, and theatres." **Raphael,** *Problems of Political Philosophy*

welfarism
POLITICAL PHILOSOPHY If the overall **good** of society is a function of the individual **welfare** of

its members, the **state** can promote its welfare by promoting the welfare of its citizens. According to welfarism, all social goods can be reduced to individual goods, and every aspect of social goods can be derived from individual goods. Hence, a state should focus on individual goods, through means such as health insurance, free education, unemployment benefits, and child allowances, to promote the good of society. This account of the role of the state contrasts with the eighteenth- and nineteenth-century view that the main function of the state is to protect the security of its citizens from both outward invasion and internal instability. The idea of welfarism, which is considered by some to be state **paternalism**, has been adopted more in Western European countries than in the United States. In recent years, with a shortage of funding and misgivings about the alleged negative effects of welfare on its recipients, the positive picture of welfare has come under pressure.

"Welfarism, requiring that the goodness of a state of affairs be a function only of the utility information regarding that state." **Sen,** *On Ethics and Economics*

well-being

ETHICS [Greek *eudaimonia*, usually translated as happiness] Some philosophers prefer the translation "well-being" to "happiness" to catch the peculiarity of what **Plato** and **Aristotle** called *eudaimonia*, in contrast to the modern notion of happiness. *Eudaimonia* as a state of satisfaction is not for one moment or one day, but a matter for one's whole life. As an important independent notion in modern ethics, well-being roughly means what it is for a single life to go well.

"I shall use the expression well-being for such a state." **B. Williams,** *Ethics and the Limits of Philosophy*

well-formed formula

LOGIC An expression or a string of **symbols** in a logical system that conforms to the formation rules of that system. It is equivalent to a grammatical sentence in natural languages. A simple well-formed formula is formed out the basic vocabulary of the formal system and its deductive **rules**, while a complicated well-formed formula is constructed out of the simple well-formed formulae of the system.

All well-formed formulae can be explained within that system. If the formula contains a **variable** not bound by a **quantifier** (a free variable), it is an open well-formed formula; otherwise, it is a closed one. "Well-formed formula" is generally abbreviated as wff. Since there is no interest in ill-formed formulae, well-formed formulae are often simply called formulae. **Axioms** and theorems of a system are among its well-formed formulae.

"Consider the class of all permutations of some set of elements of a language we shall use 'L'. The formation rules of L divides the class of all possible permutations into two mutually exclusive subclasses, one of which will comprise all of the grammatically permissible or well-formed formulations (for short, 'wffs') of L; the other subclass will comprise the expressions which, made up of elements of L, are nevertheless not grammatically correct expressions of L." **Rudner,** *Philosophy of Social Science*

well-founded phenomena

METAPHYSICS Also called true phenomena or real phenomena, **Leibniz**'s term for material **bodies**. In his later metaphysics, only **monads** exist in **nature**, and all other things are not true **substances** but only phenomena. Their unity can not be explained merely in terms of the modification of extension. Thus material bodies do not form a part of Leibniz's fundamental **ontology**. Instead, they are composed of monads and their individual modifications. Their existence is to be explained in terms of the existence of monads and their **properties**, which are the foundations of the phenomenal derivative **force** exerted by material things in **motion**. Material bodies are aggregates of true substances (or monads). On this basis, Leibniz called material bodies well-founded phenomena or the result of monads.

"I showed that bodies are only aggregates that constitute a unity accidentally, or by extrinsic denomination and, to that extent, are all well-founded phenomena." **Leibniz,** *Philosophical Essays*

Weyl, Hermann (1885–1955)

German mathematician and philosopher of mathematics and science, born in Hamburg, Professor at University of Göttingen, University of Zurich, and Princeton University. Weyl contributed to the development of the general theory of relativity and later advocated Brouwer's intuitionism within a unified philosophy of mathematics and science. His major works include *Space-Time-Matter* (1921), *Philosophy of Mathematics and Natural Science* (1949), and *Symmetry* (1952).

wff, abbreviation of well-formed formula

what-it-is
ANCIENT GREEK PHILOSOPHY, METAPHYSICS [Greek *ti esti,* the essential nature of a thing or the object of a definition, from the question *ti esti,* what is this thing?, what is it? as used to seek the general and essential nature of a thing]

The philosophy of **Socrates** consists in seeking the what-it-is of such things as **justice** and **courage**. Finding out what-it-is depends on what is. Only when a thing is, can one ask what it is.

Aristotle classified ten kinds of **being** or **categories**. In the broad sense, each kind of being has its what-it-is, for example, Socrates is a man or white is a kind of color. In a narrow sense, what-it-is is only used for the category of substance because in Aristotle's theory of being, the existence of all secondary categories depends on substance. Just as he distinguished being in its primary sense from being in secondary senses, he also distinguished what-it-is in its primary sense from what-it-is in its subordinate senses. The primary sense belongs to substance, and the subsidiary senses belong to the other categories. On this basis Aristotle usually used what-it-is as a synonym of substance.

> "For in one sense the being meant is what it is or a this." **Aristotle,** *Metaphysics*

Whewell, William (1794–1866)
British philosopher of science, born in Lancaster, Master of Trinity College, Cambridge. In *History of the Inductive Sciences,* 3 vols. (1837) and *Philosophy of the Inductive Sciences* (1840), Whewell rejected establishing a logic of induction to parallel the logic of deduction and argued that to understand induction we must examine how it works in history. Induction requires non-inferential acts to colligate or bind together observed facts. He introduced the notion of consilience to describe how, in the course of induction, seemingly diverse phenomena provide evidence that suggests an unforeseen scientific hypothesis. Against J. S. Mill, he took a Kantian view that some principles are presuppositions, rather than results, of empirical knowledge.

Whitehead, Alfred North (1861–1947)
English philosopher and mathematician, born in Ramsgate, Kent, taught at Cambridge, London, and Harvard. In *Principia Mathematica* (1910–13), Russell and Whitehead sought to reduce mathematics to logic. After he moved to Harvard in 1924, Whitehead's interest turned from logic and philosophy of science to metaphysics. *Process and Reality* (1929) developed the philosophy of organism into a comprehensive metaphysical system of "process philosophy." In opposition to the modern tendency to the "bifurcation of nature," in which philosophers divide reality into different parts with different degrees of reality, Whitehead sought to develop a single system encompassing all the interrelations of all objects. He understood nature in terms of a process of becoming and held that the most fundamental metaphysical component of reality is an actual occasion in this process, while a nexus of actual occasions can inherit characteristics in serial order to become enduring objects. Applying this theory to theology, he initiated **process theology**. His other important books include *Science and the Modern World* (1925), *Adventures of Ideas* (1933), and *Modes of Thought* (1938).

wide content, see narrow content

wide states, see narrow states

Wiggins, David (1933–)
English philosopher of metaphysics, mind, and ethics, born in London, Professor of Philosophy, Birkbeck College, London and Professor of Logic, University of Oxford. Wiggins's discussion of identity, sortals, and substances led to a moderate essentialism in which individuals must belong to kinds but do not have individual essences. He holds that persons are animals who are conscious of themselves as conscious continuants and interpret one another according to norms that can be compared to Grice's conventions of implicature and Quine and Davidson's principle of charity. His major works

include *Identity and Spatio-Temporal Continuity* (1967), *Sameness and Substance* (1980), and *Needs, Values and Truth* (1987).

will

PHILOSOPHY OF MIND, PHILOSOPHY OF ACTION, ETHICS The human ability to **desire** something, to **choose** and **decide** courses of action and to initiate actions according to one's choice or decision. The will is a **wish** that we **believe** we are capable of realizing through effort. The act of will, or **volition**, contains both **cognitive** and conative elements. Will has been a puzzling topic for philosophers. **Plato** first characterizes it as a part of the **soul**, along with **reason** and appetite (or bodily desire), although philosophers disagree whether Greek philosophy had a fully developed conception of the will. **Descartes** considered the will to be a **faculty** of **mind**. This traditional faculty view was rejected by **Ryle**, who provided a **behaviorist** account of will. Consistency between will and reason is often seen to be a **virtue**. If will fails to follow reason, it is called **weakness of will** [Greek *akrasia*]. Weakness of will, **free will** and **determinism**, and free will and moral **responsibility** have been major issues in ethics. **Hume** claimed that passion rather than reason mainly determines one's behavior and that reason alone could never be a sufficient **motive** for any action of the will. For **Kant**, a **good will**, which is reason in its **practical** employment, is the basis for rational ethics. **Schopenhauer** sees will as the first principle in his *The World as Will and Idea*. Will remains a subject of intense interest and controversy in contemporary philosophy.

"Willing, then, can be defined as wishing, involving a decision, that has as its object something that is to be realized by ourselves and that we confidently expect to take place as a result of our desiring it." **Brentano,** *The Foundation and Construction of Ethics*

will (Kant)

ETHICS **Kant** distinguished between *Wille* and *Willkür*, although both are translated as will in English. As the power of **self-determination**, *Wille* is the source of **ought** and **obligation**. It is not a product or discovery of the **understanding**, but is a faculty of acting according to a conception of **law**. It is generally associated with **freedom**, **autonomy**, and **spontaneity**, and as **practical reason** itself it is the home of the moral law. *Willkür* is the capacity for **decision** or **choice**, which is both determined by *Wille* and affected by sensuous **inclinations**. It is thus **heteronomous**. It chooses between the **imperatives** stemming from *Wille* and the **desires**. With this distinction, Kant set aside the traditional problem about the relation between **free will** and **determinism**. His separation between the will as practical reason and the will capacity for choice was claimed by **Nietzsche** to make the will only a **hypostatization**.

"Insofar as it is combined with the consciousness of the capacity of its action to produce its object, it is called will, or choice [Willkur], if not so combined, its act is called a wish. The faculty of desire whose internal ground of determination and consequently, even whose likings are found in the reason of the subject is called the Will [der Wille]." **Kant,** *The Metaphysics of Morals*

will of all

POLITICAL PHILOSOPHY **Rousseau**'s term for the aggregate of the private and individual **wills** of members of a society. The will of all is the total of what all persons individually want. A particular will involves what one wants for oneself alone and does not take into consideration the interests of others. Since each private will conflicts with other private wills, a **civil society** needs a **general will** that is directed to the common interest. A general will is not the will of all, but Rousseau claims that it can be determined from the will of all by finding what is common to all once the conflicting elements in the will of all are cancelled. It is not clear that we can determine the general will in this way or that the general will is a good basis for deciding the policy of a **state**. Possibly a state should allow a certain amount of conflict. Critics of Rousseau argue that his emphasis on the general will would allow intolerance through a form of **totalitarian democracy**.

"There is often a great deal of difference between the will of all and the general will; the latter considers only the common interest, while the former takes private interest into account, and is no more than a sum of particulars." **Rousseau,** *The Social Contract*

will to believe

EPISTEMOLOGY A term introduced by William **James** in 1897 as the title for one of his most influential essays. He argued that on many occasions we are forced to choose one of two alternatives, where there are no intellectual grounds for choosing one rather than the other. Then we must let **emotion** or **passion** determine our decision in terms of the effect that each choice would have upon our states of mind or subsequent life. Accordingly, we have no rational basis for deciding the question whether **God** exists, but we tend to believe in God's existence because this would provide us with a ground for **optimism**. The same applies to the choice between **believing** in **free will** and believing in **determinism**. Critics argue that the lack of a rational basis for choice does not legitimate a non-rational basis and that the **burden of proof** is not satisfied by determining emotional consequences.

"I have brought with me tonight . . . an essay in justification of faith, a defence of our right to develop a believing attitude in religious matter, in spite of the fact that our merely logical intellect may not have been coerced. 'The will to believe', accordingly, is the title of my paper." **W. James, *The Will to Believe and Other Essays***

will to power

ETHICS, METAPHYSICS **Nietzsche**'s term for the most basic human drive to attain a higher and more perfect state, an insatiable **desire** to manifest **power** and a drive to employ and exercise power. For him, life itself is the will to power. This drive is characterized by self-overcoming and **sublimation**. It is a **disposition** to get power in self-control, art, and philosophy. It is life-affirming rather than a desire to **dominate** others. For Nietzsche, philosophy is the most spiritual expression of the will to power. Nietzsche's book *The Will to Power* was edited by his sister from a series of fragments, headings, and reflections. It was once regarded as a source of **fascist ideology**, but this view is untenable upon serious scholarly examination.

The will to power as a **hypothesis** to explain the world and the nature of **reality** is also a metaphysical doctrine. Nietzsche claimed that the world is the will to power. The world is viewed as a monster of **energy**, eternally **self-creating** and eternally self-

destroying. The will of power is meant to be the basis for explaining all **changes**. It is neither being nor becoming, but is a tendency of all forces to extend their influence in relation to all other forces in determining the **intelligible** character of the world. The will to power is also called "efficient force," "quanta of force," or "driving force." Despite Nietzsche's attack on metaphysics, **Heidegger** held that the will to power is Nietzsche's answer to the metaphysical question about the **essence** of what is.

"Indeed life itself has been defined as an increasingly efficient inner adaptation to external circumstances (Herbert Spencer). But this is to misunderstand the essence of life, its will to power. We overlook the prime importance which the spontaneous, aggressive, expansive, re-interpreting, re-directing and formative powers have, which 'adaptation' follows only when they have had their effect." **Nietzsche, *On the Genealogy of Morals***

William of Ockham (*c.*1285–1347)

English scholastic philosopher, born in Ockham, Surrey. Ockham was the father of nominalism, according to which universals are only names invented by the mind to talk about similarities. He claimed that everything that exists is particular and emphasized empirical methods. "Ockham's razor," that is, the principle of parsimony requiring us to avoid positing the existence of unnecessary entities, is drawn from Ockham's nominalism. His writings include *Summa Logicae* and the *Treatise on Predestination and God's Foreknowledge of the Contingent Future*.

Williams, Bernard (1929–2003)

British philosopher, born in Westcliff, Essex, educated at Oxford, and taught at Oxford, London, Cambridge, and University of California, Berkeley. Williams distinguished modern moral philosophy from a more general conception of ethics. He criticized both Kantian and utilitarian moral philosophy because they claimed objective universality for their principles and pursued moral theory rather than taking account of each person's integrity and the projects central to individual ethical lives. He held that ethics should answer the Greek question of how we should live, and was influenced by Nietzsche's naturalism in working out his own response. His discussions on moral luck, integrity, the distinction

738   Winch, Peter

between internal and external reasons, the distinction between thick and thin ethical concepts, personal identity and the self have initiated significant debates that have helped to shape contemporary ethics. His most important work is *Ethics and the Limits of Philosophy* (1985) and other books include *Morality: An Introduction to Ethics* (1972), *Utilitarianism: For and Against* (with J. J. C. Smart) (1973), *Problems of the Self* (1973), *Descartes: The Project of Pure Enquiry* (1978), *Moral Luck* (1981), *Shame and Necessity* (1993), and *Truth and Truthfulness* (2002).

Winch, Peter (1926–97)

British philosopher of social science, born in London, Professor of Philosophy, King's College, London and University of Illinois, Urbana/Champaign. Winch is best known for his use of themes from Wittgenstein's later philosophy to reject a social science modeled on natural science. He held that to understand another society one must understand the practices in which its concepts and the criteria of their legitimate application are entrenched. His main works include *The Idea of a Social Science* (1958) and *Ethics and Action* (1972).

wisdom

ANCIENT GREEK PHILOSOPHY, EPISTEMOLOGY [Greek *sophia*] In a popular sense, skillfulness in some craft. A wise person is the master of any skill, in contrast to an unskilled laborer, and this is a practical aspect to its meaning. However, **Aristotle** offered a technical account of wisdom as **knowledge** of general **principles** and absolutely **first causes**. This wisdom is concerned with permanent **truths**, including both **demonstrative** knowledge and knowledge of undemonstrable premises. In this use, wisdom is contrasted with craft and **practical reason**. In the *Metaphysics*, Aristotle claimed that he was seeking wisdom in this sense. Hence, *sophia* is equivalent to **first philosophy**. In the *Nicomachean Ethics*, Aristotle considered wisdom to be a higher kind of **intellectual virtue** than practical reason.

> "Wisdom is the most exact form of knowledge."
> **Aristotle,** *Nicomachean Ethics*

Wisdom, John (1904–93)

British philosopher, born in London, Professor of Philosophy at University of Cambridge and University of Oregon. Wisdom was deeply influenced by the philosophy of Wittgenstein, first through the early Wittgenstein's notion of logical analysis and then through the later Wittgenstein's conception of philosophical theories as verbal recommendations. He shared Wittgenstein's perplexity at what philosophers say, but held that this puzzlement responded to real insight into the diversity and complexity of logic as well as arising from confusion. He, nevertheless, adopted Wittgenstein's concentration on concrete examples and suspicion of general theories. His main works include *Other Minds* (1952) and *Philosophy and Psycho-Analysis* (1953).

Wittgenstein, Ludwig (1889–1951)

Austrian-British philosopher, born in Vienna, Professor of Philosophy at Cambridge. Wittgenstein's philosophical career was divided into two periods. The early period, culminating in the *Tractatus Logico-Philosophicus* (1922), was concerned with the logical structure of language and the relation between language and reality. Wittgenstein held that the world is a world of facts rather than things and that a perspicuous representation of facts required a language in which every genuine proposition is a truth-function of elementary propositions. Propositions can picture facts in virtue of facts and propositions having the same logical form. Logical form itself can not be said, but, like the propositions of metaphysics, ethics, and religion, can only be shown. Philosophy is an activity of clarifying thought and of distinguishing between what can be said and what can only be shown. The *Tractatus* ends with the injunction: "Whereof one cannot speak, thereof one must be silent." Another work of his early period is *Notebooks 1914–1916* (1961).

Works of the transition between Wittgenstein's early and later philosophy include "Some Remarks on Logical Form" (1966), *Wittgenstein's Lectures, Cambridge, 1930–1932* (1980), *Ludwig Wittgenstein and the Vienna Circle: Conversations Recorded by Friedrich Waismann* (1979), and *Philosophical Remarks* (1975).

The main work of Wittgenstein's later period is the posthumously published *Philosophical Investigations* (1953), in which Wittgenstein was mainly concerned with how ordinary language works, the philosophy of psychology, and the philosophy of mathematics. To replace the unified account of language in the *Tractatus*, Wittgenstein saw language as comprising a variety of radically diverse "language-games" that are grounded in practices constituting a form of life. Rather than asking for meaning as a psychological or abstract entity, we should attend to the use of words and sentences. Since language use involves following rules in a public practice, there cannot be a private language that only the speaker can understand. All of these views have initiated intense discussion in epistemology, metaphysics, philosophy of mind, philosophy of language, and other philosophical fields. Other works of his later period include *The Blue and Brown Books* (1961), "Notes for Lectures on 'Private Experience' and 'Sense-data'" (1968), *Remarks on the Foundations of Mathematics* (1968), *Wittgenstein's Lectures on the Foundations of Mathematics* (1975), *On Certainty* (1969), and *Zettel* (1967).

There are significant differences between Wittgenstein's early philosophy and his later philosophy, but philosophers disagree about how to judge their continuity and discontinuity of purpose, method, and philosophical outcome.

Wolff, Christian (1679–1754)

German rationalist philosopher, born in Breslau, a follower of Leibniz. Wolff formulated a comprehensive metaphysical system that elaborated Leibniz's doctrines within the framework of the principal notions of the Aristotelian scholastic tradition. In his system, Wolff took ontology, the science of being in general, as first philosophy and emphasized the role of natural reason in setting out three special disciplines: rational cosmology, rational psychology, and rational theology. His work shaped later German philosophy, especially through its influence on Kant and Hegel. Kant, in particular, sought to reconcile insights drawn from Hume with those he derived from Wolff's Leibnizian system. Wolff's most important philosophical work was *First Philosophy or Ontology* (1729).

Wollheim, Richard (1923–2003)

British philosopher of art, mind, and psychoanalysis, born in London, Professor of Philosophy, University College, London, Columbia University, University of California, Berkeley and Davis. Wollheim held that pictorial representation can be understood in terms of "seeing in." We both see the marks on a flat canvas and see in these marks

three-dimensional scenes. He argued that the intentions of artists to cause particular experiences in the viewers of their work can not be eliminated from our understanding of art. Wollheim introduced concepts from psychoanalytic theory into his aesthetics, moral philosophy, and philosophy of mind, and he was a sympathetic philosophical commentator on Freud. His major works include *Art and Its Objects* (1968), *The Thread of Life* (1984), and *The Mind and its Depths* (1993).

Wollstonecraft, Mary (1759–97)

English radical social philosopher and feminist. Wollstonecraft rejected Edmund Burke's criticism of the French Revolution and argued that equality and freedom from false authority are the basis for the full development of men and women. She held that women were excluded from this fulfillment through the enforcement of social subservience and lack of education, but also through an incomplete and distorted conception of reason. Her major works include *A Vindication of the Rights of Men* (1790) and *Vindication of the Rights of Women* (1792).

World 1, see World 3

World 2, see World 3

World 3

EPISTEMOLOGY According to **Popper**, traditional philosophy has recognized two worlds. The first is **material** and the second is **conscious** and **mental**. Popper developed a new conceptual schema of a threefold world. World 1 is the material world, which includes all physical **objects** and **states**. World 2 is the mental world, which includes immediate perceptual **experiences**, other **mental states**, and **behavioral dispositions**. World 3 includes **objective contents** of **thought**, including problems, **theories**, criticisms and their unintended consequences. World 3 is essentially a world of storage, including the records of human intellectual efforts that are preserved in libraries and museums. The content of thought is the product of individual human **minds**, but once thoughts are produced, they transcend their producers, and are independent of anybody who thinks or expresses them. They bring with themselves all sorts of consequences and problems which we, their makers, do not intend or foresee and cannot control. They **causally** affect us and become **objects** of our **knowledge** and even the main object of World 2. In this sense, the contents of thought are autonomous and have their own logic of development that cannot be reduced to either World 1 or World 2. Although World 3 is human-made, its **autonomy** makes it similar to **Plato**'s world of **forms** or **ideas**. This world is **timeless** and results in the **evolution** of human language. Through his account of World 3, Popper developed not only a new **ontological** classification, but also a new **justification** for the **objectivity** of knowledge. World 3 provides an argument against sociological **relativism** and **psychologism**. The account of the nature and existence of such a separate world has provoked critical discussion, some of which focuses on the relation between World 3 and World 2.

"We can call the physical world 'World 1', the world of our conscious experience 'World 2', and the world of the logical *contents* of books, libraries, computer memories, and suchlike 'World 3'." **Popper,** *Objective Knowledge*

world agent, another term for ideal observer

world soul

PHILOSOPHY OF RELIGION, PHILOSOPHY OF MIND [Latin *anima mundi*] Some philosophers argue that if the universe is in harmonious celestial **motion**, there must an animating principle or **soul** to control it, just as the human soul controls the human body. Accordingly, the world should be viewed as an animated living organism, the soul of which is the world soul. The idea of a world soul was popular in **pre-Socratic** philosophy and was well elaborated in **Plato**'s *Timaeus*, in which the world is endowed with a soul by a creator or **Demiurge**. The human soul should be modeled on the world soul to achieve **harmony** among its different parts. This doctrine of the world soul was developed in Stoicism and **Neoplatonism** and through them in medieval philosophy. It was revived by **Schelling** and plays a role in contemporary environmental philosophy.

"Already in the most ancient times it was believed that the world was pervaded by an animating principle, called the world-soul." **Schelling,** *Ideas for a Philosophy of Nature*

Wright, Crispin (1942–)
British philosopher of mathematics, logic, language, and metaphysics, born in Bagshot, Professor at University of St Andrews and University of Michigan. Wright has pursued a philosophical program based on intuitionist logic and anti-realist semantics in parallel to similar work by Michael Dummett. His writings on Frege, Wittgenstein, meaning, truth, identity, and vagueness demonstrate his technical skills and philosophical insight. His major works include *Wittgenstein on the Foundations of Mathematics* (1980), *Frege's Conception of Numbers as Objects* (1983), *Realism, Meaning and Truth* (1986), *Truth and Objectivity* (1993), and *Realism: Rules and Objectivity* (1993).

Wright, G(eorg) H(enrik) von (1916–2003)
Finnish philosopher, born in Helsinki, educated at Helsinki and Cambridge, taught at Cambridge (as successor to Wittgenstein as Professor of Philosophy) and Helsinki, a member of the Academy of Finland. As an original analytic philosopher, von Wright made significant philosophical contributions in several fields. He significantly developed the theory of eliminative induction pioneered by Bacon and Mill and modern modal logic, and founded deontic logic by extending the formalism of modal logic to ethics. He contributed to ethics and value theory, and explored differences between natural causation and human action and related differences between the methods of physical sciences and those of the social sciences. He criticized the misuse of science in modern culture and society and sought a return to a more humanistic tradition. His works include: *The Logical Problem of Induction* (1941), *A Treatise on Induction and Probability* (1951), *An Essay on Modal Logic* (1951), *The Varieties of Goodness* (1963), *Norm and Action* (1963), *Explanation and Understanding* (1971), *Causality and Determinism* (1973), *The Tree of Knowledge and Other Essays* (1993), and *In the Shadow of Descartes* (1998).

X, Y, Z

Xenophanes (*c.*560–*c.*470 BC)
Pre-Socratic Greek philosopher, born in Colophon, Ionia. Xenophanes rejected traditional accounts of the gods and initiated philosophical theology by arguing that God is single, motionless, and unlike human beings. He held that God shapes all things by the thought of his mind. Xenophanes, the first known epistemologist, sharply distinguished between knowledge and opinion and held that reality is uniformly concealed from men. His philosophical thought was traditionally seen to have led on to the doctrines of Parmenides.

Xenophon (*c.*430–*c.*350 BC)
Greek historian and essayist, born in Athens, a follower of Socrates. Xenophon's writings, including *Memorabilia* ("Memoirs of Socrates"), *Apology of Socrates*, *Symposium*, and *Oeconomicus*, are a major source of our knowledge of the historical Socrates, supplementing the picture that emerges from Plato's dialogues. Xenophon sought to defend Socrates against the charges of impiety and corrupting the Athenian youth and portrayed Socrates as a teacher of virtue. His writings offer anecdotes expressing Socrates' personality rather than his philosophical thought and do not explore Socrates' irony.

Zeno of Citium (334–262 BC)
Hellenistic philosopher, born in Citium, founder of Greek Stoicism. Zeno accepted the Cynic principles that one should live in accord with nature and that one should act as a citizen of the universe rather than of a particular city, but provided positive interpretations of these principles. He held *logos* to be the dominating force of the physical universe and human nature to be rational, with virtue as the only good. He initiated the division of philosophy into logic, physics, and ethics. Because only a few fragments of his work survived, it is difficult to distinguish his contributions to Stoicism from those of other leading Stoics, such as Cleanthes and Chrisippus.

Zeno of Elea (born around 470 BC)
Greek philosopher, disciple of Parmenides. In pursuing Parmenides' rejection of change, Zeno advanced several arguments involving paradox to reject the possibility of plurality and motion. These arguments involve fundamental concepts, such as time, space, infinity, and divisibility, and demonstrate the power of speculative reasoning. Zeno's arguments, which are known through Aristotle's discussion of them, still excite the interest of philosophers and mathematicians.

Zeno's paradoxes
ANCIENT GREEK PHILOSOPHY, LOGIC, METAPHYSICS, PHILOSOPHY OF MATHEMATICS **Zeno of Elea** established a series of arguments against plurality and motion; these arguments are mutually related, with the aim of defending the thesis of his teacher

Parmenides that what is is one and unchanging. These arguments are preserved by **Aristotle** in the *Physics* and by the Greek commentators on this book. Most of these discussions, however, are very compressed, and this has given rise to very diverse interpretations. As a result there are various versions of each argument.

The two main arguments against plurality are as follows: (1) If there is a plurality of things, they are both (a) so small as to have no magnitude, and (b) so large as to be **infinite**. The proof of (a) is: the plurality must be composed of a number of indivisible units; but if the unit has magnitude, it must be divisible; if it is indivisible, it has no magnitude; and the composite of a number of non-magnitude units has no magnitude. The proof of (b) is: if there are many things, each must have magnitude; otherwise neither their addition nor their subtraction will make any difference to another thing, and will be nothing at all; if there is a plurality of things with magnitude, then a thing composed of them must have at least two separate magnitudes, and each of them has magnitude and can be further divisible; since this process can go on forever, a thing will be unlimitedly large. (2) If there is a plurality of things, they must be both (a) **limited** and (b) unlimited. The proof of (a) is: if there are many things, there must be just as many of them as they are, and neither more nor less; but if there are just as many as they are, they are limited. The proof of (b) is: if there are many things, there are always other things between things that are there; and between these in turn other things; thus the things that are are unlimited.

The paradoxes against motion are four: the **Dichotomy, Achilles and the Tortoise**, the **Flying Arrow**, and the **Moving Rows**; the so-called Stadium paradox is ambiguous in that some think it is a reworking of the Dichotomy, and others that it is a reworking of the Moving Rows. Sometimes just these four paradoxes are called Zeno's paradoxes.

The general implication of Zeno's paradoxes is that they expose the intrinsic difficulties in the instinctive assumptions of ordinary human experience about plurality, **motion**, **space**, and **time**, though some argue that he has a particular target, which is the confusion between the geometrical point, arithmetical unit, and the physical magnitude in the **Pythagoreans**. These paradoxes involve the problem of whether space and time are infinitely divis-

ible, and whether they are composed of indivisibles. These are basic philosophical conceptions and are also the fundamental mathematical conceptions, so Zeno's paradoxes attract endless interest from both philosophers and mathematicians; and there is still dispute as to whether Zeno's arguments are valid, and how to refute them. The method used by Zeno in these paradoxes is *reductio ad absurdum*, which had great influence on the development of **dialectic** and philosophical reasoning.

> "At some time in the first half of the fifth century BC, Zeno invented the set of paradoxes on which his successors have sharpened their wits."
> **G. Owen,** *Logic, Science and Dialectic*

zero method

LOGIC, PHILOSOPHY OF LANGUAGE A method manifesting the underlying **form** of language by constructing a **tautology** through a combination of **signs**. Because of their tautologous form, these signs completely cancel out the significance of their material **content**. The zero method is a logical method of constructing a **model** on the assumption of complete **rationality**. Someone who is imperfectly rational might consider that the **propositions** have content even though they are tautologies.

> "The propositions of logic demonstrate the logical properties of propositions by combining them so as to form propositions that say nothing. This method could also be called Zero-method."
> **Wittgenstein,** *Tractatus*

Zoroastrianism

PHILOSOPHY OF RELIGION A Persian religion that started in the sixth century BC and whose dominance in that area was not replaced until the rise of Islam in the seventh century AD. Its scriptures are called the *Avesta*, and its founder was the prophet Zarathustra (Greek *Zoroaster*). Its characteristic feature is its **dualism**. The force of darkness and **evil** (*Angra Mainyu*) is equally matched with the force of light and **goodness** (*Ahura Mazda*), and they are locked in a struggle from the beginning of the world to its end. Hence Zoroastrianism is not troubled by the **paradox** that arises from attempting to reconcile **God**'s **omnipotence** and evil in the world. Parts of its teachings were assimilated by Mithraism and

Manichaeism. There are still Zoroastrian believers around Bombay, India. The term is familiar in the contemporary philosophical world largely because **Nietzsche** employed Zarathustra as his spokesman in *Thus Spoke Zarathustra*.

"The religion of struggle is dualistic. Zoroastrianism is the classic example, and in this type man participates in the cosmic conflict." **Macquarrie,** *Twentieth-Century Religious Thought*

References

Ackermann, R. J., *Belief and Knowledge*. New York: Anchor Books, 1972.

Ackrill, J., *Aristotle the Philosopher*. Oxford: Oxford University Press, 1981.

Acton, H. B. (ed.), *Philosophy of Punishment: A Collection of Papers*. London: Macmillan, 1969.

Adams, E. M., *The Fundamentals of General Logic*. New York: Longmans Green, 1954.

Adams, E. M., "Motive Utilitarianism," *Journal of Philosophy*, 73 (1976), pp. 67–81.

Adorno, T. W. and Horkheimer, M., *Dialectic of Enlightenment*, trs. J. Cumming. New York: Herder & Herder, 1972.

Ajdukiewicz, K., *Problems and Theories of Philosophy*, trs. H. Skolimowski and A. Quinton. London: Cambridge University Press, 1973.

Ajdukiewicz, K., *Pragmatic Logic*, trs. O. Wojtasiewicz. Dordrecht: D. Reidel, 1974.

Alexander, P., *A Preface to the Logic of Science*. London: Sheed & Ward, 1963.

Alexander of Aphrodisias, *On Aristotle's Topics*, trs. J. M. Van Ophuijsen. London: Duckworth, 2001.

Alston, W. P., *Philosophy of Language*. Englewood Cliffs, NJ: Prentice-Hall, 1964.

Alston, W. P., *Epistemic Justification: Essays in the Theory of Knowledge*. Ithaca, NY: Cornell University Press, 1989.

Anderson, C. A. and Owen, J. (eds.), *Propositional Attitudes: The Role of Content in Logic, Language and Mind*. Stanford, CA: Center for the Study of Language and Information, 1990.

Anscombe, G. E. M., *Intention*. Ithaca, NY: Cornell University Press, 1957.

Anscombe, G. E. M., "The First Person," in S. Guttenplan (ed.), *Mind and Language*. Oxford: Clarendon Press, 1975.

Anselm, *Proslogion*, trs. S. N. Deane. La Salle, IL: Open Court, 1954.

Aquinas, T., *Summa Theologiae*, trs. T. McDermott. London: Methuen, 1989.

Arendt, H., *The Human Condition*. Chicago, IL: University of Chicago Press, 1958.

Aristotle, *Categories*, in J. Barnes (ed.), *The Complete Works of Aristotle*, 2 vols. Princeton, NJ: Princeton University Press, 1984.

Aristotle, *De Anima*, in J. Barnes (ed.), *The Complete Works of Aristotle*, 2 vols. Princeton, NJ: Princeton University Press, 1984.

Aristotle, *De Caelo*, in J. Barnes (ed.), *The Complete Works of Aristotle*, 2 vols. Princeton, NJ: Princeton University Press, 1984.

Aristotle, *De Interpretation*, in J. Barnes (ed.), *The Complete Works of Aristotle*, 2 vols. Princeton, NJ: Princeton University Press, 1984.

Aristotle, *Eudemian Ethics*, in J. Barnes (ed.), *The Complete Works of Aristotle*, 2 vols. Princeton, NJ: Princeton University Press, 1984.

Aristotle, *Metaphysics*, in J. Barnes (ed.), *The Complete Works of Aristotle*, 2 vols. Princeton, NJ: Princeton University Press, 1984.

Aristotle, *Nicomachean Ethics*, in J. Barnes (ed.), *The Complete Works of Aristotle*, 2 vols. Princeton, NJ: Princeton University Press, 1984.

Aristotle, *On Democritus*, in J. Barnes (ed.), *The Complete Works of Aristotle*, 2 vols. Princeton, NJ: Princeton University Press, 1984.

Aristotle, *Physics*, in J. Barnes (ed.), *The Complete Works of Aristotle*, 2 vols. Princeton, NJ: Princeton University Press, 1984.

Aristotle, *Posterior Analytics*, in J. Barnes (ed.), *The Complete Works of Aristotle*, 2 vols. Princeton, NJ: Princeton University Press, 1984.

Aristotle, *Prior Analytics*, in J. Barnes (ed.), *The Complete Works of Aristotle*, 2 vols. Princeton, NJ: Princeton University Press, 1984.

Aristotle, *Rhetoric*, in J. Barnes (ed.), *The Complete Works of Aristotle*, 2 vols. Princeton, NJ: Princeton University Press, 1984.

Aristotle, *Topics*, in J. Barnes (ed.), *The Complete Works of Aristotle*, 2 vols. Princeton, NJ: Princeton University Press, 1984.

Armstrong, A. H., *An Introduction to Ancient Philosophy*. London: Methuen, 1947.

Armstrong, D. M., *Perception and the Physical World*. London: Routledge, 1961.

Armstrong, D. M., *A Materialist Theory of the Mind*. London: Routledge & Kegan Paul, 1968.

Armstrong, D. M., *Universals and Scientific Realism*, vol. 1: *Nominalism and Realism*. Cambridge: Cambridge University Press, 1978.

Armstrong, D. M., *What is a Law of Nature?* Cambridge: Cambridge University Press, 1983.

Armstrong, D. M., *Universals: An Opinionated Introduction*. Boulder, CO: Westview Press, 1989.

Armstrong, S. J. and Botzler, R. (eds.), *Environmental Ethics: Divergence and Convergence*. New York: McGraw-Hill, 1993.

Aronson, J. L., *A Realist Philosophy of Science*. New York: St. Martin's Press, 1984.

Atkinson, R. F., *Knowledge and Explanation in History: An Introduction to the Philosophy of History*. London: Macmillan, 1978.

Augustine, *City of God*, trs. D. Knowles. Harmondsworth: Penguin Books, 1977.

Augustine, *Confessions*, trs. H. Chadwick. Oxford: Oxford University Press, 1991.

Austin, J., *Lectures on Jurisprudence*. London, 1911.

Austin, J. L., *How to Do Things with Words*. London: Oxford University Press, 1962.

Austin, J. L., *Philosophical Papers*, 2nd edn. Oxford: Oxford University Press, 1970.

Ayer, A. J., *Language, Truth and Logic*. London: Victor Gollancz, 1946.

Ayer, A. J., *The Problem of Knowledge*. Harmondsworth: Penguin, 1956.

Ayer, A. J. (ed.), *Logical Positivism*. New York: Free Press, 1959.

Ayer, A. J., *The Concept of a Person and Other Essays*. Cambridge: Cambridge University Press, 1963.

Ayer, A. J., *The Origins of Pragmatism*. London: Macmillan, 1968.

Ayer, A. J., *Russell and Moore: The Analytical Heritage*. Cambridge, MA: Harvard University Press, 1971.

Ayer, A. J., *Probability and Evidence*. New York: Columbia University Press, 1972.

Ayer, A. J., *Metaphysics and Common Sense*. London: Macmillan, 1973.

Ayer, A. J., *Philosophy in the Twentieth Century*. London: Weidenfeld & Nicolson, 1982.

Bacon, F., *The Philosophical Works of Francis Bacon*, ed. John M. Robertson. London: G. Routledge & Sons, 1905.

Baker, L. R., *Saving Belief: A Critique of Physicalism*. Princeton, NJ: Princeton University Press, 1987.

Bambrough, R., *Reason, Truth and God*. London: Methuen, 1969.

Bar-Hillel, Y., *Language and Information: Selected Essays on their Theory and Application*. Reading, MA: Addison-Wesley, 1964.

Barnes, J., *The Presocratic Philosophers*. London: Routledge & Kegan Paul, 1979.

Barry, B., *Political Argument*. London: Routledge & Kegan Paul, 1965.

Barwise, J., *The Situation in Logic*. Stanford, CA: Center for the Study of Language and Information, 1989.

Battin, M. P., *The Least Worst Death: Essays in Bioethics on the End of Life*. Oxford: Oxford University Press, 1994.

Baylis, C. A., *Ethics: The Principles of Wise Choice*. New York: Holt, 1958.

Beardsley, M. C., *Aesthetics: Problems in the Philosophy of Criticism*. Indianapolis, IN: Hackett, 1981.

Bell, C., *Art*. London, 1914.

Benhabib, S., "The Generalized and the Concrete Other," in E. F. Kittay and D. Meyers (eds.), *Women and Moral Theory*. Totowa, NJ: Rowman & Littlefield, 1987.

Benhabib, S., *Situating the Self: Gender, Community and Postmodernism in Contemporary Ethics*. Cambridge: Polity Press, 1992.

Benjamin, M., *Splitting the Difference: Compromise and Integrity in Ethics and Politics*. Lawrence, KS: University Press of Kansas, 1990.

Benson, D. and Hughes, J. A., *The Perspectives of Ethnomethodology*. London: Longman, 1983.

Bentham, J., *An Introduction to the Principles of Morals and Legislation*, ed. J. H. Burns, vol. III. London: Athlone Press, 1970.

Berger, P. L. and Luckmann, T., *The Social Construction of Reality*. Garden City, NY: Doubleday, 1966.

Bergmann, G., *Meaning and Existence*. Madison, WI: University of Wisconsin, 1960.

Bergson, H., *Creative Evolution*. New York: Henry Holt, 1911.

Bergson, H., *Time and Free Will*, trs. F. L. Pogson. London: Allen & Unwin, 1950.

Berkeley, G., *Passive Obedience*, in *Works of George Berkeley, Bishop of Cloyne*, ed. A. A. Luce and T. E. Jessop. London: Nelson, 1948–51.

Berkeley, G., *An Essay Towards a New Theory of Vision*, in *George Berkeley: Philosophical Works*, ed. M. Ayers. London: Dent, 1975.

Berkeley, G., *The Principles of Human Knowledge*, in *George Berkeley: Philosophical Works*, ed. M. Ayers. London: Dent, 1975.

Berkeley, G., *Three Dialogues Between Hylas and Philonous*, in *George Berkeley: Philosophical Works*, ed. Ed. M. Ayers. London: Dent, 1975.

Berlin, I., *Four Essays on Liberty*. London: Oxford University Press, 1969.

Berlin, I., *The Magus of the North: J. G. Hamann and the Origins of Modern Irrationalism*, ed. H. Hardy. London: John Murray, 1993.

Beth, E. W., *Aspects of Modern Logic*. Dordrecht: D. Reidel, 1967.

Bhaskar, R., *The Possibility of Naturalism*. Brighton: Harvester, 1979.

Bird, G., *Philosophical Tasks: An Introduction to Some Aims and Methods in Recent Philosophy*. London: Hutchinson, 1972.

Blanshard, B., *Reason and Goodness*. London: Allen & Unwin, 1961.

Bloomfield, L., *Language*. New York: Henry Holt, 1933.

Boden, M. A., *Artificial Intelligence and Natural Man*. Brighton: Harvester Press, 1977.

Boehner, P. (ed.), *Ockham: Philosophic Writing*. Edinburgh: Nelson, 1957.

Boer, S. E. and Lycan, W., *Knowing Who*. Cambridge, MA: MIT Press, 1986.

Bok, S., *Lying*. New York: Pantheon, 1978.

Bollinger, D. and Sears, D. A., *Aspects of Language*. New York: Harcourt Brace Jovanovich, 1981.

Bostock, D., *Intermediate Logic*. Oxford: Clarendon Press, 1997.

Bradley, F. H., *Essays on Truth and Reality*. Oxford: Clarendon Press, 1914.

Brailsford, H. N., *Voltaire*. London: Butterworth, 1935.

Brandt, R. B., *Ethical Theory: The Problems of Normative and Critical Ethics*. Englewood Cliffs, NJ: Prentice-Hall, 1959.

Brentano, F. C., *The Foundation and Construction of Ethics*, ed. and trs. Elizabeth Hughes Schneewind. London: Routledge & Kegan Paul, 1973.

Brentano, F. C., *Psychology from an Empirical Standpoint*, trs. L. L. McAlister. London: Routledge & Kegan Paul, 1973.

Brentano, F. C., *Descriptive Psychology*, trs. and ed. B. Müller. The Hague: M. Nijhoff, 1982.

Broad, C. D., *Examination of McTaggart's Philosophy*, 2 vols. London: Cambridge University Press, 1933.

Broad, C. D., *The Mind and its Place in Nature*, Tarner Lectures delivered in Trinity College, Cambridge, 1923. London: Routledge & Kegan Paul, 1962.

Broad, C. D., *Scientific Thought*. New York: Prometheus Books, 1969.

Broadie, A., *Introduction to Medieval Logic*. Oxford: Clarendon Press, 1987.

Brody, B. A., *Identity and Essence*. Princeton, NJ: Princeton University Press, 1980.

Brown, H. L., *Perception, Theory and Commitment*. Chicago, IL: University of Chicago Press, 1977.

Brown, J. B., *The Laboratory of the Mind*. London: Routledge, 1991.

Buber, M., *I and Thou*, trs. J. Kaufman. New York: Charles Scribner's Sons, 1970.

Bunge, M., *Causality*. Cambridge, MA: Harvard University Press, 1959.

Bunge, M., *Philosophy of Physics*, Dordrecht and Boston: D. Reidel, 1973.

Bunnin, N. and Tsui-James, E. P. (eds.), *The Black-well Companion to Philosophy*, 2nd edn. Oxford: Blackwell Publishers, 2003.

Burleigh, M., *The City of God: A Study of St. Augustine's Philosophy*. London: Nisbet, 1949.

Butler, J., *Fifteen Sermons*, Preface. London, 1726.

Callicott, J. B., *In Defense of the Land Ethic: Essays in Environmental Philosophy*. Albany, NY: State University of New York Press, 1989.

Campbell, C. A., *On Selfhood and Godhood*. London: Allen & Unwin, 1957.

Campbell, R. and Sowden, L. (eds.), *Paradoxes of Rationality and Cooperation: Prisoner's Dilemma and Newcomb's Problem*. Vancouver: University of British Columbia Press, 1985.

Camus, A., *The Myth of Sisyphus*, trs. Justin O'Brien. London: Hamish Hamilton, 1955.

Cann, R., *Formal Semantics: An Introduction*. Cambridge: Cambridge University Press, 1993.

Card, C. (ed.), *Feminist Ethics*. Lawrence, KS: University Press of Kansas, 1991.

Carnap, R., *The Logical Syntax of Language*. London: Kegan Paul Trench, 1937.

Carnap, R., *Meaning and Necessity: A Study in Semantics and Modal Logic*. Chicago, IL: University of Chicago Press, 1947.

Carnap, R., *Logical Foundations of Probability*. Chicago, IL: University of Chicago Press, 1950.

Carnap, R., "The Methodological Character of Theoretical Concepts," in H. Feigl and M. Scriven (eds.), *Minnesota Studies in the Philosophy of Science*, vol. i: *Foundations of Science and Concepts of Psychology and Psychoanalysis*. Minneapolis, MN: University of Minnesota Press, 1956, pp. 38–76.

Carnap, R., *Introduction to Symbolic Logic and its Applications*, trs. W. H. Meyer and J. Wilkinson. New York: Dover, 1958.

Carnap, R., "The Elimination of Metaphysics through Logical Analysis of Language," in A. J. Ayer (ed.), *Logical Positivism*. New York: Free Press, 1959.

Carnap, R., *Philosophical Foundations of Physics: An Introduction to the Philosophy of Science*, ed. M. Gardner. New York and London: Basic Books, 1966.

Carnap, R., *The Logical Structure of the World: Pseudoproblems in Philosophy*, trs. R. A. George. London: Routledge & Kegan Paul, 1967.

Carney, J. D. and Scheer, R. K., *Fundamentals of Logic*. London: Collier Macmillan, 1974.

Carruthers, P., *Human Knowledge and Human Nature: A New Introduction to an Ancient Debate*. New York: Oxford University Press, 1992.

Carruthers, P. and Smith, P. K. (eds.), *Theories of Theories of Mind*. New York: Cambridge University Press, 1996.

Casey, J., "The Autonomy of Art," in G. Vesey (ed.), *Philosophy and the Arts*. Royal Institute of Philosophy Lectures, vol. 6. London: Macmillan, 1973.

Cassirer, E., *An Essay on Man: An Introduction to a Philosophy of Human Culture*. New Haven, CT: Yale University Press, 1944.

Castles, S. with Booth, H. and Wallace, T., *Here for Good: Western Europe's New Ethnic Minorities*. London: Pluto, 1984.

Caws, P., *The Philosophy of Science*. Princeton, NJ: Van Nostrand, 1965.

Champlin, T. S., *Reflexive Paradoxes*. London: Routledge, 1988.

Chellas, B. F., *Modal Logic: An Introduction*. Cambridge: Cambridge University Press, 1980.

Child, W., *Causality, Interpretation and the Mind*. Oxford: Oxford University Press, 1994.

Chisholm, R. M., *Theory of Knowledge*, 2nd edn. Englewood Cliffs, NJ: Prentice-Hall, 1966.

Chisholm, R. M., *Person and Object: A Metaphysical Study*. London: George Allen & Unwin, 1976.

Chisholm, R. M., *The Foundations of Knowing*. Brighton: Harvester, 1982.

Chisholm, R. M., *Brentano and Intrinsic Value*. Cambridge: Cambridge University Press, 1986.

Chomsky, N., *Syntactic Structures*. The Hague: Mouton, 1957.

Chomsky, N., *Aspects of the Theory of Syntax*. Cambridge, MA: MIT Press, 1965.

Chomsky, N., *Studies on Semantics in Generative Grammar*. The Hague: Mouton, 1972.

Chomsky, N. and Halle, M., *The Sound Pattern of English*. New York: Harper & Row, 1968.

Christensen, S. M. and Turner, D. R. (eds.), *Folk Psychology and the Philosophy of Mind*. Hillsdale, NJ: Lawrence Erlbaum Associates, 1993.

Chrysippus, in Galen, *On the Doctrines of Hippocrates and Plato*, trs. P. de Lacy. Berlin: Academie-Verlag, 1978–84.

Church, A., *Introduction to Mathematical Logic*, rev. edn. Princeton, NJ: Princeton University Press, 1956.

Churchland, P., *Neurophilosophy: Towards a Unified Science of the Mind-Brain*. Cambridge, MA: MIT Press, 1988.

Cicero, Marcus Tullius, *De Natura Deorum/Academica*, trs. H. Rackham. London: William Heinemann, 1967.

Clarke, S. G. and Simpson, E. (eds.), *Anti-Theory in Ethics and Moral Conservatism*. Albany, NY: State University of New York Press, 1989.

Cohen, G. A., *Self-Ownership, Freedom and Equality*. Cambridge: Cambridge University Press, 1995.

Cohen, L. J., *The Dialogue of Reason: An Analysis of Analytical Philosophy*. Oxford: Clarendon Press, 1986.

Cohen, L. J., *An Introduction to the Philosophy of Induction and Probability*. Oxford: Clarendon Press, 1989.

Cohen, M. R. and Nagel, E., *An Introduction to Logic and Scientific Method*. New York: Harcourt Brace, 1934.

Cohen, P. J., *Set Theory and the Continuum Hypothesis*. New York: W. A. Benjamin, 1966.

Collingwood, R. G., *An Essay on Metaphysics*. Oxford: Clarendon Press, 1940.

Cooper, N., *The Diversity of Moral Thinking*. Oxford: Clarendon Press, 1981.

Copi, I. M., *Symbolic Logic*, 3rd edn. London: Collier Macmillan, 1967.

Copi, I. M., *The Theory of Logical Types*. London: Routledge & Kegan Paul, 1971.

Copi, I. M., *Introduction to Logic*, 7th edn. New York: Macmillan, 1986.

Copleston, F. C., *A History of Philosophy*, vol. 2: *Mediaeval Philosophy, Augustine to Scotus*. London: Burns, Oates & Washbourne, 1950.

Copleston, F. C., *A History of Philosophy*, vol. 3: *Ockham to Suárez*. London: Burns, Oates & Washbourne, 1953.

Copleston, F. C., *A History of Philosophy*, vol. 7: *Fichte to Nietzsche*. London: Burns, Oates & Washbourne, 1963.

Copleston, F. C., *A History of Medieval Philosophy*. London: Methuen, 1972.

Cornman, J. W., *Materialism and Sensations*. New Haven, CT: Yale University Press, 1971.

Cornman, J. W., *Perception, Common Sense, and Science*. New Haven, CT: Yale University Press, 1975.

Crombie, I. M., *An Examination of Plato's Doctrines*. London: Routledge & Kegan Paul, 1962.

Cross, R., *Precedent in English Law*, 3rd edn. Oxford: Clarendon Press, 1977.

Cummins, R., *Meaning and Mental Representation*. Cambridge, MA: MIT Press, 1989.

Curry, H. B., *Outlines of a Formalist Philosophy of Mathematics*. Amsterdam: North Holland, 1951.

D'Agostino, F., *Chomsky's System of Ideas*. Oxford: Clarendon Press, 1986.

Dahrendorf, R., *Essays in the Theory of Society*. London: Routledge & Kegan Paul, 1968.

Dancy, J., *An Introduction to Contemporary Epistemology*. Oxford: Basil Blackwell, 1985.

Dancy, J., *Moral Reasons*. Oxford: Blackwell Publishers, 1993.

Daniels, N., *Justice and Justification: Reflective Equilibrium in Theory and Practice*. Cambridge: Cambridge University Press, 1996.

Danto, A. C., "What We Can Do," *Journal of Philosophy* 60 (1963), pp. 435–45.

Danto, A. C., *Analytical Philosophy of Knowledge*. Cambridge: Cambridge University Press, 1963.

Danto, A. C., *Analytical Philosophy of Language*. Cambridge: Cambridge University Press, 1963.

Danto, A. C., "Artworld," *Journal of Philosophy* 61 (1964), pp. 571–84.

Danto, A. C., *Analytical Philosophy of History*. Cambridge: Cambridge University Press, 1965.

Danto, A. C., *Analytical Philosophy of Action*. London: Cambridge University Press, 1973.

Danto, A. C., *The Philosophical Disenfranchisement of Art*. New York: Columbia University Press, 1986.

Davidson, D., *Essays on Actions and Events*. Oxford: Clarendon, 1980.

Davidson, D., *Inquiries into Truth and Interpretation*. Oxford: Clarendon Press, 1984.

Davidson, D. and Harman, G. (eds.), *Semantics of Natural Language*. Dordrecht: D. Reidel, 1972.

Davidson, D. and Hintikka, J. (eds.), *Words and Objections*. Dordrecht: D. Reidel, 1975.

Davies, P. C. W., *The Physics of Time Asymmetry*. Berkeley, CA: University of California Press, 1974.

Delphy, C., *Close to Home: A Materialist Analysis of Women's Oppression*, trs. and ed. Diana Leonard. London: Hutchinson, 1984.

Democritus, in Sextus Empiricus, *Against the Grammarians (Adversus Mathematicos I)*, trs. D. L. Blank. Oxford: Oxford University Press, 1996.

Dennett, D. C., *Content and Consciousness*. London: Routledge & Kegan Paul, 1969.

Dennett, D. C., *Brain Storms: Philosophical Essays on Mind and Psychology*. Hassocks: Harvester Press, 1979.

Dennett, D. C., *Consciousness Explained*. Harmondsworth: Penguin, 1991.

Dennett, D. C., *Kinds of Minds: Toward an Understanding of Consciousness*. New York: Basic Books, 1996.

Derrida, J., *Of Grammatology*, trs. G. C. Spivak. Baltimore, MD: Johns Hopkins University Press, 1974.

Derrida, J., *Margins of Philosophy*, trs. Alan Bass. Chicago, IL: University of Chicago Press, 1982.

Derrida, J., "Letter to a Japanese Friend," in D. Wood and R. Bernasconi (eds.), *Derrida and Différance*. Evanston, IL: Northwestern University Press, 1988.

Descartes, R., *Discourse on Method*, in R. Descartes, *The Philosophical Writings of Descartes*, vol. 1.

Descartes, R., *Meditations on First Philosophy*, in *The Philosophical Works of Descartes*, vol. 1.

Descartes, R., *Principles of Philosophy*, in R. Descartes, *The Philosophical Writings of Descartes*, vol. 1.

Descartes, R., *The Passions of the Soul*, in R. Descartes, *The Philosophical Writings of Descartes*, vol. 1.

Descartes, R., *Meditations: Reply to Objection V*, in *The Philosophical Works of Descartes*, vol. 2, trs. E. S. Haldane and G. R. T. Ross. Cambridge: Cambridge University Press, 1967.

Descartes, R., *The Philosophical Writings of Descartes*, vol. 1: *Early Writings; Rules for the Direction of the Mind; The World; Treatise on Man; Discourse on the Method; Optics; Principles of Philosophy; Comments on a Certain Broadsheet; Description of the Human Body; The Passions of the Soul*, trs. J. Cottingham, R. Stoothoff and D. Murdoch. Cambridge: Cambridge University Press, 1984.

Descartes, R., *The Philosophical Writings of Descartes*, vol. 3: *The Correspondence*, trs. J. Cottingham et al. Cambridge: Cambridge University Press, 1991.

Devlin, P., *The Enforcement of Morals*. London: Oxford University Press, 1965.

Dewey, J., *Essays in Experimental Logic*. Chicago, IL: Chicago University Press, 1916.

Dewey, J., *Logic: The Theory of Inquiry*. New York: Holt, Rinehart & Winston, 1938.

Dewey, J., *Theory of Evaluation*. Chicago, IL: Chicago University Press, 1939.

Dickie, G., *Art and the Aesthetic: An Institutional Analysis*. Ithaca, NY: Cornell University Press, 1974.

Diels, H. and Kranz, W., *Die Fragmente Der Vorsokratiker*. Berlin: Weidmann, 1954.

Dilthey, W., in P. Gardiner (ed.), *Theories of History*. Glencoe, IL: Free Press, 1959.

Dilthey, W., *Selected Works*, vol. 1, ed. R. a. Makkreel and F. Rodi. Princeton, NJ: Princeton University Press, 1989.

Dilthey, W., *The Construction of the Historical World in the Human Studies*, in W. Dilthey, *Selected Works*.

Diogenes Laertius, *Lives of Eminent Philosophers*, Book 7, ed. R. D. Hicks. Cambridge: Cambridge University Press, 1970.

Donagan, A., *The Theory of Morality*. Chicago, IL: University of Chicago Press, 1977.

Donnellan, K. S., "Reference and Definite Descriptions," in S. P. Schwarz (ed.), *Naming, Necessity, and Natural Kinds*. Ithaca, NY: Cornell University Press, 1977.

Downie, R. S. and Telfer, E., *Caring and Curing: A Philosophy of Medicine and Social Work*. London: Methuen, 1980.

Dray, W., *Philosophy of History*. Englewood Cliffs, NJ: Prentice-Hall, 1964.

Dretske, F., *Explaining Behavior: Reasons in a World of Causes*. Cambridge, MA: MIT Press, 1988.

Ducasse, C. J., *The Philosophy of Art*. London: Allen & Unwin, 1929.

Duhem, P. M. M., *Essays in the History and Philosophy of Science*, trs. and ed. R. Ariew and P. Barker. Indianapolis, IN: Hackett, 1996.

Dummett, M., "Bringing about the Past," *Philosophical Review* 73 (1964), pp. 338–59.

Dummett, M., *Frege: Philosophy of Language*. London: Duckworth, 1973.

Dummett, M., *Truth and Other Enigmas*. London: Duckworth, 1978.

Dummett, M., *The Interpretation of Frege's Philosophy*. Cambridge, MA: Harvard University Press, 1981.

Dummett, M., *The Logical Basis of Metaphysics*. London: Duckworth, 1991.

Dummett, M., *Origins of Analytical Philosophy*. London: Duckworth, 1993.

Dummett, M., *The Seas of Language*. Oxford: Oxford University Press, 1993.

Durkheim, E., *The Rules of Sociological Method*. Glencoe, IL: Free Press, 1938.

Dworkin, R. M., *Taking Rights Seriously*. Cambridge, MA: Harvard University Press, 1977.

Dworkin, R. M. (ed.), *The Philosophy of Law*. Oxford: Oxford University Press, 1977.

Dworkin, R. M., *A Matter of Principle*. Cambridge, MA: Harvard University Press, 1986.

Dworkin, R. M., *Law's Empire*. Cambridge, MA: Harvard University Press, 1986.

Edel, A., Flower, E., and O'Connor, F. W. (eds.), *Morality, Philosophy, and Practice: Historical and Contemporary Readings and Studies*. New York: Random House, 1989.

Edgley, R. and Osborne, R. (eds.), *A Radical Philosophy Reader*. London: Verso, 1985.

Elster, J., *Ulysses and the Sirens: Studies in Rationality and Irrationality*. Cambridge: Cambridge University Press, 1979.

Engelhardt, H. T., *The Foundations of Bioethics*. New York: Oxford University Press, 1986.

Engels, F., *Socialism: Utopian and Scientific*. London: Bookmarks, 1995.

Evans, C. O., *The Subject of Consciousness*. London: George Allen & Unwin, 1970.

Evans, J. L., *Knowledge and Infallibility*. London: Macmillan, 1978.

Farganis, S., *Situating Feminism*. London: Sage, 1994.

Feinberg, J., *Harm to Others*. Oxford: Oxford University Press, 1984.

Feinberg, J., *Offense to Others*. Oxford University Press, 1985.

Feldman, F., *Introductory Ethics*. Englewood Cliffs, NJ: Prentice-Hall, 1978.

Feldman, R. and Conee, E., "Evidentialism," *Philosophical Studies* 48:1 (1985), pp. 15–34.

Ferré, F., *Basic Modern Philosophy of Religion*. London: George Allen & Unwin, 1968.

Feyerabend, P. K., *Against Method: Outline of an Anarchistic Theory of Knowledge*. London: NLB, 1975.

Feyerabend, P. K., *Problems of Empiricism*. Cambridge: Cambridge University Press, 1981.

Feyerabend, P. K., "Against Method," in H. Feigl and G. Maxwell (eds.), *Minnesota Studies in the Philosophy of Science*, vol. iii: *Scientific Explanation, Space, and Time*. Minneapolis, MN: University of Minnesota Press, 1962, pp. 28–97.

Field, G. L. and Higley, J., *Elitism*. London: Routledge & Kegan Paul, 1980.

Findlay, J. N., *Ascent to the Absolute: Metaphysical Papers and Lectures*. London: George Allen & Unwin, 1970.

Findlay, J. N., *Axiological Ethics*. London: Macmillan, 1970.

Firth, R., "Ethical Absolutism and the Ideal Observer," *Philosophy and Phenomenological Research* 12:3(1952), pp. 317–45.

Flathman, R. E., *Political Obligation*. London: Croom Helm, 1972.

Fletcher, J., *Situation Ethics: The New Morality*. London: SCM Press, 1966.

Flew, A. (ed.), *Logic and Language* (first series). Oxford: Basil Blackwell, 1951.

Fodor, J. A., in W. G. Lycan (ed.), *Mind and Cognition: A Reader*. Oxford: Basil Blackwell, 1990.

Fodor, J. A., *The Language of Thought*. Brighton: Harvester Press, 1976.

Fodor, J. A., *Modularity of Mind: An Essay on Faculty Psychology*. Cambridge, MA: MIT Press, 1983.

Fodor, J. A., *Psychosemantics*. Cambridge, MA: MIT Press, 1988.

Fodor, J. A. and Lepore, E., *Holism: A Shopper's Guide*. Oxford: Basil Blackwell, 1992.

Foot, P. (ed.), *Theories of Ethics*. London: Oxford University Press, 1967.

Foot, P., *Virtues and Vices and Other Essays in Moral Philosophy*. Cambridge, MA: Harvard University Press, 1971; 2nd edn., 1978.

Forbes, G., *Language of Possibility*. Oxford: Basil Blackwell, 1989.

Forbes, G., *Modern Logic*. Oxford: Oxford University Press, 1994.

Foster, H. (ed.), *Postmodern Culture*. London: Pluto Press, 1985.

Foucault, M., *The Archaeology of Knowledge*, trs. A. M. Sheridan Smith. London: Tavistock Publications, 1972.

Foucault, M., *Power/Knowledge: Selected Interviews and Other Writings*, ed. C. Gordon. Brighton: Harvester Press, 1980.

Frank, P., *Philosophy of Science*. Englewood Cliffs, NJ: Prentice-Hall, 1957.

Frankena, W., "Naturalist Fallacy," *Mind* XLVIII (1939).

Frankena, W., *Ethics*. Englewood Cliffs, NJ: Prentice-Hall, 1973.

Frankfurt, H., *Demons, Dreamers and Madmen*. Indianapolis, IN: Bobbs-Merrill, 1970.

Frege, G., "Function and Concept," in *Translations from the Philosophical Writings of Gottlob Frege*, 1960.

Frege, G., "On Sense and Reference," in *Translations from the Philosophical Writings of Gottlob Frege*, 1960.

Frege, G., *Translations from the Philosophical Writings of Gottlob Frege*, ed. P. Geach and M. Black. Oxford: Basil Blackwell, 1960.

Frege, G., "The Thought: a Logical Inquiry," in P. F. Strawson (ed.), *Philosophical Logic*. Oxford: Oxford University Press, 1967.

Frege, G., *The Foundations of Arithmetic*, trs. J. L. Austin. Oxford: Basil Blackwell, 1968.

Frege, G., *Begriffsschrift: Conceptual Notation and Related Articles*, trs. T. W. Bynam. Oxford: Clarendon Press, 1972.

Frege, G., *Philosophical and Mathematical Correspondence*, ed. G. Gabriel et al. Oxford: Basil Blackwell, 1980.

Frege, G., *Collected Papers on Mathematics, Logic and Philosophy*, ed. B. McGuinness, trs. Max Black et al. Oxford: Basil Blackwell, 1984.

Freud, S., *Standard Edition of the Complete Psychological Works of Sigmund Freud*, vol. 9.

Freud, S., *Standard Edition of the Complete Psychological Works of Sigmund Freud*, vol. 18.

Freud, S., *Standard Edition of the Complete Psychological Works of Sigmund Freud*, vol. 23.

Friedmann, W. (ed.), *Legal Theory*, 5th edn. New York: Columbia University Press, 1987.

Furley, D., *The Greek Cosmologists*. Cambridge: Cambridge University Press, 1987.

Gadamer, H.-G., *Truth and Method*, ed. G. Doepel, trs. G. Barden and J. Cumming. London: Sheed & Ward, 1975.

Gans, C., *Philosophical Anarchism and Political Disobedience*. Cambridge: Cambridge University Press, 1992.

Garber, D., "Old Evidence and Logical Omniscience in Bayesian Confirmation Theory," in J. S. Earman (ed.), *Minnesota Studies in the Philosophy of Science*, vol. x: *Testing Scientific Theories*. Minneapolis, MN: University of Minnesota Press, 1983, pp. 9–132.

Gardiner, P. (ed.), *Theories of History*. New York: Free Press, 1959.

Gardiner, P. (ed.), *The Philosophy of History*. London: Oxford University Press, 1974.

Garnham, A., *Psycholinguistics: Central Topics*. London: Methuen, 1985.

Gatens, M., *Feminism and Philosophy: Perspectives on Difference and Equality*. Bloomington, IN: Indiana University Press, 1991.

Gauthier, D., *Morals by Agreement*. Oxford: Oxford University Press, 1986.

Geach, "Ascriptivism," *Philosophical Review* 69 (1960), pp. 221–5.

Geach, P. T., *Logic Matters*. Oxford: Basil Blackwell, 1972.

Geach, P. T., *Truth, Love and Immortality*. Berkeley, CA: University of California Press, 1979.

Geach, P. T., *Reference and Generality*. Ithaca, NY: Cornell University Press, 1980.

Gert, B., *The Moral Rules: A New Rational Foundation for Morality*. New York: Harper & Row, 1973.

Gewirth, A., *Reason and Morality*. Chicago, IL: University of Chicago Press, 1978.

Gibbins, P., *Particles and Paradoxes: The Limits of Quantum Logic*. Cambridge: Cambridge University Press, 1987.

Gilson, E., *The Spirit of Medieval Philosophy*. London: Sheed & Ward, 1936.

Ginet, C., *Knowledge, Perception and Memory*. Oxford: Oxford University Press, 1995.

Glover, J., *Causing Death and Saving Lives*. Harmondsworth: Penguin, 1977.

Glover, J., *What Sort of People Should There Be?* Harmondsworth: Penguin, 1977.

Glymour, C., *Thinking Things Through*. Cambridge, MA: MIT Press, 1992.

Goldman, A., *A Theory of Human Action*. Englewood Cliffs, NJ: Prentice-Hall, 1970.

Goldman, A., *Justice and Reverse Discrimination*. Princeton, NJ: Princeton University Press, 1979.

Goodman, N., *Fact, Fiction and Forecast*. New York: Bobbs-Merrill, 1973.

Goodman, N., *Languages of Art*. Indianapolis, IN: Bobbs-Merrill, 1968.

Goodman, N., *Of Mind and Other Matters*. Cambridge, MA: Harvard University Press, 1984.

Goodman, N., *Problems and Projects*. Indianapolis: Bobbs-Merrill, 1972.

Goodpaster, K. and Sayre, K. (eds.), *Ethics and Problems of the 21st Century*. Notre Dame, IN: Notre Dame University Press, 1979.

Goodstein, R. L., *Development of Mathematical Logic*. New York: Springer, 1971.

Gracia, J. E., *Individuality: An Essay on the Foundations of Metaphysics*. Albany, NY: State University of New York, 1988.

Gracia, J. E., *Metaphysics and Its Task: The Search for the Categorical Foundation of Knowledge*. Albany, NY: State University of New York, 1999.

Graham, G., *Philosophy of Mind: An Introduction*, 2nd edn. Oxford: Blackwell Publishers, 1998.

Gramsci, A., *Selections from the Prison Notebooks*, ed. Q. Hoare and G. Nowell-Smith. New York: International Publishers, 1971.

Grandy, R., "Reference, Meaning and Belief," *Journal of Philosophy* 70 (1973), pp. 439–52.

Grant, R. M., *Gnosticism and Early Christianity*, 2nd edn. New York: Columbia University Press, 1966.

Grave, S. A., *The Scottish Philosophy of Common Sense*. Oxford: Clarendon Press, 1960.

Grayling, A. C., *An Introduction to Philosophical Logic*. Brighton: Harvester Press, 1982.

Grice, H. P., *Studies in the Ways of Words*. Cambridge, MA: Harvard University Press, 1989.

Griffin, N., *Relative Identity*. Oxford: Oxford University Press, 1977.

Griffin, R., *The Nature of Fascism*. London: Routledge, 1991.

Grover, D., *A Prosentential Theory of Truth*. Princeton, NJ: Princeton University Press, 1992.

Guthrie, W. K. C., *A History of Greek Philosophy*. Cambridge: Cambridge University Press, 1969.

Guthrie, W. K. C., *The Sophists*. Cambridge: Cambridge University Press, 1971.

Guttenplan, S. (ed.), *Mind and Language*. Oxford: Clarendon Press, 1975.

Haack, S., *Evidence and Inquiry: Towards Reconstruction in Epistemology*. Oxford: Blackwell Publishers, 1995.

Haack, S., *Philosophy of Logics*. Cambridge University Press, 2000.

Haakonssen, K., "Republicanism," in R. E. Goodin and P. Pettit (eds.), *A Companion to Contemporary Political Philosophy*. Oxford: Blackwell Publishers, 1995.

Haber, J. G. (ed.), *Absolutism and its Consequentialist Critics*. New York: Rowman & Littlefield, 1994.

Habermas, J., *Justification and Application*. Cambridge, MA: MIT Press, 1993.

Habermas, J., *Theory and Practice*, trs. J. Viertel. Boston, MA: Beacon Press, 1973.

Habermas, J., *The Theory of Communicative Action*, 2 vols. Cambridge: Polity Press, 1984.

Habermas, J., *The Philosophical Discourse of Modernity*. Cambridge: Polity Press, 1984.

Hacking, I., *The Emergence of Probability: A Philosophical Study of the Early Ideas about Probability, Induction and Statistical Inference*. Cambridge: Cambridge University Press, 1975.

Hacking, I., *Representing and Intervening: Introductory Topics in the Philosophy of Nature Science*. Cambridge: Cambridge University Press, 1983.

Haksar, V., *Equality, Liberty and Perfectionism*. Oxford: Oxford University Press, 1979.

Hall, D. L., *Richard Rorty: Prophet and Poet of the New Pragmatism*. Albany, NY: State University of New York, 1994.

Hall, J. C., *Rousseau*. London: Macmillan, 1973.

Hamblin, C. L., *Fallacies*. London: Methuen, 1970.

Hamlyn, D. W., *Metaphysics*. Cambridge: Cambridge University Press, 1984.

Hampshire, S. (ed.), *Public and Private Morality*. Cambridge: Cambridge University Press, 1978.

Hampshire, S., *Morality and Conflict*. Cambridge, MA: Harvard University Press, 1983.

Hancock, R., *Twentieth-Century Ethics*. New York: Columbia University Press, 1974.

Hanfling, O. (ed.), *Essential Readings in Logical Positivism*. Oxford: Basil Blackwell, 1981.

Hanson, N., *The Patterns of Discovery*. Cambridge: Cambridge University Press, 1958.

Harding, S., *The Science Question in Feminism*. Ithaca, NY: Cornell University Press, 1986.

Hare, R. M., *The Language of Morals*. Oxford: Oxford University Press, 1952.

Hare, R. M., *Freedom and Reason*. Oxford: Oxford University Press, 1963.

Hare, R. M., *Essays on Political Morality*. Oxford: Oxford University Press, 1989.

Hare, R. M., *Essays in Ethical Theory*. Oxford: Oxford University Press, 1989.

Haren, M., *Medieval Thought: The Western Intellectual Tradition from Antiquity to the Thirteenth Century*. Toronto: University of Toronto Press, 1992.

Harré, R., *The Philosophies of Science*. Oxford: Oxford University Press, 1972.

Harré, R., *Laws of Nature*. London: Duckworth, 1993.

Harrison, R., *On What There Must Be*. Oxford: Oxford University Press, 1974.

Hart, H. L. A., *The Concept of Law*. Oxford: Oxford University Press, 1961.

Hart, H. L. A., *Punishment and Responsibility*. Oxford: Oxford University Press, 1968.

Hart, H. L. A. and Honoré, T., *Causation in the Law*, 2nd edn. Oxford: Oxford University Press, 1985.

Hartshorne, C., *Creative Synthesis and Philosophical Method*. London: SCM Press, 1970.

Hatch, E., *Culture and Morality: The Relative Values of Anthropology*. New York: Columbia University Press, 1983.

Hayek, F. A., "Scientism, Historicism and the Problem of Rationality," in J. O'Neill (ed.), *Modes of Individualism and Collectivism*. London: Heinemann, 1973, pp. 91–110.

Heal, J., "Simulation, Theory and Content," in P. Carruthers and P. K. Smith (eds.), *Theories of Theories of Mind*. Oxford: Blackwell Publishers, 1996, pp. 33–52.

Hegel, G. W. F., *Philosophy of Right*, trs. T. M. Knox. Oxford: Clarendon Press, 1942.

Hegel, G. W. F., *Phenomenology of Mind*, trs. J. B. Baillie. London: George Allen & Unwin, 1949.

Hegel, G. W. F., *Die Vernunft in der Geschichte*, ed. J. Hofmeister. Hamburg: Felix Meiner, 1955.

Hegel, G. W. F., *Science of Logic*, trs. A. V. Miller. London: George Allen & Unwin, 1969.

Hegel, G. W. F., *Philosophy of Nature*, trs. A. V. Miller. Oxford: Clarendon Press, 1970.

Hegel, G. W. F., *Logic*, trs. W. Wallace. Oxford: Clarendon Press, 1975.

Hegel, G. W. F., *Phenomenology of Spirit*, trs. A. V. Miller. Oxford: Clarendon Press, 1977.

Heidegger, M., *Being and Time*, trs. J. Macquarrie and E. Robinson. Oxford: Basil Blackwell, 1962.

Held, V., *Feminist Morality: Transforming Culture, Society and Politics*. Chicago, IL: University of Chicago Press, 1993.

Helm, P., *Eternal God: A Study of God without Time*. Oxford: Oxford University Press, 1988.

Hempel, C. G., *Aspects of Scientific Explanation*. New York: Free Press, 1965.

Hempel, C. G., *Philosophy of Natural Science*. Englewood Cliffs, NJ: Prentice-Hall, 1966.

Hempel, C. G., "The Theoretician's Dilemma," in H. Feigl, M. Scriven, and G. Maxwell (eds.), *Minnesota Studies in the Philosophy of Science*, vol. ii: *Concepts, Theories, and the Mind–Body Problem*. Minnesota, MN: University of Minnesota Press, 1958, pp. 37–98.

Hempel, "The Function of General Law in History," in P. Gardiner (ed.), *Theories of History*. London: Free Press, 1959.

Heraclitus, in H. Diels and W. Kranze (ed.), *Die Fragmente Der Vorsokratiker*. Berlin: Weidmann, 1954.

Hick, J., *Arguments for the Existence of God*. London: Macmillan, 1970.

Hirst, R. J., *The Problems of Perception*. London: George Allen & Unwin, 1959.

Hoagland, S. L., *Lesbian Ethics: Toward New Value*. Palo Alto, CA: Institute of Lesbian Studies, 1988.

Hobbes, T., *Leviathan*, trs. C. B. MacPherson. Harmondsworth: Penguin Books, 1968.

Hodges, W., *Logic: An Introduction to Elementary Logic*. Harmondsworth: Penguin, 1977.

Hodgson, D., *The Mind Matters*. Oxford: Oxford University Press, 1991.

Hofstadter, A., *Truth and Art*. New York: Columbia University Press, 1965.

Honderich, T., *A Theory of Determinism*, vol. 2: *The Consequence of Determinism*. Oxford: Clarendon Press, 1990.

Honderich, T., *Punishment: The Supposed Justifications*, 4th edn. Cambridge: Polity Press, 1989.

Horwich, P., *Truth*. Oxford: Basil Blackwell, 1990.

Hospers, J., *Human Conduct: An Introduction to the Problems of Ethics*. New York: Harcourt Brace, 1961.

Hospers, J., *An Introduction to Philosophical Analysis*. Englewood Cliffs, NJ: Prentice-Hall, 1967.

Howson, C. and Urbach, P., *Scientific Reasoning: The Bayesian Approach*. LaSalle, IL: Open Court, 1989.

Hughes, G. E. and Cresswell, M. J., *An Introduction to Modal Logic*. London: Methuen, 1968.

Hume, D., *Dialogues Concerning Natural Religion*, in R. Wollheim (ed.), *Hume on Religion*. London: Collins, 1963.

Hume, D., "On Suicide," in R. Wollheim (ed.), *Hume on Religion*. London: Collins, 1963.

Hume, D., *Enquiries Concerning the Human Understanding and Concerning the Principles of Morals*, 3rd edn., ed. P. H. Nidditch. Oxford: Clarendon Press, 1975.

Hume, D., *A Treatise of Human Nature*, 2nd edn., ed. P. H. Nidditch. Oxford: Clarendon Press, 1978.

Hurley, P. J., *A Concise Introduction to Logic*. Belmont, CA: Wadsworth, 1982.

Hursthouse, R., *On Virtue Ethics*. Oxford: Oxford University Press, 1999.

Husserl, E., *Logical Investigation*, 2 vols., trs. J. N. Findlay. New York: Humanities Press, 1970.

Husserl, E., *The Crisis of European Sciences and Trans-cendental Phenomenology*, trs. D. Carr. Evanston, IL: Northwestern University Press, 1970.

Husserl, E., *Husserl: Shorter Works*, trs. D. Willard, P. McCormick and F. A. Elliston. Notre Dame, IN: University of Notre Dame Press, 1981.

Husserl, E., *Ideas Pertaining to a Pure Phenomenology and to a Phenomenological Philosophy*, trs, F. Kersten. The Hague: Martinus Nijhoff, 1982.

Huxley, A., *The Perennial Philosophy*. New York: Harper & Row, 1945.

Jackson, F., "Epiphenomenal Qualia," *Philosophical Quarterly* 32 (1982), pp. 127–36.

Jackson, F., *Perception: A Representative Theory*. Cambridge: Cambridge University Press, 1977.

James, E. O., *The Concept of Deity*. London: Hutchinson's University Library, 1950.

James, W., *The Will to Believe and Other Essays*. New York: Longmans, Green, 1897.

James, W., *The Meaning of Truth*. New York: Macmillan, 1909.

James, W., *Pragmatism: A New Name for Some Old Ways of Thinking – Together with Four Related Essays Selected from the Meaning of Truth*. New York: Longmans, Green, 1943.

James, W., *Essays in Pragmatism*. New York: Hafner, 1948.

James, W., *The Varieties of Religious Experience: A Study in Human Nature*. London: Collins, 1960.

James, W., *Principles of Psychology*, vols. 1–3. Cambridge, MA: Harvard University Press, 1981.

Jaspers, K., *Philosophy*, 3 vols. London, 1932.

Jaspers, K., *The Philosophy of Karl Jaspers*, ed. P. A. Schilpp. LaSalle, IL: Open Court, 1957.

Johnson, W. E., *Logic*, vol. 2: *Demonstrative Inference*. Cambridge: Cambridge University Press, 1922.

Joseph, H. W. B., *An Introduction to Logic*. Oxford: Clarendon Press, 1916.

Joske, W. D., *Material Objects*. London: Macmillan, 1967.

Jowett, B. (ed.), *The Dialogues of Plato*. Oxford University Press, 1924.

Joyce, G. H., *Principles of Natural Theology*. London: Longmans, Green, 1923.

Kagan, S., "Additive Fallacy," *Ethics* 99 (1988), pp. 5–31.

Kant, I., *Critique of Judgement*, trs. J. C. Meredith. Oxford: Clarendon Press, 1952.

Kant, I., *Prolegomena*, trs. P. G. Lucas. Manchester: Manchester University Press, 1953.

Kant, I., *Observations on the Feelings of the Beautiful and Sublime*, trs. J. Goldthwait. Berkeley, CA: University of California Press, 1960.

Kant, I., *Critique of Practical Reason*, trs. T. K. Abbott, 6th edn. London: Longman, 1963.

Kant, I., *Critique of Pure Reason*, trs. N. Kemp Smith. London: Macmillan, 1968.

Kant, I., *Logic*, trs. R. S. Hartman and W. Schwartz. Indianapolis, IN: Bobbs-Merrill, 1974.

Kant, I., *Groundwork for the Metaphysics of Morals*, trs. J. W. Ellington. Indianapolis, IN: Hackett, 1981.

Kant, I., *Lectures on Logic*, trs. and ed. J. M. Young. Cambridge: Cambridge University Press, 1992.

Kant, I., *The Metaphysics of Morals*, trs. M. Gregor. Cambridge: Cambridge University Press, 1996.

Kant, I., *Theoretical Philosophy, 1755–1770*, trs. and ed. D. Walford and R Meerbote. Cambridge: Cambridge University Press, 1992.

Katz, J. J., *Linguistic Philosophy*. London: George Allen & Unwin, 1971.

Katz, J. J., *Semantic Theory*. New York: Harper & Row, 1972.

Katz, J. J., *Cogitations*. Oxford: Oxford University Press, 1986.

Keat, R. and Urry, J., *Social Theory as Science*. London: Routledge, 1975.

Kelsen, H., *General Theory of Law and State*, ed. A. Wedberg. New York: Russell & Russell, 1945.

Kenny, A., *Will, Freedom and Power*. Oxford: Basil Blackwell, 1975.

Kenny, A., *The Legacy of Wittgenstein*. Oxford: Oxford University Press, 1984.

Kenny, A., *The Ivory Tower: Essays in Philosophy and Public Policy*. Oxford: Blackwell Publishers, 1985.

Keynes, J. N., *Studies and Exercises in Formal Logic*, 4th edn. London: Macmillan, 1906.

Keynes, J. M., *A Treatise on Probability*. London: Macmillan, 1921.

Kierkegaard, S., *Concluding Unscientific Postscript to Philosophical Fragments*, trs. and ed. H. V. Hong and E. H. Hong. Princeton, NJ: Princeton University Press, 1992.

Kierkegaard, S., *Kierkegaard's Writing*, vol. 19: *Sickness unto Death*, trs. and ed. H. V. Hong and E. H. Hong. Princeton, NJ: Princeton University Press, 1983.

Kittay, E. and Meyers, D. T. (eds.), *Women and Moral Theory*. Savage, MD: Rowman & Littlefield, 1987.

Kneale, W. and Kneale, M., *The Development of Logic*. Oxford: Clarendon Press, 1962.

Kneale, W., *Probability and Induction*. Oxford: Clarendon Press, 1949

Kolakowski, L., *The Alienation of Reason: A History of Positivist Thought*, trs. N. Guterman. Garden City, NY: Doubleday, 1968.

Kosso, P., *Reading the Book of Nature: An Introduction to the Philosophy of Science*. Cambridge: Cambridge University Press, 1992.

Kretzmann, N., *The Metaphysics of Theism: Aquinas's Natural Theology of Summa Contra Gentiles*. Oxford: Oxford University Press, 1997.

Kretzmann, N., et al. (eds.), *The Cambridge History of Later Medieval Philosophy*. Cambridge: Cambridge University Press, 1982.

Kripke, S. A., *Naming and Necessity*. Cambridge, MA: Harvard University Press, 1972; 2nd edn. 1980.

Kristeller, P. O., *Renaissance Thought and its Sources*. New York: Columbia University Press, 1979.

Kuhn, T., *The Structure of Scientific Revolutions*. Chicago, IL: University of Chicago Press, 1962.

Kvanvig, J. L., *The Problem of Hell*. Oxford: Oxford University Press, 1993.

Ladd, A., *The Structure of a Moral Code: A Philosophical Analysis of Ethical Discourse Applied to the Ethics of Navaho Indians*. Cambridge, MA: Harvard University Press, 1957.

Lakatos, I., in I. Lakatos and A. Musgrave (eds.), *Criticism and the Growth of Knowledge*. Cambridge: Cambridge University Press, 1970.

Langer, S. K., *An Introduction to Symbolic Logic*. New York: Dover, 1937.

Langer, S. K., *Feeling and Form*. New York: Charles Scribner's Sons, 1953.

Langford, C. H., "Moore's Notion of Analysis," in P. Schilpp (ed.), *Philosophy of G. E. Moore*. Evanston, IL: Northwestern University Press, 1942.

Larrain, J., *The Concept of Ideology*. New York: Longman, 1992.

Le Doeuff, M., *Hipparchia's Choice*. Oxford: Basil Blackwell, 1991.

Lee, S., *Law and Morals*. Oxford: Oxford University Press, 1986.

Leff, G., *Medieval Thought: St. Augustine to Ockham*. London: Penguin, 1958.

Leibniz, G. W., *Principles of Nature and Grace*, in *Leibniz: Philosophical Writings*, trs. M. Morris. London: Dent, 1934.

Leibniz, G. W., *Theodicy*. London: Routledge & Kegan Paul, 1951.

Leibniz, G. W., *The Leibniz–Clarke Correspondence*, ed. H. G. Alexander. Manchester: Manchester University Press, 1956.

Leibniz, G. W., *Philosophical Papers and Letters*, ed. L. Loemker. Dordrecht: D. Reidel, 1969.

Leibniz, G. W., *Discourse on Metaphysics*, trs. R. Martin and S. Brown. Manchester: Manchester University Press, 1988.

Leibniz, G. W., *Philosophical Essays*, ed. R. Ariew and D. Garber. Indianapolis, IN: Hackett, 1989.

Leibniz, G. W., *New Essays on Human Understanding*, ed. P. Remnant and J. Bennett. Cambridge: Cambridge University Press, 1990.

Lenin, V. I., *Collected Works*, 4th edn. Moscow: Progress Publishers, 1963.

Lenin, V. I., *Materialism and Empirio-Criticism*. Moscow: Progress Publishers, 1964.

Lennon, K. and Whitford, M. (eds.), *Knowing the Difference: Feminist Perspectives in Epistemology*. London: Routledge, 1994.

Leopold, A., *A Sand County Almanac*. Oxford: Oxford University Press, 1949.

Leslie, J., *Value and Existence*. Oxford: Basil Blackwell, 1979.

Levinas, E., *Totality and Infinity*, trs. A. Lingus. Pittsburgh, PA: Duquesne University Press, 1969.

Lévi-Strauss, C., *Structural Anthropology*. London: Allen Lane, 1968.

Lewis, C. I., *Mind and the World-Order: Outline of a Theory of Knowledge*. New York: Charles Scribner's Sons, 1929.

Lewis, C. I., *An Analysis of Knowledge and Valuation*. La Salle, IL: Open Court, 1946.

Lewis, C. I. and Langford, C. H., *Symbolic Logic*. New York: Dover, 1932.

Lewis, D., *Convention*. Cambridge, MA: Harvard University Press, 1969.

Lewis, D., *Counterfactuals*. Cambridge, MA: Harvard University Press, 1973.

Lewis, D., *Philosophical Papers*, vol. 1. Oxford: Oxford University Press, 1983.

Lewis, D., *On the Plurality of Worlds*. Oxford: Basil Blackwell, 1986.

Lewis, D., *Parts of Classes*. Oxford: Basil Blackwell, 1991.

Lewis, F. A., *Substance and Predication in Aristotle*. Cambridge: Cambridge University Press, 1992.

Lichtheim, G., *Imperialism*. Harmondsworth: Penguin, 1971.

Little, D., *Varieties of Social Explanation: An Introduction to the Philosophy of Social Science*. Boulder, CO: Westview Press, 1991.

Lloyd, G. E. R., *Aristotle: The Growth and Structure of his Thought*. Cambridge: Cambridge University Press, 1968.

Locke, J., *A Letter Concerning Toleration*, in *The Works of John Locke*, vol. 5, 12th edn. London: C. and R. Rivington, 1824.

Locke, J., *Two Treatises on Government*, ed. P. Laslett. Cambridge: Cambridge University Press, 1960.

Locke, J., *An Essay Concerning Human Understanding*, ed. P. H. Nidditch. Oxford: Clarendon Press, 1975.

Logue, J., *Projective Probability*. Oxford: Oxford University Press, 1995.

Long, A. A., *Hellenistic Philosophy: Stoics, Epicureans and Sceptics*. London: Duckworth, 1986.

Long, A. A. and Sedley, D., *The Hellenistic Philosophers*, vol. 1: *Translations of the Principal Sources*. Cambridge: Cambridge University Press, 1987.

Lossky, V., *The Mystical Theology of the Eastern Church*. Cambridge: James Clarke, 1957.

Lovejoy, O., *The Great Chain of Being: The Study of the History of an Idea*. Cambridge, MA: Harvard University Press, 1936.

Lovelock, J., *Gaia: A New Look at Life on Earth*. Oxford: Oxford University Press, 1987.

Lowe, E. J., *Kinds of Being: A Study of Individuation, Identity and the Logic of Sortal Terms*. Oxford: Basil Blackwell, 1989.

Lucas, J., *The Freedom of the Will*. Oxford: Clarendon Press, 1970.

Lucas, J., *The Concept of Probability*. Oxford: Clarendon Press, 1970.

Lucas, J., *The Principles of Politics*. Oxford: Clarendon Press, 1985.

Lucas, J., *Responsibility*. Oxford: Clarendon Press, 1993.

Lukes, S. M., *Individualism*. Oxford: Basil Blackwell, 1973.

Lycan, W., *Consciousness*. Cambridge, MA: MIT Press, 1987.

Lyons, W., *Approaches to Intentionality*. Oxford: Oxford University Press, 1995.

MacCormick, N., *Legal Reasoning and Legal Theory*. Oxford: Oxford University Press, 1978.

MacCormick, N., *H. L. A. Hart*. Stanford, CA: Stanford University Press, 1981.

MacCormick, N., *Legal Right and Social Democracy: Essays in Legal and Political Philosophy*. Oxford: Clarendon Press, 1982.

Macdonald, G. and Pettit, P., *Semantics and Social Science*. London: Routledge & Kegan Paul, 1981.

Macquarrie, J., *Twentieth-Century Religious Thought: The Frontiers of Philosophy and Theology*. London: SCM Press, 1971.

McAlister, L. (ed.), *The Philosophy of Brentano*. London: Duckworth, 1976.

McCall, R. J., *Basic Logic: The Fundamental Principles of Formative Deductive Reasoning*. New York: Barnes & Noble, 1963.

McDowell, J., "Functionalism and Anomalous Monism," in E. Lepore and B. P. McLaughlin (eds.), *Actions and Events: Perspectives on the Philosophy of Donald Davidson*. Oxford: Basil Blackwell, 1985.

McGinn, C., *The Character of Mind*. Oxford: Oxford University Press, 1982.

McGinn, C., *The Problem of Consciousness*. Oxford: Basil Blackwell, 1991.

McIntyre, A., *After Virtue: A Study of Moral Theory*. London: Duckworth, 1981.

McLean, I., *Public Choice*. Oxford: Basil Blackwell, 1987.

McNaughton, D., *Moral Vision: An Introduction to Ethics*. Oxford: Basil Blackwell, 1988.

McPherson, T., *The Philosophy of Religion*. New York, 1965.

McTaggart, J. M. E., *The Nature of Existence*, 2 vols. Cambridge: Cambridge University Press, 1927.

Mackie, J. L., *Ethics: Inventing Right and Wrong*. Harmondsworth: Penguin, 1977.

Maddy, P., *Realism in Mathematics*. Oxford: Oxford University Press, 1990.

Mandelbaum, M., *The Problem of Historical Knowledge: An Answer to Relativism*. New York: Harper, 1938.

Martin, G., *An Introduction to General Metaphysics*. London: George Allen & Unwin, 1961.

Martin, M. M., *Atheism: A Philosophical Justification*. Philadelphia, PA: Temple University Press, 1990.

Martin, R., *Historical Explanation*. Ithaca, NY: Cornell University Press, 1977.

Martin, R. M., *The Meaning of Language*. Cambridge, MA: MIT Press, 1987.

Marx, K., Preface to *A Contribution to the Critique of Political Economy*. London: Lawrence & Wishart, 1971.

Mascall, E. L., *He Who Is: A Study of Traditional Theism*. London: Longmans, Green, 1943.

Mates, B., *Elementary Logic*, 2nd edn. Oxford: Oxford University Press, 1972.

Maxwell, G., "Structural Realism and the Meaning of Theoretical Terms," in M. Radner and S. Winoker (eds.), *Minnesota Studies in the Philosophy of Science*, vol. iv: *Analyses of Theories and Methods of Physics and Psychology*. Minneapolis, MN: University of Minnesota Press, 1970.

May, L., *The Morality of Groups: Collective Responsibility, Group-based Harm and Corporate Rights*. Notre Dame, IL: University of Notre Dame Press, 1987.

Mayo, B., *The Philosophy of Right and Wrong*. London: Routledge & Kegan Paul, 1986.

Melden, A., *Rights and Persons*. Berkeley, CA: University of California Press, 1977.

Mellor, D. H., *The Matter of Chance*. Cambridge: Cambridge University Press, 1977.

Merleau-Ponty, M., *The Visible and the Invisible*, trs. A. Lingis. Evanston, IL: Northwestern University Press, 1968.

Merleau-Ponty, M., *Phénoménologie de la Perception*. Paris: Gallimard, 1945; trs. by C. Smith as *Phenomenology of Perception*. London: Routledge & Kegan Paul, 1962.

Midgley, M., *Evolution as a Religion: Strange Hopes and Strange Fears*. London: Methuen, 1985.

Mill, J. S., *Utilitarianism*, vol. X of *The Collected Works of John Stuart Mill*.

Mill, J. S., *On Liberty*, vol. XVIII of *The Collected Works of John Stuart Mill*.

Mill, J. S., *The Collected Works of John Stuart Mill*, 33 vols., ed. J. M. Robson. Toronto: University of Toronto Press, 1963–.

Mill, J. S., "On the Logic of the Moral Sciences," Book VI of *A System of Logic*, ed. A. J. Ayer. London: Duckworth, 1988.

Miller, D., *Critical Rationalism: A Restatement and Defence*. La Salle, IL: Open Court, 1994.

Miller, D., *On Nationality*. Oxford: Oxford University Press, 1995.

Miller, D. and Siedentop, L. (eds), *The Nature of Political Theory*. Oxford: Clarendon Press, 1983.

Mischel, T. (ed.), *Human Action: Conceptual and Empirical Issues*. New York: Academic Press, 1969.

Mitchell, B., *Morality: Religious and Secular*. Oxford: Oxford University Press, Englewood Cliffs, NJ: Prentice-Hall, 1985.

Mitchell, D., *An Introduction to Logic*. London: Hutchinson, 1972.

Montague, R., *Formal Philosophy*, ed. R. Thomason. New Haven, CT: Yale University Press, 1974.

Moore, G. E., *Principia Ethica*. London, 1903.

Moore, G. E., *Philosophical Studies*. London: Kegan Paul, 1922.

Moore, G. E., *Some Main Problems of Philosophy*. London: George Allen & Unwin, 1959.

Moore, G. E., "The Subjectivity of Psychology," in G. Vesey (ed.), *Body and Mind: Readings in Philosophy*. London: George Allen & Unwin, 1964.

Moore, G. H., *Zermelo's Axiom of Choice: Its Origin, Development and Influence*. New York: Springer-Verlag, 1982.

Moore, G. H., "The Emergence of First Order Logic," in W. Asprey and P. Kitcher (eds.), *Minnesota Studies in the Philosophy of Science*, vol. xi: *History and Philosophy of Modern Mathematics*. Minneapolis, MN: University of Minnesota Press, 1988.

Moore, T. W., *Philosophy of Education: An Introduction*. London: Routledge, 1982.

Moser, P. (ed.), *A Priori Knowledge*. Oxford: Oxford University Press, 1987.

Moser, P., *Philosophy after Objectivity*. Oxford: Oxford University Press, 1993.

Moser, P. and Nat, A. van der, *Human Knowledge: Classic and Contemporary Approaches*. Oxford: Oxford University Press, 1987.

Mothersill, M., *Beauty Restored*. Oxford: Oxford University Press, 1984.

Moya, C. J., *The Philosophy of Action*. Cambridge: Polity Press, 1990.

Murphy, J. and Coleman, J., *The Philosophy of Law: An Introduction to Jurisprudence*. Totowa, NJ: Rowman & Allanheld, 1984.

Naess, A., *Scepticism*. New York: McGraw Hill, 1968.

Nagel, E., "The Meaning of Reduction in the Natural Sciences," in A. Danto and S. Morgenbesser (eds.), *Philosophy of Science*. Cleveland, OH: Meridian, 1960.

Nagel, E., *The Structure of Science: Problems in the Logic of Scientific Explanation*. New York: Harcourt, Brace & World, 1961.

Nagel, T., *Mortal Questions*. Cambridge: Cambridge University Press, 1979.

Nagel, T., *The Possibility of Altruism*. Princeton, NJ: Princeton University Press, 1970.

Nagel, T., *The View from Nowhere*. Oxford: Oxford University Press, 1985.

Neisser, U., *Cognitive Psychology*. New York: Appleton-Century-Crofts, 1967.

Nelson, R. J., *The Logic of Mind*. Dordrecht: D. Reidel, 1989.

Newton, I., *Mathematical Principles of Natural Philosophy*, trs. A. Motte. Berkeley, CA: University of California Press, 1947.

Nietzsche, F., *Thus Spoke Zarathustra*, trs. R. J. Hollingdale. Harmondsworth: Penguin, 1961.

Nietzsche, F., *The Birth of Tragedy*, trs. W. Kaufmann. New York: Vintage Books, 1967.

Nietzsche, F., *The Gay Science*, trs. W. Kaufmann. New York: Vintage Books, 1967.

Nietzsche, F., *On the Genealogy of Morals and Other Writings*, ed. C. Diethe. Cambridge: Cambridge University Press, 1994.

Nowell-Smith, P. H., *Ethics*. Harmondsworth: Penguin, 1954.

Nozick, R., *Anarchy, State and Utopia*. Oxford: Basil Blackwell, 1974.

Nozick, R., *Philosophical Explanations*. Oxford: Oxford University Press, 1984.

Nussbaum, M. and Glover, J. (eds.), *Women, Culture and Development*. Oxford: Oxford University Press, 1995.

Nussbaum, M. and Sen, A. (eds.), *The Quality of Life*. Oxford: Oxford University Press, 1993.

Nye, A., *Feminist Theory and the Philosophy of Man*. London: Routledge, 1988.

Oakeshott, M., *Experience and its Modes*. Cambridge: Cambridge University Press, 1933.

O'Connor, J. D. and Carr, B., *Introduction to the Theory of Knowledge*. Minneapolis, MN: University of Minnesota, 1982.

O'Hear, A., *Experience, Explanation and Faith: An Introduction to the Philosophy of Religion*. London: Routledge & Kegan Paul, 1984.

Otto, R., *The Idea of the Holy: An Inquiry into the Non-Rational Factor in the Idea of the Divine*, 2nd edn., trs. and ed. J. W. Harvey. Oxford: Oxford University Press, 1950.

Owen, Gwilym. *Logic, Science and Dialectic: Collected Papers in Greek Philosophy*, ed. M. Nussbaum. London: Duckworth, 1986.

Owen, H. P., *Concepts of Deity*. London: Macmillan, 1971.

Owens, J., *An Elementary Christian Metaphysics*. Houston, TX: Center for Thomist Studies, 1985.

Padgett, A., *God, Eternity and the Nature of Time*. Basingstoke: Macmillan, 1992.

Pap, A., *Elements of Analytic Philosophy*. New York: Macmillan, 1949.

Pap, A., *Semantics and Necessary Truth: An Inquiry into the Foundations of Analytic Philosophy*. New Haven, CT: Yale University Press, 1958.

Pap, A., *An Introduction to the Philosophy of Science*. London: Eyre & Spottiswoode, 1963.

Parfit, D., *Reasons and Persons*. Oxford: Oxford University Press, 1984.

Parfit, D., "Personal Identity," *Philosophical Review* 80 (1971), pp. 3–27.

Parker, W. H., *The Principles of Aesthetics*. New York: Reinhold, 1947.

Passmore, J., *Philosophical Reasoning*, 2nd edn. London: Duckworth, 1970.

Peacocke, C., *Thoughts: An Essay on Content*. Oxford: Basil Blackwell, 1986.

Pears, D. F., *Motivated Irrationality*. Oxford: Oxford University Press, 1984.

Pears, D. F., "Is Existence a Predicate?," in P. F. Strawson (ed.), *Philosophical Logic*. Oxford: Oxford University Press, 1967.

Peirce, C. S., *The Collected Papers of Charles Sanders Peirce*, ed. C. Hartshorne, P. Weiss and A. Burks. Cambridge, MA: Belknap Press of Harvard University Press, 1931–58.

Penelhum, T., *Problems of Religious Knowledge*. London: Macmillan, 1971.

Perry, R. B., *Realms of Value*. Cambridge, MA: Harvard University Press, 1954.

Pettit, P., *Judging Justice: An Introduction to Contemporary Political Philosophy*. London: Routledge & Kegan Paul, 1980.

Piaget, J., *Structuralism*, trs. C. Maschler. New York: Basic Books, 1971.

Piaget, J., *The Principles of Genetic Epistemology*. New York: Basic Books, 1972.

Pieper, J., *Scholasticism: Personalities and Problems of Medieval Philosophy*. New York: Pantheon Books, 1960.

Pinson, K., *Pietism as a Factor in the Role of German Nationalism*, 2nd edn. New York: Octagon Books, 1968.

Pitcher, G. W. (ed.), *Truth*. Englewood Cliffs, NJ: Prentice-Hall, 1964.

Pitcher, G. W., *A Theory of Perception*. Princeton, NJ: Princeton University Press, 1971.

Plamenatz, J., *Karl Marx's Philosophy of Man*. Oxford: Clarendon Press, 1975.

Plant, R., *Modern Political Thought*. Oxford: Basil Blackwell, 1991.

Plantinga, A., *The Nature of Necessity*. Oxford Clarendon Press, 1974.

Plantinga, A., *God, Freedom and Evil*. Grand Rapids, MI: William B. Eerdmans, 1975.

Plato, *Euthyphro*, in *The Collected Dialogues of Plato*, ed. E. Hamilton and H. Cairns. Princeton, NJ: Princeton University Press, 1961.

Plato, *Meno*, in *The Collected Dialogues of Plato*, ed. E. Hamilton and H. Cairns. Princeton, NJ: Princeton University Press, 1961.

Plato, *Phaedo*, in *The Collected Dialogues of Plato*, ed. E. Hamilton and H. Cairns. Princeton, NJ: Princeton University Press, 1961.

Plato, *Phaedrus*, in *The Collected Dialogues of Plato*, ed. E. Hamilton and H. Cairns. Princeton, NJ: Princeton University Press, 1961.

Plato, *Republic*, in *The Collected Dialogues of Plato*, ed. E. Hamilton and H. Cairns. Princeton, NJ: Princeton University Press, 1961.

Plato, *Sophist*, in *The Collected Dialogues of Plato*, ed. E. Hamilton and H. Cairns. Princeton, NJ: Princeton University Press, 1961.

Plato, *Symposium*, in *The Collected Dialogues of Plato*, ed. E. Hamilton and H. Cairns. Princeton, NJ: Princeton University Press, 1961.

Plato, *Theatetus*, in *The Collected Dialogues of Plato*, ed. E. Hamilton and H. Cairns. Princeton, NJ: Princeton University Press, 1961.

Plato, *Timaeus*, in *The Collected Dialogues of Plato*, ed. E. Hamilton and H. Cairns. Princeton, NJ: Princeton University Press, 1961.

Plotinus, *Enneads*, trs. S. MacKenna. London: Faber, 1969.

Podro, M., *The Manifold in Perception: Theories of Art from Kant to Hildebrand*. Oxford: Clarendon Press, 1972.

Polanyi, M., *Personal Knowledge: Towards a Post-Critical Philosophy*. New York: Harper & Row, 1958.

Pollock, J. L. and Cruz, J., *Contemporary Theories of Knowledge*. Totowa, NJ: Rowman & Allenheld, 1986.

Popper, K. R., *The Open Society and Its Enemies*, 2 vols. London: Routledge & Kegan Paul, 1945.

Popper, *The Poverty of Historicism*. London: Routledge & Kegan Paul, 1957.

Popper, K. R., *The Logic of Scientific Discovery*. New York: Harper & Row, 1968.

Popper, K. R., *Objective Knowledge: An Evolutionary Approach*. Oxford: Clarendon Press, 1972.

Popper, K. R., *Conjectures and Refutation: The Growth of Scientific Knowledge*. London: Routledge & Kegan Paul, 1972.

Popper, K. R., *The Philosophy of Karl Popper*, ed. P. A. Schilpp. La Salle, IL: Open Court, 1974.

Popper, K. R., *Realism and the Aims of Science*. London: Hutchinson, 1983.

Prevost, R., *Probability and Theistic Explanation*. Oxford: Oxford University Press, 1990.

Priest, G., *Beyond the Limits of Thought*. Cambridge: Cambridge University Press, 1990.

Price, H., *Facts and the Function of Truth*. Oxford: Basil Blackwell, 1988.

Price, H. H., *Perception*. London: Methuen, 1932.

Price, H. H., *Thinking and Experience*. London: Hutchinson, 1969.

Price, H. H., *Belief*. London: George Allen & Unwin, 1969.

Prior, A. N., *Formal Logic*, 2nd edn. Oxford: Clarendon Press, 1962.

Putnam, H., "The Analytic and the Synthetic," in H. Feigl and G. Maxwell (eds.), *Minnesota Studies in the Philosophy of Science*, vol. iii: *Scientific Explanation, Space and Time*. Minneapolis, MN: University of Minnesota Press, 1962.

Putnam, H., "The Meaning of 'Meaning'," in K. Gunderson (ed.), *Minnesota Studies in the Philosophy of Science*, vol. vii: *Language, Mind, and Knowledge*. Minneapolis, MN: University of Minnesota Press, 1970.

Putnam, H., *Mind, Language and Reality*, 2 vols. Cambridge: Cambridge University Press, 1975.

Putnam, H., "Is Semantics Possible?," in S. P. Schwartz, *Naming, Necessity and Natural Kinds*. Ithaca, NY: Cornell University Press, 1977.

Putnam, H., *Meaning and the Moral Sciences*. London: Routledge & Kegan Paul, 1978.

Putnam, H., *Realism and Reason*. Cambridge: Cambridge University Press, 1983.

Quine, W. V. O., *Mathematical Logic*, 2nd edn. Cambridge, MA: Harvard University Press, 1951.

Quine, W. V. O., *From a Logical Point of View: Nine Logico-philosophical Essays*. Cambridge, MA: Harvard University Press, 1953.

Quine, W. V. O., *Word and Object*. Cambridge, MA: MIT Press, 1960.

Quine, W.V. O., *Methods of Logic*, 2nd edn. London: Routledge & Kegan Paul, 1962.

Quine, W. V. O., *Set Theory and its Logic*. Cambridge, MA: Harvard University Press, 1963; rev. edn., 1969.

Quine, W. V. O., *Selected Logical Papers*. New York: Random House, 1966.

Quine, W. V. O., *Ontological Relativity and Other Essays*. New York: Columbia University Press, 1969.

Quine, W. V. O., *Philosophy of Logic*. Englewood Cliffs, NJ: Prentice-Hall, 1970.

Quine, W. V. O., *Theories and Things*. Cambridge, MA: Harvard University Press, 1981.

Quine, W. V. O., *From Stimulus to Science*. Cambridge, MA: Harvard University Press, 1995.

Quinton, A., "Spaces and Times," *Philosophy* 37 (1962), pp. 130–47.

Quinton, A., *The Nature of Things*. London: Routledge & Kegan Paul, 1973.

Rachels, J., *The Elements of Moral Philosophy*. New York: Random House, 1986.

Randall, J. H., *Aristotle*. New York: Columbia University Press, 1960.

Raphael, D. D., *Problems of Political Philosophy*, 2nd edn. London: Macmillan, 1990.

Rawls, J., *A Theory of Justice*. Oxford: Clarendon Press, 1972.

Rawls, J., "Two Concepts of Rule," in H. B. Acton (ed.), *Philosophy of Punishment*. New York: St. Martin's Press, 1969, pp. 105–14.

Raz, J. (ed.), *Practical Reason*. Oxford: Oxford University Press, 1978.

Raz, J., *The Authority of Law*. Oxford: Oxford University Press, 1979.

Read, S., *Thinking about Logic: An Introduction to the Philosophy of Logic*. Oxford: Oxford University Press, 1994.

Regan, T., *The Case for Animal Rights*. London: Routledge & Kegan Paul, 1983.

Regan, T. (ed.), *Matters of Life and Death: New Introductory Essays in Moral Philosophy*. New York: McGraw Hill, 1993.

Reichenbach, H., *Experience and Prediction: An Analysis of the Foundations and the Structure of Knowledge*. Chicago, IL: University of Chicago Press, 1938.

Reichenbach, H., *The Rise of Scientific Philosophy*. Berkeley, CA: University of California Press, 1951.

Reiss, S., *The Basis of Scientific Thinking*. New York: Philosophical Library, 1961.

Rescher, N., *Distributive Justice: A Constructive Critique of the Utilitarian Theory of Distribution*. Indianapolis, IN: Bobbs-Merrill, 1966.

Rescher, N., *Topics in Philosophic Logic*. Dordrecht: D. Reidel, 1968.

Rescher, N., *The Coherence Theory of Truth*. Oxford: Oxford University Press, 1973.

Rescher, N., *A Theory of Possibility*. Oxford: Basil Blackwell, 1975.

Rescher, N., *Methodological Pragmatism*. Oxford: Basil Blackwell, 1977.

Rescher, N., *Cognitive Systematization: A Systems-theoretic Approach to a Coherent Theory of Knowledge*. Oxford: Basil Blackwell, 1979.

Rescher, N., *Empirical Inquiry*. Totowa, NJ: Rowman & Littlefield, 1982.

Rescher, N., *Pascal's Wager: A Study of Practical Reasoning in Philosophical Theology*. Notre Dame, IN: University of Notre Dame Press, 1985.

Rescher, N., *Rationality*. Oxford: Oxford University Press, 1988.

Richards, S., *Philosophy and Sociology of Science: An Introduction*. Oxford: Basil Blackwell, 1983.

Richards, T. J., *The Language of Reason*. Oxford: Pergamon Press, 1978.

Richter, P. E. (ed.), *Utopias: Social Ideals and Communal Experiment*. Boston, MA: Holbrook Press, 1971.

Robinson, R., *Definition*. Oxford: Clarendon Press, 1950.

Rorty, A. O. (ed.), *Explaining Emotions*. Berkeley, CA: California University Press, 1980.

Rorty, R., "Pragmatism, Relativism, Irrationalism," *Proceedings and Address of the American Philosophical Association* 53 (1980), pp. 719–38.

Ross, W. D., *The Right and the Good*. Oxford: Oxford University Press, 1930.

Rousseau, J.-J., "Discourse on Inequality," in A. Ritter and J. C. Bondanella (eds.), *Rousseau's Political Writings*. New York: W. W. Norton, 1987.

Rousseau, J.-J., *The Social Contract*, in V. Gourevitch (ed.), *Rousseau: The Social Contract and Other Later Political Writings*. Cambridge: Cambridge University Press, 1997.

Routley, R. and Routley, V., "Against the Inevitability of Human Chauvinism," in K. E. Goodpaster and K. M. Sayre (eds.), *Ethical Problems of the 21st Century*. Notre Dame, IN: University of Notre Dame Press, 1979, pp. 36–59.

Rudner, R., *Philosophy of Social Science*. Englewood Cliffs, NJ: Prentice-Hall, 1966.

Ruse, M., *Taking Darwin Seriously: A Naturalistic Approach to Philosophy*. Oxford: Basil Blackwell, 1986.

Russell, B., *The Problems of Philosophy*. London: Home University Library, 1912.

Russell, B., *Mysticism and Logic*. London: Unwin, 1917.

Russell, B., *Introduction to Mathematical Philosophy*. London: Macmillan, 1919.

Russell, B., *The Analysis of Mind*. London: George Allen & Unwin, 1921.

Russell, B., *The Analysis of Matter*. London: Kegan Paul, 1927.

Russell, B., *The Principles of Mathematics*, 2nd edn. London: George Allen & Unwin, 1937.

Russell, B., *An Inquiry into Meaning and Truth*. London: George Allen & Unwin, 1940.

Russell, B., *Human Knowledge: Its Scope and Limits*. London: George Allen & Unwin, 1948.

Russell, B., *Our Knowledge of the External World*. London: George Allen & Unwin, 1948.

Russell, B., *Logic and Knowledge*, ed. R. C. Marsh. London: Routledge, 1956.

Russell, B., *Logic and Knowledge*. London: George Allen & Unwin, 1956.

Russell, B., *Collected Papers of Bertrand Russell*, the McMasters University Edition, R. A. Remple (director). London: Routledge, 1983–.

Ryle, G., *The Concept of Mind*. London: Hutchinson, 1949.

Ryle, G., *Collected Papers*, 2 vols. London: Hutchinson, 1971.

Sachs, M., *Ideas of the Theory of Relativity*. Jerusalem: Israel University Press, 1974.

Sainsbury, M., *Logical Form*. Oxford: Basil Blackwell, 1991.

Sainsbury, M., *Paradoxes*. Cambridge: Cambridge University Press, 1988; 2nd edn., 1995.

Salmon, W., *The Foundations of Scientific Inference*. Pittsburgh, PA: University of Pittsburgh Press, 1966.

Salmon, W., *Logic*. Englewood Cliffs, NJ: Prentice-Hall, 1966.

Sartre, J.-P., *Being and Nothingness: An Essay on Phenomenological Ontology*, trs. H. E. Barnes. London: Methuen, 1957.

Sartre, J.-P., *Existentialism and Humanism*, trs. P. Mairet. London: Methuen, 1989.

Sarup, M., *An Introductory Guide to Post-Structuralism and Post-Modernism*. Athens, GA: University of Georgia Press, 1993.

Saw, R. L., *Aesthetics: An Introduction*. London: Macmillan, 1972.

Sayer, A., *Method in Social Science: A Realistic Approach*, 2nd edn. London: Routledge, 1992.

Schapiro, L., *Totalitarianism*. London: Pall Mall, 1972.

Scheffler, S., *The Rejection of Consequentialism: A Philosophical Investigation of the Considerations Underlying Rival Moral Conceptions*. Oxford: Clarendon Press, 1994.

Schelling, F. W. J., *Ideas for a Philosophy of Nature*, trs. P. Heath, ed. E. E. Harris. Cambridge: Cambridge University Press, 1988.

Schelling, F. W. J., *On the History of Modern Philosophy*, ed. A. Bowie. Cambridge: Cambridge University Press, 1994.

Schilcher, F. von and Tennant, N., *Philosophy, Evolution and Human Nature*. London: Routledge & Kegan Paul, 1984.

Schlick, M., *General Theory of Knowledge*, trs. A. E. Blumberg. New York: Springer-Verlag, 1977.

Schlick, M., *Philosophical Papers*, 2 vols. Dordrecht: D. Reidel, 1979.

Schilpp, P. A. (ed.), *The Philosophy of G. E. Moore*. La Salle, IL: Open Court, 1968.

Schmitter, P. C., "Still the Century of Corporatism?," in P. C. Schmitter and G. Lehmbruch (eds.), *Trends Toward Corporatist Intermediation*. London: Sage, 1984, pp. 1–48.

Schopenhauer, A., *The World as Will and Representation*, trs. E. F. J. Payne. New York: Dover, 1966.

Scotus, in *Duns Scotus: Metaphysician*, ed. D. A. Frank and A. B. Wolter. West Lafayette, IN: Purdue University Press, 1995.

Searle, J. R., *Speech Acts*. Cambridge: Cambridge University Press, 1969.

Searle, J. R., *The Rediscovery of the Mind*. Cambridge, MA: MIT Press, 1992.

Searle, J. R., *The Construction of Social Reality*. New York: Free Press, 1995.

Sellars, R. W., "Knowledge and its Categories," in D. Drake et al. (eds.), *Essays in Critical Realism*. London: Macmillan, 1920.

Sellars, W., *Science, Perception and Reality*. London: Routledge & Kegan Paul, 1963.

Sen, A. K., *On Ethics and Economics*. Oxford: Basil Blackwell, 1987.

Sextus Empiricus, *Against the Grammarians* (*Adversus Mathematicos I*), trs. D. L. Blank. Oxford: Oxford University Press, 1996.

Sextus Empiricus, *The Skeptic Way: Sextus Empiricus' Outline of Pyrrhonism*, trs. B. Mates. Oxford: Oxford University Press, 1996.

Sheen, F. J., *Philosophy of Religion*. London: Longmans, Green, 1952.

Sheppard, A. D. R., *Aesthetics: An Introduction to the Philosophy of Art*. Oxford: Oxford University Press, 1987.

Shimony, A. and Nails, D. (eds.), *Naturalistic Epistemology: A Symposium of Two Decades*. Dordrecht: D. Reidel, 1987.

Shoemaker, S., *Self-Knowledge and Self-Identity*. Ithaca, NY: Cornell University Press, 1963.

Shusterman, R., *Pragmatist Aesthetics: Living Beauty, Rethinking Art*. Oxford: Basil Blackwell, 1992.

Sidgwick, H., *The Methods of Ethics*. London: Macmillan, 1874.

Simon, R. J., *Abortion: Statutes, Policies and Public Attitudes the World Over*. New York: Praeger, 1998.

Simplicius, *On Aristotle's Physics*, trs. B. Fleet. London: Duckworth, 1997.

Singer, M. (ed.), *American Philosophy*. Cambridge: Cambridge University Press, 1985.

Singer, P. (ed.), *Applied Ethics*. Oxford: Oxford University Press, 1986.

Singer, P., *Animal Liberation: A New Ethic for Our Treatment of Animals*, 2nd edn. London: Cape, 1990.

Singer, P., *Practical Ethics*, 2nd edn. Cambridge: Cambridge University Press, 1993.

Singer, M., *Generalization in Ethics: An Essay in the Logic of Ethics*. New York:

Singer, P., "Animals and the Value of Life," in T. Regan (ed.), *Matters of Life and Death: New*

Introductory Essays in Moral Philosophy. New York: McGraw-Hill, 1993.

Singer, P. and Wells, D., *The Reproduction Revolution: New Ways of Making Babies*. Oxford: Oxford University Press, 1984.

Sinnott-Armstrong, W., *Moral Dilemmas*. Oxford: Basil Blackwell, 1988.

Skinner, B. F., *Science and Human Behaviour*. New York: Macmillan, 1953.

Skinner, B. F., *About Behaviourism*. London: Jonathan Cape, 1974.

Sklar, L., *Philosophy of Physics*. Boulder, CO: Westview Press, 1992.

Slote, M., *Metaphysics and Essence*. Oxford: Basil Blackwell, 1974.

Slote, M., *Goods and Virtues*. Oxford: Oxford University Press, 1983.

Slote, M., *Beyond Optimising: A Study of Rational Choice*. Cambridge, MA: Harvard University Press, 1989.

Slote, M., *From Morality to Virtue*. Oxford University Press, 1992.

Smart, J. J. C. (ed.), *Problems of Space and Time*. New York: Macmillan, 1968.

Smart, J. J. C., *Essays Metaphysical and Moral: Selected Philosophical Papers*. Oxford: Basil Blackwell, 1987.

Smart, J. J. C., *Our Place in the Universe: A Metaphysical Discussion*. Oxford: Basil Blackwell, 1989.

Smart, J. J. C. and Williams, B., *Utilitarianism: For and Against*. Cambridge: Cambridge University Press, 1973.

Smart, N., *Historical Selections in the Philosophy of Religion*. London: SCM Press, 1962.

Smart, N., *The Philosophy of Religion*. New York: Random House, 1970.

Smith, A., *The Theory of Moral Sentiments*, ed. D. D. Raphael and A. L. Macfie. Oxford: Oxford University Press, 1976.

Smith, P. and Jones, O. R., *The Philosophy of Mind: An Introduction*. Cambridge: Cambridge University Press, 1986.

Sober, E., *Philosophy of Biology*. Oxford: Oxford University Press, 1993.

Sober, E., *Simplicity*. Oxford: Oxford University Press, 1975.

Solomon, R. C., *Introducing Philosophy*. New York: Harcourt Brace Jovanovich, 1989.

Sorenson, R., *Thought Experiments*. Oxford: Oxford University Press, 1992.

Sosa, E., *Knowledge in Perspective: Selected Essays in Epistemology*. Cambridge: Cambridge University Press, 1991.

Sparshott, F. E., *The Structure of Aesthetics*. Toronto: Toronto University Press, 1963.

Spinoza, B., *Ethics*, trs. W. H. White and A. H. Stirling. New York: Hafner, 1949.

Sprigge, T. L. S., *The Rational Foundations of Ethics*. London: Routledge & Kegan Paul, 1988.

Stalnaker, R., *Inquiry*. Cambridge, MA: MIT Press, 1984.

Stebbing, L. S., *A Modern Introduction to Logic*. London: Methuen, 1950.

Stepelevich, L. S. (ed.), *The Young Hegelians: An Anthology*. Cambridge: Cambridge University Press, 1983.

Stevenson, C. L., *Ethics and Language*. New Haven, CT: Yale University Press, 1944.

Stevenson, C. L., *Facts and Values: Studies in Ethical Analysis*. New Haven, CT: Yale University Press, 1963.

Stich, S. P., *Deconstructing the Mind*. Oxford: Oxford University Press, 1996.

Stiver, D., *The Philosophy of Religious Language: Sign, Symbol and Story*. Oxford: Blackwell Publishers, 1996.

Strawson, P. F., *Introduction to Logical Theory*. London: Methuen, 1952.

Strawson, P. F., *Individuals: An Essay in Descriptive Metaphysics*. London: Methuen, 1959.

Strawson, P. F., *The Bounds of Sense: An Essay on Kant's "Critique of Pure Reason."* London: Methuen, 1966.

Strawson, P. F. (ed.), *Philosophical Logic*. Oxford: Oxford University Press, 1967.

Strawson, P. F., *Logico-Linguistic Papers*. London: Methuen, 1971.

Strawson, P. F., *Freedom and Resentment and Other Essays*. London: Methuen, 1974.

Strawson, P. F., *Analysis and Metaphysics: An Introduction to Philosophy*. Oxford: Oxford University Press, 1992.

Stroud, B., *The Significance of Philosophical Scepticism*. Oxford: Oxford University Press, 1984.

Sullivan, D. J., *Fundamentals of Logic*. New York: McGraw-Hill, 1963.

Sullivan, T. V., "The Immorality of Euthanasia," in M. Kohl (ed.), *Beneficent Euthanasia*. Amherst, MA: Prometheus Books, 1975.

Suppes, P., *Introduction to Logic*. New York: Van Nostrand Reinhold, 1957.

Swinburne, R., *Space and Time*. London: Macmillan, 1968.

Swinburne, R., *An Introduction to Confirmation Theory*. London: Methuen, 1973.

Swinburne, R., *The Coherence of Theism*. Oxford: Clarendon Press, 1977.

Syre, K. M., *Cybernetics and the Philosophy of Mind*. London: Routledge & Kegan Paul, 1976.

Taliaferro, C., "Philosophy of Religion," in N. Bunnin and E. P. Tsui-James (eds.), *The Blackwell Companion to Philosophy*. Oxford: Blackwell Publishers, 1996.

Tarski, A., "The Semantic Conception of Truth," in H. Feigl and W. Sellars (eds.), *Readings in Philosophical Analysis*. New York: Appleton-Century-Croft, 1949.

Tarski, A., *Logic, Semantics and Metamathematics*. Oxford: Oxford University Press, 1956; 2nd edn, ed. J. Corcoran, trs. J. H. Woodger. Indianapolis, IN: Hackett, 1983.

Taylor, C., *Sources of the Self: The Making of the Modern Identity*. Cambridge, MA: Harvard University Press, 1989.

Taylor, P. W., *Respect for Nature: A Theory of Environmental Ethics*. Princeton, NJ: Princeton University Press, 1986.

Teichman, J., *Pacifism and the Just War: A Study in Applied Philosophy*. Oxford: Basil Blackwell, 1986.

Temkin, L., *Inequality*. Oxford: Oxford University Press, 1993.

Thomas, P., "Marx Now and Then," in T. Carver (ed.), *The Cambridge Companion to Marx*. Cambridge: Cambridge University Press, 1991.

Thomson, J. J. and Parent, W., *Rights, Restitution and Risk: Essays in Moral Theory*. Cambridge, MA: Harvard University Press, 1986.

Tiles, M. and Tiles, J., *An Introduction to Historical Epistemology: The Authority of Knowledge*. Oxford: Basil Blackwell, 1993.

Tillich, P., *Ultimate Concern*. London: SCM Press, 1965.

Tillich, P., *What is Religion?* New York: Harper & Row, 1969.

Tillich, P., *Love, Power and Justice: Ontological Analyses and Ethical Applications*. Oxford: Oxford University Press, 1975.

Toews, J. E., *Hegelianism: The Path Toward Dialectical Humanism*. Cambridge: Cambridge University Press, 1980.

Tomas, V. (ed.), *Creativity in the Arts*. Englewood Cliffs, NJ: Prentice-Hall, 1964.

Toulmin, S., *Human Understanding*, 3 vols. Oxford: Clarendon Press, 1972.

Troelstra, A. S. and Dalen, D. van, *Constructivism in Mathematics: An Introduction*. Amsterdam: North-Holland, 1988.

Valberg, J. J., *The Puzzle of Experience*. Oxford: Oxford University Press, 1992.

Valdes, M., "Commentary on Julia Annas: Women and the Quality of Life – Two Norms or One?," in M. Nussbaum and A. Sen (eds.), *The Quality of Life*. Oxford: Oxford University Press, 1993.

Veatch, H., *For an Ontology of Morals: A Critique of Contemporary Ethical Theory*. Evanston, IL: Northwestern University Press, 1971.

Velasquez, M. G., *Business Ethics: Concepts and Cases*, 5th edn. Englewood Cliffs, NJ: Prentice-Hall, 2001.

Vignaux, P., *Philosophy in the Middle Ages: An Introduction*, trs. E. C. Hall. New York: Meridian, 1959.

Vincent, A., *Modern Political Ideologies*, 2nd edn. Oxford: Blackwell Publishers, 1995.

Vlastos, G., "The Socratic Elenchus," in *Oxford Studies in Ancient Philosophy*. Oxford: Oxford University Press, 1984.

von Schilcher, F. and Tennant, N., *Philosophy, Evolution and Human Nature*. London: Routledge & Kegan Paul, 1984.

von Wright, G. H., *An Essay in Modal Logic*. Amsterdam: North-Holland, 1951.

von Wright, G. H., *Norm and Action*. London: Routledge & Kegan Paul, 1963.

von Wright, G. H., *Explanation and Understanding*. London: Routledge & Kegan Paul, 1971.

von Wright, G. H., *Causality and Determinism*. New York, NY: Columbia University Press, 1974.

von Wright, G. H., *Philosophical Logic: Philosophical Papers*, vol. 2. Oxford: Basil Blackwell, 1983.

von Wright, G. H., *Truth, Knowledge and Modality: Philosophical Papers*, vol. 3. Oxford: Basil Blackwell, 1984.

von Wright, G. H., *Realism, Meaning and Truth*, 2nd edn. Oxford: Basil Blackwell, 1993.

Wallis, R. T., *Neo-platonism*. London: Gerald Duckworth, 1972.

Walsh, W. H., *Reason and Experience*. Oxford: Clarendon Press, 1947.

Walton, D., *Informal Logic: A Handbook for Critical Argument*. Cambridge: Cambridge University Press, 1989.

Walton, D., *Slippery Slope Arguments*. Oxford: Oxford University Press, 1992.

Walzer, M., *Spheres of Justice: A Defence of Pluralism and Equality*. New York: Basic Books, 1983.

Ware, R. and Nielsen, K. (eds.), *Analysing Marxism: New Essays on Analytical Marxism*. Calgary: University of Calgary Press, 1989.

Weatherford, R., *Philosophical Foundations of Probability Theory*. London: Routledge & Kegan Paul, 1982.

Weber, M., *The Theory of Social and Economic Organisation*, trs. A. R. Henderson and T. Parsons. London: Oxford University Press, 1947.

Weber, M., *The Methodology of the Social Sciences*, ed. E. Shils and H. Finch. New York: Free Press, 1949.

Weber, M., *Economy and Society: An Outline of Interpretative Sociology*, ed. G. Roth and C. Mittich. Berkeley, CA: University of California Press, 1978.

Werkmeister, W. H., *A History of Philosophical Ideas in America*. New York: Ronald Press, 1949.

Whewell, W., *Philosophy of the Inductive Sciences*, 2nd edn. London: Cass, 1967.

White, M., *Foundations of Historical Knowledge*. New York: Harper & Row, 1965.

Whitehead, A. N., *Process and Reality*. New York: Free Press, 1929.

Whitehead, A. N., *The Concept of Nature*. Cambridge: Cambridge University Press, 1930.

Whitehead, A. N. and Russell, B., *Principia Mathematica*. Cambridge: Cambridge University Press, 1960.

Wiggins, D., *Needs, Values, Truth*, 2nd edn. Oxford: Basil Blackwell, 1991.

Williams, B. in J. J. C. Smart and B. Williams (eds.), *Utilitarianism: For and Against*. Cambridge: Cambridge University Press, 1973.

Williams, B. A. O., *Problems of the Self: Philosophical Papers, 1956–1972*. London: Cambridge University Press, 1973.

Williams, B. A. O., *Descartes: The Project of Pure Enquiry*. Hassocks: Harvester Press, 1978.

Williams, B. A. O., *Ethics and the Limits of Philosophy*. Cambridge, MA: Harvard University Press, 1985.

Williams, C. J. F., *What is Existence?* Oxford: Clarendon Press, 1981.

Williams, C. J. F., *What is Identity?* Oxford: Oxford University Press, 1989.

Williams, C. J. F., *Being, Identity and Truth*. Oxford: Oxford University Press, 1992.

Williams, D. C., *Principles of Empirical Realism*. Springfield, IL: Charles C. Thomas, 1966.

Wisdom, J., *Problems of Mind and Matter*. Cambridge: Cambridge University Press, 1934.

Wittgenstein, L., *Philosophical Investigations*, trs. G. E. M. Anscombe. Oxford: Basil Blackwell, 1953.

Wittgenstein, L., *Notebooks, 1914–1916*, trs. G. E. M. Anscombe. Oxford: Basil Blackwell, 1961.

Wittgenstein, L., *Tractatus Logico-Philosophicus*, trs. D. F. Pears and B. McGuinness. London: Routledge, 1961.

Wittgenstein, L., "Manuscript 219," in *Wittgenstein's Nachlass: The Bergen Electronic Edition*. Oxford: Oxford University Press, 1998–2000.

Wolff, R. P., *In Defense of Anarchism*. New York: Harper & Row, 1970.

Wollheim, R., *The Mind and its Depths*. Cambridge, MA: Harvard University Press, 1993.

Woodfield, A., *Teleology*. Cambridge: Cambridge University Press, 1976.

Yearley, S., *Science and Sociological Practice*. Milton Keynes: Open University Press, 1984.

Yolton, J., *Metaphysical Analysis*. Toronto: Toronto University Press, 1967.

Zeller, E., *Outlines of the History of Greek Philosophy*, 13th edn., ed. W. Nestle. New York: Dover, 1980.